Mental Illness and Crime

Mental Illness and Crime

Robert A. Schug
California State University, Long Beach

Henry F. Fradella
Arizona State University

SAGE

Los Angeles | London | New Delhi
Singapore | Washington DC

SAGE

Los Angeles | London | New Delhi
Singapore | Washington DC

FOR INFORMATION:

SAGE Publications, Inc.
2455 Teller Road
Thousand Oaks, California 91320
E-mail: order@sagepub.com

SAGE Publications Ltd.
1 Oliver's Yard
55 City Road
London EC1Y 1SP
United Kingdom

SAGE Publications India Pvt. Ltd.
B 1/I 1 Mohan Cooperative Industrial Area
Mathura Road, New Delhi 110 044
India

SAGE Publications Asia-Pacific Pte. Ltd.
3 Church Street
#10-04 Samsung Hub
Singapore 049483

Publisher: Jerry Westby
Publishing Associate: MaryAnn Vail
Production Editor: Melanie Birdsall
Copy Editor: Karen E. Taylor
Typesetter: C&M Digitals (P) Ltd.
Proofreader: Laura Webb
Indexer: Sheila Bodell
Cover Designer: Anupama Krishnan
Marketing Manager: Terra Schultz

Library of Congress Cataloging-in-Publication Data

Schug, Robert A.

Mental illness and crime / Robert A. Schug, Henry F. Fradella.

pages cm
Includes bibliographical references and index.

ISBN 978-1-4129-8707-3 (pbk)
1. Mentally ill offenders—United States. 2. Criminals—Mental health—United States. I. Fradella, Henry F. II. Title.

HV6133.S38 2014
364.3′80973—dc23 2013039271

14 15 16 17 18 10 9 8 7 6 5 4 3 2 1

Brief Contents

Detailed Contents

Preface

This book began as a series of lectures that I hastily prepared for my first teaching job—an undergraduate course in abnormal psychology that I taught at California State University, Los Angeles, in the fall of 2004. I took this job (during the first semester of my PhD program at the University of Southern California) having no previous teaching experience, no prepared materials, and three weeks until the first class meeting.

In fact, about all I did have was a passion for the topic of mental illness and crime, which I had been researching as a student since the beginning of the millennium, and a desire to share this enthusiasm with others. In a sudden moment of clarity (much like that experienced by Cesare Lombroso, I imagine, though I was not peering into the opened skull of a dead Italian serial killer at the time), I came up with the bright idea of teaching abnormal psychology from a criminological perspective. I had been horribly disappointed with my own undergraduate abnormal psychology experience—a course taught by a tired elderly ex-clinician who, for the entire quarter, sat motionless on a desk in the front of the room and rambled on in a monotone voice about patients he had treated decades ago. In my opinion, a class in abnormal psychology should not only hold the students' attention but also be a captivating, unforgettable, and even life-changing experience. I knew somehow that I could "sell" abnormal psychology to students if I taught it using material that I was interested in—material relating different forms of mental illness to criminal and violent behavior. And that's just what I did.

Over the next several years, I taught as an adjunct professor at that university in *two* departments, bringing the study of crime and violence to students in the Department of Psychology and the fundamentals of abnormal psychology to students in the Department of Criminal Justice. The material worked surprisingly well in both contexts, and I was excited to encounter so many students who were as interested in the topic as I was. I had made mental illness and crime accessible to two different audiences and bridged a pedagogical gap between psychology and criminal justice.

I can't remember the exact day that I first met Jerry Westby, Acquisition Editor for Sage, but I remember clearly how our first meeting went. It was a couple of years into my doctoral program, and I had been teaching regularly at CSULA. I remember Dr. Adrian Raine, my PhD supervisor, brought Jerry and his colleague around to the door of my office—a small, cramped, closet-like space on the sixth floor of the SGM building at the University of Southern California. Jerry had been visiting with USC professors, soliciting authors and inquiring about possible course textbook adoptions. We talked about my teaching load. I asked him if he knew of any good books about mental illness and crime—as the lecture material from my courses remained cobbled together from numerous clinical textbooks, scientific journal articles, and research projects of my own from my doctoral training. He replied he did not, and, with what was in all likelihood a throwaway line, he said, "Why don't you write one?" The rest, as they say, is history. After my graduation in 2009 I formalized an agreement with Jerry to write *Mental Illness and Crime* for Sage, and I spent the next four years laboring to pull it all together.

In the end, *Mental Illness and Crime* became the book that I wished I had been able to use in my teaching all along—a culmination of over a decade's worth of my own work and of sharing my passion with others. And yet it ended up being so much more. It is not an ordinary college course textbook, for the information presented within is multilayered and rich on many levels. It is instead a resource, one—it is hoped—that will remain on the shelves of students of both psychology and criminal justice for long after their coursework is completed. Although the book is a comprehensive review of research on the relationship between mental illness and criminality and violence, it is also an archive—a library, so to speak—of existing research studies in this subject area, and it presents original research that to date has not been published. It combines the clinical with the theoretical and policy with practice. It integrates biological, psychological, social, and legal viewpoints and is framed within an overarching understanding of the intersection between human behavior and law. Thus, the reader is invited to return to *Mental Illness and Crime* again and again, each time gleaning something new and undiscovered from the time before. Perhaps it is even a book that will ignite the sparks of curiosity and passion in others for years to come.

I would like to extend my deepest gratitude to the following individuals, without whom this book would not have been possible. First, my thanks go to Jerry Westby, for his unending support, patience, and belief in the book—even as a seemingly endless series of unmet writing deadlines came and went over the years. Next, I thank my amazing group of young, talented, and energetic research assistant scholars—who are now embarking upon their own graduate school experiences. Gianni Geraci was the first, a delightful young woman who mercifully came to my aid in the beginning and unquestioningly stuck with the project to the very end (despite having to delve into some unsavory and even shocking subject matter—which she undertook admirably with professionalism and grace). Equally as delightful were Heather McClernon, Gabriel Marmalejo, and Samantha Holdren, who contributed a significant amount of their own time, effort, and enthusiasm. Also my thanks go to George Nguyen, an undergraduate student who assisted me toward the end of the writing process, and to graduate student Ramin Moghadam, for his essential work on the glossary. Additionally, I humbly thank the panel of esteemed academics who contributed their own time and effort to reviewing the book in its earlier versions and whose thoughtful recommendations significantly added to the finished product. Furthermore, I am eternally indebted to my coauthor, Dr. Hank Fradella, who—when I was drowning in an ocean of mounting pressure and frustration—not only threw me a lifeline but, with his knowledge, experience, guidance, and unbelievably prolific writing output, fabricated a world-class seafaring vessel on the spot. His contributions no less than catapulted *Mental Illness and Crime* into the stratosphere in terms of its quality, scope, and overarching message; and I am proud to have my name next to his on the cover.

In addition, I would like to acknowledge the others who have helped me along the way and have contributed meaningfully to my ability to take on an endeavor of this magnitude. Many thanks to Dr. Fary Cachelin for providing me the opportunity to plant the seeds of my interest in this field and for nurturing them in the early years of my graduate work. To my academic "soul sisters," Drs. Andrea Glenn, Yu Gao, and Yaling Yang—members of the "Gang of Four" from USC and the University of Pennsylvania, know that you continually inspire me with your incredible work and productivity. Also, my thanks go to those who have played key roles in my development as a junior researcher—Dr. Charles Hinkin, Dr. Ramani Durvasula, and Dr. Laura Baker—and to my colleagues who have offered much-needed encouragement and support over the course of writing this book—Dr. Dave Kosson and Dr. Paul Babiak. Finally, I wish to express my deepest gratitude to my PhD supervisor Dr. Adrian Raine—a mentor and friend in the truest sense of both words—whose gifts to me of confidence, endless opportunity, and scientific curiosity are surpassed only by his most valuable lesson: "Never give up."

This book is dedicated to those with a passion. Follow your dreams, believe, and fight on. . . .

—Robert A. Schug

Publisher's Acknowledgments

SAGE gratefully acknowledges the contributions of the following reviewers:

Tiffiney Barfield-Cottledge, University of North Texas

Melissa Berry, University of Dayton

Patricia Brennan , Emory University

Tod W. Burke, Radford University

Joseph R. Carlson, University of Nebraska at Kearney

Tomasina L. Cook, Erie Community College

Gerald Patrick Fisher, Georgia College and State University

Margie Keaton, University of Indianapolis

Shawn Keller, Florida Gulf Coast University

Travis Langley, Henderson State University

Cathy A. Levey, University of Massachusetts–Lowell

Barbara Lewis, University of West Florida

Carina Ljungwald, Holy Names University

Catherine Orban, Marygrove College

Dario Rodriguez, University of Dayton

Darren K. Stocker, Cumberland County College

Emily M. Sweitzer, California University of Pennsylvania

Aviva Twersky Glasner, Bridgewater State College

Myths and Realities

Introduction and Scope of the Problem

ADAM PETER LANZA

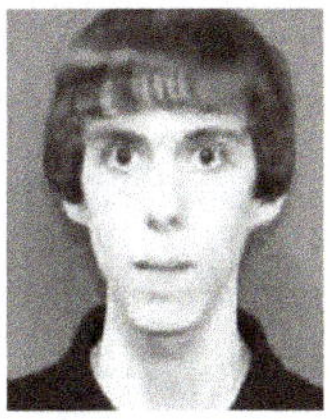

Adam Lanza was born in Exeter, New Hampshire, on April 22, 1992. On December 14, 2012, Lanza—wearing black clothing and a green utility vest—used an assault-style rifle to shoot his way through the locked front door of Sandy Hook Elementary School in the town of Newtown, Connecticut. He proceeded to shoot and kill 20 first-grade children and 6 adult staff members (wounding 2 additional individuals). Prior to doing so, he had shot and killed his mother, Nancy Lanza, in their nearby home. As emergency personnel arrived at the school, Lanza committed suicide by shooting himself in the head—marking the second-deadliest school shooting in U.S. history (behind the 2007 Virginia Tech massacre) and the second-deadliest mass murder at a U.S. elementary school (behind the 1927 Bath School bombings in Michigan).

At the time of this writing, details about Lanza's potential suffering from mental illness are uncorroborated and based on conjecture and hearsay. However, the limited available information from various media outlets—based on reports from individuals who purportedly knew him or had contact with him in various areas of his life—is highly consistent with indicators of psychiatric disorder.

As a child, he briefly attended Sandy Hook Elementary School and then a Catholic elementary and middle school and a high school in Newtown, where he was an honors student. He subsequently was removed from the public school system by his mother (who was unhappy with the district's plans for her son) and was homeschooled by her, eventually earning a GED. High school classmates and teachers described him as "intelligent, but nervous and fidgety" and having "flat affect." He had no close friends in school and avoided attention and socialization.

Lanza's brother reportedly told law enforcement that Adam was thought to have a personality disorder and to be "somewhat autistic." Others have alleged that he had been diagnosed with Asperger's disorder (see Chapter 3) and sensory processing disorder. Lanza's parents were divorced, and his mother did not work due to a settlement that left her financially stable. Conflicting reports indicate that she may have worked as a volunteer at Sandy Hook Elementary School. She has been described as a firearms enthusiast who owned at least a dozen guns, and she reportedly often took her sons to a local shooting range. Lanza had no criminal record.

Because Lanza is deceased and details of his mental functioning are sketchy, we can only speculate as to the nature of his disorders and what role they may have played in his crimes. Did he keep to himself because he was unable to socialize? Did violence become an outlet for him? Was he delusional? Had he remained in school, might special educational interventions have helped Lanza to develop coping mechanisms that might have prevented the Newtown tragedy? Questions like these motivated the authors to write this book examining the intersection of mental illness and crime.

Mentally ill criminal offenders often attract substantial attention from a broad cross section of society, particularly in the media. Perhaps the most famous case in recent history involving a mentally ill offender is the 1981 assassination attempt on President Ronald Reagan by John Hinckley Jr. Hinckley, who was diagnosed with schizophrenia, was found not guilty by reason of insanity in 1982 and has remained under institutional care at St. Elizabeth's Hospital in Washington, DC, since that time. It does not take an assassination attempt on a U.S. president, however, for the media to devote significant attention to the crimes committed by mentally ill offenders or even by those who are merely presumed to be. Aside from Adam Lanza, consider the following cases:

- In the summer of 2012, James Holmes killed 12 people and wounded 58 others inside an Aurora, Colorado, movie theater during a screening of "The Dark Knight Rises." His case is pending as of the writing of this chapter, but his defense attorneys represented to the court that Holmes was mentally ill at the time of the shooting massacre. In fact, before Holmes dropped out of a PhD program in neuroscience at the University of Colorado's Anschutz campus, he sought mental health assistance from the university's mental health service professionals. Details of Holmes's mental status have not yet been made public, but any mental illnesses he may have are likely to play a central role in his defense. Moreover, there are likely to be significant questions about the civil liability of the university-employed mental health professionals for their actions (or inaction) after meeting with Holmes and assessing his potential dangerousness.
- In 2011, Jared Loughner opened fire on a crowd of people in a Tucson, Arizona, shopping-center parking lot. The shooting killed 6, including a federal judge, and injured 13 others, including U.S. Representative Gabrielle Giffords, whose treatment was followed intently by the media up until her resignation from her congressional seat in 2012. Loughner had been diagnosed with schizophrenia. He spent more than a year and a half in a secure mental hospital during which time mental health professionals worked to restore his competency to stand trial. In August 2012, a federal judge found that his competency had been restored through treatment and then accepted Loughner's guilty plea. He was subsequently sentenced to life in prison without the possibility of parole.
- In April 2007, Seung Hoi Cho, who had been treated over a period of time for a variety of psychiatric symptoms, embarked on a shooting spree at the Virginia Polytechnic Institute and State University (commonly known as Virginia Tech), killing 32 people and injuring dozens more. At various times in his life, Cho had been diagnosed with major depression, social anxiety disorder, selective mutism, and a mood disorder not otherwise specified.
- In 2001, Andrea Yates killed her five children by drowning them in the bathtub. Although diagnosed with postpartum depression and postpartum psychosis, Yates was initially convicted of five counts of murder. Her convictions were set aside by an appellate court when it was revealed that a mental health expert falsified evidence in the case. On retrial, she was found guilty by reason of insanity and committed to the North Texas State Hospital, where she remained until 2007 before being transferred to a minimum-security hospital.

The interplay between the media and criminal justice may be greater today than ever before between the 24-hour news cycle's unquenchable thirst for reporting sensational crimes and Hollywood's seemingly endless depiction of crime stories in television and film (Surette, 2011). But other factors beyond the news media contribute to the pervasive narratives that perpetuate the myth that mental illness causes criminal offending.

The Myth That Mental Illness Causes Crime

It is well documented that the mass media often present inaccurate and sensationalized depictions of violent crimes committed by people with mental illnesses (Corrigan, 2005; Wahl, 1995). The crimes outlined previously are tragic, but they are also unrepresentative of the ways in which those with mental illness typically become involved in the criminal justice system. But it is not just the news media that contribute to common misperceptions and myths concerning mental illness, crime, and violence. Across the decades, entertainment media routinely portray characters with mental illnesses as being violently sadistic. Consider such movies as *Psycho*, *Repulsion*, *Halloween*, *The Silence of the Lambs*, and *Batman Begins*, all of which graphically depict a direct link between mental illness and serious violence (Kondo, 2008).

Given the media's distortion of the facts, it should come as no surprise that an ever-increasing number of laypersons equate mental illness with dangerousness, violence, and unpredictability—especially because the combination of factual and fictional media are the primary source of information concerning mental illness for the general public (Philo et al., 1994). Consider that in 1950, "when asked what 'mental illness' means to them, about 7% of respondents mentioned violent manifestations or symptoms, compared to 12% in 1996" (Markowitz, 2011, p. 39, citing Pescosolido, Monahan, Link, Stueve, & Kikuzawa, 1999). That percentage has increased in the past 15 years in light of the intense media coverage devoted to acts committed by Andrea Yates, Seung Hoi Cho, Jared Loughner, and Adam Lanza, just to name a few (see Kaminski, Koons-Witt, Thompson, & Weiss, 2010). For example, a whopping 60% of respondents in a national survey conducted in 2006 reported that they believed people with schizophrenia were likely to be violent, and 32% thought the same about people with major depression (as reported in the Harvard Mental Health Letter, 2011).

Such a fear of violent victimization at the hands of those with mental disorders has real consequences, perhaps the most important of which is the stigmatization of the mentally ill. Stigma contributes to a number of factors that can exacerbate mental illness, including poor self-esteem; lack of satisfaction with life; increased levels of isolation as a function of decreased social contacts and social rejection; and lack of employment opportunities that can lead to low income, unemployment, homelessness, and lack of access to health care (Bos, Kanner, Muris, Janssen, & Mayer, 2009; Markowitz, 1998). Moreover, such stigma has also contributed to decreased funding for mental health services, which, in turn, has contributed to the criminal justice system becoming a de facto mental health system—a fact that will be explored in greater detail in Chapter 12. For now, consider that the largest psychiatric facility in the United States is New York City's Rikers Island, a jail estimated to hold 3,000 mentally ill offenders at any given time (Stephey, 2007); the next two largest providers of psychiatric care in the United States are the Illinois Cook County Jail and California's Los Angeles Jail (Slate & Johnson, 2008). While incarcerated, mentally ill persons experience significant levels of victimization that exacerbate their mental illnesses and contribute to their reoffending upon being released (Gur, 2010; Human Rights Watch, 2009).

In spite of the presumably unintended consequences of the stigmatization of those with mental illnesses, in some ways, public perception about the link between mental illness and violence has a significant basis in reality. Consider that researchers in one of the most comprehensive, large-scale studies of the link between mental illness and violence found that roughly 25% of people who met the diagnostic criteria for a mental disorder had engaged in some form of violent behavior within a one-year period, including hitting, throwing things, and the use of weapons; in contrast, only 2% of those people who did not meet the diagnostic criteria for any mental disorder committed such acts (Swanson, Holzer, Ganju, & Jono, 1990). Still, it is overly simplistic to conclude from such data that mental illness alone *causes* violence. The reality is far more complex, as illustrated by the following four points.

First, the overwhelming numbers of people with psychiatric illness are not violent (Lamberg, 1988). Stuart and Arboleda-Flórez (2001) estimated that less than 3% "of violent crimes could be attributed to persons with a principal diagnosis reflecting a nonsubstance use disorder—that is, a mood, psychotic, anxiety, adjustment, or miscellaneous other axis I disorder or an axis II personality disorder" (p. 658). But their methodology, like those of most studies that attempt to estimate the prevalence rate of violence among the mentally ill, leaves some room for skepticism. Consider, for example, that many acts of violence are never reported to law enforcement, especially those perpetrated by persons with mental illness against their own family members. In an attempt to address this shortcoming, Steinwachs, Kasper, and Skinner (1992) examined violence among 1,404 families who were members of the National Alliance for the Mentally Ill and found that 11% of individuals in the study had harmed another person within a one-year period. Still, the sample size and the population from which the sample was drawn limit the generalizability of the findings. Perhaps the best study from which such an estimate can be drawn comes from Denmark. That study found that between 1978 and 1990, 6.7% of males and 0.9% of females with **serious mental illnesses (SMIs)**[1] were convicted of a violent offense, compared with 1.5% of males and 0.1% of females among individuals with no psychiatric diagnosis (Hodgins, Mednick, Brennan, Schulsinger, & Engberg, 1996). But these results may not be generalizable to other countries. In short, the methodological limitations of most research clearly constrain our ability to estimate the prevalence rate of violence among the mentally ill. What is clear, however, is that the rate is much lower than the general public believes it to be, an error likely fueled by both news and popular media.

Second, consider the prevalence rates of mental illness among criminal and incarcerated populations. Most studies find that between 16% and 30% of offenders have SMIs such as schizophrenia, schizophrenia spectrum disorder, schizoaffective disorder, bipolar disorder, brief psychotic disorder, delusional disorder, or a psychotic disorder not otherwise specified (James & Glaze, 2006; Skeem, Manchak, & Peterson, 2010; Steadman, Osher, Robbins, Case, & Samuels, 2009; Veysey & Bichler-Robertson, 2002). Thus, it is clear that a relationship between mental illness and violence exists that should not be ignored or minimized. However, the necessary correlate to the statistical findings of these prevalence studies is that more than two-thirds of offenders do not have an SMI. Clearly, other factors significantly affect violent behaviors, some of which appear to be much more salient than a psychiatric diagnosis.

Third, it is important to recognize that offenders with SMIs are a heterogeneous group whose criminal offending may stem from the same root causes as the crimes of offenders without mental illness. Some of the most pertinent of these are youthful age; antisocial cognition; deviant peers; personal stressors such as divorce, bereavement, unemployment, and homelessness; childhood exposure to violence; and, most especially, substance abuse disorders (Bonta, Law, & Hanson, 1998; Fazel, Långström, Hjern, Grann, & Lichtenstein, 2009; Fazel, Lichtenstein, Grann, Goodwin, & Långström, 2010; Fischer, Silver, & Wolff, 2006; Joyal, Côté, Meloche, & Hodgins, 2011; Junginger, Claypoole, Laygo, & Crisanti, 2006; Yee, Large, Kemp, & Nielssen, 2011). For example, Swanson (1994) found that people with mental illnesses were more than twice as likely to be involved in assaultive acts as people with no such illnesses; however, those with substance abuse disorders were more than twice as likely to have committed assaults than those diagnosed with psychiatric disorders unrelated to substance abuse (see also Elbogen & Johnson, 2009). But even among those with a substance abuse disorder, "there is a statistically significant, yet modest relationship between recent SMIs (within 12 months) and violence" (Van Dorn, Volavka, & Johnson, 2012, p. 501; see also Yee, et al., 2011). This statement appears to have particular applicability for those people who suffer from select "positive" psychotic symptoms, especially delusional thinking and command hallucinations (Elbogen & Johnson, 2009, Swanson, 1994). As we will explore in more detail in Chapter 5, it may be that "persons experiencing these symptoms may accept irrational thoughts as real, misperceiving the actions of others (including family members or police officers) as threatening and respond aggressively" (Markowitz, 2011, p. 40; see also Link, Monahan, Steuve, & Cullen, 1999; Teasdale, 2009).

Finally, to the modest extent that mental illness affects violent tendencies, the threat is generally small. In fact, the risk is significantly more likely to manifest as violence against family members than strangers (Solomon, Cavanaugh, & Gelles, 2005). Given the often confusing results of studies examining the link between mental illness and crime, we have included throughout this book tables that present the reported prevalence rates of specific mental illnesses and their correlates with specific types of crime. But to truly understand mental illness and crime, we must understand the legal and public policy implications of behavioral scientific research relevant

---

1. A note on using this book: Throughout the text, we have indicated significant words by using a combination of bold, bold italics, and italics. Terms in **bold** are "key terms"; these are listed at the end of each chapter and defined in the glossary. Terms in ***bold italics*** are "foundational terms," which, although not considered as significant to the learning objectives of each chapter as "key" terms, are important in themselves. These, too, are defined in the glossary for your convenience. We have placed other terms (ones that are defined in the chapters themselves but not in the glossary) in *italics*, to help you easily refer to these definitions. For more on the organization and pedagogy of this text, see the section in this chapter entitled "How to Use This Book."

to crimes perpetrated by those with mental disorders. Chapters 11 and 12 are devoted to those ends in some detail. In the next section of this chapter, though, we offer an overview of the often strained connections between law and behavioral science so that the reader might better grasp why the disciplines are sometimes at odds with each other—especially when, as explored in Chapters 11 and 12, the law must make use of behavioral scientific information as part of adjudication processes concerning criminal or otherwise dangerous persons.

An Overview of Some Foundational Concepts Across Disparate Disciplines

Studying the connections between mental illness and crime frequently involves two frustrations that are mirror images of each other. Nearly all aspects of the study of mental illness are the province of social and behavioral scientists, many of whom lack education or training about the law, crime, and criminal justice. Conversely, crime is defined by law and applied by justice practitioners, many of whom have no education or training in the behavioral sciences. To address potential gaps in knowledge, we feel it necessary to devote a portion of this chapter to outlining some foundational concepts and explaining some of the pitfalls of communicating across the disciplines.

The Link Between Behavioral Sciences and Law

The intersections of behavioral science and the legal system are broad and not particularly well defined (Fradella, 2008). Recognition of the intersection of disciplines such a psychology, psychiatry, and the law as distinct fields of study has been fairly recent. In fact, most scholarship in the area has been written since the 1970s (Melton, 1992). Specialized journals in the intersection of these fields began to appear in that same period. These included the *Bulletin of the American Academy of Psychiatry and the Law* in 1973 (renamed the *Journal of the American Academy of Psychiatry and the Law* in 1997), the *Law and Psychology Review* in 1975, and *Law and Human Behavior* in 1977. Over the past 40 years or so, the field has continued to grow. For example, additional specialized journals were created such as *Behavioral Sciences and the Law* in 1983, the *Journal of Police and Criminal Psychology* in 1985, and *Psychology, Public Policy, and Law* in 1995. Similarly, specialized joint-degree programs were developed in this time period that provided for interdisciplinary training between law and the mental health fields (Crane, 1999; Tomkins & Ogloff, 1990; Weinstein, 1999). This trend of creating new specialized interdisciplinary degree programs continues to grow today (Sloan, 2011). With such growth, definitions evolve, boundaries change, and areas of specialization and subspecialization develop (Haney, 1993). Perhaps this explains why it is often hard to define the various terms related to the forensic behavioral sciences.

Some Background on the Social and Behavioral Sciences

The social and behavioral sciences consist of an array of disciplines that are concerned with the actions and reactions of humans and animals, which are studied through observational and experimental methods. The National Institutes of Health ([NIH], 2010) recognizes that, although the behavioral sciences and the social sciences are inextricably tied together, fine distinctions exist between the terms:

> Behavioral and social sciences research is a large, multifaceted field, encompassing a wide array of disciplines. The field employs a variety of methodological approaches including: surveys and questionnaires, interviews, randomized clinical trials, direct observation, physiological manipulations and recording, descriptive methods, laboratory and field experiments, standardized tests, economic analyses, statistical modeling, ethnography, and evaluation. Yet, behavioral and social sciences research is not restricted to a set of disciplines or methodological approaches. Instead, the field is defined by substantive areas of research that transcend disciplinary and methodological boundaries. In addition, several key cross-cutting themes characterize social and behavioral sciences research. These include: an emphasis on theory-driven research; the search for general principles of behavioral and social functioning; the importance ascribed to a developmental, lifespan perspective; an emphasis on individual

> variation, and variation across sociodemographic categories such as gender, age, and sociocultural status; and a focus on both the social and biological contexts of behavior. . . . For . . . [definitional purposes], the term "behavioral" refers to overt actions; to underlying psychological processes such as cognition, emotion, temperament, and motivation; and to biobehavioral interactions. The term "social" encompasses sociocultural, socioeconomic, and sociodemographic status; to biosocial interactions; and to the various levels of social context from small groups to complex cultural systems and societal influences (NIH, 2010, paras. 3–5).

Applying the NIH criteria, one could argue that the behavioral sciences conventionally include biology, neuroscience, physical anthropology (including archaeology and paleontology), and several branches of medical science, such as psychiatry and neurology (see Gintis, 2007). Similarly, a defensible list of the social sciences could include cultural anthropology, economics, political science, sociology, and, depending on the methods of inquiry employed, even some of the disciplines traditionally classified as humanities, such as history, legal studies, and philosophy (Gintis, 2007). Some fields, such as criminology and psychology, clearly encompass both social and behavioral scientific aspects.

An Overview of the Forensic Behavioral Sciences. This book concerns the in-depth study of mental illness and crime. As such, it draws primarily on criminology, law, and three behavioral sciences: psychology, psychiatry, and neuroscience. Sometimes, these fields are sloppily lumped together under the term "forensic psychology." For reasons that should become clear in the following sections, it is inappropriate to use that term generically as a catchall for referring to a broader scope of disciplines than just psychology. Accordingly, we use the term **forensic behavioral science** to subsume the fields of forensic psychology, forensic psychiatry, and forensic neuroscience because they all employ the scientific application of methods, procedures, and techniques to investigate human behavior relevant to problems found in criminal law and, to a lesser degree, in civil law.

Forensic Psychology. The first word in the phrase "forensic psychology" comes from the Latin word "*forensis*," which means "of the market or forum." The forum was an active place in ancient Rome. Trials, theatrical performances, and political debates all occurred in the forum (see Pound, 1953). Accordingly, the word "forensic" is sometimes used to refer to rhetoric or debate skills. More commonly today, though, because trials occurred in the forum, the word is typically used to mean "of or pertaining to the law," especially in terms of the application of science or technology in the investigation of the facts or evidence relevant in a court of law.

The second part of the term "forensic psychology" refers to the behavioral science that deals with mental processes and behavior. The word "psychology" is derived from two Greek terms, "*logos*," from which comes the suffix "-ology," meaning the study of something, and "*psyche*," referring to the soul or the mind (Colman, 1999). Psychology consists of many subdisciplines, including cognitive, developmental, evolutionary, personality, occupational and industrial-organizational, and social psychology—just to name a few (for a complete description of the dozens of psychological specialties, see Pawlik & Rosenzweig, 2000). The two branches of psychology most relevant to this book are clinical psychology and neuropsychology. **Clinical psychology** is devoted to the study of psychopathology and to providing psychological diagnostic and treatment services to patients. **Neuropsychology** concerns the structure and function of the brain in relation to behaviors and psychological processes.

Entry into the field of psychology normally requires between four and seven years of graduate study. The two most typical doctoral degree programs in psychology are the PhD (doctor of philosophy) and PsyD (doctor of psychology). In addition, some school psychology programs culminate in the award of an EdD (doctor of education). The PhD in all areas of psychology requires a heavy emphasis on social scientific research methods and statistics, neuroscience, and the empirically based study of human behavior. People specializing in clinical psychology, though, are also required to learn specific techniques during their graduate studies and while working as postdoctoral interns in a clinical setting. These include not only the assessment and diagnosis of mental illness but also the treatment of psychopathology using psychotherapy. Additionally, clinical psychologists are usually well trained in psychometrics—the subfield of psychology concerned with the design, administration, and interpretation of tests that measure psychological variables such as intelligence, aptitude, and personality traits. The PsyD and EdD degrees generally involve curricula similar to that of the PhD, but they place more of an emphasis on practical skills than on research. Some master's programs in clinical social work and counseling psychology offer a clinical education similar to that of the PhD or PsyD but without the heavy emphasis on research (see Kring, Johnson, Davison, & Neale, 2012).

At its core, then, forensic psychology is a behavioral science specialty in which psychology is applied to the law. But such a generic definition is a bit misleading, for the field is more complicated than this simple definition would suggest. Indeed, the broadest use of forensic psychology encompasses numerous subfields. For example, police psychology involves research and clinical practice with those who work in law enforcement; it includes investigative work, such as criminal profiling, as well as providing psychological counseling services to police officers. Similarly, correctional psychology concerns research and clinical practice with correctional officers, as well as the treatment of both inmates in institutional correctional settings and those sentenced to community corrections. Forensic psychology also encompasses a specialized branch of applied social psychology in which empirical psychological research is conducted as it relates to the law and its processes; research areas could include juror understanding of jury instructions, the reliability of eyewitness testimony, or suggestibility and coercion in interview tactics, just to name a few. Finally, forensic psychology includes a specialized practice within clinical psychology and, ever increasingly, neuropsychology as well, a practice involving the psychological or neuroscientific assessment of persons under the jurisdiction of a court of law, whether criminal or civil, as part of the judicial process.

Forensic Psychiatry. Psychology and psychiatry are not the same; they are distinct fields. Although psychology and psychiatry share the Greek base "*psyche*," the latter combines the root with the Greek word "*iatros*," meaning "doctor."

> Psychiatry refers to a branch of medical science concerned with mental disorders—the classification, etiology, diagnoses, treatment, and prevention. Anyone intending to qualify as a psychiatrist must first undergo a full medical training and then specialize in psychiatry. . . . (Colman, 1999, p. 8)

Thus, there are two notable differences between psychology and psychiatry. First, in contrast to psychiatry's focus on mental disorders, most psychologists are concerned with normal human behavior. For the most part, only clinical psychology is concerned with mental illness. Second, psychiatrists are physicians who earn a medical degree, either the MD (doctor of medicine) or DO (doctor of osteopathy) degree, and then engage in four to six years of postgraduate clinical training in a residency program.

Although psychiatrists can diagnose and treat mental disorders in the same ways clinical psychologists do, they are usually not trained in psychometrics. Moreover, psychiatrists function in their full capacity as physicians by conducting physical examinations, ordering medically diagnostic tests, and prescribing drugs. Given their lack of biochemical and physiological training, psychologists are not permitted to conduct most of these tasks, although two U.S. states—Louisiana and New Mexico—grant clinical psychologists the limited ability to prescribe certain psychotropic medications after additional clinical training in physiology and pharmacology (Stambor, 2006).

Forensic Neuroscience. One burgeoning area of forensics is the application of neuroscience techniques to criminal justice processes. These techniques are based upon neurobiological theories of criminal behavior, which link crime and violence to abnormalities in the structure and functioning of the brain. Such techniques may involve brain imaging and indirect measures such as neuropsychology—paper-and-pencil type tests that measure behaviors associated with brain dysfunction—and psychophysiology, which measures peripheral physiological processes associated with specific areas of brain functioning (see Chapter 2 for more details on each of these techniques).

Popma and Raine (2006) propose a role for the forensic application of neuroscience techniques in areas of diagnostic identification, providing treatment options, risk assessment, and treatment evaluation. Although forensic neuroscience is still in its infancy, it has already raised significant philosophical, ethical, and political considerations related to the implications of its use in criminal law, much of which stem from the law's assumption that behavior is a product of free will.

The Ways in Which Forensic Behavioral Science Interacts With Law

One of the more thoughtful analyses of the ways in which psychology and law interact was written by Craig Haney in 1980. He conceptualized three distinct realms of interaction. His approach has been praised and adopted by other psycholegal scholars (e.g., Bartol & Bartol, 2012). Here, we adapt Haney's original typology applicable to law's intersection with psychology to fit the more inclusive intersections of law with the forensic behavioral sciences of psychology, psychiatry, and neuroscience.

Behavioral Science in the Law. Behavioral science *in* the law refers to the legal system's selective use of the behavioral sciences to answer questions posed by the law itself. In other words, the legal realm not only defines the question but also limits the scope of the answer. For example, is someone legally competent to stand trial? Is someone legally insane? Does someone pose a substantial risk to himself or to others? Although the law is clearly the dominant discipline in this relationship, behavioral science plays significant and important roles in these specified legal contexts, especially because the law is often highly deferential to psychological or psychiatric expert opinion. Yet it is clear that the decisions to be made are prescribed by the law and are often vested with either a judge or a jury.

Behavioral Science and the Law. Unfortunately, when law defines the scope of the question to be answered, it often does not avail itself of the benefits of the body of knowledge that the behavioral sciences can offer. The second adaptation of Haney's (1980) typology, behavioral science *and* the law, does this much better. Here, the fields are balanced in a partnership. Experimental behavioral science, as its own discipline, examines legal processes and offers informed opinions about their operations. For example, instead of answering the question "What is in the best interest of the child?" to determine which parent gets custody of a child upon divorce (a question in the realm of behavioral science *in* the law), behavioral science *and* the law might challenge the very assumption that there is a "best interest" by empirically demonstrating significant differences in placement outcomes.

Ideally, this relationship between the law and behavioral science causes the law to change in response to the data offered by psychological research. Reflecting on roughly a decade of progress after he originally set forth his classification, Haney (1993) offered several examples of cases in which the law did, in fact, evolve based on empirical research, such as how police conduct certain eyewitness identification procedures and how such identifications are subsequently handed in court, why certain mental conditions warrant legal recognition, how jury instructions are worded to promote better juror understanding of the law, and how predictions of future dangerousness are made if they are to be admissible in court. To be sure, though, the law is often slow to change in response to research. That is not necessarily a bad thing, though, because empirical research needs to be replicated and, perhaps, theory subsequently refined before laws and policies are changed to reflect research results. Just because research suggests that something is or is not so does not mean it is so (or not). But it is also clear that the law can be obstinate in coming to terms with reliable, valid, and replicated behavioral science research that challenges the status quo, especially when the challenge involves dealing with constitutional adjudication. Haney (1993) offered two stark examples of this fact:

> Anyone who thought that data alone could carry the day in constitutional jurisprudence, or that the last 10 years of psycholegal reform had educated the Court about social science and won us a hard fought, grudging respect among the Justices need only look at *Lockhart v. McCree* (1986), where the Court expressed "serious doubts about the value" of the social science research to predict actual behavior in the legal system (p. 171), despite virtual unanimity in the social science community about the biasing effects of death qualification. Or, look carefully at *McCleskey v. Kemp* (1987), where the Court rejected a veritable mountain of data documenting the discriminatory impact of capital punishment because the data were, in essence, not perfect and because the Court changed the applicable legal standard in such a way as to make social science data rarely if ever relevant to this issue in the future. (pp. 376–377)

Behavioral Science of the Law. The final adaptation of Haney's (1980) classifications is referred to as the behavioral science *of* the law. It seeks to address abstract questions regarding the role of law in society as a tool in regulating individual and collective behaviors. For example, does the mandatory minimum sentencing of first-time drunk driving offenders lower recidivism for the crime? Does the mandatory arrest of interpersonal violence offenders prevent further domestic victimization? Do brain abnormalities in the frontal lobe of the brain cause violent behaviors?

This dimension of transdisciplinary inquiry lies more in the philosophical than the practical realm because judges are quite skeptical about behavioral scientific research on how laws and policies affect human behavior and vice versa (see Fradella, 2004). There are likely numerous reasons as for this skepticism, many of which stem from a range of differences between the epistemologies, theories, and methods of the law and of the behavioral sciences—differences that we will now explore.

Some Background on the Law

Defining the law is no easy task. As legal and social scholar Steven Vago (2009) commented, "comprehensive reviews of the literature . . . indicate that there are almost as many definitions of law as there are theorists" (p. 8). One of the most influential definitions of law comes from sociologist Max Weber (1954). Weber conceptualized law as a rule of conduct that is "externally guaranteed by the probability that coercion (physical or psychological), to bring about conformity or avenge violation, will be applied by a staff of people holding themselves specially ready for that purpose" (p. 5). Davis (1962) modified Weber's definition of law, producing three distinct elements for the sake of clarity: The law is comprised of (1) explicit rules of conduct, (2) planned use of sanctions to support the rules, and (3) designated officials to interpret and enforce the rules, and often to make them.

Categorizing the Law. The law can be substantive or procedural. *Substantive law* sets forth legal prescriptions and proscriptions—the rules of what one must do and may not do. *Procedural law* sets forth the mechanisms through which substantive laws are administered. Homicide statutes are examples of substantive laws. The rules regulating trial procedure and the way in which evidence may be introduced in a homicide trial, in contrast, are examples of procedural laws.

Another way of categorizing law makes a distinction between civil and criminal law. Wrongs committed against an individual, called torts, are the realm of civil law. But civil law encompasses more than just torts; it includes many areas that regulate the relationships between individuals, such as business law (e.g., corporate and contract law); family law (e.g., marriage, divorce, child custody); and property or estate law (e.g., the law of wills, trusts, and inheritance and the law of landlord–tenant relations). In contrast, *criminal law*, also referred to as penal law, is that body of law that defines conduct criminally punishable by the government as a wrong committed against the people in society as a whole. This book is concerned with violations of the criminal law by people with mental illnesses.

The Social Objectives of Law. We often conceptualize the law as a tool by which we control human behaviors. But such a conceptualization is naïve, as the relationship between law and human behavior is complex and subject to debate (Black, 1993, 1984). Law can be both cause and effect—both independent and dependent variable (Davis, 1962; Gottfredson & Hindelang, 1979). More often than not, sociologists of law view the opinions of society—especially strongly held social mores and customs—as being the guiding force of human behavior and the law as having to be in accordance with such beliefs in order for it to be effective (Ross, 1901). Erlich (1936/1975) went so far as to say that the "center of gravity of legal development lies not in legislation, nor in juristic science, nor judicial decision, but in society itself" (forward). Yet in spite of the limited role that positive law might have on human behavior, there is no denying that one of the primary purposes of law is **social control**—controlling the behaviors of members of society. Criminal law, for example, is designed to control behavior by deterring crime through the threat of punishment. It then actually punishes those who commit offenses, thereby achieving both retribution and specific deterrence in which the punished wrongdoer is expected to learn his or her lesson.

But social control is only one of the social objectives of law. Carter and Burke (2010) set forth a typology that includes four additional objectives that law is designed to achieve: to coordinate for the collective advantage of society (e.g., laws regulating radio and television broadcasting, contract law); to support the operations of government itself (e.g., the IRS Code, elections laws); to promote health, safety, and welfare (e.g., building and sanitation codes); and to remedy social ills that face society as a whole (e.g., laws to remedy various forms of discrimination). Several of these objectives promote the peaceful and orderly resolution of disputes, while others promote social change (Vago, 2009).

Law's Adversarial System. When we think of the judicial process in the United States, we often think of a courtroom in which lawyers for two sides of a dispute argue their points to a judge and jury. We call this battle the adversarial system. Under this system, the parties to a legal dispute are each given an opportunity to "make their case." We assume, at least at the philosophical level, that pitting adversaries against each other in a winner-take-all courtroom battle will encourage both parties to gather the best evidence they can and make their best arguments.

The adversarial process, of course, is guided by many rules of procedure. The judge is supposed to act as the interpreter and enforcer of these rules and in a neutral, disinterested manner. Sometimes, the judge also serves as the trier of fact, the decision maker with regard to the factual issues disputed in a case. More frequently, however, a jury serves as the trier of fact, and the judge is left to make purely legal decisions. This approach is especially true in criminal cases as the right to trial by a jury of one's peers is guaranteed by the Sixth Amendment to the U.S. Constitution in most criminal cases.

A common misperception of law is that the adversarial legal system will lead to the uncovering of the truth. But the judicial process is not about uncovering truth. In fact, there are a number of evidentiary and procedural mechanisms applicable in the judicial process that can prevent the trier of fact from knowing the truth. The exclusionary rule is a good example. This rule operates to exclude from trial physical evidence and confessions that were obtained in violation of defendants' constitutional rights. When such evidence is excluded on legal grounds, the jury will not get to know of its existence at trial, thereby preventing jurors from knowing the truth concerning the existence of such evidence and the inferences that may be deduced from it.

If not uncovering truth, then what is the goal of the adversarial process? Although the answer to this question is open to debate, a good response would be "to achieve resolution of a legal dispute using fair procedures." How the trier of fact does so may or may not concern uncovering the truth; rather, it involves whether the legal standards of knowledge called the "burden of proof" was met. How the trier of fact comes to have sufficient knowledge to render its decision, however, is of direct relevance to us here. "Knowing," for legal decision-making purposes, is a far cry from "knowing" for scientific purposes.

The legal system asks the trier of fact to use the *a priori* method of knowledge. "*A priori*" is Latin for "it stands to reason." Using primarily deductive reasoning skills, one draws a logical conclusion after analyzing the facts presented. But since the facts presented to the trier of fact may be incomplete or inaccurate, knowledge under this method is not about arriving at truth but rather about coming to a logical conclusion that might be right or wrong.

There are other ways of knowing that come into play in the law, some of which are more embraced than others. The *method of tenacity* is frowned upon by the law. Following this method, people claim to know not because of any fact or piece of evidence but rather because of their personal belief system.

The *method of authority* is the process of coming to know something because someone in authority has told us that something is so. The law often embraces this type of knowledge when expert testimony is used. The trier of fact learns that something is so from an expert in the relevant field. Of course, this method of knowledge is limited as well. If the expert is not a true authority, or is just plain wrong, then the so-called knowledge passed along is flawed.

Finally, there is the *method of science*, the method used by the behavioral sciences. The scientific method involves formulating hypotheses from prior scientific knowledge and then testing those hypotheses using systematic experimentation and observation. The goal of the scientific method is to identify, as best as possible, objective reality or, more simply, truth. For something to have objective truth, it must be able to be tested empirically under conditions that allow for both falsification—a way to disprove a hypothesis—and replication—a way for others to verify the outcome of the research by repeated testing (Popper, 1989).

The Study and Practice of Law. Law is practiced by attorneys. Attorneys are lawyers who have been admitted to the practice of law in a given jurisdiction, usually because they have taken and passed the bar exam—a test of various fields of law designed to ensure that lawyers have a minimum level of competency and knowledge before they are allowed to represent another as an attorney. One becomes a lawyer by going to law school. Traditionally, law school is a three-year, postbaccalaureate degree program that culminates in the award of the JD degree (juris doctor or doctor of jurisprudence). One does not become an attorney, however, until one passes the bar exam and is sworn in as an officer of the court.

Although there are differing approaches to the study of law, the education at law school has historically been doctrinal and continues to be so today in large part, although broader perspectives have been gaining acceptance since the 1990s (Feinman, 1998; Sonsteng, Ward, Bruce, & Petersen, 2007). Under the doctrinal approach to the study of law, rather than learning legal skills (something that lawyers are supposed to gain in practice, after law school), students learn legal theory and reasoning via the case method, a method that combines "conceptions of legal reasoning and legal doctrine with a pedagogical technique" (Feinman, 1998, p. 476). Students are taught how to decipher the rule of law by extrapolating it from a published judicial opinion using logic and inductive, deductive, and analogical reasoning skills. Then students are asked to apply the rule of law to hypothetical fact patterns, both orally during in-class Socratic dialogues and in writing on exams. Historically, this approach to the study of law was devoid of the study of legal processes and their relationship to law's impact on society via the lenses of the humanities and social sciences; at best, such disciplines were mentioned peripherally. The goal of such a legal education, whether undertaken in the past or currently, is to make students learn to think like a lawyer—to acquire knowledge of specialized legal vocabulary; to understand the operation of differing sets of legal rules; to learn how to read various sources of law, such as cases, constitutions, statutes, and administrative regulations; and to apply the law in a persuasive form of appropriate argumentation.

Law school often leaves its graduates with a highly doctrinal approach to law in which the unit of analysis is always the case. The participants in a case each have differing views of reality rather than a shared objective one. And the behavior of those participants is assumed to be a product of free will guided by the principles of individual autonomy and rational decision making. Thus, the views of those who are a product of law school, and arguably the views of the law itself, stand in sharp contrast to the more deterministic views of those trained in the behavioral sciences.

Lawyers Are From Mars, Behavioral Scientists From Venus

The intersection of the law and behavioral science sometimes makes cooperation strained, even when accompanied by the best of intentions. In 1987, Melton and colleagues made a number of observations as to why this is the case. Sadly, many of their observations still hold true today.

First, lawyers and behavioral scientists speak different languages; they use the vocabularies that are native to their respective disciplines. As explained earlier in this chapter, a legal education is quite different from a behavioral scientific education, and very few who enter either professional realm do so with the benefit of interdisciplinary training.

Second, the fields involve socialization into very different worlds with value systems that are often in conflict. Lawyers tend to be concerned with doctrinal rules, civil rights, precedent, and helping a client achieve the desired outcome in a particular case. Behavioral scientists tend to be less concerned with such abstractions and focus instead on the therapeutic needs of the individual, often to the exclusion of macrolevel considerations such as whether doing something might set an adverse precedent or whether procedural due process protections were strictly adhered to in a particular case. As a result, while both professions ostensibly are there to help, they do so in very different ways and from perspectives that are often at odds with each other.

Third, law asks very different types of questions from those asked by the behavioral sciences. What is established as a fact for one may not be sufficient for the other. Law determines fact by relevant evidence admissible under the rules of evidence. Credibility is often key to determining whether proffered evidence will be accepted by the trier of fact. In sharp contrast, behavioral scientific methods for determining the existence of a fact are quite different; they depend on experimentation, systematic observation, and the replicability of reliable and valid conclusions. Moreover, in seeking to answer questions of fact, each discipline employs fundamentally different methods of acquiring knowledge. Law is doctrinal and grounded in logic, whereas the behavioral sciences are concerned with contributions to scientific theory via the application of scientific methods. Statistical probabilities and their corresponding uncertainties are inherent to empirical methodologies. The law, however, does not concern itself with statistical probability but rather with levels of proof that are not only often arrived at in very nonscientific ways but also significantly beyond the limits of empirical design. Uncertainty requiring further study is simply not an option in a trial. So the law asks experts to offer their conclusions to a reasonable degree of scientific certainty. This ambiguous standard may cause behavioral scientists to overstate the level of certainty they have in their factual determinations in order to fit into the model the law may be unreasonably asking of them. Similarly, the law asks the triers of fact to base their conclusions on burdens of proof, which, unlike error rates and alpha levels that are calculable in behavioral scientific research, are generally impossible to quantify.

Finally, behavioral science offers a number of theoretical models for explaining human behavior. The law, in contrast, is rarely concerned with the deterministic explanations of behavior. Quite the contrary, the law presumes behavior is a product of an autonomous free will guided by rational decision making—a premise that is seemingly flawed in most criminal cases involving a defendant with mental illness. This fundamental difference alone—a philosophical one that concerns the very basis of human nature—is significant enough to explain why the disciplines often have difficulty with each other.

The Contributions of This Book

In the following chapters, we attempt to provide the most comprehensive and accurate view possible of the current state of the literature on the relationship between crime and mental illness. Meeting that objective involves a thorough review of the studies conducted to date. However, we also attempted to provide a foundation for the advancement of knowledge in this area by (1) conducting a "metasummary" of sorts of the various studies of the prevalence rates of mental illness and crime performed to date, (2) providing a critical review of the limitations of the literature in its present form, and (3) offering a novel, more balanced perspective on which to base future empirical investigations of mental illness and crime. Ultimately, we fully appreciate that we are likely to raise more questions than answers with a book such as this. That is its purpose—and should it prove to be the case, we would consider the book a success.

Studies of Prevalence and Incidence Rates

Studies of the prevalence and incidence rates of mental disorders among the criminal population can reveal much about the relationship between mental disorders and crime. A good portion of the work undertaken in preparing this book involved an examination of these rates. For this book, we have reviewed hundreds of such studies to look for any discernible patterns in both prevalence rates and research methodologies. These studies have traditionally focused on (1) the arrest rates of patients discharged from psychiatric facilities, (2) jailed detainees and incarcerated prisoners, (3) homicide offenders, (4) birth cohorts, (5) psychiatric inpatient samples, and (6) community samples, often consisting of epidemiological catchment area survey studies and outpatient psychiatric patients (see Asnis et al., 1997). In the chapters that follow, we have provided summaries of these prevalence-rate studies—for both disorder in crime and crime in disorder. (In other words, this research considers both the prevalence of mental disorders among those committing particular crimes and the prevalence of criminal and violent behavior among those diagnosed with particular mental disorders.) These summaries are arranged according to each mental disorder discussed in this book. Summaries are presented in tabular format in boxes entitled "A Closer Look." Descriptions of the specific elements found in these boxes, along with some considerations for the critical evaluation of the studies summarized therein, are listed in the following exemplar:

A few words of caution about these collections of studies must be made. Although painstaking efforts were made to locate and catalogue them, the lists should not be considered comprehensive or even representative of the complete body of empirical and clinical work on prevalence rates. From a research methodological perspective, these collections of studies are samples of convenience—obtained through computerized database searches and what would be considered "snowball" sampling techniques (i.e., locating additional studies through the references of available studies). As such, generalizations about the overall state of the

A Closer Look: Mental Disorder and Crime

Prevalence of the Disorder in Crime

Study Type	Number	Prevalence Rates
Arrest rates Birth cohorts Community samples Homicide offenders Jailed detainees and prisoners Psychiatric inpatients Adjudicated juvenile delinquents	Numbers of studies of various types reporting the prevalence rates of mental disorders among those who have committed crimes and violence are listed here. Study type may affect generalizability of results and cross-study comparisons.	Prevalence rates are reported as ranges from lowest to highest values across studies. Rates may be affected by factors such as the operational definition of a mental disorder or the study procedure (e.g., interview versus self-report versus official file data), which may produce diagnoses of varying quality or validity.
Total Number of Studies	This number indicates the total number of prevalence-rate studies of mental illness in criminal populations. It is important to note that a greater quantity of studies does not necessarily translate into greater quality.	

Sample Characteristics	
Size	Sample size affects generalizability of results, with larger numbers of participants generally being more favorable. Here, the range of sample sizes across studies is provided to give the reader an idea of the numbers of individuals actually studied in this area.
Gender	Gender is believed to affect the presentations of both mental illness and criminal and antisocial behavior, and it may also affect the generalizability of results (i.e., to the opposite gender). Summaries of gender distributions of study participants are provided here.
Age	Age may also affect the presentations of both mental illness and criminal and antisocial behavior, and it may also affect the generalizability of results (i.e., to different age groups). Summaries of age distributions of study participants are provided here (e.g., youth, adult).
Location	Study location may affect the generalizability of results due to cultural, geopolitical, economic, and other factors characterizing different countries. The distributions of the national origins of the studies and their participants are presented here.
Diagnostic Systems	Mental disorders are conceptualized in research studies by the specific diagnostic system utilized by the researcher. Thus, the diagnostic system in any given study is important to note and critical to consider when comparing findings across studies and time periods. Historically, diagnostic systems have not been specified in a number of studies, making cross-study comparisons difficult. Even comparisons made across studies using different editions of the same system (e.g., the DSM-III and the DSM-IV) may be limited in validity.

(Continued)

(Continued)

Prevalence of Crime in the Disorder

Study Type	Number	Prevalence Rates	Crime Definition
Arrest rates Birth cohorts Community samples Homicide offenders Jailed detainees and prisoners Psychiatric inpatients	Numbers of studies of various types reporting the prevalence rates of crime and violence in individuals with mental disorders are listed here.	(See above.)	Definitions of "crime" may vary markedly across studies and can affect the generalizability of results as well as cross-study comparisons. Summaries of the operational definitions of crimes are provided here.
Total Number of Studies	This number indicates the total number of prevalence-rate studies of crime, violence, and antisocial behavior in populations with mental disorders. It is important to note that a greater quantity of studies does not necessarily translate into greater quality.		
	Sample Characteristics		
Size	(See above.)		
Gender	(See above.)		
Age	(See above.)		
Location	(See above.)		
Diagnostic Systems	(See above.)		

Nondisordered or community resident comparison group or general population baseline rates for either disorder or crime provided: **Total number of studies reporting these rates and percentage that these studies comprise of total studies located (in parentheses) are provided here.**

literature in this area or about the prevalence rates of mental disorders in criminal populations (and vice versa) must be made carefully, and any tentative conclusions drawn must take into account the inherent limitations of this "sampling" method. This book is, in part, an archive but one that is woefully incomplete and destined—due to the immense scope and ongoing nature of efforts in this area—to be a "work in progress." Our intent here is to inspire researchers to come up with new ideas, perhaps by identifying patterns within these collections.

From a qualitative point of view, some of the numbers in these tables are staggering. These should not mislead readers and should be interpreted with a critical eye. It must be remembered that this book provides merely a qualitative review, as opposed to a quantitative synthesis (i.e., meta-analysis), of the literature. From a qualitative point of view, these collections are indeed rich and speak volumes. Readers may appreciate the diversity of locations—in many instances worldwide—in which these studies of mental illness and crime have taken place.

However, some general observable points can be made. First and foremost, overall prevalence rates of mental disorders among criminal populations do appear to be higher—in most cases—relative to those observed in the general population, as do rates of criminal, violent, and antisocial behaviors among populations with mental illness. This statement—based on the work done here—cannot, however, be made without a whole host of caveats and acknowledged limitations. That being said, a confluence of these two lines of evidence has been used in the past to suggest the existence of a relationship between crime and schizophrenia specifically (Raine, 2006), and we are suggesting here that this phenomenon may extend into other mental illness categories as well—for what could be similar or entirely different reasons. Ultimately, this evidence is not definitive proof but merely one indicator of a potential relationship between mental illness and crime—a "red flag," of sorts, to call the attention of researchers and clinicians to an area worthy of further study (see below). It is also not necessarily an indication—due to methodological limitations—that either mental illness or crime *causes* the other (see below).

Second, some studies have examined the prevalence rates of multiple disorders within their sample populations. These may be multiple disorders within the same class (e.g., disorders of infancy, childhood, or adolescence; mood disorders; anxiety disorders; impulse control disorders; or personality disorders). However, a look at the prevalence-rate tables at the end of the chapters will also reveal that other authors have examined the prevalence rates of disorders from different classes (e.g., Langevin et al., 1982). This is an important step in understanding which types of mental disorders may be more common among criminal populations and may eventually speak to which sorts of disorders show stronger relationships with crime and violence. However, the literature in its current state does not yet allow for such conclusions to be reached, as studies reporting prevalence rates of disorders across classes do not generally use statistical techniques to ascertain which, if any, disorders are significantly more common.

Third, examination of prevalence-rate studies in this fashion allows the reader to gain an understanding of how the diagnostic nomenclature has evolved in the empirical literature and in clinical practice over the past several decades, as well as an appreciation for how the diagnostic terminology of one era can become significantly antiquated—and even wildly (almost embarrassingly) politically incorrect—in the years that follow. An example of an embarrassing and obsolete term is the clinical or medical use of the word "moron" (e.g., Szymusik, 1972)—a diagnostic label once used to represent intellectual disability and conceptually somewhat similar to what would be known in today's diagnostic systems as mental retardation. Although a reader may find the use of this term insensitive and even insulting, it must be remembered that these terms are often contextualized within a unique historical period, that their meanings have since changed.

Fourth, examination of prevalence-rate studies in this fashion allows the reader to gain an understanding of the types of samples (each with its own strengths and limitations) used in understanding the relationship between mental illness and crime, and of which type has been used more frequently.

Psychiatric Inpatient Studies. Are the rates of mental disorders in criminal populations highest among psychiatric inpatient studies? If so, one intuitive explanation might be that this merely reflects the nature of the individuals treated in these institutions (i.e., one would naturally expect to find higher rates of mental illness among psychiatric inpatients). That being said, it must be remembered that the facilities and institutions from which these samples are culled are forensic hospitals (called "special hospitals" in England) or specialized units rather than general psychiatric hospitals per se—indicating that these inpatients are characterized by some form of interaction with the criminal justice system. However, knowing the prevalence rates of these disorders among nonforensic inpatients within general psychiatric hospitals and units (i.e., including comparison groups from these facilities in psychiatric inpatient studies of crime and violence) would assist in ascertaining whether these rates reflect a specific criminal mental health population or the nature of psychiatric inpatients in general. Consequently, results from the numerous psychiatric inpatient studies (on which a sizeable portion of the current understanding of the relationship between mental illness and crime has been based) should be interpreted with this important caveat.

Do prevalence rates merely reflect deinstitutionalization or the criminalization of the mentally ill? One argument about findings of increased rates of individuals with mental illness among jail and prison populations could be that these figures merely represent the large numbers of deinstitutionalized mentally ill. One relatively simple way to crosscheck this assertion would be to examine the prevalence rates of mentally ill persons among incarcerated population samples in the United States in studies published before the 1980s (the beginning of the Reagan-era deinstitutionalization in the third wave of mental health reform efforts—see Chapter 12) and compare them with the rates in studies published since. Doing so using the studies catalogued in this book does not necessarily support this argument. For example, the prevalence rates of schizophrenia in studies of criminal populations in the United States before 1980, identified in Table 5.5, range (across study types) from 23.0 to 43.6%; after 1980, they range from 3.8 to 28.8%—suggesting rather a *reduction* in crime after deinstitutionalization. Although this approach is not incredibly scientific (as mentioned before, the sample of studies provided is not comprehensive or representative, so results must be interpreted with caution), it does suggest that the deinstitutionalization argument (an interesting one, admittedly) requires further empirical validation.

Another argument about these findings could be that they merely reflect the criminalization of the mentally ill—that is to say, they reflect contact with the criminal justice system involving crimes that may unfairly target the mentally ill (e.g., vagrancy, loitering) in an effort to rid the streets of those society finds undesirable (see Fradella & Smith-Casey, 2013). Although there may be some truth to this argument, one counter to it would be found if one were to examine the studies catalogued in this book to determine the types of charges and convictions among persons with mental illnesses. An overwhelming number of misdemeanor charges and convictions among the mentally ill would certainly support the assertion that they are being unfairly targeted by the criminal justice system (Fradella & Smith-Casey, 2013). In actuality, this endeavor is much more difficult than it sounds. On one hand, Table 5.5 indicates that individuals with schizophrenia are present among samples of homicide offenders, which suggests a capability of acts of extreme violence. On the other hand, Table 5.6 indicates that definitions of criminal behavior in populations of individuals with schizophrenia are often vague (e.g., charges or convictions for unspecified offenses). Lower-level misdemeanor offenses such as loitering or vagrancy are not separately specified in these studies. As such, this book may be ill-equipped to address this question, though future research should examine if the rates of arrests and convictions for such offenses are significantly increased among individuals with mental illness compared to those in the non–mentally ill population.

Problems With the Study of Crime and Violence in the Mentally Ill

A true understanding of the nature of the relationship between mental illness and crime remains—in its current state—in its infancy. Moving forward requires dispelling two assumptions that seem to have permeated throughout the public consciousness. The first is that all individuals with mental illness are criminal and violent. This dangerous assumption is not in any way helped by the sensationalized media coverage of acts of extreme violence by mentally ill individuals.

However, equally dangerous—and detrimental to the further understanding of the relationship between crime, violence, and mental illness—is the presumption that there is *no* relationship between mental illness and violence. This position is often a knee-jerk reaction by mental health professionals in response to highly publicized acts of extreme violence by individuals with mental illness. Such a reaction was observed in Adam Lanza's case, even though details of his mental health were sketchy. Eventually, after a brief period of public grieving, discussions of the contributions of mental illness to violence were silenced as the public conversation (arguably motivated by political reasons—another unfortunate influence in this area) morphed into a debate on the issue of gun control. An excellent opportunity for the beginnings of a rational, informed discussion about the relationship between mental illness and crime was sadly lost.

The Relationship

The first problem in the study of crime and violence in the mentally ill is the need for an appreciation of the tremendous complexity of this relationship. To that end, some general conceptual relationships based on the *role* of mental illness symptoms in crime and violence are suggested below:

Mental Illness Causes Crime and Violence. This statement is a tremendous oversimplification. That being said, according to this view, symptoms of mental illness are the motivations of criminal and violent behavior. Examples would be command auditory hallucinations to kill (which are not always followed) or religious delusions about sexual offending against children.

Mental Illness Contributes to (but Does Not Directly Cause) Crime and Violence. According to this view, the symptoms of mental illness are not the direct cause of criminal and violent behavior but contribute to it by impairing the processes that may have prevented—under normal circumstances—such behaviors from occurring. In other words, the symptoms of mental illnesses facilitate crime but are not the impetus for it. The symptoms did not cause the behaviors but certainly did nothing to help the individual *not* do them. Examples would be impaired judgment, impulsivity, and paranoia. This category would also include situational factors and preexisting (yet unrealized) tendencies toward crime and violence that are exacerbated by mental illness symptomatology. Examples of the former might be racism or having a "bad temper"; an example of the latter might be homelessness. One hypothesis from this perspective might be that, although mental illnesses in and of themselves do not contribute to crime and violence in any qualitative or quantitative way (e.g., schizophrenia more than depression), life is simply more difficult in general when one suffers from a mental disorder—of any kind—so the additive effects of these difficulties contribute to criminal and violent behavior.

Crime and Violence Occur in Spite of Mental Illness. According to this view, crime and violence occur independently from the influences of a mental disorder. Applicable here are the contributions of traditional and contemporary criminology to our understanding of criminal and violent behavior and its causes—social disorganization, differential association and social learning, anomie and strain theories, and labeling theory, to name a few. Such theories can certainly apply to individuals with full-blown mental illnesses, but they can also explain criminal and violent behavior occurring before the onset of mental disorder (a nuanced phenomenon not always addressed in studies of mental illness and crime).

Finally, it must be emphasized and understood that individuals with mental illness may commit crimes or engage in violent behavior for exactly the same banal reasons that people without mental illness do. Examples might include economic hardship (i.e., they needed money), getting into an argument with a family member or loved one (i.e., they got angry), or simply choosing this behavior (i.e., they wanted to and thought they could get away with it). Individuals with even the most severe forms of mental illness may have periods of lucidity, clarity, and symptom remission. In fact, when adhering to prescribed medication regimens, these individuals may even function at relatively normative levels. Crime, violence, and antisociality occurring during these periods thus cannot be directly attributed to the effects and influences of mental illness.

Methodological Limitations

The question about the relationship between mental illness and crime will ultimately be answered through research—results from scientific studies that are replicated over and over in different populations and across methods. One reason the "answer" is so elusive currently is that an enormous variety of studies have been conducted in this area, and these vary in levels of methodological quality and are inherently limited in various ways in terms of generalizability. Such methodological limitations should be kept in mind and hopefully corrected in future research efforts. Listed below are some methodological considerations:

Evolution of Methodologies. Examination of the collection of accumulated empirical work on mental illness and crime reveals a trend that occurs, more often than not, within the study of each individual illness category. Over decades of research, studies in any given subarea tend to "evolve" methodologically—usually progressing in level of sophistication from published clinical case studies (beginning with single cases and at times including small groups of cases) to more advanced descriptive studies (usually of modest-sized samples) and, ultimately, to the pinnacle of methodological sophistication—comparative studies. This "evolution" of sorts likely reflects the growth of scientific interest in any given disorder, beginning with its initial conceptualization or "discovery." It is only logical that this process would begin at a microlevel and progress with time to a more macrolevel—particularly in cases of rare disorders (which most mental disorders, in fact, are) wherein individuals presenting with those disorders would first need to be identified for study. Other factors may also contribute to the rate of methodological "growth" in studies of any given disorder, such as public need or interest in general, which may affect funding decisions by government agencies for more large-scale research endeavors.

This is not to say that empirical work representing the previous methodological stages is invalid or devoid of scientific merit. In fact, the roots of any solid comparative investigation lie in the rich clinical information provided by its case-report and descriptive-study predecessors. Moreover, there is arguably a trade-off that occurs within the methodological evolution of studies of mental illness, wherein the richness of singular clinical material must necessarily be sacrificed for the presentation of information from larger numbers of individuals in the more methodologically advanced comparative studies (i.e., a sort of a qualitative-quantitative compromise). Nonetheless, studies from earlier stages are limited in terms of generalizability—the highly sought-after brass ring that researchers reach for in their attempts to apply their findings to the larger problem at hand. Unfortunately, the current evolutionary "status" of the research of many mental disorders has not yet moved into the last stage, which limits our understanding of much of the earlier work in each illness subarea because, without a more developed understanding of these mental illnesses, we lack the context from which to evaluate the significance and generalizability of previous studies.

Even some contemporary research, however, suffers from limitations that may diminish the generalizability of salient findings. Many studies examining the link between mental illness and crime, for example, use participants from high-risk populations, which might involve selection bias (Walsh, Bachanan, & Fahy, 2002). This concern is magnified for studies using participants who are incarcerated because sampling from correctional institutions necessarily means drawing from a population of unsuccessful criminals—those who are caught and convicted. Offenders with SMIs are likely to be overrepresented in correctional populations because their disorders make it more difficult for them to evade capture.

Problematic Definitions of Criminal and Violent Behavior. Empirical work in any area of study relies heavily upon the proper identification and operationalization of key variables of interest. In the accumulated body of work on mental illness and crime, definitions of crime and violence in the literature are heterogeneous and inconsistent—even unclear and problematic. One common example is the study of violence in mentally ill persons who are high-security psychiatric inpatients. In this case, it would be very wrong to assume that just because a patient is detained in a high-security psychiatric facility she or he is violent. Many may not have a history of direct interpersonal violence (D. Murphy, personal communication, February 5, 2007; see Schug & Raine, 2009). Many other examples like this can be found; and a top priority for research in this area should be to ensure that concepts of crime, violence, aggression, and other forms of antisocial behavior are properly operationalized by its purveyors and critically examined by its consumers.

Lack of Comparison and Control Groups. Empirical work in many areas of the social sciences often requires the inclusion of comparison or control groups into research methodologies, which largely serve to ensure that any observable group characteristics are not caused or influenced by an intrinsic property of the study sample or some extraneous third variable. Studies of mental illness and crime have historically been notorious for their lack of proper comparison and control groups—a significant limitation to work in this area. In fact, reporting of baseline or comparison rates of mental illness in prevalence-rate studies of each of the classes of mental disorders has been abysmal (in Chapters 3 through 10, see the sections on the prevalence of crime in the disorder and of the prevalence of the disorder in crime). Although the provision of data for comparison has been improving with the advancing quality of studies conducted more recently in this area, much work is still needed to ensure sound research designs are employed, ones that include proper control groups.

The DSM

An inherent and necessary evil to the study of mental illness in general—and of mental illness and crime in particular—is the ever-changing nature of the major diagnostic systems in psychiatry. In the United States, the ***Diagnostic and Statistical Manual of Mental Disorder*** **(DSM)** is the primary tool used to define and diagnose mental illnesses. The DSM was first created by the American Psychiatric Association (APA) in 1952. Prior to its publication, the *Statistical Manual for the Use of Institutions for the Insane* (1918) was used. By design, the DSM has intentional, built-in obsolescence, with each version having a sort of "shelf life" while the next upgraded version is developed using new scientific knowledge acquired through research. Since the first edition of the DSM, it has gone through five major revisions: the DSM-II in 1968, the DSM-III in 1980, the DSM-IV in 1994, and the DSM-5 in 2013 (note the change from Roman to Arabic numerals in 2013). There have also been three minor revisions to the DSM over the years: the seventh printing of the DSM-II (1974), the DSM-III revised edition (1987), and the DSM-IV text revision (2000).

Structure of the DSM. First introduced in the DSM-III (1980) and included in each DSM edition through the DSM-IV-TR (2000) was a classification system that rated an individual on five separate axes or dimensions. The principal diagnosis occurred on either Axis I or Axis II. Axis I contained all of the clinical disorders and conditions other than personality disorders and mental retardation (renamed "intellectual disability" in the DSM-5), both of which were classified as Axis II disorders. The remaining axes were not necessary to make a diagnosis. Rather, they were used to assess other variables that should be taken into account during the clinical assessment of a patient. Specifically, Axis III contained diagnosis codes for general medical conditions, such as parasitic diseases; diseases of the blood, nervous, circulatory, respiratory, or digestive systems; injuries; or poisoning. Axis IV was reserved for reporting psychosocial and environmental problems that might have been influential factors for either diagnosis or treatment, such as educational problems, unemployment, homelessness, poverty, and inadequate access to health care. Finally, Axis V was reserved for reporting an individual's overall global assessment of functioning. Clinicians determined this by using the Global Assessment of Functioning (GAF) Scale. The scale ranges from 1, usually corresponding to an immediate suicide threat, to 100, indicating the possession of positive qualities and superior functioning. The DSM-5 has abandoned this multiaxial structure and replaced it with chapters containing disorders with common traits.

Diagnoses of disorders in the DSM are assigned identifying diagnostic and statistical numerical codes, which are fundamental to medical record keeping and which facilitate data collection and retrieval and the compilation of statistical information (these numerical codes are listed before the disorder names—a standard practice in clinical report writing and recordkeeping—when diagnostic criteria are presented in this book). The DSM-5 has also included identifying numerical codes from the World Health Organization's International Classification of Diseases (ICD), listed in parentheses and to be used upon publication of the ICD-10-CM. These codes are also provided in this book where appropriate (i.e., listed in parentheses after the DSM-5 codes and beginning with the letter "F"). Disorders may be further described using subtypes (mutually exclusive and jointly exhaustive phenomenological subgroupings within categories), as well as severity (e.g., mild, moderate, severe) and course specifiers (e.g., in partial remission, in full remission, prior history). Most classes of disorders outlined in the DSM (e.g., mood, psychotic, substance use, and anxiety disorders) have a "Not Otherwise Specified" (NOS) category in which the symptom presentation conforms to the general guidelines for a mental disorder in the diagnostic class, but the symptomatic picture does not meet the criteria for any of the specific disorders. In the DSM-5, the NOS category has been expanded into "other specified" disorders and "unspecified" disorders. The former applies to conditions that cause clinically significant distress or impairment yet do not meet full criteria for any of the disorders in that disorder class, and for which the clinician wishes to communicate the specific reason for which it does not. The latter is for conditions that are associated with impairment, do not meet full criteria for any of the other class disorders, and for which the clinician chooses *not* to communicate the reason that criteria are not met.

Two other key terms are important in the understanding of the diagnosis of mental illness with the DSM. The DSM's **polythetic approach** means that, to be diagnosed with a mental disorder, a person must meet a particular number of criteria out of a larger set of possible criterion symptoms. Finally, **comorbidity** is defined as the coexistence of mental disorders in one individual. Some researchers refer to lifetime comorbidity, meaning a diagnosis of two or more mental illnesses over the course of an individual's life span, regardless of age (e.g., a diagnosis of a major depressive disorder in one's early 20s and a later diagnosis of alcohol abuse in one's 50s). Others refer to the comorbidity of disorders occurring at a single point in time, as in an individual diagnosed with both bipolar disorder and cocaine dependence.

Common Criticisms of the DSM. The slow, deliberate revision process for the DSM is supposed to ensure that diagnostic practices reflect the most current, up-to-date, and empirically based conceptualizations of mental illness possible. But many critics challenge that assumption on numerous grounds.

Several commentators have derided the fact that approximately 70% of the APA's task force members for the DSM-5 are associated with the pharmaceutical industry (Cosgrove & Krimsky, 2012). Might market forces be driving the creation of diagnoses for the benefit of the profession and the pharmaceutical industry such that these "disorders" can be treated with the products sold by the companies with which the APA's DSM task force members are affiliated (Frances, 2012; Lafrance & McKenzie-Mohr, 2013; Sachdev, 2013)?

Another frequent criticism of the DSM is that it almost completely ignores the underlying causes of mental illness. Instead, the DSM defines mental disorders based on symptoms that are manifest, to statistically significant degrees, in clinical practice. Although this approach has led at least one critic to compare the DSM to a naturalist's field guide to birds (McHugh, 2005), three real problems result from focusing on symptomology to the exclusion of etiology: (1) the underlying pathology might be overlooked and, therefore, go untreated; (2) diagnosing people by symptomology undermines research, especially in behavioral genetics, by grouping patients together under a label even though they might otherwise have little in common; and (3) decisions regarding symptoms involve subjective judgment in both the patient and the clinician, leading to a lack of reliability in diagnoses.

The focus on symptomology over etiology notwithstanding, some challenge the APA's assertion that reliable and valid measures are being used to assemble the diagnostic symptoms for each disorder (Kendell & Jablensky, 2003). "[D]espite assurances that only data-driven modifications would be made, with each new edition of the DSM we have witnessed repeated instances of changes being made in the absence of sufficient data demonstrating that the new criteria are superior to the prior criteria" (Zimmerman, 2012, p. 444). This criticism is particularly acute for the DSM-5's classification of personality disorders (Verheul, 2012) and autism spectrum disorders (Ghaziuddin, 2010). Flaskerud (2010) summarized these concerns by asking, "do the diagnostic disorders defined by the DSM correspond or match up with the conditions that people in the real world have" (p. 687)?

> It has been argued that the DSM system of classification uses arbitrary cut-offs between normal and abnormal symptoms and behavior. The inability to establish validity lies partly with the fact that the DSM is a classification system without a theoretical (explanatory) basis or an agreed upon scientific model. Although DSM supporters claim a biopsychosocial model, these are actually three distinct and separate fields of thought. Currently mental disorders are conceptualized as biological conditions—they correspond, for example, to changes in the brain; as psychological conditions—we experience them cognitively and emotionally; and as sociocultural conditions—they involve our norms, values, character, and ideology. The DSM to date has not been able to integrate these different viewpoints to form a coherent framework for its diagnostic categories. (p. 687)

Flaskerud (2010) hints at another common criticism of the DSM—namely, that it is not value free. Civil rights activists have demonstrated repeatedly that many diagnoses have, over time, turned human differences into pathology because of stereotypes and cultural, political, and religious biases (Alarcón et al., 2009; Kleinplatz & Moser, 2005). Consider that "magical thinking" is a diagnostic criterion for schizophrenia. Yet "belief in clairvoyance, telepathy, or a 'sixth sense'" is viewed with esteem, if not reverence, in some cultures (Heitzeg, 1996, p. 225). Similarly, the DSM-II listed both homosexuality and "premenstrual dysphoric disorder" as mental illnesses; both were removed in subsequent editions, though premenstrual dysmorphic disorder is included in the DSM-5. Even in the most recent version of the DSM, "sexual dysfunctions and paraphilias utilise, refract, and ultimately naturalise troubling societal assumptions about gender" (Duschinsky & Chachamu, 2013, p. 49).

Medicalization. Behavioral and social scientists from a variety of disciplines, including psychiatry itself, have criticized the DSM for many years for its seemingly ever-expanding volume of diagnoses. The *Statistical Manual for the Use of Institutions for the Insane* identified 22 illnesses in 1918. The first DSM (1952) identified 106 mental disorders. By 2000, the DSM-IV-TR contained diagnostic criteria for 365 disorders, representing more than a three-fold increase. Does this massive expansion of diagnoses actually represent legitimate advances in psychiatric research and clinical practice, or is psychiatry creating diagnoses for a range of human behaviors that get labeled as disorders through a process referred to as **medicalization** (see Conrad & Schneider, 1992; Lane, 2007)?

Thomas Szasz, himself a medical doctor with a specialization in psychiatry, is one of the most outspoken critics of medicalization. Indeed, since the publication of his book *The Myth of Mental Illness: Foundations of a*

Theory of Personal Conduct in 1961, Szasz has been considered the father of the so-called anti-psychiatry movement in the United States. As the title of his book suggests, Szasz does not believe there is such a thing as mental illness. Rather, he feels that medicine, as a powerful institution of social control, has simply labeled everyday problems of living as mental illnesses and done so within the cloak of science that makes it nearly impossible for laypersons to understand what has truly transpired.

Szasz does not dispute that there are organic illnesses, such as brain lesions, that cause behaviors that appear to be deviant to those without such organic diseases. Nor does Szasz contend that such diseases cause real suffering. Instead, he asserts that "most psychological disorders do not exist at all, and those that do are actually physical diseases with mental consequences" (Szasz, 1994, p. 34). In other words, he takes issue with calling organic illnesses diseases of the *mind* rather than physical diseases of the *brain*.

Szasz is not alone in his critique of mental illness. Consider the landmark study conducted by Rosenhan (1973), which led to the publication of his famous article "Being Sane in Insane Places." In it, Rosenhan and seven colleagues, all of whom were ostensibly in good mental health, got admitted to psychiatric hospitals by complaining they heard voices. They did not exhibit any other signs of psychosis. And, once admitted, they behaved perfectly normally. Yet hospital staff detected none of these perfectly healthy people. "Once a person is designated abnormal, all of his other behaviors and characteristics are colored by that label. Indeed, the label is so powerful that many of the pseudopatients' normal behaviors were overlooked or profoundly misinterpreted" (Rosenhan, 1973, p. 253).

In support of the argument that mental illness is socially constructed, Szasz points to the history and development of the DSM. Its evolution is largely political. Today, for example, definitions are arrived at after consensus is reached by the committees and subcommittees comprised of representatives from various stake-holding groups. Accordingly, Szasz views the DSM

> not [as a] classification of mental disorders that "patients have," but [as] rosters of officially accredited psychiatric diagnoses. This is why in psychiatry, unlike in the rest of medicine, members of "consensus groups" and "task forces," appointed by officers of the APA, make and unmake diagnoses, the membership sometimes voting on whether a controversial diagnosis is or is not a disease. For more than a century, psychiatrists constructed diagnoses, pretended that they are diseases, and no one in authority challenged their deceptions. The result is that few people now realize that diagnoses are not diseases. (Szasz, 1994, p. 34)

Examining any number of diagnoses can offer support for Szasz's critique of the DSM. As one article in *The New York Times* (Sharkey, 1999) put it, "a good percentage of any prison's criminal population would seem to fit the criteria for Antisocial Personality Disorder"; yet "how could Hollywood or Sunday morning television media-punditry thrive without personalities who exhibit the symptoms of Histrionic Personality Disorder" (paras. 5–6)? Even the most recent edition of the DSM contains a host of diagnoses that give pause for thought to both laypeople and clinicians alike. For example, normal grief qualifies for a diagnosis of a major depressive disorder; The label generalized anxiety disorder obscures the "already fuzzy boundary" between this diagnosis and "the worries of everyday life" (Frances, 2012, para. 19); and "the everyday forgetting characteristic of old age will now be misdiagnosed as Minor Neurocognitive Disorder, creating a huge false positive population of people who are not at special risk for dementia" (Frances, 2012, para. 13).

Given the backlash against the ever-growing number of diagnoses, the chairperson of the APA's DSM-5 task force promised that it would not increase the number of mental disorders. But the raw numbers may not tell the whole story. The DSM-5 has added some very controversial diagnoses, such as gambling addiction, binge eating, and disruptive mood dysregulation disorder (DMD)—a diagnosis that has the potential to pathologize childhood temper tantrums (Frances, 2012). The DSM-5 also added "'caffeine withdrawal' as a diagnosis—characterized by a withdrawal headache plus at least one other symptom, such as drowsiness, that interferes with some aspect of functioning" (Rosenberg, 2013, para. 13). Other disorders, however, have been collapsed, the most controversial of which concerns Asperger's syndrome. Asperger's—a label that some claimed pathologized quirkiness—was classified as a distinct disorder from autism in the DSM-IV. In the DSM-5, however, it is now "a subtype of a newly consolidated single diagnosis of 'autism spectrum disorder'" (Rosenberg, 2013, para. 11).

Finally, it should be noted that, with the notable exception of autism, which is now harder to diagnose, many of the changes contained in the DSM-5 actually loosen psychiatric diagnoses, which not only contributes to ever-increasing medicalization but also threatens such diagnostic hyperinflation (Frances, 2012) that upwards of half the U.S. population could qualify for having a diagnosable mental disorder (Rosenberg, 2013).

Painful experience with previous DSMs teaches that, if anything in the diagnostic system can be misused and turned into a fad, it will be. Many millions of people with normal grief, gluttony, distractibility, worries, reactions to stress, the temper tantrums of childhood, the forgetfulness of old age, and "behavioral addictions" will soon be mislabeled as psychiatrically sick and given inappropriate treatment (Frances, 2012, para. 22).

Using the DSM to Evaluate the Link between Mental Illness and Crime. All of the previously mentioned criticisms need to be kept in mind when studying the intersection of mental illness and crime, especially because, to a large degree, the evolution of the predominant diagnostic systems are inextricably tied to research (the tables at the end of Chapters 3 through 8 illustrate this phenomenon). Consequently, a limitation to consider is the difficulty of comparing studies using more recent versions of the DSM to earlier studies that used older versions. Given the fact that the diagnostic conceptualization of some disorders has changed markedly over the years—along with the nomenclatures in many cases—such comparisons may be invalid, or (at the very least) they need to be entertained with caution.

Overwhelming, the information in this book is based predominantly upon the DSM-IV-TR. Although the DSM-5 incorporates some significant paradigm shifts in its conceptualization of various disorders, it will be several years before research is published examining crime within the framework of new DSM-5 diagnostic criteria. We look forward with great excitement to how the DSM-V will be applied and incorporated into the study of the potential relationships between mental illness and criminal, violent, and antisocial behavior. For now, this edition is constrained by the availability of the published research that, for the past two decades, has been predominantly linked to the DSM-IV's diagnostic system. Hence, the material presented in this edition of the book draws upon that work, although we have integrated DSM-5 diagnostic criteria throughout Chapters 3 through 10 and commented, when applicable, about how changes might affect future research on mental illness and crime. Like the disorders contained in any edition of the DSM, research that utilizes the DSM-5 may alter our understanding of how mental illness and crime are linked. Some older ideas about how crime and violence relate to mental illness may fall by the wayside while other novel ideas may emerge. In the end, this book can only be a "work in progress" (much like the DSM itself) rather than an ultimate, definitive statement about the relationship between mental illness and crime.

The Ones That Are

A final problem in the study of mental illness and crime is the manner in which the topic has been perceived and misperceived (and to a fair degree outright resisted) by others. One of the authors of this book, in his career as an educator and researcher, has given numerous professional talks and trainings about the relationship between schizophrenia and crime. This topic is generally considered a "hard sell"; on many occasions, in front of audiences containing a fair number of semihostile mental health professionals and researchers, he has felt as if he had to avoid this "third rail" of research while convincing others that it is an important area of study with significant implications. Along the way, he has developed a philosophy about the relationship between schizophrenia and crime and violence that has allowed him to break through some of the resistance—effectively enabling him to become an ambassador of sorts when it comes to the topic of mental illness and crime. The concept of the "three ironies" of schizophrenia and crime research has served him well as an introduction to the topic, and he has begun many lectures with the following information:

Current understanding of the link between schizophrenia and violence across empirical and public spheres is characterized by three ironies. First, although significant empirical evidence indicates a strong relationship between schizophrenia and crime and violence, scientists appear transfixed upon the reification of this relationship rather than moving forward with a new generation of research into common risk factors and etiological mechanisms (Raine, 2006). Second, although researchers are hesitant to address this relationship, possibly due to fears of amplifying negative stigmatization (Arseneault, Moffitt, Caspi, Taylor, & Silva, 2000; Raine, 2006), public opinion appears guided by the misperception that *all* individuals with schizophrenia are violent and dangerous (Schwartz, Petersen, & Skaggs, 2001), a view attributable largely to the sensationalized accounts of schizophrenia-associated violence that have proliferated through the popular media (Junginger, 2006; Raine, 2006). Third, although the public maintains this grossly distorted view of violence in schizophrenia, most schizophrenic individuals, in fact, pose no risk for violence (Joyal, Putkonen, Paavola, & Tiihonen, 2004). Together, these "ironies" indicate an urgent need for clarification, and the failure to address one important question: What causes only *some* individuals with schizophrenia to become violent? Ignoring this question, it seems, precludes both reducing the stigma unjustly attached to schizophrenic persons who are not violent and advancing the understanding of those who are.

Thus, the concept of *the ones that are* (meaning the small number of individuals with mental illness who actually become criminally violent) has become a mantra in Schug's work. Focusing on *the ones that are* addresses the problem of crime and violence in mental illness head-on—showing a curiosity and desire to understand it in its true form (in the spirit of Baltes and Staudinger [2000], who assert that true wisdom involves the acknowledgement and acceptance of the limitations of our own knowledge). This approach involves neither hiding our collective heads in the sand and pretending the problem does not exist nor sensationalizing and overgeneralizing it into something that it is not. Focusing on *the ones that are* allows us to bypass the negative feelings associated with stigmatizing an already vulnerable population and goes a long way toward reducing and possibly even ending that stigma altogether. Focusing on *the ones that are* allows us an opportunity as researchers and clinicians to move past the intractable stalemate that has impeded progress in this area of knowledge for far too long. It is with this philosophy and spirit that we humbly present the information in the following chapters.

Organization of the Book

This book is not intended solely as a review of the literature related to mental illness and crime; rather, it serves as a proposed framework for conceptualizing and understanding the relationship between mental disorders and various forms of antisocial behavior, a framework that (hopefully) facilitates and encourages future study. Chapter 2 is, in essence, an abnormal psychology "primer," designed to provide readers (who may or may not have experience in this discipline) with the more basic terminology and concepts for understanding the rest of the material.

Chapters 3 through 10 cover the major classes of mental disorders in the order that they are presented in the DSM IV-TR (2000). Each of these chapters begins with an opening vignette illustrating how criminal or violent behavior may present itself within the context of a disorder from that chapter. Diagnostic criteria from the DSM-5 are presented for each disorder, followed by conceptualizations from various theoretical perspectives that are useful in the understanding of that particular disorder. Prevalence-rate studies of the "disorder in crime" (i.e., the disorder in populations committing crime) and of the "crime in disorder" (i.e., the criminal behavior in populations with that disorder) are presented separately for each disorder, either in boxes or in tables.

Also included in each chapter are reviews of studies related to different aspects of the relationship between the various disorders and criminal and violent behavior, along with "origins of crime and violence" sections that present theoretical explanations for how and why these behaviors may manifest in individuals with mental disorders. The final three chapters discuss legal applications and implications: Chapter 11 covers issues related to the intersection of mental illness and law in terms of competency to stand trial and criminal responsibility, and Chapter 12 provides a discussion of other legal and public policy issues concerning the social control of dangerousness. Finally, Chapter 13 serves as an epilogue on mental illness and criminal justice policy.

How to Use This Book

Although this book was intended for traditional use as an undergraduate or graduate textbook, its multilayered content can serve a variety of purposes. Additionally, it offers several key features that are intended to be useful to readers of different types. First, key terms and review questions at the end of each chapter are included to assist students in organizing and retaining the large quantities of information within each chapter. These study aids will be particularly useful for those who are being exposed to concepts related to mental illness or criminal justice for the first time. For students and researchers, chapters on the mental disorders are presented with a very logical and consistent structure. Case vignettes are presented first, giving a human "face" to each disorder. Disorders are defined up front and historically, and then theoretical conceptualizations and diagnostic criteria are presented. This thorough investigation of how each disorder has been described and understood is followed by a compendium of research on that disorder (and crime) organized into tables; these tables are also summarized in "A Closer Look" boxes, and various concepts and topics related to the relationships between the individual disorders and crime are presented.

Readers wanting to delve deeper into what is empirically known about the relationship between mental illness and crime are encouraged to spend more time with the compendiums in each chapter—gaining a greater appreciation for the types of studies conducted in these areas and for their strengths and weaknesses. We hope that these compendiums may even serve as a beacon, guiding interested readers toward consulting original research—and even toward formulating critical opinions and hypotheses of their own about the relationship between mental illness and crime.

KEY TERMS

clinical psychology

comorbidity

Diagnostic and Statistical Manual of Mental Disorder (DSM)

forensic behavioral science

medicalization

neuropsychology

polythetic approach

serious mental illnesses

social control

REVIEW QUESTIONS

1. Describe the major methodological limitations of research on crime and mental illness.
2. Compare and contrast behavioral science "in," "and," and "of" the law.
3. Other than medicalization, summarize the major criticisms of the DSM.
4. What is medicalization? Evaluate the evidence of medicalization. Integrate the critiques of medicalization from both the anti-psychiatry movement and from opponents of at least three disorders contained in the DSM-5.

2

Abnormal Psychology Primer

EDWARD THEODORE GEIN

Ed Gein was born in La Crosse, Wisconsin, on August 6, 1906. Once known as America's most famous murderer, he and his crimes served as inspiration for the movies *Psycho*, *The Texas Chainsaw Massacre*, and *The Silence of the Lambs*.

Gein was raised in an oppressive home environment dominated by a devoutly religious mother. Additionally, beginning in childhood, Gein was ambiguous about his masculinity. He had considered amputation of his penis on several occasions and had also considered transsexual surgery—though this process at the time was very costly and frightening. Given these circumstances, Gein needed another way of "turning female" on a part-time basis.

Between 1947 and 1954, Gein opened an estimated 40 graves in nocturnal raids of local cemeteries. He removed whole corpses, as well as select bits and pieces. From these, he made domestic decorations (skulls mounted on bedposts, severed skullcaps as bowls, mobiles out of noses, lips, and labia, and a belt out of nipples), and from human skin he upholstered chairs and fashioned lampshades and wastebaskets. For ceremonial occasions, such as dancing underneath the moon, he wore a woman's scalp and face, a skinned-out "vest" complete with breasts, and female genitalia strapped above his own. Gein found a small degree of contentment by donning this other sex and personality, though his grave robbing eventually failed to satisfy deeper needs.

On December 8, 1954, 51-year-old Mary Hogan disappeared from her job at a tavern in Pine Grove, Wisconsin; and, three years later, on November 16, 1957, 58-year-old Bernice Worden disappeared from her Plainview hardware store under suspiciously similar circumstances. Both crime scenes displayed obvious evidence of foul play; and, though Gein was considered a suspect in the first crime, no charges were filed at that time. Evidence from the second murder, however, led police directly to Gein's home, where his grisly collection of macabre human remains was discovered—along with Worden's headless, disemboweled, and mutilated body hanging like a deer-hunter's kill from the rafters of a shed behind the house.

Gein willingly confessed to both murders and was found innocent by reason of insanity. He spent the remainder of his life in Central State Hospital at Waupin, Wisconsin. He is thought to be linked to at least two additional murders.

Grave robbing, murder, postmortem mutilation, and the manipulation of human remains could all be considered behaviors that are outside the normal range of human experience. Some crimes are so horrific and unspeakable that many feel the individuals who commit them *must* be deranged, sick, or mentally ill. Was Ed Gein mentally ill? On one hand, most of us would not have the mind to even comprehend the reasoning behind his crimes, or to plan them—let alone the heart, "stomach," or will to carry them off. On the other hand, as horrific and incomprehensible as Gein's crimes may seem, evidence for some degree of normalcy cannot be ignored. For example, a decade of these sorts of behaviors could not go unnoticed without at least a minimum level of mental functioning, intellectual ability, and capacity for reasoning on the part of the offender. Additionally, Gein's crimes were at least in part based upon what may be considered a practical and even rational solution to a very significant problem: a lifelong desire to become a member of the opposite sex coupled with the complete lack of financial, social, and psychological resources to do so. Though Gein's crimes are clearly inexcusable, in his own mind, they likely made sense, served a purpose, and helped satisfy a very basic need—the need to feel genuine about one's own existence. Ironically, Gein's behaviors may ultimately have been the one thing that made him feel more normal—more "human." Furthermore, it must be remembered that crimes equally as horrific as those listed here have been committed by others for what appears to be no reason at all. Ultimately, it is important to understand that the most bizarre, unexplainable, and even horrific acts committed by human beings in actuality merely represent the extreme ends of thought, emotion, and behavior that exist on a continuum with normative human experience. Was Ed Gein mentally ill? An answer to this question may only come after answering an even more important, over-arching question: What is mental illness?

What Is Mental Illness?

Any discussion of the relationship between mental illness and criminal behavior must first begin with a firm understanding of the concept of mental illness. Unfortunately, this concept can still prove to be rather elusive, despite the thousands of years of references to various forms of abnormal behavior from around the world, numerous attempts to categorize and classify different forms of mental illness, and significant efforts from a variety of schools of thought to devise theoretical frameworks for understanding how these illnesses develop and persist over the course of the lifetime. Even one of the most widely used psychiatric classification systems in the world, the fourth edition (with text revision) of the *Diagnostic and Statistical Manual of Mental Disorders* (DSM-IV-TR; APA, 2000), admits the difficulty of arriving at a definition: "The term ['mental disorders'] appears in the title because we have not found an appropriate substitute . . . no definition adequately specifies the precise boundaries for the concept of 'mental disorder' (p. xxx)." Although no such overt statements are included in its recently published successor, the DSM-5 (APA, 2013), the difficulties in effectively conceptualizing mental disorders are nonetheless implied in the introductory material of this new diagnostic nosology (a word used often in this book, referring to a type of disease classification system—see below).

Yet, philosophically speaking, the elusiveness of mental illness is what contributes to its intrigue and mystery. A common virus can be diagnosed and treated rather easily by a visit to a doctor, undertaking conventional medical tests of bodily functioning, and the administration of the appropriate antiviral medication. Mental illness, however, is different. The "mind," as it were, is not necessarily subject to the laws and principles of physics, chemistry, and biology that govern physical medicine. The mind remains an abstract concept, and our understanding of the seat of the mind (at least in Western views)—the brain—remains largely a mystery even to advanced neuroscientists. So anything attributed to the mind, particularly illness, remains shrouded in a veil of secrecy—a daunting thought given the near century and a half of scientific efforts devoted to its study and how much of the nature of its functioning still remains behind the veil.

One problem with the term mental illness is that it implies some form of suffering that is localized only to the "mind"—as if physical causes or symptoms would be absent and attributable more so to physical or medical conditions. Although, historically, there have been documented conditions that appeared to be derived from purely psychological causes (e.g., hysteria—see below), it is now generally believed that there is just as much "physical" to mental illness as there is "mental."

The range of human experience—our thoughts, behaviors, and emotions—is largely dimensional; that is to say, it is largely experienced on a continuum or spectrum (in fact, the DSM-5 has made a bold move toward this dimensional conceptualization of mental disorders). We are, for the most part, never entirely rational or completely absent of rational thought, never entirely happy or completely absent of happiness, and never entirely frightened or completely absent of fear. Rather, our experiences tend to exist somewhere in the middle, in the varying degrees of rationality, happiness, and fear. This circumstance allows for the wide range of human cognitive abilities, behaviors, and emotions that characterize us as a species and differentiate between us as individuals, and it also accounts for both the dramatic fluctuations and subtle differences within ourselves in thought, behavior, and emotion that we experience in our day-to-day lives. Mental illness is a combination of outward behavioral expression and inner experience; and these behaviors and experiences also exist on a continuum or dimensional model. Therefore, these pathological processes may exist in all of us to some degree, though, in many, they are at such small degrees as to be imperceptible to one's self or to others.

One helpful way to grasp the concept of mental illness may be to examine the different ways in which it has been defined historically in the literature. These definitions, as will be seen, comprise different attitudes and points of view and still affect, in varying degrees, conceptualizations of mental illness today. In all, there are five general ways in which mental illness has been defined throughout history.

Mental Illness Is a Deviation From Social Expectations

Mental illness has been defined as "quantitative deviations from the normal"—that is, behaviors or characteristics that deviate (in the statistical sense) from the population norm. Typically, this deviation is conceptualized as being in the negative direction from expectations; otherwise, any unusual quality (such as high intelligence or outstanding memory abilities) would be classified as a disorder. For example, Michael Kearney has an IQ that reportedly exceeds 200 (exceptionally high and statistically deviant, given that the mean of traditionally defined IQ is 100 and the standard deviation is 15); he graduated from the University of South Alabama with honors when he was only 10 years old, at the age when most children are finishing the fifth grade. These abilities and characteristics are extremely rare, but, because our culture values achievements such as these, they are not viewed as signs of mental disorder. Usually, behaviors that deviate from social expectations (such as Ed Gein's grave robbing, manipulation of human remains, and even homicides) are also statistically rare. Interestingly, when a formerly unusual behavior becomes too frequent, it stops being a sign of nonconformity and starts becoming the expected behavior or norm (Nietzel, Speltz, McCauley, & Bacon, 1997).

Any discussion of "abnormality" (i.e., in the context of, say, abnormal psychology) must be superseded by the answering of a more fundamental question—what is normal? Normality is clearly a relative concept, based upon comparisons with others in a group, culture, or society. In this sense, "normal" becomes nothing more than what occurs most frequently in others. If we examine a frequency distribution of traits or behaviors observed in society, this becomes clearer (see Figure 2.1). In this illustration, the trait or behavior could be depression, anxiety, or even sex drive; and "normal" becomes what is the same or similar to what most others experience.

Deviation from social expectations as a definition of mental illness is problematic in several aspects. First, there are many behaviors that are statistically deviant and undesirable but are not disorders (e.g., behavior that is criminal, discourteous, ignorant, morally repugnant, or disadvantageous). For a man, being five feet tall is statistically deviant and is presumably undesirable, but it is not considered a disorder. Second, this definition ignores characteristics that are not rare but are still problematic and require treatment. Third, it does not account for how rare a condition must be in order to qualify as a disorder. For example, schizophrenia is thought to be present in 1% of adults in North America—a reasonable definition of rare. Alcohol abuse, however, may be present in 10% of American adults—a less adequate definition of rare, though both are considered disorders. Finally, deviation-based definitions imply that conformity to social expectations is the equivalent of mental health, which is not necessarily true in all cases.

Mental Illness Is What Mental Health Professionals Treat

Mental illness has also been defined historically as what mental health professionals treat. This definition is commonly used in *epidemiology*, or the scientific study of the onset and frequency of disorders in certain populations. Problems also exist with this definition. First, not everyone who consults a clinician is suffering symptoms. For example, individuals may consult mental health professionals to learn how to communicate better with their spouses, improve the quality of their relationships, be more effective parents, or be happier in their jobs. Second, this definition assumes that all people—regardless of the symptoms of their mental illness, the availability of treatment, or their ability to pay for it—are equally likely to seek treatment. This assumption is incorrect: for example, it would underestimate the frequency of a disorder among the poor (who are least likely to receive treatment) or among individuals whose cultures look negatively upon those who seek mental health services.

Mental Illness Is Subjective Distress

A third definition for mental illness is that it is subjective distress; in other words, mental illness can be defined as the personal experience of suffering by an individual. Personal distress and unhappiness often accompany mental

Figure 2.1 What Is Normal? Frequency Distribution

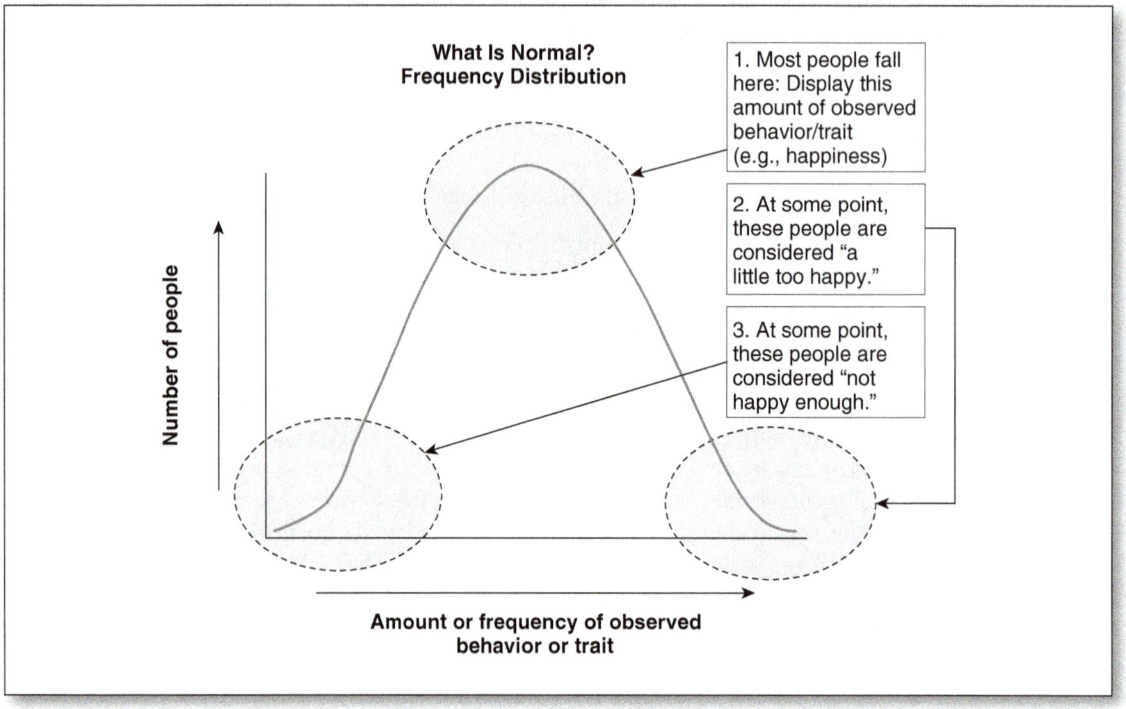

disorders; however, these alone cannot define disorder. One major criticism of this definition is that it does not distinguish between a temporary upset that may accompany stressful events and distress that is chronic, intense, and seemingly unrelated to external stressors. Furthermore, certain patterns of behavior (i.e., personality disorders) cause little or no apparent distress for the individuals suffering from them but may create immense problems and distress for the people in their lives. Although subjective distress may appear to be absent in these cases, such conditions should not be disqualified as mental disorders.

Mental Illness Is a Label for Disliked Actions

Fourth, mental illness has been defined as a label for disliked actions. There are those who argue that most mental disorders represent nothing more than labels assigned by mental health professionals to individuals whose behavior is disturbing to others. For example, recall from Chapter 1 that Thomas Szasz argued that mental illness should only refer to those relatively few behavioral problems that are clearly traceable to organic or biological causes. Labeling as mentally ill those who fall outside this category causes harm by stigmatizing them; and labels may lead to the imposition of treatment, which invades people's privacy and limits their freedom. This skeptical view has declined in influence recently because it appears to trivialize the problems of people in whom no specific biological malfunction has been found but whose troubles are very real to them. On balance, this view fails to account for the fact that behavioral problems often do not go away, sometimes worsen if unlabeled, and often improve when treated.

Mental Illness Is a Dysfunction That Causes Harm

Finally and perhaps most suitably, mental illness can be defined as a dysfunction that causes harm (i.e., harmful dysfunction). In this two-pronged approach, "dysfunction" refers to the failure of a biological or psychological mechanism to operate as it is designed. Consequently, there is a failure of a person's internal mechanisms (e.g., thought, emotions, or perceptions of the world) to perform their designated functions. "Dysfunction" is a *scientific* term, based in evolutionary biology. "Harm," on the other hand, refers to the consequences of dysfunction that a society or individual considers as negative. It is, in contrast to "dysfunction," a *value* term—a social construct based upon what we as society decide. Wakefield (1992) argues that disorder, as a concept, lies on the boundary between the given natural world and a constructed social world. The order that is disturbed when one has a disorder is simultaneously biological and social, and neither alone is sufficient to justify the label "disorder." Defining mental disorders as harmful dysfunction is not ideal for all circumstances and purposes, and it is not always entirely clear. For example, how much impairment must appear before it becomes "dysfunction"? Are some psychological conditions dysfunctional in one culture but functional in others? When do the consequences of dysfunction cease to be merely annoying and become harmful? Defining mental disorders as harmful dysfunction appears to be the most workable, least arbitrary approach, and the one that captures both the objective impairment and the subjective harm that is usually associated with the concept of mental disorders.

Mental Disorder and the DSM

Clinicians and other mental health professionals require a more practical definition of mental illness in order to diagnose and treat effectively individuals suffering from these conditions. The DSM and other diagnostic systems attempt to provide such a definition, though even the APA admits that the concept of mental disorder—similar to many other concepts in medicine and science—lacks a consistent operational definition that is appropriate for all situations. Although many of the concepts traditionally used to define mental disorder (e.g., distress, dysfunction, dyscontrol, disadvantage, disability, inflexibility, irrationality, syndromal pattern, etiology, and statistical deviation) are useful indicators for mental disorder, none is equivalent to the concept, and different situations call for different definitions (APA, 2000).

Impairment: The "I" Word

The DSM-IV-TR defines mental disorder as a clinically significant behavioral or psychological pattern that occurs in an individual and that is associated with present distress (e.g., a painful symptom) or disability (i.e., impairment in one or more important areas of functioning) or with a significantly increased risk of suffering death, pain, disability, or an important loss of freedom (APA, 2000). Crucial to this definition is the word **impairment**—to be considered a mental disorder the condition and its symptoms must cause significant difficulties in a major area or areas of an individual's life, such as school, work, family, or social relationships. By incorporating the term impairment, the DSM-IV-TR definition addresses Wakefield's (1992) argument for a socially determined objective criterion for harm.

In the DSM-5, this definition has been modified slightly. In it, a mental disorder is defined as the following:

> . . . a syndrome characterized by clinically significant disturbance in an individual's cognition, emotion regulation, or behavior that reflects a dysfunction in the psychological, biological, or developmental processes underlying mental functioning. Mental disorders are usually associated with significant distress or disability in social, occupational, or other important activities. (APA, 2013, p. 20)

Thus, the current DSM-5 definition remains consistent with that of the previous edition and congruent with Wakefield's (1992) conceptualization of a mental disorder as harmful dysfunction.

Additionally, this syndrome or pattern must not be merely an expectable and culturally sanctioned response to a particular event, for example, the death of a loved one. Whatever its original cause, it must currently be considered a manifestation of a behavioral, psychological, or biological dysfunction in the individual. Neither deviant behavior (e.g., political, religious, or sexual) nor conflicts that are primarily between the individual and society are mental disorders unless the deviance or conflict is a symptom of a dysfunction in the individual, as described previously (APA, 2000, p. xxxi; APA, 2013).

Misconceptions and Limitations

According to the DSM, a common misconception is that a classification of mental disorders classifies people when, actually, what are being classified are disorders that people have. For this reason, the text of the DSM avoids

Figure 2.2 Dimensional Conceptualization of Abnormality

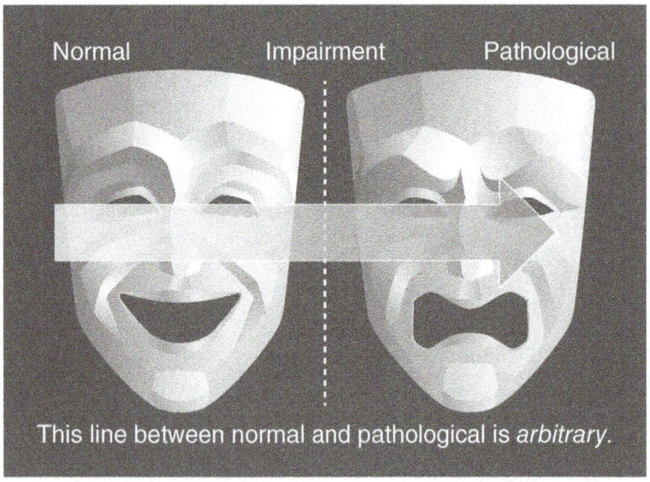

the use of such expressions as "a schizophrenic" or "an alcoholic" and instead uses the more accurate, but admittedly more cumbersome, "an individual with schizophrenia" or "an individual with alcohol dependence." Another misconception is the implied distinction between "mental" disorders and "physical" disorders. There is much "physical" symptomatology in "mental" disorders, and much "mental" symptomatology in "physical" disorders.

Furthermore, the DSM adopts a categorical approach—operating under the assumption that mental disorders are discreet illnesses or circumscribed pathological entities that are either present or absent—much in the same way conditions are conceptualized under the medical model (though, as stated before, the newly published DSM-5 has made efforts toward incorporating a dimensional approach to diagnosis). The aforementioned example of the virus helps to illustrate this point. A virus is either present in the human body, or it is not, and the characteristic symptomatic manifestations of that virus will similarly be either present or absent. Mental disorders, however, generally describe patterns of thoughts, feelings, or behaviors that exist on a continuum with normal human experience at one end and pathological experience at the other. A person may experience these patterns at different levels of intensity or severity: they may feel slightly sad or tense or be literally immobilized by weeks of deep depression or gripped by unimaginable anxiety. They cannot, however, "slightly" have a cold, the flu, a heart condition, or cancer. Importantly, the border or line designating impairment is an arbitrary one—a boundary socially constructed on the basis of what we as society consider to be normative experience (see Figure 2.2). Fortunately, the DSM acknowledges the significant limitations of its own categorical approach (APA, 2000, 2013).

Mental Illness: A Historical Overview

The concept of mental illness has evolved and changed throughout history, and some of the earliest evidence of our species suggests mankind's continual struggle with abnormalities in behavior and attempts to understand and ameliorate them. Consequently, a historical overview of the evolution of mental illness as a concept is helpful here.

Ancient Times and Supernatural Forces

Prior to the Egyptian and Mesopotamian cultures of around 3500–3000 BCE, it was believed that abnormal behavior reflected the presence of evil spirits or other overpowering supernatural forces. Human skulls dating back to the Stone Age have been found with evidence of trephining, a crude form of surgery practiced during this period that involved boring a hole through a person's cranium in order to allow evil spirits a means to escape. Evil spirits and demons were also blamed for abnormal behavior in ancient Chinese, Egyptian, and Hebrew civilizations. For example, according to the biblical account, Israel's first king, Saul, was said to be troubled by evil spirits and was treated with calming music. "David took the lyre and played it . . . so Saul was refreshed, and was well, and the evil spirit departed from him (I Samuel 16: 23 Revised Standard Version). Abnormality was sometimes interpreted as divine punishment for disobedience or other misbehavior. For example, Nebuchadnezzar, King of Babylon, was said to be stricken with lycanthropy (the belief that one is a wolf) as divine retribution for his boastfulness (Daniel 4: 28–33). The king had to live in the wild until, after acknowledging God's power, his reason was restored, and he was reinstated. Treatments in these civilizations included prayer and faith healing, possibly coinciding with the movement of planets or stars in hopes of enhancing results; exorcism rituals designed to scare, drown, pummel, or whip evil spirits out of the host body; the use of mixtures of animal excrement and blood, concocted to poison evil spirits; and treatments designed to correct biological processes related to abnormality, such as rest, exercise, peaceful activities, and improved diet (Nietzel et al., 1997).

The Birth of the Medical Tradition: The Classical Period

The development of philosophy by the Greeks around 600–500 BCE introduced the belief that humans were capable of understanding and taking control of themselves and their world; and with this came the Greeks' increasing knowledge of the human body. Hippocrates (ca. 460–377 BCE), known as the "father of medicine," argued that all illnesses had physical causes. In his treatise, *On the Nature of Man*, he concluded that mental disorders were also biological in nature and could be traced to imbalances among the four major fluids, or *humors*, of the body: black bile, yellow bile, blood, and phlegm. Even within the long medical tradition that preceded Hippocrates, the humors were considered to be causes of illness (e.g., by Pythagorean scholars from the sixth century BCE). There were other humors as well, but these four came to be regarded as primary. In Greek medicine, it was understood that food digested in the body was transformed into blood, bones, and muscle. It was conceived that the humors developed from material that was indigestible or surplus. Excesses or deficiencies in the humors caused illness (Stelmack & Stalikas, 1991). If humors became visible as in the color of yellow bile in vomiting or in the expectoration of mucus through coughing, they served as symptoms of illness.

In a complex theory of humors, Hippocrates linked the four primary elements of matter, the four qualities (hot, cold, wet, and dry), the four seasons of the year, and the four ages of man (childhood, youth, prime, and old age). He believed that the four humors, and the manner in which they combined, determined an individual's illness or health, course of life, behavior, and character. Blood was seen as the manifestation of air, as having the qualities of warmth and moistness, and as predominating in childhood and during the springtime. A "sanguine" or "blood red" personality represented an individual who was amorous, happy, and generous. Yellow bile was seen as the manifestation of fire, as having the qualities of warmth and dryness, and as predominating in youth and during the summertime. Excessive yellow bile was thought to cause the overexcitement of mania. This color was also associated with negative qualities such as jealousy, cowardice, and treachery. For this reason, in medieval paintings, Judas Iscariot was invariably represented clothed in yellow, and, during periods of persecution, Jews were ordered to wear yellow, as betrayers of Christ (Howells & Osborn, 1984). A "choleric" or "yellow bile" personality described an individual who was violent and vengeful. Black bile was seen as the manifestation of earth, as having the qualities coldness and dryness, and as predominating in the prime of life and during the autumn. It was linked with melancholia and suicidal thoughts, but early writers could not decide whether black bile was the cause of depression or whether depression caused an excess of black bile. Democritus agreed with Hippocrates that it indirectly caused madness as a carrier of warmth and cold. If the black bile were too warm, it would cause fury; if too cold, stupor and melancholia (Howells & Osborn, 1984). A "melancholic" personality, one with an excess of black (*melas*) bile (*kholē*), represented an individual who was gluttonous, lazy, and sentimental. Finally, phlegm was seen as the manifestation of water, as having the qualities of coldness and moistness, and as predominating in old age and during the winter season. A "phlegmatic" personality represented an individual who was sluggish, dull, pale, and cowardly. Treatment consisted of efforts to restore balance among the humors, usually through special diets, laxatives, purgatives, and by bloodletting.

Galen of Pergamum (130–201) later refined humoral theory and used it to explain differences in character or personality. In his treatise *On the Natural Faculties*, he defined human temperaments and "diseases of the soul" and emphasized the role of the brain in controlling mental processes. According to Galen, rebalancing of the humors could be accomplished by prescribed medicine, special diets, and physical therapy, such as showers, sunbathing, and sneezing bouts. The legacy of Galen's theory is a descriptive typology of personality that emerged in the eighteenth and nineteenth centuries, which also bears a remarkable resemblance to the ***extraversion*** and ***neuroticism*** dimensions of personality proposed by the more recent theorist Hans Eysenck (Eysenck & Eysenck, 1985).

Taoism, an ancient Chinese philosophy, emphasized the desirability of physical balance. Normal behavior was thought to depend on the proper balance between *yin* and *yang*, the two major opposing forces in the universe. Yin was usually associated with nurturance, darkness, and femininity; yang was associated with power, light, and masculinity. Furthermore, from antiquity, physicians, philosophers, and clerics have believed that the skillful use of words—a "talking cure"—could soothe troubled minds and alter disordered behavior. Epictetus (ca. 55–135), a Stoic philosopher, stated "Men are disturbed, not by things, but by the principles and notions which they form concerning things" (*Enchiridion* 5:1, trans. Elizabeth Carter). Plato believed that the power of reason could control emotions. Galen argued that a physician could, through persuasion and advice, help patients overcome anger, anxiety, and other emotional problems. In summary, thinkers from ancient China, Egypt, Greece, and Rome began to emphasize natural over supernatural causes of mental disorders, paving the way for later biological and psychological theories of abnormality. This shift also established in Western minds the idea that medical doctors (as opposed to priests and religious healers) were the experts responsible for understanding and treating mental disorders.

The Middle Ages and the Return of the Demons: The European Tradition

The Greek and Roman civilizations began to decline around 200 CE and continued to deteriorate until the fall of the Roman Empire in 476 CE. During the next 500 years, a period known as the early Middle Ages, reliance on rationalism and empiricism as sources of knowledge were replaced by the belief that, through faith and meditation, God would reveal divine truths. Although contemporary mental health fields grew largely from Western European origins (and are thus the focus of this discussion), it is important to note that non-European cultures from Middle Eastern and African regions also influenced the understanding and treatment of abnormal behavior.

Science was de-emphasized in the Middle Ages; and, once again, supernatural forces, especially the devil and his demons and witches, were believed to be responsible for disordered behavior—requiring treatment with exorcisms or other religious rituals. For example, during this time, it was believed that an incubus or succubus actually sat on a sleeper and caused frightening dreams. Also, magical potions were concocted as a cure for behavioral abnormalities: e.g., mixing a testicle of a goat that had been killed on a Tuesday at midnight during the first quarter of the moon, the heart of a dog, and the excrement of a newborn babe, then, after pulverizing, taking an amount equivalent to half an olive twice a day (Nietzel et al., 1997).

Greek and Roman traditions did not disappear completely. Avicenna, an Islamic physician who wrote *The Canon of Medicine*, described humane procedures that preserved the philosophical traditions of Aristotle and the medical practices of Galen. Islamic physicians also pioneered the use of hospitals in which mentally disordered people received special treatment. In Europe, monasteries also served as sanctuaries for the mentally disordered. By providing a place where disturbed persons could be isolated from stress and treated kindly, these facilities represented a continuation of the Greek medical tradition. Asylums were also built for detention rather than treatment. These buildings seem to have been especially numerous in Germany, where they were called *Narrentürme* (towers of fools). Other abnormal behaviors were also observed in medieval society. For example, *St. Vitus's Dance* or *tarantism* was a phenomenon in which groups of men and women would suddenly begin frenzied jumping and dancing, tearing off their clothes as they frolicked in the streets. The afflicted were tolerated or taken to chapels until they stopped or died. This phenomenon was widely blamed on demonic possession, but others attributed it to the bite of the tarantula. Modern scholars still cannot agree on an explanation.

In the late Middle Ages, the influence of the Christian church on politics and philosophy began to weaken. The church intensified its use of power in a search for suspected heretics and witches. Thousands of suspects were tortured, and many were burned at the stake in the name of religious orthodoxy. Physician-priests "diagnosed" the "possessed" by looking for signs of the devil (*stigmata diaboli*) on their skin. Dominican monks Heinrich Kraemer and Johan Sprenger wrote *Malleus Maleficarum* (*The Witches' Hammer*) in 1486–87, which was regarded as the definitive treatise on the links between sin, demonic possession, witchcraft, and disordered behavior. In it, these authors described magical methods for detecting demonic possession as well as many gruesome methods for extracting confessions from witches (Vandermeersch, 1991).

The Renaissance and the Rise of Humanism

The fall of Constantinople to the Turks in 1453 ended the Byzantine Empire and signaled the dawn of the period known as the Renaissance. This period was characterized by **humanism**, or a secularization (i.e., away from religion) of life and values. With the advent of the printing press in 1440, books became more accessible, and people came in contact with ideas other than those authorized by the Church. For example, Copernicus (1473–1543) theorized that the sun, not the earth, was the center of the universe, and this idea paved the way for later scientific discoveries that demystified all aspects of nature. People began to see the study of individuals and human nature—including behavior and social relations—not as a way to discover or honor God but as a worthy topic in its own right. This period may have been the first era in which psychological concerns equaled or surpassed theological issues as the dominant questions of the day.

Physicians again came to view the body as a biological machine to be studied empirically, rather than as an inviolate creation of God. For example, René Descartes (1596–1650) sought to explain a great deal of human mental activity in physical, mechanical terms. Descartes suggested much could be learned about human minds by studying animal behavior, a view shared by many modern psychologists. Paracelsus (1493–1541) championed naturalistic explanations of mental disorders that included both biological and psychological factors (though he retained the supernatural belief that the brain was influenced by the moon). Johann Weyer (1515–1588), often considered the first psychiatrist, made careful descriptions of various mental disorders. He believed that treatment required a "therapeutic relationship marked by understanding and kindness," and he ridiculed beliefs in witches and condemned the brutal treatments supported by many theologians. Treatment of mental disorders during the Renaissance gradually took the form of confinement in hospitals and asylums, many of which had once been monasteries. The "insane" in the hospitals of the Renaissance were usually treated as prisoners and had to endure abominable conditions.

The Enlightenment and the Rise of Science

The seventeenth and eighteenth centuries, which became to be known as the Enlightenment, were characterized by an unshakable confidence in human reason and especially in science. With this confidence came the assumption that empirical research would reveal the mathematical or mechanical principles that governed all phenomena. This attitude made it possible, late in the 1800s, for psychology to become a scientific discipline. Initially, in this new era, the deplorable conditions in European and North American asylums had not changed much. Until the beginning of the nineteenth century, asylum visiting was actually considered a legitimate form of entertainment. Whole families would go to stare and to tease the unfortunate inmates. Admission tickets were issued, and attendants and porters regarded the tips they received from the visitors as a considerable part of their earnings. In 1799, Immanuel Kant warned those of nervous disposition against such visits, lest they become similarly affected. The display of the insane was sometimes taken to extremes, even to the extent of placing these individuals in publicly located cages for spectators to observe (Howells & Osborn, 1984).

In the latter half of the 1700s, a group of reformers tried to improve the living conditions and treatment in asylums. Philippe Pinel (1745–1826), a French physician, was one such reformer, and he became the inspirational leader of the moral treatment movement. When placed in charge of the Bicêtre asylum in Paris in 1793, Pinel unchained its inmates and insisted they be treated with kindness and consideration. As he replied to a critic, "Citizen, it is my conviction that these mentally ill are intractable only because they are deprived of fresh air and of their liberty" (quoted in Ronningstam, 2000, p. 203).

Moral treatment tried to instill in patients the expectation that they could alter their disordered behavior, learn to manage daily stress, find useful employment, and get along better with others. After years of being treated as wild beasts and acting accordingly, many of the inmates at Bicêtre and other moral treatment centers transformed almost overnight into well-behaved human beings. Pinel pioneered important methods such as taking notes to document his observations of patients.

Unfortunately, moral treatment waned by the late 1800s, especially in the United States. Ironically, its own success was partially responsible, as many believed that hospital care could help more patients if hospitals were larger than the traditional moral treatment centers. Crusaders such as Boston schoolteacher Dorothea Dix (1802–1887) and former mental patient Clifford W. Beers (1876–1943) became tireless agitators for the construction of large, public mental hospitals—though these hospitals were so understaffed that they could offer little more than custodial care to the large number of patients they housed. Moral treatment approaches were also overshadowed in the late 1800s because of the belief that disorder was caused by biological rather than social factors and thus required treatment based on biology and medicine. This view was largely fueled by the emergence of a disease called "general paresis" (labeled in 1825), a deteriorative brain syndrome characterized by ever-worsening delusions, muscle paralysis, and death. Throughout the remainder of the nineteenth century, physicians searched for its cause, which ultimately turned out to be syphilitic infection of the brain. With this mental disorder traced to a biological cause, the search was on to find other links between mental disorders and physical causes.

Classification systems for mental disorders began to be developed via psychiatrists' comparisons of individual patterns of abnormal behavior. The most prominent of these systems was developed by Emil Kraeplin (1856–1926) in Germany and Eugen Bleuler (1857–1939) in Switzerland. Effective treatments, however, remained scarce. American psychiatrist Benjamin Rush treated mental patients with bleedings and purges. Physicians often sought to tranquilize agitated patients by binding them in chairs, confining them in narrow cribs, dunking them in water, or wrapping them tightly in sheets. Using the rationale that shock would improve circulation and circulation disorders caused insanity, physicians subjected mental patients to rapid gyration by rotatory machines. Horace Fletcher, believing that mental health depended on proper digestion, advocated chewing each mouthful of food hundreds of times before swallowing.

The Psychoanalytic Revolution

During the Enlightenment, hypnotism (first known as mesmerism) was developed and popularized as a quasi-magical cure by a French physician, Franz Anton Mesmer (1734–1815), who believed it could realign magnetic forces in the body. French psychiatrists such as Jean Charcot, Pierre Janet, and Hippolyte Bernheim discovered that hypnosis could be helpful in the treatment of *hysteria*, a disorder in which patients with normal physical abilities appear unable to see or walk (hysteria comes from the Greek word "*hystera*," meaning "womb"; and the early conception of hysteria was that the womb wandered around in some females, and, in trying to displace some other organ, it caused the development of the disease; Brown, 1940). Success in treating hysteria with hypnotism helped reawaken the idea that at least some mental disorders might be caused by psychological factors as well as, or instead of, biological dysfunctions.

Sigmund Freud (1856–1939), a Viennese neurologist, successfully used hypnosis and other "talking cures" to cure cases of hysteria. His clinical experience led him to conclude that many forms of abnormal behavior were caused by intense, prolonged, and largely unconscious mental struggles between instinctual desires and concern over social prohibitions against fulfilling those desires. He synthesized ideas about unconscious processes into a coherent theory of personality and behavior that suggested *how* and *why* unconscious conflicts and other psychological processes create disordered behavior. He subsequently applied his theory of abnormality in *psychoanalysis*, the first modern psychological treatment of mentally disturbed people. Through Freud's work, the seeds were sown of a new mental health profession and branch of psychology devoted to studying mental disorders scientifically as well as assessing, diagnosing, and treating them—clinical psychology.

Theoretical Conceptions: The Biological Model

Different theories have been proposed to explain abnormal behavior, and these theories also apply to crime and violence. Here we will use them to explain criminal behavior occurring within the context of mental illness. The basic premise of the biological model is that the nervous system—particularly the brain—controls all thoughts and behaviors, both normal and abnormal.

Interestingly, the roots of biological explanations for crime and violence can actually be traced back to early contributions from criminology, to the work of Cesare Lombroso (considered by many to be its founding father). Lombroso, an Italian army medic turned psychiatrist turned criminologist, was working as a prison doctor in an asylum for the criminal insane in the eastern Italian coastal town of Pesaro one November morning in 1871 when he made a landmark discovery. While performing a routine postmortem examination on an infamous Calabrian brigand named Giuseppe Villella (an Italian Jack the Ripper), Lombroso peered into his opened skull and experienced an epiphany:

> At the sight of that skull, I seemed to see all at once, standing out clearly illumined as in a vast plain under a flaming sky, the problem of the nature of the criminal, who reproduces in civilised times characteristics, not only of primitive savages, but of still lower types as far back as the carnivora. (Lombroso-Ferrero, 1911/1972, pp. 6–7)

Lombroso identified an anomaly at the base of Villella's skull (the median occipital fossa): an indentation that suggested a shrunken cerebellum and features consistent with those observed in lower apes, rodents, and birds.

Lombroso's subsequent theory of crime centered on ***biological determinism*** and focused on the idea that many of the characteristics present in savage races are often found in born criminals (identified through atavistic stigmata—signs of human de-evolution such as a large jaw, sloping forehead, and single palmar crease; Lombroso-Ferrero, 1911/1972). In essence, Lombroso proposed a biological basis of crime, theorizing that it originated in the brain and that criminals represented an evolutionary throwback to more primitive species (see Raine, 2013). Other notable pseudoscientific offerings from eighteenth- and nineteenth-century ***positivism*** include phrenology, the popular study—pioneered by Franz Joseph Gall (1758–1828) and Johann K. Spurzheim (1776–1832)—of the relationship between physical attributes of the skull (i.e., "bumps" and recesses on the cranium) and behavior and personality characteristics, as well as physiognomy, the proposed relationship of a person's personality or character to his or her outer appearance, championed by J. K. Lavater (1741–1801) and Samuel R. Wells (1820–1875).

Abnormal behaviors, thought processes, and emotional experiences are presumed to be rooted in structural anomalies (e.g., differences in volume of material in the brain—such as gray or white matter—compared to that of normal individuals) and functional ***deficits*** (i.e., differences in activity, such as glucose metabolism or regional blood flow) in the various components of the nervous system, which may arise from the influences of traumatic life events, drugs, hormone imbalances, environmental toxins, head trauma, major infections, genetic defects, or other biological factors.

The Nervous System

The nervous system is divided into the **central nervous system**—consisting of the brain and spinal cord (see Figure 2.3)—and the **peripheral nervous system**. The latter is comprised of the *somatic nervous system*, which is largely concerned with the voluntary control of the muscles, and the *autonomic nervous system*, which controls the cardiovascular system, raises and lowers body temperature, and sends signals to other organs of the body.

The autonomic nervous system consists of two parts (see Figure 2.4). The **sympathetic nervous system** prepares the body for action by increasing physiological and psychological arousal—usually by stimulating heart rate and increasing blood pressure and respiration as preparation for fighting or fleeing a threat (known as the fight-or-flight response). Conversely, the **parasympathetic nervous system** decreases arousal in order to conserve the body's energy and resources. This system balances the sympathetic system by slowing heart rate and decreasing blood pressure and respiration.

Figure 2.3 The Central Nervous System

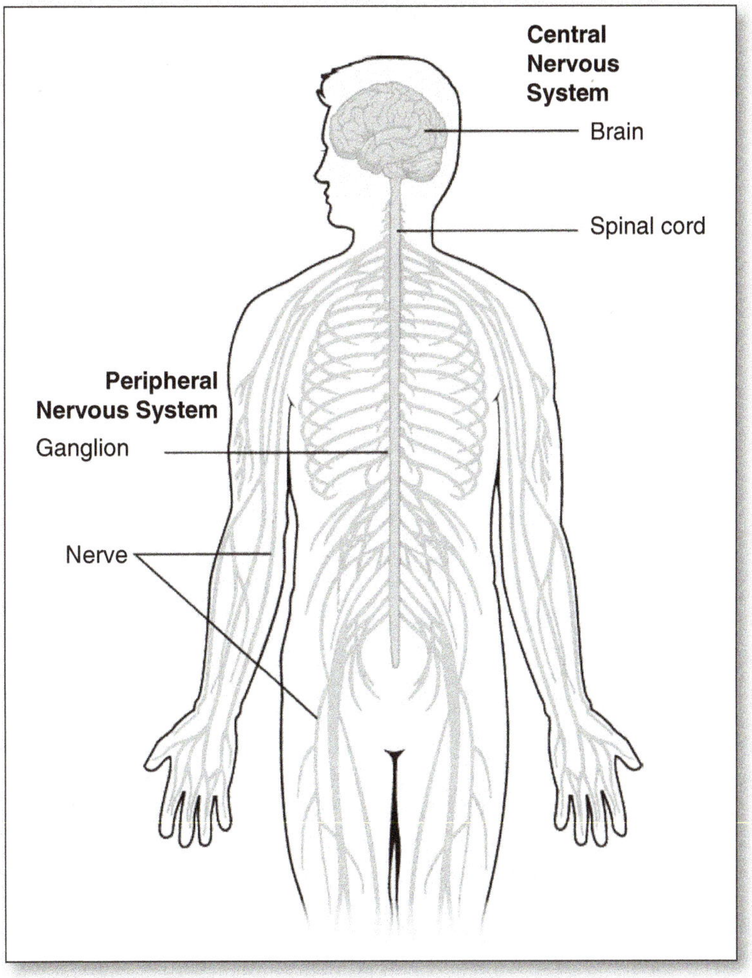

Source: http://en.wikipedia.org/wiki/File:1201_Overview_of_Nervous_System.jpg

Figure 2.4 The Autonomic Nervous System

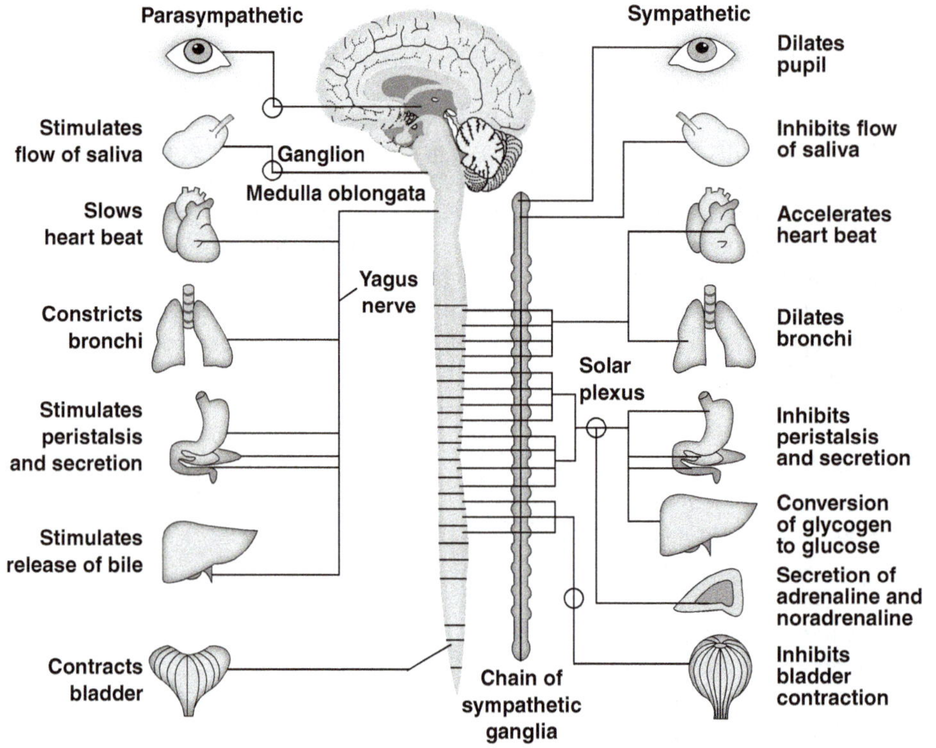

Source: http://users.rcn.com/jkimball.ma.ultranet/BiologyPages

Our understanding of the fundamental relationship between the brain and behavior is still very limited (Lezak, Howieson, Loring, Hannay, & Fischer, 2004). The brain, while considered a single organ, is in fact not one unitary structure but a complex combination of components and regions that are thought to be responsible for a multitude of different functions essential to life. The divisions of the brain are thought to reflect evolutionary progress and development over time. The oldest sections are located in the lower and more central regions, with the lowest sections being the most simply organized (Lezak et al., 2004), and the newer sections are in the upper and more superficial areas. Amongst the former are the *thalamus*, a relay station of sorts that receives, analyzes, and sends information from all the senses (except the sense of smell) to processing centers higher in the cerebral cortex; it plays a significant role in regulating higher-level brain activity. The *hypothalamus* (located just below the thalamus) regulates appetite, sexual arousal, thirst, and other motivated behaviors. It also receives information from the autonomic nervous system about the functioning of internal organs and helps regulate the activity of those organs. Additionally, it responds to chemical messengers called **hormones** that are secreted by the endocrine system, a network of glands that affect organs throughout the body by releasing hormones into the bloodstream. The hypothalamus connects to the *pituitary gland*, which, in turn, serves as the director of the endocrine system. The hypothalamus and pituitary gland are key elements of our physiological responses to stressful events. The **limbic system** is a "claw"-shaped network of smaller structures located toward the center of the brain and is important in emotional responses, drive-related behavior, and memory. Included within this system are the **amygdala** (an almond-shaped body located in both right and left sides of the brain and thought to be associated with aggression) and the *hippocampus* (see Figure 2.5).

Figure 2.5 The Limbic System

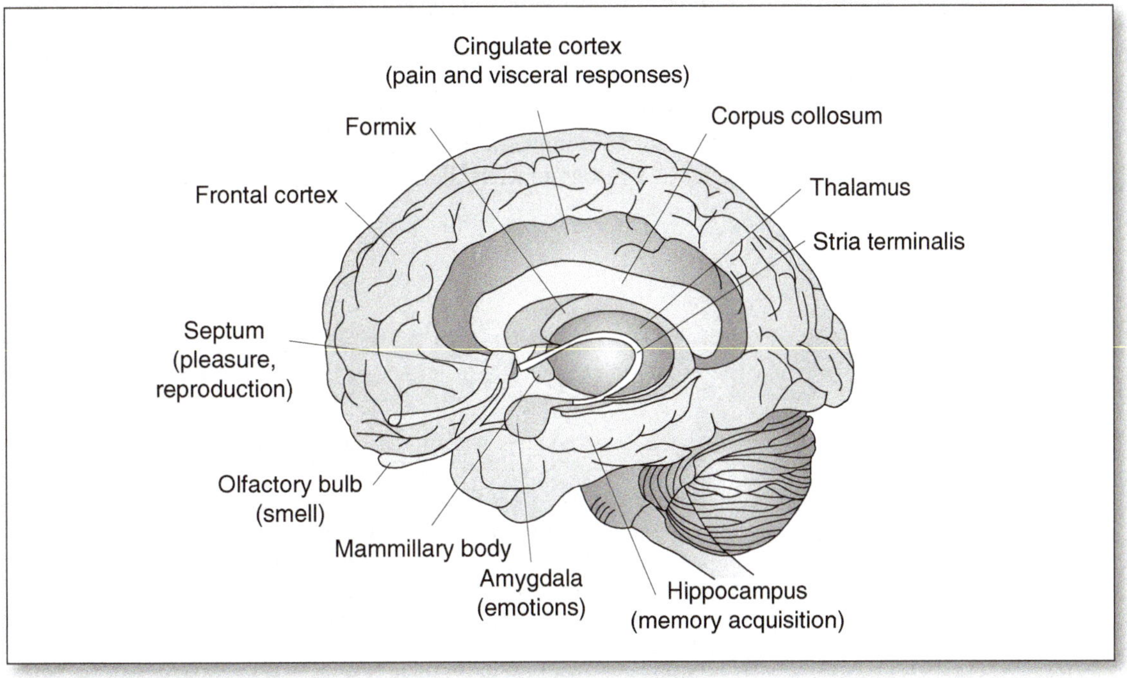

Source: http://neuroanatomy.wikispaces.com/F+Limbic+System

The *cerebrum*, and especially its outer covering, the ***cerebral cortex***, is the part of the human brain that is the most distinct from the brains of other mammals and the most active in such distinctively human capabilities as abstract thought and complex language. The cerebral cortex is divided into two ***hemispheres***, which are individually associated with different aspects of broader ***cognitive*** abilities. Additionally, each hemisphere is divided into regions, called lobes. Each ***lobe*** is thought to be involved in somewhat specialized aspects of information processing. The ***frontal lobe***, which constitutes approximately one-third of the cerebrum, extends from the ***anterior*** (forward) tip of the brain to the central ***sulcus*** (see Figure 2.6). Its surface consists of several subregions, which have distinctive patterns of connection with other areas of the cerebral cortex and with structures deep below the surface of the brain. Due to its unique composition, placement, and ***connectivity***, the frontal lobe is thought to play a key role in various forms of aggressive, violent, and antisocial behavior.

Figure 2.6 Lobes of the Brain

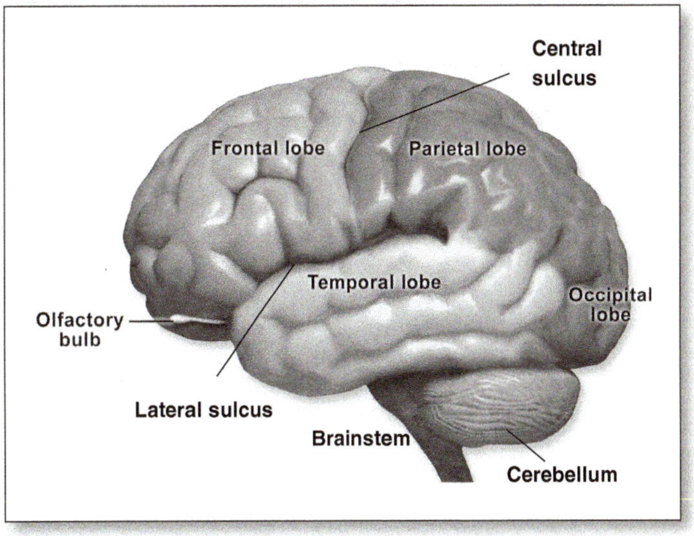

Source: http://en.wikipedia.org/wiki/File:Blausen_0111_BrainLobes.png

Neuroscience Approaches: Brain Imaging

Extensive research in multiple areas of the neurosciences—brain imaging, neurology, neuropsychology, and psychophysiology—continues to produce evidence that more and more clearly defines the role of the frontal lobe and other brain regions in aggression, violence, and antisociality. Until recently, evidence of a direct link between abnormal behavior and the structural components of the brain depended upon actual physical examination—either through autopsies or, perhaps, neurosurgery. As explained in Box 2.1, advances in technology have now allowed scientists and clinicians to examine the brains of both normal and disordered individuals in vivo (in the living body), and have led to a greater understanding of the complex relationship between brain and behavior.

BOX 2.1 BRAIN IMAGING

An array of technologies allows us to "see" into the brain without surgery. Most brain imaging methods fall into one of two broad categories: structural and functional imaging. Structural neuroimaging modalities use computers and select imaging devices to map the anatomical architecture of the brain. The two leading technologies for doing so are **computed tomography (CT)** and **magnetic resonance imaging (MRI)**. Like x-rays, these two imaging techniques produce a snapshot of the brain at the time the images are taken; unlike simple x-rays, however, CT and MRI allow for the accurate differentiation and measurement of the various brain components. The automated computation used in these techniques not only offers the benefit of being relatively straightforward but also minimizes the need for expert-user intervention.

The basic premise of **structural brain imaging** is to make inferences about the brains of different groups using comparisons with normative individuals. Clinicians look for a number of brain tissue differences, generally targeting characteristics such as size (e.g., length, thickness), volume, and shape of specific brain regions or components in both the ***gray matter*** (the physical material comprising a particular area of the brain) and the ***white matter*** (the connectivity between brain areas). Abnormalities (structural deficits) such as reduced volume of a given area (amount of material) or a misshapen appearance, allow inferences of potential functional limitations that may adversely affect normative cognitive, behavioral, or emotional functioning.

CT uses highly focused x-ray beams that delineate the distribution of tissue structures based on regional radio density in order to take images from multiple angles around a central point. These multiple images are then reconstructed by a computer to form a composite three-dimensional image of the brain. CT scans reveal the gross features of the brain but do not reveal brain structure well.

MRI uses a powerful magnetic field along with a radio-frequency stimulus (a short burst of radio waves that causes hydrogen nuclei protons in the brain–spinning in unison and aligned to the magnetic field–to resonate and emit brief radio signals of their own). Together, these construct images that contrast different types of brain tissue (gray matter, white matter, and cerebrospinal fluid) due to the unique proton density of each tissue.

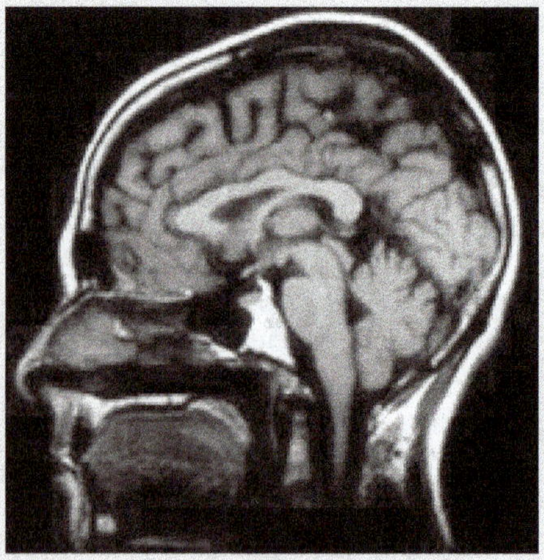

Functional brain imaging techniques are used to observe and record brain activity rather than to image the structural anatomy of the brain (although some recent techniques can accomplish both simultaneously).

One of the earliest methods for observing brain function was **electroencephalography (EEG)**, a technique developed in 1920, which uses electrodes placed on the scalp to measure the electrical responses of a large number of neurons inside the brain directly. The EEG to the right, for example, shows seizure activity.

Magnetoencephalography (MEG) is a very similar technique that measures the magnetic fields produced by electrical brain activity. Because the electrical activity measured by EEG has different physical properties than the magnetic waves MEG measures, MEG provides different information that can complement EEG data. MEG is used primarily to localize areas in which seizure activity occurs, as well as to identify areas of normal brain functioning in patients about to undergo brain surgery.

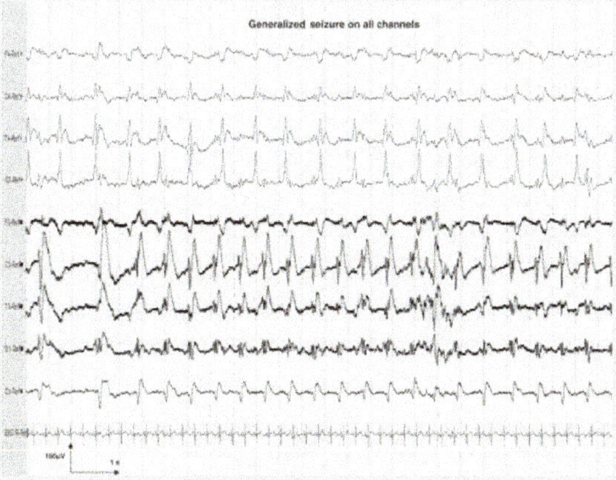

Although advances in EEG and MEG technologies have led to increases in the spatial resolution of resulting brain "images," three modern techniques for observing and recording brain function provide much richer data: **positron emission tomography (PET)**, ***single-photon emission computed tomography (SPECT)***, and **functional magnetic resonance imaging (fMRI)**. All three methods measure changes in regional blood flow and metabolism associated with changes in neural activity. And all three techniques generally involve the presentation of a visual or auditory stimulus and the subsequent measurement of the brain's functional response as indicated by regional blood flow or glucose metabolism after the stimulus, which, in turn, indicates different levels of neural activity in those regions.

Both PET and SPECT involve injecting a radioactive tracer compound bound to glucose (F-labeled fluorodeoxyglucose, or FDG) into the bloodstream. The brain metabolizes glucose to support neural activity, so wherever the glucose goes the radioactive material also goes. A scanner is able to pick up the brain regions where glucose is metabolized, indicating brain activity. For FDG PET, 30–40 minutes was generally used for image acquisition, though later methods measuring blood flow (as opposed to glucose metabolism, using a radiopharmaceutical H215O) were much speedier. SPECT is similar to PET but uses a tracer that emits only a single photon. SPECT can produce a three-dimensional representation of regional cerebral blood flow in the brain and is generally less expensive than PET, but its spatial resolution is poor compared to the images that PET produces. Regardless of which technique is used, clinicians infer "that the areas with the highest observed metabolic activity are the regions of greatest brain activation during the task under study." Although both PET and SPECT allow for very specific areas of the brain to be studied, both suffer from three significant limitations—the need to inject radioactive material, high cost, and overall poor resolution. These shortcomings have led most neuroscientists to rely on fMRI even though the latter technique does not allow, through the manipulation of specialized radioactive tracer compounds, for the study of specific metabolic or pharmacological activities in the brain (or for examining specific neurotransmitter systems).

Functional magnetic resonance imaging (fMRI) is based on the concept of neural coupling—the fact that increased neuronal activity in a brain region is followed by a local increase in blood flow through the region, a phenomenon first reported in 1894. This result leads to an increase in the ratio of oxygenated to deoxygenated hemoglobin, which can be detected because the magnetic resonance of blood differs slightly depending upon the level of oxygen within it. This hemodynamic effect can be recorded using a special magnetic resonance pulse signal called BOLD (blood oxygen level dependent) contrast, which is used to form images of activity within the brain.

First, fMRI has better spatial resolution than CT or PET; fMRI can provide details measured in millimeters, while CT and PET measure in centimeters. Thus, fMRI scans provide excellent spatial resolution. Second, fMRI offers increased temporal resolution compared to PET, measuring in seconds rather than minutes. But it can still take up to thirty seconds after the presentation of a stimulus to detect physiological responses in the brain using fMRI, whereas electrophysiological methods, such as MEG or scalp event-related potentials (ERPs), are capable of providing even finer temporal resolution—on the order of milliseconds to seconds. Third, fMRI it is noninvasive. Unlike SPECT and PET, it does not require the injection of a radioactive tracer, and, unlike CT, it does not involve the use of x-rays. Not only does this reduce potential risk to humans to nearly zero, but also it enhances the potential reliability and validity of the results because fMRI is not limited by the number of injections that may be administrated to a person in a given time frame.

Source: Schug, R. A., & Fradella, H. F. (2013). *The potential uses and misuses of fMRI in criminal justice: Implications for law, policy, and clinical practice.* Unpublished manuscript in preparation. Used with permission.

Findings from recent brain imaging studies suggest that frontal lobe deficits play a crucial role in the neurobiological mechanisms underlying violent behavior. Structural MRI studies have revealed gray matter volume reductions in the frontal lobe of violent individuals, particularly in two subregions of the **prefrontal cortex** (an area of the frontal lobe): the *orbitofrontal cortex* (OFC), located at the bottom and toward the middle of the brain, and the *dorsolateral prefrontal cortex* (DLPFC), located at the top, or ***dorsal***, and toward the sides, or the ***lateral*** portion, of the brain (see Figure 2.7; Yang & Raine, 2006). In addition, white matter abnormalities in the frontal lobe have also been associated with violent behavior. Functional brain imaging studies, using methods such as fMRI, SPECT, and PET, have suggested a link between violence and frontal dysfunction. Specifically, studies have found abnormal neural activity in the OFC, the medial frontal cortex, and the anterior cingulate cortex (ACC) during cognitive tasks in violent subjects compared to in controls. Several PET studies (e.g., Raine, Buchsbaum, & LaCasse, 1997) have also reported that murderers were characterized by significantly reduced glucose metabolism in the frontal cortex, particularly in the anterior medial frontal region (***medial*** means toward the middle). Also, MRI studies have shown prefrontal gray matter volume reductions in individuals with antisocial personality disorder (a psychiatric disorder strongly associated with criminal behavior—see Chapter 10).

Figure 2.7 Lateral and Medial Views of the Frontal Lobe With OFC, DLPFC, and ACC Subregions

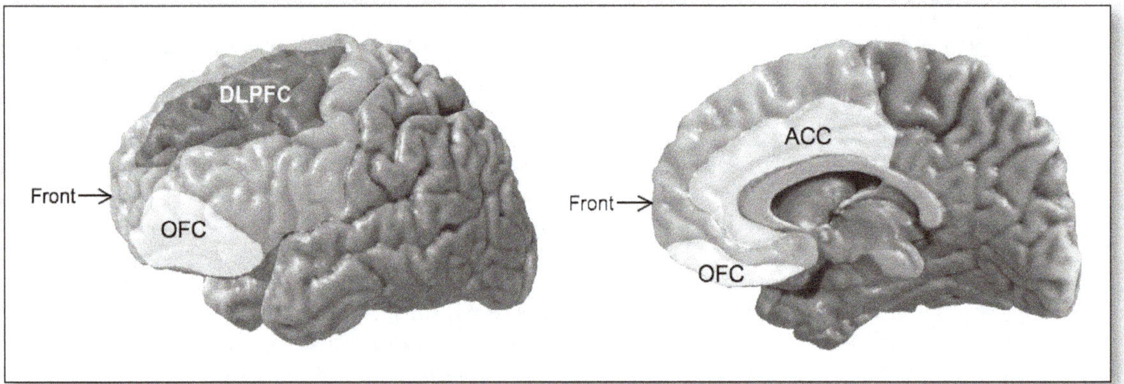

Source: Schug, R. A., Gao, Y., Glenn, A. L., Yang, Y., & Raine, A. (2009). Role of the frontal lobe in violence. In *McGraw-Hill yearbook of science and technology* (pp. 326–328). Hightstown, NJ: McGraw-Hill, Inc. Used with permission.

These findings echo what is known about frontal lobe functioning. Rich in ***intercortical*** and ***intracortical*** neuron connections with cortical and ***subcortical*** regions, the frontal lobe is closely linked to the emotional and behavioral aspects of violence. The OFC is involved in processing the reward-punishment value of the stimulus to guide behavior and is crucial to the control of violent acts. The DLPFC is critical in executive functions such as ***inhibitory control***, which is necessary for moral conduct and moral cognition development. The ACC plays an important role in regulating the intensity of response to emotional stimuli, which—when impaired—gives rise to aggression and hostility. Reduced functioning in these frontal and prefrontal areas can result in a ***dyscontrol*** of the aggressive feelings and impulses from the deeper, more emotional and primitive areas of the brain. Prefrontal damage also facilitates risk taking, irresponsibility, rule breaking, emotional and aggressive outbursts, and argumentative behavior that can predispose an individual to violence and criminality.

Other brain regions have been implicated in criminal behavior. For example, brain-imaging studies also indicate that violent offenders have structural and functional deficits in the temporal lobe (near the ears). PET studies have also indicated that the brains of murderers are characterized by deficits in key areas, such as in the left angular gyrus and corpus callosum. The left angular gyrus plays a key role in integrating information from the ***temporal*** (side of head), ***parietal*** (top and back of head) and ***occipital*** (very back of head) lobes, and it has been associated with reading and arithmetic. (A ***gyrus*** is a ridge on the surface of the brain; the plural is ***gyri***.) Impairments in such areas could lead to school failure, occupational failure, and, consequently, a criminal career. The *corpus callosum*, a thick band of fibers connecting the brain hemispheres, enables interhemispheric communication, and damage to it has been linked to inappropriate emotional expression and lack of long-term planning. Furthermore, the limbic system has been associated with violent and aggressive impulses, and the hippocampus and amygdala have demonstrated functional impairments in studies of violent individuals.

Neurology

Patients suffering damage to both gray and white matter within the prefrontal region of the brain may acquire an antisocial, psychopathic-like personality. A famous example is the nineteenth-century case of Phineas P. Gage (1823–1860), a responsible, well-liked, 25-year-old American railroad construction foreman whose personality became markedly antisocial after he suffered the passage of an iron rod through his skull in an accidental explosion in 1848—effectively destroying a portion of his prefrontal cortex. Although afterwards, his physical and intellectual abilities appeared to recover fully, he was unable to obtain similar employment again and spent the rest of his life wandering. He became irreverent, impatient, capricious, and vacillating, with no control over his instincts. His employers considered the changes so prominent that they refused to rehire him, and, to his friends, he was "no longer Gage." A similar injury and outcome involving a 21-year-old Barcelona university student who, in 1937, fell from a drainpipe and impaled his head on the spike of an iron gate was reported by Mataró and colleagues (2001).

Comparable personality changes have been observed in other case studies involving frontal lobe damage. Common features following injury include lack of empathy, difficulties with emotion regulation, impulsivity, disinhibited behavior, poor planning, and blunted emotions; and antisocial characteristics seem to develop particularly when damage occurs to the orbitofrontal region of the frontal lobe. For example, aggressive and violent attitudes were heightened in Vietnam War veterans who had suffered ***lesions*** to the orbitofrontal region of the frontal lobe when compared to controls and to individuals with lesions in other brain regions (Grafman et al., 1996). Additionally, patients who sustain damage very early in life (i.e., before the age of 16 months), develop antisocial tendencies very similar to those observed in individuals who sustain damage as adults, but the tendencies are often more severe and persist throughout development. Together, these neurological studies corroborate evidence from brain imaging studies suggesting that impairments in frontal lobe functioning are involved in the development of antisocial or violent behavior.

Neuropsychology

Neuropsychology is the study of how the brain's structure and function relate to behavior and psychological processes. Tests are considered to be an indirect measure of brain functioning in that they measure the behavioral expression of brain dysfunction (i.e., the behaviors associated with or indicative of it). Frontal lobe activity, for example, is thought to be best represented by executive functioning, an umbrella term referring to the cognitive processes necessary for socially and contextually appropriate behavior and effective self-serving conduct. Test performance errors involving poor strategy formation, ***cognitive inflexibility***, or impulsiveness all indicate deficits in executive functioning.

Neuropsychological examinations of executive functioning in those exhibiting antisocial behavior have traditionally focused on both populations diagnosed with categorical clinical syndromes and populations characterized by a particular legal grouping or judicial status (i.e., criminality and delinquency). Clinical syndromes of study have included antisocial personality disorder, conduct disorder, or psychopathy—a condition frequently associated with violence and characterized by persistent antisocial, impulsive, and irresponsible behavior and a profound lack of empathy, loyalty, and guilt (see Chapter 10). A quantitative review of these types of examinations indicates that antisocial individuals perform poorly on executive functioning measures relative to comparison groups (Morgan & Lilienfeld, 2000). Additionally, specific executive functioning deficits have been reported in both incarcerated and non-incarcerated samples of violent persons, and these deficits have been found in relationships with various forms of aggression.

Psychophysiology

Psychophysiology, defined as the study of brain-behavior relationships in the framework of central and peripheral physiological responses, addresses how mental events (e.g., emotions and thoughts) could affect bodily processes (e.g., heart rate, respiration, pupil dilation, perspiration, and the electrical activity of the brain). Like neuropsychological tests, psychophysiological recordings are an indirect measure of brain functioning, though they are often thought of as a "window" into the brain and mind (Hugdahl, 1995). Psychophysiological studies have provided additional evidence of the role of the frontal lobe and other areas in violence and antisociality. Skin conductance (SC) activity, one important area of psychophysiological research, reflects very small changes in the electrical activity of the skin—with increased sweating (i.e., imperceptible rising of sweat levels within the eccrine sweat ducts—not overt sweating from the pores per se) leading to increased SC activity. Skin conductance is considered a "pure" measure of sympathetic nervous system activity (given there are no parasympathetic connections with the eccrine sweat glands) and is thought to be controlled via a neural network involving the prefrontal cortex, hypothalamus, amygdala, and ***reticular formation***. As such, it is considered a measure of the body's state of arousal and responsivity.

The strongest research findings in this area are of poorer SC classical conditioning and quasi-conditioning in psychopaths, criminals, delinquents, and those exhibiting antisocial behaviors as compared to control groups in child and adult populations. Individuals are thought to develop a conscience that deters antisocial responding through successful classical fear conditioning, and their failure to do so may predispose some individuals to aggression and antisociality. There is also evidence for SC underarousal (e.g., reduced SC response frequency or lower SC level) in antisocial individuals. In theory, individuals with chronically low levels of arousal may seek out stimulating events (including risky or antisocial acts) in order to increase their arousal to more optimal levels. Additionally, patients with orbitofrontal injuries do not demonstrate any anticipatory SC responses—which is consistent with the somatic marker hypothesis (Damasio, 1994) and further underscores the link between neuropsychological performance, electrical activity of the skin, and antisocial behavioral tendencies (i.e., poor decision making), all stemming from orbitofrontal damage.

As explained in Box 2.1, an EEG reflects the regional electrical activity of the brain as recorded from electrodes placed at different locations on the scalp. Enhanced EEG slow-wave activity (reflecting low arousal) and abnormal frontal EEG ***asymmetry*** appear to be related to aggressive and violent behavior. The event-related potential (ERP), another psychophysiological measure, refers to averaged changes of electrical activity in the brain in response to specific stimuli; and reduced ***P300 ERP amplitude*** has been found consistently in antisocial and aggressive individuals. For example, Bernat, Hall, Steffen, and Patrick (2007) reported that the number of violent offenses, but not nonviolent offenses, is associated with reduced P300 amplitude in inmates. It is worth noting, however, that P300 amplitude reduction may reflect a disposition toward externalizing problems in general rather than to any specific behavior problems.

In aggregate, recent research from various branches of the neurosciences (brain imaging, neurology, neuropsychology, and psychophysiology) provides extensive and overlapping evidence for a link between frontal lobe dysfunction and aggressive, violent, and antisocial behavior.

Neurotransmitters

Neurotransmitters—chemicals stored in the ***synaptic vesicles*** of communicating nerve cell axons—form the basis of the transmission of information throughout the brain. Researchers have also investigated the possibility that disorders such as schizophrenia might be linked not only to problems in particular brain structures but also to breakdowns in communication among the brain's millions of nerve cells, or neurons. For example, the neurotransmitters *dopamine* and *norepinephrine* are thought to be involved in schizophrenia (Arnsten, 2004). They are also believed to lower the threshold for an aggressive response to environmental stimuli, to provocation (Volavka, Bilder, & Nolan, 2004). Another inhibitory neurotransmitter, *gamma-aminobutyric acid (GABA)*, is thought to affect anxiety disorders (Arnsten, 2004). Other biological research indicates that reduced *serotonin* and norepinephrine levels appear to be related to antisocial behavior, and some initial evidence also indicates relationships between antisocial behavior and other neurotransmitters, including dopamine, *acetylcholine*, and GABA. For example, Lande (2003) found increased levels of whole blood serotonin in a sample of

20 pretrial murder defendants compared to the levels of 93 laboratory reference group individuals; levels were particularly high for men who had been arrested as juveniles or had set fires (i.e., arsonists). Furthermore, *vasopressin* has been indicated as a key component in aggressive behavior in studies of animals and humans (Coccaro et al., 1998), and interesting work with hamsters by Ferris and colleagues (e.g., Delville, Mansour, & Ferris, 1996) has demonstrated how serotonin may also work against vasopressin to inhibit offensive aggression. Key to understanding the relationship between neurotransmitters and the expression of behavior—including violence and aggression—are receptor sites and the specific location within the brain of these receptor sites. Receptor sites are where the neurotransmitters bind to or "land" after crossing the ***synapses*** between nerve cells during the transmission of neuronal signals, so knowing whether or not this binding is blocked by other neurotransmitters or agents is significant.

Hormones

Hormonal influences upon criminal behavior have also been examined. Abnormal levels of male sex hormones (androgens) such as *testosterone* have been shown to produce aggressive behavior; and *cortisol*, a hormone believed to index arousal of the hypothalamus, pituitary, and adrenal glands (the HPA axis), may play a role in mediating antisociality, criminality, and violence. Although normal individuals who are aroused or stressed show an increase in cortisol levels, antisocial individuals demonstrate lower cortisol levels (thought to represent underarousal and fearlessness). Some biological research has also suggested a controversial link between aggression in females and the group of symptoms known as premenstrual syndrome, but this result requires replication.

Researchers have examined other biological factors that may play a role in crime. Scientists in the field of ***behavior genetics*** use specialized research methods to study genetic influences on behavior and to understand the combined influences of nature and nurture on normal and abnormal behavior, and a new generation of neurogenetic studies is now beginning to identify specific genes (e.g., monoamine oxidase A) that predispose adults to antisocial behavior when combined with negative environmental influences, such as a past experience of child abuse. Birth complications such as anoxia (getting too little oxygen), forceps delivery, and preeclampsia (hypertension leading to anoxia) are thought to contribute to brain damage and have been related to later conduct disorder, delinquency, impulsive crime, and adult violence. This is especially true when birth complications co-occur with social risk factors for violence, such as maternal rejection of the child. Additionally, minor physical anomalies (MPAs) have been associated with pregnancy complications and are thought to reflect fetal maldevelopment (including brain maldevelopment) toward the end of the first trimester of pregnancy. Other anomalies (e.g., low-seated ears, adherent ear lobes, furrowed tongue, curved fifth finger, single transverse palmar crease, gaps between the first and second toes, unusually long third toes, and fine hair), though not stigmatizing, have been found to characterize preadult antisocial behavior and temperament.

Nutritional factors, which have demonstrated effects upon human behavior in general, have shown relationships to aggression and crime. For example, some claim that hypoglycemia (low blood sugar) is linked to impaired brain function and violent crime. Lower cholesterol levels and deficiencies in vitamins (B3, B6, and C), minerals (iron, zinc), and proteins have also shown relationships with various forms of antisocial behavior. Children with poor nutrition early in life have been found to develop antisocial and aggressive behavior in late childhood and late adolescence, independent of social risk factors. Furthermore, environmental pollutants (i.e., heavy metals such as lead and manganese that have neurotoxic effects) have been implicated as biological factors in crime.

Theoretical Conceptions: The Sociocultural Model

In the sociocultural model, the basic assumption is that abnormality is the result of external forces. There are many schools of thought within the sociocultural model. Social disorganization approaches focus on environmental conditions that lead to antisocial and criminal behavior, especially at the neighborhood level (e.g., Bursik, 1988; Shaw & McKay, 1942). Subcultural theories (Cohen, 1955; Miller, 1958) explain deviance as a function of cultural traditions and values that influence the frequency and form of disorders. Strain theories (e.g., Agnew,

1992; Merton, 1968) emphasize how dysfunctional social structures and their associated factors, such as poverty and inferior school systems, interfere with people's ability to function in ways that society expects. Conflict theory argues that crime is a function of conflicts between the social classes (Quinney, 1970). And social control theory asserts that deviance occurs when an individual's bonds to society—including a variety of social bonds to family, religion, school, friends, work, and community—are either weak or broken (Hirschi, 1969; Gottfredson & Hirschi, 1990). Because we are primarily concerned with medical and psychological approaches to mental illness and crime, further explication of the sociocultural model is beyond the scope of this book.

Theoretical Conceptions: The Behavioral Model

In the behavioral model, the basic assumption is that abnormality is caused by learning experiences, which involve the conditions that precede behavior, the rewards or punishments that follow behavior, or the psychological or physiological pairing of various sensations or emotions with situations and events. Essentially, people *learn* how to behave based upon previous experiences with the world, and these forms of learning are also responsible for normal behavior and provide the basis for treatment with behavioral therapy of individuals exhibiting abnormal behavior. *Conditioning* is a term used to describe learning through paired experiences (Bandura, 1974). The two major forms of learning frequently discussed in the literature are classical conditioning and operant conditioning.

Classical conditioning is rooted in the work of Ivan Pavlov (1849–1936) and describes behavior based on reflexes that are automatically elicited by the environment. In his famous experiment with dogs (Figure 2.8), Pavlov repeatedly paired an *unconditioned stimulus* such as food, which elicits a reflexive (or *unconditioned response*) such as salivation, with a neutral stimulus such as a tone. Eventually, the neutral stimulus became a *conditioned stimulus* that elicited salivation as a *conditioned response*; the dogs learned to salivate in response to the tone.

Figure 2.8 Classical Conditioning

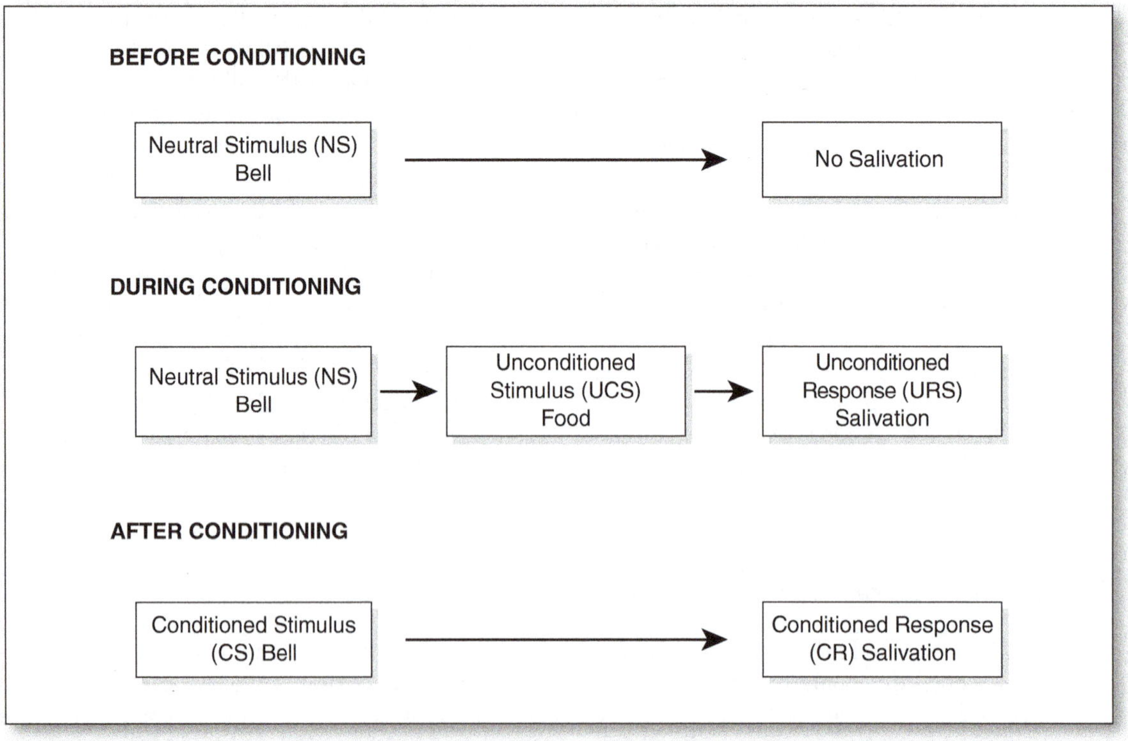

Source: Adapted from http://www3.niu.edu/acad/psych/Millis/History/2003/ClassicalConditioning.htm

The case of "Little Albert" illustrates how symptoms of mental illness can be classically conditioned in humans. In their now-famous experiment, Watson and Rayner (1920) exposed a normal, well-adjusted nine-month-old infant named Albert B. to repeated paired presentations of a white rat (which initially elicited no fear response) and the sound of a hammer striking a steel bar (which was suspended behind Albert's head). Subsequent presentations of the rat alone made him cry, and the conditioned fear response transferred to other similar objects (i.e., a rabbit, dog, fur coat, cotton wool, and a Santa Claus mask). These authors concluded it was probable that many phobias were actually conditioned emotional reactions either of the direct or the transferred type, and other authors have subsequently supported this notion (Fyer, 1998).

Operant conditioning is rooted in the work of Edward L. Thorndike (1874–1949), an American psychologist who proposed that learning follows the *law of effect*, in other words, that behaviors followed by pleasurable outcomes are more likely to be repeated. B. F. Skinner (1904–1990) expanded upon this proposition and stated that all behavior is learned as a function of the antecedent conditions in which it is displayed and the consequences that follow it. Thus, according to Skinner, behavior can be explained by looking at the functional relationships between operant behavior—acts, such as crying, that "operate" on the environment—and its observable antecedents and consequences. Behavior is strengthened through reinforcement, that is, when positive consequences follow the behavior. Any type of reinforcement makes behavior more likely to occur on appropriate occasions in the future. **Positive reinforcement** is the appearance of something pleasant, such as food or praise. **Negative reinforcement** is the disappearance of something unpleasant, such as an electric shock or an annoying sound. Additionally, behavior is *less* likely to occur when it is followed by negative consequences—a process called **punishment**. Negative consequences can take two forms: the appearance of something unpleasant, such as pain (positive), or the loss of something valued, such as privileges (negative). Behavior can also be made less likely to occur through *extinction*, or the absence of *any* notable consequences. Importantly, reinforcements and punishments may be external or internally, self-produced consequences that can serve to motivate and inform future behavior (Bandura, 1974). In the (albeit extreme) case of Ed Gein, these operant conditioning concepts are relatively easily applied and understood. For example, Gein's grave digging and manipulation of human remains may have served to increase his self-esteem or to produce sexual arousal (positive reinforcement); or they may have reduced anxieties associated with his gender identity issues or calmed—in a way unique to Gein—his feelings of isolation or inadequacy (negative reinforcement). As both were followed by favorable outcomes for Gein, both increased the likelihood of him continuing the behavior.

Behavioral theorists pioneered the theory of *social learning*, which explains many aspects of criminal behavior (Akers, 1973; Burgess & Akers, 1966; Southerland, 1947). Under this theory, crime is acquired through our observations of individuals around us and maintained through reinforcements. In a series of studies on the social learning of aggression, for example, Bandura and colleagues (Bandura & Huston, 1961; Bandura et al., 1961; Bandura et al., 1963) demonstrated how nursery school children learned—through imitation—aggressive behaviors such as assaulting inflatable or rubber dolls by watching adults (on film or in person) engaged in the same activity.

Theoretical Conceptions: The Psychoanalytic Model

Psychoanalytic theory is actually a group of theories that emphasize the effects of **unconscious processes** on human behavior—both normal and abnormal (Gabbard, 2005). Sigmund Freud proposed that the real meaning of many of our thoughts, feelings, and behaviors is determined unconsciously, outside of our awareness (Mitchell & Black, 1995), and a significant body of research supporting the existence of unconscious cognitive, ***affective***, and motivational processes has been generated (Westen, 1999). Ego psychology (e.g., Sigmund Freud, Heinz Hartmann, Anna Freud, Margaret Mahler) focuses upon abnormality determined by unconscious conflicts between personal impulses (i.e., sexual and aggressive instincts) and social rules (i.e., the moral demands and realistic constraints of society). Each individual thus faces a lifelong struggle to find ways of expressing these instincts without suffering punishment, anxiety, or guilt. Object relations theory (e.g., Melanie Klein, Otto Kernberg, W. R. D. Fairburn, D. W. Winnicott) emphasizes the internalized relationships between representations of self and object and how these later affect adult development. Self psychology (e.g., Heinz Kohut) stresses how external relationships help maintain self-esteem and self-cohesion. Attachment theory (e.g., John Bowlby)

Figure 2.9 Freud's Structural Model of the Mind (circa 1923)

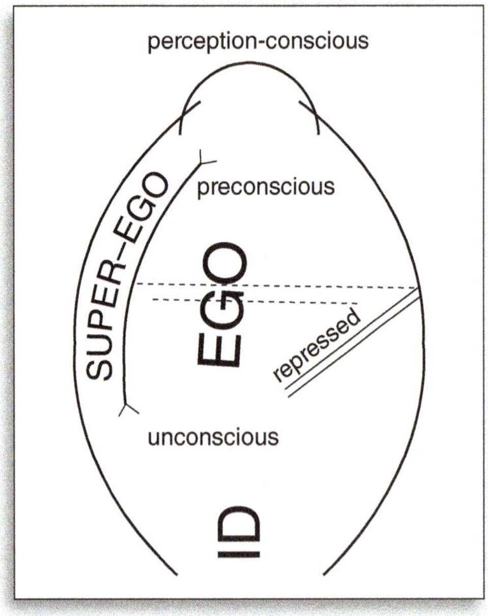

Source: Freud (1923/1961).

emphasizes the biologically based bond between child and caregiver and proposes that the child's goal is not to seek an object but rather a physical state (achieved by nearness to the mother or object), which is later transformed into a psychological state of closeness to the mother or caregiver. Attachment strategies in infancy (i.e., secure, avoidant, anxious-ambivalent, or disorganized-disoriented attachment) lead to the development of internal working models and subsequent mental schemas of relationships, which become the basis for relatively stable behavioral and interactional styles throughout life (Gabbard, 2005).

Sigmund Freud's classic psychoanalytic theory evolved and developed over the course of his several-decade career, from first an affect-trauma model focusing on traumatic events leading to symptoms of hysteria; to a topographical model identifying the unconscious, conscious, and preconscious systems; and, finally, to a structural model addressing the interplay of three mental "structures." These Freud called the **id**, a reservoir of raw, unstructured, impulsive energies seeking immediate gratification of its needs, desires, and impulses; the **ego**, a collection of regulatory functions that constrains the impulses of the id by acting as a sort of mediator; and the **superego**, a set of moral values and self-critical attitudes, internalized primarily from the parents, which assumes the role of stern taskmaster (see Figure 2.9). All of these systems and structures are theoretical concepts and not actual physical components.

Freud also proposed a developmental sequence of **psychosexual stages** (***oral***, ***anal***, ***phallic***, ***latency***, and ***genital***) based upon the anatomical structure most associated with pleasurable sensations at that given age, and he suggested that a "fixation," or failure to advance developmentally through any one stage, could result in one reverting back to behavioral patterns characteristic of that stage during times of stress or crisis later in life (e.g., "oral" behaviors such as nail-biting or smoking, or "anally retentive" personality styles characterized by excessive cleanliness and rigidity). Freud (and later his daughter Anna) also proposed an arsenal of mostly unconscious **defense mechanisms** employed by the ego to relieve the anxiety, guilt, and other unpleasant emotional problems occurring when unconscious desires and impulses approach consciousness. Anna Freud (1936/1946) originally articulated ten defense mechanisms, though more recent authors (e.g., Blackman, 2004) have described over one hundred. Table 2.1 lists a selection of the most common defense mechanisms in hierarchical fashion (i.e., from primitive to mature). Defense mechanisms require significant mental energy and can ultimately fail. If they do, the person retreats (or regresses) to even more primitive, immature behaviors reminiscent of early childhood. In extreme cases, the regression may result in incontinence, mutism, and other infantile behaviors associated with severe mental disorders. Variants of psychoanalytic theory have been employed in understanding animal phobias and obsessive-compulsive disorders, for example, Freud's "Little Hans" and "Ratman" (Freud 1909/2003); various forms of personality ***pathologies***, for example, schizoid, paranoid, and masochistic personalities (McWilliams, 1994); and other disorders of the self, for example, narcissistic behavior and personality disorders and borderline and psychotic personality states (Kohut & Wolf, 1978).

Psychoanalytic Explanations of Crime

Psychoanalysts were among the first of the psychological theorists offering explanations of criminal behavior. These began appearing in the psychiatric literature toward the first half of the twentieth century and consisted largely of psychoanalytic interpretations of crime and criminality (Holmes & Holmes, 1998; Wittels, 1937), murder cases (Abrahamsen, 1973; Arieti & Schreiber, 1981; Bromberg, 1951; Cassity, 1941; Evseef & Wisniewski, 1972; Karpman, 1951a, 1951b; Lehrman, 1939; Morrison, 1979; Revitch & Schlesinger, 1981, 1989; Wertham, 1941/1950, 1949; Wittels, 1937), and even homicide wound patterns (DeRiver, 1951). Some theorists proposed that crime results from

Table 2.1 Defense Mechanisms

	Defense Mechanism	Description
Primitive Defenses	Splitting	Compartmentalizing experiences of the self and the other such that integration is not possible. This defense prevents conflict stemming from the incompatibility of the two polarized aspects of the self or the other: the positive and the negative.
	Projective identification	Both an intrapsychic defense mechanism and an interpersonal communication, this phenomenon involves behaving in such a way that subtle interpersonal pressure is placed on another person to take on characteristics of an aspect of the self or an internal object that is projected onto that person. The person who is the target of the projection begins to behave, think, and feel in keeping with what has been projected.
	Projection	Perceiving and reacting to unacceptable inner impulses and their derivatives as though they were outside the self. Projection differs from projective identification in that the target of the projection is not changed.
	Denial	Avoiding awareness of aspects of external reality that are difficult to face by disregarding sensory data.
	Idealization	Attributing perfect or near-perfect qualities to others as a way of avoiding anxiety and negative feelings, such as contempt, anger, or envy.
	Acting out	Enacting an unconscious wish or fantasy impulsively as a way of avoiding painful affect.
	Regression	Returning to an earlier phase of development or functioning to avoid the conflicts and tensions associated with one's present level of development.
Higher-Level Neurotic Defenses	Introjection	Internalizing aspects of a significant person as a way of dealing with the loss of that person. Introjection occurs in nondefensive forms as a normal part of development.
	Identification	Internalizing the qualities of another person by becoming like the person. Whereas introjection leads to an internalized representation experienced as an "other," identification is experienced as part of the self. This, too, can serve nondefensive functions in normal development.
	Intellectualization	Using excessive and abstract ideation to avoid difficult feelings.
	Rationalization	Justification of unacceptable attitudes, beliefs, or behaviors to make them tolerable to oneself.
	Reaction formation	Transforming an unacceptable wish or impulse into its opposite.
	Repression	Expelling unacceptable ideas or impulses or blocking them from entering consciousness. This defense differs from denial in that the latter is associated with external sensory data whereas repression is associated with inner states.
	Undoing	Attempting to negate sexual, aggressive, or shameful implications from a previous comment or behavior by elaborating, clarifying, or doing the opposite.
Mature Defenses	Suppression	Consciously deciding not to attend to a particular feeling, state, or impulse. This defense differs from repression and denial in that it is conscious rather than unconscious.
	Sublimation	Transforming socially objectionable or internally unacceptable aims into socially acceptable ones.

unconscious processes (i.e., drives, instincts, and motivations and the defense mechanisms used to control them), which are maladaptive and result in antisocial behavior. Offenders may not be able to articulate fully the causal explanations for their own criminal behaviors, as these may be outside of their awareness and thus unknown to them (Alexander & Staub, 1931). For example, an individual might have unconscious aggressive and even homicidal impulses (Freud, 1913/1950). Another example would be unconscious guilt. According to Freud (1916/1961), criminal acts are performed to provide psychological relief from an "oppressive feeling of guilt," which is lessened after the crime—thus, it is the sense of guilt that precedes the criminal act and not vice versa. He proposed that preexisting guilt was derived from the ***Oedipus complex***, a normative childhood phase in which a boy develops sexual feelings for his mother and rivalries with his father (Friedman & Schustack, 1999), and that the actual criminal offense is carried out as a representation or disguised form of this forbidden Oedipal "crime" (Alexander & Straub, 1931). In other words, the criminal commits the criminal act *in order to be caught and punished*—the crime becomes a physical, tangible, and real act to which the unconscious guilt can become "attached" and for which the individual can be subsequently punished. Interestingly, the idea of unconsciously motivated errors in criminal behavior serving as clues for authorities has been discussed in the literature (Indira, 1987).

Other unconscious motivational processes might include overcompensation for a sense of inferiority; spite reactions toward others (e.g., a mother figure—perhaps applicable in the case of Ed Gein); a need for gratifying infantile, parasitic, dependent tendencies (i.e., by getting locked up in jail); masculine protest reactions against female identification or female passive tendencies (Alexander & Healy, 1969); a need to be caught and protected (Adler, 1982); or a regression to the phallic phase (Wittels, 1937). Freud (1930/1961) also later proposed aggression as an instinctual drive and discussed the ***death instinct*** or Thanatos, an impulse to return to the inorganic state, whose goal was to oppose the ***life instinct*** or Eros (Freud 1933/1964). Kohut specifically mentioned delinquency among the "perverse" behaviors characterizing narcissistic behavior disorder (Kohut & Wolf, 1978). He also discussed destructive, violent, and murderous responses to narcissistic injury, in other words, to a psychological "assault" that results in the fragmentation or loss of one's sense of self—such as disapproval, betrayal, deprivation, exploitation and manipulation, frustration, violence, and humiliation (see Chapter 10). In this circumstance, aggression serves the purpose of preserving the self. Outbursts of rage and violent behavior have also been discussed as resulting from the breakdown or dyscontrol of ego function (i.e., the ego was unsuccessful in restraining, diverting, or neutralizing dangerous impulses, or it suspended efforts to control an aggressive behavior in the interests of self-preservation). Rage responses can be significantly exacerbated when the narcissistically injured individual has access to weapons coupled with a disregard for behavioral consequences (which enhances the individual's sense of potency and capacity to respond). This combination of circumstances can result in acts of extreme violence such as mass shootings (Menninger, 2007). Additionally, from an attachment perspective, psychoanalytic writers (Bowlby, 1969, 1973, 1980; Freud, 1936/1966) have discussed the ***pathogenic*** effects of failed attachments between infants and mothers (e.g., social isolation; emotional coldness; or the sense of being weak, insignificant, unimportant, and lacking in worth), and later writers have speculated that these may be the origins of the psychological dynamics in serial murder (Whitman & Akutagawa, 2004). Finally, from an object relations' perspective, homicidal individuals can be seen as those in which the aggressive or destructive elements of the early mother-child relationship are introjected (mentally internalized) as "unmetabolized" (dissociated or separated) elements. These individuals subsequently split the introjected "badness" from their self and project it onto the female victim (Liebert, 1985).

Psychoanalytic writers have also proposed crime as being caused by defective psychological equipment. For example, in his pioneering work on the application of psychoanalytic theory to juvenile delinquency, August Aichhorn (1935) emphasized the role of maladaptive parenting practices on the development of a psychological apparatus that is prone to delinquent behavior. Through excess of parental love or parental severity, the ego may develop so that it is unable to repress instinctual urges. Additionally, identification with an antisocial parent may lead to the development of a superego that is fully functional yet characterized by an antisocial value system; or, alternatively, a weak and defective superego may arise out of early childhood deprivations (Friedlander, 1947). Bernabeu (1958) proposed that delinquency is rooted in a constricted ego, one limited to the use of reversal and projection defense mechanisms, that has developed in response to unmet unconscious needs for dependence. Alexander and Straub (1931) proposed a biopsychosocial typology of offenders consisting of the *normal criminal* who possesses normal psychological equipment—id, ego, superego—yet identifies with criminal prototypes (i.e., a sociological etiology); the *organic criminal* characterized by organic brain damage from which criminal behavior is derived (i.e., a biological etiology); and the *neurotic criminal* characterized by an unconscious sense of guilt and an excessively strong superego (i.e., a psychological etiology). According to these authors, the neurotic utilizes atonement (suffering or punishment) as a license for criminal transgressions, as it frequently serves only to lift moral inhibitions. As such, the neurotic criminal is neither frightened away nor inhibited nor made a better person by punishment because punishment in these individuals acts as a temptation to crime, and criminality is thus perpetuated rather than stopped.

Integrative and Interactional Models: Diathesis Stress and "Triple Vulnerability"

Other models of abnormality have emphasized the interaction or integration of multiple factors, such as biological, psychological, and social influences. For example, according to the ***diathesis-stress model***, abnormality is the product of two interacting factors: a biological or psychological predisposition to disorder (***diathesis***) and stressors arising from the family, environment, or the person's own behavior that translate the diathesis into an actual disorder. Stressors and diatheses can also influence each other. A diathesis can make people more likely to encounter stressors, and a stressor can intensify a diathesis. In the case of Ed Gein, it would be easy to speculate how a preexisting biological diathesis toward anxiety (perhaps inherited from his mother, who reportedly had obsessive religious concerns) and gender identity issues (thought by many to be biological in nature) may have been coupled with significant environmental stressors (i.e., an isolative, oppressive religious upbringing and the eventual death of his mother, who was arguably his primary, if not sole, social support system) to trigger Gein's downward spiral into aberrant behavior. Allen, McHugh, and Barlow (2008) discuss a triple vulnerability model relevant to the development of various anxiety and emotional regulation disorders. Its three components are generalized biological vulnerability, generalized psychological vulnerability, and specific psychological vulnerability emerging from early learning experiences.

Classification and Assessment

Terminology

Several key terms are important in the discussion of classification and assessment. **Assessment** itself is defined as the collection of information for the purposes of making an informed decision, and **diagnosis** is the classification of mental disorders by determining which of several possible descriptions best fits the nature of the problem or problems. **Nosology** is a term meaning a classification system containing a set of categories of disorder and rules for categorizing disorders based on the signs and symptoms that appear. **Prevalence** is the total number of people who suffer from a disorder in a specific population, and **incidence** is the number of people who develop a disorder in a specific time period, usually the previous six or twelve months. Assessment tools include life records (e.g., school grades, court records, police reports, and medical records), interviews (e.g., structured clinical interviews such as the Structured Clinical Interview for DSM [SCID]), psychological tests (e.g., intelligence tests, neuropsychological tests, and personality tests), observations, and biological measures.

A History of Classification Systems for Psychological Disorders

According to Netherton and Walker (1999), the description and classification of mental disorders began in ancient times (3000–2000 BCE) with Egyptian and Sumerian references to senile dementia, melancholia, and hysteria. Hippocrates (ca. 460–377 BCE) expanded on this system with the addition of phrenitis, an acute mental disease associated with fever or with another disease (Sedivec, 1989); mania; epilepsy; and Scythian disease (akin to transvestism). These diagnostic categories were included under the medical domain and based on empirical observation. Plato (ca. 427–347 BCE), in contrast, advocated an approach to the categorization of mental disorders couched in rational and logical thought.

During the Renaissance and the Enlightenment periods, Thomas Sydenham (1624–1689) proposed that different individuals with the same disease would have a similar presentation of symptoms. Thus, classification of mental disorders could be approached best through the systematic observation and description of symptom patterns. Jean Colombier and François Doublet published the *Instruction* in psychiatry in 1785 on the basis of information compiled from a group of physicians who were involved in the treatment of the mentally ill in France. Categories included *manie* (mania), *mélancolie* (melancholy), *frénésie* (frenzy), and *imbécillité* (stupidity)—strikingly similar to those described by Hippocrates more than 2000 years before this publication. This represented one of the first diagnostic systems to be sanctioned by a group of professionals, and the descriptive approach is still used in DSM and ICD development. Advances toward defining discreet diseases were made through the advent of the autopsy. (Greek physicians performed autopsies 2,500 years ago, but it wasn't until 1761 that the first comprehensive pathology text was written by *Italian physician* Giovanni Battista Morgagni). Additionally, nineteenth-century innovations such as X-rays and biological tests, as well as Louis Pasteur's identification of microorganisms, gave medicine a scientific basis.

Several nineteenth-century European physicians, including Antoine Laurent Bayle (1799–1858) and Wilhelm Griesinger (1817–1868), also proposed classification systems. Emil Kraepelin made one of the most substantive contributions to the development of a nosology of mental disorders. Kraepelin believed that the thousands of mental patients observed throughout the world could be placed in three categories: dementia praecox (now called schizophrenia), manic-depressive psychosis (now called bipolar disorder), and organic brain disorders (now called dementia, delirium, amnestic, and other cognitive disorders). Freud (1894/1962) discussed conversion hysteria, obsessional neurosis, and hallucinatory psychosis as defense neuroses (i.e., as ways of coping with or defending against incompatible ideas or sets of ideas), and, later, he attempted to distinguish between the "actual neuroses," which were without psychic causation, and the "psychoneuroses," which were based on psychic causation (PDM Task Force, 2006).

In 1853, the modern history of the International Classification of Diseases (ICD) began at the meeting of the first International Statistical Conference in Brussels, where William Farr (a medical statistician from England) and Marc d'Espine (of Geneva) were assigned the task of developing a nomenclature of causes of death that would be applicable to all countries. In the United States, the initial impetus for developing a classification of mental disorders was the need to collect statistical information (APA, 2000). The 1840 Census adopted a frequency of "idiocy/insanity" category—the first official attempt to gather information about mental illness in the United States, and, in the 1880 Census, seven categories of mental illness were distinguished: mania, melancholia, monomania, paresis, dementia, dipsomania, and epilepsy. In 1917, the Bureau of Census implemented a plan developed by both the APA Committee on Statistics and the National Commission on Mental Hygiene to gather uniform statistics across mental hospitals (a simple and not clinically useful classification system). The APA subsequently developed the first edition of the American Medical Association's Standard Classified Nomenclature of Disease, designed primarily for diagnosing inpatients with severe psychiatric and neurological disorders. In subsequent decades (1920s–1950s), discoveries such as Down's syndrome facilitated the application of discreet categorization to psychology. The DSM-I and DSM-II originated out of the experiences of military psychiatry in World War II and were guided by the application of psychoanalytic theory to the understanding and treatment of combat stress (PDM Task Force, 2006).

During the 1950s, the American Psychiatric Association (APA) sought to update its own diagnostic system and came up with the first DSM in 1952. This system was not compatible with ICD-6 (current at that time), yet it was still firmly entrenched in the medical model. During the 1960s, several challenges to the medical model as outlined in the DSM were offered from various sources. First, as explained in Chapter 1, the anti-psychiatrists, led by Thomas Szasz, challenged the very idea of mental disorders—asserting they were not true illnesses (given the absence of biological abnormality) and were nothing more than attempts to control social deviance. An additional group advocating *labeling theory*—which argues that efforts at social control (not the behavior of the criminal) ultimately trigger the processes trapping individuals in life trajectories of criminal offending—also argued this latter point (e.g., Lemert, 1951; Tannenbaum, 1938). Dimensional theorists disagreed with the narrow and categorical nature of the medical model, advocating for a dimensional approach that recognized the rarity of sharp boundaries between the normal and pathological; they argued that, in many cases, diagnoses are extensions of normal phenomenon (e.g., Widiger, 1993).

In a sense, the DSM-I and DSM-II could be considered "warm-up" efforts. The much more descriptive, precise, research-oriented DSM-III was intended as an atheoretical document (PDM Task Force, 2006). Not included in this version, however, were the neuroses—an enormous defeat for psychoanalysts, which was indicative of the difficulties (at that time) of fitting psychoanalytic conceptualizations into the framework of mental disorders determined by organized psychiatry's classificatory and research needs (PDM Task Force, 2006). Interestingly, up until DSM-III, there was never a psychologist on the committee for the DSM. Theodore Millon was the first, and, in this third edition, the personality disorders category was added. Ultimately, it is important to remember that all classification efforts are products of time and place in human history and context, making regular revision a scientific requirement (PDM Task Force, 2006). As well, consider that the extensive DSM revision process consists of distinct phases of literature reviews, data reanalysis, and field trials—historically taking in its entirety several years or more to complete.

Conclusion

In the preceding chapter, we provided a "crash course" of sorts in the fundamentals of abnormal psychology. This is an ambitious task, particularly given the multitudes of available well-written textbooks dedicated solely to this topic (which—as can be seen—is essentially a collection of topics encompassing many different areas of scientific study). Due to the scope of this book, numerous very important concepts may have received only modest amounts of attention here (and some, admittedly, even the briefest of mention); so readers are encouraged to pursue further reading about concepts of interest in the existing volumes of work that provide more extensive and in-depth coverage. That being said, the primer material amassed in this chapter should provide readers with a solid foundation for understanding the disorders and their relations to legal concepts presented in the chapters that follow, as well as with tools that will aid in the critical examination of the intersection between mental illness and crime.

For centuries, attempts have been made both to explain thoughts, feelings, and behaviors that appear to fall outside of the normal range of human experience and to quantify and categorize them in order to help those who are suffering. History is replete with examples of how this has been done with varying levels of success, and the struggle to do so effectively continues to the present day. Although some approaches to understanding abnormal behavior have fallen completely by the wayside (e.g., those blaming supernatural forces or based on rudimentary understandings of human anatomy), others (e.g., those emphasizing social or environmental influences, learning mechanisms, or unconscious processes) have waxed and waned in favorability over time but have nonetheless provided and continue to provide important contributions. Still others represent themes that appear to cycle through history—incorporating the legacies of past theorists with exciting new technology. For example, are neurobiologists and neurocriminologists the "new Lombrosians," or is brain imaging techniques merely modern-day phrenology? Perhaps one take-home message from this chapter is that all of these approaches (even those proven inadequate, as science advances through both successes and failures) have provided important pieces to the abnormal psychology puzzle, with none solving it (or even coming close to doing so) in its entirety.

Incomprehensible and aberrant as the inner experiences and behaviors of Ed Gein may seem to most of us, it must be remembered that his mind (and brain alike)—though somewhat mysterious and veiled in secrecy from our current perspective—should not be considered ultimately "unknowable." Inevitably, with time and continued research efforts, explanations for his enigmatic existence (and for those of others who have suffered similarly) will most assuredly be brought to bear. Moving forward into the subsequent chapters of this book, we challenge readers to examine the individuals presented—like Gein—from the various theoretical perspectives outlined here and to think critically about how mental illness may or may not have contributed to their criminal and violent deeds.

KEY TERMS

amygdala

assessment

central nervous system

classical conditioning

computed tomography (CT) scanning

defense mechanisms

diagnosis

ego

electroencephalography (EEG)
functional brain imaging
functional magnetic resonance imaging (fMRI)
hormones
humanism
id
impairment
incidence
limbic system
magnetic resonance imaging (MRI)
magnetoencephalography (MEG)
negative reinforcement
neuropsychology
neurotransmitters
nosology
operant conditioning
parasympathetic nervous system
peripheral nervous system
positron emission tomography (PET)
positive reinforcement
prefrontal cortex
prevalence
psychophysiology
psychosexual stages
punishment
structural brain imaging
superego
sympathetic nervous system
unconscious processes

REVIEW QUESTIONS

1. Identify the different ways in which mental illness has been defined historically. Compare and contrast the strengths and weaknesses of each. Is Wakefield's biological dysfunction truly the best definition? Why or why not?
2. By comparing and contrasting their respective methodologies, critically evaluate the different neuroscientific methods (i.e., structural and functional brain imaging, neurology, neuropsychology, and psychophysiology) for collecting information about the brain. Identify the strengths and weakness of each, as well as the underlying conceptual presuppositions of each. What is the appropriateness of each method in the study of both mental illness and crime?
3. Compare and contrast Freud's structural model of the mind with the current neurobiological understanding of the brain. Examine Figures 2.5 and 2.9. How are the two proposals visually similar? How are they analogous conceptually?
4. Provide explanations for Ed Gein's bizarre and aberrant behavior using each of the theoretical models presented in this chapter: neurobiological, sociocultural, behavioral, psychoanalytic, and integrative or interactional. What are the strengths and weaknesses of each, and which model performs the best in this case? Identify the difficulties and limitations in applying each model.
5. Construct arguments both for and against the classification of psychological disorders. How might a particular classification system affect the study of mental illness and crime? Given the dissent among different theorists about how (and even why) these disorders are classified, is the classification of mental illness even an appropriate area of study? Why or why not?

3

Disorders of Infancy, Childhood, or Adolescence

(Neurodevelopmental Disorders)

JOEL DAVID RIFKIN

Joel Rifkin was born in New York on January 20, 1959. Rifkin is considered New York's most prolific serial killer, convicted of murdering 9 women—mostly drug addicted prostitutes—from 1989 to 1993 (though it is believed he killed as many as 17).

Rifkin was adopted at three weeks of age (not much is known of his biological parents, other than they were young college students). A shy and awkward young boy, Rifkin was teased and harassed by classmates (who nicknamed him "the Turtle") when he entered school. Though he had an above-average IQ, he struggled academically because of severe dyslexia. He had an intense interest in collecting and storing objects. Later in high school, despite attempts to fit in via yearbook photography and the track team, he was considered by his peers as odd and a "loner": he remained a social outcast who behaved unusually, dressed awkwardly, and was frequently bullied. As a disorganized and disheveled young adult, he failed to find steady work but later became profoundly interested in horticulture, working in his late twenties as an intern groundskeeper and a self-employed landscaper. At age 18, he began having sex with female prostitutes. Living in his mother's suburban East Meadow, New York home, he often hired prostitutes in New York City.

When Rifkin was 28, his father, suffering from unbearable pain from prostate cancer, committed suicide (a significant stressor possibly related to his killings). Rifkin committed his first murder at age 30 in his bedroom: a prostitute whose body he subsequently dismembered with a hobby knife and distributed in surrounding areas. He killed his victims—often in his bedroom or car—by beating and strangling or suffocating them during or shortly after sexual intercourse.

Rifkin has been described as emotionally detached, with abnormal nonverbal social expressions, awkward bodily postures, clumsy movements, and flat and monotone speech. His mother once stated that "he never seemed to be aware that people were angry and annoyed with him," summing up his difficulties with social and emotional interactions. He was also described as very routine oriented and terrified of change.

Rifkin was apprehended with his final victim's body in the back of his pickup truck on June 28, 1993, after a police pursuit (initiated because his vehicle had no license plates). As of the writing of this book, Rifkin was serving 203 years to life in prison at Clinton Correctional Facility in upstate New York.

The idea that various forms of mental illness may have their developmental underpinnings in the early stages of life is likely relatively easy to grasp. However, the notion that some of these illnesses may present in their full-blown forms during the years of childhood and adolescence can be much more difficult to entertain. As human beings, these early formative years become the crucial foundation upon which our lives are subsequently laid; and navigating them successfully while challenged with symptoms that fall outside of the normal range of human experience (i.e., in terms of cognitions, emotions, behaviors, and social interactions) can be quite challenging for the individual and his or her family. Especially difficult are those cases—like Joel Rifkin's—in which symptoms may lead to decades of mounting frustration and social isolation and possibly (eventually) to acts of extreme violence and aggression.

The DSM-IV-TR (APA, 2000) outlines an entire class of disorders that are usually diagnosed in the earlier developmental stages of the human life course. These include mental retardation; learning disorders (reading disorder, mathematics disorder, disorder of written expression, learning disorder NOS); motor skills disorder (including developmental coordination disorder); communication disorders (expressive language disorder, mixed receptive-expressive language disorder, phonological disorder, stuttering, communication disorder NOS); pervasive developmental disorders (autistic disorder, Rett's disorder, childhood disintegrative disorder, Asperger's disorder, pervasive developmental disorder NOS); attention-deficit and disruptive behavior disorders (attention-deficit/hyperactivity disorder or ADHD, conduct disorder, oppositional defiant disorder or ODD, ADHD NOS and ODD NOS); feeding and eating disorders of infancy or early childhood (pica, rumination disorder, feeding disorder of early infancy or early childhood); tic disorders (Tourette's disorder, chronic motor or vocal tic disorder, transient tic disorder, tic disorder NOS); elimination disorders (encopresis, enuresis); and other disorders of infancy, childhood, or adolescence (separation anxiety disorder, selective mutism, reactive attachment disorder of infancy or early childhood, stereotypic movement disorder, and disorder of infancy, childhood, or adolescence NOS).

The DSM-IV-TR cautions that the inclusion of a class of disorders usually diagnosed first in infancy, childhood, or adolescence is not meant to suggest any clear distinction between disorders of childhood and of adulthood. In fact, although many individuals with these disorders present for clinical attention in earlier years, some may not be diagnosed until adulthood.

In the DSM-5 (APA, 2013), this class of disorders has been renamed neurodevelopmental disorders, and several key changes have been made in both conceptualization and diagnostic nomenclature. Disorders now include intellectual disability (intellectual developmental disorder), communication disorders, autism spectrum disorder, ADHD, neurodevelopmental motor disorders, and specific learning disorder. Specific changes will be discussed below.

As an aside, the case of Joel Rifkin holds particular significance for author Robert Schug, as he had the good fortune to interview Rifkin in person in Clinton Correctional Facility in the spring of 2007, for a television documentary about the brain. The chance to speak face-to-face with an individual with such a violent past was a career highlight for Schug—a brief but unforgettable firsthand glimpse into the dark recesses of the mind of a prolific serial killer, as well as an opportunity to understand and appreciate the inner human experience of a very unique and troubled individual.

Mental Retardation (Intellectual Disability or Intellectual Developmental Disorder)

The term **mental retardation**, which was used in the DSM-IV-TR, has been replaced with "intellectual disability (intellectual developmental disorder)" in the DSM-5, reflecting language more recently used in federal statutes, research journals, and by medical and educational professionals, the lay public, and advocacy groups (APA, 2013). Diagnostic criteria for the category intellectual disability are listed in Table 3.1.

Prevalence and Incidence Rates of Mental Retardation

Prevalence rates for mental retardation have been estimated at approximately 1% of the U.S. population. Of these people, approximately 85% are diagnosed with mild mental retardation, 10% with moderate mental

Table 3.1 DSM-5 Diagnostic Criteria for Intellectual Disability

Intellectual Disability

Intellectual disability (intellectual developmental disorder) is a disorder with onset during the developmental period that includes both intellectual and adaptive functioning deficits in conceptual, social, and practical domains. The following three criteria must be met:

A. Deficits in intellectual functions, such as reasoning, problem solving, planning, abstract thinking, judgment, academic learning, and learning from experience, confirmed by both clinical assessment and individualized, standardized intelligence testing.

B. Deficits in adaptive functioning that result in failure to meet developmental and sociocultural standards for personal independence and social responsibility. Without ongoing support, the adaptive deficits limit functioning in one or more activities of daily life, such as communication, social participation, and independent living, across multiple environments, such as home, school, work, and community.

C. Onset of intellectual and adaptive deficits during the developmental period.

Specify current severity:

(F70) Mild

(F71) Moderate

(F72) Severe

(F73) Profound

Source: APA (2013, p. 33). Reprinted with permission from the *Diagnostic and Statistical Manual of Mental Disorders*, Fifth Edition (Copyright © 2013). American Psychiatric Association. All rights reserved.

retardation, 3–4% with severe mental retardation, and 1–2% with profound mental retardation (APA, 2000). More recent estimates are similar, with a prevalence rate for intellectual disability in the general population of approximately 1% (varying by age) and, for severe intellectual disability, a rate of approximately 6 per 1,000 (APA, 2013).

Theoretical Conceptualizations

Mental retardation was operationalized in the DSM-IV-TR using neuropsychological measures of intelligence such as the **intelligence quotient (IQ)**—indirect indices of brain function (or dysfunction) that speak largely to a neurobiological conceptualization of this disorder. In fact, mental retardation was the only disorder within the DSM-IV-TR that used IQ scores as primary criteria for diagnosis. (For mental retardation, significantly subaverage intellectual functioning was defined as an IQ of approximately 70 or below). The DSM-5 continues to use IQ as part of the diagnostic criteria, but IQ is no longer the exclusive measure; IQ has been coupled with a requisite assessment of deficits in adaptive functioning. To that end, brain neurobiological studies have investigated the link between mental retardation and *fragile X syndrome.* (FraX, a mutation occurring on the *FMR1* gene on chromosome Xq27.3, is the most common known cause of genetically transmitted neurodevelopmental disability.) Specifically, structural brain imaging studies have identified FraX-associated abnormalities in each general cortical lobe region (frontal, temporal, parietal, and occipital), as well as in the caudate nucleus, small superior temporal gyrus, posterior (cerebellar) vermis, amygdala, and cerebellum. (Remember from the primer on the brain's structure in Chapter 2 that many of these terms are directional: ***posterior*** means "behind" or "toward the rear" and is the opposite of *anterior*, and ***superior*** and ***inferior*** are opposites meaning "above" and "below," respectively.) These abnormalities include brain asymmetry. Additionally, functional imaging studies have demonstrated abnormal anterior cerebral-caudate connectivity and function in individuals with FraX (Gothelf et al., 2008). Moreover, though neurobiological explanations appear suitable for conceptualizing this disorder, the characteristic cognitive deficits of mental retardation would likely not be readily explained by unconscious processes (i.e., psychoanalytic theory) or conditioning or learning (i.e., behavioral theory).

The Relationship Between Mental Retardation and Crime

While we await forthcoming studies of mental illness and crime and violence using the new DSM-5 nomenclature, the term mental retardation will be retained here to refer to the body of research already conducted using the previous diagnostic terminology. Tables 3.2 and 3.3 list a number of investigations, in chronological order, that have examined both prevalence rates of crime and violence in individuals with mental retardation and rates of mental retardation in criminal populations.

General Studies. First references to relationships between intellectual disabilities (IDs) and criminal behavior appear in the criminological literature dating back to the nineteenth century. Pioneering Italian criminologist Cesare Lombroso, in his classical text *Criminal Man*, alludes to two such relationships in his discussions of the evolutionary and biological roots of criminality. Under what he terms "general forms of lunacy," Lombroso designates the *idiot*, who is "prompted by paroxysms of rage to murder," as well as the *imbecile*, which he defines as "weak-minded" (Lombroso-Ferrero, 1911/1972). Appalling as these terms may seem today, in historical context, they were not intended as pejorative and merely reflected the standard diagnostic nomenclature of the period. Deficits in general intelligence (e.g., IQ or Full Scale IQ) are the best-replicated cognitive correlate of antisocial, violent, and criminal behavior among non-mentally ill individuals (Wilson & Herrnstein, 1985).

To date, studies of intellectual disabilities and mental retardation and crime have been limited overall and have focused largely on the qualitative nature of antisocial behavior in individuals with IDs. In their landmark study from Germany of mentally ill, mentally defective, and mentally abnormal offenders located through searches of criminal records and a regional psychiatric hospital register, (see Table 3.2), Häfner and Böker (1982) found that, compared to those with other mental illnesses (e.g., schizophrenia, mood disorders, and epilepsy), individuals with mental deficiency were more likely to attack persons outside of the family and intimate social circle. In fact, 39.7% (27 of 68) attacked acquaintances, neighbors, or other inmates while 25% (17 of 68) violently assaulted complete strangers. However, they were less likely than those with schizophrenia to attack individuals in authority (i.e., 7.9% or 3 of 68)—which may have been due in some way to their subordinate social status. According to Read and Rendall (2007), individuals with IDs are more vulnerable to aggressive and disruptive behaviors and are quite difficult to manage. In fact, a meta-analysis of 22 studies (McClintock et al., 2003) found males with IDs were significantly more likely to demonstrate aggression than females and that individuals with severe or profound IDs were significantly more likely to be characterized by self-injury and stereotypy than individuals with mild or moderate levels of IDs.

Other studies have noted a variety in the frequency of particular offense types among offenders with IDs. According to Barron and colleagues (2002), although property crimes are quite common in this population, sexual offending and fire setting are more often linked to offenders with ID. In fact, these authors report that sex offending is four to six times higher in those with ID than in the general population. However, studies have also shown other offenses to be common in this population, and ID offenders are also more likely to commit property crimes, as well as violent crimes and arson. Additionally, re-offense rates among ID offenders have been shown to be quite high in studies in the United Kingdom (e.g., over 50% reported in Barron et al., 2004).

Origins of Crime and Violence in Mental Retardation: Theoretical Explanations and Etiological Mechanisms

Comparatively few researchers have made efforts to understand how and why crime and violence may manifest in individuals with mental retardation or other intellectual disabilities. Though ID-associated impairments in cognitive problem solving and impulse control might intuitively seem blameworthy at first, neither would explain why *all* individuals with IDs do not become criminal or violent. From a neurobiological perspective, Isir and colleagues (2010), in a first-of-its-kind study, failed to find a significant association between a polymorphism

(Text continues on page 71)

Table 3.2 Prevalence of Mental Retardation in Criminal Populations

Mental Retardation								
Source	**N**	**Gender**	**Age**	**Study Type**[a1]	**Sample Description**	**Disorder**	**Diagnostic System**	**Prevalence/ Incidence**
Cohen & Freeman (1945)	(1) 320 (2) 87	M, F	Adult?	AR	Police records of arrested patients from 1,676 patients paroled/ discharged from Norwich State Hospital (Connecticut), 1940–1944: (1) Arrested before hospitalization (2) Arrested after hospitalization	Psychosis with mental deficiency	?	(1) 5.9% (n = 19) (2) 4.6% (n = 4)
Pfeiffer, Eisenstein, & Dabbs (1967)	85	2/3 M, 1/3 F	17–63	JD	Federal prisoners referred for mental competency evaluations, at the USPHS Hospital in Lexington, Kentucky, 1960–1965	Mental deficiency	?	9.4% (n =8)
Kahn (1971)	43	41 M, 2 F	11–74	HO	Interviews and psychiatric examinations of individuals who made pleas of insanity to charges of first- or second-degree murder.	Mental deficiency	?	9.3% (n =4)
Szymusik (1972)	50	M	16–68	HO	Murderers, Poland, 1955–1969	Mental dullness	?	18.0% (n =9)
						Borderline moron		20.0% (n =10)
						Moron		18.0% (n =9)
Frazier (1974)	31	?	?	HO	Murderers in prisons in Texas, Minnesota, New Jersey, and New York and in mental hospitals in Texas, Minnesota, Saskatchewan, Massachusetts, and New York	Idiopathic mental retardation	?	6.5% (n = 2)
Okasha et al. (1975)	(1) 60 (2) 20	(1) 50 M, 10 F (2) ?M, ?F	25–35[a]	HO	"Socio-psychiatric study" of (1) Murderers in Abou-Zabel and Kanater prisons, Egypt (2) Murderers in Egyptian State Mental Hospital	Mental subnormality	?	(1) 16.7% (n = 10) (2) 23.3% (n = 7)

(Continued)

(Continued)

Mental Retardation								
Source	**N**	**Gender**	**Age**	**Study Type**[a1]	**Sample Description**	**Disorder**	**Diagnostic System**	**Prevalence/ Incidence**
Pétursson & Gudjónsson (1981)	47	44 M, 3 F	Adult[ai]	HO	File review of cases of intentional and unintentional homicide in Iceland, 1900–1979	Mental subnormality	?	6.4% (n = 3)
Häfner & Böker (1982)	(1) 533 (2) 3392	M, F	14–60+	PI	(1) Mentally ill and mentally defective offenders from records searches of German federal and regional criminal bureaus, 1955–1964 (2) Mentally abnormal non-offenders (every fifth admission to regional psychiatric hospital, from register search, 1955–1964)	Mental deficiency (mental retardation)	Not IQ-based (i.e., IQ < 70), but rather "substantial degree of defect" and diminished responsibility	(1) 12.8% (n = 68)[c] (2) 5.0% (n = 171)
Langevin et al. (1982)	(1) 109 (2) 38	?	Adult?	PI	File record review of minimum-security forensic ward psychiatric hospital cases, 1969–1979 (Clarke Institute in Toronto, Ontario, Canada) (1) Killers (2) Nonviolent offenders	Mental retardation	Feighner et al. (1972) psychiatric research diagnostic criteria	(1) 4.0% (2) 3.0%
Dell & Smith (1983)	253	M	15 and under to 70+[d]	HO	File review of men convicted of manslaughter on the grounds of diminished responsibility, 1966–1977	Mental handicap (including borderline cases)	?	5.1% (n = 13)
Seltzer & Langford (1984)	85	M, F	15–25 (Median = 18)	PI	Interviews of individuals referred by courts or legal counsel to psychiatry department of large regional hospital in Northwest Territories, calendar year 1981	Mental retardation	DSM-III, MMPI	7.1% (n = 6)
Reich & Wells (1985)	390	325 M, 65 F	M = 30.9	JD	Record review of defendants evaluated for competency to stand trial by the Yale-New Haven Psychiatric Court Clinic, 1980–1982.	Mental retardation	DSM-III	5.9% (n = 23)[bc]

Mental Retardation								
Source	**N**	**Gender**	**Age**	**Study Type**[a1]	**Sample Description**	**Disorder**	**Diagnostic System**	**Prevalence/ Incidence**
Zagar et al. (1989)	1,956	1,572 M, 384 F	6–17 (*M* = 13.9, *SD* = 1.9)	AJ[bq]	Adjudicated child and adolescent delinquents referred by Circuit Court of Cook County Juvenile Division for clinical evaluation, 1981–1986	Mental retardation	DSM-III	15.0%
Rath & Dash (1990)	15	10 M, 3 F[p]	20–29[p]	JD	Interviews, file reviews, and clinical observation of prisoners (murderers) referred for psychiatric evaluation, India	Mental subnormality	ICD-9	6.7% ($n = 1$)
Yarvis (1990)	100	88 M, 12 F	33% < 25, 85% < 40	HO	Diagnostic interviews and record reviews of a series of murderers referred for psychiatric evaluation in California, 1980–1988	Mental retardation/ developmental disorder (Axis I)	DSM-III	2.0% ($n = 2$)[j]
						Developmental disorder (Axis II)	DSM-III	1.0% ($n = 1$)[j]
Siponmaa et al. (2001)	126	123 M, 3 F	15–22 (Median = 20)	JD	Interviews with young offenders consecutively referred for presentencing psychiatric investigation, Stockholm, Sweden, 1990–1995	Organic syndrome, mental retardation, neuropsychiatric developmental disorder	ICD-9	5% ($n = 7$)
Hanlon et al. (2010)	77	69 M, 8 F	*M* = 31.92, *SD* = 11.5	JD	Clinical interviews, file and record reviews of indigent men and women charged with or convicted of first-degree murder in Illinois and Missouri	Developmental disorder (MR, learning disorder)	?	49.4% ($n = 38$)
Catanesi et al. (2011)	103	85.44% M	53.41% 25–54, 22.73% 45–65, 13.64% 18–24, 5.68% <18	HO	Psychiatric and psychological evaluations on perpetrators of homicide and attempted homicide, Italy	Mental retardation	DSM-IV-TR	8.7%

(Continued)

(Continued)

Asperger's Syndrome and Autistic Spectrum Disorders								
Source	**N**	**Gender**	**Age**	**Study Type[a1]**	**Sample Description**	**Disorder**	**Diagnostic System**	**Prevalence/ Incidence**
Scragg & Shah (1994)	392	M	Adult?	PI	Diagnostic interviews of maximum-security hospital patients (Broadmoor)	Asperger's syndrome	Gillberg & Gillberg (1989)	1.5% ($n = 6$)
Hare et al. (2000)	1305	?M, ?F	Adult	PI	Residents in one of three special hospitals (Ashworth, Broadmoor, & Rampton) in England	Autistic spectrum disorders	HBS schedule	2.4% ($n = 31$)
Siponmaa et al. (2001)	126	123 M, 3 F	15–22 (Median = 20)	JD	Case record reviews of young offenders consecutively referred for presentencing psychiatric investigation, Stockholm, Sweden, 1990–1995	Asperger syndrome	DSM-IV	10% ($n = 13$)
ADHD								
Source	**N**	**Gender**	**Age**	**Study Type[a1]**	**Sample Description**	**Disorder**	**Diagnostic System**	**Prevalence/ Incidence**
Zagar et al. (1989)	1,956	1,572 M, 384 F	6–17 ($M = 13.9$, $SD = 1.9$)	AJ[bq]	Adjudicated child and adolescent delinquents referred by Circuit Court of Cook County Juvenile Division for clinical evaluation, 1981–1986	ADD-H	DSM-III	9.0%
						ADD		46.0%
Myers et al. (1990)	15	F	Juveniles	PI	Diagnostic interviews with juvenile delinquents committed to a residential treatment program, Florida	ADD	DSM-III (DICA)	20% ($n = 3$)
Haapasalo & Hämäläinen (1996)	89	?	16–22 ($M = 20.21$, $SD = 1.37$)	JD	Structured clinical interviews with offenders randomly selected among prison inmates, Finland (1) Property offenders (2) Violent offenders	ADHD	DSM-IV (DICA-R-A)	(1) 51.4% (2) 48.1%

ADHD								
Source	**N**	**Gender**	**Age**	**Study Type**[a1]	**Sample Description**	**Disorder**	**Diagnostic System**	**Prevalence/ Incidence**
Galli et al. (1999)	22	M	13–17 (*M* = 15.9, *SD* = 1.1)	PI, CS	Interviews with adolescents admitting to sexually assaulting another child, referred from a juvenile rehabilitation center, the juvenile court system, and an inpatient adolescent psychiatric unit, Hamilton County, Ohio	ADHD	DSM-III-R (DICA)	71.0% (*n* = 12)[by]
Pliszka et al. (2000)	50	45 M, 5 F	*M* = 15.4, *SD* =1.4	JD	Interviews with adolescents consecutively admitted to the Bexar County, Texas Juvenile Detention Center	ADHD	DSM-IV (DIS-C)	18.0% (*n* = 9)
Siponmaa et al. (2001)	126	123 M, 3 F	15–22 (Median = 20)	JD	Case record reviews of young offenders consecutively referred for presentencing psychiatric investigation, Stockholm, Sweden, 1990–1995	ADHD	DSM-IV	25% (*n* = 31)
Lindgren et al. (2002)	45	M	19–51 (*M* = 32.0, *SD* = 8.3)	JD	Standardized clinical interviews and questionnaire data from prison inmates in the two prisons of the island of Gotland, Sweden	AD/HD	DSM-III-R (SCID-II-Screen, WURS)	55.0% (*n* = 25)
Teplin et al. (2002)	1829	1172 M, 657 F	10–18	JD	Diagnostic interviews of youths randomly sampled from intake into the Cook County Juvenile Temporary Detention Center, Nov. 1995–June 1998	ADHD	DSM-III-R	M: 16.6% F: 21.4%
Rösler et al. (2004)	129	M	*M* = 19.5, *SD* = 2.0	JD	Clinical interviews, record reviews, and rating scales conducted on inmates of a German offender facility (JSA Ottweiler)	Disturbance of activity and attention	ICD-10	5.4%[bx]
						ADHD-CT[bw]	DSM-IV	21.7%[bx]*
						ADHD-IT[bw]		1.6%[bx]
						ADHD-HIT[bw]		21.7%[bx]*

(Continued)

(Continued)

ADHD								
Source	**N**	**Gender**	**Age**	**Study Type**[a1]	**Sample Description**	**Disorder**	**Diagnostic System**	**Prevalence/ Incidence**
Langevin (2003)	(1) 33 (2) 80 (3) 23 (4) 611	M	(1) $M = 32.06$ (2) $M = 27.58$ (3) $M = 27.57$ (4) $M = 31.42$	PI	Interviews with convicted sex offenders ($n = 747$) belonging to one of four groups: (1) sex killers, (2) nonhomicidal sexually aggressives, (3) nonhomicidal sadists, and (4) general sex offenders. Participants were chosen from a database of more than 2,800 minimum-security forensic ward psychiatric hospital cases (Clarke Institute in Toronto, Ontario, Canada) seen since 1973.	ADHD	?	(1) 6.1% (2) 7.5% (3) 4.4% (4) 2.6%
Hanlon et al. (2010)	77	69 M, 8 F	$M = 31.92$, $SD = 11.5$	JD	Clinical interviews, file and record reviews of indigent men and women charged with or convicted of first-degree murder in Illinois and Missouri	ADHD or disruptive behavior disorder	?	36.4% ($n = 28$)
Conduct Disorder								
Source	**N**	**Gender**	**Age**	**Study type**[a1]	**Sample Description**	**Disorder**	**Diagnostic System**	**Prevalence/ Incidence**
Reich & Wells (1985)	390	325 M, 65 F	$M = 30.9$	JD	Record review of defendants evaluated for competency to stand trial by the Yale-New Haven Psychiatric Court Clinic, 1980–1982	Conduct disorders	DSM-III	3.1% ($n = 12$)
Myers et al. (1990)	15	F	Juveniles	PI	Diagnostic interviews with juvenile delinquents committed to a residential treatment program, Florida	Conduct disorder	DSM-III (DICA)	100% ($n = 15$)
Yarvis (1990)	100	88 M, 12 F	33% < 25, 85% < 40	HO	Diagnostic interviews and record reviews of a series of murderers referred for psychiatric evaluation in California, 1980–1988	Explosive/conduct disorder	DSM-III	4.0% ($n = 4$)[j]

Conduct Disorder								
Source	**N**	**Gender**	**Age**	**Study type**[a1]	**Sample Description**	**Disorder**	**Diagnostic System**	**Prevalence/ Incidence**
DeJong, Virkkunen, & Linnoila (1992)	(1) 248 (2) 100	M	16–68, (*M* = 31.2, *SD* = 11.9)	JD	Criminals ordered for forensic psychiatric examination at initial incarceration in Finland (1) Murders and attempted murderers (2) Arsonists	Conduct disorder	DSM-III	(1) 4.0% (2) 3.0%
Haapasalo & Hämäläinen (1996)	89	?	16–22 (*M* = 20.21, *SD* = 1.37)	JD	Structured clinical interviews with offenders randomly selected among prison inmates, Finland (1) Property offenders (2) Violent offenders	Conduct disorder	DSM-IV (DICA-R-A)	(1) 100.0% (2) 100.0%
Galli et al. (1999)	22	M	13–17 (*M* = 15.9, *SD* =1.1)	PI, CS	Interviews with adolescents admitting to sexually assaulting another child, referred from a juvenile rehabilitation center, the juvenile court system, and an inpatient adolescent psychiatric unit, Hamilton County, Ohio	Conduct disorders	DSM-III-R (DICA)	94.0% (n = 16)[by]
Pliszka et al. (2000)	50	45 M, 5 F	*M* = 15.4, *SD* = 1.4	JD	Interviews with adolescents consecutively admitted to the Bexar County, Texas Juvenile Detention Center	Conduct disorder	DSM-IV (DIS-C)	60.0% (n = 30)
Teplin et al. (2002)	1829	1172 M, 657 F	10–18	JD	Diagnostic interviews of youths randomly sampled from intake into the Cook County Juvenile Temporary Detention Center, November 1995—June 1998	Conduct disorder	DSM-III-R	M: 37.8% F: 40.6%

(*Continued*)

(Continued)

Conduct Disorder								
Source	**N**	**Gender**	**Age**	**Study type**[a1]	**Sample Description**	**Disorder**	**Diagnostic System**	**Prevalence/ Incidence**
Rösler et al. (2004)	129	M	*M* = 19.5, *SD* = 2.0	JD	Clinical interviews, record reviews, and rating scales conducted on inmates of a German offender facility (JSA Ottweiler)	Hyperkinetic conduct disorder	ICD-10	16.3%[bx*]
Oppositional-Defiant Disorder								
Source	**N**	**Gender**	**Age**	**Study Type**[a1]	**Sample Description**	**Disorder**	**Diagnostic System**	**Prevalence/ Incidence**
Haapasalo & Hämäläinen (1996)	89	?	16–22 (*M* = 20.21, *SD* = 1.37)	JD	Structured clinical interviews with offenders randomly selected among prison inmates, Finland (1) Property offenders (2) Violent offenders	Oppositional defiant disorder	DSM-IV (DICA-R-A)	(1) 24.3% (2) 23.1%
Pliszka et al. (2000)	50	45 M, 5 F	*M* = 15.4, *SD* = 1.4	JD	Interviews with adolescents consecutively admitted to the Bexar County, Texas Juvenile Detention Center	Oppositional-defiant disorder	DSM-IV (DIS-C)	24.0% (n = 12)
Teplin et al. (2002)	1829	1172 M, 657 F	10–18	JD	Diagnostic interviews of youths randomly sampled from intake into the Cook County Juvenile Temporary Detention Center, November 1995—June 1998.	Oppositional-defiant disorder	DSM-III-R	M: 14.5% F: 17.5%

Miscellaneous Disorders								
Source	**N**	**Gender**	**Age**	**Study Type[a1]**	**Sample Description**	**Disorder**	**Diagnostic System**	**Prevalence/ Incidence**
Siponmaa et al. (2001)	126	123 M, 3 F	15–22 (Median = 20)	JD	Case record reviews of young offenders consecutively referred for presentencing psychiatric investigation, Stockholm, Sweden, 1990–1995	PDD	DSM-IV	27% ($n = 34$)
						PDD NOS		17% ($n = 21$)
						Tourette syndrome		2% ($n = 3$)
Epilepsy								
Source	**N**	**Gender**	**Age**	**Study Type[a1]**	**Sample Description**	**Disorder**	**Diagnostic System**	**Prevalence/ Incidence**
Cohen & Freeman (1945)	(1) 320 (2) 87	M, F	Adult?	AR	Police records of arrested patients from 1,676 patients paroled or discharged from Norwich State Hospital, Connecticut, 1940–1944 (1) Arrested before hospitalization (2) Arrested after hospitalization	Psychosis with epilepsy	?	(1) 3.1% ($n = 10$) (2) 2.3% ($n = 2$)
Stierlin (1956, in Schipkowensky, 1968)	773	?	?	PI	Statistical data from aggressive inmates in 73 psychiatric clinics and mental hospitals in Europe	Epilepsy	?	12.4% ($n = 94$)
Lanzkron (1964, in Schipkowensky, 1968)	150	?	?	HO	Murderers in Matteawan State Hospital, New York	Epilepsy (psychoses)	?	2.7% ($n = 4$)
Kalashnik (1966, in Schipkowensky, 1968)	271	?	?	HO	Murderers in the Moscow Forensic Psychiatric Institute	Epilepsy	?	4.4% ($n = 12$)
Rachev (1966, in Schipkowensky, 1968)	100	?	?	HO	Murderers in custodial care at Lovech Mental Hospital Forensic Department, Bulgaria, 1933–1965	Epilepsy	?	16.0% ($n = 16$)

(Continued)

(Continued)

Miscellaneous Disorders								
Source	**N**	**Gender**	**Age**	**Study Type**[a1]	**Sample Description**	**Disorder**	**Diagnostic System**	**Prevalence/ Incidence**
Schipkowensky (1968)	194	?	?	HO	Murderers at the Psychiatric Clinic of the University of Sofia, Bulgaria, 1926–1965	Epilepsy (psychoses)	?	13.8% (n = 25)
Szymusik (1972)	50	M	16–68	HO	Murderers, Poland, 1955–1969	Epilepsy	?	2.0% (n =1)
Frazier (1974)	31	?	?	HO	Murderers in prisons in Texas, Minnesota, New Jersey, and New York and in mental hospitals in Texas, Minnesota, Saskatchewan, Massachusetts, and New York	Temporal lobe epilepsy	?	6.5% (n = 2)
Okasha et al. (1975)	(1) 60 (2) 20	(1) 50 M, 10 F (2) ?M, ?F	25–35[a]	HO	"Socio-psychiatric study" of (1) Murderers in Abou-Zabel and Kanater prisons, Egypt (2) Murderers in Egyptian State Mental Hospital	Epilepsy	?	(1) 3.3% (n = 2) (2) 10.0% (n = 3)
Langevin et al. (1982)	(1) 109 (2) 38	?	Adult?	PI	File record review of minimum-security forensic ward psychiatric hospital cases, 1969–1979 (Clarke Institute in Toronto, Ontario, Canada) (1) Killers (2) Non-violent offenders	Epilepsy	Feighner et al. (1972) psychiatric research diagnostic criteria	(1) 1.0% (2) 0.0%
Dell & Smith (1983)	253	M	15 and under to 70+[d]	HO	File review of men convicted of manslaughter on the grounds of diminished responsibility, 1966–1977	Brain damage or epilepsy	?	7.9% (n = 20)
Seltzer & Langford (1984)	85	M, F	15–25 (Median = 18)	PI	Interviews of individuals referred by courts or legal counsel to psychiatry department of large regional hospital in Northwest Territories, calendar year 1981	Epilepsy	?	1.2% (n = 1)
Taylor & Gunn (1984)	2,743	M	Adult	JD	File review of men remanded to Brixton prison, South London (June, September, December 1979 and March 1980)	Epilepsy	ICD	1.5% (n = 40)

Miscellaneous Disorders								
Source	N	Gender	Age	Study Type[a1]	Sample Description	Disorder	Diagnostic System	Prevalence/ Incidence
Taylor (1986)	183	175 M, 8 F	18–73	JD	Record review of life-sentenced men and women, supervised by the Inner London Probation Service (inside prison and on license in the community)	Epilepsy	ICD-9	4% ($n = 8$)
Rath & Dash (1990)	15	10 M, 3 F[p]	20–29[p]	JD	Interviews, file reviews, and clinical observation of prisoners (murderers) referred for psychiatric evaluation, India	Epilepsy	ICD-9	6.7% ($n = 1$)
Baillargeon et al. (2000)	170,215	155,949 M; 14,268 F	32% 18–29, 60% 30–49, 8% 50+	JD	File review of Texas Department of Criminal Justice inmates incarcerated August 1997—July 1998	Epilepsy	ICD-10	1.9%

Notes: *Significant increase in comparison to control group.

**Significant decrease in comparison to control group.

[a1]AR = arrest rates of patients discharged from psychiatric facilities, JD = jailed detainees and incarcerated prisoners, HO = homicide offenders, BC = birth cohort study, PI = psychiatric inpatient sample, CS = community sample (i.e., epidemiological catchment area survey studies and outpatient psychiatric patients).

[a]Highest percentage of subjects in this age range.

[c]Rate per 1,000 of Mannheim's inhabitants, 1965: 1.52.

[d]Group mean ages: 1966–1969 ($M = 36.1$, $SD = 15.8$), 1970–1973 ($M = 36.2$, $SD = 14.9$), 1974–1977 ($M = 37.1$, $SD = 16.9$).

[j]Community sample comparative data (six-month prevalence rates from NIMH Community Survey data): Data not reported.

[p]Psychotic group ($n = 13$)—including schizophrenia, drug-related psychosis, epilepsy, affective psychosis (depression), mental subnormality, and paranoid illness.

[ai]Group means and standard deviations: Psychotic illness (35.7, 8.8), personality disorder and alcohol use disorders (24.4, 8.2), no psychiatric abnormality (34.0, 12.4).

[bc]Rates of mental retardation in comparison outpatient and inpatient samples from same catchment area: 2.8% ($n = 259$) and 0.3% ($n = 3$).

[bq]Adjudicated juvenile delinquents.

[bw]CT = combined type, IT = predominantly inattentive type, HIT = predominantly hyperactive-impulsive type.

[bx]Prevalence rates for controls ($n = 54$ males without history of delinquency): ADHD-CT = 1.9%, ADHD-IT = 3.7%, ADHD-HIT = 1.9%.

[by]Only 17 participants completed this section of the DICA.

Table 3.3 Prevalence of Crime in Disordered Populations

Mental Retardation

Source	N	Gender	Age	Study Type[a1]	Sample Description	Disorder	Crime Definition	Prevalence/Incidence
Tardiff & Koenigsberg (1985)	(1) 2,106 (2) 810	(1) 842 M, 1256 F (2) 354 M, 453 F	(1) \leq 20–65+[aa] (2) \leq 20–65+[aa]	CS	Psychiatric outpatients evaluated during a 1.5 year period at two New York hospitals, diagnosed using DSM II and DSM II criteria (1) Payne Whitney Clinic (2) Westchester Division of NY Hospital	Childhood and adolescent disorders or mental retardation (1) $n = 84$ (2) $n = 42$	Presence of assaultive behavior toward others in hospital records	(1) 14.3% ($n = 12$) (2) 7.1% ($n = 3$)

Asperger's Syndrome

Source	N	Gender	Age	Study Type[a1]	Sample Description	Disorder	Crime Definition	Prevalence/Incidence
Wing (1981)	34	?M, ?F	?Adult, ?Children	CR[br]	Published case series (with six case histories included) of patients examined and diagnosed by author	Asperger's syndrome	"Bizarre antisocial acts"	11.8% ($n = 4$)
Scott (1985)	10	6M, 4F	16–26 ($M = 18.9$, $SD = 2.8$)	PI	Patients in behavior modification units who have been diagnosed by consulting psychiatrists; diagnostic system not reported	Asperger's syndrome or "Asperger-like"	Physical aggression and "acting out"	Not reported[bs]
Woodbury-Smith et al. (2006)	25	6M, 1F	$M = 29.8$, $SD = 7.9$	CS	Community men and women, FSIQ ≥ 70, diagnosed using ICD-10 criteria	High-functioning autistic spectrum disorders (including AS)	Law breaking: Self-reported and official statistics	Burglary: 4% ($n = 1$)
								Robbery: 0% ($n = 0$)
								Theft (handling stolen goods): 9% ($n = 2$)

Asperger's Syndrome								
Source	**N**	**Gender**	**Age**	**Study Type**[a1]	**Sample Description**	**Disorder**	**Crime Definition**	**Prevalence/ Incidence**
								Theft (shoplifting): 11% ($n = 3$)
								Theft (other): 0% ($n = 0$)
								Drug offenses: 11% ($n = 3$)**
								Criminal damage: 19% ($n = 5$)*
								Violent offenses: 30% ($n = 8$)
								History of convictions: 7% ($n = 2$)
Mauridsen et al. (2008)	313	235 M, 78 F	25–59	AR	Follow-up screening through nationwide Danish Criminal Register of inpatient children at University Clinic of Child Psychiatry of Copenhagen & Aarhus, 1960–1984, diagnosed using ICD-9 criteria	PDDs (Childhood Autism, $n = 113$; Atypical Autism, $n = 86$; Asperger's Syndrome, $n = 114$)	Court convictions	9% ($n = 29$)[bv]**

Notes: *Significant increase in comparison to control group.

**Significant decrease in comparison to control group.

[a1] AR = arrest rates of patients discharged from psychiatric facilities, JD = jailed detainees and incarcerated prisoners, HO = homicide offenders, BC = birth cohort study, PI = psychiatric inpatient sample, CS = community sample (i.e., epidemiological catchment area survey studies and outpatient psychiatric patients).

[a] Highest percentage of subjects in this age range.

[aa](1) 12.4% ($n = 261$) 20 years and younger, 30.7% ($n = 647$) 21–30, 23.6% ($n = 496$) 31–40, 24.3% ($n = 511$) 41–64, 7.5% ($n = 158$) 65 years and older, 1.6% ($n = 33$) unknown; (2) 18.0% ($n = 146$) 20 years and younger, 31.4% ($n = 254$) 21–30, 18.0% ($n = 146$) 31–40, 27.0% ($n = 219$) 41–64, 5.0% ($n = 41$) 65 years and older, 0.5% ($n = 4$) unknown.

[br]Published case reports.

[bs]Non-Asperger's syndrome control group ($n = 10$) also characterized by physical aggression and "acting out" (prevalence rate not reported).

[bt]Comparison group data (large company employee volunteers; $n = 20$; male/female ratio 2:1): Burglary, 0% ($n = 0$); robbery, 0% ($n = 0$); theft—handling stolen goods, 10% ($n = 2$); theft—shoplifting, 20% ($n = 4$); theft—other, 0% ($n = 0$); drug offenses, 55% ($n = 11$); criminal damage, 0% ($n = 0$); violent offenses, 25% ($n = 5$); history of convictions, NA.

[bv]Control group drawn from Danish Central Persons Register: 18% ($n = 168$).

A Closer Look: Mental Retardation and Crime

Prevalence of the Disorder in Crime

Study Type	Number	Prevalence Rates
Arrest rates	1	4.6–5.9%
Birth cohorts	0	–
Community samples	0	–
Homicide offenders	8	2.0–23.3%
Jailed detainees and prisoners	5	5.9–49.4%†
Psychiatric inpatients	3	3.0–12.8%
Adjudicated juvenile delinquents*	1	15.0%
Total Number of Studies	**18**	

Sample Characteristics

Size	21–3,392
Gender	Male only (2 studies); male and female but unbalanced, predominantly males (14 studies); not reported (2 studies)
Age	Youth, adult
Location	Countries worldwide (e.g., Canada, Egypt, Germany, Iceland, India, Italy, Poland, Sweden, United States)
Diagnostic Systems	Not specified in earlier studies (i.e., before 1982). DSM (various editions), ICD (various editions), other research diagnostic criteria.

Notes: *A rarer category of studies somewhat unique to this chapter.

†Latter figure possibly artificially inflated due to categorization method in Hanlon (2010). Rates are 5.9–9.4% without this study.

Prevalence of Crime in the Disorder

Study Type	Number	Prevalence Rates	Crime Definition
Arrest rates	0	–	–
Birth cohorts	0	–	–
Community samples	1*	7.1–14.3%	Presence of assaultive behavior towards others in hospital records.
Homicide offenders	0	–	–
Jailed detainees and prisoners	0	–	–
Psychiatric inpatients	0	–	–
Total Number of Studies	**1**		

Sample Characteristics

Size	2,916
Gender	Male and female
Age	Youth, adult.
Location	United States
Diagnostic Systems	DSM I and DSM II.

Note: *Psychiatric outpatients with "childhood and adolescent disorders or mental retardation."

Nondisordered or community resident comparison group or general population baseline rates for either disorder or crime provided: **2 studies (10.5%)†**

Note: †In both studies, rates of mental retardation are elevated in criminal populations relative to comparison groups.

(Continued from page 56)

of the *catechol-O-methyltransferase (COMT)* gene and violent offending in a sample of Turkish participants with mental retardation. However, from a social learning perspective, Novaco and Taylor (2008) identified a significant relationship between childhood exposure to parental anger or aggression and anger and assaultiveness in adulthood in a sample of male forensic patients with developmental disabilities (with average Full Scale IQ scores of 67.5); and Hayes (2009) found increased self-reports of childhood physical abuse victimization in sex offenders with IDs relative to those without and increased threatening and violent behavior and weapon use in those who had been abused. Finally, crime and violence occurring in individuals with IDs may be attributable to comorbid psychiatric conditions associated with antisociality. For example, Lund (1990) found that 87.5% of inmates with ID also were characterized by an antisocial-aggressive type of behavioral disorder; and Alexander and colleagues (2010) found significantly increased rates of legal detentions and histories of convictions for violent offenses and fire setting in secure hospital offenders with IDs and comorbid personality disorders relative to those with IDs and no personality disorders. Ultimately, although each perspective makes unique contributions to an initial understanding of the origins of crime and violence in mental retardation, more work is needed in this area.

Pervasive Developmental Disorders: Autistic Disorder (Autism Spectrum Disorder)

One of the more significant changes in the DSM-5 is the reclassification of previous DSM-IV-TR disorders of infancy, childhood, or adolescence (i.e., autistic disorder, Asperger's disorder, child disintegrative disorder, Rhett's disorder, and PDD not otherwise specified) into autism spectrum disorder—a condition marked by **social communication and interaction deficits** as well as **restricted repetitive patterns of behavior, interests, and activities** (APA, 2013, p. 809). In fact, the DSM-5 specifies that well-established DSM-IV diagnoses of these disorders should be given the diagnosis of autism spectrum disorder. DSM-5 diagnostic criteria for autism spectrum disorder are listed in Table 3.4.

Prevalence and Incidence Rates of Autistic Disorder

According to the DSM-IV-TR, prevalence rates reported in epidemiological studies are 5 cases per 10,000 individuals (i.e., 0.0005%), with reported rates ranging from 2–20 cases per 10,000 individuals (i.e., 0.0002—0.0020%; APA, 2000). The DSM-5 reports rates of autism spectrum disorder that approach 1% of the population of the United States and of other countries, though this increased rate may reflect factors such as an expansion of the diagnostic criteria, increased awareness, or research methodological differences (APA, 2013).

Theoretical Conceptualizations

Well-known psychological theorists eloquently captured the essence of **autistic disorder** (or autism) in their early nineteenth-century descriptions. Eugen Bleuler, for example, described autism as "the living inside oneself" (Kretschmer, 1925). Kretschmer later noted other authors' almost poetic descriptions; individuals with this disorder were said to "close the shutters of their houses in order to lead a dream-life . . . in the soft muffled gloom of the interior" or to "spin themselves into the silk of their own souls" (p. 157). Infantile autism was first described by Kanner in 1943 (Simblett & Wilson, 1993).

Neurobiological theorists have proposed that the core structural and functional abnormalities in autism are located in the amygdala and other structures within the limbic system, as well as in the corpus callosum. Damage to the amygdala has been linked to social cognition deficits and difficulties in interpreting emotions; and autism has also been associated with abnormalities in the amygdala, temporal lobes, hippocampi, and striatum. Other areas further down the central nervous system also appear to be relevant, as autism has been associated with abnormalities in the brain stem (where the monoaminergic system's nuclei and cranial nerves are located) and in the cerebellum. Additionally, the frontal cortex, with its interconnections with the limbic system, is thought to play a key role in the abnormal processing of **mentalizing** (i.e., attending to mental states) associated with autism (Anckarsäter, 2006).

Initial neurobiological conceptualizations viewed autism as a developmental disorder characterized by neuronal disorganization, leading to impairment of the ability to process complex information. Earlier reports

Table 3.4 DSM-5 Diagnostic Criteria for Autism Spectrum Disorder

A. Persistent deficits in social communication and social interaction across multiple contexts, as manifested by the following, currently or by history (examples are illustrative, not exhaustive):

1. Deficits in social-emotional reciprocity, ranging, for example, from abnormal social approach and failure of normal back-and-forth conversation; to reduced sharing of interests, emotions, or affect; to failure to initiate or respond to social interactions.
2. Deficits in nonverbal communicative behaviors used for social interaction, ranging, for example, from poorly integrated verbal and nonverbal communication; to abnormalities in eye contact and body language or deficits in understanding and use of gestures; to a total lack of facial expressions and nonverbal communication.
3. Deficits in developing, maintaining, and understanding relationships, ranging, for example, from difficulties adjusting behavior to suit various social contexts; to difficulties in sharing imaginative play or in making friends; to absence of interest in peers.

Specify current severity:

Severity is based on social communication impairments and restricted, repetitive patterns of behavior.

B. Restricted, repetitive patterns of behavior, interests, or activities, as manifested by at least two of the following, currently or by history (examples are illustrative, not exhaustive):

1. Stereotyped or repetitive motor movements, use of objects, or speech (e.g., simple motor stereotypies, lining up toys or flipping objects, echolalia, idiosyncratic phrases).
2. Insistence on sameness, inflexible adherence to routines, or ritualized patterns of verbal or nonverbal behavior (e.g., extreme distress at small changes, difficulties with transitions, rigid thinking patterns, greeting rituals, need to take same route or eat same food every day).
3. Highly restricted, fixated interests that are abnormal in intensity or focus (e.g., strong attachment to or preoccupation with unusual objects, excessively circumscribed or perseverative interests).
4. Hyper- or hyporeactivity to sensory input or unusual interest in sensory aspects of the environment (e.g., apparent indifference to pain/temperature, adverse response to specific sounds or textures, excessive smelling or touching of objects, visual fascination with lights or movement).

Specify current severity:

Severity is based on social communication impairments and restricted, repetitive patterns of behavior.

C. Symptoms must be present in the early developmental period (but may not become fully manifest until social demands exceed limited capacities, or may be masked by learned strategies in later life).

D. Symptoms cause clinically significant impairment in social, occupational, or other important areas of functioning.

E. These disturbances are not better explained by intellectual disability (intellectual developmental disorder) or global developmental delay.

Source: APA (2013, p. 50–51). Reprinted with permission from the *Diagnostic and Statistical Manual of Mental Disorders*, Fifth Edition (Copyright © 2013). American Psychiatric Association. All rights reserved.

of morphological (structural) observations in patients with autism describe *histoanatomical abnormalities* (i.e., microscopic cellular and tissue abnormalities such as a reduced number of Purkinje cells and other neurons) in the limbic system and cerebellar circuits, the areas of the brain associated with social interaction, language, and learning (Bauman, 1996). Studies using evoked potential, oculomotor, and neuropsychological methods have consistently identified cognitive processing, neocortical circuitry, and higher order cognitive ability abnormalities in people with autism. Three *neuropathic abnormalities* (observed in autopsy brain specimens) have been described in autism: increased brain weight, shortened dendritic tree development of neurons in limbic structures, and decreased number of Purkinje cells in the cerebellum—defining autism as a disorder of neuronal disorganization (Minshew, 1996). Earlier imaging studies have identified increased supratentorial brain volume (consistent with increased brain weight and head circumference) in autism (Minshew, 1996). Other earlier PET studies have shown decreased functional connectivity between cortical and subcortical regions and delayed maturation of the frontal cortex (Minshew, 1996). These structural and functional abnormalities have been described as "too much brain" in some areas and "too little brain" in others (Minshew, 1996).

A sizeable body of brain imaging work on autism has already been conducted, and some authors have begun to apply meta-analytic techniques to gain a further understanding of the links between autism and brain structure and function. For example, in a meta-analysis of 46 structural MRI studies of individuals with autism (which included over 800 individuals with autism, a similar number of controls, and structural imaging data on 20 brain regions), Stanfield and colleagues (2008) found—across studies—volumetric increases in the total brain, the cerebral hemispheres, the cerebellum, and the caudate nucleus and volumetric reductions in the corpus callosum. These authors conclude that autism may result from structural abnormalities in key brain areas and a global lack of integration due to an enlargement of the brain.

Philip and colleagues (2012) recently conducted a meta-analysis of 90 fMRI studies of individuals with autism spectrum disorders (ASDs—autism, Asperger's disorder, and PDD-NOS). These studies included a total of 1083 individuals with ASDs. Results indicated functional abnormalities during *motor* behaviors, visual processing, executive functioning, auditory and language behaviors, basic social processing, and complex social cognition tasks, and these were associated with ASDs in the brain regions consistent with their hallmark symptomatic features. In individuals with ASDs, abnormal brain activations during motor tasks were observed in "traditional" motor regions (anterior cerebellum, precentral gyrus, basal ganglia) as well as in other areas, including the cerebellum (consistent with motor coordination impairments associated with ASDs). Reduced activity in visual processing areas (the lingual and occipital gyri) but similar visual processing performance in individuals with ASDs was interpreted as more efficient processing of visual stimuli in these areas in ASD individuals (consistent with the idea that these individuals show enhanced perceptual abilities). *Executive dysfunction*, a well-established important feature of ASDs, was indicated by the reduced activations in the brain regions associated with executive function that were observed in individuals with ASDs; reductions particularly involved those regions in control of attention, including the dorsolateral prefrontal cortex, the inferior parietal lobe, the insula, and the posterior cingulate gyrus. During auditory and language tasks, abnormalities in brain activation in individuals with ASDs were observed in regions associated receptive language and other language functioning (e.g., the bilateral superior temporal gyri, the left middle cingulate gyrus, the motor cortex, and the cerebellum). These abnormal patterns were in line with the communication dysfunction that characterizes autism spectrum disorders. Other differences in brain activation were congruent with the social interaction impairments characteristic of ASDs. Regarding basic social processing, individuals with ASDs are characterized by abnormalities in brain networks that enable face perception and the interpretation of facial expressions and emotions (e.g., the fusiform face area). Finally, during complex cognition tasks, individuals with ASDs were characterized by aberrant activations in the brain regions associated with social cognition tasks such as mentalizing or ToM. These regions include the superior temporal gyri and those areas thought to comprise part of the mirror neuron system (MNS) in humans. The MNS is a neuronal network shown in animal studies to activate both when one performs a particular motor action and in response to one's observation of another performing the same motor action. It is thought to be crucial for successful complex mentalizing (i.e., assessing and re-representing another's cognitive perspective following the observation of her or his actions) and to enable emotional understanding via action representation. Overall, functional deficits in social brain regions were among the most well-replicated findings, though abnormal activations in these regions may be attributable more to a lack of preference for social stimuli rather than to primary dysfunction in these areas. Studies in this area are limited by small sample sizes and a primary focus upon high-functioning males with autism. Limitations of this meta-analysis may include the combining of autism, Asperger's syndrome, and PDD-NOS for most analyses (though groups comprised solely of individuals with autism were utilized in analyses of motor tasks). Such a combination of disorders may be too heterogeneous, given the potential variation in presentation and level of functioning among them.

The Relationship Between Autistic Disorder and Crime

With studies of mental illness and crime and violence using the new DSM-5 nomenclature still forthcoming, we will use the DSM-IV-TR terms "autistic disorder" and "Asperger's disorder" here in order to examine the research already conducted using this previous diagnostic terminology. Tables 3.2 and 3.3 list a number of investigations, in chronological order, that have examined the prevalence rates of crime and violence in individuals with autistic disorder and the prevalence rates of autistic disorder in criminal populations.

A Closer Look: Autistic Disorder and Crime

Prevalence of the Disorder in Crime

Study Type	Number	Prevalence Rates
Arrest rates	0	–
Birth cohorts	0	–
Community samples	0	–
Homicide offenders	0	–
Jailed detainees and prisoners	0	–
Psychiatric inpatients	1*	2.4%
Total Number of Studies	**1**	

Sample Characteristics

Size	1,305
Gender	Male and female (numbers not specified)
Age	Adult
Location	England
Diagnostic Systems	HBS Schedule

Note: *Exact number of individuals with autistic disorders (as opposed to those with other disorders on the autistic spectrum) not specified.

Prevalence of Crime in the Disorder

Study Type	Number	Prevalence Rates	Crime Definition
Arrest rates	1*	9.0%†	–
Birth cohorts	0	–	–
Community samples	0	–	Court convictions
Homicide offenders	0	–	–
Jailed detainees and prisoners	0	–	–
Psychiatric inpatients	0	–	–
Total Number of Studies	**1**		

Sample Characteristics

Size	313
Gender	235 males, 75 females
Age	Adult
Location	Denmark
Diagnostic Systems	ICD-9

Note: * Pervasive developmental disorders, including childhood autism, atypical autism, and Asperger's syndrome (Mauridsen et al., 2008).

†Rates significantly decreased for individuals with PDDs relative to controls drawn from a national registry, though conviction rates for each PDD type are not individually reported.

Nondisordered or community resident comparison group or general population baseline rates for either disorder or crime provided: **1 study (50.0%)**

Case Material. In the literature on crime and violence, autistic disorder does not appear to be examined singularly so much as it is studied in combination with the other disorders in the autistic spectrum. That being said, some case material exists demonstrating autism's potential relationship with criminal and violent behavior. For example, Mukaddes and Topcu (2006) present the case of a 10-year-old girl (O. G.), diagnosed with autistic disorder, who killed her 6-month-old sister by throwing her out of a fifth-floor window. According to the report, O. G. had a history of significant behavioral problems, including irritability and sleep problems from late infancy and impulsive-aggressivity and hyperactivity beginning at 18 months; for example, she exhibited behaviors such as breaking toys and glass, tearing papers, hitting and biting people, yelling, and climbing on top of doors. *Stereotypical behaviors* (rocking, spinning, tearing papers) began around the same time, and she developed *circumscribed interests*, spending her time playing with soap and a Coca Cola bottle. Despite pharmacological treatment, her behaviors persisted. She set fire to a neighbor's balcony at age 8, and she became hostile toward and began hitting her 6-month-old sister one month before killing her. The authors emphasize the potential role of adverse environmental factors on this child: she was the product of an unwanted, unplanned pregnancy; grew up in an unsupervised, disorganized family environment where she was neglected and physically and emotionally abused; and she was not referred for psychiatric evaluation until age 7).

Realmuto and Ruble (1999) discuss potential abnormalities in the sexual behavior development of those with autism. They present the case of an adult male with autism (diagnosed at age 6) who engaged in persistent masturbation at age 24; the behavior was elicited by young children. His sexual preferences were both conventional (he was attracted to a young woman therapist) and deviant (he exhibited predatory behaviors toward young children). According to these authors, in the absence of more traditional causal mechanisms, such as childhood sexual victimization, his behavior could have resulted from missed opportunities while growing up with rich and complex social experiences (like most developmentally delayed individuals), reduced exposure to erotic material during puberty, the unavailability of an appropriate sexual partner, and significant social skills deficits. Ultimately, although other case and descriptive studies of criminal offending in ASDs may be limited because their retrospective designs lack detailed developmental histories, making diagnosis impossible (Woodbury-Smith et al., 2005), both cases here demonstrate the qualitative nature of how criminality may present in individuals with autistic disorder.

Autism and Violent Crime. Other descriptive and comparative research has also spoken to the qualitative nature of violent behavior within the context of autism. For example, Hare and colleagues (2000) examined the prevalence of ASDs in three English special hospitals (see Table 3.2). Of the 31 individuals diagnosed with ASDs, 8 had committed homicide. Using a small sample of Swedish offenders convicted for lethal violence and referred for psychiatric evaluation, Wahlund and Kristiansson (2006) compared the characteristics of those with autism spectrum disorder (ASD; $n = 8$) to those with impulsive and controlled antisocial personality disorder (ASPD; $ns = 14$ and 13, respectively). Results indicated that although ASPD groups were more likely to use firearms or knives to kill victims, ASD offenders were more likely to use other methods such as blunt violence, strangulation, or poison. Furthermore, ASD offenders were less likely to be intoxicated at the time of the offense. Finally, in the aforementioned meta-analysis of 22 studies, McClintock and colleagues (2003) found that individuals diagnosed with autism were significantly more likely to be characterized by self-injury, aggression, and disruption to the environment, while individuals with receptive and expressive communication deficits were more likely to show self-injury. Such studies may begin to suggest how violence may look in those with autism compared to in those with other conditions, but more work is clearly needed.

The Origins of Crime and Violence in Those With Autistic Disorders: Theoretical Explanations and Etiological Mechanisms

Several authors have suggested factors that may underlie the manifestation of criminal and violent behavior in those with autistic disorders. For example, Anckarsäter (2006) conceptualizes autism and ASDs as *social brain disorders*, which are defined by early developmental abnormalities in social interaction, in communication (verbal and non-verbal), and in the ability to adjust one's behavior and thinking flexibly to other individuals. Deficits or abnormalities in the mentalizing abilities of autistic individuals has been linked to abnormalities in the perception of human faces and gazes. According to Anckarsäter, social brain dysfunction also makes up the core features of criminogenic mental disorders—such as psychopathy and aggressive personality disorders—and these disorders may all share common underlying deficits in brain structure and functioning. Similarly, in an attempt to identify a pattern of cognitive deficits associated with criminal offending in those with ASDs, Woodbury-Smith and colleagues (2005) examined 21 ASD adults (18 men and 3 women) with criminal histories, 23 ASD adults with no criminal histories, and 23 control subjects with neither ASDs nor criminal histories. Results indicated that ASD offenders were characterized by significantly increased impairment in the recognition of emotional expressions of fear compared to non-offender groups, but were similar in executive functioning, in the recognition facial expressions indicating sadness, and in theory of mind (ToM), or the ability to recognize that others have mental states such as beliefs and desires that influence their behavior.

Other etiological mechanisms have also been explored. Some have suggested an overlap between ASDs and criminogenic personality disorders such as psychopathy (see Chapter 10). Rogers and colleagues (2006), however, report different findings in a study of 28 boys with ASDs who were selected for behavioral problems related to aggression: 3 were diagnosed with *high-functioning autistic spectrum disorders*, or hfASDs, and 25 with Asperger's disorder. The study used a series of social cognitive and neuropsychological measures to demonstrate how psychopathic (i.e., callous and unemotional) traits are independent from severity of autistic behavior. Additionally, these traits appear unrelated to the core cognitive deficits associated with ASDs (i.e., "mind reading" and executive function). According to these authors, callous or psychopathic acts committed by individuals with ASDs likely represent a "double hit" of additional deficits in empathy, ones not directly part of the ASDs themselves, rather than the shared cognitive underpinnings of both psychopathy and ASDs. Finally, Stokes and Newton (2004) suggest that individuals with ASDs may be particularly prone to stalking behaviors. Although they have normative sexual desires in terms of intensity and deviancy, they are also characterized by cravings for and persistent seeking out of intimacy and a lack of social competence to initiate intimate relationships. These authors relate ASD individuals with a type of stalker identified as the "incompetent stalker," who is characterized by isolation, loneliness, social ineptness, and—in someone who is obsessive—a sense of entitlement to the victim. To date, research findings have not supported this possibility, and the etiological mechanisms underlying crime and violence in those with ASDs have yet to be definitively identified.

Pervasive Developmental Disorders: Asperger's Disorder[1]

Asperger's disorder, as a term and a separate diagnostic entity, has been removed from the DSM-5; the features of this disorder are now incorporated into the diagnostic category "autism spectrum disorders." This is not a radical shift conceptually, however, given researchers and theorists have historically considered Asperger's disorder to be a higher-functioning variant of the disorders on the autism spectrum. Nonetheless, given the significant amount of literature produced on this disorder and its relationship with crime and violence over the past several decades, its retention as a separate diagnostic category for discussion in this book seemed warranted. The diagnostic criteria for DSM-IV-TR Asperger's disorder are listed in Table 3.5.

Asperger's disorder was originally known as "autistic psychopathy,"[2] a term coined by Austrian physician Hans Asperger who first described the disorder while working on the habilitation of children with behavior problems (Ghaziuddin et al., 1991; Newman & Ghaziuddin, 2008). Asperger (1944, in Mnukhin & Isaev, 1975) noted the tendency of autistic psychopaths to show motor incoordination, marked scattering of abilities, impoverished affect, thought disturbance, and an inability to put themselves in the state of mind of others. His clinical descriptions were published one year after Kanner's description of infantile autism, which received the lion's share of international recognition and influence because it contributed to the scholarship of developmental disorders, a pervasive interest until recent decades (Simblett & Wilson, 1993). Asperger's findings were later refined and popularized in a seminal paper by Lorna Wing (1981). Symptoms of Asperger's disorder include

1. Much of the published material on Asperger's disorder also utilizes the term "Asperger's syndrome." For purposes of simplification, in this chapter, both terms have been subsumed under the term "Asperger's disorder."

2. The latter term was used by Asperger in the technical sense of an abnormality of personality (Wing, 1981).

Table 3.5 DSM-IV-TR Diagnostic Criteria for Asperger's Disorder

299.80 Asperger's Disorder

A. Qualitative impairment in social interaction, as manifested by at least two of the following:
   1. marked impairment in the use of multiple nonverbal behaviors such as eye-to-eye gaze, facial expression, body postures, and gestures to regulate social interaction
   2. failure to develop peer relationships appropriate to developmental level
   3. a lack of spontaneous seeking to share enjoyment, interests, or achievements with other people (e.g., by a lack of showing, bringing, or pointing out objects of interest to other people)
   4. lack of social or emotional reciprocity

B. Restricted repetitive and stereotyped patterns of behavior, interests, and activities, as manifested by at least one of the following:
   1. encompassing preoccupation with one or more stereotyped and restricted patterns of interest that is abnormal either in intensity or focus
   2. apparently inflexible adherence to specific, nonfunctional routines or rituals
   3. stereotyped and repetitive motor mannerisms (e.g., hand or finger flapping or twisting, or complex whole-body movements)
   4. persistent preoccupation with parts of objects
   C. The disturbance causes clinically significant impairment in social, occupational, or other important areas of functioning.

D. There is no clinically significant general delay in language (e.g., single words used by age 2 years, communicative phrases used by age 3 years).

E. There is no clinically significant delay in cognitive development or in the development of age-appropriate self-help skills, adaptive behavior (other than in social interaction), and curiosity about the environment in childhood.

F. Criteria are not met for another specific Pervasive Developmental Disorder or Schizophrenia.

Source: APA (2000, p. 80). Reprinted with permission from the *Diagnostic and Statistical Manual of Mental Disorders,* Fourth Edition, Text Revision

social isolation, odd and pedantic speech, poor verbal communication, and a preoccupation with certain idiosyncratic interests. Additionally, these individuals are frequently physically clumsy and, as children, have a reduced or lack of interest in or capacity for imaginative play (Wing, 1981). They may also be described as egocentric and unable to understand and relate to others (Barry-Walsh & Mullen, 2004). Haskins and Silva (2006) describe a triad of deficits, including (1) deficient reciprocal social behavior; (2) verbal and nonverbal communication deficits (i.e., the inability to respond appropriately in social interactions, which impairs the capacity for social reciprocity); and (3) abnormalities or deficiencies related to the pursuance of flexible, imaginative activities. Communication abnormalities could involve inappropriate gestures, personal space, timing, and topic selection; difficulty recognizing humor, irony, or sarcasm; and abnormal prosody and pedantic language. Yet marked heterogeneity in the presentation of this disorder has been noted: some individuals may appear aloof and indifferent to others while some may passively accept social approaches. Some may make intrusive, odd, or one-sided approaches to social interaction (Haskins & Silva, 2006).

The features of Asperger's disorder do overlap largely with those of autism and, to some degree, with the features of schizoid personality disorder (Ghaziuddin et al., 1991). In fact, some authors (e.g., Wolff & Cull, 1986) have suggested that schizoid personality disorder—when occurring in childhood in a severe form—corresponds with Asperger's syndrome, thus reflecting a different theoretical conceptualization linking Asperger's disorder with schizophrenia spectrum disorders rather than with autism (Simblett & Wilson, 1993).

Prevalence and Incidence Rates of Asperger's Disorder

According to the DSM-IV-TR, there are no definitive data regarding the prevalence of Asperger's disorder (APA, 2000). Early studies estimated the prevalence of all ASDs to be approximately 0.05%, but more recent data suggests 0.60%, and one large epidemiological study of twin data reported rates of 1.4% for males and 0.3% for females (Constantino & Rodd, 2003, in Haskins & Silva, 2006). Rates for PDD-NOS (.31%) and Asperger's disorder (0.095%) have been reported more recently by other sources (Haskins & Silva, 2006).

Theoretical Conceptualizations

Brain imaging data have suggested a neurobiological component to Asperger's disorder. For example, functional imaging using SPECT of a patient described by Chen and colleagues (2003) revealed decreased blood flow in the bilateral frontal, temporal, and posterior parietal lobes, a finding consistent with earlier reports suggesting that a precise frontal lobe region (i.e., the medial frontal region or *Brodmann's area 18*) may, if impaired in childhood, produce the characteristic behavioral and cognitive symptoms of Asperger's disorder. Earlier reports describe microscopic morphological abnormalities in patients with Asperger's disorder. These abnormalities included small neuronal cell size, increased cell packing density, and reduced numbers of *Purkinje cells* in the amygdala and entorhinal cortex and were similar to the abnormalities observed in people with autism in that they were confined to the limbic system and cerebellar circuits (see above). In the population with Asperger's disorder, however, the degree of abnormality was comparatively limited (Bauman, 1996; see Silva et al., 2002). Functional imaging studies have revealed abnormalities in the brains of individuals with hfASDs, in areas associated with social cognition such as the amygdala, prefrontal cortex, and fusiform gyrus (Haskins & Silva, 2006). Furthermore, several studies of Asperger's syndrome have reported significant discrepancies between verbal IQ and performance IQ, with verbal IQ abilities being better than performance IQ abilities, or VIQ > PIQ (Chesterman & Rutter, 1993). This finding may suggest right hemispheric dysfunction. Interestingly, however, it is the PIQ > VIQ discrepancy that has shown associations with antisocial behavior in the literature (Schug et al., 2010).

One concept commonly discussed in relation to the abnormal behaviors associated with Asperger's disorder is **theory of mind (ToM)**. Primatologists Premack and Woodruff (1978) originally coined the term "theory of mind" in their seminal article on the mental abilities of chimpanzees. Subsequently, empirical evidence has indicated the universal capacity in humans to estimate and appreciate other people's mental states (to engage in "mind reading"). Humans need this ability in order to understand the different beliefs, attitudes, and intentions that determine the behavior of others, and to subsequently predict their behavior. Theory of mind (or mentalization) is defined as the ability to estimate the cognitive, perceptual, and emotional experiences of others as well as of one's self. The relative inability to do so has been called **mindblindness** (Haskins & Silva, 2006).

It has been proposed that individuals with Asperger's disorder either lack ToM altogether or lack the ability to apply it (Bowler, 1992, in Chesterman & Rutter, 1993). According to Bowler (1992, in Blackshaw et al., 2001), individuals with Asperger's disorder acquire ToM later in development rather than lacking it altogether. Consequently, their underdeveloped, "untuned" theory of mind—a result of their missing a critical developmental period—causes them to acquire social rules in an overlearned and rigid fashion. This, in turn, leads them to struggle with the subtleties of social communication, as they attempt to attribute mental states to others by using rigid, learned rules.

The Relationship Between Asperger's Disorder and Crime

Tables 3.2 and 3.3 list a number of investigations, in chronological order, that have examined both the prevalence rates of crime in individuals with Asperger's disorder and the prevalence of Asperger's disorder in criminal populations.

Case Material. Much of what is known about the relationship between Asperger's disorder and criminal and violent behavior is derived from published case descriptions and reports. A sizeable case literature has been developed (one of the largest, a fact perhaps due to the more recent clinical conceptualization of Asperger's disorder). This literature describes the socially deviant, destructive, and antisocial behaviors of individuals with this condition. In fact, Asperger (1944) himself, in his original paper, noted that some of the children with his

A Closer Look: Asperger's Disorder and Crime

Prevalence of the Disorder in Crime

Study Type	Number	Prevalence Rates
Arrest rates	0	–
Birth cohorts	0	–
Community samples	0	–
Homicide offenders	0	–
Jailed detainees and prisoners	1	10.0%
Psychiatric inpatients	1	1.5%
Total Number of Studies	**2**	

Sample Characteristics

Size	126–392
Gender	Male only (1 study); male and female but almost exclusively males (1 study)
Age	Youth, adult
Location	England, Sweden
Diagnostic Systems	DSM-IV, other research diagnostic criteria (Gillberg & Gillberg, 1989)

Prevalence of Crime in the Disorder

Study Type	Number	Prevalence Rates	Crime Definition
Arrest rates	1*	9.0%	Court convictions
Birth cohorts	0	–	–
Community samples	1	0.0–30.0%	Law breaking: self-reported and official statistics†
Homicide offenders	0	3.4–62.1%	–
Jailed detainees and prisoners	0	–	–
Psychiatric inpatients	1	Present but rates not reported	Physical aggression and "acting out"
Total Number of Studies	**4**		

Sample Characteristics

Size	10–313
Gender	Male and female (4 studies)
Age	Youth, adult
Location	Denmark, unspecified
Diagnostic Systems	ICD, not reported

Notes: *Asperger's disorder, childhood autism, and atypical autism.

†Depending on offense category—highest for violent offenses, lowest for robbery and miscellaneous theft.

Nondisordered or community resident comparison group or general population baseline rates for either disorder or crime provided: **2 studies (33.3%)**[‡]

Note: [‡]Rates of crime significantly increased relative to comparisons in some cases (i.e., for criminal damage in Woodbury-Smith et al., 2006) and significantly decreased in others (i.e., for drug offenses in Woodbury-Smith et al., 2006 and for court convictions in Mauridsen et al., 2008).

disorder perpetrated "mischievous, malicious acts" without regard for the consequences for others (in Hare et al., 2000). For example, he described Fritz V. as "quickly becoming aggressive" and "attack[ing] other children," and Harrow L. as "attack[ing] other children" and showing "social unconcern in sexual play with other boys, allegedly going so far as homosexual acts, coitus attempt" (in Barry-Walsh & Mullen, 2004, p. 97). Baron-Cohen (1988) discusses the case of "John," a 21-year old man with Asperger's disorder (see Table 3.6) and an obsessional interest in his own jaw. John would physically strike—without provocation—his 71-year-old girlfriend, "Betty," up to three times per day. Here is John's description of one such incident:

> Immediately before hitting her I felt angry and bitter about my jaw . . . I felt boiled up inside. I then asked her if my jaw was alright. She said it was, in a deep tone of voice. Immediately, I hit her hard. I enjoy attacking Betty because she is vulnerable and weak. It makes me feel powerful. (Baron-Cohen, 1988, p. 356)

Baron-Cohen provides a *functional analysis* of John's violence, explaining this behavior in terms of precursors and reinforcers using this common CBT technique. Antecedents include historical factors, such as his mother's suicide; internal states, such as anxiety (about his jaw and social contact), anger, and frustration; and changes in routine. Targets included family members, his family's property, Betty, and others (nursing staff and patients). Reinforcing factors include his social-cognitive deficits (i.e., in appreciating others' mental states, in solving interpersonal problems, and in knowledge of social norms), internal consequences (i.e., feelings of power), and responses from others (i.e., Betty providing no corrective feedback).

Wolff and Cull (1986) conducted a *retrospective analysis* of the case notes on 30 boys diagnosed with "schizoid" personality (the term used by these authors to indicate Asperger's disorder) matched with those on 30 boys with other psychiatric diagnoses. This sample was drawn from a larger cohort of 111 boys seen in a psychiatric clinic. Case description examples are presented in Table 3.6. Results indicated that, although there was no difference in the prevalence of conduct disorders between the two groups, each group was characterized by qualitatively different antisocial behaviors. Children with "schizoid" personality less often committed thefts compared to those without, had fewer alcohol problems in young adulthood, and less often were exposed to loss of a parent and socioeconomic difficulties. In fact, in "schizoid" boys, antisocial behavior appeared to be related less to adverse environmental influences, such as family disruption and social disadvantage, and more to an unusual and even violent fantasy life that featured, for example, Zulu wars, abattoirs, Fascists and communists, and a collection of knives. The boys would tell fantastic stories with these themes, and sometimes they would appear to believe in them and translate them into action. Wolff and Cull (1986) also discussed 13 girls with "schizoid" personality who were also described as "seriously antisocial": nine were characterized with aggression (one put her jump rope around the neck of a neighbor's baby), nine expressed unusual fantasies, seven were pathological liars (two used aliases and five falsely reported their parents as cruel), seven wandered, six had committed property crimes, two had stolen babies, and three made suicidal threats or attempts.

Although one appealing feature of published case reports is the richness of information generally presented within each case, it is only by examining case reports collectively that one can begin to observe patterns and suggest possible relationships that may generalize to others in a given population (i.e., those with Asperger's disorder in this case). To that end, we searched the literature using computerized databases and references from other articles in an attempt to locate a sizeable collection of published case reports of individuals with Asperger's disorder who are characterized by antisocial, criminal, and violent behavior. Table 3.6 lists 54 such cases published in 20 separate reports between 1975 and 2006. Although the information presented in these reports varies in level of detail, some noticeable patterns can be observed. For example, within the published cases, the individuals with Asperger's disorder who engaged in antisocial behaviors were mostly male (88.9%), which could reflect differential rates in the gender of those with Autistic spectrum disorders (Gothelf et al., 2008) or in those committing crime (Raine, 1993), or perhaps a factor unique to antisocial Asperger's disordered individuals. These individuals were also mostly adult (75.9%). In fact, cases of children and adolescents appeared predominantly in earlier studies. Also, although previous literature suggested an expectation of higher intelligence, these individuals were actually characterized by a wide range of intellectual abilities. More specifically, of the 31 cases in which IQ scores or information about intellectual or cognitive functioning was presented, only 8 (25.8%) had above-average intelligence. In fact, 16 (51.6%) were characterized by average intellectual abilities, and 7 (22.6%) were described as having below-average intelligence.

Table 3.6 Case Reports of Asperger's Disorder (AD) and Antisocial Behavior

Source	Gender	Age	Noted Symptoms	Antisocial Behaviors	Crime?*	Notes
Mnukhin & Isaev (1975)	M	12	Early learning difficulties, social isolation, behavioral abnormalities. Inappropriate affect. Good expressive language. General hypotonia and motor incoordination.	Irritability, aggressive outbursts at age 12 (no details reported).	No	Case histories ($n = 4$). S. M. Psychiatric inpatient. Subnormal intellect.
	M	14	"Dragged" right foot until age 5. No speech until age 4. Quick tempered, distractible, uncooperative. No friends, played with younger children. Odd behaviors (no details reported).	Threatening behaviors at age 7.5 (no details reported).	No	I.I. Psychiatric inpatient.
Wing (1981)	M	24	Pedantic speech beginning in childhood. Social isolation until age 14. Odd appearance, posture, and gait; movement abnormalities. Preoccupation with time. Social ineptitude.	Suicide attempt at age 24 (attempted to drown and then strangle himself) in response to possible reorganization at his job.	No	Case series ($n = 34$). Six case histories in article. Mr. L. P. Psychiatric inpatient. Average intelligence.
Mawson et al. (1985)	M	44	Marked interest in chemistry, radio, and mechanical subjects. Socially isolated, odd social manner. Stereotyped movements. Speech abnormalities (including over-precise speech and speaking during inspiration). Walks with odd, stiff gait; rocks while sitting. Admitted to extreme dislike for high-pitched sounds. Preoccupations with poisons and poisoning.	Age 16: Absconding from school, attempted to steal chemical, strangle a girl; "lying in wait" for schoolgirls. Age 18: Dropped firework into girl's car and stabbed her in the wrist with a screwdriver. Age 22: Entered neighbor's house with knife because of a noisy dog; kicked the dog and struck the owner—a girl—with a screwdriver. Age 25: Assaulted crying child at railway station by putting his hands over its mouth to stop noise. Age 29: Attempted to stab a girl with a hacksaw blade because he thought she was indecently dressed. Attacked crying baby in supermarket.	No	Psychiatric inpatient. Above-average intelligence (IQ = 133).

(Continued)

(Continued)

Source	Gender	Age	Noted Symptoms	Antisocial Behaviors	Crime?*	Notes
Wolff & Cull (1986)	M	13	Constantly hitting other children and having no friends at age 6. Diagnosed as "schizoid" at age 13.	Threatened parents with knife at age 13. Threatened to kill family dog. Expressed fear of getting into fight and strangling opponent.	No	"Seriously antisocial boys": (i) Psychiatric inpatient.
	M	10	Social isolation. Failing in school.	Markedly aggressive behavior: kicked and bit teacher; physically attacked nurses and children; forcefully hit doctor over head without warning; hurled easel over bannister. Expelled from several schools due to unexpected attacks on teachers and children.	No	(ii) Psychiatric inpatient. Highly intelligent.
	M	15	Loner. Serious expressive, developmental language delay in early childhood. Preoccupied with fantasies of sex and violence in adolescence; read avidly about violent crimes; collected photographs of notorious murderer and anarchic literature, posters, and paraphernalia depicting callous brutality (which frightened his family).	Bit staff member in residential school; cut fellow pupil with scissors (charged with assault).	Yes	(iii) Psychiatric inpatient.
	M	Child	Marked obsessive-compulsive rituals; suspended from several schools.	Threatened to kill housefather at residential school; threatened to kill psychiatrist.	No	(iv) Psychiatric inpatient.
	M	Adult	Flamboyant and compulsive wanderer as child; obsessive ruminations about sex and sin at age 10. Social isolation in childhood and adulthood. Spent time in psychiatric inpatient unit and boarding school for maladjusted children. Had sex with his only school friend's mother.	Compulsive gambler during late adolescence. As adult, charged (with sister) with conspiracy to defraud a bank by cashing checks at casinos.	Yes	"Fraudulent boys": (i)

Source	Gender	Age	Noted Symptoms	Antisocial Behaviors	Crime?*	Notes
	M	Adult	Solitary in childhood with vivid fantasy life. Garbled talk in early childhood; poor educational and social progress.	Charged with fraud at age 23. Used aliases; several serious suicide attempts; drinking and thieving; getting into fights.	Yes	(ii)
	F	Adolescent	Solitary, somewhat paranoid. Recurrent wanderer in late adolescence.	Threatened suicide intermittently since middle childhood; frightened young cousin by carrying an open sheathed knife, slashing bathroom curtains with razor, showing cousin book about sex with medieval torture.	No	"Seriously antisocial girls": (i) Psychiatric inpatient. High intelligence.
	F	10	Stuffed her nostrils with paper in class; chased other children with dog feces; forced a new blazer down a toilet; broke her eyeglasses and put pieces in her mouth.	Frequent running away; escaped inpatient child psychiatric unit, charged with theft.	Yes	(ii) Psychiatric inpatient.
	F	Adult	Frequently admitted to hospital in adolescence, diagnosed with Munchhausen's syndrome. In hospital, impersonated doctor.	Used aliases in adulthood. Suspected of setting small, unexplained fires in gynecological unit in hospital.	No	(iii)
	F	Child	In school, emitted sudden loud calls or whistles, threw equipment around the room.	At age 10, stole baby and wandered around town for hours. Started fire in child psychiatric unit. Classroom misbehavior. Stabs other pupils with sewing pins or needles.	No	(iv) Psychiatric inpatient
Baron-Cohen (1988)	M	21	Non-affection-seeking as infant; hand flapping age 3; conversational language difficulties; obsessional knowledge about "Top 40" lists, automobile details, radio stations; difficulties in adapting to change, fitting into social groups; obsessional interest in his jaw in adulthood.	Occasional masturbation in public, age 11. Arrested for stealing at age 17; frequent violent attacks (i.e., hitting, slapping, pushing, 2–3 times per day) against his 71-year-old live in "girlfriend"; repeated assaults on hospital nursing staff and patients; violence toward objects; attempted to strangle brother.	Yes	John. Psychiatric inpatient. Below-average intelligence (FSIQ = 80).

(Continued)

(Continued)

Source	Gender	Age	Noted Symptoms	Antisocial Behaviors	Crime?*	Notes
Everall & LeCouteur (1990)	M	17	Pedantic speech, monotonous tone, idiosyncratic use of phrases. Socially "remote" and isolated. Stereotyped and repetitive play with toys. No fantasy play. Preoccupations with water, plastic pipes, sailing ships, trees and tree felling. Disruptive, bizarre, abnormal behavior when stressed beginning age 5.	Fire setting—mostly hay and straw stack fires (at least nine separate fires) beginning age 16. Perhaps in response to new/stressful situation (i.e., uncertainty about future placement after full-time education ended).	No	DH.
Littlejohns et al. (1990)	M	15	Socially isolated. Preoccupations with inanimate objects (vacuum cleaners, musical boxes, insectivorous plants) at age 7. Ritualistic touching of objects at age 8. Marked writhing movements of limbs and trunk, fidgeting, ran in circles at age 11. Tourette-like syndrome at age 11.	Aggressive and destructive at age 5. Frequent temper outbursts, agitation, and aggressive behavior at age 7/8 (no details reported). Tantrums provoked by others' attempts to change order of objects in environment.	No	A. Psychiatric inpatient. Low intelligence (FSIQ = 65).
Chesterman & Rutter (1993)	M	22	As child, speech and conversational abnormalities; lack of empathy/interest in others; preoccupation with valves of automobile tires; resistant to change; repeatedly pinching other children.	As adolescent, history of inappropriate sexual behavior toward classmates. As adult, made anonymous bomb threat to coworkers. Age 21: exposed himself to sister. Age 22: guilty of several counts of theft and criminal damage. History of stealing cotton lingerie, masturbating while holding women's nightdresses, and watching clothes spinning in washing machine. Assaulted police officer who accused him of intent to commit burglary. Aggressive outbursts resulting in property damage, physical assaults, and sexual offenses usually precipitated by mother not accepting his need to adhere to rigid routines.	Yes	RM. FSIQ = 90.

Source	Gender	Age	Noted Symptoms	Antisocial Behaviors	Crime?*	Notes
Cooper et al. (1993)	M	38	Always had been socially isolated, excessively shy and lonely, no close friends, virgin; spends several hours per day on personal hygiene; developed interest in cross-dressing in female underwear (in home only); poor social skills (evades eye contact, lacks normative facial expressions and body movements, invades personal space of others).	Assaulted daughter of a neighbor. Several sexual assaults (i.e., touching) and physical assaults against women. Failure to attend outpatient clinics as required by conditions of probation.	Yes	PM. IQ (age 15) = 54.
Simblett & Wilson (1993)	F	27	"Odd"; socially isolated; concretized speech and thought; interpersonal difficulties; obsessively enamored of Catholic priest; preoccupation with physical health and food additives.	Temper tantrums ages 17–19 (no details reported).	No	Ms. A. Mental handicap hospital patient. Intelligence in "dull normal range."
	F	22	Diagnosis of autism at age 7. As adult inpatient, interpersonal difficulties, language lacking pragmatics, poor response to social cues, preoccupation with Down's syndrome, sexually active and manipulative.	At age 7, long history of temper tantrums with bizarre, often violent behavior; impulsive aggressive acts in school. As adult inpatient, violent and destructive behavior, unpredictable violent rages (no details reported).	No	Ms. B. Mental handicap hospital patient.
	M	23	Good academic skills; concretized language lacking pragmatics; naïve conversations; preoccupations with soccer; lacking common sense; interpersonal difficulties.	Severe temper tantrums as toddler, uncontrollable and violent in school, age 5. Aggression, violent and destructive behavior at age 19 (no details reported).	No	Mr. C. Mental handicap hospital patient. Average intelligence.
Scragg & Shah (1994)	M	Adult	Unable to pretend; monotonous voice noted since age 3; touching people's hair as a child; odd social manner since age 5; preoccupations with poisons, chemistry, water pipes.	Extreme reaction to certain sounds, leading to violence.	Yes	Case 1. Broadmoor Special Hospital patient. FSIQ = 113. Possible R. prefrontal pathology. Normal EEG.

(Continued)

(Continued)

Source	Gender	Age	Noted Symptoms	Antisocial Behaviors	Crime?*	Notes
	M	Adult	Delayed speech; clumsy; indiscriminate attachments; no concept of reciprocal relationships; preoccupations with staff rotation schedules, collecting bottles.	Fire setting.	Yes	Case 2. Broadmoor Special Hospital patient. FSIQ = 93. R. temporal lobe problems. EEG & CT normal.
	M	Adult	Repetitive questioning; touching and following people; preoccupations with reading pop music and football magazines (to the exclusion of other activities).	Feigning punches.	Yes	Case 3. Broadmoor Special Hospital patient. FSIQ = 111. Mild EEG abnormality.
	M	Adult	Delayed speech; intense one-sided attachments; preoccupations with military, cryogenics; erotomania.	Wounding with intent.	Yes	Case 4. Broadmoor Special Hospital patient. FSIQ = 126. Brain scan indicating R. temporal lobe atrophy.
	M	Adult	Loner; preoccupations with scientific matters, murder books, collecting maps.	Unlawful killing.	Yes	Case 5. Broadmoor Special Hospital patient. Abnormal EEG R. hemisphere.
	M	Adult	Lacked interest in communication (babbling and gesturing); one-sided social interaction; erotomanic attachment; preoccupations with Ohm's Law, martial arts.	Threats to kill.	Yes	Case 6. Broadmoor Special Hospital patient. FSIQ = 79. Prefrontal pathology suggested by neuropsychology.

Source	Gender	Age	Noted Symptoms	Antisocial Behaviors	Crime?*	Notes
	M	Adult	Ritualistic self-care since age 16; rigid meal-eating schedule; difficult peer interactions; little understanding that his interests may alienate peers; preoccupations with discoveries in medicine, science, archeology; precise memory for dates; erotomania.	Unlawful killing.	Yes	Case 7. Broadmoor Special Hospital patient. FSIQ = 93.
	M	Adult	Obsessive hand washing in childhood; avoids eye contact; loner; preoccupations with weapons (collecting knives, air pistols).	Unlawful killing (matricide).	Yes	Case 8. Broadmoor Special Hospital patient. FSIQ = 128.
	M	Adult	Special routines at school; social isolation; conversation one-sided and repetitive; preoccupations with building electric circuits, poisons, chemistry.	Physical aggression.	Yes	Case 9. Broadmoor Special Hospital patient. FSIQ = 94.
Kohn et al. (1998)	M	16	In childhood, described as "egotistical and shameless," unable to relate to other children; strong verbal and math skills; circumscribed interests focused only on math, chemistry, and computers; skilled at chess; stereotyped movements (rocking, banging head on pillow).	From age 4, aggressive toward other children and lacked empathy. Committed 3 sexual assaults at age 14 (in one, he approached an unknown girl on the street, grabbed her, attempted to undress her, touched her breasts and genitals). Habit of grabbing and fondling women in an attempt to make them his "girlfriends." Expelled from school for numerous thefts and violent fights. Other violent assaults.	Yes	N. Psychiatric inpatient. WISC-R IQ = 120.
Bankier et al. (1999)	M	25	History of selective mutism, severe social withdrawal. Described as "difficult" child by mother; developed waggling tic (shaking head) at age 8. As adult inpatient, language very precise and speech inaccuracies in others irritated him. Preoccupations with technology, science, and science fiction.	Outbursts of violence (in adulthood) with attacks against his mother (no details reported).	No	M. Psychiatric inpatient. FSIQ = 123. Some SPECT and slight EEG abnormalities, normal cranial CT and brain MR.

(Continued)

(Continued)

Source	Gender	Age	Noted Symptoms	Antisocial Behaviors	Crime?*	Notes
Milton et al. (2002)	M	Early 30s	In childhood, no close friends; emotionally detached; lacked social understanding; neologisms; long-standing preoccupation with women's genitalia (image of woman's gynecological examination—aroused by women disliking having to remove their clothing in these situations). In adulthood, cleansing rituals and obsessional symptoms; difficulties with social interactions; excessive masturbation.	In childhood, shoplifting surgical appliance (thought to have a gynecological purpose) from pharmacy at age 13. Theft of women's underwear and voyeurism in early teenage years. In adulthood, indirect sexual assaults upon women (obscene phone calls pretending to be a gynecologist, voyeurism), beginning age 17. Thefts and direct sexual assaults. Convicted for theft of a telephone and making obscene phone calls.	Yes	B. Psychiatric inpatient. FSIQ = 80.
Murrie et al. (2002)	M	31	In childhood, shy and quiet, considered "peculiar" by teachers; preoccupations with fish, birds, ancient castles; strict adherence to routines (e.g., mealtime "ceremonies"), became very irritated with attempts to change routines; some friendships (one at a time). In adulthood, occupational problems centered on his inflexibility; lived with parents and no sexual/romantic relationships; socially isolated, irritable, and verbally aggressive before crimes.	Charged with 11 cases of arson at age 31. When arrested, confessed and explained crimes were revenge against classmates who harassed him in youth (details of houses reminded him of peers who harassed him).	Yes	AB. Referred for forensic evaluation. IQ scores in borderline to low range.
	M	27	In childhood, described as "oblivious to everyone around him"; marked social impairments and verbal communication deficits; history of compulsive masturbation beginning age 10; collection of "artificial vaginas." In adulthood, intense preoccupation with having sexual intercourse, but naïve and passive courtship strategies—resulted in being used and exploited by others.	In adulthood, repeated sexual contact with a 15-year-old male.	Yes	CD. Referred for forensic evaluation.

Source	Gender	Age	Noted Symptoms	Antisocial Behaviors	Crime?*	Notes
	M	44	In childhood, developed special routines regarding everyday activities at age 8; no friendships or romantic relationships. In adulthood, excellent academic performance in college, but occupational problems due to his idiosyncratic routines; primary interest photography—using computer to modify photos to create "perfect pictures" of women; rigid facial expression ("odd smile").	Charged with attempted murder: Shot psychologist who was taking part in custody examination of his 2-year-old daughter.	Yes	EF. Referred for forensic evaluation. Cognitive skills above average but variable.
	M	33	In childhood, shy and reserved; difficulties establishing relationships. In adulthood, interest in photographing and filming children since age 25; fantasies about having sex with children; preoccupation with paper dolls (i.e., collected thousands in his home, played sexual games and masturbated with them). Showed no remorse for sexual offense.	Charged with showing pornographic films to, and then filming, his 9-year-old daughter and peer. Minor property crimes in childhood (while attempting to make friendships).	Yes	GH. Referred for forensic evaluation. IQ in average range.
	M	22	In childhood, isolated, one close friend; interests in computer games and rearranging baseball card collection; preoccupation with memorizing notes for complex pieces of classical music. In adulthood, difficulties making friends and communicating with women; avoided eye contact; spoke in flat tone; conversational difficulties.	Found peeping at girls in women's locker room of university fitness center through small holes he had made in a supply closet. When apprehended, denied sexual motivation and related offense to school difficulties and feeling isolated from peers.	Yes	IJ. Referred for forensic evaluation. Intellectual functioning normal.

(Continued)

(Continued)

Source	Gender	Age	Noted Symptoms	Antisocial Behaviors	Crime?*	Notes
	M	31	In adulthood, living with mother; blank, emotionless facial expression; movement abnormalities when walking; inappropriate expression to others of active and aggressive fantasies; reported feelings of loneliness and isolation; excessive masturbation and sexual fantasies of themes related to his offense (following strange women, binding them, and cutting their breasts with a knife).	Assaulted two women in the female restroom at a local zoo (i.e., followed victims into bathroom, threatened them with a knife, bound them with rope, then subsequently cut the ropes and allowed them to escape).	Yes	KL. Referred for forensic evaluation.
Chen et al. (2003)	M	21	In childhood, socially remote/isolated, socially naïve; stereotyped/repetitive play; unusual preoccupations; disliked changes in environment; good academic skills. In adolescence, deterioration in academic performance after moving to new city; collected paper, boxes, cups, plastic bags. In adulthood, physically clumsy/awkward; marked sexual interest.	Repeated thefts, age 17 (beginning after move to new city). Collected/hoarded stolen items in living room. Stole letters from mailboxes in neighborhood. Aggressive behaviors (unspecified).	No	Psychiatric inpatient. FSIQ = 111.
Barry-Walsh & Mullen (2004)	M	26	In childhood, inability to relate with other children; fascination with moving object; generally slow to learn but skilled in mathematics. In adolescence, preoccupations with words and dictionaries. History of interest in flickering flames (e.g., watching the pilot flame in the gas heater for long periods).	Charged with arson (set fire to a hedge, causing considerable damage). Reportedly lit fire in order to watch the fascinating flickering of flames.	Yes	Mr. BD. Referred for forensic evaluation. Normal intelligence.
	M	Adult	In childhood, no development of interpersonal/social skills; preoccupation with words and their meanings; isolated and nonresponsive to discipline in school; obsessional-like symptoms with checking and rituals. In adolescence, movement disorder with catatonic symptoms; preoccupation with thresholds and inability to cross thresholds of rooms; rigid routines.	Repeated convictions for public nuisance and minor assaults. Convicted of stalking and threatening professionals involved in his care.	Yes	KD. Referred for forensic evaluation.

Source	Gender	Age	Noted Symptoms	Antisocial Behaviors	Crime?*	Notes
	M	24	In childhood, fascination with moving objects; slow motor skill development, precocious language skills; absence of interpersonal/social skills. In adulthood, preoccupation with armaments of WWII aircraft and listening to a particular music radio station; no friendships.	Arson: Family moved to a new city and a local religious station's new broadcast interfered with listening to his favored station. Became frustrated and burned new station down. Showed no remorse and was puzzled what all the fuss was about.	Yes	KA. Referred for forensic evaluation.
	M	24	In childhood, disinterest in social interaction with other children; clumsy and idiosyncratic speech; preoccupation with electronics. Lifelong rigidity and inflexibility in thinking. Tolerated change poorly and had restricted routine.	Assaulted father, who had confronted him about lighting a fire on the back lawn. Previously charged for willful trespass.	Yes	NY. Referred for forensic evaluation.
	M	16	In childhood, clumsy, unsettled, and noncompliant with instructions; poor social interactions with other children; social isolation. History of behavioral problems associated with anger and aggression. Good memory skills but language abnormalities. Preoccupations with sex and naïveté of sexual matters.	Charged twice with minor sexual offending: once sexually propositioned a 7-year-old girl and her 5-year-old brother, and once made sexual advances toward a girl in a library. In the latter case, he grabbed the victim by the throat when she declined.	Yes	TE. Referred for forensic evaluation. Normal intelligence.
Palermo (2004)	M	33	In childhood, described by mother as temperamentally "stubborn," rigid, and extremely anxious. Preoccupations with Internet, chemical weapons, and "firebombs." Comorbid depressive disorder NOS.	Threatened to burn down his grandmother's home.	?	Patient 2. IQ in normal range.

(Continued)

(Continued)

Source	Gender	Age	Noted Symptoms	Antisocial Behaviors	Crime?*	Notes
	M	30	In childhood, no close friends, described as temperamentally hyperexcitable with low tolerance for frustration. In adulthood, odd, effeminate mannerisms and severe degree of interpersonal intrusiveness. Comorbid bipolar disorder (became hypersexual during manic phases).	Exposed himself and touched a prepubescent boy at a playground.		Patient 3.
Schwartz-Watts (2005)	M	22	Prior diagnosis of pervasive developmental disorder. Military family, as a child moved often: teachers noted impaired performance each time he attended a new school. Stereotyped interests including Game Boy games, weapons (guns and swords), and Legos. As adult, hospitalized for Tylenol overdose, homeless at time of crime; "tactile defensiveness."	Charged with murdering an 8-year-old boy. Shot victim after victim ran over his foot with a bicycle; used a gun he always carried for protection.	Yes	Case 1. Average intelligence.
	M	35	No prior diagnosis of pervasive developmental disorder. In childhood, parents maintained something was wrong with him; "savant" in mathematics; repetitive interests in collecting items (health club memberships, bicycles, refrigerators, textbooks, guns, jobs) in multiples of two, and in World War II, Adolf Hitler, numbers, and television shows. In adulthood, oversensitivity to/irritability associated with having his head or glasses touched.	Charged with murdering a neighbor, who entered his apartment attempting to intervene in an argument. Overkill: Shot victim repeatedly with revolver, subsequently retrieved a second gun from a bedroom and shot victim in the head.	Yes	Case 2.

Source	Gender	Age	Noted Symptoms	Antisocial Behaviors	Crime?*	Notes
	M	20	Previous psychiatric treatments but no previous diagnosis of autistic spectrum disorder; diagnosed with schizoaffective disorder at time of offense (a diagnosis not confirmed by neuropsychological testing or neurological examination). In childhood, intolerance of or hypersensitivity to specific noise (parents talking on telephone downstairs)—on hearing noise would become aggressive towards others and bang his head against the wall; idiosyncratic collections (tire stem valves); impaired relationships and few friends.	Charged with murdering his girlfriend's father. Shot victim with a shotgun after being asked to remove his belongings from the victim's beach house. Reported having difficulty recognizing the facial expression and nonverbal cues of victim.	Yes	Case 3.
Haskins & Silva (2006)	M	Adult	As a child, problems relating to other children; bullied; described as "backwards." As adult, poor social skills; difficulty maintaining employment; no adult friends; displayed little emotion; "cold and calculating."	Charged with capital murder. Accused of starting fire in his apartment to obtain insurance money—the fire killed his daughter and critically injured his wife. Stole credit card to purchase fire-fighting supplies.	Yes	Mr. A. Young volunteer fireman.
	M	Adult	No friends during childhood/adolescence, but good student. Obtained degree in engineering, but failed graduate examination five times. Obtained master's degree in chemistry, but alienated professors and others because of rigid, pedantic approach and poor social skills.	Convicted of two counts of child annoyance. Accused of inappropriately touching numerous adolescent female students (i.e., in the shoulder area).	Yes	Mr. B. Middle-aged substitute teacher.
	M	Adult	Deaf. History of poor socialization, no friends, inability to keep a job. Preoccupations with black men, elevators, computer labs, construction sites.	Compulsively propositioned male strangers for sex in public restrooms. Two trespassing charges.	Yes	Mr. C. Outpatient psychotherapy patient.

Note: *Behavior or action for which the individual was arrested, charged, and/or convicted.

Regarding any identifiable relationships between symptoms of Asperger's disorder and motivations for antisocial behavior, results were quite mixed. For example, in some cases, direct links between symptoms and antisocial acts were explicitly reported, such as violence in direct response to anxiety associated with changes in the environment or routines (e.g., KA in Barry-Walsh & Mullen, 2004; Chen et al., 2003; Chesterman & Rutter, 1993; Everall & LeCouteur, 1990; Littlejohns et al., 1990; Wing, 1981—see discussion below), violence in response to disliked stimuli such as high-pitched sounds (Mawson et al., 1985), or crimes directly related and linked to preoccupations such as sex or fire (BD and TE in Barry-Walsh & Mullen, 2004; Milton et al., 2002; CD, GH, and KL in Murrie et al., 2002). However, in other cases, changes in routines or intolerance for change did not appear directly related to subsequent criminal behavior (e.g., NY in Barry-Walsh & Mullen, 2004; Baron-Cohen, 1988; AB in Murrie et al., 2002). Most limiting, however, is the fact that many studies (e.g., Bankier, 1999; Mnukhin & Isaev, 1975) did not include sufficient information about symptoms, motivations, or antisocial behaviors to make any inferences about how they may (or may not) be related in any meaningful way. Ultimately, though examining case report data in aggregate may be useful in hypothesis generation, comparison studies are the most desirable next step in gaining a further understanding of the etiological factors of crime and violence in individuals with Asperger's disorder.

Asperger's Disorder and Violent Offending. Several authors (e.g., Mawson et al., 1985; Schwartz-Watts, 2005; Silva et al., 2005) suggest that the relationship between Asperger's disorder and violence and aggression is more common than has been recognized and call for further research into this relationship. Attempts have been made to synthesize this literature and examine published case material collectively. For example, a review by Ghaziuddin and colleagues (1991) of 21 published case series and case reports of patients with Asperger's disorder indicated that only 3 of 132 patients (2.27%) were characterized by histories of violence—rates markedly lower than point-prevalence rates of violent crimes in the United States, which, at that time, were 6–7% for rape, robbery, and assault for individuals aged 12–24 years (as reported by the U.S. Bureau of Justice Statistics in 1987). From a qualitative perspective, violence in individual with Asperger's disorder has been described in some studies as "domestic in nature" (Tantam, 1988a), and "morbid fascinations" for violence in some of these individuals has also been reported (Tantam, 1988b).

Silva and colleagues (2002, 2003, 2004, 2005) have proposed that Asperger's disorder may play a key role in the pathogenesis of various forms of serial homicidal behavior. More specifically, serial killing has been linked in the literature to schizoid personality disorder (i.e., a pervasive pattern of emotional coldness and preference for social isolation—see Chapter 10), and several authors have made a case for the close conceptual and symptomatic relationship between Asperger's disorder and schizoid personality disorder (Silva et al., 2003). Silva and colleagues proposed a **neuropsychiatric developmental model (NDM) for serial murder**, taking into account five causative components: neuropsychiatric development (i.e., autism spectrum disorders such as Asperger's disorder), psychopathy, aggressive behavior, sexual psychopathology (i.e., fetishism such as partialism or necrophilia), and environmental stressors. These authors have used the NDM to analyze separately the cases of multiple murderers Jeffrey Dahmer, Theodore Kaczynski (the Unabomber), and Joel Rifkin from neuropsychiatric developmental and ecological perspectives (see Box 3.1 and Table 3.7).

Asperger's Disorder and Sexual Offending. Some evidence for a link between Asperger's disorder and the perpetration of sexual crimes has been reported in the literature. Mauridsen and colleagues (2008; see Table 3.2) used the nationwide Danish Criminal Register to examine rates of criminal convictions in a follow-up study of 313 former child psychiatric inpatients with PDDs (113 with childhood autism, 86 with atypical autism, and 114 with Asperger's disorder). Results indicated that individuals with Asperger's disorder were characterized by increased convictions for sexual offending, which approached significance relative to controls. (Sexual offending was one of the two crimes across all criminal categories for which the offense rate of the diagnostic group was differentiated from that of the control group. The other was arson—see discussion below.)

The nature of the association between Asperger's disorder and sexual offending may be better understood by examining the problems of sexuality that have been described in published cases of individuals with Asperger's disorder. For example, Asperger (1944, in Chesterman & Rutter, 1993) reported early signs of strong

BOX 3.1 ASPERGER'S DISORDER AND MULTIPLE MURDER

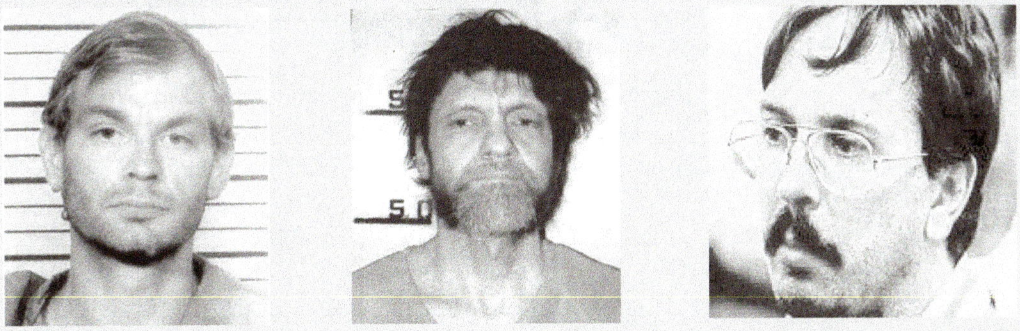

Silva and colleagues, using a neuropsychiatric developmental model, discuss the applicability of DSM-IV-TR diagnostic criteria for Asperger's disorder to the cases of three multiple murderers: serial killer Jeffrey Dahmer (left), "Unabomber" Theodore Kaczynski (middle), and Joel Rifkin (right), who was convicted of killing 9 prostitutes in New York (though it is believed it may have been as many as 17).

sexual activity with public masturbation, exhibitionism, and sadism in many of his subjects. Wing (1981) explains how sexual offending may derive from the social skills deficits of individuals with Asperger's disorder. A young man with this disorder may have poor relations with the opposite sex due to a general social ineptitude; he may have no idea how to communicate his interest appropriately and attract a partner. If he is characterized by an increased sex drive, he may sexually offend by approaching and touching or kissing a stranger. In a case series of 34 individuals with Asperger's disorder, Wing (1981) found 4 to have a history of "bizarre antisocial acts" (no details reported), with one individual injuring another boy while conducting chemical experiments. Cooper and colleagues (1993) describe the case of PM, an adult male with Asperger's disorder who committed a series of sexual touching offenses against women (see Table 3.6). In one instance, as a passenger on a bus, PM stared at a woman (another standing passenger), moved toward her, and rubbed himself against her bottom. Failing to detect her fear or recognize the consequences of his actions, he touched her again. According to the authors, PM's offending behavior becomes understandable in the context of his social deficits: Ill-equipped to navigate the proper channels for friendship and intimacy, he merely touches what he desires and relies upon immature interpersonal strategies, which happen to involve illegal behavior. Other case material has suggested that the sexual preoccupations and excessive or abnormal sexual interests of Asperger's disordered individuals may contribute to their sexual and nonsexual offending behavior (e.g., Barry-Walsh & Mullen, 2004; Chesterman & Rutter, 1993; Kohn et al., 1998; Milton et al., 2002).

According to Silva and colleagues (2004), individuals with ASDs are also likely to suffer from paraphilias associated with fetishism (see Chapter 8 for more detailed descriptions of these disorders; see also Milton et al., 2002 for a case example). Those diagnosed with paraphilias such as *partialism* (focusing on body parts), *fetishism* (focusing on physical symbolic extensions of the body proper), and *necrophilia* (exclusive focus on the physical as opposed to psychological make-up of the eroticized—albeit deceased—person) are characterized by the strong tendency to be sexually aroused by physical hyperrepresentations of the body. This may involve dehumanizing the object of their sexual desire by deconstructing that person into physical characteristics or by systematically constraining that person's intentionality and autonomy. These behaviors are consistent with reports of the relative inability of individuals with ASDs such as Asperger's disorder to distinguish between people and things, focusing on others' component parts while neglecting their mental qualities.

Table 3.7 Silva and Colleagues' Neuropsychiatric Developmental Model: Three Multiple Murderers

Symptom/Factor	Jeffrey Dahmer	Theodore Kaczynski	Joel Rifkin
DSM-IV-TR Diagnostic Criteria for Asperger's Disorder			
A. Qualitative impairment in social interaction			
1. Marked impairment in the use of multiple nonverbal behaviors . . . to regulate social interaction	[+]	[l], [l] *	[+], [+], [+], [+]**
2. Failure to develop peer relationships appropriate to developmental level	[+]	[+], [+]	[+], [+], [+], [+]
3. Lack of spontaneous seeking to share enjoyment, interests, or achievements with other people	[+]	[+], [+]	[l], [l], [l], [l]
4. Lack of social or emotional reciprocity	[+]	[+], [+]	[+], [+], [+], [+]
B. Restricted repetitive and stereotyped patterns of behavior, interests, and activities			
1. Encompassing preoccupation with stereotyped and restricted patterns of interest that is abnormal either in intensity or focus	[+] Animal and human bodies and parts	[+], [+] Mathematics, bomb-making, impact of technology on society	[+], [+], [+], [+]
2. Apparently inflexible adherence to specific, nonfunctional routines or rituals	[+] Ritualistic processing and arrangement of bones	[l], [l]	[+], [+], [+], [+]
3. Stereotyped and repetitive motor mannerisms	[–] Unusual rigid body kinetics. Listening to internal body sounds.	[–], [–]	[–], [–], [–], [–]
4. Persistent preoccupation with parts of objects	[+]	[+], [+]	[l], [l], [l], [l]
C. Clinically significant impairment in social, occupational, or other important areas of functioning	[+] School, military, occupational, social	[+], [+] Occupational, social	[+], [+], [+], [+]
D. No clinically significant general delay in language	[+]	[+], [+]	[+], [+], [+], [+]
E. No clinically significant delay in cognitive development or in the development of age-appropriate self-help skills, adaptive behavior, . . . and curiosity about the environment in childhood	[+]	[+], [+]	[+], [+], [+], [+]
F. Criteria not met for another specific PDD or schizophrenia	[+]	[+], [+]	[+], [+], [+], [+]
Axis I diagnoses	1. Asperger's disorder 2. Paraphilia NOS (necrophilia) 3. Alcohol abuse 4. Depressive disorder NOS	1. Asperger's disorder	1. Asperger's disorder 2. Fetishism 3. Paraphilia NOS (partialism)

Symptom/Factor	Jeffrey Dahmer	Theodore Kaczynski	Joel Rifkin
Axis II diagnoses	1. Personality disorder NOS (with antisocial, schizoid, and schizotypal personality disorder traits)	1. Personality disorder NOS (with schizoid, paranoid, schizotypal, narcissistic, obsessive compulsive, and antisocial personality traits)	1. Personality disorder NOS (with schizoid, antisocial, and schizotypal personality traits)
Axis III	None	None	None
Axis IV	1. Legal problems 2. Interpersonal problems 3. Occupational problems	1. Legal problems 2. Interpersonal problems 3. Unemployment	1. Legal problems 2. Interpersonal problems 3. Occupational problems
Global Assessment of Functioning (GAF)	1. GAF = 5 (highest level during year preceding his final arrest) 2. GAF = 5 (at time of arrest)	1. GAF = 35 (current) 2. GAF = 35 (highest level past year) 3. GAF = 5 (during instant offense)	1. GAF = 8 (highest level during year preceding his final arrest) 2. GAF = 5 (at time of arrest)

Source: Adapted from Silva, Ferrari, and Leong (2002, pp. 4–5); Silva, Ferrari, and Leong (2003, pp. 18, 32); and Silva, Leong, Smith, Hawes, and Ferrari (2005).

Notes: + = present; – = absent; I = insufficient data.

*For Theodore Kaczynski, the first bracket refers to childhood and adolescence combined, and the second bracket refers to adulthood.

**For Joel Rifkin, the first bracket refers to childhood (approximately birth to age 12 years), the second bracket to adolescence (approximately ages 13 to 17), the third to adulthood (approximately ages 18 years and above), and the fourth to the holistic DSM-IV-TR rating.

Kohn and colleagues (1998) suggest that the reason only some individuals with Asperger's disorder are violent or offend sexually is linked to individual differences in areas such as impulsivity, aggression, and sexuality (similar to individual differences in these areas observed in those without the disorder). Asperger's disorder patients with high levels of these traits, however, would not be able to control their behavior in accordance with social norms, as it is possible for aggressive individuals not diagnosed with Asperger's to do.

Asperger's Disorder and Arson. Criminal fire setting by those with Asperger's disorder has been reported in the literature. For example, in a retrospective study of 126 young Swedish offenders (aged 15–22 years) referred for presentencing forensic psychiatric evaluation (most because of serious or violent offenses), Siponmaa and colleagues (2002) found that of the 16 individuals that had committed arson as a main crime, 2 (12.5%) were diagnosed with ADHD, 2 with mental retardation, and 10 (63%) with PDD (Asperger's syndrome and PDD-NOS). Additionally, the diagnoses of Asperger's syndrome and PDD-NOS were significantly more frequent in the arson group than in any other crime group—the only statistically significant relationship between crime type and diagnosis revealed. Mauridsen and colleagues (2008) also found that individuals with Asperger's disorder were characterized by significantly more convictions for arson than controls—the only significant increase in crime across all crime categories and diagnostic groups relative to controls. In the case of arson described by Murrie and colleagues (2002), social disappointments led to rumination, which subsequently resulted in crime. Interestingly, others have noted that individuals with Asperger's disorder have experienced depression and anxiety resulting from disappointment at failed attempts at social relationships (Tantam, 1991).

Asperger's Disorder and Property Crime. Published case material suggests how Asperger's disorder may relate to property offending. Chen and colleagues (2003) reported the case of a 21-year-old man with Asperger's disorder and previous diagnoses of schizophrenia (based on idiosyncratic interests, affective disturbance, and withdrawn attitude at home) and *kleptomania* (a disorder discussed in Chapter 9). Beginning at age 17, he stole compulsively from elder classmates in school and also hoarded objects such as paper, boxes, cups, and plastic bags. He was eventually expelled from high school for his repeated stealing. In his early adult years, he stole from neighborhood mailboxes, continued his collecting behaviors, and was characterized by temper tantrums, aggressive behavior, and poor self-care. It was at this point (after professionals reconsidered from a longitudinal view the symptoms he had displayed in adolescence) that his diagnosis was revised to Asperger's disorder. Haskins and Silva (2005) suggest that the Chen et al. (2003) case represents a combination of kleptomania and schizoid traits reported elsewhere in the literature, which may indicate the presence of a pervasive developmental disorder (PDD).

Origins of Crime and Violence in Asperger's Disorder: Theoretical Explanations and Etiological Mechanisms

Theory of Mind. Theory of mind deficits are often cited as causal mechanisms in the criminal and violent behavior of Asperger's disordered individuals. As stated, these individuals have significant difficulties with reading social cues, and perpetrators with this disorder frequently cannot understand that another person may have a different emotional or cognitive experience of a shared event, or they may be unable to read the necessary interpersonal cues notifying them to disengage from particular social interactions (Haskins & Silva, 2006). Chesterman and Rutter (1993) provide an excellent example—describing how an inability to appreciate another's point of view led to an Asperger's disorder patient (RM in Table 3.6) assaulting a police officer, who discovered him inside someone else's home and assumed he was committing a burglary. From RM's point of view, he merely intended to borrow a washing machine and steal a worthless article (i.e., lingerie) in order to act out his sexual fantasy. Burglary—in his mind—meant the theft of valuable items such as jewelry.

Preoccupations or Restricted Interests. Silva and colleagues (2005) propose that aggression may stem from preoccupations or restricted interests involving potentially dangerous subjects, such as setting fires, making explosives, or the martial arts. According to Haskins and Silva (2006), criminal behaviors associated with Asperger's disorder may be attributable to abnormal, repetitive interests. For example, fire setting in one of Barry-Walsh and Mullen's (2004) cases reflected a typical, narrow, all-absorbing interest (i.e., in fire). Of the 26 individuals in the sample of English special hospital residents (almost exclusively violent offenders) who had their circumscribed interests reported (Hare et al., 2000), 12 had interests with antisocial or violent themes (e.g., toy soldiers, cowboys and Indians, Nazism, dictators, World War II, militaria, violent films, knives, bombs, harm to women, martial arts, morbid offenses, and breaking windows). Others had circumscribed interests in rather benign areas such as chess, railways, flushing toilets, touching walls, and Chinese food. Additionally, preoccupations or narrow interests may combine with other factors contributing to the origins of criminal behavior in Asperger's disordered persons. For example, these individuals may engage in sexual crimes that are closely linked to their repetitive, stereotyped, and excessively focused interests; and their ToM deficits also place them at risk for engaging in unwelcome sexual behaviors (Haskins & Silva, 2006).

Deficient Empathy. Deficient empathy and, in turn, lack of remorse due to difficulties appreciating the subjective experiences of others have been discussed in relation to the crime, violence, and aggression associated with Asperger's disorder (Haskins & Silva, 2006; Silva et al., 2005). In fact, case material (e.g., Murrie et al., 2002) appears to support Wing's (1981) earlier suggestion that deficient empathy is a central feature among individuals with Asperger's disorder who engage in criminal and antisocial acts. Such empathy deficits may also profoundly impact the interactions of Asperger's disordered offenders with the criminal justice system. Some authors (e.g., Murrie et al., 2002) have proposed that the deficient empathy characterizing Asperger's disorder could provide the basis for an insanity defense for an individual with this disorder. These authors discuss how, in terms of criminal justice applications, deficient empathy can be said to limit an offender's ability to judge right from wrong or to recognize culpability, which could affect whether that individual is fit to stand trial. Also, given the importance of expressing remorse during sentencing procedures, Asperger's disordered individuals may be at substantial risk for offending judges and juries during the legal process (Haskins & Silva, 2006). Ultimately, a provocative question is raised by Barry-Walsh and Mullen (2004): How can individuals with Asperger's disorder be expected to authentically appreciate the moral wrongfulness of their actions (and thus be responsible for their social behaviors, including criminality), given their difficulties with social conventions and connectedness?

Social and Interpersonal Deficits. The characteristic interpersonal deficits of Asperger's disorder may also contribute in some way to the crime, violence, and antisocial behavior observed in these individuals. Murrie and colleagues (2002) discuss the roles of interpersonal naïveté in offending associated with Asperger's disorder. Such naïveté leaves individuals with Asperger's disorder vulnerable to mistreatment by others and leads them to seek interpersonal contact in inappropriate and misguided ways. Similarly, Tantam (1999, in Woodbury-Smith et al., 2006) proposed that some individuals with Asperger's disorder and other hfASDs may—due to feelings of powerlessness—engage in behaviors deliberately intended to shock and disrupt, behaviors best characterized as malicious. According to Tantam, these behaviors do not stem from social exclusion but instead indicate a subgroup of ASD individuals who are characterized by malice, immaturity, and naiveté (rather than eccentricity and clumsiness).

Other relationships between criminality and interpersonal deficits have been proposed. Woodbury-Smith and colleagues (2006) note that several of their study participants appear to have perpetrated their crimes in response to perceived victimization. For example, one woman damaged a female neighbor's automobile because she was jealous of her "normality"; one man damaged toilets at his work when his job was eliminated; another man—when younger—ripped seats of a bus with a knife because he believed the bus deliberately failed to stop for him the previous day. Wing (1997, in Woodbury-Smith et al., 2006) have also proposed that unprovoked assaults perpetrated by individuals with hfASDs may be due to their feelings of resentment. Additionally, interpersonal deficits may lead to sexual frustration (i.e., being ill-equipped interpersonally to initiate or sustain intimate relationships associated with consensual sexual contact), which may contribute to the sexual offending associated with Asperger's disorder (Murrie et al., 2002). Sexual offending in one published case study (Barry-Walsh & Mullen, 2004) was attributed to the individual's age (16 years), burgeoning libido, and crippling inability either to transact sexual activity (i.e., he made direct and blunt sexual advances) or to establish normal relationships with peers. However, in the published case study of a different individual, charges of public nuisance and minor assaults stemmed from his catatonic behaviors, which drew attention to himself when he was in public and resulted in his making angry and aggressive responses to members of the public who attempted to assist him.

Social and interpersonal deficits may also affect the interactions of Asperger's disordered individuals with law enforcement. For example, Hare and colleagues (2000) propose that offenders with Asperger's disorder may be more likely to be detected, compared to other offenders, because of their impaired social skills (e.g., their inability to understand and use deception while engaged in criminal activity). Furthermore, Murrie and colleagues (2002) propose that individuals with Asperger's disorder may also be more likely to provide immediate confessions to the police when apprehended.

Cognitive and Behavioral Factors. Several authors have explored the contributions of unusual or abnormal thought processes and learning experiences to the criminal and violent behaviors of those with Asperger's disorder. For example, Frith (1989, in Haskins & Silva, 2006) proposed the concept of *central coherence*, a natural tendency in human beings to construct their view of the world as a rich but unified tapestry of lived experience. For many individuals with Asperger's disorder, however, key aspects of their lives (e.g., social, moral, and physical environments) are lived outside of this unified experience. Consequently, those with deficits in central coherence may engage in crime because they focus excessively on their internal preoccupations while ignoring social and legal consequences. *Top-down modulation* (i.e., making behavioral choices based on long-term goals that prevent one from being distracted by or overloaded with stimuli) is another model for this process. Failure of top-down modulation in Asperger's disorder has been noted by Frith (2004, in Haskins & Silva, 2006) and others. Asperger's disordered individuals may also be predisposed to develop a psychological niche for growing inner preoccupations and *fixations* due to their deficits in internal coherence and associated *compartmentalization* characteristics. Subsequently, these fixations may (if left unchecked by a normal understanding of morals and societal constraints) lead to maladaptive fantasies (Silva et al., 2005). This characteristic is demonstrated by serial murderers with Asperger's disorder who compartmentalize their lives into a "prosocial" component (functioning as law-abiding citizens) and an "antisocial" component (functioning as sexual predators; Silva, Leong, & Ferrari, 2004; Silva et al., 2000, in Haskins & Silva, 2006).

Some authors have speculated about how thought and behavioral rigidity in Asperger's disorder may contribute to criminal offending. For example, fire setting in another of Barry-Walsh and Mullen's (2004) cases was the product of lateral, concrete logical thought processes.[3] Murrie and colleagues (2002) also note that in some cases, there appears to be a rigid sense of right and wrong (which otherwise may have served to deter criminality) that leads individuals with Asperger's disorder to feel exceptionally frustrated when they believe they have been wronged and to subsequently act out aggressively.

Paranoid thought processes may contribute significantly to violent and aggressive behavior (see Chapter 5), and investigators have examined paranoia within the context of Asperger's disorder. Blackshaw and colleagues (2001) looked at 25 individuals with Asperger's disorder recruited through the UK National Autistic Society and from residential houses for individuals with learning disabilities. These subjects were characterized by both reduced ToM abilities and increased self-reported paranoia compared to normal controls—though, in this study, ToM abilities and paranoia were not related to causal attributions (i.e., blaming others versus blaming oneself). This finding may have important implications, as, in one theory (Bentall & Kinderman, 1989, in Blackshaw et al., 2001), paranoia is derived from external, other-blaming attributions used to explain the occurrence of negative events that threaten a fragile self-concept ("these bad things are not my fault, someone else is responsible")—allowing these individuals closure of the discrepancies between the way they see themselves (*self-ideal*) and who they actually are (*self-actual*). Blackshaw and colleagues (2001) propose that, although this theory may explain the persecutory delusions observed in schizophrenia (see Chapter 5), their results here suggest that the paranoia observed in those with Asperger's disorder may be qualitatively different—more a confusion originating in not understanding the subtleties of social interactions and rules rather than a defensive strategy. Ultimately, more research is needed to determine if and how abnormal thought processes may contribute to the crime and violence observed in individuals with Asperger's disorder.

Comorbidity. The comorbidity of Asperger's disorder with other psychiatric conditions such as psychotic and mood disorders and Tourette syndrome has been demonstrated in the literature (Simblett & Wilson, 1993). Palermo (2004) emphasizes the role of comorbid psychopathology (i.e., mood disorders) as the driving force for offending behaviors in individuals with Asperger's disorder and other PDDs. Palermo (2004) also states that the multifaceted deficits associated with PDDs might make individuals with these disorders more vulnerable to overreacting to frustrating situations or sudden environmental stimulation while interpersonal and internal rigidity might leave them vulnerable to frustration, which could contribute to aggression or violence. In a review of 17 publications describing 37 cases of individuals with both Asperger's disorder diagnoses and histories of violence, Newman and Ghaziuddin (2008) found 11 cases (29.7%) to have definite evidence and 20 cases (54%) to have probable evidence of a comorbid psychiatric disorder. In fact, only 6 cases demonstrated no clear evidence of a comorbid psychiatric condition, suggesting that psychiatric comorbidity may play a role in the violent behaviors observed in individuals with Asperger's disorder. Unfortunately, these authors do not explain either if or how this comorbidity contributes more to criminality than does the Asperger's disorder. Finally, antisocial behavior in individuals with Asperger's disorder and other hfASDs may be attributable to comorbidity with criminogenic disorders such as antisocial personality disorder (Haskins & Silva, 2006).

Other Social and Gender Factors. Other social and gender-related factors may explain the occurrence of Asperger's disorder–associated crime and violence. For example, although estimates of the genetic heritability of ASD are as high as 90%, environmental influences such as bullying by others, excessive noise level, and family instability may lead to a vulnerability to antisocial behavior in individuals with hfASDs (Haskins & Silva, 2006).

---

3. An example of concrete thought process is the following, from Everall and LeCoutier's (1990) case of an adolescent fire setter with Asperger's disorder (see Table 3.6): Asked the meaning of the proverb "people who live in glass houses should not throw stones," he stated "if you throw stones at a glass house it will let cold air in and it will spoil the ceilings" (p. 286).

Evidence also indicates that aggression in individuals with Asperger's disorder may be due, in part, to frustration associated with low tolerance for change, particularly social change (Silva et al., 2005). Finally, Wolff (1995, in Hare et al., 2000) found the risk of delinquency in boys with "schizoid personality of childhood" (which overlaps largely with Asperger's disorder) to be only slightly higher than the risk in same-aged boys in the general population. However, for girls with Asperger's disorder, rates of delinquency were significantly increased compared to those of controls, which suggests that this disorder may contribute differentially to the presentation of criminal behavior among men and women.

Attention-Deficit and Disruptive Behavior Disorders: Attention-Deficit/Hyperactivity Disorder

In the DSM-IV, ADHD was discussed in a subgroup of attention-deficit and disruptive behavior disorders, along with conduct disorder and oppositional defiant disorder. In the DSM-5, the latter two have been reclassified into a new group of disorders known as disruptive, impulse-control, and conduct disorders—now separate from neurodevelopmental disorders. Nonetheless, conduct disorder and oppositional defiant disorder will be discussed below according to how they were defined within their original DSM-IV-TR organizational grouping because the literature on mental illness and crime (at the time of this writing) is still transitioning from the DSM-IV-TR to the DSM-5.

According to Pratt and colleagues (2002), 20 different labels have been used to describe inattentive, impulsive, and hyperactive youth over the past century (including such terms as "Fidgety Phils" and "hyperkinesis"). What is currently referred to as **attention-deficit/hyperactivity disorder (ADHD)** was first introduced in the DSM-III (APA, 1980). Diagnostic criteria for DSM-5 ADHD (which have remained largely unchanged from those of the DSM-IV) are listed in Table 3.8. ADHD's three main features include **inattention** (a lack of attention, notice, or regard); **hyperactivity** (being abnormally active); and **impulsivity** (a tendency to act on a whim, engaging in behavior characterized by little or no forethought, reflection, or consideration of the consequences). This disorder may be coded as a combined type (DSM-IV-TR) or a combined presentation (DSM-5), when both criteria A1 and A2 have been met for the past six months; as a predominantly inattentive type or presentation, when criterion A1 but not A2 has been met for the past six months; or as a predominantly hyperactive-impulsive type or presentation, when criterion A2 but not A1 has been met for the past six months.

Prevalence and Incidence Rates of ADHD

The DSM-IV-TR reports rates of ADHD ranging from 3% to 7% in school-aged children, depending upon the type of sample and method of assessment (APA, 2000). Slightly higher rates have been reported elsewhere (see Fergusson et al., 2010). According to the DSM-IV-TR, only limited data exist on the prevalence of ADHD in adolescents and adults (APA, 2000) though rates of about 5% for children and 2.5% for adults are reported in the DSM-5 (APA, 2013). Other more recent prevalence estimates within adult populations range from 1.0% in Holland to 10.0% in South America (Ebejer et al., 2012); and Ebejer and colleagues found lifetime prevalence rates of ADHD of 0.9% for women and 2.1% for men in a large Australian twin registry study.

Theoretical Conceptualizations

The DSM-IV-TR defines the diagnostic criteria for ADHD almost exclusively in terms of behavioral symptoms. In fact, according to Gabbard (2005), what is rarely discussed is the *mental* experience of individuals with ADHD, a gap partially due to the fact that few psychoanalytic contributions have been made to the understanding of ADHD and learning disabilities. Gabbard provides a rare thoughtful discussion of how unconscious processes (in conjunction with neurobiological factors) have been suggested in recent years in the etiology of ADHD, which also may be applied to the other disorders in this chapter. For example, drive theorists have proposed that an understanding of adult patients with congenital forms of brain dysfunction involves the understanding of how this dysfunction impacts the achievement of normal developmental tasks. As the infant grows,

Table 3.8 DSM-5 Diagnostic Criteria for Attention-Deficit/Hyperactivity Disorder

Attention-Deficit/Hyperactivity Disorder

A. A persistent pattern of inattention and/or hyperactivity-impulsivity that interferes with functioning or development, as characterized by (1) or (2):

1. *Inattention:* Six (or more) of the following symptoms have persisted for at least 6 months to a degree that is inconsistent with developmental level and that negatively impacts directly on social and academic/occupational activities:

Note: The symptoms are not solely a manifestation of oppositional behavior, defiance, hostility, or failure to understand tasks or instructions. For older adolescents and adults (age 17 and older), at least five symptoms are required.

a. Often fails to give close attention to details or makes careless mistakes in schoolwork, work, or other activities (e.g., overlooks or misses details, work is inaccurate).
b. Often has difficulty sustaining attention in tasks or play activities (e.g., has difficulty remaining focused during lectures, conversations, or lengthy reading).
c. Often does not seem to listen when spoken to directly (e.g., mind seems elsewhere, even in the absence of any obvious distraction).
d. Often does not follow through on instructions and fails to finish schoolwork, chores, or duties in the workplace (e.g., starts tasks but quickly loses focus or is easily sidetracked).
e. Often has difficulty organizing tasks and activities (e.g., difficulty managing sequential tasks; difficulty keeping materials and belongings in order; messy, disorganized work; has poor time management; fails to meet deadlines).
f. Often avoids, dislikes, or is reluctant to engage in tasks that require sustained mental effort (e.g., schoolwork or homework; for older adolescents and adults, preparing reports, completing forms, reviewing lengthy papers).
g. Often loses things necessary for tasks or activities (e.g., school materials, pencils, books, tools, wallets, keys, paperwork, eyeglasses, mobile telephones).
h. Is often distracted by extraneous stimuli (for older adolescents and adults, may include unrelated thoughts).
i. Is often forgetful in daily activities (e.g., doing chores, running errands; for older adolescents and adults, returning calls, paying bills, keeping appointments).

2. *Hyperactivity and impulsivity:* Six (or more) of the following symptoms have persisted for at least 6 months to a degree that is inconsistent with developmental level and that negatively impacts directly on social and academic/occupational activities:

Note: The symptoms are not solely a manifestation of oppositional behavior, defiance, hostility, or failure to understand tasks or instructions. For older adolescents and adults (age 17 and older), at least five symptoms are required.

a. Often fidgets with or taps hands or feet or squirms in seat.
b. Often leaves seat in classroom or in other situations in which remaining seated is expected (e.g., leaves his or her place in the classroom, in the office or other workplace, or in other situations that require remaining in place).
c. Often runs about or climbs in situations where it is inappropriate. (*Note:* In adolescents or adults, may be limited to feeling restless.)
d. Often unable to play or engage in leisure activities quietly.
e. Is often "on the go," acting as if "driven by a motor" (e.g., is unable to be or uncomfortable being still for extended time, as in restaurants, meetings; may be experienced by others as being restless or difficult to keep up with).
f. Often talks excessively.
g. Often blurts out an answer before a question has been completed (e.g., completes people's sentences; cannot wait for turn in conversation).

h. Often has difficulty awaiting his or her turn (e.g., while waiting in line).

i. Often interrupts or intrudes on others (e.g., butts into conversations, games, or activities; may start using other people's things without asking or receiving permission; for adolescents and adults, may intrude into or take over what others are doing).

A. Severe inattentive or hyperactive-impulsive symptoms were present prior to age 12 years.

B. Several inattentive or hyperactive-impulsive symptoms are present in two or more settings (e.g., at home, school, or work; with friends or relatives; in other activities).

C. There is clear evidence that the symptoms interfere with, or reduce the quality of, social, academic, or occupational functioning.

D. The symptoms do not occur exclusively during the course of schizophrenia or another psychotic disorder and are not better explained by another mental disorder (e.g., mood disorder, anxiety disorder, dissociative disorder, personality disorder, substance intoxication or withdrawal).

Source: APA (2013, p. 59–61). Reprinted with permission from the *Diagnostic and Statistical Manual of Mental Disorders*, Fifth Edition (Copyright © 2013). American Psychiatric Association. All rights reserved.

he or she struggles daily as the pressure of drives and emotions is pitted against cortical control. Mastery of these drive pressures, in turn, becomes much more difficult without a functioning cortex.

Object relations theorists have speculated on how biologically based cognitive deficits may adversely affect the development of the self and the *internalization* of relations with other objects. Daniel Stern (2004, in Gabbard, 2005) notes that the development of the self begins with an *intersubjective matrix* between the infant and the mother or caregiver. Children with biologically based cognitive deficits cannot accurately perceive or effectively integrate the emotional signals from the mother. A child's failure to respond to the mother as she expects may cause anxiety, tension, and discord in mother-infant interactions. Parents may subsequently recoil from the child, and interactions with him or her may be tainted with disappointment and anxiety, causing disturbances in the child's self-esteem (Abams & Kaslow, 1976, in Gabbard, 2005). Parents may also become overinvolved and overprotective, placing unattainable expectations upon these children as they grow and develop, which results in further feelings of failure and humiliation. Such children have poor impulse control, leading to a cycle of parental reprimands, angry and punitive interactions, and suggestions by parents (through their excessive anxiety) that separation from them is dangerous (Pickar, 1986, and Weil, 1978, in Gabbard, 2005). These children cannot understand cause and effect sequences, do not link rejection from others to their own behavior, and subsequently feel victimized and helpless (Bryan, 1977, in Gabbard, 2005).

Furthermore, deficits in visual and auditory perception and memory make it difficult for those with ADHD to achieve object constancy. Children with learning disabilities and ADHD often lack the ability to self-soothe because they have never internalized and maintained comforting, emotionally meaningful images of the mother; thus, they struggle with maintaining a stable sense of self. Furthermore, they are unable to perceive social cues from others accurately and hence relate to them in a socially appropriate manner (Bryan et al., 1980, in Gabbard, 2005).

According to Gabbard, some individuals with biologically based cognitive deficits (e.g., those with ADHD) can compensate for them by overdeveloping other areas of ego functioning (for example, the inventor Thomas Edison had learning disabilities). However, such compensatory efforts may fail, causing the youth to avoid the enormous frustration of repeated failure by turning to juvenile delinquency (Pickar, 1986, in Gabbard, 2005) and to develop contempt toward the values of parents, teachers, and society instead of dealing with the shame and humiliation associated with failing to meet the expectations of others (Gabbard, 2005).

"Pure" neurobiological explanations for the development of ADHD have also been offered. For example, abnormalities in dopamine functioning, particularly in prefrontal regions, have been proposed to play a role in symptoms of ADHD (Anckarsäter, 2006). A strong genetic component has also been suggested, as heritability estimates are in the range of 60–90%. Birth complications, maternal smoking, and family adversity have also been suggested as etiological factors (Savolainen et al., 2010).

A Closer Look: ADHD and Crime

Prevalence of the Disorder in Crime

Study Type	Number	Prevalence Rates
Arrest rates	0	–
Birth cohorts	0	–
Community samples	1*	71.0%
Homicide offenders	0	–
Jailed detainees and prisoners	7	1.6–55.0%
Psychiatric inpatients	3*	2.6–71.0%
Adjudicated juvenile delinquents	1	46.0%†
Total Number of Studies	**11**	

Sample Characteristics

Size	15–1,956
Gender	Male only (4 studies); female only (1 study); male and female but unbalanced, predominantly males (5 studies); not reported (1 study)
Age	Youth, adult
Location	Several North American and European countries (e.g., Canada, Germany, Sweden, United States)
Diagnostic Systems	DSM, ICD. Not specified in some more recent studies.

Notes: *One psychiatric inpatient study (Galli et al., 1999) also included community individuals. No "pure" community samples were located.

†For ADD hyperactive type: 9.0%.

Prevalence of Crime in the Disorder

Total Number of Studies **0**

Nondisordered or community resident comparison group or general population baseline rates for either disorder or crime provided: **1 study (9.1%)**†

Note: †In this study, Rösler et al. (2004) found rates of ADHD nearly 11 times higher for both combined and hyperactive-impulsive types relative to controls. Rates were decreased relative to controls for the inattentive type, though this difference was not significant.

The Relationship Between ADHD and Crime

Table 3.2 lists a number of investigations, in chronological order, that have examined the prevalence rates of ADHD in criminal populations. No studies reporting prevalence rates of crime and violence in individuals with ADHD were located.

General Studies. Numerous studies have established a statistical association between ADHD and various form of misconduct (Pratt et al., 2002; Savolainen et al., 2010), and ADHD is often associated with symptoms of maladaptive aggression in children and adolescents (Patel & Barzman, 2013). Recent and compelling examples include a study of adults from a large Australian twin registry; Ebejer and colleagues (2012) found the lifetime prevalence of conduct problems for those with ADHD was 57.8%, compared to 6.9% in those without ADHD.

Additionally, Fergusson and colleagues (2010) recently examined adolescent behavior disorders in a large birth cohort of 995 New Zealand–born individuals ("followed" until age 25). Results indicated a significant linear relationship between ADHD diagnosis in adolescence and adult outcomes of criminality, with more property and violent crime incidents and arrests in individuals with ADHD compared to those with subclinical ADHD and, in turn, to those without ADHD. However, similar linear relationships were observed with adult outcomes of substance use (legal and illegal), mental health issues (depressive or anxiety disorders, antisocial personality disorder, suicide attempts), pregnancy by age 20, interpersonal violence, and education and employment difficulties (quantified according to achievement and income). After adjusting for comorbid disorders and other confounding factors, however, associations remained significant only for education and employment difficulties—a distinct pattern of associations differing from those found with CD and ODD. Results also indicated that dimensional measures of behavior disorders were more strongly correlated with outcomes than categorical measures—emphasizing the need to consider subclinical symptoms in this area of research.

Origins of Crime and Violence in ADHD: Theoretical Explanations and Etiological Mechanisms

A link between ADHD and antisocial behavior is not a difficult one to imagine, given the hallmark impulsivity characterizing some forms of this disorder. However, theoretical explanations for crime and violence in ADHD offered in the literature have expanded far beyond simply "blaming" impulsivity. Recent reviews (e.g., Thapar et al., 2006) have suggested the significance of ADHD symptom severity and pervasiveness, genetic factors, family adversity, and peer rejection in the development of antisocial behavior (implicating neurobiological and social theories, as well as the effects of psychological symptoms). In a unique crossover between psychological or neurobiological and criminological approaches, Savolainen and colleagues (2010) attempted to apply two key theories of life-course criminology toward understanding the etiology of criminal behavior in ADHD: Moffitt's (1993) *dual developmental taxonomy*, which accounts for both life-course persistent and adolescent-onset criminal offending, and Sampson and Laub's (1993) *age-graded theory of informal social control*, which argues that crime is caused by weak bonds to prosocial entities. Data from the 1986 Northern Finland Birth Cohort Study (n = 5,010) provided support for Moffitt's theory (there was a substantial effect of ADHD on crime, moderated by verbal cognitive deficits) but not for Sampson and Laub's (adolescent social bonds had no mediating effect). However, adolescent social marginalization appeared to play a significant role in the development of criminal behavior, independent of early childhood measures of criminal propensity.

From a "pure" neurobiological perspective, Huebner et al. (2008) found a 6% gray matter volumetric reduction in the bilateral temporal lobes, left amygdala, left hippocampus, and orbitofrontal and ventromedial regions in boys with CD and ADHD, as well as volumetric increases in cerebellar gray matter. Temporal but not frontal or prefrontal lobe reductions have also been observed in adolescents diagnosed with early-onset CD and histories of ADHD (Kruesi et al., 2004). Finally, as for other disorders covered in this book, the role of comorbidity has been discussed. For example, in a study of 129 male prison inmates in a German facility, Röser and colleagues (2004) found comorbid psychiatric conditions in all but 1 of the 7 inmates who had been diagnosed with disturbance of activity and attention (an ICD-10 analogue for a type of ADHD). These comorbid conditions included alcoholism, substance use disorders, and personality disorders. Given the increased attention being paid of late to ADHD and its apparent proliferation among our youth (whether or not these in fact represent valid diagnoses in all cases), a more complete understanding of its relationship with crime and violence is a suitable priority for researchers.

Attention-Deficit and Disruptive Behavior Disorders: Conduct Disorder

As stated, **conduct disorder** and oppositional defiant disorder are no longer considered neurodevelopmental disorders but have been reclassified in the DSM-5 into the new category of disruptive, impulse-control, and conduct disorders; these disorders are characterized by problems stemming from behaviors violating the rights of others and bringing the individual into significant conflict with societal norms or authority figures (APA, 2013). The DSM-5 diagnostic criteria for conduct disorder are listed in Table 3.9.

Table 3.9 DSM-5 Diagnostic Criteria for Conduct Disorder

Conduct Disorder

A. A repetitive and persistent pattern of behavior in which the basic rights of others or major age-appropriate societal norms or rules are violated, as manifested by the presence of at least three of the following 15 criteria in the past 12 months from any of the categories below, with at least one criterion present in the past 6 months:

Aggression to People and Animals

1. Often bullies, threatens, or intimidates others.
2. Often initiates physical fights.
3. Has used a weapon that can cause serious physical harm to others (e.g., a bat, brick, broken bottle, knife, gun).
4. Has been physically cruel to people.
5. Has been physically cruel to animals.
6. Has stolen while confronting a victim (e.g., mugging, purse snatching, extortion, armed robbery).
7. Has forced someone into sexual activity.

Destruction of Property

8. Has deliberately engaged in fire setting with the intention of causing serious damage.
9. Has deliberately destroyed others' property (other than by fire setting).

Deceitfulness or Theft

10. Has broken into someone else's house, building, or car.
11. Often lies to obtain goods or favors or to avoid obligations (i.e., "cons" others).
12. Has stolen items of nontrivial value without confronting a victim (e.g., shoplifting, but without breaking and entering; forgery).

Serious Violations of Rules

13. Often stays out at night despite parental prohibitions, beginning before age 13 years.
14. Has run away from home overnight at least twice while living in parental or parental surrogate home (or once without returning for a lengthy period).
15. Is often truant from school, beginning before age 13 years.

B. The disturbance causes clinically significant impairment in social, occupational, or other important areas of functioning.

C. If the individual is age 18 years or older, criteria are not met for Antisocial Personality Disorder.

Source: APA (2013, pp. 469–471). Reprinted with permission from the *Diagnostic and Statistical Manual of Mental Disorders*, Fifth Edition (Copyright © 2013).

Prevalence and Incidence Rates of Conduct Disorder

According to the DSM-IV-TR, recent decades have shown an increase in prevalence rates of conduct disorder, and rates may be elevated in urban compared to rural settings. These rates are widely variable, depending upon sample types and assessment methods. Studies of the general population have reported prevalence rates of conduct disorder ranging from less than 1% to over 10%, and rates are higher for males relative to females.

Conduct disorder is one of the most frequently diagnosed disorders among children in outpatient and inpatient mental health facilities (APA, 2000).

Theoretical Conceptualizations. The phenomenon of clinically significant conduct problems in childhood has been largely conceptualized as a precursor to adult criminogenic personalities such as antisocial personality disorder and psychopathy (see Chapter 10). Conduct disorder was only recently introduced (comparatively speaking) as a criterion for antisocial personality disorder in the DSM-III in 1980 and clarified and simplified in the DSM-IV in 1994. Thus, it has not yet been afforded the opportunity to develop a rich tradition of theoretical conceptualization, unlike many of the other disorders described in this book.

Viewed as a behavioral or experiential precursor to antisocial personality disorder, conduct disorder can likely be explained, in part, through some of the neurobiological and psychoanalytic conceptualizations outlined in Chapter 10. Viewed as a separate "disease entity," conduct disorder may be conceptualized theoretically using social approaches. Renowned personality theorist Theodore Millon acknowledges the applicability in this area of the juvenile delinquency literature (too long and detailed to be presented here) and discusses an earlier historical distinction between aggressive and nonaggressive types of conduct disorders, a distinction that has disappeared in recent versions of the DSM (Millon & Davis, 1996). Millon, however, emphasizes its importance conceptually, and states that the nonaggressive variant may be further broken down into two categories: 1) a "delinquent and partially socialized syndrome," which occurs most frequently in peer contexts and involves the chronic violation of social rules (e.g., truancy, substance abuse, persistent lying, nonconfrontive stealing) and 2) a "rebellious syndrome," which is a direct and challenging assault on authority and the establishment and includes vigorous attacks on established societal norms via intentional antisocial acts targeting societal symbols. He articulates a spectrum of rebellious behaviors through which young people react to the strains of growing up: from milder forms such as running away from home (often triggered by intolerable parental conflict) to more serious forms such as truancy, vandalism, and sexual promiscuity (signifying contempt for what are seen as the oppressive rules and customs of a hypocritical society).

The Relationship Between Conduct Disorder and Crime

Table 3.2 lists a number of investigations, in chronological order, which have examined the prevalence rates of CD in criminal populations. No studies reporting the prevalence rates of crime and violence in individuals with CD were located.

Origins of Crime and Violence in Conduct Disorder: Theoretical Explanations and Etiological Mechanisms

Unlike many of the other disorders presented in this book, a discussion of how and why criminal, violent, and antisocial behavior may develop within the context of CD is—in many respects—conceptually redundant. This is because the essence of the disorder itself, at least in its current conceptualization, is a list of specific antisocial behaviors—what Millon refers to as "a rather broadly encompassing collection of repugnant behaviors as seen by society" (Millon & Davis, 1996, p. 450). Items on this list serve as diagnostic criteria.

Attention-Deficit and Disruptive Behavior Disorders: Oppositional Defiant Disorder

The diagnostic criteria for **oppositional defiant disorder**, as outlined in DSM-5, are listed in Table 3.10.

Prevalence and Incidence Rates of Oppositional Defiant Disorder

According to the DSM-IV-TR, studies have reported prevalence rates of oppositional defiant disorder ranging from 2% to 6%, depending upon the type of sample and method of assessment (APA, 2000). The DSM-5

A Closer Look: Conduct Disorder and Crime

Prevalence of the Disorder in Crime

Study Type	Number	Prevalence Rates
Arrest rates	0	–
Birth cohorts	0	–
Community samples	1*	94.0%
Homicide offenders	1	4.0%
Jailed detainees and prisoners	6	3.0–100.0%
Psychiatric inpatients	2*	94.0–100.0%
Total Number of Studies	**9**	

Sample Characteristics

Size	15–1,829
Gender	Male only (3 studies); female only (1 study); male and female but unbalanced, predominantly males (4 studies); not reported (1 study)
Age	Youth, adult
Location	North American and European countries (e.g., Finland, Germany, United States)
Diagnostic Systems	DSM, ICD

Note: *One psychiatric inpatient study (Galli et al., 1999) also included community individuals. No "pure" community samples were located.

Prevalence of Crime in the Disorder

Study Type	Number	Prevalence Rates	Crime Definition
Total Number of Studies	0		

Nondisordered or community resident comparison group or general population baseline rates for either disorder or crime provided: **0 studies (0.0%)**

reports prevalence rates ranging from 1% to 11%, with an average of around 3.3% (APA, 2013). Prevalence rates as high as 15% have been reported in one urban New Zealand birth cohort study (Fergusson et al., 2010).

Theoretical Conceptualizations

Psychoanalytic theorists have speculated that a child raised in an environment that is neither warm nor with firm, consistent limits (or with limits that are capriciously and abusively imposed) will develop sensation seeking characterized by rage and indiscriminate, aggressive acting out (PDM Task Force, 2006). In a classic study of institutionalized children deprived of affection in infancy, Spitz (1945, in PDM Task Force, 2006, p. 329) identified one group that became withdrawn, depressed, apathetic, or failed to thrive physically (some did not survive) and another group characterized by sensation seeking, aggression, promiscuity, and indifference to others.

Speltz and colleagues (1999) found that preschool boys with early-onset conduct problems who were diagnosed with both ODD and ADHD demonstrated reduced verbal and executive functioning abilities compared to

Table 3.10 DSM-5 Diagnostic Criteria for Oppositional Defiant Disorder

313.81 Oppositional Defiant Disorder

A. A pattern of angry/irritable mood, argumentative/defiant behavior, or vindictiveness lasting at least 6 months as evidenced by at least four symptoms from any of the following categories, and exhibited during interaction with at least one individual who is not a sibling.

Angry/Irritable Mood

1. Often loses temper.
2. Is often touchy or easily annoyed.
3. Is often angry and resentful.

Argumentative/Defiant Behavior

4. Often argues with authority figures or, for children and adolescents, with adults.
5. Often actively defies or refuses to comply with requests from authority figures or with rules.
6. Often deliberately annoys others.
7. Often blames others for his or her mistakes or misbehavior.

Vindictiveness

8. Has been spiteful or vindictive at least twice within the past 6 months.

Note: The persistence and frequency of these behaviors should be used to distinguish a behavior that is within normal limits from a behavior that is symptomatic. For children younger than 5 years, the behavior should occur on most days for a period of at least 6 months unless otherwise noted (Criterion A8). For individuals 5 years or older, the behavior should occur at least once per week for at least 6 months, unless otherwise noted (Criterion A8). While these frequency criteria provide guidance on a minimal level of frequency to define symptoms, other factors should also be considered, such as whether the frequency and intensity of the behaviors are outside a range that is normative for the individual's developmental level, gender, and culture.

B. The disturbance in behavior is associated with distress in the individual or others in his or her immediate social context (e.g., family, peer group, work colleagues), or it impacts negatively on social, educational, occupational, or other important areas of functioning.

C. The behaviors do not occur exclusively during the course of a psychotic, substance use, depressive, or bipolar disorder. Also, the criteria are not met for disruptive mood dysregulation disorder.

Specify current severity:

Mild: Symptoms are confined to only one setting (e.g., at home, at school, at work, with peers).

Moderate: Some symptoms are present in at least two settings.

Severe: Some symptoms are present in three or more settings.

Source: APA (2013, pp. 462–463) . Reprinted with permission from the *Diagnostic and Statistical Manual of Mental Disorders*, Fifth Edition (Copyright © 2013). American Psychiatric Association. All rights reserved.

those with ODD alone. In children, hormones, including testosterone and cortisol, have consistently shown associations with aggressive behavior, CD, and ODD (Cohen-Bendahan, Buitelaar, van Goozen, Orlebeke, & Cohen-Kettenis, 2005; Dorn et al., 2009; McBurnett, Lahey, Rathouz, & Loeber, 2000; Pajer et al., 2006; Shoal, Giancola, & Kirillova, 2003).

The Relationship Between ODD and Crime

Table 3.2 lists a number of investigations, in chronological order, that have examined the prevalence rates of ODD in criminal populations. No studies reporting the prevalence rates of crime and violence in individuals with ODD were located.

A Closer Look: Oppositional Defiant Disorder and Crime

Prevalence of the Disorder in Crime

Study Type	Number	Prevalence Rates
Arrest rates	0	–
Birth cohorts	0	–
Community samples	0	–
Homicide offenders	0	–
Jailed detainees and prisoners	3	14.5–23.3%
Psychiatric inpatients	0	–
Total Number of Studies	**3**	

Sample Characteristics

Size	50–1,829
Gender	Male and female but mostly males (2 studies); not reported (1 study)
Age	Youth, adult
Location	Finland, United States
Diagnostic Systems	DSM

Prevalence of Crime in the Disorder

Study Type	Number	Prevalence Rates	Crime Definition
Total Number of Studies	**0**		

Nondisordered or community resident comparison group or general population baseline rates for either disorder or crime provided: **0 studies (0.0%)**

Epilepsy

A surprising number of researchers examining the relationship between mental illness and crime have included **epilepsy** alongside other disorders of interest in their investigations. In fact, references to a potential link between epilepsy and crime have appeared in classical criminological texts dating back over a century. Cesare Lombroso (Lombroso-Ferrero, 1911/1972), for example, provides a discussion of the "born criminal and his relation to moral insanity and epilepsy." Under the category of "insane criminal," Lombroso classifies epilepsy, along with alcoholism and hysteria, as being among the "special [as opposed to general] forms of lunacy" (Lombroso-Ferrero, 1911/1972—see Box 3.2). Interestingly, although the hallmarks of epilepsy as a disease and a symptom largely mirror conceptualizations of other forms of abnormal behavior over the past centuries (Diamantis et al., 2010; Magiorkinis et al., 2010; Sidiropoulou et al., 2010), it is nonetheless considered a medical rather than a mental disorder. However, its inclusion here seemed appropriate given its prominent presence in the mental illness and crime literature over the years. Its prevalence among children (as well as adults) also appeared to make it a suitable fit for a chapter on disorders commonly diagnosed in childhood.

Because epilepsy is not considered a psychiatric disorder, the DSM-IV-TR does not specify criteria for its diagnosis. However, the DSM has a history of including listings of many major disease categories in its previous editions and revisions, to aid in multiaxial diagnostic conceptualization. These have been traditionally derived from another major classification system, the International Classification of Diseases (ICD), developed by the World Health Organization. For example, the DSM-II (APA, 1968) includes the major disease categories of ICD-8, which lists epilepsy (classification code 345) under "other diseases of the central nervous system." The International Classification of Diseases, 10th Revision, Clinical Modification (ICD-10-CM) is the official coding system in use at the time of this writing. Its predecessor, the ICD-9-CM is acknowledged in Appendix G of the DSM-IV-TR for the coding of general medical conditions. The ICD-10-CM classifies numerous forms of epilepsy under "diseases of the nervous system" (G00–G99), in the subcategory "episodic and paroxysmal disorders" (G40–G47). Diagnostic criteria for epilepsy are listed in Table 3.11.

Prevalence and Incidence Rates of Epilepsy

Prevalence rates for epilepsy have been reported as varying from 0.4–1.0% in the general population, in samples from around the world (Chen et al., 2012; D'Souza et al., 2012; Kobau et al., 2007; Picot et al., 2008).

BOX 3.2 EARLY CRIMINOLOGICAL REFERENCES TO EPILEPSY AND CRIME

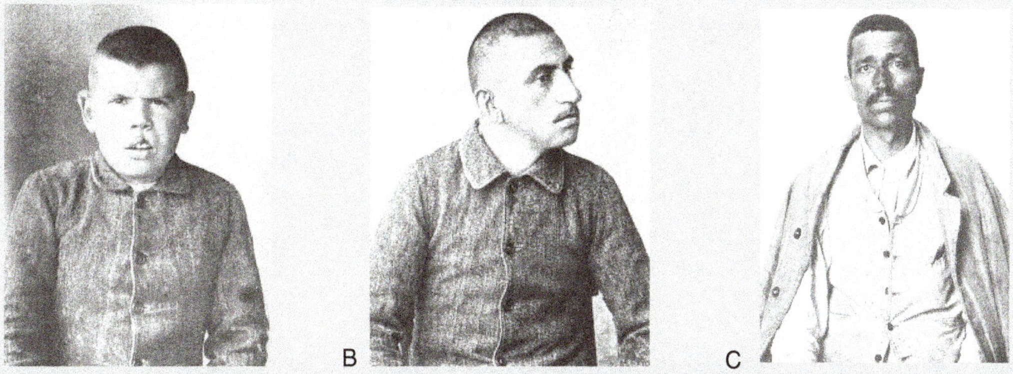

A B C

Early Italian criminologist Cesare Lombroso was among the first to discuss a possible relationship between epilepsy and criminal behavior. In his classical criminological text *Criminal Man*, he suggests indicators of criminality in the physical characteristics of individuals with epilepsy and other conditions. Lombroso's captions for these images read as follows: (A) "Figure 14. An Epileptic Boy"; (B) "Figure 15. Fernando. Epileptic"; and (C) "Figure 26. Head of a Criminal. Epileptic." The latter was further described as "A.D., a morally insane epileptic, the perpetrator of three murderers" (Lombroso-Ferrero, 1911/1972).

Table 3.11 ICD-10-CM Diagnostic Criteria for Epilepsy and Recurrent Seizures

Epilepsy and Recurrent Seizures G40

- A brain disorder characterized by episodes of abnormally increased neuronal discharge resulting in transient episodes of motor or sensory neurological dysfunction, or psychic dysfunction. These episodes may or may not be associated with loss of consciousness or convulsive movements.
- A group of disorders marked by problems in the normal functioning of the brain. These problems can produce seizures, unusual body movements, a loss of consciousness or change in consciousness, as well as mental problems or problems with the senses.

Source: 2014 ICD-10-CM Diagnosis Codes, http://www.icd10data.com

A Closer Look: Epilepsy and Crime

Prevalence of the Disorder in Crime

Study Type	Number	Prevalence Rates
Arrest rates	1	2.3–3.1%*
Birth cohorts	0	–
Community samples	0	–
Homicide offenders	8	2.0–16.0%
Jailed detainees and prisoners	4	1.5–6.7%
Psychiatric inpatients	3	0.0–12.4%
Total Number of Studies	**16**	

Sample Characteristics

Size	50–170,215
Gender	Male and female but mostly males (2 studies); not reported (1 study)
Age	Youth, adult. Age not specified in several earlier studies.
Location	Several countries worldwide (e.g., Bulgaria, Canada, Egypt, England, India, Poland, Russia, United States)
Diagnostic Systems	ICD, other research diagnostic criteria. Diagnostic systems generally not specified in earlier studies.

Note: *Psychosis with epilepsy.

Prevalence of Crime in the Disorder

Total Number of Studies	**0**

Nondisordered or community resident comparison group or general population baseline rates for either disorder or crime provided: **0 studies (0.0%)**

The Relationship Between Epilepsy and Crime

Table 3.2 lists a number of investigations, in chronological order, that have examined the prevalence rates of epilepsy in criminal populations. No studies reporting the prevalence rates of crime and violence in individuals with epilepsy were located.

Origins of Crime and Violence in Epilepsy: Theoretical Explanations and Etiological Mechanisms

Neurobiological explanations for criminal and violent behavior in individuals with epilepsy have been proposed and tested using brain imaging methods. For example, Juhász et al. (2001) found a significant correlation between a higher severity of aggression and lower metabolism in the bilateral medial prefrontal and left temporal cortex in aggressive children with epilepsy.

Treatment Implications

Treatment of individuals with the disorders presented in these chapters is associated with a very unique set of challenges, especially within the limited confines of the criminal justice and correctional systems. For example, Simblett and Wilson (1993) express the frustrations of planning interventions for individuals with Asperger's disorder, in that they are "(1) not autistic enough for autistic services; (2) not ill enough for psychiatric services; and (3) not learning disabled enough for mental handicap services. In fact, one mother of a young man with Asperger's disorder told the authors: 'If he had been a bit worse we would have got some help, if he'd been a bit better we wouldn't have needed it'" (p. 93). Research studies from the United Kingdom have articulated how ineffectively the criminal justice system (from law enforcement to corrections) interacts with individuals with intellectual and learning disabilities, and several consistent themes have emerged, including (1) the lack of a standardized definition of the disorders, (2) the lack of screening and assessment during the initial point of contact, (3) the lack of experience or knowledge among criminal justice professionals when they are required to respond to the needs of challenged offenders, (4) the lack of access to programming and services (including diversionary interventions) for offenders with these disabilities, and, most important, (5) problems related to identifying offenders with these disabilities (Barron et al., 2002; Hayes, 2007; Talbot & Riley, 2007). As an example of potential areas of abuse, studies have demonstrated that LD offenders have more difficulty understanding open-answered questions and are more likely to give confessions—both true and false (Gendle & Woodhams, 2005).

Regarding correctional treatment approaches for those with specific disorders, Woodbury-Smith and colleagues (2005) suggest that strategies such as "teaching" empathy skills may be appropriate for individuals with ASDs, given their problems with recognizing others' distress. Such strategies might include using individual or group treatment to attempt to develop in the offender an understanding of the victims' feelings, as has been done in sex offender treatment. Other approaches may involve teaching empathy in a more concrete way, for example, through role playing or the use of computer software packages to develop an understanding of emotions. For offenders with intellectual disabilities, interventions aimed at improving competencies and skills have been recommended, including using cognitive-behavioral approaches and token economies (Barron et al., 2002). Furthermore, applications of *pharmacological treatments* in correctional settings have been explored for some neurodevelopmental disorders. For example, stimulants are the most common treatment for pediatric ADHD, and several studies have demonstrated their effectiveness in the treatment of ADHD-associated aggression in children (Patel & Barzman, 2013). Also shown to be effective in treating children with ADHD and CD are *second-target treatments*, which specifically target the aggression instead of the disorder symptoms if the severity of aggression is too high or the disorder-oriented medications are ineffective (these medications might include antipsychotics such as risperidone or mood stabilizers such as lithium). The potentially problematic nature of the use of prescription stimulants for individuals with ADHD in correctional settings has been noted (e.g., medication misuse, security concerns, demands on psychiatrists for dealing with malingerers and on nurses for storing, monitoring, and distributing medications). However, a recent examination of a monitored stimulant medication protocol in the Massachusetts state prison system demonstrated that a very small number of inmates (less than 1%) met criteria for treatment with stimulants (Appelbaum, 2011). Future research is needed to ascertain if stimulant medication treatment is an effective approach for ADHD in correctional settings, if only for a limited number of special cases.

Conclusion

The DSM-IV-TR disorders of infancy, childhood, or adolescence outlined in this chapter, which have been reclassified as DSM-5 neurodevelopmental disorders, have received varying levels of empirical attention in terms of understanding their potential relationships with crime, violence, and antisociality. Although the state of the literature has moved into more advanced methodological forms (e.g., comparative studies) for some disorders such as ADHD, for other disorders (e.g., Asperger's disorder) published clinical case material forms the lion's share of what is currently known. A variety of theoretical perspectives—psychoanalytic, cognitive-behavioral, neurobiological, and social—have been applied to understanding these disorders and how crime and violence may develop within them. Some may be hesitant or even resistant to probe the potential relationships between these disorders and crime; they may fear demonizing this already vulnerable population or branding people diagnosed with these illnesses with a highly stigmatizing (and in many cases permanent) label so early in life. Although this concern is paramount, perhaps another way of viewing the issue would be to emphasize early detection and prevention—to seize the opportunity presented in the early years of development to recognize and address responsibly any signs of future violence and aggression, and to stop the crimes perpetrated by people like Joel Rifkin before they are allowed to happen.

KEY TERMS

attention-deficit/hyperactivity disorder (ADHD)

Asperger's disorder

autistic disorder

conduct disorder

deficient empathy

epilepsy

hyperactivity impulsivity

inattention

intelligence quotient (IQ)

mental retardation

mentalizing

mindblindness

neuropsychiatric developmental model (NDM) for serial murder

oppositional defiant disorder

restrictive repetitive patterns of behavior, interests, or activities

social communication and interaction deficits

theory of mind (ToM)

REVIEW QUESTIONS

1. Examine Table 3.2 and 3.3 and the summaries of research studies in the "A Closer Look" sections for each disorder in this chapter. Discuss how the prevalence rates outlined in this chapter differ among these disorders, if at all. Using the information in the tables, speculate as to how methodological approaches may have occasioned differences in prevalence rates (e.g., in terms of study types, sample characteristics, methodological issues, or other concerns).

2. Choose one DSM-IV-TR pervasive developmental disorder (i.e., mental retardation, autistic disorder, or Asperger's disorder) and one attention-deficit/disruptive behavior disorder (ADHD, CD, or ODD). Compare and contrast the two in terms of symptomatology and how the characteristic symptoms of each may contribute to crime and violence.

3. Discuss the ways in which Asperger's disorder explains the criminal behavior of serial murderer Joel Rifkin, and the ways in which it does not. What are the strengths and weaknesses of an argument for a link between this disorder and violence in Rifkin's case?
4. Examine the case reports of Asperger's disorder and antisocial behavior listed in Table 3.6. What are some of the similarities observed among cases in terms of symptoms and antisocial behaviors? What are some of the differences?
5. Critically evaluate the theorized origins of crime and violence in the disorders presented in this chapter. In your opinion, which perspectives offer the most promising explanations, and which do not? Discuss the reasons for your opinion.

4

Substance-Related Disorders

ANTRON SINGLETON

Antron Singleton was born in Dallas, Texas, on September 15, 1976. An aspiring rap musician, Singleton stood at 6'6" tall and was better known by the stage name "Big Lurch."

In 2002, 21-year-old mother of two, Tynisha Ysais, and her boyfriend, Thomas Moore, had been living with Singleton in a Los Angeles apartment. On April 10, while under the influence of phencyclidine (PCP), 25-year-old Singleton murdered Ysais in their apartment and ate parts of her body. Moore later testified that he and Singleton had spent the evening prior to the murder smoking PCP.

Singleton's PCP use was described as habitual. He reportedly began using the substance to ease the pain from a broken neck—an injury he previously sustained when he was hit by a drunk driver in a traffic collision. He was also known to praise PCP and its effects in the lyrics of his songs.

Ysais's body was discovered in her apartment by a friend. A three-inch paring knife had been used to tear open her chest—its blade was discovered broken off in her shoulder blade. Bite marks covered her face and were found on her lungs, which had been torn from her chest. According to one eyewitness report, Singleton was apprehended by police in the Watts area at 2 o'clock in the afternoon. He was found in the middle of the street naked, covered in blood, and screaming at the sky. A subsequent medical examination identified in his stomach human flesh that was not his own. In a later video documentary, Ysais's mother reported that Singleton had eaten part of her daughter's intestines. Reports from investigators indicated that Singleton had also broken her neck and fractured one of her eye sockets. Other reports indicate blunt trauma had been inflicted to the back of her head with a scooter.

Singleton pled not guilty by reason of insanity at the time of the murder (see Chapter 11). Although one psychiatrist testified that Singleton's PCP use caused mental impairment, another court-appointed psychiatrist who evaluated him found him to be of sound mind. As in most states, California law specifies that defendants cannot wage an insanity defense if their purported mental illness is due to substance addiction or use. It took less than an hour for a Compton jury to find Singleton guilty of first-degree murder, torture, and aggravated mayhem. Singleton was sentenced to life in prison on November 7, 2003.

The use of mind- and mood-altering substances dates back to the origins of human existence. Psychoactive substances have historically been consumed medicinally or recreationally to regulate emotions, stimulate arousal, increase perceptual awareness, or ease physical pain. The effects of some substances may even mimic the symptoms of mental illness, and maladaptive patterns of substance use may become mental disorders in and of themselves.

The relationship between substance-related disorders and criminal behavior is a bit different from that noted for the other disorders covered in this book. Certain substances are regulated by law and controlled by governmental agencies. In such cases, the mere possession of the substance (either for personal use or for manufacture, distribution, or sales) is considered a criminal act. In other cases—such as with alcohol—the possession or even use of a substance may not be prohibited by law, but legal parameters may dictate who may possess or use it (i.e., those of legal drinking age as defined by law) and when and where it may be used. The Penal Code of the State of California articulates numerous laws related to the possession or use of illicit substances. The case of Antron Singleton is extreme and unusual, but it nonetheless begs the question: Was the potent substance he consumed the *cause* of the nightmarish murderous impulses, or did the drug merely free up the expression of violent tendencies that were already there?

According to the DSM-IV-TR, substance-related disorders include those related to (1) the taking of a drug of abuse (including alcohol), (2) the side effects of a medication, and (3) prescribed and over-the-counter medications. Additionally, exposure to a wide range of other chemical substances can also lead to the development of a substance-related disorder. Toxic substances that may cause substance-related disorders include, but are not limited to, heavy metals (e.g., lead or aluminum); rat poisons containing strychnine; pesticides containing nicotine; or acetylcholinesterase inhibitors, nerve gas, ethylene glycol (antifreeze), carbon monoxide, and carbon dioxide. The DSM-5 has incorporated some significant modifications to this class of disorders, which are discussed below.

Terminology

Addictive behaviors are defined as any compulsive habit pattern in which the individual seeks a state of immediate gratification. Gratification may occur because of relief from discomforts such as tension, negative mood, or withdrawal states or because of the introduction of pleasure or euphoria. Addiction involves continued involvement with the behavior despite adverse consequences and attempts to stop. Addictive behaviors include excessive use of psychoactive substances (drugs that affect thought, emotion, and behavior) or excessive, unhealthy levels of other behaviors with compulsive characteristics, such as gambling, eating, or sexual acts (Tapert et al., 2001). **Substance dependence** and **substance abuse** are defined as clinical disorder diagnoses of the DSM-IV-TR that require fulfilling specific criteria. Substance dependence implies an addiction to the drug. Substance abuse refers to a less severe condition involving continued use of a mind-altering substance despite problems caused by such use. **Psychological dependence** refers to users' perceptions that they need the substance to feel or function optimally. For example, regular marijuana smokers who feel they cannot relax at the end of the day without an evening joint have developed psychological dependence on marijuana. **Physical dependence** indicates the physiological adaptation of the body to prolonged exposure to the substance. **Tolerance** refers to cellular and metabolic adaptations in response to the continued presence of the substance. As tolerance develops, more of the drug is necessary to obtain the desired effects, and use becomes more frequent. **Cross-tolerance** occurs when tolerance to one drug has developed and more of any drug in that class is necessary to produce comparable effects; the condition occurs because the similar organic structure of the active ingredients in these drugs creates a similar nervous-system response. **Potentiation** refers to the additive or synergistic effects of multiple drugs of the same class administered simultaneously, which can result in an overdose. **Withdrawal** is experienced when the supply of a substance to a physically dependent organism is halted. Characteristic withdrawal syndromes ensue, depending on the drug class used, and the withdrawal syndromes tend to involve symptoms opposite to the intoxication effects of the substance (Tapert et al., 2001).

Theoretical Conceptualizations

Various models of addiction have been proposed that are not grounded in psychological theory but nonetheless demonstrate attempts to conceptualize certain types of substance-related disorders theoretically. These include (1) the **moral model**—exemplified historically by the perspectives of the temperance movement and the "War on Drugs"—wherein addiction and relapse are a sign of character or moral weakness for which the individual is responsible, must be overcome by willpower, and can foster guilt for initial development and failure to change;

(2) the **medical model**—the most common view in the United States—which attributes the addiction and relapse to physiological factors (e.g., family history of addiction or pathological metabolism) beyond the individual's control, thus alleviating blame and encouraging professional help-seeking; and (3) the **spiritual model**—espoused by twelve-step programs such as Alcoholics Anonymous and Narcotics Anonymous—wherein addiction and relapse are attributed to spiritual weakness, must be overcome by admission of helplessness over the problem and submission to a "higher power," and in which addicts are aided by social supports (i.e., group meetings) that are advantageous but may alienate nonspiritual individuals and that utilize peers or paraprofessionals with addiction histories rather than addiction-trained professionals. Other *biobehavioral and interactionist models*, however, incorporate biological, psychological, and cultural components into a multifaceted understanding of addiction (Tapert et al., 2001).

Psychoanalytic theorists have emphasized the role of unconscious processes in the initiation and maintenance of addiction. According to Blum (1966), psychoanalytic authors do not use the term addiction in the narrow sense, i.e., physiological dependence upon a pharmacologically active substance. Rather, psychoanalysts use this term more broadly, referring to dependence upon some entity (e.g., a substance, an activity, or a person) that serves two purposes: providing pleasure as well as relief from psychic pain (e.g., anxiety). Addictive behaviors (which historically have included alcoholism and drug addictions but also cultism, kleptomania, pyromania, gambling, bulimia, addiction to surgery, and sexual addictions) are, in essence, repetitive and maladaptive attempts to master actively situations from the past that were suffered passively. In earlier writings, Freud suggested that addictions to substances such as alcohol, morphine, and tobacco served as a substitute and replacement for masturbation, which he referred to as a "primary addiction" (Blum, 1966). From a psychoanalytic perspective, addiction may be rooted in psychosocial developmental failure (i.e., fixation at a particular stage of psychosexual growth or regression to a previously outgrown stage). Many psychoanalytic authors have argued that alcoholism is rooted in a fixation in the oral stage (in fact, many have compared the alcoholic's pleasure in the bottle, as well as his or her enjoyment of satiation followed by drowsiness or unconsciousness, as comparable to the characteristics of an infant). According to Blum (1966), however, fixation at this stage may actually produce only one type of a variety of observed alcohol addictions. For example, the *essential* or *primary alcoholic* is fixated at or regressed to the oral stage and may be characterized by (infant-like) narcissism, emotional or economic dependency, passivity, and defense mechanisms of denial (e.g., the unpleasant reality that the individual has a drinking problem) and projection (e.g., blaming the wife, parent, boss, for the drinking problem). The *reactive* and *secondary* (or *neurotic*) *alcoholic* are fixated at or regressed to the anal stage and are characterized by latent homosexuality and the defense mechanisms of sublimation and repression. (For example, the addict may sublimate homosexuality into same-sex friendships, although undisguised homosexual tendencies may be observed when the pathological drinker is intoxicated; and repression can be inferred from the individual's irrational persecutory ideas about and hatred of same-sex individuals, suggesting an inability to hold his or her "unacceptable" attraction in check.) A third type of alcoholic is described as fixated at or regressed to the phallic stage, as unable to master the original Oedipal conflict and emerging sexual feelings toward the mother. These individuals are characterized by difficulties with authority figures, the repression of painful and conflictual feelings, and hysterical symptoms. They are described as friendly, affable, and anxious, with many superficial relationships, but also as rebellious and afraid of sexual inadequacy, with repressed anger and low self-esteem, and as overactive and competitive to compensate for these perceived weaknesses.

Other psychoanalytic theories have also been offered. Shapiro (1999), for example, discusses alcoholics and drug addicts within the context of a larger group of individuals characterized by impulsive modes of functioning. These include impulsive, psychopathic, passive-neurotic, and narcissistic personalities, along with "certain kinds of male homosexuals" (p. 134). According to Shapiro, in addition to readily giving in to whims, urges, and impulse, alcoholics may also possess a passive "weak" character. These individuals may report a marionette-style of existence—that they are victims of their irresistible impulses and "just can't help it"—though they do not appear to regret completely what their impulses choose to do with them. According to the PDM (PDM Task Force, 2006), at the heart of addictive behavior is acute and chronic distress. Vulnerabilities to addiction result from the developmental ego and self-organization deficits associated with neglect, abuse, and chaos and, often, with substance abuse by others in early family environments. These deficits significantly impact the ability to regulate emotions, self-esteem, relationships, and self-care; and substances are used to ameliorate, control, change, or mute intense and confusing emotions. A particular class of substance may be preferred for specific types of painful emotions. Opiates may offer calming, mellowing, or normalizing effects, while stimulants may counter feelings of low energy, weakness, or being unloved (or to augment hypomanic symptoms in high-energy individuals). High doses of sedatives may eliminate negative, unwelcome feelings; while low doses may help to overcome feelings of isolation and permit feelings of closeness and warmth (e.g., feeling like "one of the guys," or "joining the human race").

Behavioral theorists have proposed the initiation, maintenance, and remission of addiction to be rooted in the processes of classical and operant conditioning. From a classical conditioning approach, drug-induced euphoria (unconditioned stimulus) over time becomes associated with environmental stimuli present during the euphoric state (conditioned stimuli), such as drug-taking paraphernalia, locations, behavior, and people. After continued pairing with the drug-induced euphoria, these associated stimuli may produce intense urges or cravings to take the substance again. Similarly, stimuli associated with unpleasant periods of abstinence may elicit withdrawal-like symptoms. This conditioning principle can be observed in individuals who attempt to quit substance use and are constantly reminded of the addictive substance by a wide range of cues in the environment. From an operant conditioning (instrumental learning) approach, any reward following a behavior will increase the chance that the behavior will occur again. With substance use, both the acute pharmacological impact and social and environmental factors may produce rewards following drug self-administration, which increase the chance that drug use will recur. For example, if individuals smoked marijuana and then experienced pleasurable pharmacological effects or social approval, they would be likely to smoke marijuana again. Additionally, relief from aversive states, such as withdrawal or distress following drug self-administration also increases the likelihood of repeated drug-taking behaviors.

Neurobiological theorists have proposed that individuals take substances because they activate the brain's endogenous reward systems. Psychologists James Olds and Peter Milner (1954, in Durrant & Thakker, 2003) first discovered these reward systems by electrically stimulating certain areas of the brains of laboratory rats, which produced specific behavioral responses. When implants allowing self-stimulation (i.e., by pressing a lever) were fitted to the rats' brains, they would reliably press the lever continuously until the point of exhaustion. Later studies showed that many other psychoactive substances activate these so-called reward systems within the brain as well (Durrant & Thakker, 2003).

The rewarding effects of many psychoactive substances have been associated with a critical brain circuit—the **mesolimbic reward pathway**—that connects areas of the frontal cortex with the nucleus accumbens and ventral tegmental area in the limbic system. (***Ventral*** is another anatomical term of location, meaning "toward the abdomen.") A variety of neurotransmitters serve this circuit, including dopamine, which appears to be the most important. Psychoactive substances act on a range of specific, *endogenous transmitters*, mimicking or blocking their effects and thus affecting central nervous system functioning (e.g., heroin and other opioids operate on natural opioid receptors, caffeine blocks adenosine receptors, and cannabis acts on cannabinoid systems). These rewarding effects, however, appear to reflect their direct or indirect influence upon *dopaminergic neurons* in the mesolimbic reward pathway (see Figure 4.1), so a single physiological effect may be common to many substances of abuse. For example,

Figure 4.1 Mesolimbic Reward Pathway

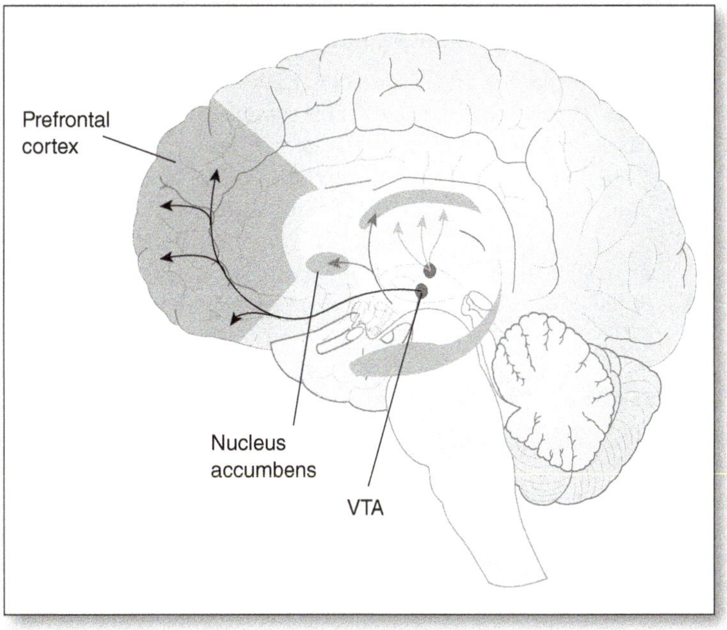

Source: http://en.wikipedia.org/wiki/File:Dopamine_Pathways.png

cocaine and amphetamines, powerful dopamine agonists, increase available dopamine levels at the synapse by blocking reuptake of dopamine; delta-9-tetrahydrocannabinol (THC), the active ingredient in cannabis, inhibits dopamine reuptake in the nucleus accumbens; and other psychoactive substances (nicotine, alcohol, and opiates) increase dopamine levels in reward pathways in the brain, along with stimulating other important neurotransmitter systems likely involved in producing their rewarding effects (Durrant & Thakker, 2003).

The rewarding effects produced by psychoactive substances likely serve as two different types of reinforcers: acting first as powerful primary reinforcers by stimulating natural reward systems and second as negative reinforcers by relieving pain associated with substance withdrawal or other substance use-related factors (Durrant & Thakker, 2003).

Finally, other theorists have proposed that several personality traits are common among people with addiction problems, such as rebelliousness, autonomy striving, liberalism, willingness to try new experiences, and independence. Similarly, research has linked sensation seeking, impulsivity, low self-esteem, reduced self-efficacy, nonconventionality, behavioral undercontrol, and aggressive tendencies to high rates of substance involvement.

Diagnostic Conceptualizations

In the DSM-IV-TR, substances are grouped into 11 classes (see Table 4.1). *Substance use disorders* consist of substance dependence and substance abuse. The former is a more chronic and debilitating condition, conceptually similar to addiction. It focuses on the physiological changes associated with prolonged substance use (i.e., symptoms of tolerance or withdrawal and impairments associated with obtaining, using, or trying to stop using substances). The latter, on balance, is a lesser condition. It focuses more on impairments that occur in various areas of psychosocial functioning and are related to substance use (i.e., within a 12-month period, at least one instance related to substance use of a failure to fulfill major work, school, or home obligations; substance use in physically hazardous situations; legal problems related to substance use; or interpersonal problems or conflict related to substance use). *Substance induced disorders* include substance intoxication and substance withdrawal. Several key changes were made to this class of disorders in the DSM-5. First, the name has been changed to "substance-related and addictive disorders." Second, the distinction between abuse and dependence has been dropped, and the new term "substance use" is now used in their place. In the DSM-5, a substance use disorder, essentially defined by a combination of the abuse and dependence symptoms in DSM-IV-TR, is differentiated in severity by the number of symptoms present. Third, diagnostic criteria have been provided for substance use disorders for each class of substances separately. Table 4.2 lists diagnostic criteria for *alcohol use disorder*, as an example (criteria for substance use disorders of most other substance classes are largely similar but replace the term "alcohol" with the name of the substance class in the criterion listings). Finally, each class of substance now has outlined separately its own set of substance-related disorders (e.g., for alcohol, there are alcohol use disorder, alcohol intoxication, alcohol withdrawal, other alcohol-induced disorders, and unspecified alcohol-related disorder). These vary slightly among substance classes (APA, 2013).

Tapert and colleagues (2001) reported that substance abuse or dependence is present in 11% of the U.S. population and that nearly 27% have met criteria during their lifetime. Prevalence and incidence rates reported in the DSM-IV-TR and DSM-5 are also compared in Table 4.1.

Substances of Abuse

Alcohol

Alcohol is the most widely used intoxicating substance. It is considered a central nervous system (CNS) depressant, which, along with other depressant drugs (i.e., sedatives—see below) reduce activity within excitable tissues at all levels of the brain, cause subjective experiences of intoxication, and lead to physical addiction (Tapert et al., 2001). The psychopharmacological effects of alcohol, however, are highly complex; at initial low doses, it appears to affect CNS inhibitory chemical processes, acting as a stimulant and producing euphoria, good cheer, and social and physical warmth (Bartol & Bartol, 2011) before its depressant effects are observed at

Table 4.1 DSM-IV-TR and DSM-5 Classes of Substances and Prevalence/Incidence of Substance-Related Disorders

	Prevalence/Incidence Rates	
Substances	**DSM-IV-TR**	**DSM-5**
Alcohol	In the mid-1990s, alcohol dependence approximately 5%, lifetime risk approximately 15% in general population.	In the United States, estimated 12-month prevalence of alcohol use disorder 4.6% among 12- to 17-year-olds, 8.5% among adults.
Amphetamines or similarly acting sympathomimetics*	In the early 1990s, a U.S. national epidemiological study found 0.14% prevalence of amphetamine use disorders in the past year, 1.5% lifetime prevalence.	In the United States, estimated 12-month prevalence of amphetamine-type stimulant use disorder 0.2% among 12- to 17-year-olds, 0.2% among adults.
Caffeine	Prevalence of caffeine-related disorders unknown in general population.	Prevalence of caffeine intoxication in general population unknown. Approximately 7% of U.S. general population may experience symptoms and impairment consistent with caffeine intoxication.
Cannabis	A1992 U.S. national survey found an approximately 5% lifetime prevalence for cannabis abuse or dependence and a 1.2% prevalence in the past year.	In the United States, estimated 12-month prevalence of cannabis use disorder 3.4% among 12- to 17-year-olds, 1.5% among adults.
Cocaine*	A1992 U.S. community study found approximately 0.2% prevalence of cocaine abuse or dependence in the past year, approximately 2% lifetime prevalence.	In the United States, estimated 12-month prevalence of cocaine use disorder 0.2% among 12- to 17-year-olds, 0.3% among adults.
Hallucinogens	A 1992 U.S. community study found lifetime prevalence of hallucinogen abuse or dependence approximately 0.6%, 12-month prevalence rate approximately 0.1%.	In the United States, estimated 12-month prevalence of hallucinogen use disorder 0.5% among 12- to 17-year-olds, 0.1% among adults.
Inhalants	Prevalence of inhalant abuse or dependence unknown in general population.	In the United States, estimated 12-month prevalence of inhalant use disorder 0.4% among 12- to 17-year-olds, 0.02% among adults.
Nicotine*	Up to 25% of U.S. population may have nicotine dependence.	In the United States, estimated 12-month prevalence of nicotine use disorder 13% among adults.
Opioids	A U.S. community study from 1980–1985 found the lifetime prevalence of opioid abuse or dependence at 0.7%.	Estimated 12-month prevalence of opioid use disorder is 0.37% among community adults.
Phencyclidine (PCP) or similarly acting arylcyclohexylamines*	Prevalence of phencyclidine abuse or dependence unknown in general population.	Prevalence of phencyclidine use disorder unknown. Approximately 2.5% of population reports ever using PCP.
Sedatives, hypnotics, or anxiolytics	A1992 U.S. national survey found the lifetime prevalence of sedative, hypnotic, or anxiolytic abuse or dependence at less than 1%, 12-month prevalence less than 0.1%.	Estimated 12-month prevalence of DSM-IV sedative, hypnotic, or anxiolytic use disorder 0.3% among 12- to 17-year-olds, 0.2% among adults.

Sources: APA (2000); APA (2013)

Note: *In the DSM-5, amphetamine-type substances and cocaine have been incorporated into a "stimulants" class of substances (while caffeine—interestingly—remains as its own class). Phencyclidine has been subsumed under hallucinogens (as a separate subcategory), and a category for "other (or unknown)" has been added (APA, 2013). The term "tobacco" has also replaced nicotine for this class of substances.

Table 4.2 DSM-5 Diagnostic Criteria for Alcohol Use Disorder

Alcohol Use Disorder

A. A problematic pattern of alcohol use leading to clinically significant impairment or distress, as manifested by at least two of the following, occurring within a 12-month period:

1. Alcohol is often taken in larger amounts or over a longer period than was intended.
2. There is a persistent desire or unsuccessful efforts to cut down or control alcohol use.
3. A great deal of time is spent in activities necessary to obtain alcohol, use alcohol, or recover from its effects.
4. Craving, or a strong desire or urge to use alcohol.
5. Recurrent alcohol use resulting in a failure to fulfill major role obligations at work, school, or home.
6. Continued alcohol use despite having persistent or recurrent social or interpersonal problems caused or exacerbated by the effects of alcohol.
7. Important social, occupational, or recreational activities are given up or reduced because of alcohol use.
8. Recurrent alcohol use in situations in which it is physically hazardous.
9. Alcohol use is continued despite knowledge of having a persistent or recurrent physical or psychological problem that is likely to have been caused or exacerbated by alcohol.
10. Tolerance, as defined by either of the following:
    a. A need for markedly increased amounts of alcohol to achieve intoxication or desired effect.
    b. A markedly diminished effect with continued use of the same amount of alcohol.
11. Withdrawal, as defined by either of the following:
    a. The characteristic withdrawal syndrome for alcohol.
    b. Alcohol (or a closely related substance, such as a benzodiazepine) is taken to relieve or avoid withdrawal symptoms.

Specify if:

In early remission: After full criteria for alcohol use disorder were previously met, none of the criteria for alcohol use disorder have been met for at least 3 months but for less than 12 months (with the exception that Criterion A4, "Craving, or a strong desire or urge to use alcohol," may be met).

In sustained remission: After full criteria for alcohol use disorder were previously met, none of the criteria for alcohol use disorder have been met at any time during a period of 12 months or longer (with the exception that Criterion A4, "Craving, or a strong desire or urge to use alcohol," may be met).

Specify if:

In a controlled environment: This additional specifier is used if the individual is in an environment where access to alcohol is restricted.

Specify current severity:

305.00 (F10.10) Mild: Presence of 2–3 symptoms.

303.90 (F10.20) Moderate: Presence of 4–5 symptoms.

303.90 (F10.20) Severe: Presence of 6 or more symptoms.

Source: APA (2013, pp. 490–491). Reprinted with permission from the *Diagnostic and Statistical Manual of Mental Disorders*, Fifth Edition (Copyright © 2013). American Psychiatric Association. All rights reserved.

higher doses. Among the more severe symptoms of alcohol withdrawal are seizures and delirium tremens, a condition appearing in about 5% of individuals withdrawing from alcohol that is characterized by increased tremor, profound confusion, and hallucinations (Tapert et al., 2001).

Amphetamines

Amphetamines are considered CNS stimulants (along with caffeine, nicotine, and tobacco), a class of substances that typically produce physiological arousal, euphoria, insomnia, and diminished appetite. Amphetamines include pharmaceutically produced substances (e.g., Benzedrine®, Dexedrine®, Ritalin®, and other drugs prescribed for obesity, ADHD, and narcolepsy) and illegally manufactured substances (methamphetamine, or "crystal meth," "speed," or "ice"). Routes of administration of these drugs include snorting them in powdered form, dissolving and injecting them, smoking them, or ingesting them orally. Effects of amphetamines include subjective experiences of euphoria, sociability, hypervigilance, anxiety, stereotyped behaviors, and impaired judgment. Like cocaine (see below), the more concentrated forms are smoked and injected, causing more dramatically altered behaviors than with other forms of the drugs. Amphetamines have a half-life of 6–12 hours, and withdrawal symptoms (e.g., depression, irritability, fatigue, hypersomnia, and potentially aggression and hallucinations) may last from one to six months (Tapert et al., 2001).

Cannabinols

The most commonly used illicit drug in the United States is marijuana. The active ingredient in this substance is THC (delta-9 tetrahydrocannabinol), ingested by smoking marijuana leaves ("pot," "weed"), smoking resin ("hashish"), or eating cannabinoids mixed in food products. Relaxation, euphoria, perceptual alteration, impaired motor coordination and judgment, the perception of slowed time, and social withdrawal are among the effects of cannabis intoxication. The half-life of THC is relatively long, at two to seven days. Acute anxiety, paranoia, attention and memory impairment, panic, and hallucinations may occur with use. Fewer physiological changes are associated with cannabis compared to other substances of abuse, though chronic use may lead to amotivational syndrome and lung diseases (similar to those found in tobacco smokers). In men, physiological changes may include impaired sperm production, decreased testosterone secretion, and decreased size of prostate and testes; in women, ovulation may be blocked (Tapert et al., 2001).

Cocaine

Also considered a CNS stimulant, cocaine can be snorted or smoked in powdered form, sprinkled and smoked in rolled cigarettes, smoked it its cooked form ("crack" or "rock"), or injected it its dissolved form. Crack cocaine is more powerful than cocaine in its powdered form and produces intense effects that rapidly diminish. Tolerance may develop rapidly—often within days of continued use. Fatigue, depressed mood, cravings, agitation, and physical aggression (in some cases) are among its withdrawal symptoms. Cocaine has a half-life of one hour, though withdrawal symptoms may last from days to months (Tapert et al., 2001).

Hallucinogens

Lysergic acid diethylamide (LSD), psilocybin (from certain mushrooms), dimethyltryptamine (DMT), mescaline (from the peyote cactus), 2,5-dimethoxy-4-methylamphetamine (DOM or STP), methylenedioxyamphetamine (MDA), methylenedioxymethamphetamine (MDMA, "ecstasy," "E," or "X"), 2C-B ("Nexus"), ibotenic acid, and muscimol are all included within this class of substances, which cause dramatic sensory-perceptual alterations. The effects of hallucinogens (which are commonly taken orally) include intensified perceptions, visual hallucinations, derealization, euphoria, alertness, and emotional lability, along with confusion, paranoia, panic, loss of control, and depression. Acting on delusional beliefs (e.g., the ability to fly) is the most imminent risk during intoxication. Younger users tend to experience more intense hallucinogenic effects than older users, and frequent use can lead to tolerance (Tapert et al., 2001).

Inhalants

This class of substances includes industrial and household compounds and products that can be inhaled, such as glues, aerosol sprays, gasoline, paints, paint thinners, nail polish remover, correction fluid, certain cleaning solvents, and nitrous oxide ("poppers," "rush"). Children, adolescents, and economically disadvantaged youth form the majority of inhalant users, given the availability and low cost of these substances. Acute effects include euphoria, sensations of floating, temporal distortions, and visual hallucinations; and apathy, confusion, irritability, assaultiveness, and panic may follow. Adverse physiological effects from chronic use include damage to the eye, nose, throat, kidney, liver, and heart, as well as to the respiratory, gastrointestinal, and nervous systems. Heart arrhythmias or suffocation (from inhaling solvents in plastic bags) may lead to serious injury and even death (Tapert et al., 2001).

Opioids

The class of opiates encompasses by-products of the opium poppy (*Papaver sominferum*; e.g., opium, morphine), semisynthetics (heroin), synthesized morphine-like medication properties (e.g., codeine, hydromorphone, methadone, oxycodone, meperidine, and fentanyl), and opiate agonist/antagonist medications (buprenorphine, pentazocine). Opiates may be prescribed as pain relievers, cough suppressants, and to alleviate the symptoms of opium withdrawal. Opiates may be injected, snorted, smoked, or swallowed; and effects include euphoria immediately following administration, along with apathy, dysphoria, impaired judgment, and relaxation. Tolerance to opiates may develop quickly, and the comparatively short half-life of heroin (30 minutes, compared to morphine's 2 to 3.5 hours) allows for addicts to commonly use heroin four times per day. Thus, obtaining and administrating opiates become the primary focus of daily activities for the addict. Nausea, vomiting, diarrhea, muscle aches, tremor, fatigue, insomnia, fever, dysphoric mood, and cravings (lasting up to eight days) comprise the withdrawal syndrome, which is generally very unpleasant. Because the purity levels of street opiates remain unknown to the user, administration of these drugs poses a particular risk for overdose. Many users of opiates inject, which makes them highly vulnerable to the additional risks of HIV infection, hepatitis, cellulitis, endocarditis, and tuberculosis. Respiratory depression is the most common cause of death from opiate overdose (Tapert et al., 2001).

PCP

Phencyclidine (PCP, Sernylan®, "Angel Dust") and related compounds (Ketamine®, Ketaject®) are considered dissociatives. These were developed originally as anesthetics but subsequently became street drugs in the 1960s because of their hallucinogenic properties. Both PCP and Ketamine® work by blocking the neurotransmitter glutamate at one of its receptors, thereby causing a feeling of being disconnected from one's body. PCP also releases dopamine, causing amphetamine-like levels of stimulation. PCP can be smoked, snorted, orally ingested, or injected; and because of its relatively low cost, drug dealers often intensify its effects by mixing it with other drugs (particularly marijuana). Marked behavioral change, assaultiveness, belligerence, unpredictability, impaired judgment, euphoria, hallucinations, intensified perceptions, and heightened emotions—along with hyperactivity, panic, paranoia, and confusion—are among the effects of PCP, which has a half-life of approximately 18 hours (Tapert et al., 2001).

Sedatives

Sedatives, another form of CNS depressants, include hypnotics (e.g., barbiturates, methaqualone, chloral hydrate), which are used to induce sleep or anesthesia, and benzodiazepines (e.g., Xanax®, Valium®, Librium®, Ativan®), which are used for anxiolytic or antianxiety purposes. Prescriptions for sedatives are fairly common in the general population (i.e., approximately 15%), and misuse is observed in 5–10% of patients who are prescribed these medications. Euphoria, disinhibition, cognitive impairment, loss of motor control, and slurred speech are among immediate effects after ingestion; and increased amounts can lead to hallucinations, paranoia, ataxia, sedation, and heightened risk for accidents (e.g., while driving a motor vehicle). Depressed heart rate, respiratory failure, coma, and even death may result from very high doses. Cross-tolerances have been shown with alcohol and other CNS depressants, which present a high risk for lethal overdose when these substances are used simultaneously. Anxiety, insomnia, headaches, tremors, muscle aches, increased heart and respiratory rates, fatigue, and, sometimes, disorientation, hallucinations, depression, and convulsions comprise the typical withdrawal syndrome, which may last from days to weeks and require monitoring by medical professionals (Tapert et al., 2001).

Historical Conceptions of Substance-Related Disorders

The use of psychoactive substances in humans far predates the advent of the formal diagnostic systems that have conceptualized substance-related disorders. However, historical references to these types of disorders—i.e., substance use patterns leading to impairment—may be inferred from indicators that earlier societies and civilizations treated these substances and the negative effects of their use with significant concern. For example, prominent beer and wine use has been noted in early Egyptian and Mesopotamian cultures over 6,000 years ago. Strict regulations for the use of alcohol have been outlined in Egyptian papyri dating back to 1,700 BCE. Evidence also indicates that early Egyptian and Babylonian civilizations employed alcohol-control measures, such as heavy taxes on alcoholic beverages and severe punishments (i.e., death by drowning) to tavern owners who degraded the quality of alcohol served to patrons. The dangers of excessive alcohol use appear to have been known by early Greek and Roman societies, wherein periods of moderation and excess and calls for temperance have been described; and authors such as Pliny (ca. 23–79 CE) identified many of the key features of alcohol dependence, such as hand tremors and alcoholic blackouts (Durrant & Thakker, 2003).

Archeological evidence indicates that opium poppies were cultivated in the region of what is now Switzerland more than 6,000 years ago, and early opium use has been described in ancient Sumerian writings, Egyptian hieroglyphs, and Greek literature (e.g., Homer's *Odyssey*). The habit-forming and tolerance-generating properties of opium were identified by Greek and Roman physicians, leading them to modify their prescriptions for this drug. Centuries later, after the advent of numerous opium derivatives in the 1800s and the introduction of the hypodermic syringe in 1853, rising levels of opium dependence from medicinal use were observed in Britain and the United States in the nineteenth century. (Morphine was introduced in 1803, followed by codeine, narvaine, thebaine, and, eventually, heroin in 1878.) In the years to follow, strict anti-opium and -morphine regulations were enacted in these countries, as a result of growing public awareness of the dangers of recreational opium smoking (which became increasingly popular) and morphine use.

The cultivation and use of cannabis extends back at least 6,000 years in China (the origin of this plant likely lies in central Asian regions), and both documentation and archeological evidence indicates its use for medicinal, ritual-religious, and social or recreational purposes dating back up to several millennia in regions such as India, Greece, Siberia, Romania, the Caucasus, and in Near and Middle Eastern cultures (Durrant & Thakker, 2003). Antimarijuana legislation began to emerge in the United States in the early to middle 1900s—largely due to the antidrug spirit of the times, and critical public awareness campaigns purporting the dangerous consequences of its use.

Archeological evidence from Peruvian mummy bundles and depictions on ancient pottery also suggest the utilization of coca in various South American regions for over 2,000 years. However, given the relatively low levels of cocaine extracted from traditional methods of coca consumption (i.e., the chewing of coca leaves), it is unlikely that many problems stemmed from its early use. Coca received little attention in early and modern Europe (although Spanish missionaries were concerned that it impeded the conversion of native "Indians" to Catholicism, and others noted its usefulness—due to its ability to stave off hunger and reduce fatigue—in promoting hard labor in South American silver mines). This circumstance changed with the isolation of cocaine—the active alkaloid in the coca leaf—by German graduate student Albert Niemann in 1859 (Durrant & Thakker, 2003). A legal and commercially available product in the mid to late 1800s, cocaine was used by authors Mark Twain and Robert Louis Stevenson, and its benefits were briefly examined and enthusiastically extolled by Sigmund Freud. (Freud prescribed liberal doses of cocaine to cure his friend and colleague, Ernst von Fleischl-Marxow, of his morphine dependence; Fleischl-Marxow rapidly became dependent and died of cocaine poisoning in 1891). Cocaine use shifted from medicinal to recreational toward the close of the nineteenth and beginning of the twentieth centuries, when increased cocaine use was observed in the United States (described as "America's first cocaine epidemic"), Canada, Germany, and the United Kingdom and reports of dependence on cocaine became widespread.

The Relationship Between Substance-Related Disorders and Crime

Any discussion of the relationship between substance-related disorders and criminal behavior should first address the legality of the substances themselves. According to Robins (1980), most drugs were not defined as illegal at the time they were discovered or synthesized—this labeling generally occurred only when evidence for problems resulting from their use became apparent. A number of drugs that are currently illegal have been both legal and popular among upper- and middle-class individuals during specific historical periods. However, once these drugs were made illegal, their clientele changed; and drugs once used for "legitimate" purposes (e.g., physical pain relief, cough medicines, cures for diarrhea, sleeping potions, health-giving "tonics," daily work performance enhancers, and cures for other substance dependencies) became valued for their ability to create illicit pleasures. Americans in the late 1800s were generally accepting of "patent medicines" (cure-alls, often containing opium, openly available from private physicians, the Sears catalog, and travelling medicine shows). More potent drugs became available with both advances in chemistry and the development of the hypodermic needle in the mid-1800s, which allowed these drugs to be delivered much more effectively (McBride & McCoy, 2006).

In the early 1900s, the opiate user was viewed in the medical and psychiatric literature as lethargic—debilitated by use of the drug and less likely to be a violent criminal. It was believed that this individual was instead more likely to engage in minor property crimes in order obtain money to buy drugs, and debauchery, laziness, and prostitution (not predatory violent crime) were noted by many observers as the main deviant consequences of opiate use (McBride & McCoy, 2006).

One often-cited historical milestone in the literature on the relationship between drugs and crime is the passage of the **Harrison Narcotic Tax Act** in the United States after World War I, which marked a major governmental attempt to make psychoactive substances illegal (Robins, 1980). A powerful (but likely oversimplified) critique of the Harrison Act is that it, in effect, made criminals out of law-abiding patent medicine users. Regardless of the validity of this argument, this legislation did serve to solidify and propel a popular social reform movement that labeled drug use as both a form of criminality and a common cause of violence and bizarre behavior (McBride & McCoy, 2006). Drug use subsequently decreased among the middle class (as physicians reduced prescriptions) and became concentrated among "outsider" groups (e.g., musicians and minorities); however, after World War II in the United States it spread from the segregated African American ghettoes to urban middle-class college students and their younger siblings to working-class youth and rural populations. Additionally, in many parts of the world a new pattern of urban youth drug use has been superimposed over the traditional pattern of middle-class and rural use, and the age of drug use initiation has declined (Robins, 1980).

A sizeable literature exists related to the relationship between substance *use* and criminal behavior. Although these studies are interesting and have provided valuable information about the various classes of substances and their differential effects upon behavior—including crime, they do not *per se* address the more limited focus of how drug use at the level of clinical disorder is related to criminality. For example, a study that examines the criminal behavioral correlates of individuals who use a particular drug—perhaps infrequently or at what would be considered subclinical levels—may not be entirely relevant to this discussion, nor would a study examining crime committed by a drug user when the criminal behavior is not a direct result of the substance or of the need to get access to the substance (i.e., the person just happened to be under the influence of the substance at the time of the crime). On balance, as substance intoxication (which produces impairment in one or more important areas of functioning) is considered a mental disorder in the DSM-IV-TR, studies that address antisocial, criminal, and violent behaviors that result specifically from the intoxication effects of a particular substance would certainly be germane here.

Substance-Related Disorders and Crime: Prevalence Studies

Comparatively speaking, few studies have examined the relationship between substance-related disorders and crime. As with the other disorders mentioned in previous chapters, however, a number of prevalence rate studies are available; and the association between substance-related disorders and crime can be at least partially understood through these studies, which examine both rates of substance-related disorders in criminal and antisocial populations and rates of crime and antisocial behavior in populations of individuals with substance-related disorders. Tables 4.3 and 4.4 list a number of investigations, in chronological order, that have

(Text continues on page 146)

Table 4.3 Prevalence of Substance Use Disorders in Criminal Populations

Alcohol								
Source	**N**	**Gender**	**Age**	**Study Type**[a1]	**Sample Description**	**Disorder**	**Diagnostic System**	**Prevalence/ Incidence**
Cohen & Freeman (1945)	(1) 320 (2) 87	M, F	Adult?	AR	Police records of arrested patients from 1,676 patients paroled or discharged from Norwich State Hospital (Connecticut), 1940–1944 (1) Arrested before hospitalization (2) Arrested after hospitalization	Alcoholism	?	(1) 33.4% ($n = 107$) (2) 47.3% ($n = 41$)
Szymusik (1972)	50	M	16–68	HO	Murderers, Poland, 1955–1969	Pathological alcoholic intoxication	?	2.0% ($n = 1$)
Schuckit et al. (1977)	199	M	Adult[b]	JD	Structured personal interviews of newly arrested prisoners at a San Diego, California, jail	Alcoholism	Brief screen for psychiatric illness (Woodruff et al., 1974)	15.0%
Pétursson & Gudjónsson (1981)	47	44 M, 3 F	Adult[ai]	HO	File review of cases of intentional and unintentional homicide in Iceland, 1900–1979	Alcoholism, drug dependence	?	12.8% ($n = 6$)
Langevin et al. (1982)	(1) 109 (2) 38	?	Adult?	PI	File record review of minimum-security forensic ward psychiatric hospital cases, 1969–1979 (Clarke Institute in Toronto, Ontario, Canada) (1) Killers (2) Nonviolent offenders	Alcoholism	Feighner et al. (1972) psychiatric research diagnostic criteria	(1) 18.0% (2) 5.0%
Seltzer & Langford (1984)	85	M, F	15–25 (Median = 18)	PI	Interviews of individuals referred by courts or legal counsel to psychiatry department of large regional hospital in Northwest Territories, calendar year 1981	Alcoholism	DSM-III, MMPI	15.3% ($n = 13$)
						Acute alcohol intoxication		85.0% ($n = 72$)

(Continued)

(Continued)

Alcohol								
Source	**N**	**Gender**	**Age**	**Study Type**[a1]	**Sample Description**	**Disorder**	**Diagnostic System**	**Prevalence/ Incidence**
Taylor & Gunn (1984)	2,743	M	Adult	JD	File review of men remanded to Brixton prison, South London (June, September, December 1979 and March 1980)	Alcoholism	ICD	4.1% (n = 113)
Reich & Wells (1985)	390	325 M, 65 F	M = 30.9	JD	Record review of defendants evaluated for competency to stand trial by the Yale–New Haven Psychiatric Court Clinic, 1980–1982	Alcohol-related substance use disorders	DSM-III	8.7% (n = 34)[bf]
Wilcox (1985, 1987)	71	62 M, 9 F	Six < 18, five > 50	HO	Record review of all individuals convicted for homicides committed in Contra Costa County, California, 1978–1980	Habituation to alcohol	?	14.1% (n = 10)
Taylor (1986)	183	175 M, 8 F	18–73	JD	Record review of life-sentenced men and women, supervised by the Inner London Probation Service (inside prison and on license in the community)	Alcoholism/ very heavy abuse	ICD-9	33% (n = 60)
Phillips et al. (1988)	1,816	1,569 M, 247 F	11–78 (M = 28)	PI, CS	Record review of psychiatric referrals from the criminal justice system of Alaska, 1977–1981	Alcohol-related disorders	DSM-II, DSM-III	21.1% (n = 383)
Bland et al. (1990)	180	M	18–44	JD	Diagnostic interviews with inmates from two correctional centers, Alberta, Canada	Alcohol abuse/ dependence	DSM-III (DIS)	78.9% (n = 142)[as*]
Coté & Hodgins (1990)	495	M	19–67 (M = 31.1)	JD	Diagnostic interviews with Quebec penitentiary inmates	Alcohol abuse/ dependence	DSM-III (DIS)	66.9% (n = 330)
Myers et al. (1990)	15	F	Juveniles	PI	Diagnostic interviews with juvenile delinquents committed to a residential treatment program, Florida	Alcohol abuse	DSM-III (DICA)	Past and current: 73.3% (n = 11)
Abram & Teplin (1991)[r]	728	M	16–68 (M = 26.3)	JD	Diagnostic interviews with jail detainees at Cook County Department of Corrections, Chicago, November 1983–November 1984	Alcohol abuse/ dependence	DSM-III-R (DIS)	Lifetime: 51.1% (n = 372) Current: 18.4% (n = 134)

Alcohol								
Source	**N**	**Gender**	**Age**	**Study Type**[a1]	**Sample Description**	**Disorder**	**Diagnostic System**	**Prevalence/ Incidence**
Côté & Hodgins (1992)	(1) 87 (2) 373	M	(1) *M* = 35.6, *SD* = 8.9 (2) *M* = 30.3, *SD*= 8.3	JD	Diagnostic interviews and file reviews of penitentiary inmates, Quebec (1) Homicide offenders (2) Non-homicide offenders	Alcohol abuse/ dependence	DSM-III (DIS)	(1) 46.0% ($n = 40$) (2) 50.4% ($n = 188$)
DeJong, Virkkunen, & Linnoila (1992)	(1) 248 (2) 100	M	16–68 (*M* = 31.2, *SD* =11.9)	JD	Criminals ordered for forensic psychiatric examination at initial incarceration in Finland (1) Murders and attempted murderers (2) Arsonists	Alcohol abuse	DSM-III	(1) 90.0% (2) 86.0%
Haapasalo & Hämäläinen (1996)	89	?	16–22 (*M* = 20.21, *SD* = 1.37)	JD	Structured clinical interviews with offenders randomly selected among prison inmates, Finland (1) Property offenders (2) Violent offenders	Alcohol abuse	DSM-IV (DICA-R-A)	(1) 97.3% (2) 100.0%
						Alcohol dependence		(1) 83.8% (2) 84.6%
Firestone et al. (1998)	48	M	*M* = 33.5, *SD* = 9.48	HO	Interviews with homicidal sex offenders assessed at the Sexual Behaviors Clinic, Royal Ottawa Hospital, Eastern Ontario, 1982–1992	Alcohol abuse	DSM III	27.1% ($n = 13$)
						Total substance abuse		39.6% ($n = 19$)
Galli et al. (1999)	22	M	13–17 (*M* = 15.9, *SD* = 1.1)	PI, CS	Interviews with adolescents admitting to sexually assaulting another child, referred from a juvenile rehabilitation center, the juvenile court system, and an inpatient adolescent psychiatric unit, Hamilton County, Ohio	Alcohol abuse/ dependence	DSM-III-R (DICA)	36.0% ($n = 8$)
						Total substance use disorders		50.0% ($n = 11$)

(Continued)

(Continued)

Alcohol								
Source	**N**	**Gender**	**Age**	**Study Type**[a1]	**Sample Description**	**Disorder**	**Diagnostic System**	**Prevalence/ Incidence**
Marshall et al. (1998)	103	M	18–56	JD	Diagnostic interviews and questionnaires administered to recently sentenced inmates (August–December 1997) at Yatala Labour Prison, South Australia	Alcoholism	(PDI-R)	38.2%
Gibson et al. (1999)	213	M	$M = 32$	JD	Structured interviews with randomly selected state prison and regional jail inmates from a rural New England state	Alcohol abuse/ dependence	DSM-III-R (DIS-III-R)	Lifetime: 82.2% ($n = 175$) Current: NA
McElroy et al. (1999)	36	M	18–47 ($M = 33$, $SD = 8$)	PI	Interviews with convicted sex offenders consecutively admitted to the New Life Program, Cincinnati, Ohio, November 1996–June 1998	Alcohol abuse	DSM-IV (SCID)	61% ($n = 22$)
						Total substance abuse		83% ($n = 30$)
Raymond et al. (1999)	45	M	$M = 37$	PI, CS	Diagnostic interviews with convicted pedophilic sex offenders in either a residential or outpatient sex-offender treatment program	Alcohol abuse	DSM-IV	51.1% ($n = 23$)
Pliszka et al. (2000)	50	45 M, 5 F	$M = 15.4$, $SD = 1.4$	JD	Interviews with adolescents consecutively admitted to the Bexar County Juvenile Detention Center, Texas	Alcohol dependence	DSM-IV (DIS-C)	28.0% ($n = 14$)
Inciardi & Surratt (2001)	708	F	Adult	CS	Interviews with women sex traders in Miami, Florida, 1994–1996.	Alcohol dependence (daily alcohol use)	—	35.3%
Siponmaa et al. (2001)	126	123 M, 3 F	15–22 (Median = 20)	JD	Interviews with young offenders consecutively referred for presentencing psychiatric investigation, Stockholm, Sweden, 1990–1995	Abuse of alcohol or drugs	ICD-9	2.0% ($n = 2$)

Alcohol								
Source	N	Gender	Age	Study Type[a1]	Sample Description	Disorder	Diagnostic System	Prevalence/ Incidence
Harris et al. (2002)	57	48 M, 9 F	20–49	JD	HIV-positive offenders seen for mental health evaluation at King County Correctional Facility, Seattle, Washington	Substance abuse history: Alcohol only	? (FAMIO)	14.0% ($n = 8$)
						Drugs and alcohol		21.1% ($n = 12$)
Teplin et al. (2002)	1829	1172 M, 657 F	10–18	JD	Diagnostic interviews of youths randomly sampled from intake into the Cook County Juvenile Temporary Detention Center, November 1995–June 1998	Alcohol use disorder	DSM-III-R	M: 25.9% F: 26.5%
Langevin (2003)	(1) 33 (2) 80 (3) 23 (4) 611	M	(1) $M = 32.06$ (2) $M = 27.58$ (3) $M = 27.57$ (4) $M = 31.42$	PI	Interviews with convicted sex offenders ($n = 747$) belonging to one of four groups: (1) sex killers, (2) nonhomicidal sexually aggressives, (3) nonhomicidal sadists, and (4) general sex offenders. Participants were chosen from a database of more than 2,800 minimum-security forensic ward psychiatric hospital cases (Clarke Institute in Toronto, Ontario, Canada) seen since 1973.	Alcohol abuse	MAST, DAST, Drug Use Survey	(1) 57.6% (2) 80.0% (3) 56.5% (4) 76.8%
						Any drug abuse		(1) 81.5% (2) 61.3% (3) 69.6% (4) 37.5%
Stuart et al. (2003)	35	F	$M = 32.6$, $SD = 8.8$	CS	Questionnaire administered to women arrested for domestic violence and court referred to batterer intervention programs, Rhode Island	Alcohol-related diagnosis	DSM-IV (PDSQ)	31%

(Continued)

(Continued)

Alcohol								
Source	**N**	**Gender**	**Age**	**Study Type**[a1]	**Sample Description**	**Disorder**	**Diagnostic System**	**Prevalence/ Incidence**
Dunsieth et al. (2004)	113	M	18–66 (*M* = 35.3, *SD* = 10.4)	PI	Diagnostic interviews with sex offenders consecutively referred to an Ohio residential sex-offender treatment program	Alcohol abuse	DSM-IV	8.0% (*n* = 9)
						Alcohol and drug abuse		61.9% (*n* = 70)
Leue et al. (2004)	55	M	Adult?	PI	Structured clinical interviews with sexual offenders hospitalized in forensic facilities in Arnsdorf, Saxony, and Moringen, Lower Saxony, Germany	Alcoholism	DSM-IV	56% (*n* = 31)
						Any substance use disorder		56% (*n* = 31)
Rösler et al. (2004)	129	M	*M* = 19.5, *SD* = 2.0	JD	Clinical interviews, record reviews, and rating scales conducted on inmates of a German offender facility (JSA Ottweiler)	Alcoholism	ICD-10	64.3%[bz*]
Stuart et al. (2006)	103	F	*M* = 31.5, *SD* = 9.6	CS	Questionnaire administered to women arrested for violence and court referred to batterer intervention programs, Rhode Island	Alcohol diagnosis	DSM-IV (PDSQ)	43%
Kraanen et al. (2010)	150	142 M, 8 F	*M* = 37.8	CS	Interviews with intimate partner violence perpetrators in an outpatient domestic-violence treatment program at forensic outpatient clinic De Waag in Amsterdam, the Netherlands	Alcohol abuse	DSM-IV-TR	28% (*n* = 42)[bn]
						Alcohol dependence		11.3% (*n* = 17)
Pham & Saloppé (2010)	84	M	Adult	PI	Psychological evaluations of forensic patients at high-security psychiatric hospital in Tomai, Belgium (Etablissement de Défense Sociale)	Alcohol abuse/ dependence	DSM-III (DISSI)	61% (*n* = 51)
						Substance-related disorders		69% (*n* = 58)

Drugs								
Source	**N**	**Gender**	**Age**	**Study Type**[a1]	**Sample Description**	**Disorder**	**Diagnostic System**	**Prevalence/ Incidence**
Cohen & Freeman (1945)	(1) 320 (2) 87	M, F	Adult?	AR	Police records of arrested patients from 1,676 patients paroled or discharged from Norwich State Hospital (Connecticut), 1940–1944 (1) Arrested before hospitalization (2) Arrested after hospitalization	Drug addiction	?	(1) 1.8% ($n = 6$) (2) 3.4% ($n = 3$)
Pfeiffer, Eisenstein, & Dabbs (1967)	85	2/3 M, 1/3 F	17–63	JD	Federal prisoners referred for mental competency evaluations, at USPHS Hospital in Lexington, Kentucky, 1960–1965	Drug addiction, heroin	?	1.2% ($n = 1$)
Schuckit et al. (1977)	199	M	Adult[b]	JD	Structured personal interviews of newly arrested prisoners at a San Diego, California, jail	Drug abuse	Brief screen for psychiatric illness (Woodruff et al., 1974)	12.0%
Langevin et al. (1982)	(1) 109 (2) 38	?	Adult?	PI	File record review of minimum-security forensic ward psychiatric hospital cases, 1969–1979 (Clarke Institute in Toronto, Ontario, Canada) (1) Killers (2) Nonviolent offenders	Drug dependence	Feighner et al. (1972) psychiatric research diagnostic criteria	(1) 2.0% (2) 15.0%
Seltzer & Langford (1984)	85	M, F	15–25 (Median = 18)	PI	Interviews of individuals referred by courts or legal counsel to psychiatry department of large regional hospital in Northwest Territories, calendar year 1981	Substance dependence	DSM-III, MMPI	3.5% ($n = 3$)

(Continued)

(Continued)

Drugs								
Source	**N**	**Gender**	**Age**	**Study Type**[a1]	**Sample Description**	**Disorder**	**Diagnostic System**	**Prevalence/ Incidence**
Taylor & Gunn (1984)	2,743	M	Adult	JD	File review of men remanded to Brixton prison, South London (June, September, December 1979 and March 1980	Drug dependency	ICD	5.4% ($n = 147$)
Reich & Wells (1985)	390	325 M, 65 F	$M = 30.9$	JD	Record review of defendants evaluated for competency to stand trial by the Yale–New Haven Psychiatric Court Clinic, 1980–1982	Drug-related substance use disorders	DSM-III	5.9% ($n = 23$)[bg]
Wilcox (1985, 1987)	71	62 M, 9 F	Six < 18, five > 50	HO	Record review of all individuals convicted for homicides committed in Contra Costa County, California, 1978–1980	Habituation to methamphetamine	?	11.3% ($n = 8$)
						Habituation to heroin		1.4% ($n = 1$)
						Habituation to cocaine		1.4% ($n = 1$)
						Methamphetamine psychosis		1.4% ($n = 1$)
Taylor (1986)	183	175 M, 8 F	18–73	JD	Record review of life-sentenced men and women, supervised by the Inner London Probation Service (inside prison and on license in the community)	Drug abuse	ICD-9	11% ($n = 21$)
Bland et al. (1990)	180	M	18–44	JD	Diagnostic interviews with inmates from two correctional centers, Alberta, Canada	Drug abuse/dependence	DSM-III (DIS)	50.6% ($n = 91$)[at*]
Coté & Hodgins (1990)	495	M	19–67 ($M = 31.1$)	JD	Diagnostic interviews with Quebec adult penitentiary inmates	Drug abuse/dependence	DSM-III (DIS)	48.9% ($n = 241$)

Drugs								
Source	**N**	**Gender**	**Age**	**Study Type**[a1]	**Sample Description**	**Disorder**	**Diagnostic System**	**Prevalence/ Incidence**
Myers et al. (1990)	15	F	Juveniles	PI	Diagnostic interviews with juvenile delinquents committed to a residential treatment program, Florida	Cocaine abuse/ dependence	DSM-III (DICA)	Past and current: 46.7% ($n = 7$)
						Marijuana abuse		Past and current: 40.0% ($n = 6$)
						Other (amphetamines, barbiturates, inhalants) abuse		Past and current: 20.0% ($n = 3$)
Yarvis (1990)	100	88 M, 12 F	33% < 25, 85% < 40	HO	Diagnostic interviews and record reviews of a series of murderers referred for psychiatric evaluation in California, 1980–1988	Substance abuse conditions	DSM-III	35.0% ($n = 35$)[k]
Abram & Teplin (1991)[r]	728	M	16–68 ($M = 26.3$)	JD	Diagnostic interviews with jail detainees at Cook County Department of Corrections, Chicago, November 1983–November 1984	Drug abuse/dependence	DSM-III-R (DIS)	Lifetime: 32.4% ($n = 236$) Current: 15.2% ($n = 111$)
Côté & Hodgins (1992)	(1) 87 (2) 373	M	(1) $M = 35.6$, $SD = 8.9$ (2) $M = 30.3$, $SD = 8.3$	JD	Diagnostic interviews and file reviews of penitentiary inmates, Quebec (1) Homicide offenders (2) Non-homicide offenders	Drug abuse/dependence	DSM-III (DIS)	(1) 26.4% ($n = 23$) (2) 37.3% ($n = 139$)
DeJong, Virkkunen, & Linnoila (1992)	(1) 248 (2) 100	M	16–68 ($M = 31.2$, $SD = 11.9$)	JD	Criminals ordered for forensic psychiatric examination at initial incarceration in Finland (1) Murders and attempted murderers (2) Arsonists	Drug dependence	DSM-III	(1) 3.0% (2) 2.0%

(Continued)

(Continued)

Drugs								
Source	**N**	**Gender**	**Age**	**Study Type[a1]**	**Sample Description**	**Disorder**	**Diagnostic System**	**Prevalence/ Incidence**
Haapasalo & Hämäläinen (1996)	89	?	16–22 (M = 20.21, SD = 1.37)	JD	Structured clinical interviews with offenders randomly selected among prison inmates, Finland (1) Property offenders (2) Violent offenders	Cannabis dependence	DSM-IV (DICA-R-A)	(1) 48.6% (2) 61.5%
						Substance abuse (street drugs)		(1) 51.4% (2) 71.2%
						Substance dependence (street drugs)		(1) 43.2% (2) 61.5%
Firestone et al. (1998)	48	M	M = 33.5, SD = 9.48	HO	Interviews with homicidal sex offenders assessed at the Sexual Behaviors Clinic, Royal Ottawa Hospital, Eastern Ontario, 1982–1992	Drug abuse	DSM III	22.9% (n = 11)
						Total substance abuse		39.6% (n = 19)
Wallace et al. (1998)	(1) 3838 (2) 1998 (3) 152 (4) 1137 (5) 876	M	Adult	AR	Case-linkage study of higher court records and psychiatric case register databases, Victoria, Australia, 1993–1995 (men) (1) Total convictions (2) Violent offenses (3) Homicide offenses (4) Property offenses (5) Sexual offending	Substance misuse	ICD-9	(1) 6.4% (n = 246) (2) 8.5% (n = 169) (3) 5.3% (n = 8) (4) 8.4% (n = 95) (5) 3.3% (n = 29)

Drugs								
Source	N	Gender	Age	Study Type[a1]	Sample Description	Disorder	Diagnostic System	Prevalence/ Incidence
	(1) 315 (2) 152 (3) 116	F	Adult		(women) (1) Total convictions (2) Violent offenses (3) Property offenses	Substance misuse	ICD-9	(1) 7.9% (n = 25) (2) 11.8% (n = 18) (3) 10.3% (n = 12)
Galli et al. (1999)	22	M	13–17 (M = 15.9, SD = 1.1)	PI, CS	Interviews with adolescents admitting to sexually assaulting another child, referred from a juvenile rehabilitation center, the juvenile court system, and an inpatient adolescent psychiatric unit, Hamilton County, Ohio	Cannabis use/ dependence	DSM-III-R (DICA)	36.0% (n = 8)
						Inhalant abuse		5.0% (n = 1)
						Total substance use disorders		50.0% (n = 11)
Gibson et al. (1999)	213	M	M = 32	JD	Structured interviews with randomly selected state prison and regional jail inmates from a rural New England state	Drug abuse/dependence	DSM-III-R (DIS-III-R)	Lifetime: 68.5% (n = 146) Current: NA
McElroy et al. (1999)	36	M	18–47 (M = 33, SD = 8)	PI	Interviews with convicted sex offenders consecutively admitted to the New Life Program, Cincinnati, Ohio, November 1996–June 1998	Drug abuse	DSM-IV (SCID)	75% (n = 27)
						Total substance abuse		83% (n = 30)
Raymond et al. (1999)	45	M	M = 37	PI, CS	Diagnostic interviews with convicted pedophilic sex offenders in either a residential or outpatient sex-offender treatment program	Any psychoactive substance use disorder	DSM-IV	60% (n = 27)

(Continued)

(Continued)

Drugs								
Source	**N**	**Gender**	**Age**	**Study Type**[a1]	**Sample Description**	**Disorder**	**Diagnostic System**	**Prevalence/ Incidence**
						Sedative/hypnotic/ anxiolytic		0%
						Cannabis		37.8% ($n = 17$)
						Stimulant		11.1% ($n = 5$)
						Opioid		4.4% ($n = 2$)
						Cocaine		17.8% ($n = 8$)
Pliszka et al. (2000)	50	45 M, 5 F	$M = 15.4$, $SD = 1.4$	JD	Interviews with adolescents consecutively admitted to the Bexar County Juvenile Detention Center, Texas	Marijuana dependence	DSM-IV (DIS-C)	46.0% ($n = 23$)
						Other substance dependence		14.0% ($n = 7$)
Siponmaa et al. (2001)	126	123 M, 3 F	15–22 (Median = 20)	JD	Interviews with young offenders consecutively referred for presentencing psychiatric investigation, Stockholm, Sweden, 1990–1995	Abuse of alcohol or drugs	ICD-9	2.0% ($n = 2$)
Teplin et al. (2002)	1829	1172 M, 657 F	10–18	JD	Diagnostic interviews of youths randomly sampled from intake into the Cook County Juvenile Temporary Detention Center, November 1995–June 1998	Marijuana use disorder	DSM-III-R	M: 44.8% F: 40.5%
						Other substance use disorder		M: 2.4% F: 6.9%
Inciardi & Surratt (2001)	708	F	Adult	CS	Interviews with women sex traders in Miami, Florida, 1994–1996	Cocaine dependence (daily crack cocaine use)	—	59.9%
Harris et al. (2002)	57	48 M, 9 F	20–49	JD	HIV-positive offenders seen for mental health evaluation at King County Correctional Facility, Seattle, Washington	Substance abuse history: Drugs only	? (FAMIO)	57.9% ($n = 33$)
						Drugs and alcohol		21.1% ($n = 12$)

Drugs								
Source	**N**	**Gender**	**Age**	**Study Type[a1]**	**Sample Description**	**Disorder**	**Diagnostic System**	**Prevalence/ Incidence**
Langevin (2003)	(1) 33 (2) 80 (3) 23 (4) 611	M	(1) $M = 32.06$ (2) $M = 27.58$ (3) $M = 27.57$ (4) $M = 31.42$	PI	Interviews with convicted sex offenders ($n = 747$) belonging to one of four groups: (1) sex killers, (2) nonhomicidal sexually aggressives, (3) nonhomicidal sadists, and (4) general sex offenders. Participants were chosen from a database of more than 2,800 minimum-security forensic ward psychiatric hospital cases (Clarke Institute in Toronto, Ontario, Canada) seen since 1973.	Amphetamine abuse	MAST, DAST, Drug Use Survey	(1) 36.4% (2) 31.3% (3) 34.8% (4) 14.9%
						Cocaine abuse		(1) 21.2% (2) 16.3% (3) 21.7% (4) 4.8%
						Hallucinogens abuse		(1) 42.4% (2) 32.5% (3) 39.1% (4)17.4%
						Marijuana abuse		(1) 69.7% (2) 56.3% (3) 52.1% (4) 29.3%
						Any drug abuse		(1) 81.5% (2) 61.3% (3) 69.6% (4) 37.5%

(Continued)

(Continued)

Drugs								
Source	**N**	**Gender**	**Age**	**Study Type**[a1]	**Sample Description**	**Disorder**	**Diagnostic System**	**Prevalence/ Incidence**
Stuart et al. (2003)	35	F	*M* = 32.6, *SD* = 8.8	CS	Questionnaire administered to women arrested for domestic violence and court referred to batterer intervention programs, Rhode Island	Drug-related diagnosis	DSM-IV (PDSQ)	26%
Dunsieth et al. (2004)	113	M	18–66 (*M* = 35.3, *SD* = 10.4)	PI	Diagnostic interviews with sex offenders consecutively referred to an Ohio residential sex-offender treatment program	Drug abuse	DSM-IV	15.0% (*n* = 17)
Leue et al. (2004)	55	M	Adult?	PI	Structured clinical interviews with sexual offenders hospitalized in forensic facilities in Arnsdorf, Saxony, and Moringen, Lower Saxony, Germany	Drug use	DSM-IV	16% (*n* = 9)
						Any substance use disorder		56% (*n* = 31)
Rösler et al. (2004)	129	M	*M* = 19.5, *SD* = 2.0	JD	Clinical interviews, record reviews, and rating scales conducted on inmates of a German offender facility (JSA Ottweiler)	Substance use disorder (SUD) abuse	ICD-10	33.3%[bz*]
						SUD dependence		55.8%[bz*]
Stuart et al. (2006)	103	F	*M* = 31.5, *SD* = 9.6	CS	Questionnaire administered to women arrested for violence and court referred to batterer intervention programs, Rhode Island	Drug diagnosis	DSM-IV (PDSQ)	24%

Drugs								
Source	**N**	**Gender**	**Age**	**Study Type**[a1]	**Sample Description**	**Disorder**	**Diagnostic System**	**Prevalence/ Incidence**
Kerridge (2009)	(1) 996 (2) 1339 (3) 1251 (4) 871	Male: (1) 93.2% (2) 85.3% (3) 83.9% (4) 89.2%	Adult: (1) 924 (2) 1276 (3) 1228 (4) 847	JD	Interviews with U.S. jail inmates (2002 Department of Justice, Bureau of Justice Statistics, Survey of Inmates of Local Jails), convicted of the following index offenses: (1) Violent (2) Property (3) Drug (4) Public order	Substance use disorder	DSM-IV-TR	(1) 58.4% (2) 70.6% (3) 70.2% (4) 63.8%
Kraanen et al. (2010)	150	142 M, 8 F	$M = 37.8$	CS	Interviews with intimate partner violence perpetrators in an outpatient domestic-violence treatment program at forensic outpatient clinic De Waag in Amsterdam, the Netherlands	Cannabis abuse	DSM-IV-TR	10.7% (n= 16)[bn]
						Cannabis dependence		6.7% (n= 10)
						Cocaine abuse		7.3% (n= 11)
						Cocaine dependence		5.3% (n= 8)
						Heroin abuse		0.0% (n= 0)
						Heroin dependence		0.0% (n= 0)
						Amphetamine abuse		1.3% (n= 2)
						Amphetamine dependence		0.0% (n= 0)
						Any drug-related abuse		16.7% (n= 25)
						Any drug-related dependence		11.3% (n= 17)
						Poly-substance abuse		5.3% (n= 8)
						Poly-substance dependence		10.0% (n= 15)

(Continued)

(Continued)

Drugs								
Source	N	Gender	Age	Study Type[a1]	Sample Description	Disorder	Diagnostic System	Prevalence/ Incidence
Pham & Saloppé (2010)	84	M	Adult	PI	Psychological evaluations of forensic patients at high-security psychiatric hospital in Tomai, Belgium (Etablissement de Défense Sociale)	Psychoactive substance abuse/dependence	DSM-III (DISSI)	33% ($n = 28$)
						Substance-related disorders		69% ($n = 58$)
Catanesi et al. (2011)	103	85.44% M	53.41% 25–54, 22.73% 45–65, 13.64% 18–24, 5.68% <18	HO	Psychiatric and psychological evaluations on perpetrators of homicide and attempted homicide, Italy	Substance abuse	DSM-IV-TR	2.9%

Notes: *Significant difference in comparison to control group.

[a1]AR = arrest rates of patients discharged from psychiatric facilities, JD = jailed detainees and incarcerated prisoners, HO = homicide offenders, BC = birth cohort study, PI = psychiatric inpatient sample, CS = community sample (i.e., epidemiological catchment area survey studies and outpatient psychiatric patients).

[b]Reported group mean ages: Antisocial personality ($M = 21.9$), drug ($M = 19.6$), alcohol ($M = 32.5$), no diagnosis ($M = 22.0$).

[k]Community sample comparative data (six-month prevalence rates from NIMH Community Survey Data): 2.2–13.4%.

[r]Other reports (Teplin, 1990b; Teplin, 1994) have been published on this sample.

[ai]Group means and standard deviations: Psychotic illness (35.7, 8.8), personality disorder and alcohol use disorders (24.4, 8.2), no psychiatric abnormality (34.0, 12.4).

[as]Lifetime prevalence rate. For community comparison sample, standardized prevalence ratio (SPR) = 2.2 (an SPR greater than 1 indicates the prevalence rate in the prison sample was greater than that in the general population).

[at]Lifetime prevalence rate. For community comparison sample, standardized prevalence ratio (SPR) = 3.5 (an SPR greater than 1 indicates the prevalence rate in the prison sample was greater than that in the general population).

[bf]Rates of alcohol use disorders in comparison outpatient and inpatient samples from same catchment area: 9.2% ($n = 852$) and 7.1% ($n = 66$).

[bg]Rates of drug-related substance use disorders in comparison outpatient and inpatient samples from same catchment area: 23.0% ($n = 2{,}136$) and 12.9% ($n = 120$).

[bn]One-month prevalence rates of substance use disorders in a large Dutch national household survey ($N = 7{,}076$): 2.5% for alcohol abuse, 2.7% for alcohol dependence, 0.3% for drug abuse, and 0.7% for drug dependence.

[bz]Prevalence rates for controls ($n = 54$ males without history of delinquency): Alcoholism = 0.0%, SUD abuse = 0.0%, SUS dependence = 0.0%.

Table 4.4 Prevalence of Crime in Substance Use Disordered Populations

Source	N	Gender	Age	Study Type[a1]	Sample Description	Disorder	Crime Definition	Prevalence/Incidence
Guze et al. (1974)	70	?M, ?F	Adult	CS	Community psychiatric clinic patients, diagnosed with Feighner diagnostic criteria (Feighner et al., 1972)	Alcoholism	Felony conviction	13.0% ($n = 9$)
	13					Drug dependency		23.0% ($n = 3$)
Tardiff & Koenigsberg (1985)	(1) 2,106 (2) 810	(1) 842 M, 1,256 F (2) 354 M, 453 F	(1) ≤ 20–65+[aa] (2) ≤ 20–65+[aa]	CS	Psychiatric outpatients evaluated during a 1.5 year period at two New York hospitals, diagnosed with DSM II and DSM II criteria (1) Payne Whitney Clinic (2) Westchester Division of NY Hospital	Alcohol or substance abuse (1) $n = 214$ (2) $n = 106$	Presence of assaultive behavior toward others in hospital records	(1) 2.3% ($n = 5$) (2) 1.9% ($n = 2$)
Swanson et al. (1990)	10,059	4,717 M, 5,306 F[f]	Adult	CS	Epidemiologic catchment area respondent data (community adults from five U.S. sites), diagnosed with DSM-III criteria (DIS)	Alcohol abuse/ dependence	Self-report violence	24.57% violent ($n = 586$[f])
						Cannabis abuse/ dependence		19.25% violent ($n = 191$[f])
						Other drug abuse/ dependence		34.74% violent ($n = 99$[f])
Asnis et al. (1994)	517	204 M, 313 F	13–87 ($M = 38.7$)	CS	Psychiatric outpatients, Montefiore Medical Center, Bronx, New York, diagnosed with DSM-III criteria	Substance abuse ($n = 38$)	Self-reported homicidal ideation and attempts	Ideation: 32% ($n = 12$) Attempts: 3% ($n = 1$)
Arsenault et al. (2000)	(1) 389 (2) 572	51.6% M, 48.4% F	Adult	BC	From a study of a total-city New Zealand birth cohort (N = 1,037)—diagnosed using DSM-III-R criteria—individuals with (1) Psychiatric disorder (2) No psychiatric disorder	Alcohol dependence disorder ($n = 94$)	Violence: Self-report and criminal convictions	(1) Convictions: 8.5% ($n = 8$), self-report: 24.5% ($n = 23$) (2) Convictions: 1.2% ($n = 7$), self-report: 3.1% ($n = 18$)

(Continued)

(Continued)

Source	N	Gender	Age	Study Type[a1]	Sample Description	Disorder	Crime Definition	Prevalence/Incidence
						Marijuana dependence disorder ($n = 91$)		1) Convictions: 17.6% ($n = 16$), self-report: 26.4% ($n = 24$)
Logan & Leukefeld (2000)	754	456 M, 298 F	Adult	CS	Crack users recruited into NIDA Cooperative Agreement Project, Lexington and Louisville, Kentucky, June 1995–January 1998	Cocaine dependence[bo]	Violence: Conflict Tactics Scale	Males: 66.9% ($n = 305$) moderate or severe violence Females: 74.8% ($n = 223$) moderate or severe violence
Zweben et al. (2004)	1,016	454 M, 562 F	Adult	CS	Methamphetamine users recruited from 8 outpatient treatment programs in California, Montana, and Hawaii, diagnosed with DSM-IV criteria	Methamphetamine dependence	Self-reported violence and crime	Attempted suicide: 27%
								Violent behavior problems: 43%
								Assault charges: $M = 0.29$
								Weapons charges: $M = 0.13$
Corrigan & Watson (2005)	5,865	?M, ?F	15–54	CS	Subset of respondents from the (U.S.) National Comorbidity Survey, diagnosed with DSM-III-R criteria (structured diagnostic interview), 1990–1992	Alcohol abuse w/wo dependence	Self-reported violence	Mental illness lifetime: 8.2% (110/133); 12 months: 9.1% (13/145)
						Drug abuse w/wo dependence		Mental illness lifetime: 10.9% (70/645); 12 months: 19.8% (10/49)
Digiusto et al. (2006)	(1) 997 (2) 300	(1) 66% M (2) 59% M	(1) $M = 30$, $SD = 8$ (2) $M = 33$, $SD = 7$	CS	Data collected from participants in the Australian National Evaluation of Pharmacotherapies for Opioid Dependence (11 clinical trials at multiple sites), diagnosed with DSM-IV criteria	(1) Heroin dependence (2) Heroin dependence (methadone patients)	Self-reported crime (property crime, drug dealing, fraud, violence)	(1) 39% (1 month incidence, previous to baseline measurement) (2) 13% (1 month incidence, previous to baseline measurement)[v]

Source	N	Gender	Age	Study Type[a1]	Sample Description	Disorder	Crime Definition	Prevalence/Incidence
Sommers et al. (2006)	106	59.4 % M, 40.6% F	18–25 (*M* = 22)	CS	Structured interviews with Los Angeles, CA, methamphetamine users from the community and from a drug treatment program (68.9% daily use, 12.2% 3–6 days/week use)	Methamphetamine dependence[bo]	Self-reported crime	Auto theft: 43%
								Shoplifting: 69%
								Forgery: 9%
								Prostitution: 1%
								Burglary: 13%
								Assault: 37%
								Robbery: 16%
								Weapons possession: 54%
								Attempted murder: 16%
								Murder: 7%
Darke et al. (2010)	(1) 118 (2) 161 (3) 121	280 M, 120 F	18–75 (*M*= 35.4)	CS	Structured interviews with community drug-user volunteers in Sydney, Australia, September 2007–November 2008, with at least weekly methamphetamine/opiate use in the preceding 12 months	(1) Methamphetamine dependence (2) Heroin dependence (3) Methamphetamine and heroin dependence	Self-reported violent offenses	(1) Lifetime = 81%, 12 months = 51% (2) Lifetime = 81%, 12 months = 35%[bm] (3) Lifetime = 84% 12 months = 41%

Notes: [f]Weighted Ns

[v]Heroin users: Property crime 22%, drug dealing 21%, fraud 7%, violence 3%. Methadone patients: Property crime 6%, drug dealing 7%, fraud 2%, violence 0%.

[aa](1) 12.4% (*n* = 261) 20 years and younger, 30.7% (*n* = 647) 21–30, 23.6% (*n* = 496) 31–40, 24.3% (*n* = 511) 41–64, 7.5% (*n* = 158) 65 years and older, 1.6% (*n* = 33) unknown; (2) 18.0% (*n* = 146) 20 years and younger, 31.4% (*n* = 254) 21–30, 18.0% (*n* = 146) 31–40, 27.0% (*n* = 219) 41–64, 5.0% (*n* = 41) 65 years and older, 0.5% (*n* = 4) unknown.

[bm]Methamphetamine > Heroin.

[bo]Suggested by use pattern but not formally diagnosed within study.

(Continued from page 126)

examined separately (or incidentally reported) prevalence rates of substance-related disorders and prevalence rates of crime in these disorders. (In Table 4.3, disorders involving the use of alcohol are presented separately from those involving the use of drugs other than alcohol.) Samples here come from several countries around the world and use a multitude of different methodologies and a number of different major diagnostic systems.

A Closer Look: Alcohol Use Disorders and Crime

Prevalence of the Disorder in Crime

Study Type	Number	Prevalence Rates
Arrest rates	1	33.4–47.3%
Birth cohorts	0	–
Community samples	7*	11.3–51.1%
Homicide offenders	4	2.0–27.1%
Jailed detainees and prisoners	17	4.1–100.0%
Psychiatric inpatients	11*	5.0–85.0%
Total Number of Studies	**37**	

Sample Characteristics

Size	15–2,743
Gender	Male only (19 studies); female only (4 studies); male and female but generally more males than females (12 studies); not reported (2 studies)
Age	Youth, adult
Location	Countries worldwide (e.g., Australia, Belgium, Canada, England, Finland, Germany, Iceland, the Netherlands, Poland, Sweden, United States)
Diagnostic Systems	DSM (various editions), ICD (various editions), other research diagnostic criteria and self-report measures. Unspecified in some studies.

Note: *Three psychiatric inpatient studies also included community individuals. "Pure" community samples included one unique community study of women sex traders (Inciardi & Surratt, 2001), with alcohol dependence suggested by daily alcohol use.

Prevalence of Crime in the Disorder

Study Type	Number	Prevalence Rates	Crime Definition
Arrest rates	0	–	–
Birth cohorts	1	8.5–24.5%	Self-reported violence, criminal convictions
Community samples	3	8.2–24.6%	Felony convictions, self-reported violence
Homicide offenders	0	–	–
Jailed detainees and prisoners	0	–	–
Psychiatric inpatients	0	–	–
Total Number of Studies	**4**		

Sample Characteristics	
Size	70–10,059
Gender	Male and female, more evenly distributed than studies of other disorders (17 studies)
Age	Youth, adult
Location	New Zealand, United States
Diagnostic Systems	DSM, other research diagnostic criteria

Nondisordered or community resident comparison group or general population baseline rates for either disorder or crime provided: **4 studies (9.8%)**†

Note: †Rates of alcohol-related disorders in criminal populations are comparable to inpatient and outpatient comparison groups (Reich & Wells, 1985) but are greater than general population rates (Bland et al., 1990; Kraanen et al., 2010) and noncriminal comparison groups (Rösler et al., 2004); and rates of crime among those with alcohol dependence appear significantly higher than those with no psychiatric disorder (Arsenault et al., 2000).

Additionally, among the seven studies of crime in substance use disorders involving specifically identified substances other than alcohol (see Table 4.4), rates of crime and violence across two studies of individuals with marijuana use disorders are 17.6–26.4%, across two studies of individuals with heroin use disorders are 13.0–81.0%, and across three studies of those with methamphetamine use disorders are 1.0%–69.0%. With continued work in this area, rates of criminal behavior across individual classes of substances may be examined to ascertain if substance-related disorders involving different substances may contribute to crime differentially.

Furthermore, 12 studies reported rates that combined alcohol-related disorders and disorders related to the use or abuse of other substances. (These rates were sometimes reported separately, along with alcohol-related or non-alcohol substance-related disorders, as "drugs and alcohol abuse," "total substance use disorders," "total substance abuse," "any substance use disorder," "substance-related disorders," or "any psychoactive substance use disorder"; or they were reported as "alcohol or substance abuse," "abuse of alcohol or drugs," "substance abuse conditions," "substance misuse," or "substance use disorders.") In these studies, rates of total substance-related disorders in criminal populations are 2.0–83.0%, and rates of crime (i.e., assaultive behavior, self-reported homicidal ideation or attempts) in substance-related disordered populations are 1.9–32.0%.

A Closer Look: Non-Alcohol Substance Use Disorders and Crime

Prevalence of the Disorder in Crime

Study Type	**Number**	**Prevalence Rates**†
Arrest rates	2	1.8–11.8%
Birth cohorts	0	–
Community samples	6*	0.0–59.9%
Homicide offenders	4	1.4–35.0%
Jailed detainees and prisoners	18	1.2–71.2%
Psychiatric inpatients	10*	0.0–75.0%
Total Number of Studies	**38**	

(Continued)

(Continued)

Sample Characteristics	
Size	15–4,457
Gender	Male only (17 studies); female only (4 studies); male and female but generally more males than females (15 studies); not reported (2 studies)
Age	Youth, adult
Location	Countries worldwide (e.g., Australia, Belgium, Canada, England, Finland, Germany, Italy, the Netherlands, Sweden, United States)
Diagnostic Systems	DSM (various editions), ICD (various editions), other research diagnostic criteria and self-report measures. Unspecified in some studies.

Notes: *Two psychiatric inpatient studies also included community individuals. "Pure" community samples included one unique community study of women sex traders (Inciardi & Surratt, 2001), with cocaine dependence suggested by daily crack cocaine use and other behavioral indicators.

†Rates of substance use disorders often vary markedly when reported separately for different substances. See Table 4.1. Prevalence rates across all 38 studies appear to be increased in most cases (and for a small number of studies, at least comparable at minimum levels) relative to estimates of non-alcohol substance-related disorders in the general population (e.g., those reported in the DSM-IV-TR; see above).

Prevalence of Crime in the Disorder

Study Type	Number	Prevalence Rates	Crime Definition
Arrest rates	0	–	–
Birth cohorts	1	17.6–26.4%	Self-reported violence, criminal convictions
Community samples	8	1.0–84.0%*	Felony convictions, self-reported crimes and violence
Homicide offenders	0	–	–
Jailed detainees and prisoners	0	–	–
Psychiatric inpatients	0	–	–
Total Number of Studies	**9**		

Sample Characteristics	
Size	13–10,059
Gender	Male and female (more evenly distributed than studies of other disorders: 9 studies)
Age	Youth, adult
Location	Australia, New Zealand, United States
Diagnostic Systems	DSM, other research diagnostic criteria

Note: *Zweben et al. (2004) also report mean number of assault and weapons charges for their study participants–*M* = 0.29 and 0.13, respectively. Asnis and colleagues (1994) reported rates of self-reported homicidal ideation (32%) and attempts (3%) in individuals diagnosed with substance abuse–without separating alcohol from non-alcohol substance-related disorders.

Nondisordered or community resident comparison group or general population baseline rates for either disorder or crime provided: **6 studies (12.8%)**†

Note: †Rates of disorders in criminal populations are increased relative to comparison groups in four studies (Bland et al., 1990; Kerridge et al., 2009; Yarvis, 1990; and, for drug-related abuse/dependence as well as most individual drug categories, Krannen et al., 2010) and decreased relative to a comparison group in one study (Reich & Wells, 1985). Rates of crime in disordered populations are increased relative to comparison groups (approximately 15 times the rate for convictions, and 8.5 times for self-reports) in one study of individuals with marijuana dependence disorder (Arsenault et al., 2000).

Case Material

Earlier interest in the relationship between substance-related disorders and crime is demonstrated by published case material from the nineteenth century. Cesare Lombroso (1876/2006), in the fourth edition of his classic work *Criminal Man* (*L'uomo delinquente*), identifies a subcategory of the insane criminal—the alcoholic criminal. According to Lombroso, these criminals "tend to impromptu murder and motiveless suicide" and are "inclined to theft" (p. 84). He writes of one chronic alcoholic criminal:

> Pietro Belm . . . , forty-one years old, had been charged with vagabondage on several occasions. Born in Sassari to parents from Nice, he wore greasy clothes, and his hair and breath smelled of alcohol. He was 5 feet 1 inch tall and weighed 128 lbs. His hands and nose were redder than normal, his eyes bulbous, and the left eye less sensitive to touch than the right. Although his pupils reacted properly, there was a blurring at the back of his eyes. His tongue trembled and his lips formed a constant smile that sometimes shifted to lament for no reason. His cephalic index was eighty-three, his cranial capacity slightly above average (1,545 cc), and his forehead sloping. (p. 279)

Lombroso also reports that, "in Africa, the explorer Stanley found a species of bandit called Ruga-Ruga, an indigenous people who made use of cannabis. He also recorded a Ugandan legend according to which crime appeared only after the introduction of beer" (p. 279).

Gaupp (1914, 1938, in Häfner & Böker, 1982) reported the well-known case of Headmaster Wagner, who committed multiple acts of sodomy while under the influence of alcohol and later (on September 4, 1913) murdered his wife and four children, went to the village of Mulhausen and committed several acts of arson, and (in delusional self-defense) shot to death 9 villagers and injured 11 more. Additionally, the contribution of problematic alcohol use to criminal and antisocial behavior has been described in case material presented in seminal works from the early and middle twentieth century; these cases describe psychiatric patients with schizophrenia (Kraepelin, 1919/2002) and psychopathy (Cleckley, 1988).

Individual Substance Classes and Criminal Behavior

To date, the lion's share of work on the relationship between substance-related disorders and crime is found in the criminological literature, in which sociological and ethnographic approaches have been used to examine the more generalized drugs-crime relationship. Many, but not all, have been descriptive in nature. Most of the different classes of substances mentioned have been examined separately in their relationship with crime and violence, and research has focused on their pharmacological effects as well as other etiological factors.

Alcohol

Alcohol is the substance most commonly associated with violence and is linked to both committing and being exposed to violent acts (Darke, 2010; Hoaken & Stewart, 2003). For example, reviews of violent offenders (i.e., homicide, sexual, and assault offenders, marital violence perpetrators, and child abusers) reveal that many are drinking at the time of their offense and that this fact holds true across various offender types (local, state, or federal offenders sentenced to either probation, jail, or prison). Violent offenders report drinking at the time of their offenses at higher rates than those reported by drug and property offenders (Bartol & Bartol, 2011). Additionally, alcohol has been shown to be the substance most related to homicides in incarcerated homicidal offenders in New York State prisons (Spunt et al., 1995). Athanasiadis (1999) describes the multifaceted relationship between drugs, alcohol, and violence in South East Asian cities (which likely rings true in other regions), where alcohol use and abuse are linked closely to intimate partner violence and violence against women and girls. Alcohol- or drug-using men tend to become physically or sexually violent, while alcohol- or drug-using women may ineffectively interpret and act upon warning signs of violence and end up in settings with potential offenders. Victims of partner violence are, in turn, more likely than other women to abuse alcohol and drugs.

Three interrelated domains of influence have been proposed in theoretical approaches to alcohol and violence: the situational context, the aggression-facilitating personality characteristics of individuals, and the effects of alcohol consumption (Leonard et al., 2003). Leonard and colleagues (2003) found the first two to be predictors of barroom violence experiences in a survey study of 368 men and 269 women. Regarding the psychopharmacological effects of alcohol, moderate and high amounts of alcohol consumption are associated with depression of the CNS inhibitory processes, impaired concentration, increased self-confidence, and the "numbing" of higher brain centers, including those processing judgment and abstract thought (Bartol & Bartol, 2011). These effects leave one vulnerable to impulsivity and poor decision making and, potentially, to crime and violence. The rewarding psychomotor effects of alcohol (including increased heart rate and novelty-seeking and approach behaviors), its ability to produce "stress-response dampening" (i.e., reducing appropriate appraisal of a stressful event), its analgesic properties (which block pain sensitivity and the punishing effects of aggressive altercations), and its cognitive effects (decreasing attention, including visuospatial attention, and verbal and spatial learning) may all elicit aggression (Hoaken & Stewart, 2003). Finally, other factors such as cultural differences may play a significant role in the relationship between alcohol and aggression (Bartol & Bartol, 2011).

Aside from the prevalence studies listed in Tables 4.3 and 4.4, qualitative studies of alcohol-related disorders and crime are somewhat limited. Some studies of prison inmates have discussed "heavy" or "problem" drinkers, which are characterized by more significant arrest histories and increased numbers of assaults (Reiss & Roth, 1993, in Bartol & Bartol, 2011). Other studies (e.g., Bland et al., 1990) have found high rates of comorbid criminogenic disorders (alcohol abuse/dependence, drug abuse/dependence, and antisocial personality disorder) in prison inmates with a history of suicide attempts. Ultimately, the exact nature of the relationship between alcohol and violence remains unclear, though it is likely that alcohol merely *facilitates* the preexisting aggressive tendencies of some individuals already prone to aggression, antisociality, and violence—rather than directly *causing* them *per se* (Bartol & Bartol, 2011).

Amphetamines

The link between amphetamines and crime in the literature appears to be focused largely on their association with violent behavior. Numerous studies have examined this link (Parker & Auerhahm, 1998), and research has led to mixed conclusions. A recent review by Darke and colleagues (2008) indicates that violent behaviors appear common among methamphetamine users and that rates of attempted suicide are substantially higher for methamphetamine users than for the general population. Some studies have reported a rare reaction associated with violence, called variously "toxic psychosis" or "amphetamine induced psychosis"; it presents very similar to schizophrenia and is characterized by sustained heavy use of amphetamines or significantly high doses (Darke et al., 2008; Parker & Auerhahn, 1998). Ethnographic and animal studies alike, however, have suggested that the amphetamines-violence association may be more the result of situational influences and social factors (i.e., in humans, a long-term solitary lifestyle in which an individual has few opportunities to cross-check delusional thinking; (Parker & Auerhahn, 1998), or that it may reflect a preexisting proneness to violence (e.g., Bartol & Bartol, 2011). Other studies have even indicated a negative relationship in specific populations (i.e., hyperactive children and brain-injured adults; Hoaken & Stewart, 2003).

At the clinical disorder level, amphetamine use and violence may be more definitively related, though actual studies of amphetamine-related disorders and violence are rare. Investigations of regular and problematic amphetamine use—which may suggest the presence of disorder—have shed some light in this area: for example, studies have shown that chronic methamphetamine use may increase aggressive behavior (Darke et al., 2008). In a mostly male Australian sample of regular drug users (n = 118 methamphetamine, n = 161 heroin, and n = 161 both substances), Darke and colleagues (2010) found high rates of both violent offending (82%) and victimization (95%); in fact, those who had committed a violent crime in the past year were also approximately 13 times more likely to have been victimized. Regular methamphetamine users were at an increased risk for offending but not for victimization compared to regular heroin users. Studying methamphetamine clinic outpatients, Zweben and colleagues (2004) found the route of amphetamine administration (i.e., injection) to be associated with a significantly increased history of assault and weapons charges and increased reports of difficulty controlling violent behavior. However, comorbid psychopathology may have also contributed to these findings, and general population comparison base rates were not reported.

Sommers and colleagues (2006) demonstrate the potential role of social and contextual factors in the amphetamine-violence relationship. In their community-outpatient study of 106 daily methamphetamine users, who were predominantly young adults, 34.9% reported committing acts of violence while under the influence of methamphetamines; this methamphetamine-based violence occurred more often within family and acquaintance relationships in private domestic situations. According to the authors, methamphetamine use turned nonthreatening everyday verbal exchanges into contests of character involving violent resolutions and exaggerated outrage over perceived violations of personal codes (respect, space, verbal challenges), which led to violent behavior for the purposes of retribution or exerting social control. Paranoia was a common effect of methamphetamine use, which contributed to hostile attributions, a threatening and dangerous air, and, ultimately, defensive or preemptive violent behavior. Numerous participants reported that, when they found themselves within violent events, their decision-making ability was compromised (most commonly, they described this as loss of control, blowing up, or having an outburst of rage). Thus, several mechanisms for facilitating violence were indicated as being associated with methamphetamine use—congruent with other studies (Darke et al., 2008), which have shown that, while individuals are acutely intoxicated, aggressive responses may be enhanced or augmented when threatened or provoked. Sommers and colleagues (2006) also found that cognitively, methamphetamine use appeared to inhibit cues that normally control behavior, to interfere with communication and interpersonal interactions, and to intensify emotions. Additionally, violent criminality for the most part *predated* the onset of methamphetamine use and *followed* the onset of alcohol and marijuana use, suggesting that the early use of other illicit substances may predispose people to later violence and criminality as well as to the use of "harder" drugs such as methamphetamines. Overall, methamphetamine-related violence may stem from an interaction between the individual, the drug itself, and the situation.

Cannabis

Discussions in the literature of the relationship between cannabis use and crime largely center upon its pharmacological effects and their influences (or, more precisely, lack thereof) upon criminal and violent behavior. The general consensus appears to be that the psychoactive ingredient of cannabis, THC, induces marked muscle weakness, promotes feelings of lethargy, and thus reduces the likelihood of violence (Bartol & Bartol, 2011; Hoaken & Stewart, 2003). In fact, studies have shown that irritability and hostility are actually reduced upon administration of the drug (Hoaken & Stewart, 2003). Some evidence may suggest a cannabis-violence relationship in rare instances or under special circumstances. For example, though it is believed that moderate and large doses of THC suppress or even eliminate violent behavior, a developing literature demonstrates an authentic cannabis withdrawal syndrome possibly characterized by the increased likelihood of interpersonal aggression. In small doses, THC may increase aggression (Hoaken & Stewart, 2003). Additionally, occasional negative experiences produced by THC have been reported (e.g., feelings of panic, hypersensitivity, feelings of disconnect with surroundings, bizarre behavior, and irrelevant thought intrusions). These may lead to the misinterpretation of the actions of others and, possibly, to aggressive outbursts; and small percentages of homicide offenders report homicides being related to the effects of marijuana (Lipton & Johnson, 1998). However, these instances appear rare, and a cannabis-violence relationship does not appear to be supported by any meaningful evidence; rare exceptions likely reflect a predisposition to violence rather than effects of the drug itself (Bartol & Bartol, 2011). On balance, studies of a potential relationship between cannabis-related disorders and violence and crime appear largely nonexistent.

Cocaine

Conclusions in the literature about a possible cocaine-crime relationship are mixed. On one hand, Bartol and Bartol (2011) report that studies have produced little evidence indicating that cocaine—in either crack or powder form—causes an individual who is nonviolent to suddenly become violent or dangerous or that it facilitates the commission of property crime; and cocaine-associated violence is likely due to an individual's preexisting vulnerability to violence (e.g., lifestyle) rather than to simply the pharmacological effects of the drug. However, recent research reports have indicated that increased use of cocaine is associated with violent confrontational crime in both men and women (McBride & McCoy, 2006) and that, across 142 U.S. cities from 1984–1992, those with increased levels of crack use were characterized by greater increases in Uniform Crime Report (UCR) rates of robbery and decreases in burglary (Baumer et al., 2006).

Paranoia is one of the most commonly reported pharmacological effects in cocaine users, and some researchers have proposed that cocaine-associated violence may be at least partially a defensive reaction to irrational fear (Miller et al., 1991, in Parker & Auerhahn, 1998). Reports of this relationship date back to the observations of medical practitioners in the early 1900s (McBride & McCoy, 2006). Furthermore, the route of cocaine administration may affect this relationship, with the methods producing the most intense and immediate effects being more strongly associated with some forms of violence. For example, Giannini and colleagues (1993, in Parker & Auerhahn, 1998) found users who smoked crack cocaine were more likely to be violent following cocaine use, followed by intravenous users and then by intranasal users—who were least likely to become violent. Additionally, "sustained activity" forms of violence (e.g., rape and robbery) were unrelated to the route of administration of cocaine and may be more related to situational variables. Other researchers have also suggested a greater influence of social and circumstantial rather than pharmacological factors in the cocaine-violence relationship, e.g., males, as opposed to females, being "big users" or crack-using women experiencing violence resulting from their involvement with prostitution (Parker & Auerhahn, 1998).

Studies of cocaine-related disorders and crime are uncommon (whether the disorder is specified or inferred from regular or problematic patterns of use). However, studies of street juvenile delinquent crack users conducted in Miami, Florida (review in Inciardi & Pottieger, 1998), have found increased involvement in the crack business to be associated with increased drug use (daily marijuana and crack use, regular consumption of alcohol and depressants); frequent crime (robberies, assaults, burglaries, motor vehicle thefts); younger age of first alcohol, marijuana, pills, and cocaine use; younger age of first drug sales; and heroin use and robbery. Studies of adult regular crack users in Miami (review in Inciardi & Pottieger, 1998) indicate differences in the criminal behaviors reported by those in treatment compared to those who were not. Varying types of nonviolent crimes (e.g., property offenses, fraud) were reported by both groups, though robberies and assaults were significantly more prominent in the former. However, women in treatment were characterized by more prostitution than those not in treatment (43.8% versus 65.5%), and mean numbers of total crimes were higher for those not in treatment (nearly 10 times higher for men and 5 times higher for women). Another treatment study (Khalsa et a., 1993a, 1993b, in Anglin & Perrochet, 1998) examined 325 cocaine-dependent men seeking treatment at the West Los Angeles Veterans Affairs Medical Center. Participants were from more socially normative backgrounds than the inner-city, lower socioeconomic status cocaine users commonly reported in other studies; one-fourth reported 16 of 33 socially deviant behaviors before the initiation of cocaine use, and stealing and shoplifting predated cocaine use onset in over half of the sample (only 25% did so after dependence-level cocaine use). After cocaine use onset, the most common criminal behaviors were carrying drugs for someone else (47%), purchasing stolen property (42%), threatening with a weapon (27%), and drug sales (64%), and over a third of those who sold or carried drugs had never done so before the onset of cocaine use.

Hallucinogens

Studies of hallucinogen use and crime are rare, and, to date, the relationship between hallucinogen-related disorders and crime and violence appears largely unexplored. According to Hoaken and Stewart (2003), MDMA ("ecstasy") use appears to be associated with a decrease rather than an increase in aggression, though long-term use may increase the propensity for violent behavior. Interestingly, Hendricks and colleagues (2014) recently conducted a unique study examining the relationship between hallucinogen use and recidivism among a large sample of 25,622 individuals under community corrections supervision. Results from this longitudinal study indicated that the presence of any hallucinogen-use disorder predicted a *reduced* likelihood of recidivism in these individuals. (Recidivism, in this study, was defined as supervision failure, e.g., the failure to report for supervision or to court or not complying with other legal requirements, including limiting alcohol and other drug use.) The authors speculate that hallucinogens might promote prosocial behavior along with abstinence from alcohol and other drugs in this highly recidivistic population. Clearly, more empirical investigations are needed in this understudied area.

Opioids

Of all the classes of substances, the opioids in general—and heroin in particular—appear to be among the most studied in their relationship with crime. A number of studies from Australia and New Zealand have demonstrated associations between heroin use and criminality (Darke et al., 2010; Digiusto et al., 2006). Mixed conclusions have been drawn as to whether a heroin-violence relationship exists. Some authors (e.g., Parker & Auerhahn) assert that virtually no evidence supports this relationship. Opioids are sedatives and do not directly facilitate violence (Darke, 2010); and opioids used regularly—unlike psychostimulants—are not associated with paranoid symptoms or violence after administration (Hoaken & Stewart, 2003). However, heroin or opiate use has been associated with violent offenses in some samples (Incaiardi & Pottieger, 1998); and, although animal studies have not generally supported a heroin-aggression relationship, several controlled studies in humans have demonstrated increased aggression in participants administered both codeine and morphine, and heroin-dependent patients undergoing methadone treatment have demonstrated increased levels of aggression relative to healthy controls (Hoaken & Stewart, 2003). Violence and aggression in opiate users likely result from a complex interplay of interpersonal and pharmacological factors (Hoaken & Stewart, 2003)—including withdrawal and distal lifestyle factors (Darke, 2010; Hoaken & Stewart, 2003)—and are likely more due to the reasons they abuse the drug rather than the drug itself (Hoaken & Stewart, 2003). Some evidence indicates a relationship between heroin use and property crime (Hoaken & Stewart, 2003); for example, studies from the 1970s found heroin users to be overrepresented among perpetrators of property crimes and underrepresented among violent criminals (McBride & McCoy, 2006).

In contrast to research focusing on the other classes of substances, studies of opioid-related disorders and crime are much more common. These have largely examined heroin "addicts" (wherein diagnostic systems or procedures are generally not specified). In studies dating back several decades, extensive ranges of crime (drunkenness, gambling, drug sales, larcenies, prostitution, property crimes, robberies) have been reported in varying degrees in samples of heroin addicts from several U.S. cities (Inciardi, Pottieger, & Pottieger, 1998; Waldorf, 1998). These addicts had early and multiple arrests and complicated incarceration histories (Waldorf, 1998). Decades of research on heroin addicts (Anglin & Perrochet, 1998; Nurco, 1998) have demonstrated differences in self-reported crime between periods of addiction and abstinence (e.g., frequency of crime is increased six-fold and crime income is increased tenfold when addicted compared to when not addicted). This crime often predated heroin use but occurred mostly within addiction periods. Additionally, research strongly suggests that heroin addicts largely do not commit violent crimes such as assault, rape, or homicide (Bartol & Bartol, 2011).

The temporal relationship between heroin use and property crime levels has been described as **approximate simultaneity**: over the span of the addiction career, increased levels of heroin use and crime appear to be somewhat episodic and sporadic (i.e., rarely lasting more than 1–2 years at a time), but they vary directly with one another, likely reflecting increased income-generating criminality motivated by the need to purchase heroin during addicted periods. Subsistence levels of criminal income common to non-addicted periods suggest that many addicts use property crime to pay for life's basic necessities (Anglin & Perrochet, 1998). Ethnographic studies have demonstrated increased criminality in heroin addicts compared to cocaine addicts (Waldorf, 1998), and clinical pharmacotherapy trials have shown increased criminality in heroin addicts compared to methadone patients (Diguisto et al., 2006). Finally, Waldorf and colleagues (in Waldorf, 1998) discovered three "addict lifestyles" in a study of Vietnam War veterans: (1) *street addicts* (often working or lower class property criminals, who were incarcerated more than the other types), (2) *middle-class counterculture addicts* or *bohemians* (not involved in crime other than drug use, who often avoided incarceration), and (3) *situational addicts* (typically women addicts who used opiates when cohabitating with addicted mates and were seldom criminal or incarcerated).

Phencyclidine (PCP)

Cases like that of Antron Singleton are extreme and thankfully rare, but they occur with enough frequency to suppose—at least in the eyes of the public—a strong relationship between PCP and violence. Exactly how accurate, however, is this supposition? PCP, 1-(1-phenylcyclohexyl)piperidine, is classified as a "dissociative anesthetic," meaning that it reduces awareness of both pain and the environment in general (Parker & Auerhahn, 1998). It was first synthesized by Parke-Davis in 1958 and tested widely in humans from 1959–1962. Its suppression of pain and other stimuli perception—without full stupor—made it ideal for surgical applications, though its tendency to cause surgery patients to become excited, delusionally fearful, and even full-blown psychotic forced its developers to curtail its clinical use. It later became available to veterinarians who discovered its utility as an anesthesia for large animals, particularly primates (Morgan & Kagan, 1980). Users and clinicians have continued to report delusions, paranoia, and psychosis (in rare cases) as often being among the effects of PCP (Parker & Auerhahn, 1998).

Headlines such as "The Devil Drug of All Time," "Violence Increases Due to Angel Dust," and "Person High on PCP Gouges Out His Own Eyes" (Morgan & Kagan, 1980) exemplify mass media representations, which would suggest that PCP is the drug most likely to produce a violent "rage." However, the empirical literature is at best inconsistent. Although PCP may indeed lead to violent behavior in some individuals, the effect appears inconsistent and may be explained by factors other than direct pharmacological action (Hoaken & Stewart, 2003). Geberth (1996) discusses a case of extreme self-mutilation following PCP use, wherein a young man under the influence of PCP used pieces of a mirror to peel his face from his skull; he subsequently fed parts of himself to his pet dogs (bits of his face, lips, and nose were later recovered when veterinarians pumped the dogs' stomachs). Due to the large quantity of PCP anesthetizing his system, the man survived.

BOX 4.1 RICKY KASSO, THE ACID KING

Richard "Ricky" Kasso (1967–1984) murdered 17-year-old Gary Lauwers in the Aztakea Woods of Northport, Long Island, New York, on June 16, 1984. Kasso, Lauwers, and two other teenage boys present at the murder were all high on what they believed to be mescaline. It was likely PCP or LSD. Over the course of several hours, Lauwers was stabbed 17–36 times, burned, had his eyeballs gouged out, and had stones shoved down his throat. The Satanic rituals and torture involved in the murder caused it to become sensational news across the nation.

Two days after his arrest, Kasso hanged himself in his jail cell.

According to Parker and Auerhahn (1998), the widely believed association between PCP and violence is based almost entirely upon case-study research, which often uses as subjects persons with psychiatric disturbances. Discussions of PCP and its effect on aggression are inconsistent in the literature (Hoaken & Stewart, 2003). However, one researcher (Siegel, 1978, in Parker & Auerhahn, 1998) has concluded that individuals who are emotionally stable and under the influence of PCP will likely not behave in a manner very different from their usual behavior. A unique link between PCP use and violent crime is not conclusively supported by official crime statistics (Parker & Auerhahn, 1998); and rates of assault charges have been shown to be increased in arrestees testing negative (by urinalysis) for illicit drugs compared to those testing positive for PCP in at least one sample (Wish, 1986, in Parker & Auerhahn, 1998). Although PCP-positive arrestees were characterized by a greater likelihood of robbery charges compared to other offenses, Wish speculates that this may be a demographically related artifact—PCP users were often younger than the average illicit drug user and coincided with the demographic most often associated with robbery arrests. On balance, others (e.g., Tapert et al., 2001) report PCP users may engage in very violent or destructive behaviors while high, due to profoundly impaired judgment and reduced fear of pain. Overall, any current understanding of the relationship between PCP and violent behavior is, at best, based upon mixed evidence and not on any body of systematized empirical research, and more work is needed to further this understanding. Furthermore, while Antron Singleton's pattern of PCP use may suggest a substance use disorder, the relationship between PCP use disorders and crime and violence remains largely unexplored.

Sedatives

To date, the literature on sedative-related disorders, crime, and violence is virtually non-existent. Some attention has been paid to the relationship between benzodiazepines and aggression, and numerous case reports have linked the two since the introduction of benzodiazepines in the 1960s. Although clinicians have dismissed the clinical evidence (even prescribing benzodiazepines as "antiaggression" medications), animal and human studies alike suggest benzodiazepines may increase aggression by interfering with the anxiety or threat-detection system. These effects, however, may be explained by individual differences or dosage levels (Hoaken & Stewart, 2003).

Other Studies

Psychosocial, Psychopathological, and Medical Correlates

Kerridge and colleagues (2009) examined psychosocial and psychopathological correlates of substance use disorders in a large representative sample (n = 6982) of U.S. local jail inmates. Results indicated high rates of substance use disorders (see Table 4.3), which were associated with homelessness in the year prior to the offense, single relationship status (i.e., never married, widowed, separated, or divorced) and ethnicity (African Americans and Caucasians were found to be at a higher risk of developing a substance use disorder compared to Hispanics). Additionally, compared to inmates without substance use disorders, those with these disorders were characterized by older age at first conviction, increased number of convictions prior to the current offense, psychosocial problems during childhood or adolescence (involvement with peers who participate in crime, peer drug use, parental substance use, physical and/or sexual abuse), having a girlfriend or boyfriend who served time (violent offenders only), diagnosis of or treatment for a mental disorder, having considered or attempted suicide prior to the current offense, and various forms of psychopathology (depression symptoms, delusions or hallucinations, anger management difficulties). Saladin and colleagues (2003) found PTSD symptom severity predicted alcohol and drug cravings following trauma and drug cues in alcohol-dependent and cocaine-dependent victims of violent crime. Additionally, substance abuse (drugs but not alcohol) significantly increased the relative risk for rearrest in HIV-positive offenders in a Seattle, Washington County, correctional facility (Harris et al., 2002); and Logan and Leukefeld (2000) found levels of recent violence to be associated with increased HIV risk behavior (more frequent sex and more sex partners, HIV sex partners, drug use, and intravenous drug-using sex partners) in a Kentucky sample of 754 crack cocaine users.

Substance-Related Disorders and Intimate Partner Violence

Studies of domestic violence perpetrators have shown high rates of substance-related disorders in these individuals (e.g., Kraanen et al., 2010; Stuart et al., 2003—see Table 4.3). Couples that enter treatment for substance abuse have very high rates of partner violence. For example, 54–66% of couples report one or more episodes of IPV in the 12 months prior to substance abuse treatment, and rates of at least one IPV episode in the previous year for married or cohabitating patients entering treatment for alcoholism are 4–6 times higher than national samples (Klostermann et al., 2010). Longitudinal day-to-day diary studies of married or cohabitating men recruited from substance abuse treatment programs (e.g., Fals-Stewart, 2003; Fals-Stewart et al., 2003) indicate a significantly higher likelihood of male-to-female physical aggression on days after substance use (11 times higher for serious physical aggression). Fals-Stewart (2003) found 60% of all episodes of aggression to occur within two hours of drinking by the male partner. Additionally, Fals-Stewart and colleagues (2003) found specific substance use (i.e., alcohol and cocaine, but not cannabis and opiates) to be associated with significantly greater daily likelihood of male-to-female physical aggression.

Kraanen and colleagues (2010) found that more than a third of 158 forensic outpatients who committed IPV were intoxicated at the time of the offense and that those with substance use disorders were more likely to be so compared to those without. Additionally, those with substance use disorders were more likely than those without to have used or threatened to use a weapon against their partners or former partners and to victimize non-family members (though differences were not statistically significant). In a sample of 72 men and 124 women from inpatient and outpatient substance use treatment programs, Parrott and colleagues (2003) found that PTSD increases the risk for partner violence more so among those with cocaine dependence compared to those with alcohol dependence. Stuart and colleagues (2003) emphasize the importance of assessing substance use and abuse as part of domestic violence intervention programs and offering adjunct or integrated treatment for alcohol use disorders (see also Klostermann et al., 2010).

Origins of Crime and Violence in Substance-Related Disorders: Theoretical Explanations and Etiological Mechanisms

Contributions from psychological and neurobiological theorists regarding the etiology of criminality and violent behavior in substance-related disorders remain largely absent, though theoretical models of drug-crime relationships have proliferated in the criminological literature. The "chicken-egg" question (i.e., which comes first in an opiate addict's career, addiction or crime?) is the most common theoretical framework in research studies on the relationship between drug use and crime, dating back to the 1920s. About half of these studies found that opiate addiction came first, a result explained by **enslavement theory**, which argued that opiate addiction enslaves otherwise law-abiding individuals to the point that they must commit crimes to support their drug use. The other studies concluded that criminality came first, with addiction being merely a later stage in a preexisting deviant lifestyle. Unfortunately, methodological shortcomings, such as focusing on addicts in treatment and forgetting those in the criminal justice system or those street addicts never receiving treatment, small sample sizes, and inadequate measures, plagued this literature for some time (Inciardi & Pottieger, 1998).

According to Inciardi and Pottieger (1998), the answer depends upon the type of measure that is used. For example, Table 4.5 lists the mean ages both at first use of various substances and at first criminal activity in a sample of 356 heroin addicts. According to lines 3 and 4, crime precedes heroin use. However, considering marijuana (almost always the first substance requiring contact with the illegal drug market), lines 2 and 3 suggest street drug use and street crime begin almost simultaneously. Finally, lines 1 and 2 suggest that alcohol use (i.e., the use of at least one type of substance) precedes crime by several years. Thus, three different answers—crime first, crime and drugs at the same time, and drugs first—become apparent even within the same data set.

Hough (1996, in Simpson, 2003) asserts that the causal process can take several forms: (1) drug dependence can predate and precipitate other forms of crime; (2) property criminality can predate drug misuse and facilitate experimental or casual misuse, which may lead to dependence; (3) drug dependence may amplify property offending; and (4) drug use and property offending may increase together in an upward spiral. Simpson (2003)

Table 4.5 Mean Ages (in Years) of Age at First Substance Use and Crime

	Males	Females
1. First alcohol use	12.8	13.8
2. First marijuana use	15.5	15.4
3. First crime	15.1	15.9
4. First heroin use	18.7	18.2

Source: Inciardi & Pottieger (1998).

argues against the established recreational versus dependent drug use dichotomy, stating that it is problematic and does not account for the concept of the "drug career," which may also include what he refers to as "persistent drug use." Although Hough (1996, in Simpson, 2003) proposed that persistent drug use (other than of heroin and cocaine) appeared unrelated to persistent predatory offending, Simpson (2003) asserts that a strong relationship exists between persistent drug use (beyond the use of heroin and cocaine) and revenue-raising crime. A simple unilateral causal explanation, according to Simpson, fails to account for the complexities of drug using careers (e.g., transitions through different forms of drug using behavior are accompanied by changes in drug-related crime); and both drug classifications and the drug use–crime relationship are produced by local social contexts and environments. Inciardi and Surratt's (2011) Miami study of cocaine-dependent women sex traders demonstrates such a complex interplay of escalating drug use and utilitarian criminality.

Parker and Auerhahn (1998) identified four recent theoretical explanations for the linkages among drugs, alcohol, and violence:

1. **Fagan's approach** theorizes that intoxication influences aggression by impacting cognitive functioning, in a manner that varies according to the substance used, so that intoxicated persons tend to have limited response sets in social situations. This effect is moderated by the context in which behavior occurs: the social and cultural meanings of how individuals behave while intoxicated, understandings about how intoxication impacts judgment, the ability to perceive social cues and to focus on both long-term and short-term desires and outcomes, the nature of the setting, and the absence or presence of formal or informal means of social control.
2. **Parker's selective disinhibition approach** suggests that internalized norms against violence may become disinhibited in certain situations and contexts.
3. Another explanation considers the cultural consequences of the availability of alcohol (i.e., the spatial and demographic distribution of alcohol outlets).
4. **Goldstein's tripartite framework** offers an explanation that considers *psychopharmacological violence*, which stems from properties of the drug itself; *economic compulsive violence*, which is associated with the high costs of the use of illicit drugs and is motivated by the need or desire to obtain especially those drugs that produce strong physical and psychological dependencies, such as opiates and cocaine; and *systemic violence*, which is associated with the traditionally aggressive interactions related to drug distribution and use.

New York homicide studies applying the tripartite model have found nearly half of the crimes (and, in some cases, over half) to be psychopharmacological in nature, followed at a distant second and third by systematic and economic compulsive crimes. Psychopharmacological homicides were most associated with alcohol, and crack was most prominent in economic compulsive and systematic homicides (Lipton & Johnson, 1998). Similar findings have been reported in street studies of drug-related violence in drug users and dealers (Goldstein, 1998). A later New York homicide study found that, among drug-related homicides, 38% were psychopharmacological, and the rest were due to drug-dealing business practices (Tardiff et al., 2002).

Hoaken and Stewart (2003) articulate four differential (but not mutually exclusive) reasons for a drugs-aggression relationship: (1) violent crimes for the purpose of gaining access to drugs or resources to purchase drugs; (2) violence to settle disputes in an illegal drug-dealing business that is unregulated and ruleless; (3) violence and drug use existing coincidentally, both being by-products of the same factors (e.g., high sensation seeking); and (4) violence as a direct effect of drugs on the individual. The latter can be classified into direct pharmacological effects (intoxication), neurotoxic effects (damage caused by sustained use), and withdrawal effects (abstinence immediately after prolonged use). According to McBride and McCoy (2006), although many studies have indicated that drug use does not initiate a criminal career, drug use—particularly its frequency—significantly impacts that career in terms of its extent, direction, and duration. Furthermore, the onset of criminal behavior may lead to subcultural participation and risky decision making that involves the use of high-risk drugs. Finally, in terms of limitations, toxicology studies of violence are limited by blood and urine testing, which only detect recent use so might not detect substances at the time of arrest and testing, and because self-reported information is vulnerable to memory recall error (Darke, 2010); and theoretical and empirical investigations of the relation of substance use and violence have been limited by lumping different forms of illicit drugs together (Parker & Auerhahn, 1998).

Sociological Theoretical Perspectives

Sociological theorists have emphasized the influences of social factors on the relationship between criminal behavior and substance use (but not necessarily substance use *disorders*, which are largely not addressed by these theories). For example, frequent drug use, crime, and high-risk sexual behavior may be integral to subcultural social roles—"taking care of business," so to speak—for the street drug user. Thus, drug use and crime may not be related in cause directly or linearly but instead be intertwined in a mutually reinforcing set of behaviors specific to a subcultural context (McBride & McCoy, 2006). Ecological theoretical analysts have proposed that the drug-crime relationship is spurious—an artifact of common etiology in both behaviors, a consequence, for example, of similar environmental conditions such as poverty and the lack of social control and economic opportunity. Radical criminological theorists maintain that the apparent drugs-crime relationship is an artifact of laws from the early 1900s that effectively criminalized a variety of behaviors associated with drug use. Although a significant amount of evidence suggests that crimes committed by drug users tend to be violations of drug laws (i.e., possession, distribution), this perspective assumes the drug-crime relationship would simply disappear if drugs were just decriminalized—ignoring the psychopharmacological aspects of the drug-crime relationship as well as evidence indicating that crime may predate drug use and that both behaviors may be mutually reinforced in development by similar etiological variables (McBride & McCoy, 2006).

Comorbidity

Darke (2010) emphasizes the need to consider the role of preexisting comorbid psychopathology (known to be strongly associated with elevated rates of psychopathology in general) in the relationship between substance use and violence. These other forms of psychopathology may themselves be associated with self-harm (e.g., major depression) or impulsivity, risk taking, and violence (e.g., ASPD, borderline personality disorder); and substance use may exacerbate other preexisting psychopathological conditions (e.g., psychosis) and increase the risk of violence. Hall and colleagues found high rates of comorbidity in a sample of 301 amphetamine users, which was significantly associated with route (i.e., injection) and frequency of amphetamine administration. Also, Zweben and colleagues (2004; see Table 4.4) found high rates of violent behavior and a wide range of comorbid psychiatric symptoms in 1016 methamphetamine users who met DSM-IV criteria for methamphetamine dependence; the study examined self-reported psychiatric comorbidity and violence in this multisite outpatient treatment sample.

Policy and Treatment Implications

The criminal justice system can become a virtual "revolving door" to substance-dependent offenders when their dependency issues are not addressed (Warner & Kramer, 2009), and the relationship between substance-related disorders and crime has already begun to have policy implications in specific jurisdictions. For example, on November 7, 2000, voters in the State of California passed Proposition 36, the Substance Abuse and Crime Prevention Act of 2000, which prohibits incarceration and mandates treatment for first-time nonviolent offenders convicted of simple drug possession. In the United States, drug offenders are the fastest-growing segment of prison populations (Auerhahn, 2004). Auerhahn (2004) used computer dynamic system simulation modeling to examine changes in the composition of the California prisons drug offender population over an 18-year period (1980–1998). Results indicated that incarcerated drug offenders increased in prevalence from 10 to 30% over this period and that conviction histories and violent convictions steadily increased among drug offenders during this time. Projections forward to the year 2020 indicate that Proposition 36 will have some impact on the composition of the population of drug offenders (i.e., age will decrease, though ethnic or racial composition will remain constant) but will not reduce the proportion of drug offenders housed in California's prison system.

A portion of the studies examining the relationship between substance-related disorders and crime have examined both the effects of drug-treatment programs on substance-abusing or substance-dependent individuals who engage in various forms of criminal behavior and how these programs—aimed primarily at reducing substance-related disorder symptomatology—may actually reduce levels of criminality indirectly. Studies of heroin addicts have shown that property crime was significantly reduced during treatment periods and that legal supervision with urine testing was ineffective compared to methadone treatment programs in reducing crime (Anglin & Perrochet, 1998). In a large Australian evaluation study of pharmacotherapies for opioid dependence (997 heroin users and 300 methadone patients participating in a national series of 11 clinical trials across multiple sites), Digiusto and colleagues (2006) found reductions in crime and heroin expenditure for those remaining in treatment at a three-month follow-up, though there were no significant differences between the effects of pharmacotherapy type (i.e., methadone, buprenorphine, LAAM, or naltrexone treatment) on criminal behavior. (Type of therapy was associated, however, with differential effects upon heroin expenditure.) Furthermore, the promising effectiveness of *multisystemic therapy* (MST), which is based on Bronfenbrenner's (1979) social ecology theory, and of intermediate-level sentencing options (i.e., Pennsylvania's Restrictive Intermediate Punishments) in substance-related disordered offenders has already been discussed (Randall & Cunningham, 203; Warner & Kramer, 2009). Finally, Leukefeld, Gallego, and Farabee (1997) suggest that the criminal justice system—if based on a model of treatment and control—could function as a means for keeping drug users in treatment in order to reduce usage, injections, and the spread of diseases such as HIV. Using criminal justice authority as external motivation for treatment compliance remains one of the most consistent indicators for increasing treatment duration for drug users, as previous studies have demonstrated that drug users in community corrections remain in treatment longer.

Conclusion

Antron Singleton perpetrated an unspeakably heinous act of violence, and it may never be known whether his pattern of substance use *caused* his murderous impulses or merely freed those already existing within him. Substance-related disorders appear to be among the least-studied disorders in the overarching topic of mental illness and crime. However, an impressive body of literature has been assembled on the relationship between drug *use* and crime for a number of different illicit substances, which is rooted largely in the disciplines of criminology and sociology. The apparent lack of studies related to substance-related disorders and crime, then, may merely reflect a differential paradigm focus rather than a lack of data *per se*. In other words, the deleterious effects of substance use have been quantified by psychologists and neuroscientists as *disorder* and by criminologists and sociologists as constructs native to their own disciplines. These studies have focused on the "chicken-egg" question and have outlined the intricate nuances surrounding the temporal relationship between drugs and crime, as well as discussing how both the pharmacological effects of substances and situational and contextual factors may play a role in drug use's relationship with crime and violence. Most of the criminological studies of substance use and crime and violence do not address the potential presence of other mental disorders, for which the substance use may be serving as self-medication. Thus, it is unknown whether the substance use or possible comorbid psychopathology may be playing more of a key role in the criminal or violent behavior in these cases.

KEY TERMS

addictive behaviors
approximate simultaneity
cross-tolerance
enslavement theory
Fagan's approach
Goldstein's tripartite framework
Harrison Narcotic Tax Act
medical model [of addiction]
mesolimbic reward pathway
moral model [of addiction]
Parker's selective disinhibition approach
physical dependence
potentiation

psychological dependence
spiritual model [of addiction]
substance abuse
substance dependence
tolerance
withdrawal

REVIEW QUESTIONS

1. Explain how an understanding of the historical conceptions of substance use disorders and the progression toward illegality of certain psychoactive substances is important for discussing the relationship between substance use disorders and crime. Does this discussion begin and end with the legality (or, rather, the illegality) of the substances themselves? Why or why not?
2. Examine Tables 4.3 and 4.4 and the summaries of the research studies in the "A Closer Look" sections for each disorder in this chapter. Discuss how prevalence rates of crimes in disordered populations and of disorders in criminal populations differ among these disorders, if at all. Using the information in the tables, speculate as to how methodological approaches may have occasioned differences in prevalence rates (e.g., in terms of study types, sample characteristics, methodological issues, or other concerns).
3. Compare and contrast the classes of substances discussed in this chapter in terms of their proposed contributions to crime and violence. In your opinion, which class is most dangerous and which is least? Explain your answer.
4. Compare and contrast approximate simultaneity with enslavement theory. In your opinion, which theory of the crime-drug chronology has more merit and why? Why is it important to understand the temporal ordering of first crime and first drug use?
5. Discuss how Parker and Auerhahn's (1998) four theoretical explanations for the relationship between drugs, alcohol, and violence may (or may not) apply to substance use at the level of clinical *disorder* (as opposed to simply at the level of *use*).

5

Schizophrenia and Other Psychotic Disorders

HERBERT WILLIAM MULLIN

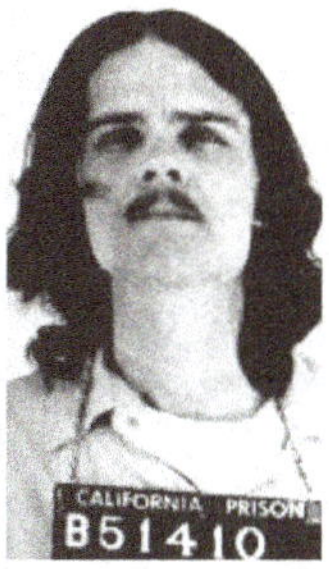

Herbert Mullin was born in Salinas, California, on April 18, 1947. The son of Catholic parents, he was raised in an oppressively religious home. As a child, he was described as bright and gentle-natured. He had many friends in high school and was envied as one of the "popular" crowd. He played varsity football, had a steady girlfriend, and was voted "most likely to succeed."

Psychological problems began for Mullin in late adolescence (a point when schizophrenia characteristically surfaces). He experienced delusions and a range of involuntary repetitive behaviors, such as echolalia and echopraxia. He was institutionalized on several occasions and diagnosed with paranoid schizophrenia. At one point, he began to hear voices commanding him to shave his head and to burn his penis with a cigarette. He also wrote dozens of letters to strangers, signing them "A human sacrifice, Herb Mullin."

On October 13, 1972, Mullin bashed the skull of Lawrence White, an alcoholic drifter, with a baseball bat. Eleven days later, he picked up coed hitchhiker Mary Guilfoyle, stabbed her in the heart, disemboweled her, and scattered her organs on the shoulder of the road. On November 2, 1972 ("All Souls' Day"), he stabbed a priest, Father Henry Tomei, to death in his confessional booth. He also shot and stabbed a drug dealer's wife and children and a young married couple. On February 6, 1973, he murdered four teenage campers execution-style. A week later, while driving through Santa Cruz, he pulled to the curb and shot a retired boxer, Fred Perez, in his front yard with a rifle. In total, Mullin brutally murdered 13 victims.

Mullin's crimes had decidedly religious overtones. He claimed he was a hero, a sacrificial scapegoat, and that his victims telepathically gave him permission to kill them. He also claimed his homicides were necessary to prevent catastrophic earthquakes from destroying California and that his war veteran father had telepathically commanded him to murder. He believed he was obeying God's "commandment" to make human sacrifices for the greater good of humanity. Mullin's birthday (April 18, 1947) held great significance for him. April 18th was the anniversary of the 1906 San Francisco earthquake and the anniversary of Albert Einstein's death. Both of these events would, in his psychotic mind, give him a cosmic duty to kill. Mullin was ultimately convicted of many of these homicides and sentenced to life imprisonment with the possibility of parole when he reaches 78 years of age.

The world of *psychosis* is one of chaos, disruption, and disorganization. In it, the psychological boundary separating one's internal experiences from external reality, a boundary that for some is a nearly solid "wall" and for others already a mere thin veil, becomes blurred, compromised, or even obliterated. Thoughts, beliefs, feelings, behaviors, and perceptions can become confusing and frightening as the barrier disintegrates and inner and outer worlds collide. This psychotic "break" from reality may occur suddenly or develop insidiously over months and even years.

Herbert Mullin suffered from an illness known as schizophrenia—one of a group of similar disorders outlined in the DSM-IV-TR, DSM-5, and other diagnostic systems. Mullin's separation from reality brought over a dozen innocent lives to a tragic end, for reasons not likely to be readily understood by others. However, as unusual and bizarre as his symptoms may seem (as psychotic symptoms often do), it must be understood that they represent his attempts to make sense of his own unraveling sense of self, the reference point for assessing our perceptions (Dorman, 2008), as he gradually descended into psychosis. Although his murderous behavior exemplifies *how* crime and violence may manifest within the context of schizophrenia and other psychotic disorders, discussions in the pages that follow will demonstrate how researchers have attempted to address a more important question about the schizophrenia-crime relationship: *why*.

Diagnostic Criteria and the Prevalence of Psychotic Disorders

Psychotic disorders are a class of illnesses characterized by delusions and hallucinations. The DSM-IV-TR defines a **delusion** as a "false belief based on an incorrect inference about external reality that is firmly sustained despite what almost everyone else believes and despite what constitutes incontrovertible and obvious proof of evidence to the contrary" (APA, 2000, p. 821). The DSM-5 states that delusions are "fixed beliefs not amenable to change in light of conflicting evidence" (APA, 2013, p. 87). The DSM-5 descriptions of delusions are listed in Table 5.1.

The DSM-IV-TR defines a **hallucination** as "a sensory perception that has the compelling sense of reality of a true sensation, but that occurs without external stimulation of the relevant sensory organ" (APA, 2000, p. 823); the DSM-5 states that hallucinations are "perception-like experiences that occur without an external stimulus" (APA, 2013, p. 87). In essence, they are sensory perception without sensory input. Hallucinations may occur along any sensory modality—sight (visual), hearing (auditory), smell (olfactory), touch (tactile), and taste (gustatory). An individual might see the Devil coming out of the ceiling, hear voices commenting on his or her

Table 5.1 DSM-5 Classifications of Delusions

Delusions
Bizarre: A delusion that is clearly implausible and not understandable to same-culture peers and does not derive from ordinary life experiences.
Nihilistic: Involves the conviction that a major catastrophe will occur.
Erotomanic: When an individual believes falsely that another person is in love with him or her.
Grandiose: When an individual believes that he or she has exceptional abilities, wealth, or fame.
Of control: The belief that one's body or actions are being acted on or manipulated by some outside force.
Referential: The belief that certain gestures, comments, environmental cues, and so forth are directed at oneself.
Persecutory: The belief that one is going to be harmed, harassed, and so forth by an individual, organization, or other group.
Somatic: A delusion that focuses on preoccupations regarding health and organ function.
Thought withdrawal: The belief that one's thoughts have been "removed" by some outside force.
Thought insertion: The belief that alien thoughts have been put into one's mind.

Source: APA (2013, p. 87). Reprinted with permission from the *Diagnostic and Statistical Manual of Mental Disorders*, Fifth Edition

behavior, smell perfumes or foul odors that are not actually present, feel insects crawling on or under his or her skin, or taste food in his or her mouth. The most common type of hallucination is the auditory type. The DSM-IV-TR distinguishes between hallucinations and illusions—the latter being actual external stimuli that are misperceived or misinterpreted (APA, 2000). Interestingly, this distinction is not made in the DSM-5; however, the newer edition does explicitly state that "hallucinations must occur in the context of a clear sensorium; those that occur while falling asleep (*hypnagogic*) or waking up (*hypnopompic*) are considered to be within the range of normal experience" (pp. 87–88).

Schizophrenia is a devastating mental illness, and only one of the larger class or spectrum of psychotic disorders. This illness is characterized by a cluster of symptoms (see Table 5.2), which are categorized into two distinct types. **Positive symptoms** represent ways of thinking and behaving that indicate something has been added to the way a person normally thinks and behaves. These include delusions, hallucinations, **catatonic behavior**, and **disorganized speech**, which is referred to by some as **thought disorder** (see Box 5.1 for explanations of different types of disorganized speech). **Negative symptoms** (i.e., *affective flattening, alogia*, and *avolition*), on the other hand, represent ways of thinking, feeling, and behaving that suggest something is missing or has been taken away from a person's normal experience. Disorganized speech patterns reflect disrupted and unorganized thoughts and may be characterized by jumping "off-track" during conversations, speaking with random and jumbled words, and the use of words that do not make sense to others. Catatonic behaviors occur when an individual moves or behaves in a disorganized manner, such as remaining completely still in unusual positions, moving in ways that do not serve a purpose, mimicking the speech or behaviors of others, or refusing to talk or respond to others. (The DSM-5 has now articulated diagnostic criteria for "Catatonia Associated With Another Mental Disorder [Catatonia Specifier]" for schizophrenia and other disorders, and these criteria explicate the various forms of catatonic behavior; see Table 5.3 and Box 5.2.). Affective flattening refers to a lack of emotional response or experience as suggested by an individual's facial expressions (as if their emotions are missing). Alogia refers to an absence of thoughts, which is indicated by "poverty of speech" (e.g., very limited talking or short, one-word responses). Finally, avolition refers to the lack of will to engage in behavior that is goal directed or purpose driven.

Other problems commonly associated with schizophrenia include isolation or withdrawal from others. Schizophrenia may develop gradually or rapidly and can begin at any point in one's life, though it is typically first seen between the late teens and the mid-30s (and, on average, slightly later in life in women than in men). Women with schizophrenia typically suffer more from affective (emotional) symptoms, paranoid delusions, and hallucinations, and men tend to express more negative symptoms. Also, schizophrenia rarely occurs alone as a diagnosis. Depression, anxiety disorders, or substance abuse often accompany schizophrenia (APA, 2000, 2013).

Prevalence and Incidence Rates of Schizophrenia

The DSM-IV-TR indicates that adult prevalence rates of schizophrenia are often reported in the 0.5% to 1.5% range (APA, 2000), and the DSM-5 reports lifetime prevalence rates of approximately 0.3% to 0.7%

Table 5.2 DSM-5 Diagnostic Criteria for Schizophrenia

295.90 (F20.9) Schizophrenia

A. Two (or more) of the following, each present for a significant portion of time during a 1-month period (or less if successfully treated). At least one of these must be (1), (2), or (3):

1. Delusions.
2. Hallucinations.
3. Disorganized speech (e.g., frequent derailment or incoherence).
4. Grossly disorganized or catatonic behavior.
5. Negative symptoms (i.e., diminished emotional expression or avolition).

(Continued)

(Continued)

B. For a significant portion of the time since the onset of the disturbance, level of functioning in one or more major areas, such as work, interpersonal relations, or self-care, is markedly below the level achieved prior to the onset (or when the onset is in childhood or adolescence, there is failure to achieve expected level of interpersonal, academic, or occupational functioning).

C. Continuous signs of the disturbance persist for at least 6 months. This 6-month period must include at least 1 month of symptoms (or less if successfully treated) that meet Criterion A (i.e., active-phase symptoms) and may include periods of prodromal or residual symptoms. During these prodromal or residual periods, the signs of the disturbance may be manifested by only negative symptoms or two or more symptoms listed in Criterion A present in attenuated form (e.g., odd beliefs, unusual perceptual experiences).

D. Schizoaffective disorder and depressive or bipolar disorder with psychotic features have been ruled out because either 1) no major depressive or manic episodes have occurred concurrently with the active-phase symptoms; or 2) if mood episodes have occurred during active-phase symptoms, they have been present for a minority of the total duration of the active and residual periods of the illness.

E. The disturbance is not due to the direct physiological effects of a substance (e.g., a drug of abuse, a medication) or another medical condition.

F. If there is a history of autism spectrum disorder or a communication disorder of childhood onset, the additional diagnosis of schizophrenia is made only if prominent delusions or hallucinations, in addition to the other required symptoms of schizophrenia, are also present for at least 1 month (or less if successfully treated).

Specify if:

The following course specifiers are only to be used after a 1-year duration of the disorder and if they are not in contradiction to the diagnostic course criteria.

First episode, currently in acute episode: First manifestation of the disorder meeting the defining diagnostic symptom and time criteria. An *acute episode* is a time period in which the symptom criteria are fulfilled.

First episode, currently in partial remission: *Partial remission* is a period of time during which an improvement after a previous episode is maintained and in which the defining criteria of the disorder are only partially fulfilled.

First episode, currently in full remission: Full remission is a period of time after a previous episode during which no disorder-specific symptoms are present.

Multiple episodes, currently in acute episode: Multiple episodes may be determined after a minimum of two episodes (i.e., after a first episode, a remission and a minimum of one relapse).

Multiple episodes, currently in partial remission

Multiple episodes, currently in full remission

Continuous: Symptoms fulfilling the diagnostic symptom criteria of the disorder are remaining for the majority of the illness course, with subthreshold symptom periods being very brief relative to the overall course.

Unspecified

Specify if:

With catatonia (refer to the criteria for catatonia associated with another mental disorder [Table 5.3] for definition).

Specify current severity:

Severity is rated by a quantitative assessment of the primary symptoms of psychosis, including delusions, hallucinations, disorganized speech, abnormal psychomotor behavior, and negative symptoms. Each of these symptoms may be rated for its current severity (most severe in the last 7 days) on a 5-point scale ranging from 0 (not present) to 4 (present and severe).

Note: Diagnosis of schizophrenia can be made without using this severity specifier.

Source: APA (2013, pp. 99–100) . Reprinted with permission from the *Diagnostic and Statistical Manual of Mental Disorders*, Fifth Edition

Table 5.3 DSM-5 Diagnostic Criteria for Catatonia Associated With Another Mental Disorder (Catatonia Specifier)

293.89 (F06.1) Catatonia Associated With Another Mental Disorder (Catatonia Specifier)

A. The clinical picture is dominated by three (or more) of the following symptoms:

1. Stupor (i.e., no psychomotor activity; not actively relating to environment).
2. Catalepsy (i.e., passive induction of a posture held against gravity).
3. Waxy flexibility (i.e., slight, even resistance to positioning by examiner).
4. Mutism (i.e., no, or very little, verbal response [exclude if known aphasia]).
5. Negativism (i.e., opposition or no response to instructions or external stimuli).
6. Posturing (i.e., spontaneous and active maintenance of a posture against gravity).
7. Mannerism (i.e., odd, circumstantial caricature of normal actions).
8. Stereotypy (i.e., repetitive, abnormally frequent, non-goal-directed behaviors).
9. Agitation, not influenced by external stimuli.
10. Grimacing.
11. Echolalia (i.e., mimicking another's speech).
12. Echopraxia (i.e., mimicking another's movements).

Coding note: Indicate the name of the associated mental disorder when recoding the name of the condition (i.e., 293.89 [F06.1] catatonia associated with major depressive disorder). Code first the associated mental disorder (e.g., neurodevelopmental disorder, brief psychotic disorder, schizophreniform disorder, schizophrenia, schizoaffective disorder, bipolar disorder, major depressive disorder, or other mental disorder) (e.g., 295.70 [F25.1] schizoaffective disorder, depressive type; 293.89 [F06.01] catatonia associated with schizoaffective disorder).

Source: APA (2013, pp. 119–120) . Reprinted with permission from the *Diagnostic and Statistical Manual of Mental Disorders*, Fifth Edition (Copyright © 2013). American Psychiatric Association. All rights reserved.

(APA, 2013). A 1% prevalence rate is often reported in textbooks and other sources (Bhugra, 2005; Bobes et al., 2009). Incidence rates are often reported in the range of 0.5 to 5.0 per 10,000 individuals per year (APA, 2000), though lower estimates have been reported (McGrath et al., 2004; Saha et al., 2005). *Birth cohort studies* suggest some geographic and historical variations in incidence. For example, an elevated risk has been reported among urban-born individuals in comparison to rural-born individuals (APA, 2000) and in richer countries in comparison to poorer countries (Saha et al., 2005).

Other Psychotic Disorders

Diagnoses of other psychotic disorders are based upon presentations of some psychotic symptoms and not others, the inclusion of mood disorder symptomatology, or variations in the length of symptom presentation. Table 5.4 lists and describes the various psychotic disorders found in the DSM-IV-TR. The DSM-5 has renamed this class of disorders "Schizophrenia Spectrum and Other Psychotic Disorders," and the disorders remain largely consistent with those in the DSM-IV-TR. Exceptions include the removal of shared psychotic disorder and the addition of substance / medication-induced psychotic disorder (formerly substance-induced psychotic disorder), psychotic disorder due to another medical condition (formerly psychotic disorder due to a general medical condition), other specified schizophrenia spectrum and other psychotic disorder, and unspecified schizophrenia spectrum and other psychotic disorder (the latter two roughly translating into the former DSM-IV-TR designation of psychotic disorder NOS). Additionally, *schizotypal personality disorder*—considered to be part of the schizophrenia spectrum—has now been included among these disorders in the DSM-5. The ICD-10

BOX 5.1 DISORGANIZED SPEECH

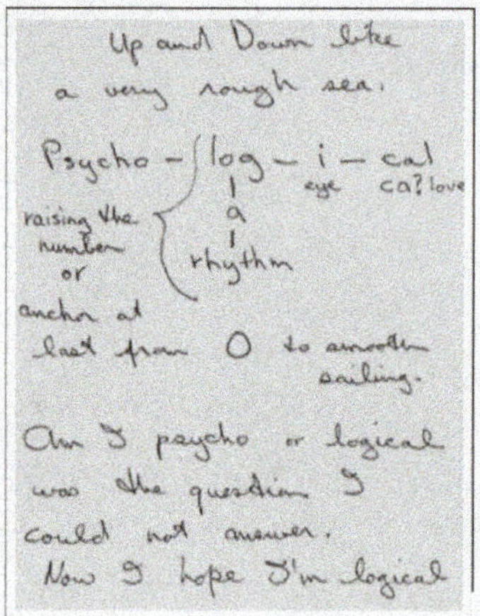

There are several types of disorganized speech patterns (Andreasen, 1979).

- **Tangentiality:** Replying to a question in an oblique, tangential, or even irrelevant manner.
- **Derailment:** A pattern of spontaneous speech in which the ideas slip off the track onto another one that is clearly but obliquely related or onto one that is completely unrelated.
- **Disorganized speech:** Speech marked by poorly organized ideas and difficult for others to understand (i.e., "**word salad**").
- **Neologisms:** New word formations. A completely new word or phrase whose derivation cannot be understood (e.g., a "geshinker").
- **Word approximations:** Old words that are used in a new and unconventional way, or new words that are developed by conventional rules of word formation (e.g., "handshoes" for gloves).
- **Circumstantiality:** A pattern of speech that is very indirect and delayed in reaching its goal idea.

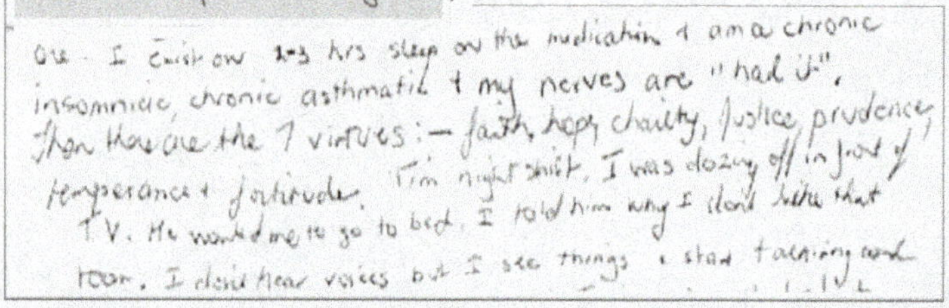

BOX 5.2 CATATONIC BEHAVIOR

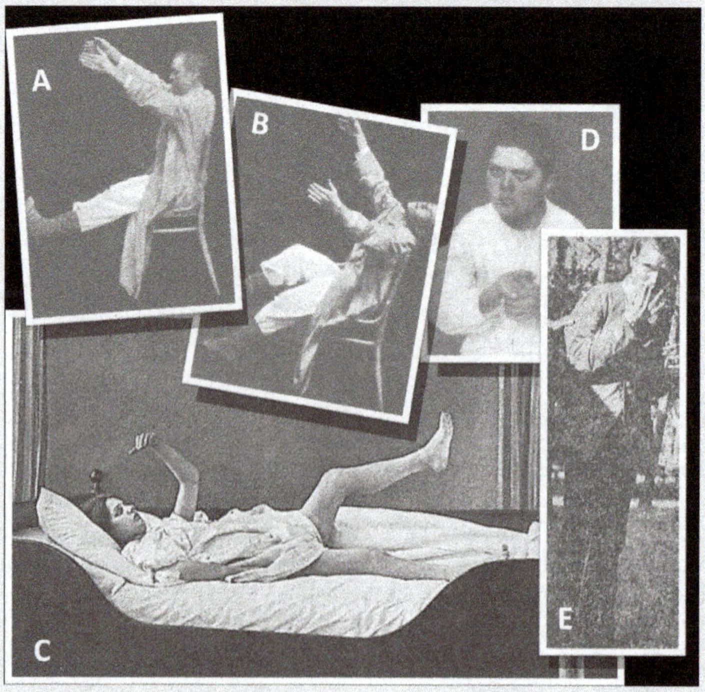

Late nineteenth- and early twentieth-century images of catatonic behavior: Catalepsy, waxy flexibility (A, B), posturing (C), stupor (D), and mannerism (E).

classifies this group of disorders under "Schizophrenia, Schizotypal and Delusional Disorders"; these include schizophrenia, schizotypal disorder, persistent delusional disorders, acute and transient psychotic disorders, induced delusional disorder, schizoaffective disorders, other nonorganic psychotic disorders, and unspecified nonorganic psychosis. The limited evidence available indicates that these other psychotic disorders are, overall, much more rare than schizophrenia (see Table 5.4), though lifetime prevalence of all psychotic disorders has been reported at rates as high as 3.48% (Perala et al., 2007).

Table 5.4 Other Psychotic Disorders

DSM-IV-TR[1]/DSM-5[2]	Description	Prevalence/Incidence
Schizophreniform Disorder	Characterized by a symptomatic presentation that is equivalent to Schizophrenia except for its duration (i.e., the disturbance lasts from 1 to 6 months) and the absence of a requirement that there be a decline in functioning.	Variable incidence across sociocultural settings. Low incidence in developed countries (i.e., five-fold less than schizophrenia), higher in developing countries.[1,2] Likely similar to that observed in schizophrenia.[2]
Schizoaffective Disorder	A disorder in which a mood episode and the active-phase symptoms of Schizophrenia occur together and were preceded or are followed by at least 2 weeks of delusions or hallucinations without prominent mood symptoms.	Detailed information lacking. Thought to be less common than schizophrenia.[1] Lifetime prevalence estimated to be 0.3%.[2]
Delusional Disorder	Characterized by at least 1 month of nonbizarre delusions without other active-phase symptoms of Schizophrenia.	Best estimate of population prevalence around 0.03%. Lifetime morbidity risk 0.05%–0.1%.[1] Lifetime prevalence estimated at around 0.2%.[2]
Brief Psychotic Disorder	A disorder that lasts more than 1 day and remits by 1 month.	Rare in clinical settings in developed countries. Overall prevalence or incidence rates largely unknown.[1] May account for 9% of cases of first-onset psychosis in U.S.[2]
Shared Psychotic Disorder (Folie à Deux)[1]	Characterized by the presence of a delusion in an individual who is influenced by someone else.	Little systematic information available. Rare in clinical settings. May be more common in women than men.[1]
Psychotic Disorder Due to a General Medical Condition[1] (Psychotic Disorder Due to Another Medical Condition[2])	The psychotic symptoms are judged to be a direct physiological consequence of a general medical condition.	Prevalence rates difficult to estimate. Psychotic symptoms can be present in ≥ 40% of individuals with certain medical conditions (i.e., temporal lobe epilepsy).[1] Lifetime prevalence estimated to range from 0.21% to 0.54%.[2]
Substance-Induced Psychotic Disorder[1] (Substance / Medication-Induced Psychotic Disorder[2])	The psychotic symptoms are judged to be a direct physiological consequence of a drug of abuse, medication, or toxin exposure.	Not specified in DSM-IV-TR.[1] Prevalence unknown.[2]
Psychotic Disorder NOS (Other Specified Schizophrenia Spectrum and Other Psychotic Disorder; Unspecified Schizophrenia Spectrum and Other Psychotic Disorder[2])	Included for classifying psychotic presentations that do not meet the criteria for any of the specific Psychotic Disorders defined in this section or psychotic symptomatology about which there is inadequate or contradictory information.	Not specified in DSM-IV-TR[1] or DSM-5.[2]

Sources: [1]APA (2000); [2]APA (2013)

Theoretical Conceptualizations

Several theoretical perspectives have proven useful in the conceptualization of schizophrenia. Psychoanalytic theorists have proposed that the psychotic individual is characterized by ego defenses that are too weak, leaving him or her helplessly overwhelmed by primitive material from the id. Freud explained symptoms of schizophrenia and psychosis as a regression to an *autoerotic stage of development* accompanied by emotional withdrawal from external figures and internal objects (the internal picture of those people and things that satisfy the instinctual drives)—as a sort of primitive, detached, self-contained state of narcissistic self-absorption (Mitchell & Black, 1995). Later, Freud saw psychosis as a conflict between the ego and the external world (in contrast to neurosis, which was a conflict between the ego and id). Others have noted a complete lack of a barrier between internal and external experiences in schizophrenia patients (Gabbard, 2005). Neurobiological theorists explain schizophrenia and other psychotic disorders as a dysfunction in neurotransmitter systems or as a series of structural or functional deficits in brain anatomical components, for example, in the frontal lobe and its subregions or in the thalamus or cingulate gyrus (Haznedar et al., 2004; Mitelman et al., 2005; Zhou et al., 2005). Proposed etiological mechanisms include genetic transmission (i.e., family history of schizophrenia), prenatal complications, and even maternal exposure to influenza (Gabbard, 2005).

It is here that an interesting conceptual overlap between psychoanalytic and neurobiological theories can be observed. The former proposes a profound confusion between the inner and outer worlds of the individual with schizophrenia, the result of ego defenses that are too weak and leave him or her helplessly overwhelmed by primitive material from the id. A conceptual analogue in neurobiological theory lies in the functioning of the thalamus, which—as stated in Chapter 2—acts as a kind of relay station that receives information from all of the senses (except the sense of smell) and sends it on to the associated regions of the cerebral cortex for processing (Mitelman et al., 2005). The thalamus is also thought to process sensory information, receiving strong "back projections" from the cerebral cortex, and to play a role in recollective and familiarity memory given its functional connections to the hippocampus (Carlesimo et al., 2011). Thus, it would not be difficult to imagine the sensory and perceptual confusion that would occur if the critical connectivity between the thalamus and other brain regions was structurally compromised, as brain imaging evidence suggests it is in schizophrenia (Mitelman et al., 2005). Processed sensory information, memory material, and external data from the senses might all become hopelessly jumbled—a profound confusion between inner and outer worlds (see Box 5.3).

Cognitive and behavioral theorists have proposed that psychotic experiences are essentially normal phenomena that occur on a continuum in the general population. Most individuals are able to reject the idea that these experiences are externally caused and personally significant, the idea that forms the basis for delusions and hallucinations (e.g., "I am being poisoned"; "God is giving me special powers"; "My voices are coming from persecutors who want to kill me"; or "A transmitter is beaming my thoughts worldwide"). They do not develop full-blown psychotic symptoms because they make protective self-correcting decisions (e.g., "I thought I was hearing the voice of God, but more likely my mind is playing tricks"; or "Things look different, somehow, I must be stressed with all that's going on"). In the individual with schizophrenia, however, this is not the case. Instead, sensory input becomes distorted, disorganized, and confused with previous material from memory, and these individuals begin to perceive their own intentions as alien and externally controlled. Experiences and distressing interpretations are sustained and made worse by cognitive and behavioral responses (e.g., selective attention, thought suppression, and safety behaviors), as well as by emotional and physiological responses and environmental factors (Garety et al., 2001; Morrison, 2008). Interestingly, it has also been proposed that schizophrenia can be "learned" through a system of rewards. For example, the thinking of aberrant, irrelevant thoughts may be rewarded by anxiety reduction by removing disturbing ideation from consciousness (Mednick, 1958). Also, the "mentally ill" schizophrenic role could be reinforced by the short-term advantages of the deviant social role, such as avoiding military service or being disturbing to others and thereby avoiding unpleasant and increasing pleasant stimuli; this role could be selectively reinforced in patients by the culture of large psychiatric hospitals (Rosenbaum, 1969).

BOX 5.3 SCHIZOPHRENIA: OVERLAPPING PSYCHOANALYTIC AND NEUROBIOLOGICAL THEORIES

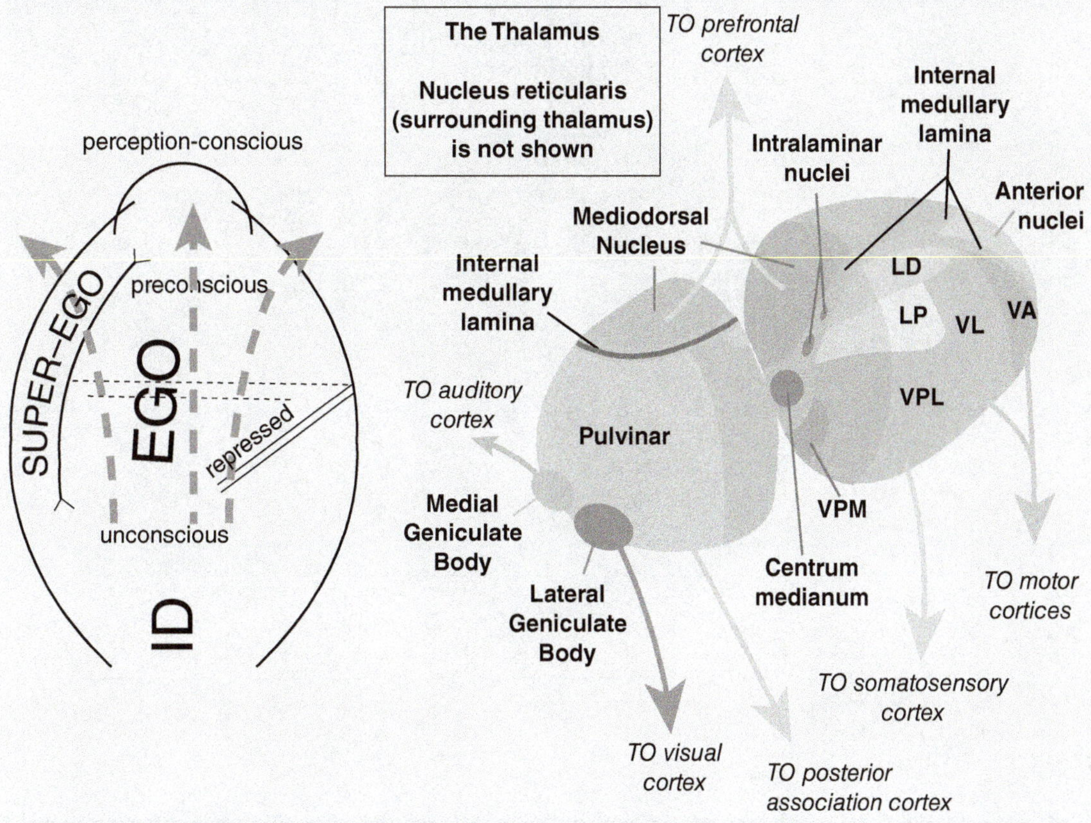

Schizophrenia: Confusion Between Internal and External Worlds?

Psychoanalytic and neurobiological theories of schizophrenia overlap. According to psychoanalytic theory (left), weak ego defenses lead to primitive material from the id overwhelming the schizophrenic individual's mind. According to neurobiological theory (right), abnormal connections between the thalamus and cerebral cortex may cause misinterpretation of sensory information. In both scenarios, the barrier between inner and outer worlds effectively disintegrates, thus explaining some of the hallmark characteristics of schizophrenia.

The Relationship Between Schizophrenia and Crime

Historically, the relationship between schizophrenia and crime has received attention from numerous authors—perhaps due to the aberrant nature of both phenomena. Cases of sexually deviant behavior in schizophrenic individuals were reported by Krafft-Ebing (1886/1965), and early psychoanalytic writers proposed an intimate relationship between crime and psychosis (Karpman, 1923). It must be remembered (as we stated in Chapter 1)

BOX 5.4 RESULTS OF NATIONAL INSTITUTE OF MENTAL HEALTH (NIMH) CLINICAL ANTIPSYCHOTIC TRIALS OF INTERVENTION EFFECTIVENESS (CATIE) STUDY

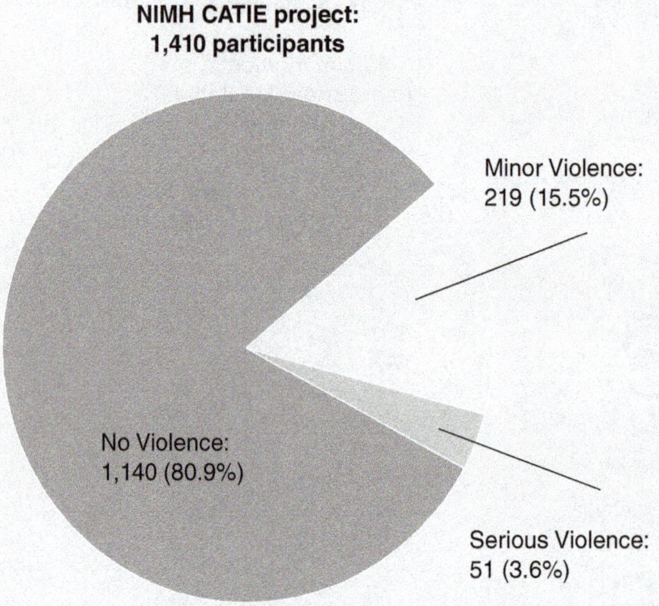

Source: Swanson et al. (2006).

that most individuals with schizophrenia are not violent. To put this point into perspective, a national multisite study investigating the cost-effectiveness of antipsychotic medications found low 6-month prevalence rates of self-reported violence (and even lower rates of serious violence) in a large sample of schizophrenia patients (n = 1,410). In short, *over 80%* of this sizeable group of individuals with schizophrenia was characterized by no violence whatsoever (Swanson et al., 2006; see Box 5.4).

That being said, multiple studies have consistently demonstrated that higher rates of psychosis and schizophrenia are found in criminal or delinquent populations and that schizophrenia patients are much more criminal and violent than the general population (Nijman, Cima, & Merckelbach, 2003; Raine, 2006; Taylor et al., 1998; Tengström, Hodgins, Grann, Langström, & Kullgren, 2004; Walsh, Buchanan, & Fahy, 2002). International studies have demonstrated that people with schizophrenia are at elevated risk for committing homicide (Schwartz, Petersen, & Skaggs, 2001) and that the prevalence rates of homicides committed by persons with schizophrenia are comparatively high (8–20% for men and 6–44% for women; Taylor & Gunn, 1999). Even the aforementioned CATIE results for serious violence are about 19 times the rates of violent crime in the general population reported to the FBI in 2008 (see below).

Tables 5.5 and 5.6 list a number of investigations, in chronological order, that have examined both prevalence rates of crime in those diagnosed with schizophrenia (and other psychotic disorders) and rates of schizophrenia in criminal populations.

Interestingly, Rabkin (1979) noted that studies before 1965 demonstrated reduced arrest rates among discharged psychiatric inpatients compared to the general population, but those findings have been the opposite in studies conducted since 1965 (with arrest ratios ranging from a low of 1.16 patients per community resident to

(Text continues on page 188)

Table 5.5 Prevalence of Schizophrenia and Other Psychotic Disorders in Criminal Populations

Source	N	Gender	Age	Study Type[a1]	Sample Description	Disorder	Diagnostic System	Prevalence/ Incidence
Cohen & Freeman (1945)	(1) 320 (2) 87	M, F	Adult?	AR	Police records of arrested patients from 1,676 patients paroled or discharged from Norwich State Hospital (Connecticut), 1940–1944 (1) Arrested before hospitalization (2) Arrested after hospitalization	Schizophrenia	?	(1) 28.1% (n = 90) (2) 23.0% (n = 20)
Stierlin (1956, in Schipkowensky, 1968)	773	?	?	PI	Statistical data from aggressive inmates in 73 psychiatric clinics and mental hospitals in Europe	Schizophrenia	?	59.6% (n = 462)
Lanzkron (1964, in Schipkowensky, 1968)	150	?	?	HO	Murderers in Matteawan State Hospital, New York	Schizophrenia	?	42.6% (n = 64)
Kalashnik (1966, in Schipkowensky, 1968)	271	?	?	HO	Murderers in the Moscow Forensic Psychiatric Institute	Schizophrenia	?	49.1% (n = 133)
Rachev (1966, in Schipkowensky, 1968)	100	?	?	HO	Murderers in custodial care at Lovech Mental Hospital Forensic Department, Bulgaria, 1933–1965	Schizophrenia	?	57.0% (n = 57; + Paranoia [13] = 70.0%)
West (1966)	148	88 M, 60 F	< 20 – 40+	HO	Homicide followed by suicide: England and Wales, 1954–1961	Schizophrenia	?	2.7% (n = 4)
						Morbid jealousy		1.4% (n = 2)
						Total psychotic disorders		4.1% (n = 6)
Pfeiffer, Eisenstein, & Dabbs (1967)	85	2/3 M, 1/3 F	17–63	JD	Federal prisoners referred for mental competency evaluations, at USPHS Hospital in Lexington, Kentucky, 1960–1965	Schizophrenia	?	37.6% (n =32)

(Continued)

(Continued)

Source	N	Gender	Age	Study Type[a1]	Sample Description	Disorder	Diagnostic System	Prevalence/ Incidence
Schipkowensky (1968)	194	?	?	HO	Murderers at the psychiatric clinic of the University of Sofia, Bulgaria, 1926–1965	Schizophrenia	?	55.0% (n = 108)
Kahn (1971)	43	41 M, 2 F	11–74	HO	Interviews and psychiatric examinations of individuals who made pleas of insanity to charges of first or second degree murder	Psychotic	?	14.0% (n =6)
Szymusik (1972)	50	M	16–68	HO	Murderers, Poland, 1955–1969	Schizophrenia	?	6.0% (n =3)
						Hallucinatory-delusional syndromes		10.0% (n =5)
						Organic psychosis		4.0% (n =2)
						Total psychotic disorders		20.0% (n =10)
Frazier (1974)	31	?	?	HO	Murderers in prisons in Texas, Minnesota, New Jersey, and New York and in mental hospitals in Texas, Minnesota, Saskatchewan, Massachusetts, and New York	Episodic psychosis	?	48.4% (n = 15)
Okasha et al. (1975)	(1) 60 (2) 20	(1) 50 M, 10 F (2) ?M, ?F	25–35[a]	HO	"Socio-psychiatric study" of (1) Murderers in Abou-Zabel and Kanater prisons, Egypt (2) Murderers in Egyptian State Mental Hospital	Schizophrenia	?	(1) 13.3% (n = 8) (2) 50.0% (n = 15)
Medlicott (1976)	38	29 M, 9 F	14–62	HO	Individuals charged with murder (n = 28) and attempted murder (n = 10) hospitalized or referred for psychiatric opinion, New Zealand	Schizophrenia	?	28.9% (n = 11)
						Mixed paranoid states		18.4% (n = 7)
						Total psychotic disorders		47.4% (n = 18)
Parker (1979)	100	79 M, 21 F	Adult?	HO	Murderers (n = 70) and attempted murderers (n = 30) examined in Brisbane, Queensland, 1956–1976	Schizophrenia	?	11.0% (n = 11)

Source	N	Gender	Age	Study Type[a1]	Sample Description	Disorder	Diagnostic System	Prevalence/ Incidence
Pétursson & Gudjónsson (1981)	47	44 M, 3 F	Adult[ai]	HO	File review of cases of intentional and unintentional homicide in Iceland, 1900–1979	Schizophrenia (paranoid)	?	8.5% ($n = 4$)
						Schizophrenia (other)		6.4% ($n = 3$)
						Psychogenic psychosis		4.3% ($n = 2$)
						Organic psychosis		2.1% ($n = 1$)
						Morbid jealousy		2.1% ($n = 1$)
						Total psychotic disorders		23.4% ($n = 11$)
Häfner & Böker (1982)	(1) 533 (2) 3,392	M, F	14–60+	PI	(1) Mentally ill and mentally defective offenders from records searches of German federal and regional criminal bureaus, 1955–1964 (2) Mentally abnormal non-offenders (every fifth admission to regional psychiatric hospital, from register search, 1955–1964)	Schizophrenias	Unspecified multiple (different and discordant) German psychiatric classification systems	(1) 53.3% ($n = 284$)[c] (2) 23.8% ($n = 807$)
Langevin et al. (1982)	(1) 109 (2) 38	?	Adult?	PI	File record review of minimum-security forensic ward psychiatric hospital cases, 1969–1979 (Clarke Institute in Toronto, Ontario, Canada) (1) Killers (2) Nonviolent offenders	Schizophrenia	Feighner et al. (1972) psychiatric research diagnostic criteria	(1) 8.0% (2) 15.0%
						Paranoid states		(1) 2.0% (2) 0.0%
Dell & Smith (1983)	253	M	15 and under to 70+[d]	HO	File review of men convicted of manslaughter on the grounds of diminished responsibility, 1966–1977	Schizophrenia	?	20.0% ($n = 51$)

(Continued)

(Continued)

Source	N	Gender	Age	Study Type[a1]	Sample Description	Disorder	Diagnostic System	Prevalence/ Incidence
Seltzer & Langford (1984)	85	M, F	15–25 (Median = 18)	PI	Interviews of individuals referred by courts or legal counsel to psychiatry department of large regional hospital in Northwest Territories, calendar year 1981	Schizophrenia	DSM-III, MMPI	2.4% ($n = 2$)
						Paranoid disorder		5.9% ($n = 5$)
						Total psychotic disorders		8.2% ($n = 7$)
Taylor & Gunn (1984)	2,743	M	Adult	JD	File review of men remanded to Brixton prison, South London (June, September, December 1979 and March 1980)	Schizophrenia	ICD	6.1% ($n = 166$)
						Schizoaffective psychosis		0.3% ($n = 8$)
						Other psychosis		1.1% ($n = 30$)
						Total psychotic disorders		7.4% ($n = 204$)
Reich & Wells (1985)	390	325 M, 65 F	$M = 30.9$	JD	Record review of defendants evaluated for competency to stand trial by the Yale-New Haven Psychiatric Court Clinic, 1980–1982	Schizophrenia	DSM-III	28.8% ($n = 112$)[bb]
						Other psychotic disorders		13.3% ($n = 52$)
						Total psychotic disorders		42.1% ($n = 164$)
Taylor (1986)	183	175 M, 8 F	18–73	JD	Record review of life-sentenced men and women, supervised by the Inner London Probation Service (inside prison and on license in the community)	Schizophrenia	ICD-9	9% ($n = 17$)
Gottlieb et al. (1987)	251	215 M, 36 F	Median = 33[aj]	HO	Record review of homicide defendants in Copenhagen, 1959–1983	Psychotic disorders, including schizophrenia	ICD-8	16.3% ($n = 41$) psychotic at the time of the crime (16.3% of males, 16.7% of females)

Source	N	Gender	Age	Study Type[a1]	Sample Description	Disorder	Diagnostic System	Prevalence/ Incidence
Wilcox (1985, 1987)	71	62 M, 9 F	Six < 18, five > 50	HO	Record review of all individuals convicted for homicides committed in Contra Costa County, California, 1978–1980	Acute and chronic paranoid schizophrenia	?	9.9% ($n = 7$)
Phillips et al. (1988)	1,816	1,569 M, 247 F	11–78 ($M = 28$)	PI, CS	Record review of psychiatric referrals from the criminal justice system of Alaska, 1977–1981	Schizophrenia	DSM-II, DSM-III	16.5% ($n = 300$)
Bland et al. (1990)	180	M	18–44	JD	Diagnostic interviews with inmates from two correctional centers, Alberta, Canada	Schizophrenia	DSM-III (DIS)	2.2% ($n = 4$) [ao]
Côté & Hodgins (1990)	495	M	19–67 ($M = 31.1$)	JD	Diagnostic interviews with Quebec adult penitentiary inmates	Schizophrenic disorder	DSM-III (DIS)	6.5% ($n = 32$)
						Schizophreniform disorder		1.2% ($n = 6$)
						Total psychotic disorders		7.7% ($n = 38$)
Rath & Dash (1990)	15	10 M, 3 F[p]	20–29[p]	JD	Interviews, file reviews, and clinical observation of prisoners (murderers) referred for psychiatric evaluation, India	Schizophrenia	ICD-9	33.3% ($n = 5$)
						Paranoid illness		13.3% ($n = 2$)
						Drug-related psychosis		23.1% ($n = 3$)
						Total psychotic disorders		66.7% ($n = 10$)
Yarvis (1990)	100	88 M, 12 F	33% < 25, 85% < 40	HO	Diagnostic interviews and record reviews of a series of murderers referred for psychiatric evaluation in California, 1980–1988	All psychoses	DSM-III	29.0% ($n = 29$)[g]

(Continued)

(Continued)

Source	N	Gender	Age	Study Type[a1]	Sample Description	Disorder	Diagnostic System	Prevalence/ Incidence
						Schizophrenia		21.0% (n = 21)[g]
						Affective psychoses		8.0% (n = 8)[g]
Côté & Hodgins (1992)	(1) 87 (2) 373	M	(1) M = 35.6, SD = 8.9 (2) M = 30.3, SD = 8.3	JD	Diagnostic interviews and file reviews of penitentiary inmates, Quebec: (1) Homicide offenders (2) Nonhomicide offenders	Schizophrenia	DSM-III (DIS)	(1) 12.6% (n = 11) (2) 5.4% (n = 20)
						Schizophreniform disorder		(1) 0.0% (n = 0) (2) 1.1% (n = 4)
						Total psychotic disorders		(1) 12.6% (n = 11) (2) 6.4% (n = 24)
Abram & Teplin (1991)[r]	728	M	16–68 (M = 26.3)	JD	Diagnostic interviews with jail detainees at Cook County Department of Corrections, Chicago, November 1983–November 1984	Schizophrenia	DSM-III-R (DIS)	Lifetime: 3.8% (n = 28) Current: 3.0% (n = 22)[s]
DeJong, Virkkunen, & Linnoila (1992)	(1) 248 (2) 100	M	16–68 (M = 31.2, SD = 11.9)	JD	Criminals ordered for forensic psychiatric examination at initial incarceration in Finland (1) Murders and attempted murderers (2) Arsonists	Schizophrenia	DSM-III	(1) 1.0% (2) 2.0%
Eronen et al. (1996)	1,423	1,302 M, 121 F	Adult	HO	File review of forensic psychiatric examinations of homicide and attempted homicide cases, Finland, 1980–1991	Schizophrenia	DSM-III, ICD-8, DSM-III-R	6.5% (6.6% of men, 5.8% of women)[ah]
Marshall et al. (1998)	103	M	18–56	JD	Diagnostic interviews and questionnaires administered to recently sentenced inmates (August–December 1997) at Yatala Labour Prison, South Australia	Schizophrenia	(PDI-R)	2.9%

Source	N	Gender	Age	Study Type[a1]	Sample Description	Disorder	Diagnostic System	Prevalence/ Incidence
Wallace et al. (1998)	(1) 3,838 (2) 1,998 (3) 152 (4) 1,137 (5) 876	M	Adult	AR	Case linkage study of higher court records and psychiatric case register databases, Victoria, Australia, 1993–1995 (men) (1) Total convictions (2) Violent offenses (3) Homicide offenses (4) Property offenses (5) Sexual offending	Schizophrenia	ICD-9	(1) 2.4% ($n = 91$) (2) 3.3% ($n = 66$) (3) 7.2% ($n = 11$) (4) 2.1% ($n = 24$) (5) 2.1% ($n = 18$)
	(1) 315 (2) 152 (3) 116	F	Adult		(women) (1) Total convictions (2) Violent offenses (3) Property offenses	Schizophrenia	ICD-9	(1) 2.5% ($n = 8$) (2) 2.6% ($n = 4$) (3) 2.6% ($n = 3$)
Gibson et al. (1999)	213	M	$M = 32$	JD	Structured interviews with randomly selected state prison and regional jail inmates from a rural New England state	Schizophrenia	DSM-III-R (DIS-III-R)	Lifetime: 6.6% ($n = 14$) Current: 5.2% ($n = 11$)
						Schizoaffective		Lifetime: 5.6% ($n = 12$) Current: NA
Baillargeon et al. (2000)	170,215	155,949 M, 14,268 F	32% 18–29, 60% 30–49, 8% 50+	JD	File review of Texas Department of Criminal Justice inmates incarcerated August 1997–July 1998	Schizophrenic disorders	ICD-10	2.0%
Baxter et al. (2001)	257	240 M, 17 F	$M = 30.6$, $M = 31.4$[bi]	HO	File review of consecutive series of patients, with index offenses of parricide or stranger killing, admitted to 1 of 3 high-secure hospitals in England and Wales, 1972–1996	Schizophrenia	?	56.8% ($n = 146$)

(Continued)

(Continued)

Source	N	Gender	Age	Study Type[a1]	Sample Description	Disorder	Diagnostic System	Prevalence/ Incidence
Siponmaa et al. (2001)	126	123 M, 3 F	15–22 (Median = 20)	JD	Interviews with young offenders consecutively referred for presentencing psychiatric investigation, Stockholm, Sweden, 1990–1995	Psychosis	ICD-9	13% (n = 16)
Teplin et al. (2002)	1,829	1,172 M, 657 F	10–18	JD	Diagnostic interviews of youths randomly sampled from intake into the Cook County Juvenile Temporary Detention Center, November 1995–June 1998	Psychotic disorders	DSM-III-R	M: 1.0% F: 1.0%
Langevin (2003)	(1) 33 (2) 80 (3) 23 (4) 611	M	(1) M = 32.06 (2) M = 27.58 (3) M = 27.57 (4) M = 31.42	PI	Interviews with convicted sex offenders (n = 747) belonging to one of four groups: (1) sex killers, (2) nonhomicidal sexually aggressives, (3) nonhomicidal sadists, and (4) general sex offenders. Participants were chosen from a database of more than 2,800 minimum-security forensic ward psychiatric hospital cases (Clarke Institute in Toronto, Ontario, Canada) seen since 1973.	Psychosis	?	(1) 27.3% (2) 18.8% (3) 30.4% (4) 12.9%
Trestman et al. (2007)	508	307 M, 201 F	18–64 (M = 31.6, SD = 9.3)	JD	Diagnostic interviews with randomly selected inmates newly admitted to one of five jail facilities, Connecticut	Psychotic disorder	DSM-IV (SCID)	1.6%
Grella et al. (2008)	280	65% M	M = 34.8	JD	Diagnostic interviews with offenders consecutively admitted to prison-based substance-abuse treatment programs at one of four research centers (Colorado, Rhode Island, Texas, California)	Schizophrenia	DSM-IV (SCID)	1.4% (n = 4)
						Psychotic disorder NOS		1.4% (n = 4)
						Any psychotic disorder		2.9% (n = 8)
Hanlon et al. (2010)	77	69 M, 8 F	M = 31.92	HO	Indigent murder defendants and death row inmates clinically interviewed while in custody in jails and maximum-security prisons (Illinois and Missouri)	Psychosis	?	14.3% (n = 11)

Source	N	Gender	Age	Study Type[a1]	Sample Description	Disorder	Diagnostic System	Prevalence/ Incidence
Pham & Saloppé (2010)	84	M	Adult	PI	Psychological evaluations of forensic patients at high-security psychiatric hospital in Tomai, Belgium (Etablissement de Défense Sociale)	Schizophrenia and other psychotic disorder	DSM-III (DISSI)	18% ($n = 15$)
Bennett et al. (2011)	435	380 M, 55 F	16-84 ($M = 34.49$, $SD = 12.57$)	HO	Database case-linkage study of offenders convicted of murder or manslaughter, 1997–2005, Victoria, Australia	Schizophrenia disorders	ICD-10	8.7% ($n = 38$)[bu]
Catanesi et al. (2011)	103	85.44% M	53.41% 25–54, 22.73% 45–65, 13.64% 18–24, 5.68% <18	HO	Psychiatric and psychological evaluations of perpetrators of homicide and attempted homicide, Italy	Schizophrenia	DSM-IV-TR	23.3%
						Delusional disorder		11.7%

Notes: [a1]AR = arrest rates of patients discharged from psychiatric facilities, JD = jailed detainees and incarcerated prisoners, HO = homicide offenders, BC = birth cohort study, PI = psychiatric inpatient sample, CS = community sample (i.e., epidemiological catchment area survey studies and outpatient psychiatric patients).

[a]Highest percentage of subjects in this age range.

[c]Rate per 1,000 of Mannheim's inhabitants, 1965: 0.51.

[d]Group mean ages: 1966–1969 ($M = 36.1$, $SD = 15.8$), 1970–1973 ($M = 36.2$, $SD = 14.9$), 1974–1977 ($M = 37.1$, $SD = 16.9$).

[g]Community sample comparative data (6-month prevalence rates from NIMH Community Survey data): 1.1–2.2% for all psychoses, 0.4–1.6% for schizophrenia, 0.4–0.9 for affective psychoses.

[p]Psychotic group ($n = 13$)—including schizophrenia, drug-related psychosis, epilepsy, affective psychosis (depression), mental subnormality, and paranoid illness.

[r]Other reports (Teplin, 1990b; Teplin, 1994) have been published on this sample. Teplin (1994) utilized the diagnostic category of schizophrenia/schizophreniform disorder.

[s]Non-jail lifetime prevalence rates from NIMH Epidemiologic Catchment Area ($n = 3,654$) = 1.7%, and current prevalence rates = 0.9% (Teplin, 1990b).

[ah]Prevalence of schizophrenia and schizophreniform disorder among general population—Males: 0.7%, females: 0.7%.

[ai]Group means and standard deviations: Psychotic illness (35.7, 8.8), personality disorder and alcohol use disorders (24.4, 8.2), no psychiatric abnormality (34.0, 12.4).

[aj]For defendants who were psychotic at the time of the crime. For those who were not, median age = 29.

[ao]Lifetime prevalence rate. For community comparison sample, standardized prevalence ratio (SPR) = 4.1 (an SPR greater than 1 indicates the prevalence rate in the prison sample was greater than that in the general population).

[bb]Rates of schizophrenia in comparison outpatient and inpatient samples from same catchment area: 8.6% ($n = 800$) and 19.9% ($n = 185$).

[br]The former value represents parricial offenders, the latter stranger killers.

[bu]General community comparison group ($n = 4,830$): 0.7% ($n = 35$).

Table 5.6 Prevalence of Crime in Schizophrenia and Psychotic Disordered Populations

Source	N	Gender	Age	Study Type[a1]	Sample Description	Disorder	Crime Definition	Prevalence/Incidence
Giovannoni & Gurel (1967)	1,142	M	Adult	AR	Functional psychotic patients released from 12 Veterans Administration hospitals	Schizophrenia (95%)	(1) Homicide (2) Negligent manslaughter (3) Aggravated assault (4) Forcible rape (5) Robbery (6) Burglary (7) Grand larceny (8) Petty larceny (9) Auto theft	Est. annual rate/100,000:[n] (1) 98.2 (2) 0.0 (3) 229.1 (4) 0.0 (5) 98.2 (6) 65.4 (7) 130.9 (8) 32.7 (9) 163.6
Guze et al. (1974)	200+	?M, ?F	Adult	CS	Community psychiatric clinic patients, diagnosed using Feighner diagnostic criteria (Feighner et al., 1972)	Schizophrenia, schizophreniform illness, primary affective disorder	Felony conviction	0.0% ($n = 0$)
Tardiff & Koenigsberg (1985)	(1) 2,106 (2) 810	(1) 842 M, 1,256 F (2) 354 M, 453 F	(1) ≤20–65+[aa] (2) ≤20–65+[aa]	CS	Psychiatric outpatients evaluated during 1.5 years at two New York hospitals, diagnosed using DSM II and DSM II criteria (1) Payne Whitney Clinic (2) Westchester Division of NY Hospital	Paranoid schizophrenia and mania (1) $n = 310$ (2) $n = 121$ Other schizophrenia and atypical psychosis (1) $n = 136$ (2) $n = 69$	Presence of assaultive behavior toward others in hospital records	Paranoid schizophrenia and mania (1) 2.3% ($n = 7$) (2) 1.7% ($n = 2$) Other schizophrenia and atypical psychosis (1) 1.5% ($n = 2$) (2) 0.0% ($n = 0$)

Source	N	Gender	Age	Study Type[a1]	Sample Description	Disorder	Crime Definition	Prevalence/Incidence
Chuang et al. (1987)	(1) 42 (2) 42	?M, ?F	$M = 34.8$, $SD = 10.9$	CS	Randomly selected hospital patients, Alberta and British Columbia, Canada, diagnosed using DSM-III criteria (1) Psychiatric outpatients (2) Nonpsychiatric inpatients	Schizophrenia	Self-reported criminal behavior	(1) Property (28.6%, $n = 12$), persons (7.1%, $n = 3$), victimless (35.7%, $n = 15$), traffic (33.3%, $n = 4$) (2) Property (14.3%, $n = 6$), persons (9.5%, $n = 4$), victimless (31.0%, $n = 13$), traffic (50.0%, $n = 21$)
Shore et al. (1990)	(1) 192 (2) 192	M	20–59	AR	(1) White House case subjects (mainly DSM-II chart diagnoses of paranoid schizophrenia) with and without prior arrests, Washington DC, 1973–1983 (2) Matched control subjects with prior arrests	(1) Schizophrenia (2) None	Arrests for violence with 10-year follow-up	(1) No prior arrest: 12.48[e] ($n = 13$), prior arrest: 38.40 ($n = 39$) (2) 24.61 ($n = 50$)
Swanson et al. (1990)	10,059	4,717 M, 5,306 F[f]	Adult	CS	NIMH Epidemiologic Catchment Area respondent data (community adults from five U.S. sites), diagnosed using DSM-III criteria (DIS)	Schizophrenia or schizophreniform disorder	Self-reported violence	12.69% violent ($n = 114$[f])
Lindqvist & Allebeck (1990)	644	330 M, 314 F	12–51	AR	Patients identified in a county inpatient register in Stockholm, Sweden, 1920–1959, diagnosed using ICD-8 criteria	Schizophrenia	Official police register with 15-year follow-up	Any crime, 1976-1986: 14.3% ($n = 92$; 22.7% or $n = 75$ of males, 5.4% or $n = 17$ of females), violent crimes, 1972-1986: 6.7% ($n = 43$)
Link et al. (1992)	(1) 521 (2) 232	?M, ?F	(1) 19–59 (2) Adult?	PI, CS	Interviews with (1) Community residents (2) Psychiatric patients (from an outpatient clinic and an inpatient community service), New York City, diagnosed using DSM-III criteria[w]	(2) 33.6% ($n = 78$) major depression, 29.9% ($n = 69$) schizophrenia /other psychotic disorders, 36.6% ($n = 85$) other diagnoses[x]	Official arrest data, self-reports of violent or illegal behavior, 1980–1983[y]	Patient groups > never-treated community residents[z]

(Continued)

(Continued)

Source	N	Gender	Age	Study Type[a1]	Sample Description	Disorder	Crime Definition	Prevalence/Incidence
Coid et al. (1993)	280	146 M, 134 F	20–80 ($M = 45.9$)	PI	Patients of twin birth seen at Bethlem and Maudsley hospitals, 1948–1988, diagnosed using DSM-III and RDC (Spitzer et al., 1978) criteria	Schizophrenia ($n = 70$)[ba]	Official criminal records	48.6% ($n = 34$)
Asnis et al. (1994)	517	204 M, 313 F	13–87 ($M = 38.7$)	CS	Psychiatric outpatients, Montefiore Medical Center, Bronx, New York, diagnosed using DSM-III criteria	Schizophrenia ($n = 46$)	Self-reported homicidal ideation and attempts	Ideation: 20% ($n = 9$) Attempts: 11% ($n = 5$)
						Psychotic disorder NOS ($n = 29$)		Ideation: 17% ($n = 5$) Attempts: 0% ($n = 0$)
Modestin & Ammann (1996)	(1) 282 (2) 282	M	18–78	PI	(1) Psychiatric patients hospitalized on at least one occasion at the Psychiatric Hospital of Berne, Switzerland, 1985–1987, diagnosed using Research Diagnostic Criteria (RDC) and DSM-III-R criteria (2) Catchment area general population controls	(1) Schizophrenia, schizophreniform disorder	National criminal register conviction records	Total criminal records: (1) 34% ($n = 97$) (2) 36% ($n = 102$)[ab]
Tiihonen et al. (1997)	(1) 86 (2) 5,285	M[ac]	(longitudinal)	BC	From a 26-year prospective study of a large unselected 1966 northern Finland birth cohort ($N = 12{,}058$) of individuals diagnosed using DSM-III-R with (1) Major mental illness (2) No mental disorder	Schizophrenia ($n = 51$)	Criminal register records	At least one registered crime: 19.6% ($n = 10$)* Violent crime: 13.7% ($n = 7$)* Property crime: 3.9% ($n = 2$)[ad]

Source	N	Gender	Age	Study Type[a1]	Sample Description	Disorder	Crime Definition	Prevalence/Incidence
						Schizophreniform and schizoaffective disorders ($n = 7$)		At least one registered crime: 28.6% ($n = 2$)* Violent crime: 0.0% ($n = 0$) Property crime: 0.0% ($n = 0$)
						Paranoid and other psychoses ($n = 9$)		At least one registered crime: 33.3% ($n = 3$)* Violent crime: 11.1% ($n = 1$) Property crime: 11.1% ($n = 1$)
Arango et al. (1999)	63	46 M, 17 F	$M = 35.2$, $SD = 10.8$	PI	Psychiatric inpatients admitted consecutively to a Madrid university general hospital, diagnosed using DSM-IV criteria	Schizophrenia and schizoaffective disorder	Checklist for aggression (OAS; verbal aggression, physical aggression against self, objects, others) administered by nursing staff	Violent: 25.4% ($n = 16$)
Arsenault et al. (2000)	(1) 389 (2) 572	51.6% M, 48.4% F	Adult	BC	From a study of a total-city New Zealand birth cohort ($N = 1,037$) of individuals diagnosed using DSM-III-R criteria with (1) Psychiatric disorder (2) No psychiatric disorder	Schizophrenia-spectrum disorder ($n = 39$)	Violence: Self-reported and criminal convictions	(1) Convictions: 15.4% ($n = 6$), self-report: 33.3% ($n = 13$) (2) Convictions: 1.2% ($n = 7$), self-report: 3.1% ($n = 18$)

(Continued)

(Continued)

Source	N	Gender	Age	Study Type[a1]	Sample Description	Disorder	Crime Definition	Prevalence/Incidence
Brennan et al. (2000)	(1) 7,692 (2) 314,715	51.7% M, 48.3% F	Adult	BC	From a study of a large Danish birth cohort (*n* = 358,180) of individuals diagnosed using ICD-8 criteria with (1) Psychiatric diagnoses (2) No diagnoses (reference group)	Schizophrenia (*n* = 1143)	Arrests for violent crime	(1) Men: 11.3%, women: 2.8% (2) Men: 2.7%, women: 0.1%
						Organic psychosis (*n* = 895)		(1) Men: 19.4%, women: 2.0%
						Affective psychosis (*n* = 729)		(1) Men: 5.2%, women: 0.5%
						Other psychosis (*n* = 1,042)		(1) Men: 10.7%, women: 1.2%
Mullen et al. (2000)	(1) 301 (2) 331	M[ae]	(1) *M* = 34.2, *SD* = 15.7 (2) *M* = 33.0, *SD* = 15.1	PI	Cases from the Victorian Psychiatric Case Register (Australia) with ICD-9 diagnoses of schizophrenia (1) First admitted in 1975 (2) First admitted in 1985 Along with matched community controls for each schizophrenia group	Schizophrenia	Criminal conviction records from police databases	Lifetime convictions: (1) Patients: 21.6% (*n* = 65), controls: 6.5% (*n* = 18)* (2) Patients: 26.3% (*n* = 87), controls: 8.6% (*n* = 19)* Convictions in 10 years after admission: (1) Patients: 13.3% (*n* = 40), controls: 2.9% (*n* = 8)* (2) Patients: 14.2% (*n* = 47), controls: 2.3% (*n* = 5)[af]*

Source	N	Gender	Age	Study Type[a1]	Sample Description	Disorder	Crime Definition	Prevalence/Incidence
Erb et al. (2001)	(1) 284 (2) 29	(1) 232 M, 52 F (2) 25 M, 4 F	(1) < 21–60+ (2) < 21–60+	HO	File review of all persons in Germany (FRG and Hessen) with schizophrenia who had committed or attempted homicide, diagnosed using DSM-III-R criteria[ag] (1) 1955–1964 (2) 1992–1996	Schizophrenia	Official criminal records	Criminal histories: (1) Violent offense: 33.5% (n = 95), murder 3.9% (n = 11), threat 41.9% (n = 119), nonviolent offense 7.4% (n = 21) (2) Violent offense: 62.1% (n = 18), murder 3.4% (n = 1), threat 13.8% (n = 4), nonviolent offense 24.1% (n = 7)
Walsh et al. (2004)	271	65% M	18–65	AR	Schizophrenia patients recruited as part of the multisite UK700 case management study, diagnosed with Research Diagnostic Criteria	Schizophrenia	Self and case manager reports and official records of assault	25.5% (n = 69) committed assault within 2-year follow-up
Corrigan & Watson (2005)	5,865	?M, ?F	15–54	CS	Subset of respondents from the U.S. National Comorbidity Survey, diagnosed using DSM-III-R criteria (structured diagnostic interview), 1990–1992	Psychosis (nonaffective disorder)	Self-reported violence	Mental illness lifetime: 11.5% (5/42); 12 months: 3.2% (1/18)
Swanson et al. (2006)	1,410	74.3% M	Adult (M = 40.5)	PI, CS	Schizophrenia patients enrolled from 56 U.S. sites in antipsychotic medication clinical trials (NIMH CATIE project), diagnosed using DSM-IV criteria	Schizophrenia	6-month prevalence of self and family reports of (1) Minor violence (2) Serious violence	(1) 15.5% (n = 219) (2) 3.6% (n = 51)

(Continued)

(Continued)

Source	N	Gender	Age	Study Type[a1]	Sample Description	Disorder	Crime Definition	Prevalence/Incidence
Bobes et al. (2009)	895	589 M, 291 F	$M = 38.7$, $SD = 11.5$	CS	Schizophrenia outpatients in Spain receiving stable pharmacological treatment, diagnosed using DSM-IV-TR criteria	Schizophrenia	Self-reports of recent (past week) aggression, using MAOS scale	Verbal aggression: 4.5% (n = 40); physical aggression against self: 0.9% (n = 8), objects: 2.9% (n = 26), others: 1.9% (n = 17)

Notes: *Significant difference in comparison to control group.

[a1]AR = arrest rates of patients discharged from psychiatric facilities, JD = jailed detainees and incarcerated prisoners, HO = homicide offenders, BC = birth cohort study, PI = psychiatric inpatient sample, CS = community sample (i.e., epidemiological catchment area survey studies and outpatient psychiatric patients).

[e]Arrest rate per 1,000 population per year. Rate for general population reported as 7.92.

[f]Weighted Ns.

[n]Based on average number of patients in community on any given day 1957–1960, N = 764; computed as (100,000) (mean annual of N of offenses divided by 764). General population average annual rate/100,000 (FBI Uniform Crime Reports for the United States, 1957–1960): Homicide (4.7), negligent manslaughter (3.1), aggravated assault (86.0), forcible rape (8.6), robbery (61.6), burglary (507.5), grand larceny (319.3), petty larceny (962.1), auto theft (237.9).

[w]Study groups formed consisting of never-treated community residents, first-contact patients, repeat-contact patients, and former patients. A portion of community members were grouped into patient groups, though diagnoses for these individuals were not reported.

[x]Separate analyses were not conducted for individual diagnoses.

[y]Six indicators: (1) self-reported arrests; (2) official arrests; and self-reports of (3) hitting others, (4) fighting, (5) weapon use in a fight, and (6) ever hurting someone badly.

[z]Patient groups collapsed into one group and percentage rates recalculated. Results (never-treated community residents/patients): all lifetime official arrests (6.7/10.6), lifetime violent arrests (1.0/4.9), lifetime self-reported arrests (9.9/18.3), hitting others—past year/month (5.2/12.3), fighting—past 5 years (15.1/25.7), weapon use—past 5 years (2.7/9.7), lifetime hurting someone badly (5.4/14.8).

[aa](1) 12.4% (n = 261) 20 years and younger, 30.7% (n = 647) 21–30, 23.6% (n = 496) 31–40, 24.3% (n = 511) 41–64, 7.5% (n = 158) 65 years and older, 1.6% (n = 33) unknown; (2) 18.0% (n = 146) 20 years and younger, 31.4% (n = 254) 21–30, 18.0% (n = 146) 31–40, 27.0% (n = 219) 41–64, 5.0% (n = 41) 65 years and older, 0.5% (n = 4) unknown.

[ab]Percentages of patients with criminal records/controls with criminal records: Violent crimes (5/1*), crimes against property (19/9*), sexual offenses (3/1), violations of drug laws (10/4*), violations of traffic laws (21/31*), other offenses (15/11).

[ac]5,217 females were also included in this study. Only one offender among the female subjects (33.3%) was diagnosed with a major mental disorder. The prevalence of offenders among women with no mental disorders was 0.8% (n = 42).

[ad]Comparison group with no mental disorder: At least one registered crime: 7.3% (n = 387), violent crime: 2.2% (n = 117), property crime: 2.5% (n = 133).

[ae]Women were included in this study but conviction rates were very low: 5 (2.4%) female patients and 3 controls from the 1975 group and similarly low numbers in the 1985 group.

[af]Schizophrenia patients were characterized by significantly increased lifetime and 10-year post-admission convictions for property, violent, and other crimes (but not for sexual crimes) compared to controls in the 1975 group and by significantly increased lifetime and 10-year post-admission convictions for property, violent, drug-related, and other crimes (but not for sexual crimes) compared to controls in the 1985 group.

[ag]1992–1996 cohort only. Proportions of persons overall who committed homicide—1955–1964: 0.11%, 1992–1996: 0.09%.

[ai]Group means and standard deviations: Psychotic illness (35.7, 8.8), personality disorder and alcohol use disorders (24.4, 8.2), no psychiatric abnormality (34.0, 12.4).

A Closer Look: Schizophrenia, Other Psychotic Disorders, and Crime

Prevalence of the Disorder in Crime

Study Type	Number	Prevalence Rates
Arrest rates	2	2.1–28.1% (2.1–28.1%)
Birth cohorts	0	–
Community samples	1*	–
Homicide offenders	21	2.7–57.0% (4.1–57.0%)
Jailed detainees and prisoners	17	1.0–37.6% (1.0–66.7%)
Psychiatric inpatients	7*	2.4–59.6% (8.2–59.6%)
Total Number of Studies	**47**	

Sample Characteristics

Size	15–170,215
Gender	Male only (12 studies); male and female but unbalanced, predominantly males (28 studies); not reported (7 studies)
Age	Youth, adult
Location	Countries worldwide (e.g., Australia, Belgium, Bulgaria, Canada, England, Egypt, Finland, Germany, Iceland, India, Italy, New Zealand, Poland, Sweden, United States)
Diagnostic Systems	Not specified in earlier studies (i.e., before 1982). DSM (various editions), ICD (various editions), other research diagnostic criteria.

Note: *One study involved both psychiatric inpatients and community individuals.

Prevalence of Crime in the Disorder

Study Type	Number	Prevalence Rates	Crime Definition
Arrest rates	4	0.1–3.8%	Violent crime
Birth cohorts	3	0.1–33.3%	Arrests, convictions, self-reported crime
Community samples	9*	0.0–35.7%	Convictions, self- and informant-reported crimes or violence
Homicide offenders	1	3.4–62.1%	Criminal histories (aside from index offense of homicide)
Jailed detainees and prisoners	0	–	–
Psychiatric inpatients	6*	15.5–48.6%	Official criminal records, convictions, self- and informant-reported violence
Total Number of Studies	**21**		

Sample Characteristics

Size	29–314,715
Gender	Male only (4 studies); male and female (17 studies)

(Continued)

(Continued)

Age	Predominantly adult, some youth and longitudinal cohort
Location	Several North American and European countries (e.g., Australia, Canada, Denmark, Finland, Germany, Spain, Sweden, Switzerland, United States)
Diagnostic Systems	DSM, ICD, and other research diagnostic criteria

Note: *Two studies involved both psychiatric inpatients and community individuals.

Nondisordered or community resident comparison group or general population baseline rates for either disorder or crime provided: **17 studies (25.0%)**[†]

Note: [†]Rates of schizophrenia and other psychotic disorders are increased relative to general population baseline rates when provided. Rates of crime are elevated relative to comparisons in most cases.

(Continued from page 170)

a high of 15 patients per community resident). The mean ratio of patient/public arrest across thirteen samples published since 1965 was reported to be 3.05 to 1 (Link et al., 1992). On balance, it does appear that the rates of crime are comparatively elevated in schizophrenia populations in these studies compared to the general population arrest rates reported in other sources (e.g., the FBI's UCR estimates of 4,437.7 arrests per 100,000 inhabitants [4.4%] and 198.2 arrests for violent crime per 100,000 inhabitants [0.2%] in 2008). Second, there are significant limitations in comparing different types of criminological data, such as official criminal records versus self-reported crime.

Finally, it must be remembered that elevated rates of either schizophrenia in criminal populations or of crime in those diagnosed with schizophrenia do not necessarily indicate that one *causes* the other, which is true, for that matter, for the other disorders discussed in this book (see Chapter 1). For example, in birth cohort studies, one must consider the chronology of offending in relation to onset of illness. Offending that occurs before the onset of schizophrenia, for example, may reflect etiological factors that are completely unrelated to schizophrenia (particularly if the offending occurs in youth or adolescence, which is before the typical age of onset for schizophrenia). Post-illness onset criminality, however, may speak more to the effects of the illness, particularly if no offending occurred before the illness began. Several studies of schizophrenia and crime have addressed this consideration (Brennan & Alden, 2006; Mullen et al., 2000).

Schizophrenia and Violent Crime

A general understanding of the timeline for the development of violence in schizophrenia has not been definitively established. Taylor (1993), for example, reports that, in schizophrenia, first violence may long postdate the illness but usually occurs once the illness is well established, the peak being 5–10 years after illness onset. *Longitudinal studies* suggest that violence largely postdates the onset of schizophrenia in schizophrenic individuals who become violent (Baxter, 1997). However, one Danish register linkage study (Gosden et al., 2005) found conviction of violence in late adolescence to be significantly associated with later schizophrenia diagnosis, suggesting that violent behavior may be conceptualized as a part of the preschizophrenia phase of young criminals.

Other emerging evidence, however, indicates a greatly increased risk of violence during the first episode of psychotic illness. Three recent studies of homicide, in fact, found 38%–61% of offenders at the time of their crimes to be in their first psychotic episode and yet to receive adequate treatment (Large & Nielssen, 2007), and the acute phase of mental illness in general is known to be associated with increased dangerous and lethal behavior (Nielssen, Westmore, Large, & Hayes, 2007). According to Nordström, Kullgren, and Dahlgren (2006), the highest probability of offending is found among young males in their early stage of the illness, and the negative impact of coexisting alcohol abuse on violent behavior has been emphasized in several studies. Hodgins and colleagues (2011) noted that a significant number of men and women contacting mental health services for a first episode of psychosis already had a prior history of criminal convictions, including those for violent crimes.

Inpatient Violence

Much of what is currently known about violence in schizophrenia is based upon studies of schizophrenia inpatients newly admitted to hospitals and other psychiatric institutions, who often experience emotional turmoil along with intense psychotic symptoms (Krakowski, 2005) and who are often first-time offenders that committed severe physical assaults against intimates (Nijman et al., 2003). A significant number of violent incidents occur on psychiatric units, and schizophrenia has been shown to be overrepresented among the diagnoses of patients involved in violence upon admission in many, but not all, studies. In fact, rates of inpatients with schizophrenia who are involved in aggressive episodes vary widely, from 9%–45% (Arango, Barba, Gonzáles-Salvador, & Ordóñez, 1999). Violence among schizophrenia inpatients has been shown to be associated with such factors as level of aggression and anxiety at referral, previous violence during admissions, positive symptoms, schizophrenia subtypes (i.e., both paranoid and nonparanoid), hospital environmental factors, neurological impairment, lack of treatment compliance, medication levels, and lack of insight into psychotic symptoms (Arango et al., 1999). As well, poor self-care and substance misuse at the time of hospital admission and medication noncompliance and substance misuse after release have been associated with homicide in hospital inpatients with schizophrenia and other psychotic disorders (Fazel, Lichtenstein, Grann, Goodwin, & Långström, 2010).

Outpatient Violence

Studies of violence and aggressive behavior in medicated schizophrenia outpatients are somewhat rare. Given the ability of many schizophrenia patients to live functional lives outside of institutions and in the community, while managing symptoms with antipsychotic medication, this area of research can be very important. Bobes and colleagues (2009) found only a small number of medication-compliant schizophrenia outpatients engaged in aggressive and violent behaviors in a one-week period prior to clinic visits (see Table 5.6). These behaviors were significantly more likely among patients with a history of violence, patients with relapses within the previous year, and those with low treatment satisfaction. In a study of 1,662 former university hospital inpatients with schizophrenia, Soyka, Graz, Bottlender, Dirschedl, and Schoech, (2007) found those with a hostility syndrome (e.g., suspiciousness, dysphoria, irritability, aggressiveness, lack of feeling of illness, lack of insight, and uncooperativeness) to be significantly more likely than those with a depressive syndrome to become criminal or violent during a 7- to 12-year period after discharge, suggesting that depressive symptoms may act as a possible protective factor against criminality in schizophrenia.

Birth Cohort Data

Birth cohort data from large national registers have also proven useful in understanding the relationship between schizophrenia and violence. Using criminal and psychiatric registers in Denmark, Brennan and Alden (2006) examined data from a Danish birth cohort of 358,180 individuals born between 1944 and 1947 to calculate odds ratios for schizophrenia and several types of violence: violence against authority, assault, robbery, rape, and murder. (An odds ratio is a statistical measure of *effect size*—a measure of the strength of a phenomenon—which describes the strength of association between two data values.) For males, *odds ratios* were significant for all categories of violence (ranging from 2.08 for assault to 3.30 for murder). For females, robbery was not linked to schizophrenia (and no cases of rape were located), though odds ratios for violence against authority and murder were quite high. In fact, females with schizophrenia were approximately 11 times more likely to commit violence against authority and over 22 times more likely to commit murder compared to females without schizophrenia (due partly to very low base rates of these crimes in nonschizophrenic controls). For males, schizophrenia diagnosis preceded arrest for violence in 50% and arrest for murder in 60% of cases. For females, the corresponding rates were 53% and 89%. This chronology of events suggests that schizophrenia may have played a role in the etiology of violence—particularly homicide—in this particular birth cohort (i.e., to the extent that it preceded the violence in a majority of cases).

Homicide

As illustrated in the Mullin case, nonhospitalized persons with schizophrenia may engage in the spectrum of violent behaviors observed in the general population, from minor assaults to brutal murders; and some speculation exists as to whether the *nature* of homicidal crimes committed by individuals with schizophrenia differs in some qualitative way from that of crimes committed by normal individuals or even by those with other forms of mental illness. In common folklore, the schizophrenic offender is depicted as "a crazed, senseless, and highly-lethal offender who preys on innocent and unsuspecting strangers in public places without apparent motive" (Steury & Choinski, 1995, p. 183). Others have reported murders by schizophrenic persons taking place more often during daytime hours on weekdays as opposed to weekends (Häkkänen & Laajasalo, 2006) or during evening and nighttime hours (Nordström & Kullgren, 2003). Another finding was that, among filicidal women, psychotic women were 11 times more likely to use a weapon to kill their children than nonpsychotic women (Lewis et al., 1998). Additional reports have indicated that psychotic murderers are less often addicted to drugs than nonpsychotic murderers (Gottlieb, Gabrielsen, & Kramp, 1987; Nijman et al., 2003) and have fewer arrest records and later onset of criminality than nonlethal psychotics (Nijman et al., 2003). Also, schizophrenic murderers may be more likely to injure the victim's face in comparison to nonschizophrenic murderers (Häkkänen & Laajasalo, 2006). Murder weapon choice has also been examined. For example, in a sample of 103 homicide perpetrators, Catanesi and colleagues (2011) found an association between delusional disorder and the use of sharp weapons, multiple (i.e., 4–10) strikes, and wounds to the thorax (depressive disorders were more associated with asphyxia, and organic disorders with blunt instruments). It may be that the characteristics of schizophrenia—unusual beliefs or disorganized thinking or behaviors—could be reflected in the motivations, behaviors, or emotional experiences of schizophrenic persons who commit crime.

In an attempt to integrate the literature in this area qualitatively, we identified 16 studies reporting on multiple variables related to the motivational, behavioral, and emotional aspects of homicide and criminal violence committed by individuals with schizophrenia and other psychotic illnesses; studies on hospital inpatient assaults, a separate but related literature, were excluded (see Table 5.7). Though some problems exist in interpreting the results from all 16 studies (from 10 different countries) in aggregate, an interesting picture related to the nature of schizophrenic and psychotic violent crime emerged.

Motivationally (see Table 5.8), 16.0–92.8% of criminally violent and homicidal psychotic offenders across 8 studies were characterized by no apparent motive, 10.4–71.0% across 11 studies by alcohol or drug use before or during the offense, and 3.7–76.9% across 10 studies by an argument or provocation that preceded the crime. Behaviorally (see Table 5.9), the crimes of 22.0–98.2% of criminally violent and homicidal psychotics across 6 studies were characterized by a public offense location, 52.7–99.4% across 5 studies by lack of offense planning, and 0.7–16.0% across 9 studies by use of a firearm. Gudjónnson and Pétursson (1982) and Pétursson and Gudjónsson (1981) reported 56.3% using a sharp instrument or shooting, and the use of sharp and blunt weapons was commonly reported across studies. Also, 0.0–8.0% of these crimes across 5 studies involved offenses with a sexual motivation or of a sexual nature, and 2.7–36.7% across all 16 studies involved victims not known to the offender, which is consistent with reports that homicidal offenders with schizophrenia and other mental illnesses often threaten or target family members and known individuals (Dolan & Parry, 1996; Gottlieb et al., 1987; Gudjónnson & Pétursson, 1982; Nestor & Haycock, 1997; Nestor et al., 1995; Torrey, 2006; Turkat & Buzzell, 1983). Interestingly, however, Nordström, Dahlgren, and Kullgren (2006) found alcohol or drug intoxication was rare for both offenders and victims in homicides involving family victims but common for both in homicides involving nonfamily victims. Finally, 22.0–100.0% of these crimes across 6 studies were excessively violent offenses, and 0.0–98.2% across 4 studies were characterized by unusual post-offense behavior (e.g., no attempt at crime concealment or escaping detection).

Emotionally (see Table 5.10), homicidal and criminally violent psychotic offenders across 3 studies were characterized by lack of emotion (73.0–97.7%), though Golenkov, Large, Nielssen, and Tsymbalova (2011) reported that 24.1% of murderers with schizophrenia were characterized by a "deficit of higher emotion"—a negative symptom of schizophrenia akin to a lack of empathy. In 1 study 100% lacked guilt or regret (Rath & Dash, 1990). These results are consistent with the emotional indifference and lack of remorse observed in violent psychotic individuals in other studies (Green, 1981; Taylor, 1993).

As can be seen, a wide variability was observed in motivational and in some behavioral aspects across studies. Behaviorally, reduced variability was seen for schizophrenic and psychotic offenders in offense planning (generally uncommon), use of firearms (decreased—perhaps due to reduced ability to purchase firearms because of government restrictions against mentally ill individuals), sexually motivated or natured crimes (generally rare), and victimology (generally not strangers). Emotionally, schizophrenic and psychotic offenders tended to be characterized by lack of emotion and guilt across studies. There were some significant methodological limitations. Some studies did not use comparison groups that were not psychotic or mentally ill (Benezech, Yesavage, Addad, Bourgeois, & Mills, 1984; Golenkov et al., 2011; Joyal, Putkonen, Paavola, Tijhonen, 2004; Laajasalo & Häkkänen, 2006; Nijman et al., 2003; Nordström and Kullgren, 2003; Nordström, Dahlgren, & Kullgren, 2006; Planansky & Johnson, 1977; Varma & Jha, 1966). Others had sample diagnostic heterogeneity (i.e., the inclusion of other mental disorders in psychotic disordered groups; Steury & Choinski, 1995). Additionally, one classic and often-cited study from this literature (Varma & Jha, 1966) used murderers with mental illness (as opposed to schizophrenia or psychotic disorders specifically) but did not define what was meant by this term. Overall, results indicate that, although the nature of homicidal and criminally violent behavior in schizophrenia may be qualitatively distinct in some respects, generalizations must be made with caution until more research in this area is completed.

Furthermore, the psychosocial backgrounds of violent schizophrenic individuals may differ from those of violent offenders who do not have schizophrenia. In a study of the forensic psychiatric reports of 183 Finnish homicide offenders, Laajasalo and Häkkänen (2004) found that schizophrenic offenders had relatively well-adjusted childhoods compared to other groups (i.e., drug addicts, alcoholics, and personality disordered offenders). They had fewer problems in school and participated less in special education, though psychopathology in their childhood family members (other than parents) was much more common. Parental alcohol abuse was actually negatively associated with later schizophrenia. Adulthood for the schizophrenic offenders, however, was characterized by more social isolation and withdrawal. Schizophrenic offenders were more likely to be living alone, were less often married, and had fewer children than did other offender groups. Though most (85.7%) had psychiatric contact as adults, only 46.3% had ongoing contact, and 38.9% had current psychiatric medication at the time of the offense. Additionally, they were more likely to be on a sickness pension than were all other groups. All demonstrated symptoms of paranoia, and two-thirds had depression (significantly more than for all groups except drug addicts—though rates were still almost double those of the latter).

Matricide

Matricide—or mother-killing—has been described as *the* "schizophrenic crime" (Gillies, 1965). This description is not surprising, given the taboo associated with mother-murder present for many ages in the mythology and legend of various cultures (Bunker, 1941; Wertham, 1941) and the case histories published beginning several decades ago that demonstrate an early and ongoing psychiatric and psychoanalytic interest in the schizophrenic mother-killer (Schug, 2011). Individuals with schizophrenia or other psychotic disorders do appear to be overrepresented among the modest number of published studies related to matricide. Schug (2011) identified 61 publications (34 case studies, 19 descriptive studies, and 8 comparison studies) involving matricidal offenders. Schizophrenia and other psychotic disorders were mentioned in 26 of the 34 case studies (76.5%), 16 of the 18 descriptive study samples (88.9%), and 7 of the 8 comparison studies (87.5%). Within these, the prevalence rates of psychotic disorders among matricidal offenders varied from 25–100% among case studies, 33.3–100% among descriptive studies, and 46.5–100% among comparison studies. Clearly, these rates are significantly higher compared to the rates of psychotic disorders in the general population and comparable or higher, in some instances, to the rates of schizophrenia observed in populations of general homicidal offenders (see Table 5.5). Negative family dynamics, pathological relationships with mothers (e.g., sexualized, hostile, or overly dependent), and excessive offense violence were commonly reported among matricidal offenders across studies. Generalizations from this integrative review must be made with caution, however, given the convenience sampling methods used to obtain these studies; and further studies of matricidal offenders are needed before any definitive conclusions about a schizophrenia-matricide relationship can be made. Luckily, a more recent publication of case material (Ogunwale & Abayomi, 2012) indicates a continuing worldwide clinical and empirical interest in this area.

Table 5.7 Nature of Violent Crime in Schizophrenia: Sample Characteristics

Source	Sample	N	Location	Offense Type(s)	Method
Varma & Jha (1966)	Criminal mental hospital patients (10:1 male/female ratio).[a] No comparison group. Mental illness not defined.	486	India	Homicide	File review
Planansky & Johnson (1977)	From a larger sample of 205 hospitalized schizophrenia patients, men who threatened to kill or attacked others at some time during their illness. No nonschizophrenic comparison group.	59	United States (New York)	Homicidal assaults, homicidal threatening	File review
Pétursson & Gudjónsson (1981); Gudjónsson & Pétursson (1982)	All known homicide cases in Iceland from 1900–1979 (6.4% female): (1) Psychotic illness,[b] mental subnormality (2) Personality disorder, drug or alcohol dependence, neurosis (3) No psychiatric abnormality	(1) 16 (2) 17 (3) 14	Iceland	Homicide	File review
Häfner & Böker (1982)	From a larger sample of mentally normal offenders (*n* = 3,808) and mentally abnormal individuals (*n* = 1,938), male and female:[c] (1) Schizophrenic violent offenders (2) Mood disordered violent offenders[d] (3) Mentally deficient violent offenders No comparisons with mentally normal offenders.	(1) 284 (2) 37 (3) 68	Germany	Homicide, attempted homicide	File review
Benezech et al. (1984)	Forensic hospital psychotic patients (93% male): (1) Schizophrenia (2) Paranoid disorder (3) Mood disorder or other No non-mentally ill comparison group.	(1) 64 (2) 37 (3) 8	France	Homicide	File review
Robertson (1988)	Male remand prisoners (1) Schizophrenia (2) Mood disorder[e] (3) Normal (violent) (4) Normal (nonviolent)	(1) 61 (2) 30 (3) 35 (4) 41	England	Acquisitive, sexual, minor violence, major violence, homicide[f]	Interview
Rath & Dash (1990)	(1) Psychotic murderers[g] referred for psychiatric evaluation (10:3 male/female ratio) (2) Randomly selected nonpsychotic murderer comparisons (12:1 male/female ratio)	(1) 13 (2) 13	India	Homicide	Interview, file review, observation

Source	Sample	N	Location	Offense Type(s)	Method
Taylor (1993)	Prison sample of men remanded on violent charges or in prison hospital wing ("interviewed sample"): (1) Psychotic men[h] (2) Nonpsychotic men	(1) 121 (2) 82	England	Personal violence (including homicide), property violence[i]	Interview, file review
Steury & Choinski (1995)	"Victim-defendant dyads" based on 100 male defendants charged with violent crimes: (1) Psychiatric inpatient/outpatients (50% schizophrenic) (2) Not patients	(1) 32 (2) 82	United States (Wisconsin)	"Dangerous and deadly felonies" (including homicide)	File review
Nijman et al. (2003)	(1) Psychotic disordered forensic hospital patients (2) Nonpsychotic disordered patients Gender not specified. No nondisordered comparison group.	(1) 111 (2) 197	Germany, the Netherlands	Homicide, sexual crimes, assault, arson	File review
Nordström & Kullgren (2003)	Court convictions of male violent offenders with schizophrenia, 1992–2000	382	Sweden	Homicide, violent assault	File review
Joyal et al. (2004)	Male forensic hospital patients—offenders with schizophrenia/ schizoaffective psychoses: (1) With ASPD (2) Without ASPD No nonschizophrenic comparison group.	(1) 35 (2) 23	Finland	Homicide	Interview, file review
Häkkänen & Laajasalo (2006)	National medicolegal archive cases (10% female): (1) Schizophrenia (2) Drug addiction (3) Alcoholism (4) Personality disorder (5) No diagnosis	(1) 43 (2) 15 (3) 43 (4) 44 (5) 37	Finland	Homicide	File review
Laajasalo & Häkkänen (2006)	National forensic examination archive cases (113 men, 12 women)—all with schizophrenia: (1) Excessive violence (2) Non-excessive violence No nonschizophrenic comparison group.	(1) 37 (2) 88	Finland	Homicide	File review
Nordström, Dahlgren, & Kullgren (2006)	Male homicide offenders diagnosed with schizophrenia during pretrial forensic psychiatric examination, 1992–2000	48	Sweden	Homicide	File review

(Continued)

(Continued)

Source	Sample	N	Location	Offense Type(s)	Method
Golenkov et al. (2011)	Homicide offenders (120 men, 13 women) with schizophrenia referred for judicial psychiatric examination in Chuvashia, 1981–2010	133	Russia	Homicide	File review

Notes: [a]Mental illness was not actually defined; and though offense characteristics (see below) reflect a disorganized quality characteristic of schizophrenia and psychotic symptoms (i.e., delusions of persecution, jealousy, and auditory hallucinations) were mentioned as motives for the murders in 17 cases, it cannot be assumed that all or even a majority of the offenders suffered from schizophrenia.

[b]Including schizophrenia (n = 7), manic-depressive illness (n = 2), psychogenic psychosis (n = 2), organic psychosis (n = 1), and morbid jealousy (n = 1).

[c]Additional analyses conducted by gender (410 male, 123 female), though exact gender composition of the smaller diagnostic groups was not reported.

[d]Including affective psychoses.

[e]Described as "usually of psychotic intensity."

[f]Homicide: 13% of schizophrenia group, 7% of mood disordered group, 24% of violent group, 0% of normal group.

[g]Including schizophrenia (n = 5), drug-related psychosis (n = 3), epilepsy (n = 1), affective psychosis—depression (n = 1), mental subnormality (n = 1), and paranoid illness (n = 2).

[h]Schizophrenia (majority), affective psychoses, paranoid disorders.

[i]Psychotic offenders: 48% personal violence, 52%* property violence.

*Significantly increased relative to comparison group.

Table 5.8 Nature of Violent Crime in Schizophrenia: Motivation

Source	Motivation	ETOH/Drugs	Argument
Varma & Jha (1966)	92.8% No apparent motive	—	"Altercations, quarrels, anger-provoking situations and jealousies" listed as motivation among 3.7% of offenders
Planansky & Johnson (1977)	39% delusional misperceptions; 15% irresistible compulsion; 12% ordered by auditory hallucinations; 10% sudden, explosive attacks in a frenzy; 5% paranoid self-defense—systematized; 19% cause unknown, insufficient data	—	—
Pétursson & Gudjónsson (1981); Gudjónsson & Pétursson (1982)	Most common motive for all groups: Quarrel/violent rage (see "Argument" column). Delusional: (1) 31.2%,* (2) 0.0%, (3) 0.0%. Robbery/financial gain: (1) 0.0%,** (2) 17.6%, (3) 28.7%	ETOH intoxication at time of offense: (1) 50.0%, (2) 70.6%, (3) 71.4%	Quarrel/violent rage as motive: (1) 43.8%, (2) 47.1%, (3) 35.7%
Häfner & Böker (1982)	No recognizable motive: (1) 18.8%, (2) 24.0%, (3) 15.0%. Most common by group: (1) Revenge (39.1%), (2) Release from feared suffering (76.0%), (3) Gain, removal of troublesome persons, concealment of offense (66.0%)	No ETOH: (1) 89.6%, (2) 95%, (3) 72% (1*, 2* > 3)	Preceding argument: (1) 26.5%, (2) 6.0%, (3) 30.0%

Source	Motivation	ETOH/Drugs	Argument
Benezech et al. (1984)	—	—	(Entire sample): "… often involved misperceived slights or threats by the victim or the exacerbation of long-standing family quarrels"
Robertson (1988)	—	No ETOH: (1) 86.0%,[a]* (2) 67.0%, (3) 45.0%, (4) 83.0%	—
Rath & Dash (1990)	(1) Not reported (2) 46.2% property dispute, 15.4% monetary gain, 30.8% sexual jealousy, 7.7% murder/suicide	(1) 23.1% cannabis and ETOH abuse-related homicides (2) Not reported	(1) 15.4% external provocation (2) 76.9% external provocation
Taylor (1993)	—	(1) 21% ETOH use before crime** (2) 55% ETOH use before crime	(1) 40% provoked by victim,** 17% history of quarreling with victim** (2) 71% provoked by victim, 38% history of quarreling with victim
Steury & Choinski (1995)	Trivial dispute (most common): (1) 44%, (2) 42%. No apparent motive: (1) 16%, (2) 7%.	(1) 63% no ETOH or drugs (2) 57% no ETOH or drugs	(1) 58% argued with victim at time (2) 49% argued with victim at time
Nijman et al. (2003)	—	—	—
Nordström & Kullgren (2003)	—	—	—
Joyal et al. (2004)	—	(1) 71% ETOH intoxicated* (2) 30% ETOH intoxicated	(1) 34% fight or argument* (2) 9% fight or argument
Häkkänen & Laajasalo (2006)	—	(1) 42% ETOH intoxicated (2, 3, 4, 5 > 1**) Drug use: (1) 24%, (5) 5%	Preceding argument: (1) 42%, (5) 63.6% (3*, 4* > 1)
Laajasalo & Häkkänen (2006)	Psychotic symptoms motivated offense: (1) 54.1%, (2) 71.6%† (total sample 66.4%)	Intoxicated: (1) 51.4%, (2) 47.7% (total sample 48.8%)	—
Nordström, Dahlgren, & Kullgren (2006)	Psychotic symptoms motivated offense: 54.2%	ETOH or drug intoxication: 27.1%	22.9% argument, typically about money
Golenkov et al. (2011)	—	ETOH intoxication: 31.3% (26/83) of positive symptom predominant, 63.8% (37/58) of negative symptom predominant (44.7% total)	—

Notes: [a]Data recoded and reanalyzed by this author. Schizophrenia group also had a significantly higher proportion of no ETOH compared to all non-mentally ill individuals when grouped together, $X^2 = 7.29$, $df = 2$, $p = .026$.

*Significantly increased relative to comparison groups.

**Significantly decreased relative to comparison groups.

†Trend toward significance.

Table 5.9 Nature of Violent Crime in Schizophrenia: Behavior

Source	Location	Planning	Method	Sex	Victimology	Excessive Violence	Post-Offense
Varma & Jha (1966)	98.2% broad daylight	99.4% no planning	Common household articles as weapons	Sexual motive inferred in 1 case	78.5% victim known	Excessive violence in most cases	98.2% no attempt at crime concealment
Planansky & Johnson (1977)	—	—	—	—	Of total threats ($n = 48$): 47.9% family, 6.3% friend or acquaintance, 4.2% stranger or non-acquaintance, 41.7% unspecified Of total attacks ($n = 24$): 62.5% family, 8.3% friend or acquaintance, 29.2% stranger or non-acquaintance	—	—
Pétursson & Gudjónsson (1981); Gudjónsson & Pétursson (1982)	—	—	Sharp instrument use or shooting: (1) 56.3%, (2) 41.2%, (3) 21.4%** Blunt instrument or other: (1) 43.7%, (2) 58.8%, (3) 78.6%	Sexual motive: (1) 0.0%, (2) 5.9%, (3) 0.0%	Blood relative: (1) 23.5%,* (2) 5.5%, (3) 7.1% Most common within-group victim: (1) Spouse/girlfriend (35.3%), (2) Stranger (38.9%), (3) Friend/acquaintance (42.8%)	—	No attempt to escape detection: (1) 50.0%, (2) 41.2%, (3) 14.3% Reported offense: (1) 12.5%, (2) 5.9%, (3) 42.9% Suicide or attempted suicide: (1) 25.0%, (2) 0.0%, (3) 7.1%
Häfner & Böker (1982)	—	Planned: (1) 47.3%, (2) 74.0%, (3) 37.0% (2* > 1, 3)	(1) Mostly blunt/sharp instruments, strangulation/choking, followed by firearms, brachial pressure, and poisoning or gas (2) Poisoning or drowning (3) Blunt/sharp instruments	(1) 95% no sex (1 < 3*, 2 < 3)	Victims only adults: (1) 81.7%, (2) 22.0%, (3) 75% (1*, 3* > 2) Victim from within intimate circle: (1) 58.1%, (2) 95.0%, (3) 31.0% (2* > 1, 2* > 3, 1* > 3) Victims strangers: (1) 8.5%, (2) 3.0%, (3) 25.0%	—	—
Benezech et al. (1984)	—	—	(Entire sample): Firearm (33%), stabbing (31%), head injury (11%), strangulation (11%)	—	Victims strangers: (1) 36.7%, (2) 28.9%, (3) 22.2%	—	—

Source	Location	Planning	Method	Sex	Victimology	Excessive Violence	Post-Offense
Robertson (1988)	Shared home of victim: (1) 18%, (2) 41%,* (3) 13%, (4) 15% Public: (1) 38%,[a]* (2) 24%, (3) 23%, (4) 18%	—	—	Sexual nature of offense: (1) 3%, (2) 0%, (3) 6%, (4) 27%	Victim family or close friend: (1) 39%, (2) 61%, (3) 15%[b]	—	Arrested at offense location: (1) 75%,* (2) 70%,* (3) 58%, (4) 32% Presented self to police: (1) 28%, (2) 17%, (3) 9%, (4) 12%
Rath & Dash (1990)	—	(1) 15.4% prior thought of murdering (2) 69.2% prior thought of murdering	(1) Beheading with heavy cutting weapons, repeated chopping; manual strangulation; crushing head with heavy stones, clubs, etc. (2) More exact forms (ropes, sticks for strangulation; stabbing) and non-mutating forms (poisoning) of violence in nonpsychotics	—	(1) Victims: 53.8% family relations, 23.1% acquaintances, 23.1% strangers (2) More family members victims of nonpsychotic murderers	(1) Excessive violence in all cases (2) Excessive violence in 30.8% of cases	—
Taylor (1993)	—	—	—	—	(1) 42% known victims (2) 59% known victims	—	—
Steury & Choinski (1995)	(1) 53% offense at home (2) 39% offense at home	Planning—10 minutes or less: (1) 67%, (2) 46% Planning—more than 2 hours: (1) 6%, (2) 7%	Firearms: (1) 16%, (2) 50% Knives: (1) 44%, (2) 18%	—	(1) 16% strangers as victims (2) 26% strangers as victims	Gratuitous violence: (1) 22%, (2) 14%	—

(Continued)

(Continued)

Source	Location	Planning	Method	Sex	Victimology	Excessive Violence	Post-Offense
Nijman et al. (2003)	—	—	—	(1) 8% sexual index offense** (2) 37% sexual index offense (co-occurring sex/violent crimes not assessed)	(1) 69% known victims.* Within psychotics, 100% of lethal offenders* (vs. nonlethal) known victims. (2) 44% known victims.	—	—
Nordström & Kullgren (2003)	57% in someone's home (27% victim's home, 11% offender's home, 15% shared home, 4% other's home)	—	Knife most common weapon (18%). 0.7% firearm.	—	31% unacquainted with victim. 82% of homicide victims known to offender.	—	—
Joyal et al. (2004)	Total sample: 78% private residence, 22% public	—	—	—	Total sample: 86% known victims, 14% strangers as victims Relatives: (1) 69%,* (2) 43% Household members: (1) 77%,* (2) 70%	—	—
Häkkänen & Laajasalo (2006)	Victim found in shared household: 1*, 5* > 2	Weapon taken to scene: (1) 30.2%, (5) 41.7	Blunt weapon: 1 > 5 (O.R. 4.9) Sharp weapon: 1 > 5 (O.R. 2.3), 3 > 5 (O.R. 3.2) No rifles or shotguns used in groups 1 and 2. More hitting and kicking in group 2 than 1. Handgun: 2 (9.3%), 5 (27.0%)	—	Victim relative: 1, 5 > 2, 4 Victim stranger: (1) 7%, (5) 10.8%	Injury to victim's face: (1) 67.9%,* (5) 32%	(1) No "abnormal" behaviors after crime, not likely to remain at crime scene after offense

Source	Location	Planning	Method	Sex	Victimology	Excessive Violence	Post-Offense
Laajasalo & Häkkänen (2006)	—	—	—	—	Victim stranger: (1) 2.7%, (2) 9.4% (total sample 6.4%)	(1) 29.6% (by definition): sadistic/sexual features (binding/ penetration), mutilation, or > 15 stab wounds	—
Nordström, Dahlgren, & Kullgren (2006)	—	—	Weapon used in 92.3% of homicides, most often a knife (also objects including dumbbells, flower pot, and frying pan). Firearm used in only 1 case (2.0%).	—	17.3% (9/52) of victims strangers. 34.6% of victims women.	22.9% extreme violence ("in some cases offender continued to violate victim after victim's death")	—
Golenkov et al. (2011)	3% in company of others	—	52% blade or knife, 21% fists or blunt objects, 11% strangulation, 7% multiple methods, 7%, method not recorded, 2% firearms	—	51% family or close relative, 43% acquaintances or neighbors, 6% strangers	—	—

Notes: [a]Data recoded and reanalyzed by this author. Schizophrenia group had a significantly higher proportion of public location compared to all non-mentally ill individuals when grouped together, $X^2 = 4.84$, $df = 1$, $p = .028$.

[b]Victimology not reported for nonviolent normal group.

*Significant increase relative to comparison groups.

**Significant decrease relative to comparison groups.

Table 5.10 Nature of Violent Crime in Schizophrenia: Affect

Source	Emotion	Regret
Varma & Jha (1966)	97.7% complete emotional indifference	—
Planansky & Johnson (1977)	—	—
Pétursson & Gudjónsson (1981)/ Gudjónsson & Pétursson (1982)	—	—
Häfner & Böker (1982)	—	—
Benezech et al. (1984)	—	—
Rath & Dash (1990)	—	(1) 100% no guilt or hostility toward victim (2) 46.2% had guilt feelings after committing act; 53.8% expressed satisfaction over the act
Robertson (1988)	—	—
Taylor (1993)	(1) 73% no feelings toward victim* (2) 48% no feelings toward victim	—
Steury & Choinski (1995)	—	—
Nijman et al. (2003)	—	—
Nordström & Kullgren (2003)	—	—
Joyal et al. (2004)	—	—
Häkkänen & Laajasalo (2006)	—	—
Laajasalo & Häkkänen (2006)	—	—
Nordström, Dahlgren, & Kullgren (2006)	—	—
Golenkov et al. (2011)	24.1% "deficit of higher emotion" (i.e., a negative symptom of schizophrenia conceptually similar to a lack of empathy)	—

Notes: *Significant increase relative to comparison groups.

Suicide

Many studies have examined rates of suicidal behaviors among individuals with schizophrenia. For example, 9.8% of subjects in a Chinese sample with lifetime schizophrenia reported suicide attempts (Xiang et al., 2008). Studies have also shown that the risk for suicide is influenced by the stage of schizophrenia and that the risk is generally highest during the early phases of the illness, during, for example, the first presentation or episode (Clarke et al., 2006). Taylor (1993), however, found even distributions of previous suicide attempts among psychotic and nonpsychotic offenders (approximately 40% of each group) in an interviewed sample.

Schizophrenia and Nonviolent Crimes

Nonviolent or property offending among schizophrenic persons has, to date, not been systematically studied. Incidental data, however, have been included in some reports of psychotic and mentally ill individuals. In a study of motives for offending among 212 hospital-remanded prisoners, Taylor (1985) describes a small subsample of 21 mentally ill nonviolent offenders (14 psychotic) who engaged in minor offenses with motivations categorized as minor material gain, trivial material gain with other primary motives (e.g., thefts of vehicles to find relatives, theft of food due to hunger, theft to spend Christmas in prison, theft of a public library psychology text for the purposes of self-psychoanalysis), vagrancy (e.g., begging, threatening), and other offenses (e.g., sending threatening letters, making inappropriate emergency services calls, cultivating cannabis, insulting behavior, indecent assault). Among those psychotic patients classified as vagrants, some were behaving in a bizarre manner. One schizoaffective man was arrested while carefully covering a motorcycle in paper while another was "touching car door handles" in an attempt to locate a place to sleep. Despite these reports, reduced property offending rates have been observed in schizophrenic individuals compared to non-mentally ill persons in at least one case linkage study (Wallace et al., 1998). In a large Massachusetts statewide cohort of adults receiving mental health services, McCabe and colleagues (2012) found that, among those with both a diagnosis of schizophrenia (or other psychotic disorders) and criminal histories, 45% were arrested for property crimes (compared to 65% for public order crimes and 50% for serious violent crimes) over a 10-year period. Overall, more work is clearly needed to understand the relationship between schizophrenia and various forms of nonviolent criminal offending.

Schizophrenia and Sexual Crimes

Despite sensationalized media accounts of violent schizophrenic sexual attackers (Phillips, Heads, Taylor, & Hill, 1999) and reports of the bizarre and terrifying nature of these attacks (Craissati & Hodes, 1992), sexual crimes appear comparatively rare among schizophrenic persons. Individuals with schizophrenia and other psychotic disorders comprise only small percentages of sexual offender populations, 2–5% according to Alish et al. (2007). They also demonstrate reduced proportional rates of sexual offense convictions in comparison to non-mentally ill individuals in case linkage studies (Wallace et al., 1998). Additionally, sexual index offenses have been found to be proportionally rare among psychotic offenders (8% of 111) compared to nonpsychotic offenders (39% of 197) in forensic psychiatric hospital samples (Nijman et al., 2003). Rare descriptive reports from small, highly selected samples suggest that the relationship between schizophrenia and sexual offending may be somewhat complex. Table 5.11 lists several descriptive studies of schizophrenia and sexual crimes; it demonstrates the variability among these types of offenders in terms of factors such as victimology, level of violence, and sexual naïveté.

In another descriptive study, Smith and colleagues (Smith, 1999, 2000; Smith & Taylor 1999a, 1999b) used clinical records and author-developed checklists to examine the cases of 80 restricted hospital order inpatients with schizophrenia, all male, who, while psychotic, committed contact sexual offenses (i.e., rape, attempted rape, indecent assault) against women. Researchers examined how specific types of psychotic symptomatology were related to sexual offending in these patients. The relationship of the delusions and hallucinations to the offense were rated as direct, indirect, or coincidental. *Direct delusions* contained sexual elements that were clearly congruent with carrying out the index sex offense (e.g., the sex attack had to be carried out as part of a mission to avert a world catastrophe). Indirect delusions contained sexual components that were not directly congruent (but not entirely unrelated) with the specific sex assault (e.g., a belief that the patient was famous and admired by all women or was developing another penis), or these delusions had no sexual component but were linked in some way to the offense (e.g., a persecutory belief regarding the victim leading to a retaliatory physical assault). *Coincidental delusions* appeared to have no connection to carrying out the sex offense (e.g., a belief that the patient was being monitored by secret governmental services). *Direct hallucinations* were imperative auditory hallucinations that instructed the patient to rape or carry out a sex attack. *Indirect hallucinations* had sexual components that were not directly congruent (but not entirely unrelated) with the sex assault (e.g., voices discussing sexual matters; an *imperative hallucination* instructing the listener to carry out a physical but not specifically sexual assault; a *tactile hallucination* perceived as sexual by the offender, such as the sensation of being

Table 5.11 Descriptive Studies of Schizophrenia and Sexual Crimes

Source	N	Sample Description	Sexual Offense Characteristics	Participant Characteristics
Craissati & Hodes (1992)	11	Psychotic sexual offender inpatients (10 with schizophrenia)	• Included rape, indecent assault, and buggery—alone or in combination with other crimes (i.e., robbery, grievous bodily harm, battery) • Overall relatively nonviolent, triggered by feelings of sexual disinhibition (some reports of pre-offense offense-related masturbatory fantasies) • Generally occurred in early phases of illness when florid symptoms remained concealed • Victims known by offenders in over 50% of cases, received minimal physical harm	• Sexual naïveté. Over 50% had either limited or no previous sexual experience with a partner. • Comparatively low antisociality • Minimal offense-related or histories of substance abuse • Often not identified as psychotic until after offense
Jones et al. (1992)	4	Male schizophrenia patients	• Attempted rape, indecent assault • In response to auditory command hallucinations	• Minimal or no sexual experience prior to assaults • Marked social or interpersonal deficits • Dominant mother and absent or emotionally distant father in childhood • Pharmacological treatment resistance
Chesterman & Sahota (1998)	20	In secure unit of hospital, mentally ill sex offender patients (17 of 20 with schizophrenia)	• Rape, indecent assault, buggery, attempted rape • Over 50% of offenders engaged in excessive violence • Victims mostly strangers, female, and over 14 years of age • Only one schizophrenia patient reported specific delusional and hallucinatory drive; others reported motivations including revenge, sexual frustration, anger and arousal	• Comparatively more violent, antisocial, and sexually knowledgeable • Most were heterosexual, and the majority had relationships lasting over 12 weeks. Only 25% of sample reported no or low numbers of sexual partners. • 30% history of drug abuse, 25% history of alcohol abuse, majority reported substance abuse at time of offense • Extensive criminal histories: most had convictions for previous violent offenses, and nearly 50% had past sexual offending history (the majority of these prior to contact with psychiatric services). • Low rates of family psychiatric and criminal history

Source	N	Sample Description	Sexual Offense Characteristics	Participant Characteristics
				• Many reported histories of childhood psychosocial deprivation (i.e., families with 5 or more children, physical and sexual abuse, parental discord, parental separation or divorce, inadequate parental nurturance), educational problems (i.e., feeling alienated and excluded by education system, attending special schools), and adult psychosocial deficits (i.e., unstable work histories, lengthy unemployment, social isolation at the time of the offense). • Majority had previous inpatient treatment; over 50% had no psychiatric contact at time of offense. • Low rates of being on medication and medication compliance at time of offense • Over 50% considered psychotic at time of offense—predominant symptoms were irritability, cognitive disturbance, and paranoid ideation
Phillips et al. (1999)	15	Male sexual offenders at secure hospital, and sexually antisocial inpatients with schizophrenia at secure hospital.	• Nonspecific definitions of sexual offenses (i.e., "of a sexual nature") and antisocial sexual behavior (i.e., "seriously disinhibited, inappropriate, or offensive sexual behavior") • In 12 of 15 cases, sexual offenses occurred after the onset of schizophrenia and in the context of psychotic symptoms.	• Relatively high rates of previous contact with psychiatric services • Low rates of medication compliance at the time of the index offense

touched in the genital region). Finally, *coincidental hallucinations* appeared to have no connection with carrying out the sex offense (Smith & Taylor, 1999a). Although half the patients had delusions or hallucinations related to the offenses, a specific delusional or hallucinatory drive was pertinent in only 18 cases. In the majority of cases, schizophrenia onset predated sexual offending, victims were complete strangers, and exclusive sexual offending was uncommon (Smith & Taylor, 1999a, 1999b).

Psychosexual, motivational, and psychosocial variables were also examined. For example, only about one-quarter of the sample was characterized by aggressive sexual fantasies at the time of their offenses, and these patients were more likely to have a history of sexual offending that predated schizophrenia onset (Smith, 1999). Clinical records indicated that, for some patients, the intensity of aggressive sexual fantasies appeared to fluctuate in unison with schizophrenia symptom severity; others experienced these fantasies only when psychotic (Smith, 1999). Primary motivations for offending among this sample were sexual (54%), opportunistic (29%), vindictive (11%), and pervasive anger (6%). Among the 18 cases in which delusional and hallucinatory drives were present during the offense, higher percentages of sexual motivations (i.e., 78%) and significantly higher proportions of sexual, non-sadistic motivations (i.e., not containing features of excessive violence or humiliation) were seen in comparison to the 62 cases in which these drives were not present (Smith, 2000). Most offenders characterized by sexual, non-sadistic motivations appeared preoccupied with feelings of sexual arousal or fantasy and with a desire to have physical contact with women. These men reportedly expressed frustration and desperation regarding their perceived social isolation, low self-esteem, inability to approach or form intimate relationships with women, and the negative impact of their illness upon their social functioning (Smith, 2000). Overall, the sample experienced significant social and sexual functional decline after the onset of schizophrenia. Preschizophrenia sex offenders were more likely to have pre-onset social and sexual impairment compared with post-onset offenders—though only pre-onset social isolation remained significantly associated with pre-onset sex offending when other variables were controlled (Smith & Taylor, 1999b).

Specific facets of sexual offending in schizophrenia also became the focus of subsequent comparative investigations. For example, in the Sahota and Chesterman (1998a) sample, both mentally ill and non-mentally ill sexual offenders were found to have similar levels of cognitive distortions, whereas mentally ill offenders were characterized by significantly higher levels of sexual obsession, sexual dysfunction, and faulty sexual knowledge and beliefs in comparison to non-mentally ill offenders. Cultural factors may be relevant, however, as the London catchment area served by this regional secure unit has a high proportion of persons of Afro-Caribbean descent, who were overrepresented in this sample (Smith & Taylor, 1999b).

More recently, in the first comparison study of its kind, Alish et al. (2007) compared 36 schizophrenic sex offenders, 80 schizophrenia patients who had committed nonsexual offenses, and 57 nonschizophrenic sex offenders on various clinical, sociodemographic, and sexual variables. Sexual offenses included those related to paraphilia (e.g., pedophilia, exhibitionism, sexual sadism—see Chapter 8), sex crimes not related to paraphilia (e.g., sexual offenses carried out under the influence of drugs or alcohol and related to general antisocial behavior), and deviant—though not necessarily illegal—sexual behaviors (e.g., compulsive masturbation, protracted heterosexual or homosexual promiscuity, pornography dependence, telephone-sex dependence, severe sexual desire incompatibility). In comparison to schizophrenic patients who had committed nonsexual offenses, schizophrenic sex offenders were (1) sociodemographically more likely to be married, employed, and nonheterosexual and (2) clinically characterized by lower percentages of psychiatric hospitalization, antisocial personality, substance abuse, negative symptoms, and less overall illness severity with more improvement over time of hospitalization. Additionally, schizophrenic sex offenders demonstrated a tendency toward female assault while their nonschizophrenic counterparts tended toward male assault. Nonschizophrenic sex offenders demonstrated a greater tendency toward nonadult (i.e., child and adolescent) victims than schizophrenic sex offenders, though differences only approached significance. Among incest offenders, schizophrenic subjects attacked higher percentages of female relatives, whereas nonschizophrenic offenders attacked male and female relatives similarly. Results appear to suggest a schizophrenic sex-offender group that is somewhat higher in functioning both socially and clinically in comparison to the group committing nonsexual offenses; or perhaps those in the first group are in earlier stages of illness than those in the second.

Theoretical explanations for the causes of sexual offending among schizophrenic persons are varied. First, one must consider etiological mechanisms not necessarily related to schizophrenia itself and thought to be involved in sexual offending in general (e.g., childhood abuse, deviant sexual preferences and behaviors, and antisocial personality traits). In such cases, offending may predate the onset of schizophrenia.

Second, schizophrenia-related factors such as psychotic symptoms, disinhibition, and psychosocial or psychosexual impairment may cause or predispose a schizophrenic individual to sexual offending. Delusions and hallucinations occurring at the time of sexual offending have been reported by almost all schizophrenic sex offenders in some samples (e.g., Smith & Taylor, 1999a). High occurrences of sexual content in schizophrenic delusions and hallucinations have been reported (e.g., Klaf & Davis, 1960), along with sexual identity confusion and genital hallucinations (Drake & Pathé, 2004). Additionally, delusions or command hallucinations may directly influence behavior and serve to exacerbate preexisting deviant sexuality in some schizophrenic sex offenders (Drake & Pathé, 2004).

Third, schizophrenia symptomatology and associated executive functioning deficits may lead to disinhibition and impulsivity, which could facilitate the expression of deviant sexual behavior or the exacerbation of preexisting deviant sexual thoughts and urges (Craissati & Hodes, 1992; Drake & Pathé, 2004; Phillips et al.,

1999; Sahota & Chesterman, 1998b). Impulsivity and disorganization may also lead to opportunistic offending. For example, Smith (2000) reports a variety of opportunistic sexual offenses among psychotic men stemming from complex situational factors—from an offender with enough behavioral control to engage in robbery or burglary before impulsively sexually offending to the more disorganized thought-disordered individual, whose impaired judgment and poor social cue-reading ability facilitate an impulsive attempt at forced sexual intercourse with a known female during a chance encounter.

Schizophrenia-related social and sexual functioning deficits may also play a role in schizophrenic sex offending. For example, schizophrenia-related attentional and verbal memory deficits associated with social cue misperception and poor social problem solving may contribute to context-inappropriate sexual behavior. Additionally, hypersexuality has been associated with early stages of schizophrenia (Phillips et al., 1999), which may contribute to sexual offending in these patients. Later stages and prolonged untreated schizophrenia have been associated with hyposexuality (Drake & Pathé, 2004; Phillips et al., 1999). Also, negative symptoms, along with schizophrenia-related psychosexual deficits (i.e., poorly communicated and primitively enacted sexual behaviors and intense confusion and preoccupation with body and boundaries) and associated pharmacotherapeutic effects (e.g., antipsychotic drug-related sexual dysfunction and unsuppressed sexual urges or behaviors), may lead to an inability to satisfy sexual needs in an appropriate manner and thus subsequent deviant sexual behavior (Drake & Pathé, 2004). In such cases, sexual offending may occur after the onset of schizophrenia; though long-standing pre-morbid social and sexual dysfunction—rather than the deleterious effects of schizophrenia—may contribute more to offending in some patients (Smith & Taylor, 1999b).

Finally, schizophrenic symptomatology may interact with other *potentiators* to sexual offending at the time of the offense rather than operating as an isolated causal factor (Sahota & Chesterman, 1998b). Other factors such as brain injury and substance misuse must be considered—though the exact nature of the combined effects of these factors with schizophrenia in sexual offending is not entirely clear. For example, though it has been suggested that deviant sexuality among schizophrenic persons may be a manifestation of more generalized antisociality, such as substance abuse or ASPD (Chesterman & Sahota, 1998; Drake and Pathé, 2004), Alish et al. (2007) report lower rates of substance abuse and ASPD among schizophrenic sex offenders in comparison to schizophrenic nonsexual offenders, and Wallace et al. (1998) found twice as many schizophrenic sexual offenders (operationalization of sexual offenses not specified) without histories of substance misuse in comparison to those with histories of substance misuse. The indirect effects of schizophrenia may increase the likelihood of general criminal offending in a number of ways, but why this results in sexual offending is only partially understood (Chesterman & Sahota, 1998). Ultimately, however, schizophrenic sex offenders comprise a small subgroup of schizophrenic criminals requiring highly specialized treatment (Drake and Pathé, 2004).

Schizophrenia and Arson

The literature on schizophrenia and the crime of arson is scant, though initial evidence suggests between the two. For example, several studies from different countries dating back to the early twentieth century have reported rates of schizophrenic individuals among samples of arsonists between 2.4 and 30.0% (Repo & Virkkunen, 1997; Virkkunen, 1974). Furthermore, in a recent national case-control study of 1,689 male and female convicted arson offenders in Sweden, Anwar and colleagues (2011) found arson offenders were likely to be diagnosed with schizophrenia (with an adjusted odds ratio of 22.6 for men and 38.7 for women) or with other psychoses (adjusted odds ratio of 14.4 for men and 30.8 for women). These risk estimates were higher than those reported for other violent crimes, making arson comparable to homicide in terms of the strength of its association with psychotic disorders.

Some attention has also been paid in the literature to motivations for arson, and a handful of studies have attempted to describe these motivations as they occur in schizophrenic persons in order to ascertain if they might be in any way qualitatively different from those of nonpsychotic arsonists. In one study, Virkkunen (1974) examined the mental examination statements of individuals who had committed the crime of arson and had been admitted to a Finnish university psychiatric hospital for evaluation between 1918 and 1972. Thirty individuals with diagnoses of schizophrenia were identified, as were 30 controls without schizophrenia (27 males and

3 females comprised each group). Results indicated that hate was the principal motive for arson in 15 (50.0%) of the schizophrenic individuals and in 18 (60.0%) of the controls (essentially equal rates, statistically speaking). However, among those where hate was present as a motive, controls were significantly more likely to direct their hate toward family, relatives, and acquaintances while individuals with schizophrenia more often directed their hate against outsiders or the entire community (fueled by aggressive reactions to difficulties with housing or work, for example). This finding would appear to be an interesting contrast to the results of studies mentioned earlier, which have shown that schizophrenic individuals are more likely to target family members and acquaintances with other violent crimes such as physical assault or homicide. One explanation may be that an individual with schizophrenia may be more likely to be living with a family member (i.e., who is acting as a caretaker) and may be reluctant to destroy with fire a residence that they both shared. Or, if the schizophrenic offender was in fact homeless and living alone at the time of the offense, the opportunity to target intimates as opposed to the community as a whole may not have presented itself.

The offenses of nonschizophrenic arsonists were significantly more likely to be associated with alcohol use compared to those of schizophrenic arsonists (70.0% versus 30.0%, respectively), and those with schizophrenia were, of course, more likely to be motivated by hallucinations and delusions (30.0%). Additionally, schizophrenic arsonists were more likely to choose uninhabited structures and objects (e.g., bars, laundry rooms, saunas, garbage heaps, forest vegetation, and, in one case, telephone poles) while controls most often targeted residential houses. For schizophrenic individuals, 43.3% remained at the scene of the fire after setting it, as did 50.0% of controls; and one third of each offender group stayed to watch the fire burn. Only two cases of schizophrenic offenders and one control case reported sexual pleasure associated with setting the fires.

Repo and Virkkunen (1997) examined criminal recidivism and family histories in a later hospital record review of 304 male fire setters referred for forensic psychiatric evaluation. Results indicated that both schizophrenic fire setters comorbid for alcohol dependence and nonschizophrenic fire setters had high rates of criminal recidivism, and the family histories of schizophrenic fire setters were more often characterized by an alcoholic father and a psychotic mother (in fact, familial alcoholism was associated with increased life-long criminal recidivism in schizophrenic fire setters). Results also indicated that a high proportion of schizophrenia patients committed violent offenses, multiple fire-setting offenses, and property offenses, suggesting that these schizophrenic fire setters are as dangerous for these other reasons as they are for fire setting. Interestingly, in contrast to the previously mentioned study, this research found that the schizophrenic fire setters in this sample targeted their own apartments as often as had nonschizophrenic fire setters.

Psychological Factors: Schizophrenia Symptoms

Individual psychological symptoms may explain the criminal and violent behavior observed in individuals with schizophrenia and other psychotic disorders, and research on delusions and hallucinations in the mentally ill have provided some evidence for this explanation. (The subjects of this research are not only schizophrenia patients but also those with mood and substance use disorders, which may also be characterized by secondary psychotic symptomatology.) Positive psychotic symptoms have been correlated with violence (Bjorkly, 2002a, 2002b; Krakowski, 2005), homicidal ideation (Schwartz et al., 2001), and homicidal aggression (Planansky & Johnston, 1977). In fact, Bo and colleagues (2011) proposed two different trajectories toward violence in individuals with schizophrenia: (1) patients with no prior history of violence or crime, for which violence appears to stem from positive symptoms, and (2) patients in whom comorbid personality pathology (e.g., psychopathy—see Chapter 10) predicts violence, regardless of other schizophrenia symptoms (see Hodgins, 2008, below). A fair amount of research in this area has focused on delusions, hallucinations, the syndrome of disorganization, and negative symptoms.

Delusions

Herbert Mullin's delusional belief systems are quite apparent and undeniable. In fact, delusional motivations for violent crimes such as homicide can seem quite bizarre. Gillies (1965), for example, lists several, including these: "I wanted to be a fourteen-year-old homosexual but my wife laughed at the idea," "Because my wife was putting powder in my tea," or "A mysterious power told me she was being unfaithful." Previous research indicates a general association between delusions and violence among individuals with mental illness; and although one hospital and criminal record review of 1,740 special high-security hospital patients found more than 75% of psychotic patients to be driven to violent offending by their delusions (Taylor et al., 1998), it is generally believed that only a small proportion of violence committed by psychotic persons appears to be driven by delusional beliefs (Appelbaum, Robbins, & Monahan, 2000; Taylor, 2006). Specific delusions may contribute more to violence risk, such as **persecutory delusions** (Bjorkly, 2002a; Catanesi et al., 2011) or *passivity delusions* (Taylor, 1998). Other symptoms, such as the perception of being threatened or harmed by others or that one's self-control is being overridden, perhaps by mind control or thought insertion (threat/control-override symptoms), have been shown to be separately associated with violent behaviors (Link, Stueve, & Phelan, 1998).

Also noted have been several rare content-specific delusional syndromes involving the reduplication of elements in the environment—such as places (e.g., *reduplicative paramnesia*, the replacement of a physical location by a duplicate) and persons. Reduplicative delusions involving people have demonstrated a relationship with violence. These **delusions of misidentification** include **Capgras syndrome** (the belief that familiar persons have been replaced by physically identical imposters), ***subjective doubles*** or **Doppelgänger syndrome** (the belief that oneself has a double or impersonator), **Fregoli syndrome** (the belief that another person has changed his or her physical identity while his or her psychological identity remains the same), and **intermetamorphosis** (the belief that others have undergone radical physical and psychological changes to become persecutors; Bullock & Arrigo, 2006; Malloy, Cimino, & Westlake, 1992). Misidentification syndromes in general are associated with anger and suspiciousness toward the misidentified other. Hostility and paranoid ideation directed toward the misidentified object have the potential to lead to violence and have been associated with completed homicides (Bullock & Arrigo, 2006). For example, in one case, a Capgras patient decapitated his father—whom he thought to be a robot imposter—in order to find the "batteries in his head" (De Pauw & Szulecka, 1988). Studies of differential diagnoses of primary and secondary Capgras syndromes (Malloy et al., 1992) indicate that the former—characterized by earlier, insidious onset and positive psychiatric history—is more associated with paranoia and violence; but the latter—characterized by later, sudden onset and neurological dysfunction—is not.

Though many patients with schizophrenia and other psychotic disorders will not act on their delusions, the risk of them doing so may increase with accompanying emotional distress (Bjorkly, 2002a), fear (Kennedy et al., 1992), sadness (Douglas & Skeem, 2005), anxiety or anger (Kennedy et al., 1992; Buchanan et al., 1993; Silva et al., 1996; Appelbaum et al., 1999), challenge to the delusion by others (Taylor, 2006), or the absence of protective social support networks and professional supervision (Douglas & Skeem, 2005). Junginger (1996) has even proposed the use of content analysis (i.e., counting the number of logical elaborations of the central theme—the who, what, where, when, why, and how) to assess the degree to which a delusion is systematized and to understand its relationship with violence.

How this body of research necessarily applies to the schizophrenia-violence relationship may still be somewhat unclear, as Bjorkly's (2002a) review largely encompasses studies with samples containing disorders other than schizophrenia (e.g., Appelbaum et al. [2000] included only 17.2 % schizophrenia or schizoaffective disordered patients). In fact, only three studies in this review utilized schizophrenia-only samples (Cheung, Schweitzer, Crowley, & Tuckwell, 1997; Humphreys, Johnstone, MacMillan, & Taylor, 1992; Smith & Taylor, 1999a, 1999b). One of these (Smith & Taylor, 1999a, 1999b) studied a sex offender population not characterized entirely by violence *per se* (see below). These three studies noted a prevalence of persecutory delusions among subjects and found a positive relationship between these delusions and violence. Furthermore, in a national case-control study of discharged patients with schizophrenia and other psychotic disorders, Fazel, Buxrud, and colleagues (2010) found no relationship between homicide and the presence of delusions or hallucinations. Controlled studies of violent persons with schizophrenia that compare those who acted upon delusions to those who did not would help to clarify the relationship of delusions and violence in schizophrenia specifically—as would comparing offender and non-offender samples. In summary, though delusions in general and persecutory delusions in particular may be related to violence in only some mentally ill patients, this relationship may be somewhat different in patients with schizophrenia specifically.

Hallucinations

The literature on **command hallucinations** (i.e., voices ordering action—either nonviolent, such as "Play the record player," or violent, such as "Kill everyone in the house!") is disparate—with some studies examining the relationship between command hallucinations and compliance, some the factors associated with acting on command hallucinations, and some the relationship between command hallucinations and dangerous behavior. Although methodological problems have been noted, evidence indicates that some individuals who experience violent command auditory hallucinations will act on them; however, these hallucinations do not produce action in isolation, and other factors mediate the process (Braham, Trower, & Birchwood, 2004). Compliance with auditory command hallucinations may depend upon a variety of different factors. Increased compliance may be associated with beliefs about the voices. Are they malevolent or benevolent, powerful, trustworthy? Whose voice is it? Is it recognizable or familiar? Also important are voice quality, such as how pressuring, persistent, or emotional it is, and voice content, such as how aggressive or self-punishing the instructions are. Other factors of significance to compliance are the person's general reasoning processes leading to action (including beliefs about disobedience in general), his or her mood, the hospital environment, the consistency of the instructions with the individual's delusional beliefs, and the presence of a concurrent delusional belief (Bjorkly, 2002b; Braham et al., 2004; Junginger, 2006). Compliance may also depend upon various personal, situational (e.g., outside versus inside hospital setting), and clinician variables (McNiel, Binder, & Greenfield, 1988).

One recent study of 75 psychotic-disordered adults recruited from community and forensic services (Shawyer et al., 2008) found compliance with harmful command hallucinations to be driven by a complex interaction of beliefs and personal characteristics. Compliance (reported by 79% of the sample) was associated with increased age, viewing the command hallucination as positive, congruent delusions, and low maternal control in childhood. Antipsychotic medication reduced the likelihood of compliance while increased anger and violence history actually reduced odds of compliance with command hallucinations viewed as threatening. Other studies have shown that most command hallucinations urge the person to commit suicide rather than attack others (Häkkänen & Laajasalo, 2006). One study using content analysis of the command hallucinations of 58 inpatients (Hellerstein, Frosch, & Koenigsberg, 1987, in Häkkänen & Laajasalo, 2006) found that, in only 5%, the instruction was to kill another person, and there is evidence that most ignore these commands.

Syndrome of Disorganization and Negative Symptoms

Delusions may not account for all of the excess violence observed in schizophrenia (Baxter, 1997). A three-syndrome model of schizophrenia based on reality distortion, disorganization, and *psychomotor poverty* (Liddle, 1987) may account for the remaining schizophrenia-associated violence; and it has been proposed that thought disorder—the primary feature of the **disorganization syndrome**—may contribute to violence in schizophrenia (Baxter, 1997), though to date this relationship has not been empirically established. Finally, one national antipsychotic clinical-trials study (Swanson et al., 2006) found that negative symptoms of schizophrenia, such as social withdrawal, actually reduced the risk of serious violence. Other authors have also reported a lower risk of violence associated with patients with negative symptoms (Markowitz, 2011).

Other Factors

Poor insight and medication noncompliance have been associated with an increased risk for violence in inpatients with schizophrenia (Arango et al., 1999; Carroll, Pantelis, & Harvey, 2004), and lack of insight at discharge has predicted criminal recidivism in released schizophrenia inpatients (Soyka et al., 2007). Carroll and colleagues (2004) administered measures of insight, hopelessness, and schizophrenia symptomatology to an Australian sample of forensic psychiatric hospital inpatients and outpatients with schizophrenia (25 men and 3 women)—23 of whom were found not guilty by reason of insanity (see Chapter 11) for the crime of murder. (The diagnoses were rendered using DSM-IV criteria for schizophrenia and made by the consulting psychiatrist using file review and interviews.) Results indicated that insight scores did not differ significantly between patients with a history of violence prior to their index offense compared to those without. Awareness of illness, but not compliance, was positively correlated with level of hopelessness; and a higher level of awareness of having a mental illness was thus related to feeling more hopeless about the future. Additionally, forensic patients demonstrated comparable levels of insight to those shown by general psychiatry (nonforensic) outpatients from samples in Canada and Taiwan (better insight, in fact, compared to the latter)—though the size and characteristics of these samples are not discussed and thus the validity of such comparisons is not entirely clear, nor is the statistical significance of the Taiwanese sample comparison.

Laajasalo and Häkkänen (2006) suggest that situational variables and violent behavioral history rather than psychotic symptomatology may be associated with excessive violence in homicidal schizophrenic persons. In a study of Florida psychiatric clinic patients with schizophrenia who underwent emergency evaluation, Schwartz, Petersen, and Skaggs (2001) found that global level of functioning, manic symptomatology (see Chapter 6), and disturbed thought processes all significantly predicted the degree of homicidal ideation. A decrease in the first and an increase in the latter two variables were associated with increased homicidality. However, correlation does not imply causation, and no nonschizophrenic control groups were used in this study. Results were replicated in a later study (Schwartz et al., 2003), where substance abuse was also found to be positively correlated with extreme homicidality.

Crime in schizophrenia and in other psychotic disorders may reflect the coexistence of additional mental illnesses associated with criminal behavior, such as psychopathy (Laajasalo, Salenius, Lindberg, Repo-Tiihonen, & Häkkänen-Nyholm, 2011; Tengström et al., 2004—see Chapter 10), substance use disorders (McCabe et al., 2012; Tengström et al., 2004—see below), conduct disorder (Hodgins, Tiihonen, & Ross, 2005), and antisocial personality disorder (ASPD; McCabe et al., 2012; Moran & Hodgins, 2004; Schug, Raine, & Wilcox, 2007—see Chapter 10). Joyal and colleagues (2004) found that homicidal offenders in Finland with both schizophrenia and ASPD were less likely to be triggered by psychotic symptoms, more likely to assault victims who were not family or household members, more likely to be intoxicated at the time of the offense, and more likely to be involved in a fight or argument with the victim prior to the homicide than were offenders without ASPD (though these results may merely reflect characteristics associated with ASPD offenders rather than with a subgroup of schizophrenic offenders with ASPD—as nonschizophrenic offenders both with and without ASPD were not used in this study). In a community sample, Schug et al. (2007) found significantly increased rates of self-reported crime in individuals with both schizophrenia-spectrum personality disorders (SSPDs) and ASPD compared to those with either condition alone and to normal controls. Also, both the SSPD and ASPD group and the ASPD-only group were characterized by significantly more official record criminal charges and convictions than were either SSPD-only individuals or normal controls. (Though the SSPD and ASPD group had almost double the number of charges and convictions as the ASPD-only group, these differences were not statistically significant.) Interestingly, Fazel, Buxrud, and colleagues (2010) found depression to be inversely associated with homicide in a national case-control study of discharged psychotic-disordered hospital patients.

Gender

Although both men and women have been included in studies of schizophrenia and crime and violence, gender-specific factors associated with schizophrenic violence have largely gone understudied. Some evidence, however, suggests that schizophrenia may interact with gender to produce elevated rates of violence in schizophrenic women. For example, in a study of a Danish birth cohort, schizophrenic men were found to be 4.6 times more likely to be convicted of violent offenses than men with no psychiatric admissions whereas schizophrenic women were 23.2 times more likely to have violent convictions than their counterparts with no psychiatric admissions (Hodgins, 2004). Similarly, rates of homicide convictions in Copenhagen over a 25-year period (Gottlieb et al., 1987) and of homicidal assaults in West Germany over a 10-year period (Häfner & Böker, 1982) appear comparatively elevated among schizophrenic women (6–44%) versus men (8–20%) and may reflect gender differences.

Studies of violence in samples of women that have included those with psychotic disorders may shed additional light on the nature of violence in women with schizophrenia. For example, in a national sample of 125 Finnish women prosecuted for homicide or attempted homicide who underwent forensic psychiatric evaluation, Putkonen, Collander, Honkasalo, and Lönnqvist (2001) found that those with personality disorders and those with psychoses formed two distinct subgroups of homicidal female offenders. Psychotic women ($n = 34$) were significantly more likely to target children, drown or suffocate victims, and engage in extended suicide;

personality disordered women ($n = 77$) more often targeted adults, stabbed victims, were involved in a quarrel with or were provoked by the victim, and were intoxicated with alcohol at the time of the offense. Finally, one prospective community study of 304 psychotic women (Dean et al., 2006) found one-fifth to have committed assault over a two-year period. Six independent risk factors predicted violence in this sample: history of violence, nonviolent conviction, African-Caribbean ethnicity, victimization, high levels of unmet need, and comorbid Cluster B personality disorder. However, no men were included for comparison, so it is difficult to know if these are gender-specific factors associated with violence in women with schizophrenia.

Origins of Crime and Violence in Schizophrenia: Theoretical Explanations and Etiological Mechanisms

Psychoanalytic Factors

Psychoanalytic interpretations of case material from schizophrenic murderers can be found in the literature (Arieti & Schreiber, 1981; Lehrman, 1939), and some authors have speculated that people with schizophrenia commit violent acts such as homicide as an unconscious defense against an oncoming outbreak of psychosis (Reichard & Tillman, 1950; Sugai, 1999; Wertham, 1937). Others do not agree, stating that *psychodynamic defense mechanisms* are usually employed habitually whereas schizophrenic violence tends to be committed only once (Guttmacher, 1960, in Arieti & Schreiber, 1981). Karpman (1951) interpreted murder within the context of psychoses as being a symbolic murder of one's own homosexuality. According to Blackman et al. (1963), the personality profiles of "sudden murderers" (i.e., individuals who, without prior history of serious aggressive antisocial acts, suddenly and intentionally kill) indicate they are dependent, schizoid, or borderline (see Chapter 10) schizophrenic males with weak masculine identification who are easily provoked into rage. Their homicides follow periods of profound struggling against dependency, feelings of helplessness, inner disequilibrium, and impending psychotic episodes.

Neurobiological Factors

Recent findings suggest that antisocial individuals with schizophrenia may represent a biologically distinct subgroup of schizophrenic individuals. For example, brain imaging studies indicate structural and functional differences in frontal and temporal regions among aggressive, violent, and antisocial schizophrenia patients in comparison to those who are not (e.g., Hoptman et al., 2005; Joyal, Putkonen et al., 2007; Kumari et al., 2006; Spalletta et al., 2001; Wong et al., 1997). Using structural magnetic resonance imaging in a Chinese forensic sample of 92 males and females, Yang, Raine, and colleagues (2010) found differential patterns of volumetric reductions among murderers with schizophrenia, murderers without schizophrenia, and nonviolent schizophrenia inpatients compared to normal controls. These reductions were found in the right hippocampus and parahippocampal gyrus for murderers with schizophrenia, in the right parahippocampal gyrus for murderers without schizophrenia, and in the bilateral medial frontal cortex for nonviolent schizophrenia patients. For murderers with schizophrenia, these gray matter reductions in the right hippocampus were also significant relative to those found in murderers without schizophrenia and in nonviolent schizophrenia inpatients.

EEG anomalies have been shown to characterize violent but not nonviolent schizophrenia patients and controls. For example, violent schizophrenia patients failed to demonstrate P50 auditory evoked potential suppression, suggesting they have disturbed information sensory gating in comparison to nonviolent patients and to controls (Fresán et al., 2007). Additionally, Schug and colleagues (2011) found murderers with schizophrenia to be characterized by increased left-hemispheric *fast-wave* resting EEG activity relative to nonviolent schizophrenia patients; instead, nonviolent schizophrenia patients demonstrated increased diffuse *slow-wave* activity compared to all other groups.

Psychophysiological investigations have produced evidence for a biologically based antisocial schizophrenia subtype. For example, in a study of 101 male schoolchildren (age 14–16 years), Raine and Venables (1984) identified a subgroup of antisocial schoolchildren with schizoid tendencies that were characterized by *skin conductance nonresponding*—suggestive of a disturbance in attentional processes—relative to other antisocial (responding) and prosocial children. In a study of 37 adult, male, top-security English prisoners, Raine (1987) found reduced skin conductance in those characterized by high schizotypy compared to those with low schizotypy. In a later prospective longitudinal study of 134 males from a Danish birth cohort, Raine, Bihrle, Venables, Mednick, and Pollock (1999) found a subgroup of schizotypal criminals in whom schizotypy was assessed at ages 18–19 and criminality at ages 30–33 years to be characterized by SC-orienting deficits relative to schizotypal noncriminals. These schizotypal criminals also had increased alcoholism relative to criminals, schizotypal noncriminals, and normal controls. Additionally, in an adult community sample, Schug, Raine, and Wilcox (2007) found reduced SC orienting to neutral tones in individuals with both schizophrenia spectrum personality disorders and antisocial personality disorder relative to those with either condition alone or to normal controls.

Specific neuropsychological deficits also appear to distinguish antisocial individuals with schizophrenia from their non-antisocial and nonschizophrenic counterparts. A recent series of meta-analyses of 45 studies (Schug & Raine, 2009) compared the neuropsychological performance of antisocial schizophrenic individuals to that of non-antisocial schizophrenic individuals and to antisocial individuals without schizophrenia. Performance was evaluated across several different domains of neuropsychological functioning for both types of comparisons. Results indicated antisocial schizophrenic individuals, compared to their antisocial counterparts, demonstrated widespread deficits across multiple domains (Full Scale IQ, Verbal and Performance IQ, attention, broadly defined executive function, and memory). However, in comparison to their schizophrenic counterparts, persons with antisocial schizophrenia were characterized instead by reduced general intellectual functioning and memory dysfunction (as opposed to hypothesized Verbal IQ and executive function deficits). More recent data continue to indicate similar deficits in murderers with schizophrenia who commit domestic homicide (Hanlon et al., 2011).

Additionally, molecular genetic studies report that homozygosity of the low-activity *catechol O-methyltransferase (COMT)* genotype differentiates schizophrenia patients characterized by aggressive, dangerous, violent, and homicidal behaviors from those who are not (Kotler et al., 1999; Lachman et al., 1998; Strous et al., 1997), and various forms of antisociality are reportedly elevated among relatives of schizophrenics compared to relatives of nonschizophrenic individuals (Hodgins, 2004). Furthermore, obstetrical factors, such as higher birth weight and larger head circumference, have been associated with later adult criminality in schizophrenia patients (Cannon et al., 2002). Last, Schug and colleagues (2010) found murderers with schizophrenia to be characterized by significantly increased (i.e., later) *birth order* relative to both nonviolent schizophrenia patients and murderers without schizophrenia. Birth order was also negatively correlated with gray matter volume in key frontal subregions for schizophrenic murderers and was negatively correlated with parental socioeconomic status. These findings may suggest that biological, psychosocial, or interactional trajectories may lead to homicidal violence in schizophrenia. Overall, although the findings are still preliminary, the prospect of identifying the distinct biological characteristics of antisocial schizophrenia appears promising.

Theory of Mind

Theory of mind (ToM) is the ability to represent the mental states of one's self and of others (Murphy, 1998; see Chapter 3). It is believed that deficits in ToM functioning might explain the social withdrawal, poverty of speech, and repetitive behaviors seen in schizophrenia. Thought insertion and delusions of control may also reflect impairments in the ability to represent one's own intentions to act, and reference and persecutory delusions may reflect difficulties in representing the mental states of others. Theory of mind research in hospitalized forensic patients has shown that violent individuals with paranoid schizophrenia demonstrated poor empathy but good mentalizing abilities compared to patients who were nonviolent (Abu-Akel & Abushua'leh, 2004). Also, in forensic samples, unique ToM deficits differentiate schizophrenia patients from those without schizophrenia (i.e., those with personality disorders or Asperger's syndrome) and differentiate among subtypes of schizophrenia patients characterized by specific symptoms (Murphy, 1998, 2006).

Substance Use

Police referred to Herbert Mullin as a "whacked-out druggie," and on his abdomen were the tattoos "LEGALIZE ACID" and "Eagle Eyes Marijuana," reflecting his consumption of both substances, which may have exacerbated his illness (Newton, 2000). In fact, rates of substance use among individuals with schizophrenia are high, possibly representing efforts to use legal and illegal substances to self-medicate and reduce psychotic symptoms. Schizophrenic persons are more likely than others to abuse substances and be criminal and violent

(Douglas & Skeem, 2005; Wallace et al., 1998), and substance abuse appears to contribute to increased crime and violence in schizophrenic individuals over and beyond levels seen in those without substance use disorders (e.g., Fazel et al., 2009b, 2009c; Yates et al., 2010). For example, though schizophrenic men without substance use disorders are more than 4 times more likely to violently offend than men with no mental illness or substance abuse, those with alcohol abuse were shown to be more than 25 times more likely to commit violent offenses in comparison to men with no mental disorders or alcohol problems (Tengström et al., 2004). Similarly, in a meta-analysis of 20 studies (incorporating a combined total of 18,423 participants), Fazel and colleagues (2009a) found a nearly four-fold increased risk of violent crime among schizophrenia patients comorbid for substance abuse compared to those without substance abuse. Furthermore, Swanson et al. (1996) found the combination of substance use disorders with **threat/control-override (TCO) symptoms** added significantly to the risk of violent behavior. Finally, Dumais and colleagues (2011) tested their "clinical specificity hypothesis" using a sample of male patients with schizophrenia-spectrum disorders. (The hypothesis is that it is possible to define a specific group of individuals with schizophrenia associated with substance use, impulsivity, and serious violence.) Four subgroups were identified, with substance use disorders being associated with risk for serious violence and incarceration. Furthermore, comorbid alcohol and substance abuse are among the five items on a novel and brief screening tool used for violence prediction in discharged hospital patients with schizophrenia; other items include male gender, previous conviction, and young age at assessment (Singh et al., 2012). Ultimately, it appears that schizophrenia and substance use are often inextricably intertwined, and the effects of such use on crime and violence in schizophrenia continues to be a promising area of study.

Psychosocial Factors

Herbert Mullin did not appear to be characterized by any significant social or interpersonal difficulties in the years leading up to his disorder; in fact—other than his oppressive religious upbringing—the opposite appears to be true. Nevertheless, evidence suggests that psychosocial factors may play a key role in the etiology of crime and violence in schizophrenia. For example, Flannery, Penk, Irvin, and Gallagher (1998) compared violent and nonviolent schizophrenia patients (and, in a subsequent analysis, interpersonally violent versus non-interpersonally violent schizophrenia patients) in several areas of social and personal adjustments in a statewide sample of 847 hospital inpatients (56% males, 44% females). Violence was defined using medical histories, as well as reports and observations made during patient hospitalization, which lasted up to one year. Violence ratings were made by treatment teams of mental health professionals. Violent schizophrenia patients—particularly those who were interpersonally violent (i.e., those that harmed others)—were characterized by deficits in basic daily self-care and in family and community social adjustment; nonviolent patients were characterized by intact social role functioning but with impairments in cognition and affect, including internal confusion, restless agitation, and depression. These authors discuss findings in terms of interpersonal skills and conflict resolution: interpersonally violent schizophrenia patients appear to lack the skills to resolve conflicts with others adaptively while non-interpersonally violent patients may be distracted by internal cognitive confusion and psychotic symptoms, which limit or preclude social interactions and opportunities for conflicts that may tax their limited social skills. In a 14-year prospective follow-up study of a rural Chinese cohort, Ran and colleagues (2010) found the risk of criminality among individuals with schizophrenia to be associated with similar psychosocial risk factors (i.e., being male, unmarried, previous violence, homelessness, no family caregivers, and illness symptom severity). Other psychosocial factors such as stress have been considered in the manifestation of aggressive and violent behaviors in schizophrenia (Volavka & Citrome, 2011). Ultimately, it may be key social factors, such as interpersonal skills and social support networks, that act as important protective mechanisms against violence in schizophrenia.

Other studies have examined psychosocial functioning and early childhood psychosocial deprivation in violent offenders with schizophrenia and other psychotic disorders. Homelessness, for example, is a noted problem among the severely and persistently mentally ill—including those with schizophrenia. Homelessness can impede access to treatment, contribute to deterioration in social functioning, and attenuate social bonds and family support (Felix, Herman, & Susser, 2008). In a sample of English prisoners, Taylor (1993) found psychotic violent offenders more likely to be socially isolated (living alone, homelessness) than their nonpsychotic counterparts. In a Chinese brain hospital sample (see Schug et al., 2011), Schug (2009) found murderers with schizophrenia to be characterized by more recent homelessness in comparison to both normal controls and to nonviolent schizophrenia patients (though group differences with the latter only approached significance) and more likely to be living alone than murderers without schizophrenia. Additionally, Moran and Hodgins (2004) used four indices of psychosocial functioning in a sample of 232 men with schizophrenic disorders (including 38 murderers). They found more deficits in the GAF (see Chapter 1, and remember that the GAF has been eliminated in the DSM-5) and in intimate relationships, employment history, and "successfully completed military service" in those with ASPD compared to those without ASPD—though these differences were not significant.

Individuals who later become schizophrenic are disproportionately likely to have suffered the disadvantages of social deprivation (i.e., to have low *SES*) both *in utero* and in early life (Venables, Raine, Dalais, Liu, & Mednick, 2006). Schizophrenic murderers in the aforementioned Chinese brain hospital sample (see Schug et al., 2011) have been characterized by significant increases in total amounts of childhood psychosocial deprivation compared to normal controls; examples of deprivation include lacking one or both parents; parental divorce, criminality, discord, alcohol use, and mental and physical health problems; having parents on welfare; large family size; childhood abuse; low parental SES, resulting in moving to many different homes; and childhood institutionalization (Schug, 2009). Indeed, childhood psychosocial deprivation has been reported in psychotic offenders in other studies (Taylor, 1993). In fact, in a 35-year longitudinal study of a Swedish male birth cohort, Eriksson and colleagues (2011) found four factors (at age 18) strongly associated with lifetime criminal offending among those later diagnosed with schizophrenia (i.e., in 377 of 49,398): poor conduct in school, contact with police or child care authorities, crowded living conditions, and arrest for public drinking. In another large Swedish cohort study, Fazel and colleagues (2009a) found parental violent crime to be associated with violent criminality in offspring hospitalized for schizophrenia. In a retrospective interview and records case-control study of English high-security hospital patients with schizophrenia, Jones and colleagues (2010) found paternal criminal convictions, larger family size, and younger age of first cigarette and illegal drug use and of maternal separation, along with younger and more frequent criminal justice system contact, to be associated with preadmission offending compared to postadmission offending (which was associated with younger and more frequent hospitalization). It is noteworthy that many of these social factors are also commonly observed among individuals in the general population who become criminal and violent—reemphasizing that potential pathways to crime and violence among those with schizophrenia may not necessarily be illness related.

Other etiological mechanisms associated with crime and violence in schizophrenia and reflecting a developmental perspective have been proposed by researchers. For example, integrative biological and social (i.e., biosocial) risk factors have been examined in longitudinal studies of crime and schizophrenia. More specifically, Finnish longitudinal health-care and criminal-register data indicate that poor educational attainment and poor grades for attention at school, along with the previously mentioned obstetric factors, were significantly associated with adult criminal offending in a sample of schizophrenia patients (Cannon et al., 2002). Additionally, several studies indicate the existence of what may be a distinct subgroup of "early start" schizophrenic offenders characterized by preschizophrenia criminality (Naudts & Hodgins, 2006). In fact, Hodgins (2008) later proposed three distinct subtypes of violent offenders with schizophrenia based upon the age of onset of antisociality and violence: (1) **early starters**, wherein antisocial behavior emerges in childhood or adolescence, well before the onset of schizophrenia, and remains stable throughout the lifespan; (2) the most common offenders, who are not violent prior to the onset of schizophrenia but are repeatedly aggressive towards others once the illness develops; and (3) a small group with chronic schizophrenia who are not aggressive for one or two decades after the illness develops but who then become seriously violent—often killing those who care for them. Overall, this developmental perspective is crucial in understanding the numerous ways in which schizophrenia and crime may be chronologically related, and it could have enormous implications in the prevention of various forms of schizophrenic violence.

Applied Issues

The last section of this chapter is devoted to various applied issues that have been addressed in the literature on the schizophrenia-crime relationship; they are related to treatment (including medication adherence and treatment alliance), involvement with the criminal justice system, and victimization. Issues related to standard biosocial treatment and management approaches (i.e., pharmacological and psychosocial therapies) may directly influence violence and criminality in individuals with schizophrenia and other psychotic disorders. Violence in schizophrenic outpatients has been associated with difficulties in basic social areas, including psychosocial treatment adherence, medication compliance, and treatment alliance (Douglas & Skeem, 2005). In fact, Yates and colleagues (2010) found medication compliance to be the single most enduring factor associated with clinical stability and the prevention of crime and violence in a long-term cognitive skills inpatient program for individuals with mental illness (including schizophrenia). Additionally, both biological and social factors are thought to affect the management and treatment of aggression and violence in schizophrenia patients (Volavka & Citrome, 2011); and new biosocial research into the prevention and treatment of schizophrenia indicates that early environmental enrichment approaches that emphasized nutritional, educational, and physical exercise enhancements at ages 3–5 reduced a mild form of schizophrenia and antisocial behavior 14–20 years later (Raine et al., 2006). Furthermore, long-term patient care and mental health service applications may play a significant role in reducing violence in schizophrenic individuals. For example, Erb, Hodgins, Freese, Müller-Isberner, and Jöckel (2001) found that the risk of homicide by persons in Germany with schizophrenia was not significantly different in time periods before and after that country instituted a policy of deinstitutionalization (in the study, 1955–1964 and 1992–1996, respectively). This result suggests that either specialized long-term care or mental health services use (which characterized the latter period) may have a preventative effect and reduce homicides by these individuals.

Researchers have also recently begun to assess the extent and nature of the involvement of schizophrenic persons with the criminal justice system. Such involvement in the United States and other countries is both highly prevalent and costly (Ascher-Svanum, Nyhuis, Faries, Ball, & Kinon, 2010). In fact, Ascher-Svanum and colleagues found being a victim of a crime and being on parole or probation to be the most common encounters with the criminal justice system among individuals with schizophrenia and that the mean annual per-patient cost of this involvement was $1,429. Schizophrenic individuals with criminal justice system involvement were more likely to be substance users and less likely to be compliant with antipsychotic medication regimes compared to those without involvement. Likewise, data from the Clinical Antipsychotic Trials of Intervention Effectiveness (CATIE), a large medication trial treating 1,460 individuals with schizophrenia, indicate several variables associated with criminal justice system involvement: past adolescent conduct disorder, being younger and male, movement disorder symptoms (*Akathisia*) developing as a side effect of antipsychotic medications, and drug abuse (Greenberg et al., 2011). Heinrichs and Sam (2012) found context variables (employment status, education, substance use) and illness symptoms (paranoia, depression, low energy) but not neuropsychological performance to predict criminal charges (i.e., contact with law enforcement). Neither predicted violence or convictions (i.e., involvement with courts) in individuals with schizophrenia, however, suggesting that specific contextual and illness aspects of schizophrenia are associated with particular criminal justice system outcomes. Ultimately, the extreme financial and personal costs related to the interactions with the criminal justice system of individuals with schizophrenia, along with the complex nature of this involvement, further underscore the dire need for a greater scientific understanding of the relationship between schizophrenia and crime.

Finally, a related literature on the association between schizophrenia and criminal victimization has burgeoned in the past decade. Self-reported data from studies in Australia and Finland indicate that patients with schizophrenia and other psychotic disorders are at an increased risk for violent and nonviolent victimization (Chapple et al., 2004; Fitzgerald et al., 2005; Honkonen, Henriksson, Koivisto, Stengård, & Salokangas, 2004). Increased odds are associated with specific victimological characteristics: female gender, homelessness, lifetime history of substance abuse, recent arrest, poorer social and occupational functioning, and increased symptoms of disorganization (Chapple et al., 2004). Furthermore, a recent first-of-its-kind Australian case-linkage study using official victimization records (Short et al., 2013) found patients with schizophrenia-spectrum disorders to be at increased risk for violent and sexually violent but not overall victimization compared to the general community. Interestingly, schizophrenia-spectrum disordered patients who had been charged with a criminal offense were also 4.80 times more likely to have a record of violent victimization and 3.07 times more likely to have a record of nonviolent victimization compared to those without criminal histories. Together, results may suggest a complex interplay between offending and victimization, psychotic illness and substance use, and psychosocial and environmental factors predisposing one to criminality and being victimized (e.g., homelessness) in the relationship between schizophrenia and crime victimization. More work is needed in this important area of research, which will contribute significantly to the current understanding of the overarching schizophrenia-crime relationship.

Conclusion

The case of Herbert Mullin illustrates how acts of extreme violence may manifest within the psychotic experience. In the study of the relationship between mental illness and crime, the scientific literature on schizophrenia is among the largest and most developed relative to that on other mental illness categories. Although prevalence-rate studies have produced variable results, overall, the rates of schizophrenia in criminal populations and of criminal behavior in schizophrenic populations appear to be elevated relative to those for comparison groups without schizophrenia and for the general population. Many studies have focused upon violence in patient samples of schizophrenic persons and on homicide within the context of the disorder. Fewer studies have addressed nonviolent crimes such as property and drug offenses or other more violent crimes such as sexual offenses and arson. Specific psychological factors—psychotic symptoms, such as delusions, hallucinations, syndrome of disorganization, and negative symptoms, along with other factors—have been examined in their relationship with crime and violence. Explanatory mechanisms for crime in schizophrenia have been offered in the form of psychoanalytic theory, neurobiological research, and social explanations. Despite this relative abundance of acquired scientific information about schizophrenia and other psychotic disorders and crime, much more research is needed to understand fully the nature, scope, and implications of the relationship between the two phenomena.

KEY TERMS

Capgras syndrome
catatonic behavior
command hallucinations
delusion
delusions of misidentification
disorganization syndrome
disorganized speech
Doppelgänger syndrome
early starters
Fregoli syndrome
hallucination
intermetamorphosis
negative symptoms
persecutory delusions
positive symptoms
psychotic disorders
schizophrenia
thought disorder
threat/control-override (TCO) symptoms

REVIEW QUESTIONS

1. Compare and contrast the theoretical perspectives regarding the etiology of schizophrenia outlined in this chapter. Identify and describe areas of conceptual overlap.
2. Examine Tables 5.5 and 5.6 and the summaries of research studies in the "A Closer Look" sections for each disorder in this chapter. Discuss how prevalence rates of crime in the disordered populations and of the disorder in criminal populations differ among these disorders, if at all. Using the information in the tables, speculate as to how these differences in prevalence rates may have been caused by methodology (e.g., in terms of study types, sample characteristics, methodological issues, or other concerns).
3. Compare and contrast the associations between schizophrenia and the crimes of homicide, arson, property offenses, and sexual crimes. Critically evaluate the research in each of these areas.
4. Compare and contrast the symptoms of schizophrenia in terms of their potentially differential contributions toward crime and violence.
5. Reflect on research that concerns the theoretical explanations of and the etiological mechanisms involved in the origins of crime and violence in schizophrenia. Identify the strengths and weaknesses of each perspective. From which theoretical perspective does the research hold up best to critical evaluation? Explain your answer.

6

Mood Disorders

BLAIR MARIE STOCKDILL

On the morning of September 20, 2010, police were called to the Ventura, California, apartment of 25-year-old Blair Marie Stockdill, where loud screams had been reported by neighbors. Officers arrived to find Stockdill holding a knife and fighting with her ex-boyfriend, who had stab wounds to his wrist and arm. Inside the apartment was the body of Alaina, her eight-year-old daughter, in the bathtub where Stockdill had drowned her several days before.

Stockdill had struggled for years with mental illness. At age 17, she had been hospitalized for bipolar disorder–police were called because she was screaming "in tongues" and holding one-year-old Alaina upside down by the calves because there were "evil spirits in her." Complaints of Stockdill's out of control behavior followed her release. Two years later, police found Alaina, three, left alone in a car while her mother visited a friend's house; and a social worker conducting a subsequent home visit found Stockdill's furniture on her lawn. At that point Alaina's father, Michael Stockdill, took guardianship.

In 2005, Blair Marie Stockdill was convicted of two petty thefts (one from a discount store and another a shopping cart from a grocery store) and for disturbing the peace–when she allegedly fought with and tossed a lit match at a police officer. An initial charge of resisting arrest was dismissed.

For a time, Stockdill had improved. She took college courses and planned to attend cosmetology school. She had been living with her daughter since 2007 and had won legal custody of her daughter less than a year before her death. In her petition, Stockdill had written "Please help me in my endeavor to become a fully productive member of society and give me the chance every American deserves." Her father believed his daughter loved Alaina and, in her right mind, would never do anything to hurt her.

Stockdill also struggled with drug addiction. Although she had been sober for two years, she stopped her psychotropic medication and starting to use methamphetamines. In the weeks that followed, some had expressed concerns about Alaina's welfare, and several had called Child Protective Services. One report alleged that Stockdill had choked her daughter. Both police and social workers investigating complaints determined Alaina was not in danger.

Stockdill eventually pled guilty to first-degree murder by reason of insanity. She was sentenced to 25 years to life, to be served at Patton State Hospital.

Emotions are as integral to and inseparable from human experience as are thoughts and behaviors, and fluctuations in moods are arguably the colors in the palette of our existence. Many of us will experience signs of mood disturbances, though most will not endure mood syndromes that reach a level of clinical significance and cause impairment in important areas of our lives. These mood disorders are often easily grasped by students in undergraduate abnormal psychology courses because the symptoms of such a disorder—at least at subthreshold levels—can be quite common and easy to relate to. How then can one's mood become so severe as to interfere with day-to-day healthy functioning and, even then, how would this cause someone to be criminal or violent? Cases of women like Blair Stockdill who, under the influence of severe mood disorders, murder their children are unfortunately not uncommon; and they speak to a need for greater understanding of the relationship between mood disorders and crime.

Diagnostic Criteria and the Prevalence of Mood Disorders

The DSM-IV-TR originally outlined an entire class of mood disorders, comprised of major depressive disorder, dysthymic disorder, bipolar I disorder, bipolar II disorder, cyclothymic disorder, mood disorder due to a general medical condition, and mood disorder NOS. Changes in the DSM-5 include the separation of bipolar and related disorders from the depressive disorders and the reordering of these disorder classes in the actual text. Although the DSM-IV-TR originally presented depressive disorders first, the DSM-5 places bipolar and related disorders before depressive disorders and right after the schizophrenia spectrum and other psychotic disorders (see Chapter 5); the newly placed category represents a "bridge" between the two disorder classes in terms of symptoms, family history, and genetics (APA, 2013, p. 123). Conceptually, however, the disorders themselves have remained largely similar across the two editions; and the DSM-IV-TR sequencing of disorders will be retained for the present chapter.

The diagnosis of mood disorders using the DSM-IV-TR and DSM-5 is essentially a two-step process. The "building blocks," so to speak, of these disorders—known as mood episodes (major depressive, manic, hypomanic, and mixed)—are first diagnosed using the criteria listed below. Table 6.1 shows the DSM-5 diagnostic criteria for a **major depressive episode**, and Table 6.2 does the same for a **manic episode**. Diagnostic criteria for hypomanic and mixed episodes are not included here. A **hypomanic episode** is considered a less severe variant of a manic episode with identical symptomatology but a four-day versus a seven-day threshold for symptom duration. A mixed episode is a one-week period in which criteria are met for both a major depressive episode and a manic episode. Mixed episodes have been deleted from the DSM-5.

In the second step, diagnosed mood episodes are subsequently combined to form the various mood disorders listed in the DSM-IV-TR and DSM-5: **major depressive disorder**, **bipolar I disorder**, and **bipolar II**

Table 6.1 DSM-5 Diagnostic Criteria for a Major Depressive Episode

Major Depressive Episode

A. Five (or more) of the following symptoms have been present during the same 2-week period and represent a change from previous functioning; at least one of the symptoms is either (1) depressed mood or (2) loss of interest or pleasure.

Note: Do not include symptoms that are clearly attributable to another medical condition.

1. Depressed mood most of the day, nearly every day, as indicated by either subjective report (e.g., feels sad, empty, or hopeless) or observation made by others (e.g., appears tearful). (*Note:* In children and adolescents, can be irritable mood).
2. Markedly diminished interest or pleasure in all, or almost all, activities most of the day, nearly every day (as indicated by either subjective account or observation).
3. Significant weight loss when not dieting or weight gain (e.g., a change of more than 5% of body weight in a month), or decrease or increase in appetite nearly every day. (**Note:** In children, consider failure to make expected weight gain).
4. Insomnia or hypersomnia nearly every day.
5. Psychomotor agitation or retardation nearly every day (observable by others; not merely subjective feelings of restlessness or being slowed down).
6. Fatigue or loss of energy nearly every day.
7. Feelings of worthlessness or excessive or inappropriate guilt (which may be delusional) nearly every day (not merely self-reproach or guilt about being sick).

(Continued)

(Continued)

8. Diminished ability to think or concentrate, or indecisiveness, nearly every day (either by subjective account or as observed by others).
9. Recurrent thoughts of death (not just fear of dying), recurrent suicidal ideation without a specific plan, or a suicide attempt or a specific plan for committing suicide.

B. The symptoms cause clinically significant distress or impairment in social, occupational, or other important areas of functioning.

C. The episode is not attributable to the physiological effects of a substance or to another medical condition.

Note: Criteria A-C represent a major depressive episode.

Note: Responses to a significant loss (e.g., bereavement, financial ruin, losses from a natural disaster, a serious medical illness or disability) may include feelings of intense sadness, rumination about the loss, insomnia, poor appetite, and weight loss noted in Criterion A, which may resemble a depressive episode. Although such symptoms may be understandable or considered appropriate to the loss, the presence of a major depressive episode in addition to the normal response to a significant loss should also be carefully considered. This decision inevitably requires the exercise of clinical judgment based on the individual's history and the cultural norms of the expression of distress in the context of loss.[1]

D. The occurrence of the major depressive episode is not better explained by schizoaffective disorder, schizophrenia, schizophreniform disorder, delusional disorder, or other specified and unspecified schizophrenia spectrum and other psychotic disorders.

E. There has never been a manic episode or hypomanic episode.

Note: This exclusion does not apply if all of the manic-like or hypomanic-like episodes are substance induced or are attributable to the physiological effects of another medical condition.

Source: APA (2013, pp. 160–161). Reprinted with permission from the *Diagnostic and Statistical Manual of Mental Disorders*, Fifth Edition (Copyright © 2013). American Psychiatric Association. All rights reserved.

Note: [1]In distinguishing grief from a major depressive episode (MDE), it is useful to consider that in grief the predominant affect is feelings of emptiness and loss, while in MDE it is persistent and depressed mood and the inability to anticipate happiness or pleasure. The dysphoria in grief is likely to decrease in intensity over days to weeks and occurs in waves, the so-called pangs of grief. These waves tend to be associated with thoughts or reminders of the deceased. The depressed mood of MDE is more persistent and not tied to specific thoughts or preoccupations. The pain of grief may be accompanied by positive emotions and humor that are uncharacteristic of the pervasive unhappiness and misery characteristic of MDE. The thought content associated with grief generally features a preoccupation with thoughts and memories of the deceased, rather than the self-critical or pessimistic ruminations seen in MDE. In grief, self-esteem is generally preserved, whereas in MDE feelings of worthlessness and self-loathing are common. If self-derogatory ideation is present in grief, it typically involves perceived failings vis-à-vis the deceased (e.g., not visiting frequently enough, not telling the deceased how much he or she was loved). If a bereaved individual thinks about death and dying, such thoughts are generally focused on the deceased and possibly about "joining" the deceased, whereas in MDE such thoughts are focused on ending one's own life because of feeling worthless, undeserving of life, or unable to cope with the pain of depression (APA, 2013, p. 161).

disorder. The combination arrived at is based upon the individual's history of mood episodes. Figure 6.1 illustrates this graphically, plotting mood level on the Y-axis over the passage of time on the X-axis. Representations of **cyclothymic disorder** and **dysthymic disorder** are also presented for comparison, though these disorders are not comprised of mood episodes. The former is defined by numerous periods of hypomanic symptoms that do not meet criteria for a hypomanic episode and numerous periods of depressive symptoms that do not meet criteria for a major depressive episode; the latter is characterized by a prolonged period of depressed mood accompanied by additional depressive symptoms that do not meet criteria for a major depressive episode (APA, 2000, pp. 345–346; APA, 2013, p. 139).

Prevalence and incidence rates of the various DSM-IV-TR mood disorders and of the DSM-5 bipolar and related disorders and depressive disorders are listed in Table 6.3.

Theoretical Conceptualizations: Depression

Several theoretical perspectives have contributed to the conceptualization of mood disorders. Historically, psychoanalytic attempts at the understanding of depression began with Freud's classic "Mourning and Melancholia"

Table 6.2 DSM-5 Diagnostic Criteria for a Manic Episode

Manic Episode

A. A distinct period of abnormally and persistently elevated, expansive, or irritable mood and abnormally and persistently increased goal-directed activity or energy, lasting at least 1 week and present most of the day, nearly every day (or any duration if hospitalization is necessary).

B. During the period of mood disturbance and increased energy or activity, three (or more) of the following symptoms (four if the mood is only irritable) are present to a significant degree and represent a noticeable change from usual behavior:

1. Inflated self-esteem or grandiosity.
2. Decreased need for sleep (e.g., feels rested after only 3 hours of sleep).
3. More talkative than usual or pressure to keep talking.
4. Flight of ideas or subjective experience that thoughts are racing.
5. Distractibility (i.e., attention too easily drawn to unimportant or irrelevant external stimuli) as reported or observed.
6. Increase in goal-directed activity (either socially, at work or school, or sexually) or psychomotor agitation (i.e., purposeless non-goal-directed activity).
7. Excessive involvement in activities that have a high potential for painful consequences (e.g., engaging in unrestrained buying sprees, sexual indiscretions, or foolish business investments).

C. The mood disturbance is sufficiently severe to cause marked impairment in social or occupational functioning or to necessitate hospitalization to prevent harm to self or others, or there are psychotic features.

D. The episode is not attributable to the physiological effects of a substance (e.g., a drug of abuse, a medication, other treatment) or to another medical condition.

Note: A full manic episode that emerges during antidepressant treatment (e.g., medication, electroconvulsive therapy) but persists at a fully syndromal level beyond the physiological effect of the treatment is sufficient evidence for a manic episode and, therefore, a bipolar I diagnosis.

Note: Criteria A-D constitute a manic episode. At least one lifetime manic episode is required for the diagnosis of bipolar I disorder.

Source: APA (2013, p. 124). Reprinted with permission from the *Diagnostic and Statistical Manual of Mental Disorders*, Fifth Edition (Copyright © 2013). American Psychiatric Association. All rights reserved.

(Freud 1917/1963). Freud proposed that early losses in childhood lead to vulnerability to depression later in adulthood and that the marked self-deprecation commonly seen in depressed patients was in fact anger turned inward. This rage, he felt, was actually directed at the lost object, which had been internalized and identified with by the patient's ego (self)—perhaps the only way some people can give up an important figure in their lives. He also proposed a severe superego in patients with *melancholia*, which was reflected in their guilt over having shown aggression toward loved ones (Gabbard, 2005). Other psychoanalytic theorists have explained depression as resulting from a present loss which reactivates a childhood blow to self-esteem (Abraham, 1924/1927); a failure during a critical phase of object-relations development known as the *depressive position* (Klein, 1940/1975); tension in the ego between ideals and reality (Bibring, 1953); helplessness in response to childhood loss of a real or imagined love object (Sandler & Joffe, 1965); loss that reactivates a feeling of being unlovable and abandoned secondary to *insecure attachment* (Bowlby, 1969); a lost love object that is transformed into a sadistic superego (Jacobson, 1971a, 1971b); and living for a dominant other (Arieti, 1977). More recently, distinctions between depression types have been proposed: dependency versus dominant goals depression (Arieti & Bemporad, 1980) and **anaclitic** versus **introjective/self-critical depression** (Blatt, 1974). According to these overlapping theories, individuals experiencing the first type of depression are vulnerable to perceived losses in relationships with others because they are dependent upon the judgments of others for self-esteem; their histories are characterized by early loss. Those experiencing the second type are exceedingly self-critical; they fail to meet their own unrealistically high

Figure 6.1 Graphic Representations of DSM-IV-TR Mood Disorders and DSM-5 Bipolar and Related Disorders and Depressive Disorders

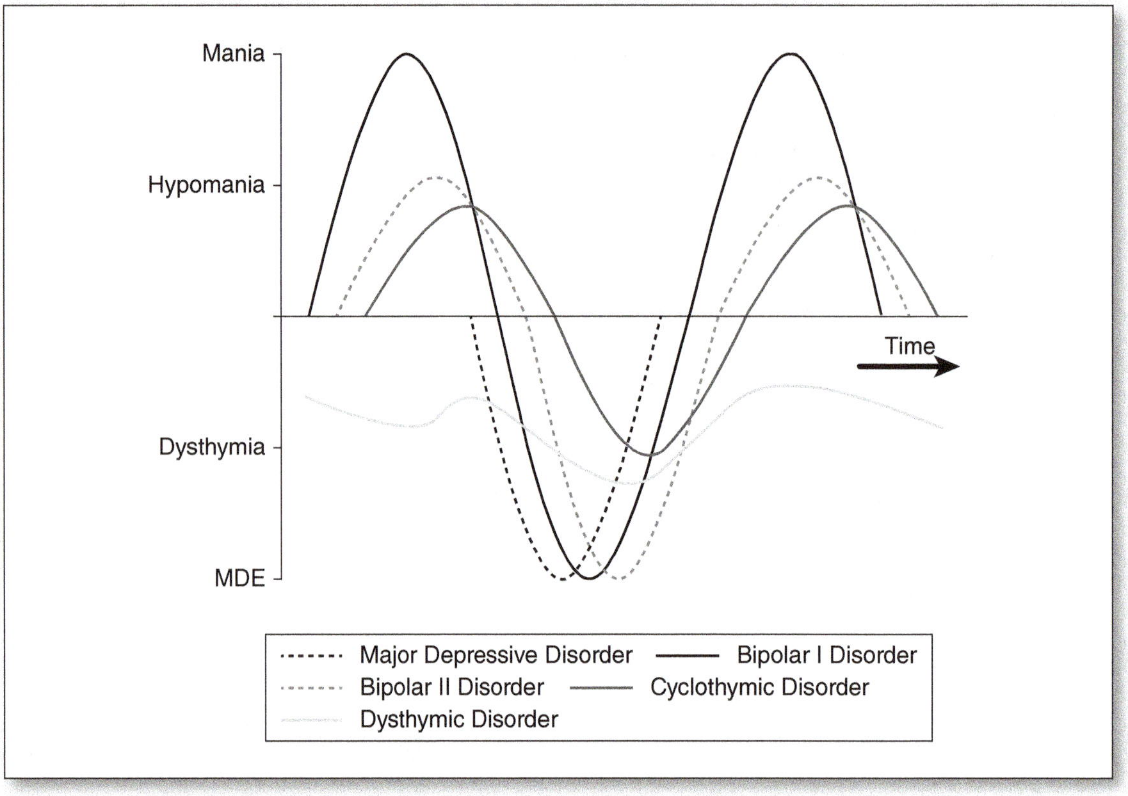

Sources: APA (2000, pp. 345–346); APA (2013, p. 139)

standards and show later acceptance of external negative evaluations (Rehm et al., 2001). In each group, unique vulnerabilities, categorized by type, trigger depression.

Cognitive theorists such as Aaron T. Beck have conceptualized depression in terms of abnormal thought processes. Beck's (1972) theory of depression is based on a cognitive triad, which he sees as comprised of the essential elements of the disorder: negative view of the self, negative view of the world, negative view of the future. Depression results from a tendency to interpret everyday events in negative ways; in a sense, the world is seen through a "blue filter" or with "tunnel vision." Depressed individuals have a set of **automatic thoughts** (schematic inferences and interpretations an individual makes in a particular situation) that intervene between outside experiences and their emotional responses to them. These thoughts are "automatic" in that the interpretive process and even the thoughts themselves may be outside of the individual's awareness—leaving only the emotional consequence of the thought known to the individual. The theme of automatic thoughts in depression is the perception of *loss*—the cognition that relates to depression. These automatic thoughts are thought to be manifestations of deeper underlying **maladaptive assumptions** (more basic interpretive rules), which drive automatic thoughts and lead us to make critical **cognitive errors** in everyday functioning. For example, *all-or-none thinking* (also known as black-and-white, polarized, or dichotomous thinking) is viewing a situation in only two categories instead of on a continuum (e.g., "If I am not completely successful, I am a total failure"). An *arbitrary inference* is an arbitrary assumption that some negative event was caused by oneself. *Selective abstraction* (also called mental filter) occurs when an individual focuses on the negative element in an otherwise positive set of information (e.g., "I received one low rating on my evaluation—which also contained several high ratings—therefore, I am doing a poor job"). *Magnification* and *minimization* also involve

Table 6.3 Diagnostic Criteria for Mood Disorders (DSM-IV-TR) and Bipolar and Related Disorders and Depressive Disorders (DSM-5)

DSM-IV-TR[1] and DSM-5[2]		
	Description	**Prevalence/Incidence**
Major Depressive Disorder	Characterized by one or more major depressive episodes (i.e., at least 2 weeks of depressed mood or loss of interest accompanied by at least four additional symptoms of depression).	Lifetime risk in community samples 10–25% for women and 5–12% for men; point prevalence is 5–9% for women and 2–3% for men. Prevalence rates appear to be unrelated to ethnicity, education, income, marital status.[1] 12-month prevalence of major depressive disorder in the United States ≈ 7%.[2]
Dysthymic Disorder **(Persistent Depressive Disorder[2])**	Characterized by at least 2 years of depressed mood for more days than not, accompanied by additional depressive symptoms that do not meet criteria for a major depressive episode.	Lifetime prevalence ≈ 6%, point prevalence ≈ 3%.[1] 12-month prevalence in the United States ≈ 0.5% for persistent depressive disorder and 1.5% for chronic major depressive disorder.[2]
Bipolar I Disorder	Characterized by one or more manic or mixed episodes, usually accompanied by major depressive episodes.	Lifetime prevalence in community samples: 0.24%[3] to 1.6%.[1] 12-month prevalence in United States ≈ 0.6%, across 11 countries: 0.0% to 0.6%.[2]
Bipolar II Disorder	Characterized by one or more major depressive episodes accompanied by at least one hypomanic episode.	Lifetime prevalence in community samples ≈ 0.5%.[1] 12-month prevalence internationally is 0.3%; in the United States, 0.8%.[2]
Cyclothymic Disorder	Characterized by at least 2 years of numerous periods of hypomanic symptoms that do not meet criteria for a manic episode and numerous periods of depressive symptoms that do not meet criteria for a major depressive episode.	Lifetime prevalence 0.4–1%. Prevalence in mood disorder clinics ≈ 3–5%.[1] Lifetime prevalence ≈ 04%–1%. Prevalence in mood disorder clinics: 3%–5%.[2]

Sources: [1]APA (2000); [2]APA (2013); [3]Perälä et al. (2007)

Note: Not listed from the DSM-IV-TR are depressive disorder NOS, bipolar disorder NOS, mood disorder due to a general medical condition, substance-induced mood disorder, and mood disorder NOS. Not listed from the DSM-5 are substance/medication-induced bipolar and related disorder, bipolar and related disorder due to another medical condition, other specified bipolar and related disorder, unspecified bipolar and related disorder, disruptive mood dysregulation disorder, premenstrual dysphoric disorder, substance/medication-induced depressive disorder, depressive disorder due to another medical condition, other specified depressive disorder, and unspecified depressive disorder.

overemphasizing negatives and underemphasizing positives (e.g., "Getting an average evaluation proves how inadequate I am, and getting high grades does not mean I am intelligent"). Finally, *inexact labeling* involves giving a distorted, global label to an event and then reacting to the label rather than the event, labeling oneself, for example, a "loser" after a perceived failure, then reacting to that distorted label: "I am a loser" (Beck, 1995; Rehm et al., 2001). Interestingly, Beck (1983) also proposed two types of depressions—**sociotropic depression** (dependency upon interpersonal relationships for positive self-evaluation) and **autonomous depression** (focused on achievement and independence)—which correspond with the two psychoanalytic types (i.e., other-oriented and self-critical) mentioned above (Rehm et al., 2001).

Behavioral theorists contend that depression arises when response-reinforcement relationships become disrupted. Ferster (1973, in Rehm et al., 2001) viewed depression as a generalized reduction of rates of response to external stimuli (analogous to the process of extinction), wherein major losses in life (e.g., loss of employment) amount to losses of important sources of reinforcement. Lewinsohn (1974) proposed that depression is a response to a loss or lack of response-contingent positive reinforcement. Reduced access to positive reinforcers in major life areas narrows behavioral repertoires and causes some behaviors to become extinct—leading to depressed mood and behavioral reduction (primary symptoms of depression). Other symptoms (e.g., low self-esteem and hopelessness) follow from this reduced level of functioning (Farmer & Chapman, 2008; Rehm et al., 2001). Depression may also arise when an individual more frequently experiences punishment rather than positive reinforcement in response to behaviors or has limited exposure to positive reinforcers due to behavioral avoidance (Martell et al., 2001).

Neurobiological evidence suggests that the causes of depression may lie in deficiencies in neurotransmitters—namely norepinephrine, dopamine, and serotonin. Studies have demonstrated that antidepressants increase norepinephrine and serotonin levels in the synaptic cleft, which probably block the movement of these chemicals back into the presynaptic axon terminal (i.e., blocking reuptake). Also, MAO inhibitor antidepressants prevent enzymes from breaking down neurotransmitters. Recent research on additional neurotransmitters (acetylcholine and gamma-aminobutyric acid, or GABA) has suggested that a more generalized neurochemical dysregulation may be at work in depression. Furthermore, diseases of the endocrine glands, which often present with symptoms of depression, suggest a role of endocrine functioning in this disorder. For example, investigations of thyroid functioning have suggested the implication of hypothyroidism in depression (Rehm et al., 2001).

Research on emotion perception has supported the idea that emotions are, in general, differentially controlled by the right hemisphere of the brain, perhaps due to this hemisphere's greater control of the subcortical systems involved in arousal and emotion. A number of skin conductance, EEG, and lesion studies have suggested increased right frontal lobe activation and increased right relative to left hemisphere activation (i.e., a hemispheric imbalance) in individuals with depression (Shenal et al., 2003). Prefrontal dysfunction has also been implicated in depression, and neuropsychological studies have identified in individuals with unipolar depression deficits in several aspects of executive functioning: working memory, *cognitive-set shifting*, planning, conflict resolution, and *emotional salience*. The problem might represent an inability to deviate from a "default mode" of repetitive behavior locked to stimuli in the environment, (e.g., depressive rumination or psychomotor retardation). Also, functional imaging studies have identified that reduced activation in the dorsolateral prefrontal cortex and the anterior cingulate cortex, as well as hyperactivation in the orbitofrontal cortex, is associated with major depression (Rogers et al., 2011). Additionally, structural imaging studies have revealed gray matter volumetric reductions in key brain regions (hippocampus, basal ganglia, orbitofrontal cortex, and anterior cingulate cortex) and white matter increases in the upper brainstem tegmentum in patients with major depressive disorder (Soriano-Mas et al., 2011).

Theoretical Conceptualizations: Mania

Various theoretical perspectives have also contributed to the understanding of mania. Psychoanalytic theorists such as Freud (1917/1947, in Rehm et al., 2001) speculated that mania was characterized by the same conflict as depression (i.e., a reaction to the loss of an unconscious object), though the anger and reproach were released outward rather than being self-directed. Abraham (1911, in Rehm et al., 2001) proposed that mania reflected an individual's failure to repress the self-hatred and guilt associated with giving up an ungratified sexual aim. Klein (1940/1975, in Gabbard, 2005) noted that manic defenses (e.g., omnipotence, denial, contempt, and idealization) result from painful emotions produced by yearning for lost love objects. These defenses are used to rescue and restore lost love objects, disavow bad internal objects, and deny slavish dependency on love objects. Expression of these manic operations may be seen as the patient denies aggression or destructiveness toward others, adopts a euphoric disposition contrary to his or her actual life situation, idealizes others, or adopts a scornful and contemptuous attitude toward others (disavowing the need for relationships). According to Klein, this manic defensive stance is often based largely upon a wish to triumph over parents and reverse the child-parent relationship. However, this wish may subsequently lead to guilt and depression—a mechanism partially responsible for the depression that often follows success or promotion.

Cognitive theorists such as Beck proposed that the manic patient is characterized by positive cognitive distortions: perceiving significant gain in life experiences, indiscriminately attributing positive value to experiences, unrealistically expecting positive outcomes for endeavors, and having exaggerated estimates of her or his abilities. These distortions occur automatically, appear plausible, and are less likely to be changed by reasoning and contradictory evidence. Additionally, they lead to feelings of euphoria and provide energy for high levels of activity (Rehm et al., 2001).

Neurobiological theorists have proposed that mania, in contrast to depression, results from an excess of neurotransmitters (Rehm et al., 2001). The integrity of white matter tracts (i.e., the neural connectivity within the brain) could be altered in bipolar disorder, and structural imaging studies have found white matter abnormalities (perhaps representing *demyelination* and/or *dysmyelination*) in bipolar I patients within major depressive episodes, which may suggest a structural marker of the illness phases of bipolar disorder (Benedetti et al., 2011). A recent multinational, multisite "mega-analysis" of structural fMRI data (Hallahan et al., 2011) revealed increased right lateral ventricular, left temporal lobe, and right putamen volumes in patients with bipolar disorder (and—interestingly—increased hippocampal and amygdala volumes in patients taking lithium compared to those not taking lithium and to normal controls). Savitz and colleagues (2011) found volumetric reductions in the habenula in unmedicated, depressed patients with bipolar disorder compared to healthy controls. (The *habenula* is a structure above the thalamus implicated in serotonin and dopamine transmission, behavioral responses to stress, and dopamine activity after the absence of an expected reward.) It has also been suggested that bipolar disorder results from a dysfunction of the brain systems that maintain emotional arousal and homeostasis (Strakowski et al., 2011), and findings from structural and functional imaging studies suggest there may be diminished prefrontal control of anterior limbic system structures (amygdala, anterior striatum, and thalamus) that results in the dysregulation of mood in those with bipolar disorder (Strakowski et al., 2005; Strakowski et al., 2011). Earlier neuropsychological findings of lower performance IQ than verbal IQ scores (thought to reflect right and left hemispheric functioning, respectively) suggested right hemispheric dysfunction in bipolar disorder, though a later critical review (Bearden et al., 2001) indicates little evidence for a specific cognitive profile in this illness. Rather, significant cognitive dysfunction in bipolar disorder may be limited to a subgroup of chronic, elderly, or multiple-episode patients and suggest a possible toxic disease process. However, more recent evidence indicates that specific neuropsychological deficits may distinguish bipolar II from bipolar I disorders; bipolar II patients performed significantly more poorly on tests of attention and reaction time. Also, those with either type of disorder may have distinct neuropsychology from healthy controls, who performed better on tests of psychomotor functioning, working memory, and impulsiveness (Harkavy-Friedman et al., 2006).

The Relationship Between Mood Disorders and Crime

The literature on mood disorders and criminal behavior is not as well-developed as that pertaining to other disorders (such as schizophrenia or psychopathy), and, to date, it remains largely unintegrated. Interesting reports of depression, mania, and various forms of criminality—dating back nearly a century and a half—have been published, though they tend to be scattered and far-flung throughout the literature and difficult to locate in many cases. However, a number of prevalence-rate studies are available; and the association between mood disorders and crime can be at least partially understood through these studies, which examine both rates of mood disorders in criminal and antisocial populations and rates of crime and antisocial behavior in populations of individuals with mood disorders. Tables 6.4 and 6.5 list a number of investigations, in chronological order, that have examined separately the prevalence rates of depressive disorders, bipolar disorders, and general *affective disorders*[1] in criminal populations and the prevalence rates of crime among those with these disorders.

1. The terms "affect," "emotion," and "mood" are often used interchangeably and have held different meanings historically with the evolution of psychiatric and psychological nomenclature. The term "affect" is traditionally used by psychologists to refer to the experience of feeling or emotion though further clarification—particularly from the cognitive psychology and neuroscience communities—has been specified. An *affect* is an automatic, physiological response to a stimulus (e.g., startle, surprise, and stun responses), which includes a basic evaluation of the stimulus as positive or negative (Reevy, Malamud Ozer, & Ito, 2010). Affects are comparable to building blocks for emotions—which are short-term, intensely felt states (Kemeny & Shestyuk, 2005) that involve further evaluation of the stimulus (i.e., beyond simply positive or negative; N. L. Stein, Hernandez, & Trabasso, 2008). Moods are longer-term affective states (Kemeny & Shestyuk, 2005).

Table 6.4 Prevalence of Mood Disorders in Criminal Populations

Depressive Disorders								
Source	**N**	**Gender**	**Age**	**Study Type**[a1]	**Sample Description**	**Disorder**	**Diagnostic system**	**Prevalence/ Incidence**
East (1936, in Good, 1978)	300	?M	?	HO	Insane murderers at Broadmoor Criminal Lunatic Asylum, England	Melancholia	?	20.7% ($n = 62$)
Rylander (1956, in Hirose, 1979)	95	M, F	?	HO	Murderers, Sweden, 1931–1945	Depression	?	16.8% ($n = 16$)
McGarry (1965, in Good, 1978)	206	183 M, 23 F	?	PI	Commitments for pretrial psychiatric evaluation at Boston State Hospital (July 1959–June 1960) and Massachusetts Mental Health Center (July–December 1957)	Psychotic depressive	?	1.5% ($n = 3$)
West (1966)	148	88 M, 60 F	< 20–40+	HO	Homicide followed by suicide: England and Wales, 1954–1961	Depressive illness	?	18.9% ($n = 28$)
Pfeiffer, Eisenstein, & Dabbs (1967)	85	2/3 M, 1/3 F	17–63	JD	Federal prisoners referred for mental competency evaluations, at USPHS Hospital in Lexington, Kentucky, 1960–1965	Psychotic depressive reaction	?	1.2% ($n = 1$)
Frazier (1974)	31	?	?	HO	Murderers in prisons in Texas, Minnesota, New Jersey, and New York and in mental hospitals in Texas, Minnesota, Saskatchewan, Massachusetts and New York	Depression	?	22.6% ($n = 7$)
Szymusik (1972)	50	M	16–68	HO	Murderers, Poland, 1955–1969	Reactive depression	?	2.0% ($n = 1$)
Okasha et al. (1975)	(1) 60 (2) 20	(1) 50 M, 10 F (2) ?M, ?F	25–35[a]	HO	"Socio-psychiatric study" of (1) Murderers in Abou-Zabel and Kanater prisons, Egypt (2) Murderers in Egyptian State Mental Hospital	Depression	?	(1) 3.3% ($n = 2$) (2) 16.7% ($n = 15$)
Medlicott (1976)	38	29 M, 9 F	14–62	HO	Individuals charged with murder ($n = 28$) and attempted murder ($n = 10$) hospitalized or referred for psychiatric opinion, New Zealand	Depressive	?	15.8% ($n = 6$)

Depressive Disorders								
Source	**N**	**Gender**	**Age**	**Study Type**[a1]	**Sample Description**	**Disorder**	**Diagnostic system**	**Prevalence/ Incidence**
Goldney (1977)	4	2 M, 2 F	31–38	HO	Case histories based upon clinical findings from coroner's reports of individuals who committed family murders followed by suicide	Depression	?	75.0% ($n = 3$)
Schuckit et al. (1977)	199	M	Adult[b]	JD	Structured personal interviews of newly arrested prisoners at a San Diego, California, jail	Affective disorder (depressive)	Brief screen for psychiatric illness (Woodruff et al., 1974)	3.0%
Good (1978)	100	11 M, 89 F	Adult	JD	Consecutive cases referred for psychiatric evaluation at a Massachusetts minimum-security prison, 1972–1975	Recurrent depression	"Unofficial" psychiatric diagnostic system (Woodruff et al., 1974)	3.0% ($n = 3$)
Parker (1979)	100	79 M, 21 F	Adult?	HO	Murderers ($n = 70$) and attempted murderers ($n = 30$) examined in Brisbane, Queensland, 1956–1976	Depression	?	23.0% ($n = 23$)
Häfner & Böker (1982)	(1) 533 (2) 3,392	M, F	14–60+	PI	(1) Mentally ill and mentally defective offenders from records searches of German federal and regional criminal bureaus, 1955–1964 (2) Mentally abnormal non-offenders (every fifth admission to regional psychiatric hospital, from register search, 1955–1964)	Affective psychoses (including manic-depressive illness and endogenous depressions)	Unspecified multiple (different or discordant) German psychiatric classification systems	(1) 6.9% ($n = 37$)[c] (2) 16.8% ($n = 571$)
Allen (1983)	104	93% M	20–40+	HO	Los Angeles Police Department record review of homicide-followed-by-suicide events in Los Angeles, 1970–1979	Despondence or depression[an]	?	18.3% ($n = 19$)

(Continued)

(Continued)

Depressive Disorders								
Source	N	Gender	Age	Study Type[a1]	Sample Description	Disorder	Diagnostic system	Prevalence/ Incidence
Dell & Smith (1983)	253	M	15 and under–70+[d]	HO	File review of men convicted of manslaughter on the grounds of diminished responsibility, 1966–1977	Depression	?	37.2% (n = 94)
Seltzer & Langford (1984)	85	M, F	15–25 (Median = 18)	PI	Interviews of individuals referred by courts or legal counsel to psychiatry department of large regional hospital in Northwest Territories, calendar year 1981	Dysthymic disorder	DSM-III, MMPI	10.6% (n = 9)
Reich & Wells (1985)	390	325 M, 65 F	M = 30.9	JD	Record review of defendants evaluated for competency to stand trial by the Yale-New Haven Psychiatric Court Clinic, 1980–1982	Major depression	DSM-III	1.0% (n = 4)[be]
						Dysthymic disorder		1.0% (n = 4)
Taylor (1986)	183	175 M, 8 F	18–73	JD	Record review of life-sentenced men and women, supervised by the Inner London Probation Service (inside prison and on license in the community)	Depression	ICD-9	13% (n = 23)
Gottlieb et al. (1987)	251	215 M, 36 F	Median = 33[aj]	HO	Record review of homicide defendants in Copenhagen, 1959–1983	Depression	ICD-8	6.3% (n = 17) depression at the time of the crime (3.3% of males, 27.8% of females)
Bland et al. (1990)	180	M	18–44	JD	Diagnostic interviews with inmates from two correctional centers, Alberta, Canada	Major depressive episode	DSM-III (DIS)	16.7% (n = 30)[ap]*
						Dysthymia		10.6% (n = 19)[aq]*

Depressive Disorders								
Source	N	Gender	Age	Study Type[al]	Sample Description	Disorder	Diagnostic system	Prevalence/ Incidence
Coté & Hodgins (1990)	495	M	19–67 (M = 31.1)	JD	Diagnostic interviews with Quebec adult penitentiary inmates	Major depression	DSM-III (DIS)	14.8% (n = 73)
Myers et al. (1990)	15	F	Juveniles	PI	Diagnostic interviews with juvenile delinquents committed to a residential treatment program, Florida	Major depressive disorder	DSM-III (DICA)	Past or current: 66.7% (n = 10)
Rath & Dash (1990)	15	10 M, 3 F[p]	20–29[p]	JD	Interviews, file reviews, and clinical observation of prisoners (murderers) referred for psychiatric evaluation, India	(1) Depression (2) Affective psychosis (depression)	ICD-9	(1) 6.7% (n = 1) (2) 6.7% (n = 1)
Yarvis (1990)	100	88 M, 12 F	33% < 25, 85% < 40	HO	Diagnostic interviews and record reviews of a series of murderers referred for psychiatric evaluation in California, 1980–1988	Dysthymic disorder	DSM-III	9.0% (n = 9)[h]
Abram & Teplin (1991)[r]	728	M	16–68 (M = 26.3)	JD	Diagnostic interviews with jail detainees at Cook County Department of Corrections, Chicago, November 1983–November 1984	(1) Major depression (2) Dysthymic disorder[u]	DSM-III-R (DIS)	(1) Lifetime: 5.1% (n = 37), Current: 3.4% (n = 25)[s] (2) Lifetime: 8.5% (n = 59)
Côté & Hodgins (1992)	(1) 87 (2) 373	M	(1) M = 35.6, SD = 8.9 (2) M = 30.3, SD = 8.3	JD	Diagnostic interviews and file reviews of penitentiary inmates, Quebec (1) Homicide offenders (2) Nonhomicide offenders	Major depression	DSM-III (DIS)	(1) 14.9% (n = 13) (2) 10.2% (n = 38)
DeJong, Virkkunen, & Linnoila (1992)	(1) 248 (2) 100	M	16–68 (M = 31.2, SD = 11.9)	JD	Criminals ordered for forensic psychiatric examination at initial incarceration in Finland (1) Murders and attempted murderers (2) Arsonists	Major depressive disorder	DSM-III	(1) 9.0% (2) 5.0%

(Continued)

(Continued)

Depressive Disorders								
Source	**N**	**Gender**	**Age**	**Study Type**[a1]	**Sample Description**	**Disorder**	**Diagnostic system**	**Prevalence/ Incidence**
Haapasalo & Hämäläinen (1996)	89	?	16–22 (*M* = 20.21, *SD* = 1.37)	JD	Structured clinical interviews with offenders randomly selected among prison inmates, Finland (1) Property offenders (2) Violent offenders	Depressive episode	DSM-IV (DICA-R-A)	Past: (1) 59.5% (2) 71.2% Current: (1) 16.2% (2) 13.5%
Marshall et al. (1998)	103	M	18–56	JD	Diagnostic interviews and questionnaires administered to recently sentenced inmates (August–December 1997) at Yatala Labour Prison, South Australia	Depression	(PDI-R)	14.7%
Galli et al. (1999)	22	M	13–17 (*M* = 15.9, *SD* = 1.1)	PI, CS	Interviews with adolescents admitting to sexually assaulting another child, referred from a juvenile rehabilitation center, the juvenile court system, and an inpatient adolescent psychiatric unit, Hamilton County, Ohio	Major depression	DSM-III-R (DICA)	23% ($n = 5$)
						Dysthymia		5% ($n = 1$)
						Total mood disorders		82% ($n = 18$)
Gibson et al. (1999)	213	M	*M* = 32	JD	Structured interviews with randomly selected state prison and regional jail inmates from a rural New England state	Major depressive	DSM-III-R (DIS-III-R)	Lifetime: 24.9% ($n = 53$) Current: 16.0% ($n = 34$)
						Dysthymia		Lifetime: 17.8% ($n = 38$) Current: 9.4% ($n = 20$)

Depressive Disorders								
Source	**N**	**Gender**	**Age**	**Study Type**[a1]	**Sample Description**	**Disorder**	**Diagnostic system**	**Prevalence/ Incidence**
McElroy et al. (1999)	36	M	18–47 (*M* = 33, *SD* = 8)	PI	Interviews with convicted sex offenders consecutively admitted to the New Life Program, Cincinnati, Ohio, November 1996–June 1998	Major depressive disorder	DSM-IV (SCID)	22% ($n = 8$)
						Total mood disorders		61% ($n = 22$)
Baillargeon et al. (2000)	170,215	155,949 M; 14,268 F	32% 18–29, 60% 30–49, 8% 50+	JD	File review of Texas Department of Criminal Justice inmates incarcerated August 1997–July 1998	Affective disorders (major depression, dysthymia)	ICD-10	3.9%
Pliszka et al. (2000)	50	45 M, 5 F	*M* = 15.4, *SD* = 1.4	JD	Interviews with adolescents consecutively admitted to the Bexar County, Texas, Juvenile Detention Center	Major depressive disorder	DSM-IV (DIS-C)	20.0% ($n = 10$)
Baxter et al. (2001)	257	240 M, 17 F	*M* = 30.6, *M* = 31.4[bi]	HO	File review of consecutive series of patients, with index offenses of parricide or stranger killing, admitted to 1 of 3 high-security hospitals in England and Wales, 1972–1996	Depression	?	5.4% ($n = 14$)
Siponmaa et al. (2001)	126	123 M, 3 F	15–22 (Median = 20)	JD	Interviews with young offenders consecutively referred for presentencing psychiatric investigation, Stockholm, Sweden, 1990–1995	Depression	ICD-9	1.0% ($n = 1$)

(Continued)

(Continued)

Depressive Disorders								
Source	**N**	**Gender**	**Age**	**Study Type**[a1]	**Sample Description**	**Disorder**	**Diagnostic system**	**Prevalence/ Incidence**
Teplin et al. (2002)	1,829	1,172 M, 657 F	10–18	JD	Diagnostic interviews of youths randomly sampled from intake into the Cook County Juvenile Temporary Detention Center, November 1995–June 1998	Major depressive episode	DSM-III-R	M: 13.0% F: 21.6%
						Dysthymia		M: 12.2% F: 15.8%
Dunsieth et al. (2004)	113	M	18–66 ($M = 35.3$, $SD = 10.4$)	PI	Diagnostic interviews with sex offenders consecutively referred to an Ohio residential sex-offender treatment program	Major depressive disorder	DSM-IV	23.9% ($n = 27$)
Leue et al. (2004)	55	M	Adult?	PI	Structured clinical interviews with sexual offenders hospitalized in forensic state hospitals in Arnsdorf, Saxony, and Moringen, Lower Saxony, Germany	Major depressive disorder	DSM-IV	53% ($n = 29$)[bk]
						Dysthymia		6% ($n = 3$)
						Any mood disorder		56% ($n = 31$)[bl]

Depressive Disorders								
Source	**N**	**Gender**	**Age**	**Study Type**[a1]	**Sample Description**	**Disorder**	**Diagnostic system**	**Prevalence/ Incidence**
Stuart et al. (2006)	103	F	$M = 31.5$, $SD = 9.6$	CS	Questionnaire administered to women arrested for violence and court referred to batterer intervention programs, Rhode Island	Depression	DSM-IV (PDSQ)	35%
Grella et al. (2008)	280	65% M	$M = 34.8$	JD	Diagnostic interviews with offenders consecutively admitted to prison-based substance-abuse treatment programs at one of four research centers (Colorado, Rhode Island, Texas, California)	Major depression	DSM-IV (SCID)	26.1% ($n = 73$)
						Dysthymia		3.9% ($n = 11$)
						Mood disorder—GMC		1.1% ($n = 3$)
						Any mood disorder		33.2% ($n = 93$)
Pham & Saloppé (2010)	84	M	Adult	PI	Psychological evaluations of forensic patients at high-security psychiatric hospital in Tomai, Belgium (Etablissement de Défense Sociale)	Depressive disorder	DSM-III (DISSI)	40% ($n = 34$)
						Mood disorders		44% ($n = 37$)
Catanesi et al. (2011)	103	85.44% M	53.41% 25–54, 22.73% 45–65, 13.64% 18–24, 5.68% < 18	HO	Psychiatric and psychological evaluations on perpetrators of homicide and attempted homicide, Italy	Depressive disorders	DSM-IV-TR	6.8%

(Continued)

(Continued)

Bipolar Disorders								
Source	**N**	**Gender**	**Age**	**Study Type[a1]**	**Sample Description**	**Disorder**	**Diagnostic System**	**Prevalence/ Incidence**
Glueck (1918, in Good, 1978)	608	M	?	JD	608 of 683 consecutive admissions to Sing Sing Prison over a 9-month period; 73 with mental illness	Manic-depressive	?	0.3% ($n = 2$)
						Cyclothymia		0.2% ($n = 1$)
Jacoby (1918, in Good, 1978)	150	M	?	JD	Psychiatric cases in Portsmouth Naval Prison, New Hampshire	Manic-depressive	?	1.3% ($n = 2$)
Hopwood (1927, in Good, 1978)	166	F	?	HO	Record review of 388 female receptions to the State Criminal Lunatic Asylum, Broadmoor, England, 1900–1924, 166 of whom were charged with infanticide or child murder	Manic-depressive	?	13.2% ($n = 22$)
Martin (1927, in Good, 1978)	103	M	?	JD	Inmates of the Illinois State Penitentiary developing a psychosis or behavior requiring isolation from general population, over a 3-year period	Manic-depressive	?	1.0% ($n = 1$)
East (1936, in Good, 1978)	300	?M	?	HO	Insane murderers at Broadmoor Criminal Lunatic Asylum, England	Mania	?	9.3% ($n = 28$)
						Alternating insanity		6.7% ($n = 20$)

Bipolar Disorders								
Source	**N**	**Gender**	**Age**	**Study Type**[a1]	**Sample Description**	**Disorder**	**Diagnostic System**	**Prevalence/ Incidence**
Foxe (1938, in Good, 1978)	3,400	M	?	JD	Consecutively examined classifications of men at the Great Meadow Prison in Comstock, New York, over a 10-year period	Manic-depressive	?	0.03% ($n = 1$)
Oltman & Friedman (1941, in Good, 1978)	100	95 M, 5 F	?	PI	Consecutive study of patients sent by court to New Hampshire State Hospital for observation	Manic-depressive	?	3.0% ($n = 3$)
Silverman (1943, in Good, 1978)	500	M	?	JD	Record review of male psychotics consecutively admitted to the Medical Center for Federal Prisoners, Springfield, Missouri	Manic-depressive	?	1.8% ($n = 9$)
Cohen & Freeman (1945)	(1) 320 (2) 87	M, F	Adult?	AR	Police records of arrested patients from 1,676 patients paroled or discharged from Norwich State Hospital, Connecticut, 1940–1944 (1) Arrested before hospitalization (2) Arrested after hospitalization	Manic-depressive psychosis	?	(1) 2.8% ($n = 9$) (2) 2.3% ($n = 2$)

(Continued)

(Continued)

Bipolar Disorders								
Source	**N**	**Gender**	**Age**	**Study Type[a1]**	**Sample Description**	**Disorder**	**Diagnostic System**	**Prevalence/ Incidence**
Stierlin (1956, in Schipkowensky, 1968)	773	?	?	PI	Statistical data from aggressive inmates in 73 psychiatric clinics and mental hospitals in Europe	Cyclophrenia	?	3.8% ($n = 29$)
Wolff & Johnston (1958, in Good, 1978)	204	147 M, 57 F	?	PI	Consecutive admissions to the Matteawan State Hospital in New York from civil state hospitals because of dangerousness, 1933–1956	Manic-depressive	?	1.0% ($n = 2$)
MacDonald (1959, in Good, 1978)	300	?	?	JD, PI	Check offenders, including mental hospital patients, penitentiary inmates, and referrals from courts for psychiatric evaluation	Manic-depressive	?	2.7% ($n = 8$)
MacDonald (1963, in Good, 1978)	100	55 M, 45 F	?	PI	Admissions over a 15-month period to the Colorado Psychopathic Hospital on civil court order or as alternative to filing a criminal charge for homicidal threats	Manic	?	2.0% ($n = 2$)
Lanzkron (1964, in Schipkowensky, 1968)	150	?	?	HO	Murderers in Matteawan State Hospital, New York	Cyclophrenia	?	4.0% ($n = 6$)

Bipolar Disorders								
Source	N	Gender	Age	Study Type[a1]	Sample Description	Disorder	Diagnostic System	Prevalence/ Incidence
Kalashnik (1966, in Schipkowensky, 1968)	271	?	?	HO	Murderers in the Moscow Forensic Psychiatric Institute	Cyclophrenia	?	0.0% ($n = 0$)
McGarry (1965, in Good, 1978)	206	183 M, 23 F	?	PI	Commitments for pretrial psychiatric evaluation at Boston State Hospital (July 1959–June 1960) and Massachusetts Mental Health Center (July–December 1957)	Manic-depressive	?	2.9% ($n = 6$)
Bearcroft & Donovan (1965, in Good, 1978)	146	M	?	PI	Consecutive psychiatric referrals for hospitalization from court or prison, Long Grove Hospital, London, 1963	Manic-depressive	?	6.8% ($n = 10$)
Bearcroft (1966, in Good, 1978)	177	M	?	PI	Consecutive psychiatric referrals for hospitalization from court or prison, Long Grove Hospital, London, 1963–1964	Manic-depressive	?	6.8% ($n = 12$)
Rachev (1966, in Schipkowensky, 1968)	100	?	?	HO	Murderers in custodial care at Lovech Mental Hospital Forensic Department, Bulgaria, 1933–1965	Cyclophrenia	?	9.0% ($n = 9$)

(Continued)

(Continued)

Bipolar Disorders								
Source	N	Gender	Age	Study Type[a1]	Sample Description	Disorder	Diagnostic System	Prevalence/ Incidence
Pfeiffer, Eisenstein, & Dabbs (1967)	85	2/3 M, 1/3 F	17–63	JD	Federal prisoners referred for mental competency evaluations, at USPHS Hospital in Lexington, Kentucky, 1960–1965	Manic-depressive, manic	?	1.2% (n =1)
Schipkowensky (1968)	194	?	?	HO	Murderers at the psychiatric clinic of the University of Sofia, Bulgaria, 1926–1965	Cyclophrenia	?	13.8% (n = 25)[am]
Guze et al. (1969, in Good, 1978)	223	M	?	CS	Consecutive series of unselected felons on probation and parole, St. Louis	Manic-depressive	?	0.0% (n = 0)
Gold (1973, in Good, 1978)	450	?	?	JD, PI	Pretrial court-ordered psychiatric evaluation of mentally disturbed offenders in 1971, Hartford, Connecticut	Manic-depressive	?	0.7% (n = 3)
Tennent et al. (1974, in Good, 1978)	178	M	?	PI	All male admissions to Broadmoor Hospital, January 1970–March 1971	Manic-depressive	?	5.0% (n = 9)
Good (1978)	100	11 M, 89 F	Adult	JD	Consecutive cases referred for psychiatric evaluation at a Massachusetts minimum-security prison, 1972–1975	Manic-depressive	"Unofficial" psychiatric diagnostic system (Woodruff et al., 1974)	7.0% (n = 7)

Bipolar Disorders								
Source	**N**	**Gender**	**Age**	**Study Type**[a1]	**Sample Description**	**Disorder**	**Diagnostic System**	**Prevalence/ Incidence**
Pétursson & Gudjónsson (1981)	47	44 M, 3 F	Adult[ai]	HO	File review of cases of intentional and unintentional homicide in Iceland, 1900–1979	Manic-depressive illness	?	4.3% ($n = 2$)
Häfner & Böker (1982)	(1) 533 (2) 3,392	M, F	14–60+	PI	(1) Mentally ill or mentally defective offenders from records searches of German federal and regional criminal bureaus, 1955–1964 (2) Mentally abnormal non-offenders (every fifth admission to regional psychiatric hospital, from register search, 1955–1964)	Affective psychoses (including manic-depressive illness and endogenous depressions)	Unspecified multiple (different or discordant) German psychiatric classification systems	(1) 6.9% ($n = 37$)[c] (2) 16.8% ($n = 571$)
Reich & Wells (1985)	390	325 M, 65 F	$M = 30.9$	JD	Record review of defendants evaluated for competency to stand trial by the Yale-New Haven Psychiatric Court Clinic, 1980–1982	Bipolar disorder	DSM-III	4.4% ($n = 17$)[be]
Bland et al. (1990)	180	M	18–44	JD	Diagnostic interviews with inmates from two correctional centers, Alberta, Canada	Manic episode	DSM-III (DIS)	4.4% ($n = 8$)[ar*]

(Continued)

(Continued)

Bipolar Disorders								
Source	**N**	**Gender**	**Age**	**Study Type**[a1]	**Sample Description**	**Disorder**	**Diagnostic System**	**Prevalence/ Incidence**
Coté & Hodgins (1990)	495	M	19–67 (M = 31.1)	JD	Diagnostic interviews with Quebec adult penitentiary inmates	Bipolar disorder	DSM-III (DIS)	3.4% (n = 17)
						Atypical bipolar disorder		3.2% (n = 16)
Abram & Teplin (1991)[r]	728	M	16–68 (M = 26.3)	JD	Diagnostic interviews with jail detainees at Cook County Department of Corrections, Chicago, November 1983–November 1984	Mania	DSM-III-R (DIS)	Lifetime: 2.2% (n = 16), Current: 1.2% (n = 9)[t]
Côté & Hodgins (1992)	(1) 87 (2) 373	M	(1) M = 35.6, SD = 8.9 (2) M = 30.3, SD = 8.3	JD	Diagnostic interviews and file reviews of penitentiary inmates, Quebec (1) Homicide offenders (2) Nonhomicide offenders	Bipolar disorder	DSM-III (DIS)	(1) 2.3% (n = 2) (2) 1.6% (n = 6)
						Atypical bipolar disorder		(1) 3.4% (n = 3) (2) 2.7% (n = 10)
DeJong, Virkkunen, & Linnoila (1992)	(1) 248 (2) 100	M	16–68 (M = 31.2, SD = 11.9)	JD	Criminals ordered for forensic psychiatric examination at initial incarceration in Finland (1) Murders and attempted murderers (2) Arsonists	Bipolar disorder	DSM-III	(1) 0.4% (2) 3.0%

Bipolar Disorders								
Source	**N**	**Gender**	**Age**	**Study Type[a1]**	**Sample Description**	**Disorder**	**Diagnostic System**	**Prevalence/ Incidence**
Marshall et al. (1998)	103	M	18–56	JD	Diagnostic interviews and questionnaires administered to recently sentenced inmates (August–December 1997) at Yatala Labour Prison, South Australia	Mania	(PDI-R)	5.9%
Galli et al. (1999)	22	M	13–17 (*M* = 15.9, *SD* = 1.1)	PI, CS	Interviews with adolescents admitting to sexually assaulting another child, referred from a juvenile rehabilitation center, the juvenile court system, and an inpatient adolescent psychiatric unit, Hamilton County, Ohio	Bipolar disorder	DSM-III-R (DICA)	27% (*n* = 6)
						Bipolar disorder NOS		27% (*n* = 6)
						Total mood disorders		82% (*n* = 18)
Gibson et al. (1999)	213	M	*M* = 32	JD	Structured interviews with randomly selected state prison and regional jail inmates from a rural New England state	Bipolar disorder	DSM-III-R (DIS-III-R)	Lifetime: 5.2% (*n* = 11) Current: 3.3% (*n* = 7)

(*Continued*)

(Continued)

Bipolar Disorders								
Source	N	Gender	Age	Study Type[a1]	Sample Description	Disorder	Diagnostic System	Prevalence/ Incidence
McElroy et al. (1999)	36	M	18–47 (M = 33, SD = 8)	PI	Interviews with convicted sex offenders consecutively admitted to the New Life Program, Cincinnati, Ohio, November 1996–June 1998	Bipolar I	DSM-IV (SCID)	17% (n = 6)
						Bipolar II		11% (n = 4)
						Bipolar NOS		8% (n = 3)
						Cyclothymia		3% (n = 1)
						Total mood disorders		61% (n = 22)
Pliszka et al. (2000)	50	45 M, 5 F	M = 15.4, SD = 1.4	JD	Interviews with adolescents consecutively admitted to the Bexar County, Texas, Juvenile Detention Center	Mania	DSM-IV (DIS-C)	20.0% (n = 10)
Baxter et al. (2001)	257	240 M, 17 F	M = 30.6, M = 31.4[bi]	HO	File review of consecutive series of patients, with index offenses of parricide or stranger killing, admitted to 1 of 3 high-security hospitals in England and Wales, 1972–1996	Mania	?	3.1% (n = 8)

Bipolar Disorders

Source	N	Gender	Age	Study Type[a1]	Sample Description	Disorder	Diagnostic System	Prevalence/ Incidence
Teplin et al. (2002)	1829	1,172 M, 657 F	10–18	JD	Diagnostic interviews of youths randomly sampled from intake into the Cook County Juvenile Temporary Detention Center, November 1995–June 1998	Manic episode	DSM-III-R	M: 2.2% F: 1.8%
Langevin (2003)	(1) 33 (2) 80 (3) 23 (4) 611	M	(1) $M = 32.06$ (2) $M = 27.08$ (3) $M = 27.57$ (4) $M = 31.42$	PI	Interviews with convicted sex offenders ($n = 747$) belonging to one of four groups: (1) sex killers, (2) nonhomicidal sexually aggressives, (3) nonhomicidal sadists, and (4) general sex offenders. Participants were chosen from a database of more than 2,800 minimum-security forensic ward psychiatric hospital cases (Clarke Institute in Toronto, Ontario, Canada) seen since 1973.	Mania	SADS, standard interview, MMPI, MCMI	(1) 3.0% (2) 1.3% (3) 4.4% (4) 1.5%
Dunsieth et al. (2004)	113	M	18–66 ($M = 35.3$, $SD = 10.4$)	PI	Diagnostic interviews with sex offenders consecutively referred to an Ohio residential sex-offender treatment program	Bipolar I	DSM-IV	24.8% ($n = 28$)

(Continued)

(Continued)

Bipolar Disorders								
Source	**N**	**Gender**	**Age**	**Study Type**[a1]	**Sample Description**	**Disorder**	**Diagnostic System**	**Prevalence/ Incidence**
						Bipolar II		5.3% ($n = 6$)
						Bipolar NOS		4.4% ($n = 5$)
						Cyclothymia		0.9% ($n = 1$)
Grella et al. (2008)	280	65% M	$M = 34.8$	JD	Diagnostic interviews with offenders consecutively admitted to prison-based substance abuse treatment programs at one of four research centers (Colorado, Rhode Island, Texas, California)	Bipolar I	DSM-IV (SCID)	3.6% ($n = 10$)
						Bipolar II		1.1% ($n = 3$)
						Other bipolar		0.7% ($n = 2$)
						Any mood disorder		33.2% ($n = 93$)
Pham & Saloppé (2 010)	84	M	Adult	PI	Psychological evaluations of forensic patients at high-security psychiatric hospital in Tomai, Belgium (Etablissement de Défense Sociale)	Bipolar disorder	DSM-III (DISSI)	7% ($n = 6$)
						Mood disorders		44% ($n = 37$)
Catanesi et al. (2011)	103	85.44% M	53.41% 25–54, 22.73% 45–65, 13.64% 18–24, 5.68% < 18	HO	Psychiatric and psychological evaluations on perpetrators of homicide and attempted homicide, Italy	Bipolar disorder	DSM-IV-TR	1.9%

Affective Disorders								
Source	**N**	**Gender**	**Age**	**Study Type**[a1]	**Sample Description**	**Disorder**	**Diagnostic System**	**Prevalence/Incidence**
Rollin (1965, in Good, 1978)	75	M	?	PI	Consecutive unprosecuted offenders sent for voluntary or compulsory psychiatric hospitalization, Horton Hospital, London	Affective disorder	?	4.0% ($n = 3$)
Langevin et al. (1982)	(1) 109 (2) 38	?	Adult?	PI	File record review of minimum security forensic ward psychiatric hospital cases, 1969–1979 (Clarke Institute in Toronto, Ontario, Canada) (1) Killers (2) Nonviolent offenders	Affective psychoses	Feighner et al. (1972) psychiatric research diagnostic criteria	(1) 4.0% (2) 2.0%
Seltzer & Langford (1984)	85	M, F	15–25 (Median = 18)	PI	Interviews of individuals referred by courts or legal counsel to psychiatry department of large regional hospital in Northwest Territories, calendar year 1981	Affective disorder	DSM-III, MMPI	3.5% ($n = 3$)

(Continued)

(Continued)

Affective Disorders								
Source	**N**	**Gender**	**Age**	**Study Type[a1]**	**Sample Description**	**Disorder**	**Diagnostic System**	**Prevalence/Incidence**
Taylor & Gunn (1984)	2,743	M	Adult	JD	File review of men remanded to Brixton Prison, South London (June, September, December 1979 and March 1980)	Affective psychosis	ICD	1.2% (n = 33)
Phillips et al. (1988)	1,816	1,569 M, 247 F	11–78 (M = 28)	PI, CS	Record review of psychiatric referrals from the criminal justice system of Alaska, 1977–1981	Affective disorders	DSM-II, DSM-III	6.6% (n = 120)
Yarvis (1990)	100	88 M, 12 F	33% < 25, 85% < 40	HO	Diagnostic interviews and record reviews of a series of murderers referred for psychiatric evaluation in California, 1980–1988	Affective psychoses	DSM-III	8.0% (n = 8)[i]
Wallace et al. (1998)	(1) 3,838 (2) 1,998 (3) 152 (4) 1,137 (5) 876	M	Adult	AR	Case-linkage study of higher court records and psychiatric case register databases, Victoria, Australia, 1993–1995 (men) (1) Total convictions (2) Violent offenses (3) Homicide offenses (4) Property offenses (5) Sexual offending	Affective psychosis	ICD-9	(1) 0.7% (n = 28) (2) 0.8% (n = 16) (3) 1.3% (n = 2) (4) 0.4% (n = 5) (5) 0.8% (n = 7)

Affective Disorders								
Source	**N**	**Gender**	**Age**	**Study Type[a1]**	**Sample Description**	**Disorder**	**Diagnostic System**	**Prevalence/Incidence**
						Affective disorders	ICD-9	(1) 1.7% (*n* = 64) (2) 2.0% (*n* = 40) (3) 2.6% (*n* = 4) (4) 1.4% (*n* = 16) (5) 1.9% (*n* = 17)
	(1) 315 (2) 152 (3) 116	F	Adult		(women) (1) Total convictions (2) Violent offenses (3) Property offenses	Affective psychosis	ICD-9	(1) 1.3% (*n* = 4) (2) 1.3% (*n* = 2) (3) 0.0% (*n* = 0)
						Affective disorders	ICD-9	(1) 3.2% (*n* = 10) (2) 3.9% (*n* = 6) (3) 0.0% (*n* = 0)
Trestman et al. (2007)	508	307 M, 201 F	18–64 (*M* = 31.6, *SD* = 9.3)	JD	Diagnostic interviews with randomly selected inmates newly admitted to one of five jail facilities, Connecticut	Affective disorder	DSM-IV (SCID)	37.1%
Hanlon et al. (2010)	77	69 M, 8 F	*M*= 31.92	HO	Indigent murder defendants and death row inmates clinically interviewed while in custody in jails and maximum-security prisons (Illinois and Missouri)	Mood disorder	?	26.0% (*n* = 20)

(Continued)

(Continued)

Notes: *Significant difference in comparison to control group.

[a1]AR = arrest rates of patients discharged from psychiatric facilities, JD = jailed detainees and incarcerated prisoners, HO = homicide offenders, BC = birth cohort study, PI = psychiatric inpatient sample, CS = community sample (i.e., epidemiological catchment area survey studies and outpatient psychiatric patients).

[a]Highest percentage of subjects in this age range.

[b]Reported group mean ages: Antisocial personality ($M = 21.9$), drug ($M = 19.6$), alcohol ($M = 32.5$), no diagnosis ($M = 22.0$).

[c]Rate per 1,000 of Mannheim's inhabitants, 1965: 0.74.

[d]Group mean ages: 1966–1969 ($M = 36.1$, $SD = 15.8$), 1970–1973 ($M = 36.2$, $SD = 14.9$), 1974–1977 ($M = 37.1$, $SD = 16.9$).

[h]Community sample comparative data (six-month prevalence rates from NIMH Community Survey Data): 1.2–5.4%.

[i]Community sample comparative data (six-month prevalence rates from NIMH Community Survey Data): 1.2–5.4%.

[p]Psychotic group ($n = 13$)—including schizophrenia, drug-related psychosis, epilepsy, affective psychosis (depression), mental subnormality, and paranoid illness.

[r]Other reports (Teplin, 1990b; Teplin, 1994) have been published on this sample.

[s]Non-jail (i.e., NIMH Epidemiologic Catchment Area, $n = 3{,}654$) lifetime prevalence rates = 3.2%, and current prevalence rates = 1.1% (Teplin, 1990b).

[t]Non-jail (i.e., NIMH Epidemiologic Catchment Area, $n = 3{,}654$) lifetime prevalence rates = 0.3%, and current prevalence rates = 0.1% (Teplin, 1990b).

[u]Teplin (1994).

[ai]Group means and standard deviations: Psychotic illness (35.7, 8.8), personality disorder and alcohol use disorders (24.4, 8.2), no psychiatric abnormality (34.0, 12.4).

[aj]For defendants who were psychotic at the time of the crime. For those who were not, median age = 29.

[am]All diagnosed as depressive ($n = 21$) committed murder; none of the patients in the manic phase of illness murdered or attempted murder.

[an]Considered unreliable data by author.

[ap]Lifetime prevalence rate. For community comparison sample, standardized prevalence ratio (SPR) = 1.8 (an SPR greater than 1 indicates the prevalence rate in the prison sample was greater than that in the general population).

[aq]Lifetime prevalence rate. For community comparison sample, standardized prevalence ratio (SPR) = 2.8 (an SPR greater than 1 indicates the prevalence rate in the prison sample was greater than that in the general population).

[ar]Lifetime prevalence rate. For community comparison sample, standardized prevalence ratio (SPR) = 5.4 (an SPR greater than 1 indicates the prevalence rate in the prison sample was greater than that in the general population).

[be]Rates of affective disorders in comparison outpatient and inpatient samples from same catchment area: 6.5% ($n = 609$) and 28.3% ($n = 263$).

[bi]The former value represents parricidal offenders, the latter stranger killers.

[bk]Comparison rates for male population reported as 10–25%.

[bl]Comparison rates for offenders in prison reported as 22%.

Table 6.5 Prevalence of Crime in Mood Disordered Populations

Source	N	Gender	Age	Study Type	Sample Description	Disorder	Crime Definition	Prevalence/Incidence
Shepherd (1961)[al]	35	M, F	Adult	PI	From case summaries of 81 psychiatric patients, mostly hospitalized	Major depressive disorder ($n = 11$), dysthymic disorder ($n = 15$), atypical depression ($n = 9$)	Histories of homicidal behavior (homicidal attacks, threats, violent assaults, and actual homicide)	60% ($n = 15$; all men)
Carlson & Goodwin (1973)	20	10 M, 10 W	Adult	PI	Patients admitted to one of two metabolic research hospitals, Washington, DC (diagnostic criteria not reported), with longitudinal follow-up data	Bipolar affective disorder	Assaultiveness or threatening behavior during hospitalization	75% ($n = 15$)
Tardiff & Koenigsberg (1985)	(1) 2,106 (2) 810	(1) 842 M, 1,256 F (2) 354 M, 453 F	(1) ≤ 20–65+[aa] (2) ≤ 20–65+[aa]	CS	Psychiatric outpatients evaluated during 1.5 years at two New York hospitals, diagnosed using DSM II and DSM II criteria (1) Payne Whitney Clinic (2) Westchester Division of NY Hospital	Depressive, schizoaffective, and dysthymic disorders (1) $n = 290$ (2) $n = 102$	Presence of assaultive behavior toward others in hospital records	(1) 1.0% ($n = 3$) (2) 1.0% ($n = 1$)
Swanson et al. (1990)	10,059	4,717 M, 5,306 F[f]	Adult	CS	Epidemiologic Catchment Area respondent data (community adults from five U.S. sites), diagnosed using DSM-III criteria (DIS)	Major depression	Self-report violence	11.68% violent ($n = 282$[f])
						Major depression with grief		10.70% violent ($n = 308$[f])

(Continued)

(Continued)

Source	N	Gender	Age	Study Type	Sample Description	Disorder	Crime Definition	Prevalence/Incidence
						Mania or bipolar disorder		11.02% violent ($n = 30$[f])
Link et al. (1992)	(1) 521 (2) 232	?M, ?F	(1) 19–59 (2) Adult?	PI, CS	Interviews with (1) Community residents (2) Psychiatric patients (from an outpatient clinic and an inpatient community service), New York City, diagnosed using DSM-III criteria[w]	(2) 33.6% ($n = 78$) major depression, 29.9% ($n = 69$) schizophrenia and other psychotic disorders, 36.6% ($n = 85$) other diagnoses[x]	Official arrest data, self-reports of violent or illegal behavior, 1980–1983[y]	Patient groups > never-treated community residents[z]
B. Coid et al. (1993)	280	146 M, 134 F	20–80 ($M = 45.9$)	PI	Patients of twin birth seen at Bethlem and Maudsley hospitals, 1948–1988, diagnosed using DSM-III and RDC (Spitzer et al., 1978) criteria	Bipolar or major affective disorder ($n = 67$)[ba]	Official criminal records	19.4% ($n = 13$)
Asnis et al. (1994)	517	204 M, 313 F	13–87 ($M = 38.7$)	CS	Psychiatric outpatients, Montefiore Medical Center, Bronx, New York, diagnosed using DSM-III criteria	Major depression ($n = 172$)	Self-reported homicidal ideation and attempts	Ideation: 17% ($n =2 9$) Attempts: 4% ($n = 7$)
						Bipolar disorder ($n = 39$)		Ideation: 21% ($n = 8$) Attempts: 5% ($n = 2$)
						Dysthymia ($n = 31$)		Ideation: 19% ($n = 6$) Attempts: 3% ($n = 1$)

Source	N	Gender	Age	Study Type	Sample Description	Disorder	Crime Definition	Prevalence/Incidence
Modestin, Hug, & Ammann (1997)	261	M	18–78 ($M = 42.2$)	PI	Psychiatric inpatients, Psychiatric University Hospital of Berne, 1985–1987, diagnosed using Research Diagnostic Criteria (RDC: Spitzer et al., 1978)[an]	Bipolar disorder ($n = 82$)	Criminal register conviction records	Total sample: 48% ($n = 39$)* Violent crimes: 5% ($n = 4$) Property crimes: 20% ($n = 16$)* Sexual offences: 2% ($n = 2$) Drug violations: 18% ($n = 15$)* Traffic violations: 34% ($n = 28$) Other offences: 22% ($n = 18$)
						Unipolar major depression ($n = 112$)		Total sample: 28% ($n = 31$) Violent crimes: 3% ($n = 3$) Property crimes: 9% ($n = 10$) Sexual offences: 1% ($n = 1$) Drug violations: 2% ($n = 2$) Traffic violations: 16% ($n = 18$) Other offences: 8% ($n = 9$)
						Unipolar minor or intermittent depression ($n = 67$)		Total sample: 60% ($n = 40$)* Violent crimes: 7% ($n = 5$) Property crimes: 30% ($n = 20$)* Sexual offences: 4% ($n = 3$) Drug violations: 10% ($n = 7$) Traffic violations: 37% ($n = 25$) Other offences: 33% ($n = 22$)*

(Continued)

(Continued)

Source	N	Gender	Age	Study Type	Sample Description	Disorder	Crime Definition	Prevalence/Incidence
Tiihonen et al. (1997)	(1) 86 (2) 5,285	M[ac]	(longitudinal)	BC	From a 26-year prospective study of a large unselected 1966 northern Finland birth cohort (N = 12,058), diagnosed using DSM-III-R criteria with (1) Major mental illness (2) No mental disorder	Mood disorders with psychotic features ($n = 6$)	Criminal register records	At least one registered crime: 33.3% ($n = 2$)* Violent crime: 16.7% ($n = 1$)* Property crime: 0.0% ($n = 0$)[ad]
Arsenault et al. (2000)	(1) 389 (2) 572	51.6% M, 48.4% F	Adult	BC	From a study of a total-city New Zealand birth cohort (N = 1,037), diagnosed using DSM-III-R criteria with (1) Psychiatric disorder (2) No psychiatric disorder	Depression disorders ($n = 172$)	Violence: Self-reported and criminal convictions	(1) Convictions: 4.1% ($n = 7$); self-reported: 15.1% ($n = 26$) (2) Convictions: 1.2% ($n = 7$); self-reported: 3.1% ($n = 18$)
						Manic disorder ($n = 19$)		(1) Convictions: 15.8% ($n = 3$); self-reported: 26.3% ($n = 5$)
Corrigan & Watson (2005)	5,865	?M, ?F	15–54	CS	Subset of respondents from the U.S. National Comorbidity Survey, diagnosed using DSM-III-R criteria (structured diagnostic interview), 1990–1992	Dysthymia	Self-reported violence	Mental illness lifetime: 4.6% (18/382); 12 months: 0.8% (13/148)
						Major depression		Mental illness lifetime: 4.6% (46/992); 12 months: 7.1% (42/586)
						Bipolar disorder		Mental illness lifetime: 12.2% (11/93); 12 months: 16.0% (11/71)

Source	N	Gender	Age	Study Type	Sample Description	Disorder	Crime Definition	Prevalence/Incidence
Barzman et al. (2007)	80	37 M, 43 F	12–21, $M = 15.6$	PI	Adolescent psychiatric inpatients from Cincinnati Children's Hospital Center and the University of Cincinnati Medical Center, 1998–2004, diagnosed using DSM-IV criteria	Bipolar I disorder	Self-reported status and criminal offenses	55.0% ($n = 44$)[bj]

Notes: *Significant difference in comparison to control group.

[f]Weighted Ns.

[w]Study groups formed consisting of never-treated community residents, first-contact patients, repeat-contact patients, and former patients. A portion of community members were grouped into patient groups, though diagnoses for these individuals were not reported.

[x]Separate analyses were not conducted for individual diagnoses.

[y]Six indicators: (1) self-reported arrests, (2) official arrests, and self reports of (3) hitting others, (4) fighting, (5) weapon use in a fight, or (6) ever hurting someone badly.

[z]Patient groups collapsed into one group and percentage rates recalculated. Results (never-treated community residents or patients): all lifetime official arrests (6.7/10.6), lifetime violent arrests (1.0/4.9), lifetime self-reported arrests (9.9/18.3), hitting others—past year or month (5.2/12.3), fighting—past 5 years (15.1/25.7), weapon use—past 5 years (2.7/9.7), lifetime hurting someone badly (5.4/14.8).

[aa](1) 12.4% ($n = 261$) 20 years and younger, 30.7% ($n = 647$) 21–30, 23.6% ($n = 496$) 31–40, 24.3% ($n = 511$) 41–64, 7.5% ($n = 158$) 65 years and older, 1.6% ($n = 33$) unknown; (2) 18.0% ($n = 146$) 20 years and younger, 31.4% ($n = 254$) 21–30, 18.0% ($n = 146$) 31–40, 27.0% ($n = 219$) 41–64, 5.0% ($n = 41$) 65 years and older, 0.5% ($n = 4$) unknown.

[ac]5,217 females were also included in this study. Only one offender among the female subjects (33.3%) was diagnosed with a major mental disorder. The prevalence of offenders among women with no mental disorders was 0.8% ($n = 42$).

[ad]Comparison group with no mental disorder: 7.3% ($n = 387$) at least one registered crime, 2.2% ($n = 117$) violent crime, 2.5% ($n = 133$) property crime.

[al]Clinical data reanalyzed in Rosenbaum & Bennett (1986).

[an]Comparison subjects with criminal record: 31% ($n = 80$) total sample, 1% ($n = 3$) violent crimes, 8% ($n = 20$) property crimes, 1% ($n = 3$) sexual offences, 3% ($n = 7$) drug violations, 24% ($n = 63$) traffic violations, 10% ($n = 27$) other offences.

[ba]Men only.

[bj]Types of offenses: Drug charges (17.5%, $n = 14$), shoplifting-larceny-theft (17.5%, $n = 14$), domestic violence (11.0%, $n = 9$), vandalism (9.0%, $n = 7$), run away (9.0%, $n = 7$), assault (9.0%, $n = 7$), probation violation (7.5%, $n = 6$), disorderly conduct (6.0%, $n = 5$), unruly (6.0%, $n = 5$), traffic violations (6.0%, $n = 5$), truancy (6.0%, $n = 5$), other (6.0%, $n < 5$). General population comparison rate: 5.3%.

Samples here come from several countries around the world and use a multitude of different methodologies and a number of different major diagnostic systems. One limitation, noted by Häfner and Böker (1982), is that poor reliability of earlier mood disorder diagnoses may have affected the rates of violence and crime and of mood disorders reported in these samples.

A Closer Look: Affective Disorders and Crime

Prevalence of the Disorder in Crime

Study Type	Number	Prevalence Rates
Arrest rates	1	0.4–2.6% (men); 0.0–3.9% (women)
Birth cohorts	0	–
Community samples	1*	6.0%
Homicide offenders	2	8.0–26.0%
Jailed detainees and prisoners	2	1.2–37.1%
Psychiatric inpatients	4*	2.0–6.6%
Total Number of Studies	**9**	

Sample Characteristics

Size	75–4,153
Gender	Male only (2 studies); male and female but generally more males than females (6 studies); not reported (1 study)
Age	Youth, adult
Location	Countries worldwide (e.g., Australia, Canada, England, and the United States)
Diagnostic Systems	DSM (various editions), ICD (various editions), other research diagnostic criteria

Note: *One study involved both psychiatric inpatients and community individuals.

Prevalence of Crime in the Disorder

Study Type	Number	Prevalence Rates	Crime Definition
Arrest rates	0	–	–
Birth cohorts	1	33.3%	At least one registered crime*
Community samples	0	–	–
Homicide offenders	0	–	–
Jailed detainees and prisoners	0	–	–
Psychiatric inpatients	0	–	–
Total Number of Studies	**1**		

Sample Characteristics

Size	5,371
Gender	Male and female

Age	Longitudinal cohort
Location	Finland
Diagnostic Systems	DSM-III-R

Note: *16.7% violent crime.

Nondisordered or community resident comparison group or general population baseline rates for either disorder or crime provided: **2 studies (20.0%)**†

Note: †Rates of affective disorders appear to be elevated in murderers relative to comparison general population base rates (Yarvis, 1990). Rates of crime are significantly elevated relative to non-mentally ill comparison group rates (Tiihonen et al., 1997).

Depressive Disorders

Although general studies of affective disorders are helpful in understanding the relationship between mood disorders and crime, the wide spectrum of these disorders—with their varied symptom presentations—make it difficult to ascertain which types of mood disorders contribute to crime, how much, and how. Studies of specific mood disorders, such as depression and depressive disorders, provide a more specific understanding of this relationship.

A Closer Look: Depressive Disorders and Crime

Prevalence of the Disorder in Crime

Study Type	Number	Prevalence Rates
Arrest rates	0	–
Birth cohorts	0	–
Community samples	2*	23.0–35.0%
Homicide offenders	15	2.0–75.0%†
Jailed detainees and prisoners	19	1.0–71.2%†
Psychiatric inpatients	9*	1.5–66.7%
Total Number of Studies	**44‡**	

Sample Characteristics

Size	4–170,215
Gender	Male only (16 studies); female only (2 studies); male and female but generally more males than females (24 studies); not reported (2 studies)
Age	Youth, adult
Location	Countries worldwide (e.g., Australia, Belgium, Canada, Denmark, England, Egypt, Finland, Germany, India, Italy, New Zealand, Poland, Sweden, the United States, and Wales)
Diagnostic Systems	Not specified in many earlier studies. DSM (various editions), ICD (various editions), other research diagnostic criteria.

Notes: *One study involved both psychiatric inpatients and community individuals.

(Continued)

(Continued)

†For jailed detainees, the latter figure represents past major depressive episodes in a sample of Finnish prison inmates, and it is significantly elevated compared to most other reports—the next-highest reported figure is 26.1%. For homicide offenders, the latter figure was reported in a sample of murderers who killed family members and subsequently committed suicide—arguably a group more likely to be associated with depressive disorders; without this study, the highest reported figure is 37.2%.

‡Prevalence rates across all 44 studies appear to be increased in most cases (and, for a small number of studies, at least comparable at minimum levels) relative to estimates of major depression in the general population (e.g., reported in the DSM-IV-TR; see above). For the ten studies reporting separate prevalence rates for dysthymic disorder, these rates (1.0–15.8%) appear elevated in comparison to those observed in the general population, with the exception of the rates reported by Reich and Wells (1985). In one study reporting separate prevalence rates for males and females (Teplin et al., 2002), rates were elevated in females compared to males for major depressive disorder (21.6% versus 13.0%) and dysthymia (15.8% versus 12.2%).

Prevalence of Crime in the Disorder

Study Type	**Number**	**Prevalence Rates**	**Crime Definition**
Arrest rates	0	–	–
Birth cohorts	2	0.0–33.3%†	Convictions and self-reports of various crime types, including violent and property crime
Community samples	4*	1.0–10.6%‡	Assaultive behavior; arrest data and self-reported violent or illegal behavior; self-reported homicidal ideation and attempts
Homicide offenders	0	–	–
Jailed detainees and prisoners	0	–	–
Psychiatric inpatients	2*	10.6–60.0%	History of homicidal behavior; arrest data and self-reported violent or illegal behavior
Total Number of Studies	**8**		

Sample Characteristics

Size	35–10,059
Gender	Male only (2 studies); male and female (6 studies)
Age	Predominantly adult, some youth and longitudinal cohort
Location	Countries worldwide (e.g., Finland, New Zealand, Switzerland, the United States)
Diagnostic Systems	DSM and other research diagnostic criteria

Notes: *Two studies involved both psychiatric inpatients and community individuals.

†For any crime, these rates are 0.0–33.3%; for violent crime, they are 4.1–16.7%.

‡For all offense types. For homicidal ideation, the latter figure increases to 17.0%, and for self-reported recent fighting, to 25.7%.

Nondisordered or community resident comparison group or general population baseline rates for either disorder or crime provided: **8 studies (15.4%)**††

Note: ††Rates of depressive disorders are increased relative to general population baseline rates when provided. Rates of crime are elevated relative to comparisons in most cases.

Depression and Crime: Connections With Violence

Although some authors (i.e., Harrer & Kofler-Westergren, 1986) have noted that a broad spectrum of crime can be observed within the context of depressive disorders (including sexual and property offenses), the literature on depressive disorders and criminality has focused predominantly upon various forms of severe violence. Historically, early writings often discussed the "extended suicide"—which almost without exception involved young mothers between the ages of 30 and 40, who, in a delusional frame of mind, included their children in their suicide in order to prevent them from a presumably unavoidable disaster. One early view suggested that violence in a depressed (melancholic) person would arise from (1) sensitive feelings and obsessive ideas, (2) anxiety affects, and (3) delusions and hallucinations (Krafft-Ebing, 1892, in Harrer & Kofler-Westergren, 1986). This view emphasized the severity of crime rather than its frequency in the relationship between depression and criminality. In the early years of the twentieth century, published case reports of "family homicide" included those committed in a state of "raptus melancholicus." Several decades later, the literature still remained focused on the extended suicide and on the relationship between homicide and suicide, though scattered references to misdemeanor crimes committed by patients with milder forms of depression began to surface (Harrer & Kofler-Westergren, 1986).

Studies in this area have largely been qualitative in nature—that is, focusing on the presentation of case material of individuals with depression who have committed acts of severe violence. Generalizing findings from these studies rather than from quantitative investigations with larger sample sizes becomes much more difficult, though the value of individual case presentations—which are often rich in clinical detail—cannot be overstated.

Case Material

Aside from Krafft-Ebbing's (1886/1965) very early published case studies, and some 255 cases of extended suicide in the German-speaking literature from 1933–1985 (Harrer & Kofler-Westergren, 1986), qualitative case reports in English-speaking publications remained scarce until the latter part of the twentieth century. One of the first of these is a psychiatric and forensic study from Japan, in which Hirose (1979) presents the cases of four murderers who suffered from depression—illustrating how different types and aspects of depression may contribute to various forms of extreme violence. The first case was of a 34-year-old woman, who suffocated her daughter several weeks after birth and attempted suicide by drowning in a creek. Hirose concludes that the woman killed her infant under the influence of a postpartum period of *endogenous depression,* provoked by psychological stress due to poor household economy and an emotionally absent and neglectful husband, whose family the couple lived with. (Endogenous depression is defined as being caused primarily by factors inside the individual, which are presumably not discernible by others; in contrast, *reactive depression* follows mental stress, as in the fourth case below.) The second case was of a 29-year-old farmer who suffered from endogenous depression accompanied by severe insomnia and anxiety. Early one morning, he struck his wife's face with an axe and strangled her and subsequently attempted suicide with a "kimono" sash. Here again, Hirose proposes that the homicidal act stemmed from a pre-existing depressive state (a depressive reaction to the death of both of his parents several months prior) and was provoked by unbearable psychological stress (the sexual advances of his half-brother toward his wife) and that the man killed his wife in a state of disturbed consciousness (referred to as "affective sleep-drunkenness"). The third case was of a 56-year-old farmer who suffered from *involutional melancholia* characterized by excessive worry, self-reproachfulness, and severe agitation. He killed his wife and son in an outburst of rage under trivial stimuli. According to Hirose, the man flew into a blind rage, triggered by his wife's words of encouragement in response to his dire financial situation, and he subsequently struck her on the head and dismembered both bodies over several hours with an axe and a kitchen knife in a psychogenic dreamy state or twilight state (events about which he subsequently had no recollection). Finally, the fourth case involved a 43-year-old tailor who suffered from *neurotic depression* following an acute grief reaction due to the sudden death of his only son, who was killed while riding a motorcycle by a reckless driver. The subsequent callousness of the driver, along with domestic difficulties with his wife, led to chronic frustration in the patient—who six months later lured his son's killer to his home and stabbed him to death. Afterwards, he made repeated unsuccessful attempts at suicide by hanging. Overall, these cases illustrate how depression—though not necessarily *causing* violence—may provide a weakened psychological state in which environmental stressors readily trigger homicidal violent outcomes.

Using clinical data from coroners' reports, Goldney (1977) presents the cases of four family murderers who committed suicide; three of the perpetrators suffered from depression. In the first case, a 34-year-old migrant woman poisoned herself, her 13-year-old son, and her 11-year-old daughter with weed killer mixed into warm milk after her husband left in the morning with a load of vegetables for the market. Only the boy survived. Goldney reports that the woman had lost her 18-month-old son in an accident five years prior and was suffering a pathological grief reaction to the anniversary of his death. In the second case, a 38-year-old woman living on an isolated farm shot and killed her 13-year-old daughter and 11-year-old son, wounded her 17-year-old daughter, and then committed suicide by ingesting rat poisoning. In the month before the murders, the woman developed symptoms of depression, weeping, irritability, insomnia, and lack of insight into her condition. Though she was found one night standing over their older son with a carving knife and hammer, and two nights later with a rifle, she refused to see a doctor. Goldney suggests that she may have experienced delusions of shame and guilt related to herself and her family. In the third case of a depressed murderer, a 31-year-old high school teacher fatally wounded his wife in the head with an axe and shot his children (ages five, four, and two years) and himself to death. The man had suffered from recurrent and worsening depressive episodes for eight years and had been treated with antidepressant medication. At the time of the murders, it had been fourteen months since the resolution of his last depressive episode, and he had not taken antidepressant medications in the year prior to the incident—most likely a result of being told by a doctor and a pharmacist that he was taking too much medication. Goldney states that individuals with severe depression are highly sensitive to rejection—real or fantasized—and that well-meaning and potentially therapeutic comments (i.e., being told by a health professional that one is taking too much medication) may be interpreted in a self-deprecatory manner.

Rosenbaum and Bennett (1986) described 7 case reports of homicidal individuals who met DSM-III criteria for major depressive disorder (6 university clinic outpatients and 1 psychiatric inpatient; 4 women and 3 men). Additionally, these authors reanalyzed data from an earlier report of 81 case studies (Shepherd, 1961), which contained 35 depressed patients. In the latter, 15 (all men) had histories of homicidal behavior (homicidal attacks, threats, violent assaults, and one actual homicide), and 10 (9 men) had histories of suicide attempts (see Table 6.5). From these cases in aggregate, Rosenbaum and Bennett concluded that depressed patients at risk for homicide were those who also had personality disorders; histories of child abuse, alcohol or drug abuse, or suicidal behavior; and depressions that were precipitated by real or fantasized sexual infidelity rather than by the loss of an object on whom the patient was dependent through death or by a real or threatened separation, in other words, more by a *narcissistic injury* (i.e., a reaction to situations that produce hurt pride, shame, and humiliation—see Chapter 10). One limitation is the discrepancies in diagnostic methods across the two samples (which used two different systems). For example, these authors report diagnosing 35 of Shepherd's original cases with depression, whereas only 31 were diagnosed with depression in the original report.

Macdonald (1986) states that the victims of homicide by severely depressed persons are almost always members of the murderer's family. The husband that is so depressed that he can see no hope for the future may take his life in order to avoid further misery. His depression may be so severe that he believes that his wife and children also face such a bleak future that life has no meaning for them. Convinced that he is conferring an advantage on them by cutting short their lives, he may kill them one by one before taking his own life (p. 186). Macdonald (1986) describes the case of a 55-year-old dentist whose depressive symptoms (forgetfulness, difficulty concentrating, insomnia, feelings of worthlessness) led to impairment in his occupational and psychological functioning. Concern for the financial security and future well-being of his wife and son, along with purported command auditory hallucinations (i.e., the voice of the devil), led him to kill his wife and son with a claw hammer. Although he planned to kill himself afterwards, he apparently lacked the energy and instead telephoned the police.

Frazier (1974) detailed the characteristics of 31 murderers in prisons and psychiatric hospitals (see Table 6.4); 7 were characterized by severe low self-esteem and depression. All had suffered severe personal losses or separations (e.g., the loss of parents or parental figures or separations from significant others) either earlier in life or in the months preceding the murders. Parker (1979), later commenting on a series of Queensland murderers he examined personally (see Table 6.4), states that the significantly depressed have a remarkable capacity to cover up their suffering. In some depressed murderers from this series, homicidal assaults arose out of despair and hopelessness. These murderers are often actively suicidal at the time of the killing. Interestingly, Parker reports these murders often occurred in the morning (i.e., at breakfast time)—a vulnerable time for those "weighed down by circumstances." Four women in this sample killed their children before attempting suicide, and two more were so attached to their spouses that they wanted to take them with them when they died—both struck their victims on the head and then took an overdose of pills. Another group of depressed murderers were those who had made extreme efforts to keep an unhappy marriage together; a love-hate relationship developed—characterized by humiliation and degradation—to the point where suicide appeared the only solution to their misery. In two cases, a chance remark or incident converted their own suicidal ideation and planning into homicidal rage against their spouses.

Finally, depression has been discussed within the context of mass murder. Palermo (1997) describes the prototypical mass murderer as being characterized by several aspects of depression and anxiety: having periods of obsessive ruminations; displaying moody, antagonistic, rebellious, frustrated, or violent behavior; being occasionally under the care of mental health personnel; and often committing suicide. In his review of mass murder, Palermo presents the case of a depressed, narcissistic, and suicidal mass murderer. On the afternoon of October 10, 1993, 33-year-old Dion Terres, dressed in military-style pants and armed with a handgun, entered a fast-food restaurant in Kenosha, Wisconsin, and began shooting. Four shots claimed four victims—a 52-year old man, who died at the scene; a 42-year-old woman, who died later in the hospital; an 18-year-old male, who survived the attack; and Torres himself, who shot himself in the forehead. Found in his car was a 40-minute videotape of a testamentary soliloquy he filmed the day before the shooting, which clearly evidenced his destructive hostility, feelings of rejection, depressed mood, and wounded narcissism, along with fetishistic and magical thinking and his prominent inner fantasy world. Terres had recently been under the care of a psychiatrist and was prescribed antidepressant medication. According to Malmquist (1995), mass homicidal violence may occur when people in states of severe depression join cults or movements. Though being indoctrinated in a cult may put a depression on hold or alleviate its extreme symptoms, it is likely to leave the person with alterations in integrative functions of identity, memory, or consciousness. In such a dissociated state, those in a group setting are more vulnerable to carry out acts of suicide or homicide (e.g., the stand-off between the Branch Davidians religious cult and the FBI in Waco, Texas, in 1993; see Malmquist, 1995, for a review). Both authors here provide compelling explanations for how depression may play a role in this particular form of homicide.

Murder-Suicide

Several authors have examined murder-suicide within the context of depressive disorders. For example, Harrer and Kofler-Westergren (1986) discuss 5 Austrian cases, occurring over a 10-year period, of unsuccessful extended suicide involving mothers and their children. These authors also summarize 255 cases of extended suicide (of both men and women) reported in the German-language literature from 1933–1985. The majority of these cases were characterized by reactive and neurotic depressions and abnormal reactions, whereas only about one-third suffered from endogenous depressions. It has been proposed that, during phases of depression, depressed individuals (regardless of which type) tend to lean on and enter into a more or less total fusion with those people close to them—who then become narcissistically integrated in the world of the patient.

According to Harrer and Kofler-Westergren (1986), anxiety, inner tension, resentfulness, and latent aggression may build up and create an indefinable need for discharge—eventually leading to a sudden release and a potentially violent expression of suppressed emotion, which is referred to by some as **catathymic crisis** (see Wertham, 1937). Most offenses related to this phenomenon occur during a shift or change in mood episodes or symptoms or in a state characterized by mixed manic and depressive features. These authors emphasize the importance of recognizing "badweather-areas" such as these, where a criminogenic "thunderstorm" may build up—much in the same way that periods with increased suicide risk have been identified, when inhibitions come loose immediately prior to a depression clearing up. Additionally, these authors differentiate between depression types with regard to perceived responsibility for criminality. Whereas individuals with endogenous depression will always blame themselves, those with reactive and neurotic depression will instead blame their environment and special circumstances for their suffering and eventual crime. Furthermore, in endogenous depression, the disorder itself is thought to play a key role in the genesis of crime, while in other depressive conditions, criminality is thought to derive more from non-depressive influences such as personality characteristics, social development, and disease-independent psychodynamics.

Rosenbaum (1990) later compared 12 couples in cases of murder-suicide with 24 couples in cases of domestic homicide. Results indicated that perpetrators of murder-suicide were depressed (75%) and men (95%), while perpetrators of homicide were not depressed and one-half were women. The data indicate that the murder-suicide and homicide groups are two different populations. Finally, Hillbrand (2001) describes the declining health type of spousal homicide-suicide in which an older male kills his physically incapacitated spouse and then himself. Hopelessness, despair, and nonpsychotic depression are common in this type. Together, these studies demonstrate how murder-suicide within the context of depression—which may sound like a unitary concept—can actually be brought about by a number of psychological, situational, and interpersonal dynamics.

Postpartum Depression

Although Blair Stockdill's illness may, in some way, be linked to her homicidal actions against her own daughter, another mood disorder has also been putatively associated with filicide. One particular form of depressive illness that has been associated with extreme forms of violence is **postpartum depression (PPD)** or "New Mother Syndrome"—also referred to clinically as "Puerperal Psychosis" and, more commonly, as the "baby blues" (Williamson, 1993). Postpartum depression is conceptualized in the DSM-IV-TR using the *postpartum onset specifier* (a *specifier* is the DSM method for defining a more homogenous subgrouping of individuals with the disorder who share certain features). This specifier is applied when the onset of the current or most recent mood episode of a mood disorder or brief psychotic disorder is within four weeks after childbirth. In the DSM-5, the *peripartum onset specifier* is used. According to the DSM-IV-TR, the presence of severe ruminations or delusional thoughts about the infant is associated with a significantly increased risk of harm to the infant. Postpartum-onset mood episodes can be accompanied by psychotic symptoms. *Infanticide* is most often associated with postpartum psychotic episodes in which command hallucinations to kill the infant or delusions that the infant is possessed are present, but it also may occur in severe postpartum mood episodes without such specific delusions or hallucinations. Postpartum mood episodes with psychotic features appear to occur in from 1 in 500 to 1 in 1,000 women who have given birth and may be more common in women having their first child. Table 6.6 lists some more recent cases of this phenomenon.

Though only a limited amount of research has been conducted in this area, postpartum depression has been used as a basis of acquittal in criminal cases as well as for reversal of convictions (Williamson, 1993). For example, Sheryl Lynn Massip of Anaheim, California, was convicted of second-degree murder in the killing of her six-week-old son (see Table 6.6 and Box 6.1). Massip testified that postpartum depression drove her to murder; and, though a jury convicted her, the conviction was later set aside by a superior court judge who found sufficient evidence supporting legal insanity. However, although the terminology used varies in legal defenses referring to PPD, these generally refer to postpartum psychosis, and milder forms of PPD have not been successfully used as defenses to crime. British law recognizes postnatal depression as a viable insanity defense under the Infanticide Act of 1938, which states that a mother cannot be found guilty of the murder of her own child within 12 months of childbirth—though she may, however, be prosecuted for manslaughter. In the United States, the postpartum psychosis defense has been asserted in comparatively fewer cases, only 18 times as of 1993 (Williamson, 1993).

Although few studies have examined homicidal violence in women with postpartum depression, comparatively more studies have examined factors related to depression and violence during the postpartum period, whether that violence is perpetrated by men or women. This is an important consideration, as violence may characterize the postpartum period and may predispose women to postpartum depression-based violence by creating an environment conducive to violent behavior. For example, studies of violence around the time of pregnancy indicate that 4–8% of women are abused during and after pregnancy, with a majority of the perpetrators being their intimate partners (Chang et al., 2005; Romito et al., 2009). Romito and colleagues (2009) found rates of postpartum family or partner violence of 10% in one Italian sample, and homicide has been shown to be a leading cause of injury deaths among pregnant and postpartum women in the United States from 1991–1999 (Chang et al., 2005). Mixed evidence across studies exists, however, for pregnant or postpartum women being at a greater

Table 6.6 Cases of Postpartum Depression (PPD) and Homicide

Name	Age	Location	Date	Victim(s)/Age(s)	Offense: Method	Suicide/ Attempt?	Diagnosis/ Indicators
Adams, Lakeisha	18	Louisiana	2005	1 son (3 months)	Homicide: Put victim in clothes dryer	No	Antidepressant medication, possible PPD
Alley, Sharon	29	Virginia	1998	1 daughter (8 months)	Homicide: Stabbing	No	PPD
Anfinson, Heidi		Iowa	1998	1 son (2 weeks)	Homicide: Drowning in bathtub	No	PPD
Baldillez, Lori	25	Texas	1992	1 son (2 weeks)	Homicide: Shaking victim to death	No	PPD
Boeskool, Cheryl Lynn	28	Virginia	1991	1 son (6 weeks)	Homicide: Suffocation	No	Depressed, antianxiety medication
Ener, Mine	38	Minnesota	2003	1 daughter (6 months)	Homicide: Cut throat	No	PPD
Feltman, Bethe	32	Colorado	1998	1 son (3 years), 1 daughter (3 months)	Homicide: Drugging and suffocation	Yes	PPD
Fleetwood, Jessica	20	New Hampshire	2000	1 son (2 months)	Homicide: Suffocation	No	PPD
Haskew, Annie Mae	22	Alabama	2003	1 son (10 weeks)	Homicide: Suffocation	No	PPD
Kemp, Karyn Louise	34	Australia	2008	1 son (7 months)	Homicide: Suffocation and gassing with exhaust fumes	Yes	PPD
Kenneally-Owens, Nollaig	33	Ireland	2007	1 son (9 months)	Homicide: Drowning	Yes	PPD
Kuether, Anne	43	Florida	2006	1 son (5 years)	Homicide: Gun shot	Yes	PPD
Ladislaw, Eileen	42	New Jersey	2000	1 daughter (5 months)	Homicide: Suffocation	Yes	PPD
Lawson, Kristen	30	California	2006	2 daughters (6 years, 5 months)	Attempted homicide: Drowning in bathtub	No	PPD
Massip, Sheryl	22	California	1987	1 son (6 weeks)	Homicide: Threw victim into oncoming traffic, hit over head with blunt object, ran over with car	No	Postpartum psychosis
Maxon, Valeria	32	Texas	2006	1 son (1 year)	Homicide: Drowned in hot tub	No	Bipolar disorder, most recent episode depressed with psychotic features

(Continued)

(Continued)

Name	Age	Location	Date	Victim(s)/Age(s)	Offense: Method	Suicide/ Attempt?	Diagnosis/ Indicators
Moffitt, Mary Ellen	37	Michigan	2004	1 daughter (5 weeks)	Homicide: Suffocation	Yes	PPD
Padron, Emiri	24	New Jersey	2004	1 daughter (10 months)	Homicide: Suffocation	Yes	Antidepressant medication, under care of psychiatrist
Palma, Sheila	22	Illinois	2005	1 son (3 months)	Homicide: Shook, punched, squeezed	No	PPD
Renubala, Nabram Ongbi	35	India	2008	1 child (6 months)	Homicide: Burned to death	Yes	Depression, medication
Rothstein, Seema	32	Virginia	2001	Husband (36 years)	Homicide: Stabbing	?[a]	PPD
Sherr, Isabel	31	Virginia	2005	1 son (4 years), 1 daughter (19 months)	Attempted homicide: Drowning in bathtub	Yes	PPD
Sidhu, Navjeet	27	England	2006	1 daughter (5 years), 1 son (23 months)	Homicide: Jumped in front of train	Yes	Depression
Topham, Yeeda	41	Australia	2007	1 son (21 months)	Homicide: Climbed eight flights of stairs holding baby and jumped	Yes	PPD
Williams, Marianne	24	England	2006	1 son (16 months)	Homicide: Poisoning	No	Antidepressants
Yates, Andrea	27	Texas	2001	4 sons (7, 5, 3, and 2 years), 1 daughter (6 months)	Homicide: Drowned in bathtub	No	PPD and psychosis

Note: [a]Self-inflicted stab wounds, but no mention of suicidal ideation or attempt.

(or lesser) risk of homicide compared to other women of reproductive age (Samandari, Martin, & Schiro, 2010). Other factors to consider are the increased rates of maternal psychological distress occurring within the postpartum period (Romito et al., 2009), as well as the supposition that a history of violence may predispose women to postpartum depression (M. Cohen et al., 2002). Overall, postpartum depression-related violence is likely a complex phenomenon, requiring more empirical work to gain a further understanding of its etiology in some women.

Other Studies

Though somewhat uncommon in the literature, other studies have examined aspects related to the relationship between depression and crime and violence. In one study, Baillargeon, Black, Contreras, Grady, and Pulvino (2001) examined antidepressant medication prescribing patterns among 5,305 inmates in the Texas

BOX 6.1 SHERYL LYNN MASSIP

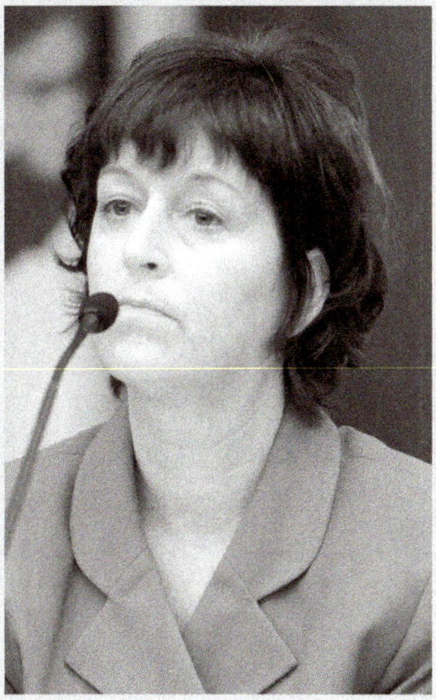

On April 29, 1987, Sheryl Lynn Massip, a 23-year-old Anaheim, California, mother (pictured here testifying during her trial), brutally murdered her six-week-old son Michael, compelled by voices in her head.

According to prosecutors, earlier that day—Massip's birthday—she threw Michael into oncoming traffic and a driver had to swerve to avoid hitting him. Massip then took Michael home and bludgeoned him with a blunt object and drove the infant, who was still alive, to a remote area in a nearby city. There Massip placed him under the front tire of her car and ran over him. Massip's attorney argued she was driven insane by postpartum psychosis, but she was nonetheless convicted of murder. A superior court judge ruled her not guilty by reason of insanity.

prison system diagnosed with depressive disorders (major depression, dysthymia, or bipolar disorder). Two broad classes of antidepressant medications were studied: tricyclic antidepressants (TCAs, such as amitripty-line, doxepin, Pamelor, Tofranil, and Surmontil) and selective serotonin reuptake inhibitors (SSRIs, such as Prozac, Celexa, Lexapro, Paxil, and Zoloft). Though both classes are reported to be similar in efficacy, the former drugs—while substantially less expensive than the latter—are reportedly associated with more side effects and thus poorer patient adherence. Results indicated that antidepressant prescribing patterns varied significantly according to several sociodemographic factors. Female inmates with depressive disorders were more frequently prescribed SSRIs but less frequently TCAs or no treatment compared to their male inmate counterparts—perhaps reflecting differential symptom presentations among genders, a propensity for practitioners to prescribe medication more readily for female inmates, or higher rates of treatment before incarceration. Hispanic inmates were characterized by a higher prevalence of no pharmacotherapy than white or black inmates, and black inmates were prescribed SSRIs less frequently compared to white and Hispanic inmates, which is possibly explained by differential symptom presentations among ethnicities, language barriers, or medication patterns that existed before inmates were incarcerated. The importance of this study is twofold: providing an understanding of how depressive disorders are managed via pharmacological methods among criminal offenders in general and illustrating how sociodemographic factors may play a role in the expression and treatment of criminal depression. Ultimately, with more studies like these, further layers of understanding may be added to our current conceptualization of the link between depression and crime.

Bipolar Disorders

Blair Stockdill suffered from bipolar disorder and tragically murdered her own daughter—but what sort of scientific evidence links this type of illness to acts of crime and violence? The literature on bipolar disorders and crime, similar to that on depressive disorders and crime, is modest and dominated by studies of prevalence rates and presentations of descriptive and qualitative data. However, rather than being centered on associations with violence, studies of bipolar disorder have also examined various aspects of mania—psychological factors such as the effects of symptom type and number, hypersexuality, aggression, psychotic symptoms, and comorbidity with other disorders—and how these relate to a broader spectrum of criminal behavior.

A Closer Look: Bipolar Disorders and Crime

Prevalence of the Disorder in Crime

Study Type	**Number**	**Prevalence Rates†**
Arrest rates	1	2.3–2.8%
Birth cohorts	0	–
Community samples	1*	27.0%
Homicide offenders	9	0.0–13.8%
Jailed detainees and prisoners	20*	0.03–20.0%
Psychiatric inpatients	16*	0.7–27.0%
Total Number of Studies	**45**	

Sample Characteristics

Size	22–3,925
Gender	Male only (22 studies); female only (1 study); male and female but generally more males than females (15 studies); not reported (7 studies)
Age	Youth, adult
Location	Countries worldwide (e.g., Australia, Belgium, Bulgaria, Canada, England, Finland, Germany, Iceland, Italy, Russia, the United States, Wales, other European countries)
Diagnostic Systems	Not specified in many earlier studies. DSM (various editions), other research diagnostic criteria, "unofficial" and unspecified psychiatric classification systems.

Notes: *Two studies involved both jailed detainees and psychiatric inpatients. One study involved both psychiatric inpatients and community individuals.

†General population prevalence rates of disorders are presented in only one study (Häfner & Böker, 1982), and rates of affective psychoses (including manic-depressive illness) appear to be elevated in this sample of German mentally ill offenders relative to comparison base rates. This finding may be misleading, however, as Häfner and Böker's sample of mentally ill offenders would be expected to have elevated rates of psychiatric illness relative to one not designated as such–and rates of affective psychoses in this sample are actually lower than those reported in a comparison group of non-offender psychiatric hospital patients. Prevalence rates across all 45 studies appear to be increased in most cases and, for a small number of studies, at least comparable at minimum levels relative to estimates of bipolar disorders in the general population (e.g., reported in the DSM-IV-TR; see above). Rates of cyclothymia, reported in only three studies, appear congruent with general population base rates (Glueck, 1918, in Good, 1978; Dunsieth et al., 2004; McElroy et al., 1999), although, in the latter study, rates are actually more comparable to those reported in mood disorder clinics. However, the rates of cyclophrenia reported in five earlier studies appear significantly higher than base rates for cyclothymia in the majority of studies.

Prevalence of Crime in the Disorder

Study Type	Number	Prevalence Rates	Crime Definition
Arrest rates	0	–	–
Birth cohorts	2	0.0–33.3%†	Criminal register records, self-reported and criminal convictions for violence
Community samples	5*	1.0–21.0%	Assaultive behavior; arrest data and self-reported violent or illegal behavior; self-reported homicidal ideation and attempts
Homicide offenders	0	–	–
Jailed detainees and prisoners	0	–	–
Psychiatric inpatients	2*	2.0–75.0%	Assaultiveness or threatening during hospitalization; self-reported crime and violence; official criminal records
Total Number of Studies	**8**		

Sample Characteristics

Size	20–10,059
Gender	Male only (1 study); male and female (7 studies)
Age	Adult, youth, and longitudinal cohort
Location	Countries worldwide (e.g., England, New Zealand, Switzerland, the United States)
Diagnostic Systems	DSM and other research diagnostic criteria

Notes: *One study involved both psychiatric inpatients and community individuals.

†For any crime, these rates are 0.0–33.3%; for violent crime, they are 15.8–26.3%.

Nondisordered or community resident comparison group or general population baseline rates for either disorder or crime provided: **8 studies (11.3%)‡**

Note: ‡Rates of bipolar disorders are increased relative to general population baseline rates when provided (with the exception of Reich & Wells, 1985, wherein rates are lower relative to inpatient and outpatient comparison rates). Rates of affective psychoses (including manic-depressive illness) appear to be elevated in Häfner and Böker's (1982) sample of German mentally ill offenders relative to comparison base rates. This finding may be misleading, however, as this sample of mentally ill offenders would be expected to have elevated rates of psychiatric illness relative to samples not designated as such–and rates of affective psychoses in this sample are actually lower than those reported in a non-offender psychiatric hospital patient comparison group. Rates of crime are significantly elevated relative to comparisons when reported.

Bipolar Disorders and Crime: Descriptive Studies and Qualitative Data

"*Le maniaque fait généralement plus de bruit que de mal* [The manic makes more noise than harm]," wrote French psychiatrist Henri Ey in 1962 (quoted in Wulach, 1983, p. 75). This dictum suggests the relative benignity of the manic individual, despite those with mania who are angry, intrusive, and considered dangerous and frightening enough to be arrested and restrained. This dictum is not universal, however, as indicated by the serious criminal charges brought against some individuals in the manic phases of bipolar disorders (including the arson, rape, and life-threatening assaults found in Wulach's own sample—see below). In fact, though it has been said that excitements with laughter are safer than those with preoccupations, for many centuries it has been recognized that there are numerous signs of mania and that these may be aggressive rather than cheerful (Good, 1978). Some authors (e.g., Thorneloe & Crews, 1981) have proposed that manic-depressive illness may be an etiological factor in the antisocial and criminal behavior of some individuals.

The qualitative nature of criminal behavior associated with bipolar disorder has been explored in descriptive studies of manic patients—though comprehensive studies of this type are uncommon. One of the most impressive studies in this area, in terms of its uncommonly large sample size and the richness of its clinical detail, is Wulach's (1983) file review of 100 consecutive cases of manic criminal defendants (adult males) discharged from a forensic psychiatric ward from 1974–1981. This sample comprised 2% of 5,081 total consecutive discharges during this time period, which is consistent with the aforementioned prevalence rates of bipolar disorders in jailed detainee and psychiatric inpatient populations. Cases were included only if they met at discharge DSM-III criteria for a manic—as opposed to a depressive—episode. Results indicated charges of crimes against persons ($n = 32$), property ($n = 49$), and sexual crimes ($n = 6$). However, although rich in qualitative and descriptive data, Wulach's study did not utilize nondisordered comparison groups. Thus, we are left wondering how, if at all, the manic criminal in this sample may differ qualitatively from the criminal without mental illness.

Nonetheless, Wulach described the average defendant in this sample as being a Caucasian male in his late thirties with both psychiatric hospitalization and incarceration histories, who typically had been arrested for simple assaults, threats, or minor property damage (e.g., destroying a window in a state of rage). His victims—except in sexual cases—were usually strangers, and he often appeared elated and nonthreatening during clinical examination, despite a history of violence. According to Wulach, this type of defendant responded better to being in a forensic hospital than in a prison. The aggressive histories of ten randomly selected manic defendants were described and included referrals to the forensic unit for the following: throwing chairs in a police station; robbery and assault, banging head against prison cell door in an agitated state; the criminal possession of a weapon, breaking down a door to an apartment while armed with several weapons (i.e., a sword, pool cue, and hammer); harassment and menacing, hitting a complainant by driving an automobile at him; assault and burglary, pushing a woman down a flight of stairs and kicking arresting officers; assault, striking and kicking a complainant; assaulting a police officer who was interceding in an argument with a landlady; being "agitated and threatening" in prison; and attempted robbery, angrily and abusively threatening a stranger. Clearly, the manic defendants in this sample were capable of both noise and harm.

More recently, Quanbeck and colleagues (2004) examined 66 male and female inmates housed in the Los Angeles County Jail psychiatric division during a 7-month period and diagnosed with DSM-IV bipolar I disorder, comparing them to a community sample of 54 non-arrested male and female county psychiatric hospital patients with discharge diagnoses of bipolar I disorder, identified during the same time period. At the time of arrest, most inmates (74.2%) were experiencing a manic or mixed episode, while approximately one-quarter were depressed. Additionally, 59% were psychotic, and more manic or mixed inmates were experiencing psychotic symptoms when arrested than were depressed inmates (63.3% versus 47.1%, respectively). Results indicated an average of 1.29 charges per inmate (85 in total), and these consisted of violent crimes (41.2%—including 3 homicide or attempted homicide charges), property crimes (20%), drug-related crimes (18.8%), noncompliance with court orders (11.8%), and miscellaneous crimes (8.2%). Narcotics possession (11/85) and terrorist threats (10/85) were the two most common charges. Bipolar illness phase (manic, mixed, or depressed) did not correlate with charge type, though a relationship between presence of psychosis and violent charges approached statistical significance. Women were more likely to be charged with a property crime, but men were *not* more likely to be charged with a violent crime. Most inmates (80%) had a previous criminal record, and 61.6% were under legal supervision at the time of their arrest. In summary, descriptive studies here suggest the bipolar disordered individual to be capable of a variety of offenses while within the manic phase, ranging in seriousness from trivial to deadly.

Violence

Although violent crimes have emerged in descriptive studies of general criminality in manic persons, several studies have examined the relationship between mania and violence specifically. These have yielded mixed evidence (Collins & Bailey, 1990a), though some consistencies have been observed. For example, according to

Hirose (1979), most psychiatrists agree that murder is rare among manic patients. In Wulach's (1983) sample of 100 discharged forensic psychiatric ward manic cases, 18% ($n = 18$) had charges for simple assault, 8% ($n = 8$) had charges for menacing, 2% ($n = 2$) had charges for assault with a weapon (no lasting injury), 2% ($n = 2$) had charges for assault causing serious injury, and 2% ($n = 2$) had charges for negligent homicide with an automobile. Rates for charges of violent crimes reported by Quanbeck et al. (2004) are slightly higher (41.2%, including 3 for homicide or attempted homicide). Though homicides do appear relatively infrequently within these two studies, rates of violent crimes overall are somewhat variable.

Violence in bipolar disorders may be directly related to the phase of the illness. For example, Good (1978) reports that, across studies, violence and homicidal behavior are more often associated with the depressive phase of manic-depressive illness, while the manic phase is more often characterized by petty theft, swindling, minor assault, fraud, and drunkenness—though he cautions that these findings may be limited because of previous ambiguity in psychiatric diagnoses. On balance, the strongest connection between bipolar disorder and violence may appear during acute episodes of illness (Feldmann, 2001). In two reports on a sample of over 200 patients hospitalized on 72-hour emergency civil commitments (diagnosed with schizophrenia, mania, or other disorders), McNiel and colleagues (Binder & McNiel, 1988; McNiel et al., 1988) found that, although both schizophrenic and manic patients were overrepresented among those who engaged in physical attacks in the community during the two weeks preceding admission, only manic patients were most likely to be physically assaultive during the first 24 hours of hospitalization (Binder & McNiel, 1988) and in the first three days (McNiel et al., 1988). Feldmann (2001) reports that targets of violence are generally random in these cases and that manic patients often become violent when they feel restricted or when limits are set by hospital staff. In all, evidence suggests that, though not all manic individuals are violent, a significant minority of forensic psychiatric ward patients and jail inmates with mania are characterized by violent behavior; and violence in bipolar disordered patients may be related to illness progression or factors related to hospitalization.

Psychological Factors: Mania Symptoms

It may be interesting to speculate if manic symptomatology such as flight of thoughts or ideas in fact *causes* criminal behavior or merely facilitates it by contributing energy and motivation to—or allowing for the expression of—preexisting criminal thoughts or tendencies (e.g., through an increase in goal-directed activity or psychomotor agitation). Previous authors have echoed this very sentiment: Wulach (1983) admitted that it cannot be determined if irritability, anger, and aggression are central features of some manic states; if these features emerge secondarily to rejection and interference with the manic individual's activities; or if these are characterological aggressive features that become disinhibited in manic episodes. Several studies have examined various psychological factors related to crime in those with bipolar disorder, beginning with the actual symptoms of a manic episode.

The symptom profile of mania can contribute to assaultive and threatening behavior and criminal offending or predispose an individual to both (Janowsky, El-Yousef, & Davis, 1974; Wulach, 1983). In a sample of psychiatric inpatients ($n = 9$ with DSM-II schizophrenia, $n = 10$ with schizoaffective disorder, and $n = 10$ with manic depression, manic phase), Janowsky and colleagues (1974) looked at particular patterns of interpersonal maneuvering, including nursing staff ratings on interactional variables of the testing of limits, the projection of responsibility, sensitivity to others' soft spots, attempts to divide staff, flattering behavior, and the ability to evoke anger. They found these to be significantly more associated with manic individuals compared to other groups. Limitations include a small sample size, no normal comparison group, and using an interpersonal interaction rating scale which—by design—appeared specific to the illness in question (mania) and based on a small sample of manic patients (Beigel & Murphy, 1971). However, the superior ability of manic patients to manipulate and evoke anger in hospital staff compared to schizophrenia patients is an interesting finding and may explain the underpinnings of threatening and assaultive behavior in these patients. For example, the authors purport the aforementioned interpersonal variables to be more associated with the manic phase of the illness rather than with any underlying personality predispositions toward interpersonal behaviors. This finding suggests that maladaptive interpersonal functioning predisposing individuals to threatening and assaultive interactions with others could be directly attributable to the illness itself.

Several authors have proposed subtypes of or variations within mania, into which they place groups of manic individuals who may be predisposed to criminality and violence. For example, Beigel and Murphy (1971) proposed two manic subgroups: (1) elated and grandiose but not paranoid and destructive and (2) paranoid and destructive but not euphoric and grandiose. Carlson and Goodwin (1973) proposed that manic patients are only assaultive and threatening during the second phase of a three-phase manic episode: euphoria, followed by hostility, anger, and aggression, and then by panic. Additionally, one factor analytic study of 576 manic patients (Sato et al., 2002) identified an aggressive mania subtype, separable from other phenomenological subtypes of mania (i.e., pure, psychotic, and depressive or mixed). To date, however, none of these proposals has been empirically validated; and Wulach's (1983) descriptive sample does not appear to support either Beigel and Murphy's (1971) manic typology or Carlson and Goodwin's (1973) phase proposal of manic illness—at least in terms of aggressive or violent behavior in mania.

Symptoms Versus Disorders

Some authors have speculated that manic *symptoms*—rather than bipolar *disorders*—are the key to understanding the association between these illnesses and crime and violence. In a sample of 325 psychiatric probation and parole clients, P. L. Solomon and Draine (1999), using hierarchical block multiple regression analysis, found the number of lifetime psychiatric hospitalizations and lifetime occurrences of mania diagnoses significantly explained self-reported lifetime arrests (though the total model explained 10% of the variance in lifetime arrests compared to opportunity variables, which explained 45%). Results were interpreted as further support that the occurrence of symptoms, not categorical disorders, explained criminal arrests.

Associations between manic symptomatology and criminal behavior may be even more specific—perhaps related to symptom number, symptom type, or both. Collins and Bailey (1990a) examined how both depressive disorders and depressive and manic symptoms were associated with several indicators of violent behavior. Participants included 1,140 adult male North Carolina prison inmates diagnosed with structured clinical interviews using DSM-III criteria (disorders used in analyses were limited to depression and dysthymia; symptom counts were used in place of disorder categories—i.e., mania—with insufficient numbers of inmates to support analysis). Violence indicators included adulthood fighting, recent arrests for violent offenses (homicide, rape, assault, robbery), current incarceration for expressive violence (homicide, rape, assault) or instrumental violence (robbery), and lifetime arrests for expressive or instrumental violence. Logistic regression analyses indicated dysthymia to be associated with arrest or incarceration history for robbery and for multiple incidents of adulthood fighting, recurrent depression to be associated with an incarceration history for robbery, and depression symptoms (whether or not a disorder diagnosis was made) to be associated with adulthood fighting. Although a statistically significant relationship was observed between two or more manic symptoms and recent arrest for a violent offense, these results became nonsignificant when depression symptoms rather than disorders were entered into the analysis. Although the validity of the expressive versus instrumental violence distinction is questionable, the comparatively low rates of actual mania in the present study make results difficult to interpret and generalize. In fact, the groupings by number of manic symptoms (i.e., one manic symptom, two or more manic symptoms) may not be entirely valid (being too "weak" in the former and perhaps too heterogeneous in the latter). Means and standard deviations for the number of manic symptoms (or depressive symptoms, for that matter) were not reported. Furthermore, the authors conclude that only some mood disorder features are related to specific types of violence indicators—but it remains unclear *which* features demonstrate this relationship. It may be that symptom type rather than mere number of symptoms is the key to understanding the association between mania and violence.

Hypersexuality: Mania and Sexual Crimes

Given the characteristic hypersexuality of mania, it is tempting to speculate whether a connection may exist between bipolar disorders and sexual offending. Dunsieth and colleagues (2004) suggest that a substantial proportion of sexual offenders may have mood disorders; and Nicolas and colleagues (2005) report that hypersexuality is a common symptom in manic episodes in teenagers with bipolar disorder, which can lead to risky behaviors that put the adolescent in dangerous situations and induce sexual delusional ideas and false allegations of sexual abuse. In a sample of adolescent patients hospitalized for bipolar I disorder, Barzman and colleagues (2007) found older age at first treatment, sexual activity in the previous month, the therapeutic use of stimulants (but not substance abuse or dependence), and anxiety disorders to be the most significant factors differentiating juvenile offenders from non-offenders (though sexual offenses—i.e., prostitution comprised less than 5% of offenses, and offenses, in general, occurred before onset of illness in approximately half of the participants). Unfortunately, this topic has gone largely unexplored in the literature, though reports of prevalence rates of bipolar disorders among sexual offenders (and vice versa) may provide some initial information.

Studies reporting the prevalence rates of sexual offenses among bipolar disordered individuals suggest some support for a relationship between the two. For example, high rates of homosexual prostitution were reported in Thorneloe and Crews' (1981) case study of six young adult males with manic-depressive illness and antisocial personality disorder. Six percent (n = 6) of Wulach's (1983) 100 people diagnosed with mania and discharged from a forensic psychiatric ward manic had sexual charges (including two rapes and three cases of fondling genitalia), as did 10% (n = 1) of Bearcroft and Donovan's (1965, in Wulach, 1983) and 20% (n = 2) of Good's (1978) samples of manic-depressive prisoners. On balance, there were two child molestation charges and one rape charge in the Quanbeck et al. (2004) sample, which together accounted for only 3.5% of the total charges. Though prevalence rates of criminality are difficult to estimate in the general population, rates of sexual offending in these samples do appear significantly elevated; for example, in 2009, the National Center for Exploited and Missing Children estimated the rate of registered sex offenders in the United States at 234 per 100,000 population (0.23%).

Studies reporting prevalence rates of bipolar disorders among sexual offenders may also indicate supporting evidence. In a sample of 22 adolescent sex offenders, Galli and colleagues (1999) found increased rates of bipolar disorders but also higher rates of major depression comparable to those of bipolar disorder and bipolar disorder NOS. In a later study, Dunsieth et al. (2004) used structured clinical interviews (supplemented with medical and legal records and polygraph examinations) to examine a sample of 113 convicted male sexual offenders in a residential sex-offender treatment program and to compare offenders with paraphilias (n = 84) to those without (n = 26). Elevated rates of bipolar disorders (35.4%) were observed in this sample, but, when rates of individual disorders were examined separately, those of major depressive disorder (23.9%) nearly matched those of bipolar I disorder (24.8%), and rates of other bipolar disorders (II, NOS, and cyclothymia) were much lower (i.e., approximately 5% or below). Furthermore, mood disorders (any type), major depressive disorder, bipolar disorder (any type) and bipolar I were significantly more prevalent among sex offenders with paraphilias compared to those without. Worth noting are two commonalities to both studies: (1) other disorders (substance use, anxiety, eating, and impulse control disorders, as well as paraphilias) were also observed at increased rates, suggesting that psychopathology in general rather than mania specifically may be related to sexual offending; and (2) rates of bipolar disorders were comparable to those of major depression, suggesting that mood disorders overall rather than bipolar disorders in particular may be associated with sexual offenses. In fact, Becker and colleagues (1991) noted markedly increased levels of self-reported depressive symptomatology in a sample of 246 male juvenile sex offenders, particularly those with histories of abuse (however, bipolar disorder was not assessed for).

Rates of bipolar disorder in these sex offender samples (27–35.4%) are among the highest compared to those observed in criminal populations overall (see Table 6.4), suggesting what may be some degree of specificity to sexual offenses. However, although an association between bipolar disorder and sexual offending is suggested by the increased rates of these illnesses among sexual offender samples, there is no way of knowing yet if these rates are due to hypersexuality in particular, to other manic symptomatology (aggression or agitation, impulsivity), to mood disorder symptoms in general (including symptoms of depression), or to psychopathology of any form. Hypersexuality may manifest in increased consensual sexual relations rather than in sexual offending *per se*. Or, sexual offending fueled by manic hypersexuality may involve only known victims, who may be less likely to report these crimes (sexual offenders in Wulach's [1983] sample of manic defendants tended to victimize known persons as opposed to strangers). Furthermore, sexual offending often is based upon motives that are not sexual in nature, such as anger, power, or naïve cognitions (Bartol & Bartol, 2008), and there is no reason to assume that a manic individual would not commit a sexual offense while motivated by these other factors. Unfortunately, without separate control groups comprised of non-offenders and nonsexual offenders (absent from both studies here), no firm conclusions can be drawn. Ultimately, more studies are needed if any association between manic hypersexuality and sexual offending is to be elucidated.

Aggression

Hostility and aggression have been characterized as particularly important core features of manic and mixed episodes (Garno, Gunawardane, & Goldberg, 2008). Good's (1978) classic review of mood disorder, aggression, and criminality indicates that numerous researchers have associated mania with aggression. It is traditionally considered that hostility only appears in mania when the patient's activities are interfered with and he or she feels threatened, unloved, and unsuccessful (Good, 1978). Several researchers have attempted to qualify the nature of aggression in bipolar disorders. For example, Blackburn (1974) used self-report questionnaires to examine the direction of hostility and aggression in patients with unipolar and bipolar disorders. Results indicated patients with mania to be the only group characterized mostly by *extrapunitiveness* (i.e., hostility directed outwards toward others or objects) over *intropunitiveness* (i.e., hostility directed toward the self) and that this characteristic may be specific to the phase of the disorder. Patients with *unipolar depression* were significantly more extrapunitive than those with bipolar depression, but less so than those with mania.

More recently, Garno and colleagues (2008) examined predictors of trait aggression in 100 hospital patients with bipolar disorders (73 with bipolar I and 27 with bipolar II). Psychiatric diagnoses were made with structured clinical interviews using DSM-IV criteria, and trait aggression, depressive and manic symptom severity, and history of childhood maltreatment were assessed via self-report questionnaires. Stepwise multiple regression analysis revealed that comorbid borderline personality disorder and current depressive and manic symptoms each significantly predicted trait aggression scores when controlled for confounding factors. No control groups were used in this study, so it is unclear if these relationships are specific to bipolar disorder or reflect a more general relationship between trait aggression and co-occurring personality pathologies and mood symptoms. Others have investigated the effects of psychotropic medications upon anger in bipolar disordered individuals. In a study of 179 patients hospitalized for manic episodes, Swann (1999) found that divalproex (an anticonvulsant or anti-seizure medication also used to treat mania) significantly reduced anger factor scores in manic patients and was superior to lithium in controlling manic episodes in patients with *dysphoric mania* who displayed hostile, aggressive, or impulsive behavior. In aggregate, evidence suggests an association between bipolar disorder and aggression, and different factors related to aggression may mediate this relationship.

Psychotic Symptoms

Before her daughter's murder, Blair Stockdill exhibited behavior that was erratic and likely difficult for others to understand. Bipolar patients may present with psychotic symptomatology (recall the new placement conceptually of bipolar disorders between psychotic disorders and depressive disorders in the DSM-5)—particularly when manic features are most intense (Binder & McNiel, 1988; Yesavage, 1983), and it may be these psychotic symptoms rather than the bipolar illness itself that contribute to violence (Binder & McNiel, 1988). According to Tardiff (1984), studies of private and public hospital inpatients have shown a high risk of assaultive behavior associated with schizophrenia- and mania-related psychotic symptoms among patients in the acute phase; and with organic disorders, mental retardation, and disorganized nonparanoid schizophrenics among chronic inpatients. Tardiff (1999) found schizophrenia and mania to be overrepresented among physically violent patients in private hospitals, and identified a positive correlation between the following symptoms and violence in bipolar patients: conceptual disorganization, auditory hallucinations, unusual thought content, suspiciousness, uncooperativeness, and hostility. In another study of 40 male inpatients from a Veteran's Administration hospital psychiatric intensive care unit in California, Yesavage (1983) found bipolar patients more likely to be violent when manic rather than when depressed; though severe childhood discipline, intensity of psychotic symptoms, and a history of pre-admission violence also predicted physical assaultiveness in this study. Additionally, the correlation of bipolar disorder with assaultiveness among hospitalized patients may vary as a function of post-admission time. Patients with mania may respond to treatment faster than schizophrenics—thus, violence related to psychotic symptoms declines more rapidly in manic patients compared to those with schizophrenia (Volavka, 1995, in Feldmann, 2001). Though more work is needed in this area, it is clear that psychotic symptoms co-occurring with mood episodes may be critical to the understanding of crime and violence in bipolar disorders.

Comorbidity With Other Disorders

In Blair Stockdill's case, the picture is complicated by her struggles with a methamphetamine use disorder. Criminality in bipolar illness may reflect the coexistence of additional mental disorders associated with criminal, antisocial, or impulsive behavior. For example, Thorneloe and Crews (1981) present the cases of six young adults with the manic type of manic-depressive illness who were also comorbid for antisocial personality disorder (diagnosed using Feighner research criteria) and suggest an association between the two disorders. However, some of the studies reviewed from the modest amount of literature available at the time of this report relied upon positive lithium responses, rather than actual psychiatric diagnoses, to indicate manic-depressive illness. Comorbidity between bipolar disorder and conduct disorder has also been demonstrated in children and adolescents (Kovacs & Pollock, 1995). In a later study involving 50 adolescents (45 boys and 5 girls) admitted to a juvenile detention center, Pliszka and colleagues (2000) found significantly increased proportions of conduct disorder and dependence on substances other than alcohol or marijuana in those diagnosed with mania ($n = 11$) compared to those diagnosed with major depressive disorder ($n = 10$) and those with no mood disorder ($n = 29$). Though substance and alcohol use were highly prevalent, no significant differences in rates of alcohol or marijuana dependence or in age at first use of any substances were observed among groups. Participants with mood disorders were much more likely to meet criteria for conduct disorder than those without; and, for those with both mood and conduct disorders, the conduct disorder symptoms predated the onset of the mood disorder. Furthermore, comorbidity with ADHD may also be a concern. It has been shown that, among children with ADHD, those with both bipolar disorder and conduct disorder appear to be at higher risk for later mood disorders than those with only conduct disorder, who are more at risk for adult antisocial personality disorder. Additionally, children having both disorders in addition to ADHD demonstrate poorer functioning and are more at risk for later hospitalization (Biederman et al., 1997). Together, these studies illustrate the importance of considering coexisting criminogenic disorders when examining crime and violence in bipolar illness, though more research is needed to ascertain which disorders contribute more to criminal outcomes when occurring together.

Other Studies

Other miscellaneous studies in this area are worth mentioning. For example, two studies conducted by Feldmann (2001) may suggest additional qualitative aspects of the relationship between affective disorders and crime. In the first, 34% of 419 individuals involved in hostage or barricade situations were found to meet DSM-IV criteria for affective disorders (31% for depression and 3% for bipolar disorder). Higher rates of violence (including suicide) were observed in the affective disordered group compared to other diagnostic groups. Furthermore, police negotiations with these individuals were less successful for subjects who were depressed compared to those who were manic. In this study, SWAT team assaults were more common in cases involving affective disorders. Unfortunately, methodological details such as diagnostic procedures and sample acquisition were not presented in this report. In the second study, 877 workplace-violence offenders were examined—of which 21.6% met DSM-IV diagnostic criteria for affective disorders (19.2% for depression and 2.4% for bipolar disorder). According to the author, workplace-violence offenders with affective disorders were characterized by decreased violence compared to offenders with personality or substance abuse disorders. Again, methodological details were not provided, and violence was not operationally defined.

Findings from other studies may assist in the understanding of crime and violence in those with bipolar disorder—such as examining the effectiveness of self-report questionnaires for screening for bipolar disorder in correctional settings (Kemp et al., 2008). Studies of suicidality may also provide valuable information. For example, in a prospective study of 216 patients diagnosed using DSM-IV with bipolar I disorder, Khalsa and colleagues (2008) found 127 to be suicidal over an average of 4.2 years at risk (14% per year). The patients' rate of completed suicides was 10 times above the incidence rate in the U.S. general population, and their rate of suicide attempts was 14 times above that estimated for the general population. The rate of accidental violent fatalities was 3 times above the current U.S. national rate. Increased mixed dysphoric agitation and depression, as well as prior suicide attempts, appeared to be associated with suicidal acts and thus may be predictive factors. Alcohol abuse, an increased number of psychotropic medications per individual, and antipsychotics or sedatives were also associated with life-threatening suicidal behaviors and accidents—perhaps representing (in the latter) either a more severe or an earlier, more acute form of the illness. Miscellaneous studies such as these underscore the complexity of the association between bipolar disorders and crime and suggest different empirical avenues to follow in pursuing its further understanding.

Origins of Crime and Violence in Mood Disorders: Theoretical Explanations and Etiological Mechanisms

Psychoanalytic Factors

Crime and violence occurring within the context of mood disorders may be explained by unconscious processes and dynamics, and psychoanalytic explanations for criminal and violent behavior in depressed individuals have been offered in the literature. For example, Harrer and Kofler-Westergren (1986) discuss the case of a 50-year-old woman diagnosed with agitated depression, who initially wanted to set her house on fire. Instead, she scratched her eyes out with her fingernails because of self-reproach over incest with her own son. The authors interpreted the self-blinding as a symbolic form of self-castration; and, afterwards, the woman experienced relief and the confidence to be forgiven.

Interestingly, psychoanalytic explanations of mood disorders and criminal behavior share a common overlapping dynamic—**unconscious guilt**. For example, Freud proposed that frequent alternations between manic and depressive episodes in the same individual indicate the alternating influences of unconscious wishes and unconscious self-punishment. The manic phase is characterized by the unbridled gratification of forbidden wishes (e.g., excessive involvement in pleasurable activities), which cause an accumulation of feelings of guilt and the need for punishment—a need that, when satisfied, relieves the individual from the feelings of guilt. According to Freud, the depression that follows a manic episode is dominated by the need for punishment. During the depressive episode, intense suffering (resulting from self-inflicted punishment and the unrestrained tormenting of conscience) leads subsequently to a fresh manic episode, which is similar to a revolution, as the once-restricted instincts now break through with renewed energy or force (Alexander & Staub, 1931). In fact, Alexander and Staub (1931) propose that the same individual who continually contemplates the idea of suicide during a severe depression may become dangerous to the lives of others during a manic episode. The unconscious need for punishment has been discussed in relationship to the general psychoanalytic theory of crime (see Chapter 2). There is an overlap here between depression and crime—perhaps both are merely potential byproducts of unconscious guilt. This theory would explain why crime and violence are possible within the context of depression, and vice versa.

In examining psychoanalytic explanations for crime and violence in those with mood disorders, a question must be asked: Is it the unconscious processes related to the disorder (i.e., depression or mania), the criminality, or a unique combination or interaction of both that leads to the criminal or violent behavior? Which contributes the most? Do these processes cause the behaviors, or predispose the individual to them? Important to remember, however, is the distinction between the unconscious processes specific to mood disorders that lead to crime and violence and the nonspecific unconscious processes occurring within the mind of the criminal, who just so happens to be depressed.

Neurobiological Factors

Earlier authors proposed that the symptoms of depression (e.g., slow perceptual-motor reaction time and physical movement and social isolation) would not intuitively predispose an individual toward violence in social settings. Some early studies on depression, however, suggested that depression may narrow the field of consciousness, sharpen focus, and stabilize attention. Thus, the depressed individual, when roused from apathy, may be more likely to disregard the broader implications of a frustrating social situation (Anthony, 1968).

One interesting approach was used by Anthony (1968) in an early study on depression and criminality. This author administered a psychomotor test of depression, along with other neuropsychological measures (including for general intelligence), to a sample of 197 young male English offenders (ages 15–21). The psychomotor test involved an apparatus that presented light signals to participants and measured control knob movement responses—a test that purportedly had differentiated depressed from nondepressed individuals in other studies (wherein the former demonstrated reduced perceptual-motor response speed). Anthony compared violent offenders convicted of assault to those convicted of property or motor vehicle offenses. The results indicated that depression (as indicated by a slower perceptual-motor response speed) was associated with violent convictions. Response speed was not significantly associated with general intelligence. Although the validity of the psychomotor test as a diagnostic measure for depression may be questionable, the author does suggest the value of nonverbal tests in the diagnostic process for depression.

Impulsive aggression in bipolar mania has been linked to decreased serotonin functioning, as well as to increased catecholaminergic function and behavioral hyperarousal (Frankle et al., 2005; Swann, 1999). In fact, low central nervous system serotonin levels may be an indicator for vulnerability to impulsive aggression across mood disorders and other psychiatric illnesses (Swann et al., 1994; Oquendo & Mann, 2000). Swann (1999) also proposed that autonomic overarousal may lead to disruptive or externalizing behaviors (including aggression, impulsivity, and anxiety) in manic patients. Though Harkavy-Friedman et al. (2006) found some neuropsychological performance differences between bipolar I and bipolar II disordered suicide attempters, comparisons were not made with nonviolent individuals with bipolar disorder in this study, and no inferences can be made from it about the neurobiological factors related to the etiology of violence in this disorder. More work is needed in this area.

Psychosocial Factors

Finally, psychosocial and environmental influences may play an important role in the etiology of crime and violence in mood disorders. For example, 80% of Wulach's (1983) sample was living alone, which suggested to him a significant amount of family instability. This, he reports, may be explained by demographic factors but also by the destructive interpersonal consequences of manic episodes—particularly among those with more severe and less manageable forms of the illness. Treatment history may be an additional important factor. Quanbeck and colleagues (2004) observed differences in treatment history among inmates in manic, mixed, and depressive episodes at the time of arrest; 62.1% of all inmates and 82.9% of manic inmates in particular were receiving inpatient treatment in the 3 months prior to arrest. Manic inmates were released from an inpatient setting significantly more recently than depressive or mixed-episode inmates. Of the inmates who were manic at the time of arrest, 60% had been hospitalized within one month prior to the arrest, and approximately half of these were released from an inpatient setting within the week prior to their arrest. Only one-third of the inmates had followed up with post-hospitalization outpatient care. Inmates were characterized by significantly increased rates of comorbid substance abuse than the community sample. Additionally, the community sample was significantly older and more likely to be female than the inmate sample. In a subsequent study (Quanbeck et al., 2005), these 66 patients were compared to matched cases of Los Angeles County bipolar I disorder patients (n = 52) with no known history of arrest. Results indicated arrested patients were more likely to be male and have a history of substance use disorder but less likely to have a history of treatment while under mental health conservatorship. Additionally, compared to the non-arrested group, the arrested group was characterized by more frequent but briefer hospitalizations. Ultimately, psychosocial and environmental factors should remain key considerations in understanding the etiology of crime and violence in mood disorders.

Conclusion

The case of Blair Stockdill demonstrates how the extreme ends of emotional experience may contribute to crime, violence, and even murder; and the dozens of other individuals discussed in this chapter—who, in similar situations, committed similarly unspeakable acts—indicate that she is not alone. Though mood disorders are among the earliest studied in relation to criminality, the literature in this area remains somewhat underdeveloped compared to that for other mental disorders (i.e., schizophrenia and psychopathy). Also, it has yet to move in any significant way beyond the prevalence rate studies or the clinical case material and descriptive studies of the previous century, which addressed the more qualitative aspects of the association between the illness and criminality. Beyond these initial invaluable qualitative contributions, studies of depressive disorders are comparatively limited in scope to relationships with violence, murder-suicide, and postpartum depression. Studies of bipolar disorders and crime have also included important qualitative data and have started to focus on understanding how psychological factors (e.g., the symptoms of mania, including hypersexuality, as well as aggression, psychotic symptoms, and comorbid disorders) may contribute to a broader variety of criminal behavior. Although psychoanalytic theory has offered explanations of the etiology of crime and violence in those with mood disorders, contributions have also been made from neurobiological research and psychosocial perspectives. Given the increasing "popularity" of mood disorder diagnoses and the seemingly never-ending stream of murder-suicides and other forms of violence related to these disorders in news media headlines, the need for more work in this understudied area appears crucial.

KEY TERMS

anaclitic depression
automatic thoughts
autonomous depression
bipolar I disorder
bipolar II disorder
catathymic crisis
cognitive errors
cyclothymic disorder
dysthymic disorder
hypomanic episode
introjective/self-critical depression
major depressive disorder
major depressive episode
maladaptive assumptions
manic episode
postpartum depression (PPD)
sociotropic depression
unconscious guilt

REVIEW QUESTIONS

1. Compare and contrast the conceptualizations of depression from the different theoretical perspectives discussed in the chapter. Discuss similarities and differences between these and the conceptualizations of mania. Why might these similarities occur (i.e., why might depression and mania be conceptually related)?
2. Examine Table 6.4 and 6.5 and the summaries of research studies in the "A Closer Look" sections for each disorder in this chapter. Discuss how prevalence rates of crime in those with mood disorders and of mood disorders in criminal populations differ among these disorders, if at all. Using the information in the tables, speculate as to how these differences in prevalence rates may have been caused by methodology (e.g., in terms of study types, sample characteristics, methodological issues, or other concerns).
3. Reflect on the case material related to depression and violence presented in the chapter. In what ways are these cases similar (i.e., in terms of types of depression, situational factors or precursors to the homicidal event, individual characteristics)? Do any patterns emerge in terms of how depression may relate to extreme violence?
4. Critically evaluate the information presented in the chapter about postpartum depression and violence. Does this information constitute strong evidence for a relationship between the two? Why or why not?
5. Compare and contrast the psychological factors associated with a putative link between mania and violence. Which mania symptoms (or other factors related to mania) demonstrate the strongest evidence for a mania-violence relationship? Explain your answer.

7

Anxiety Disorders

ROBERT CAMERON HOUSTON

In February 2006, Robert Cameron Houston, age 17, brutally murdered 22-year-old youth counselor Raechale Elton. Elton worked at an independent living center contracted by the State of Utah to reform young offenders. Houston had been placed there by authorities for two previous sexually motivated knife assaults, one on a younger relative and one on an adult aunt.

Elton was killed after driving Houston back to the center during an intense snowstorm—a violation of the center's rules. After raping Elton at knifepoint, Houston stabbed her multiple times and tried to break her neck and spine in several different ways. He also slit Elton's throat and tried to rip out her trachea because she would not stop screaming. Houston subsequently crashed Elton's car into a nearby house in an apparent attempt to kill himself. He told the owner of the house, "You should stab me, kill me now."

Houston was reportedly physically abused by his mother and sexually abused by an older male as a child. Born without one ear canal—which caused deafness in one ear and problems learning to walk and talk—and overweight, he was constantly teased and suffered from enuresis (bed wetting) until age 10. As a child, Houston once witnessed his father hold a knife to his mother's throat, and, at age 8, Houston allegedly put a knife to his own throat and told his older brother he wanted to die.

Though reportedly Houston was a good student when in a structured group home, a psychologist testified for the defense that Houston suffered from an undiagnosed and untreated obsessive-compulsive disorder that overwhelmed his mind with uncontrollable thoughts of sexual violence. His condition may have been exacerbated by lax supervision (which allowed him to be sexually active with a girlfriend and to hear an adult supervisor at the home have sex with his girlfriend on numerous occasions) and stimulated by treatment (i.e., talking about his fantasies with a female therapist instead of receiving needed medication). Houston later confessed to police that he was infatuated with Elton.

On April 13, 2007, Houston was sentenced to life in prison without parole.

Fear—of an unknown danger or of an immediate threat—is a basic element of human survival. Worry, fear, and anxiety are all woven into the tapestry of human experience. To a large extent, these experiences are adaptive, allowing us to anticipate and avoid physical and emotional harm, adverse situations, and other negative consequences and outcomes. For some, anxiety can be a powerful ally—for others, the most debilitating of enemies. Understanding how the inner experience of anxiety is related to the outward manifestation of behavior can be relatively straightforward, at times. However, the case of Robert Cameron Houston demonstrates how the two can be linked in subtle, even imperceptible ways. Furthermore, the ways in which clinically significant anxiety symptoms may predispose an individual to violent, criminal, or antisocial behavior (or vice versa) have received comparatively little attention in the literature, at least relative to the other mental disorders presented in this book, and Houston's heinous act of violence speaks to a greater need to explore this relationship further.

The DSM-IV-TR outlines an entire class of anxiety disorders, which are somewhat varied, both conceptually and in symptom presentation. These include generalized anxiety disorder, panic disorder (with and without agoraphobia), agoraphobia without history of panic disorder, specific phobia, social phobia, obsessive-compulsive disorder, post-traumatic stress disorder, acute stress disorder, anxiety disorder due to a general medical condition, substance-induced anxiety disorder, and anxiety disorder NOS (APA, 2000). In the DSM-5, anxiety disorders have been arranged developmentally (i.e., in sequence according to age of onset) and include separation anxiety disorder, selective mutism, specific phobia, social anxiety disorder (social phobia), panic disorder, agoraphobia, generalized anxiety disorder, substance- or medication-induced anxiety disorder, anxiety due to another medical condition, other specific anxiety disorder, and unspecified anxiety disorder (APA, 2013). Interestingly, in the DSM-5, obsessive-compulsive disorder, post-traumatic stress disorder, and acute stress disorder are no longer found within the anxiety disorders. The first has been reclassified under obsessive-compulsive and related disorders and the last two under trauma- and stressor-related disorders. However, these disorders and their relationship with crime will be covered here according to the previous DSM-IV-TR categories.

Diagnostic Criteria and the Prevalence of Anxiety Disorders

Unlike in the other chapters of this book, the specific diagnostic criteria for each DSM-5 disorder will not be presented in this chapter. Doing so for anxiety disorders was decided against because of (1) the comparatively larger number of disorders contained within the DSM-5 anxiety disorders class (i.e., nearly a dozen), (2) the large number of diagnostic criteria for each disorder, (3) the sheer amount of space required to present them all here, and (4) the fact that a significant amount of literature has not been developed to date on each disorder individually, in terms of its relationship with crime and violence (see below). Nonetheless, the essential features and characteristics of these disorders, along with their known prevalence and incidence rates, are presented in Table 7.1 in both DSM-IV-TR and DSM-5 formulations but, again, using the original DSM-IV-TR grouping for anxiety disorders. The reader should gain an adequate understanding of the characteristic symptoms of these disorders via these descriptions and the sections below related to theoretical conceptualizations.

Theoretical Conceptualizations: Anxiety Disorders

Anxiety

Anxiety is commonly defined as a diffuse, vague, and extremely unpleasant feeling of fear and apprehension (Saranson & Saranson, 2002). Historically, the word "anxiety" is derived from "*anxius*"—a Latin term dating back at least to the year 1661 for a condition associated with mood (agitation and depression) and physiological symptoms (a sensation of tightness and distress in the region over the heart and lower chest) or for a state of concern, solicitude, or disturbing suspense (Marks, 1969). **Physiological symptoms** may include combinations of rapid heart rate, shortness of breath, diarrhea, loss of appetite, fainting, dizziness, sweating, sleepiness, frequent urination, and tremors (Saranson & Saranson, 2002).

Discussions within the literature have differentiated **fear** from **anxiety**, which appear to be interrelated on several different levels. It is generally held that individuals experiencing fear are easily able to articulate what they are afraid of, but those experiencing anxiety are not. For the latter, expressing the cause of their distress is difficult because the source of danger is unknown, not obvious, or outside of their awareness (PDM Task Force, 2006; Saranson & Saranson, 2002). Psychodynamic clinicians have also clarified differences between potential and present danger, between the evaluation of and response to danger, and between adaptive responses to actual danger (possibly but not necessarily including fear and anxiety) and anxiety responses associated with the activation of the human fight-or-flight response in expectation of disaster (PDM Task Force, 2006).

Freud originally coined the term "anxiety neurosis" in 1895, and over the next several decades he refined his conceptualization of anxiety. For him, anxiety was the result of conflict between the id's unconscious sexual or

Table 7.1 Descriptions and Prevalence Rates of DSM-IV-TR and DSM-5 Anxiety Disorders

Anxiety Disorder	Description: DSM-IV-TR[1]	Description: DSM-5[2]	Prevalence/Incidence
Panic Attack	A discrete period in which there is the sudden onset of intense apprehension, fearfulness, or terror, often associated with feelings of impending doom. During these attacks, symptoms such as shortness of breath, palpitations, chest pain or discomfort, choking or smothering sensations, and fear of "going crazy" or losing control are present.	Abrupt surges of intense fear or intense discomfort that reach a peak within minutes and are accompanied by physical or cognitive symptoms.	12-month community prevalence in U.S. adults ≈ 11.2%, in other countries ≈ 2.7%–3.3%.[2]
Agoraphobia	Anxiety about, or avoidance of, places or situations from which escape might be difficult (or embarrassing) or in which help may not be available in the event of having a panic attack or panic-like symptoms.	(see below)	(see below)
Panic Disorder with Agoraphobia (300.21) or without Agoraphobia (300.01)[1] **Panic Disorder without Agoraphobia (300.01 [F41.0])**[2]	Characterized by recurrent unexpected panic attacks about which there is persistent concern (can occur either with or without agoraphobia).	In panic disorder, the individual experiences recurrent unexpected panic attacks and is persistently concerned or worried about having more panic attacks or changes his or her behavior because of panic attacks (e.g., avoidance of exercise or of unfamiliar locations).	Community samples: Lifetime prevalence rates 1–3.5%, one-year prevalence rates 0.5–1.5%. Clinical samples: Prevalence rates 10–60% (the latter in cardiology clinics).[1] 12-month community prevalence in the United States and other countries ≈ 2%–3%.[2]
Agoraphobia without History of Panic Disorder (300.22)[1] **Agoraphobia (300.22 [F40.00])**[2]	Characterized by the presence of agoraphobia and panic-like symptoms without a history of unexpected panic attacks.	Individuals with agoraphobia are fearful and anxious about two or more of the following situations: using public transportation, being in open spaces, being in enclosed places, standing in line or being in a crowd, or being outside of the home alone in other situations. The individual fears or avoids these situations because of thoughts that escape might be difficult or help might not be available in the event of developing panic-like symptoms or other incapacitating or embarrassing symptoms.	Epidemiological samples: prevalence higher than panic disorder with agoraphobia, though assessment problems appear to have inflated these rates.[1] Every year approximately 1.7% of adolescents and adults have a diagnosis of agoraphobia.[2]

(Continued)

(Continued)

Anxiety Disorder	Description		Prevalence/Incidence
	DSM-IV-TR[1]	DSM-5[2]	
Specific Phobia (300.29)[1] **Specific Phobia (300.29 [F40.2xx])**[2]	Characterized by clinically significant anxiety provoked by exposure to a specific feared object or situation, often leading to avoidance behavior.	Individuals with specific phobia are fearful or anxious about or avoidant of circumscribed objects or situations.	Community samples: current prevalence rates 4–8.8%, lifetime prevalence rates 7.2–11.3%. Prevalence rates decline in the elderly, and vary for different types of specific phobias.[1] 12-month community prevalence in the United States ≈ 7%–9%, in other countries ≈ 2%–6%.[2]
Social Phobia (300.23)[1] **Social Anxiety Disorder (300.23 [F40.10])** [2]	Characterized by clinically significant anxiety provoked by exposure to certain types of social or performance situations, often leading to avoidance behavior.	In social anxiety disorder (social phobia), the individual is fearful or anxious about or avoidant of social interactions and situations that involve the possibility of being scrutinized.	Epidemiological or community-based studies: Lifetime prevalence 3–13%. In the general population, most with social phobia fear public speaking. Social phobia is rarely the reason for inpatient admissions. Outpatient clinics: 10–20% of individuals with anxiety disorders.[1] 12-month community prevalence in the United States ≈ 7%, in other countries ≈ 0.5%–2.0%.[2]
Obsessive-Compulsive Disorder (300.3)[1] **Obsessive-Compulsive Disorder (300.3 [F42])**[2]	Characterized by obsessions (which cause marked anxiety or distress) and/or by compulsions (which serve to neutralize anxiety).	Characterized by the presence of obsessions (recurrent and persistent thoughts, urges, or images that are experienced as intrusive and unwanted) and compulsions (repetitive behaviors or mental acts that an individual feels driven to perform in response to an obsession or according to rules that must be applied rigidly).	Community studies estimate lifetime prevalence of 2.5% and 1-year prevalence of 0.5–2.1% in adults, and lifetime prevalence of 1–2.3% and 1-year prevalence of 0.7% in children and adolescents.[1] 12-month community prevalence in the United Sates ≈ 1.2%, in other countries ≈ 1.1%–1.8%.[2]
Post-traumatic Stress Disorder (309.81)[1] **Post-traumatic Stress Disorder (309.81 [F43.10])**[2]	Characterized by the reexperiencing of an extremely traumatic event accompanied by symptoms of increased arousal and by avoidance of stimuli associated with the trauma.	The essential feature of post-traumatic stress disorder is the development of characteristic symptoms following exposure to one or more traumatic events.	Community-based studies indicate a lifetime prevalence rate ≈ 8% in U.S. adults.[1] 12-month community prevalence in U.S. adults ≈ 3.5%, in adults in other countries ≈ 0.5%–1.0%.[2]

Anxiety Disorder	Description		Prevalence/Incidence
	DSM-IV-TR[1]	DSM-5[2]	
Acute Stress Disorder (308.3)[1] **Acute Stress Disorder (308.3 [F43.0])**[2]	Characterized by symptoms similar to those of post-traumatic stress disorder that occur immediately in the aftermath of an extremely traumatic event.	The essential feature of acute stress disorder is the development of characteristic symptoms lasting from 3 days to 1 month following exposure to one or more traumatic events.	Prevalence unknown in general population. Rates from 14–33% reported in individuals exposed to severe trauma.[1] Varies in recently trauma-exposed populations (i.e., within one month of trauma exposure) according to the nature of the event and the context in which it is assessed.[2]
Generalized Anxiety Disorder (300.02)[1] **Generalized Anxiety Disorder (300.02 [F41.1])**[2]	Characterized by at least 6 months of persistent and excessive anxiety and worry.	The key features of generalized anxiety disorder are persistent and excessive anxiety and worry in various domains, including work and school performance, that the individual finds difficult to control.	In one community sample, 1-year prevalence ≈ 3% and lifetime prevalence was 5%. In anxiety clinics, up to 25% have GAD as a presenting or comorbid diagnosis.[1] 12-month community prevalence in the United States ≈ 0.9% for adolescents and 2.9% for adults, in other countries ≈ 0.4%–3.6%.[2]

Sources: APA (2000, pp. 429–430); APA (2013, pp. 189–190, 235, 274, 281)

Note: Not listed are anxiety disorder due to a general medical condition,[1] substance-induced anxiety disorder,[1] anxiety disorder NOS,[1] separation anxiety disorder,[2] selective mutism,[2] substance/medication-induced anxiety disorder,[2] anxiety disorder due to another medical condition,[2] other specified anxiety disorder,[2] and unspecified anxiety disorder.[2]

aggressive wishes and the superego's corresponding threats of punishment. Freud understood anxiety as a signal indicating danger within the unconscious. The ego, in response to this **signal anxiety**, marshaled its defensive resources to prevent unacceptable thoughts and feelings from entering conscious awareness. Failure to block these thoughts and feelings resulted in intense, more persistent anxiety or other **neurotic** symptoms (Gabbard, 2005). Subsequent psychoanalytic theorists have differentiated between separate forms of conscious and unconscious anxiety. These include the fear of losing a love object (*separation anxiety*); the fear of damage to the body in general or to the genitals specifically (*castration anxiety*); the fear of being punished for transgressing one's values (*moral anxiety*); the fear of being devastatingly overwhelmed, merged, invaded, and destroyed (*annihilation anxiety*); and the fear of self-disintegration (*fragmentation anxiety*). All of these anxieties, in certain situations and bearable amounts, are considered normal, but they are considered psychopathology when disproportionate or unceasing (PDM Task Force, 2006). Furthermore, variants of anxiety have been organized hierarchically according to level of psychological development: with *superego anxiety* (guilt about not living up to an internalized moral standard) being at the most mature level and persecutory and disintegration anxiety being the most primitive (Gabbard, 2005).

Anxiety researchers have also distinguished between trait and state anxiety. **Trait anxiety** is considered long lasting; it refers to either an individual's typical anxiety level or to her or his general vulnerability or predisposition to becoming anxious. **State anxiety**, on the other hand, is considered transient; it refers to an individual's level of anxiety over shorter periods of time (e.g., seconds, minutes, and hours; Wilt et al., 2011). Anxiety, then, may be thought of as both an enduring pattern of personality functioning and an in-the-moment cognitive, emotional, or behavioral experience.

Panic Disorder and Agoraphobia

The DSM-IV-TR specifies a trio of disorders related to recurrent, unexpected panic attacks and agoraphobia (i.e., the fear of having difficulty escaping from, or being extremely embarrassed in, a location or situation in which a panic attack occurs). Both conditions may occur in isolation (i.e., panic disorder without agoraphobia, agoraphobia without a history of panic disorder) or in combination with one another (i.e., panic disorder with agoraphobia; APA, 2000). In the DSM-5, panic disorder and agoraphobia are diagnosed independently from one another, and an individual may be assigned both diagnoses if criteria are met for each disorder (APA, 2013). One psychoanalytic theory proposes an inborn temperamental characteristic termed "behavioral inhibition to the unfamiliar," in which children are easily frightened by anything strange in their environment. Other approaches based in attachment theory have also been proposed. These suggest, for example, that panic disordered patients are unable to modulate the normal oscillation between separation and attachment or that threats to attachment trigger overwhelming panic (Gabbard, 2005). Additionally, some forms of agoraphobia may stem from interpersonal dysregulation—from conflicting desires for both autonomy and dependency in interpersonal relationships. Finally, neurobiological, cognitive, and behavioral theorists have proposed panic disorder to be an acquired fear of bodily sensations, particularly those related to autonomic arousal. A **triple vulnerability theory** explains the psychological and biological predispositions that enhance an individual's vulnerability to acquiring this fear. These include (1) genetics and temperament (a biologically based "fear of fear"), (2) anxiety sensitivity (the belief that anxiety causes negative physical, social, and psychological consequences beyond the immediate physical discomfort experienced during a panic or anxiety episode), and (3) early learning experiences (i.e., a history of medical illness and abuse) focusing anxiety on particular areas of concern (Craske & Barlow, 2008).

Phobias

The term **phobia** is derived from the Greek word "*phobos,*" defined as flight, panic, fear, or terror. Phobos was also the name of the Greek deity who had the power to cause fear and panic in one's enemies, and his likeness was depicted on weapons such as shields to be used as "fear masks," examples of which appear on ancient Greek vase paintings (Errera, 1962, in Marks, 1969). Doctors from Hippocrates onward described morbid fears, though the only medical usage for the term "phobia" before the nineteenth century was *hydrophobia*—Celsus's term for a prominent symptom of rabies. It is noteworthy that clinical descriptions of phobias have remained largely unchanged from their earliest portrayals.

Psychoanalytic theorists have conceptualized phobias as being rooted in unconscious processes. According to Freud, phobias are merely symptoms caused by neurotic anxiety, which itself is rooted in unconscious conflicts involving drives, wishes, and desires related to sex and aggression (Mavissakalian & Barlow, 1981). A classic battle between two opposing theoretical orientations over the conceptualization of phobias quite literally erupted in the literature at the beginning of the twentieth century. The battle began with Freud's (1909/2003) publication of *Analysis of a Phobia in a Five-Year-Old Boy* in 1909. In it, Freud relates the analysis of "Little Hans" (Herbert Graf), age five, conducted by his father, Max Graf, an early follower of Freud. Hans developed a fear of horses, in particular, of being bitten by one or seeing one fall, which was interpreted as his internal Oedipal conflict and fear of castration psychically transformed into an external danger (which he could escape by fleeing or avoidance).

Behavioral theorists responded by proposing phobias to be a product of conditioning processes. In fact, Watson and Rayner (1920), in a classic experiment, successfully conditioned a fear response in an otherwise well-adjusted young boy. "Little Albert," as he was called (a direct retaliatory response to Freud's case of "Little Hans") was conditioned to fear a small white rat, as well as other furry objects. In this controlled experiment, Albert B., a well-adjusted nine-month-old infant, was first presented with a white rat and other animals (a rabbit, dog, and monkey) and objects (masks with and without hair, cotton wool, and burning newspapers) to which he showed no fear. Subsequently, a conditioned emotional response was established by presenting the white rat (the neutral stimulus) along with a loud noise made by striking a hammer on a suspended four-foot-long steel bar (the unconditioned stimulus), which previously had produced a fear reaction in Albert, making him cry, jump violently, fall forward, and bury his face in a mattress (the unconditioned response); ironically, this was the second historical instance in which a metal bar of similar dimensions has significantly impacted our understanding of human behavior—see the case of Phineas Gage in Chapter 2. Subsequent simultaneous presentations of both the rat and the noise led to the rat (now the conditioned stimulus) producing a fear reaction in Albert (conditioned response) when presented alone. Additionally, the conditioned fear response transferred to other objects (e.g., a rabbit, dog, fur coat, cotton wool, and a Santa Claus mask). The presentations of these objects would cause him to cry, but presenting blocks in between would not. Commenting critically on the prevailing psychoanalytic view of phobias, Watson and Rayner (1920) wrote,

> The Freudians twenty years from now, unless their hypotheses change, when they come to analyze Albert's fear of a seal skin coat—assuming that he comes to analysis at that age—will probably tease from him the recital of a dream which upon their analysis will show that Albert at three years of age attempted to play with the pubic hair of the mother and was scolded violently for it. (p. 14)

Watson and Rayner also suggested that many phobias were likely direct or transferred true conditioned emotional reactions. Five types of phobias are identified in the DSM-IV-TR and specified in diagnosis. These are the animal type, the natural environment type (e.g., fear of heights, storms, or water), the blood-injection-injury type, the situational type (e.g., fear of airplanes, elevators, or enclosed places), and the category other type (e.g., fear of choking, vomiting, or contracting an illness; in children, fear of loud sounds or costumed characters). These types have been retained in the DSM-5 as coding specifiers.

Obsessive-Compulsive Disorder

Historically, compulsive states (as they are currently known) were first portrayed by early nineteenth-century German and French clinicians. The German term for "compulsion"—"*Zwang*" (from "*zwingen*," meaning "to force"; Freud, 1909/2003)—was first employed in a manner consistent with contemporary usage by Griesinger, in a posthumous paper published in 1868 (Millon & Davis, 1998). In 1875, Legrand du Saulle described "*la folie du doute*"—mental "interrogations" resulting from doubt and the fear of touching external objects (Lopez-Ibor, 1990). A debate arose in the late 1800s as to whether compulsions indeed indicated the presence and operation of hidden emotions, with theorists such as Emil Kraepelin (1877, in Millon & Davis, 1996) being convinced of their central involvement.

Obsessions are defined in the DSM-IV-TR as persistent ideas, thoughts, impulses, or images that are experienced as intrusive and inappropriate and that cause marked anxiety or distress (APA, 2000). This definition has remained largely consistent in the DSM-5 (APA, 2013; see Table 7.1). They are primarily *ego-dystonic*—meaning the individual senses the obsession's content to be alien, outside of his or her control, and uncharacteristic of him or her. Repeated thoughts about becoming contaminated (e.g., by shaking hands), repeated doubts (e.g., about performing some act such as hurting someone in a traffic accident or leaving a door unlocked), orderliness (e.g., intense distress associated with disordered or asymmetrical objects), impulses to commit aggressive or horrifying acts (e.g., hurting one's child or shouting an obscenity in church), and recurrent sexual (e.g., pornographic) imagery are among the most commonly reported obsessions.

Compulsions are defined in the DSM-IV-TR as repetitive behaviors or mental acts that are employed to prevent or diminish anxiety, tension, or distress (APA, 2000), a definition that has remained relatively unchanged conceptually in the DSM-5 (APA, 2013; see Table 7.1). Compulsive behaviors are not goal oriented or rewarding in and of themselves (Carter, Pauls, & Leckman, 1995). They may be linked functionally to obsessive thoughts (e.g., checking the stove to make sure that it is turned off in response to an obsessional thought that it was left on), but they are usually not realistically connected to the source of the distress (e.g., counting up to 100 four times in four minutes in response to disturbing mental images involving sexual themes). According to Turner and colleagues (2001), the most frequently reported compulsive behaviors are repetitive washing (e.g., hand washing, showering, house cleaning) and checking (e.g., of locks, appliances, numerical figures, or mathematical calculations). Other common forms of compulsions include repeating rituals (e.g., repeatedly getting up and down from a chair, repeatedly entering and exiting doorways), ordering and arranging behaviors, hoarding, and cognitive compulsions (e.g., mental counting or the repetition of certain words, phrases, or images). **Obsessive-compulsive disorder (OCD)**, in its current DSM-5 formulation, is characterized by the presence of both obsessions and compulsions.

Psychoanalytic theorists understand obsessive-compulsive disorder as being rooted in unconscious processes. Freud originally termed this condition as *obsessional neurosis* (Rycroft, 1995), and described it as a *regression* (reversion to an earlier state or mode of functioning) to the anal psychosexual stage of development.

BOX 7.1 TWO THEORIES OF PHOBIAS

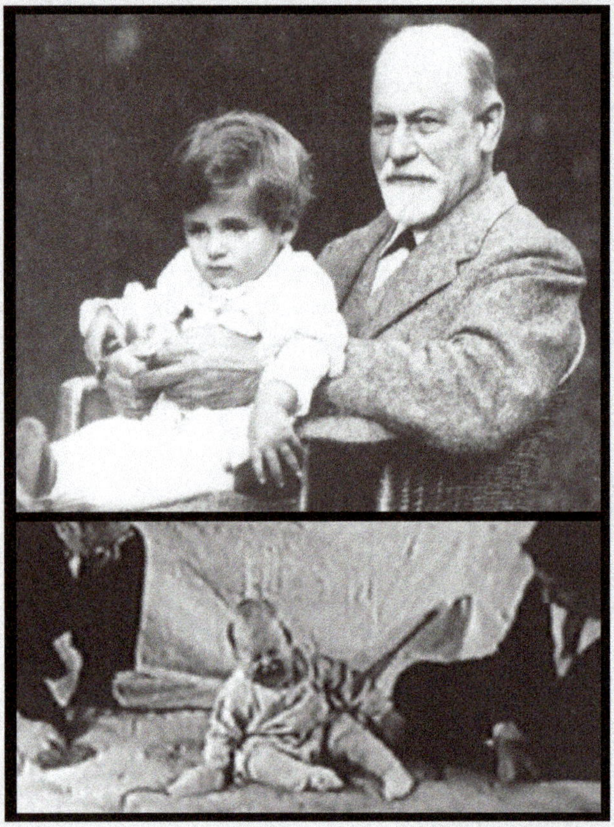

Rival theories of phobias from early twentieth-century cases: Freud's "Little Hans" (above) and Watson and Rayner's "Little Albert" (below).

His published case of the "Ratman," a man with an obsessive-compulsive neurosis involving a violent fear of rats gnawing into his father and his romantic partner, demonstrates the complexities of unconscious conflicts in this type of disorder (Freud, 1909/2003). Obsessive-compulsive symptoms indicate a range of unconscious concerns, such as fear of losing control (especially regarding aggression, contamination, and shame; PDM Task Force, 2006), and they are produced by ego-dystonic negative impulses (e.g., to hurt, soil, or control) and by defenses against these impulses (Carter et al., 1995). Preventing OCD individuals from carrying out their compulsions may cause them to become diffusely terrified. Compulsive behaviors can be the "leftovers" of the *magical thinking* of early childhood, when impulses and actions are, to the child, indistinguishable from each other. (Children around ages 6–9 often develop minor rituals and magical ideation to control frightening aggressive ideas, such as "If I don't step on a crack, I won't break my mother's back.") Thus, individuals with OCD symptoms have unconsciously convicted themselves of "thought crimes" (hostile and selfish cognitions), are tormented and persecuted by mental representations of them (by obsessive images and ideas), and subsequently attempt to expiate their guilt with cleansing and undoing rituals (PDM Task Force, 2006). One type of psychological defense mechanism that nicely exemplifies the compulsive aspects of this condition is *undoing*—wherein an individual, through thought or action, makes as though some previous thought or action had not occurred (Rycroft, 1995; see Chapter 2). For example, a young child who experiences anxiety about his hostile wishes toward a sibling or parent may first hit the object of his anger and then kiss it. The second action *undoes* the first.

Cognitive and behavioral theorists have also provided several different conceptualizations of obsessive-compulsive disorder. These involve mechanisms such as maladaptive conditioning processes, information processing deficits, and fear responses associated with mistaken beliefs or meanings (Franklin & Foa, 2008; Turner et al., 2001). In one prominent theoretical model proposed by Salkovskis (1985; see Figure 7.1), the OCD process begins first with an intrusive thought or image (e.g., killing one's spouse). These are thought to be everyday occurrences, experienced by almost everyone. Second, the intrusive thought is evaluated by a preexisting cognitive schemata as unacceptable. In some individuals, the intrusive thoughts activate preexisting cognitive schemata, which, in turn, evaluate the intrusive thoughts in a negative light (e.g., "It is bad to have a thought about killing my spouse"). Third, the individual believes that he or she has the "pivotal power" to bring about or prevent the negative consequences of intrusive thought (i.e., responsibility—in this example, for either killing the spouse or preventing the killing of his or her spouse). Salkovskis draws upon Beck's concept of "dysfunctional assumptions" to explain how this connection is made in the person's thoughts (Beck, 1976, in Salkovskis, 1985). These include the assumptions that (1) having a thought about an action is like performing the action, (2) failing to prevent (or failing to try and prevent) harm to self or others is the same as having caused the harm in the first place, (3) responsibility is not attenuated by other factors (e.g., a low probability of occurrence), (4) not neutralizing when an intrusion has occurred is similar to or equivalent to seeking or wanting the harm involved in that intrusion to happen, and (5) one should (and can) exercise control over one's thoughts (see Table 7.2). In this manner, the original obsession, which is ego dystonic, elicits an automatic thought, which is ego syntonic (Franklin & Foa, 2008). Fourth, efforts to control or undo the intrusive thoughts increase the salience (prominence) of these thoughts. Beliefs and cognitive schemata generate distress that leads to efforts to control or undo the thoughts (i.e., avoidance and ritualistic behavior). Fifth, efforts to control or undo lead to more thoughts and distress. Efforts (1) increase the salience and frequency of the thoughts and (2) create emotional distress. Finally, beliefs are reinforced because engagement in rituals prevents disconfirmation of the belief. Thus, a feedback loop is created: beliefs about "pivotal power" or responsibility become reinforced because the person *does* follow the rituals designed to undo both the intrusive thoughts and their supposed consequences, which prevents responsibility beliefs from being refuted (Salkovskis, 1985).

According to Salkovskis (1985), there are three main consequences of this neutralization process. First, neutralizing usually results in reduced discomfort, which allows the development of obsessional behavior as a strategy for coping with stress. This eventuality not only increases the probability of subsequent neutralizing but may also result in the generalization of this strategy to other circumstances. Second, neutralization will consistently be followed by non-punishment. Rewarding non-punishment is a powerful reinforcement in its own right and will also be expected to have an effect on the perceived validity of the beliefs described above (e.g., "I acted on my belief and felt better; therefore the belief must have some basis in truth" or "The disaster I attempted to forestall has not come about, which may mean that my neutralization was a reasonable and effective thing to do"). Third, performance or completion of neutralizing will be, in itself, a powerful and unavoidable triggering stimulus. Turner and colleagues (2001) assert that the main criticism of the cognitive theory of obsessive-compulsive disorder is that it does not recognize the emotional and motivational components of the disorder—that is to say, even though cognitive theories generally conceptualize intrusive thoughts as emotionally neutral, the content of these thoughts nearly always relates to harm happening to oneself or others.

Neurobiological findings include increased glucose metabolic rates in the left orbital gyrus, which is implicated in mood regulation and in integrating the perception of complex temporal relationships by inhibiting interfering external stimuli. These appear to be coupled with dysfunction in the caudate nuclei, which serve as a sensory information gate station or processor of sorts, and in other basal ganglia in OCD. Additionally, reduced brain serotonin (5-HT) metabolism ("turnover") and decreased cerebrospinal fluid (CSF) levels of 5-HIAA (a major 5-HT metabolite), common to other impulse-control disorders, have been associated with OCD, as has increased concentrations of CSF noradrenaline (Braun et al., 2008; Leckman et al., 1990; Lopez-Ibor, 1990). Other studies have found abnormally elevated levels of urinary and plasma cortisol in OCD patients, and associations between OCD and gene alleles regulating neurotransmitter metabolism have been examined—with the most significant findings involving those that code for serotonin (Braun et al., 2008).

Post-Traumatic Stress Disorder

The condition known currently as **post-traumatic stress disorder (PTSD)** has been identified formally for nearly a century and, arguably, has been encountered—whether identified or not—as far back as human beings have placed themselves in combat situations. Historic terms for PTSD include "war neurosis," "combat fatigue,"

Figure 7.1 A Theoretical Model of OCD

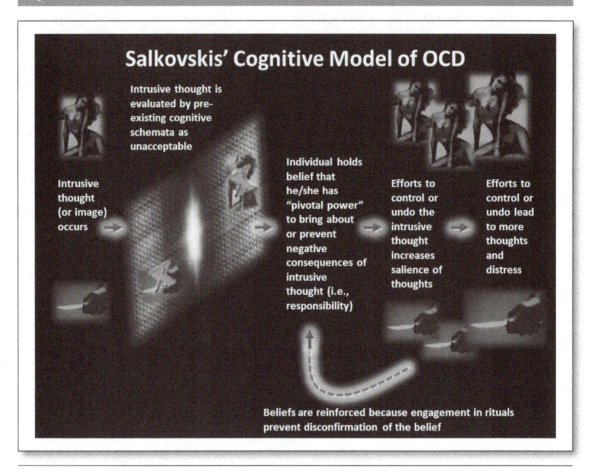

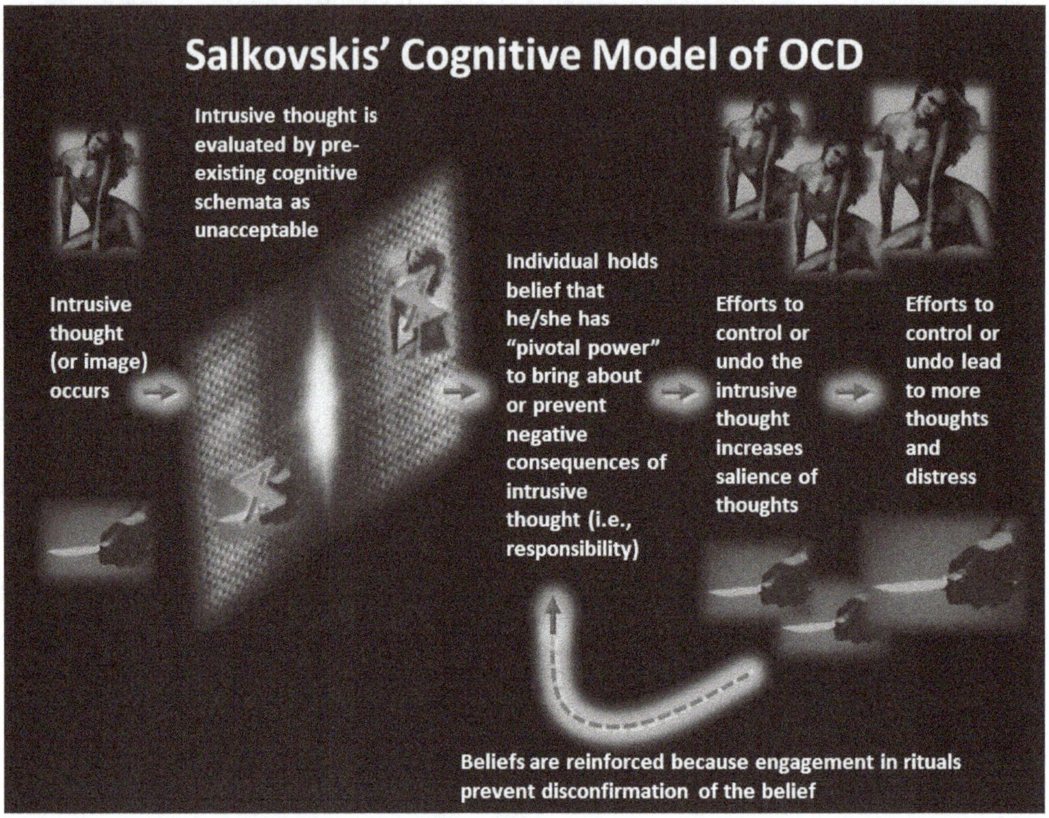

Source: Adapted from Salkovskis (1985).

and "shell shock." Since the beginnings of the psychoanalytic movement, psychic trauma has been an important diagnostic and clinical consideration for psychoanalytic clinicians (PDM Task Force, 2006). Freud (1917/1966) noted that an individual may be "brought so completely to a stop by a traumatic event which shatters the foundations of his life that he abandons all interest in the present and future and remains permanently absorbed in mental concentration upon the past" (p. 342). Several decades of evidence from concentration camp survivors, Vietnam War veterans, and victims of childhood sexual and physical abuse, torture, and terrorism indicate high rates of trauma-related psychopathology, of which PTSD is only one potential outcome. This condition has been classified as an anxiety disorder in the DSM-IV-TR, a trauma- and stressor-related disorder in the DSM-5, a dissociative disorder, and a stress disorder, which speaks to its complexity and the reason some conceptualize it as a spectrum of conditions associated with different levels of impairment and individual meanings. Psychoanalytic theorists have long emphasized the shock, helplessness, vulnerability, and terror associated with trauma. Trauma contributes to the breakdown of meaning; to an interference in cognitions, emotions, and memory; to changes in one's sense of self and ego functions (e.g., a blurring between past and present); to the presence of adverse somatic states; and to a decline in interpersonal relationships (PDM Task Force, 2006).

According to Gabbard (2005), the mind of the trauma victim attempts to process and organize overwhelming stimuli by alternating between denying the event (i.e., memory loss) and compulsively repeating it (i.e., flashbacks or nightmares). Eight common psychological themes following severe trauma have been identified by Horowitz (1976, in Gabbard, 2005): (1) grief or sadness, (2) guilt about one's angry or destructive impulses,

Table 7.2 Cases of Obsessions and Their Associated Ideation

Gender	Duration (Years)	Type of Intrusion	Ideation	Behavior
F	5	Blasphemous thoughts	"I won't be forgiven for these thoughts; I have sinned by having them."	Avoids churches, prays
F	7	Thoughts of having picked up someone's money or set fire or made a person lose a purse	"I might have done something which will make me a thief; the thought might mean I want to be a thief."	Asks if people have their purses, seeks reassurance, avoids tills and purses
F	14	Thoughts of harming her children; images of strangling them or of them dead by her hand	"This means that I want to do these things; having such thoughts means I am evil; having the picture may make it happen."	Avoids being on her own with children, tries to think good thoughts
F	2	Thoughts of having contaminated others, especially her children, by touching them	"I will have caused people or my children to get cancer; they'll get sick because of me."	Avoids touching anything that others may touch, washes, checks for reassurance

Source: Adapted from Salkovskis (1985).

(3) fear of one's own capabilities for being destructive, (4) guilt about surviving, (5) fear of identification with the victims, (6) shame about feeling helpless and empty, (7) fear that one will repeat the trauma, and (8) intense anger directed at the trauma's source. Response to trauma may vary with an individual's mental and physical state, personality resources, and trauma history effects (Gabbard, 2005; PDM Task Force, 2006). Other predisposing vulnerability factors have been identified, such as genetic vulnerability to mental illness, adverse or traumatic childhood experiences, recent life stressors or changes, failure of social support networks, recent heavy use of alcohol, limited cognitive abilities, and a perception of external rather than internal locus of control (Gabbard, 2005). Cognitive and behavioral theoretical models of PTSD have focused on classical and operant conditioning processes in the development and maintenance of fear and avoidance symptoms. The content of PTSD cognitions have been emphasized by other social-cognitive theorists and researchers, who have proposed that basic assumptions about oneself and the world are "shattered" in PTSD. Additionally, others have focused on maladaptive emotional processing and memory disturbances (Resick et al., 2008).

Generalized Anxiety Disorder

Some psychoanalytic theorists view **generalized anxiety disorder (GAD)** as a personality disorder rather than a syndrome of symptoms, given that some individuals suffer anxieties that are pervasive, chronic, and disabling (PDM Task Force, 2006). The neurobiological literature on GAD remains largely in its infancy, though limited brain-imaging data suggest deficits in a brain circuit comprised of the amygdala and several other regions in the prefrontal cortex. Specifically, hyperreactivity of the amygdala to anticipatory signals and to uncertainty in general appears to be a key factor in the pathophysiology of this disorder (Schienle et al., 2011).

The Relationship Between Anxiety Disorders and Crime

Tables 7.3 and 7.4 list a number of investigations, in chronological order, that have examined both the prevalence rates of crime in those diagnosed with anxiety disorders and the rates of anxiety disorders in criminal populations.

Table 7.3 Prevalence of Anxiety Disorders in Criminal Populations

Source	N	Gender	Age	Study Type[a1]	Sample Description	Disorder	Diagnostic System	Prevalence/Incidence
Cohen & Freeman (1945)	(1) 320 (2) 87	M, F	Adult?	AR	Police records of arrested patients from 1,676 patients paroled or discharged from Norwich State Hospital (Connecticut), 1940–1944 (1) Arrested before hospitalization (2) Arrested after hospitalization	Psychoneuroses	?	(1) 1.8% ($n = 6$) (2) 1.1% ($n = 1$)
West (1966)	148	88 M, 60 F	< 20 – 40+	HO	Homicide followed by suicide: England and Wales, 1954–1961	Severe neurotic instability	?	4.7% ($n = 7$)
Pfeiffer, Eisenstein, & Dabbs (1967)	85	2/3 M, 1/3 F	17–63	JD	Federal prisoners referred for mental competency evaluations at the USPHS Hospital in Lexington, Kentucky, 1960–1965	Neurotic depressive reaction	?	1.2% ($n = 1$)
						Anxiety reaction		1.2% ($n = 1$)
						Psychoneurotic reaction, other		1.2% ($n = 1$)
Kahn (1971)	43	41 M, 2 F	11–74	HO	Interviews and psychiatric examinations of individuals who made pleas of insanity to charges of first or second degree murder	Psychoneurotic	?	4.7% ($n = 2$)
Pétursson & Gudjónsson (1981)	47	44 M, 3 F	Adult[ai]	HO	File review of cases of intentional and unintentional homicide in Iceland, 1900–1979	Neurosis	?	2.1% ($n = 1$)
Langevin et al. (1982)	(1) 109 (2) 38	?	Adult?	PI	File record review of minimum-security forensic ward psychiatric hospital cases, 1969–1979 (Clarke Institute in Toronto, Ontario, Canada) (1) Killers (2) Nonviolent offenders	Depressive neurosis	Feighner et al. (1972) psychiatric research diagnostic criteria	(1) 13.0% (2) 16.0%

Source	N	Gender	Age	Study Type[a1]	Sample Description	Disorder	Diagnostic System	Prevalence/Incidence
Seltzer & Langford (1984)	85	M, F	15–25 (Median = 18)	PI	Interviews of individuals referred by courts or legal counsel to psychiatry department of large regional hospital in Northwest Territories, calendar year 1981	Anxiety disorder	DSM-III, MMPI	2.4% (*n* = 2)
Taylor & Gunn (1984)	2,743	M	Adult	JD	File review of men remanded to Brixton prison, South London (June, September, December 1979 and March 1980)	Depressive neurosis	ICD	2.4% (*n* = 67)
						Other neurosis		0.9% (*n* = 24)
Reich & Wells (1985)	390	325 M, 65 F	*M* = 30.9	JD	Record review of defendants evaluated for competency to stand trial by the Yale-New Haven Psychiatric Court Clinic, 1980–1982	Generalized anxiety disorders	DSM-III	0.5% (*n* = 2)
Bland et al. (1990)	180	M	18–44	JD	Diagnostic interviews with inmates from two correctional centers, Alberta, Canada	Panic disorder	DSM-III (DIS)	7.2% (*n* = 13)[av]*
						Agoraphobia		5.6% (*n* = 10)[aw]*
						Social phobia		1.7% (*n* = 3)[ax]
						Simple phobia		4.4% (*n* = 8)[ay]
						OCD		9.4% (*n* = 17)[az]
Myers et al. (1990)	15	F	Juveniles	PI	Diagnostic interviews with juvenile delinquents committed to a residential treatment program, Florida	Separation anxiety disorder	DSM-III (DICA)	Past and current: 33.3% (*n* = 5)
						OCD		Current: 6.7% (*n* = 1)
						Phobia		Current: 20.0% (*n* = 3)
						Overanxious disorder		Current: 6.7% (*n* = 1)

(Continued)

(Continued)

Source	N	Gender	Age	Study Type[a1]	Sample Description	Disorder	Diagnostic System	Prevalence/Incidence
Yarvis (1990)	100	88 M, 12 F	33% < 25, 85% < 40	HO	Diagnostic interviews and record reviews of a series of murderers referred for psychiatric evaluation in California, 1980–1988	Other neurotic and adjustment disorders	DSM-III	3.0% (*n* = 3)[j]
Marshall et al. (1998)	103	M	18–56	JD	Diagnostic interviews and questionnaires administered to recently sentenced inmates (August–December 1997) at Yatala Labour Prison, South Australia	Generalized anxiety	(PDI-R)	5.9%
						OCD		8.8%
						Panic disorder		8.8%
						Phobic disorder		5.9%
						PTSD		8.8%
Galli et al. (1999)	22	M	13–17, (*M* = 15.9, *SD* = 1.1)	PI, CS	Interviews with adolescents admitting to sexually assaulting another child, referred from a juvenile rehabilitation center, the juvenile court system, and an inpatient adolescent psychiatric unit, Hamilton County, Ohio	Panic disorder	DSM-III-R (DICA)	1.0% (*n* = 2)
						PTSD		32.0% (*n* = 7)
						OCD		27.0% (*n* = 6)
						Total		55.0% (*n* = 12)
Gibson et al. (1999)	213	M	*M* = 32	JD	Structured interviews with randomly selected state prison and regional jail inmates from a rural New England state.	OCD	DSM-III-R (DIS-III-R)	Lifetime: 12.2% (*n* = 26) Current: 6.6% (*n* = 14)
						Panic disorder		Lifetime: 8.5% (*n* = 18) Current: 4.7% (*n* = 10)
						GAD		Lifetime: 11.3% (*n* = 24) Current: 5.6% (*n* = 12)

Source	N	Gender	Age	Study Type[a1]	Sample Description	Disorder	Diagnostic System	Prevalence/Incidence
						PTSD		Lifetime: 32.4% ($n = 69$) Current: 21.1% ($n = 45$)
McElroy et al. (1999)	36	M	18–47 ($M = 33$, $SD = 8$)	PI	Interviews with convicted sex offenders consecutively admitted to the New Life Program, Cincinnati, Ohio, November 1996–June 1998	GAD	DSM-IV (SCID)	3% ($n = 1$)
						Panic disorder		6% ($n = 2$)
						Social phobia		17% ($n = 6$)
						Simple phobia		3% ($n = 1$)
						OCD		11% ($n = 4$)
						PTSD		17% ($n = 6$)
						Total anxiety disorders		36% ($n = 13$)
Teplin et al. (2002)	1829	1,172 M, 657 F	10–18	JD	Diagnostic interviews of youths randomly sampled from intake into the Cook County Juvenile Temporary Detention Center, November 1995–June 1998	Panic disorder	DSM-III-R	M: 0.3% F: 1.5%
						Separation anxiety disorder		M: 12.9% F: 18.6%
						Overanxious disorder		M: 6.7% F: 12.3%
						Generalized anxiety disorder		M: 7.1% F: 7.3%
						OCD		M: 8.3% F: 10.6%

(Continued)

(Continued)

Source	N	Gender	Age	Study Type[a1]	Sample Description	Disorder	Diagnostic System	Prevalence/Incidence
Dunsieth et al. (2004)	113	M	18–66 ($M = 35.3$, $SD = 10.4$)	PI	Diagnostic interviews with sex offenders consecutively referred to an Ohio residential sex-offender treatment program	Generalized anxiety disorder	DSM-IV	2.7% ($n = 3$)
						Panic disorder		5.3% ($n = 6$)
						Social phobia		9.7% ($n = 11$)
						Simple phobia		6.2% ($n = 7$)
						OCD		5.3% ($n = 6$)
						PTSD		8.8% ($n = 10$)
Stuart et al. (2006)	103	F	$M = 31.5$, $SD = 9.6$	CS	Questionnaire administered to women arrested for violence and court referred to batterer intervention programs, Rhode Island	PTSD	DSM-IV (PDSQ)	44%
						GAD		34%
						Panic disorder		28%
Trestman et al. (2007)	508	307 M, 201 F	18–64 ($M = 31.6$, $SD = 9.3$)	JD	Diagnostic interviews with randomly selected inmates newly admitted to one of five jail facilities, Connecticut	Anxiety disorders (excluding PTSD)	DSM-IV (SCID)	43.6%
						PTSD		28.6%
Grella et al. (2008)	280	65% M	$M = 34.8$	JD	Diagnostic interviews with offenders consecutively admitted to prison-based substance-abuse treatment programs at one of four research centers (Colorado, Rhode Island, Texas, California)	Panic disorder	DSM-IV (SCID)	10.4% ($n = 29$)
						Agoraphobia w/o panic		1.4% ($n = 4$)
						OCD		4.6% ($n = 13$)
						PTSD		11.4% ($n = 32$)
						Generalized anxiety		5.4% ($n = 15$)

Source	N	Gender	Age	Study Type[a1]	Sample Description	Disorder	Diagnostic System	Prevalence/Incidence
						Anxiety disorders GMC		0.4% ($n = 1$)
						Anxiety Disorders NOS		2.5% ($n = 7$)
						Any anxiety disorder		23.9% ($n = 67$)
Pham & Saloppé (2010)	84	M	27–69 ($M = 43.6$, $SD = 9.87$)	PI	Diagnostic interviews with forensic patients at a high-security psychiatric hospital in Toumai, Belgium	Anxiety disorders	DSM-III (DISSI)	57% ($n = 47$)
						Generalized anxiety disorder		21% ($n = 18$)
						Panic disorder		4% ($n = 3$)
						Phobic disorder		40% ($n = 34$)
						OCD		8% ($n = 7$)

Notes: *Significant difference in comparison to control group.

[a1]AR = arrest rates of patients discharged from psychiatric facilities, JD = jailed detainees and incarcerated prisoners, HO = homicide offenders, BC = birth cohort study, PI = psychiatric inpatient sample, CS = community sample (i.e., epidemiological catchment area survey studies and outpatient psychiatric patients).

[j]Community sample comparative data (six-month prevalence rates from NIMH Community Survey data): Data not reported.

[ai]Group means and standard deviations: Psychotic illness (35.7, 8.8), personality disorder and alcohol use disorders (24.4, 8.2), no psychiatric abnormality (34.0, 12.4).

[av]Lifetime prevalence rate. For community comparison sample, standardized prevalence ratio (SPR) = 6.8 (an SPR greater than 1 indicates the prevalence rate in the prison sample was greater than that in the general population).

[aw]Lifetime prevalence rate. For community comparison sample, standardized prevalence ratio (SPR) = 5.6 (an SPR greater than 1 indicates the prevalence rate in the prison sample was greater than that in the general population).

[ax]Lifetime prevalence rate. For community comparison sample, standardized prevalence ratio (SPR) = 4.4 (an SPR greater than 1 indicates the prevalence rate in the prison sample was greater than that in the general population).

[ay]Lifetime prevalence rate. For community comparison sample, standardized prevalence ratio (SPR) = 1.8 (an SPR greater than 1 indicates the prevalence rate in the prison sample was greater than that in the general population).

[az]Lifetime prevalence rate. For community comparison sample, standardized prevalence ratio (SPR) = 4.4 (an SPR greater than 1 indicates the prevalence rate in the prison sample was greater than that in the general population).

Table 7.4 Prevalence of Crime in Anxiety Disordered Populations

Source	N	Gender	Age	Study Type[a1]	Sample description	Disorder	Crime Definition	Prevalence/Incidence
Guze et al. (1974)	62	?M, ?F	Adult	CS	Community psychiatric clinic patients, diagnosed with Feighner diagnostic criteria (Feighner et al., 1972)	Anxiety neurosis	Felony conviction	2.0% (n = 1)
Swanson et al. (1990)	10,059	4,717 M, 5,306 F[f]	Adult	CS	Epidemiologic Catchment Area respondent data (community adults from five U.S. sites), diagnosed using DSM-III criteria (DIS)	Phobia	Self-reported violence	4.97% violent (n = 1,323[f])
						Obsessive-compulsive disorder		10.66% violent (n = 182[f])
						Panic disorder		11.56% violent (n = 90[f])
Asnis et al. (1994)	517	204 M, 313 F	13–87 (M = 38.7)	CS	Psychiatric outpatients, Montefiore Medical Center, Bronx, New York, diagnosed using DSM-III criteria	Panic disorder (n = 38)	Self-reported homicidal ideation and attempts	Ideation: 18% (n =7) Attempts: 3% (n = 1)
						Generalized anxiety disorder (n = 34)		Ideation: 3% (n =1) Attempts: 0% (n = 0)
Arsenault et al. (2000)	(1) 389 (2) 572	51.6% M, 48.4% F	Adult	BC	From a study of a total-city New Zealand birth cohort (N = 1,037), diagnosed using DSM-III-R with (1) Psychiatric disorder (2) No psychiatric disorder	Anxiety disorders (n = 170)	Violence: Self-reported and criminal convictions	(1) Convictions: 5.9% (n = 10); self-reported: 9.4% (n = 16) (2) Convictions: 1.2% (n = 7); self-reported: 3.1% (n = 18)
Corrigan & Watson (2005)	5,865	?M, ?F	15–54	CS	Subset of respondents from the U.S. National Comorbidity Survey, diagnosed using DSM-III-R criteria (structured diagnostic interview), 1990–1992	Simple phobia	Self-reported violence	Mental illness lifetime: 4.9% (32/654); 12 months: 5.8% (30/515)

Source	N	Gender	Age	Study Type[a1]	Sample description	Disorder	Crime Definition	Prevalence/Incidence
						Social phobia		Mental illness lifetime: 5.7% (45/795); 12 months: 7.7% (36/474)
						Agoraphobia		Mental illness lifetime: 6.0% (23/386); 12 months: 7.8% (17/214)
						Generalized anxiety disorder		Mental illness lifetime: 4.2% (12/294); 12 months: 6.4% (11/171)
						Panic disorder		Mental illness lifetime: 6.1% (12/200); 12 months: 8.4% (11/129)
						PTSD		Mental illness lifetime: 5.8% (25/429); 12 months: 7.5% (17/223)
Barret et al. (2011)	124	62.7% F	$M = 33.8$, $SD = 7.9$	CS	Diagnostic interviews with current (past month) substance users recruited from substance-use treatment centers and the community, Sydney, Australia, diagnosed using DSM-IV criteria	PTSD	Self-reported violent crime	Lifetime = 54.7% Past month = 15.7%

Note: [a1]AR = arrest rates of patients discharged from psychiatric facilities, JD = jailed detainees and incarcerated prisoners, HO = homicide offenders, BC = birth cohort study, PI = psychiatric inpatient sample, CS = community sample (i.e., epidemiological catchment area survey studies and outpatient psychiatric patients).

[f]Weighted Ns.

A Closer Look: Anxiety Disorders and Crime

Prevalence of the Disorder in Crime

Study Type	Number	Prevalence Rates
Arrest rates	1	1.1–1.8
Birth cohorts	0	–
Community samples	2*	1.0–55.0%†
Homicide offenders	4	2.1–4.7%
Jailed detainees and prisoners	9	0.3–43.6%
Psychiatric inpatients	7*	1.5–57.0%
Total Number of Studies	**22**	

Sample Characteristics

Size	15–2,743
Gender	Male only (8 studies); female only (2 studies); male and female but generally more males than females (11 studies); not reported (1 study)
Age	Youth, adult
Location	Countries worldwide (e.g., Australia, Canada, England, Iceland, the United States, Wales)
Diagnostic Systems	Not specified in many earlier studies. DSM (various editions), ICD (various editions), other research diagnostic criteria.

Notes: Early studies utilized a variety of terms reflecting the diagnostic nomenclature of the time, which largely conceptualized these disorders as neuroses (e.g., psychoneurosis, severe neurotic instability, anxiety reaction), and specific diagnostic systems are often not specified in this early work (e.g., Cohen & Freeman, 1945; West, 1966). In some cases, lower prevalence rates represent less common anxiety disorders (e.g., anxiety disorders due to a general medical condition–Grella et al., 2008) or somewhat unconventional sample characteristics (e.g., panic disorder in male juveniles–Teplin et al., 2002). Additionally, studies on anxiety disorders and crime (at least in recent decades), when compared to the studies linking crime and the other disorders covered in this book, have done notable work in terms of separating out individual disorders within the class and reporting prevalence rates for each. As such, it is possible to compare–to a limited degree–prevalence rates of individual disorders across these studies of jailed detainees and prisoners, psychiatric inpatients, and community individuals. For example, rates of panic disorder across ten studies are 0.3–28.0%. Rates of OCD across ten studies are 4.6–27.0%. Rates of PTSD across eight studies are 1.0–44.0%. Rates of generalized anxiety disorder across nine studies are 0.5–34.0%. Rates of social phobia across three studies are 1.7–17.0%; and, across six studies, rates of simple phobias and phobic disorders are 3.0–40.0%. For panic disorder, the lower prevalence rates are comparable to those seen in community samples (see Table 7.1), and the higher rates appear elevated in comparison. Rates for OCD overall appear elevated compared to those for community samples. Rates for PTSD and GAD appear reduced in the lower ranges and increased in the higher ranges compared to those found in community samples. Finally, rates of social phobia appear comparable to those reported in epidemiological and community-based studies; and rates of simple phobias and phobic disorders appear elevated.

*One study involved both psychiatric inpatients and community individuals.

†One of these studies (Galli et al., 1999) also included psychiatric inpatients; rates in the sample comprised solely of community individuals (Stuart et al., 2006) were 28.0–44.0%.

Prevalence of Crime in the Disorder

Study Type	Number	Prevalence Rates	Crime Definition
Arrest rates	0	–	–
Birth cohorts	1	5.9–9.4%	Violent crime convictions; self-reported violent crime

Prevalence of Crime in the Disorder

Community samples	5	0.0–54.7%*	Felony convictions; self-reported violence; self-reported homicidal ideation and attempts
Homicide offenders	0	–	–
Jailed detainees and prisoners	0	–	–
Psychiatric inpatients	0	–	–
Total Number of Studies	**6**		

Sample Characteristics

Size	62–10,059
Gender	Male and female (6 studies)
Age	Predominantly adult, some youth
Location	Countries worldwide (e.g., Australia, New Zealand, the United States)
Diagnostic Systems	DSM and other research diagnostic criteria

Note: *Rates of crime and violence could only be compared across studies for panic disorder. Highest rates of (lifetime) violence were observed in a single community study of PTSD (Barrett et al., 2011).

Nondisordered or community resident comparison group or general population baseline rates for either disorder or crime provided: **2 studies (7.1%)†**

Note: †Rates of panic disorder, agoraphobia, and OCD were significantly higher in jailed detainees than were those in a community comparison sample (Bland et al., 1990), and rates of violence were nearly five times higher for convictions and three times higher for self-reports in those with anxiety disorders compared to those without psychiatric disorders (Arsenault et al., 2000).

Anxiety Disorders and Crime: Clinical Presentation and Case Material

Although cases of violent individuals with anxiety disorders, like Robert Cameron Houston's, may be found in the popular media, published case studies of individuals characterized by both anxiety disorders and criminality are somewhat less common in the empirical literature relative to those for the other disorders covered in this book (e.g., mood and psychotic disorders). Cesare Lombroso (1876/2006) was among the first to discuss the clinical presentation of anxiety disorders within the context of criminality, identifying in the fourth edition of his seminal work, *Criminal Man*, "multiple phobias" as a type of insanity among Italian criminals.

Subsequent published case material related to anxiety disorders and crime has focused largely on individuals with OCD. For example, McDermott (2006) describe the case and treatment of Mr. G., a 38-year-old man diagnosed with OCD and troubled by intrusive, violent images of grabbing a kitchen knife and walking into his sleeping children's bedroom (which subsequently became an overall anxiety about knives). Leckman and colleagues (1990) discuss two cases of OCD individuals with low cerebrospinal fluid 5-HIAA and a significant preoccupation with violent thoughts and images. The first, a 24-year-old man with a history of motor and vocal tics and compulsive behaviors (including touching objects, other people, and inappropriately touching his genitals) was preoccupied for three years with images of using military survival techniques to injure others, usually strangers, such as individuals waiting at the bus stop. Although he never acted out violently or aggressively, the images—which appeared so realistic that he often wondered if he had actually committed the acts—caused clinically significant impairment leading to the loss of his job as a design engineer. The second, a 24-year-old woman, experienced for three years highly disturbing and intrusive thoughts of acting on unwanted impulses to kill household pets and vulnerable individuals (such as children, the elderly, and the physically disabled). She went so far as to consult with a surgeon, requesting to have both of her arms amputated to prevent her from bludgeoning, stabbing, or strangling others to death; shortly after being denied the operation, she took a nonfatal overdose of psychotropic medication. Across all three cases, though the content of obsessions was highly violent and aggressive, no real behavioral manifestations of violence or aggression were reported (perhaps because the impulses were so ego dystonic and caused so much distress that the individuals sought treatment before acting out violently).

As a balance to these cases, Kramer and Zimmerman (2009) present one about an OCD individual who engaged in repeated criminal behavior but whose obsessions were not related to crime or violence. This 14-year-old Swiss boy was characterized by criminality beginning at age 11 (including theft, physical violence, and multiple threats with knives against other adolescents and younger children). His OCD symptoms (involving obsessions about contamination, which developed initially after engaging in oral sex with a female fellow gang member) developed two years later. These authors propose fear and anxiety to be the basis of adolescent externalizing behaviors (e.g., juvenile delinquency). Overall, this material demonstrates how the content of obsessions in OCD—however related or unrelated to crime and violence—is not often congruent with the manifestation of behavior in published case histories. The congruence of Houston's obsessions and violent behavior, along with the purported exacerbating effects of treatment, perhaps speak to a more case-specific link between OCD and violence.

Anxiety Disorders and Violent Crime

A growing body of literature continues to demonstrate a relationship between anxiety disorders and various forms of violence. For example, an analysis of data from the National Comorbidity Survey by Corrigan and Watson (2005) showed that people with an anxiety disorder were almost four times more likely to engage in violent behavior than people who did not have a psychiatric diagnosis. Regarding specific anxiety disorders such as OCD, Arai and colleagues (2006) found violence and significant involvement behaviors directed toward family members to be among the clinical features of inpatient children and adolescents with OCD admitted to the Tokyo Metropolitan Umegaoka Hospital. These behaviors were related to OCD symptoms. According to Lopez-Ibor (1990), OCD patients may at times lose control and become extremely violent or suicidal, and they are capable of the most violent and dramatic types of suicide attempts. Other empirical contributions to the understanding of the anxiety disorders–violence relationship have been in the areas of suicidality, OCD and serial homicide, and PTSD and homicidal (and other forms of) violence.

Suicidality

One specific form of violence that has captured the attention of researchers in terms of its association with anxiety disorders is suicide. In fact, particularly salient in the public consciousness as of late are the increased rates of suicides among U.S. war veterans suffering from PTSD. For example, a report from RAND Corporation (Tanielian & Jaycox, 2008) identified prevalence rates of PTSD of approximately 5–15% across studies of deployed U.S. service members. The rates on the higher end are nearly double the lifetime prevalence rates and quadruple the 12-month prevalence rates of those reported in U.S. community populations (see Table 7.1). Also, according to a recent report from the U.S. Department of Veterans Affairs (2012), a military veteran commits suicide every 65 minutes (amounting to 22 per day). These numbers are alarming and certainly justify further examination as to why suicide may be overrepresented among this population and what its potential connections with PTSD may be.

Clinical and epidemiologic studies have actually demonstrated positive associations between suicidal ideation and behavior and *several* anxiety disorders (GAD, agoraphobia, simple phobia, social phobia, PTSD, and panic disorder—the most extensively studied), though it is unclear whether these associations are unique to individual anxiety disorders or are driven more by comorbidity with other mental disorders—particularly major depression (Boden et al., 2007; Sareen et al., 2005). Using data from a large scale national survey of community individuals, Sareen and colleagues (2005) found that, among all of the anxiety disorders (with the exception of

OCD, which was not studied), only PTSD was associated with suicidal ideation or attempts when they controlled for comorbid psychiatric disorders (though the temporal sequencing of the disorder and suicidality onset were not examined). Boden, Fergusson, and Horwood (2007) examined the relationship between anxiety disorders and suicidal behaviors in a 25-year longitudinal study of 1,265 children in an urban New Zealand birth cohort. Anxiety disorders (GAD, phobias—including social phobia, agoraphobia, and specific phobia—and panic disorder) were assessed via structured clinical interviews using DSM-IV criteria at three points for ages 16–25. Suicidal behaviors were also assessed by interview. Results indicated that, after data were controlled for co-occurring mental disorders, life stress, and other non-observed, fixed confounding factors (i.e., common genetic and environmental influences), any single anxiety disorder increased the odds of suicidal ideation by 2.80 and the odds of suicide attempts by 1.90. Additionally, rates of suicidal behavior increased in those diagnosed with multiple anxiety disorders. However, despite this more sophisticated methodology, these authors were also unable to determine the temporal sequencing of the onset of anxiety disorders and suicidality. Neither could they rule out the possibility that suicidal behavior may increase an individual's risk for the development of anxiety disorders.

Studies of incarcerated sample populations have produced similar findings. For example, Bland and colleagues (1990) found that prison inmates who attempted suicide had increased rates of major depression, antisocial personality, and anxiety or somatoform disorders compared to those that did not. In a sample of delinquent youth seen at a justice system assessment center for juveniles, Nolen and colleagues (2008) found lifetime suicide attempts to be related to age (older), gender (female), not living with both parents, and arrest for a felony or violent crime, as well as with mood, substance use, or behavior disorder. However, results also indicated anxiety disorders were associated with increased rates of suicide attempts for boys but not girls. As with research using individuals outside the criminal justice system, studies of anxiety disorders and suicidal behaviors using those within it have mainly utilized statistical techniques such as stepwise logistic regression to examine potential associations between anxiety disorders, recent or lifetime suicidality, and other potential confounding factors; they have largely not focused upon causal relationships or which condition predates the other.

Obsessive-Compulsive Disorder and Serial Murder

Some discussion by law enforcement professionals has suggested a relationship between OCD traits and behaviors and serial homicide. For example, several decades ago, the Federal Bureau of Investigation—using a convenience sample of 36 sexual homicide and serial homicide offenders—developed an *organized/disorganized typology* of offending based upon behaviors and personality traits inferred from crime-scene evidence for the purpose of criminal investigative profiling. According to Ressler and colleagues (1988), the organized offender is characterized by marked fantasy and ritual, and obsessive and compulsive traits become apparent in the behavior and/or crime scene patterns of these individuals. The literature on serial murder, which is largely quasi-empirical or based on nonscientific anecdotal accounts, often refers to serial killing being a compulsive behavior and describes the killer's actions as "obsessive-compulsive aggressivity." However, interpreting this too literally may be problematic (see Ferreira, 2000, for a review), particularly with regard to the gratification associated with the purported "compulsive" behaviors linked to serial murder. More specifically, in actual OCD, the goal of the behaviors is "to prevent or reduce anxiety, not to provide pleasure or gratification" (APA, 2000, p. 457). The DSM-5 retains this distinction, stating, "compulsions are not done for pleasure, although some individuals experience relief from anxiety or distress" (APA, 2013, p. 238). In serial killing, however, the behaviors (based on available accounts) appear more akin to pleasurable activities that the killer may wish to resist engaging in only because of deleterious consequences (see APA, 2000, pp. 461–462), which negates an OCD diagnosis.

Post-Traumatic Stress Disorder, Homicide, and Other Forms of Violence

The relationship between PTSD and violence has been established in the literature largely through studies of combat veterans, nonveteran men and women within the criminal justice system, and nonveteran individuals not in prison. Interestingly, recent arrest data is beginning to elucidate a relationship between PTSD and criminal and violent behavior in combat veterans. For example, in a recent study of 1,388 veterans from the era of the Iraq and Afghanistan wars, Elbogen and colleagues (2012) found a subset of veterans—characterized by both PTSD or traumatic injury and anger or irritability—that were at an increased risk for criminal arrest (i.e., nearly twice as likely) compared to other veterans. In another recent study of 2,102 Maricopa County (Arizona) booked arrestees, White and associates (2012) found military veterans comprised 6.3% of the arrestee population; more than half of these individuals reported at least one combat-related problem (e.g., physical injury, mental health problems, substance abuse)—including PTSD. Further analyses indicated veterans were characterized by more arrests for violent offenses and greater crack cocaine and opiates use compared to nonveterans.

Several other investigators have examined the association between PTSD and aggression, hostility, and violence in samples of combat veterans. Research includes case studies describing anger regulation deficits in Korean and Vietnam War combat veterans (Chemtob et al., 1997); increased self-reported anger and hostility in Iraq and Afghanistan War combat veterans with PTSD compared to those without (Jakupcak et al., 2007); increased self-reported acts of violence, specifically, property destruction, threats of violence without a weapon, physical fighting, and violent threats with a weapon, in inpatient Vietnam War combat veterans with PTSD compared to both non-inpatient veterans with PTSD and psychiatric inpatients without PTSD (McFall et al., 1999); and indirect association between combat exposure and aggression (i.e., via PTSD symptoms) and direct and indirect (i.e., via dysphoric symptoms) associations between PTSD symptoms and aggression in combat veterans (Taft et al., 2007). One notable limitation of these studies is an overall lack of assessment for pre-trauma levels of aggression and hostility or for a possible predisposition to violence in combat veterans, because of brain injuries or personality characteristics, for example. Additionally, the chronological sequencing of trauma and PTSD symptoms and of the onset of violent behavior in these individuals remains largely unexamined (see below).

Although empirical studies on the relationship between PTSD and extreme (homicidal) violence in combat veterans are currently lacking, *The New York Times* (2008) located 121 cases of Iraq and Afghanistan War veterans who either committed or were charged with committing a homicide in the United States after returning home from war. In many cases, homicides were attributed to combat trauma and the stress of deployment, along with alcohol abuse, family discord, and other problems. Nearly 75% were still in the military at the time of the homicides—over half of which involved guns, with the remaining being stabbings, beatings, strangulations, bathtub drowning, and fatal automobile accidents resulting from drunken, reckless, or suicidal driving. Cases were located in most U.S. states. Seventy-six were from the army, 37 from the marines, and 8 from other branches of the military. One hundred and eight served in Iraq and 13 in Afghanistan (two Iraq War veterans also served in Afghanistan). Forty-one killed family members or girlfriends (in four cases, the victim was also in the military), 32 killed service members, and 59 killed other types of victims. Seventy-nine were charged with murder, 12 with manslaughter, 16 with other types of homicide, and 14 were not charged (i.e., they committed suicide or were killed by law enforcement officers). Unfortunately, *The New York Times* did not report rates of PTSD among these combat veterans, and the assumption that the killings resulted directly or indirectly from PTSD symptoms cannot be made definitively.

Nonveteran sample populations have also been investigated. Elevated rates of PTSD have been reported in samples of male prison and jail inmates (e.g., Gibson et al., 1999), and PTSD has demonstrated relationships with arrest and incarceration for violent offenses in male prison inmates (Collins & Bailey, 1990b). Neller and colleagues (2006) found that, among 93 maximum-security detention center inmates—67% of which reported violent behavior in the year before incarceration—96% reported previously witnessing traumatic events; and McFarlane and colleagues (2006) found psychiatric inpatients who reported previous victimization (nearly half of which met diagnostic criteria for PTSD) were characterized by increased self-reported aggression, anger, and hostility compared to those who did not (none of which had PTSD diagnoses). In a sample of 239 male prisoners from a rural New England state (the majority of whom had no military experience), Gibson et al. (1999) found witnessing someone being seriously injured or killed, being sexually abused, and being physically assaulted to be the three antecedent traumas most commonly reported in those diagnosed with PTSD (33% had lifetime and 21% had current diagnoses). Other areas of focus have been intimate partner violence (IPV) perpetrators and victims of crime. For example, women arrested for intimate partner violence are approximately 7 times more likely than those in the general population to have PTSD, as well as 7.2 times more likely to have depression, 12.4 times more likely to have GAD, and 12.6 times more likely to have panic disorder (Stuart et al.,

BOX 7.2 PTSD AND HOMICIDE IN COMBAT VETERANS

Josiah Sher, age 27, slashed and shot two people to death; he served several tours in Pakistan, Afghanistan, and Iraq between 2005 and 2009 and was institutionalized and taking medications for severe PTSD. Jessie Bratcher, age 27, shot six times with hollow-point bullets and killed a man who had consensual sexual intercourse with his fiancée; he served 11 months in Iraq and was the first in the State of Oregon successfully to claim PTSD as a defense for murder and be sentenced to a psychiatric hospital. Steven Russell (pictured) shot four times and killed his girlfriend in a cold-blooded, premeditated fashion; he served in Iraq in 2003 and suffered from PTSD, according to defense attorneys. Matthew Sepi shot and killed one gang member and wounded another at a convenience store in self-defense with an AK-47 assault rifle; he served in Iraq in 2003 and allegedly suffered from PTSD-like symptoms; Seth Strasburg, age 29, shot and killed a stranger–a young male college student; Strasburg served in Iraq from 2003–2005 and allegedly suffered from PTSD-like symptoms.

2006). No significant differences in PTSD symptom levels were revealed, however, between incarcerated battered women who killed or seriously assaulted their spouses and those who committed other offenses (O'Keefe, 1998). In non-incarcerated samples, elevated anger has been shown to be positively associated with the development of PTSD in female victims of crime (Riggs et al., 1992), and victimization from partners and childhood abuse have been associated with PTSD and depression symptoms in women in court-mandated domestic violence programs who perpetrated IPV (Swann et al., 2005).

Few studies have examined the chronological relationship between PTSD and violence. Collins and Bailey (1990b) found first arrests for homicide, rape, or assault to happen before or during the same year as the first PTSD symptoms in only 27.5% of incarcerated male felons. In 18.7% of inmates, first violent arrests happened over a decade after PTSD symptom onset. In an Australian sample of 124 current substance users diagnosed with PTSD, Barrett and colleagues (2011) found over half had committed a violent crime in their lifetime, and 15.7% had done so in the past month. This study's sample population was unique in that 62.7% were women; both men and women in the sample were either from the community or undergoing substance-use treatment as outpatients. The mean ages of first intoxication, first trauma, and first violent crime were 12.8 years ($SD = 3.3$), 8 years (range 1–44) and 21.6 years ($SD = 7.8$), respectively. Both violent and nonviolent participants had similar trauma histories; most commonly, they witnessed serious injury or death, threat with a weapon, or physical assault, and 50% or more were victims of rape or sexual molestation. Also, participants had experienced a mean of 6.0 (*SD* = 1.7) different types of traumatic events over the course of their lifetime. In terms of the temporal sequence of events, the majority (95.7%) committed their violent crime after the age of first intoxication and after experiencing their first trauma; the rest experienced their first trauma after the age of first intoxication and after committing their violent crime. Backward stepwise logistic regression analysis indicated that increased trait physical aggression and more severe PTSD hyperarousal symptoms significantly predicted violent crime perpetration. Those who committed a violent crime in the past month presented with more severe symptoms (specifically, symptoms of hyperarousal), which is consistent with prior research.

Several theoretical explanations have been offered for the association between PTSD and violence. The **"cycle of violence" theory**, based on research demonstrating that the experience of violent trauma may contribute to the perpetration of future violent behavior, has been referenced by some researchers (O'Keefe, 1998). Interestingly, prevalence rates of PTSD in trauma populations such as women victimized by intimate partner violence are quite high (Johnson et al., 2008). These women often find themselves in cyclical patterns of violence: they are initially abused by their partners, have subsequent psychological difficulties, and are unable to curtail their partners' future violence. Battered women's syndrome is largely considered to be a subtype of PTSD in which the cycle of violence plays a particularly important role (Walker, 2009). In fact, such women may kill their partners after years of severe abuse, usually in self-defense (O'Keefe, 1998), or even murder their own children (Kachaeva et al., 2010).

Other studies have applied the **survivor mode theory**, which suggests that PTSD individuals have a reduced threshold for the perception of situations as threatening so that any perception of threat activates a biological survival response possibly accompanied by anger regulation deficits (i.e., the "ball of rage") (Chemtob et al., 1997). The **fear avoidance theory**, on the other hand, proposes that some PTSD individuals may be characterized by feelings of anger and avoid intrusive, fear-related thoughts and feelings activated by reminders of the trauma through the expression of physical aggression (Riggs et al., 1992).

Anxiety Disorders and Other Types of Crime

Shoplifting

Although shoplifting as a behavior is not considered a mental disorder, kleptomania is defined as an impulse control disorder in the DSM-IV-TR (discussed in Chapter 9) and has been reclassified in the DSM-5 to be under disruptive, impulse-control, and conduct disorders (APA, 2013). Kleptomania is a recurrent failure to resist impulses to steal objects not needed for personal use or their monetary value; those with this disorder experience increased tension before and pleasure, gratification, and relief after the theft (APA, 2000). Although kleptomania is rare compared to shoplifting in general, with fewer than 5% of identified shoplifters meeting the criteria for kleptomania (APA, 2000), some authors have commented on the aspects of kleptomanic stealing that appear related to anxiety disorders in general and compulsions in particular. For example, it is thought that kleptomanic stealing is similar to a classic compulsion in that the urge to steal is experienced as intrusive and senseless, with an individual feeling a build-up of anxiety or tension before the act or while resisting the urge and tension relief afterwards. The stealing, therefore, is ego dystonic (i.e., incongruent with or contrary to one's sense of self—the individual is aware it is wrong and senseless), and some authors have proposed kleptomania to be a variant of OCD (McElroy, 1991). Gudjónsson (1990) describes kleptomania as a "compulsive" behavior whose primary motive is the enhancement of arousal (i.e., increased subjective and physiological arousal occurring before the behavior that serves to make the person feel excited and more alive or to allow avoidance of some other ongoing activity—such as worrying—that is perceived as aversive), followed by the reduction of anxiety (i.e., the completion of stealing is associated with lowered arousal levels and a feeling of relief).

Comorbidity with other anxiety disorders may also speak to the anxiety-related aspects of kleptomania. Other studies have identified the comorbidity of kleptomania with anxiety disorders, mood disorders, eating disorders, substance use disorders, personality disorders, and even other impulse control disorders (APA, 2000; Gudjónsson, 1990; Lamontagne et al., 2000). For example, in a study of 20 psychiatric hospital inpatients and outpatients (15 women and 5 men) diagnosed with DSM-III-R kleptomania and assessed with structured clinical interviews, McElroy and colleagues (1991) found all 20 to also have a lifetime diagnosis of mood disorders (12 with bipolar disorders and 8 with major depression); 8 (40%) were also diagnosed with panic disorders, 1 (5%) with agoraphobia without panic disorder, 8 (40%) with social phobia, 6 (30%) with simple phobia, and 9 (45%) with OCD. Additionally, 12 (60%) were diagnosed with eating disorders and 8 (40%) with other impulse control disorders such as pathological gambling, pyromania, trichotillomania, and intermittent explosive disorder. Interestingly, the rates of comorbid OCD in this kleptomanic sample are 18 times those reported in community studies (see Table 7.1), and rates of other comorbid anxiety disorders are also significantly increased in comparison.

Lamontagne and colleagues (2000) examined the relationship between demographic factors and anxiety, significant losses, depression, and irrational beliefs in a sample of 106 adult male and female first-offense shoplifters at a Montreal municipal court. All data were collected using self-report questionnaires (including the BDI and Zung's Self-Rating Anxiety Scale)—a limitation, though self-report questionnaires of anxiety and depression are often used in research studies examining symptomatology but not necessarily clinical disorders. Results indicated that 23.3% reported extreme anxiety and 42.9% reported moderate or severe depression. Depressed subjects presented the greatest number of shoplifting-related irrational beliefs. Unfortunately, BDI data were missing in 43 cases, so rates of depression may have been underestimated in this sample. Additionally, no non-shoplifting control group was utilized in this study (perhaps many individuals at the court were depressed and anxious), and there is no way of knowing if the depression or anxiety preceded the shoplifting or was involved in any way in the etiology of the shoplifting. Nonetheless, the authors purport their findings support Gudjónsson's (1990) proposed dichotomy of shoplifters: those who shoplift out of rational choice and those that do because of depression.

Sexual Crimes

The relationship between anxiety disorders and sexual offending has received comparatively little attention in the literature. Nonetheless, some evidence suggests an association worthy of investigation. For example, the OCD nature in which certain types of sex offenders catalog child pornographic images has been noted anecdotally (Roger Pimentel, Senior U.S. Pretrial Services Officer, Sex Offender Specialist, Central District of California, personal communication, March 20, 2012). Studies of sex offender populations have reported markedly increased rates of anxiety disorders in these individuals, particularly in those also diagnosed with paraphilias (see Chapter 8). For example, in a study of 45 male sex offenders with pedophilia (Raymond et al., 1999), 64% ($n = 29$) were also diagnosed with a history of anxiety disorder. Social phobia ($n = 17$) and PTSD ($n = 15$) were the most common anxiety disorders. Dunsieth and colleagues (2004), in a study of 113 convicted male sex offenders in a residential treatment program, found anxiety disorders to be significantly more prevalent among those with paraphilias than those without. Additionally, a much more recent Dutch study of juvenile sex offenders (Hart-Kerkhoffs et al., 2011) found that 75% met criteria for at least one psychiatric disorder and more than 50% were comorbid for other disorders. Child molesters were characterized by the highest rates of internalizing disorders (i.e., mood and anxiety disorders) and showed the most core symptoms of autism spectrum disorder. Compared to those with single offenses, multiple sex offenders demonstrated increased rates of disruptive behavioral disorders and anxiety disorder. Ultimately, though initial evidence is interesting, more work is needed in this area to determine if and exactly how anxiety disorder symptomatology may manifest in sex offenders or contribute to the commission of sexual offenses.

Origins of Crime and Violence in Anxiety Disorders: Theoretical Explanations and Etiological Mechanisms

Psychoanalytic Factors

As stated in Chapter 2, Alexander and Straub (1931) distinguish between the neurotic criminal, whose criminality is based in an intrapsychic conflict between the prosocial and antisocial components of his or her personality (i.e., in a psychological etiological process), and the normal and organic criminal types, whose criminality is based in sociological and biological etiological processes, respectively. In fact, these authors use the psychoanalytic theory of neurotic symptom formation as the basis for understanding criminal behavior, describing psychoneurosis as the "parody of primitive criminality" in which the primal crime (i.e., murder of the father and incest with the mother) and its punishment (i.e., castration) are central (Alexander and Straub, 1931, p. 56). For the neurotic patient, anxiety symptoms are a form of unconscious self-punishment meant to satisfy internalized moral demands (evidenced by neurotic patients whose symptoms become worse when they begin to notice small levels of improvement). For the neurotic criminal, punishment (either forthcoming or already served) frequently only lifts moral inhibitions by relieving the anxiety associated with criminal transgressions, and it allows for criminal offending in general and repeated criminality in particular.

Comorbidity

Significant comorbidity has been observed between anxiety disorders and mood, substance use, and borderline and antisocial personality disorders within both incarcerated and non-incarcerated populations (Gibson et al., 1999; Grella et al., 2008; Mitchell et al., 2007; Trestman et al., 2007). Further understanding of the relationship between anxiety disorders and crime may be gained by looking at studies that have examined anxiety and anxiety disorders within the context of criminogenic disorders such as antisocial personality disorder, conduct disorder, and psychopathy. For several decades, a sizeable amount of literature has been dedicated to understanding how (and if) anxiety manifests in these disorders, and how its presence or absence may contribute to the development and maintenance of antisocial behavioral patterns. One prominent hypothesis derived from studies of psychopaths and other antisocial personalities is the **low-fear hypothesis** (Lykken, 1995). According to this hypothesis, certain types of psychopaths (known as "primary" psychopaths—see below) are characterized by attenuated experiences of anxiety and fear; and, because of their "below average endowment of innate fearfulness" (Lykken, 1995, p. 154), they are more difficult to socialize using conventional parenting methods, which are based on a child's motivation to avoid punishment (Newman, 1998). For several decades, a debate in the literature has centered on whether persistently antisocial individuals are characterized by such reduced fear (Dolan & Rennie, 2007; Lykken, 1995) or even by the absence of anxiety (Cleckley, 1988)—or whether these individuals have comparatively high levels of negative emotions (including anxiety) resulting from antisocial behavior (Dolan & Rennie, 2007). Some have suggested the existence of subgroups of antisocial individuals marked by either low or high levels of anxiety and ***neuroticism***, such as "primary" versus "secondary" psychopaths or "undersocialized" versus "neurotic" delinquents (Blackburn, 1990 and Quay, 1987, in Dolan & Rennie, 2007). A classic experiment by Lykken (1957) demonstrated physiological correlates to these subgroup distinctions. "Primary" (non-anxious) psychopaths were characterized by lower self-reported anxiety, reduced skin conductance reactivity to a conditioned stimulus associated with an electric shock, and reduced performance on an avoidance learning task when compared to controls. "Neurotic" psychopaths demonstrated avoidance learning at levels between the other groups and scored higher on anxiety measures. Subsequent studies of psychopathic adults and juveniles, however, have produced mixed findings, though particular aspects of anxiety and fearfulness have shown relationships with specific components of psychopathy (Dolan & Rennie, 2007).

At the clinical disorder level, the significant overlap between criminogenic personality pathologies and anxiety disorders may also speak to a relationship between the two. Grant and colleagues (2005) examined the comorbidity between 12-month mood and anxiety disorders and personality disorders using data from a large U.S. epidemiological study sample. Results indicated significant associations between various anxiety, mood, and personality disorders; but, of all the personality disorders, histrionic and antisocial personality disorder were most strongly related to mania and to panic disorder with agoraphobia. A review by Nichita and Buckley (2007) indicates major mental disorders such as schizophrenia, mood disorders, substance abuse, and anxiety disorders are commonly found in patients with antisocial personality disorder. Large national comorbidity study samples (Goodwin & Hamilton, 2003; Sareen et al., 2004) have shown nearly half of individuals diagnosed with antisocial diagnoses (i.e., ASPD, CD, or adult antisocial behavior, but not psychopathy) also had diagnoses of anxiety disorders. Across these studies, social phobia and PTSD had the strongest relationships with antisocial behavior, and increased levels of disability, psychological distress, comorbid depression, substance dependence, and suicidality and lower quality of life have been observed among individuals with both anxiety disorders and antisocial diagnoses compared to those with either condition alone (Goodwin & Hamilton, 2003; Sareen et al., 2004). Stinson and colleagues (2005) found elevated rates of depression and anxiety disorder symptomatology (42% and 26%, respectively) in a sample of 68 civilly committed adult male sex offenders also characterized by high rates of psychopathy. However, Pham and Saloppé (2010) found no significant comorbidity between psychopathy and psychotic, mood, and anxiety disorders in a sample of 84 Belgian adult male forensic patients (although, for anxiety disorders, analyses were conducted separately only for two disorders, GAD and phobic disorder, and not for anxiety disorders in general or for panic disorder or OCD separately). Overall, evidence—though somewhat mixed—may suggest a specific relationship between anxiety disorders and antisocial personalities, though the overlap with other DSM Axis I mental disorders indicates that comorbidity with more generalized psychopathology may also explain this relationship.

Neurobiological Factors

Braun and colleagues (2008) propose an interesting conceptual and neurobiological framework for understanding the relationship between OCD and antisocial personality disorder. These authors propose that the two disorders are at opposite ends of a morality continuum. At one end, ASPD represents "dysfunctional *hypo*moralism" while, at the other, OCD represents "dysfunctional *hyper*moralism." As such, the two disorders are in a sense reversed mirror images of each other in terms of behavioral and biological traits. The behaviors of those with ASPD include aggressiveness, insensitivity to punishment, impulsivity and agitation as compared to phobia or passivity, excessive sensitivity to punishment, rigidity, and paralyzing lethargy in those with OCD. Biologically, ASPD is related to cortical orbitofrontal *hypo*metabolism, *hypo*cortisolism, *hyper*dopaminergism, and *hypo*serotoninergism and OCD to cortical orbitofrontal *hyper*metabolism, *hyper*cortisolism, *hypo*dopaminergism, and *hyper*serotoninergism in OCD. A comparison of 25 published cases of post-lesion ASPD and 39 published cases of acquired OCD indicated that patients with ASPD presented most often with lesions in putamenal or pallidal regions, and that contrasting patterns of neurobiological, endocrine, and behavioral traits in both groups suggests an orbitofrontostriatopallidal neural circuit in the brain underlying morality (Braun, Léveillé, and Guimond, 2008). Unfortunately, these authors did not explore neurobiological characteristics of individuals with *both* disorders, which may suggest common neurobiological underpinnings for both conditions within the same individual or perhaps a neurobiologically distinct form of antisocial OCD.

Conclusion

Anxiety disorders in general are among the first mental disorders to be recognized historically and have a rich tradition in conceptualization from a variety of theoretical perspectives. Nonetheless, their relationship with crime and violence remains largely underexplored. Nevertheless, the literature in this area has moved to some degree past both qualitative clinical case studies and prevalence rate studies, which, despite methodological limitations, appear to show increased rates of anxiety disorders in criminal populations and more criminal and violent behavior among those diagnosed with anxiety disorders. Current studies have moved into the investigation of the criminogenic etiological mechanisms specific to certain anxiety disorders. For example, OCD and PTSD have received the lion's share of empirical attention in this area, and numerous studies have examined relationships between these disorders (and other anxiety disorders, to some extent) and suicidal behaviors and various forms of violence (including homicide), as well as comorbidity with criminogenic conditions such as ASPD and psychopathy. The case of Robert Cameron Houston highlights the need for further understanding of the association between anxiety disorders and crime and violence, and the ever-growing number of cases in the popular media of combat veterans with PTSD committing acts of extreme violence only underscores how grave this need actually is.

KEY TERMS

anxiety

"cycle of violence" theory [of PTSD]

compulsions

fear

fear avoidance theory [of PTSD]

generalized anxiety disorder (GAD)

low-fear hypothesis

neurotic

obsessions

obsessive-compulsive disorder (OCD)

phobia

physiological symptoms [of anxiety]

post-traumatic stress disorder (PTSD)

signal anxiety

state anxiety

survivor mode theory [of PTSD]

trait anxiety

triple vulnerability theory

REVIEW QUESTIONS

1. Compare and contrast the conceptualizations from the different theoretical perspectives discussed in the chapter for each of the following anxiety disorders: panic disorder/agoraphobia, phobias, OCD, and PTSD. What are some of the similarities and differences in the way pathological anxiety is conceptualized across disorders?
2. Examine Tables 7.3 and 7.4 and the summaries of research studies in the "A Closer Look" sections for each disorder in this chapter. Discuss how prevalence rates of crime in those with anxiety disorders and of anxiety disorders in criminal populations differ among these disorders, if at all. Using the information in the tables, speculate as to how these differences in prevalence rates may have been caused by methodology (e.g., in terms of study types, sample characteristics, methodological issues, or other concerns).
3. Reflect on the case material related to anxiety disorders and crime presented in the chapter. In what ways are these cases similar (i.e., in terms of types of anxiety symptoms, situational factors, individual characteristics)? Do any patterns emerge in terms of how anxiety may relate to criminal behavior?
4. Explain conceptual arguments for and against a relationship between OCD and serial homicide.
5. Compare and contrast (1) the low-fear hypothesis and its relationship to antisocial personalities or individuals (i.e., primary or secondary psychopaths and undersocialized or neurotic delinquents) and (2) Braun and colleagues' (2008) proposed morality continuum of OCD and antisocial personality disorder. Both conceptualize relationships between anxiety and criminogenic personality pathologies. Which hypothesis is more convincing, and why?

8

Sexual Disorders

JEFFREY LIONEL DAHMER

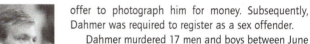

Jeffrey Dahmer was born in West Allis, Wisconsin, on May 21, 1960. Dahmer was emotionally distant as a child and socially withdrawn and uncommunicative in early adolescence. Although he demonstrated some interests in high school (playing clarinet, tennis, writing for the school newspaper) and received decent grades, he had no friendships and was an alcoholic by his high school graduation. He dropped out of college after one year and was dishonorably discharged from the army because of alcoholism.

Throughout his childhood, Dahmer collected dead animals found by the roadside, using a chemistry set to cure their skins or burying them in backyard graves. He did not enjoy torturing animals to death but was merely obsessed with observing and feeling their internal organs. This fascination became sexualized in adolescence when Dahmer began engaging in compulsive masturbation—at times while dissecting dead animals.

In his twenties, Dahmer was arrested for exposing himself to children and masturbating in front of two 12-year-old boys, and he admitted to several incidents of public masturbation. At age 28, he was arrested for drugging and sexually fondling a 13-year-old boy, whom he had lured to his apartment with an offer to photograph him for money. Subsequently, Dahmer was required to register as a sex offender.

Dahmer murdered 17 men and boys between June 1978 and July 1991. Often he picked up his victims in gay bars and had sex with them before killing them. Relatives and neighbors complained about Dahmer's unusual apartment, police found skulls, preserved body parts, and an organized scrapbook of photographs of dead and dismembered victims—items with which Dahmer would masturbate. He kept an additional victim's head in a locker at the chocolate factory where he worked. While he often sedated and killed his victims quickly, some he attempted to turn into obedient sex "zombies" by drilling and injecting acid or boiling water into their frontal lobes.

A human head and heart were discovered in his refrigerator, and patties of chopped human flesh were kept in his freezer. Dahmer felt eating his victims made them forever a part of him, and he achieved sexual gratification from doing so.

Dahmer was eventually arrested and stood trial on 15 counts of murder in 1992. His insanity defense was unsuccessful (see Chapter 11). His convictions resulted in him being sentenced to 15 life terms—the maximum under Wisconsin law. Two years later, he was beaten to death by a fellow inmate while imprisoned.

Sexual interests, fantasies, and behaviors—like other aspects of the human experience discussed in this book—exist in the general population along a continuum. What is sexually arousing or fulfilling to one individual may seem too safe, tame, or boring to another, and too wild, extreme, or "kinky" to yet another. Among the mental disorders outlined in the DSM-IV-TR and DSM-5, few are as interwoven with morality and moral judgment as those involving sexual deviancy. The identification of a class of sexual disorders implies the establishment of clear norms for sexual behavior and, moreover, that psychiatrists are the moral guardians of sexual behavior. Definitions for perversions have evolved historically as psychiatric classification systems mirror the societies from which they are derived. Between 1905 and 1962, psychiatry used late-Victorian conceptualizations of perversions (traces of which could be found in everyone); the DSM-III presented nonjudgmental—some say "sanitized"—classifications of paraphilias, and Stoller (1975, 1985, in Gabbard, 2005) narrowed sexual disorders using the idea of "erotic hatred," which required a sense of sinning to create erotic excitement. Additionally, evolving terms such as "sexual deviation," "perversion," and even "paraphilia" may become associated with pejorative overtones (Gabbard, 2005). Although the sexual excitement and pleasure derived by Jeffrey Dahmer from his activities is beyond the comprehension of most people, his behavior still constitutes the extreme end of a spectrum of human experience. His fantasies of violence became intermingled with sex in early adolescence, and his paraphilias included **necrophilia**, cannibalism (anthropophagy), pedophilia, and exhibitionism.

Diagnostic Criteria and the Prevalence of Sexual Disorders

The DSM-IV-TR classifies several disorders under the umbrella term "sexual and gender identity disorders." There are three main categories: sexual dysfunctions, gender identity disorders, and paraphilias (APA, 2000). Sexual dysfunctions involve abnormalities in the sexual response cycle or painful sexual intercourse and include sexual desire disorders (hypoactive sexual desire disorder, sexual aversion disorder), sexual arousal disorders (female sexual arousal disorder, male erectile disorder), orgasmic disorders (female orgasmic disorder, male orgasmic disorder, premature ejaculation), and sexual pain disorders (dyspareunia, vaginismus). Gender identity disorders involve strongly and persistently identifying with the opposite gender—not merely desiring the perceived cultural advantages of being the other sex; people with these disorders feel persistent discomfort with their own sex or a sense of inappropriateness in the gender role of that sex. Paraphilias involve a dependency on fantasizing about or engaging in sexual behavior that is atypical and extreme. In the DSM-5, these disorders have been reclassified into the following three diagnostic classes. *Sexual dysfunctions* (1) deal predominantly with clinically significant disturbances in sexual responsivity or in the ability to experience pleasure from sexual activity: delayed ejaculation, erectile disorder, female orgasmic disorder, female sexual interest or arousal disorder, genito-pelvic pain or penetration disorder, male hypoactive sexual desire disorder, premature [early] ejaculation, substance or medication-induced sexual dysfunction, other specified sexual dysfunction, and unspecified sexual dysfunction. *Gender dysphoria* (2) is "distress that may accompany the incongruence between one's experienced or expressed gender and one's assigned gender" (APA, 2013, p. 451). And *paraphilic disorders* (3) involve functional impairments associated with specific types of intense sexual desires or behaviors. The order of presentation of the paraphilic disorders listed in the DSM-5 corresponds generally to classification schemes commonly used with these disorders. The first group is based on *anomalous activity preferences* and is subdivided into *courtship disorders* (voyeuristic disorder, exhibitionistic disorder, and frotteuristic disorder) and *algolagnic disorders* (sexual masochism disorder and sexual sadism disorder). The first disorders resemble distorted elements of human courtship behavior, and the second involve pain and suffering. This second group is further subdivided according to *anomalous target preferences*: pedophilic disorder, fetishistic disorder, and transvestic disorder (APA, 2013).

Paraphilia literally means "abnormal love" ("*para*" is a Greek term for "beyond or outside the usual," and "*philia*" is a Greek term for "love"). According to the DSM-IV-TR, the essential features of a paraphilia are recurrent, intense sexually arousing fantasies, sexual urges, or behaviors—occurring over a period of at least six months—and generally involving 1) nonhuman objects, 2) the suffering or humiliation of oneself or one's partner, or 3) children or other nonconsenting persons (APA 2000). These include **exhibitionism**, **fetishism** (which involves the use of nonliving objects, such as women's underpants, bras, stockings, shoes, boots, or other apparel), frotteurism, **pedophilia**, **sexual masochism**, **sexual sadism**, **transvestic fetishism**, and **voyeurism**. DSM-5 diagnostic criteria for the major classifications of paraphilic disorders are listed in Table 8.1. (Note: Table 8.3 lists other paraphilias associated with crime, violence, and antisocial behavior; these disorders will be discussed later in this chapter.)

Limited data on the prevalence of the various DSM-IV-TR sexual dysfunctions suggest rates from 3–33% among adults in the United States. In the DSM-5, reported prevalence rates of sexual dysfunctions—when known—vary from as little as 1% to as much as 80%, depending on age and other factors. Additionally, though no recent data on the prevalence of DSM-IV-TR gender identity disorder are available, studies from smaller

Table 8.1 DSM-5 Diagnostic Criteria for Paraphilic Disorders

Paraphilic Disorders

302.82 (F65.3) Voyeuristic Disorder

A. Over a period of at least 6 months, recurrent and intense sexual arousal from observing an unsuspecting person who is naked, in the process of disrobing, or engaging in sexual activity, as manifested by fantasies, urges, or behaviors.

B. The individual has acted on these sexual urges with a nonconsenting person, or the sexual urges or fantasies cause clinically significant distress or impairment in social, occupational, or other important areas of functioning.

302.4 (F65.2) Exhibitionistic Disorder

A. Over a period of at least 6 months, recurrent and intense sexual arousal from the exposure of one's genitals to an unsuspecting person, as manifested by fantasies, urges, or behaviors.

B. The individual has acted on these sexual urges with a nonconsenting person, or the sexual urges or fantasies cause clinically significant distress or impairment in social, occupational, or other important areas of functioning.

302.89 (F65.81) Frotteuristic Disorder

A. Over a period of at least 6 months, recurrent and intense sexual arousal from touching or rubbing against a nonconsenting person, as manifested by fantasies, urges, or behaviors.

B. The individual has acted on these sexual urges with a nonconsenting person, or the sexual urges or fantasies cause clinically significant distress or impairment in social, occupational, or other important areas of functioning.

302.83 (F65.51) Sexual Masochism Disorder

A. Over a period of at least 6 months, recurrent and intense sexual arousal from the act of being humiliated, beaten, bound, or otherwise made to suffer, as manifested by fantasies, urges, or behaviors.

B. The fantasies, sexual urges, or behaviors cause clinically significant distress or impairment in social, occupational, or other important areas of functioning.

302.84 (F65.52) Sexual Sadism Disorder

A. Over a period of at least 6 months, recurrent and intense sexual arousal from the physical or psychological suffering of another person, as manifested by fantasies, urges, or behaviors.

B. The individual has acted on these sexual urges with a nonconsenting person, or the sexual urges or fantasies cause clinically significant distress or impairment in social, occupational, or other areas of functioning.

302.2 (F65.4) Pedophilic Disorder

A. Over a period of at least 6 months, recurrent, intense sexually arousing fantasies, sexual urges, or behaviors involving sexual activity with a prepubescent child or children (generally age 13 years or younger).

B. The individual has acted on these sexual urges, or the sexual urges or fantasies cause marked distress or interpersonal difficulty.

C. The individual is at least age 16 years and at least 5 years older than the child or children in Criterion A.

Note: Do not include an individual in late adolescence involved in an ongoing sexual relationship with a 12- or 13-year-old.

302.81 (F65.0) Fetishistic Disorder

A. Over a period of at least 6 months, recurrent and intense sexual arousal from either the use of nonliving objects or a highly specific focus on nongenital body part(s), as manifested by fantasies, urges, or behaviors.

B. The fantasies, sexual urges, or behaviors cause clinically significant distress or impairment in social, occupational, or other important areas of functioning.

C. The fetish objects are not limited to articles of clothing used in cross-dressing (as in transvestic disorder) or devices designed for the purposes of tactile genital stimulation (e.g., vibrator).

(Continued)

(Continued)

302.3 (F65.1) Transvestic Disorder

A. Over a period of at least 6 months, recurrent and intense sexual arousal from cross-dressing, as manifested by fantasies, urges, or behaviors.

B. The fantasies, sexual urges, or behaviors cause clinically significant distress or impairment in social, occupational, or other important areas of functioning.

302.89 (F65.89) Other Specified Paraphilic Disorder

This category applies to presentations in which symptoms characteristic of a paraphilic disorder that cause clinically significant distress or impairment in social, occupational, or other important areas of functioning predominate but do not meet full criteria for any of the disorders in the paraphilic disorders diagnostic class. The other specified paraphilic disorder category is used in situations in which the clinician chooses to communicate the specific reason that the presentation does not meet the criteria for any specific paraphilic disorder. This is done by recording "other specified paraphilic disorder" followed by the specific reason (e.g., "zoophilia").

Examples of presentations that can be specified using the "other specified" designation include, but are not limited to, recurrent and intense sexual arousal involving *telephone scatologia* (obscene phone calls), *necrophilia* (corpses), *zoophilia* (animals), *coprophilia* (feces), *klismaphilia* (enemas), or *urophilia* (urine) that has been present for at least 6 months and causes marked distress or impairment in social, occupational, or other important areas of functioning. Other specified paraphilic disorder can be specified as in remission and/or as occurring in a controlled environment.

302.9 (F65.9) Unspecified Paraphilic Disorder

This category applies to presentations in which symptoms characteristic of a paraphilic disorder that cause clinically significant distress or impairment in social, occupational, or other important areas of functioning predominate but do not meet the full criteria for any of the disorders in the paraphilic disorders diagnostic class. The unspecified paraphilic disorder category is used in situations in which the clinician chooses *not* to specify the reason that the criteria are not met for a specific paraphilic disorder, and includes presentations in which there is insufficient information to make a more specific diagnosis.

Source: APA (2013, pp. 686–705). Reprinted with permission from the *Diagnostic and Statistical Manual of Mental Disorders*, Fifth Edition (Copyright © 2013).

European countries suggest that approximately 1 in 30,000 adult males and 1 in 100,000 adult females seek sex-reassignment surgery (APA, 2000). The DSM-5 lists prevalence rates of gender dysphoria of 0.005% to 0.014% for natal adult males and 0.002% to 0.003% for natal females (APA, 2013).

Specific prevalence rates for paraphilias are not reported in the DSM-IV-TR (as no epidemiological data are available), and population prevalence rates are reported as unknown for each of the paraphilic disorders in the DSM-5 although "highest possible lifetime prevalence" rates are predicted for some paraphilic disorders (e.g., voyeuristic disorder—12% in males and 4% in females) and rates found in specialized populations (i.e., outpatient or forensic settings) are listed for others. According to the DSM-IV-TR, although paraphilias are rarely diagnosed in clinical settings, the actual prevalence in the community is likely to be higher given the extensive commercial proliferation of paraphilic pornography and paraphernalia (APA, 2000). Other authors have attempted to quantify the prevalence of specific paraphilias using alternative methods. For example, rates of pedophilia—the paraphilia most commonly discussed in the forensic and clinical literatures (Seto, 2004)—have been estimated using victim reports of adult-child sexual activity (with widely variable rates reported but more recent U.S. studies suggesting 17–27% of women and 12–16% of men being sexually touched or abused as children; McConaghy, 1998), surveys of sexual fantasies in college students (with 3–62% of college males across three studies reporting fantasies of having sex with young children—though, in some studies, the child's age was unspecified), and self-report data from non-incarcerated college samples (i.e., in one study of college males, 3% reported having a sexual experience with a child when they themselves were over 16 years of age—see review in Seto, 2004). In fact, using victimological, demographic, and population data, McConaghy (1998) estimated that 5% of men and 0.5% of women molest preadult females. Finally, others have attempted to estimate the prevalence using criminal justice statistics such as sexual offense convictions—with 1–2% of the male population estimated to be convicted of a sexual offense eventually (Bradford et al., 2007). Holmes (1991) reports that the average number of paraphilias is 4.8 per person; and other authors have suggested that, although multiple paraphilias are often present in a single individual, one paraphilia typically becomes and remains dominant until another replaces it (Arrigo & Purcell, 2001). The case of Jeffrey Dahmer appropriately illustrates how the coexistence of multiple paraphilias may progress over time.

Theoretical Conceptualizations

Though the paraphilias are considered only one type or group of sexual disorders, their overrepresentation among sexual disorders in the literature on crime and violence will make them the focus of the present chapter. Furthermore, it is beneficial to examine their theoretical conceptualizations separately, as etiological mechanisms—from different theoretical perspectives—can actually vary quite markedly.

Voyeurism (Voyeuristic Disorder)

For the voyeur, the focus of the paraphilia is the act of observing others (usually strangers) who are nude, undressing, or engaging in sexual activity. Generally, no sexual interaction with the observed other is sought—the act of observation ("peeping") alone is for sexual gratification. Orgasm (usually achieved through masturbation) may occur during the voyeurism or afterwards in response to the memory of the event, and, though the voyeur often fantasizes about a sexual encounter with the observed other, this rarely occurs in reality. In severe forms of voyeurism, peeping becomes the sole form of sexual behavior. Voyeurism tends to be chronic, with onset generally occurring before 15 years of age (APA, 2000, 2013). According to Aggrawal (2009), voyeurs may be male or female and may observe either male or female victims. This author also proposes a theoretical classification system of voyeurism based on a continuum from innocuous to dangerous: pseudovoyeurs (who are content with fantasies of voyeurism but not bold enough to engage in the actual activity), opportunistic voyeurs (who take some risk of peeping to satisfy their latent desires when an opportunity arises), computer voyeurs (who use computers to engage in online sexual activities and view explicit images on the Internet—often breaking various laws in doing so), video voyeurs (who set up complicated equipment to view victims naked, disrobing, or engaging in sexual intercourse in bathrooms, bedrooms, or other intimate places—a criminal offense in most jurisdictions), classical voyeurs (who meet the DSM-IV-TR criteria for voyeurism), and criminal voyeurs (who also engage in serious sexual offenses and become aggressive sexually with women and children). In an earlier review, Smith (1976) characterized the voyeur as male—relatively young and of low socioeconomic status—who is not sociosexually retarded but a sociosexual "late bloomer" and prone to minor rather than major crimes.

Paraphilias in general, and voyeurism in particular, likely develop from a complex interplay of biological, psychological, and social factors—no single factor seems to account for their etiology (Aggrawal, 2009). The classical psychoanalytic view of perversions is rooted in drive theory. Freud (1905/1962) originally defined perversions as the negative of neuroses, with the latter representing transformed (desexualized) unconscious perverse fantasies and the former being conscious fantasies expressed directly in ego-syntonic (compatible with the self), pleasurable behaviors. Others viewed perversions as fixations or regressions to infantile stages of psychosexual development, which persist into adulthood (as ritualized procedures that become the only means for genital orgasm). They proposed that castration anxiety prevents orgasm through conventional genital intercourse, and perversions thus serve to deny castration (Gabbard, 2005).

According to Freud (1905/1962), perversions are complex and multilayered, and "active" perversions may unconsciously co-occur with their "passive" counterparts—like opposite sides of the same coin: e.g., the sadist has a masochistic core, and the voyeur is unconsciously an exhibitionist (Gabbard, 2005). Other psychoanalytic explanations include paraphilias as fantasies of adult triumph over childhood humiliation and degradation by parents or as instances of defiance and independence—through sexual expression—from an overbearing and controlling internal representation of the mother. Paraphilias have also been explained as the acting out of the unconscious psychological drama stemming from the parents' erotic desires and conflicts—"scripts" that are "written" by the parents and internalized by the child (object relations). Additionally, paraphilias have been seen, from the psychoanalytic perspective, as an attempt to restore the integrity and cohesiveness of the self when threatened by abandonment or separation, by a sense of inner deadness and fear of self-disintegration, or by another painful emotional state (self psychology) or as the consequence of an inability to tolerate the "otherness" of a separate person (i.e., as complex, real, and different from oneself), wherein the perversion becomes a way to relate to yet bypass a genuine connection with another using seduction, domination, and exploitation. Many such individuals experienced intimacy as dangerous or deadly during childhood, and avoid it for the rest of their lives. An example is *infantilism*, or adult baby syndrome (dressing as a baby, wearing diapers, and acting as a child), which is performed to coerce others into a quasi-maternal role that utterly negates their subjectivity (Gabbard, 2005). Recent research has also shown that perverse fantasies are actually common in women. It is thought that female paraphilias involve unconscious themes of separation, abandonment, and loss; as an example, some women who suffered childhood sexual abuse may adopt an exaggerated stereotype of female sexiness in an attempt to inflict vengeance upon men and reassure themselves of their femaleness (Gabbard, 2005). The reasons an individual may prefer one perverse fantasy or behavior are not entirely clear. Different paraphilias may be present simultaneously in the same person, and some individuals shift from one paraphilia to another sequentially over time (Gabbard, 2005).

Behavioral theorists have attempted to explain the development of paraphilias (in general) in terms of classical and operant conditioning processes. Krafft-Ebing (1886/1965) observed that many male sexual offenders had a fear of adult women that precluded them from utilizing normal sexual outlets. According to behavioral theory, sexual deviations such as paraphilias may be explained by conditioning processes. Any stimulus—whether circumstantial (e.g., the particular time or place that masturbation or intercourse is usually engaged in) or deliberate (e.g., the real or fantasized sexual situation, such as normal intercourse or wearing female undergarments)—that regularly precedes orgasm by the appropriate time interval becomes more and more sexually exciting. It is believed that the prospective paraphiliac chooses to masturbate to his or her particular fantasy rather than that of more normative intercourse because the precipitating incident has stronger initial stimulus value as a masturbatory fantasy. Its power might derive from being the individual's first *real* sexual experience (as opposed to accounts from others) or from the fact that the individual believes a normal sex life is not possible for him or her. Additionally, normal interests during regular masturbation may develop into deviant ones because memory-based fantasies are subject to the usual distortions and selection of cues that occur during the usual psychological processes of recall. Certain cues become more and more dominant (and thus more stimulating) during the conditioning process while other sexual stimuli become deconditioned, so the sexual interest becomes more and more specific (McGuire et al., 1965).

From a neurobiological perspective, brain damage stemming from biological processes can lead to a multitude of sexual abnormalities depending on the location and extent of the brain tissue involved. These include hypersexuality (e.g., promiscuity, seductiveness, excessive or public masturbation, exhibitionism, rape, voyeurism, and even penile mutilation), as well as sexual jealousy, homosexual aggression, sodomy, and even violent and aggressive sexual behavior. Biological processes can include neuropathologies such as the Kluver-Bucy syndrome (resulting from bilateral lesions to the temporal lobe), Huntington's disease, epilepsy (especially of the temporal lobes), and traumatic brain injury (Britton, 1998; Graber et al., 1982; Hucker et al., 1988). Neurobiological explanations for paraphilias in general have been based partially upon studies of sexual offenders (including those with paraphilias—e.g., Graber et al., 1982), which demonstrated structural, functional, and neuropsychological deficits in frontal and temporal lobe regions. Additionally, studies of individuals with brain injury who later became hypersexual or sexually disinhibited have reported injuries to medial basal-frontal or diencephalic regions of the brain (Miller et al., 1986) and have presented imaging findings of periventricular white matter abnormalities and widespread cerebral atrophy (Britton, 1998). Furthermore, altered sexual preference may also follow injuries to limbic system structures (Britton, 1998). Animal studies have also suggested increased sexual drive to be associated with neurotransmitters such as norepinephrine and dopamine and with stimulation within areas of the brain such as the septal region (Miller et al., 1986).

Several theoretic perspectives contribute to an understanding of voyeurism in particular. Considered the reverse side of exhibitionism, voyeurism also involves violating a strange woman's privacy and is a secret and aggressive victory over the female sex. Psychoanalytic theorists such as Fenichel (1945, in Gabbard, 2005) propose that voyeurism stems from a fixation on witnessing or overhearing parental sexual intercourse (the primal scene) in childhood—a traumatic event that causes castration anxiety and leads the child to reenact the event over and over in an attempt to master the passively experienced trauma. Others (see R. S. Smith, 1976) have proposed that the voyeur searches from woman to woman trying to find a woman with a penis, in order to deny that castration exists. Voyeurism may also be a displaced form of aggression—an unconscious defense mechanism against guilt for wanting to be directly destructive to women (Gabbard, 2005). Furthermore, Smith (1976) emphasizes the voyeuristic characteristics of troilism (the sharing of a sexual partner with another person while one looks on) and coprophilia (an affinity for filth, feces, and urine), wherein sexual gratification is achieved from looking rather than doing. From a psychoanalytic standpoint, troilism may represent heterosexual identification with the person performing the sexual act on another, the homosexual identification with the woman in receiving the phallus of the man, or an incestuous identification (i.e., vicariously partaking of mother, sister, or daughter through identification with the involved male). The classical psychoanalytic interpretation of coprophilia is that feces represent the penis (Smith, 1976).[1] Behavioral theorists propose that voyeurism can be explained through classical and operant conditioning processes (Aggrawal, 2009). For example, the viewing of a naked woman (unconditioned stimulus) through a window (conditioned stimulus) causes sexual arousal (initially an unconditioned but, subsequently, a conditioned response), or masturbating to the point of orgasm when viewing the woman in that situation can be positive reinforcement in terms of sexual gratification or negative reinforcement in terms of the reduction of stress or negative emotion.

Exhibitionism (Exhibitionistic Disorder)

For the exhibitionist, the focus of the paraphilia is the exposure of his or her genitals to a stranger. Individuals may masturbate while exposing themselves or while fantasizing about doing so; if an individual acts on these urges, further attempts at sexual contact with the stranger is generally not likely. The individual may have a desire to surprise and shock the stranger or may fantasize that the stranger will also become sexually aroused. Exhibitionism usually begins before 18 years of age though onset may occur later. The condition may decline in severity after age 40, as few arrests for exhibitionism are made in older age groups (APA, 2000; in the DSM-5, the course of exhibitionistic disorder is reported to likely vary with age; APA, 2013).

From a psychoanalytic perspective, the exhibitionist reassures himself that he is not castrated by exposing his genitals to female strangers. Shock reactions produced by his behaviors reduce castration anxiety and provide a feeling of power over women. In fact, exhibitionism may often follow a humiliating situation at the hands of a woman after which the man avenges the humiliation by shocking women strangers. Also, the exhibitionist may regain a sense of self-worth and masculinity by exposing his genitals; frequently, these men admit to being profoundly insecure about their masculinity. Others (Stoller, 1985, in Gabbard, 2005) suggest "existence anxiety"—not castration anxiety—as a motivation for exhibitionism; according to this idea, humiliation becomes a threat to core gender identity. Exhibitionists, feeling they have made no impact on family members, resort to exhibitionism to be noticed and to reverse traumatic situations in childhood (Gabbard, 2005).

Comparatively few studies have examined biological bases for exhibitionism, and results are mixed. However, some evidence indicates that monoamines—particularly dopamine—may play a role in exhibitionism (Aggrawal, 2009). McGuire and colleagues (1965) discuss the cases of two patients who became exhibitionistic through conditioning processes. According to these authors, the two patients separately reported being surprised by passing women while urinating in semipublic areas. Each felt embarrassed and left hurriedly but later realized the sexual significance of the encounter and masturbated frequently to the memory of the incident. Over time, by conditioning, the thought of self-exposure acquired such strong sexual stimulus value that each patient subsequently engaged in public exposure, even though neither had done so before the incident.

---

1. According to a secret wartime report on Adolph Hitler (Lancer, 1972, in Smith, 1976), informants indicated that Hitler, a coprophiliac, never was known to have had sexual intercourse with a woman. Instead, he required his intimate female friends to degrade him, kick him, and especially squat over him and urinate and defecate on him. Lancer reports that Hitler's niece, Geli Raubal, indicated how extremely important it was for him that she squat over him in a manner that allowed him to "see everything." Lancer interprets this as a feces equals fetus equation, derived from Hitler's childhood when his mother was pregnant with his younger brother, Edmund.

BOX 8.1 COURTSHIP DISORDER THEORY

According to courtship disorder theory, a normal individual spends roughly equal time, resources, and energy in each of these four stages. The paraphiliac spends all energies in one stage, "shortcircuiting" the other three stages.

	Normal Courtship Stage	Normal Behavior	Abnormal (Paraphilic) Behavior
Precontact Stages of Courtship	1. Search for a partner	Suitable partner searched for and selected by viewing multiple prospective partners	**Voyeur** masturbates while surreptitiously viewing partner.
	2. Pretactile interaction	Looking, smiling, posturing, and talking to a prospective partner	**Exhibitionist** masturbates while showing his genitals. **Telephone scatologist** masturbates while talking to prospective partner.
Contact Stages of Courtship	3. Tactile interaction	Petting, touching, kissing	**Toucher** grabs intimate parts of prospective partner. **Frotteur** rubs penis against victim's buttocks or other body part.
	4. Genital union	Normal penile-vaginal copulation	**Biastophile** or **preferential rapist** rapes prospective partner immediately.

Source: Adapted from Aggrawal (2009).

Frotteurism (Frotteuristic Disorder)

The term **frotteurism** is derived from "*frotter*," a French word of unknown origin that means "to rub, chafe, stroke, or caress" (Aggrawal, 2009). For the frotteur (i.e., one who performs the activity), the focus of the paraphilia is the touching and rubbing against a nonconsenting person. Often the behavior occurs in crowded places (e.g., shopping malls, elevators, public transportation vehicles, busy sidewalks, and public festivals)—which allow the frotteur to easily conceal his rubbing behavior under the pretext of navigating through a large crowd or a crowded bus or train and to more easily escape detection and arrest. The frotteur's activities generally include either rubbing his genitals against the thighs or buttocks of the victim or fondling her genitalia or breasts with his hands (though some refer to this latter behavior as *toucherism*); he usually fantasizes an exclusive, caring relationship with the victim while doing so. However, once the act is completed, he realizes escape is necessary to avoid prosecution. Frotteurism usually begins by adolescence and is typically performed by a young male, aged 15–25, toward a female (gradually, frequency declines after 25). In fact, the behavior is not described in females in the literature though there is thought to be no reason precluding a female counterpart (Aggrawal, 2009; APA, 2000, 2013).

Most scholars think that the best etiological explanation for frotteurism is courtship disorder theory (see Box 8.1), though other theoretical explanations have been offered. For example, psychoanalytic theorists have proposed that an individual may develop frotteurism as a reaction to the trauma of having been inappropriately touched or rubbed at an earlier age. From a neurobiological perspective, Simpson and colleagues (1999) found that 6.5% ($n = 29$) of an Australian sample of traumatic brain injury patients ($n = 445$) committed a total of 128 sexual offenses after injury—most commonly frotteurism and toucherism (i.e., 64.8% of the offenses). All offenders had sustained closed head injuries to various brain regions, including the frontal, temporal, and parietal lobes, as well as other subcortical structures. Additionally, the published case of a man with Parkinson's disease who developed frotteurism after dopaminergic treatment suggests—along with other preliminary evidence—that dopaminergic medications may disinhibit preexisting sexual fantasies that could lead to frotteuristic (and other paraphilic) behaviors (Wilson, 2010).

Sadism (Sexual Sadism Disorder)

The term "sadism" is derived from the name of the eighteenth-century French aristocrat and writer, Donatien Alphonse François, Marquis de Sade—most known for his erotic works and libertine sexual lifestyle involving the abuse and mistreatment of others. According to the DSM-IV-TR, the sexual sadist derives sexual excitement from behaviors involving the physical or psychological suffering (including humiliation) of the victim. These sadistic fantasies may bother some individuals with this paraphilia, who may invoke them during sexual activity but otherwise not act on them, relying for gratification on fantasies of complete control over the victim, who is terrified while anticipating the forthcoming sadistic behavior. Others do act on them, either with a consenting partner (perhaps a sexual masochist) who is willingly harmed or humiliated or with nonconsenting victims. Sadistic fantasies or behaviors may involve dominance (e.g., forcing the victim to crawl or be caged), restraint, blindfolding, and physical violence (e.g., paddling, spanking, whipping, pinching, beating, burning, administering electrical shocks, raping, cutting, stabbing, strangling, torture, mutilation, or killing). Sexual sadism is generally chronic, with sadistic sexual fantasies likely present in childhood and the onset of behaviors by early adulthood. When practiced with nonconsenting partners, the behaviors will likely continue until the sexual sadist is apprehended. Although some sexual sadists may not escalate the potential for inflicting more serious physical harm as time goes on, it is common for others to increase the severity of their sadistic behaviors over time. Severe forms of this paraphilia, especially when combined with antisocial personality disorder, are associated with serious injury and death of victims (APA, 2000). Like other paraphilic and normophilic behavior, increased age is likely to have a reducing effect on this disorder (APA, 2013).

Psychoanalytic writers have proposed that sexual sadists are often unconsciously attempting to reverse childhood scenarios of physical or sexual abuse victimization. By inflicting their own childhood experiences onto others, they are able to gain both revenge and a sense of mastery over the childhood trauma. Stoller (1991, in Gabbard, 2005) found a majority of sadomasochistic club members who practiced body piercing to have been hospitalized as children for illnesses that required treatment involving continual injections. Object relations theorists propose that sadism stems from an internal object relationship wherein the self-representation must forcefully overcome the resistance of a withholding and distant object (Gabbard, 2005).

From a behavioral perspective, Krafft-Ebing (1886/1965) earlier proposed a factor in some sexual deviations that is strikingly similar to what has more recently been referred to as **accidental conditioning**. For example, boys when spanked may experience penile sensations by chance because of being held face down across an adult's lap, for example, or simply from friction against their own clothing. These can subsequently lead to an associative pairing of erotic pleasure with spanking, then to a spanking fetish, and, in some cases, to sadism or masochism. Most boys who do experience such sensations, however, do not become fixated on these incidental experiences and progress toward normative sexuality. MacCulloch and colleagues (1983) argue that the *wish to control* is the primary motivating force in sadism. Based upon their examination of 16 male psychiatric hospital patients, these authors propose that the sadistic offender's repetitive sadistic masturbatory fantasies transform into overt behavior as the individual feels impelled to seek and create increasingly dangerous real-life rehearsals or behavioral "try-outs" of the fantasies, which progressively intensify in order to remain a source of arousal and pleasure. Typically, in the case of a fantasy-rape sequence, several months or years of masturbation (several times a week) preceded a try-out of an early part of the fantasy sequence, such as following a girl on a dark night or in a lonely place. Subsequently, that real-life vignette is incorporated in further self-masturbatory fantasy and used in the complete fantasy sequence, which might end in a serious assault or murder. Most offenders were characterized by a significant lack of sexual experience and social contact with the preferred sex, to the point that their sexual fantasy lives and behavioral try-outs were their only source of sexual arousal. Others had no such deficits yet still masturbated to the sadistic fantasies and required the use of the fantasies to become sexually aroused during normal intercourse with their partners.

From a neurobiological perspective, Hucker and colleagues (1988) examined brain damage and dysfunction in a Canadian sample of 51 men with charges or convictions of sexual assaults on adult women and 36 offender controls who were charged or convicted of nonviolent, nonsexual crimes. Sexual offenders were grouped as sadists ($n = 22$), nonsadistic sexual aggressors ($n = 21$), and unclassified ($n = 8$); and all participants received a CT scan and were administered the Luria-Nebraska Neuropsychological Battery (LNNB). Results indicated a greater proportion of right temporal lobe abnormalities (i.e., right temporal horn dilatations) in sadistic sexual offenders compared to in nonsadists and controls. Additionally, nonsadistic sexual offenders demonstrated more global neuropsychological impairment than both other groups (though no group differences in IQ were revealed). Despite the nonoverlapping imaging and neuropsychological findings, results provide additional support for underlying cerebral dysfunction in some forms of sexually aberrant behavior, including sadistic sexual offending. Furthermore, Money (1990) proposes that, in sexual sadism, limbic system dysfunction may cause the brain to transmit messages of attack simultaneously with messages of sexual arousal and mating behavior. According to Money, sexual sadism is an episodic (paroxysmal) dysfunction rather than continuous—parallel in many ways to nonconvulsive epileptic seizures (i.e., psychomotor or temporal lobe seizures). In fact, epilepsy is found comorbid with sexual sadism (as well as with other paraphilias) in some individuals. Money also identifies contributing causes to sexual sadism as genetic predisposition, hormonal functioning, pathological relationships, sexual abuse, and syndrome overlap (i.e., with temporal lobe epilepsy, bipolar disorder, schizoid and antisocial personality traits, and dissociative identity disorder).

Masochism (Sexual Masochism Disorder)

The term "masochism" was coined by Krafft-Ebing and derived from the name of a nineteenth-century Austrian writer, Leopold von Sacher-Masoch, who himself was both a poet and practitioner of male masochism (Gabbard, 2005; Krafft-Ebing, 1886/1965). The sexual masochist, on balance, derives sexual excitement from acts involving humiliation, restraint, beating, or other forms of suffering. These masochistic fantasies may bother some individuals with this paraphilia, who may not act on them but only invoke them during sexual activity (e.g., in fantasies of being raped while restrained by others without possibility of escape). Others act on them by themselves (e.g., binding themselves, piercing themselves with needles, shocking themselves with electricity, or self-mutilation) or with a partner. Partnered activities involve restraint (physical bondage); blindfolding (sensory bondage); physical violence, such as paddling, spanking, whipping, beating, electrical shocks, cutting, and "pinning and piercing" (infibulations); and humiliation, for example, being urinated or defecated on, forced to crawl and bark like a dog, forced to cross-dress, treated like a helpless infant and clothed in diapers (infantilism), or verbally abused. *Hypoxyphilia*—one particularly dangerous type of sexual masochism—involves sexual excitement through oxygen deprivation (i.e., via chest compression, noose, ligature, plastic bag, mask, or chemical), which may be practiced alone or with a partner. Accidental deaths may occur, resulting from equipment malfunction, improperly placed nooses or ligatures, or other mistakes. Some sexually masochistic males may also have other types of fetishism and even sadism. Sexual masochism is generally chronic, with the individual usually repeating the same masochistic act, and masochistic sexual fantasies are likely present in childhood, with the onset of behaviors by early adulthood. Although some sexual masochists may not escalate the potential for self-injury as time goes on, others may increase the severity of their masochistic behaviors over time or during stressful periods, potentially resulting in serious injury or death (APA, 2000).

From a psychoanalytic perspective, self psychologists would explain sexual masochism as a frantic attempt to avoid a sense of inner deadness and self-disintegration. Though masochists may appear self-destructive, their masochistic behaviors may actually be experienced as self-restorative, in that physical pain and abuse at the hands of others allows them to feel as though they exist and are connected to others. Object relationists propose masochism to be an acting out of an internal object relationship wherein the object only responds when the self is humiliated. Those requiring humiliation or pain for sexual arousal may also be reenacting childhood experiences of abuse. Other psychoanalytic writers have proposed sexual masochism to be a sacrifice: a "lesser evil" in place of castration, a deserved punishment for conflictual sadistic desires, or a defense against separation anxiety—an abusive relationship being better than no relationship at all (Gabbard, 2005).

Fetishism (Fetishistic Disorder)

Fetishism involves the sexualization of inanimate or nonliving objects (the "fetish"), which commonly include women's undergarments, stockings, shoes, boots, other types of clothing and apparel, or a nongenital body part (APA, 2000; Gabbard, 2005). The fetishist often masturbates with the fetish object (i.e., while holding, rubbing, or smelling it) or may ask a sexual partner to wear it during their sexual activities. The fetish is usually required or strongly preferred for sexual arousal, and males may experience erectile dysfunction in its absence (APA, 2000). Some persons with fetishistic disorder may procure extensive collections of highly desired fetish objects (APA, 2013). Fetishism tends to be chronic once established, and it usually begins by adolescence, though the object may have acquired special significance earlier in childhood (APA, 2000). Fetishism tends to fluctuate in intensity and frequency of urges or in terms of behavior over time (APA, 2013).

Psychoanalytic and neurobiological contributions to the understanding of fetishism have been offered. Some psychoanalytic theorists viewed castration anxiety as being at the root of fetishism. Freud proposed that the chosen fetish object unconsciously symbolized the "female penis," a displacement used to overcome castration anxiety wherein a man's awareness of the female genitals increased his fear of losing his own genitals and becoming a woman (Gabbard, 2005). Grenacre (1970, 1979, in Gabbard, 2005) also proposed castration anxiety to be central to fetishism, though stating that its origins were much earlier: Traumatic and severely problematic mother-infant relationships in the first months of life produced an infant unable to be soothed by the mother or transitional objects (e.g., blankets), and the child thus requires a reliable, durable, unyielding and unchanging object to experience body integrity. Later in life, when the boy or adult male is concerned about genital integrity, the fetish functions much like a transitional object. Similarly, but from a self-psychology perspective, Kohut (1977, in Gabbard, 2005) proposed the fetish (e.g., women's undergarments) to be a substitute for an earlier unavailable self object (i.e., a traumatically unavailable mother in childhood). Although the patient experiences helplessness about his actual mother, he is able to maintain total control over this nonhuman substitute so that, outwardly, though there appears to be an intense sexual need for the fetish object, inside this is actually severe anxiety about the loss of one's sense of self (Gabbard, 2005). Finally, earlier studies have suggested fetishism and transvestism are the paraphilias most commonly associated with temporal lobe abnormalities (Hucker et al., 1988), though the specific neurobiological mechanisms underlying fetishism remain largely unexplored.

Pedophilia (Pedophilic Disorder)

For the pedophile, sexual excitement stems from sexual activity with a prepubescent child usually 13 years of age or younger; by definition, the pedophile is16 years of age or older and at least 5 years older than the child (APA, 2000). According to the DSM-IV-TR, persons with pedophilia usually report being aroused by children of a particular age, and they may be attracted to only males, females, or children of both genders. Those preferring females generally favor 8- to 10-year-olds; those attracted to boys prefer them slightly older. Female-victim pedophilia is more commonly reported than male-victim pedophilia. Some pedophilic persons are sexually aroused only by children while others may also be attracted to adults. Pedophilic individuals who act on their urges may engage in the full range of sexual behaviors with children: some limiting their behaviors to milder sexual acts such as undressing, touching, or fondling the child and others engaging in more severe forms, such as oral copulation, genital intercourse, or rape with foreign objects, with varying degrees of force. Such behaviors are often rationalized by the pedophilic individual as being beneficial to the child (having educational value or being sexually pleasurable) or as having been deserved because the child was behaving in a seductive manner. As pedophilia is generally ego-syntonic (i.e., psychologically compatible with the self), those with this disorder do not often experience significant distress (APA, 2000). Furthermore, because individuals with pedophilic disorder may deny having impulses or fantasies involving children, they may also deny feelings of subjective distress (APA, 2013).

According to the DSM-IV-TR, pedophilic individuals may victimize their own children or other children inside or outside their families. They may use complicated schemes to gain access to children (e.g., befriending or marrying the child's mother, taking in foster children from third-world countries, or kidnapping). To prevent disclosure, they may use threats or be especially attentive to gain a child victim's trust and loyalty. Pedophilia usually begins in adolescence (though some report not becoming aroused by children until middle adulthood), and it is generally chronic—especially when involving an attraction to males. Those with a preference for males are characterized by recidivism rates that are approximately twice the rates of those preferring females. Pedophilic behaviors often covary with psychosocial stress (APA, 2000). Some have proposed a distinction between pedophilia and hebephilia—sexual attraction toward postpubescent children (Marshall, 2006, in Bradford et al., 2007).

Historically, adult-adolescent heterosexual interactions have been not only tolerated but actually normative during some periods—with reported practitioners including St. Augustine, the prophet Muhammad, and Gandhi. Romeo and Juliet—history's archetypal heterosexual lovers—would be classified as pedophile and victim by current standards, as Romeo was an adult, according to scholars, and Juliet was 13 years of age. In fact, until 1929, the age of sexual consent and marriage for girls set by the English legal code was 12; until more recently, it was 14 in most U.S. states (McConaghy, 1998). Today, most U.S. states set their age of consent at 16, although a few states use 14, 17, or 18 as their official ages of consent. In countries around the world, the age of consent varies from 12 to 18. Several authors have discussed the occurrence of sanctioned adult-child sex in different cultures and time periods. For example, the Sambian tribe in Papua, New Guinea, subjects its prepubescent boys to an initiation process involving ritualistic fellatio on older boys. In this tribe, it is believed that semen assists in building up the boy's life force (*tingus*) and is necessary to reach puberty. Younger boys are coerced to participate due to fear of punishment, and, eventually (when older), expect to receive fellatio from younger boys beginning their own initiation. Other tribal groups in Micronesia, such as the Etoro and the Kaluli, are reported to engage in a similar practice (Seto, 2004).

The existence of historical Western laws against adult-child sex suggests that it occurred and concerned those attempting to regulate such behavior. Ancient Roman law, for example, fixed the minimum age for marriage at 12 and 14 for girls and boys, respectively—the same minimum ages fixed by the Roman Catholic Church. Adult-child sex, child prostitution, and incest have also been documented in the (post-Roman) Byzantine Empire (Seto, 2004).

In the classical psychoanalytic view, the pedophilic individual is impotent and weak, seeking child sexual objects because relations with children involve less resistance or anxiety than those with adult partners, which allows the individual to avoid castration anxiety. Additionally, the child may be a narcissistic object choice for the pedophilic individual—that is, the individual may see a child as a mirror image of himself as a child (Gabbard, 2005). A pedophile may engage in sexual activity with a prepubescent child to strengthen his own fragile self-esteem. These individuals may choose professions dealing with children in order to maintain positive self-regard through the idealization from the children—who are often idealized by the pedophile in return. Sexual activity with children thus involves the unconscious fantasy of merging with an ideal object or the restoration of a young, idealized self; and it may become a way to ward off anxiety about aging and death (Gabbard, 2005). The unconscious processes underlying pedophilia may also be closely related to those of sadism. The vehicle of vengeance is the sexual conquest of the child—pedophiles themselves were often sexually abused as children (Fagan et al., 2005, in Gabbard, 2005), and transforming passive traumas into actively perpetrated victimizations may contribute to their sense of triumph and power (Gabbard, 2005).

Power and aggression also figure prominently in the concerns of pedophiles who engage exclusively in incestuous sexual relationships with their own children or stepchildren. Often feeling unloved by their wives, these men portray themselves as victims in order to elicit caretaking responses from their children. Appearing as martyrs on the surface, they are characterized underneath by a desire for control and power over sexual partners. They harbor extreme hostility toward women and often think of their penis as a weapon to be used in vengeful acts against them. Some report erections produced by feelings of intense anger (Gabbard, 2005).

Various authors have made distinctions between the characteristics of victims and offenders, on the one hand, and offense behaviors, on the other, in fixated versus regressed pedophilia (Gabbard, 2005) and in heterosexual versus homosexual pedophilia (McConaghy, 1998). Others distinguish between the definitional features of pedophilia and of child sexual abuse and child molestation (Aggrawal, 2009; see Table 8.2). Further proposed subtypes of pedophilia include true versus opportunistic (including fixated versus regressed pedophilia and pedophilic versus nonpedophilic child molesters), exclusive versus nonexclusive, and incest versus nonfamilial (Cohen & Galynker, 2002). Some evidence suggests that number of victims and frequency of acts may vary according to pedophilia subtype. For example, in a study of 453 pedophilic offenders recruited via outpatient sex offender programs, Abel and Osborne (1992, in Cohen & Galynker, 2002) found offenders admitted to, on average, 236 acts

Table 8.2 Pedophilia Comparisons

Fixated Versus Regressed Pedophiles[a]	
Fixated	**Regressed**
• Sexually attracted to younger individuals from the time of adolescence	• Not demonstrating sexual attraction to younger individuals until adulthood
• Generally offends against boys (usually tending to have many victims and preying upon boys who live outside the home)	• More often offends against girls (typically having fewer victims and carrying out offenses in the home as part of an incestuous relationship)
• Focuses primarily on boys	• May also demonstrate sexual attraction toward adult women
• Prognosis considered worse	• Prognosis considered better
Heterosexual Versus Homosexual Pedophiles[b]	
Heterosexual	**Homosexual**
• Few victims	• Many victims (up to hundreds)
• Offenses repeated with same victim for months or years	• Offenses commonly occur only once with same victim
• Offenses occur in victim's home	• Offenses occur outside of victim's home
• Mean age of victim is 8 years	• Mean age of victim is 10 years
• Offender attracted to older women	• Offender not attracted to adults of either sex
• Offender commonly married	• Offender single
• Behavior commenced in adulthood	• Behavior commenced in adolescence
• Often low SES, unemployed, alcoholic, lower IQ, psychopathic	• Stable or employed, average IQ but "immature," prefers company of children, not interested in friendships with adults
Pedophilia Versus Child Sexual Abuse[c]	
Pedophilia	**Child Sexual Abuse/Child Molestation**
• Pedophilia represents a mental disorder, listed in the DSM-IV-TR	• Child sexual abuse and child molestation do not represent mental disorders. The former is a V Code in the DSM-IV-TR while the latter is not mentioned.
• Interest of the pedophile is fixated on prepubescent children; the pedophile shows no or minimal sexuo-erotic interest in adults	• Sexuo-erotic interest is primarily in adults, but this individual molests children, if given an opportunity
• Refers to psychological propensities only; the pedophile's psychological propensity may or may not have been acted upon; not all pedophiles actually molest children	• Refers to actual sexual contact
• Pedophile has an ongoing pattern of sexual attraction to children	• Child sexual abuse is situational; may be a one-time incident; does not manifest an ongoing pattern of sexual attraction to children

Sources: [a]Adapted from Gabbard (2005). [b]Adapted from McConaghy (1998, p. 259). [c]Adapted from Aggrawal (2009, p. 48).

and 148 victims per offender. Those who molested nonrelated boys committed a median of 10.1 acts, incest offenders a median of 4.4 acts against females and 5.2 acts against males, and offenders against unrelated girls a median of 1.4 acts per offender. Means were much larger than medians: molesters of unrelated boys averaged 150.2 victims, molesters of unrelated girls averaged 19.8 victims, and incest offenders averaged 1.7 male victims and 1.8 female victims per offender.

The pathological nature of pedophilia—from a biological standpoint—derives from its causing the individual to be uninterested in those who are reproductively viable (i.e., sexually mature, opposite-sex partners). A preference for infertile sexual partners could be considered evolutionarily disadvantageous and represent a disruption in the mechanisms underlying sexual age preferences; thus, pedophilia, in its stronger forms, would meet Wakefield's (1992—see Chapter 2) conceptualization of a mental disorder (Seto, 2004). A modest but growing body of literature has examined biological factors associated with pedophilia, which may provide clues into how this disorder develops. For example, alterations in hormonal functioning related to cortisol, serotonin, and luteinizing hormone-releasing hormone (LHRH) have characterized pedophiles compared to nonpedophilic men (Aggrawal, 2009). Regarding LHRH, Gaffney and Berlin (1984) found increased sensitivity to this hormone in the pituitary glands of pedophilic men, suggesting a hypothalamic-pituitary-gonadal dysfunction. Compared to men with nonpedophilic paraphilias and to normal controls, pedophiles had significantly increased responses to administered doses of LHRH, which resulted in marked elevations of luteinizing hormone (LH) in this group. This finding is noteworthy, given the role of LH in the stimulation and release of testosterone from the Leydig cells of the testes (Aggrawal, 2009). Interestingly, Schiffer and colleagues (2009), after treating a pedophilic individual for three years with a long-acting LHRH agonist, found in this individual a reduction in deviant fantasies and masturbatory frequency over time (more than 90% of baseline measures) and reduced neuronal responses to visual sexual stimuli using fMRI. Results are among the first evidence for the potential effectiveness of LHRH agonists in the suppression of paraphilic urges and arousal.

Other studies have suggested a neurological component to pedophilia. For example, Cantor and colleagues (2005) found in individuals with pedophilia increased rates of non-right-handedness, which, when not inherited, may be a marker for developmental neuropathology associated with prenatal or perinatal biological stressors (see also Cantor et al., 2004). These rates were two-fold higher than those seen in men who sexually offended against adults and comparable to rates observed in those with pervasive developmental disorders such as autism. Associations between pedophilia and abnormalities in the ***frontal*** and ***temporal lobes*** have been identified (Aggrawal, 2009), though some authors (e.g., Joyal, Black, & Dassylva, 2007) have noted that basal frontotemporal abnormalities are also associated with other forms of sexual offending and with delinquency and criminality in general. Several ongoing imaging studies have also focused on other brain regions, and more recent work implicates subcortical regions rather than cortical areas. Schiffer and colleagues (2008) compared regional fMRI activations in homosexual pedophiles and healthy homosexual individuals as they viewed sexually arousing images of homosexual and pedophilic content. Results indicated that, although both groups responded to respective stimuli with activations in brain regions associated with processing visual stimuli and emotional content (i.e., occipitotemporal and prefrontal cortices), pedophiles were also characterized by anomalous brain activations in the "reward areas" of the brain (i.e., the thalamus, globus pallidus, caudate nucleus, substantia nigra, and striatum). These brain areas are associated with addictive and stimulus-controlled behavior. Interestingly, in the case reported by Schiffer and colleagues (2009), LHRH agonist treatment of the pedophile appeared to affect functioning in subcortical brain regions associated with the emotional and autonomic aspects of sexual behavioral processing (e.g., the hypothalamus, amygdala, and hippocampus, but not the prefrontal and temporal regions). In a later study, Schiffer and Vonlaufen (2011) found differential patterns of executive dysfunction in pedophilic and nonpedophilic child molesters (*ns* = 15 and 15, respectively). Pedophilic child molesters demonstrated deficits in response inhibition compared to healthy controls ($n = 17$) and to nonsexual offenders ($n = 16$); nonpedophilic child molesters were characterize by more severe executive dysfunction, especially on tests of cognitive flexibility and verbal memory. These results may suggest differential patterns of prefrontal dysfunction in each condition, with the former having more orbitofrontal deficits and the latter deficits in the dorsolateral prefrontal region. Though results may partially explain the behavior of pedophiles and different types of child molesters, further research is needed to understand why, in pedophiles, specific reward areas of the brain are stimulated during pedophilic activities, and why deficits in specific areas of the prefrontal cortex may differentiate pedophilic from nonpedophilic sexual offending against children.

Using a German sample, Sartorius and colleagues (2008) found that, compared to heterosexual male controls ($n = 10$), convicted sex offenders attracted exclusively to young boys ($n = 10$) demonstrated abnormal fMRI amygdala activations when exposed to sexually non-explicit images of adults and children in swimsuits. Although controls had increased amygdala activations in response to images of adult women, pedophilic sex offenders instead were characterized by increased activations to images of children, especially boys in swimsuits. Given the amygdala's role in processing fear and sexual arousal, results may speak to the pedophiles' sexual desire for children or may indicate a fearful reaction to images of boys because sexual desire for them is legally and socially forbidden.

Cooper and colleagues (1990) describe the psychological, psychophysiological, and endocrine characteristics of Ms. K, a 20-year-old female with multiple paraphilias (pedophilia, sexual sadism, zoophilia) and hypersexuality who sexually assaulted two young sisters. Though results indicated normal endocrine functioning, her psychological and physiological arousal profiles were similar to those of a sizable proportion of male child molesters, especially those who perpetrated incest. Hormonal and endocrine factors associated with sexual offending have been discussed. For example, hyperthyroidism has been associated with increased libido, though Ms. K's thyroid appeared to be functioning normally. A weak correlation between increased serum testosterone and physical aggression—with or without a sexual component—has been reported in male offenders. However, in females, a more tenuous relationship between androgens and physical and sexual aggression is evident. For example, Ms. K's serum testosterone levels were within normal limits—though it has been suggested that female hypersexuality may be more caused by "super-sensitive" androgen receptors or the proliferation of these receptors than by testosterone levels per se (Cooper et al., 1990).

Lachman and colleagues (1991) discuss the case of a repeat sexual offender with three abnormalities: Klinefelter's syndrome with karyotype 48, XXXY, a rare condition characterized by two extra X chromosomes; genetically caused mental retardation; and *hypogonadism* (i.e., decreased testicular/endocrine functioning). Reports from several decades ago discussed social and sexual maladjustment associated with Klinefelter's syndrome in its more common variant (karyotype 47, XXY); these maladjustments are thought to arise secondarily from the mental retardation and personality disorders co-occurring with the condition. Interestingly, this particular individual (V.S.) sexually offended against a 13-year-old boy almost two decades after a testicular pulpectomy, a form of castration, and he demonstrated testosterone levels nearly four times those reported in castrated males though still only about half of those reported in normal controls (his level was comparable to that commonly found in pubertal boys). The authors discuss why these abnormally elevated testosterone levels may have occurred after castration but do not specifically implicate testosterone in the patient's sexual offending.

Hendricks and colleagues (1988) compared 16 male psychiatric inpatients charged with sexual molestation of children (aged 14 or younger) to 16 patient controls and 10 volunteer controls using CT head scans and regional cerebral blood flow (rCBF), measured using a Xenon inhalation technique. Results indicated child molesters were characterized by significantly reduced white and gray matter rCBF, particularly in anterior (frontal) compared to posterior sites, and by skulls that were significantly thinner and less dense compared to volunteer controls.

In a recent pilot study using neuropsychological tests of various domains of cognitive functioning, Joyal, Black, and Dassylva (2007) examined 20 male forensic psychiatric hospital patients who were pedophiles ($n = 12$) and rapists ($n = 8$); each had sexually assaulted at least two people. Results indicated that offenders in general demonstrated verbal deficits and lower-order executive dysfunctions, such as impairments in sustained attention and inhibition, but intact higher-order executive functions (i.e., reasoning and cognitive flexibility) and visuospatial processing. Pedophiles were characterized by more severe cognitive impairments than rapists. These results are consistent with a basal frontotemporal deficit profile; however, these authors suggest that this profile is characteristic of delinquency and criminality in general rather than being specific to sexual deviance. Methodological strengths of this study include its comparisons of each offender group's performance to several sources of published normative data across domains of neuropsychological functioning.

Finally, from a behavioral perspective, McGuire and colleagues (1965) present the case of a 40-year-old male patient who became a pedophile through conditioning processes. This patient had normal sexual interests until age 20 but experienced impotency when sexual intercourse was first attempted. While he was in the military in Asia during World War II, his sexual desires were conditioned through masturbation performed by others, his only sexual outlet because of his fear of venereal disease. First prostitutes performed these acts; then, when he moved into the jungle and no prostitutes were available, he used native children of both sexes (he had scruples about having relations with the native married women). Returning home after three years of service, his self-masturbatory fantasies continued to be of masturbation by children, which he eventually succumbed to and acted out with young boys. Married five years later, he had no interest in adult heterosexual relations. Hence, what began as a substitutive sexual behavior eventually became dominant through frequent positive sexual reinforcement.

Transvestism (Transvestic Disorder)

For the transvestic fetishist (traditionally described only in males), sexual excitement is derived from cross-dressing in women's clothing. For most of these men, sexual arousal is produced by the accompanying thought or image of themselves as a female (known as "autogynephilia")—by either fantasizing that they actually are women (with female genitalia) or by merely being dressed as women (with no attention to genitalia). The transvestic male usually keeps a collection of female garments that he uses intermittently to cross-dress, which are arousing primarily as symbols of his femininity. A wide range of transvestic phenomena have been noted—from the wearing of a single item underneath masculine attire (e.g., women's underwear or hosiery) to dressing entirely as females, wearing makeup, and being extensively involved in transvestic subculture. Mannerisms, body habitus, and cross-dressing skill all contribute to how successfully the cross-dressed individual appears to be female; and, when not cross-dressed, these men usually appear unremarkably masculine. The transvestic fetishist prefers heterosexual relations, though he typically has had few sexual partners and may have participated in occasional homosexual acts. Sexual masochism may also be associated with this disorder. Typically, the age of onset for transvestic fetishism is childhood or early adolescence, though cross-dressing behaviors are often not done in public until adulthood. Initially, transvestic fetishism may involve partial or total cross-dressing, and the progression from partial to total cross-dressing is common. The transvestic fetishist's favored article of clothing may become eroticized and used habitually, in masturbation at first and subsequently in intercourse. For some, the motivation for cross-dressing may change temporarily or permanently over time, and sexual arousal in response to cross-dressing may diminish or disappear. In these cases, cross-dressing alleviates anxiety or depression and has a calming effect. Gender dysphoria may emerge in others, especially if they are affected by situational stress. In a small number of individuals, it becomes fixed and can be accompanied by the wish to seek hormonal or surgical reassignment to dress and live permanently as females (APA, 2000). Interestingly, transvestism is defined in almost all studies as psychopathological only in terms of male cross-dressing, suggesting that the phenomenon does not exist in females or is not a problem that is psychopathological in nature (Aggrawal, 2009). Furthermore, paraphilias such as transvestic fetishism appear in more normative contexts for entertainment purposes, such as live performances featuring male cross-dressers (e.g., drag shows).

The classical psychoanalytic view of cross-dressing centers on the idea of identification with the phallic mother. A male child imagines his mother possesses a penis (even if it is not directly observable) and thus overcomes his own castration anxiety by identifying with her (Fenichel, 1945, in Gabbard, 2005). At a more primitive level, the young boy may also identify with the mother to avoid separation anxiety (i.e., the anxiety that he will lose his mother caused by his awareness of genital differences between them and thus their being separate individuals). Transvestites in clinical work have revealed experiencing some degree of fusion with an internal mother object when they cross-dress, which reassures them that they will not lose the soothing maternal presence within. Without exception, these men are heterosexual, and most are well-adjusted in all other respects (Gabbard, 2005). According to Stoller (1968, in Aggrawal, 2009), male transvestites tend to have (1) a mother with an unconscious wish to feminize her young son, possibly as an unconscious expression of her own homosexuality; (2) a father (in such cases) who is either a coconspirator by remaining silent and passive or absent entirely; (3) castration anxiety, compensated for by transforming themselves into phallic women; and (4) an efficient way (transvestism) of dealing with very strong feminine identification (i.e., channeling it through feminine dress) without altogether losing a sense of masculinity (i.e., the "insignia of maleness," or the penis).

BOX 8.2 TRANSVESTISM AND SERIAL MURDER

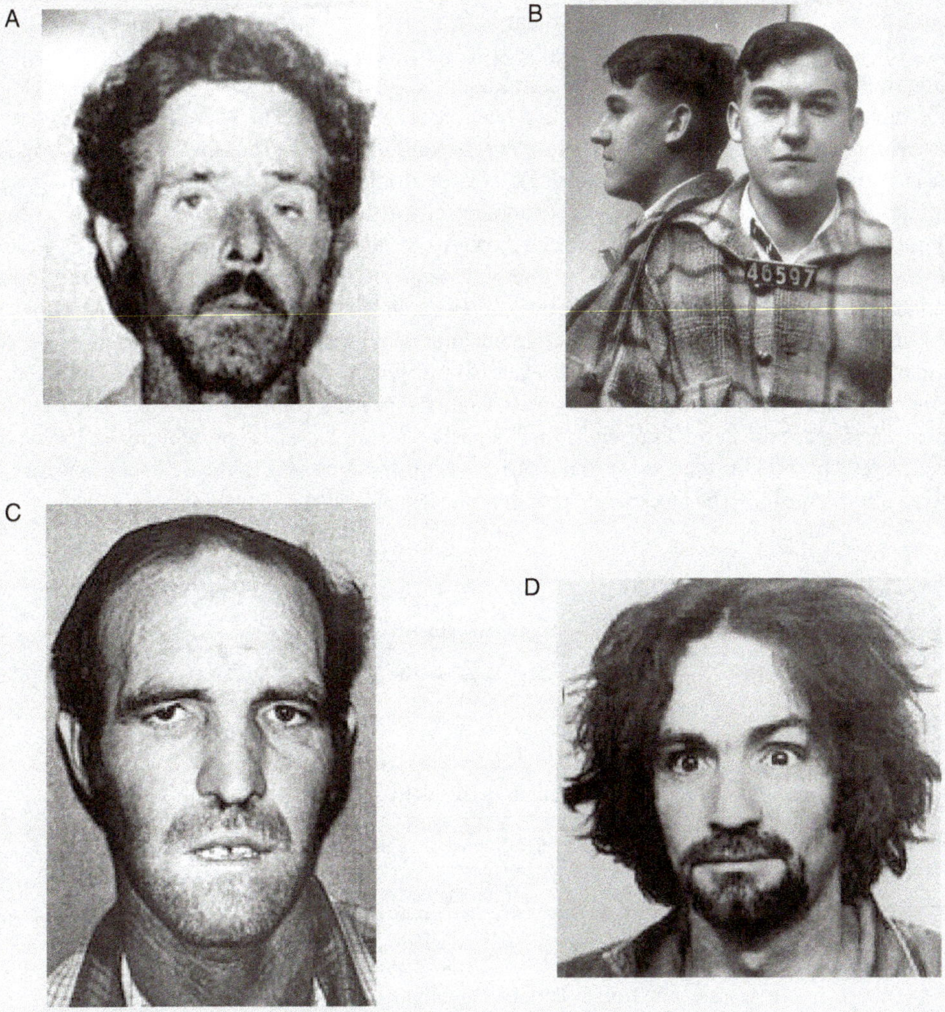

Friedrich "Fritz" Haarmann (1879–1925) enjoyed dressing as a girl throughout his school life—a behavior that later ceased (Aggrawal, 2009). (A) Henry Lee Lucas (1936–2001), (B) Gordon Northcott (1906–1930), (C) Ottis Toole (1947–1996), (D) murder conspirator Charles Manson (1934–), Carroll Cole (1938–1985), and Daniel Barbosa (1930–1994) were forced by relatives (often mothers) to dress as girls during childhood, though this trend continued into adolescence and adulthood voluntarily for Toole (Newton, 2000). Although it may be tempting to conceptualize these behaviors as paraphilic, cases in which cross-dressing is purely involuntary (i.e., not involving recurrent, intense sexual fantasies) would not meet diagnostic criteria for transvestism. They may, however, speak to an early form of trauma or humiliation, which may factor into the etiology of extreme forms of serial sexual violence.

Biological explanations of transvestism have centered largely upon published case studies that mention similar forms of brain abnormalities, such as postencephalitic states or temporal lobe lesions, among transvestic individuals (Aggrawal, 2009). How exactly these abnormalities relate to transvestism and their possible role in the development of this paraphilia are not yet explained.

Other Paraphilias

Other paraphilias (some of which are subsumed under the label "paraphilia NOS" in the DSM-IV-TR and under "other specified paraphilic disorder" and "unspecified paraphilic disorder" in the DSM-5) have also been the focus of clinical attention. Beetz (2004) presents a review of the literature on zoophilia, or sexual arousal by contact with animals, from a more-balanced and less-vilifying perspective (see Table 8.3). This literature, according to Beetz, is larger than expected but limited by its prevalence of pseudoscientific reports and lack of scientific research. It often mentions zoophilia in relation to law, homosexuality, sexual offending, or pornography. Sexual contact with animals has been prevalent throughout history, from the Bronze and Iron Age people, whose cave paintings depict the penile penetration of large animals by men, to ancient Greek, Egyptian, Roman, and Indian societies, which had rituals and ceremonies of worship involving sexual contact with snakes, bulls, or stallions or copulation with goats, dogs, or birds, to the Middle Ages, when witchcraft trials were often connected to capital punishment for bestiality. Literature and art from numerous historical periods have also depicted sexual contact between animals and humans (who, incidentally, appear to be almost without exception women), and religious texts such as the Old Testament and Talmud, as well as older legal codes, have condemned this form of behavior and assigned differential levels of punishment according to the species involved, with some acts being punished by death. Currently, laws on bestiality vary from country to country. Some countries, such as Germany and approximately half of the United States, no longer have laws prohibiting bestiality; others have laws that directly prohibit it, subsume it under "crimes against nature" (as in the State of California, where it is considered a misdemeanor), or incorporate it with homosexuality as "sodomy."

Table 8.3 Paraphilias Related to Violent, Criminal, or Antisocial Behavior

Paraphilia	Definition
Acousticophilia	Arousal from certain sounds, particularly someone screaming in agony
Agonophilia	Arousal by a partner pretending to struggle (to be free), pseudo-rape
Agoraphilia	Arousal from open spaces or having sex in public
Algolagnia	Arousal from both inflicting pain or humiliation, as well as receiving pain or humiliation
Algophilia	Arousal from pain or humiliation inflicted on oneself
Amokoscisia	Arousal or sexual frenzy with the desire to slash or mutilate women (proposed name: Jack the Ripper syndrome)
Anonraptus	A rapist who attacks only elderly women
Anthropophagy	Pleasure derived from the ingestion of human flesh
Asthenolagnia	Arousal from being humiliated or weakened
Autoassassinophilia	Arousal from putting oneself in a position in which one might be killed; arousal from orchestrating one's death by the hand of another
Autodermatophagia	Eating one's own flesh as a form of automasochism
Autoflagellation	Arousal from self-inflicted whipping
Autohaemofetishism	Sexual arousal by the sight of one's blood; usually seen in intravenous drug users filling a syringe

Paraphilia	Definition
Automasochism	Inflicting intense pain on one's own body; different from masochism in which a partner inflicts pain. Also sometimes referred to as autosadism
Autosadism	Generic term for paraphilias involving the self-infliction of pain
Autovampirism	Arousal by drinking one's own blood obtained by inducing scrapes and cuts on self
Avisodomy	Breaking the neck of a bird while penetrating it for sex
Barysadism	Severe sexual sadism. Individuals suffering from this disorder seriously injure or kill their victims
Bestiality	Sexual intercourse with animals
Bestialsadism	Torture of animal during sexual contact
Biastophilia	Arousal from raping someone or from the idea of being raped
Bondage	Physical or mental restriction of partner
Chrematistophilia	Arousal from being charged for sex or being robbed by sex partner
Clinical vampirism (Renfield's syndrome)	Arousal by drinking blood of others (human or animal)
Cordophilia	Arousal from being bound with ropes or chains and sometimes suspended
Corephallism	Anal sex with a young girl
Crush fetish	Sexual arousal from seeing small creatures being crushed by members of the opposite sex, or being crushed oneself
Cryptoscopophilia	Desire and arousal from seeing the behavior of others in the privacy of their home, not necessarily sexual
Dacnolagnomania	Sexually sadistic murder; sexual arousal and gratification are found in the act of killing; lust murder
Dippoldism	Sexual arousal from abusing children
Dystychiphilia	Deriving pleasure from accidents
Ecorchement	Arousal from flagellation
Ederacinism	To tear out sex organs by the roots as in a frenzy or to punish oneself for sexual cravings
Electra complex	Intended sex between father and daughter
Ephebophilia	Sexual arousal from adolescent sex partners; same as phebophilia, hebephilia, or Lolita syndrome
Erotophonophilia	Sexual satisfaction from murdering strangers; lust murder
Exhibitionism	Sexual arousal through sexual behavior in view of third parties
Frotteurism	Sexual arousal from rubbing against or touching a nonconsenting person

(Continued)

(Continued)

Paraphilia	Definition
Frottophilia	Being aroused by being touched or rubbed by strangers in a public place
Ganyphilia	Sexual interest in and preference for adolescent boys by adolescent men
Grapholagnia	An urge to look at sexually explicit, obscene, scatological, lewd, vulgar, pornographic, or offensive pictures
Gynophagia	Sexual fetish involving fantasies of cooking and consuming human females; literally "woman eating"
Harpaxophilia	Getting pleasure by robbery or being robbed
Homicidophilia	Arousal and gratification through the murder, real or imagined (stage-managed and acted out), of one's partner or a stranger
Hybristophilia	Sexual arousal due to the knowledge that one's partner has committed an act of violence
Infantophilia (nepiophilia)	Sexual attraction towards babies and toddlers, aged from 0 to about 5 years
Leptosadism	Mild form of sadism
Lolita syndrome	Sexual arousal from adolescent sex partners; same as ephebophilia, phebophilia, or hebephilia
Maniaphilia	Attraction to insane people
Masochism	Reverse of sadism; sexual arousal through getting pain inflicted on oneself through another person, usually a partner of the opposite sex; also known as passive algolagnia
Mastigophilia	Arousal from pain or humiliation inflicted on oneself
Mazoperosis	Sexual gratification received from the mutilation of female breasts
Necroacrotomophilia	Arousal from having sex with a dead amputee
Necrobestialism (necrobestiality)	Arousal from having sex with dead animals
Necrochlesis	Sex with a female corpse
Necrophagia	Sexual gratification through eating the flesh of dead people
Necrophilia (necrophilism, necrolagnia, thanatophilia)	Sexual gratification only by having sex with the dead
Necrophiliapediobeastophile	Sexual gratification by having sex with dead baby animals
Necrocoitus	Sexual penetration of a corpse
Necrosadism	Arousal from mutilating a corpse
Necropedophilia	Sexual attraction to the corpses of children
Necrozoophilia	Sexual attraction to dead animals
Oedipus complex	Intended sex between mother and son
Pecattiphilia	Arousal from sinning or having committed an imaginary crime

Paraphilia	Definition
Pederasty	An abnormal sexual desire towards young children; same as pedophilia
Pedohebephilia	Sexual interest in persons with the body shape of under 11-year-olds as well as pubescent persons between 11 and 14 years for females and 11 and 16 years for males
Phalloorchoalgolagnia	Sexual arousal by the experiencing of painful stimuli being administered to the male genitals
Phygephilia	Arousal from being a fugitive
Piquerism	Arousal from penetrating one's body with sharp objects (e.g., pins, razors, knives)
Pornolagnia	Desire for prostitutes
Pyrolagnia	Sexual gratification from witnessing, making, or extinguishing fires
Raptophilia	Arousal from raping a victim; acquiescence on the part of the victim may cause the paraphiliac to lose interest or, more often, to increase the threats and violence
Rhabdophilia	Arousal from being flagellated
Sadism (tyrannism)	Sexual arousal through inflicting pain on another person; also known as algolagnia
Scatologia (scatophilia)	Arousal from making obscene phone calls
Symphorophilia	Arousal from stage-managing or arranging a disaster, crash, or explosion; arousal by accidents or catastrophes
Tamakeri	Arousal when a female kicks a man in the testicles; a variant of masochism, prevalent in Japan
Thygatrilagnia	A father's sexual love for his daughter
Tit torture	Sexual gratification from any of the several erotic BDSM activities focusing solely on inflicting pain on the breast, nipples, and areola
Traumaphilia	Sexual arousal from wounds or trauma
Toucherism	Touching a nonconsenting person's intimate parts in a crowd (see, for example, frotteurism, in which the frotteur rubs his male organ against the nonconsenting person)
Vorarephilia	Sexual attraction to being eaten by or eating another person or creature
Voyeurism	Observing nude individuals without their knowledge
Zoolagnia	Sexual attraction towards animals, sexual bestiality, or sexual desire for animals
Zoonecrophilia	Having sex with dead animals
Zoophagia	Eating live animals for erotic arousal
Zoophilia	Sexual arousal by contact with animals
Zoophilic exhibitionism	Exposure of genitals in front of animals with concomitant masturbation
Zoophilic frottage	Rubbing one's genitals on the furs of live animals
Zoosadism	Sexual arousal by causing pain and suffering to animals

Source: Adapted from Aggrawal (2009).

BOX 8.3 THE ACHILLES COMPLEX

DeLia (2004) proposes the Achilles complex, an intrapsychic complex characterized by

1. Prenatal or neonatal trauma
2. Physical injury in infancy or childhood
3. A physically or emotionally absent father along with a controlling, ambivalent mother
4. Cruelty to animals
5. A period of isolation in an attempt to control sadistic murderous impulses
6. Sexual perversion or paraphilia
7. Accumulation of murderous rage, which may take the form of sadistic homicide

DeLia refers to Jeffrey Dahmer as the "modern day Achilles" because he and the mythological figure had similar case histories (Achilles's paraphilia was described in myth as cross-dressing). DeLia offers the Achilles complex as an explanation for the cases of serial murderers Henry Lee Lucas and Ted Bundy. Although it is a psychoanalytic formulation, the Achilles complex integrates biological and psychosocial developmental components.

The relationship between bestiality and violence may seem intuitive, as violence toward the animal is automatically implied. In fact, in a review of an impressive 750 cases of Austrian men convicted of sexual activity with animals between 1923 and 1937, Grassberger (1968, in Beetz, 2004) reported smaller animals (e.g., sheep, goats, foals, calves, and dogs) sometimes being strangled to death in connection with the sexual acts and many larger animals suffering severe injuries in the genital area. Other smaller animals (e.g., fowl or rodents) usually did not survive the sexual abuse. From cases in which the animal was injured by the sexual act or out of anger when the animal did not comply, Grassberger inferred the offender was characterized by a cold and uncaring personality and assumed a poor relapse prognosis. Other studies of violent juvenile offenders and adult sex offenders have found rates of bestiality that are—depending upon offender type—at least similar to and more often elevated (e.g., 8.3–37%) in comparison to those found in the general population (i.e., 8.3%). Community studies of zoophiles, though less common, have reported cases of extreme violence. For example, one participant in a study by Miletski (2002, in Beetz, 2004) reported that he had raped dogs and killed them afterwards and that he had fantasies of cruelty and killing.

Several authors have speculated that bestiality could be a rehearsal for violence directed toward humans, and others have proposed a blurred line between bestiality and sadism, hypothesizing that some individuals who practice bestiality may actually be latent sadists and lust murderers (Beetz, 2007). An earlier report (Masters & Lea, 1963, in Beetz, 2007) described the case of a male necrophiliac whose necrophilia began with the mutilation of dead animals while he masturbated; he subsequently killed the animals himself for mutilation and masturbation. This case has striking similarities with and is an eerie foreshadowing of another case occurring several decades later—that of Jeffrey Dahmer.

On balance, sexual interests in animals may vary in form and intensity and exist on a continuum—from an interest in watching animals mate to a proposed emotional and sexual attraction or relationship to animals, or zoosexuality (Beetz, 2004). Studies of human-animal sexual contact using larger community samples recruited predominantly from the Internet (Beetz, 2002, and Miletski, 2002, in Beetz, 2004) has demonstrated that the emotional attachment to the animal is important—if not more important than the sexual interaction—for many zoophiles. Ultimately it may be that zoophilia in and of itself, aside from being a violation of the legal codes of certain regions, may not predispose an individual to crime and violence. Rather, it may be the contributions of other forms of paraphilic interests or personality traits (e.g., sadism) that contribute to the violence seen in some individuals who engage in sexual acts with animals.

A less-often discussed paraphilia related to criminal behavior is scatalogia (or scatophilia)—sexual arousal from making obscene telephone calls. Pakhomou (2006) presents a rare case study of a 39-year-old male telephone scatologist who harassed approximately 3,000 victims over a period of 16 months in 1997–1998.

Typically, the offender would mimic a female voice, pretending to be either a mother claiming she had observed her son masturbating while wearing the victim's underwear, stolen from the victim's home, or an athletic coach who was having strong sexual urges toward female teenage athletes while observing them in the shower. Victims were identified by name, as was the legitimate local coach's name in the latter scenario. The offender reported masturbating after sexual phone conversations though no physical contact was made with victims, and telephone calls lasted, on average, from 2 to 4 minutes (ranging, overall, from 1–10 minutes). Finally, newer forms of paraphilias related to criminality have been proposed based upon similar patterns of sexually deviant behavior observed in offenders. For example, using the MTC:R3 typology that was developed for classifying rapists (Prentky & Knight, 1991), Burgess and colleagues (2007) examined and classified 77 cases of offenders convicted of raping elderly women (aged 60 years and older). The authors suggest the term "gerontophilia" to describe this proposed paraphilic subtype but acknowledge that further research is needed.

The Relationship Between Sexual Disorders and Crime

A Closer Look: Sexual Disorders and Crime

Prevalence of the Disorder in Crime

Study Type	Number	Prevalence Rates‡
Arrest rates	0	–
Birth cohorts	0	–
Community samples	2*	8.5–100.0%†
Homicide offenders	1	3.0%
Jailed detainees and prisoners	1	0.5%
Psychiatric inpatients	5*	1.8–100.0%
Total Number of Studies	**8**	

Sample Characteristics

Size	22–747
Gender	Male only (5 studies); male and female but generally more males than females (3 studies)
Age	Youth, adult
Location	North America (i.e., Canada and the United States)
Diagnostic Systems	DSM (various editions). Not reported in one study (Langevin, 2003).

Notes: *One study involved both psychiatric inpatients and community individuals. Pedophilia and paraphilia NOS represent the most common disorder in three psychiatric inpatient studies of multiple paraphilias (Dunsieth et al., 2004; Galli et al., 1999; McElroy et al., 1999); and prevalence rates of gender identity problems are 8–13%.

†In the only "pure" community sample (Kingston et al., 2010), rates of sexual sadism are 8.5%.

‡ General population or comparison group prevalence rates of disorders are not presented in any of these studies, and, given the lack of general population estimates for paraphilias specifically in the DSM-IV-TR (see above), determining if rates of these disorders are elevated in these criminal populations becomes difficult. Rates of pedophilia across studies are 0.5% (Reich & Wells, 1985), 37.2% (Dunsieth et al., 2004), 47% (McElroy et al., 1999), and 100.0% (Galli et al., 1999), which are mostly elevated in comparison to estimates of the rates of pedophilia provided by McConaghy (1998; see above). The three latter studies, however, utilize samples of sex offenders, and Galli and colleagues (1999) specifically studied adolescents who sexually assaulted another child, which may have inflated rates of these disorders artificially above what might characterize criminal offenders in general.

(Continued)

(Continued)

Prevalence of Crime in the Disorder

Study Type	Number	Prevalence Rates	Crime Definition
Total Number of Studies	**0**		

Note: Studies of the prevalence of criminal behavior among those with sexual disorders in general and among those with paraphilias in particular appear to be very rare, and we were unable to locate any such studies at the time of this writing. One exception, in some respects, is a study by Smallbone and Wortley (2004) who reported rates of convictions for 15 different offense types in an Australian sample of men convicted of sexual offenses against children. Although a broad range of criminal offenses characterized this group, no comparison groups for conviction rates were utilized. Also, though some men were characterized by a variety of clinical and subclinical paraphilic interests, pedophilia was not examined. Unfortunately, the presence of pedophilia cannot be inferred based solely upon criminal offense history (see below), thus the Smallbone and Wortley study cannot effectively be used to indicate the prevalence of crime in those with pedophilia.

Nondisordered or community resident comparison group or general population baseline rates for either disorder or crime provided: **0 studies (0.0%)**

Psychological Factors: Comorbidity With Other Disorders

The influence of concurrent psychiatric diagnoses must also be considered in the association between paraphilias and crime. Comorbidity with other criminogenic disorders may contribute directly to criminal and antisocial behavior, or—as in the case of paraphilic sexual offenders—multiple comorbidities may represent compounded psychological and psychosocial difficulties in an individual, which may decrease quality of life and predispose that person to sexual offending. It is known that the paraphilic individual may present with a wide variety of other mental disorders and levels of personality organization. For example, perversions have been observed in psychotic, personality disordered, and relatively intact or neurotic patients. Thus, understanding any individual involved in perverse sexual behavior—from a psychoanalytic perspective—requires a thorough understanding of how the perversion interacts with the individual's underlying personality structure. For example, neurotic patients may use paraphilias to facilitate a general sense of potency while those near the psychotic border may use the same paraphilias to fight off a feeling of the complete breakdown of the self (Gabbard, 2005).

Studies of various types of individuals with paraphilias in or seeking treatment, including juveniles and adults, offenders and non-offenders, and inpatients and outpatients, have revealed significant comorbidity with major mental disorders and personality disorders previously classified on Axis I and Axis II of the DSM-III-R and DSM-IV (Dunsieth et al., 2004; Galli et al., 1999; Kafka & Hennen, 2002; Raymond et al., 1999). Across studies, rates of mood disorders range from 58–82%, anxiety disorders from 39.1–64% (with social phobia and PTSD being among the most common, when specified), substance use disorders from 50–85%, and impulse control disorders from 26.6–55%. Rates of ADHD (71%), conduct disorder (94%; Galli et al., 1999), and antisocial personality disorder (56%; Dunsieth et al., 2004) have also been reported. In one of the rare examinations of comorbid sexual disorders, Raymond and colleagues (1999) reported prevalence rates of general sexual dysfunction (current 15.6%, $n = 7$; lifetime 24.4%, $n = 11$), sexual aversion (current 0.0%; lifetime 2.2%, $n = 1$), and erectile dysfunction (current 4.4%, $n = 2$; lifetime 4.4%, $n = 2$) in paraphilic sex offenders. Furthermore, these authors reported that 93% ($n = 42$) of these offenders were diagnosed with some form of comorbid psychiatric disorder and 56% ($n = 25$) with five or more disorders in addition to pedophilia. Other studies have shown that multiple paraphilias are often present in any given individual diagnosed with a paraphilia (Bradford et al., 2007; Cohen & Galynker, 2002). Finally, Cohen and Galynker (2002) note that pedophiles in particular may present with pervasive and severe forms of Axis II psychopathology, especially schizotypy, antisocial, and Cluster C personality disorders (see Chapter 10).

Additionally, studies of sexual offenders in treatment programs have reported higher rates of comorbid psychiatric disorders in offenders with paraphilias compared to those without. McElroy and colleagues (1999) found significantly elevated rates of mood, anxiety, and eating disorders, as well as significantly increased rates of childhood sexual abuse in inpatient sex offenders with paraphilias compared to those without. Dunsieth et al. (2004) found inpatient sexual offenders with paraphilias were characterized by significantly higher rates of mood disorders (i.e., any mood disorder, any bipolar disorder, and major depressive and bipolar I disorders, when examined separately), anxiety disorders, impulse control disorders (i.e., any impulse control disorder and compulsive buying, when examined separately), and avoidant personality disorder than those without. Sex offenders without paraphilic diagnoses were characterized by increased rates of drug abuse without alcohol abuse. In a sample of 60 outpatient treatment-seeking males (42 with paraphilias—grouped as sex offenders and non-offenders—and 18 with paraphilia-related disorders), Kafka and Prentky (1998) found that, though childhood ADHD distinguished those with paraphilias from those without, lifetime comorbid mood and anxiety disorders, impulse disorders NOS, and substance abuse did not. Additionally, childhood ADHD distinguished paraphilic sex offenders from non-offenders. In a later extension of this study, Kafka and Hennen (2002) found childhood ADHD to be one of the most prominent developmental and demographic variables differentiating paraphilic from non-paraphilic individuals, along with a history of hospitalization for substance abuse or psychiatric reasons, contact with the criminal justice system (including arrest and incarceration), higher rates of current unemployment or disability status, and reduced current earnings. The combined subtype of ADHD (ADHD-C) was often present with persistent socially deviant sexual arousal, conduct disorder, and multiple hypersexual disorders (i.e., multiple paraphilias). Specific paraphilias (frotteurism, fetishism, paraphilia NOS) and paraphilia-related disorders (compulsive masturbation and pornography dependence) were significantly associated with ADHD. Paraphilic sex offenders were characterized by increased school-related learning and behavioral problems, psychiatric hospitalization, and arrests and incarcerations compared to paraphilic and non-paraphilic non-offenders, though these groups were similar on all other demographic variables. Interestingly, Cohen and Galynker (2002) propose an impulsive subtype of pedophilia and suggest that impulse control disorders may be nonspecific indicators of severe psychopathology and that compulsive behavior in pedophiles may be misidentified as impulsive behavior.

Other evidence suggests a relationship between paraphilias, comorbid psychiatric disorders, and traumatic brain injury (TBI). In a sample of sexual offenders recruited from an Ohio inpatient biopsychosocial treatment program, DelBello and colleagues (1999) found increased rates of traumatic brain injury (TBI) in those diagnosed with bipolar disorder (n = 9) compared to both those without (n = 16) and to offender controls with bipolar disorder convicted of nonsexual crimes (n = 15). Results also indicated that, for most participants, TBI predated the first sexual offense and the onset of bipolar disorder. Additionally, rates of paraphilias (pedophilia, sadism, voyeurism, paraphilia NOS, and frotteurism) were increased in offenders with bipolar disorder compared to those without (78% vs. 56%), though these differences were not statistically significant. Rates of paraphilias did not differ among offenders with and without TBI.

Additional evidence suggests a relationship with psychopathy (see Chapter 10). The literature on the comorbidity of paraphilias and psychopathy has centered largely on recidivism studies of sexual offenders with certain paraphilias (see review in Bradford et al., 2007). Across studies, the Psychopathy Checklist—Revised (PCL-R), a validated measure of psychopathy (see Chapter 10) appears effective in differentiating recidivists from non-recidivists in samples of pedophiles (i.e., incest offenders and extrafamilial child molesters) and exhibitionistic offenders, with higher PCL-R scores associated with higher recidivism or risk of violence. Psychopathy has also differentiated homicidal from nonhomicidal child molesters (Firestone et al., 1998). Interestingly, while mean PCL-R scores reported in the Bradford et al. (2007) review are somewhat elevated for extrafamilial child molester groups (15.6–22.1), they do not meet the clinical diagnostic threshold for psychopathy outlined by Hare (2003), which is 30. However, it is generally thought that rapists are characterized by increased psychopathy or antisocial traits compared to incest perpetrators and extrafamilial child molesters (Bradford et al., 2007). To date, prevalence rates of paraphilias among individuals with psychopathy appear unexamined.

Origins of Crime and Violence in Sexual Disorders: Using Paraphilias to Understand, Manage, and Predict Crime

This discussion of the theoretical explanations and etiological mechanisms of crime and violence in those with sexual disorders takes a slight departure from the discussions found in most of the other chapters in this book because some of these disorders (i.e., select paraphilias) may be criminal in and of themselves if the behavioral manifestation or acting out of intense sexual fantasies or urges constitutes an act that is explicitly prohibited by law. In such specific cases, the disorder itself could be the predominant criminogenic factor. The acting out of other paraphilias, however, does not violate any penal code but might, nonetheless, influence criminal offending. For example, according to Mann and colleagues (2010), it is possible for a paraphilia to be legal but offense related: An offender may coerce another into performing sexual acts for which finding a consenting partner is difficult (e.g., certain forms of coprophilia). These authors also report being unable to locate any studies examining the recidivism rates of sexual offenders characterized by noncriminal paraphilias, such as transvestism or shoe fetishism.

A separate but relevant discussion here may be of how paraphilias can serve as etiological factors in crime and violence. The literature on paraphilias encompasses published case material, studies of violent and sexual offending, and studies of crime management and crime prediction, which speak to the contributions these disorders may make to criminal behavior.

Case Material

Richard von Krafft-Ebing's (1886/1965) classic work *Psychopathia Sexualis* is one of the earliest and most comprehensive collections of case material in the area of sexual deviancy. It remains a landmark in the literature and is often cited even to this day. Krafft-Ebing intended the book for doctors, lawyers, and judges exclusively; consequently, in the earlier German language editions, he used technical language and described specific sexual behaviors in Latin so as to prevent the common reader from understanding the material. Within the book, 238 cases are presented that are relevant to areas of general pathology and special pathology and to the legal aspects related to sexual disorders.

Under general pathology, Krafft-Ebing presents cases involving sexual instinct outside the period of the anatomical-physiological processes of reproduction, for example, sexual desire in early childhood or old age (paradoxia); the absence of sexual instinct (anaesthesia sexualis); pathologically exaggerated sexual instinct (hyperesthesia); sadism (including lust murder, anthropophagy, corpse mutilation, cutting and flogging women, the defilement of women by urination or defecation, flogging boys, and sadistic acts on animals); masochism (including passive flagellation and sexual bondage); fetishism (including fetishes for specific female body parts such as hands or hair, for physically handicapped persons, for despoiling or cutting off young girls' hair, for women's clothing such as undergarments or handkerchiefs or shoes, and for domestic animals); and various conditions falling under the umbrella term "antipathic sexual instinct" (eviration and defemination). Some disorders in this last category were considered "congenital" (hermaphroditism, homosexuality, and effemination), and others appear to represent, in varying degrees, what are currently referred to as gender identity disorders.

Several cases from Krafft-Ebing's book illustrate various aspects of the relationship between sexual disorders and crime. A 30-year-old soldier (Case 27) achieved sexual gratification at different times and places by stabbing girls with pocketknives or penknives in the abdomen or genitals. A man (Case 28) attacked young girls on the street by stabbing them in the upper arm with a dagger, which caused him to ejaculate. A man (Case 23) repeatedly dug up human corpses, removed the entrails, and then masturbated. A 20-year-old man (Case 15), when arrested, was found with the forearm of a missing 4-year-old girl in his pocket, her partially cooked head and entrails on the stove, and other body parts in the bathroom. Evidence, including an obscene poem found on the man, indicated that he had sexually assaulted the child and murdered her. In fact, a broad spectrum of sexual offenders, including rapists and lust murderers, are described within this book. Eleven lust murderers are portrayed, 10 of whom engaged in postmortem mutilation. Of these, 4 also committed anthropophagy and 2 who also engaged in necrophilia. In one case (Jack the Ripper), the offender did not have sexual intercourse with the victims, though it is believed that the homicide and subsequent mutilation of the corpses were substitutes for the sexual act. There were also four cases of men who cut or stabbed girls and women (often in public) for sexual gratification.

Sexual Disorders and Violence

The association between lust and violence has long been discussed in the literature. Krafft-Ebing (1886/1965) provides numerous examples of aggressive and violent behavior occurring within the context of sexual activity (i.e., for sexual pleasure), and he also describes several historical references to powerful sexual desires manifesting during and after acts of extreme violence.

A review by Cohen and Galynker (2002) indicates that the behavioral patterns of pedophiles are largely premeditated, not impulsive, and mostly nonviolent and that the ease of access to victims affects the frequency and severity of the abuse as well as the number of victims. Additionally, pedophiles tend to be characterized by a lack of insight and cognitive distortions, which allow them to deny or minimize the deviancy of their behavior and the destructive impact it has upon their child victims. Regarding violence, Gebhard and colleagues (1967, in Cohen & Galynker, 2002) found that sexually aggressive child molesters, compared to nonviolent pedophiles, were characterized by more impulsive offenses, stranger victims, and higher incidence of completed intercourse.

Arrigo and Purcell (2001) propose an integrated conceptual model of how paraphilias may play a motivational role in lust murder, based upon a synthesis of earlier motivational and trauma-control formulations (Burgess et al., 1986; Hickey, 1997). According to the model, paraphilias begin during formative development; predispositional factors such as dysfunctional family surroundings affect early attachments with primary caregivers in childhood, or an individual experiences sexual, psychological, or physical trauma. These lead to unsuccessful psychosocial development, low self-esteem, and an inability to form social relationships. Fantasies become a substitute for relationships and the basis for paraphilic behaviors. These behaviors manifest through a cyclical paraphilic process, beginning with paraphilic stimuli and fantasy; images provide relief from internal failures and become a safe, private, yet isolated world for the individual. Next is an orgasmic conditioning process that begins with compulsive genital stimulation in order to achieve sexual gratification. Successive fantasies, rehearsals of the paraphilia, and orgasms achieved through masturbation (which serve as reinforcers) condition the individual to lose all sense of normalcy and depend upon the paraphilic fantasy for erotic arousal and satisfaction. Though comparatively normal paraphilias may be experienced initially, these may become increasingly violent and sexual in nature and content—possibly intensifying and becoming more frequent. Finally, facilitators such as drugs, alcohol, and pornography manifest as addictions for the sexually deviant individual, who becomes increasingly desensitized to them, and these further fuel the cycle. Environmental stressors (e.g., rejection, isolation, ridicule) act as triggers that affect the paraphilic cycle by way of a feedback loop, which also encourages behavioral manifestations (i.e., acting out) and increasingly violent fantasies. The cycle continues to escalate and may ultimately culminate in the acting out of depraved and erotically charged fantasies in the form of sexual homicide or lust murder.

Langevin (2003) compared the psychosocial characteristics of 33 sex killers to 80 nonhomicidal sexually aggressive men and 611 general sex offenders (all from a database of more than 2,800 Canadian cases seen by the author and colleagues since 1973). Sex killers were characterized by earlier criminal careers, increased rates of reform school, criminal gang membership, fire setting, drug abuse, neuropsychological impairment, grades failure, and learning disabilities relative to other groups. Furthermore, they demonstrated more sadism, fetishism, and voyeurism, and more often collected (non-offense related) pornography.

According to Arrigo and Purcell (2001), sexual homicide (or lust murder) can itself be considered a paraphilia—known as **erotophonophilia**. Other paraphilias have been identified in association with lust murder: **flagellationism** (an intense desire to beat, whip, or club someone), **anthropophagy** (an intense desire to eat the flesh or body parts of another—see Box 8.4), **piquerism** (the intense desire to stab, wound, or cut the flesh of another person—often these stab wounds are inflicted near the genitals or breasts in the act of lust killing), and **necrosadism** (sexual contact with a dead body; see Table 8.3). This is an example of how multiple paraphilic interests may coexist in the same individual, with one or more perhaps operating in the service of another, either in fantasy or behavior. According to Stein and colleagues (2010), many reported cases of sexual murderers who engaged in post-offense necrophilia indicate the offender often suffered from erectile dysfunction and feelings of sexual inadequacy. Necrophiles may be more likely to seek employment at morgues and funeral parlors to facilitate solitary access to dead bodies, and some may kill in order to get a corpse. However, in a descriptive case-file review study of 16 necrophiles culled from a sample of 211 sexual murderers, these authors found that the common conception of individuals with necrophilia—that of requiring an unresisting and unrejecting partner—may not be true for all cases.

BOX 8.4 ANTHROPOPHAGY: ARMIN MEIWES AND BERND JÜRGEN BRANDES

Armin Meiwes (left), also known as the Rotenburg Cannibal or *Der Metzgermeister* (The Master Butcher), is a German man who became internationally known for killing and eating a voluntary victim that he located using an advertisement on an Internet website called the Cannibal Cafe. Bernd Jürgen Brandes (right) answered the ad ("looking for a well-built 18- to 30-year-old to be slaughtered and then consumed"). Many others had answered the ad but had backed out. After Meiwes and Brandes met in Meiwes's home in March of 2001 and together attempted to eat Brandes's severed penis, Meiwes killed him and proceeded to eat up to 44 pounds of his flesh over the next 10 months. He was arrested in December of 2002, after police were notified he had been placing new advertisements for victims and was describing the killing online. Prosecutors claimed Meiwes committed the act for sexual enjoyment.

Paraphilias and Sexual Offending

What may seem counterintuitive is that all sexual offenders are not characterized by paraphilias or other sexual disorders. In fact, paraphilias are nonexistent or not mentioned in some studies of sexual offenders that report rates of mental disorders and other psychopathology (Grossman & Cavanaugh, 1990; Lewis et al., 1979), and rates of paraphilias across other studies of sexual offenders are highly variable (see Table 8.4). However, many sexual offenders may often minimize and deny symptoms of severe psychopathology—including deviant sexual desires and behaviors—in clinical evaluations (Grossman & Cavanaugh, 1990), and many studies do not use operational diagnostic criteria or structured clinical interviews to assess for mental disorders (Galli et al., 1999). Furthermore, the relationship between paraphilia and sexual criminality is a nuanced one—for the behavior that forms the *corpus delicti* (Latin meaning "body of crime") of a sexual offense may be motivated by non-paraphilic factors, such as environmental opportunities and cues or absence of a capable guardian (Smallbone & Wortley, 2004), or may not have persisted for the requisite six-month diagnostic time period (First & Hanlon, 2008). Conversely, paraphilic urges may not necessarily lead to an acted out, punishable sexual behavior. Stated another way, not all child molesters, for example, have pedophilia, and not all pedophiles commit contact sexual offenses against children although they may or may not engage in other related illegal activities, such as the possession and distribution of child pornography.

Table 8.4 Prevalence of Sexual Disorders in Criminal Populations

Source	N	Gender	Age	Study type[a1]	Sample Description	Disorder	Diagnostic System	Prevalence/ Incidence
Seltzer & Langford (1984)	85	M, F	15–25 (Median = 18)	PI	Interviews of individuals referred by courts or legal counsel to psychiatry department of large regional hospital in Northwest Territories, calendar year 1981	Psychosexual disorder	DSM-III, MMPI	4.7% (*n* = 4)
Reich & Wells (1985)	390	325 M, 65 F	*M* = 30.9	JD	Record review of defendants evaluated for competency to stand trial by the Yale-New Haven Psychiatric Court Clinic, 1980–1982	Pedophilia	DSM-III	0.5% (*n* = 2)
Yarvis (1990)	100	88 M, 12 F	33% < 25, 85% < 40	HO	Diagnostic interviews and record reviews of a series of murderers referred for psychiatric evaluation in California, 1980–1988	Sexual sadism	DSM-III	3.0% (*n* = 3)[j]
Galli et al. (1999)	22	M	13–17 (*M* = 15.9, *SD* = 1.1)	PI, CS	Interviews with adolescents admitting to sexually assaulting another child, referred from a juvenile rehabilitation center, the juvenile court system, and an inpatient adolescent psychiatric unit, Hamilton County, Ohio	Pedophilia	DSM-III-R (DICA)	100.0% (*n* = 22)
						Frotteurism		86.0% (*n* = 19)
						Voyeurism		50.0% (*n* = 11)
						Exhibitionism		41.0% (*n* = 9)
						Paraphilia NOS		64.0% (*n* = 14)
						Total		100.0% (*n* = 22)
McElroy et al. (1999)	36	M	18–47 (*M* = 33, *SD* = 8)	PI	Interviews with convicted sex offenders consecutively admitted to the New Life Program, Cincinnati, Ohio, November 1996–June 1998	Frotteurism	DSM-IV (SCID)	25% (*n* = 9)

(Continued)

(Continued)

Source	N	Gender	Age	Study type[a1]	Sample Description	Disorder	Diagnostic System	Prevalence/ Incidence
						Pedophilia		47% ($n = 17$)
						Sexual sadism		11% ($n = 4$)
						Voyeurism		8% ($n = 3$)
						Paraphilia NOS		8% ($n = 3$)
						Total paraphilias		58% ($n = 21$)
						Sexual disorder NOS		8% ($n = 3$)
Langevin (2003)	(1) 33 (2) 80 (3) 23 (4) 611	M	(1) $M = 32.06$ (2) $M = 27.58$ (3) $M = 27.57$ (4) $M = 31.42$	PI	Interviews with convicted sex offenders ($n = 747$) belonging to one of four groups: (1) sex killers, (2) nonhomicidal sexually aggressives, (3) nonhomicidal sadists, and (4) general sex offenders. Participants were chosen from a database of more than 2,800 minimum-security forensic ward psychiatric hospital cases (Clarke Institute in Toronto, Ontario, Canada) seen since 1973.	Sadomasochism	?	70% 30% 100% 4%
						Voyeurism		42% 34% 35% 21%
						Transvestism		15% 18% 26% 20%
						Fetishism		18% 5% 13% 4%

Source	N	Gender	Age	Study type[a1]	Sample Description	Disorder	Diagnostic System	Prevalence/ Incidence
						Gender identity problems		12% 9% 13% 8%
Dunsieth et al. (2004)	113	M	18–66 (M = 35.3, SD = 10.4)	PI	Diagnostic interviews with sex offenders consecutively referred to an Ohio residential sex-offender treatment program	Frotteurism	DSM-IV	16.8% (n = 19)
						Voyeurism		14.2% (n = 16)
						Exhibitionism		5.3% (n = 6)
						Fetishism		3.5% (n = 4)
						Transvestic fetishism		2.7% (n = 3)
						Pedophilia		37.2% (n = 42)
						Sexual sadism		13.3% (n = 15)
						Masochism		1.8% (n = 2)
						Paraphilia NOS		44.2% (n = 50)
						Sexual disorder NOS		35.4% (n = 40)
Kingston et al. (2010)	586	M	18–78 (M = 38.1, SD = 12.0)	CS	Evaluations of sex offenders (convicted of an intrafamilial offense against a child, an extrafamilial offense against a child, or rape) from an outpatient sexology clinic, Canada, 1982–1992	Sexual sadism	DSM-III, DSM-III-R	8.5% (n=50)

Notes: [a1] AR = arrest rates of patients discharged from psychiatric facilities, JD = jailed detainees and incarcerated prisoners, HO = homicide offenders, BC = birth cohort study, PI = psychiatric inpatient sample, CS = community sample (i.e., epidemiological catchment area survey studies and outpatient psychiatric patients).

[j] Community sample comparative data (six-month prevalence rates from NIMH Community Survey data): Data not reported

Sex offenders may be a criminally diverse group with multiple forms of paraphilias, which may relate more so to general rather than sexual offending. Smallbone and Wortley (2004) examined nonpedophilic paraphilic interests and previous criminal behavior in an Australian sample of adult men convicted of sexual offenses against children ($n = 221$). Results indicated that offenders' criminal histories were characterized by a considerably diverse array of offense categories and that most previous convictions were for nonsexual offenses. Approximately half reported at least one subthreshold paraphilic interest (most commonly voyeurism), and about one-quarter reported multiple subthreshold paraphilias. Prevalence rates for threshold-level paraphilias and multiple paraphilias were 11.6% ($n = 25$) and 9.2% ($n = 11$), respectively. (These rates are downplayed by the authors but seem consistent with rates of paraphilias reported in other studies of sexual offenders—see Table 8.4). No significant relationship was revealed between paraphilias and sexual offending. However, specific paraphilias (voyeurism, frotteurism, sexual masochism, telephone scatologia, and sexual sadism) significantly correlated with nonsexual offending. According to the authors, results indicate the need to emphasize general crime factors rather than the traditionally held link between sexual crimes and sexual psychopathology to better conceptualize sexual offending. The authors admit the questionable reliability of their own paraphilic interest assessment questionnaire, and it is unclear if pedophilia diagnoses are implied from previous convictions for sexual offenses against children (only 22.3% of the sample) or merely an index offense of the same type. Neither would be entirely valid (see below), and the reasons for not considering pedophilia in the present study are not made clear—and this omission is particularly unfortunate given the authors' stance that links between sexual offending and paraphilias should be de-emphasized.

Specific paraphilias may contribute to particular forms of criminal and violent sexual behavior. Richards and Jackson (2011) examined possible offense behavioral indicators unique to sexual sadism. Using a sample of sex offenders in a northwest civil commitment program ($n = 39$ diagnosed with sexual sadism, $n = 39$ with paraphilia NOS), these authors found the behaviors of sexual sadists to be severely violent and controlling—characterized by the digital penetration of a male victim, violent sexual acts, strangling or choking after the sex act, cutting or stabbing the victim, inflicting cut wounds requiring stitches, breaking one or more of the victim's bones, confining the victim during an offense lasting longer than 90 minutes, beating the victim, and using restraints. Those with paraphilia NOS were characterized by taking items of personal importance to the victims and keeping offense trophies. The researchers concluded that, although there were several items that discriminated between the two groups, there were also many similarities, and further research is necessary to determine whether or not these two disorders fall on opposite ends of the same continuum or if, in fact, they are completely separate. In a sample of 113 male sex offenders in an 18-month residential sex-offender treatment program, Dunsieth et al. (2004) found that although non-paraphilic offenders were imprisoned longer than paraphilic offenders, those with paraphilias were associated with having more victims, being younger at first offending, and being more likely to perpetrate incest. The latter were also more likely to victimize minors, according to self-reports or convictions while the former were more likely to victimize adults exclusively, have a prior conviction for theft, and have a juvenile offending history.

Paraphilias and Crime Management

From a crime management perspective, researchers have investigated paraphilias because of legislation permitting the civil commitment of sexually violent predators (SVPs). These laws passed originally in the state of Washington in 1990 and were subsequently enacted in similar forms in 19 other states (at the time of this writing). Using a Florida sample of 450 incarcerated male sexual offenders, Levenson and Morin (2006) examined factors essential in determining recommendations for civil commitment as an SVP. Results of discriminant function analysis indicated the following significant predictors of civil commitment among these offenders: diagnoses of specific paraphilias (pedophilia and paraphilia NOS), psychopathy, actuarial risk assessment scores (evaluated using Static-99 and MnSOST-R, risk assessment measures developed for sex-offender populations), younger victim age, and nonminority race. First and Hanlon (2008), however, discuss the psychiatric community's concern about the constitutionality of SVP commitment statutes, which are based on the criteria that the sexual offender has a "mental abnormality" that makes the commission of violent predatory sexual offending more likely. Although paraphilias are the most common form of mental disorder used to address the statutes' version of mental abnormality, they are commonly misdiagnosed. These authors propose that, for judicious applications of the paraphilia diagnosis within SVP commitment evaluations, the following should occur: (1) establishing the presence of a paraphilia (having an offense history does not mean the individual's offense was motivated by a paraphilia), (2) determining if the crime was a consequence of the paraphilia (ruling out any other cause for the behavior), and (3) demonstrating volitional impairment (rather than assuming that the diagnosis of paraphilia is sufficient alone). Ultimately, this approach emphasizes the importance of not making paraphilia diagnoses based solely on the sexual offenses themselves.

Paraphilias and Crime Prediction

From a crime prediction perspective, researchers also study risk factors leading to recidivism for sexual offenders. In a recent review of psychologically meaningful risk factors for sexual-offender recidivism, Mann and colleagues (2010) list as significant risk factors the presence of multiple paraphilias (which, in sex offenders, are most commonly pedophilia, exhibitionism, voyeurism, and paraphilic rape), as well as other empirically supported considerations: sexual preoccupation, any deviant sexual interest, offense-supportive attitudes, emotional congruence with children, lack of emotionally intimate relationships with adults, lifestyle impulsivity, general self-regulation problems, poor cognitive problem solving, resistance to rules or supervision, grievance or hostility, and negative social influences. Kingston and colleagues (2010) examined indicators of sexual sadism as predictors of adult male sexual-offender recidivism. Their longitudinal study considered 586 males convicted of contact sexual offenses who were evaluated at an outpatient sexology clinic in Canada; behaviors included intrafamilial offenses against a child, extrafamilial offenses against a child, and rape. These authors compared offenders with DSM-III and DSM-III-R diagnoses of sexual sadism to those without. Results indicated that, compared to nonsadistic offenders, sexually sadistic offenders were significantly younger, more violent during the index offense, and demonstrated increased phallometrically assessed sexual arousal to violence and higher actuarial risk scores (i.e., on the Sex Offender Risk Appraisal Guide, or SORAG). In terms of their victims, sexually sadistic offenders predominantly offended against unrelated adults (66%), followed by extrafamilial children (24%), and related children (10%). In fact, those offending against adult women were significantly more likely to be diagnosed with sexual sadism, while those offending against related children were less likely. Furthermore, criminal record data at 20-year follow-up indicated that behavioral indicators, especially sexual arousal measured by phallometric assessment, were a greater predictor of future sexual and violent recidivism than a psychiatric diagnosis of sexual sadism alone.

Conclusion

Sexual deviancy has captured the attention of psychological theorists, clinicians, researchers, and criminologists for well over a century. Definitions of deviancy have changed with the evolving moral fabric of society, and, because of the advent of a class of sexual psychiatric disorders, some argue that psychiatrists have become the new guardians of sexual morality. Though much theoretical and empirical work has been done to understand the etiological mechanisms underlying paraphilias, in particular, the literature on their relationship with crime, violence, and other antisocial behavior remains, to a large degree, in its infancy. Prevalence rate studies of paraphilias in criminal populations are few and far between, and studies of crime in paraphilic populations appear nearly nonexistent at this time. Published case material, studies of violent and sexual offending, and studies of crime management and crime prediction have illustrated the contributions that paraphilias may make to criminal behavior. However, the case of Jeffrey Dahmer underscores the need for more work in this area—particularly if we are to understand how the most extreme ends of the human sexual experience may manifest in unspeakable acts of violent sexual depravity toward others.

KEY TERMS

accidental conditioning

anthropophagy

erotophonophilia

exhibitionism

fetishism

flagellationism

frotteurism

necrophilia

necrosadism

paraphilia

pedophilia

piquerism

sexual masochism

sexual sadism

transvestic fetishism

voyeurism

REVIEW QUESTIONS

1. Compare and contrast the conceptualizations from the different theoretical perspectives discussed in the chapter for each of the following paraphilias: voyeurism, exhibitionism, frotteurism, sadism, masochism, fetishism, pedophilia, and transvestism. What are some of the similarities and differences in the way pathological sexual desires, urges, and behaviors are conceptualized across disorders?
2. Examine Table 8.4 and the summaries of research studies in the "A Closer Look" section for the disorders in this chapter. Discuss how prevalence rates of crime in those with sexual disorders differ among these disorders, if at all. Using the information in the tables, speculate as to how these differences in prevalence rates may have been caused by methodology (e.g., in terms of study types, sample characteristics, methodological issues, or other concerns).
3. Reflect on how pedophilic behavior has been tolerated and even normative during some historical periods and how culturally sanctioned pedophilia (i.e., behaviors that would resemble disorders according to definitions in the DSM) still exists in certain societies or regions today. This cultural interpretation of behavior, in essence, forms the line between normalcy and abnormality. Can this be the case for any of the other disorders discussed in this chapter? Explain your answer.
4. Discuss Arrigo and Purcell's (2001) integrated model of how paraphilias may play a motivational role in lust murder. How might this model be applied to the case of Jeffrey Dahmer? What are the strengths and weaknesses in this application?
5. Explain the relationship between paraphilias and sexual offending, as discussed in the chapter.

9

Impulse Control Disorders Not Elsewhere Classified

(Disruptive, Impulse Control, and Conduct Disorders)

PAUL KENNETH KELLER

Paul Kenneth Keller was born in Everett, Washington, on January 6, 1966. He is a serial arsonist, convicted of setting 32 fires and admitting to setting 44 more. His fires, set during a six-month period from August 1992 to February 1993, killed at least three people (including three women at the Four Freedoms Retirement Home in Seattle, Washington), and they caused more than 30 million dollars in property damage.

Though Keller had a religious upbringing and education and volunteered with the elderly through his church as a young man, he was described as a hyperactive child (possibly with undiagnosed attention-deficit disorder) who was fascinated with fire at a young age. He reportedly set many nuisance fires in childhood—even torching a vacant house next to his own at age eight or nine. This fire setting continued even after he was lectured by firemen about his dangerous behavior. He chased fire vehicles (fascinated by their lights and sirens) and would later begin riding along with firefighter friends. Listening for emergency broadcasts on his own scanner, he would race fire trucks to the scene. At the time, his family believed his behavior to be an appropriate release for his excess energy (he had stopped taking his medication for hyperactivity and refused personal counseling).

As a young adult, Keller worked as a bookkeeper but was fired when his desk mysteriously caught fire. He subsequently began working for his father's advertising agency, where he reportedly found targets for his fires. An upper-middle-class professional, he later divorced and filed for bankruptcy, becoming troubled and abusing drugs and alcohol.

A clinical psychologist who later examined Keller diagnosed him with pyromania, writing, "Fire endowed the weak child, Paul Keller, with power." Keller claimed feeling sadness, confusion, and remorse—not enjoyment or excitement—from setting fires. Admitting to being drunk and sometimes on drugs before setting each fire, he also admitted remaining at the scenes of the fires to watch firefighters put them out because he was "interested in the methodology" of extinguishing them.

Keller was turned in to authorities by his parents and arrested in March of 1993. He is currently serving 99 years in prison without the possibility of parole.

Similar to the other aspects of the human experience mentioned in this book thus far, the ability to control one's impulses exists on a continuum, varying from individual to individual. Most impulses involve the immediate gratification of needs and may be in line with what many others experience. The need to eat, have sex, possess a material object, rid oneself of negative thoughts and emotions, feel in control, and even act out aggressively in response to frustration or threat can all be relatively normative, and most individuals are able to control their impulses while navigating solutions to getting their needs met in a socially acceptable manner. For others, having their needs met can be more difficult—even impossible—causing impairment in important areas of their lives.

The DSM-IV-TR classifies several disorders under the umbrella term "impulse-control disorders not elsewhere classified"; these include intermittent explosive disorder, kleptomania, pyromania, pathological gambling, trichotillomania, and "impulse-control disorder NOS" (APA, 2000). The category is a catchall for conditions marked by the inability to resist an impulse, drive, or temptation to engage in a behavior that is harmful to one's self or others—a behavior that is not due more to the other disorders mentioned in this book, which may also involve problems with impulse control (e.g., substance-related disorders, paraphilias, antisocial personality disorder, schizophrenia, and mood disorders). One of the more prominent conceptual shifts in the DSM-5 is the renaming of this disorder class—it is now "disruptive, impulse-control, and conduct disorders"—and the reclassification of disorders to include the following conditions involving problems in emotional and behavioral self-control: oppositional defiant disorder; intermittent explosive disorder; conduct disorder; antisocial personality disorder; pyromania; kleptomania; other specified disruptive, impulsive-control, and conduct disorder; and "unspecified disruptive, impulse-control, and conduct disorder" (APA, 2013). Furthermore, the DSM-IV-TR category "pathological gambling," an impulse control disorder, has been renamed "gambling disorder" and is now reclassified under DSM-5 as a substance-related and addictive disorder; also, trichotillomania, an impulse control disorder according to DSM-IV-TR, has been relocated under DSM-5 and is now categorized under "obsessive-compulsive and related disorders." For the purposes of this book, coverage of these disorders remains consistent with the DSM-IV-TR configuration—oppositional defiant disorders and conduct disorders are discussed in Chapter 3, and antisocial personality disorder is presented in Chapter 10.

Interestingly, approximately half of the DSM-IV-TR impulse control disorders are among the very limited number of disorders in that edition in which violations of the laws of society make up actual diagnostic criteria for the disorders themselves—rendering them, in a sense, inextricably bound to criminal behavior by definition. Other such disorders include conduct disorders (Chapter 3), illegal substance use disorders (Chapter 4), and, to a large extent, antisocial personality disorder (Chapter 10). The DSM-5 even notes that "disruptive, impulse-control, and conduct disorders" are unique in that their associated problems "are manifested in behaviors that violate the rights of others (e.g., aggression, destruction of property) and/or bring the individual into significant conflict with societal norms or authority figures" (APA, 2013, p. 461). Paul Keller was tormented with irresistible urges to set fires, though it is likely that his behaviors served much deeper psychological needs than simply a desire to cause destruction and harm. In this chapter, we will discuss the relationship between the maladaptive patterns of uncontrolled impulses of various types and criminal behavior and how common underlying processes—biological, psychological, and social—may be at the root of them all.

Intermittent Explosive Disorder

Although aggression may be a normative and perhaps essential component of the human experience, repeated failures to control anger-based aggressive impulses, which result in the destruction of property or in physical and emotional interpersonal harm, are considered extreme and beyond the scope of normal behavior. **Intermittent explosive disorder** represents a pattern of recurrent, unplanned outbursts of verbal or physical aggression, outbursts that are disproportionately intense relative to the situation and cause significant distress or have markedly deleterious consequences in the individual's life. DSM-5 diagnostic criteria for intermittent explosive disorder are listed in Table 9.1.

Table 9.1 DSM-5 Diagnostic Criteria for Intermittent Explosive Disorder

312.34 (F63.81) Intermittent Explosive Disorder

A. Recurrent behavioral outbursts representing a failure to control aggressive impulses as manifested by either of the following:

1. Verbal aggression (e.g., temper tantrums, tirades, verbal arguments or fights) or physical aggression toward property, animals, or other individuals, occurring twice weekly, on average, for a period of 3 months. The physical aggression does not result in damage or destruction of property and does not result in physical injury to animals or other individuals.
2. Three behavioral outbursts involving damage to destruction of property and/or physical assault involving physical injury against animals or other individuals occurring within a 12-month period.

B. The magnitude of aggressiveness expressed during the recurrent outbursts is grossly out of proportion to the provocation or to any precipitating psychosocial stressors.

C. The recurrent aggressive outbursts are not premeditated (i.e., they are impulsive and/or anger-based) and are not committed to achieve some tangible objective (e.g., money, power, intimidation).

D. The recurrent aggressive outbursts cause either marked distress in the individual or impairment in occupational or interpersonal functioning, or are associated with financial or legal consequences.

E. Chronological age is at least 6 years (or equivalent developmental level).

E. The recurrent aggressive outbursts are not better accounted for by another mental disorder (e.g., major depressive disorder, bipolar disorder, disruptive mood dysregulation disorder, a psychotic disorder, antisocial personality disorder, borderline personality disorder) and are not attributable to another medical condition (e.g., head trauma, Alzheimer's disease) or to the physiological effects of a substance (e.g., a drug of abuse, a medication). For children ages 6–18 years, aggressive behavior that occurs as part of an adjustment disorder should not be considered for this diagnosis.

Note: This diagnosis can be made in addition to the diagnosis of attention-deficit/hyperactivity disorder, conduct disorder, oppositional defiant disorder, or autism spectrum disorder when recurrent impulsive aggressive outbursts are in excess of those usually seen in these disorders and warrant independent clinical attention.

Source: APA (2013, p. 466). Reprinted with permission from the *Diagnostic and Statistical Manual of Mental Disorders*, Fifth Edition (Copyright © 2013). American Psychiatric Association. All rights reserved.

Prevalence and Incidence Rates of Intermittent Explosive Disorder

The DSM-IV-TR notes the paucity of reliable information about prevalence rates for intermittent explosive disorder (IED) but acknowledges that it is apparently rare (APA, 2000). The DSM-5 reports one-year prevalence rates for narrowly defined IED in the United States of approximately 2.7% (APA, 2013). More recently, Coccaro (2012) identified 12 community-sampling studies of IED, which reported weighted prevalence rates of 5.4–6.9% in the United States (using narrow and broad definitions, respectively), and rates of 1.4–3.0% in other countries (see also Fincham et al., 2009). Rates as low as 1–2% have been reported in psychiatric populations and up to 11.1% in some adult populations (Dell'Osso et al., 2006).

Theoretical Conceptualizations

According to Coccaro (2012), the first use of the term "intermittent explosive disorder" appeared in the DSM-III (APA, 1980), though the condition was known as "passive-aggressive personality, aggressive type" in the DSM-I (APA, 1952) and "explosive personality" in the DSM-II (APA, 1968). Post–DSM-IV-TR conceptualizations later emphasized verbal aggression and forms of relational aggression such as social exclusion

(McCloskey et al., 2008a; Murray-Close et al., 2010). Coccaro (2012) subsequently provided an expanded phenomenological clinical description of IED, which included aggressive outbursts typically having a rapid onset without a prodromal period and lasting less than 30 minutes. Assaults occurring within these episodes may be verbal, destructive or nondestructive against property, or injurious or non-injurious against people. Outbursts of aggression usually are responses to minor provocations by close intimates or associates, and individuals with IED commonly have "milder" episodes of verbal and nondestructive property assaults between the more intense episodes. Research criteria developed by Coccaro operationalize these episodes of aggression in even further detail, stating that they must involve either (1) verbal or physical aggression against people, animals, or property occurring at least twice a week on average for one month or (2) three episodes characterized by physical assault against others or property destruction over a one-year period (p. 578).

Anand and Malhi (2009) make a case for the conceptualization of a separate class of anger disorders. According to these authors, anger has only been vaguely defined within the changing versions of the DSM—usually as an aspect of other disorders rather than as a stand-alone entity. In fact, the only disorder solely pertaining to anger in the DSM-IV-TR (and, now, the DSM-5) is IED, which integrates aggression with an impulsive component and thus fails to capture the full range of anger-related phenomenon. According to these authors, attempts to include anger disorders among Axis I psychopathology have been unsuccessful due to anger being conceptualized from an environmental rather than a biological perspective.

Some evidence indicates that a history of exposure to trauma—either in the form of interpersonal trauma in childhood (Nickerson et al., 2012) or multiple traumatic life events (Fincham et al., 2009)—may contribute to the etiology of IED. Additionally, studies from South Africa and Japan indicate that employment and good educational background have shown associations with increased risk for IED, which suggests that job-related stress among educated groups might be one of the environmental triggers of impulsive aggression (Fincham et al., 2009; Yoshimasu & Kawakami, 2011). Finally, Coccaro (2012) reviews evidence of a neurobiological basis for IED. Recent studies have suggested a relationship between aggression and serotonin, and global serotonergic abnormalities have been identified in the brains of individuals with IED, along with specific abnormalities in the limbic system (i.e., the anterior cingulate) and orbitofrontal cortex. Furthermore, twin studies have suggested a genetic component to IED.

The Relationship Between Intermittent Explosive Disorder and Crime

A Closer Look: Intermittent Explosive Disorder and Crime

Prevalence of the Disorder in Crime

Study Type	Number	Prevalence Rates
Arrest rates	0	–
Birth cohorts	0	–
Community samples	1*	45.0%
Homicide offenders	0	–
Jailed detainees and prisoners	1	20.0–25.0%
Psychiatric inpatients	3*	19.0–45.0%
Total Number of Studies	**4**	

Sample Characteristics

Size	22–348
Gender	Male only (4 studies)

Age	Youth, adult
Location	United States
Diagnostic Systems	DSM (various editions)

Note: *One study involved both psychiatric inpatients and community individuals.

Prevalence of Crime in the Disorder

Study Type	Number	Prevalence Rates	Crime Definition
Total Number of Studies	**0**		

Nondisordered or community resident comparison group or general population baseline rates for either disorder or crime provided: **0 studies (0.0%)**

Origins of Crime and Violence in Those With IED: Theoretical Explanations and Etiological Mechanisms

Intermittent explosive disorder is another of the rare disorders covered in this book, rare because antisocial behavior (i.e., aggression) is inextricably bound to its diagnostic criteria. In other words, IED *is* aggression—thus rendering a discussion of how and why aggressive behavior may develop within the context of IED conceptually redundant. That being said, some evidence to date may suggest a role for co-occurring psychiatric disorders in the aggressive behavior characterizing IED. According to Coccaro (2012), community studies indicate that depressive, anxiety, and substance use disorders are three to four times more prevalent in individuals with IED but that the age of onset for IED is generally earlier than for the other disorders. Comorbidity with bipolar disorder has also been noted, with the aggressive episodes in some individuals resembling "micromanic episodes" accompanied by irritability, increased energy, and racing thoughts. Additionally, initial evidence indicates that comorbid antisocial and borderline personality disorders are more common among individuals that have IED compared to those that do not. Ultimately, however, the specific contribution made by other comorbid disorders toward aggression in those with IED still requires clarification.

Kleptomania

The urge to take what does not belong to us likely dates back to the beginnings of human existence. Most individuals (through socialization and the development of empathy) are able to resist impulses to steal the property of others; but, for some, these impulses can be overwhelming, leading to a pattern of stealing and to clinically significant impairment. This condition is known as **kleptomania**, a disorder characterized by the repeated inability to resist the impulsive stealing of objects (even though they are not needed by the individual or are of trivial monetary value). These thefts are preceded by an increasing sense of tension and followed by relief. Interestingly, individuals with kleptomania often are able to afford the items they steal and usually discard stolen goods or give them away afterwards (though they may hoard items or even secretly return them). They also are aware of the wrongfulness and senselessness of their behavior, are afraid of being caught, and often feel depressed or guilty about the thefts (APA, 2000). Diagnostic criteria from the DSM-5 for kleptomania are listed in Table 9.2.

Table 9.2 DSM-5 Diagnostic Criteria for Kleptomania

312.32 (F63.3) Kleptomania

A. Recurrent failure to resist impulses to steal objects that are not needed for personal use or for their monetary value.

B. Increasing sense of tension immediately before committing the theft.

C. Pleasure, gratification, or relief at the time of committing the theft.

D. The stealing is not committed to express anger or vengeance and is not in response to a delusion or a hallucination.

E. The stealing is not better accounted for by conduct disorder, a manic episode, or antisocial personality disorder.

Source: APA (2013, p. 478). Reprinted with permission from the *Diagnostic and Statistical Manual of Mental Disorders,* Fifth Edition

Prevalence and Incidence Rates of Kleptomania

Originally, in the DSM-IV-TR, prevalence rates of kleptomania in the general population were reported as unknown; estimated rates were less than 5% among identified shoplifters (APA, 2000). According to the DSM-5, kleptomania is very rare among the general population, with prevalence rates estimated at 0.3–0.6%. Among individuals arrested for shoplifting, prevalence rates of kleptomania are approximately 4– 24% (APA, 2013).

Theoretical Conceptualizations

Though kleptomania involves the act of stealing (most often from retail stores, but occasionally from family members and friends), it has been differentiated conceptually on several levels from shoplifting in general. For example, kleptomaniacs represent only a minority of shoplifters (i.e., approximately 4–8%) and, unlike most shoplifters, steal over extended periods of time (Fullerton, 2007). In fact, one recent study (Grant, 2003), the duration of shoplifting behavior in a sample of individuals with kleptomania ranged from 12.1 to 28.7 years ($M = 20.4$).

Kleptomania has been acknowledged in the medical literature for nearly two centuries. In fact, it was first described in 1816 by Swiss physician Andre Matthey, who originally used the term *klopemania.* Early writers who discussed the condition noted that the sufferer experienced uncontrollable urges to steal senseless items; and these impulses generated a frisson (similar to a sexual tension) that triggered a rush of exhilaration and relief when surrendered to. Early investigators have agreed that most kleptomaniacs from that era were females, particularly of elevated social status (Fullerton, 2007). A large body of case material was developed over the course of the 1800s, predominantly by French psychiatrists. Though theoretical explanations lagged, a focus became the irrational choice of objects stolen by kleptomaniacs, which was attributed to hysteria, imbecility, cerebral defects, menopause, and department store atmospherics, among other explanations. Nineteenth-century psychiatrists noted that infants naturally tend to take whatever they want whenever they want it—observations that became central to later psychoanalytic explanations of kleptomania.

Psychoanalytic theorists led the initial charge in the formal theoretical conceptualization of kleptomania, which evolved over approximately 50 years beginning in the early 1900s. With Sigmund Freud providing encouraging suggestions, proposals were offered by early renowned psychoanalytic thinkers such as Wilhelm Stekel, Fritz Wittels, and Alfred Adler. Stekel emphasized the sexual symbolism of the objects stolen by the female kleptomaniac—candles represented penis symbols, music boxes represented female genitalia, umbrellas represented erections, and gloves were symbolic or either condoms or female sex organs. Wittels proposed stealing constituted the sex lives of kleptomaniacs, who were sexually underdeveloped and inexperienced people feeling deprived of love. Adler instead focused on feelings of physical and social inferiority, proposing that self-aggrandizing rather than sexual pleasure drove people to compulsive stealing or kleptomania. A second generation of psychoanalytic literature proffered by Franz Alexander, Otto Fenichel, and Sandor Rado introduced concepts such as penis envy and the castration complex to the understanding of kleptomania (Fullerton, 2007).

In the mid-twentieth century, Charles Socarides (1954, in Fullerton, 2007) produced an article considered by the psychoanalytic literature to be the last word on kleptomania. In it, he summarized the various psychoanalytic explanations for this disorder that had amassed over the previous decades: (1) kleptomania represented striving for lost sexual satisfaction; (2) stealing in kleptomania represented secretly engaging in a forbidden act, such as masturbation; (3) stealing could have the symbolic meaning of stealing a penis, particularly in women who feared open displays of aggression and who considered themselves deprived in childhood; (4) stolen property symbolically represented mother's milk, which the kleptomaniac believed was unfairly withheld from him or her early in life; and (5) kleptomania is the "regressive expression of a desire for objects corresponding to a higher level of organization: feces, penis, or child" (Fenichel, 1933, p. 577). According to Fenichel (1933), these three items may be supposed to be inside the mother, so the theft represented the kleptomaniac's desire to seize the contents of his or her mother's body.

Compared to the rather extensive history of psychoanalytic contributions to the understanding of kleptomania, relatively little empirical work has been done to understand the potential neurobiological underpinnings of this disorder. However, damage to orbitofrontal-subcortical circuits has been proposed as a factor in the *neuropathogenesis* of kleptomania, which would be consistent with an inability to control irresistible impulses to steal. In a pilot study using *diffusor tension imaging* (DTI), an MRI technique that measures the self-diffusion of water in brain tissue, Grant and colleagues (2006) identified decreased white matter microstructural integrity in inferior frontal brain regions in 10 women with kleptomania compared to 10 female controls (presumably due to axonal degeneration and evidence that supports the notion of structural compromise in brain circuitry associated with behavioral regulation). In a subsequent pilot study of neuropsychological functioning in those with kleptomania, Grant, Odlaug, and Wozniak (2007) found that, although individuals with kleptomania did not demonstrate neuropsychological dysfunction as a group, greater kleptomania symptom severity was associated with below-average performance on measures of executive functioning (it should be noted, however, that no control group was utilized in this study). Furthermore, in a subsequent neurobiological study, the opiate antagonist naltrexone demonstrated effectiveness in reducing obsessive and compulsive thoughts, stealing urges, and stealing behavior in individuals with kleptomania (Grant, Kim, & Odlaug, 2009).

Finally, from a cognitive and behavioral perspective, Bohne and Stevens (2009) propose a model of kleptomania based on learning theory in which the disorder is viewed as developing from and maintained through a vicious cycle of inner experiences, behaviors, and reinforcements. The central components of this model include an initial state of inner tension, environmental cues triggering impulses to steal, and negative reinforcement in the form of tension reduction occurring after the act of stealing. These authors propose specific cognitive-behavioral interventions for the treatment of this disorder. Interestingly, it has also been proposed that kleptomanic stealing is similar to a classic compulsion in that the urge to steal is experienced as intrusive and senseless, with a build-up of anxiety or tension before the act or while resisting the urge and tension relief afterwards. The stealing, therefore, is ego-dystonic, and some authors have proposed kleptomania to be a variant of OCD (McElroy, 1991).

The Relationship Between Kleptomania and Crime

A Closer Look: Kleptomania and Crime

Prevalence of the Disorder in Crime

Study Type	Number	Prevalence Rates
Arrest rates	0	–
Birth cohorts	0	–
Community samples	1*	18.0%
Homicide offenders	0	–

(Continued)

(Continued)

Jailed detainees and prisoners	0	–
Psychiatric inpatients	3*	2.7–18.0%
Total Number of Studies	**3**	

Sample Characteristics

Size	22–113
Gender	Male only (3 studies)
Age	Youth, adult
Location	United States
Diagnostic Systems	DSM-III-R and DSM-IV

Note: *One study involved both psychiatric inpatients and community individuals.

Prevalence of Crime in the Disorder

Study Type	Number	Prevalence Rates	Crime Definition
Total Number of Studies	**0**		

Nondisordered or community resident comparison group or general population baseline rates for either disorder or crime provided: **0 studies (0.0%)**

General Studies

Though general studies of the relationship between kleptomania and crime appear somewhat rare in the literature, some empirical attention has been directed towards understanding the implications of this disorder within the criminal justice system. For example, Grant, Odlaug, Davis, and Kim (2009) were the first to examine the legal consequences associated with kleptomania in a sample of 101 outpatient adults (27 men and 74 women) previously diagnosed with kleptomania. Results from this study indicated that 69 participants (68.3%) had been arrested at least once; of these, 37 (approximately half of those arrested) had been arrested but not convicted, 21 had been convicted and incarcerated after conviction, and 11 had been convicted and not incarcerated. Somewhat surprising is the sizeable minority that had never actually been apprehended for shoplifting (particularly given that many participants had been shoplifting at least twice a week for 20 or 30 years), and it is not known whether these findings reflect general criminal justice system attitudes toward property offending.

Origins of Crime and Violence in Kleptomania: Theoretical Explanations and Etiological Mechanisms

Although a discussion of kleptomania as a disorder causing crime may be conceptually redundant, some investigators have noted its comorbidity with other psychiatric disorders. These may contribute in some meaningful way to the etiology of this disorder's characteristic stealing behaviors. In a small sample of male and female adult psychiatric hospital inpatients and outpatients, McElroy and colleagues found significant lifetime comorbidity with mood disorders (bipolar disorders and depression), anxiety disorders (panic disorders, agoraphobia, social and simple phobias, and OCD), eating disorders, and other impulse control disorders (pathological gambling, pyromania, trichotillomania, and IED). Grant and colleagues (2009), in their aforementioned study of

101 adult outpatients with kleptomania, found lifetime comorbidity with other impulse control disorders (mostly compulsive buying) in 42 participants and at least one other Axis I disorder in 64 participants. Furthermore, Grant (2004) emphasizes the forensic implications of a possible association between shoplifting and personality disorders. However, in a small sample of individuals with kleptomania, this author found a high prevalence of comorbid personality disorders but very little overlap between kleptomania and criminogenic personality disorders (comorbidity with antisocial personality disorder in this sample was only 3.6%).

Earlier writers on kleptomania emphasized its predominance among females (Fullerton, 2007), which, interestingly, runs contrary to the known and well-established gender distributions of crime, violence, and antisocial behavior in general, as these appear skewed heavily toward males. Recent evidence supports that kleptomania is a predominately feminine disorder. For example, a significant majority (73.3%) of the participants in the study by Grant, Odlaug, and colleagues (2009) of adult outpatients with kleptomania were female. In a sample of 95 adults with kleptomania, Grant and Potenza (2008) found men to have an earlier onset of kleptomania compared to women, though women appeared to develop kleptomania at a faster rate than men. Additionally, women more often stole from household item stores and men from stores selling electronics (see also Roncero et al., 2009). Furthermore, men were more likely to have a comorbid impulse control disorder, while women more often were characterized by a comorbid eating disorder. Ultimately, more work is needed to disentangle the potential influences of gender upon the development and presentation of kleptomania.

Pyromania

Though a curiosity about or even a fascination with fire may be considered within the normal range of human experience, an inability to resist impulses to set fires is clearly problematic given this behavior's significant potential to result in the destruction of property and the loss of human life. Individuals with **pyromania** (like Paul Keller) repeatedly engage in deliberate and purposeful fire setting, and, much as those with other impulse control disorders, they experience tension and emotional arousal before the act and pleasure or relief afterwards. They may be indifferent to the damage caused by the fires they set, at times even deriving satisfaction from the resulting destruction of property (APA, 2000). Diagnostic criteria for pyromania, taken from the DSM-5, are listed in Table 9.3.

Table 9.3 DSM-5 Diagnostic Criteria for Pyromania

312.33 (F63.1) Pyromania

A. Deliberate and purposeful fire setting on more than one occasion.

B. Tension or affective arousal before the act.

C. Fascination with, interest in, curiosity about, or attraction to fire and its situational contexts (e.g., paraphernalia, uses, consequences).

D. Pleasure, gratification, or relief when setting fires, or when witnessing or participating in their aftermath.

E. The fire setting is not done for monetary gain, as an expression of sociopolitical ideology, to conceal criminal activity, to express anger or vengeance, to improve one's living circumstances, in response to a delusion or hallucination, or as a result of impaired judgment (e.g., in major neurocognitive disorder, intellectual disability [intellectual developmental disorder], substance intoxication).

F. The fire setting is not better accounted for by conduct disorder, a manic episode, or antisocial personality disorder.

Source: APA (2013, p. 476). Reprinted with permission from the *Diagnostic and Statistical Manual of Mental Disorders*, Fifth Edition (Copyright © 2013). American Psychiatric Association. All rights reserved.

Prevalence and Incidence Rates of Pyromania

The DSM-IV-TR does not report prevalence rate estimates for pyromania, noting only that it is "apparently rare" (APA, 2000, p. 670); and the DSM-5 acknowledges that population prevalence of pyromania is unknown (APA, 2013). Rates of 2.4–3.5% have been reported in samples of children and adolescents (Dell'Osso et al., 2006) and of 3.3% in individuals who were in contact with the criminal justice system for repeated fire setting (APA, 2013).

Theoretical Conceptualizations

Fire setting, even fire setting that is deliberate and purposeful, is not in and of itself a criminal act. Rather, fire setting typically only becomes criminal if it either intentionally or recklessly results in damage to property (arson or the malicious destruction of property) or harm to people (aggravated assault or a form of homicide). Furthermore, numerous authors have made key conceptual distinctions between fire setting, arson, and pyromania. According to Burton and colleagues (2012), not all fire setters have committed arson, and most arsonists do not meet criteria for pyromania. However, given the theoretical and empirical efforts made to differentiate between these concepts, it is somewhat difficult to understand why even the best-written samples of this literature (e.g., Horley & Bowlby, 2011) keep them largely interwoven. Perhaps the reason is, in part, a comparative lack of studies on pyromania in particular or that each of the concepts represents a different lexicon (i.e., *fire setting* from human behavior, *arson* from law, and *pyromania* from psychiatry) and so describes distinct but necessarily overlapping phenomenon.

Historically, physicians from Germany, Prussia, and France in the late eighteenth and early nineteenth centuries provided the initial medical models for understanding fire setting. "Pyromania" is derived from the Greek terms for "fire (*πυρ*)" and "mania (*μανί*)." French psychiatrist Charles Chrétien Henri Marc (1833, in Andrews, 2010a) is often accredited with coining this term (see also Horley & Bowlby, 2011)—though it is actually an inaccurate English translation of his original term "*monomanie incendiare*" (Andrews, 2010a), which represented fire setting that was repetitive and "bizarre" (i.e., not stemming from common motives such as revenge; Horley & Bowlby, 2011). In fact, several German and Prussian writers had recognized and addressed the problem of "insane incendiarism" in the decades before, using terms such as the "*Feuerlust*," or "fire lust" and "delight in seeing a fire burning" (often seen in "imbeciles"), and "*Brandstiftungstrieb*," meaning "impulsive incendiarism." Early theorists noted that insane incendiarism was especially common among young females, and they attributed impulses for fire setting to disturbed or irregular somatic and psychosexual development, often associating it with menstrual and reproductive disorders around puberty (Andrews, 2010a). Franz Josef Gall, founder of phrenology (see Chapter 2), believed that murderers and arsonists were of similar mental dispositions (Gall, 1833, in Horley & Bowlby, 2011). Later, James Cowles Prichard was the first British psychiatrist to recognize that fire setting could be exclusively indicative of a mental illness (1835, in Andrews, 2010a), and the term "insane arson" has been used to describe its medicolegal conceptual development in Britain, the United States, and Europe during the nineteenth and early twentieth centuries (Andrews, 2010a,b).

Psychoanalytic interpretations of pyromania began when Stekel (1943, in Horley & Bowlby, 2011) described it as a form of paraphilia caused by impeded or unfulfilled sexual tension. He proposed three distinct sexual motives behind pyromania: sexual sadism (wherein the pyromaniac enjoys the pain experienced by victims and typically masturbates at the scene), arson committed to enforce abstinence from masturbation, and arson intended to end the habit of masturbation. Freud (1932, in Horley & Bowlby, 2011) later elaborated on the theme of pyromania as a sexual disorder, using the myth of Prometheus to propose that pyromania represented a homosexual conflict related to the primitive desire of men to extinguish fire with their own urine. Thus, fire was symbolic of lust, and fire setting was a sexual, specifically, a homoerotic symbolic act. Other psychoanalytic writers proposed strong connections between fire and water (i.e., "urethral eroticism" or the "urethra-erotic character trait") and, later, observed connections between enuresis, or the involuntary and inappropriate voiding of urine, and fire setting. They also explained fire setting as a substitution for masturbation and suggested that oral fixations were among the unconscious processes associated with pyromania (Horley & Bowlby, 2011).

Learning theorists have proposed that fire setting is a much-needed outlet for the expression of negative emotions and sexual frustrations when appropriate outlets for the expression of these or of arousal are never learned. Individuals who are socially or interpersonally inept, are poorly educated, or who grew up in dysfunctional or abusive home environments are particularly in need of these outlets. Thus, fire setting becomes a learned behavior used to gain control and relieve sexual tension for those who deliberately set fires. Finally, dynamic-behavioral theory, which takes into account societal, environmental, and personality characteristics that lead to fire setting, emphasizes nonemotional factors (family history, school functioning, previously enacted behaviors, organic and physical problems), environmental factors (modeling, imitation, and inconsistent parenting), and other factors such as stress, peer pressure, and emotional distress (Horley & Bowlby, 2011; see also MacKay et al., 2012; and Tyler & Gannon, 2012). This theory coincides with others noted in the literature on the common triggers for fire setting, which include stress, boredom, feelings of inadequacy, and interpersonal conflict (Burton et al., 2012).

Neurobiological conceptualizations of pyromania have been offered (see Horley & Bowlby, 2011) but are comparatively rare. For example, Grant (2006) presents the case of an 18-year-old man diagnosed with pyromania. Though this man had above-average intelligence, brain imaging using single photon emission computed tomography (SPECT) revealed a left inferior frontal perfusion deficit. According to this author, some researchers have speculated about the role of the corticomesolimbic dopamine function in pyromania.

Furthermore, the neurobiological mechanisms of pyromania may be better understood by examining the neuroanatomical pleasure response systems thought to underlie impulse-control disorders as a whole. More specifically, Schmitz (2005) proposes that, in people with impulse-control disorders, the neurocircuits (i.e., the amygdala and mesocortical tract) and the neurochemical mediation of pleasure and reward responses via dopamine and HPA axis functioning may be the same as those in people with substance-related disorders. Thus, impulse-control disorders such as IED, kleptomania, pyromania, and pathological gambling may be conceptually linked and neurobiologically akin to substance addictions (remember how pathological gambling has recently been renamed gambling disorder and put under the substance-related and addictive disorders classification in the DSM-5)—a conceptualization that could have significant implications for the treatment of these disorders.

The Relationship Between Pyromania and Crime

A Closer Look: Pyromania and Crime

Prevalence of the Disorder in Crime

Study Type	**Number**	**Prevalence Rates**
Arrest rates	0	–
Birth cohorts	0	–
Community samples	1*	23.0%
Homicide offenders	0	–
Jailed detainees and prisoners	2	4.0–19.0%
Psychiatric inpatients	2*	1.8–23.0%
Total Number of Studies	**4**	

Sample Characteristics

Size	22–126
Gender	Male only (2 studies); female only (1 study); male and female (1 study)
Age	Youth, adult

(Continued)

(Continued)

Location	Sweden, United States
Diagnostic Systems	DSM (various editions), ICD-9

Note: *One study involved both psychiatric inpatients and community individuals.

Prevalence of Crime in the Disorder

Study Type	Number	Prevalence Rates	Crime Definition
Total Number of Studies	**0**		

Nondisordered or community resident comparison group or general population baseline rates for either disorder or crime provided: **0 studies (0.0%)**

General Studies

Relatively few studies have actually examined the relationship between the *disorder* of pyromania and the *crime* of arson. Empirical studies of pyromania appear somewhat rare relative to the body of work dedicated to the other disorders examined in this chapter. Some attention, however, has been paid to the phenomenological features of individuals with this disorder. For example, Grant and Kim (2007) examined the clinical characteristics of 21 adult inpatients with pyromania (including 10 women), and found the mean age of onset of the disorder to be 18.1 $\pm$ 5.8 years. Most (85.7%) reported urges to set fires, and participants reported setting 1 fire every 5.9 $\pm$ 3.8 weeks. Interestingly, a slight majority of these individuals (n = 12; 57.1%) set fires that did not meet the legal definition of arson (these were, arguably, "controlled" fires in dumpsters, their bathrooms, backyards, or vacant lots). Additionally, Horley and Bowlby (2011) reviewed research and classification systems related to arson and pyromania (see Table 9.4). Remarkably, these classification systems, as a whole, have not incorporated pyromania into their typologies; however, some categories in some systems include categories that could be conceptually similar to features of pyromania—though further clarification is needed.

One area of the literature that may be germane to research into pyromania is the number of studies conducted on juvenile or childhood or adolescent fire setting (remember, however, that many juvenile fire setters do not go on to develop pyromania). Interestingly, juvenile fire setters account for over half of all arrests for arson in the United States and for 45% of all arson cases solved by arrest (Kolko, 2002, in Dolan et al., 2010). An interest in fire is thought to be nearly universal in children, and fire setting in this age group is often due to curiosity (Burton et al., 2012). Fires set by individuals in this age group, however, even when unintentional, can be quite damaging and often go undetected or unsolved (Dolan et al., 2010). Most researchers have found useful Gaynor's (1996) proposed three stages of fire related behaviors—fire interest, fire play, and fire setting—which reflect both the severity of the behavior as well as age-associated developmental changes (Dolan et al., 2010)

Much of the literature on juvenile fire setting has focused on rates of this behavior among different youth samples and on factors associated with fire setting when it occurs in these particular age ranges. Other studies of intentional fire setting in childhood have suggested individual features of temperament, parental psychopathological factors, social and environmental factors (e.g., large family size and low SES), and possibly neurochemical predispositions to be among causes of childhood fire setting; and anger, sadness, depression, and feeling ignored have commonly been reported before fire setting among fire setters in this age group (Chen et al., 2003). Chen and colleagues (2003) used epidemiological evidence from a large U.S. national sample survey (the 1995 National Household Survey on Drug Abuse) to examine factors related to fire setting in adolescence. Results indicated that, of the 4,595 respondents (ages 12 to 17), 284 reported fire setting, and 6% reported doing

Table 9.4 Incorporating the Concept of Pyromania Within Classification Systems for Arson

Earliest Attempts: Presence or Absence of Mental Disorder							**Incorporation of Pyromania?**
Lewis & Yarnell (1951): Arsonists who set fires due to diminished mental capacity	Accidental or unintentional	Delusional	Erotically motivated	Revenge motivated	Children who light fires		Unclear: Possibly "erotically motivated"
Second Stage: Inferred Motivation							**Incorporation of Pyromania?**
Barker (1994), Douglas et al., (1992), others: Motivational categories	Revenge	Excitement	Profit	Vandalism	Crime concealment	Extremist	Unclear: Possibly "excitement"
Davis & Lauber (1999), Prins et al. (1985): Added categories	Cry for help	Vagrancy	Heroism	Unknown reasons			Unclear (see above)
Third Stage: Behavior							**Incorporation of Pyromania?**
Douglas et al. (1992): Behavior	Organized • Elaborate incendiary devices • Methodological approach to fire setting • Leaves little evidence at crime scene	Disorganized • Uses materials found at crime scene • Common ignition devices • Physical evidence often left at crime scene					No
Canter & Fritzon (1998): Behavioral indicators	Instrumental person (conflicts between arsonist and victim)	Instrumental object (opportunistic style—no apparent purpose)	Expressive person (heroic or attention-seeking motivation)	Expressive object (arson committed to achieve emotional relief)			Unclear: Possibly "expressive object"
Kocsis (2004, 2006): Behavioral patterns linked to offender characteristics	Anger	Thrill	Resentment	Sexual			Unclear: Possibly "thrill" or "sexual"

Source: Adapted from Horley & Bowlby (2011).

so recently. Strong associations between fire setting and shyness, aggressiveness, and peer rejection were also observed. Looking at samples including children and adolescents from around the world, other authors have reported relationships between fire setting and such factors as childhood traumatic experiences (Lyons et al., 2010), maltreatment history (Root et al., 2008), alcohol intoxication (Lindberg et al., 2005), suicidal ideation and behavior, and antisocial behavior and risk-taking activities (Martin et al., 2004).

Del Bove and MacKay (2011) noted the significant dearth of empirically based classification systems in the literature on juvenile fire setting. Within a sample of 240 child and adolescent fire setters, these authors used cluster analysis to differentiate three distinct subtypes based on fire-specific characteristics, individual and environmental variables, and fire-setting recidivism and general outcome. These subtypes are conventional-limited fire setters (with the lowest fire-setting incidence, the oldest age of fire-setting onset, and the fewest ignition sources), home-instability-moderate fire setters (with more fire-setting episodes; a younger age of onset behavior; and more curiosity, targets, and ignition sources), and multi-risk-persistent fire setters (with the most fire-setting episodes, the youngest age of onset, the most resources and curiosity, and having experienced significantly more abuse than conventional-limited but less than home-instability-moderate groups).

Origins of Crime and Violence in Pyromania: Theoretical Explanations and Etiological Mechanisms

In small inpatient and outpatient sample populations, pyromania has demonstrated high rates of comorbidity both with various impulse-control disorders (Grant & Kim, 2007; Schmitz, 2005) and with other—though not necessarily criminogenic—Axis I psychopathologies, such as mood disorders (Grant & Kim, 2007). Additionally, some authors (e.g., Gelhorn et al., 2009) have found juvenile fire setting to be a strong predictor of conduct disorder while others have questioned whether or not pyromania can be better explained as a conduct disorder, an antisocial personality disorder, or a manic state.

The potential role of gender in pyromania has been explored to some degree in the literature, at least to the extent that differential rates of fire setting between genders have been reported across studies. For example, in a large national epidemiological sample, Chen and colleagues (2003) found boys to be 3.8 times more likely to be fire setters than girls, and Lyons and colleagues (2010) found rates of childhood fire setting to be twice as high in males compared to females in a large Illinois Department of Children and Family Services sample. Males have comprised up to 90% of fire-setting youth in other epidemiological samples (Del Bove & MacKay, 2011). Although there is more literature on males diagnosed with pyromania, examining pyromania in females is equally important. In a rare study of the characteristics of incarcerated women who were fire setters, Coid and Coid (1999) compared female inmates with a history of self-mutilation ($n = 74$) to those without ($n = 62$). Results indicated 19% ($n = 14$) of the former were diagnosed with pyromania while the disorder was not at all present in the latter; the findings suggest a relationship between pyromania and self-injurious behavior in women.

BOX 9.1 JOHN LEONARD ORR: FIRE DEPARTMENT CAPTAIN AND SERIAL ARSONIST

John Leonard Orr, former fire captain and arson investigator for the Glendale Fire Department in Southern California and novelist, was convicted of arson for setting a series fires in the 1980s and 1990s; these fires caused millions of dollars in damages and claimed four lives.

Pathological Gambling (Gambling Disorder)

The excitement of risking one's own wealth in the hopes of a possible immediate and substantial monetary gain is certainly an understandable experience to many individuals (with the impulsivity of such behavior arguably adding to the thrill). For some, however, the inability to control impulses to gamble can create the potential for significant personal and financial consequences. **Pathological gambling (gambling disorder)** is a problematic pattern of persistent and repeated gambling behavior leading to disruptions in personal, family, or vocational endeavors (APA, 2000). DSM-5 Diagnostic criteria for gambling disorder (previously known as pathological gambling in the DSM-IV-TR) are listed in Table 9.5.

Table 9.5 DSM-5 Diagnostic Criteria for a Gambling Disorder

312.31 (F63.0) Gambling Disorder

A. Persistent and recurrent problematic gambling behavior leading to clinically significant impairment or distress, as indicated by the individual exhibiting four (or more) of the following in a 12-month period:

1. Needs to gamble with increasing amounts of money in order to achieve the desired excitement.
2. Is restless or irritable when attempting to cut down or stop gambling.
3. Has made repeated unsuccessful efforts to control, cut back, or stop gambling.
4. Is often preoccupied with gambling (i.e., having persistent thoughts of reliving past gambling experiences, handicapping or planning the next venture, thinking of ways to get money with which to gamble).
5. Often gambles when feeling distressed (e.g., helpless, guilty, anxious, depressed).
6. After losing money gambling, often returns another day to get even ("chasing" one's losses).
7. Lies to conceal the extent of involvement with gambling.
8. Has jeopardized or lost a significant relationship, job, or educational or career opportunity because of gambling.
9. Relies on others to provide money to relieve desperate financial situations caused by gambling.

B. The gambling behavior is not better explained by a manic episode.

Specify if:

Episodic: Meeting diagnostic criteria at more than one time point, with symptoms subsiding between periods of gambling disorder for at least several months.

Persistent: Experiencing continuous symptoms, to meet diagnostic criteria for multiple years.

Specify if:

In early remission: After full criteria for gambling disorder were previously met, none of the criteria for gambling disorder have been met for at least 3 months but for less than 12 months.

In sustained remission: After full criteria for gambling disorder were previously met, none of the criteria for gambling disorder have been met during a period of 12 months or longer.

Specify current severity:

Mild: 4–5 criteria met.

Moderate: 6–7 criteria met.

Severe: 8–9 criteria met.

Source: APA (2013, pp. 585–586). Reprinted with permission from the *Diagnostic and Statistical Manual of Mental Disorders*, Fifth Edition (Copyright © 2013). American Psychiatric Association. All rights reserved.

Prevalence and Incidence Rates of Pathological Gambling

According to the DSM-IV-TR, prevalence rates of pathological gambling vary directly with the availability of legalized gambling. Lifetime prevalence rates of 0.4% to 3.4% have been estimated in community studies of adults although increased rates have been reported in specific areas (e.g., 7% in Puerto Rico and Australia) and in other populations (e.g., 2.8–8% in adolescents and college students). Furthermore, treatment-seeking individuals with a substance use disorder may also be characterized by higher rates of pathological gambling (APA, 2000). According to the DSM-5, past-year prevalence rates of gambling disorder in the general population are reported at approximately 0.2–0.3% and lifetime prevalence rates at approximately 0.4–1.0% (APA, 2013).

Theoretical Conceptualizations

From a neurobiological perspective, pathological gambling has been examined within the context of **information processing theory**, which incorporates the concept of neural or memory networks (Walters & Contri, 1998). These are networks of interrelated elements or nodes that provide structure to the ways in which we think about and observe the world around us. An individual's neural network for gambling may include elements or nodes that represent what they experience when they sit down at a blackjack table or place a bet on a sports match; these include feelings (e.g., excitement or other bodily sensations), thoughts (e.g., perceived odds of winning or how others will react when they win), and expectancies (e.g., winning, losing, feeling exhilarated or depressed). Pathological gamblers often report experiencing an unanticipated "big win" toward the beginning of their gambling careers. This success is thought to affect future gambling behavior in several ways: (1) winnings are viewed by the individual as less significant than money earned through hard work and are subsequently more likely to be spent frivolously, (2) prior gambling successes may encourage future risk-taking behavior, and (3) unanticipated "big wins" may create expectancies for future success in gambling—all of these may allow some individuals to believe that gambling will provide financial and psychological rewards that cannot be obtained elsewhere (Walters & Contri, 1998). From a cognitive perspective, factors such as *attributional style*, *cognitive bias*, and *illusions of control* may also play key roles in pathological gambling behavior. For example, the roulette wheel gambler could irrationally assume that the outcome of a spin is dependent upon the outcomes of previous spins or could discount gambling failures while focusing on gambling successes to prove the validity of a problem gambler's methods or the depth of his or her insight. These views may lead the problem gambler to focus too much on anticipated positive gambling outcomes while largely ignoring the potential negative outcomes (Walters & Contri, 1998). In fact, outcome expectancies for gambling (i.e., positive-negative and arousal-sedating dimensions) have shown similarities to those for alcohol in some studies (Walters & Contri, 1998).

Brain-imaging studies have also revealed some potential neurobiological underpinnings of pathological gambling. In one fMRI study, Crockford and colleagues (2005) found not only increased cravings for gambling in 13 men with pathological gambling compared to 10 controls but also increased activity during alternating visual presentations of a gambling-related video and a video of nature scenes. This increased activity occurred in several of their key brain regions: the right dorsolateral prefrontal cortex (DLPFC), the right inferior medial and frontal gyri, the right parahippocampal gyrus, and the left occipital cortex.

These findings may represent a cue-induced or conditioned craving response that underlies pathological gambling. In another fMRI study, Reuter and colleagues (2005) found reduced activation in the ventral striatum and ventromedial prefrontal cortex in 12 pathological gamblers compared to 12 matched controls. Reduced activity in these two areas are hallmarks of drug addiction and impulse-control deficits, respectively, suggesting that pathological gambling is a form of "non-substance-related addiction." Unfortunately, brain-imaging studies on pathological gambling are few and far between, and more work is needed to understand fully the neurobiological mechanisms that might underlie this disorder.

The Relationship Between Pathological Gambling and Crime

A Closer Look: Pathological Gambling and Crime

Prevalence of the Disorder in Crime

Study Type	Number	Prevalence Rates
Arrest rates	0	–
Birth cohorts	0	–
Community samples	3*	22.0–34.0%
Homicide offenders	0	–
Jailed detainees and prisoners	16	5.0–33.0%†
Psychiatric inpatients	3	6.2–18.0%
Total Number of Studies	**21**	

Sample Characteristics

Size	36–2,307
Gender	Male only (13 studies); male and female (5 studies); not reported (3 studies)
Age	Youth, adult
Location	Several countries worldwide (e.g., Australia, Belgium, England, New Zealand, and the United States)
Diagnostic Systems	DSM (various editions), South Oaks Gambling Screen (SOGS), other research diagnostic measures

Notes: *One study involved both psychiatric inpatients and community individuals.
†Lifetime prevalence rates reported separately at 2.0–39.0%.

Prevalence of Crime in the Disorder

Study Type	Number	Prevalence Rates	Crime Definition
Total Number of Studies	**0**		

Nondisordered or community resident comparison group or general population baseline rates for either disorder or crime provided: **0 studies (0.0%)**

General Studies

Much of the literature on the relationship between pathological gambling and crime and violence has been dedicated to studying prevalence rates of pathological gambling and the frequency and severity of problematic gambling behaviors among incarcerated inmates (e.g., Templer et al., 1993; Walters, 1997—see Table 9.6). Gambling activities such as the lottery, card and dice games, and gambling on sports outcomes can be quite common in correctional settings (Walters, 1997). A sizeable number of studies have been generated from male and female prison populations in New Zealand (e.g., Abbott & McKenna, 2000; Abbott, McKenna, & Giles, 2000; Sullivan et al., 2008), Australia (e.g., Marshall, Balfour, & Kenner, 1998), and the State of Texas (e.g., Kerber, 2001a, 2001b; Kerber & Harris, 2001; Kerber, Maxwell, & Wallisch, 2001). These have demonstrated significant rates of pathological and problematic gambling in these populations (see Table 9.6). Common measures utilized in such studies are the **South Oaks Gambling Screen** (SOGS; Lesieur & Blume, 1987) and the Revised South Oaks Gambling Screen (SOGS-R; Abbott & Volberg, 1991, 1996), which calculate a score based on gambling-related behaviors such as chasing losses, lying about winning, losing time from school or work because of gambling, and borrowing money for gambling from household sources, relatives, financial institutions, and other sources. Furthermore, studies of youth in correctional facilities and serving community sentences in Texas and New Zealand have also reported significant rates of pathological and problematic gambling (Brown, 1998; Wallisch & Kerber, 2001).

Origins of Crime and Violence in Pathological Gambling: Theoretical Explanations and Etiological Mechanisms

Little empirical attention has been paid to understanding factors related to the expression of crime and violence within individuals with pathological gambling. Some of the previously mentioned prison studies, however, have gone beyond the reporting of prevalence rates of pathological or problematic gambling and have examined potential mechanisms that may—at the very least—underlie the basic association between pathological gambling and crime. For example, reduced intelligence and elevated MMPI psychopathic deviate and hypomania scale scores have been reported among inmates who score higher on the SOGS (Templer et al., 1993). (MMPI stands for the Minnesota Multiphasic Personality Inventory—a frequently used self-report measure of personality.) Others have found associations between pathological and problematic gambling and substance abuse and dependence (Kennedy & Grubin, 1990; Kerber, 2001b; Maxwell & Wallisch, 1998; McCorkle, 2002). Furthermore, rather significant gender differences in pathological gambling behavior have been noted in studies of inmates. For example, in a sample 440 male and 419 female offenders from the Texas Department of Justice's Substance Abuse Felony Punishment program, Kerber, Maxwell, and Wallisch (2001) found that men were more likely than women to engage in some form of gambling (68% versus 43%, respectively). Also, men were also more likely than women to gamble on a weekly basis (37% versus 11%, respectively) or to have a gambling problem compared to women. In aggregate, evidence presented here (i.e., in the form of personality functioning, substance use, or gender influences) may begin to suggest the underlying etiological mechanisms of crime and violence in pathological gambling, though work in this area to date remains in its nascent stages and requires further attention from researchers.

Trichotillomania (Hair-Pulling Disorder)

The purposeful pulling out of one's own hair (for reasons other than enhancing cosmetic appearance) may seem a bit unusual on its face, and perhaps even more difficult to fathom is the inability to resist *impulsively* doing so. Individuals with **trichotillomania**, however, do in fact repeatedly pull out their own hair—to the point that hair loss becomes noticeable, and they experience significant distress or impairment. According to the DSM-IV-TR, those with this disorder commonly pull hair from the scalp, eyebrows, and eyelashes (see Box 9.2), though sites may include anywhere on the body that hair is found, such as the axillary, pubic, and perirectal regions (APA, 2000). DSM-5 diagnostic criteria for trichotillomania (hair-pulling disorder) are listed in Table 9.7.

Prevalence and Incidence Rates of Trichotillomania

While the DSM-IV-TR originally reported that no systematic data were available on the prevalence rates for trichotillomania (APA, 2000), the DSM-5 has since reported 12-month estimates of 1– 2% in adolescents and adults in the general population, with females being affected at a ratio of 10:1 relative to males (APA, 2013). Rates among college students have also been reported at 1.5% for males and 3.4% for females (Dell'Osso et al., 2006).

Table 9.6 Prevalence of Impulse Control Disorders in Criminal Populations

Source	N	Gender	Age	Study Type[a1]	Sample Description	Disorder	Diagnostic System	Prevalence/ Incidence
Royal College of Psychiatrists (1977, in Lesieur, 1993)	1,058	M	Adult	JD	Prison inmates, United Kingdom (London)	Pathological gambling	Clinical assessment	5%
Lesieur & Klein (1985, in Williams et al., 2005)	448	?M, ?W	Adult	JD	Prison inmates, United States (New Jersey)	Pathological gambling (lifetime)	South Oaks Gambling Screen (SOGS)	30%
Jones (1990, in Williams et al., 2005)	60	M	Adult	JD	Remand center prisoners in Western Australia	Pathological gambling (lifetime)	SOGS	22%
Kennedy & Grubin (1990)	51	M	Adult	JD	Interviews and questionnaires administered to prison sex offenders, United Kingdom	Pathological gambling (lifetime)	DSM-III-R	18%
DeJong, Virkkunen, & Linnoila (1992)	(1) 248 (2) 100	M	16–68 (*M* = 31.2, *SD* =11.9)	JD	Criminals ordered for forensic psychiatric examination at initial incarceration in Finland (1) Murders and attempted murderers (2) Arsonists	Intermittent explosive disorder	DSM-III	(1) 20.0% (2) 25.0%
Maden et al. (1992)	404	M	*M* = 19	JD	Inmates of youth custody centers, United Kingdom	Pathological gambling (lifetime)	Gambling caused problems; DSM-III-R	2%
Templer et al. (1993)	136	M	Adult	JD	Recently sentenced prison inmates, United States (Nevada)	Pathological gambling (lifetime)	SOGS	24%
Marshall et al. (1998)	103	M	18–56	JD	Diagnostic interviews and questionnaires administered to recently sentenced inmates (August–December 1997) at Yatala Labour Prison, South Australia	Pathological gambling (past 6 months)	SOGS	33%

(Continued)

(Continued)

Source	N	Gender	Age	Study Type[a1]	Sample Description	Disorder	Diagnostic System	Prevalence/ Incidence
Walters (1997)	363	M	Adult	JD	Interviews with medium-security federal prison inmates, United States (northeastern region)	Pathological gambling (lifetime)	SOGS	5%
Brown (1998, in Williams et al., 2005)	100	?	Adult	CS	Offenders serving community sentences, New Zealand	Pathological gambling (lifetime)	SOGS	26%
Walters & Contri (1998)	316	M	Adult	JD	Questionnaires administered to randomly selected medium security federal facility prison inmates	Probable pathological gambling (lifetime)	SOGS	18.0% (n = 57)
Westphal et al. (1998, in Williams et al., 2005)	(1) 1,673 (2) 310	(1) 61% M (2) 72% M	(1) Adult (2) Median = 16	JD	Representative sample of (1) Adult Indiana inmates (2) Juvenile Indiana inmates	Pathological gambling (lifetime)	(1) SOGS (2) SOGS-R	(1) 19% (2) 39%
Anderson (1999)	233	M	Adult	JD	Questionnaire administered to prison inmates participating in prerelease programing, United States (Midwest)	Pathological gambling (lifetime)	SOGS	38%
Coid et al. (1999)	74	F	M = 23.3, SD = 6.9	JD	Subgroup of remanded female prisoners with a history of self-mutilation	Pyromania	DSM-III	19% (n = 14)
Galli et al. (1999)	22	M	13–17 (M = 15.9, SD =1.1)	PI, CS	Interviews with adolescents admitting to sexually assaulting another child, referred from a juvenile rehabilitation center, the juvenile court system, and an inpatient adolescent psychiatric unit, Hamilton County, Ohio	Intermittent explosive disorder	DSM-III-R	45.0% (n = 10)
						Kleptomania		18.0% (n = 4)
						Pyromania		23.0% (n = 5)
						Impulse-control disorder NOS		0.05% (n = 1)
						Total		55.0% (n = 12)
McElroy et al. (1999)	36	M	18–47 (M = 33, SD = 8)	PI	Interviews with convicted sex offenders consecutively admitted to the New Life Program, Cincinnati, Ohio, November 1996–June 1998	Kleptomania	DSM-IV (SCID)	3% (n = 1)
						Pathological gambling		8% (n = 3)

Source	N	Gender	Age	Study Type[a1]	Sample Description	Disorder	Diagnostic System	Prevalence/ Incidence
						Trichotillomania		3% (n = 1)
						Compulsive buying		14% (n = 5)
						Compulsive skin picking		3% (n = 1)
						Intermittent explosive disorder		19% (n = 7)
						Impulsive-control disorder NOS		3% (n = 1)
						Total impulse-control disorders		39% (n = 14)
Abbott & McKenna (2000, in Williams et al., 2005)	100	?	Adult	CS	Offenders serving community sentences, New Zealand	Pathological gambling	SOGS-R	22% (6 months) 33% (lifetime)
Abbott et al. (2000, in Williams et al., 2005)	357	?	Adult	JD	Recently sentenced prison inmates, New Zealand	Pathological gambling	SOGS-R	16% (6 months) 21% (lifetime)
Siponmaa et al. (2001)	126	123 M, 3 F	15–22 (Median = 20)	JD	Interviews with young offenders consecutively referred for presentencing psychiatric investigation, Stockholm, Sweden, 1990–1995	Pyromania	ICD-9	4% (n = 5)
McCorkle (2002, in Williams et al., 2005)	2,307	75% M	Adult	JD	Recent arrestees, United States (Las Vegas and Des Moines)	Pathological gambling (past year)	DSM-IV	9%
Queensland Government (2002, in Williams et al., 2005)	178	59% M	Adult	JD	Inmates in secure and open custody facilities, Queensland, Australia	Pathological gambling (1 year prior to incarceration)	Canadian Problem Gambling Index	17%

(Continued)

(Continued)

Source	N	Gender	Age	Study Type[a1]	Sample Description	Disorder	Diagnostic System	Prevalence/ Incidence
Australian National University Centre for Gambling Research (2003, in Williams et al., 2005)	102	95% M	Adult	JD, CS	Offenders in remand, serving weekend sentences, on bail, on parole, or serving community orders, Australian Capital Territory, Australia	Pathological gambling (lifetime)	SOGS	34%
Dunsieth et al. (2004)	113	M	18–66 (*M* = 35.3, *SD* =10.4)	PI	Diagnostic interviews with sex offenders consecutively referred to an Ohio residential sex-offender treatment program	Kleptomania	DSM-IV	2.7% ($n = 3$)
						Pathological gambling		6.2% ($n = 7$)
						Pyromania		1.8% ($n = 2$)
						Trichotillomania		2.7% ($n = 3$)
						Compulsive buying		9.7% ($n = 11$)
						Compulsive skin picking		1.8% ($n = 2$)
						Intermittent explosive disorder		20.4% ($n = 23$)
						Impulse-control disorder NOS		2.7% ($n = 3$)
Sullivan et al. (2008)	100	M	Adult?	JD	Screening measures and clinical assessment of medium-security prison inmates, North Island of New Zealand	Pathological gambling	DSM-IV, Eight Screen, SOGS	11% ($n = 11$)
Pham & Saloppé (2010)	84	M	Adult	PI	Psychological evaluations of forensic patients at a high-security psychiatric hospital in Tomai, Belgium (Etablissement de Défense Sociale)	Pathological gambling	DSM-III (DISSI)	18% ($n = 15$)

Note: [a1]AR = arrest rates of patients discharged from psychiatric facilities, JD = jailed detainees and incarcerated prisoners, HO = homicide offenders, BC = birth cohort study, PI = psychiatric inpatient sample, CS = community sample (i.e., epidemiological catchment area survey studies and outpatient psychiatric patients).

Table 9.7 DSM-5 Diagnostic Criteria for Trichotillomania (Hair-Pulling Disorder)

312.39 (F63.2) Trichotillomania (Hair-Pulling Disorder)

A. Recurrent pulling out of one's hair, resulting in hair loss.
B. Repeated attempts to decrease or stop hair pulling.
C. The hair pulling causes clinically significant distress or impairment in social, occupational, or other important areas of functioning.
D. The hair pulling or hair loss is not attributable to another medical condition (e.g., a dermatological condition).
E. The hair pulling is not better explained by the symptoms of another mental disorder (e.g., attempts to improve a perceived defect or flaw in appearance in body dysmorphic disorder).

Source: APA (2013, p. 251). Reprinted with permission from the *Diagnostic and Statistical Manual of Mental Disorders*, Fifth Edition (Copyright © 2013). American Psychiatric Association. All rights reserved.

Theoretical Conceptualizations

Recent brain-imaging studies have provided evidence for a possible neurobiological underpinning of trichotillomania. For example, several structural and functional imaging studies have revealed evidence of frontostriatal grey matter abnormalities in individuals with trichotillomania (Roos et al., 2013), though results have been mixed. Other investigators have focused on white matter structural deficits. For example, using MRI, Olza-Fernández and colleagues (2012) identified structural white matter abnormalities (i.e., hyperintensities) in various brain regions in the case of a six-year-old girl with trichotillomania who repeatedly pulled out her eyebrows and eyelashes. She was also diagnosed with pediatric bipolar disorder and ADHD. Using diffusion tensor

BOX 9.2 HAIR-PULLING PATIENT

Pathological hair pulling has been noted in the psychiatric literature for many years. This photograph of a "hair-pulling patient" comes from Emil Kraepelin's classic text on schizophrenia, *Dementia Praecox and Paraphrenia*, first published nearly a century ago. As the hair pulling in this case is likely more because of a psychotic disorder (the patient presented with stereotyped/catatonic behavior), a diagnosis of trichotillomania was precluded (see the diagnostic criteria for trichotillomania listed in Table 9.7). Nonetheless, it remains a good example of the marked degree to which hair pulling can occur in an individual suffering from mental illness.

Source: Kraepelin (1919/2002).

imaging (DTI), Roos and associates (2013) also found white matter abnormalities in a sample of women with trichotillomania ($n = 16$) and adult female controls ($n = 13$). Although the former was characterized by more anxiety, the groups did not differ on DTI measures. However, results indicated that increased white matter mean diffusivity (suggesting damaged or disorganized white matter tracts) in the frontostriatal-thalamic pathway was significantly associated with longer and more severe hair pulling.

The Relationship Between Trichotillomania and Crime

A Closer Look: Trichotillomania and Crime

Prevalence of the Disorder in Crime

Study Type	Number	Prevalence Rates
Arrest rates	0	–
Birth cohorts	0	–
Community samples	0	–
Homicide offenders	0	–
Jailed detainees and prisoners	0	–
Psychiatric inpatients	2	2.7–3.0%
Total Number of Studies	**2**	

Sample Characteristics

Size	36–113
Gender	Male only
Age	Adult
Location	United States (Ohio)
Diagnostic Systems	DSM-IV

Prevalence of Crime in the Disorder

Study Type	Number	Prevalence Rates	Crime Definition
Total Number of Studies	**0**		

Nondisordered or community resident comparison group or general population baseline rates for either disorder or crime provided: **0 studies (0.0%)**

Origins of Crime and Violence in Trichotillomania: Theoretical Explanations and Etiological Mechanisms

To date, evidence for a potential relationship between trichotillomania and crime remains virtually non-existent, partially due to the dearth of studies conducted in this area. However, the appearance of trichotillomania in at least a small number of studies of criminal populations, together with its inclusion in a class of disorders that has demonstrated associations with crime and violence, warrants a brief discussion of it here.

Among the limited evidence in this area, Olza-Fernández and colleagues (2012) report that the six-rear old girl with comorbid trichotillomania, pediatric bipolar disorder, and ADHD mentioned above was characterized by irritability, tantrums, and aggressive behaviors (unspecified) while under observation in a psychiatric hospital. Though trichotillomania often presents with other comorbid impulse control disorders (e.g., Lejoyeux et al., 2006; Müller et al., 2011), this case may demonstrate how comorbid psychiatric conditions associated with aggression and impulsivity (see Chapters 3 and 6) may contribute to the potential association of trichotillomania and antisocial behavior. Furthermore, the cyclical phenomenon of tension build-up, hair pulling, and release characterizing this disorder mirrors directly that of the other disorders discussed in this chapter. This cycle may also speak to a relationship between crime, violence, and a more general inability to regulate tension rather than to the association of crime and violence with specific disorders *per se*, or even with behaviors, such as stealing, fire setting, hair pulling, or outbursts of aggression.

Treatment Implications

A key implication of this research for the treatment of some impulse control disorders (e.g., IED, kleptomania, and pyromania) is that reductions in the symptomatic features of the disorders themselves, in effect, become reductions in criminal and violent behavior. For example, regarding IED, though no single medication has yet been approved by the U.S. government for the treatment of aggression (Felthous et al., 2013), some studies have indicated that reductions in impulsivity and aggression may be achieved by using medications such as mood stabilizers, phenytoin, selective serotonin reuptake inhibitors (SSRIs), ß-blockers, α2-agonists, and antipsychotics (Olivera, 2002). Group and individual cognitive-behavioral therapy approaches have shown effectiveness in reducing aggression, anger, hostile thinking, and depressive symptoms in individuals with IED (McCloskey et al., 2008b); and other behavioral interventions such as behavior management therapy and social skills training have also demonstrated usefulness in controlling aggression (Olivera, 2002). Additionally, approaches such as child-centered play therapy have also reportedly met with some success in children with IED (Paone & Douma, 2009). Other evidence indicates that the aforementioned treatment strategies—pharmacotherapy and cognitive-behavior therapy—have also demonstrated effectiveness in reducing stealing behaviors in those with kleptomania (Grant & Odlaug, 2008; Grant et al., 2013; Talih, 2013) and fire setting in those with pyromania (Burton et al., 2012; Grant, 2006). Though controlled, randomized trials of therapies for these conditions are still lacking (e.g., Burton et al., 2012) and more work is clearly needed, the successful treatment of these disorders has the potential for profoundly diminishing the crime and violence often associated with their core symptomatology.

Conclusion

The DSM-IV-TR's classification of impulse control disorders not elsewhere classified is, in a sense (and by name), a catchall for disorders that do not fit neatly into other disorder classes and that seem to share the underlying theme of an inability to control impulses of various types. In the DSM-5, this class of disorders has been refined somewhat and now includes disorders related to problematic emotional and behavioral self-control and associated with the violation of others' rights and significant conflict with societal norms or authority figures. As with the disorders covered in other chapters of this book, the disorders in this chapter have received varying levels of empirical attention in terms of their potential relationship with criminal, violent, and antisocial behavior. Unlike many of the disorders covered in this book, however, impulse control disorders (at least in the cases of IED, kleptomania, and pyromania) are, on some levels, intimately connected with criminality and actually form the basis of crime, violence, and aggression (to varying degrees) simply because of their diagnostic criteria. That being said, the state of the literature in this area is woefully embryonic, at least in terms of the paucity of studies striving for a deeper qualitative and quantitative understanding of the connections these disorders may have with criminal behavior beyond diagnostic conceptualizations. Paul Keller's impulse to destroy, possibly stemming from his own feelings of powerlessness, found release in uncontrollable acts of violent devastation. The fires he set accentuate the harm and damage possible to life, safety, and property when people are unable to control their impulses. So despite impulse control disorders being, arguably, in a "catchall" category of mental illness, the potential of those diagnosed with these disorders to do harm should compel researchers to greater empirical efforts in this area.

KEY TERMS

information processing theory

intermittent explosive disorder

kleptomania

pathological gambling (gambling disorder)

pyromania

South Oaks Gambling Screen

trichotillomania [hair-pulling disorder]

REVIEW QUESTIONS

1. Compare and contrast the conceptualizations from the different theoretical perspectives discussed in the chapter for each of the following impulse control disorders: intermittent explosive disorder, kleptomania, pyromania, pathological gambling (gambling disorder), and trichotillomania (hair-pulling disorder). What are some of the similarities and differences in the way pathological deficiencies in impulse control are conceptualized across disorders?
2. Examine Table 9.6 and the summaries of research studies in the "A Closer Look" section for the disorders in this chapter. Discuss how prevalence rates of crime in those with impulse control disorders differ depending upon disorder, if they do. Using the information in the tables, speculate as to how these differences in prevalence rates may have been caused by methodology (e.g., in terms of study types, sample characteristics, methodological issues, or other concerns).
3. Reflect on the material presented in Chapter 4 about substance-related disorders (substance-related and addictive disorders). In what ways do the impulse control disorders found in this chapter resemble conceptually those in Chapter 4? In what ways are they different? How might this affect treatment implications?
4. Examine the classification systems for arson listed in Table 9.4. How have these systems evolved conceptually over time? Has pyromania been successfully incorporated into these classification systems? If not, can you identify ways in which it could be? Is it even important to do so? Explain your answer.
5. Differentiate conceptually the crime of assault from IED, the crime of stealing from kleptomania, and the crime of arson from pyromania.

10

Personality Disorders

THEODORE ROBERT "TED" BUNDY

Theodore Robert "Ted" Bundy was born in Burlington, Vermont, on November 24, 1946. Bundy was an American serial killer who committed acts of murder, rape, kidnapping, and necrophilia against numerous young women and girls during (and possibly before) the 1970s. Known for his chameleon-like ability to blend in and his talent for belonging, he confessed to 30 homicides committed in seven states between 1974 and 1978—though the true total remains unknown.

Fatherless, Bundy spent his early childhood living in the home of his maternal grandparents, believing that his biological mother was actually his sister (a family ruse designed to avoid the social stigma of his illegitimate birth). At an early age, he exhibited disturbing behavior, on one occasion (at age three) reportedly surrounding his napping aunt with butcher knives and standing by the bed, smiling, as she awoke.

In his late teens, he had an explosive temper, was a compulsive masturbator, and a night-prowling peeping tom. Initially a college dropout, he eventually adopted a more civic-minded façade: he was commended by police for chasing down a purse-snatcher, became a well-regarded honors student and psychology major, and worked on a suicide hotline. After college, he even appeared to be headed for a successful career in law and politics.

Bundy's first series of known murders occurred in Washington and Oregon—while he worked at the government agency searching for the victims. Eluding capture, he later killed in Idaho, Utah, and Colorado. He exploited his good looks and charisma to win the trust of his young female victims, typically feigning disability or impersonating authority figures before overpowering them.

Arrested in Utah for a traffic violation, he was eventually convicted there for kidnapping as a consequence of evidence from his notorious Volkswagen Beetle. Extradition to Colorado to face murder charges followed. After two escapes and a series of violent and lethal assaults in Florida, he was finally apprehended. During his trial, Bundy insisted upon acting as his own defense counsel. Later, in prison, he offered his "expertise" on serial killers to assist investigators working on the famous Green River Killer case. Psychiatric examinations indicated a diagnosis of antisocial personality disorder though he is also considered by some to be the prototypical psychopath—charming, narcissistic, manipulative, and completely devoid of remorse. Florida executed Bundy in the electric chair on January 24, 1989.

Ted Bundy's lifelong pattern of disturbing and violent behavior, as incomprehensible as it may seem to others, was likely not experienced as unusual by him. It was instead a normative mode of functioning—predictable and familiar—due to its roots deep within the foundational recesses of his personality. What is personality? The question is easily asked but difficult to answer. Historically, the word itself is derived from "*persona*," the Greek term originally representing the theatrical mask used by actors on the stage. Today, personality is viewed as a complex pattern of deeply embedded psychological characteristics—intrinsic, pervasive, largely unconscious, and resistant to change—that are automatically expressed in just about every area of functioning. It is thought that personality traits emerge from a complicated mixture of biology and experience to form a pattern of perceiving, feeling, thinking, coping, and behaving that is unique to each and every individual (Millon & Davis, 1996).

The personality has been compared to an impressionistic painting: from afar a cohesive image but up close a complex array of moods, cognitions, and motives. From an ecological and evolutionary point of view, **personality disorders** are not human perversities but problematic styles of human adaptation. Individuals with these disorders are intriguing and unique, but their biological makeup and early life experiences combined to misdirect development, so their sense of self, the expression of their thoughts and feelings, and their ways of behaving are constructed as unsatisfying, problematic, and troublesome (Millon & Davis, 1996). The disorder represents, in a sense, the way the individual has found to "get through life." Symptoms of the disorder are ego-syntonic—embodying the only "normal" the individual has ever known or experienced.

Personality traits are defined in the DSM-IV-TR and DSM-5 as enduring patterns of perceiving, relating to, and thinking about the environment and self that are present across a wide range of contexts and situations. However, these traits do not represent disorders *per se* until they become inflexible and maladaptive, causing significant functional impairment or subjective distress (APA, 2000, 2013). In fact, several authors have emphasized that personality disorders may be better understood as dimensions of general personality functioning rather than as discrete illness categories (Millon & Davis, 1996; Vachon et al., 2013). Interestingly, the characteristic impairment associated with many of the disorders in the DSM-IV-TR and DSM-5 is often *not* experienced subjectively by the individual with a personality disorder; instead, it is the people around him or her that are chronically subjected to the difficult and frustrating nature of the illness. Furthermore, while the DSM-IV-TR and DSM-5 both outline ten personality disorders, Millon and Davis (1996) assert that this list of personality constructs is *not* exhaustive and that many more likely exist.

Personality disorders, which are categorized as Axis II disorders in the DSM-IV-TR, may coexist with other mental disorders, for example, Axis I disorders in the DSM-IV-TR (see Chapter 2 about the multiaxial diagnostic nature of the DSM-IV-TR). And some have speculated as to how these two types of disorders may be related. For example, the **vulnerability model** considers personality as the equivalent of an immune system (or "force field"), with personality disorders predisposing an individual, because of his or her limited or impoverished coping responses, to the development of an Axis I disorder such as anxiety or depression. Interestingly, it is thought that personality disorders themselves may evoke the very stressors that will promote the development of an Axis I disorder, so the process becomes, in a sense, a vicious circle that continues to perpetuate stressful conditions, which further weaken the "immune system" and lead to more severe clinical conditions. According to the **complication model**, this vulnerability relationship is reversed; the Axis I disorder, however it began, creates a predisposition for personality change. For example, a man may experience a schizophrenic episode and become greatly depressed afterwards as he realizes the significance of this disorder for his life. He may then become pessimistic and hopeless (i.e., his personality traits change) as a result of a change in his self-concept and self-efficacy. Under the **pathoplasty model**, personality influences the course of the Axis I disorder without itself disposing toward the development of the disorder. Finally the **spectrum model** proposes a continuum of increasing trait or symptom severity (from normal personality to subclinical traits to full-blown Axis I disorders), wherein the entire personality is organized around subclinical traits (Millon & Davis, 1996).

Although the ten different personality disorders listed in the DSM-IV-TR and DSM-5 differ in varying degrees from each other in terms of symptom expression, all must first meet the DSM-IV-TR general diagnostic criteria for a personality disorder or the DSM-5 diagnostic criteria for a general personality disorder. DSM-5 diagnostic criteria for a general personality disorder are listed in Table 10.1.

Furthermore, the DSM-IV-TR and DSM-5 outline a clustering system for personality disorders, based on descriptive similarities, which has proven useful in some research and educational situations. **Cluster A** includes the paranoid, schizoid, and schizotypal personality disorders (individuals described as odd or eccentric); **Cluster B** includes the antisocial, borderline, histrionic, and narcissistic personality disorders (individuals often appearing dramatic, emotional, or erratic); and **Cluster C** includes the avoidant, dependent, and obsessive-compulsive personality disorders (individuals often appearing anxious or fearful). It must be noted that this

Table 10.1 DSM-5 Diagnostic Criteria for a General Personality Disorder

General Personality Disorder*

A. An enduring pattern of inner experience and behavior that deviated markedly from the expectations of the individual's culture. This pattern is manifested in two (or more) of the following areas:
   1. Cognition (i.e., ways of perceiving and interpreting self, other people, and events)
   2. Affectivity (i.e., the range, intensity, lability, and appropriateness of emotional response)
   3. Interpersonal functioning
   4. Impulse control

B. The enduring pattern is inflexible and pervasive across a broad range of personal and social situations.

C. The enduring pattern leads to clinically significant distress or impairment in social, occupational, or other important areas of functioning.

D. The pattern is stable and of long duration, and its onset can be traced back at least to adolescence or early adulthood.

E. The enduring pattern is not better accounted for as a manifestation or consequence of another mental disorder.

F. The enduring pattern is not due to the direct physiological effects of a substance (e.g., a drug of abuse, a medication) or another medical condition* (e.g., head trauma).

Source: APA (2013, pp. 646–647). Reprinted with permission from the *Diagnostic and Statistical Manual of Mental Disorders*, Fifth Edition (Copyright © 2013). American Psychiatric Association. All rights reserved.

Note: *In the DSM-IV-TR, the title was just "Personality Disorder" and the wording "another medical condition" was "a general medical condition" (APA, 2000, p. 689).

clustering system has serious limitations and has not been consistently validated. Also, individuals may often present with coexisting personality disorders from different clusters (APA, 2000, 2013).

Finally, the DSM-5 has proposed an alternative model for conceptualizing personality disorders, which focuses on both *personality functioning* and pathological *personality traits*. Rather than being based on the traditional categorical approach, this alternative model uses a *dimensional perspective* in which personality disorders are maladaptive variations of personality traits that gradually merge into normality and into each other. Under this model, level of personality functioning is evaluated on a continuum for self (identity and self-direction) and for interpersonal elements (empathy and intimacy), with disturbances in these areas forming the core of personality disorders. Pathological personality traits for each disorder are represented by a taxonomy of 25 specific trait facets (a catalogue of sorts of pathological personality trait descriptors), which are subsumed under five domains—negative affectivity, detachment, antagonism, disinhibition, and psychoticism.[1] According to the DSM-5, this model is useful in categorizing only the antisocial, avoidant, borderline, narcissistic, obsessive-compulsive, and schizotypal personality disorders (APA, 2013). While this alternative model is an exciting addition to the DSM-5, the traditional model will be used in this chapter as the framework for the presentation of the personality disorders, and for our discussion of their relationships with crime and violence.

Theoretical Conceptualizations

The various personality disorders outlined in the DSM have been conceptualized according to numerous theoretical perspectives. Personality theorist Theodore Millon (see Box 10.1) proposed a unique theory-driven

1. As an example, for avoidant personality disorder, theDSM-5 proposed diagnostic criteria include four possible pathological personality traits: anxiousness (an aspect of negative affectivity), withdrawal (an aspect of detachment), anhedonia (an aspect of detachment), and intimacy avoidance (an aspect of detachment).

framework that draws heavily from biosocial learning and evolutionary principles (Millon & Davis, 1996). The foundation of Millon's personality theory is comprised of three polarities of behavior and motivation: active-passive, pleasure-pain, and self-other. These can be used to derive personality coping patterns that correspond rather well with the official DSM personality disorders. Rather than articulating specific diagnostic criteria, Millon identifies *personality prototypes* representing each pattern and discusses each within clinical diagnostic domains at the behavioral (expressive behavior, interpersonal conduct), phenomenological (cognitive style, self-image, object representation), intrapsychic (regulatory mechanisms, morphological organization), and biophysical levels (mood or temperament).[2] Because Millon's model is an integrated approach involving biological, psychological, and social perspectives, it will be used in this chapter as the primary basis for the theoretical conceptualizations of personality disorders.

BOX 10.1 THEODORE MILLON'S BIOSOCIAL LEARNING (EVOLUTIONARY) THEORY OF PERSONALITY

Personality theorist Theodore Millon was one of the first appointees in 1974 to the APA's Task Force responsible for developing the DSM-III, and he served as a full member of the DSM-IV Axis II Work Group. He has been editor in chief of the *Journal of Personality Disorders* and has authored numerous personality assessment inventories.

Millon proposed a biosocial learning theory (subsequently identified as an evolutionary model), identifying personality patterns based on a threefold framework of behavioral and motivational polarities: *active-passive, pleasure-pain,* and *self-other.*

The Relationship Between Personality Disorders and Crime

The prevalence rates of personality disorders in studies of criminal populations tend to be reported in the literature in one of two ways. First, they are often listed in aggregate, using more generic terms such as "personality disorder" (e.g., Medlicott, 1976), "any personality disorder" (e.g., Grella et al., 2008; Pham & Saloppé, 2010), or "other character disorder" (e.g., Kahn, 1971). Sometimes, the aforementioned clustering system is used (e.g., McElroy et al., 1999; Catanesi et al., 2011). In fact, 17 of the studies of personality disorders in criminal populations listed in Table 10.2 utilize the aggregate approach while 5 use the clustering system. Although prevalence rates of general personality disorders in populations of criminal and violent individuals are helpful to some extent in understanding the relationship between these disorders and crime, the differential rates of presentation of these disorders suggests that a better understanding may be gained by examining them separately.

The prevalence rates of specific personality disorders are indeed reported in studies of criminal populations. Sometimes, a study will focus solely on one given personality disorder (e.g., Schuckit et al., 1977), and sometimes one will examine various personality disorders together but differentiate between them and list the prevalence rates of each disorder separately (e.g., DeJong et al., 1992).

Although two prevalence rate studies of criminal and violent behavior in populations with personality disorders are identified in Table 10.3 (Asnis et al., 1994; Tardiff & Koenigsberg, 1985), these studies appeared to examine personality disorders in the general sense without reporting rates for specific personality disorders individually. As can be seen by examining the "A Closer Look" boxes that follow in this chapter, studies reporting rates of criminal behavior among populations with specific personality disorders are exceedingly rare.

2. Note the incorporation of a domain approach into the alternative model for personality disorders proposed in the DSM-5.

Table 10.2 Prevalence of Personality Disorders in Criminal Populations

Antisocial Personality Disorder								
Source	**N**	**Gender**	**Age**	**Study Type**[a1]	**Sample Description**	**Disorder**	**Diagnostic System**	**Prevalence/Incidence**
Schuckit et al. (1977)	199	M	Adult[b]	JD	Structured personal interviews of newly arrested prisoners at a San Diego, California jail	Antisocial personality	Brief screen for psychiatric illness (Woodruff et al., 1974)	16.0%
Langevin et al. (1982)	(1) 109 (2) 38	?	Adult?	PI	File record review of minimum-security forensic ward psychiatric hospital cases, 1969–1979 (Clarke Institute in Toronto, Ontario, Canada) (1) Killers (2) Nonviolent offenders	Antisocial personality	Feighner et al. (1972) psychiatric research diagnostic criteria	(1) 8.0% (2) 8.0%
Seltzer & Langford (1984)	85	M, F	15–25 (Median = 18)	PI	Interviews of individuals referred by courts or legal counsel to psychiatry department of large regional hospital in Northwest Territories, calendar year 1981	Antisocial personality	DSM-III, MMPI	12.9% ($n = 11$)
Reich & Wells (1985)	390	325 M, 65 F	$M = 30.9$	JD	Record review of defendants evaluated for competency to stand trial by the Yale–New Haven Psychiatric Court Clinic, 1980–1982	Antisocial personality disorder	DSM-III	1.0% ($n = 4$)[bh]
Wilcox (1985, 1987)	71	62 M, 9 F	Adult, juvenile (six < 18, five > 50)	HO	Record review of all individuals convicted for homicides committed in Contra Costa County, California, 1978–1980	Antisocial personality	?	35.2% ($n = 25$)[o]

(Continued)

(Continued)

Antisocial Personality Disorder								
Source	**N**	**Gender**	**Age**	**Study Type**[a1]	**Sample Description**	**Disorder**	**Diagnostic System**	**Prevalence/Incidence**
Bland et al. (1990)	180	M	18–44	JD	Diagnostic interviews with inmates from two correctional centers, Alberta, Canada	Antisocial personality	DSM-III (DIS)	56.7% (n = 102)[au*]
Coté & Hodgins (1990)	495	M	19–67 (M = 31.1)	JD	Diagnostic interviews with Quebec penitentiary inmates	Antisocial personality disorder	DSM-III (DIS)	61.5% (n = 303)
Yarvis (1990)	100	88 M, 12 F	33% < 25, 85% < 40	HO	Diagnostic interviews and record reviews of a series of murderers referred for psychiatric evaluation in California, 1980–1988	Antisocial disorder	DSM-III	38.0% (n = 38)[m]
Abram & Teplin (1991)	728	M	16–68 (M = 26.3)	JD	Diagnostic interviews with jail detainees at Cook County Department of Corrections, Chicago, November 1983–November 1984	Antisocial personality	DSM-III-R (DIS)	Lifetime: 50.1% (n = 371) Current: 49.9% (n = 363)
Côté & Hodgins (1992)	(1) 87 (2) 373	M	(1) M = 35.6, SD = 8.9 (2) M = 30.3, SD = 8.3	JD, HO	Diagnostic interviews and file reviews of penitentiary inmates, Quebec (1) Homicide offenders (2) Nonhomicide offenders	Antisocial personality disorder	DSM-III (DIS)	(1) 35.6% (n = 31) (2) 47.7% (n = 178)
DeJong, Virkkunen, & Linnoila (1992)	(1) 248 (2) 100	M	16–68 (M = 31.2, SD =11.9)	JD	Criminals ordered for forensic psychiatric examination at initial incarceration in Finland (1) Murders and attempted murderers (2) Arsonists	Antisocial personality disorder	DSM-III	(1) 32.0% (2) 16.0%
Marshall et al. (1998)	103	M	18–56	JD	Diagnostic interviews and questionnaires administered to recently sentenced inmates (August–December 1997) at Yatala Labour Prison, South Australia	Antisocial personality	DSM-III-R (PDI-R)	47.1%

Antisocial Personality Disorder								
Source	N	Gender	Age	Study Type[a1]	Sample Description	Disorder	Diagnostic System	Prevalence/Incidence
Aromäki et al. (1999)	(1) 15 (2) 13 (3) 15 (4) 16	M	(1) M = 33.8, SD = 7.3 (2) M = 38.0, SD =5.8 (3) M = 39.5, SD = 7.7 (4) M = 31.7, SD = 6.9	JD, CS	Blood samples, questionnaires, and interviews with volunteers, consisting of (1) Imprisoned violent men (2) Nonimprisoned violent men (3) Nonviolent alcoholics (4) Community controls	Antisocial personality disorder	DSM-III-R	(1) 92%* (2) 73%* (3) 0.0% (4) 0.0%
Gibson et al. (1999)	213	M	M = 32	JD	Structured interviews with randomly selected state prison and regional jail inmates from a rural New England state	Antisocial personality	DSM-III-R (DIS-III-R)	Lifetime: 54.5% (n = 116) Current: NA
McElroy et al. (1999)	36	M	18–47 (M = 33, SD = 8)	PI	Interviews with convicted sex offenders consecutively admitted to the New Life Program, Cincinnati, Ohio, November 1996–June 1998	Antisocial personality disorder	DSM-IV (SCID)	72% (n = 26)
						Total Cluster B personality disorders		92% (n = 33)
Langevin (2003)	(1) 33 (2) 80 (3) 23 (4) 611	M	(1) M = 32.06 (2) M = 27.58 (3) M = 27.57 (4) M = 31.42	PI	Interviews with convicted sex offenders (n = 747) belonging to one of four groups: (1) sex killers, (2) nonhomicidal sexually aggressives, (3) nonhomicidal sadists, and (4) general sex offenders. Participants were chosen from a database of more than 2,800 minimum-security forensic ward psychiatric hospital cases (Clarke Institute in Toronto, Ontario, Canada) seen since 1973.	Antisocial personality disorder	?	51.2% 41.3% 39.1% 10.6%
Rosler et al. (2004)	(1) 129 (2) 54	M	M = 19.2	PI	Diagnostic interviews with (1) prisoners and (2) controls in a German offender facility	Definite antisocial personality disorder	DSM-IV	9.3% 0%

(Continued)

(Continued)

Antisocial Personality Disorder								
Source	**N**	**Gender**	**Age**	**Study Type**[a1]	**Sample Description**	**Disorder**	**Diagnostic System**	**Prevalence/Incidence**
Stuart et al. (2006)	103	F	*M* = 31.5, *SD* = 9.6	CS	Questionnaire administered to women arrested for violence and court referred to batterer intervention programs, Rhode Island	Antisocial personality disorder	DSM-IV (PDSQ)	7%
Huchzermeier et al. (2007)	(1) 141 (2) 111 (3) 47	M	Adult, youth	JD, PI	Diagnostic interviews with three different samples of incarcerated male violent offenders in Germany (1) Adult prison inmates, years 2000–2004 (2) Youth custody, 2001–2003 (3) Adults in a psychiatric hospital	Antisocial personality disorder	DSM-IV(SCID)	50.8%
Trestman et al. (2007)	(1) 218 (2) 177 (3) 110	307 M, 201 F	*M* = 31.6	JD	Diagnostic interviews with both male and female offenders categorized by race: (1) white, (2) black, and (3) Hispanic, in three male jails and one female jail (Connecticut)	ASPD	DSM-IV (SCID)	34.6%
Grella et al. (2008)	280	65% M	*M* = 34.8	JD	Diagnostic interviews with offenders consecutively admitted to prison-based substance abuse treatment programs at one of four research centers (Colorado, Rhode Island, Texas, California)	Antisocial personality disorder	DSM-IV (SCID)	42.1% (*n* = 118)
						Any personality disorder		45.4% (*n* = 127)
Pham & Saloppé (2010)	84	M	Adult	PI	Psychological evaluations of forensic patients at high-security psychiatric hospital in Tomai, Belgium (Etablissement de Défense Sociale)	Antisocial personality disorder	DSM-IV (SCID II)	48% (*n* = 40)

Other/General Personality Disorders								
Source	**N**	**Gender**	**Age**	**Study Type**[a1]	**Sample Description**	**Disorder**	**Diagnostic System**	**Prevalence/Incidence**
Pfeiffer, Eisenstein, & Dabbs (1967)	85	2/3 M, 1/3 F	17–63	JD	Federal prisoners referred for mental competency evaluations, at the USPHS Hospital in Lexington, Kentucky, 1960–1965	Schizoid personality	?	3.5% (n =3)
						Paranoid personality		1.2% (n = 1)
						Emotionally unstable personality		15.3% (n = 13)
						Inadequate personality		4.7% (n = 4)
						Passive-aggressive personality		7.1% (n = 6)
						Passive-dependent personality		3.5% (n = 3)
						Hysterical personality		2.4% (n = 2)
Kahn (1971)	43	41 M, 2 F	11–74	HO	Interviews and psychiatric examinations of individuals who made pleas of insanity to charges of first- or second-degree murder	Other character disorder	?	18.6% (n =8)
Medlicott (1976)	38	29 M, 9 F	14–62	HO	Individuals charged with murder (n = 28) and attempted murder (n = 10) who were hospitalized or referred for psychiatric opinion, New Zealand	Personality disorder	?	34.2% (n = 13)
Pétursson & Gudjónsson (1981)	47	44 M, 3 F	Adult[ai]	HO	File review of cases of intentional and unintentional homicide in Iceland, 1900–1979	Personality disorder	?	21.3% (n = 10)
Langevin et al. (1982)	(1) 109 (2) 38	?	Adult?	PI	File record review of minimum-security forensic ward psychiatric hospital cases, 1969–1979 (Clarke Institute in Toronto, Ontario, Canada) (1) Killers (2) Nonviolent offenders	Schizoid personality	Feighner et al. (1972) psychiatric research diagnostic criteria	(1) 5.0% (2) 3.0%

(Continued)

(Continued)

Other/General Personality Disorders								
Source	N	Gender	Age	Study Type[a1]	Sample Description	Disorder	Diagnostic System	Prevalence/Incidence
						Immature or other personality		(1) 8.0% (2) 15.0%
Dell & Smith (1983)	253	M	15 and under–70+[d]	HO	File review of men convicted of manslaughter on the grounds of diminished responsibility, 1966–1977	Personality disorder	?	26.9% (n = 68)
Seltzer & Langford (1984)	85	M, F	15 and under–25 (Median = 18)	PI	Interviews of individuals referred by courts or legal counsel to psychiatry department of large regional hospital in Northwest Territories, calendar year 1981	Personality disorder	DSM-III, MMPI	28.2% (n = 24)
Taylor & Gunn (1984)	2,743	M	Adult	JD	File review of men remanded to Brixton Prison, South London (June, September, and December 1979 and March 1980)	Personality disorder	ICD	13.8% (n = 379)
Reich & Wells (1985)	390	325 M, 65 F	M = 30.9	JD	Record review of defendants evaluated for competency to stand trial by the Yale–New Haven Psychiatric Court Clinic, 1980–1982	Personality disorders (other than antisocial)	DSM-III	1.3% (n = 5)[bh]
Wilcox (1985, 1987)	71	62 M, 9 F	Adult, juvenile (six < 18, five > 50)	HO	Record review of all individuals convicted for homicides committed in Contra Costa County, California, 1978–1980	Passive-dependent personality	?	1.4% (n = 1)
Taylor (1986)	183	175 M, 8 F	18–73	JD	Record review of life-sentenced men and women, supervised by the Inner London Probation Service (inside prison and on license in the community)	Personality disorder	ICD-9	33% (n = 61)
Phillips et al. (1988)	1,816	1,569 M, 247 F	11–78 (M = 28)	PI, CS	Record review of psychiatric referrals from the criminal justice system of Alaska, 1977–1981	Personality disorders	DSM-II, DSM-III	15.2% (n = 276)

Other/General Personality Disorders								
Source	N	Gender	Age	Study Type[a1]	Sample Description	Disorder	Diagnostic System	Prevalence/Incidence
Yarvis (1990)	100	88 M, 12 F	33% < 25, 85% < 40	HO	Diagnostic interviews and record reviews of a series of murderers referred for psychiatric evaluation in California, 1980–1988	Borderline disorder	DSM-III	18.0% (n = 18)[j]
						Histrionic, narcissistic		2.0% (n = 2)[j]
						Paranoid, schizoid, schizotypal		5.0% (n = 5)[j]
						Avoidant or dependent, compulsive, or passive-aggressive		10.0% (n = 10)[j]
DeJong, Virkkunen, & Linnoila (1992)	(1) 248 (2) 100	M	16–68, (M = 31.2, SD = 11.9)	JD	Criminals ordered for forensic psychiatric examination at initial incarceration in Finland (1) Murders and attempted murderers (2) Arsonists	Borderline	DSM-III	(1) 58.0% (2) 65.0%
						Narcissistic		(1) 2.0% (2) 3.0%
						Paranoid		(1) 13.0% (2) 6.0%
						Passive-aggressive		(1) 10.0% (2) 6.0%
						Schizoid		(1) 1.0% (2) 4.0%
						Schizotypal		(1) 0.4% (2) 0.0%

(Continued)

(Continued)

Other/General Personality Disorders								
Source	N	Gender	Age	Study Type[a1]	Sample Description	Disorder	Diagnostic System	Prevalence/Incidence
Wallace et al. (1998)	(1) 3,838 (2) 1,998 (3) 152 (4) 1,137 (5) 876	M	Adult	AR	Case linkage study of higher court records and psychiatric case register databases, Victoria, Australia, 1993–1995 (men) (1) Total convictions (2) Violent offenses (3) Homicide offenses (4) Property offenses (5) Sexual offending	Personality disorders	ICD-9	(1) 1.7% ($n = 67$) (2) 2.6% ($n = 51$) (3) 3.9% ($n = 6$) (4) 1.4% ($n = 16$) (5) 2.1% ($n = 18$)
	(1) 315 (2) 152 (3) 116	F	Adult		(women) (1) Total convictions (2) Violent offenses (3) Property offenses	Personality disorders	ICD-9	(1) 2.9% ($n = 9$) (2) 4.6% ($n = 7$) (3) 2.6% ($n = 3$)
McElroy et al. (1999)	36	M	18–47 ($M = 33$, $SD = 8$)	PI	Interviews with convicted sex offenders consecutively admitted to the New Life Program, Cincinnati, Ohio, November 1996–June 1998	Paranoid	DSM-IV (SCID)	28% ($n = 10$)
						Schizoid		0% ($n = 0$)
						Schizotypal		0% ($n = 0$)
						Total Cluster A personality disorders		28% ($n = 10$)
						Borderline		42% ($n = 15$)
						Histrionic		6% ($n = 2$)
						Narcissistic		17% ($n = 6$)

Other/General Personality Disorders								
Source	N	Gender	Age	Study Type[a1]	Sample Description	Disorder	Diagnostic System	Prevalence/Incidence
						Total Cluster B personality disorders		92% ($n = 33$)
						Avoidant		22% ($n = 8$)
						Dependent		8% ($n = 3$)
						Obsessive-compulsive		25% ($n = 9$)
						Total Cluster C personality disorders		36% ($n = 13$)
Baxter et al. (2001)	257	240 M, 17 F	$M = 30.6$, $SD = 31.4$[bi]	HO	File review of consecutive series of patients with index offenses of parricide or stranger killing admitted to 1 of 3 high-security hospitals in England and Wales, 1972–1996	Personality disorder	?	35.4% ($n = 91$)
Siponmaa et al. (2001)	126	123 M, 3 F	15–22 (Median = 20)	JD	Interviews with young offenders consecutively referred for presentencing psychiatric investigation, Stockholm, Sweden, 1990–1995	Personality disorder	ICD-9	53% ($n = 67$)
Rösler et al. (2004)	(1) 129 (2) 54	M	$M = 19.2$	PI	Diagnostic interviews with (1) prisoners and (2) controls in a German offender facility	Definite personality disorder	DSM-IV	(1) 21.1% (2) 0%
						Definite impulsive personality disorder		(1) 10.1% (2) 0%
						Other definite personality disorder		(1) 14.7% (2) 0%
Stuart et al. (2006)	103	F	$M = 31.5$, $SD = 9.6$	CS	Questionnaire administered to women arrested for violence and court referred to batterer intervention programs, Rhode Island	Borderline personality disorder	DSM-IV (PDSQ)	27%

(Continued)

(Continued)

Other/General Personality Disorders								
Source	**N**	**Gender**	**Age**	**Study Type**[a1]	**Sample Description**	**Disorder**	**Diagnostic System**	**Prevalence/Incidence**
Huchzermeier et al. (2007)	(1) 141 (2) 111 (3) 47	M	Adult, youth	JD, PI	Diagnostic interviews with three different samples of incarcerated male violent offenders in Germany (1) Adult prison inmates, years 2000–2004 (2) Youth custody, 2001–2003 (3) Adults in a psychiatric hospital	Paranoid	DSM-IV (SCID)	9.0%
						Schizotypal		1.3%
						Schizoid		1.7%
						Cluster A		11.4%
						Histrionic		1.3%
						Narcissistic		11.6%
						Borderline		15.2%
						Cluster B		57.2%
						Avoidant		5.1%
						Dependent		2.0%
						Obsessive-compulsive		4.0%
						Cluster C		9.0%
						Negativistic		7.4%
						Depressive		3.7%
Trestman et al. (2007)	(1) 218 (2) 177 (3) 110	307 M, 201 F	$M = 31.6$	JD	Diagnostic interviews with both male and female offenders categorized by race: (1) white, (2) black, and (3) Hispanic, in three male jails and one female jail (Connecticut)	Cluster A	DSM-IV (SCID)	11.4%
						Cluster B		40.7%

Other/General Personality Disorders								
Source	N	Gender	Age	Study Type[a1]	Sample Description	Disorder	Diagnostic System	Prevalence/Incidence
						Cluster C		14.1%
						Borderline PD		16.9%
Grella et al. (2008)	280	65% M	*M* = 34.8	JD	Diagnostic interviews with offenders consecutively admitted to prison-based substance-abuse treatment programs at one of four research centers (Colorado, Rhode Island, Texas, California)	Borderline personality disorder	DSM-IV (SCID)	13.2% (n = 37)
						Any personality disorder		45.4% (n = 127)
Hanlon et al. (2010)	77	69 M, 8 F	*M*= 31.92	HO	Indigent murder defendants and death row inmates clinically interviewed while in custody in jails and maximum-security prisons (Illinois and Missouri)	Personality disorder	?	54.5% (n = 42)
Pham & Saloppé (2010)	84	M	Adult	PI	Psychological evaluations of forensic patients at high-security psychiatric hospital in Tomai, Belgium (Etablissement de Défense Sociale)	Cluster A	DSM-IV (SCID II)	29% (n = 24)
						Paranoid PD		24% (n = 20)
						Schizoid PD		6% (n = 5)
						Schizotypal PD		5% (n = 4)
						Cluster B		62% (n = 52)
						Borderline PD		25% (n = 21)
						Narcissistic PD		18% (n = 15)
						Histrionic PD		2% (n = 2)

(Continued)

(Continued)

Other/General Personality Disorders								
Source	N	Gender	Age	Study Type[a1]	Sample Description	Disorder	Diagnostic System	Prevalence/Incidence
						Cluster C		23% (n = 19)
						Avoidant PD		4% (n = 3)
						Dependent PD		2% (n = 2)
						Obsessive-compulsive PD		19% (n = 16)
						Any PD		71% (n = 60)
Catanesi et al. (2011)	103	85.44% M	53.41% 25–54, 22.73% 45–65, 13.64% 18–24, 5.68% <18	HO	Psychiatric and psychological evaluations on perpetrators of homicide and attempted homicide, Italy	Personality disorder Cluster A	DSM-IV-TR	6.8%%
						Personality disorder Cluster B		16.5%

Notes: *Significant difference in comparison to control group.

[a1]AR = arrest rates of patients discharged from psychiatric facilities, JD = jailed detainees and incarcerated prisoners, HO = homicide offenders, BC = birth cohort study, PI = psychiatric inpatient sample, CS = community sample (i.e., epidemiological catchment area survey studies and outpatient psychiatric patients).

[b]Reported group mean ages: Antisocial personality (M = 21.9), drug (M = 19.6), alcohol (M = 32.5), no diagnosis (M = 22.0).

[d]Group mean ages: 1966–1969 (M = 36.1, SD = 15.8), 1970–1973 (M = 36.2, SD = 14.9), 1974–1977 (M = 37.1, SD = 16.9).

[j]Community sample comparative data (six-month prevalence rates from NIMH Community Survey Data): data not reported.

[m]Community sample comparative data (six-month prevalence rates from NIMH Community Survey data): 0.6–2.1%.

[o]Reported as n = 23 in Wilcox (1985).

[ai]Group means and standard deviations: Psychotic illness (35.7, 8.8), personality disorder and alcohol use disorders (24.4, 8.2), no psychiatric abnormality (34.0, 12.4).

[au]Lifetime prevalence rate. For community comparison sample, standardized prevalence ratio (SPR) = 6.6 (an SPR greater than 1 indicates the prevalence rate in the prison sample was greater than that in the general population).

[bh]Rates of personality disorders in comparison outpatient and inpatient samples from same catchment area: 4.3% (n = 401) and 2.3% (n = 21).

[bi]The former value represents parricidal offenders, the latter, stranger killers.

Table 10.3 Prevalence of Crime in Personality Disordered Populations

Source	N	Gender	Age	Study Type[a1]	Sample Description	Disorder	Crime Definition	Prevalence/ Incidence
Tardiff & Koenigsberg (1985)	(1) 2,106 (2) 810	(1) 842 M, 1,256 F (2) 354 M, 453 F	(1) ≤ 20 – 65+[aa] (2) ≤ 20 – 65+[aa]	CS	Psychiatric outpatients evaluated during 1.5 years at two New York hospitals, diagnosed using DSM II and DSM II criteria (1) Payne Whitney Clinic (2) Westchester Division of NY Hospital	Personality disorder (1) n = 372 (2) n = 130	Presence of assaultive behavior toward others in hospital records	(1) 1.3% (n = 5) (2) 6.9% (n = 9)
Asnis et al. (1994)	517	204 M, 313 F	13–87, M = 38.7	CS	Psychiatric outpatients, Montefiore Medical Center, Bronx, New York, diagnosed using DSM-III criteria	Personality disorder (n = 14)	Self-reported homicidal ideation and attempts	Ideation: 14% (n =2) Attempts: 7% (n = 1)

Note: [a1]AR = arrest rates of patients discharged from psychiatric facilities, JD = jailed detainees and incarcerated prisoners, HO = homicide offenders, BC = birth cohort study, PI = psychiatric inpatient sample, CS = community sample (i.e., epidemiological catchment area survey studies and outpatient psychiatric patients).

[aa](1) 12.4% (n = 261) 20 years and younger, 30.7% (n = 647) 21–30, 23.6% (n = 496) 31–40, 24.3% (n = 511) 41–64, 7.5% (n = 158) 65 years and older, 1.6% (n = 33) unknown; (2) 18.0% (n = 146) 20 years and younger, 31.4% (n = 254) 21–30, 18.0% (n = 146) 31–40, 27.0% (n = 219) 41–64, 5.0% (n = 41) 65 years and older, 0.5% (n = 4) unknown.

Cluster A Personality Disorders

Paranoid Personality Disorder

Paranoid personality disorder is a pervasive, inflexible, and enduring pattern of distrust and suspiciousness of others (APA, 2000, 2013). DSM-5 diagnostic criteria for paranoid personality disorder (PPD) are listed in Table 10.4. Except when noted, the language outlining the diagnostic criteria for PPD (and the other personality disorders in the DSM-5) remains unchanged from the DSM-IV-TR.

Prevalence and Incidence Rates of Paranoid Personality Disorder. Prevalence rates for PPD have been reported in the general population at 0.5%–2.5% (APA, 2000) and at 10%–30% in inpatient psychiatric settings and 2%–10% in outpatient mental health clinics (APA, 2000). More recent national survey data suggests rates between 2.3% and 4.4% (APA, 2013).

Theodore Millon refers to paranoid personality disorder (PPD) as the "suspicious pattern." Individuals having this disorder are characterized by defensive expressive behaviors, provocative interpersonal conduct, and a suspicious cognitive style. The primary regulatory (defense) mechanisms involved in the development and maintenance of this disorder are projection and fantasy—wherein the individual actively disowns undesirable aspects of himself or herself (i.e., personal traits and motives) and attributes them to other people, consequently remaining blind to these undesirable characteristics while being overly alert to and hypercritical of them in others (Millon & Davis, 1996).

Table 10.4 DSM-5 Diagnostic Criteria for Paranoid Personality Disorder

301.0 (F60.0) Paranoid Personality Disorder

A. A pervasive mistrust and suspiciousness of others such that their motives are interpreted as malevolent, beginning by early adulthood and present in a variety of contexts, as indicated by four (or more) of the following:

1. suspects, without sufficient basis, that others are exploiting, harming, or deceiving him or her
2. is preoccupied with unjustified doubts about the loyalty or trustworthiness of friends or associates
3. is reluctant to confide in others because of unwarranted fear that the information will be used maliciously against him or her
4. reads hidden demeaning or threatening meanings into benign remarks or events
5. persistently bears grudges, i.e., is unforgiving of insults, injuries, or slights
6. perceives attacks on his or her character or reputation that are not apparent to others and is quick to react angrily or to counterattack
7. has recurrent suspicions, without justification, regarding fidelity of spouse or sexual partner

B. Does not occur exclusively during the course of schizophrenia, a bipolar disorder or depressive disorder with psychotic features, or another psychotic disorder and is not attributable to the physiological effects of another medical condition.*

Note: If criteria are met prior to the onset of schizophrenia, add "premorbid," e.g., "paranoid personality disorder (premorbid)."

Source: APA (2013, p. 649). Reprinted with permission from the *Diagnostic and Statistical Manual of Mental Disorders*, Fifth Edition (Copyright © 2013). American Psychiatric Association. All rights reserved.

Note: *In the DSM-IV-TR, this section reads "Does not occur exclusively during the course of Schizophrenia, a Mood Disorder With Psychotic Features, or another Psychotic Disorder and is not due to the direct physiological effects of a general medical condition" (APA, 2000, p. 694).

The Relationship Between Paranoid Personality Disorder and Crime and Violence

Though symptoms of extreme paranoia have shown empirical associations with violent behavior (see Chapter 5), systematic studies examining the relationship between PPD and crime and violence are rare; and what is known about this relationship appears largely based on clinical lore or information obtained from published biographical works and case studies. According to Tardiff (2007), individuals with PPD, particularly men, may be members of militaristic organizations or preoccupied with military themes. These individuals tend to be preoccupied with guns and often possess firearms. A history of violent episodes is usually rare; however, a history of violent threats against others is common (e.g., threatening human resources personnel after being fired from a job). Most PPD patients will not become physically violent, although, when they do, violence is often lethal and targeted against multiple individuals, such as in the work environment. Stone (1998) echoes these thoughts in his discussion of the relationship of PPD to homicide, suggesting that it may operate down any one of a number of pathways as a predisposing factor to the crime of murder. These include paranoid political and religious fanaticism, pathological jealousy of estranged spouses or lovers, or smoldering rage and resentment combined with a sense of righteous indignation. (Individuals with this disposition who are fired from their jobs feel unjustly picked on or mistreated and subsequently kill coworkers and bosses in acts of extreme retaliatory workplace violence.)

One rare example of a more systematic study in this area is a recent large-scale national survey of male prisoners in England and Wales conducted by Roberts and Coid (2010). They used multiple regression analyses to examine the independent associations between lifetime criminal offending and personality disorders in

A Closer Look: Paranoid Personality Disorder and Crime

Prevalence of the Disorder in Crime

Study Type	Number	Prevalence Rates
Arrest rates	0	–
Birth cohorts	0	–
Community samples	0	–
Homicide offenders	0	–
Jailed detainees and prisoners	3*	1.2–13.0%
Psychiatric inpatients	3*	9.0–28.0%
Total Number of Studies	**5†**	

Sample Characteristics

Size	36–348
Gender	Male only (4 studies); male and female (1 study)
Age	Adult, youth
Location	North American and European countries (e.g., Belgium, Finland, Germany, and the United States)
Diagnostic Systems	DSM-III, DSM-IV, not reported in one study

Notes: *One study involved both jailed detainees or prisoners and psychiatric inpatients.

†One additional study (Yarvis, 1990) listed paranoid personality disorder but included it with other Cluster A personality disorders.

Prevalence of Crime in the Disorder

Study Type	Number	Prevalence Rates	Crime Definition
Total Number of Studies	**0**		

Nondisordered or community resident comparison group or general population baseline rates for either disorder or crime provided: **0 studies (0.0%)**

391 of 3,563 prisoners who completed both of two surveys. Results indicated PPD was positively correlated with robbery and blackmail but negatively associated with driving offenses (differential associations between offense types and other personality disorders are listed in their respective sections in this chapter). Clearly, more work is needed to substantiate and qualify a putative relationship between PPD and various forms of criminal and violent behavior.

Schizoid Personality Disorder

Schizoid personality disorder is a pervasive, inflexible, and enduring pattern of social detachment and limited range of emotional expression (APA, 2000, 2013). DSM-5 diagnostic criteria for schizoid personality disorder are listed in Table 10.5.

Table 10.5 DSM-5 Diagnostic Criteria for Schizoid Personality Disorder

301.20 (F60.1) Schizoid Personality Disorder

A. A pervasive pattern of detachment from social relationships and a restricted range of expression of emotions in interpersonal settings, beginning by early adulthood and present in a variety of contexts, as indicated by four (or more) of the following:

1. Neither desires nor enjoys close relationships, including being part of a family.
2. Almost always chooses solitary activities.
3. Has little, if any, interest in having sexual experiences with another person.
4. Takes pleasure in few, if any, activities.
5. Lacks close friends or confidants other than first-degree relatives.
6. Appears indifferent to the praise or criticism of others.
7. Shows emotional coldness, detachment, or flattened affectivity.

B. Does not occur exclusively during the course of schizophrenia, a bipolar disorder or depressive disorder with psychotic features, another psychotic disorder, or autism spectrum disorder and is not attributable to the physiological effects of another medical condition.*

Note: If criteria are met prior to the onset of schizophrenia, add "premorbid," e.g., "schizoid personality disorder (premorbid)."

Source: APA (2013, pp. 652–653). Reprinted with permission from the *Diagnostic and Statistical Manual of Mental Disorders*, Fifth Edition (Copyright © 2013). American Psychiatric Association. All rights reserved.

Note: *In the DSM-IV-TR, the wording is "Does not occur exclusively during the course of Schizophrenia, a Mood Disorder With Psychotic Features, or another Psychotic Disorder, or a Pervasive Developmental Disorder and is not due to the direct physiological effects of a general medical condition" (APA, 2000, p. 697).

Prevalence and Incidence Rates of Schizoid Personality Disorder

Regarding prevalence rates for schizoid personality disorder, the DSM-IV-TR and DSM-5 simply state that this disorder is "uncommon in clinical settings" (APA, 2000, p. 696; APA, 2013, p. 654). More recent national survey data suggests rates between 3.1% and 4.9% (APA, 2013).

Theoretical Conceptualizations

Millon refers to schizoid personality disorder as the asocial pattern, with individuals having this disorder being characterized by impassive expressive behaviors (they are unsusceptible to pain or emotion), unengaged interpersonal conduct, and an impoverished cognitive style. The primary regulatory (defense) mechanism involved in the development and maintenance of this disorder is intellectualization—describing interpersonal and emotional experiences in a matter-of-fact, impersonal, or mechanical manner and focusing on the formal and objective aspects of these experiences (Millon & Davis, 1996).

The Relationship Between Schizoid Personality Disorder and Crime

Of the three Cluster A personality disorders, schizoid personality disorder appears to have received the most clinical and empirical interest in terms of its relationship with criminal and violent behavior, perhaps due to its earlier proposed (but unsubstantiated) conceptual overlap with psychopathy (Raine, 1986). References to the schizoid criminal can be found in the writings of earlier criminological theorists (e.g., Kretschmer, 1945); and Wolff found relationships between schizoid personality disorder and both antisocial conduct in childhood and criminality in adulthood, though this author appeared to use the term "schizoid personality disorder" interchangeably with

A Closer Look: Schizoid Personality Disorder and Crime

Prevalence of the Disorder in Crime

Study Type	Number	Prevalence Rates
Arrest rates	0	–
Birth cohorts	0	–
Community samples	0	–
Homicide offenders	0	–
Jailed detainees and prisoners	3*	1.0–4.0%
Psychiatric inpatients	4*	0.0–6.0%
Total Number of Studies	**6†**	

Sample Characteristics

Size	36–348
Gender	Male only (4 studies); male and female (1 study); not reported (1 study)
Age	Adult, youth
Location	North American and European countries (e.g., Belgium, Canada, Finland, Germany, and the United States)
Diagnostic Systems	DSM (various editions), other psychiatric research diagnostic criteria, not reported in one study

Notes: *One study involved both jailed detainees or prisoners and psychiatric inpatients.

†One additional study (Yarvis, 1990) listed paranoid personality disorder but included it with other Cluster A personality disorders.

Prevalence of Crime in the Disorder

Study Type	Number	Prevalence Rates	Crime Definition
Total Number of Studies	**0**		

Nondisordered or community resident comparison group or general population baseline rates for either disorder or crime provided: **0 studies (0.0%)**

"Asperger's disorder" (i.e., in Wolff & Cull, 1986, but not in Wolff, 1992—see Chapter 3). Additionally, Stone (1998) proposes that, although most individuals with schizoid personality disorder are not criminal and instead live in the margins of society working at certain reclusive occupations, some become capable of crimes and even extreme acts of violence due to their extreme detachment from human emotions. Stone notes, however, that paranoid traits are important factors in murders committed by schizoid individuals.

Other studies have compared the relationship between crime and schizoid personality disorder to that between crime and other personality disorders. In a longitudinal study of 168 Swedish offenders referred for presentencing forensic psychiatric evaluation, Hiscoke and colleagues (2003) found self-reported personality disorder symptoms to be related to subsequent violent criminal reoffending only for antisocial and schizoid personality traits. Roberts and Coid (2010), in their recent large-scale national survey of male prisoners in England and Wales (see above), found schizoid personality disorder to be positively correlated with kidnapping, burglary, and theft. Interestingly, the lion's share of the empirical work on the relationship between schizoid personality disorder and crime and violence appears to have been conducted in neurobiological studies. For example, reduced skin conductance (SC) amplitudes to orienting stimuli have been found in secondary schizoid psychopaths relative to primary psychopaths (Blackburn, 1979) and in schizoid antisocial 15-year-old males relative to their nonschizoid antisocial counterparts (Raine & Venables, 1984—see Chapter 5). In fact, Fowles (1993) speculated that there might be a detached schizoid subgroup of antisocial individuals characterized by electrodermal hyporeactivity. Furthermore, in a sample of 32 prison inmates, Raine and Venables (1990) tested a stimulation-seeking theory of psychopathy and found schizoid criminals (defined by poor eye tracking), but not psychopaths, to be characterized by event-related potential (ERP) nonaugmenting/reducing (a psychophysiological profile characteristic of schizophrenia in which ERP amplitudes show no increase or actually decrease in response to visual stimuli of increasing intensity, in this case, brief flashes of white light). This finding suggests that the etiological mechanisms underlying schizoid criminality are different from those underlying other forms of criminality. Though the collective body of work in this area is comparatively larger than that on the other Cluster A personality disorders, more investigative efforts are needed to clarify the nature of the relationship between schizoid personality disorder and crime.

Schizotypal Personality Disorder

Schizotypal personality disorder is a pervasive, inflexible, and enduring pattern of intense discomfort in close relationships, distorted thinking and perceptions, and eccentric behavior (APA, 2000, 2013). DSM-5 diagnostic criteria for schizotypal personality disorder are listed in Table 10.6.

Table 10.6 DSM-5 Diagnostic Criteria for Schizotypal Personality Disorder

301.22 (F21) Schizotypal Personality Disorder

A. A pervasive pattern of social and interpersonal deficits marked by acute discomfort with, and reduced capacity for, close relationships as well as by cognitive or perceptual distortions and eccentricities of behavior, beginning in early adulthood and present in a variety of contexts, as indicated by five (or more) of the following:

1. Ideas of reference (excluding delusions of reference)
2. Odd beliefs or magical thinking that influences behavior and is inconsistent with subcultural norms (e.g., superstitiousness, belief in clairvoyance, telepathy, or "sixth sense"; in children and adolescents, bizarre fantasies or preoccupations).
3. Unusual perceptual experiences, including bodily illusions.
4. Odd thinking and speech (e.g., vague, circumstantial, metaphorical, overelaborate, or stereotyped).
5. Suspiciousness or paranoid ideation.
6. Inappropriate or constricted affect.
7. Behavior or appearance that is odd, eccentric, or peculiar.
8. Lack of close friends or confidants other than first-degree relatives.
9. Excessive social anxiety that does not diminish with familiarity and tends to be associated with paranoid fears rather than negative judgments about self.

B. Does not occur exclusively during the course of schizophrenia, a bipolar disorder or depressive disorder with psychotic features, another psychotic disorder, or autism spectrum disorder.*

Note: If criteria are met prior to the onset of schizophrenia, add "premorbid," e.g., "schizotypal personality disorder (premorbid)."

Source: APA (2013, pp. 655–656). Reprinted with permission from the *Diagnostic and Statistical Manual of Mental Disorders*, Fifth Edition (Copyright © 2013). American Psychiatric Association. All rights reserved.

Note: *In the DSM-IV-TR, this wording was "Does not occur exclusively during the course of Schizophrenia, a Mood Disorder With Psychotic Features, or another Psychotic Disorder, or a Pervasive Developmental Disorder " (APA, 2000, p. 701).

Prevalence and Incidence Rates of Schizotypal Personality Disorder

Prevalence rates for schizoid personality disorder have been reported to be 3% in the general population (APA, 2000); more recently reported community rates for Norway and the United States are 0.6% and 4.6%, respectively (APA, 2013).

Theoretical Conceptualizations

Millon refers to schizotypal personality disorder as the eccentric pattern, with individuals having this disorder being characterized by eccentric expressive behaviors, secretive interpersonal conduct, and a disorganized cognitive style. The primary regulatory (defense) mechanism involved in the development and maintenance of this disorder is undoing; the individual uses bizarre mannerisms and idiosyncratic thoughts to retract or reverse previous acts or ideas that cause that individual feelings of anxiety, conflict, or guilt, and he or she uses ritualistic or magical behaviors to repent for or nullify misdeeds or thoughts assumed to be "evil" (Millon & Davis, 1996). Schizotypal personality disorder has been classified under the schizophrenia spectrum and other psychotic disorders in the DSM-5 (APA, 2013).

A Closer Look: Schizotypal Personality Disorder and Crime

Prevalence of the Disorder in Crime

Study Type	Number	Prevalence Rates
Arrest rates	0	–
Birth cohorts	0	–
Community samples	0	–
Homicide offenders	0	–
Jailed detainees and prisoners	2*	0.0–1.3%
Psychiatric inpatients	3*	0.0–5.0%
Total Number of Studies	**4†**	

Sample Characteristics

Size	36–348
Gender	Male only
Age	Adult, youth
Location	North American and European countries (e.g., Belgium, Finland, Germany, and the United States)
Diagnostic Systems	DSM-III and DSM-IV

Notes: *One study involved both jailed detainees or prisoners and psychiatric inpatients.

†One additional study (Yarvis, 1990) listed paranoid personality disorder but included it with other Cluster A personality disorders.

Prevalence of Crime in the Disorder

Study Type	Number	Prevalence Rates	Crime Definition
Total Number of Studies	**0**		

Nondisordered or community resident comparison group or general population baseline rates for either disorder or crime provided: **0 studies (0.0%)**

The Relationship Between Schizotypal Personality Disorder and Crime

Much of the work concerning the association between schizotypal personality disorder and criminal and violent behavior has focused on schizophrenia and crime (see Chapter 5). In fact, the relationship between schizotypal personality disorder (schizotypy) and aggression in children has been considered by researchers to be a nonclinical "downward extension" of the schizophrenia-crime relationship (Raine et al., 2011). Nonetheless, some studies have examined how this personality disorder may relate to crime and violence in its own unique way. For example, Roberts and Coid (2010), in their recent large-scale national survey of male prisoners in England and Wales (see above), found schizotypal personality disorder to be strongly associated with arson but negatively associated with robbery and blackmail. Additionally, neuroscience research studies have identified neurobiological deficits characterizing the schizotypal criminal. For example, recall from Chapter 5 Raine's (1987) finding of reduced skin conductance (SC) in high-schizotypy compared to low-schizotypy individuals in his study of 37 adult male prisoners in top-security English prisons; and consider the later findings from the prospective longitudinal Danish birth-cohort study that showed SC-orienting deficits in schizotypal criminals relative to schizotypal individuals who were not criminals, as well as this group's increased alcoholism relative to criminals, schizotypal individuals who were not criminals, and normal controls (Raine et al. 1999). Furthermore, Raine and colleagues (2011) found schizotypy to be related to certain types of aggression (i.e., total and reactive but not proactive aggression) in a sample of 3,804 Hong Kong schoolchildren (ages 8–16) and that peer victimization accounted for nearly 60% of this relationship. Finally, Wilkinson and colleagues (2011) found qualitative differences in reasoning about criminal behavior in high-schizotypal individuals compared to those with low schizotypy. Overall, though schizotypy research has proven helpful in understanding the relationship between schizophrenia and crime, this disorder's own relationship with criminal, violent, and aggressive behavior continues to be an important area of study.

Moreover, other researchers have examined the relationship between crime or violence and Cluster A personality disorders in aggregate. For example, Warren and colleagues (2002), in a sample of 261 incarcerated women, found Cluster A personality disorders to be significantly associated with prostitution. Furthermore, recall from Chapter 5 that Schug and colleagues (2007) examined schizophrenia-spectrum personality disorders (SSPDs—paranoid, schizoid, and schizotypal) and comorbidity with antisocial personality disorder in relation to self-reported criminal behaviors and psychophysiological functioning in an adult community sample. They found increased criminality in the comorbid group relative to each group having been diagnosed with one disorder alone and relative to controls, as well as significantly reduced SC orienting to neutral tones in the comorbid group relative to all other groups. These initial findings lend support for an association between schizotypal personality disorder—either alone or together with other SSPDs—and various forms of criminal, violent, and antisocial behavior; and research efforts should continue in this area of study.

Cluster B Personality Disorders

Antisocial Personality Disorder

Antisocial personality disorder is a pervasive, inflexible, and enduring pattern of disregarding and violating the rights of others (APA, 2000, 2013). DSM-5 diagnostic criteria for antisocial personality disorder (ASPD) are listed in Table 10.7.

Prevalence and Incidence Rates of Antisocial Personality Disorder

According to the DSM-IV-TR, prevalence rates for ASPD in community samples are 3% for males and 1% for females (APA, 2000), and more recent data indicate 12-month prevalence rates of 0.2–3.3% (APA, 2013). Within clinical settings, rates have been estimated between 3% and 30%, depending upon the type of population being studied. Substance-abuse treatment settings, prisons, and forensic settings are associated with even higher prevalence rates of ASPD (APA, 2000)—i.e., greater than 70% in some of these samples (APA, 2013).

Table 10.7 DSM-5 Diagnostic Criteria for Antisocial Personality Disorder

307.1 (F60.2) Antisocial Personality Disorder

A. There is a pervasive pattern of disregard for and violation of the rights of others occurring since age 15 years, as indicated by three (or more) of the following:

1. Failure to conform to social norms with respect to lawful behaviors, as indicated by repeatedly performing acts that are grounds for arrest.
2. Deceitfulness, as indicated by repeated lying, use of aliases, or conning others for personal profit or pleasure.
3. Impulsivity or failure to plan ahead.
4. Irritability and aggressiveness, as indicated by repeated physical fights or assaults.
5. Reckless disregard for safety of self or others.
6. Consistent irresponsibility, as indicated by repeated failure to sustain consistent work behavior or honor financial obligations.
7. Lack of remorse, as indicated by being indifferent to or rationalizing having hurt, mistreated, or stolen from another.

B. The individual is at least age 18 years.

C. There is evidence of conduct disorder [see Chapter 3] with onset before age 15 years.

D. The occurrence of antisocial behavior is not exclusively during the course of schizophrenia or bipolar disorder.*

Source: APA (2013, p. 659). Reprinted with permission from the *Diagnostic and Statistical Manual of Mental Disorders*, Fifth Edition (Copyright © 2013). American Psychiatric Association. All rights reserved.

Note: *In the DSM-IV-TR, this wording is "Does not occur exclusively during the course of Schizophrenia or a Manic Episode" (APA, 2000, p. 706).

Theoretical Conceptualizations

Historically, the theoretical and diagnostic roots of ASPD run deep, and this disorder shares a rich ancestry with another psychiatric illness—psychopathy—which will be covered extensively later in this chapter. Also worth noting is that some authors (e.g., Lykken, 1995) have proposed a group or spectrum of *antisocial personalities* rather than representing this particular constellation of traits and behaviors as a singular disease entity. Millon refers to ASPD as the aggrandizing pattern: individuals having this disorder are characterized by impulsive expressive behaviors, irresponsible interpersonal conduct, and a deviant cognitive style. The primary regulatory (defense) mechanisms involved in the development and maintenance of this disorder are acting out and projection; the individual rarely constrains inner tensions that might build up by postponing expressions of offensive thoughts and malevolent action, and she or he directly and precipitously discharges—usually without guilt or remorse—socially repugnant impulses instead of refashioning them into socially acceptable forms (Millon & Davis, 1996).

The Relationship Between Antisocial Personality Disorder and Crime or Violence

Given the current diagnostic conceptualization of ASPD in the DSM-IV and DSM-5, with its emphasis on criminal, violent, aggressive, impulsive, and remorseless behavior, a relationship between this disorder and crime and violence seems unsurprising, if not intuitive. Indeed, some personality theorists such as Millon (Millon & Davis, 1996) have criticized the current DSM-IV criteria for ASPD (which have been retained in the DSM-5) as being merely a laundry list of undesirable, unlawful behaviors. In fact, the examination of an ASPD-crime relationship immediately gives rise to an inherent conceptual dilemma—a "chicken and egg" enigma of sorts: Is ASPD *related to* or *defined by* criminal behavior? Millon's criticisms suggests the latter view, which appears to predominate in the justice system as the overwhelming number of U.S. states specifically exclude

A Closer Look: Antisocial Personality Disorder and Crime

Prevalence of the Disorder in Crime

Study Type	Number	Prevalence Rates
Arrest rates	0	–
Birth cohorts	0	–
Community samples	1	7.0%
Homicide offenders	3*	35.2–38.0%
Jailed detainees and prisoners	13*	1.0–61.5%
Psychiatric inpatients	7*	8.0–72.0%
Total Number of Studies	**22**	

Sample Characteristics

Size	36–747
Gender	Male only (14 studies); female only (1 study); male and female (6 studies); not reported (1 study)
Age	Adult, youth
Location	North American and European countries (e.g., Australia, Belgium, Canada, Finland, Germany, and the United States)
Diagnostic Systems	DSM (various editions), other psychiatric research diagnostic criteria, not reported in two studies

Notes: *One study involved both jailed detainees or prisoners and psychiatric inpatients, and another study involved both jailed detainees or prisoners and homicide offenders.

†ASPD is the most "popular" among the personality disorders in studies of this type.

Prevalence of Crime in the Disorder

Study Type	Number	Prevalence Rates	Crime Definition
Total Number of Studies	**0**		

Nondisordered or community resident comparison group or general population baseline rates for either disorder or crime provided: **5 studies (22.7%)‡**

Note: ‡Rates of ASPD appear markedly (if not significantly) elevated relative to comparison group rates when rates are provided.

ASPD as a qualifying "mental disease or defect" for insanity and diminished capacity purposes (see Chapter 11). However, if ASPD is thought of as a suitable and accommodating "psychological terrain" for the progression toward crime and violence, a more complex relationship is not difficult to fathom.

Conceptual dilemmas notwithstanding, studies have attempted to go beyond establishing the mere presence of an ASPD-crime relationship and have made efforts toward a qualitative understanding of the nature of criminality in those with ASPD. For example, Roberts and Coid (2010) found conduct disorder and ASPD to be associated with a wide range of criminal offenses, including firearm possession, robbery and blackmail, escape and breach of parole, arson, kidnapping, fraud, burglary, and violence. Additionally, in a sample of 261 incarcerated women, Warren and colleagues (2002) found ASPD to be significantly associated with institutional violence.

The association between ASPD and homicidal violence appears well supported in the literature; according to Stone (1998), ASPD (including its "semantic close cousin," dissocial personality) is significantly overrepresented among samples of homicide offenders. For example, in an extensive review of serial killers, the editors of Time-Life Books (1992, in Ferreira, 2000) reported that 90% were deemed to be suffering from personality disorders, namely ASPD. In a study of serial sexual homicide, Geberth and Turco (1997) found all 68 (100%) of the serial murderers with sufficient data to complete research protocols met DSM-IV diagnostic criteria for ASPD. In a study of 693 homicide offenders in Finland (Eronen, Hakola, & Tiihonen, 1996), antisocial personality disorder was found to increase the odds ratio of homicidal violence over 10-fold in men and over 50-fold in women (odds ratios are calculated using prevalence rates of mental disorders). In sum, a further understanding of the qualitative nature of crime and violence in ASPD (i.e., the crucial next step beyond merely establishing the existence of a relationship based on prevalence rate studies) continues to be gained by empirical efforts in this area.

The Origins of Crime and Violence in Those With Antisocial Personality Disorder

Neurobiological Factors. Evidence from studies employing various neuroscience methods indicates structural and functional deficits in the brains of individuals with ASPD. In one of the earlier of these imaging studies, Raine and colleagues (2000) found individuals with ASPD (n = 21) had a 11.0% reduction in prefrontal gray matter volume compared to healthy controls (n = 34) and a 13.9% reduction compared to individuals with substance dependence (n = 26). Individuals with ASPD also demonstrated reduced autonomic reactivity during a stressor task, and results provided the first evidence for the structural brain deficits in ASPD that might underlie the characteristic low arousal, poor fear conditioning, lack of conscience, and decision-making impairments of this disorder.

Regarding psychophysiological findings, Lindberg and colleagues (2005) found quantitative EEG abnormalities (i.e., reduced overall alpha power and bilaterally increased occipital delta and theta power) in the waking EEG of 16 detoxified male homicidal offenders with ASPD when comparing these to the EEG's of 15 healthy controls. This result indicates that the ASPD group has difficulties in maintaining normal daytime arousal. Also, Lijffijt and colleagues (2009) found impaired P50 gating in ASPD individuals (n = 9) compared both to those with adult-onset antisocial behavior (n = 7) and to controls (n = 15), suggesting abnormal pre-attentive filtering in ASPD-related impulsive behavior. Finally, regarding hormone evidence, Aromäki and colleagues (1999) found significantly elevated rates of ASPD in men convicted of violent crimes (both in and out of prison—see Table 10.2) compared to controls and that unweighted ASPD symptom count was significantly and positively correlated with testosterone levels in these violent men. Overall, neurobiological studies continue to be among the more promising inquires regarding the etiological mechanisms underlying ASPD.

Psychological Factors: Comorbidity. Although ASPD may be criminogenic in and of itself, studies have demonstrated how its co-occurrence with other psychiatric conditions can contribute to crime and violence over and above what might normally be seen in those with this disorder alone. Evidence to date indicates that ASPD commonly presents with other personality disorders (see review in Blackburn, 2000), but its comorbidity with Axis I disorders such as schizophrenia has been observed to increase criminality. For example, in a multisite study of 232 men with schizophrenia and other psychotic disorders, Moran and Hodgins (2004) found those with a comorbid diagnosis of ASPD were characterized by early attention and concentration problems, below-average performance in school, and a greater likelihood of institutionalization before the age of 18. These individuals also committed more nonviolent crimes relative to those without ASPD. Furthermore, ASPD has demonstrated significant comorbidity with anxiety disorders among community adults (Goodwin & Hamilton, 2003); and, in a subsequent study of 279 male penitentiary inmates with ASPD, Hodgins and colleagues (2010) found two-thirds to have comorbid anxiety disorders, half of which with an onset before age 16 years. Most prisoners with anxiety disorders had been convicted of serious (interpersonal) violent crimes, and these authors suggest comorbidity with anxiety disorders may represent a distinct subgroup of ASPD offenders characterized by unique mechanisms underlying violent behavior.

Comorbid substance use disorders may also play a role in the etiology of crime and violence in those with ASPD. For example, in a longitudinal record-linkage study of 1,052 drug abusers recruited from a Swedish detoxification and short-term rehabilitation unit, Fridell and colleagues (2008) found those diagnosed with ASPD were 2.16 times more likely to be charged with theft and 2.44 times more likely to be charged with multiple types of crime (including violent and drug offenses) during a given year of observation. Of those with ASPD, 38% were readmitted to the facility within one year after their first admission. In a study of 41 mid-sentence female felons diagnosed with ASPD, Lewis (2011) found significant comorbidity with alcohol, opiate, and cocaine dependence, as well as an association between symptom severity and violent behavior among women with comorbid substance dependence. Finally, McCabe and colleagues (2012), in a sample of 1,530 individuals with psychotic disorders from a large-state cohort of adults receiving psychiatric services, found comorbid ASPD and substance use disorders to be associated with the greatest increase in risk for arrest. Overall, findings here suggest that the comorbidity of other psychological illnesses, including Axis I psychotic, anxiety, and substance use disorders, may contribute to an increased expression of criminal and violent behavior in individuals with ASPD.

Psychosocial Factors. Empirical evidence to date has also implicated environmental and family influences in the etiology of crime and violence in those diagnosed with ASPD. In a study of 54 men serving prison sentences for violent crimes, Hill and Nathan (2008) found a predictive pathway involving childhood conduct disorder (CD) and adulthood ASPD associated with interparental discord, as well as a separate predictive pathway associated with witnessing interparental violence in childhood. However, the CD-ASPD pathway was associated with social but not interpersonal violence, suggesting differential pathways to later serious violence depending upon the social context in which the violence occurs. More work is needed to further understand how these psychosocial factors may play a role in the relationship between ASPD and crime.

Applied Issues: Criminal Responsibility

Although the historical antecedents of ASPD have been discussed in theoretical relation to guilt or innocence in criminal legal matters, recent decades have demonstrated how the criminal justice system has attempted to incorporate ASPD into the determination of criminal responsibility (see Chapter 11). Even within the past decade, more and more authors have referred to how various judicial entities from around the world appear increasingly open to absolving individuals with ASPD from criminal guilt. For example, Palermo (2007) discusses the current willingness among forensic psychiatrists, psychologists, criminologists, and jurists in Europe to consider some personality disordered offenders (including those with ASPD) mentally and emotionally ill enough to be deemed not guilty by reason of insanity (NGRI). In fact, in a Dutch file-review study of 1,209 defendant pretrial reports, Spaans and colleagues (2011) found that a diagnosis of ASPD was associated with diminished criminal responsibility and a recommendation for forensic treatment. It will be interesting indeed to see in the coming years how criminal justice systems around the world, including in the United States, view individuals with this disorder in terms of guilt or innocence and how ASPD may factor into other criminal justice decisions, such as sentencing and conditional release.

Borderline Personality Disorder

Borderline personality disorder is a pervasive, inflexible, and enduring pattern of instability in relationships with others, self-image, and emotions, along with significant impulsivity (APA, 2000, 2013). DSM-5 diagnostic criteria for borderline personality disorder (BPD) are listed in Table 10.8.

Prevalence and Incidence Rates of Borderline Personality Disorder

Prevalence rates for BPD have been estimated at approximately 2% of the general population (APA, 2000), with more recent estimates of 1.6% to as high as 5.9% for median population prevalence (APA, 2013). Increased rates have been reported in other sample populations, such as in outpatients in mental health clinics or primary care settings (10%), in psychiatric inpatients (20%), and among clinical populations with personality disorders (30–60%; APA, 2000, 2013).

Table 10.8 DSM-5 Diagnostic Criteria for Borderline Personality Disorder

301.83 (F60.3) Borderline Personality Disorder

A pervasive pattern of instability of interpersonal relationships, self-image, and affects, and marked impulsivity, beginning in early adulthood and present in a variety of contexts, as indicated by five (or more) of the following:

1. Frantic efforts to avoid real or imagined abandonment. (*Note:* Do not include suicidal or self-mutilating behavior covered in Criterion 5.)
2. A pattern of unstable and intense interpersonal relationships characterized by alternating between extremes of idealization and devaluation.
3. Identity disturbance: markedly and persistently unstable self-image or sense of self.
4. Impulsivity in at least two areas that are potentially self-damaging (i.e., spending, sex, substance abuse, reckless driving, binge eating). (*Note:* Do not include suicidal or self-mutilating behavior covered in Criterion 5.)
5. Recurrent suicidal behavior, gestures, threats, or self-mutilating behavior.
6. Affective instability due to marked reactivity of mood (e.g., intense episodic dysphoria, irritability, or anxiety usually lasting a few hours and rarely more than a few days).
7. Chronic feelings of emptiness.
8. Inappropriate, intense anger or difficulty controlling anger (e.g., frequent displays of temper, constant anger, recurrent physical fights).
9. Transient, stress-related paranoid ideation or severe dissociative symptoms.

Source: APA (2013, p. 663). Reprinted with permission from the *Diagnostic and Statistical Manual of Mental Disorders*, Fifth Edition

Theoretical Conceptualizations

Writers from the earliest literary and medical history (including Homer, Hippocrates, and Aretaeus) have identified within single individuals intense and divergent moods, such as euphoria, irritability, and depression, that coexist (Millon & Davis, 1996). The concept of a "borderline" personality has evolved significantly from its early modern formulations by psychoanalytic theorists, who called this behavioral pattern "pseudoneurotic schizophrenia," "as-if personality," and "borderline state." The term "borderline" itself originally meant an individual who appeared to have a level of disturbance somewhere between the neurotic and psychotic. Kernberg (1967, in Bradley et al., 2007) later conceptualized "borderline personality organization" and subsequently identified three criteria for its structural diagnosis: (1) identity diffusion, i.e., the lack of a self or having an ego not performing its function; (2) lack of defensive operations, i.e., having more primitive defenses centering on the mechanism of splitting—of viewing others as all good or all bad; and (3) capacity for reality testing, i.e., having perceptions that are problematic but not psychotic and mostly intact (Kernberg et al., 1989). Research studies have since identified several mechanisms potentially at work in the etiology of BPD, including biological and genetic factors, separation and loss, childhood abuse, family environment, and attachment issues (Bradley et al., 2007).

Millon refers to BPD as the unstable pattern; individuals having this disorder are characterized by spasmodic expressive behaviors, paradoxical interpersonal conduct, and a capricious cognitive style. The primary regulatory (defense) mechanism involved in the development and maintenance of this disorder is regression—the individual retreats to earlier developmental states of anxiety tolerance, impulse control, and social adaptation (often evidencing immature if not increasingly infantile behaviors) during times of stress (Millon & Davis, 1996).

Borderline Personality Disorder and Crime, Violence, and Stalking

Until the end of the twentieth century, the relationship between BPD and crime and violence had gone largely unexplored. One of the initial empirical investigations of this relationship was a study by Raine (1993), who was

A Closer Look: Borderline Personality Disorder and Crime

Prevalence of the Disorder in Crime

Study Type	Number	Prevalence Rates
Arrest rates	0	–
Birth cohorts	0	–
Community samples	1	27.0%
Homicide offenders	1	18.0%
Jailed detainees and prisoners	4*	13.2–65.0%
Psychiatric inpatients	3*	15.2–42.0%
Total Number of Studies	**8**	

Sample Characteristics

Size	36–505
Gender	Male only (4 studies); female only (1 study); male and female (3 studies)
Age	Adult, youth
Location	North American and European countries (e.g., Belgium, Finland, Germany, and the United States)
Diagnostic Systems	DSM-III and DSM-IV

Note: *One study involved both jailed detainees or prisoners and psychiatric inpatients.

Prevalence of Crime in the Disorder

Study Type	Number	Prevalence Rates	Crime Definition
Total Number of Studies	**0**		

Nondisordered or community resident comparison group or general population baseline rates for either disorder or crime provided: **0 studies (0.0%)**

among the first to propose that the unique personality constellation of BPD, which includes unstable and intense interpersonal relationships, impulsivity, intense anger, and emotional instability, made an individual with this disorder particularly susceptible to violent behavior. In this study of 37 prisoners in an English top-security facility, a study that included 13 murderers, 5 violent offenders, and 19 nonviolent offenders, Raine found significantly increased borderline personality scores in murderers relative to nonviolent offenders. Specifically, affective instability and unstable, intense relationships represented the specific borderline traits elevated in the murderer group. According to Tardiff (2007), individuals with BPD engage in frequent displays of anger and violence towards others and, in between violent episodes, engage in a wide range of impulsive behaviors putting them at risk for crime and more violence. These include suicidal or self-mutilating behaviors, excessive spending, indiscreet sexual behavior, drug abuse, shoplifting, and reckless driving. Typically violence in these individuals is accompanied by intense displays of emotion and affective instability and is in response to feelings of abandonment or rejection from another—usually from someone from whom the individual wants love, care, or attention. In fact, in a small sample of personality disordered patients, Martins de Barros and de Pádua Serafim (2008) found those with

ASPD ($n = 11$) to be characterized as cold and to involve themselves more in crimes requiring detailed planning and those with BPD ($n = 19$) to be impulsive and to engage in explosive episodes of physical violence. Interestingly, however, Roberts and Coid (2010) found no associations between any offense types and BPD.

In a review of fairly recent research, Sansone and Sansone (2009) concluded that, aside from the increased rates of BPD observed in prison samples (see above), rates of BPD in female offenders are consistently higher than those in male offenders in studies that have compared both. In fact, among inmates, factors associated with an increased likelihood of BPD include being female, childhood sexual abuse, violent offenses, comorbid ASPD, and domestic violence. According to this review, several studies of homicide offenders have reported individuals with BPD and borderline characteristics within their samples (see also Table 10.2), and a number of authors have speculated that subtypes of BPD may be associated with homicidal acts. For example, some have suggested that serial murderers may represent a highly manipulative form of BPD, whereas others have argued that rage-based murders are related to an overcontrolled form of BPD. Stone (1998) discusses several additional cases of murderers with BPD (see Table 10.9) and notes the 3:1 ratio of female-to-male murderers with BPD in his long-term follow-up study of 206 BPD patients. He also notes that more than half (i.e., 8 of 15) of the women with BPD in his biographical series of murderers were victims of incest.

Table 10.9 Cases of Murderers With Borderline Personality Disorder

Source	Age	Gender	Details/Description
Long-term follow-up study of 206 BPD patients (Stone, 1990)	Adult	M	In a lifelong battle with parents who humiliated him constantly; killed his mother when he was 40 after she had refused him his favorite meal at Thanksgiving.
Long-term follow-up study of 206 BPD patients (Stone, 1990)	15	M	Burned down the house of a family whose son, the patient assumed, had sexually molested his sister.
Kaplan et al. (1990)	Adult	F	Laurie Wasserman Dann: bizarre descent after divorce with husband, whom she stabbed with an icepick while he slept; consulted with famous psychiatrist in Chicago area, whose recommendations she ignored; sent him container of fruit juice laced with poison; barged into kindergarten of a school in Winnetka, Illinois, killing one child and wounded several others; killed herself when police later closed in.
Biographical series (Stone, 1998)	Adult	F	Velma Barfield, North Carolinian farm girl: father had intercourse with her from age 13 until age 17, when she married; became addicted to psychotropic drugs after her husband died a few years later; at first, falsified checks or stole small amounts to support her drug habit; eventually, faked her mother's signature on a loan against her mother's house and then poisoned her mother to prevent her from learning of the forgery; not antisocial until she became addicted after the death of her husband.
Hughes (1992)	Adult	F	Darci Pierce, Oregon adoptee: early rage outbursts at home; developed pseudologia fantastica, cunningly manipulative, and carried on sexual relationships with several relatives from age 6 on; in adolescence, mutilated herself and made up stories of living in mansions and taking fantastic trips; obsessed with having a baby and proving herself a better mother than either of hers, so fooled her boyfriend into marrying her because she was "pregnant"; grew desperate and killed a woman who was nine months pregnant, upon whom she did a cesarean section off a deserted highway using a car key as a scalpel, and then drove to the hospital, as though the hastily delivered baby was hers.

Source: Adapted from Stone (1998, pp. 41–42).

In a later review, Sansone and Sansone (2010) discuss the relationship between BPD and stalking behaviors. These authors pay brief homage to a well-known cinematic stalker with BPD, Alex Forrest (played by actress Glenn Close), who stalked and ultimately violently assaulted her married, one-night-stand lover, Dan Gallagher (played by actor Michael Douglas) in the movie *Fatal Attraction.* Sansone and Sansone review five studies reporting the prevalence rates of BPD among stalkers: a small minority (i.e., 4–15%) is characterized by this disorder. However, these authors note a significantly increased rate of BPD in a less forensically focused sample of stalkers (i.e., > 45%), and suggest that, overall, the unusual and intense attachment dynamics of BPD lend themselves particularly to the crime of stalking. Ultimately, although the relationship between BPD and crime and violence has received a modest amount or empirical attention, more research is needed to understand the mechanisms underlying this association.

Histrionic Personality Disorder

Histrionic personality disorder is a pervasive, inflexible, and enduring pattern of excessive emotionality and seeking of attention (APA, 2000, 2013). DSM-5 diagnostic criteria for histrionic personality disorder are listed in Table 10.10.

Prevalence and Incidence Rates of Histrionic Personality Disorder

Prevalence rates for histrionic personality disorder have been estimated at approximately 2–3%, with increased rates (i.e., 10–15%) reported in inpatient and outpatient mental health settings (APA, 2000). More recent national survey data indicate rates of 1.84% (APA, 2013).

Theoretical Conceptualizations

Millon refers to histrionic personality disorder as the gregarious pattern: individuals having this disorder are characterized by dramatic expressive behaviors, attention-seeking interpersonal conduct, and a flighty cognitive style. The primary regulatory (defense) mechanisms involved in the development and maintenance of this disorder are dissociation and repression—the individual regularly changes self-presentations to create a series of socially desirable but altering facades and engages in activities that distract them from reflection on and the integration of unpleasant thoughts and emotions (Millon & Davis, 1996).

Table 10.10 DSM-5 Diagnostic Criteria for Histrionic Personality Disorder

301.50 (F60.4) Histrionic Personality Disorder

A pervasive pattern of excessive emotionality and attention seeking, beginning by early adulthood and present in a variety of contexts, as indicated by five (or more) of the following:

1. Is uncomfortable in situations in which he or she is not the center of attention.
2. Interaction with others is often characterized by inappropriate sexually seductive or provocative behavior.
3. Displays rapidly shifting and shallow expression of emotions.
4. Consistently uses physical appearance to draw attention to self.
5. Has a style of speech that is excessively impressionistic and lacking in detail.
6. Shows self-dramatization, theatricality, and exaggerated expression of emotion.
7. Is suggestible, i.e., easily influenced by others or circumstances.
8. Considers relationships to be more intimate than they actually are.

Source: APA (2013, p. 667). Reprinted with permission from the *Diagnostic and Statistical Manual of Mental Disorders*, Fifth Edition (Copyright © 2013).

A Closer Look: Histrionic Personality Disorder and Crime

Prevalence of the Disorder in Crime

Study Type	Number	Prevalence Rates
Arrest rates	0	–
Birth cohorts	0	–
Community samples	0	–
Homicide offenders	0	–
Jailed detainees and prisoners	1*	1.3%
Psychiatric inpatients	3*	1.3–6.0%
Total Number of Studies	**3†**	

Sample Characteristics

Size	36–299
Gender	Male only (3 studies); male and female (1 study)
Age	Adult, youth
Location	North American and European countries (e.g., Belgium, Germany and the United States)
Diagnostic Systems	DSM-III and DSM-IV

Notes: *One study involved both jailed detainees or prisoners and psychiatric inpatients.

†One additional study of homicide offenders (Yarvis, 1990) listed histrionic personality disorder but included it with narcissistic personality disorder.

Prevalence of Crime in the Disorder

Study Type	Number	Prevalence Rates	Crime Definition
Total Number of Studies	**0**		

Nondisordered or community resident comparison group or general population baseline rates for either disorder or crime provided: **0 studies (0.0%)**

The Relationship Between Histrionic Personality Disorder and Crime

To date, the relationship between histrionic personality disorder and crime and violence has gone largely unexamined with the exception of Roberts and Coid (2010) who found no associations between histrionic personality disorder and any offense types. What is known about this relationship can be gleaned only from limited reports concerning the prevalence rates of histrionic personality disorder in criminal populations and vice versa.

Narcissistic Personality Disorder

Narcissistic personality disorder is a pervasive, inflexible, and enduring pattern of grandiosity, need for admiration, and lack of empathy for others (APA, 2000, 2013). DSM-5 diagnostic criteria for narcissistic personality disorder (NPD) are listed in Table 10.11.

Table 10.11 DSM-5 Diagnostic Criteria for Narcissistic Personality Disorder

301.81 (F60.81) Narcissistic Personality Disorder

A pervasive pattern of grandiosity (in fantasy or behavior), need for admiration, and lack of empathy, beginning in early adulthood and present in a variety of contexts, as indicated by five (or more) of the following:

1. Has a grandiose sense of self-importance (e.g., exaggerates achievements and talents, expects to be recognized as superior without commensurate achievements).
2. Is preoccupied with fantasies of unlimited success, power, brilliance, beauty, or ideal love.
3. Believes that he or she is "special" and unique and can only be understood by, or should associate with, other special or high-status people (or institutions).
4. Requires excessive admiration.
5. Has a sense of entitlement, i.e., unreasonable expectations of especially favorable treatment or automatic compliance with his or her expectations.
6. Is interpersonally exploitative, i.e., takes advantage of others to achieve his or her own ends.
7. Lacks empathy: is unwilling to recognize or identify with the feelings and needs of others.
8. Is often envious of others or believes that others are envious of him or her.
9. Shows arrogant, haughty behaviors or attitudes.

Source: APA (2013, pp. 669–670). Reprinted with permission from the *Diagnostic and Statistical Manual of Mental Disorders*, Fifth Edition (Copyright © 2013). American Psychiatric Association. All rights reserved.

Prevalence and Incidence Rates of Narcissistic Personality Disorder

Prevalence rates for NPD have been estimated at less than 1% in the general population. Increased rates (i.e., 2–16%) have been reported in clinical populations (APA, 2000), but rates appear to vary according to the clinical setting and type of practice (Levy et al., 2007). More recent community estimates range from 0% to 6.2% (APA, 2013).

Theoretical Conceptualizations

The term "narcissism" is derived from the Greek myth of Narcissus, originally written as Homeric hymns in the seventh or eighth century BCE and made popular in Ovid's *Metamorphoses*. Narcissus mistook his own reflected image in a lake for that of another, fell in love with it, and died when the image failed to love him back (Levy et al., 2007). Pioneering English psychologist and sex researcher Havelock Ellis first applied this myth clinically in an 1898 case study of a man characterized by excessive masturbation (Levy et al., 2007), conceptualizing narcissism as autoeroticism or sexual gratification without stimulation by another person (Millon & Davis, 1996). Decades later Otto Kernberg, in his paper proposing borderline personality organization, described "narcissistic personality structure" and distinguished between normal and pathological narcissism (1967, 1970, in Levy et al., 2007). Around the same time Heinz Kohut introduced the term "narcissistic personality disorder" (one of the proposed primary disorders of the self—see Chapter 2), and these writings led to an increased interest in the topic (Levy et al., 2007). Millon refers to NPD as the egotistic pattern; individuals having this disorder are characterized by haughty expressive behaviors, exploitive interpersonal conduct, and an expansive cognitive style. The primary regulatory (defense) mechanisms involved in the development and maintenance of this disorder are rationalization and fantasy—the individual is self-deceptive and adept at concocting plausible reasons justifying behaviors that are self-centered and socially inconsiderate, and despite obvious shortcomings or failures, offers excuses to place himself or herself in the best possible light (Millon & Davis, 1996).

From a psychoanalytic perspective, self psychologists have made important contributions to the understanding of both normative and pathological narcissism. Kohut proposed the concept of the "selfobject": objects (i.e., people) that we experience early in our lives as part of ourselves (e.g., the mother to the three-month-old infant) and experience later in life in terms of the functions or services they originally performed (Kohut & Wolf, 1978). Two kinds of selfobjects are the *mirroring selfobject*, which responds to and confirms the child's innate sense of vigor, greatness, and perfection, and the *idealized parent imago*, which is perceived as a calm, infallible, and omnipotent person whom the child can admire and merge with when she or he needs soothing. In fact, Kohut proposed that a lack of mirroring and idealizing experiences from parents leads to the impairments and deficits in self-soothing and self-esteem that characterize the primary disorders of the self (including narcissistic personality disorder and narcissistic behavior disorder—see Chapter 2). Currently, though there is a broad theoretical and empirical literature on narcissism, some authors feel that it remains poorly calibrated across the disciplines of clinical psychology, psychiatry, and social or personality psychology (Pincus & Lukowitsky, 2010).

A Closer Look: Narcissistic Personality Disorder and Crime

Prevalence of the Disorder in Crime

Study Type	Number	Prevalence Rates
Arrest rates	0	–
Birth cohorts	0	–
Community samples	0	–
Homicide offenders	1	2.0%
Jailed detainees and prisoners	2*	2.0–11.6%
Psychiatric inpatients	3*	7.0–11.6%
Total Number of Studies	**4**	

Sample Characteristics

Size	36–348
Gender	Male only
Age	Adult, youth
Location	North American and European countries (e.g., Belgium, Finland, Germany, and the United States)
Diagnostic Systems	DSM-III and DSM-IV

Notes: *One study involved both jailed detainees or prisoners and psychiatric inpatients.

†One additional study of homicide offenders (Yarvis, 1990) listed histrionic personality disorder but included it with narcissistic personality disorder.

Prevalence of Crime in the Disorder

Study Type	Number	Prevalence Rates	Crime Definition
Total Number of Studies	**0**		

Nondisordered or community resident comparison group or general population baseline rates for either disorder or crime provided: **0 studies (0.0%)**

The Relationship Between Narcissistic Personality Disorder and Crime and Violence

Aside from a few exceptions, the literature on the relationship between NPD and crime in general has not extended much beyond prevalence rate studies. One exception is Millon's discussion of a variant of the narcissistic personalities—the unprincipled narcissist—found more commonly as of late in drug rehabilitation programs, youth offender centers, and jails and prisons (Millon & Davis, 1996). Two other exceptions are Roberts and Coid's (2010) recent large-scale national survey of English and Welsh male prisoners (see above), which found NPD to be associated with drug offenses and fraud, and Warren and colleagues' (2002) finding of a significant association between NPD and incarceration for violent crime in a sample of 261 female prison inmates. Nonetheless, a fair amount of literature has been dedicated to examining the association between extreme forms of narcissism and violent behavior in particular. For example, numerous authors have presented theoretical and clinical formulations of narcissism and murder (see Table 10.12). Two concepts describing pathological forms or expressions of narcissism have been discussed in the literature, and these may be key in understanding the relationship between NPD and violent offending: narcissistic rage and malignant narcissism.

Narcissistic rage is one of two forms of aggression proposed by Kohut (1972, 1971, 1977, and 1984, in Kieffer, 2003). The first, *competitive (instrumental) aggression*, is directed at removing barriers to goals. **Narcissistic rage**, on balance, is directed toward the selfobjects that threaten or are perceived to threaten the self. It represents a need for avenging a previous *narcissistic injury*, a perceived harm or emotional insult that may seem ever so slight and almost imperceptible to others (e.g., when an acquaintance we like momentarily forgets our name) but that, nonetheless, exposes the vulnerable underbelly of the grandiose, primitively omnipotent and idealized self. Unlike competitive aggression, which dissipates immediately after the barrier is removed, narcissistic rage persists long after the threat is eliminated and may endure—smoldering and even increasing—with the passage of years. According to Kieffer (2003), patients with chronic narcissistic rage become preoccupied with malice and spite and may even "erupt in cold fury" and plan acts of revenge (p. 736; see also Harrang, 2012). Furthermore, some authors (e.g., Ornstein, 1998) have suggested that narcissistic rage may be expressed in behavior that is sadistic (i.e., direct behavior such as physical or verbal assault) or masochistic and paranoid (i.e., indirect behavior such as arrogant withdrawal, holding grudges, collecting injustices, self-mutilation or cutting, and suicidal threats). Fox (1974) even proposed a link between narcissistic rage and the forms of aggression observed in combat soldiers, aggression that is often the consequence of the death of a combat buddy—a circumstance that can be equated to the loss of a mirror relationship.

Malignant narcissism was originally described by Kernberg (1984, 1992, in Pollock, 1995), who proposed the term to represent an extreme variant of NPD and an intermediate or "hybrid" personality disorder between NPD and ASPD. Characteristics include typical NPD along with unrestrained "characterologically anchored" aggression (i.e., a "self-righteous aggression" that has "infiltrated" the pathologically grandiose self), unregulated antisocial behavior, "joyful cruelty" and ego-syntonic sadism, a lack of conscience, a need for power and significance, and paranoid interactions with others. According to Kernberg, malignant narcissism reflects a defense against feelings of inferiority, rejection, and insignificance. It develops through pathological self and object representations (i.e., through experiencing parental or other objects as omnipotent, cruel, attacking, and destructive originally), and it manifests as a ruthless desire to become superior and triumphant over life, death, fear, and pain through cruelty toward others or self-mutilation. Pollock (1995) indicates that the severe narcissistic and antisocial tendencies in this disorder may be expressed in extreme forms of sadism and violence and presents as an exemplar the case of a British spree serial killer whose behavior and history suggest the contributory role of malignant narcissism.

Interestingly, Stone (1998) alludes to the concept of malignant narcissism by discussing the trait overlap of NPD, ASPD, and psychopathy. Specifically, he notes egocentricity, or adhering only to one's own rules while being contemptuous of the rules or needs of others, as one of the core features of antisociality and psychopathy and states that, though many individuals with NPD are neither antisocial nor psychopathic, those who attempt or commit murder are more often narcissistic than antisocial personality disordered or psychopathic. He further notes that the blending of narcissistic and psychopathic traits form a personality configuration that is "almost ubiquitous among murderers of almost every type" (p. 36).

Table 10.12 Theoretical and Clinical Formulations of Narcissism and Murder

Fromm (1973)	Relationship between malignant aggression, narcissism, and symbiotic relationships and human destructiveness.
McCarthy (1978)	Homicidal behavior in young males due to narcissistic insults and anger.
Liebert (1985)	The use of borderline and narcissistic disorder in profiling of serial murderers.
Morohn (1987)	Narcissistic personality disorder in case of John Wesley Hardin and his murders.
Stone (1989)	Concept of malignant narcissism: Coexistence of narcissistic and antisocial traits in personalities of serial murderers.
Hickey (1991)	Highly developed narcissistic qualities present in personalities of serial murderers.
Gacono (1992)	Reported a Rorschach analysis of a sexual murderer indicating borderline personality, sadism, and narcissism.
Lowenstein (1992)	Borderline personality, pathological omnipotence, and antisocial behavior in personalities of serial murderers.
Palermo & Knudten (1994)	History of interpersonal sensitivity, feelings of inadequacy, and fear of rejection associated with fantasies of power and control over others in the case of Jeffrey Dahmer.

Source: Adapted from Pollock (1995, p. 259).

Other authors have proposed etiological mechanisms underlying associations between NPD and criminal offending. In a study of 51 male inpatients at two German maximum-security forensic hospitals, Dudeck and colleagues (2007) found significantly increased rates of NPD (but not other personality disorders) among sexual offenders compared to other offenders. The authors suggest an incapability to care for and exhibit empathy for others prevents these offenders from developing stable relationships. Because of their grandiose sense of importance combined with their lack of respect for the needs of others, those with NPD, it could be argued, are at greater risk of committing sexual crimes; they may respond to personal insults—real or imagined—with vindictive rage in the form of sexual violence, oblivious to the feelings or needs of their victims. Furthermore, Tardiff (2007) proposed that individuals with NPD feel as though they have the right to control others and demand their attention and admiration. Still, though this individual exploits others and has little or no remorse doing so, he or she exhibits little flagrant criminal behavior. When present, violence usually results from the individual's frustration and anger with others when they do not give the individual what he or she thinks is deserved. Ultimately, the understanding of the relationship between NPD and crime and violence to date remains largely theoretically based, and more work is needed to ground this relationship in empirical findings.

Cluster C Personality Disorders

Avoidant Personality Disorder

Avoidant personality disorder is a pervasive, inflexible, and enduring pattern of inhibited social interactions, feelings of inadequacy, and hypersensitivity to criticism or rejection (APA, 2000, 2013). DSM-5 diagnostic criteria for avoidant personality disorder are listed in Table 10.13.

Table 10.13 DSM-5 Diagnostic Criteria for Avoidant Personality Disorder

301.82 (F60.6) Avoidant Personality Disorder

A pervasive pattern of social inhibition, feelings of inadequacy, and hypersensitivity to negative evaluation, beginning in early adulthood and present in a variety of contexts, as indicated by four (or more) of the following:

1. Avoids occupational activities that involve significant interpersonal contact, because of fears of criticism, disapproval, or rejection.
2. Is unwilling to get involved with people unless certain of being liked.
3. Shows restraint within intimate relationships because of the fear of being shamed or ridiculed.
4. Is preoccupied with being criticized or rejected in social situations.
5. Is inhibited in new interpersonal situations because of feelings of inadequacy.
6. Views self as socially inept, personally unappealing, or inferior to others.
7. Is unusually reluctant to take personal risks or to engage in any new activities because they may prove embarrassing.

Source: APA (2013, pp. 672–673). Reprinted with permission from the *Diagnostic and Statistical Manual of Mental Disorders*, Fifth Edition

Prevalence and Incidence Rates of Avoidant Personality Disorder

Estimates of prevalence rates for avoidant personality disorder are between 0.5% and 1% for the general population and are approximately 10% among individuals in outpatient mental health clinics (APA, 2000). More recent national survey data suggests community rates of 2.4% (APA, 2013).

Theoretical Conceptualizations

Millon refers to avoidant personality disorder as the withdrawn pattern; individuals having this disorder are characterized by fretful expressive behaviors, aversive interpersonal conduct, and a distracted cognitive style. The primary regulatory (defense) mechanism involved in the development and maintenance of this disorder is fantasy—the individual achieves gratification of needs, confidence building, and conflict resolution primarily through the use of imagination and safely discharges frustrated affectionate and angry impulses by withdrawing into reveries (Millon & Davis, 1996).

The Relationship Between Avoidant Personality Disorder and Crime

To date, systematic empirical investigations of the relationship between avoidant personality disorder and crime and violence are scarce. One rare exception is the recent large-scale national survey of male prisoners in England and Wales conducted by Roberts and Coid (2010), which found avoidant personality disorder scores to be negatively correlated with firearm offenses but positively correlated with criminal damage. Unfortunately, the best source of information about the relationship between this personality disorder and crime remains that which can be gleaned from the limited reports of prevalence rates of avoidant personality disorder in criminal populations and of crime or violent behavior in those with this disorder.

Dependent Personality Disorder

Dependent personality disorder is a pervasive, inflexible, and enduring pattern of submissiveness, clinging behavior, and excessive need to be cared for (APA, 2000, 2013). DSM-5 diagnostic criteria for dependent personality disorder are listed in Table 10.14.

A Closer Look: Avoidant Personality Disorder and Crime

Prevalence of the Disorder in Crime

Study Type	Number	Prevalence Rates
Arrest rates	0	–
Birth cohorts	0	–
Community samples	0	–
Homicide offenders	0	–
Jailed detainees and prisoners	1*	5.1%
Psychiatric inpatients	3*	4.0–22.0%
Total Number of Studies	**3†**	

Sample Characteristics

Size	36–299
Gender	Male only
Age	Adult, youth
Location	North American and European countries (e.g., Belgium, Germany, and the United States)
Diagnostic Systems	DSM-IV

Notes: *One study involved both jailed detainees or prisoners and psychiatric inpatients.

†One additional study of homicide offenders (Yarvis, 1990) listed avoidant personality disorder but included it with dependent, compulsive, and passive-aggressive personality disorders.

Prevalence of Crime in the Disorder

Study Type	Number	Prevalence Rates	Crime Definition
Total Number of Studies	**0**		

Nondisordered or community resident comparison group or general population baseline rates for either disorder or crime provided: **0 studies (0.0%)**

Prevalence and Incidence Rates of Dependent Personality Disorder

The DSM-IV-TR reports that dependent personality disorder is one of the most frequently reported personality disorders among individuals in mental health clinics (APA, 2000). It does not, however, identify specific prevalence rates. More recent national survey data suggest rates between 0.49% and 0.6% (APA, 2013).

Theoretical Conceptualizations

Millon refers to dependent personality disorder as the submissive pattern; individuals having this disorder are characterized by incompetent expressive behaviors, submissive interpersonal conduct, and a naïve cognitive

Table 10.14 DSM-5 Diagnostic Criteria for Dependent Personality Disorder

301.6 (F60.7) Dependent Personality Disorder

A pervasive and excessive need to be taken care of that leads to submissive and clinging behavior and fears of separation, beginning by early adulthood and present in a variety of contexts, as indicated by five (or more) of the following:

1. Has difficulty making everyday decisions without an excessive amount of advice and reassurance from others.
2. Needs others to assume responsibility for most major areas of his or her life.
3. Has difficulty expressing disagreement with others because of fear of loss of support or approval. *Note:* Do not include realistic fears of retribution.
4. Has difficulty initiating projects or doing things on his or her own (because of a lack of self-confidence in judgment or abilities rather than a lack of motivation or energy).
5. Goes to excessive lengths to obtain nurturance and support from others, to the point of volunteering to do things that are unpleasant.
6. Feels uncomfortable or helpless when alone because of exaggerated fears of being unable to care for himself or herself.
7. Urgently seeks another relationship as a source of care and support when a close relationship ends.
8. Is unrealistically preoccupied with fears of being left to take care of himself or herself

Source: APA (2013, p. 675). Reprinted with permission from the *Diagnostic and Statistical Manual of Mental Disorders*, Fifth Edition (Copyright © 2013). American Psychiatric Association. All rights reserved.

style. The primary regulatory (defense) mechanism involved in the development and maintenance of this disorder is introjection—the individual strengthens the belief that an inseparable bond exists between himself or herself and another through firm devotion to that person, forgoing independent views in favor of those of others to avoid conflicts and threats to this relationship (Millon & Davis, 1996).

A Closer Look: Dependent Personality Disorder and Crime

Prevalence of the Disorder in Crime

Study Type	Number	Prevalence Rates
Arrest rates	0	–
Birth cohorts	0	–
Community samples	0	–
Homicide offenders	1	1.4%
Jailed detainees and prisoners	2*	2.0–3.5%
Psychiatric inpatients	3*	2.0–8.0%
Total Number of Studies	**5†**	

Sample Characteristics

Size	36–299
Gender	Male only (3 studies); male and female (2 studies)
Age	Adult, youth

Location	North American and European countries (e.g., Belgium, Germany, the United States)
Diagnostic Systems	DSM-IV, not reported in earlier studies‡

Notes: *One study involved both jailed detainees or prisoners and psychiatric inpatients.

†One additional study of homicide offenders (Yarvis, 1990) listed dependent personality disorder but included it with avoidant, compulsive, and passive-aggressive personality disorders.

‡Earlier studies (Pfieffer et al., 1967; Wilcox, 1985, 1987) utilize the term "passive dependent personality."

Prevalence of Crime in the Disorder

Study Type	Number	Prevalence Rates	Crime Definition
Total Number of Studies	**0**		

Nondisordered or community resident comparison group or general population baseline rates for either disorder or crime provided: **0 studies (0.0%)**

The Relationship Between Dependent Personality Disorder and Crime

To date, the relationship between dependent personality disorder and crime and violence remains largely unexamined. One rare exception is, again, the recent large-scale national survey of male prisoners in England and Wales conducted by Roberts and Coid (2010). This study found dependent personality disorder scores to be significantly and positively correlated with firearm and violent offenses but negatively associated with criminal damage. Unfortunately, as is the case for avoidant personality disorder, the best source of information about the relationship between dependent personality disorder and crime remains the limited studies examining the prevalence rates of this disorder in criminal populations and of crime or violence in those with this disorder.

Obsessive-Compulsive Personality Disorder

Obsessive-compulsive personality disorder is a pervasive, inflexible, and enduring pattern of concern for orderliness, perfectionism, and control (APA, 2000, 2013). DSM-5 diagnostic criteria for obsessive-compulsive personality disorder (OCPD) are listed in Table 10.15.

Prevalence and Incidence Rates of Obsessive-Compulsive Personality Disorder

Prevalence rates for OCPD have been estimated at approximately 1% in the general population and 3–10% in mental health clinic samples (APA, 2000). More recent community estimates have been reported at 2.1% to 7.9% (APA, 2013).

Theoretical Conceptualizations

Millon refers to obsessive-compulsive personality disorder as the conforming pattern; individuals having this disorder are characterized by disciplined expressive behaviors, respectful interpersonal conduct, and a constricted cognitive style. The primary regulatory (defense) mechanisms involved in the development and maintenance of this disorder are reaction-formation and identification—the individual repeatedly presents thoughts and behaviors that are positive and socially commendable but also diametrically opposite to her or his deeper contrary and forbidden feelings. For example, a person may appear reasonable and mature when faced with circumstances that cause others to become angered or dismayed (Millon & Davis, 1996).

Table 10.15 DSM-5 Diagnostic Criteria for Obsessive-Compulsive Personality Disorder

301.4 (F60.5) Obsessive-Compulsive Personality Disorder

A pervasive pattern of preoccupation with orderliness, perfectionism, and mental and interpersonal control, at the expense of flexibility, openness, and efficiency, beginning by early adulthood and present in a variety of contexts, as indicated by four (or more) of the following:

1. Is preoccupied with details, rules, lists, order, organization, or schedules to the extent that the major point of the activity is lost.
2. Shows perfectionism that interferes with task completion (e.g., is unable to complete a project because his or her own overly strict standards are not met).
3. Is excessively devoted to work and productivity to the exclusion of leisure activities and friendships (not accounted for by obvious economic necessity).
4. Is overconscientious, scrupulous, and inflexible about matters of morality, ethics, or values (not accounted for by cultural or religious identification).
5. Is unable to discard worn-out or worthless objects even when they have no sentimental value.
6. Is reluctant to delegate tasks or to work with others unless they submit to exactly his or her way of doing things.
7. Adopts a miserly spending style toward both self and others; money is viewed as something to be hoarded for future catastrophes.
8. Shows rigidity and stubbornness.

Source: APA (2013, pp. 678–679). Reprinted with permission from the *Diagnostic and Statistical Manual of Mental Disorders*, Fifth Edition

A Closer Look: Obsessive-Compulsive Personality Disorder and Crime

Prevalence of the Disorder in Crime

Study Type	Number	Prevalence Rates
Arrest rates	0	–
Birth cohorts	0	–
Community samples	0	–
Homicide offenders	0	–
Jailed detainees and prisoners	1*	4.0%
Psychiatric inpatients	3*	4.0–25.0%
Total Number of Studies	**3†**	

Sample Characteristics

Size	36–299
Gender	Male only
Age	Adult, youth
Location	North American and European countries (e.g., Belgium, Germany, and the United States)
Diagnostic Systems	DSM-IV

Notes: *One study involved both jailed detainees or prisoners and psychiatric inpatients.

†One additional study of homicide offenders (Yarvis, 1990) listed compulsive personality disorder but included it with avoidant, dependent, and passive-aggressive personality disorders.

Prevalence of Crime in the Disorder

Study Type	Number	Prevalence Rates	Crime Definition
Total Number of Studies	0		

Nondisordered or community resident comparison group or general population baseline rates for either disorder or crime provided: **0 studies (0.0%)**

The Relationship Between Obsessive-Compulsive Personality Disorder and Crime

To date, systematic empirical investigations of the relationship between OCPD and crime and violence have, for the most part, not been undertaken. In fact, this disorder is rarely mentioned within any criminological context, though Ferreira (2000) did state that there was no reported relationship between OCPD and serial murder. Once again, the rare exception is the recent large-scale national survey of male prisoners in England and Wales conducted by Roberts and Coid (2010), which found OCPD to be positively associated with firearm offenses. Unfortunately, like the other Cluster C personality disorders, the strongest argument to be made for a relationship between OCPD and crime remains that based on information gleaned from studies reporting on the prevalence rates of OCPD in criminal populations and of crime in disordered populations.

Multiple Personality Disorder and Dissociative Identity Disorder

Multiple personality disorder was first introduced in the DSM-III as "300.14 Multiple Personality," and it was classified under "Hysteria," one of the "Neurotic Disorders"(APA, 1980). Maintaining its original numerical code, it was renamed "Multiple Personality Disorder" in the DSM-III-R (APA, 1987) and then reconceptualized as a dissociative disorder and renamed in the DSM-IV (APA, 1994). **Dissociative identity disorder** is its current name in the DSM-5 at the time of this writing. According to the DSM-III-R, in classic cases of MPD, an individual has at least two fully developed personalities, with each having its own unique memories, behavior patterns, social relationships, styles of dress, and so on (APA, 1987; Carlisle, 1991). In adults, the number of personalities may range from 2 to over 100, but approximately half of the cases have 10 personalities or fewer. Transition from one personality to another—often triggered by psychosocial stress, environmental cues, or conflicts among personalities—usually happens within seconds or minutes but may occur gradually over hours or days. Studies demonstrated that different personalities might have different physiological characteristics (e.g., eyeglass prescriptions or medication responses) or responses to psychological tests. Also these personalities may or may not have an awareness of or be in communication with each other (APA, 1987). In terms of prevalence rates for MPD, the DSM-III-R merely states that "recent reports suggest that this disorder is not nearly so rare as it has commonly been thought to be" (p. 271). The DSM-IV-TR recognizes a recent "sharp rise" in the reported rates of dissociative identity disorder in the United States—attributable perhaps to a greater awareness of the diagnosis resulting in the identification of previously undiagnosed cases or to its being overdiagnosed in individuals that are highly suggestible. It does not mention any specific prevalence rates (APA, 2000). The DSM-5 mentions 12-month prevalence rates of 1.5% in a small U.S. community study (APA, 2013).

Diagnostic criteria multiple personality disorder, as outlined in the DSM-III-R, and for dissociative identity disorder, as outlined in the DSM-5, are listed in Tables 10.16 and 10.17, respectively.

Table 10.16 DMS III-R Diagnostic Criteria for Multiple Personality Disorder

300.14 Multiple Personality Disorder

A. The existence within the person of two or more distinct personalities or personality states (each with its own relatively enduring pattern of perceiving, relating to, and thinking about the environment and self).

B. At least two of these personalities or personality states recurrently take full control of the person's behavior.

Source: APA (1987, p. 272). Reprinted with permission from the *Diagnostic and Statistical Manual of Mental Disorders,* Third Edition (Copyright © 1980). American Psychiatric Association. All rights reserved.

Table 10.17 DSM-5 Diagnostic Criteria for Dissociative Identity Disorder

300.14 (F44.81) Dissociative Identity Disorder

A. Disruption of identity characterized by two or more distinct personality states, which may be described in some cultures as an experience of possession. The disruption of identity involves marked discontinuity in sense of self and sense of agency, accompanied by related alterations in affect, behavior, consciousness, memory, perception, cognition, and/or sensory-motor functioning. These signs and symptoms may be observed by others or reported by the individual.

B. Recurrent gaps in the recall of everyday events, important personal information, and/or traumatic events that are inconsistent with ordinary forgetting.

C. The symptoms cause clinically significant distress or impairment in social, occupational, and other important areas of functioning.

D. The disturbance is not a normal part of a broadly accepted cultural or religious practice. *Note:* In children, the symptoms are not better explained by imaginary playmates or other fantasy play.

E. The symptoms are not attributable to the physiological effects of a substance (e.g., blackouts or chaotic behavior during alcohol intoxication) or another medical condition (e.g., complex partial seizures).

Source: APA (2013, p. 292). Reprinted with permission from the *Diagnostic and Statistical Manual of Mental Disorders*, Fifth Edition (Copyright © 2013). American Psychiatric Association. All rights reserved.

Theoretical Conceptualizations

A DID process generally begins before the age of five and is the result of overwhelming trauma, which the mind of the child cannot tolerate. For emotional survival, the child dissociates self from the mental or physical pain. Depending upon the personality makeup of the child and the nature of the trauma, the event may be blocked from the awareness of the child. The structuring of this dissociated material leads to alter personalities or personality states (less fully developed personalities), which result in the DID process (see Carlisle, 1991, for a review). ***Dissociation***, the process of blocking out unwanted stimuli from awareness, occurs on a continuum from day-dreaming to the more serious pathological form, dissociative identity disorder (Chu, 1988, in Carlisle, 1991).

The Relationship Between Dissociative Identity Disorder and Crime

It has been suggested that offender dissociation is common in violent crimes (Carlisle, 1991). The dissociative process is a protective psychological process that reduces depression, pain, and anxiety. Coons (1991) noted that between 1977 and 1990, at least 18 accounts of murder defendants with alleged DID appeared in both the scientific literature and the lay press. Other cases, chronicled in local newspapers, undoubtedly exist. Of the cases reviewed by Coons, over two-thirds were thought by someone to be feigning DID, and only two were found NGRI. Most of the defendants showed a simplistic good/bad dichotomy or split between at least two personality states.

DID and Malingering. The possibility that the offender is feigning DID must always be considered. One of the most famous cases of malingering was that of American serial killer Kenneth Bianchi (the Los Angeles "Hillside Strangler"), who murdered—with his cousin Angelo Buono—10 young women (ages 12–28) and who appeared to manifest multiple personalities while under hypnosis. His claims of DID were eventually repudiated, and he was subsequently diagnosed as an antisocial personality (Watkins, 1984). Evidence of multiple personality symptomatology prior to the offense supports an argument for DID (see Lewis, Yeager, Swica, Pincus, & Lewis, 1997). Hall (1989) presents the case of John Jason Davis, a 46-year-old divorced male who murdered his live-in girlfriend. After Davis murdered the victim, he dismembered her body and scattered the body parts in plastic bags throughout the county. He was not arrested until 17 days later because his carefully calculated disposal of the remains made identification of the body nearly impossible. He had severed the fingertips from the hands, which eliminated fingerprint identification, and removed all the teeth so that dental records were useless (the victim was identified via the manufacturer's identification number on a steel plate that had been previously surgically implanted in her right forearm to mend a fracture). Davis had an extensive history of psychiatric hospitalizations and had been in outpatient therapy for eight months prior to the murder, to address his DID diagnosis.

In one interesting study of 12 murderers with DID, Lewis et al. (1997) demonstrated that DID can be differentiated from malingering by utilizing objective data (related to time periods before the offense) gathered from medical, psychiatric, social service, school, military, and prison records and from records of interviews with subjects' family members and others. In a novel approach, handwriting samples (e.g., old journals, letters) produced before the participants' psychiatric evaluations were also examined. Results indicated that symptoms and signs of DID in both childhood and adulthood were corroborated independently from multiple sources in all cases, and, in 10 cases, significant changes in writing style or signatures were documented. These authors conclude by asserting that it is possible to distinguish DID from malingering accurately, though this process requires great effort and ample amounts of objective evidence. Ultimately, more work is needed in this very under-researched area, which may further elucidate the nature of the relationship between MPD or DID, crime, and violence.

Psychopathy

Ted Bundy is often referred to as the prototypical psychopath. Unfortunately, though this assertion seems difficult to contest given the nature of his personality, history, and behavior, significant confusion related to the term "psychopathy" exists among both mental health professionals and the general public. This confusion is partly due to the fact that, literally translated, the term "psychopathy" means "mental illness" (from "*psyche*," or "mind," and "*pathos*," or "disease"). The news and popular media's use of the term as an equivalent for "insane" or "crazy" also confuses. How often do we hear "The police say a 'psycho' is on the loose," or "The guy that killed her must be a 'psycho'" Newton, 2000)? Furthermore, the term is often used to describe an individual who commits criminal acts that are unspeakable, horrific, or too difficult for most others to understand (Lykken, 1995). For example, murderers such as Ed Gein (see Chapter 2) may be thought of as psychopaths (Newton, 2000). Unfortunately, applying this label is a gross misrepresentation. Gein's behavior was admittedly bizarre—and he may have, in fact, possessed psychopathic traits to some degree—but, overall, he does not appear to meet the diagnostic criteria for psychopathy using today's standards (see below).

A Definition

One of the factors contributing to the confusion about psychopathy is the fact that a standardized definition has not yet permeated, in any official way, through the world of mental health clinicians or of the public at large.

However, Brinkley and colleagues (2004) provide a relatively comprehensive definition that has been cobbled together from other sources. **Psychopathy**, as it is currently defined, is a personality disorder that manifests early and persists throughout life (Hare, 1996). Psychopathic individuals have been traditionally described as lacking in empathy, loyalty, and guilt and engaging in persistent antisocial, impulsive, and irresponsible behavior (Cleckley, 1976). Such individuals typically do not evidence impaired intelligence but appear unable to make use of their intelligence to learn from mistakes (Hart & Hare, 1989). This discrepancy between ability and performance led Cleckley (1976) to conclude that psychopathic individuals suffer from a condition as debilitating as schizophrenia.

Historical Conceptions of Psychopathy

Psychopathy was the first personality disorder to be recognized in psychiatry (Millon et al., 1998, in Hare, 2003). It is important to note that the term "psychopathic" has been a generic label for all personality disorders until recent decades and was originally selected by German psychiatrist Julius Ludwig August Koch (1841–1908) in 1891 to indicate a physiological basis for these specific impairments in functioning (Millon & Davis, 1998). For centuries, psychopathy has shared a common lineage with antisocial personality disorder, which only recently (comparatively speaking) diverged when the DSM in 1980 moved away from focusing on the internal processes and personality traits of psychopathy and concentrated instead on the behavioral characteristics of this disorder—conceptualizing those characteristics as ASPD (see Figure 10.1).

The clinical and empirical discussion of psychopathy dates back many centuries and extends throughout many different cultures and societies. In fact, researchers have found references to psychopathic individuals in biblical, classical, and medieval texts (Arrigo & Shipley, 2001). For example, Theophrastus, Aristotle's student, describes the "Unscrupulous Man"—an individual who corresponds closely to modern conceptualizations of psychopathy:

> The Unscrupulous Man will go and borrow more money from a creditor he has never paid. . . . When marketing he reminds the butcher of some service he has rendered him and, standing near the scales, throws in some meat, if he can, and a soup-bone. If he succeeds, so much the better; if not, he will snatch a piece of tripe and go off laughing. (Millon & Davis, 1998, p. 430)

Numerous formal conceptualizations of psychopathy have been proposed over the past two centuries (see Figure 10.1). In 1801, Philippe Pinel (1745–1826) described *manie sans délire* or "insanity without delirium," noting that some patients engaged in impulsive acts and episodes of violence while still understanding the irrationality of their actions and having intact reasoning abilities. Though Pinel's *manie sans délire* label was intended as morally neutral, in 1812, American psychiatrist Benjamin Rush (1746–1813) reconceptualized Pinel's idea for this disorder—with its defects in "passion and affect"—as socially condemnable and pejorative. In 1835, James Cowles Prichard (1786–1848) introduced the term "moral insanity," an overly broad (as well as pejorative) term, which became a major source of contention and preoccupation in England and continental Europe for more than 70 years. Prichard even maintained that moral insanity reduced criminal culpability and should be employed as a legal defense. In 1874, another leading British psychiatrist of the period, Henry Maudsley (1835–1918), described the condition as a sort of moral "colorblindness": "As there are persons who cannot distinguish certain colours, having what is called colour blindness, so there are some who are congenitally deprived of moral sense" (Millon & Davis, 1998, p. 432).[3] Maudsley later described individuals with this disorder as "moral imbeciles" (Maudsley, 1895, in Saleh et al., 2010).

In the late nineteenth and early twentieth centuries, a move back toward moral neutrality can be observed in scholars' descriptions of the conceptual precursors of psychopathy. German psychiatrists turned attention

---

3. Johns and Quay (1962) coined a phrase that is often repeated in the literature on psychopathy: the psychopath, they said, "knows the words but not the music" (p. 217). In a sense, the idea is that psychopaths understand the lexical meaning of emotional words but do not experience their emotional value. It is interesting that both semantic "tone deafness" and moral "color blindness" have been used to describe deficits in those with psychopathy. These sensory analogues are elegantly understated yet eloquently capture the true essence of this disorder.

away from British value-laden theories and towards what they believed to be observational research. Koch (1891) introduced the term "psychopathic inferiority" (see above)—with *psychopathic* indicating a physical basis for these impairments and *inferiority* implying nothing more than a deviation from the norm. Unfortunately, Koch's efforts to obviate the pejorative label of Prichard's conceptions were slowly undermined, and, gradually, his term evolved to mean the opposite of what he had originally intended.

German psychiatrist Emil Kraepelin expanded on Koch's psychopathic inferiority terminology in 1915, moving it back toward moral judgment and social condemnation and including within it categories of criminal offenders of arguably the most vicious and wicked disordered sorts. These included "morbid swindlers and liars," who were manipulative, glib, charming, and unconcerned for others; "criminals by impulse," who were overcome by uncontrollable desires to commit offenses like arson or rape for purposes unrelated to material gain; "professional criminals," who acted out of cold, calculated self-interest rather than an uncontrollable impulse; and "morbid vagabonds," who wandered through life with neither self-confidence nor responsibility (Millon & Davis, 1998).

In the 1940s after World War I, an American psychiatrist named Hervey Cleckley published a hallmark book entitled *The Mask of Sanity* (1941), which marked the beginning of the modern clinical construct of psychopathy. Based on his own clinical observations, Cleckley proposed that psychopaths wear a "mask" of seeming emotional health, referring to them as "automatons" who appear outwardly normal but who are nonetheless internally devoid of the human emotional experience. Cleckley clearly stated his belief that criminal behavior was not inherent to the definition of psychopathy, but he noted that "when serious criminal tendencies do emerge in the psychopath, they gain ready expression" (1976, p. 262). In other words, the disinhibited nature of psychopathic individuals causes the behaviors toward which they might otherwise be inclined to become excessive (Brinkley et al., 2004). The diagnostic criteria for the "Cleckley psychopath" are listed in Table 10.18.

Table 10.18 Diagnostic Criteria for Psychopathy

The Mask of Sanity[1]	PCL-R[2]
"Cleckley's Psychopath"	**"Hare's Psychopath"**
Superficial charm and good intelligence	Item 1: Glibness/superficial charm
Absence of delusions and other signs of irrational thinking	Item 2: Grandiose sense of self-worth
Absence of nervousness or psychoneurotic manifestations	Item 3: Need for stimulation/proneness to boredom
Unreliability	Item 4: Pathological lying
Untruthfulness or insincerity	Item 5: Conning/manipulative
Lack of remorse or shame	Item 6: Lack of remorse or guilt
Inadequately motivated antisocial behavior	Item 7: Shallow affect
Poor judgment and failure to learn from experience	Item 8: Callous/lack of empathy
Pathologic egocentricity and incapacity for love	Item 9: Parasitic lifestyle
General poverty in major affective relations	Item 10: Poor behavioral controls
Specific loss of insight	Item 11: Promiscuous sexual behavior
Unresponsiveness in general interpersonal relations	Item 12: Early behavioral problems
Fantastic and uninviting behavior with drink and sometimes without	Item 13: Lack of realistic, long-term goals
Suicide rarely carried out	Item 14: Impulsivity
Impersonal, trivial, and poorly integrated sex life	Item 15: Irresponsibility
Failure to follow any life plan	Item 16: Failure to accept responsibility for own actions
	Item 17: Many short-term marital relationships
	Item 18: Juvenile delinquency
	Item 19: Revocation of conditional release
	Item 20: Criminal versatility

Sources: [1]Cleckley (1941); [2]Hare (2003)

Cleckley's work was a milestone in the understanding of psychopathy. His published clinical observations served as an anchor in the tumultuous seas of diagnostic confusion existing for clinicians encountering and working with psychopathic clients at that time. However, as much as *The Mask of Sanity* provided a standardized clinical view of psychopathy, an empirically validated measurement tool was still desperately needed for research studies. In 1980, Canadian psychologist Robert Hare developed the "Psychopathy Checklist" in an attempt to operationalize the construct of psychopathy based on Cleckley's clinical material and formulations. After years of refinement, the **Psychopathy Checklist—Revised** (PCL-R; Hare, 2003) is now considered the "gold standard" of psychopathy measures, and, although it was developed initially for use with Canadian offender populations, it has since demonstrated sound psychometric properties (i.e., good reliability and validity) in a multitude of sample types in locations around the world. The term "checklist" is actually somewhat of a misnomer, as the standard PCL-R assessment procedure consists of a semi-structured interview and a review of available file and collateral information. Unlike the polythetic diagnostic approach of the DSM, the PCL-R is based on a numerical scoring system in which each of its 20 items (see Table 10.18) is assigned a value of 0–2 based on the "goodness of fit" of that item to the individual being assessed. Scores for all items are summed, and a PCL-R total score 30 out of a possible of 40 points is considered the diagnostic threshold for psychopathy. Factor-analytic studies of these 20 items have since identified subcomponents of the higher-order construct of psychopathy; and individual PCL-R scores are now represented in either a two-factor structure, with interpersonal or affective elements comprising Factor 1 and social deviance, Factor 2, or, more recently, a four-facet structure, with Facet 1 being interpersonal, Facet 2 affective, Facet 3 lifestyle, and Facet 4 antisocial elements (Hare, 2003). Other researchers (Cooke & Michie, 2001) have also proposed a three-factor model, and, to date, a spirited debate continues in the literature regarding which model, the two-factor/four facet or the three-factor model, best captures the underlying structure of psychopathy (see Cooke et al., 2007; Hare, 2003).

Psychopathy Versus Antisocial Personality Disorder. Throughout the history of the DSM, nomenclature and the definitions of antisocial personality disorder, psychopathy, sociopathy, and the like have continued to evolve. In the first DSM (1952), this collection of personality characteristics was termed "Sociopathic Personality Disturbance," and, in the DSM-II (1968), it was termed "Antisocial Personality." The definitions for both included many of the personality characteristics set forth by Cleckley in his descriptions of the psychopath and were focused on internal processes and personality traits. However, as mentioned, a paradigm shift occurred in 1980 with the release of the DSM-III. In this and subsequent editions of the DSM, the term "Antisocial Personality Disorder" was adopted, and the focus was no longer on personality traits. The DSM-III task force felt that the clinical inferences necessary to determine the personality characteristics of the psychopath lowered the reliability of the diagnosis. Therefore, a diagnostic shift toward assessing the behavioral characteristics commonly associated with the disorder was made; and these diagnostic criteria were considered more reliable for identification purposes than were the personality factors explaining why the behaviors occurred. However, the new criteria were so broad they included almost every known criminal offense. In fact, Theodore Millon argued against the behavior-based conceptualization of ASPD, describing the diagnostic criteria as "merely a sequence of picayunish specifics (e.g., thefts, three or more traffic arrests, etc.)" (Millon & Davis, 1998, p. 430) and as a shift from the level of focus used to outline all of the other personality disorders.

Unfortunately, the DSM-IV (APA, 1994), DSM-IV-TR (APA, 2000), and DSM-5 (APA, 2013) have inadvertently compounded the confusion associated with this diagnostic terminology by adding, in the ASPD section, this note: "This pattern has also been referred to as psychopathy, sociopathy, or dissocial personality disorder" (APA, 2000, p. 702; APA, 2013, p. 659). Designations such as ASPD, sociopathy, and the like are erroneously used as synonyms for psychopathy, and each of these diagnostic constructs can represent a different constellation of personality traits and behaviors. For example, although approximately 90% of the criminals classified as psychopathic using the PCL-R are diagnosed with ASPD, only 30% of those with ASPD diagnoses meet criteria for psychopathy. In offender populations, the base rate for ASPD ranges from 50% to 80%, although the base rate for psychopathy is much lower at 15% to 25%. Most individuals with ASPD are not psychopaths; however, most psychopaths do engage in antisocial behaviors. More recent authors have proposed that ASPD is on a continuum with psychopathy and that psychopathic ASPD is a more severe form—with a greater risk for violence—than ASPD alone (Coid & Ullrich, 2010). Others see these as overlapping constructs with differential patterns of criminal behavior, comorbidity with other personality disorders, victimization, and institutional adjustment (Warren & South, 2006). Furthermore, the designation of psychopathy is routinely equated with being untreatable (see below), and the consequences of diagnostic misidentification can be severe, substantial, and enduring. Regrettably, mental health professionals continue to remain perplexed when diagnosing, treating, or making recommendations to the court system about psychopathic individuals (Shipley & Arrigo, 2001).

Interestingly, the DSM-5 has made a significant step toward the recognition of psychopathy by incorporating it into its alternative model for personality disorders (see above). Under this new proposed model, the designation "psychopathic features" has been added as a specifier for ASPD:

> A distinct variant often termed psychopathy (or "primary" psychopathy) is marked by a lack of anxiety or fear and by a bold interpersonal style that may mask maladaptive behaviors (e.g., fraudulence). This psychopathic variant is characterized by low levels of anxiousness (Negative Affectivity domain) and withdrawal (Detachment domain) and high levels of attention seeking (Antagonism domain). High attention seeking and low withdrawal capture the social potency (assertive/dominant) component of psychopathy, whereas low anxiousness captures the stress immunity (emotional stability/resilience) component. (APA, 2013, p. 765)

In essence, using this proposed model, a clinician can now diagnose an individual with ASPD as having psychopathic features or not. It will be interesting to see how researchers and mental health professionals apply this new model in research, clinical, and forensic arenas and if it contributes at all to reducing the conceptual and diagnostic confusion (and "healing" the rift—so to speak—among nomenclatures) related to psychopathy and ASPD.

Relationship Between Psychopathy and DSM-IV-TR Personality Disorders. Psychopathy is not included in recent editions of the DSM as a distinct disorder, though psychopathic features have been proposed as a specifier for ASPD in the DSM-5. This change does not mean that psychopathy is a completely different diagnostic phenomenon from the personality disorders currently outlined within the DSM-IV-TR and DSM-5. Rather, it is merely a different conceptualization, a different constellation or subset of the limited number of traits and behaviors that form the basis of the human experience and the foundations of the other DSM personality patterns and disorders. As such, a conceptual overlap between many of the PCL-R traits of psychopathy and the traits of personality disorders in the DSM-IV-TR and DSM-5 should not be surprising. In fact, recent research (Vachon et al., 2013) demonstrates how psychopathy and other personality disorders may be understood theoretically using basic traits such as impulsiveness, warmth, straightforwardness, modesty, and deliberation. From a theoretical standpoint, Lykken (1995) proposes a group of "psychopathies" and Millon (Millon & Davis, 1998) identifies 10 theoretical subtypes of psychopathy, which overlap, in different aspects, with the various personality disorders outlined in DSM-IV-TR and DSM-5. In order of severity, these subtypes are unprincipled, disingenuous, risk-taking, covetous, spineless, explosive, abrasive, malevolent, tyrannical, and malignant. For example, according to Millon, the "unprincipled psychopath" is seen most commonly in conjunction with narcissistic personality patterns and the "disingenuous psychopath" with a variant of histrionic personality disorder (the individual has a veneer of friendliness and sociability and pursues a strong need for attention and approval). The category "spineless psychopath" is a derivative of the "avoidant and dependent personality" diagnosis, and the "abrasive psychopath" has negativistic and paranoid personality patterns. The "malevolent psychopath" displays the patterns of sadistic or paranoid personalities, the "tyrannical psychopath" those of sadistic and negativistic personalities, and the "malignant psychopath" those of individuals diagnosed with paranoid personality disorder. Furthermore, some psychopathy researchers have advanced the notion that certain of the disorders that are diagnosed more commonly in women, including borderline personality disorder, histrionic personality disorder, and somatization disorder, may represent female expressions of psychopathy (Verona & Vitale, 2006).

Figure 10.1 History of Psychopathy

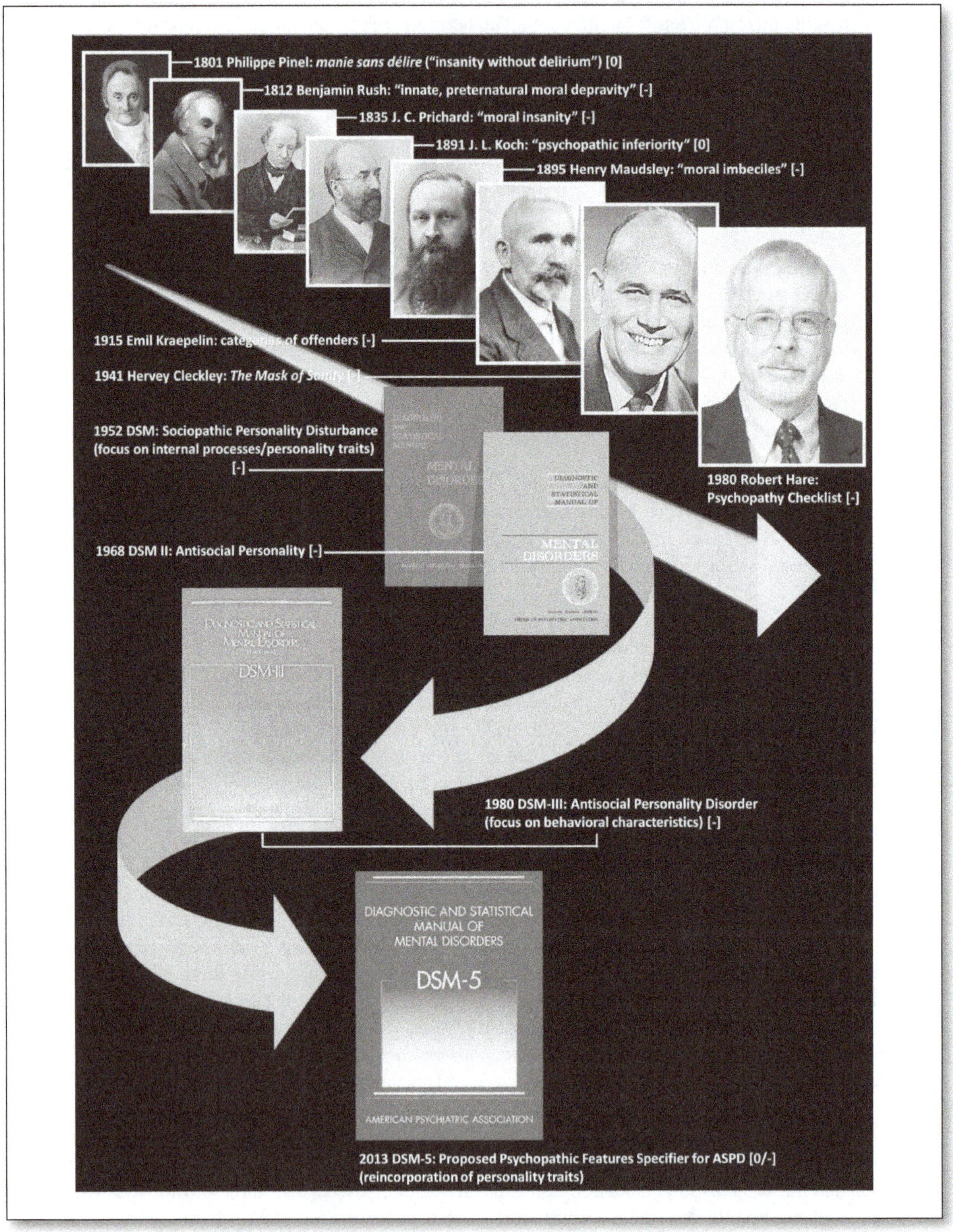

Notes: [0] = morally neutral; [-] = moral censorious or indicative of social depravity, pejorative (Arrigo & Shipley, 2001; Millon & Davis, 1998).

Researchers have also recently sought to extend former theoretical speculations and clarify this overlap using empirical rather than theoretical approaches. For example, in a sample of 299 German violent offenders, Huchzermeier and colleagues (2007) found significant associations between Factor 2 of PCL-R-measured psychopathy and antisocial and borderline personality disorders; they also found a significant correlation between narcissistic personality disorder and Factor 1 of the PCL-R. In a sample of 84 Belgian adult male forensic patients, Pham and Saloppé (2010) found significant positive relationships between ASPD and (a) PCL-R total scores, (b) Factor 1 and 2 scores, and (c) Facet 1, 3, and 4 scores. They also found a significant positive correlation between narcissistic personality disorder and PCL-R Factor 1 and Facet 1 scores.

Psychopathy and Sociopathy

The term **sociopathy** was first coined in 1914 by German psychiatrist Karl Birnbaum, who attributed the causes of this disorder to societal forces. This social conditioning thesis became prominent among psychiatrists later in the 1920s (Millon & Davis, 1998), and the label "sociopath" gained widespread popularity in the 1950s when social constructivism was the dominant paradigm (Fersch, 2006). In fact, the first DSM (APA, 1952) reflects this social constructivism zeitgeist in its use of the term "sociopathic personality disturbance." Some theorists have proposed a theoretical distinction between sociopathy and psychopathy. In perhaps one of most well known of these theoretical differentiations, Lykken (1995) discusses the "family of antisocial personalities," consisting of sociopathic personality, psychopathic personality, and character neurosis, a "wastebasket collection of persons who break the rules, usually in a rather minor way" and, incidentally, the group most likely to benefit from treatment (p. 39). Lykken relates inadequate socialization to both sociopathic and psychopathic personalities but proposes that, in those with sociopathic personalities—the largest group—this lack of socialization is due to neglectful or incompetent parenting while in those with psychopathy, it is overridden by innate biological (i.e., genetic) characteristics (see also Lykken, 2000). However, Lykken admits that his proposed taxonomy was not derived from empirical data but rather "concocted . . . from the armchair" (Lykken, 1995, p. 41). Other theorists have even proposed a conceptual continuum of psychopaths, sociopaths, normal criminal offenders (i.e., neither psychopaths nor sociopaths), and non-offenders—based on biological predispositions and parenting competency (Walsh & Wu, 2008).

Although a theoretical distinction between sociopathy and psychopathy may be helpful in terms of understanding the etiology of the behavior associated with these disorders, in practice, this distinction has gained little—if any—scientific traction. For example, to date there are no empirically validated methods for measuring sociopathy in research studies, and no one has articulated how the outward clinical presentation of sociopathy might be distinguishable from that of psychopathy. So, from a scientific standpoint, "sociopathy" is an antiquated term, lacking clear definition and remaining largely unsuitable for technical use.

Theoretical Conceptualizations

Meloy and Shiva (2007) discuss how several psychoanalytic theories may help us understand psychopathy. These authors quote Freud (1928/1961) to eloquently summarize the psychoanalytic conceptualization of the psychopathic mind:

> two traits are essential in a criminal: boundless egoism and a strong destructive urge. Common to both of these, and a necessary condition for their expression, is absence of love, lack of an emotional appreciation for (human) objects. (p. 178)

According to Meloy and Shiva (2007), the foundation on which the "house of psychopath" is constructed is comprised of three elements: no attachment, underarousal, and minimal anxiety. The psychopath's mind is characterized predominantly by a dismissive attachment style or a chronic emotional detachment from others (which includes elements such as apathy, self-absorption, preoccupation with nonhuman objects, and no displays of emotion). British psychoanalyst John Bowlby initially described this condition as "affectionless psychopathy" in a study of 44 juvenile thieves (Bowlby, 1944). He believed it was caused by constant maternal rejection in infancy and early childhood. In fact, early skin contact with the mother may be the first means of affectional relatedness and the beginnings of secure attachment, which may be absent in the psychopath (Meloy & Shiva, 2007).

Other unconscious processes have been proposed to be at work in the etiology and maintenance of the psychopathic personality. For example, psychopaths may be characterized by failures of internalization—meaning failures in the transference of external means of biological and psychological regulation and functioning to their inner worlds. These failures begin with an organism's distrust of the environment and deficits in incorporation (e.g., the infant's developmentally primitive instinct and desire to "take in" everything—from the mother's nipple to a piece of lint on the floor—through its mouth). Two kinds of internalizations, *identifications* (ways of modifying the self or behavior to resemble the object) and *introjections* (internalized representations of objects that become part of the superego) thus become, in the psychopath, absent, unavailable when wanted, or harsh and unpleasant. Lacking internalized processes for self-soothing, the child anticipates hard, aggressive objects from the outside world and identifies with them for adaptation and defense. Anna Freud (1936/1966) called this phenomenon "identification with the aggressor," when abused children closely bond to their abusive parent; Meloy (2001, in Meloy & Shiva, 2007) termed it a "predator part-object" in psychopathy. According to Meloy and Shiva (2007), the central motivation of the psychopath is to dominate his objects (p. 339); thus, the psychopath operates from within a dominance-submission (prey-predator) paradigm, desiring neither affectional relating nor reciprocal altruism.

Furthermore, psychopaths are characterized by a grandiose self structure comprised of (1) a "real self," the actual specialness of the child; (2) the "ideal self," a fantasized image compensating for oral rage and envy; and (3) an "ideal object," a fantasized image of a parent who is completely loving and accepting—often contrasting with the behavior of the devalued actual parent. They also have primitive object relations, with a personality organized at the preoedipal or borderline level and no tripartite structure (id, ego, superego), and unintegrated good and bad part-objects maintained through primitive defenses. Finally, the psychopath is thought to be characterized by sadistic superego precursors, which are projected aspects of early persecutory objects; narcissistically defined affects, which create an emotional world similar to that of a presocialized young toddler—in fact, psychopathic men are said to modulate emotions like five- to seven-year-old boys (Meloy & Shiva, 2007, p. 342); and two ego-syntonic modes of aggression: affective and predatory.

From an evolutionary perspective, some theorists have proposed how the behavioral traits of psychopathy may be transmitted intergenerationally. For example, Dawkins (1989, in Raine, 1993) proposes the notion of the "selfish gene," wherein genes struggle selfishly and ruthlessly for their only goal—survival—and humans are merely containers to serve this purpose. Individuals may die, but genes are passed on from generation to generation. Furthermore, behaviors evolve if they increase the "reproductive fitness" (ability to have more offspring) of the individual. Resources (e.g., food and access to mates) are crucial to reproductive fitness, and, in humans, such fitness stems from power, money, and social class. Furthermore, although reciprocal altruism (e.g., sharing food with hungry neighbors) provides an evolutionary advantage, so, in fact, does antisocial behavior, in the form of a "cheating" strategy involving lying and property crime. In fact, sexual infidelity and rape can be seen as the "ultimate" reproductive cheating strategies; hence psychopaths (from an evolutionary perspective) become the "ultimate cheats" (Raine, 1993).

Some have proposed that psychopathic traits may develop at the "macro" level, necessitated by the location, ecological niche, and social climate of a given society. For example, Raine (1993) contrasts the characteristic psychopathic and nonpsychopathic qualities of two relatively geographically isolated groups of people in different parts of the world: the !Kung bushmen of the Kalahari desert and the Mundurucu of the Amazon basin (see Box 10.2). Another often-cited example is the Yanomamo Indians of southern Venezuela and northern Brazil. Chagnon (1988, in Raine, 1993) found the men of this tribe to be characterized by significant psychopathic features: they broke rules when doing so was in their interest, forcibly appropriated women, and were fearless and highly aggressive. Of all male deaths in this group, 30% are due to violence. In fact, the term "*unokais*" is bestowed upon any tribal member who has committed homicide, and Chagnon reported nearly half (44%) of all Yanomamo males over the age of 25 have killed (one *unokais* killed 16 times). Murders are motivated by fighting over women, and violence translates directly into reproductive fitness. Specifically, *unokais*—compared to men

BOX 10.2 PSYCHOPATHIC AND NONPSYCHOPATHIC SOCIETIES

	!Kung Bushmen	Mundurucu
Location	Kalahari desert	Amazon basin
Ecological Niche	Harsh	Rich
Social Climate	Cooperative	Competitive
Parental Investment	High	Low
Fertility	Low	High
Male Activities	Group hunting	Competition, raids
Favored Traits	Reciprocal altruism, careful mate selection, good parenting	Manipulative behavior, fearlessness, fighting

Source: Adapted from Raine (1993).

who have not killed—have more wives (1.63 vs. 0.63) and children (4.91 vs. 1.59), and villages containing *unokais* are attacked less frequently and have lower death rates.[4]

From a neurobiological perspective, imaging studies have identified abnormalities in brain structure and function that may point toward underlying neurobiological mechanisms in the development of psychopathy. More specifically, these abnormalities are in the cortical regions, such as the prefrontal regions, and the subcortical regions, such as the amygdala and other limbic structures (Glenn & Raine, 2009). For example, fMRI evidence indicates deficient fear conditioning in psychopathic individuals in the limbic-prefrontal circuit: the amygdala, orbitofrontal cortex, insula, and anterior cingulate (Birbaumer et al., 2005). Also abnormalities in emotion processing exist in the cortical and subcortical brain regions of criminal psychopaths (Müller et al., 2003). Structural imaging studies have identified corpus callosum abnormalities (e.g., in white matter volume, thickness, and length) in the brains of psychopathic antisocial individuals (Raine et al., 2003) and an exaggerated structural asymmetry between the right and left hippocampi, with the right hemisphere's volume greater than the left's, in unsuccessful psychopaths (Raine et al., 2004). Finally, Yang and colleagues (2005a) found white matter structural increases in the prefrontal region of the brains of pathological liars, which may explain why psychopathic individuals can become such adept and proficient (i.e., pathological) liars. Furthermore, researchers have examined genetic influences on psychopathy and antisocial behavior, particularly as they may relate to or interact with influences from the environment. Twin and adoption studies tend to define psychopathy via related personality traits rather than the PCL-R (Waldman & Rhee, 2006). A meta-analysis of 51 twin and adoption studies (Waldman & Rhee, 2006) indicates evidence for genetic and non-shared environmental influences (i.e., nearly 50% for each) but not for shared environmental influences. Overall, neurobiological research has become one of the most impassioned and promising areas of investigation in the study of psychopathy.

---

4. Similar cross-cultural examples of psychopathic individuals have been identified in cultures from around the world. For example, the Yoruba, a rural tribe from Nigeria, has a syndrome known as *arankan*—a person "who always goes his own way regardless of others, who is uncooperative, full of malice, and bullheaded." The Alaskan Inuit have a word, "*kunlangeta*," that refers to an individual whose "mind knows what to do but he does not do it." This individual may repeatedly lie, cheat, steal, and refuse to go hunting; and when the other men are away from the village, he takes sexual advantage of many women. He does not pay attention to reprimands, and is always being brought before the elders for punishment (Murphy, 1976, p. 1026).

Contributions from other theoretical perspectives have also aided in our current understanding of the etiological mechanisms underlying psychopathy. From a cognitive and information processing perspective, numerous studies have identified a broad array of deficits in attention, language, and behavioral inhibition among psychopathic individuals (Hiatt & Newman, 2006). Psychosocial theorists have emphasized the role of family background in the development of psychopathy. Early psychosocial research in psychopathy began with the pioneering work of Bowlby (1944) on the relationship between prolonged maternal deprivation and "affectionless psychopathy" and delinquency (see above). Also, McCord and McCord (1964) emphasized the influence of parental rejection, having an antisocial parent, erratic discipline, and poor parental supervision on the development of psychopathy. Subsequent researchers have linked the etiology of psychopathy to family factors such as childrearing problems (meaning the supervision and monitoring of children), with poor supervision being the strongest predictor of offending among all childrearing deficits; discipline or parental reinforcement, with harsh or punitive discipline, erratic or inconsistent discipline, and low parental reinforcement (i.e., not praising) predicting offending; the warmth or coldness of emotional relationships, with cold, rejecting parents tending to have delinquent children; parental involvement with children, with low parental involvement in the child's activities predicting offending; child abuse and neglect; parental conflict and disrupted families; and large family size. This last factor might need some explanation: as the number of children in a family increases, the amount of parental attention given to each child decreases; and as the number of children increases, the household tends to become more overcrowded, possibly leading to increases in frustration, irritation, and conflict. Other family factors associated with the development of psychopathy are having criminal or antisocial parents or siblings; other parental features such as mothers who bear children early or in their teens or who are unwed, high parental stress, parental anxiety or depression, or parental substance use; and socioeconomic factors.

The Relationship Between Psychopathy and Crime

The Prevalence of Psychopathy in Criminal Populations. Studies of prevalence rates of psychopathy in criminal populations are somewhat unique relative to those for the other personality disorders covered in this chapter in that they tend to appear in one of two forms: (1) with rates of psychopathy reported as present or absent or (2) with rates of psychopathy reported as actual PCL-R scores. Given the enormous number of studies of psychopathy in criminal populations published over the past several decades and the sheer numbers of prevalence rates that could be gleaned from each, we did not attempt to present a comprehensive or even a representative list of such studies here. Rather, a comparatively modest number of studies were identified to demonstrate how our general organizational framework for understanding the relationship between mental illness and crime (i.e., via the examination of reported prevalence rates) could be applied to the literature on psychopathy (see Tables 10.19 and 10.20).

The Relationship Between Sociopathy and Crime

For posterity's sake, examples of studies examining the prevalence rates of sociopathy and crime were also identified here (see Tables 10.19 and 10.20). Interesting (but not surprising) is their publication before the formal research operationalization of psychopathy in the PCL in the year 1980 (and before the move toward ASPD in the DSM-III). Also interesting is the fact that the specific method used to produce a diagnosis of sociopathy in these studies (with the exception of the study by Guze et al., 1974) is conspicuous in its absence (as it is in most of the pre-1980 studies of psychopathy discussed above).

Psychopathy and Risk for Recidivism

The area of psychopathy research that predominates the literature on the relationship between psychopathy and crime addresses how psychopathy might relate to criminal recidivism. This research has had and will continue to have significant practical implications, particularly given the criminal justice system's strong demand for predictions of criminal and violent behavior (e.g., by the parole boards, courts, and clinicians responsible for releasing clients). Dozens of studies utilizing an array of different methodological approaches have examined the utility of psychopathy in criminal recidivism prediction. These studies have varied in aspects such as research design (i.e., prospective designs versus postdictive analyses), psychopathy measurement (i.e., PCL-defined measures versus

Table 10.19 Prevalence of Psychopathy and Sociopathy in Criminal Populations

Psychopathy								
Source	**N**	**Gender**	**Age**	**Study Type**[a1]	**Sample Description**	**Disorder**	**Diagnostic System**	**Prevalence/Incidence**
Cohen & Freeman (1945)	(1) 320 (2) 87	M, F	Adult?	AR	Police records of arrested patients from 1,676 patients paroled or discharged from Norwich State Hospital (Connecticut), 1940–1944 (1) Arrested before hospitalization (2) Arrested after hospitalization	Psychopathic personality	?	(1) 3.7% ($n = 12$) (2) 4.6% ($n = 4$)
West (1966)	148	88 M, 60 F	< 20 – 40+	HO	Homicide followed by suicide, subjects in England and Wales, 1954–1961	Aggressive psychopaths	?	2.7% ($n = 4$)
Okasha et al. (1975)	(1) 60 (2) 20	(1) 50 M, 10 F (2) ?M, ?F	25–35[a]	HO	"Socio-psychiatric study" of (1) Murderers in Abou-Zabel and Kanater prisons, Egypt (2) Murderers in Egyptian State Mental Hospital	Psychopathy	?	(1) 50.0% ($n = 30$) (2) 0.0% ($n = 0$)
Heilbrun 1979	76	?	$M = 30.14$	JD	Prisoners in Georgia state system (inclusion in study required at least grade 6 reading level)	Psychopathy	MMPI-Pd scale & CPI-So scale	50% scores of 32+
Grann et al. (1999)	401	M/F?	?	JD (and post-detainment follow up)	Individuals convicted of violent crime and court-ordered to evaluation	Psychopathy	PCL-R	43% scores of 22+ 32% scores of 26+ 10% scores of 32+

(Continued)

(Continued)

Psychopathy								
Source	**N**	**Gender**	**Age**	**Study Type[a1]**	**Sample Description**	**Disorder**	**Diagnostic System**	**Prevalence/Incidence**
Långström & Lindblad (2000)	56	M = 54 F = 2	15–20	JD	Adolescents who committed a crime severe enough to receive detainment and be ordered to forensic psychiatric investigations	Psychopathy	PCL-R	16% ($n = 9$) Score of 26+
Langevin (2003)	(1) 33 (2) 80 (3) 23 (4) 611	M	(1) $M = 32.06$ (2) $M = 27.58$ (3) $M = 27.57$ (4) $M = 31.42$	PI	Interviews with convicted sex offenders ($n = 747$) belonging to one of four groups: (1) sex killers, (2) nonhomicidal sexually aggressives, (3) nonhomicidal sadists, and (4) general sex offenders. Participants were chosen from a database of more than 2,800 minimum-security forensic ward psychiatric hospital cases (Clarke Institute in Toronto, Ontario, Canada) seen since 1973	PCL-R > 30	PCL-R	15.2% 15.0% 17.4% 4.8%
Porter et al. (2003)	38	M	41.42	JD/HO	Sexual homicide offenders taken from a group of 125 homicide offenders, from a larger group of about 800 incarcerated offenders in Canadian federal prisons	Psychopathy	PCL-R	52.6 % ($n = 20$) scores of 30+
Hervé et al. (2004)	90	M	$M = 30.6$	JD	Archival study of incarcerated federal offenders who had committed acts of unlawful confinement (hostage takers), 1960s–1998, Pacific region of Canada	Psychopathy	PCL-R	48.9 % ($n = 44$) PCL-R ≥ 30
Vitacco et al. (2007)	168	M	M=16.40	PI	Offenders placed at the Medota Juvenile Treatment Center in Wisconsin	Psychopathy	PCL-YV	$M = 19.10$

Psychopathy								
Source	**N**	**Gender**	**Age**	**Study Type[a1]**	**Sample Description**	**Disorder**	**Diagnostic System**	**Prevalence/Incidence**
Walsh & Kosson (2007)	199	M	17–40	JD	Offenders serving 1 or less years at a county jail	Psychopathy	PCL-R	33.2% (n = 66) scores of 30+
Fougere, Potter & Boutilier (2009)	40	M	13–19	JD, CS	File review of court-ordered assessments or of aggression risk assessments in Nova Scotia	Psychopathy	PCL-YV	Median score in violent group = 21 Median score of sexual offender group = 17.5
Sociopathy								
Source	**N**	**Gender**	**Age**	**Study Type[a1]**	**Sample Description**	**Disorder**	**Diagnostic System**	**Prevalence/Incidence**
Pfeiffer, Eisenstein, & Dabbs (1967)	85	2/3 M, 1/3 F	17–63	JD	Federal prisoners referred for mental competency evaluations, at the USPHS Hospital in Lexington, Kentucky, 1960–1965	Sociopathic personality	?	2.4% (n =2)
Kahn (1971)	43	41 M, 2 F	11–74	HO	Interviews and psychiatric examinations of individuals who made pleas of insanity to charges of first- or second-degree murder.	Sociopathic	?	32.6% (n =14)

Notes: [a1]AR = arrest rates of patients discharged from psychiatric facilities, JD = jailed detainees and incarcerated prisoners, HO = homicide offenders, BC = birth cohort study, PI = psychiatric inpatient sample, CS = community sample (i.e., epidemiological catchment area survey studies and outpatient psychiatric patients).

[a] Highest percentage of subjects in this age range.

Table 10.20 The Prevalence of Crime in Psychopathic Populations

Source	N	Gender	Age	Study Type	Sample Description	Disorder	Crime Definition	Prevalence/Incidence
Guze et al. (1974)	35	?M, ?F	Adult	CS	Community psychiatric clinic patients, diagnosed using Feighner's diagnostic criteria (Feighner et al., 1972)	Sociopathy	Felony conviction	37.0% (*n* = 13)
Ishikawa et al. (2001) and Yang et al. (2005b)	29	M	21–45	CS	Interviews and collateral file reviews of 91 adult males recruited from five temporary employment agencies in the greater Los Angeles area, diagnosed with the PCL-R (using a tertile split)	Psychopathy	Criminal convictions (court records and self-report)	"Unsuccessful psychopaths": 55.2% (*n* = 16)

A Closer Look: Psychopathy and Crime

Prevalence of the Disorder in Crime

Study Type	Number	Prevalence Rates
Arrest rates	1	3.4–4.6%
Birth cohorts	0	–
Community samples	1*	(see below)‡
Homicide offenders	2	0.0–50.0%
Jailed detainees and prisoners	7*	10.0–52.6%‡
Psychiatric inpatients	2	4.8–17.4%†
Total Number of Studies	**12**	

Sample Characteristics

Size	38–747
Gender	Male only (6 studies); male and female but generally more males than females (5 studies); not reported (1 study)
Age	Youth, adult

Location	North American and European countries (e.g., Canada, England, Egypt, the United States, and Wales)
Diagnostic Systems	PCL-R, PCL-YV, MMPI-Pd scale, and CPI-So scale, not reported in earlier studies

Notes: *One study (Fougere et al., 2009) involved both jailed detainees or prisoners and community individuals.

†Rates reported in Langevin (2003). In another psychiatric inpatient study (Vitacco et al., 2007), the mean PCL-YV score was 19.10.

‡Fougere et al. (2009) reported mean PCL-YV scores of 21.0 for violent offenders and 17.5 for sexual offenders.

Prevalence of Crime in the Disorder

Study Type	Number	Prevalence Rates	Crime Definition
Arrest rates	0	–	–
Birth cohorts	0	–	–
Community samples	1	55.2%	"Unsuccessful psychopaths" (criminal convictions)
Homicide offenders	0	–	–
Jailed detainees and prisoners	0	–	–
Psychiatric inpatients	0	–	–
Total Number of Studies	**1**		

Sample Characteristics

Size	29
Gender	Male only
Age	Adult
Location	United States
Diagnostic Systems	PCL-R

Nondisordered or community resident comparison group or general population baseline rates for either disorder or crime provided: **0 studies (0.0%)**

self-reports), and settings (i.e., prison and correctional settings, forensic psychiatric settings with insanity acquittees as subjects, and civil psychiatric settings). Also, they have taken into account—to varying degrees—factors such as gender, ethnicity, country of study, and age (Douglas et al., 2006). Overall, results from a series of meta-analyses of these studies conducted within the past two decades have (with some caveats) generally supported an association between measures of psychopathy and criminal re-offending, across contexts and types of people (Gendreau et al., 2002; Hemphill et al., 1998; Salekin et al., 1996; and Walters, 2003, in Douglas et al., 2006). Efforts to further refine our understanding of this relationship continue (e.g., Walters, 2012). In fact, PCL measures of psychopathy continue to play a prominent role in contemporary risk assessment instruments (Douglas et al., 2006) and have demonstrated comparatively more predictive power than other recidivism-related variables, such as substance abuse, early behavioral problems, age, number of convictions, elementary school maladjustment, early separation from a parent, never having been married, and failure on prior conditional release (e.g., Grann et al., 1999; Harris et al, 1993).

A Closer Look: Sociopathy and Crime

Prevalence of the Disorder in Crime

Study Type	Number	Prevalence Rates
Arrest rates	0	–
Birth cohorts	0	–
Community samples	0	–
Homicide offenders	1	32.6%
Jailed detainees and prisoners	1	2.4%
Psychiatric inpatients	0	–
Total Number of Studies	**2**	

Sample Characteristics

Size	43–85
Gender	Male and female (predominantly male)
Age	Youth, adult
Location	United States
Diagnostic Systems	Not specified

Prevalence of Crime in the Disorder

Study Type	Number	Prevalence Rates	Crime Definition
Arrest rates	0	–	–
Birth cohorts	0	–	–
Community samples	1*	37.0%	Felony convictions
Homicide offenders	0	–	–
Jailed detainees and prisoners	0	–	–
Psychiatric inpatients	0	–	–
Total Number of Studies	**1**		

Sample Characteristics

Size	35
Gender	Male and female
Age	Adult
Location	Not specified
Diagnostic Systems	Feigner diagnostic criteria

Note: *Community psychiatric patients.

Nondisordered or community resident comparison group or general population baseline rates for either disorder or crime provided: **0 studies (0.0%)**

More recent work has focused on how different factors—such as socioeconomic status and ethnicity—may interact with psychopathy in the prediction of violence. For example, in a sample of county jail inmates in the United States, Walsh and Kosson (2007) found psychopaths to be nearly twice as likely to reoffend violently than those without a psychopathy diagnosis; also, although psychopathy predicted recidivism at lower but not higher levels of socioeconomic status (SES) for European American inmates, its predictive power was stable across SES levels for African American inmates. Furthermore, a recent meta-analysis by Hawes and colleagues (2013) has shown the effectiveness of a combination of psychopathy and measures of sexual deviance as predictors of sexual recidivism.

Psychopathy, Homicide, and Other Violent Crimes

A fair amount of empirical attention has been directed toward understanding the nature of violence and aggression in individuals with psychopathy, and evidence suggests that the violent crimes committed by psychopaths exhibit a more complex and distinctive form of violence than do those of other violent offenders (O'Toole, 2007).

Motivation: Instrumental Homicides. Studies of homicide offenders have demonstrated how psychopaths may have different motives for murder than do those who are not psychopaths. Specifically, distinctions have been made between instrumental and reactive homicides. According to Woodworth and Porter (2002), *instrumental homicides* are "cold blooded"—associated with premeditation, motivated by an external goal, and not preceded by a strong emotional reaction (e.g., an offender carefully plans, carries out, and conceals a homicide in order to steal from the victim). *Reactive homicides*, however, are "crimes of passion"—associated with high levels of impulsivity, reactivity, and emotions (e.g., a stranger verbally insults the perpetrator, who, in a rage, immediately starts a fight and proceeds to stab the victim to death with a weapon of "convenience," such as a broken bottle in a bar). It has been proposed that violence and aggression in psychopaths is motivated by primitive or weak rather than intense or emotional states and thus is more instrumental in nature (Hare, 2003). Others argue that, although psychopaths are certainly capable of both instrumental and reactive violence, they are prone to the former (Glenn & Raine, 2009).

In fact, many studies involving different sample types (i.e., incarcerated offenders and community individuals) and methodologies (e.g., the coding of offense histories, psychological tests, and computer tasks) have shown relationships between various forms of instrumental aggression and psychopathy (Cornell et al., 1997; Glenn & Raine, 2009; Hare, 2003; Serin, 1991). However, some of these (e.g., Glenn & Raine, 2009; Serin, 1991) are not based on criminal offending. Regarding homicide offenders, Woodworth and Porter (2002), for example, found nearly all (93.3%) of homicides committed by psychopaths in a sample of 125 Canadian offenders to be instrumental in nature, compared to approximately half (48.4%) of those committed by offenders who were not psychopaths. Williamson and colleagues (1987) found that, among offenders from five Canadian correctional institutions convicted of violent crimes (including murder, violent assaults, robbery, kidnapping, and sexual assault), psychopaths were significantly more likely motivated by material gain, while those not psychopathic were more often motivated by strong emotional arousal (i.e., jealousy, rage, or intense argument). In fact, most homicides committed by nonpsychopaths—but none of those committed by psychopaths—occurred during a domestic dispute or an intensely emotional event. Cornell and colleagues (1997) found that instrumental (and more psychopathic) violent offenders were significantly more often not provoked by the behavior of the victim and not acting in a state of anger compared to reactive violent offenders. Studies have also demonstrated that instrumental violence and homicide may be more related to the interpersonal and affective (i.e., Factor 1) features of psychopathy (Dempster et al., 1996, in Hare, 2003; Porter et al., 2001; Woodworth & Porter, 2002), though psychopathic murderers may be unwilling (or perhaps or unable) to recognize the instrumental nature of their own violence. For example, Porter and Woodworth (2007) compared the official accounts and self-reported descriptions of homicides committed by 50 incarcerated offenders and found that psychopaths exaggerated the reactivity of their homicides to a greater degree than nonpsychopaths (even though the homicides of psychopaths were primarily instrumental). Finally, although the aggression of psychopaths often appears to be used for instrumental gain, recent evidence suggests that aggression by psychopaths may also have more self-gratifying aspects, as evidenced by thrill-seeking and sadistic motivations (Porter & Woodworth, 2006).

Victimology. Perhaps due to the interpersonal deficits associated with psychopathy (i.e., little familial contact, reduced relationship intensity, frequent changes in residence), some researchers have speculated that psychopaths would victimize known individuals such as family members or friends less often when committing acts of violence (Williamson et al., 1987). In fact, barring some rare exceptions (e.g., Laurell & Dåderman, 2005), one of most consistent findings across studies is that victims are generally not family members but rather are unknown to the psychopathic violent offender (e.g., Cornell et al., 1997; Weizman-Henelius et al., 2002). Some evidence suggests that victim gender may also be somehow related to psychopathy in violent offending. For example, Williamson and colleagues (1987) found that nonpsychopaths were more likely to victimize females that were known to them, but psychopaths more often victimized males who were not known to them. Interestingly, Hervé and colleagues (2004) found that violent Canadian hostage takers were more likely to have victimized female strangers. In the most comprehensive study to date of the relationship between crime scene behavioral characteristics and psychopathy, Häkkänen-Nyholm and Hare (2009), using retrospective file-based PCL-R assessments, national legal registry data, and computerized police crime report data in a sample of 546 Finnish homicide offenders, found that offenders with higher PCL-R scores were more likely to kill males as well as nonfamily members or ex-partners.[5] Other aspects of the victimology of psychopathic violent criminals have also been examined. For example, offenders whose victims include both children and adults are more likely than not to be psychopaths (O'Toole, 2007).

Offense Behavior. Other researchers have examined potential relationships between psychopathy and specific offense-related behaviors. Regarding offense planning, Williamson and colleagues (1987) suggest that psychopaths often engage in criminal behavior that lacks purpose and long-range planning, but Cornell and colleagues (1997) found instrumental violent offenders (who are, by and large, more psychopathic) had significantly higher proportions of offense planning and goals present than did reactive violent offenders. Studies have also shown that a psychopathic offender is more likely to commit a sexually motivated homicide and to engage in significantly more gratuitous or excessive violence, including sadistic violence, than is a nonpsychopathic offender (Porter et al., 2003). Juodis and colleagues (2009) found psychopathic murderers were more likely to act alone when perpetrating sexual homicides but tended to involve an accomplice in other types of homicides. Additionally, psychopaths were likely to commit gratuitous acts of violence against women, regardless of whether or not they were acting alone. Regarding other offense-related behaviors, homicidal offenders with increased levels of psychopathy have demonstrated a greater likelihood of being under the influence of alcohol while killing and of leaving their crime scenes without informing anyone (Häkkänen-Nyholm & Hare, 2009); and male psychopaths have been shown to be more geographically mobile than nonpsychopaths (O'Toole, 2007). Finally, psychopathic traits may be inferred from the crime scene behaviors of serial violent offenders. Impulsivity and sensation seeking may be evidenced by the variation among the crime scenes of one offender (e.g., in victim age, race, and physical appearance; in method of assault; in types of injuries to victims; and in weapon choice). There may be risky behavior over and beyond what is needed to commit the crime, and glibness or superficial charm and conning and manipulative behavior may be indicated by the killer's various approaches to accessing victims, which might include a con, ruse, or surprise or a blitz assault (O'Toole, 2007).

Psychopathy and Serial Murder. Ted Bundy's pattern of heinous violent behavior may be very difficult for some to understand. Many serial killers like Bundy perpetrate multiple acts of extreme violence against others, which—on their face—would seem to indicate that some form of severe personality pathology (such as psychopathy) is at work in these individuals. It seems tempting, then, if not intuitive, to assume a strong

---

5. The past decade (with the exception of rare examples such as Taylor et al., 2012) has, disappointingly, yielded a near dearth of systematic empirical studies into the effectiveness of criminal investigative psychological techniques such as criminal profiling. Schug thinks that studies such as this—linking measurable personality constructs to documented crime scene behaviors—are among the most promising lines of inquiry to date for advancing the current (and, arguably, floundering) scientific state of the practice of criminal profiling.

association between serial murder and psychopathy. In fact, frequent references are made in the serial murder literature to these killers being "psychopathic sexual sadists" (Geberth & Turco, 1997). Furthermore, criminal profiling methods developed by the FBI have relied heavily upon differentiating both crime scenes and offenders into psychopathic (organized) and psychotic (disorganized) types, especially in serial and sexual homicide cases (Turvey, 2008), and the presence of psychopathy has been noted in published case assessment reports of sexual murderers (e.g., Gacono, 1997). Moreover, one statistic that is commonly proffered in media and law enforcement circles is that over 90% of all serial killers are psychopaths. Though this figure is impressive and even sounds reasonable, one must be cautioned that the "science" behind it is actually somewhat dubious.

In fact, to date, very few empirical investigations into the relationship between psychopathy and serial murder have been undertaken. Geberth and Turco (1997), for example, used a case history evaluation protocol (including psychiatric and law enforcement data) on a sample of 248 identified serial sexual killers in the United States. They found that all of those with complete protocols ($n = 68$) met a rigorous DSM-IV criteria for ASPD and sexual sadism (psychopathy, however, was not assessed). The widely publicized "90%" figure mentioned above appears to be derived from a study by Stone (1998), who—in an admittedly novel approach—reviewed 279 "true crime" biographies of murderers. Results indicated that 74 out of 77 (or 96%) of the male serial killers in this sample met PCL-R criteria for psychopathy (using PCL-R scores of 25 or higher). Stone acknowledges some of the methodological weaknesses of this approach, admitting that his biographical series is not representative of murderers in the United States in general. (In fact, according to Stone, only about 1 murderer in 1,100 becomes the subject of a full-length book.) He also appears to acknowledge that detailed information obtained from direct clinical interviews would be more desirable than that derived from biographical novels.

Other studies, on balance, have demonstrated how individuals who commit horrific homicidal acts against others may not necessarily be psychopathic. For example, in a study of 14 juvenile offenders who had committed simultaneous sexual assault and homicide or attempted homicide, Myers and Blashfield (1997) found mean PCL-R scores to be 22.4 (range 7.1–30.6). In a later study of 25 nonfamily child abductors who murdered their victims, Beyer and Beasley (2004) reported mean PCL-R scores of 17.6 (range 5–37). In fact, only four of the offenders (19%) in this study exceeded the cutoff score that would classify them as psychopaths; this finding was consistent with the overall lack of glibness or superficiality or of conning or manipulation among this group and with the presence of appropriate affect and expressions of remorse and even of victim empathy observed in many of these participants.

In sum, what is known about the relationship between psychopathy and serial murder is actually very limited. Widely disseminated characterizations of this relationship are based on less-than-scientific data collection methods, systematic studies are few and far between, and studies of individuals who commit reprehensible acts of sexualized lethal violence demonstrate that these individuals often do not necessarily meet diagnostic criteria for psychopathy.

Psychopathy and "White-Collar" Crimes

In a casual response to a journalist's question at the end of a 2002 address to the Canadian Police Association meeting in St. John's, Newfoundland, Robert Hare astutely noted, "Not all psychopaths are in prison. Some are in the boardroom" (Babiak et al., 2010). In fact, recent decades have witnessed the growth of target-rich environments in which white-collar or corporate psychopaths are able to thrive: business, financial institutions, organized religion, politics, social organizations, and the Internet are now fertile and lucrative "kill zones," with Ponzi schemes, insider trading, and mortgage and Internet frauds their weapons of economic assault.

Lykken (1995) linked the concepts of psychopathy and white-collar criminality by first noting the importance of examining the white-collar criminal within the context of his proposed classification of criminal types, referring to them as "people with 'broadly normal temperaments and backgrounds [who] are sometimes lured into crime by environmental circumstances that constitute a kind of Devil's offer that they cannot (or do not choose) to refuse'" (p. 20). He subsequently stated that these are the politicians, police officers, businessmen, lawyers, company executives, or stock speculators who, on one hand, may feel normative shame and guilt if caught and, on the other, may be more likely to succumb to this "Devil's offer" if they possess a psychopathic personality. Hare (1993) discusses how psychopathic individuals may con or manipulate their way into desirable and profitable professional roles. Using their masterful skills as imposters, these individuals may forge and brazenly use impressive credentials (often faked and unchecked, in professions with easy-to-learn jargon) to adopt or acquire positions that offer prestige and power, such as the professional position of financial consultant, minister, counselor, psychologist, medical doctor, and even surgeon.

Though it makes sense that many psychopaths would likely not possess a common work ethic, the corporate environment of large organizations can be a prime hunting ground for entrepreneurial psychopaths with the necessary skills and attributes to fool others; especially useful are psychopathic traits that equate to "talents" in the business world (Babiak & Hare, 2006). Other researchers have even suggested that there are specific behavioral manifestations of corporate psychopathy, including features such as the harsh treatment of employees, the sudden termination of employee contracts, unhealthy and environmentally damaging production practices, dangerous working conditions, the violation of human rights conventions and employment laws, and bullying (Boddy, 2011).

The fact remains, however, that there is little empirical data on the role of psychopathy in corporate crime (Babiak et al., 2010). One notable exception is a first-of-its-kind study of 203 U.S. corporate professionals, in which Babiak and colleagues (2010) used in-house "360°" assessments and performance ratings to determine the applicability of PCL measures of psychopathy in a corporate sample, as well as the prevalence of psychopathic traits. Results indicated that the performance of PCL measures was comparably to that observed in studies of offenders and community members: the prevalence rate of psychopathy in this sample was higher than reported rates in community samples (5.9% compared to 1.2% for "potential" or "possible" psychopathy and 3.0% compared to 0.2% for a PCL-R-comparable cut score of 30). Furthermore, psychopathy scores were associated with peer ratings of creativity and good strategic thinking and communication skills (charisma and good presentation style) but negatively associated with ratings of being a team player, management skills, and overall accomplishments (responsibility and performance). Further research (Mathieu et al., 2013) has demonstrated the utility and effectiveness of the B-Scan 360, a promising measure of psychopathy for use in corporate settings. Other methods of operationalizing corporate psychopathy have been proposed (e.g., Boddy, 2011), but these require empirical validation.

Psychopathy and Sexual Crimes

Sex for the psychopath is characteristically impersonal, casual, and trivial (Hare, 2003)—a state of affairs that might seem to encourage sexual offending. However, much of the literature on the relationship between psychopathy and sexual crimes presents a somewhat mixed picture. For example, a review by Vitacco and Rogers (2009) indicates that, although sexual offending recidivists are characterized by increased PCL-R scores relative to sexual offenders who do not reoffend, in general, most sex offenders—including recidivists—are not psychopaths (see Table 10.21). According to Vitacco and Rogers (2009), this is because sex offenders often have multiple motivations for deviant behavior. However, in a small subset of sex offenders, psychopathic traits do appear to play a contributory role in sex offending.

Table 10.21 Psychopathy and Recidivism in Sex Offenders

	PCL-R Total Scores	
Study	**Sex Offenders Who Reoffend**	**Sex Offenders Who Do Not Reoffend**
Langevin et al. (2004)	21.4	15.7
Hanson & Harris (2000)	23.4	16.7
Dempster (1998), Simourd & Malcomb (1998)	21.5, 23.2	13.3
Firestone et al. (1999)	21.7	16.3

Source: Vitacco & Rogers (2009).

Regarding recidivism studies in particular, Bradford and colleagues (2007) report that PCL-R studies of sex offenders have also shown mixed results. In fact, although the PCL-R has demonstrated strong correlations with general and violent criminal behavior (see above), it appears less strongly correlated with sexual offending behavior (Hare, 2003). However, the PCL-R appears important in differentiating recidivists from nonrecidivists across offender and paraphilia types (Bradford et al., 2007). In fact, the importance of considering the comorbidity of psychopathy and paraphilias in predicting the risk of recidivism has been emphasized in the literature, and psychopathy has historically been factored into various formulations of sexual predator laws (Saleh et al., 2010).

Interestingly, studies have also shown mixed results for the PCL-R's ability to distinguish among sex-offender subtypes. For example, a review by Bradford and colleagues (2007) indicates that PCL-R scores do not appear to differentiate significantly between sex offender and paraphilia types (i.e., between incest offenders, child molesters, rapists, homicidal sex offenders, and homicidal child molesters). In fact, the majority of child molesters are not psychopathic. Nonetheless, PCL-R scores do appear to be comparatively elevated in groups characterized by more violence (see Figure 10.2). In a subsequent study, however, Porter and colleagues (2009) found rapists, a mixed group of rapists and molesters, and offenders convicted of nonsexual crimes had significantly increased mean PCL-R total scores compared to child molesters (with PCL-R scores reported in the child molester and rapist groups similar to those reported by Bradford et al., 2007). But psychopathy was associated with an increased number of previous sex offenses within the child molester group. Clearly, more work is needed to ascertain if specific subtypes of sex offenders are, in fact, characterized by differential levels of psychopathy.

Figure 10.2 Mean PCL-R Scores in Different Sex Offender Types

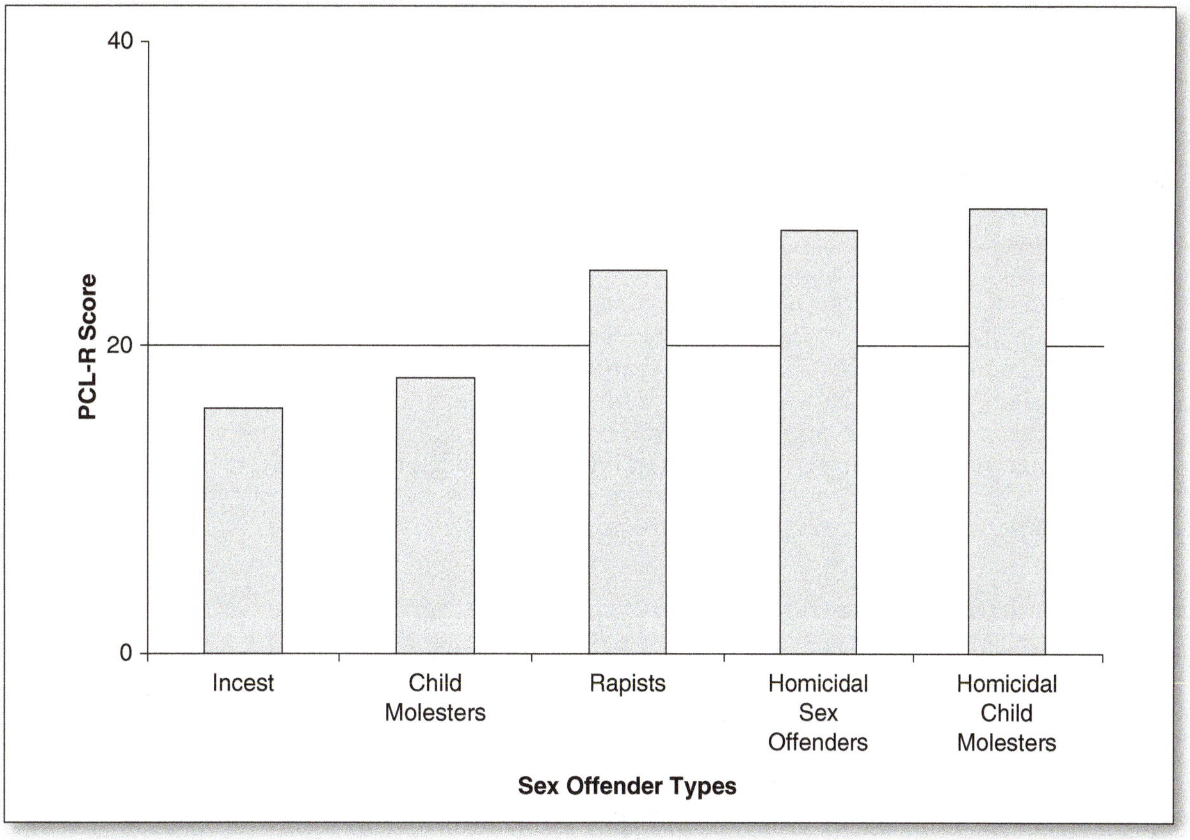

Source: Adapted from Bradford et al. (2007, p. 288).

Other studies have examined how sexual offending may relate to violence in psychopathic individuals. For example, Porter and colleagues (2003) found that psychopaths committed sexual homicides more often than their nonpsychopathic counterparts and that most sexual murderers (84.7%) had moderate to high scores on the PCL-R. This finding is consistent with other data suggesting increased levels of psychopathy in offenders whose crimes are characterized by both sexual and violent components (see above), though more work is needed to understand the interplay of sex, violence, and psychopathy in the more extreme end of the offending spectrum.

Psychopathy may have important implications in clinical settings involving sexual offenders. For example, Oliver and Wong (2011) examined predictors of treatment dropout in a sample of 154 federally incarcerated sex offenders in a high-intensity sex-offender treatment program. Results from logistic regression and discriminant function analyses indicated that the emotional facet (Facet 1) of the PCL-R and having never being married were the most salient predictors of treatment dropout; this research correctly identified about 70% of the dropout cases. In terms of clinical recommendations, Vitacco and Rogers (2009) suggest that psychopathy should be considered only as a peripheral issue in sexually violent predator (SVP) determinations and that, beyond SVP determinations (e.g., institutional placement or treatment development), psychopathy should be evaluated selectively. These authors recommend considering the complex interplay of paraphilias, psychopathology, and facets of psychopathy in program development and emphasize the fact that measurements of psychopathy may not be precise. In terms of treatment considerations, the following guidelines for the treatment of psychopathic sex offenders have been offered: (1) target cognitive distortions frequently employed to minimize responsibility, (2) target affective deficits that impair ability to experience emotions of others (victims), (3) employ long term components aimed at improving psychopathic personality traits, and (4) target issues related to general recidivism (Vitacco & Rogers, 2009). Overall, the relationship between psychopathy and sexual offending appears to have captured the attention of researchers and clinicians alike, and understanding this relationship could have significant implications in the conceptualization, management, and treatment of this potentially more dangerous and psychopathic sex offender.

Subcriminal Psychopathy

Though psychopaths may be at high risk for engaging in criminal behavior, not all of them succumb to that risk. In fact, for some careers (e.g., bomb disposal technician, test pilot, race car driver), certain levels of psychopathic traits such as fearlessness would seem advantageous—if not necessary. Several authors have discussed the concept of the "successful" psychopath: individuals in the general population whose psychopathy appears in adaptive and subclinical manifestations (Hall & Benning, 2006). Examples from history include, according to some, Oskar Schindler (savior of hundreds of Krakow Jewish concentration camp victims and protagonist of Steven Spielberg's *Schindler's List*), President Lyndon Johnson, Prime Minister Winston Churchill, explorer Sir Richard Burton, and test pilot Chuck Yeager—the first man to break the sound barrier (Lykken, 1995). The term "successful psychopath" may have different connotations, however. For example, Ishikawa and colleagues (2001) utilize the term "successful" psychopath to represent a psychopathic individual who has avoided criminal conviction (but not criminal behavior *per se*). In all, a better understanding of the relationship between psychopathy and crime is achieved by understanding why some psychopaths may avoid committing crimes and, of course, how some are able to commit crimes without being caught.

Psychopathy and the Legal System

According to Lyon and Ogloff (2000), American case law is replete with examples of expert evidence about psychopathy, ASPD, and sociopathy being offered in both criminal and civil courts on a wide array of legal issues. In criminal settings, information about or evidence of psychopathy has been applied to areas such as witness credibility, competency to stand trial, insanity, capital sentencing, and sexual psychopath and habitual offender laws. Within the civil context, evidence of psychopathy has emerged in areas such as child custody disputes and civil commitment procedures. Viljoen and colleagues (2010) reviewed 111 American and Canadian adolescent offender cases, which included 143 separate evaluations involving psychopathy, and found the introduction of psychopathy evidence to be increasingly common in a sizeable number of cases. Results indicated that, although judges did not make ultimate legal decisions based on psychopathy evidence, this evidence was influential in some cases. Evidence of psychopathy was also used to infer that the treatment of these youths would be difficult or impossible, and the absence of psychopathy was, at times, interpreted as a sign of amenability that supported more lenient sanctions. Juvenile psychopathy is itself a largely unexplored and controversial topic (Salekin, 2006), particularly given the implications of applying the psychopathy label to youth (Viljoen et al., 2010). In fact, some researchers have conceptualized milder forms of psychopathy and developed measures for these; for example, measuring "callous-unemotional (CU) traits" (Frick et al., 2003) might be more appropriate when dealing with youth offender populations. Overall, research indicates that the use of psychopathy in courtroom applications is limited but growing, and it will be interesting to see how psychopathy may factor into legal decision-making processes in the future.

Perhaps alarmingly, recent evidence also suggests that psychopathic individuals may be effective at "working the system"—manipulating decision makers in criminal justice and correctional settings to receive more favorable treatment. For example, Häkkänen-Nyholm and Hare (2009; see above) found psychopathic homicidal offenders to be more likely to deny criminal charges, to be convicted of lesser charges (i.e., involuntary manslaughter as opposed to manslaughter or murder), and to be granted permission from the Supreme Court to appeal their lower court sentence. In a study of 310 male Canadian offenders, Porter and colleagues (2009) found that high-psychopathy sexual and nonsexual offenders (despite significant criminal histories and high rates of recidivism) were two-and-a-half times more likely to be granted conditional release than nonpsychopathic offenders, suggesting their greater proficiency in convincing parole boards to release them into the community.

Origins of Crime and Violence in Psychopathy: Theoretical Explanations and Etiological Mechanisms

Although Cleckley (1941) emphasized that criminal behavior was not inherent to the definition of psychopathy, he admitted that the disorder provided fertile ground for manifestations of crime to occur. Consequently, psychopathy may be considered "criminogenic" in the sense that it allows for the easy expression of crime and violence because of its key characteristic personality traits (e.g., impulsivity and lack of remorse and empathy. In fact, the PCL-R incorporates elements of criminality (i.e., items 18–20) that need not be present to meet the diagnostic threshold for psychopathy but that suggest important relationships to the construct. Nonetheless, other factors should be taken into account, factors that may impact the origin, maintenance, and modes of expression of criminal and violent behavior within the psychopathic individual.

Gender. Newer research is beginning to elucidate gender differences in psychopathy, which may contribute to differential forms of antisocial and criminal behavior among psychopathic men and women. Cleckley (1988) originally presented the cases of two female psychopathic individuals ("Roberta" and "Anna") in *The Mask of Sanity*; and despite the fact that women who met the criteria for the "Cleckley psychopath" were appearing in clinical settings as early as the 1940s, few active attempts were made to study female psychopathy until the 1960s and 1970s, when the number of incarcerated females increased dramatically (Vitale & Newman, 2001). Though available evidence suggests slightly lower base rates of psychopathy in incarcerated women compared to men (Vitale & Newman, 2001; Vitale & Verona, 2006; Warren et al., 2003), prevalence rates in the general population might not necessarily be comparable. For example, female psychopathic behaviors may be less overt and less likely to result in incarceration compared to those of male psychopaths (e.g., a female psychopathic individual who neglects her children may do so without drawing the attention of authorities). The processes underlying the behavioral symptoms of psychopathy (e.g., of impulsivity and lack of inhibition) also appear to differ between women and men, and studies comparing male and female offenders have revealed salient differences in the expression of psychopathy in women—including less evidence of early behavioral problems, less disinhibition, and less overtly violent aggression. In fact, covert relational aggression involving social network manipulations, such as gossip, the refusal of friendship, and ostracism, is more common in females and contrasts to the overt physical aggression often seen in males. On balance, emotional reactivity and "mood-anxiety" may be more strongly associated with antisociality in women, and female psychopaths have been characterized by increased sexual misbehavior such as prostitution (Verona & Vitale, 2006). Furthermore, the lower reported base rates of psychopathy in women may simply be due to the inability of the PCL-R to measure female manifestations of psychopathy adequately; for example, the rates of juvenile delinquency—assessed in item 18—are lower in females relative to males (Vitale & Newman, 2001).

Comorbidity, Culture, and Cognitive Ability. Other factors may contribute to crime and violence in psychopathy. For example, the comorbidity of psychopathy with childhood-onset disorders such as ADHD (Langevin & Curnoe, 2010), CD, autism spectrum disorders, mental retardation, and tic disorders—symptoms of which have been associated with increased levels of aggression in some sample groups (e.g., Anckarsäter, 2005)—may play a role in psychopathic criminality. Ethnic and cultural variations in psychopathy may also affect how and how often crime and violence occur within psychopathic individuals. Although the majority of the research to date on psychopathy has been conducted in North America on European American prisoners, a recent review (Sullivan & Kosson, 2006) indicates evidence for the reliability and partial-construct validity of psychopathy across ethnicity. However, numerous studies of offenders in incarcerated, psychiatric, and forensic settings from around the world suggest what may be cross-cultural variations in levels of psychopathy among these offenders. Finally, expressions of criminal behavior in psychopathy may be affected in some way by cognitive ability. For example, Heilbrun (1979) found psychopathic offenders with lower intelligence to be characterized by more violent criminal behaviors than those with higher intelligence. Ultimately, though it is tempting merely to assume that the psychopath will be criminal and violent due to the nature of his or her disorder, proposals from earlier authors (e.g., Cleckley) and evidence from recent studies indicates that factors not related to this disorder contribute to psychopathic crime and violence and must also be considered.

Treatment of Psychopathy

Much of the literature on clinical and applied issues related to psychopathy has been devoted to understanding what—if any—treatments may be effective for psychopathic populations. Cleckley (1988) originally suggested that psychopaths would neither benefit from nor be capable of forming the emotional bonds required for effective therapy; and subsequent clinical evidence and research findings in this area have left little room for optimism (Harris & Rice, 2006).

One of the more ubiquitous examples in this literature of an unsuccessful attempt to treat psychopathy is the therapeutic community method. Rice and colleagues (in Harris & Rice, 2006) evaluated an intensive therapeutic community for mentally disordered offenders thought to be especially suitable for psychopaths. It operated for over 10 years in a maximum-security psychiatric hospital during the latter part of the twentieth century, and it was known worldwide for its novel approach. Largely peer operated, this therapeutic community involved up to 80 hours of weekly intensive group therapy sessions, which had the goal of fostering empathy and responsibility for peers. Results, however, were shocking to investigators—the program *actually made psychopaths worse.* A follow-up evaluation (M = 10.5 years post-treatment) of 146 treated and 146 untreated offenders (matched on recidivism-related variables such as age, criminal history, and index offense) indicated that, compared to no program (in most cases, untreated offenders went to prison), treatment was associated with lower violent recidivism for nonpsychopaths but *higher recidivism for psychopaths.* Psychopaths, while in the program, also showed poorer adjustment in terms of behavioral problems, even though they were just as likely as nonpsychopaths to achieve positions of trust and early recommendations for release.

Harris and Rice suggest that this therapeutic community, in which participants learned more about the feelings of others and were tasked with taking others' perspectives, using emotional language, behaving in socially skilled ways, and delaying gratification, actually aided psychopaths in their criminal endeavors, emboldening them and equipping them with new skills for the manipulation and exploitation of others. Despite similar results being reported in other therapeutic community programs, their popularity in prisons, secure hospitals, and other institutions in Europe (in which some participants are likely to be psychopaths) has unfortunately not waned. Furthermore, other approaches have provided little to no evidence of treatment effect for psychopaths; these include cognitive-behavioral therapy (CBT) targeting criminogenic needs, e.g., antisocial attitudes and cognitions, pro-criminal associates, and personality factors such as impulsiveness and self-control (see Gendreau, Goggin, French, & Smith, 2006); behavioral modification using token economies; and multisystemic therapy (MST). These dismal results have led some to suggest that discussing the management rather than the treatment of psychopathic offenders may be more warranted and that programs benefitting other offenders may actually increase the risk represented by psychopaths. Ultimately, psychopaths may be fundamentally different from other offenders in that they possess no deficit or impairment that is "fixable" by therapy—having instead an evolved and viable life strategy that incorporates lies, cheating, and the manipulation of others (Harris & Rice, 2006).

Conclusion

As a group, personality disorders are among the most studied psychiatric illnesses in terms of their relationships to violence, crime, aggression, and antisociality. Most of the work in this area has focused on psychopathy and the Cluster B personality disorders and on theoretical conceptualization, diagnostic clarification, etiological mechanisms, and clinical and applied issues. Additionally, a fair amount of work—particularly that using neuroscience approaches—has been conducted on the Cluster A (or schizophrenia spectrum) personality disorders and their relationships with criminal and violent behavior. Studies relating Cluster C personality disorders (avoidant, dependent, and obsessive-compulsive personality disorders) to crime and violence, however, are virtually nonexistent.

Because of their enduring and ubiquitous nature, personality disorders pose a unique and challenging problem with regard to crime and violence. These behaviors are likely to manifest as ingrained patterns and across situations and contexts—thus extending the scope and time frame in which they may occur. Moreover, as they are ego-syntonic and viable (yet maladaptive) strategies that individuals have adopted to "get through life," insight into these disorders may be rare—and the affected individual's willingness to change even rarer. For Ted Bundy, this strategy was a deadly combination of lying, manipulation, emotional coldness, and violence—it was perfectly suited to a multiple killer, but it ultimately led to his death and to the destruction of innocent lives around him.

KEY TERMS

antisocial personality disorder
avoidant personality disorder
borderline personality disorder
Cluster A [personality disorders]
Cluster B [personality disorders]
Cluster C [personality disorders]
complication model
dependent personality disorder
dissociative identity disorder
histrionic personality disorder
multiple personality disorder
narcissistic personality disorder
narcissistic rage
obsessive-compulsive personality disorder
paranoid personality disorder
pathoplasty model
personality disorders
personality traits
psychopathy
Psychopathy Checklist—Revised (PCL-R)
schizoid personality disorder
schizotypal personality disorder
sociopathy
spectrum model
vulnerability model

REVIEW QUESTIONS

1. Using the different theoretical perspectives discussed in the chapter, compare and contrast the conceptualizations of the personality disorders outlined in DSM-5. What are some of the similarities and differences in the way pathological patterns of inner experience and behavior are conceptualized across disorders?
2. Examine Tables 10.2, 10.3, 10.19, and 10.20 and the summaries of research studies in the "A Closer Look" sections for each personality disorder in this chapter. Discuss how prevalence rates of crime in those with personality

disorders and of these disorders in criminal populations differ among these specific disorders, if at all. Using the information in the tables, speculate as to how these differences in prevalence rates may have been caused by methodology (e.g., in terms of study types, sample characteristics, methodological issues, or other concerns).

3. Describe multiple personality disorder and dissociative identity disorder and critically evaluate the evidence for a relationship between these disorders and crime and violence.
4. Discuss the evolution of the term "psychopathy" in terms of its conceptualization and meaning relative to social condemnation. How are psychopathy, antisocial personality disorder, and sociopathy differentiated from one another? Explain the reasons for the differences in diagnostic nomenclature.
5. Hervey Cleckley argued that criminality is not necessarily a component of psychopathy, and, though a significant amount of research has been conducted using the PCL-R to understand criminal behavior, it is also technically possible to render a psychopathy diagnosis when no criminality is present using this measure. Should criminality be conceptually distinct from psychopathy? Why or why not?

11

Mental Illness and Criminal Law

Applications and Implications

JARED LEE LOUGHNER

On January 8, 2011, Jared Loughner was 22 years of age. He woke up that morning, got into a taxi, and went to a local grocery store in Tucson, Arizona. After calmly waiting for change from the $20 bill he used to pay his fare, Loughner exited the cab and opened fire in the parking lot killing 6 people, including a federal judge, and injuring U.S. Congresswoman Gabrielle Giffords and 13 others. After initial outrage, many members of the public began to express sympathy for Loughner when details of his mental illness emerged. This man whom many had assumed to be a cold-blooded killer was actually seriously mentally ill with schizophrenia.

Sadly, there were many warning signs that Loughner was seriously mentally ill and dangerous, but nothing was done about it. Loughner had dropped out of high school before his senior year. He began to self-medicate using alcohol and marijuana. He began to speak in random jumbles of words. He grew paranoid that the government was trying to control him. His ability to function deteriorated so badly that he was unable to maintain his jobs working in a sandwich shop and at a local animal shelter. Loughner displayed several classic symptoms of psychosis, ranging from paranoia and disorganized thoughts and speech to nonsensical outbursts and the inability to function in social situations. In fact, Pima Community College, where Loughner had been a student, dismissed him for behavior that scared his professors and fellow students alike. But he never got any help.

Loughner was determined to be incompetent to stand trial because his mental illness prevented him from grasping the nature of the charges against him and assisting his lawyers in his own defense. He was subsequently confined to the psychiatric wing of the U.S. Medical Center for Federal Prisoners in Springfield, Missouri, where he was forcibly medicated with antipsychotic drugs in an attempt to restore his mental faculties sufficiently, so he could be ruled competent to stand trial.

Loughner was ruled competent to stand trial in early August 2012 and pled guilty in exchange for a life sentence. Had his case gone to trial, he likely would have pled not guilty by reason of insanity. The insanity defense is one of the most hotly debated topics in criminal law. This defense is rooted in a fundamental concept of Anglo-American law: a person should not be punished for conduct not rooted in criminal intent. But what degree of mental illness renders some insane and, therefore, legally blameless for otherwise criminal acts?

The legal system recognizes that the law should take into account a variety of situations in which a person's ability to function within the law's mandate is impaired by mental illness. In civil law, issues surrounding mental illness frequently concern a variety of competencies. **Competency** is a legal term that refers to the possession of sufficient mental faculties to understand problems and make decisions. When a mental disability interferes with a person's ability make the decisions that the law presumes a person of legal age should be able to make—such as entering into a contract, creating a valid will, caring for one's own health or finances, or making decisions regarding how to raise one's children—formal judicial proceedings may be necessary to determine the actor's competency or fitness. Although such civil law issues are challenging, they tend to be less controversial than the concerns that arise when a mentally ill person violates one of the proscriptions of the criminal law. Indeed, as Hafemeister, Garner, and Bath (2012) note, "for almost as long as there has been a criminal justice system, society has struggled with how to respond to offenders . . . whose criminal behavior has been shaped and driven by their mental disorder" (p. 148). This chapter explores two of the most vexing questions with which the justice system struggles when dealing with mentally ill offenders: competency to stand trial and the criminal responsibility under the insanity and diminished capacity defenses.

Competency to Stand Trial

In the criminal law context, one of the most important competencies is the **competency to stand trial**. Simply put, criminal defendants must be able to understand the nature of the charges against them and assist counsel in their own defense (*Dusky v. United States*, 1960; Meyers, 1997; Pirelli, Gottdiener, & Zapf, 2011).

Justifications for the Competency to Stand Trial Doctrine

The legal bar against trying incompetent defendants dates back to common law England, probably back to the time of Edward I in the thirteenth and early fourteenth century (Roesch & Golding, 1980).

> Blackstone wrote that a defendant who becomes "mad" after the commission of an offense should not be arraigned "because he is not able to plead . . . with the advice and caution that he ought," and should not be tried, for "how can he make his defense?" The ban on trial of an incompetent defendant stems from the common law prohibition on trials in absentia, and from the difficulties the English courts encountered when defendants frustrated the ritual of the common law trial by remaining mute instead of pleading to charges. Without a plea, the trial could not go forward. (Winick, 1995b, p. 574)

At that point in the history of English common law, a person rarely had the right to counsel; in fact, counsel was prohibited in many cases. A defendant, therefore, usually had to represent himself (*Faretta v. California*, 1975; Neubauer & Fradella, 2013). As a result, "the defendant stood alone before the court, and trial was merely 'a long argument between the prisoner and the counsel for the Crown.' Thus, it was imperative that defendants be competent because they were required to conduct their own defense" (Winick, 1995b, p. 575).

Today, however, the Sixth Amendment to the U.S. Constitution is interpreted to guarantee the right to the effective assistance of counsel to all felony defendants (*Gideon v. Wainwright*, 1963) and to most misdemeanor defendants (*Argersinger v. Hamlin*, 1972). As a result, the common law rationale underlying the doctrine of competency to stand trial is no longer applicable. But there are still important justifications for the doctrine in modern times, not the least of which that the U.S. Supreme Court has repeatedly reasoned that the U.S. Constitution's guarantee of due process in both the Fifth and Fourteenth Amendment prohibits the trying of an incompetent defendant for several reasons.

> First, it increases the accuracy and reliability of the trial since an incompetent defendant cannot, for example, adequately testify on his behalf. The requirement also enhances fairness, since an incompetent defendant cannot make decisions regarding the course and nature of his defense. In addition, it maintains the "dignity" of the trial, in that an incompetent defendant may behave in an offensive or inappropriate manner. Finally, a competent defendant's comprehension of why he is being punished makes the punishment more just. (Meyers, 1997, p. 1017)

In short, competency to stand trial is an essential part of due process because "the rights deemed essential to a fair trial—including the right to effective assistance of counsel, the rights to summon, to confront, and to cross-examine witnesses, and the right to testify on one's own behalf or to remain silent without penalty for doing so"—depend, in large part, upon a defendant's ability to cooperate with counsel and participate in the criminal trial process (*Riggins v. Nevada*, 1992, pp. 139–140).

Competency Differentiated From Insanity

Competency to stand trial is often confused with insanity. Although the two legal doctrines are related insofar as both are concerned with the mental status of a criminal defendant, they are quite different.

First, timing is a critical distinction between the two doctrines. Competency to stand trial concerns itself with a criminal defendant's mental state at the time of trial (Herseth, 1996; Meyers, 1997). In contrast, insanity is concerned with the defendant's state of mind at the time the criminal offense is alleged to have taken place (Fradella, 2007).

Second, insanity must generally be asserted by the defendant, usually through defense counsel, in a timely manner in order to be litigated as a criminal defense at trial. If insanity is not pled at arraignment (or by whatever time specified in a jurisdiction's rules of criminal procedure), the defense is deemed waived (e.g., *People v. Low*, 1987). Competency to stand trial, though, may be raised at any time in the criminal process, even after conviction (Winick, 1995b). Moreover, although the issue of competency to stand trial is usually raised by the defense, the prosecution can raise the issue, as can the court on its own (*Pate v. Robinson*, 1966). Once the issue has been raised, *Pate v. Robinson* (1966) guarantees defendants a constitutionally based due process right to an adversarial hearing to determine his or her competency to stand trial; in contrast, the U.S. Supreme Court has never held there is a constitutional right to present an insanity defense. Indeed, the high courts of last resort in several states have held no such right exists (*State v. Bethel*, 2003; *State v. Herrera*, 1995; *State v. Korell*, 1984; *State v. Searcy*, 1990).

Third, there are significant differences in proving competency to stand trial and insanity. Modern formulations of the insanity defense in most U.S. jurisdictions require the defense to prove the defendant's insanity at trial by clear and convincing evidence, although a handful of jurisdictions require the defendant to prove his or her insanity by only a preponderance of the evidence (Fradella, 2007). In contrast, at a competency hearing, the prosecution typically bears the burden of persuasion to prove that the defendant is competent to proceed with the criminal trial, usually by a preponderance of the evidence (King, 2008). There are some jurisdictions that have shifted the burden of persuasion to the defense to prove the incompetency of the defendant by a preponderance of the evidence, a practice the U.S. Supreme Court approved in *Medina v. California* (1992). In *Cooper v. Oklahoma* (1996), however, the Court invalidated statutory schemes that required the defendant to prove incompetence by clear and convincing evidence, finding such a requirement violated the guarantee of due process.

When Is a Competency Hearing Required?

If there are no objective grounds for a judge to order a competency determination, it is highly unlikely that a judicial refusal to hold a competency hearing will have any outcome on a case. On the other hand, if there are reasons that call into question the defendant's competency and the trial court judge fails to order a competency evaluation, then serious constitutional concerns can be raised that could invalidate a conviction on appeal or via some post-conviction relief mechanism such as a *habeas corpus* proceeding. Thus, most requests for a clinical determination of competency to stand trial go unopposed by opposing counsel and are routinely granted by judges (Melton, Petrila, Poythress, & Slobogin, 2007; Roesch, Zapf, Golding, & Skeem, 1999). Consider the case of Jared Loughner. After his arrest, the judge ordered that he undergo psychological evaluation based on evidence submitted by the prosecution, including largely incoherent Internet postings by Loughner, many of which referenced Loughner being a "conscience dreamer," becoming a treasurer of a new currency, and controlling "English grammar structure." Others referenced brainwashing and suggested that Loughner possessed mind control abilities.

Judicial willingness to have criminal defendants evaluated for competency to stand trial is likely a function of clear appellate rulings on the consequences of neglecting to conduct such an inquiry. A failure to conduct an evidentiary hearing when evidence before a trial court raises a "bona fide doubt" about the defendant's competency to stand trial violates due process (*Medina v. California*, 1992, p. 452; *Pate v. Robinson*, 1966, p. 378). Although this may appear to be a concise rule, what constitutes a "bona fide doubt" often proves ambiguous, especially since reasonable people can differ with respect to whether such a doubt exists given the facts of any particular case. There are no "fixed or immutable signs which invariably indicate the need for further inquiry to determine fitness to proceed" (*Drope v. Missouri*, 1975, p. 180). Rather, a wide range of factors can give rise to the need for a formal inquiry into a defendant's competency. Consider the case of *United States v. Loyola-Dominguez* (1997), summarized in Box 11.1.

Psycholegal Focus of the Inquiry Into Competency

Once a bona fide issue regarding the defendant's competency has been raised, the court must then determine whether the defendant is competent to stand trial. According to the Supreme Court's landmark decision in *Dusky v. United States* (1960), competency to stand trial requires a defendant to possess (1) "a rational as well as factual understanding of the proceedings against him" and (2) "sufficient present ability to consult with his lawyer with a reasonable degree of rational understanding" (p. 402). *Dusky*'s formulation of competency to stand trial was reaffirmed by the U.S. Supreme Court in *Medina v. California* (1992), although several states use slight variations in this language, which can muddy the waters regarding the degree of rational understanding that is required (for a critique, see Felthous, 2011).

The first question under *Dusky*—can the defendant understand the proceedings against him or her?—is not directed at whether the defendant understands the intricacies of the criminal process. Rather, it concerns whether the defendant has a basic understanding of the circumstances in which he or she finds himself or herself. More simply, does the defendant understand that he or she has been charged with a crime and faces government-imposed punishment if convicted (American Bar Association, 1989; Bonnie, 1993)? Although not technically a requirement of the test for competency, whether the defendant is oriented with respect to time, place, and situation is often considered by mental health professionals in this phase of the competency evaluation (Grisso, 2003; Melton et al., 2007). In other words, does the defendant know who and where he or she is? Without such orientation, it is unlikely that a defendant understands, even in a basic way, the proceedings against him or her. As a result, it should come as no surprise that most criminal defendants determined to be incompetent to stand trial are diagnosed with severe mental disorders, such as schizophrenia, bipolar disorder, or schizoaffective disorder (Cox & Zapf, 2004; Hubbard, Zapf, & Ronan, 2003; Rogers, Gillis, McMain, & Dickens, 1988).

The second line of inquiry under *Dusky* is whether the defendant is capable of assisting in his or her own defense. If the defendant cannot communicate with his or her attorney in a manner that permits the defense lawyer the ability to formulate a defense, there is little likelihood that the defendant will be found competent (Grisso, 2003; Melton et al., 2007).

The competency standard as applied in any particular case tends to be flexible; there is no set of fixed diagnostic criteria that, if satisfied, renders a person either competent of incompetent. In *Wieter v. Settle* (1961), a federal district court attempted to operationalize *Dusky* by setting forth a list of factors to guide judges in competency decisions. The court stated a defendant would be competent to stand trial if that defendant

1. has the "mental capacity to appreciate his presence in relation to time, place, and things";
2. has "elementary mental processes . . . such that he apprehends (i.e., seizes and grasps with what mind he has) that he is in a Court of Justice, charged with a criminal offense";
3. understands "there is a Judge on the Bench";
4. understands there is "a prosecutor present who will try to convict him of a criminal charge";
5. understands "he has a lawyer (self-employed or Court-appointed) who will undertake to defend him against that charge";

BOX 11.1 *UNITED STATES V. LOYOLA-DOMINGUEZ*

125 F.3d 1315 (9th Cir. 1997).

On the night before his trial for being a deported alien found in the United States following an aggravated felony, Jacobo Loyola-Dominguez tried to commit suicide by hanging himself in his jail cell. In court the next morning, defense counsel advised the judge of the attempted suicide and moved for a hearing to determine competency to stand trial. Defense counsel elaborated on his concerns regarding his client's competency by explaining that Loyola-Dominguez's had been in isolation for more than five months and speculated that such long-term deprivation from social interactions may have contributed to the suicide attempt. The judge then briefly questioned the defendant:

Court: Mr. Loyola, your attorney asked to continue this matter and send you away for a psychiatric examination. Is it your desire to be examined by a psychiatrist or are you ready to go to trial today?

Defendant: I don't know. Whatever they want to do, because they've already—I've been abused a lot already. What I want to do is get away from here, get out of here.

Court: Well, then, you want to go ahead with the trial today?

Defendant: Yeah, whatever.

Court: Well, do you feel—do you know what's going on? Do you know what's going on at the trial?

Defendant: I don't know. I've never been here like this, so I don't know.

Court: Well, do you feel that you're competent to understand what's going on?

Defendant: How long would it take? Because I just can't stand anymore, the way they have me there. I feel desperate.

Court: Well, what does it usually take, a 90-day study for psychiatric study?

Defense: I've had one done since I've been here, and it's more than 90 days.

Gov't: I'm not sure if he's asking how long the trial was going to take.

Court: No, no, how long the psychiatric examination would take. Is it 120 days now?

Defense: I had one done, your Honor, with Judge Coyle approximately a year ago, and it was about 120 days before he came back. He went to Springfield Medical - Federal Hospital in Missouri.

Court: Well, he's always appeared mentally competent when he's been in court as far as I'm concerned and this is the first time that anything like this has happened, and he's been in custody for over a year in the state system without any problem.

Following this brief discussion, the court determined that there was no cause to question Loyola-Dominguez's competency. It denied the motion for a hearing and summoned the jurors. After Loyola-Dominguez was convicted, his lawyer appealed, arguing that the trial court's failure to grant a competency hearing following his suicide attempt on the eve of trial violated his right to due process of law. The appellate court agreed, reasoning as follows:

> An attempted suicide is an extremely serious action. While we do not believe that every suicide attempt inevitably creates a doubt concerning the defendant's competency, we are persuaded that, under the circumstances of this case, such a doubt existed. Of particular significance to our decision are the timing of the attempt and the fact that the trial court did not elicit adequate information, from either defense counsel or Loyola-Dominguez, that would have dispelled the concerns that would ordinarily arise regarding competency. Loyola-Dominguez's responses to the trial court's four questions simply provided further cause to doubt his competency. Especially troubling is Loyola-Dominguez's expressed desire to "get out of here," which, in light of the government's open-and-shut case against him, suggests that he may not have had a full grasp of the nature of the proceedings. Also of concern is his response to

(Continued)

(Continued)

the question from the court, "Do you know what's going on?" Loyola-Dominguez answered, "I don't know. I've never been here like this, so I don't know." Indeed, none of Loyola-Dominguez's answers demonstrates that he understood the nature and consequences of the proceedings or that he could assist properly in his own defense.

In explaining why a competency hearing was unnecessary, the trial court noted that Loyola-Dominguez had always seemed fine in the past. However, given his suicide attempt the night before trial, his performance during previous court appearances is at best inconclusive, particularly in view of defense counsel's explanation that Loyola-Dominguez's mental state was probably the result of recent events that had occurred at the jail. Without a meaningful inquiry to determine whether the suicide attempt evidenced a severe decline in Loyola-Dominguez's mental health, the court simply did not have enough information to conclude that a hearing regarding his competency was not warranted. (*United States v. Loyola-Dominguez*, 1997, pp. 1318–1319)

1. The evidence of incompetency in *Loyola-Dominguez* was the defendant's suicide attempt on the night before trial. Do you agree with the court that "not every suicide attempt inevitably creates a doubt concerning the defendant's competency"? Does this invite defendants seeking to avoid trial to feign mental illness in the hopes that they can avoid criminal trial and punishment?

2. Given the result in *Loyola-Dominguez*, why wouldn't a trial court judge routinely order a competency hearing using a "better safe than sorry" approach? Do you think the time factors discussed in *Loyola-Dominguez* might have some impact on that decision? What about the fact that there is much evidence that suggests nonpsychological factors, such as trial strategy, are often the motivating factors in a request for a determination of competency to stand trial?

6. understands "he will be expected to tell his lawyer the circumstances, to the best of his mental ability, (whether colored or not by mental aberration) the facts surrounding him at the time and place where the law violation is alleged to have been committed";
7. understands "there is, or will be, a jury present to pass upon evidence adduced as to his guilt or innocence of such charge"; and
8. has "memory sufficient to relate those things in his own personal manner." (pp. 321–322)

Although the factors specified in *Wieter v. Settle* have proven helpful over the years, the court has been criticized for using the term "understanding" without incorporating *Dusky*'s use of both the words "rational" and "factual" to modify it (see Felthous, 2011). The inclusion of both words indicates that competency "demands more than simple knowledge of facts and factors relevant to the proceedings, but also an ability to appreciate and consider those facts that is not significantly impaired by mental disorder" (Otto, 2006, p. 84; see also Felthous, 2011). Professor Richard Bonnie (1993) distinguished factual understanding from rational understanding using the terms *basic adjudicative competency* and *decisional adjudicative competency*. Basic competency includes a cognitive understanding of the charges and of the nature of a criminal prosecution and defense, as well as a general ability to work with defense counsel. Decisional competence, in contrast, is concerned with the quality of the defendant's understanding and reasoning processes. Marcus and colleagues (2010) offer the following example to illustrate the difference between basic competency evidencing a mere factual understanding of the criminal trial process and rational competency:

> [A] defendant who shot a police officer believing him to be the devil could well understand that he is being tried for murder. If, however, he also suffers from companion delusions that as a special agent of God he will receive special consideration by the judge or jury, such delusions would indicate an irrational appraisal of the adjudicative process and of his actual legal jeopardy. (pp. 716–717)

To assist a court in determining whether a defendant possesses sufficient factual and rational understanding to be deemed competent to stand trial under *Dusky*, defendants should be evaluated clinically by qualified mental health experts. All criminal defendants have a Sixth Amendment right to consult with defense counsel before submitting to a court-ordered psychiatric examination (*Estelle v. Smith*, 1981). There is no right, however, to have counsel present during the examination (*Buchanan v. Kentucky*, 1987).

Clinical Evaluation and Assessment Instruments

The assessment of a criminal defendant for competency to stand trial is one of the most important roles mental health professionals play in the criminal process. Clinicians evaluating a defendant's competency to stand trial rely heavily on medical histories, clinical interviews, observations and reports from collateral sources, and a combination of clinical and forensic assessment instruments (Acklin, 2012; Melton, et al., 2007; Pirelli, Gottdiener, & Zapf, 2011). Many clinicians rely heavily on traditional assessment instruments designed to measure intelligence and personality, such as the Wechsler Adult Intelligence Scale and the Minnesota Multiphasic Personality Inventory, as well as instruments designed to detect the presence of mental disorders such as psychopathy, e.g., the Brief Psychiatric Rating Scale and the Hare Psychopathy Checklist—Revised (Pirelli, Gottdiener, & Zapf, 2011). But most also utilize specialized forensic assessment instruments that, starting in the early 1970s, were developed to assist clinicians conducting competency to stand trial evaluations. Table 11.1 presents an overview of the forensic assessment instruments most commonly used for this purpose.

Bonnie and Grisso (2000) estimate that roughly 60,000 clinical assessments of competency to stand trial occur each year in the United States (see also Melton, et al., 2007). The assessment of the defendant is normally conducted by clinicians appointed by the court who examine the defendant and then submit written reports to the court. The court then decides the issue either based on the stipulation of the parties or after a competency hearing.

Competency Hearings

At the outset, it should be noted that, although statutes or court rules require a formal, adversarial hearing in court to determine competency to stand trial per the mandate of *Pate v. Robinson* (1966), the parties often agree to waive a competency hearing and stipulate to the incompetency of a defendant based on the recommendation of the clinical evaluators (Melton, et al., 2007). When the prosecution and defense disagree on a defendant's competency to stand trial, though, *Pate* requires the trial court judge to conduct an adversarial hearing at which clinical "examiners testify and are subject to cross-examination" (Winick, 1995b, p. 572).

In such proceedings, the judge acts as both the arbiter of law and the trier of fact, meaning that the ultimate decision regarding a defendant's competency is a judicial one.

Although the determination of competency to stand trial is purely a legal determination, not a clinical one, the importance of the role of the evaluating clinicians cannot be overstated. Most competency determinations are based on the clinical assessment of a single clinician (Gowensmith, Murrie, & Boccaccini, 2012; Melton, et al., 2007; Roesch & Golding, 1980). Even when multiple clinicians evaluate a defendant's competency to stand trial, they agree unanimously in their initial competency assessments in more than 70% of cases and in 61% of subsequent evaluations (Gowensmith, et al., 2012). Second, and arguably more important, judges routinely adopt the recommendation of clinical evaluators in more than 90% of cases (Cruise & Rogers, 1998; Hart & Hare, 1992). One study even reported a judicial concurrence rate with clinical evaluators' recommendations as high a 99.6% (Zapf, Hubbard, Galloway, Cox, & Ronan, 2004). In the rare cases in which several clinicians differ in their respective assessments of a defendant's competency to stand trial, judges defer to the majority evaluator opinion nearly 90% of the time (Gowensmith, et al., 2012).

Competency Determinations

In spite of the fact that it may seem the various criteria used to assess competency to stand trial are complex, the overall determination on competency is not all that complicated. The threshold for finding a defendant to be competent to stand trial is quite low (Melton, et al., 2007). Although the frequency of both referrals and ultimate decisions regarding competency vary across jurisdictions and situations (Murrie, Boccaccini, Zapf, Warren, & Henderson, 2008), between 20% to 30% of those referred for evaluation are found to be incompetent to stand trial (Gowensmith, et al., 2012; Pirelli, et al., 2011; Roesch, et al., 1999).

Table 11.1 Forensic Assessment Instruments for Competency to Stand Trial

Assessment Instrument	Source	Description
Competency Screening Test (CST)	Lipsitt, P. D., Lelos, D., & McGarry, A. L. (1971). Competency for trial: A screening instrument. *American Journal of Psychiatry, 128,* 105–109.	An approximately 25-minute test that evaluates the level of defendant legal comprehension. Scores between 0 and 2 are given in response to each of 22 sentence-completion-style questions (e.g., "When I go to court, my lawyer will..." or "When they say a man is innocent until proven guilty, I..."), with a score of 20 or less indicating that further assessment by the CAI should be administered. Though popular, standardized, and easily administered, the validity of this test is questionable, as it often produces false positives—especially as a function of defendants who are cynical about legal procedures. Quantitative scores do not capture a quantitative assessment of a defendant's specific capabilities. Reliability is also a concern.
Competency to Stand Trial Assessment Instrument (CAI)	Laboratory of Community Psychiatry, Harvard Medical School (1973). *Competency to stand trial and mental illness.* Rockville, MD: NIMH, DHEW Publication No. (AMD) 77–103.	A follow-up test for the CST, the CAI is a semi-structured comprehensive interview evaluating 13 areas of competence to stand trial, developed in addition to the CST by the National Institute of Mental Health. While varying in duration of administration, the test uses a five-point Likert scale (1=total incapacity; 5=no incapacity), with a majority of scores 3 or lower indicating inpatient clinical treatment would be beneficial. Though useful, the CST has proved to be difficult to validate as a function of there being no normed responses and no standardized methods for administration or scoring.
Computer-Assisted Determination of Competency to Proceed	Barnard, G. W., Thompson Jr., J. W., Freeman, W. C., Robbins, L., Gies, D., Hankins, M. A., & Hankins, G. C. (1991). Competency to stand trial: Description and initial evaluation of a new computer-assisted assessment tool (CADCOMP). *Journal of the American Academy of Psychiatry and the Law, 19*(4), 367–381.	This 90-minute screening instrument is comprised of 272 items that explore a defendant's mental abilities, social and environmental background, and grasp of the legal system. Not considered a valid measure in and of itself, it indicates whether further assessment may be needed. Its main drawback is its length of administration, though inaccurate self-reporting by defendants and its lack of adaptability to administration in various settings (e.g., prison) also contribute to unreliable results. Reading levels and lack of computer proficiency can also skew results.
Georgia Court Competency Test (GCCT)	Nicholson, R. A., Briggs, S. R., & Robertson, H. C. (1988). Instruments for assessing competence to stand trial: How do they work? *Professional Psychology: Research and Practice, 19*(4), 383–394.	Designed to screen defendants who are clearly competent from those who may need further evaluation in less than 15 minutes, the GCCT consists of 21 questions that address three dimensions of competency: general legal knowledge (e.g., the respective jobs of the judge, prosecutor, and defense lawyer), courtroom layout (e.g., where the judge and jury are located in the courtroom), and specific legal knowledge (e.g., how to interact with defense counsel). This instrument displays high levels of reliability and validity. One of the major drawbacks of this tool, however, is its focus on cognition rather than on affective and other psychopathological issues. Additionally, it focuses on foundational competencies and ignores many of the more important decisional competencies stressed in other instruments.

Assessment Instrument	Source	Description
Competence Assessment for Standing Trial for Defendants with Mental Retardation (CAST-MR)	Everington, C. T., & Dunn, C. (1995). A second validation study of the Competence Assessment for Standing Trial for Defendants with Mental Retardation (CAST-MR). *Criminal Justice and Behavior, 22*(1), 44–59.	This 50-item test, administered in under an hour, determines adjudicative competence for defendants with mental retardation. Simplified from the CAI, it uses multiple-choice questions to improve respondent accuracy while assessing respondents' comprehension of concepts related to the courtroom, their knowledge of the law and of legal procedures, as well as their contextual knowledge of the situations related to their charges. Though preferred to the CAI for the mentally impaired, this test only measures legal knowledge superficially and tends to overattribute defendant capabilities.
Evaluation for Competency to Stand Trial—Revised (ECST-R)	Rogers, R., Sewell, K. W., Grandjean, N. R., Vitacco, M. (2002). The detection of feigned mental disorders on specific competency measures. *Psychological Assessment, 14*(2), 177–183.	A test designed for English-speaking adults aged 18+ with an IQ over 60, the ECST-R utilizes both semi-structured and unstructured interviews, creating a "hybrid" format to measure a defendant's cognitive grasp of legal rules and proceedings, as well as "feigned incompetence." The duration of administration varies. Similar to the MacCAT-CA, the test is known to produce strong results, yet it also falls short of properly assessing defendants' knowledge of legal terminology and procedures.
Fitness Interview Test Revised (FIT-R)	Zapf, P. A., Roesch, R., & Viljoen, J. L. (2001). Assessing fitness to stand trial: The utility of the Fitness Interview Test (revised version). *Canadian Journal of Psychiatry, 46*(5), 426–432.	Used either for initial or in-depth competency assessments, this 30-minute test was developed in Canada and adapted for use in the United States. The FIT-R uses 70 structured interview questions to assess a defendant's understanding of legal proceedings, possible trial outcomes, and interactions with legal counsel. The measures of this test suffer from limited standardization and unsatisfactory criterion and construct validity, but the original FIT, though revised numerous times, helped serve as a launching point for Canadian psychometric and competency evaluations.
Interdisciplinary Fitness Interview Revised (IFI-R)	Golding, S. L., Roesch, R., & Schreiber, J. (1984). Assessment and conceptualization of competency to stand trial: Preliminary data on the IFI. *Law and Human Behavior, 8*(3–4), 321–334.	Designed for administration either by a sole mental health professional or by a mental health professional and an attorney together, the test measures a defendant's ability to aid in his or her own defense and to understand legal proceedings (e.g., how to act while in court and whether charges are understood) in less than an hour. Psychiatrists rate defendants on a scale from zero to two (0, 1, or 2), with zero showing no or minimal incapacity and 2 substantial incapacity, according to how important they deem each aspect of the case given the specific facts of that case. Though its basis as an interdisciplinary test is viewed as a positive and outcomes of the IFI-R seem to align fairly often with legal professionals' evaluations of adjudicative incompetence, there is little data to support either the IFI-R's validity or reliability.
MacArthur Competence Assessment Tool—Criminal Adjudication (MacCAT-CA)	Otto, R. K., Poythress, N. G., Edens, J. F., Nicholson, R. A., Monahan, J., Bonnie, R. J., Hoge, S. K., & Eisenberg, M. (1998). Psychometric properties of the MacArthur Competence Assessment Tool—Criminal Adjudication. *Psychological Assessment, 10*(4), 435–443.	The MacCAT-CA is considered to be one of the strongest evaluative tools available for determining a defendant's reasoning abilities. Designed to be administered in 25 to 45 minutes, this 22-item assessment evaluates competence-related abilities concerning the understanding, reasoning, and appreciation of the criminal legal process based on a defendant's responses to a series of vignettes. Normative interpretations of scores are categorized as minimal or no, mild, and clinically significant impairment. The vignettes are both the greatest strength and weakness of the test, allowing for wide respondent interpretation and sensitivity of response. Scores are easily normalized and compared. The major drawback is the test's lack of sampling of defendant's knowledge of legal terms and procedures.

(Continued)

(Continued)

Assessment Instrument	Source	Description
Metropolitan Toronto Forensic Service Fitness Questionnaire	Nussbaum, D., Mamak, M., Tremblay, H., Wright, P., & Callaghan, J. (1998). The METFORS Fitness Questionnaire (MFQ): A self-report measure for screening competency to stand trial. *American Journal of Forensic Psychology, 16*(3), 41–65.	Utilizing a self-report method of assessment, the MFQ presents 19 measures of legal problems characteristically found in fitness interviews. Coupled with post-assessment interviews, this test has been found to be a valid measure of competency, though its reliability is still in the process of being evaluated. Early uses of the test indicate that it is a good screening tool to see whether more complex assessment measures are needed.
Mosley Forensic Competency Scale (MFCS)	Mosley, D., Thyer, B. A., & Larrison, C. (2001). Development and preliminary validation of the Mosley Forensic Competency Scale. *Journal of Human Behavior in The Social Environment, 4*(1), 41–48.	Using 21 true-false questions, the MFCS is an initial screening mechanism for adjudicative competency. With a score of 17 and above indicative of competency, the test is widely regarded as being a valid assessment tool possessing especially strong predictive validity.
Test of Malingered Incompetence (TOMI)	Colwell, K., Colwell, L. H., Perry, A. T., Wasieleski, D., & Billings, T. (2008). The Test of Malingered Incompetence (TOMI): A forced-choice instrument for assessing cognitive malingering in competence to stand trial evaluations. *American Journal of Forensic Psychology, 26*(3), 17–42.	TOMI is divided into two subtests: General Knowledge (TOMI-G) and Legal Knowledge (TOMI-L). Both are forced-choice scales comprised of 25 questions. Validated against existing malingering scales (Rey-FIT and TOMM), this test is still relatively new, though it shows promise in distinguishing honest responses from those that are feigned through malingering.

Pirelli and colleagues (2011) conducted a meta-analysis of 68 studies published between 1967 and 2008 that compared competent and incompetent defendants on a number of demographic, psychiatric, and criminological variables. Highlights of their results are presented in Table 11.2.

As Table 11.2 illustrates, the most significant correlates among defendants found incompetent to stand trial are not demographic characteristics but rather clinical ones. These data lend further support to prior research that found those incompetent to stand trial frequently performed poorly on tests specifically designed to assess legally relevant functional abilities, were diagnosed with psychotic disorders, and exhibited psychiatric symptoms indicating severe psychopathology (e.g., Nicholson & Kugler, 1991). Given the low threshold for competency to stand trial, it is unsurprising that such substantial mental impairment must be present as a prerequisite to a finding of incompetency.

Psychosis and Competency. As was the case with Jared Loughner, whose diagnosis of schizophrenia led him to be declared incompetent to stand trial early in the judicial proceedings against him, the most pervasive form of mental illness found in those adjudicated incompetent to stand trial is psychosis (Melton, et al., 2007; Pirelli et al., 2011).

Table 11.2 Variables Related to Competency to Stand Trial

Factor	Competent	Incompetent	Major Finding
Sex	81.9% male	84.1% male	Female defendants were essentially equally as likely as male defendants to be found incompetent.
Age	31.8 years	35 years	Incompetent defendants tend to be slightly older than competent ones.
Race	43.1% not white	52.3% not white	Non-white defendants were approximately one and a half times more likely to be found incompetent than white defendants.
Education	10.5 years average educational level	10.4 years average educational level	The mean age of competent and incompetent defendants did not differ significantly.
Employment	58.2% unemployed	70.8% unemployed	Unemployed defendants were twice as likely to be found incompetent as employed defendants.
Marital Status	77.3% unmarried	84% unmarried	Defendants who were not married were approximately one and a half times more likely than married defendants to be found incompetent.
Previous Psychiatric Hospitalization	32.3% previously hospitalized	53.4% previously hospitalized	Defendants who had a previous psychiatric hospitalization were nearly twice as likely as defendants without such a history to be found incompetent.
Psychiatric Disorder Diagnosis	22.2% diagnosed with psychotic disorder; 27.9% diagnosed with personality disorder	66.5% diagnosed with psychotic disorder; 8.2% diagnosed with personality disorder	Defendants diagnosed with a psychotic disorder were nearly eight times more likely to be found incompetent than those without such a diagnosis. In contrast, personality disorder diagnoses rarely rendered a defendant incompetent to stand trial.
Intelligence	Mean Wechsler Full Scale IQ 86.8	Mean Wechsler Full Scale IQ 80.6	Competent defendants scored approximately six Mean Wechsler Full Scale IQ points higher than their incompetent counterparts.
Prior Arrest	63.4% with prior arrest history	59.6% with prior arrest history	Competent and incompetent defendants both have prior criminal arrest records that do not differ significantly.
Current Violent Crime Charge	55.1% currently charged with violent crime	50.8% currently charged with violent crime	Defendants with a current violent criminal charge were 1.25 times more likely to be found competent than those with a current nonviolent charge.

Source: Pirelli et al. (2011).

Psychosis is a common finding in those ruled incompetent because, for some people with psychotic thinking, the interference with reality perception is blatantly obvious. For instance, the commonly thought of psychotic who is attending to voices in his/her head rather than to the examiner is easy to identify as impaired. Thus, in one of the few studies comparing competency referred and non-referred clients, the most important predictor of referral was disorganized speech [Berman & Osborne, 1980]. Disorganized speech is a difficult symptom to overlook, even for attorneys who have essentially no training in mental health. Yet, what of more difficult symptoms to identify? (Freedman, 2009, p. 131)

Freedman's question about other symptoms that suggest significant impairment is not easily answered because, unlike differential diagnoses of mental illnesses that hinge on the presence or absence of specific symptoms, competency to stand trial is functionally based. Freedman (2009) explored this difference in the context of another hallmark of psychosis—formal thought disorder:

> Thought disorder may show itself as a poverty of speech (a restriction in the amount of spontaneous speech, often coinciding with the negative symptoms of schizophrenia) or as pressured speech (an increase in the amount of spontaneous speech and the pace of that speech) or as poverty of content (where there is sufficient or extra production of words but they are unnecessary or not useful in conveying an idea). The observable symptoms are very different and the difficulties faced in the interactive dialogue are very different, but the potential for interference in specific settings (and therefore the question of competence) is the same. Thus, how the symptom interferes or does not interfere with the interactive dialogue is critical. (p. 132).

In a meta-analysis of more than 30 studies comparing competent and incompetent defendants, Nicholson and Kugler (1991) found that disorganized communication and thoughts were reported in approximately 25% of defendants found incompetent to stand trial. Other symptoms associated with both psychosis and incompetency to stand trial included disorientation ($r = .43$), delusions ($r = .36$), hallucinations ($r = .29$), disturbed behavior ($r = .25$), and impaired memory ($r = .28$).

Other Mental Disorders and Competency. In contrast to psychotic disorders, few other forms of mental disability support a finding of incompetence to stand trial. For example, Otto (2006) reported that less than 10% of adults found incompetent have a diagnosis of mental retardation. Maroney (2006) reported that courts have all but rejected the notion that depression and other mood disorders (other than bipolar disorders with psychotic features) are significant contributors to incompetence. The same holds true for most anxiety disorders—including PTSD (see e.g., *United States v. Tracy, 1994; Warren v. Schriro*, 2006), although such mental illnesses may be relevant to adjudicating criminal responsibility or for the purposes of mitigation at sentencing (see, e.g., *Porter v. McCollum*, 2009). Thus, although a broad range of significant psychiatric diagnoses may impair both cognition and affect in ways that might run afoul of the mandates of *Dusky v. United States*, the threshold for competency to stand trial is so low that only a narrow class of severe mental illnesses typically renders a defendant incompetent to stand trial. Absent a psychotic disorder or a severe organic brain deficit, such as dementia, courts usually find defendants competent to stand trial.

After a Competency Determination

If, after evaluation and a hearing, the defendant is found competent, the case proceeds. Such a determination of competency does not prevent the defendant from asserting the insanity defense for many of the reasons discussed above, the most important of which is the issue of timing since competency deals with the defendant's state of mind at the time of trial and insanity deals with the defendant's state of mind at the time of the alleged offense.

The more difficult scenario occurs when a defendant is adjudicated incompetent. The normal course of events in such a case is that the court "suspends the criminal proceedings and remands the defendant for treatment, typically on an inpatient basis. Treatment is designed not to cure the defendant, but to restore competency" (Winick, 1995b, p. 572). If, after a period of evaluation often set by statute (often between three and six months), the psychiatric staff believes that the defendant can be restored to competency, the defendant will remain for treatment and the government must report to the court on the defendant's progress at regular intervals. Assuming the original belief of the psychiatric staff was correct and the defendant is restored to competency, he or she will then face trial.

On the other hand, if the defendant's condition is unchanging and the psychiatric staff does not believe it will improve, the defendant may not be held indefinitely. This was not always the case, though. Until the Supreme Court's decision in *Jackson v. Indiana* (1972), defendants found incompetent to stand trial were routinely kept hospitalized indefinitely, often for a period of time that was in excess of the maximum sentence that could have been imposed had they been convicted (a fact especially so for defendants charged with misdemeanors). And, in some cases, such defendants were kept hospitalized for the remainder of their lives (Gobert, 1973). *Jackson* changed that by holding a defendant committed after a finding of incompetency to stand trial could not "be held more than a reasonable period of time necessary to determine whether there is a substantial probability that he will attain that capacity in the foreseeable future" (p. 738). This is what occurred in Jared Loughner's case. After the court initially determined he was incompetent to stand trial, Loughner was sent to the U.S. Medical Center for Federal Prisoners in Springfield, Missouri. The court reviewed Loughner's progress on two occasions and determined that, although he remained incompetent to stand trial, progress was being made in restoring him to competency. It was not until the summer of 2012 that Loughner was ruled competent to stand trial. He then pled guilty to the charges against him, sparing the community the trauma of a trial that would have reopened healing wounds and sparing himself a possible death sentence.

Since *Jackson*, a defendant found incompetent to stand trial can only be kept confined if the treatment he or she is receiving while committed is likely to restore capacity in the foreseeable future—not at some distant time. Most research suggests that six months is a sufficient period of time to restore a criminal defendant to competence if restoration appears possible (Miller, 2003; Noffsinger, 2001; Pinals, 2005), although many state laws provide up to one, three, or even five years to restore competency (for a review, see Rosinia, 2012).

If the treatment being provided to the defendant either does not advance the defendant toward competency or advances the defendant only marginally without a fair probability that competency will be restored within the foreseeable future, "then the state must either institute customary civil commitment proceedings to detain the defendant, or release the defendant" (Winick, 1995b, p. 580). To prevent such a person from being released, the state must show that a person poses a danger to himself or herself or to others (*O'Connor v. Donaldson*, 1975). Without proving such dangerousness by clear and convincing evidence, the state cannot have the individual civilly committed and must therefore release him or her (*Addington v. Texas*, 1979; *United States v. Comstock*, 2010).

The Quandary Presented by Synthetic Competency

The issue of competency has been greatly affected by the advent of antipsychotic medications. Antipsychotic drugs are frequently used, often in an inpatient setting, in an attempt to restore an incompetent defendant to competency (Winick, 1995b). The first generation of these drugs, sometimes called "typical" antipsychotics (e.g., Haldol, Mellaril, Moban, Navane, Trilafon, Prolixin, Stelazine, and Thorazine), were introduced in the 1950s and 1960s. These drugs caused significant adverse side effects, including *extrapyramidal symptoms* (involuntary movements), which could become irreversible after long-term use—a condition termed *tardive dyskinesia* (Adkins, et al., 2011).

Clozapine, the first of the second generation of antipsychotic medications, often called *atypical neuroleptics*, was developed in 1989. Through selective targeting of certain neurotransmitter receptors, clozapine produced greater therapeutic effects in patients who responded poorly to treatment with typical antipsychotics while carrying a significantly lower risk of extrapyramidal side effects; however, it carried the risk of causing severe agranulocytosis—a potentially life-threatening condition in which a major class of infection-fighting white blood cells are reduced to the point that the immune system is unable to fight a wide range of infections (Adkins, et al., 2011). In the 1990s, though, other atypical neuroleptics (e.g., risperidone and olanzapine) became available that carry an even "lower incidence of extrapyramidal symptoms/tardive dyskinesia and do not share clozapine's risk of agranulocytosis (Adkins, et al., 2011, p. 322). These drugs do, however, cause a variety of metabolic side effects ranging from weight gain to hypertension, coronary artery disease, and diabetes (Henderson & Doraiswamy, 2008).

Both first- and second-generation antipsychotics alter brain chemistry by regulating neurotransmitters. In doing so, these drugs can "enable the incompetent individual affected by psychosis to possibly think more clearly or control his emotions in such a way as to prevent them from interfering with his rational thinking process" (Byers, 1994, p. 376). This process of using antipsychotics drugs to restore competency, which has been termed both **synthetic competency** and *artificial competency* by different commentators (e.g., Fradella, 2005; Gutheil & Appelbaum, 1983), raises clinical and ethical issues that are beyond the scope of this book (see, e.g., Schaefer, 1994/1995; Siegel, 2008; Slobogin, 2006). Synthetically restoring competency also raises legal policy concerns of constitutional dimensions.

Synthetic Competency as a Function of Controlling a Dangerous Inmate. In *Washington v. Harper* (1990), the U.S. Supreme Court grappled with whether a correctional inmate may be forcibly medicated while imprisoned. Given the adverse side effects the drugs can cause, the Court recognized that an individual possesses a significant, constitutionally protected liberty interest in "avoiding the unwanted administration of antipsychotic drugs" (p. 221). But this interest yields to the government's legitimate penological interests in protecting correctional staff, other inmates, and mentally ill offenders themselves, provided that psychiatrists determine that inmates are "gravely disabled or represent a significant danger to themselves or others" due to mental illness (p. 226). Under such circumstances, the forced administration of antipsychotics is constitutionally permissible "if treatment is in the inmate's medical interest" (p. 227).

Forced medication under *Harper*'s dangerousness standard is what occurred in Jared Loughner's case. Loughner declined to take antipsychotic medication voluntarily. But psychiatric staff at the Federal Medical Center in Springfield authorized his being forcibly medicated on the grounds of dangerousness because

> Loughner had become enraged while being interviewed and yelled obscenities; had thrown objects, including plastic chairs and toilet paper; had spat on his attorney, lunged at her, and had to be restrained by staff; and his behavior had been characterized by indications that he was experiencing auditory hallucinations, including inappropriate laughter, poor eye contact, yelling "No!" repeatedly, and covering his ears. . . . [Psychiatrists] rejected other, less intrusive measures (e.g., psychotherapy, minor tranquilizers, seclusion and restraints) because they "are not practicable," "do not address the fundamental problem," "have no direct effect on the core manifestations of the mental disease," or "are merely temporary protective measures with no direct effect on mental disease." (*United States v. Loughner*, 2012, p. 737)

Both the federal district court and the Ninth Circuit Court of Appeals upheld the forced administration of four medications to Loughner under the *Harper* framework: the antipsychotic medication risperidone, the antidepressant bupropion, the anticholinergic benztropine (to control the side effects of the antipsychotic), and the tranquilizer clonazepam (p. 739). The medication also improved Loughner's cognitive and behavioral condition: "his thoughts are more rational and organized, he is better able to concentrate and hold conversations, and he is becoming more aware of how others perceive him. . . . [Although] Loughner is still depressed, . . . his cognitive abilities and functioning have improved, and he is more oriented, less delusional, and less obsessed" (p. 741). Based on these observations, psychiatrists testified that they believed Loughner could be restored to competency, and the court ruled that he was competent by the summer of 2012.

Synthetic Competency Beyond *Harper*. Having recognized a constitutionally protected liberty interest in "avoiding the unwanted administration of antipsychotic drugs," the U.S. Supreme Court held in *Riggins v. Nevada* (1992) that due process prohibits the state from forcibly medicating a criminal defendant during an insanity defense trial without a judicial determination that there were no "less intrusive alternatives," that the antipsychotics were "medically appropriate," and that forced administration of the drug was "essential" for the sake of the defendant's safety or the safety of others (p. 135). Although Riggins did not squarely address competency to stand trial, the decision intonated that forcibly medicating a criminal defendant to restore competency to stand trial would be constitutionally permissible under some circumstances (see Winick, 1993). The Supreme Court specifically held so in *Sell v. United States* (2003), but it set forth criteria designed to protect the interests of both the state and the defendant.

Under *Sell*, antipsychotic drugs can be forcibly administered to a criminal defendant to restore his or her competency to stand trial only if the trial court issues findings that four criteria are met. First, important governmental interests must be at stake. With *Sell*, the Court recognized an "important" governmental interest in trying a defendant accused of "a serious crime against the person or a serious crime against property" in light of the criminal law's fundamental purpose of protecting "the basic human need for security" (*Sell*, 2003, p. 180). The Court cautioned, however, that

> [s]pecial circumstances may lessen the importance of that interest. The defendant's failure to take drugs voluntarily, for example, may mean lengthy confinement in an institution for the mentally

> ill—and that would diminish the risks that ordinarily attach to freeing without punishment one who has committed a serious crime. . . . And it may be difficult or impossible to try a defendant who regains competence after years of commitment during which memories may fade and evidence may be lost. The potential for future confinement affects, but does not totally undermine the strength of the need for prosecution. The same is true of the possibility that the defendant has already been confined for a significant amount of time (for which he would receive credit toward any sentence ultimately imposed . . .). Moreover, the Government has a concomitant, constitutionally essential interest in assuring that the defendant's trial is a fair one. (p. 180)

Second, involuntary medication must "significantly further" the government's concomitant interests insofar as being "substantially likely to render the defendant competent to stand trial" while simultaneously being "substantially unlikely to have side effects that will interfere significantly with the defendant's ability to assist counsel in conducting a trial defense, thereby rendering the trial unfair" (*Sell*, 2003, p. 181).

Third, involuntary medication must be "*necessary* to further those interests" (p. 181). Thus, trial courts must find that "any alternative, less intrusive treatments"—such as nondrug therapies—"are unlikely to achieve substantially the same results" (p. 181). This criterion is likely to be satisfied only in cases in which the defendant presents with one of "three types of psychological conditions: (1) schizophrenia, schizoaffective disorder, and other psychotic disorders; (2) bipolar and other mood disorders; and (3) melancholic depression" (*Harvard Law Review*, 2008, p. 1122).

Finally, administration of the antipsychotic drugs must be "medically appropriate" insofar as they are "in the patient's best medical interest" in light of his or her psychiatric condition (p. 181).

Applying *Sell v. United States.* *Sell* did not establish any standards of proof. At least two circuit courts of appeal have ruled, though, that the clear and convincing evidence standard applied in *Riggins* extends to *Sell* (*United States v. Gomes*, 2004; *United States v. Valenzuela-Puentes*, 2007). But problems with *Sell* go beyond the burden of persuasion. Perhaps as a function of balancing the tests embedded in each of *Sell*'s criteria, the lower courts applying them have ruled inconsistently on all four of *Sell*'s factors (*Harvard Law Review*, 2008; Preston-Baecht, 2009). Consider the question of whether "important governmental interests" justify forcibly medicating a defendant.

In violent felony cases, the first *Sell* factor almost always tips in favor of forcibly medicating a defendant to restore competency. The designation as a felony, however, is not necessarily determinative, as some courts have held that select nonviolent felonies are not the serious charges described under *Sell* (e.g., *United States v. Barajas-Torress*, 2004; for an in-depth analysis of several such cases, see Preston-Baecht, 2009). Moreover, even when select nonviolent felonies such as conspiracy, fraud, and identity theft are deemed to be serious crimes, special circumstances may undermine the government's interest in prosecution (see *United States v. White*, 2010). Similarly, a misdemeanor designation does not necessarily rule out the designation of a serious crime. Although courts have ruled that misdemeanor offenses are not serious crimes and that, therefore, the governmental interest at stake in trying an incompetent defendant is diminished (e.g., *United States v. Kourey*, 2003), other courts have decided that a misdemeanor offense for which a defendant could be sentenced to six months or more of imprisonment constitutes a "serious crime" even though it is not a felony (e.g., *United States v. Evans*, 2003; see also Preston-Baecht, 2009). "Given the conflicting interpretations across jurisdictions, mental health clinicians are in an uncomfortable, if not untenable, position" (Preston-Baecht, 2009, p. 429).

Even when the *Sell* factors balance clearly in favor of forcibly medicating a defendant to restore competency to stand trial, *Riggins v. Nevada* (1992) remains a concern. The case involved a defendant who had been found mentally competent to stand trial after being treated with Mellaril (an antipsychotic) and Dilantin (an anticonvulsant). But he did not want to be on any psychotropic medication during his trial during which he had asserted the insanity defense. In ruling for the defendant, the Court reasoned that the Mellaril could have prejudicially affected his attitude, appearance, and demeanor at trial (p. 131). Further, the drug's side effects may have gone beyond impacting his outward appearance by impairing "content of his testimony on direct or cross examination, his ability to follow the proceedings, or the substance of his communication with counsel" (p. 137), thereby creating an "unacceptable risk" that forced medication compromised his trial rights (p. 138).

Riggins made clear that due process could be satisfied if forced administration of antipsychotic medication was both "medically appropriate and, considering less intrusive alternatives, essential for the sake of [the defendant's] own safety or the safety of others" (p. 135). *Riggins* foreshadowed the *Sell* holding on synthetically restoring competency when medically appropriate if the government cannot obtain adjudication of a defendant's guilt or innocence by using "less intrusive means" than forced administration of antipsychotics (p. 135). What "less intrusive means," though, might keep a person with a psychotic disorder competent to stand trial without running afoul of the due process concerns raised in *Riggins* is unclear. Reconciling *Riggins* and *Sell* would have been nearly impossible prior to the advent of today's second-generation antipsychotics. The comparably low risk of experiencing significant side effects when using atypical neuroleptics such as risperidone and olanzapine might permit the harmonization of *Riggins* and *Sell* in some cases, but because they are not without significant health risks, such drugs are not a complete solution to the problem.

Mental Illness and Criminal Responsibility: Insanity

Insanity is a legal term—not a psychological or medical one. Unlike competency to stand trial, which examines the state of mind of the defendant at the time of the criminal prosecution of a case, insanity refers to the defendant's state of mind at the time of the offense. Thus, the very nature of an insanity defense is retrospective. The law requires the trier of fact (usually a jury) to go back in time to evaluate the defendant's state of mind in the past. Accordingly, mental health experts are used to assist the trier of fact in reconstructing the defendant's past mental state.

Why do we have an insanity defense? Though answers to this question could fill several volumes, a simplified response can be given in three parts. First, it is unfair to punish people for acts that result from mental illness. The rational decision-making model of a person of free will is inapplicable when dealing with someone who is severely mentally ill (see Arenella, 1982). A severely mentally ill person may not act from free will or act rationally. Such an actor is not morally blameworthy (see Plaut, 1983). Hence, the criminal law's reasons for imposing a sanction are no longer applicable.

Second, as Grachek (2006) and Pustilnik (2005) explain, all of the major theoretical justifications for punishment are inapplicable to the mentally ill criminal offender. From the standpoint of retribution theory, what evil is there to punish if someone acts not out of criminal intent, but rather out of a delusionary or otherwise psychotic thought process? Punishment of the mentally ill also cannot be justified under deterrence theory because it is nearly impossible to deter acts resulting from mental illness. Deterrence as a theory is predicated on the utilitarian notion of rational choice, a presupposition that is not applicable to the insane defendant. Because the treatment of the mentally ill in the correctional setting leaves much to be desired, charitably speaking, both rehabilitation and incapacitation are better accomplished through the mental health system rather than in jails or prisons.

Third, those who commit criminal acts as a result of their mental illness do not fit nicely into the criminal law's doctrinal definitions of *mens rea*. ***Mens rea*** means "a guilty mind," "a guilty or wrongful purpose," or "a criminal intent" (Garner, 2004, p. 999). With the exception of a small number of offenses called strict liability crimes that punish criminal acts without regard to criminal intent, the union of *mens rea* (criminal intent) with ***actus reus*** (the criminally prohibited act) is an essential element of all crimes (see LaFave, 2011). But those who commit criminal acts while they are mentally ill may or may not have formed *mens rea*. Even if they did, their *mens rea* may have been formed defectively under circumstances that do not manifest any true, morally blameworthy criminal intent. This distinction was recognized as early as the thirteenth century in English common law when, as explained by Henry de Bracton, a noted English jurist, the courts excused a "madman" who lacked "mind and reason" because he was "not much removed from a brute" (Bracton, as quoted in Elkins, 1994, p. 162).

Common Misperceptions Regarding the Insanity Defense

The insanity defense is controversial for many reasons, not the least of which is that the public labors under a series of myths and misperceptions about the defense, muddles arising from a small number of highly publicized cases that are not representative of the way this defense is used (Daftary-Kapur, Groscup, O'Connor, Coffaro, & Galietta, 2011; Perlin, 1997).

In a two-year research study on insanity defense, Professor Michael Perlin (1997) found not only that people believed the defense was much more widely used than it really is but also that public sentiment toward the defense was overwhelmingly negative:

> According to the news media, the allegedly "popular" insanity defense—nothing more than a "legalistic slight of hand" and a "common feature of murder defenses"—is a reward to mentally disabled defendants for "staying sick," a "travesty," a "loophole," a "refuge," a "technicality," one of the "absurdities of state law," perhaps a "monstrous fraud." It is used—again, allegedly—in cases involving "mild disorders or a sudden disappointment or mounting frustrations . . . or a less-than-perfect childhood." It is reflected in "pseudoscience [that] can only obfuscate the issues," and is seen as responsible for "burying the traditional Judeo-Christian notion of moral responsibility under a tower of psychobabble." (p. 1403)

In fact, the insanity defense is used quite rarely. It is raised in fewer than 1% of all felony cases, and, when invoked, it is successful less than 25% of the time (Callahan, Steadman, McGreevy, & Robbins, 1991; Janofsky, Vandewalle, & Rappeport, 1989; Kirschner & Galperin, 2001; Silver, Cirincione, & Steadman, 1994). It is used nearly twice as much for nonhomicide offenses as it is for those offenses involving a human death (Perlin, 1997; Silver et al., 1994). Thus, contrary to popular misperceptions, insanity is pled infrequently and, in the rare instances when it is raised, the defense is unsuccessful three-quarters of the time.

Additionally, Perlin reports much public concern about defendants who waste time and resources hiring clinicians to engage in expert battles with the prosecution at trial. But such cases are the rare exception and not the rule. Studies repeatedly demonstrate that between 75% and 82% of defendants who plead insanity have been diagnosed with a major psychotic disorder (Callahan, Steadman, McGreevy, & Robbins, 1991; Rice & Harris, 1990). And between 44% and 80% of those who plead insane have a history of prior psychiatric hospitalizations for their illnesses (Callahan, Steadman, McGreevy, & Robbins, 1991; Jeffrey, Pasewark, & Bieber, 1988).

Perlin also found that the public fears the insanity defense will be used by defendants to fake mental illnesses in order to escape convictions. Hollywood storylines in movies such as *Primal Fear* (1996) exacerbate these fears. They are, however, ill founded. Clinicians on both sides of the criminal dispute overwhelmingly agree on a clinical diagnosis. One study put the clinician agreement rate at 88% (Rogers, Bloom, & Manson, 1984) and another study at 92% (Fukunaga, Pasewark, Hawkins, & Gudeman, 1981). Moreover, modern diagnostic instruments and procedures allow clinicians to distinguish correctly those who are truly mentally ill and those who are faking between 92% and 95% of the time (Cornell & Hawk, 1989; Grossman & Wasyliw, 1988). Thus, when defendants fake mental illness, it is extraordinarily difficult for them to "get away with it" (see also Franklin, 2008; Resnick & Harris, 2002).

Evolution of the Insanity Defense

The Wild Beast Defense. The insanity defense has a long history, having roots in Muslim, Hebrew, Greek, and Roman law (Moore, 1984). Justice Tracy, a judge in King Edward's court, first formulated the foundation of an insanity defense when he

> [i]nstructed the jury that it should acquit by reason of insanity if it found the defendant to be a madman which he described as "a man that is totally deprived of his understanding and memory, and doth not know what he is doing, no more than an infant, than a brute, or a wild beast, such a one is never the object of punishment." (Perlin, 1990, p. 632, quoting *Rex v. Arnold*, 1724)[1]

---

1. Perlin goes on to explain that the word "brute" as used in Arnold's case referred to "farm animals such as 'badgers, foxes, deer, and rabbits.' . . . Thus, the emphasis was apparently meant to focus on a lack of intellectual ability, rather than the savage beast-like image the phrase calls to mind." (p. 632)

Justice Tracy's wild beast test "set the standard which would be applied in English courts throughout the eighteenth century" (Gresham, 1993, p. 194). There are few records about how the wild beast test was actually applied, but "commentators of the period consistently spoke of a requirement that the defendant lack understanding of good and evil or be devoid of all reason, and often equated the insane with animals or infants" (Slobogin, 2000, p. 1208). Interestingly, there was no separate or special verdict that excused a defendant on the basis of his insanity. Rather, after conviction, an appeal was made to the king for a pardon (Maeder, 1985).

The defense evolved significantly in 1800 when James Hadfield, believing he was acting on orders from God, shot King George III (Maeder, 1985; Robin, 1997). At Hadfield's trial for treason, his defense counsel argued that Hadfield's delusions, stemming from head trauma suffered during battle, caused his actions. Several physicians offered testimony corroborating Hadfield's head trauma claims. The jury acquitted Hadfield because "the prisoner appear[ed] to be under the influence of insanity at the time the act was committed" (Robin, 1997, p. 226; see also Moran, 1985).

The Hadfield case represented a departure from the "wild beast" test in two ways. First, "it rejected the argument that the defendant 'must be totally deprived of all mental faculty before acquitt[al]'" (Gresham, 1993, p. 194). Second, it was the first time that a verdict of not guilty by reasons of insanity (NGBRI) "became a separate verdict of acquittal" (Robin, 1997, p. 226). However, within a few years of the Hadfield decision, English jurisprudence reverted to using Justice Tracy's wild beast test, which did require a near complete deprivation of mental faculties for an acquittal (Gresham, 1993; see also Simon, 1967).

The *M'Naghten* Rule. In 1843, the *M'Naghten* case[2] set forth a legal standard for insanity that many U.S. states—indeed many common law jurisdictions around the world—still use today. M'Naghten was indicted for the first-degree murder of Edward Drummond, the secretary to the English Prime Minister Sir Robert Peel. M'Naghten had intended to kill Peel, but mistook Drummond for him. He explained to the police that he wanted to kill the Prime Minister because he believed that the Tories in his city followed him around, persecuting and harassing him (Moran, 1981).

At M'Naghten's trial, his defense attorneys argued that he suffered from paranoid persecutory delusions. To support this defense, M'Naghten was represented by four well-respected barristers and nine prominent medical experts (Moran, 1981). In contrast, the prosecution put on no experts. Lord Chief Justice Tindal charged the jury as follows:

> The question to be determined is whether at the time the act in question was committed, the prisoner had or had not the use of his understanding, so as to know that he was doing a wrong or wicked act. If the jurors should be of opinion that the prisoner was not sensible, at the time he committed it, that he was violating the laws of both God and man, then he would be entitled to a verdict in his favour; but if, on the contrary, they were of opinion that when he committed the act he was in a sound state of mind, then their verdict must be against him. (*M'Naghten*, 1843, p. 718)

The jury found M'Naghten not guilty by reason of insanity. M'Naghten was committed to Bedlam, the notorious asylum, where he lived until his death. Much public outrage over the acquittal followed, including condemnation of the case from Queen Victoria, who herself had been the target of assassination attempts. The House of Lords subsequently enacted what became known as the ***M'Naghten* rule**—a test for criminal insanity. It provides that

1. A person is not responsible for criminal conduct if, at the time of the offense,
2. the defendant suffered from a mental disease or defect
3. that caused the defendant either
   a. not to know the nature and quality of the act he or she committed or,
   b. knowing the quality or nature of the act, nonetheless not to know that the act was wrong.

---

2. There are at least twelve different spellings of M'Naghten's last name, something that he himself likely contributed to as he spelled his own name differently on several occasions (Moran, 1981).

The first *M'Naghten* rule element illustrates that the insanity defense is concerned with a defendant's mental state at the time the criminal act is alleged to have taken place. The second element requires that the defendant suffer from a "mental disease or defect," a concept explored in detail later in this chapter. The third part of the test concerns the legal doctrine of *causation.*

The doctrine of causation applicable in criminal law requires two distinct types of causation: cause in fact and proximate cause (see LaFave, 2011). The *M'Naghten* rule is concerned with the former. Cause in fact is what we normally think of as "causing": if a person does some act that directly brings about a particular result, then that person is said to have caused the result. If the result would not have occurred but for the defendant's conduct, then the defendant's conduct is the cause in fact of the result (see Johnson, 2005). The relevant question concerning causation for insanity purposes is this: "But for the mental disease or defect, would the criminal act have occurred?" If the answer to that question is "yes," then the mental illness was not the cause in fact of the crime; only if the answer to the question is "no" is insanity considered causative. This factual question must be resolved at trial by the trier of fact.

Under the *M'Naghten* rule, the mental disease or defect that existed at the time of the offense must have caused one of two things: *cognitive incapacity*, the inability to know the nature and quality of the act committed, or *moral incapacity*, the inability to know that the act committed was wrong (see *Clark v. Arizona*, 2006, pp. 748–752). The cognitive incapacity part of the test relieves the defendant of liability when the defendant is incapable of forming *mens rea*. For example, if a man strangled another person believing that he was squeezing the juice out of a lemon, he did not understand the nature and quality of his act (Rosen, 1999). Finding cognitive incapacity is rare because it requires that a person suffer from a psychotic disorder of such severity that he or she is removed from reality and unaware of his or her actions. For example, M'Naghten knew the nature and quality of his act. He wanted to kill the Prime Minister and attempted to do so. He was, therefore, not cognitively incapacitated under the first prong of the *M'Naghten* rule. The same can be said for Jared Loughner; his actions on the morning of the Tucson shooting clearly indicate that he knew what he was doing.

The second part of the *M'Naghten* rule—the lack of moral capacity to distinguish right from wrong—is usually at the crux of an insanity defense. This part of the insanity test relieves a defendant from criminal liability even if the person formed the requisite *mens rea* (as M'Naghten formed an intent to kill) so long as the actor did not understand that his or her act was wrong.

For years, scholars have criticized the *M'Naghten* rule because it only looked at the cognitive and moral aspects of the defendant's actions. The test had no element that evaluated the volition of the defendant. The *M'Naghten* rule's focus on the cognitive, to the full exclusion of the affective and volitional elements of human behavior, failed to consider "that mentally ill offenders might be aware that their behavior is wrong, yet nonetheless be emotionally unable to restrain themselves or control their conduct" (Robin, 1997, p. 227). Thus, to many scholars and practitioners of the mental health sciences, the test was incomplete and "scientifically outdated" (Dressler, 1995, p. 321). Practitioners and scholars also criticized this test for being too rigid. "Even if one accepts the premise that cognitive dysfunction is the only appropriate focus of the insanity defense, the *M'Naghten* rule . . . did not fairly pose the question. . . . '[I]f the test language were taken seriously . . . it would excuse only those totally deteriorated, drooling hopeless psychotics of long-standing and congenital idiots'" (Zilboorg, 1943, p. 273, as quoted in Melton et al., 2007, p. 206). Finally, the *M'Naghten* rule was criticized for its focus on "right" and "wrong," a standard that often required clinicians to make moral judgments about defendants (see *Durham v. United States*, 1954). Some of these problems led to the development of other formulations of the insanity defense—one's that included an affective component.

The Short-Lived *Durham* Rule. Dissatisfied with the *M'Naghten* rule, the U.S. Court of Appeals for the District of Columbia Circuit formulated a new insanity test in relation to *Durham v. United States* (1954). In this case, the court held that "an accused is not criminally responsible if his unlawful act was the product of a mental disease or defect" (pp. 874–875). This finding came to be known as the *Durham* "product test" or the "***Durham* rule.**"

Although the *Durham* rule did away with both the cognitive focus and the moral judgments embedded in the *M'Naghten* rule, it proved to be an unworkable standard. The rule led to an "influx" of expert witnesses whose testimony largely narrowed the jury's role as fact finders (Robin, 1997). Additionally, the number of criminal acquittals on the basis of the *Durham* rule rose dramatically (Arens, 1974; Simon, 1967). Although this increase was not necessarily problematic, some viewed it as having the effect of abolishing the notion of insanity as a *limited* excuse by judicially legislating a rule that excused all mentally ill persons from criminal responsibility, regardless of the type or degree of impairment (Wechsler, 1955). The *Durham* rule was eventually overruled by the D. C. Court of Appeals in 1972 in *United States v. Brawner*, which adopted a formulation of the insanity defense based on the standards suggested by the American Law Institute (ALI) in its 1962 Model Penal Code.

The ALI/Model Penal Code Affective Test for Insanity. The ALI, a prestigious, nonpartisan group of judges, lawyers, and scholars from both law and related disciplines, developed a Model Penal Code (MPC) in 1962. Its formulation of the insanity defense is usually referred to as the **ALI/MPC affective test** and provides that "a person is not responsible for criminal conduct if, at the time of such conduct as of a result of a mental disease or defect, he [or she] lacks the substantial capacity to appreciate the criminality of his [or her] conduct or to conform his [or her] conduct to the requirements of law" (Model Penal Code § 4.01[1]). Although the ALI/MPC formulation of the insanity defense did not define mental diseases or defects (just as the *M'Naghten* rule failed to do), it did include a provision that purposefully excluded those who were suffering from antisocial personality disorder and related disorders, such as psychopathy, from being considered to have a mental disease or defect. For the sake of being able to make element-by-element comparisons among the various formulations of the insanity defense, the ALI/MPC Affective Test can be expressed in this way:

1. A person is not responsible for criminal conduct if, at the time of the offense
2. the defendant suffered from a mental disease or defect (other than antisocial personality disorder or any other abnormality manifested only by repeated criminal or otherwise antisocial conduct)
3. that caused the defendant to lack either
   a. the substantial capacity to appreciate the criminality (wrongfulness) of his or her conduct or
   b. the substantial capacity to conform his conduct to the requirements of law.

The first two elements of the ALI/MPC Affective Test are the same as those required under the *M'Naghten* rule. Both look at the defendant's conduct at the time of the offense, and both require a mental disease or defect. However, a slight difference is that the ALI/MPC formulation for insanity specifically excludes antisocial personality disorder and psychopathy. The principal difference between the two is in the third element. As discussed earlier, the *M'Naghten* rule focused on the cognitive aspects of behavior—did the defendant *know* what he or she was doing, and, if so, did the defendant *know* it was wrong? It was an all-or-nothing standard that required total (or nearly total) impairment. The ALI/MPC formulation avoided a purely cognitive focus by adding a volitional element. Further, the ALI/MPC test replaced the *M'Naghten* rule's focus on lacking a pure and almost complete cognitive knowledge of the wrongfulness of one's acts with a less stringent test requiring that the defendant lack the "substantial capacity to appreciate" the wrongfulness of his or her actions. As a result, mental health experts and, ultimately, juries were permitted to "consider the defendant's moral, emotional, and legal awareness of the consequences of his or her behavior . . . [in recognition that] there are gradations of criminal responsibility and that the defendant need not be totally impaired to be absolved of such responsibility" (Robin, 1997, p. 230).

Additionally, the ALI/MPC test was less strict than the *M'Naghten* rule because it allowed even those who knew and appreciated that their acts were wrong to assert the insanity defense by claiming they were unable to abide by the law. This aspect came to be known as the *irresistible impulse test*. The ALI sought to implement the irresistible impulse test nationwide in response to its recognition that the evolving state of behavioral science knowledge clearly acknowledged that one's volition was often impacted by mental illness, especially in the presence of compulsions. As a result, the inability to control one's actions became a basis for legal insanity.

The ALI/MPC formulation of the insanity defense was repeatedly criticized by scholars, lawyers, and psychiatrists for the inclusion of the irresistible impulse test (e.g. Morse, 1994). These critics argued that an irresistible impulse was really just an impulse that was not, in fact, resisted. For example, would a criminal defendant have committed the crime if a police officer had been next to him? That the answer to this hypothetical question in all likelihood would be "no" suggests that the impulse was not truly irresistible. Moreover, allowing volitional impairment to qualify as the basis of a defense of excuse is inconsistent "with a criminal justice system premised on free will" (Slobogin, 2003a, p. 320). In spite of the criticisms, a majority of the states and all but one federal circuit eventually adopted the ALI/MPC formulation of the insanity defense (Robin, 1997).

The John Hinckley Case. In the late 1970s, John Hinckley, an obsessed fan of actress Jodie Foster's, made several attempts to woo Foster while she was a first-year student at Yale University (Low, Jeffries, & Bonnie, 1986). When Foster rebuffed his overtures, Hinckley decided he needed to do something that would make an impression on her—some "historic deed [that would] finally gain her respect and love for him" (p. 32). On March 30, 1981, he carried out his plan by attempting to assassinate the president, then Ronald Reagan, as he was leaving the Washington Hilton Hotel in Washington, DC.

At his trial for attempted murder, Hinckley asserted the insanity defense; the ALI/MPC formulation of the insanity defense governed his trial. In response to this defense, the government had to prove that Hinckley was sane, beyond a reasonable doubt, at the time he made his assassination attempt on President Reagan. "After weeks of conflicting testimony by defense and prosecution psychiatrists—testimony that struck some as an affront to common sense—the jury found Hinckley not guilty by reason of insanity" (Robin, 1997, p. 231). At least for some jurors, the ALI/MPC formulation of the insanity defense determined the outcome of the case. One juror reported feeling "trapped" by the test: "My conscience had me voting one way, but the law would not allow me to vote that way" (as quoted in Robin, 1997, p. 231). Hinckley's acquittal using the insanity defense sparked a furor over the defense and focused critical national attention on it (Blau & Pasewark, 1994). "Within days [of the verdict], the most 'celebrated' insanity trial in American history had instantly become the most 'outrageous' verdict" (Perlin, 1990, p. 637).

In the wake of the *Hinckley* verdict, the insanity defense underwent sweeping reforms in both the federal system and in many states (Callahan, Mayer, & Steadman, 1987). After twenty-six different pieces of legislation were introduced in Congress to either abolish or restrict the insanity defense at the federal level (Perlin, 1985), Congress enacted the **Insanity Defense Reform Act of 1984 (IDRA).** In doing so, Congress codified the federal insanity defense for the first time and legislatively overruled the application of the ALI/MPC insanity test in all federal cases.

The Provisions of the IDRA. A defense based on IDRA will prevail if, "at the time of the commission of the acts constituting the offense, the defendant, as a result of a severe mental disease or defect, was unable to appreciate the nature and quality or the wrongfulness of his acts. Mental disease or defect does not otherwise constitute a defense" (18 U.S.C. § 17). Again, it is helpful to consider the requirements of IDRA in terms of its specific elements:

1. A person is not responsible for criminal conduct if, at the time of acts constituting the offense
2. the defendant suffered from a *severe* mental disease or defect
3. that caused the defendant to be unable to appreciate either
    a. the nature and quality of his or her acts or
    b. the wrongfulness of his or her acts.

In effect, IDRA returns the law of insanity to where it was at the time the *M'Naghten* rule was adopted. Like the previous insanity defense formulations, the first element looks at the mental state of the defendant at the time of the commission of the offense. The second element, just like the *M'Naghten* rule and the ALI/MPC formulation of the insanity defense, requires a mental disease or defect. But IDRA added the requirement that the mental disease or defect be "severe." This requirement effectively limited the applicability of the defense to people suffering from psychoses and mental retardation, thereby effectively eliminating neuroses, disabilities, and personality disorders as predicate mental diseases or defects (Perlin, 1990).

The third element is similar to all prior formulations of the insanity defense insofar as there must be a causal nexus between the mental illness and the crime committed. However, the third element changed the insanity defense as it existed in the federal courts quite significantly in two important ways.

First, the third element effectively abolished the volitional aspect of the ALI/MPC insanity defense as expressed in the irresistible impulse test. Thus, under the IDRA, an inability to conform one's conduct to the requirements of the law no longer qualifies as the basis of an insanity defense. Second, the third element effectively reinstated the *M'Naghten* rule with a slight modification. Instead of requiring a lack of knowledge that one's conduct is wrong to qualify a person as legally insane, IDRA requires an inability to "appreciate" the wrongfulness of one's conduct. This leaves the slightest door open for the defense to introduce some affective component rather than having to focus exclusively on the defendant's cognitive incapacities.

In addition to changing the elements of the insanity defense and standardizing the defense for the federal system, IDRA also made a critical procedural change to how the insanity defense is litigated. Up until the IDRA, once the defense announced its intention to use the insanity defense (i.e., once the defense met its burden of production), the prosecution bore the burden of persuasion to prove that, beyond a reasonable doubt, the defendant was legally sane at the time of a criminal offense. But the IDRA shifted the burden of persuasion, so the defense must now prove, by clear and convincing evidence, that the defendant was insane at the time of the criminal offense.

Callahan and colleagues (1987) reported that, by 1985, 33 states had followed the lead of Congress and reevaluated the insanity defense as it applied in their respective state jurisdictions. Many states followed IDRA and made insanity an affirmative defense, thereby shifting the burden of persuasion from the prosecution to the defense, which was required to prove the defendant's insanity by a preponderance of the evidence, usually. Other states left the burden of persuasion with the government, which had to show the defendant's sanity, but tightened the substantive test for insanity by requiring a severe mental disease or defect or something equivalent. Twelve states replaced the insanity defense with some variant of the "guilty, but mentally ill" verdict. And four states—Utah, Montana, Idaho, and Kansas—abolished the insanity defense altogether.

Alternative Verdicts for Defendants Claiming Mental Illness

Guilty but Mentally Ill. Some states provide juries with a number of verdicts to consider in cases that rely on insanity defenses. For example, in August 1975, Michigan was the first U.S. state to supplement its NGBRI verdict (not guilty by reason of insanity) by adding another verdict alternative termed **guilty but mentally ill (GBMI)**. The impetus for enacting the new verdict came largely from the case of John Bernard McGee. McGee was found NGBRI at his murder trial and was committed to a mental institution. While institutionalized, he admitted to 25 additional killings. Two months later, in a civil commitment hearing mandated for NGBRI acquittees by an unrelated Michigan Supreme Court case, McGee was found "not presently insane" and was released (Mickenberg, 1987). He again was arrested one month later for beating his wife to death. Public outcry led the state legislature to adopt the GBMI verdict in an effort "to reduce the number of successful [NGBRI] pleas and insure lengthy confinement for those defendants who are found insane" (p. 974).

Under Michigan law (Mich. Comp. Laws § 768.36(1), 1975), a jury would return a verdict of GBMI if the following three criteria were found beyond a reasonable doubt:

1. The defendant is guilty of an offense;
2. The defendant was mentally ill at the time of the commission of the offense;
3. The defendant was *not* legally insane at the time of the commission of the offense.

This verdict was, in effect, a compromise. It allowed juries to acquit those defendants who were clearly insane under a traditional NGBRI verdict while also giving jurors a "middle ground" verdict to convict those who were not clearly insane but who did suffer from a mental illness at the time of the commission of a criminal offense (Perlin, 1997).

Under the Michigan GBMI scheme, a defendant so adjudicated would be sentenced just as if he or she had been found guilty of the crime, with one exception: a court must make a determination as to whether the GBMI defendant needs treatment. If a court finds the defendant does need treatment, then the defendant would be remanded into the custody of either the department of corrections or the state's department of mental health services for treatment. Interestingly, after treatment, the defendant must serve whatever time remains on his or her sentence in a correctional facility. The law, however, provides that a judge can order the remainder of the term to be served on probation if the defendant continues with mandatory mental health treatment.

Other states followed Michigan's lead and adopted the GBMI verdict. This movement was largely in response to NGBRI verdicts in those states that brought public outcry over the insanity defense.

The very phrase "guilty, but mentally ill" is an oxymoron, however. It allows jurors to affix guilt while simultaneously allowing a finding that excuses that guilt. This contradiction—between a lack of moral blameworthiness due to mental illness and a determination of factual guilt—should be intellectually irreconcilable. But supporters argue that it has a two-fold benefit: it allows jurors to feel better about returning NGBRI verdicts when someone is truly mentally ill, and, conversely, it allows jurors to convict those who are mentally ill, but not insane, while still recognizing mental illness as a contributing factor that mitigates the need for punishment (see Mickenberg, 1987).

The GBMI verdict received much criticism from scholars (for a summary, see Slobogin, 1985). Notably, empirical research demonstrated that the verdict had little if any effect on the NGBRI adjudication rate. For example, Smith and Hall (1982) found that NGBRI acquittals represented .026% of all arrests before the GBMI law went into effect and .024% of all arrests in the six years after the new verdict was available. They concluded that the new GBMI verdict "merely substituted a new name for certain defendants who, in the absence of the new statute, probably would have been found guilty" (p. 80).

Moreover, one of the primary objectives of the GBMI verdict was to get treatment for those defendants who, although mentally ill, were not so cognitively impaired as to be rendered legally insane. In reality, however, "GBMI prisoners are treated like any other prisoners; they will get extra treatment if they need it, but that's the same treatment [the prison will] give everyone else" (p. 106). In fact, Smith and Hall (1982) reported that 75% of GBMI defendants in Michigan received no psychiatric treatment at all, usually due to financial constraints. But even when treatment is provided in states using the GBMI approach, whether such treatment produces effective outcomes is questionable. As the former chair of the parole board in Kentucky stated, "From psychological evaluations and treatment summaries, the Board can detect no differences in treatment or outcome for [inmates adjudicated as GBMI] from those who have been adjudicated as simply 'guilty'" (Greene & Heilbrun, 2011, p. 220).

Guilty Except Insane. Not all states structured their variations to the NGBRI verdict along the line of the GBMI verdict. Consider Arizona's approach. Under it, a person may be found **guilty except insane (GEI)** if

1. at the time of the commission of the criminal act
2. the person was afflicted with a mental disease or defect of such severity
3. that the person did not know the criminal act was wrong.
4. A mental disease or defect constituting legal insanity is an affirmative defense. . . . The defendant shall prove the defendant's legal insanity by clear and convincing evidence.
5. Mental disease or defect does not include disorders that result from acute voluntary intoxication or withdrawal from alcohol or drugs, character defects, psychosexual disorders or impulse control disorders. Conditions that do not constitute legal insanity include but are not limited to momentary, temporary conditions arising from the pressure of the circumstances, moral decadence, depravity or passion growing out of anger, jealousy, revenge, hatred or other motives in a person who does not suffer from a mental disease or defect or an abnormality that is manifested only by criminal conduct. (Ariz. Rev. Stat. Ann. § 13–502, 1997)

The GEI verdict abolished the NGBRI verdict in its entirety. It holds the person responsible (i.e., "guilty"), but simultaneously exempts the legally insane (under the narrow definition set forth in the statute) from criminal punishment. But, as at least one critic of the statute has said, "the 'guilty but insane verdict' is a contradiction in terms. . . . [O]ne cannot be both guilty from a legal standpoint and insane from a legal standpoint" (Melançon,

1998, p. 313). This conflict aside, the statute is one of the most restrictive insanity-related statutes in the United States in some aspects, though being arguably one the most progressive in other ways.

Arizona's statute returns to the *M'Naghten* rule's concept of defining insanity as not knowing right from wrong. As a result, the statute suffers from the same criticisms levied against this earlier formulation: its exclusive focus on the cognitive aspects of thought and behavior to the exclusion of affective elements. But Arizona's GEI statute is more restrictive than both the *M'Naghten* rule and the modern federal variation of this rule for two reasons.

First, like the modern federal formulation of the insanity defense under the IDRA, a "severe" mental disease or defect is required. Another likeness is that Arizona's GEI statute makes the defense an affirmative one, placing the burden of persuasion on the defendant to prove his or her insanity by clear and convincing evidence. But, unlike previous formulations of the insanity defense, Arizona's formulation contains the most restrictive exclusions of mental disorders. Not qualifying as a "mental disease or defect" for insanity purposes are antisocial personality disorders, psychosexual disorders, and impulse control disorders; also excluded are "disorders that result from acute voluntary intoxication or withdrawal from alcohol or drugs, character defects, . . . momentary, temporary conditions arising from the pressure of the circumstances, moral decadence, depravity or passion growing out of anger, jealousy, revenge, hatred or other motives."

The second major change to the traditional *M'Naghten* rule is that Arizona's GEI law eliminates the cognitive incapacity prong of that rule (i.e., not knowing the nature and quality of one's acts) from the definition of legal insanity. This omission narrows the definition of insanity. The change appears to be one merely of form rather than substance, as the first part of the *M'Naghten* rule was the much more stringent. Indeed, the U.S. Supreme Court recognized the overlap between the two prongs of the *M'Naghten* rule in *Clark v. Arizona* (2006) noting that, "[i]n practical terms, if a defendant did not know what he was doing when he acted, he could not have known that he was performing the wrongful act charged as a crime" (p. 753).

Although Arizona's GEI approach seems harsher than the GMBI approach taken by other states, the treatment of the offender after a GEI verdict is actually more humane than in other jurisdictions. In Arizona, a defendant found GEI of a crime involving a death or physical injury does not go to a correctional institution but rather enters the custody of a state-run mental health facility. The person remains confined until it is shown by clear and convincing evidence that he or she no longer suffers from the mental disease or defect. However, a conditional release is available if the person is still mentally ill but the illness is under control and the person poses no danger to self or others. Additionally, if the person's crime did not involve a death or physical injury, then a court must release the person upon a judicial determination that he or she poses no risk of danger to self or to others. On the other hand, if there is a risk of dangerousness, then civil commitment proceedings are instituted, and their strict due process supervision requirements must be met.

These post-verdict procedures are among the most progressive in the United States. Arizona's statute is clearly designed to ensure that those who need mental health care actually get it—quite a different result than appears to occur in GBMI jurisdictions. Equally important, the length of any period of detention in the mental health facility is not tied to any potential criminal sentence but rather to the person's recovery. Finally, someone adjudicated GEI does not serve any time in a correctional institution, even if a fast recovery is made. Thus, although the law labels someone "guilty," its aim is clearly not to punish someone who is insane under its quirky definition of insanity, a fact further demonstrated by the provision of the law that specifies that a GEI verdict does not constitute a criminal conviction for sentencing-enhancement purposes for any future crimes.

Abolition of the Insanity Defense: The *Mens Rea* Approach

Montana, Idaho, Utah, and Kansas have no insanity defense and allow the introduction of mental illness evidence only to show that the level of *mens rea* the state requires was not possessed by the defendant due to his or her mental condition. Normally, the insanity defense would apply to the same types of cases as does the ***mens rea* approach**. However, the technicalities of a true insanity defense function quite differently than the *mens rea* approach when dealing with a delusional defendant. For example, suppose a defendant killed another person because of his delusional belief that God had ordered him to kill that person. Under a traditional insanity defense, the psychosis responsible for such a delusionary belief system would likely excuse the defendant's criminal act because the defendant did not know that what he did was wrong if he believed he was doing God's will (see Morris & Haroun, 2001). But under the *mens rea* approach, the defendant could be convicted of premeditated murder because he acted purposefully when killing his victim. The fact that a serious mental illness was responsible for forming the defendant's specific intent to kill would be irrelevant for determining his guilt. The defendant's mental illness would, however, be relevant in sentencing.

Ambiguities Common to All Insanity Defense Formulations

What Is a "Mental Disease or Defect"? What constitutes a **mental disease or defect** for the purposes of the insanity defense? Unfortunately, the question is difficult to answer. Rarely does an answer to this question turn on a pure matter of law. Courts have consistently refused to define precisely the term "mental disease or defect." Instead, they have held that the issue of whether a person is suffering from a mental disease is a question of fact to be decided at trial.

The DSM-5 (APA, 2013) contains a cautionary section regarding its use and application in forensic settings. After acknowledging that the DSM is frequently used "as a reference for the courts and attorneys in assessing the forensic consequences of mental disorders," the APA warns that the definitions and classifications of mental disorders in the DSM-5 were "developed to meet the needs of clinicians, public health professionals, and research investigators rather than all of the technical needs of the courts and legal professionals" (p. 25). The cautionary statement goes on to say that, although the DSM may assist judges making legal decisions that turn, in part, on understanding psychiatric diagnoses,

> there is a risk that diagnostic information will be misused or misunderstood. These dangers arise because of the imperfect fit between the questions of ultimate concern to the law and the information contained in a clinical diagnosis. In most situations, the clinical diagnosis of a DSM-5 mental disorder such as intellectual disability (intellectual developmental disorder), schizophrenia, major neurocognitive disorder, gambling disorder, or pedophilic disorder does not imply that an individual with such a condition meets legal criteria for the presence of a mental disorder or a specified legal standard (e.g., for competence, criminal responsibility, or disability). For the latter, additional information is usually required beyond that contained in the DSM-5 diagnosis, which might include information about the individual's functional impairments and how these impairments affect the particular abilities in question. It is precisely because impairments, abilities, and disabilities vary widely within each diagnostic category that assignment of a particular diagnosis does not imply a specific level of impairment or disability.
>
> Use of DSM-5 to assess for the presence of a mental disorder by nonclinical, nonmedical, or otherwise insufficiently trained individuals is not advised. Nonclinical decision makers should also be cautioned that a diagnosis does not carry any necessary implications regarding the etiology or causes of the individual's mental disorder or the individual's degree of control over behaviors that may be associated with the disorder. Even when diminished control over one's behavior is a feature of the disorder, having the diagnosis in itself does not demonstrate that a particular individual is (or was) unable to control his or her behavior at a particular time. (p. 25)

The above warning notwithstanding, court actors are routinely guided by the medical categories of mental illnesses as defined by the psychiatric community in the DSM when they decide the factual question of which mental illnesses will qualify as the basis for an insanity plea. However, it is clear that courts do not rely on medical labels exclusively. "[W]hat definition of 'mental disease or defect' is to be employed by courts enforcing the criminal law is, in the final analysis, a question of legal, moral and policy—not of medical—judgment" (*United States v. Murdoch*, 1996, p. 478). Although the law does not recognize every psychiatric condition in the DSM as a mental disease or defect that qualifies for the purpose of mounting an insanity defense, without a bona fide psychiatric diagnosis, courts rarely allow defendants to plead insane.

Psychotic Disorders. A literal reading of the insanity defense would mean that any "mental disease or defect" would qualify. Such a reading, however, is not warranted, as neither courts nor clinicians read the insanity defense literally. Professor Bruce Winick (1995a), one of the foremost scholars on the intersection of law and mental health, suggests that courts view mental diseases and defects within the framework of "a traditional medical model of illness—one that may be limited to conditions that until recently were labeled psychoses. These major mental disorders—schizophrenia, major depressive disorders, and bipolar disorder—seem to be the paradigmatic cases of mental illness" (pp. 558–559). In support of the proposition that the modern conceptualization of mental illness involves psychoses, Winick cited the American Psychiatric Association's *American Psychiatric Glossary*, which defined a psychosis as follows:

> A major *mental disorder* of *organic* or *emotional* origin in which a person's ability to think, respond emotionally, remember, communicate, interpret reality, and behave appropriately is sufficiently impaired so as to interfere grossly with the capacity to meet the ordinary demands of life. Often characterized by *regressive* behavior, inappropriate *mood*, diminished impulse control, and such abnormal mental content as *delusions* and *hallucinations*. The term is applicable to conditions having a wide range of severity and duration. See also *schizophrenia, bipolar disorder, depression, organic mental disorder*, and *reality testing*. (Stone, 1988, p. 139)

Although courts generally accept psychoses as "mental diseases or defects" relevant to an insanity defense, not all psychotic disorders are significantly correlated with violence. Mania, for example, has been reported to be a risk factor for aggression and violence in psychiatric hospitals but is not strongly associated with severe violence in community settings (Nielssen, Malhi, & Large, 2012). Beyond the specific diagnosis, it is important to keep in mind that the existence of a psychosis is not, in itself, sufficient to establish insanity. Other criteria—notably the psychosis being the cause of the defendant's inability to distinguish right from wrong—must also be satisfied.

Courts rarely have problems determining how true psychoses fit within the frameworks of the varying forms of the insanity defense. The more problematic situation for courts is deciding whether other psychiatric disorders qualify as a "mental disease or defect" under the insanity defense. Perhaps the most challenging of these other diagnoses are the personality disorders.

Personality Disorders. Some federal circuit courts of appeals have specifically held that personality disorders are not "mental diseases or defects" within the meaning of the insanity defense (e.g., *United States v. Bilyk*, 1994; *United States v. Prescott*, 1990). Other federal circuit courts have determined that, although personality disorders are mental diseases or defects, they are not "severe enough" under the modern federal formulation of the insanity defense to serve as the basis for an insanity defense (e.g., *United States v. Salava*, 1992; *United States v. Shlater*, 1996). It appears that at least one federal circuit (the ninth refuses to adopt a rule covering personality disorders as a class of psychiatric diagnoses, considering instead the specific diagnosis on a case-by-case basis (*United States v. Murdoch*, 1996).

There is a similar split of authority at the state level regarding whether personality disorders qualify as mental diseases or defects for insanity defense purposes. At least two states, California and Alabama, exclude personality disorders entirely. Other states exclude only certain types of personality disorders, most notably antisocial personality disorder and psychopathy. On the other hand, some states have very broad definitions of which mental illnesses qualify for the purposes of an insanity defense. For example, the Alaska law seemingly encompasses all personality disorders while Kentucky specifically excludes antisocial personality disorder but appears to allow all other types of personality disorders to qualify as the basis of an insanity defense.

As mentioned, both the federal system and several states refuse to consider antisocial personality disorder as a mental disease or defect for insanity defense purposes. Winick (1995a) suggests there are three issues concerning this disorder that might justify the law's refusal to treat it as a qualifying mental disease or defect. First, he reasons that antisocial personality disorder is "exclusively behavioral in nature, involving certain behavioral manifestations and personality traits" (p. 560). Second, unlike psychoses, antisocial personality disorder does not appear "to be biochemical in etiology" (p. 560). And third, the disorder is not treatable in any predictable way. Winick posits that these same criteria also explain why psychopathy and other personality disorders, as well as impulse control disorders such as kleptomania, pyromania, and the paraphilias, also do not qualify as mental diseases or defects for insanity defense purposes. Although Winick's explanations are debatable in light of the APA's behaviorally based operationalization of antisocial personality disorder in 1980 to address the previously poor reliability of such diagnoses by clinicians (Arrigo & Shipley, 2001) and in light of growing evidence indicating biological factors associated with antisocial personality disorder (Yang, Glenn,

& Raine, 2008), they are nonetheless well-reasoned and consistent with logic, precedent, and significant clinical evidence.

Alcohol and Drug Addiction. The DSM classifies alcoholism and numerous drug addictions as "substance related disorders." Involuntary intoxication on drugs or alcohol was a complete defense to a crime at common law and continues to be so in many U.S. jurisdictions today (Ingle, 2002). Voluntary intoxication, however, has never been a complete defense under the criminal law. At common law, voluntary intoxication was a partial defense that mitigated a crime of specific intent down to one of general intent if the defendant was so intoxicated that he or she could not form specific intent (see LaFave, 2011). Today, some jurisdictions still follow this old common law approach while other jurisdictions have abolished the defense of voluntary intoxication entirely.

Separate and apart from the criminal defense of intoxication are two issues regarding intoxication and insanity that continue to divide U.S. courts. The first is whether an addiction to drugs or alcohol can qualify as a mental disease or defect for the purposes of an insanity defense. The second is whether *settled insanity*—a drug- or alcohol-induced psychosis (when unaccompanied by some other mental illness)—is a qualifying mental disease or defect for an insanity defense. The overwhelming number of U.S. jurisdictions answer both questions in the negative, even though psychiatry recognizes a host of substance abuse disorders as mental illnesses in the DSM (see *People v. Bieber*, 1993). This is true even for cases involving iatrogenic addictions (i.e., those that resulted from medical treatment).

Alcohol or drug addiction is not a mental illness usable in an insanity defense for several reasons, but the primary justification is the voluntariness of the person's addiction. People cannot choose whether to have schizophrenia. But people can choose whether they will drink or take drugs. Biological predispositions to alcoholism and addiction aside, the law takes the view that one should seek treatment for an illness that one has brought upon oneself rather than seeking excuse from the harm caused by failing to control one's own behavior (see *United States v. Lyons*, 1984; *People v. Bieber*, 1993).

What Is "Wrong"? What is right, just, good, moral, and so on is a question that has perplexed philosophers for eons. The counterquestion, what is bad, wrong, or immoral is not much easier to answer. The law, however, often avoids complex philosophical issues, leaving them to scholars to debate. It certainly does so in defining what is meant by "wrong" for the purposes of the insanity defense, which requires that a mental disease or defect render a defendant unable to "know right from wrong" or to "appreciate the wrongfulness" of his or her acts. The law simply looks at whether the defendant knew the act was wrong by societal or legal standards. Imagine the consequences if a person could argue that, because she or he was a member of a particular religion, killing was not wrong; rather, offering human sacrifice was a sacred act under the tenets of that belief system. To avoid the possibility of a defendant succeeding with such an argument, jurors aim to use an objective societal standard of right and wrong (*State v. Crenshaw*, 1983).

There is a narrow exception to the rule disallowing distinctions between legal and moral wrongs for insanity defense purposes; this occurs when a defendant understands that his or her action was unlawful but nonetheless believes it to have been the morally correct action as a function of command delusions from God. Imagine, for example, that a delusional defendant kills to obey an order she or he believes came from God. In such a situation, referred to as the *deific exception*, a defendant may be able to secure a NGBRI verdict because a severe mental illness caused a delusional belief in the moral "rightness" of one's acts in spite of legal prohibitions to the contrary (see *State v. Worlock*, 1990).

The Roles of Clinicians in Insanity Defense Cases

Given the nature of the insanity defense in terms of its focus on a mental state existing at the time of the commission of an offense, insanity cases pose a challenge for mental health clinicians who must attempt to evaluate a defendant's mental state at some time in the past, in other words, retrospectively. Studies assessing the reliability of retrospective mental-state examinations are rare, and those assessing their validity are practically nonexistent. The few studies examining the validity of such evaluations typically do so by comparing the evidence reported by expert witnesses and case outcomes in terms of the NGBRI verdict and find concordance rates between 88% and 93% (Daniel & Harris, 1981; Fukunaga, Pasewark, Hawkins, & Gudeman, 1981).

Although both psychiatrists and clinical psychologists are recognized as suitable expert witnesses in insanity defense cases (as are select other mental health professionals, albeit less frequently), they tend to approach criminal responsibility evaluations differently as a function of their respective training and theoretical backgrounds. "Clinical interviews tend to be utilized more readily by psychiatrists, while psychologists seek to obtain their information through interviews, observations, obtainment of collateral information, . . . and the use of objective tests" (Ferguson & Ogloff, 2011, p. 87). Regardless of which type of mental health professional is conducting a criminal responsibility evaluation, some generalizations can be made about best practices.

First, although both the Rorschach and the Minnesota Multiphasic Personality Inventory-2 are commonly used in retrospective mental-state assessment, both fare "poorly at distinguishing between groups of offenders found guilty and those found not criminally responsible" (Ferguson & Ogloff, 2011, p. 87), although the latter test is quite useful in detecting malingering. In contrast, two assessments have been shown to be reliable measures "for retrospectively assessing symptoms and characteristics that are associated with criminal responsibility assessments (p. 87): the Rogers Criminal Responsibility Assessment Scale (R-CRAS; see Rogers, 1984) and the Schedule of Affective Disorders and Schizophrenia (SADS; see Rogers and Cavanaugh, 1981).

Second, completing a responsibility assessment requires numerous steps. Psychiatrists James Knoll IV and Phillip Resnick (2008) developed a framework for mental health clinicians to use while conducting insanity defense evaluations within an evidence-based practice model. Their suggested procedures are presented in Box 11.2.

Third, psychiatrist Alan Felthous (2010) adds another recommendation for clinicians conducting insanity evaluations concerning statutory exclusions. As discussed in detail above, the IDRA and the contemporary insanity defense laws of many states contain specific exclusions of certain diagnoses from qualifying as a "mental disease or defect" for insanity defense purposes. The most common of these exclusions include prohibitions against antisocial, psychopathic, and other forms of moral depravity disorders. Some states specifically exclude other personality disorders as well. Felthous cautions clinicians to be careful not to espouse positions supporting claims of insanity based on these types of psychopathology because doing so "could contribute to the further erosion of the insanity defense" at the expense "of those whose criminal acts are due to psychosis" (p. S140).

Finally, select studies suggest that biological evidence is often persuasive in court rather than psychological evidence (e.g., Rendell, Huss, & Jensen, 2010). Indeed, data suggest that neuroimaging evidence can powerfully affect insanity adjudications. Defendants who demonstrate the existence of a brain lesion, for example, are significantly more likely to be found NGBRI than defendants who do not present any neurological testimony (Gurley & Marcus, 2008). Evidence of brain trauma or significant brain abnormality has also been documented to influence plea bargaining negotiations and mitigate sentences, even in death penalty cases in which the insanity plea was ultimately rejected by the jury (Kulynych, 1997). But care should be taken when presenting neuroimaging evidence because "not all brain lesions and abnormalities indicate a compromised mental state that is relevant to knowing whether the act was wrong at the time of commission, and juries may be swayed by neuroscientific evidence that is not relevant to the determination of the legal question before them" (Batts, 2009, p. 261). Still, as roughly 10% of all insanity acquittees have a diagnosis of a neurologically based psychosis (see Cochrane, Grisso, & Frederick, 2001; Warren, Murrie, et al., 2006), best practices in criminal responsibility evaluations might soon come to include neurological evaluation in addition to psychological assessment.

Post-Verdict Consequences of Insanity Acquittals

The public bases its primary criticism of the insanity defense on the misperception that people found NGBRI go free. Such is not the case; in fact, only about 1% of insanity acquittees are immediately released without any conditions (Silver et al., 1994). In contrast, between 84% and 95% of those found NGBRI are hospitalized, often for very long periods of time (Pasewark, Pantle, & Steadman, 1982; Silver et al., 1994). For example, John Hinckley was acquitted and institutionalized via a NGBRI verdict in 1981. As of the writing of this book more than 33 years later, he is still housed at St. Elizabeth's Hospital in its wing for the criminally insane. John Hinckley's lengthy post-acquittal confinement is the rule, not the exception. Consider that in New York, fewer than 8% of insanity acquittees are released within seven years (New York State Office of Mental Health, 2007).

Most states automatically commit someone found NGBRI for at least a 60-day period and then place the burden on the person committed to show when they are no longer mentally ill and dangerous. The overwhelming

BOX 11.2 STEPS FOR CONDUCTING A CRIMINAL RESPONSIBILITY EVALUATION

Obtain initial fact pattern from consulting agent

Determine if case falls within area of expertise

Obtain correct legal standard

Review collateral data (Review all relevant sources of information)

- Police reports, narratives, interrogations
- Audio or videotape of defendant immediately before, during, or after offense
- Victim and witness statements
- Other relevant observations of the defendant made at the time of the offense
- Crime scene photos and/or visual inspection of crime scene if necessary
- Autopsy report and photos
- Defendant's medical records
- Defendant's psychiatric records
- Other expert evaluations, testimony
- School records
- Military records
- Work records
- Financial records
- Correctional records
- Personal communications (journals, letters, Emails, etc.)
- Collateral interviews if necessary

Forensic interview

- Inform defendant of limits of confidentiality
- Conduct forensic psychiatric evaluation of defendant

Apply relevant legal standards to the facts of the case

Formulate opinion on insanity

Prepare clear, concise report . . .

1. Identification
2. Statement of nonconfidentiality
3. Sources of information
4. Social history
5. Educational history
6. Occupational history
7. Legal history
8. Medical history
9. Family psychiatric history
10. Psychiatric history
11. Substance use history
12. Current medications
13. Current mental status examination

(Continued)

(Continued)

14. Current diagnosis
15. Prior relationship of defendant to victim
16. Defendant's account of offense
17. Witness/victim account of offense
18. Summary of police records
19. Relevant collateral information
20. Opinion on sanity

Give objective testimony. . .

- Educate the court
- Clarify psychiatric issues
- Be honest and objective
- Strive for accuracy
- Offer opinions based on factual data and sound reasoning
- Readily acknowledge limitations

Source: Knoll and Resnick (2008). For the procedure, see Table 2 (p. 96); for the report format, see Table 5 (p. 101); for the method of giving objective testimony, see Table 1 (p. 93).

number of people found NGBRI are confined in mental hospitals for years beyond what they would have served in prison had they been criminally convicted. For example, in New York and California, defendants found NGBRI serve more than double the average length of criminal incarceration (Morris, 1997). And insanity acquittees who committed nonviolent crime are incarcerated for nine times longer than those convicted of similar crimes (Steadman, et al., 1993).

States differ markedly on how long an insanity acquittee may be incarcerated (Davoli, 2005). Some states limit the period of confinement in a mental health facility to no long than the maximum potential sentence would have been if the defendant had been convicted of the offense. But other states impose an indefinite period of treatment, sometimes referred to as a sentence of "one day to life" (see Caffrey, 2005). Under this standard, the defendant who is committed as mentally ill and posing a risk of danger to himself or to others remains committed in that mental institution until he or she is no longer mentally ill or no longer dangerous. Normally, state law presumes a person so committed remains both mentally ill and dangerous and places the burden of proving otherwise on the person committed. Notably, once released from treatment, insanity acquittees recidivate at rates far lower than those convicted of criminal offenses and released from correctional institutions. Miraglia and Hall (2011) found that, in contrast to two-year rearrest rates in New York for 42% of females and 56% males after their release from prison, only 2% of females and 14% of males were rearrested after their release from psychiatric hospitals. Moreover, the years immediately after release are the salient ones; the risk of rearrest drops by half within two years of release, by two-thirds within five years of release, and approached zero by the tenth year.

Summary of the State of the Insanity Defense

Whether the changes that occurred in the aftermath of *Hinckley* have had any significant impact on the rate of acquittals on the basis of insanity is questionable. Most empirical research suggests that changes in the law have had little impact on the overall rate of NGBRI verdicts (e.g., Borum & Fulero, 1999; Finkel, Shaw, Bercaw, & Koch, 1985).

One study by Finkel (1989) that compared the rate of insanity acquittals in California under the ALI/MPC formulation of the insanity defense to the rate following the state's return to the *M'Naghten* rule after the *Hinckley* case found the acquittal rate to have remained relatively constant before and after the legislative change. Finkel used an experimental design in which undergraduate students were presented with scripts whereby five female defendants, each with a unique diagnosis, had been charged with a homicide and pled insanity in her defense. He found that the particular version of the insanity defense that the evaluating students were told to apply did not significantly alter the proportion of defendants determined to be insane in each diagnostic category.

In a simulated trial study, Ogloff (1991) altered not only the actual insanity test used as an experimental condition but also the level of proof required and the side bearing the burden of persuasion. He found no significant differences for the acquittal rate among the experimental conditions. On the other hand, in contrast to those studies examining acquittal rates, at least one study found that the post-*Hinckley* statutory changes to the insanity defense in Georgia and New York resulted in fewer defendants entering insanity pleas in both jurisdictions (Steadman, et al., 1993).

The lack of empirical evidence to support the proposition that IDRA and state changes modeled after it, either in whole or in part, have actually had an effect on the incidence and success rates of the insanity defense is not surprising for a few reasons. First, "generally, in the absence of either exceptionally persuasive or 'objective' evidence, jurors reject the notion that an alleged mental disorder is severe enough to excuse criminal behavior" (Perlin 1990, p., 721). Thus, regardless of the actual formulation of the insanity defense, juries tend to view the defense with skepticism.

Second, when faced with evidence of insanity, jurors, it appears, use their own views or constructs regarding what insanity is:

> [P]erceptions of the defendant's incapacity, awareness, clarity of thinking, ability to control behavior, capability of evil motive, and whether any other person or persons were at fault for the criminal act. . . . Essentially, jurors resort to their own common sense definition of insanity, one that seem[s] much more complex than the simplistic conceptualization of the insane person embodied in the major rules. (Blau & Pasewark, 1994, p. 85)

Finally, and perhaps most important, jurors bring "their own personal sense of justice" to their insanity defense deliberations, including their attitudes "about the morality of the insanity defense and the punishment of mentally ill offenders" (Greene & Heilbrun, 2011, p. 212; see also Finkel, 1995). If so, perhaps there are crimes so heinous that it offends one's sense of justice to the point where one cannot excuse criminal responsibility even in the face of strong evidence of insanity. Consider the sensational criminal prosecutions of Jack Ruby, Sirhan Sirhan, John Wayne Gacy, Jeffrey Dahmer, Charles Manson, Colin Ferguson, and John Salvi. All pled insanity; all were convicted. In contrast, Andrea Yates killed her children by drowning them in a bathtub and was found insane after a second trial. The outcome in her case, however, is the exception and not the rule.

In discussing Jeffrey Dahmer's case, Greene and Heilbrun (2011) wrote that the careful manner in which Dahmer killed his victims so as to reduce his chances of being caught must have left the jury unconvinced that he suffered from a mental disease or defect sufficiently severe to rise to the level of insanity: "This cautiousness suggested that he appreciated the wrongfulness of his behavior *and* could control it when it was opportune for him to do so" (p. 213). Though this explanation of Dahmer's conviction is plausible, it is equally plausible that jurors found what Dahmer did to be so heinous that they refused to acquit him using one of the most liberal of all the formulations of the insanity defense—the one that included the irresistible impulse test. Consider one commentator's summary of the Dahmer case:

> [A]ssuming that there might be degrees of insanity, I do not find it hard to accept that a jury might distinguish between Dahmer and Gacy. Gacy was an otherwise industrious, capable businessman, who carefully prepared in advance to commit numerous murders in secrecy, successfully hiding the bodies and his crimes for years. On the other hand, Dahmer was a maladjusted weirdo who drilled holes in the heads of his living victims for his own scientific purposes, killed a man after police responded to his apartment building and confronted him and his naked and bleeding victim, kept body parts in his closet and refrigerator for extended periods of time, and cannibalized his victims. (Kunkle, 1997, p. 335)

Keep in mind, for comparison purposes, that John Hinckley was acquitted after being found insane under the same formal test for insanity that was rejected in Dahmer's case. The resulting harm in the two cases, however, was quite different. Although John Hinckley tried to kill the president, he did not succeed. His trial was, therefore, one of attempted murder. In contrast, Dahmer killed and dismembered fifteen victims, often had sex with their corpses, and, in some cases, ate parts of their bodies. In spite of the bizarre behaviors exhibited by Dahmer, he was convicted. But if Jeffery Dahmer was not insane, then who is?

Mental Illness and Criminal Responsibility: Diminished Capacity

The insanity defense is one way the law operates to relieve from criminal responsibility those who, as a result of mental illness, do not act with true moral culpability. But there are significant restrictions on the availability of the insanity defense. Consider people who are mentally ill but not "severely" enough to qualify as legally insane under IDRA and its progeny. Alternatively, consider people who are severely mentally ill but still knew both the nature and quality of their acts and the difference between right and wrong. Although the law generally does not recognize such conditions as qualifying for a total excuse defense, defendants with such impairments may not be as culpable as those who are not mentally ill. For such persons, the doctrine of **diminished capacity** might be available to mitigate their criminal responsibility or their sentence; in some circumstances, it might even excuse their criminal responsibility altogether.

Attempting a Definition of Diminished Capacity

Unfortunately, there is no standard definition of diminished capacity. Yet the doctrine exists, either statutorily or in case law, in more than half of all U.S. jurisdictions. Although diminished capacity is often referred to as a defense, this label is somewhat inappropriate. As commentators have often pointed out, it is not a defense at all but rather deals with the admissibility of evidence concerning the accused's mental state (Morse, 1984; Sullivan, 2000). It is most frequently invoked in first-degree murder cases to negate premeditation (Inman, 1989).

Although there are clearly "differing views regarding the meaning and application of the diminished capacity concept," the favored view is that it is "a type of evidence . . . admitted to rebut the specific intent required to convict the defendant of the crime charged" (Falk, 1995, p. 383). In other words, a defendant invoking the diminished capacity doctrine asserts that his or her mental state prevented him or her from forming the requisite *mens rea* for the crime. Without proof of the required *mens rea* element, the defendant should not be convicted of that crime. But the use of diminished capacity evidence to negate the existence of *mens rea* "is not an affirmative defense and does not result in an acquittal unless there is a failure to establish intent for the offense and for all of its lesser-included counterparts" (*State v. Phipps*, 1994, p. 143). Thus, in terms of proving intent, the burden of persuasion remains with the prosecution when a defendant argues diminished capacity; the defendant needs only to create a reasonable doubt with regard to state of mind in order to be acquitted (Sullivan, 2000). Accordingly, diminished capacity is not only easier to use but also much "more likely to succeed than the insanity defense" (Inman, 1989, p. 1299)—a fact may be largely responsible for the trend over the past decade or so for states to restrict or even reject all diminished capacity evidence shy of insanity (see *Clark v. Arizona*, 2006; *People v. Carpenter*, 2001).

The term "diminished capacity" is often used to encompass the related concept of **diminished responsibility**, but they are technically distinct concepts in criminal law. Diminished responsibility is concerned not with whether the defendant had the capacity to form intent but rather with the propriety of his or her punishment (Morse, 2003). Diminished responsibility allows either a jury or a judge to mitigate the punishment of a defendant who is not legally insane but who, as a result of some mental illness or disability, is morally less culpable than someone who commits the same criminal act in the absence of psychiatric impairment.

Diminished responsibility has not been embraced by the courts of the United States but has been in England (Compton, 1997). However, a number of U.S. jurisdictions, the Model Penal Code, and the federal sentencing guidelines allow for the admission of mental abnormality evidence in sentence mitigation. Sentencing courts retain the discretion, however, to discount or even reject evidence of diminished responsibility and to impose punitive sentences from perspectives that favor retribution and incapacitation over deterrence, rehabilitation, or restoration (see *United States v. Garthus*, 2011).

Applying Diminished Capacity

Jurisdictions that recognize diminished capacity vary greatly in the ways in which they permit the doctrine to be used. Some jurisdictions restrict the use of diminished capacity evidence to specific intent crimes. Other states further limit its use to cases in which evidence of diminished capacity might negate the specific intent requirement for murder only. Still other jurisdictions have adopted the Model Penal Code's approach, which allows diminished capacity evidence in any case in which the defendant's mental state is at issue. This approach has been endorsed by the American Bar Association and is the one most frequently followed in those U.S. states recognizing diminished capacity (Compton, 1997; Fradella, 2007). Some states, however, bar all evidence of mental illness for diminished capacity purposes, allowing expert testimony on a defendant's mental state only for insanity defense purposes, as illustrated by *Clark v. Arizona* (2006), summarized in Box 11.3.

Before the defense may introduce any evidence of diminished capacity in jurisdictions that allow courts to consider such evidence, the defendant must first meet a burden of production by providing sufficient evidence of a mental disease or defect that would causally interfere with the ability to form the requisite *mens rea*. Once the burden of production is met, the evidence used to show diminished capacity is essentially the same as the evidence that would be used to show insanity. Generally, the testimony of a mental health clinician is offered at trial to show that the defendant's capacity to form the requisite *mens rea* was "diminished" at the time of the crime due to some mental disease or defect. Such expert testimony must not only be offered by a properly qualified expert but also conform to the other applicable rules of evidence with regard to expert testimony (see Fradella, Fogarty, & O'Neill, 2003).

What Counts as a Predicate Mental Disorder for Diminished Capacity Purposes?

What qualifies as a mental disease or defect in the mounting of an insanity defense is often quite different from what qualifies as a mental disorder when a defendant is claiming diminished capacity. In light of IDRA and the majority of states that adopted its approach, it is clear that significant cognitive impairment is necessary to support a finding of insanity in most of the United States today. In contrast, the spectrum of disorders that potentially qualify as determining diminished capacity is significantly broader. For example, a learning disability generally does not constitute a "mental disease or defect" for insanity purposes. But if a learning-disabled person strikes someone and is unable to know that the blow could kill as a result of his or her disability, he or she might be able to assert diminished capacity to negate the *mens rea* of intent to kill if charged a crime (*State v. Breakiron*, 1987).

The broad scope of what can qualify as diminished capacity is illustrated by *United States v. McBroom* (1997). The defendant in *McBroom* pled guilty to possessing child pornography. At sentencing, he argued for mitigation in his sentence because "he suffered from a significantly reduced mental capacity due to the sexual abuse he had endured as a child, and that this reduced capacity compelled him to possess child pornography" (p. 539). Although the trial court agreed that the defendant had fallen victim to repeated sexual abuse, and suffered from bipolar disorder and multiple impulse control disorders, the circuit court determined that neither the abuse nor the disorders impacted the defendant's cognitive ability (i.e., knowing right from wrong). Therefore, the court held that a downward departure in sentencing was unwarranted. The Third Circuit Court of Appeals reversed, holding that volitional impairment (including impulse control personality disorders) should be considered as evidence of diminished capacity under the U.S. sentencing guidelines when determining the appropriateness of sentence mitigation. However, as stated earlier, once such evidence is considered, it is within a court's discretion to discount or reject such diminished capacity evidence and sentence a defendant from a perspective that embraces retribution and incapacitation over rehabilitation and deterrence perspectives (see *United States v. Garthus*, 2011).

Some jurisdictions have adopted such broad definitions of diminished capacity that a qualifying "mental disease or defect" need not even be recognized by the DSM. One of the leading cases in this area is the New Jersey Supreme Court's opinion in *State v. Galloway* (1993). In *Galloway*, the defendant was convicted of murder and endangering the welfare of a child when he caused the death of his girlfriend's baby by shaking the baby. The intermediate appellate court upheld the conviction, holding that the defendant's borderline personality disorder,

BOX11.3 *CLARK V. ARIZONA*

548 U.S. 735 (2006)

In the early morning hours of June 21, 2000, 17-year-old Eric Clark was driving his pickup truck around a residential neighborhood in Flagstaff, Arizona, with the radio blaring loud music. Police Officer Jeffrey Moritz pulled over Clark's truck in response to complaints. Less than a minute after having approached Clark and having told Clark to "stay where he was," Clark shot the officer and ran away. Before he died, the officer contacted the police dispatcher for help. Clark was apprehended later that day with gunpowder residue on his hands. The gun used to kill the officer was subsequently found close to where Clark had been arrested.

At Clark's trial, friends, family, classmates, and school officials all testified about his "increasingly bizarre behavior over the year before the shooting."

> Witnesses testified, for example, that paranoid delusions led Clark to rig a fishing line with beads and wind chimes at home to alert him to intrusion by invaders, and to keep a bird in his automobile to warn of airborne poison. There was lay and expert testimony that Clark thought Flagstaff was populated with "aliens" (some impersonating government agents), the "aliens" were trying to kill him, and bullets were the only way to stop them. A psychiatrist testified that Clark was suffering from paranoid schizophrenia with delusions about "aliens" when he killed Officer Moritz, and he concluded that Clark was incapable of luring the officer or understanding right from wrong and that he was thus insane at the time of the killing. In rebuttal, a psychiatrist for the State gave his opinion that Clark's paranoid schizophrenia did not keep him from appreciating the wrongfulness of his conduct, as shown by his actions before and after the shooting (such as circling the residential block with music blaring as if to lure the police to intervene, evading the police after the shooting, and hiding the gun). (p. 745)

At trial, Clark admitted that he shot and killed Moritz but contended that he should be excused from criminal responsibility because he suffered from paranoid schizophrenia. Specifically, Clark sought to offer psychiatric evidence both to support an insanity-based defense and to prove that he failed to act with the *mens rea* required for a murder conviction because he was delusional and thought he was shooting an alien. Relying on Arizona state precedent that prohibited diminished capacity evidence, the trial court refused to allow Clark to present evidence of mental illness to rebut *mens rea*, limiting such evidence strictly to consideration of his insanity claim.

Although the trial court determined that Clark "was indisputably afflicted with paranoid schizophrenia at the time of the shooting," it found him guilty nonetheless, concluding that his mental illness "did not . . . distort his perception of reality so severely that he did not know his actions were wrong" (p. 746). The court thus determined Clark had failed to prove he was insane by clear and convincing evidence as required under Arizona's narrow formulation of the "guilty except insane" (GEI) defense. Given the state's bar on diminished capacity evidence, Clark was convicted and sentenced to life in prison with the possibility of parole until after serving 25 years.

Clark challenged his conviction on due process grounds, arguing that Arizona's bar on relevant psychiatric evidence interferes with a criminal defendant's "meaningful opportunity to present a complete defense" (p. 789). Over a strong dissent, a majority of the U.S. Supreme Court rejected this argument and affirmed Clark's conviction. The Court reasoned that the nature of the evidence regarding mental disease and capacity gives rise to several risks that can be diminished "by channeling the consideration of such evidence to the insanity"—namely the "controversial character of some categories of mental disease," "the potential of mental-disease evidence to mislead," and "the danger of according greater certainty to capacity evidence than experts claim for it" (p. 774).

1. Do you agree or disagree with the Court's holding in *Clark* that due process is not violated by forcing criminal defendants to focus all evidence of mental impairment into an insanity defense or otherwise forfeit any defense that might cast reasonable doubt on a defendant's ability to form *mens rea*? Explain your reasoning.
2. Few people, if any, would argue that Clark belongs on the streets. At issue is whether he belongs in prison or in a secure mental hospital where he might receive treatment for his schizophrenia. Unfortunately, Clark now is one of the many severely mentally ill people who will be incarcerated in an inappropriate venue in which his condition is likely only to deteriorate. Mentally ill criminal offenders often receive inadequate treatment for their mental illnesses while incarcerated and, as a result, fail to adapt to life in jail or prison on every measure of psychological adaptation. What can be done to prevent similar outcomes in cases like Eric Clark's in the future?

3. Recall from the materials on insanity that Arizona's "GEI" defense is a very restrictive test for insanity. Do you think the outcome of Clark's case would have been different in a jurisdiction that subscribed to a different test for insanity? If so, explain your reasons for believing a different formulation of the insanity defense would have been to Eric Clark's advantage. If not, however, explain why you believe different formulations of the insanity defense would not have made a difference for Eric Clark.

4. What do you make of the Supreme Court's reasoning that casts doubt on both mental health diagnostic standards and mental health clinicians when it states that evidence concerning psychiatric diagnoses could "mislead jurors"?

even though it rendered the defendant unable to control his impulses, was not a sufficient "mental disease or defect" for diminished capacity purposes. The state high court reversed, holding that "all mental deficiencies, including conditions that cause a loss of emotional control, may satisfy the diminished-capacity defense if the record shows that experts in the psychological field believe . . . that kind of mental deficiency can affect a person's cognitive faculties" (p. 743). As such, whether a mental disease or defect works to impair cognitive function is decided on a case-by-case basis in New Jersey and states that take such a broad approach to diminished capacity evidence.

Finally, it should be noted that some extensions of diminished capacity have led to a backlash against the use of such evidence. The best example of this might be the steps taken in the aftermath of *People v. White* (1979).

> The defendant, Dan White, had been a member of the San Francisco Board of Supervisors. He resigned his position on the Board, but then sought to be reinstated by San Francisco Mayor George Moscone who was responsible for filling vacancies on the Board. Initially, Moscone had assured White that he would be reappointed, but he subsequently wrote White to inform him that "he had made no commitment of any kind to reappoint [White]." Apparently, Moscone changed his mind because one of the other members of the Board of Supervisors, Harvey Milk, opposed White's reappointment. Shortly thereafter, Moscone made arrangements to hold a press conference announcing the appointment of someone else to fill the vacancy created by White's resignation. But, Moscone never had the chance to make the announcement because, less than one hour prior to the time the press conference was scheduled to occur, White repeatedly shot and killed both Mayor Moscone and Supervisor Milk. He was charged with two counts of murder in the first-degree.
>
> At White's trial, three psychiatrists and a psychologist testified that White had become clinically depressed. As part of White's depression, he gorged himself on Twinkies and Coca-Cola. But White was hypoglycemic (a low blood-sugar condition). The sugar and caffeine he ingested caused a brief reactive psychosis that rendered White unable to control his actions. His defense was dubbed the "Twinkie Defense" and it worked! The jury did not convict White of murder, but rather of manslaughter, apparently believing that his capacity was, in fact, diminished as a result of his hypoglycemic reaction to the sugar and caffeine. The public outrage at the successful extension of diminished capacity in the White case eventually led California to statutorily abolish the diminished capacity doctrine in that state. (Fradella, 2007, pp. 66–67)

Other high-profile examples of diminished capacity defenses include the cases of Lorena Bobbit and the Menendez brothers, all of whom argued their formation of *mens rea* was defective in light of their respective histories of abuse. Professor Alan Dershowitz (1994) of Harvard Law School termed these defenses "abuse excuses." He defined an abuse excuse as "the legal tactic by which criminal defendants claim a history of abuse as an excuse for violent retaliation" (p. 3). Such defenses have met with varying success. It worked for Lorena Bobbit in her trial for cutting off her husband's penis after what she described as years of abuse at his hands. In contrast, an abused-based diminished capacity defense was unsuccessful for Lyle and Eric Menendez, both of whom were convicted of killing their parents in spite of their allegations that their father had physically and sexually abused them both for many years. That they shot their parents after lying in wait for them to return home one evening and that they stood to inherit a substantial sum of money upon their parents' death undoubtedly affected the jury's decision.

Proving Diminished Capacity

It is important to note the quickly evolving ways in which diminished capacity and diminished responsibility may be proven. Through the mid- to late-2000s, the overwhelming majority of diminished capacity evidence stemmed from clinical psychological assessments and opinions derived from them. Today, however, clinical neuroscience increasingly provides insight into a person's psychological functioning. For example, PET and fMRI scans (see Chapter 2) can reveal deficits in brain functioning, such as frontal lobe disorders, that are directly relevant to impulse control, aggression, and violence (see Lamparello, 2011–2012). Although people with such impairments still possess the ability to appreciate the wrongfulness of criminal conduct and, therefore, are not legally insane, their capacity to conform their conduct to the requirements of the law is diminished in comparison to those who do not have such disorders.

Neuroscientific evidence has the potential to open new frontiers in determining criminal responsibility. Consider, for example, that an appellate court in Italy reduced a murder sentence after reviewing behavioral genetic data and brain-imaging scans and determining that the evidence demonstrated the defendant's propensity for violence (Feresin, 2009). Whether such evidence meets relevant legal tests for admissibility in the United States remains an open question (see Goldberg, 2012). But the time may be approaching when courts in the United States routinely consider brain-imaging scans, and perhaps even behavioral genetic information as well, to resolve questions of criminal responsibility and determine appropriate sentences.

Conclusion

The interplay between mental illness and the criminal law presents a number of troublesome issues for courts and behavioral scientists alike. The lexicon used by psychologists and psychiatrists differs significantly from that used by judges and lawyers, which often results in confusion over what constitutes a bona fide mental illness and what the impact of any particular diagnosis might be on criminal responsibility. One thing is quite clear, though. The criminal justice system has become more and more hostile to behavioral science evidence offered in support of a claim of incompetency to stand trial, insanity, or diminished capacity, or offered as mitigation evidence at sentencing. This hostility has resulted in some odd situations that range from the ironic to the downright counterproductive and inhumane.

Consider the fact that the diagnoses that support findings of an incapacity to stand trial or that qualify as "mental disease or defects" for insanity defense purposes are quite narrow. Conversely, in many U.S. jurisdictions, a broad range of mental illnesses can be used to support a diminished capacity defense or a diminished responsibility argument in sentencing. This is ironic because it is much easier for a criminal defendant to obtain an acquittal by using diminished capacity evidence to create reasonable doubt concerning *mens rea* than it is to get one through proving insanity by clear and convincing evidence. Moreover, as discussed earlier, insanity acquittees rarely go free; they are usually incarcerated in facilities for the criminally insane—often for much longer than they would have been incarcerated in prison had they been convicted of the crime for which they were charged. In contrast, those who successfully assert diminished capacity evidence can be found "not guilty" in many U.S. jurisdictions, and, as a result, they can be set free.

The public policy and humanitarian impact of the continued narrowing of defenses based on mental illness should also be considered. As the insanity defense becomes narrower (or, in some jurisdictions, nonexistent), there has been a sharp increase in the number of mentally ill people in prisons. Given how the *Clark* Court further limited criminal defendants' ability to argue defenses of excuse within a diminished capacity framework, there is every reason to believe the sad trend of increasingly incarcerating mentally ill people in prisons will continue.

One can only hope that because *Clark* upheld a provision in Arizona law, the decision will have little impact beyond the State of Arizona. But, both the language used in *Clark* and the case's underlying rationale do not bode well for the future of defenses based on mental illness. Indeed, the *Clark* decision calls into question the admissibility of and weight to be accorded to forensic behavioral science evidence. And although that is a shame as the behavioral sciences have much to offer the law, the real tragedy concerns Eric Clark and those like him—mentally ill inmates who burden the correctional system rather than being treated in secure mental hospitals.

KEY TERMS

actus reus

ALI/MPC affective test

competency

competency to stand trial

diminished capacity

diminished responsibility

Durham rule

guilty but mentally ill (GBMI)

guilty except insane (GEI)

insanity

Insanity Defense Reform Act of 1984 (IDRA)

M'Naghten rule

mens rea

mens rea approach

mental disease or defect

synthetic competency

REVIEW QUESTIONS

1. Define competency to stand trial. Explain the legal and practical reasons for continuing to require competency to stand trial today. Given the low threshold for adjudicative competency, do you think the doctrine is serving its intended purposes? Why or why not?
2. Critically evaluate the process of restoring someone to competency to stand trial using psychotropic medications. How might synthetic competency run afoul of the constitutional rights of the accused in insanity defense cases that proceed to trial?
3. Compare and contrast the *M'Naghten* rule, the ALI/MPC affective test for insanity, and the modern federal test for insanity in the IDRA. How are these alike? How are they different? Which do you think is the wisest formulation of the insanity defense? Explain your reasoning.
4. Several states have abolished the insanity defense, limiting evidence of mental disease or defect to the question of formation of criminal intent. Evaluate the *mens rea* approach as it may apply in cases in which the defendant suffered from severe delusions.
5. Reflecting on the research presented in Chapters 3 through 10, critique the concept of "mental disease or defect" as used in both the insanity and diminished capacity contexts.

12

Law and the Control of "Dangerousness"

Applications and Implications

MICHAEL CRANE

On January 6, 1993, Michael Crane exposed himself to an attendant at a tanning salon, which subsequently resulted in his being convicted of lewd and lascivious conduct. On the same afternoon as the tanning salon incident, Crane went into a video store and waited until he was the only customer in the store. He then grabbed the clerk and, with his genitals exposed, he lifted and pushed her and squeezed her neck with his hands. Three times, Crane ordered her to perform oral sex on him. He also told the clerk that he was going to rape her. At one point, though, Crane stopped his attack and ran out of the store. He was arrested and subsequently pled guilty to aggravated sexual battery.

After Crane served four years of a prison sentence, Kansas sought to have him civilly committed under the state's Sexually Violent Predator Act. The Act provides for the commitment of persons determined to be sexually violent predators. A "sexually violent predator" is defined in the statute as "any person who has been convicted of or charged with a sexually violent offense and who suffers from a mental abnormality or personality disorder which makes the person likely to engage in repeat acts of sexual violence." At a hearing, a psychologist testified that Crane met the diagnostic criteria for both exhibitionism and antisocial personality disorder. Although exhibitionism alone does not necessarily render someone dangerous, the combination of the two disorders supported a finding that Crane was a sexual predator as evidenced by the "increasing frequency of incidents involving Crane, increasing intensity of the incidents, Crane's increasing disregard for the rights of others, and his increasing daring and aggressiveness" (*In re Crane*, 2000, p. 287). A psychiatrist testified that he concurred with the assessment of dangerousness as a function of the antisocial finding based upon substantial evidence that a defendant such as Crane "cannot control his dangerous behavior" (p. 290). Since Crane "did not admit that his sexual behavior was on account of an irresistible urge," and because there was no finding that Crane was "unable to control his behavior," the court concluded Crane could not be committed as a sexual predator.

The U.S. Supreme Court then reviewed the case and determined that the Kansas high court had construed this self-governing precedent too narrowly. The Court acknowledged that the "inability to control behavior" is not "demonstrable with mathematical precision." However, the Court concluded, "It is enough to say that there must be proof of serious difficulty in controlling behavior. And this, when viewed in light of such features of the case as the nature of the psychiatric diagnosis, and the severity of the mental abnormality itself, must be sufficient to distinguish the dangerous sexual offender whose serious mental illness, abnormality, or disorder subjects him to civil commitment from the dangerous but typical recidivist convicted in an ordinary criminal case" (*Kansas v. Crane*, 2002, p. 413). Because Crane admitted that he had previously molested children and could not "control the urge" to do so, the U.S. Supreme Court vacated the decision of the Kansas Supreme Court and remanded the case to the state courts for disposition.

As explored in Chapter 11, people with seriously mentally illnesses (SMIs) who commit crimes can avail themselves of defenses of criminal excuse, such as insanity or diminished capacity. But these cases are few and far between. Recall that insanity is pled in less than 1% of felony cases and is unsuccessful the vast majority of the time (Chapter 11). What should be done with mentally ill offenders for whom defenses of excuse are either unavailable (as a function of non-qualifying diagnoses) or unsuccessful? Upon release from criminal incarceration, some of these offenders, like Michael Crane, still pose a high risk of dangerousness to the community. What should be done with such people? And might there be interventions that can be applied to prevent people who are mentally ill and dangerous from committing crimes in the first place? This chapter explores how both the civil and criminal justice systems attempt to control socially people with mental illness who are dangerous but not legally insane.

Civil Commitment

When mentally ill people are arrested for committing criminal offenses, they are taken into custody pursuant to the state's **police power**—the authority of the state to confine those who endanger society (Dubber, 2005). The exercise of police power has a long history of due process protections when used in the criminal setting, such as trials and the associated protections afforded the criminal defendant both statutorily and constitutionally (see Ferdico, Fradella, & Totten, 2013). The same, however, cannot be said for the exercise of state power when the government seeks to hospitalize a mentally ill person against his or her will—a process known as **civil commitment**.

The word "civil" is part of the term "civil commitment" because the procedures for the involuntary commitment of someone are civil procedures not criminal ones. The government's authority to commit a person stems from not only its police power but also its ***parens patriae*** power (Cornwell, 1998; *Kansas v. Hendricks*, 1997). Literally translated from the Latin as "the state as parent," *parens patriae* has historically been "premised on the presumed incapacity of minors and mentally disabled persons to protect or care for themselves" (Winick, 1992, p. 1772). The doctrine provides the state with the ability to impinge upon the autonomy rights of minors and incompetent people because such people are ostensibly incapable of engaging in the rational decision-making processes in which the law presumes people engage (*Addington v. Texas*, 1979; Cornwell, 1998). Although the exercise of this power is presumably beneficent (i.e., in the best interest of the person), it is an inherently coercive power as evidenced by the fact that is has been used to justify the forced medication of inmates (*Washington v. Harper*, 1990) and the involuntary civil commitment of the mentally ill who pose a danger to themselves or to others (*In re Oakes*, 1845; *O'Connor v. Donaldson*, 1975).

Historical Background of Civil Commitment[1]

Since the founding of the United States, people with mental illnesses were often confined in jails rather than hospitals. That slowly began to change in the 1820s and 1830s with early reform efforts in Massachusetts. Between 1840 and 1880, the first wave of major reforms to the way the mentally ill were treated had taken firm root.

1. This section is adapted from Fradella, H. F., & Smith-Casey, R. (2013). Criminal justice responses to the mentally ill. In S. A. Mallicoat & C. Gardiner (Eds.), *Criminal justice policy* (pages 201–224). Thousand Oaks, CA: Sage.

Advances in the behavioral sciences in the early twentieth century spurred a second wave of reforms that produced little fruit. Advances in psychiatry in the 1950s and 1960s ushered in a third wave of reform efforts that produced profound effects; most notable was the advent of psychotropic medication that allowed the mentally ill to lead lives outside the walls of institutions.

First-Wave Reform Efforts: From Jails and Prisons to Asylums. In the early 1800s, Louis Dwight, a Massachusetts minister, began a crusade to improve the shockingly inhumane conditions in which he saw mentally ill offenders living when he delivered Bibles to prisoners. His efforts led the state legislature first to appoint a commission to investigate his claims and then to enact a law making it illegal to confine the mentally ill in jails rather than in hospitals (Grob, 1966, as cited in Torrey, Kennard, Eslinger, Lamb, & Pavle, 2010). A few years later, Massachusetts constructed the Worcester Lunatic Hospital to house up to 120 patients.

In the early 1840s, Dorothea Dix began to build upon Dwight's early efforts. As a nurse, she witnessed the atrocious conditions under which inmates with mental illnesses lived, such as people experiencing psychotic symptoms being caged and whipped in futile efforts to control their behavior (Viney & Zorich, 1982). Dix eventually visited upwards of 300 jails and 18 state prisons, documenting the cruel treatment of the mentally ill incarcerated therein (Dix, 1975, as cited in Torrey et al., 2010). Although her views were radical for the time—largely as a function of her era predating the dawn of modern psychology and psychiatry—through her presentation of detailed case studies, Dix successfully convinced policy makers that more human conditions for the mentally ill could lead to their improved functioning. By the time she died in 1887, she had visited every state east of the Mississippi River and 13 European countries (Viney & Zorich, 1982). Dix's efforts on both sides of the Atlantic are credited with facilitating the construction of 32 psychiatric hospitals and 15 schools for the "feeble minded" across the eastern United States. She also had a great impact on reform efforts in Europe (Viney & Zorich, 1982). According to Torrey and colleagues (2010), her reform efforts were so successful that by 1880, the U.S. Census "identified 40,942 'insane persons' in 'hospitals and asylums for the insane'" but only "397 'insane persons' in jails and prisons, constituting less than1 percent (0.7 percent) of the jail and prison population" at that time (p. 14). Largely as a result of her accomplishments, the *Encyclopedia of Human Behavior* describes Dorothea Dix as "the most effective advocate of humanitarian reform in American mental institutions during the nineteenth century" (Goldenson, 1970, p. 341).

The reforms championed by Dwight, Dix, and their colleagues were based primarily on moral arguments about the ethical treatment of people with mental illness. These reform efforts brought long-lasting changes. The movement's emphasis on caring for the mentally ill fostered acceptance of a medical-psychological model of mental illness, which replaced theories of demonic possession that had prevailed until that time (Grob, 1966; Morrissey & Goldman, 1986). This change, in turn, led to the establishment of **asylums** that were supposed to offer compassionate treatment of the mentally ill.

Asylums. The spread of asylums was effective in moving those with mental illnesses out of jails and prisons and into treatment facilities. Indeed, until the 1960s, most studies found similar prevalence rates (i.e., less than 2%) of the mentally ill in jails and prisons as were reported in the 1880 Census (e.g., Bromberg & Thompson, 1937). Those with mental illnesses "were treated as patients, not as criminals, and were sent to mental hospitals [even though] the hospitals had little treatment to offer them at that time" (Torrey et al., 2010, p. 14). Sadly, though, the goal of providing compassionate treatment to people with mental illness was never fully realized.

Asylums actually predate the first-wave reform movement. The first public asylum, Eastern State Hospital, was created in 1773 in Williamsburg, Virginia (*The New York Times*, 1900). But most early asylums established in the United States were created by Protestants whose religious convictions led them to believe that it was their religious duty to care for "the less fortunate members of society" (Morrissey & Goldman, 1986, p. 14). Many of these asylums established a patient-care model based on the principles espoused by the Quakers at the time, who believed that people with SMIs should be treated "in a comfortable, clean, family atmosphere, in the tranquil surroundings of a country house" (Parry-Jones, 1988, p. 408). Indeed, the term "asylum" stems from the notion of a place of refuge—"a quiet haven in which the shattered bark might find a means of reparation or of safety" (p. 408). This philosophy guided most of the private asylums throughout the 1800s. Public asylums generally were created with the expectation that this same patient-care model would exist within them. But lack of public funding and insufficient staffing led public asylums to become sprawling, overcrowded places in which people with mental illnesses lived in "bleak, impoverished wards" that served merely as custodial institutions rather than treatment facilities (p. 408; see also Morrissey & Goldman, 1986). Moreover, as the U.S. population increased, demand for the custodial placement of those with mental illnesses rose. As a result, the wealthy largely turned to the private, pastoral facilities while the poor filled public asylums, which became human warehouses that served as "a general-purpose solution to the welfare burdens of a society undergoing rapid industrialization and stratification along social, class, and ethnic lines" (Morrissey & Goldman, 1986, p. 17). In other words, treatment became a concern secondary to low-cost custody and community protection (Rothman, 1970).

Second-Wave Reform Efforts: The Rise of Psychiatry and Psychology. Around the turn of the twentieth century, a scientific approach to mental illness began to take firm hold. Scientific advances in neurology, psychiatry, psychology, and social work were spawned as a result of the work of researchers such as Adolf Meyer and William James. Their work focused on the therapeutic treatment of mental disorders, "especially by early intervention in acute cases" (Morrissey & Goldman, 1986, p. 18; see also Deutsch, 1944).

Second-wave reform efforts led to the creation of "psychopathic hospitals" for the acute treatment of people with mental illnesses; most of these hospitals were affiliated with research universities (Morrissey & Goldman, 1986). Other mental health facilities, mostly clinics, were created as a result of the increasing medicalization of mental illness care. But these facilities, like the psychopathic hospitals, were designed to provide acute care; patients who needed long-term care were eventually sent to state asylums where they received little, if any, real care.

Some have argued that the various forms of mental institutions that operated between the late 1800s and the mid-1900s were driven primarily by the humanitarian concern of caring for those with mental illness (e.g., Grob, 1994; Ziff, 2004). Others, however, have argued that asylums and mental hospitals primarily served the social control function of reinforcing individual conformity with prevailing societal expectations—especially in poor, immigrant populations (e.g., Foucault, 1965; Rothman, 1970; Scull, 1991). Whatever the motivations of reformers, public mental hospitals proliferated in the first half of the twentieth century, and their patient population ballooned from 150,000 in 1903 to 512,000 in 1950—"a rate of growth nearly twice as large as the rate of increase in the U.S. population as a whole" (Morrissey & Goldman, 1986, p. 19). Moreover, in spite of scientific advances in the behavioral sciences, most state facilities remained primarily custodial in nature, providing long-term custody not only to those with mental illnesses but also to the poor and disabled who could not care for themselves.

Third-Wave Reform Efforts: The Community Mental Health Movement. The third wave of reform is referred to as the **community mental health (CMH) movement**. CMH efforts emerged in the aftermath of World War II as a function of several significant factors. First, new psychosocial techniques developed during the war to provide acute care for those in military service proved to be successful on the front lines (Morrissey & Goldman, 1986). Psychiatrists who returned to practice after serving in the military brought these techniques back and taught others in state mental hospitals how to use them. Second, an increased understanding of the importance of aftercare led mental hospitals to open outpatient clinics to serve those who were discharged after inpatient treatment while, at the same time, regular hospitals opened acute psychiatric care units (Linn, 1961; Morrissey & Goldman, 1986). Third, the federal government enacted a series of laws that not only established the National Institute of Mental Health but also created far-reaching policies to foster mental health in the United States (Foley & Sharfstein, 1983; Morrissey & Goldman, 1986). Fourth, charges of neglect, abuse, and dehumanizing conditions in many state-run mental hospitals—like those described in landmark sociological studies such as Ervin *Goffman's Asylums* (1961) and those depicted in the movie *One Flew Over the Cuckoo's Nest* (Douglas, Zaentz, & Forman, 1975)—led civil libertarians and other activists to advocate for sweeping reforms in the ways in which those with mental illnesses were treated. And perhaps most important, new psychotropic medications were introduced in the 1950s and 1960s (Talbott, 1982). These antipsychotic drugs—including Haldol, Mellaril, Moban, Navane, Trifalon, Prolixin, Stelazine, and Thorazine—altered brain chemistry by regulating neurotransmitters. In doing so, these drugs enhanced clarity of thought in those affected by psychosis while also permitting them to control emotions so as to prevent these from interfering with rational thought processes. These developments led to the widespread release of the mentally ill through deinstitutionalization policies, which sought to reintroduce these patients to the community for supportive services.

The CMH movement spurred civil liberties activists to seek tightening of the means by which the mentally ill could be involuntarily committed, in other words, changes to civil commitment legislation. Prior to the 1950s, most states had only loose protections for a person others sought to have involuntarily hospitalized for psychiatric treatment. "Some jurisdictions statutorily authorized civil commitment for those persons defined as being a 'social menace' or 'a fit and proper candidate for institutionalization'" (Fradella, 2008, p. 1972). Others authorized the "confinement of insane persons 'manifestly suffering from want of proper care or treatment'" (Cornwell, 1998, pp. 380–381). Indeed, this "in need of treatment" standard was adopted in roughly half the states between 1869 and the 1960s (p. 381). It should come as no surprise that, under such amorphous standards, there was much discretion built into the system to confine people involuntarily (Grob, 1973), which, in turn, often resulted in arbitrary and unnecessary commitments (Winick, 1999). Moreover, this broad authority was frequently used, as is illustrated by the statistic that more than a half a million people were civilly confined in 1955 (Goldman, Adams, & Taube, 1983).

The advent of antipsychotic medicines and the social movements of the 1960s, of which the CMH movement was just one, fostered both legislatures and the courts to begin recognizing that people with mental illnesses possessed a range of liberty interests protected by the U.S. Constitution, including "community-situated treatment, due process procedural protections, the right to treatment, medical and constitutional minimal standards in treatment, and the right to refuse treatment" (Arrigio, 1992/1993, pp. 139–140). By the 1970s, most states had tightened their civil commitment laws such that mental illness alone, even if serious, would not suffice. Rather, someone could only be involuntarily committed for treatment if a court found, by clear and convincing evidence, that the person represented a danger to himself or herself or to others (see *Addington v. Texas*, 1979).

Contemporary Civil Commitment Standards

Involuntary civil commitment serves two goals: (1) the rehabilitation or care of people who are mentally ill, an aim stipulated by the state's *parens patriae* power, and (2) the protection of society from the potential harms such a person may cause, a purpose required under the state's police power (Levy, Rubenstein, Ennis, & Friedman, 1996). But confining someone against his or her will raises serious due-process concerns. After all, civil commitment involves not only the "massive curtailment of liberty" attendant to involuntary hospitalization but also significant restrictions on patients within the hospital (*Humphrey v. Cady*, 1972, p. 509). In light of these significant infringements of a person's liberty interests, the U.S. Supreme Court held in *O'Connor v. Donaldson* (1975) that due process prohibits the involuntary hospitalization of any person who is not both mentally ill and dangerous. In *Zinermon v. Burch* (1990), the Court reaffirmed the principle that the involuntary confinement of a mentally ill individual who does not pose a threat of harm and who can survive outside of a mental hospital is unconstitutional. Although seemingly straightforward, many of the terms used in the cases setting the constitutional boundaries of civil commitment are quite nebulous. In fact, debates permeate both civil commitment case law and scholarship about who is mentally ill, what constitutes dangerousness, what procedural rights must be honored during litigation over these standards, and what protections apply after judicial determinations on civil commitment.

Mental Illness in the Eyes of the Law. What is a mental illness? How does it differ from a "mental disorder" or a "mental disease or defect," or a "mental abnormality"? That theorists, researchers, and practitioners in the field of psychology have struggled with finding suitable and appropriate definitions is illustrated by the five ways in which mental illness has been defined throughout history: deviation from social expectations, what mental health professionals treat, subjective distress, a label for disliked actions, and a dysfunction that causes harm (see Chapter 2). Differing definitions in the legal arena demonstrate that the concept of mental illness has been equally elusive in the law.

Unfortunately, both civil and criminal law in the United States often use differing terms. Sometimes, those terms are used interchangeably to mean the same thing; at other times, a specific term is used in either a more expansive or more restrictive way than is another term (Slobogin, 2003b). The result is a hodgepodge of labels that can be at odds with the language used by psychiatry and psychology (see Winick, 1995a).

Recall from Chapter 1 that the American Psychiatric Association's listing of diagnoses is titled the *Diagnostic and Statistical Manual of Mental Disorders* (or, currently, DSM-5: APA, 2013). As the title indicates, "mental disorders" is the preferred term of the behavioral sciences. But, as explained in Chapter 11, the criminal law uses different terms when assessing competency to stand trial, insanity, and diminished capacity. In contrast, most civil commitment statutes use the term "mental illness" (Cohen, Bonnie, & Monahan, 2009). But even that term is defined differently across U.S. jurisdictions. Consider, for example, the variability in the definitions used in four U.S. states:

- "Mental illness" means an organic disorder of the brain or a clinically significant disorder of thought, mood, perception, orientation, memory, or behavior that is listed in the clinical manual of the *International Classification of Diseases* (ICD-9-CM), current edition, code range 290.0 to 302.99 or 306.0 to 316.0 or the corresponding code in the American Psychiatric Association's *Diagnostic and Statistical Manual of Mental Disorders*, current edition, Axes I, II, or III, and that seriously limits a person's capacity to function in primary aspects of daily living such as personal relations, living arrangements, work, and recreation. (Minnesota Statutes Annotated § 245.462[20], Supp. 2012)
- "Mental illness" means a current, substantial disturbance of thought, mood, perception or orientation which significantly impairs judgment, capacity to control behavior or capacity to recognize reality, but does not include simple alcohol intoxication, transitory reaction to drug ingestion, organic brain syndrome or developmental disability unless it results in the severity of impairment described herein. The term mental illness is not limited to "psychosis" or "active psychosis," but shall include all conditions that result in the severity of impairment described herein. (New Jersey Statutes Annotated § 30:4–27.2, Supp. 2012)
- "Mental illness" means an illness, disease, or condition, other than epilepsy, senility, alcoholism, or mental deficiency, that: (A) substantially impairs a person's thought, perception of reality, emotional process, or judgment; or (B) grossly impairs behavior as demonstrated by recent disturbed behavior. (Vernon's Texas Statutes and Codes Annotated, Health & Safety Code § 571.003, Supp. 2012)
- "Mental illness" means a substantial disorder of thought, mood, perception, orientation, or memory, any of which grossly impairs judgment, behavior, capacity to recognize reality, or ability to meet the ordinary demands of life, but shall not include mental retardation. (18 Vermont Statutes Annotated § 7101[14], Supp. 2012)

Major Clinical Disorders. As with laws governing competency to stand trial, insanity, and diminished capacity (Chapter 11), the four statutes quoted above should make clear that most major clinical disorders—such as schizophrenia, major depression, bipolar disorder, dissociative disorders, and anxiety disorders—qualify as mental illnesses for civil commitment purposes. It is important to note, though, that any such diagnosis must produce impairment that is significant enough to meet the relevant statutory requirement.

> For example, the symptoms of depression (such as sadness, nihilistic thinking, suicidal thoughts, and cognitive impairment) in major depressive disorder can range in severity, from being so mild that the individual is able to continue to meet all social and occupational demands to being so severe that the individual is acutely psychotic or catatonic. In addition, some mental illnesses (such as panic disorder) can present with symptoms that are more circumscribed, such that they are severe but nonetheless do not impair judgment, behavior, the capacity to recognize reality, etc. Therefore, an individual would not be subject to civil commitment unless (1) he or she has a mental illness, (2) the symptoms of the illness are significant enough to impair the individual's functioning as described above, and (3) he or she presents a risk of harm, specifically "as a result of mental illness" (as opposed to posing a chronic threat of harm for unrelated reasons). (Cohen, Bonnie, & Monahan, 2009, pp. 129–130)

Notably, there are a number of major clinical disorders—including adjustment disorders, eating disorders, impulse control disorders, and sexual disorders—that do not qualify as "mental diseases or defects" for insanity-defense purposes but do qualify as "mental illnesses" for the purposes of civil commitment. For example, a diagnosis of pyromania or pedophilia would not provide a basis to invoke the insanity defense in an attempt to excuse the crimes of arson or child molestation. However, because civil commitment is targeted at preventing harms that are caused by people who are both mentally ill and dangerous, such diagnoses constitute mental illnesses for civil commitment purposes (see *Kansas v. Hendricks*, 1997).

Substance-Related Disorders. Just as the Texas statute quoted above specifies, most states exclude drug and alcohol abuse, without more, from qualifying as "mental illnesses" for the purposes of civil commitment, even though they are recognized "mental disorders" in the DSM. However, as Cohen, Bonnie, and Monahan (2009) explain,

> chronic substance use, acute substance intoxication, and/or substance withdrawal all constitute important risk factors in assessing an individual's risk either of causing serious physical harm to himself or others or suffering serious harm due to a lack of capacity to protect himself from harm or provide for his basic human needs. . . . Substance abuse in its more severe forms can cause mood swings similar to those seen in major depressive disorder (including hopelessness and suicidal ideation), can cause psychotic symptoms (including voices telling one to kill himself), and can cause cognitive impairment as severe as that seen in other forms of dementia. (p. 130)

New Jersey's statute explicitly recognizes this point by excluding substance-related disorders from qualifying as mental illnesses for civil commitment purposes unless they are severe enough to cause significant impairment along the lines of other qualifying mental illnesses.

In contrast, a few states specifically include substance abuse in their civil commitment statutes, as illustrated by Minnesota's statute, quoted above. Hawaii also includes substance-related disorders but limits civil commitment only to those who are "imminently dangerous to self or others" or "gravely disabled," provided that "the person is in need of care or treatment, or both, and there is no suitable alternative available through existing facilities and programs which would be less restrictive than hospitalization" (Hawaii Revised Statutes § 334–60.2, Supp. 2012).

Developmental Disabilities. Many states have adopted statutes that specifically exclude the diagnosis of intellectual disability (formerly mental retardation) from the definition of mental illness for civil commitment. The Vermont and Texas statutes quoted above illustrate this approach. Other states, as demonstrated by New Jersey's statute, exclude developmental disabilities unless they are severe enough to cause significant impairment along the lines of other qualifying mental illnesses. And still other states, such as Minnesota, include developmental disabilities as qualifying mental illnesses for the purpose of civil commitment.

Personality Disorders. Most states either specifically include personality disorders, as the New Jersey and Minnesota statutes quoted above do, or, like the Texas and Vermont statutes, do not specifically exclude personality disorders from qualifying as mental illnesses for civil-commitment purposes. Accordingly, people with severe personality disorders who are significantly impaired qualify for civil commitment in most states. Cohen, Bonnie, and Monahan (2009) illustrate the propriety of this approach using borderline personality disorder.

> A severe personality disorder, such as borderline personality disorder, is associated with marked instability in interpersonal relationships, self-image, moods, and impulse-control. While most individuals with the diagnosis of borderline personality disorder are treated as outpatients, during periods of interpersonal crisis and/or in the context of other superimposed psychiatric problems such as mood disorder or substance abuse, they pose an increased risk of engaging in potentially harmful behavior toward themselves or others. Twenty percent of psychiatric inpatients meet the diagnostic criteria for borderline personality disorder, and 10% of individuals with borderline personality disorder ultimately die by suicide. An individual with a more severe form of personality disorder who is experiencing impairment in "judgment, behavior, capacity to recognize reality, or ability to address basic life necessities," therefore, would be potentially appropriate for civil commitment. (p. 130)

In contrast to personality disorders capable of causing the type of impairment that is possible with borderline personality disorder, antisocial personality disorder generally does not cause grave disability. Thus, antisocial personality disorder, in itself, would not qualify as a mental illness for civil commitment purposes. Accordingly, some states, e.g., Kansas and Arizona, have specifically excluded this diagnosis from their civil commitment statutes (Arizona Revised Statutes § 36–501[26][c], Supp. 2012; Kansas Statutes Annotated § 59–2646[f][1], Supp. 2012]).

Medical Conditions With Psychiatric Symptoms. Some medical conditions, such as various types of dementia or select traumatic brain injuries, can cause severe impairment of psychological functioning. "Medical conditions and psychiatric diagnoses are not mutually exclusive under the modern understanding that mental illnesses (the more severe ones at least) have a biological basis" (Cohen, Bonnie, & Monahan, 2009, p. 131). Accordingly, some states have enacted statutes, like Minnesota's, that specifically include such medial conditions in the definition of what constitutes mental illness for the purpose of civil commitment. Other states, like Texas, exclude "senility" from their statutes.

Dangerousness. As mentioned, *O'Connor v. Donaldson* (1975) established the "danger to self or others" standard used in civil commitments. The case illustrates the need for reform that existed in the 1970s. Kenneth Donaldson had been committed to a state mental hospital for 15 years after a judge determined that he suffered from paranoid schizophrenia. During his confinement, Donaldson repeatedly, but unsuccessfully, sought release by presenting his case to hospital staff. When he finally turned to the courts, testimony established that he did not pose any danger to others, had never been suicidal, and had responsible people willing to help him if he were released. Ultimately, these facts led the Supreme Court to conclude that "a State cannot constitutionally confine, without more, a nondangerous individual who is capable of surviving safely in freedom by himself or with the help of willing and responsible family members or friends" (p. 576). Within a few years, the Court clarified its decision in *Donaldson* by holding that the Due Process Clause of the Fourteenth Amendment prohibits the involuntary hospitalization of anyone who is not both mentally ill and dangerous (*Jones v. United States, 1983*). But the Court never defined what "dangerous" means in the context of civil commitments, leading states to adopt varying approaches to the determination.

Traditional Dangerousness. The traditional approach to determining **dangerousness** in support of a civil commitment uses one or more of three distinct criteria: the type of danger, the immediacy of the danger, and the likelihood of the danger.

> The *type of danger* refers to the category of the harm. Examples include bodily harm, threat of bodily harm, and property damage. *Immediacy* accounts for when the danger will occur. Some statutes, for example, require "imminent" danger or danger in the "near future." As these forecasts project further into the future, uncertainty and the risk of error increase. The *likelihood of the danger* refers to the accuracy of the dangerousness prediction. Because studies have found that such predictions are more accurate when based on prior overt acts, some states require evidence of similar dangerous behavior in the respondent's recent past. (Ferris, 2008, pp. 966–967; italics added and internal citations omitted)

Applying these three dimensions of dangerousness can be a confounding process that blends legal standards with the art and science of clinical evaluation, two perspectives that do not mesh well. Until fairly recently, "'imminent dangerousness' was the gold standard for defining the criteria for civil commitment" (Klein, 2012, p. 567). But such a restrictive standard can have disastrous consequences, as the case of Seung Hui Cho demonstrates.

At age 23, Seung Hui Cho went on a shooting spree at the campus of Virginia Tech, killing 32 students and faculty members and injuring 17 others before killing himself (Report of the Virginia Tech Review Panel, 2007). Approximately 16 months prior to the shooting, Cho's strange behavior led the Virginia Tech Police Department to have Cho temporarily detained as an "imminent danger to self or others" and transported to a state psychiatric hospital "for an overnight stay and mental evaluation" (p. 23). Both a psychologist and a psychiatrist at this hospital, however, concluded that, although Cho needed treatment, he did not present an imminent danger to himself or others that was sufficient to warrant involuntary hospitalization (p. 23). A judicial officer adopted the recommendations of the mental health experts that Cho not be committed but rather receive follow-up treatment as an outpatient. Cho resumed classes at Virginia Tech, where he continued to manifest inappropriate behavior ranging from heated arguments with professors to creative writing assignments about "a young man who hates the students at his school and plans to kill them and himself" (p. 23). On April 16, 2007, he committed the worst school shooting in U.S. history.

Seung Hui Cho, like many—if not most—people released to the community with orders for treatment, often failed to receive that treatment. In some ways, Cho's case is somewhat distinct insofar as his troubling behavior while he was a student at Virginia Tech prompted police to take him into custody and send him for psychiatric evaluation. The panel investigating the Virginia Tech shootings concluded that university officials could and should have done more to protect their students by making legal use of the documented risks Cho posed to their campus community (Report of the Virginia Tech Review Panel, 2007). Perhaps the behaviors exhibited by people like Adam Lanza and James Holmes (Chapter 1) should have caused people in their lives to ask questions and seek appropriate treatment for them, even if that meant seeking their involuntary civil commitment; tragically, that did not occur for either of them. But even if people close to Lanza or Holmes had taken such steps, there can be no doubt that families and friends of people with SMIs experience major challenges in securing the treatment they feel is necessary—a situation that is exacerbated to almost inordinately difficult proportions when they seek civil commitment, "even when their families or caregivers feel threatened and patients appear extremely sick" (Cornell, as cited in Szabo, 2013; see also Husted & Nehemkis, 1995).

In some ways, it is unfair to focus on people such as Lanza, Holmes, and Cho because so few people with untreated SMIs commit mass killings. On the other hand, research suggests that the high standards for civil commitment, the shortage of access to psychiatric inpatient beds, and poor community mental health services all contribute to higher homicide rates (Segal, 2012). In Virginia, these conditions certainly served as a barrier to Seung Hui Cho getting the treatment he desperately needed—treatment that may have prevented the Virginia Tech tragedy. Indeed, a blue-ribbon review panel concluded that the "imminent danger" standard employed under Virginia law not only prevented Cho from receiving effective treatment but also failed to protect the community. Accordingly, the panel recommended that the state adopt a less restrictive commitment standard and replace the "imminent danger" threshold with "language requiring 'a substantial likelihood' or 'significant risk' that the person will cause serious injury to himself or others 'in the near future'" (Report of the Virginia Tech Review Panel, 2007, p. 56). In the wake of the Virginia Tech shooting, Virginia adopted the panel's recommendation and removed the statutory requirement of imminent danger; all but four other states have done the same (Klein, 2012; Mossman, Schwartz, & Elam, 2012; Pfeffer, 2008).

Although the focus on "imminent danger" in the case of Seung Hui Cho may have been largely responsible for his not being involuntarily hospitalized for treatment, determinations of dangerousness under other legal standards are still fraught with the possibility of error (Levy et al., 1996). Of course, psychiatry and psychology are not exact sciences. Nonetheless, for many years, unstructured clinical assessments of future dangerousness were the norm in risk assessment (Campbell, French, & Gendreau, 2009). Numerous studies indicated that such unstructured clinical predictions of dangerousness were incorrect two out of three times, yielding an error rate worse than that predicted by chance (for a review, see Monahan, 1981; see also Faust & Ziskin, 1988; Monahan & Steadman, 1994). But since the time these studies were published, risk assessment has improved and, as a result, recent violence risk prediction studies provide cause for some optimism (Grisso & Tomkins, 1996). The improved outlook is, in large part, a function of tools providing more structural decision making in clinical assessments and of integrating actuarial risk assessments into clinical practice (Monahan, 2002; Otto, 1994). Forensic risk assessment is explored in great detail later in this chapter.

Passive Dangerousness. Approximately 44 U.S. states interpreted the *O'Connor v. Donaldson*'s (1975) "danger to self" standard as encompassing various types of self-inflicted harm and, therefore, included so-called "passive dangerousness" provisions in their civil commitment statutes. These provisions allow for the involuntary hospitalization of people who are **gravely disabled**. The American Psychiatric Association (1983) defines a gravely disabled person as someone who

> is substantially unable to provide for some of his basic needs, such as food, clothing, shelter, health, or safety or [who] will, if not treated, suffer or continue to suffer severe mental and abnormal mental, emotional, or physical distress, and this distress is associated with significant impairment of judgment, reason, or behavior causing a substantial deterioration of his previous ability to function on his own. (p. 673)

Just as many states have abandoned the imminent dangerousness requirement for traditional dangerousness determinations, many states have also revised their approaches to passive dangerousness as well. Gravely disabled provisions in about 17 states' civil commitment laws now include "need for treatment" provisions (Mossman et al., 2012); reflect "an understanding that people who are mentally ill are a danger to themselves if they are unable to provide for their basic needs or if they are likely to deteriorate without treatment" (Klein, 2012, p. 569). For example, roughly one-third of U.S. states allow people to be involuntarily hospitalized to prevent deterioration of their mental state, such as "escalating loss of cognitive or volitional control" (Mossman et al., 2012, p. 384).

The Process That Is Due. Recall that *Addington v. Texas* (1979) requires the state seeking an involuntary commitment to prove that a mentally ill person is either dangerous or gravely disabled by at least clear and convincing evidence; a few states employ an even higher burden of persuasion—proof beyond a reasonable doubt (Tsesis, 2011). Such evidentiary standards clearly presuppose a judicial proceeding at which evidence is presented. *Addington* also made clear that, as with all adversarial hearings, due process requires that the notice of the commitment hearing be given in sufficient time to allow the respondent to prepare for the hearing. Beyond notice, the specific procedural rights guaranteed to those facing civil commitment vary by jurisdiction; however, the basic procedural due process protections to which respondents are generally entitled include "a hearing presided over by a fair and impartial judge, at which the respondent can be present, offer evidence, and cross-examine witnesses" and the right to privately retained counsel or, if the respondent is indigent, appointed counsel (Ferris, 2008, p. 968; see also Wright, 2004). Some states have also established the right to a court-appointed clinical evaluator (Ferris, 2008). And all states provide civilly committed persons with the right to a periodic judicial review of the commitment, often every three to six months (Reisner, Slobogin, & Rai, 2009).

Even when sufficient proof of mental illness and dangerousness is adduced at a commitment hearing, the laws of most states do not allow a person to be involuntarily hospitalized unless doing so would be the *least restrictive means* of protecting the person from himself or herself or of protecting society from the person (Klein, 2012). Because psychiatric hospitals offer the benefit of treatment in a "safe, secure, structured, and supervised environment while reducing stress on both patients and family members," (Herz & Marder, 2002, p. 42), most courts consider involuntary confinement to be less restrictive than involuntary medication (Klein, 2012, p. 571). For patients who are in active psychotic episodes, though, both hospitalization and forced administration of antipsychotic medications are likely to be required to help the person (p. 572; see also Corrigan, Mueser, Bond, Drake, & Solomon 2008).

Unless specifically guaranteed by the provisions of a particular state law, a number of procedural due process rights that exist in the criminal law context are notably absent from civil commitment proceedings; these range from a right to jury determination with regard to civil commitment criteria (Wright, 2004) to the protections of legal privileges, including the privilege against self-incrimination (*Allen v. Illinois*, 1986). On the other hand, to protect the privacy rights of the person whose commitment is being sought, most states not only allow commitment proceedings to be closed to the public upon the request of the respondent but also require courts to keep medical records and reports pertaining to civil commitments confidential (Hickey, Tysinger, & Mims, 2007/2008; Stevens & Pullen, 2005).

Civil Commitment in Action. Although some civil commitments begin when the families or friends of people with mental illnesses seek to have them involuntarily hospitalized, most civil commitments are instituted by the police, emergency room physicians, psychiatrists, psychologists, and sometimes even psychiatric nurses or licensed clinical social workers who make relatively quick and often inaccurate judgments based on how patients present at the time of an emergency (Janofsky & Taburell, 2006; Tsesis, 2011; Woo, Sevilla, & Obrocea, 2006). Indeed, nearly all states permit, under appropriate circumstances, the emergency hospitalization of an individual without any prior formal legal hearing. The formal civil commitment due process protections described previously do not attach until a person is hospitalized or until more than a temporary, emergency commitment is being sought. In contrast, at the emergency detention phase, most jurisdictions only require two decision makers (usually a police officer and a clinician) to have probable cause to believe the person is mentally ill and is a danger to self or to others. Such minimal processes are rarely challenged because any more restrictive standards would be counterproductive in emergency situations, especially since a person subject to such an emergency detention still has due process rights to more formal adjudication proceedings, usually within a very short period of time such as 48 to 72 hours (Tsesis, 2011).

In spite of the due process protections afforded to people with mental illness facing full-blown civil commitment, legal commentators and civil rights advocates continue to assert that the judicial process is overly deferential to the behavioral sciences (e.g., Brooks, 2010; Collins, 2009). Indeed, judges defer to the judgment of clinicians between 90 and 100% of the time (Bursztajn, Hamm, & Gutheil, 1997; Pincus, 1995; cf. Morris, 2009). But recall that even using the best-structured clinical assessment practices, "clinicians are able to distinguish violent from nonviolent patients with [only] a modest, better-than-chance level of accuracy" (Monahan, 2000, p. 915).

Brooks (2010) offers several explanations as to why forensic behavioral scientists have not been able to predict dangerousness with a reasonable degree of scientific certainty. These include the previously described legal ambiguities in the definition of dangerousness, the shortcomings of clinical judgments, and biases in favor of a finding of dangerousness because of fears of civil liability for failing to do so or because "the medical imperative is to presume sickness" that requires treatment (p. 274). The field of forensic risk assessment, though, may temper the inclination of behavior scientists and courts alike to make determinations of dangerousness and, in turn, help to prevent the unnecessary civil commitment of people who are not dangerous to themselves or to others.

Forensic Risk Assessment and the Prediction of Dangerousness

Forensic risk assessment involves a determination as to the likelihood that a person poses a particular type of recognized threat, such as whether the person is at risk for committing a future act of violence (Kemshall, 1996). As previously mentioned, forensic risk assessment methods have improved over the past two decades as a result of two significant advances in violence prediction: (1) clinical assessments have moved from unstructured to structured decision-making formats and (2) actuarial risk assessments have been developed that can be used in clinical practice (Monahan, 2002; Otto, 1994; Scurich & John, 2011).

> Clinical predictions and actuarial assessments use different inferential processes. The first entails review of disparate information about a given individual, followed by the exercise of judgment about the risk of danger that individual might pose. The second entails the identification of specific characteristics of the individual that have been statistically correlated with a specified risk of violence. Clinical predictions make statements about the individual; actuarial assessments make statements about a group with which the individual shares characteristics, and from which one might draw inferences about the individual. (Scherr, 2003, p. 15)

Both clinical and actuarial risk assessments play important roles in the legal system. In fact, forensic risk assessments significantly influence a range of legal determinations beyond civil commitments, such as sentencing decisions, especially in capital cases, and judgments about release and case management after release (Campbell et al. 2009; Cunningham, Sorensen, & Reidy, 2009; *Jurek v. Texas*, 1976; Sorensen, Cunningham, Vigen, Woods, 2011). Accordingly, a brief review of the leading forensic risk assessment instruments is in order.

Forensic Risk Assessment Instruments

In the mid-twentieth century, assessments of dangerousness were "based on unstructured clinical judgments of risk that were prone to error and bias" (Campbell et al., 2009, p. 568). Unstructured clinical assessments were grounded in the clinician's background and experience and affected by his or her ability to make inferences from interviews, case histories, current mental status, and performance on tests that were not designed to predict dangerousness, such as intelligence tests and a variety of personality tests: e.g., the Minnesota Multiphasic Personality Inventory (MMPI), the Rorschach inkblot test, the Thematic Apperception Test, and the Children's Apperception Test (Grove, Zald, Lebow, Snitz, & Nelson, 2000). Thus, most empirical studies of such unstructured clinical methods unsurprisingly demonstrated that clinicians were wrong two out of three times, yielding an error rate significantly worse than that predicted by chance (Faust & Ziskin, 1988; Monahan, 1981; Monahan & Steadman, 1994).

The landmark decision in *Lessard v. Schmidt* (1972) significantly influenced the assessment of risk in the 1970s. The case was decided at a time before many of the modern due process protections discussed earlier in this chapter were enacted. Indeed, *Lessard* was largely responsible for transforming the legal landscape concerning due process in civil commitments (Mossman et al., 2012). The case centered on a woman was involuntarily hospitalized following an *ex parte* hearing of which she never received notice. She won her class action suit enjoining the state of Wisconsin from enforcing its involuntary commitment statute. One of the provisions the court ordered as part of its remedy in the case was to require evidence of risk as demonstrated by an actual threat or an *overt act*—some observable behavior from which dangerousness could be inferred. Several states subsequently adopted the overt act requirement as part of their own due process reforms while other states declined to require proof of an overt act (Mossman et al., 2012). But the tightening of legal standards for civil commitment with regard to both risk and other due process concerns did not produce any evidentiary restrictions on behavioral scientific testimony in spite of the profound reliability and validity limitations of dangerousness predictions (Mossman et al., 2012). In fact, Scherr (2003) reported that "no appellate court ha[d] ever ordered exclusion of expert psychiatric testimony about danger in a civil commitment case" (pp. 26–27). Rather, it was introspection from within the mental health profession concerning the high error rates of unstructured clinical assessments of risk that led to the creation of "second-generation risk instruments." These focused on the standardized assessment of static risk factors that had been statistically demonstrated to predict future violence, such as sex, age, criminal history, psychopathy, low socioeconomic status, family criminality, and DSM diagnosis (Campbell et al., 2009).

Second-generation risk assessment instruments had higher levels of predictive validity than did unstructured clinical judgments (Campbell et al., 2009; Monahan, 2002; Monahan & Steadman, 1994; Mossman et al., 2012). But recidivism is complex; risk factors are not static; rather, they are dynamic insofar as they change over time in response to a number of criminogenic attributes. Thus, "third-generation risk instruments" were developed that targeted empirically supported, dynamic risk factors, such as substance use, interpersonal conflicts, anxiety, and antisocial attitudes (Campbell et al., 2009; Singh, Grann, & Fazel, 2011).

> The latest evolution in risk instruments (i.e., fourth generation) are those specifically designed to be integrated into (a) the process of risk management, (b) the selection of intervention modes and targets for treatment, and (c) the assessment of rehabilitation progress. These instruments are administered on multiple occasions and are particularly informative because they document changes in specific criminogenic needs that might occur between an offender's entrance into the criminal justice system through his or her exit from the criminal justice system. Fourth-generation instruments are intended to identify areas of success within a case management plan as well as areas in which intervention strategies need to be modified to maximize their potential for risk reduction. . . . (Campbell et al., 2009, p. 569)

Table 12.1 presents information about the leading clinical and actuarial risk assessment techniques. When reviewing the table, keep in mind that each generation of actuarial risk assessment does not necessarily correspond to improved predictive validity in the evaluation of dangerousness. "The predictive validity of commonly used risk assessment measures varies widely" (Singh et al., 2011, p. 12). Moreover, there may be insufficient data about most fourth-generation risk assessment instruments to conclude that they are superior to those in the third generation (Campbell et al., 2009).

The Impact and Future of Risk Assessment

Advances in actuarially derived risk assessment instruments have improved the ability to predict dangerousness. And advances in cognitive neuroscience hold great promise for supplementing the ability of behavioral scientists to predict dangerousness with even greater accuracy in the future (see Lamparello, 2011). For now, the best prediction methods might blend structured clinical evaluation with the risk assessment instruments that have been empirically demonstrated to be reliable and valid predictors of violence using both static, actuarially derived factors (Kumar & Simpson, 2005), as well as theory-driven, dynamic risk assessments. Still, prediction is a difficult and inherently uncertain practice. Yang, Wong, and Coid (2010) warn that "[e]ven with a moderately accurate method of prediction, predicting low- or very-low-frequency events, such as serious violence . . . will inevitably result in a high false-positive error rate" (p. 741).

Table 12.1 Risk Assessment Instruments

Assessment		Source	Description
Clinical	Psychopathy Checklist-Revised (PCL-R)	Hare, R. D. (2003). *The Hare Psychopathy Checklist–Revised* (2nd ed.). Toronto, ON: Multi-Health Systems.	Though intended to indicate psychopathy in an individual, the PCL-R has also been used to predict violent behavior and recidivism through a 20-item scale, providing a score from 0 to 40. Predicting violence better than its predecessor (the PCL-SV), comparison with other risk assessment instruments has shown the PCL-R to perform less successfully as a catchall risk assessment measure, though it is comparable to the LSI-R.
	Sexual Violence Risk-20 (SVR-20)	Boer, D. P., Hart, S. D., Kropp, P. R., & Webster, C. D. (1997). *Manual for the Sexual Violence Risk-20. Professional guidelines for assessing risk of sexual violence.* Burnaby, BC: Simon Fraser University, Mental Health, Law, and Policy Institute.	Measuring the risk of violence in sex offenders through 20 factors, this test is reliable for predicting sexual recidivism for general sex crimes and rape, though it is not as reliable among nonsexual offenders. Additionally, the test does not differentiate well between sexual and nonsexual recidivist violence.
	Spousal Assault Risk Assessment (SARA)	Kropp, P. R., Hart, S. D., Webster, C. D., & Eaves, D. (1995). *Manual for the Spousal Assault Risk Assessment guide* (2nd ed.). Vancouver, BC: British Columbia Institute of Family Violence.	The SARA guide measures men's likeliness of committing subsequent domestic violence post arrest. It is comprised of 20 interview-based questions that address criminal history, psychosocial adjustment, spousal assault history, and details of the current offense. Multiple studies demonstrate high levels of both inter-rater reliability and predictive validity against comparable assessment tools.
	Structured Assessment of Violence Risk in Youth (SAVRY)	Borum, R., Bartel, P., & Forth, A. (2002). *Manual for the structured assessment of violence risk in youth (SAVRY).* Tampa, FL: University of South Florida.	Notable for including both dynamic and protective factors in youth, the SAVRY test is considered one of the most reliable predictors of violence for its intended group. However, it has only been validated with adolescent offenders, limiting its generalizability.
Second Generation Actuarial: Statistically derived; standardized; static risk items	General Statistical Information on Recidivism (GSIR)	Nafekh, M., & Motiuk, L. L. (2002). *The statistical information on recidivism–revised 1 (SIR-R1) scale: A psychometric examination.* Correctional Service of Canada, Research Branch.	GSIR is designed to predict recidivism within three years after release through 15 items measuring prior criminality and demographic data. Data are statistically calculated, and it has found the most success predicting violent and sexual recidivism. The test possesses internal reliability and validity among men but has been little tested among female offenders.

Assessment		Source	Description
	Sex Offender Risk Assessment Guide (SORAG)	Quinsey, V. L., Harris, G. T., Rice, M. E., & Cormier, C. A. (2006). *Violent offenders: Appraising and managing risk* (2nd ed.). Washington, DC: American Psychological Association.	Reserved generally for recidivating sex offenders, the SORAG utilizes 14 static predictive items, ranging from childhood family experiences to offender history. SORAG is accurate approximately 69% of the time for sexual recidivism, a figure that increases to 88% for violent recidivism. Therefore, it is considered a reliably predictive tool.
	Static-99	Hanson, R. K., & Thornton, D. (1999). *Static-99: Improving actuarial risk assessments for sex offenders* (User Report 99–02). Ottawa, ON: Department of the Solicitor General of Canada.	The Static-99 predicts sexual recidivism among previously convicted offenders through 10 items drawn from previous sexual recidivism studies. Validity and reliability results have been replicated multiple times for this study, making it a popular choice for assessors.
	Statistical Information on Recidivism (SIR)	Nuffield, J. (1989). The 'SIR Scale': Some reflections on its applications. *Forum on Corrections Research, 1*, 19–22.	Similar to the GSIR, SIR uses 15 items to predict recidivism within three years of release; however, unlike the GSIR, SIR does not predict violence or sexual recidivism with any kind of reliability. Indeed, because the items are all static (e.g., age, criminal history) and derived statistically, this instrument varies widely on the probabilistic certainty provided.
	Violence Risk Assessment Guide (VRAG)	Harris, G. T., Rice, M. E., & Quinsey, V. L. (1993). Violent recidivism of mentally disordered offenders: The development of a statistical prediction instrument. *Criminal Justice and Behavior, 20*, 315–335.	Utilizing statistical data, the VRAG is composed of 12 items taken from PCL-R scores, school problems, substance abuse, and age, among other dimensions of life, and is intended to predict violence from inmates released from maximum-security institutions. It is generally considered factually invalid because of a contradiction with clinical assessments on three of the items, and it is not a good predictor of institutional violence. But it tends to perform well compared to its nonstatistically based counterparts in predicting violent recidivism. However, some note that these interpretations could be attributable to sampling error in the evaluating studies.
Third Generation Actuarial: Theory-driven; statistically derived; standardized; include static and dynamic risk factors.	Bröset Violence Checklist (BVC)	Almvik, R., & Woods, P. (2003). Short-term risk prediction: The Bröset Violence Checklist. *Journal of Psychiatric & Mental Health Nursing, 10*(2), 236–238.	This short-term predictor of inmate violence measures irritability, verbal and physical aggression, the physical assault of objects, and boisterousness. Assessment takes about five minutes and is intended for those aged 20 through 50. Though possessing strong inter-rater reliability and criterion validity, the test was evaluated in Norway, a fact that could affect its generalizability across international borders.

(Continued)

(Continued)

Assessment		Source	Description
	Classification of Violence Risk (COVR)	Monahan, J., Steadman, H., Appelbaum, P., Grisso, T., Mulvey, E., Roth, L. et al. (2005). *COVR Classification of Violence Risk.* Lutz, FL: Psychological Assessment Resources.	Interactive software coming as a direct result of the Macarthur study that evaluates acute psychiatric patients' likelihood of violence toward others post release. Intended for 18- to 60-year-olds, personality characteristics, personal history, and clinical history are all included within its calculations. Though it was tested in an acute psychiatric community, results have varied even amongst acute psychiatric groups. Some scholars caution against relying solely on COVR's results, especially if results indicate a high risk of violence.
	Historical, Clinical, and Risk Management Violence Risk Assessment Scheme (HCR-20)	Webster, C. D., Douglas, K. S., Eaves, D., & Hart, S. D. (1997). Assessing risk of violence to others. In Webster, C. D., & Jackson, M. A. (eds.) *Impulsivity: Theory, assessment, and treatment.* New York, NY: Guildford Press.	Composed of 20 questions intended to evaluate violent behavior, the HCR-20 assesses the biographical history of the individual through five clinical and five actuarial risk-management items. The test constructs scenarios not considered statistically generalizable; for instance, this test has statistically significant predictive abilities with men, but results are questionable among women. It is consistently reliable when predicting institutional violence as well as post-release violent recidivism.
	Self-Appraisal Questionnaire (SAQ)	Loza, W., Neo, L. H., Shahinfar, A., & Loza-Fanous, A. (2005). Cross-validation of the Self-Appraisal Questionnaire: A tool for assessing violent and nonviolent recidivism with female offenders. *International Journal of Offender Therapy and Comparative Criminology, 49*(5), 547–560.	For an instrument that relies on self-reported data, the SAQ scores surprisingly high for predictive ability in both institutional and recidivist violence. Its 72 questions about current and past illegal behavior, antisocial tendencies, behavioral problems, substance abuse, and close associates drive the success of this test. However, further empirical validation is needed to make it more generalizable.
	Violence Risk Scale (VRS)	Wong, S. C. P., & Gordon, A. (2006). The validity and reliability of the Violence Risk Scale: A treatment-friendly violence risk assessment tool. *Psychology, Public Policy, and Law, 12*(3), 279–309.	Grounded in criminological and psychological theories, the VRS measures risk of violence through a multitude of antisocial personality characteristics by way of 6 static and 20 dynamic risk-assessment items. High inter-rater reliability and empirical support have validated this test, and it can be used either as a stand-alone measurement tool or to select clients for treatment. Results of this test often correlate well with results obtained from the LSI-R.

Assessment		Source	Description
Fourth Generation Actuarial: Integration of risk management and case management principles and practices	Correctional Assessment and Intervention System (CAIS)	National Council on Crime and Delinquency. (2004). *Correctional assessment and intervention system.* Oakland, CA: Author.	To facilitate offenders' relationship with correctional supervisor post release, this semi-structured interview evaluates the needs, strengths, and criminal motivations of inmates. Widely validated in the United States, it is constantly revalidated for each agency utilizing it to ensure maximum predictive capabilities.
	Correctional Offender Management Profile for Alternative Sanctions (COMPAS)	Brennan, T., & Oliver, W. L. (2000). *Evaluation of reliability and validity of COMPAS scales: National aggregate sample.* Traverse City, MI: Northpointe Institute for Public Management.	Nineteen items evaluating criminogenic needs pair with statistics scoring violence, recidivism, and absences from mandatory court appearances to help create a positive supervision experience for offenders. Though it is currently in the process of being validated across the country, early reports show promise of moderate generalizability and validity. It is used by the California Department of Corrections and Rehabilitation (CDCR).
	Level of Service/ Case Management Inventory (LS/ CMI)	Andrews, D. A., Bonta, J., & Wormith, J. S. (2004). *The Level of Service/Case Management Inventory (LS/CMI).* Toronto: Multi-Health Systems.	Created to both assess risk and help practitioners manage caseloads, its risk assessment items are based on those found in the LSI-R; however, it has pared down the number of assessment items from 54 to 43 and added 10 other sections covering a wide variety of risk factors. It is considered both strong internally and externally, making it a useful risk management tool.
	Level of Supervision Inventory-Revised (LSI-R)	Andrews, D. A., & Bonta, J. (1995). *Level of Service Inventory–Revised.* Toronto, ON: Multi-Health Systems.	Comprised of 54 items across 10 subscales that include both dynamic and static factors, the LSI-R scored weakly when evaluated against similar tests in terms of predicting institutional violence (approximately .14); however, the LSI-R and the PCL-R scored comparably well (.28 and .27, respectively) when predicting violent recidivism. One of the most popular risk assessment tools, the LSI-R is difficult to validate because it is used on offenders who have committed a wide variety of crimes.
	Violence Prediction Scheme (VPS)	Webster, C. D., Harris, G. T., Rice, M. E., Cormier, C., & Quinsey, V. L. (1994). *The violence prediction scheme–Assessing dangerousness in high risk men.* Toronto: Centre of Criminology, University of Toronto.	The VPS combines the VRAG with 10 widely ranging dynamic assessment items, spanning self-presentation to treatment progress. A critique of this instrument holds that the dynamic items do not add significant predictive validity to the results, leaving its reliability and accuracy approximately on par with the VRAG.

Most third- and fourth-generation actuarial risk assessment instruments have *group* accuracy rates in the 70 to 80% range (Coid, Yang, Ullrich, Zhang, Sizmur, Farrington, & Rogers, 2011; Janus & Meehl, 1997). However, actuarial methods may or may not be accurate when applied to any particular person. Thus, courts sometimes reject purely actuarial methods and evaluate them only when combined with clinical methods to support predictions concerning a particular person's dangerousness, especially in the civil commitment context (see Scherr, 2003). Researchers have found, however, that when actuarial assessments are used in court, they tend to be more persuasive than purely clinical assessments (Mossman et al., 2012; Yang, Wong, & Coid, 2010).

That being said, clinical assessments continue to hold a great deal of utility and are often favored when dealing with youths, individuals who comorbidly possess psychopathic traits, and those whose behavior is not accurately encompassed by predetermined actuarial factors (Singh et al., 2011). For example, the Structured Assessment of Violence Risk in Youth (SAVRY) is a clinical assessment tool that works reasonable well among youth—the group for whom it was intended; in contrast, it has unacceptably low predictive validity for adults (Singh, et. al, 2011). This illustrates what some might consider a self-evident point, but one that merits explicit mention. Forensic risk assessment instruments retain their highest rates of predictive accuracy when they are used to evaluate the populations for which they were validated. Thus, it is crucial that clinicians use forensic risk assessment instruments that are appropriate not only for the person being evaluated but also for the type of offenses for which the instrument was designed to have predictive validity. This task, however, is complicated by the fact that several risk assessments were validated against racially or ethnically homogenous groups, which, in turn, limits the overall generalizability of these assessments when they are used on individuals whose race or ethnicity falls outside of that comprising the majority of the validation groups (DeMatteo, Batastini, Foster, & Hunt, 2010; Singh et al., 2011).

From Preventative Detention to Preemptive Incarceration?

Up to this point in the chapter, we have explored civil commitment in its traditional context in which the state seeks to hospitalize mentally ill people involuntarily to prevent them from harming themselves or others. But modified versions of traditional civil commitment are also used to control those who commit crimes. The two most notable uses of such preventative detention techniques involve those acquitted of criminal charges on the basis of insanity and **sexually violent predator (SVP) laws** targeting those who, after serving a prison sentence for certain types of sex offenses, are determined to be at high risk for reoffending.

Jones and *Foucha*: The Preventive Detention of Insanity Acquittees

As explained in Chapter 11, people charged with crimes who successfully assert the insanity defense rarely go free upon a "not guilty by reason of insanity" verdict. Between 84% and 95% of insanity acquittees are hospitalized for treatment of their mental illness, often for periods of time that exceed the maximum period of time for which they could have been imprisoned had they been convicted (Pasewark, Pantle, & Steadman, 1982; Silver, Cirincione, & Steadman, 1994). In *Jones v. United States* (1983), the U.S. Supreme Court held that, because involuntarily hospitalization after an insanity acquittal does not constitute punishment but rather is imposed for the dual purposes of providing treatment to those adjudicated insane and protecting society from the risk of danger posed by such people, states may civilly commit insanity acquittees and hold them in preventative detention for longer periods of time than the prison sentences authorized for the original crimes.

In *Foucha v. Louisiana* (1992), the U.S. Supreme Court held that, even if an insanity acquittee is predicted to remain dangerous, it violates the Constitution to keep that person committed after she or he has recovered from mental illness. In that case, the defendant had been acquitted on insanity grounds due to a drug-induced psychosis. After being treated, he recovered from that illness and sought to be released accordingly.

At his release hearing, there was no dispute that Foucha no longer suffered from any psychosis. He had been diagnosed, though, with antisocial personality disorder. At the hearing, physicians testified that Foucha was dangerous but no longer mentally ill. "One of the doctors testified . . . that he evidenced no signs of psychosis or neurosis and was in 'good shape' mentally [but] that he had, however, an antisocial personality, a condition that is not a mental disease and that is untreatable" (*Foucha v. Louisiana*, 1992, p. 75). The trial court, relying on the fact that he was dangerous, denied Foucha's petition for release because Louisiana law authorized the continued commitment of insanity acquittees if they were dangerous, even if not mentally ill. The Supreme Court ultimately ruled in Foucha's favor, holding that his continued involuntary hospitalization violated due process because he was no longer mentally ill—a necessary prerequisite to involuntary hospitalization. The Court specifically relied on the testimony at the trial: "According to the testimony given at the hearing in the trial court, Foucha is not suffering from a mental disease or illness" (p. 79).

In rejecting Louisiana's rationale that it could hold an insanity acquittee who was dangerous even though not mentally ill, the Supreme Court said that such logic "would permit the state to hold indefinitely any other insanity acquittee not mentally ill who could be shown to have a personality disorder that may lead to criminal conduct" (p. 82). This sentence is troubling because it suggests that "the Court regarded personality disorder and mental illness as being two mutually exclusive categories" (Winick, 1995a, p. 543). Moreover, it suggests that antisocial personality disorder and indeed all personality disorders are not mental illnesses sufficient to justify commitment as a constitutional matter (p. 548).

Professor Winick (1995a) actually voiced agreement with this proposition. He argued that a medical model of deviance ought to guide the legal definition of mental illness. Thus, he asserted that mental illness, for the purposes of law, ought to be limited to those disorders that meet three criteria: (1) their etiology is organic in nature (rather than psychosocial), (2) their treatment follows some reasonably predicable course, and (3) they render the individual incapable of rational decision making or behavior control (pp. 558–559). Since antisocial personality disorder fails to meet these criteria, he argued, it should not be considered a mental illness. As explained in Chapter 11, nearly all states and the American Law Institute agree with Winick when it comes to the definition of mental illness for the purposes of the insanity defense. But as the statutes cited above in this chapter illustrate, the states are divided on that matter when it comes to civil commitment.

It should be noted that the Supreme Court's ruling in *Foucha* that antisocial personality disorder is not a mental illness for civil commitment purposes does not necessarily mean it will never qualify as such. For one thing, Foucha was not claiming he was mentally ill, nor was the state of Louisiana. The matter, therefore, was not truly at issue in this case, and the Supreme Court's handling of the disorder may therefore be regarded as dicta. Second, the decision was only a plurality one, meaning only four justices joined in the majority opinion. Justice O'Connor voted with the majority in terms of the result but filed a separate concurring opinion in which she equated the constitutional standard for "mental illness" with a "medical justification" for confinement (*Foucha v. Louisiana*, 1992, p. 88, O'Connor, J., concurring). The Louisiana statute did not meet this standard because it allowed the continued commitment of insanity acquittees who were no longer mentally ill. Thus, the diagnosis at issue in *Foucha* was not relevant to her rationale. Accordingly, *Foucha* should be read narrowly given the limited confines of the unique facts of the case and its plurality status.

Hendricks and *Crane*: The Preventative Detention of Sexually Violent Offenders

After a series of high-profile crimes committed by sex offenders after their release from prison, Washington enacted the Community Protection Act, the first law in the United States to authorize the indefinite civil commitment of sexually violent predators after their release from prison, provided that they suffer from a mental abnormality or personality disorder that makes them likely to engage in future sexually violent acts (Lave, 2011). Twenty U.S. jurisdictions followed Washington's lead, including the state of Kansas.

In *Kansas v. Hendricks* (1997), the U.S. Supreme Court upheld a Kansas statute that provided for the civil commitment of *sexually violent predators* upon the completion of their period of criminal incarceration. The Kansas statute authorized the civil commitment of

> any person who has been convicted of or charged with a sexually violent offense and who suffers from a mental abnormality or personality disorder which makes the person likely to engage in the predatory acts of sexual violence, if not confined in a secure facility. (Kansas Statute Annotated § 59–29a02[a], Supp. 1996)

Hendricks, diagnosed a pedophile, served 10 years in prison for molesting two 13-year-old boys. When he was scheduled to be released from prison, the state sought to have him committed because he had admitted to abusing children repeatedly whenever he was free (*Kansas v. Hendricks*, 1997, pp. 354–355). After Hendricks was ordered committed, he challenged the constitutionality of the statute because it allowed preventive detention based on a finding of "mental abnormality" rather than the more narrow determination of "mental illness" used in *Addington* and *Foucha*. Specifically, Hendricks argued that, even though he might be dangerous, he was not mentally ill under *Foucha*, and, therefore, he could not be detained consistent with *Foucha*'s constitutional teaching. The Kansas Supreme Court sided with Hendricks, finding that the law unconstitutionally authorized the commitment of people with mere mental abnormalities or personality disorders in violation of *Foucha*.

The U.S. Supreme Court reversed. It reasoned that the "mental abnormality" requirement of the Kansas statute, combined with a finding of dangerousness, was constitutionally sufficient to involuntarily commit a sex offender. The Court distinguished the case from *Foucha* stating that the additional factor of "mental abnormality" in the statute effectively limited "involuntary civil confinement to those who suffer from a volitional impairment rendering them dangerous beyond their control" (*Kansas v. Hendricks*, 1997, p. 358). Thus, *Hendricks* upheld specialized civil commitment statutes for sexually violent predators so long as such laws combine the traditional "dangerousness" criterion with some "mental illness" or "mental abnormality" that impairs, at minimum, volition (i.e., the ability to control oneself). For Hendricks, that disorder was pedophilia.

Hendricks did not address an evidentiary issue that became evident as the Kansas courts began to apply their statute within the framework of the Supreme Court's decision. Specifically, the Supreme Court's focus on a defendant's inability to control behavior left open the question of whether that was a necessary precondition to involuntary civil commitment for sexually dangerous predators. And, if it were, what levels of proof would be required for due process mandates to be satisfied? The Court addressed these questions in *Kansas v. Crane* (2002). In *Crane*, the petitioner had been committed after a trial court determined he suffered from a mental abnormality that made it likely he would reoffend. Crane, however, insisted that was an insufficient basis under *Hendricks* because the state had not proven that Crane lacked volitional control. The Kansas Supreme Court sided with Crane in light of the emphasis the Supreme Court had placed on volitional control in the *Hendricks* opinion. On appeal, the U.S. Supreme Court constitutionalized the requirement of proof of volitional impairment on due process grounds. The Court noted that the state need not prove a "total or complete" lack of control because such a standard would be unworkable (p. 411). Rather, the Court explained that the

> "inability to control behavior" will not be demonstrable with mathematical precision. It is enough to say that there must be proof of serious difficulty in controlling behavior. And this, when viewed in light of such features of the case as the nature of the psychiatric diagnosis, and the severity of the mental abnormality itself, must be sufficient to distinguish the dangerous sexual offender whose serious mental illness, abnormality, or disorder subjects him to civil commitment from the dangerous but typical recidivist convicted in an ordinary criminal case. (p. 413)

The ambiguity of the Supreme Court's standard for proving volition impairment was quickly criticized. As professor Stephen J. Morse (2002), one of the leading scholars on the intersection of law and psychology, commented, "There will be much legislative and judicial activity in the states about the definition of lack of control . . . ; the Supreme Court will ultimately have to provide more precise guidance" (p. 1033). From a clinical standpoint, it is important to note that judgments regarding "volitional impairments lead to psychiatric disagreement, error, and inter-rater reliability issues as there is 'no way to calibrate the degree of impairment of behavioral controls'" (Fabian, 2012, p. 322). Thus, as is often the case with questions of behavioral science *in* the law (see Chapter 1), mental health professionals will undoubtedly find it challenging, if not impossible, "to accurately differentiate the typical recidivist who chooses to commit crimes and is willfully dangerous and unwilling to restrain himself, versus the recidivist who cannot control his behaviors and who suffers from volitional impairments" (p. 364).

Comstock and Preemptive Incarceration

In *United States v. Comstock* (2010), the Supreme Court upheld the Adam Walsh Child Safety and Protection Act of 2006 as a constitutional exercise of congressional authority. The Court's decision was very narrow and did not consider a host of constitutional challenges that could be levied against one of the Act's more controversial provisions: "that people can be indefinitely committed to a locked facility as sexually dangerous persons even though they were never convicted of, or even charged with, a sex crime" (Lave, 2011, p. 408).

The Adam Walsh Act significantly expands the class of people who may be involuntarily committed under federal law. It stands in sharp contrast to the sexually violent predator laws of all but two states by not first requiring that, to be committed, a person must have been convicted of a sexually violent offense or acquitted of such a charge on insanity grounds (Lave, 2011). Rather, the civil commitment provision of the Adam Walsh Act

> authorized federal authorities to divert someone to a sex offender detention facility if: (1) he or she was "in the custody of the Bureau of Prisons"; (2) "the Attorney General or any individual authorized by the Attorney General or the Director of the Bureau of Prisons [certified] that the person is a sexually dangerous person"; and (3) "after the hearing, the court finds by clear and convincing evidence that the person is a sexually dangerous person." To prove that a person was "sexually dangerous," the Government needed to show that "a person [had] engaged or attempted to engage in sexually violent conduct or child molestation and . . . suffers from a serious mental illness, abnormality, or disorder as a result of which he would have serious difficulty in refraining from sexually violent conduct or child molestation if released." (Yung, 2011, p. 978)

Most commentators who have analyzed the statute concur with Justice Thomas, who dissented in *Comstock*, that no enumerated power in the U.S. Constitution could support this civil commitment provision (*United States v. Comstock*, 2010, pp. 159–172, Thomas, J., dissenting; see also Melcher, 2012; Lave, 2011; Yung, 2011). Some lower courts have invalidated the civil commitment provisions of the Adam Walsh Act on due process grounds while others have upheld the law's constitutionality (Burke, 2012). As a result of these conflicting decisions, the U.S. Supreme Court may need to adjudicate the constitutionality of preemptive incarceration on due process grounds soon.

Conclusion

How civil commitment statutes are drafted and applied raise significant public policy questions. As the Report of the Virginia Tech Review Panel (2007) made clear, when the legal criteria for the involuntary civil commitment of people with SMIs are particularly stringent and restrictive, people in need of treatment may not receive the help they require before they pose an imminent danger to themselves or to others—a point at which it may be too late to prevent tragedy. On the other hand, the civil liberties of each person need to be protected, as the involuntary commitment to a psychiatric hospital represents "a massive curtailment of liberty" (*Humphrey v. Cady*, 1972, p. 509).

The scope of due process rights in the areas of civil commitment and preventative detention are not clear. We know from *Jackson v. Indiana* that mental illness alone, without an individual showing some dangerousness to self or others, is a constitutionally insufficient basis for involuntary civil commitment and is in violation of liberty rights under the Fourteenth Amendment's Due Process Clause. Conversely, from *Foucha v. Louisiana*, we thought we knew that, if one is dangerous but not mentally ill, involuntary commitment is not constitutional. But *Kansas v. Hendricks* and *Kansas v. Crane* created a great uncertainly somewhere in between the two extremes of *Jackson* and *Foucha*, allowing for the involuntary civil commitment of dangerous people who have some sort of "mental abnormality" that impairs volition, at least when dealing with sex offenders. Not only has a precise definition of "mental abnormality" yet to be reached but also the degree of volitional impairment required is nebulous. Moreover, it remains an open question whether such volitional impairment will be able to be inferred from diagnoses alone or whether some quantum of independent proof will be necessary to satisfy the due process mandates of *Crane*. To date, states have taken conflicting approaches on these questions.

Seemingly in direct contradiction of *Crane*, some states require no separate finding of volitional control impairment; these states appear to permit a lack of control to be presumed from the determinations of mental abnormality and dangerousness (Pierson, 2012). Other states "explicitly require the mental abnormality to cause a lack of control by reading this requirement into the statutory definition of 'mental abnormality'" (p. 1543). And still other states require a separate factual finding on a sex offender's lack of control, although there is great variability regarding what evidence suffices to support such a factual finding (pp. 1547–1550). Clearly, *Crane's* volitional impairment standard needs to be better operationalized (see Mercado, Bornstein, & Schopp, 2006; Pierson, 2012).

Separate and apart from issues of proof, it should be noted that sexually violent predator laws are only needed in states with determinate sentencing. In states with indeterminate sentencing, as well as in states that provide up to life for violent sex offenses, there is no need to resort to special types of civil commitment to keep these offenders incapacitated. But in states that employ determinate sentencing and then turn to SVP laws to control violent sex offenders after the conclusion of criminal sentences, the process of post-sentence civil commitment raises another concern. Mental Health America (2011), formerly the National Mental Health Association, argues that the "mental health system is not the appropriate place for long-term confinement of sexual predators," especially because the civil commitment of sex offenders adds to the state's already limited ability "to provide treatment to people who need it" (para. 4). Winick and LaFond (2003) concur with this point not only because inpatient psychiatric beds are already at or beyond capacity (see the epilogue) but also because these types of former prisoners pose serious safety risks to the other patients. "If the societal goal of sexual predator laws is incapacitation and incarceration of potentially dangerous offenders, the criminal justice system is the appropriate place to pursue that goal. If current criminal justice statutes do not allow for sufficient periods of incarceration because of the widespread repeal of indeterminate sentencing laws, then those statutes should be changed" (Mental Health America, 2011, para. 4).

Mental Health America (2011) also asserts that the involuntary civil commitment of sex offenders after release from prison increases the stigma of mental illness by associating sexual predatory behavior with treatment in the mental health system. But its primary criticism of sexually violent predator laws is that they distort the nature of civil commitment.

> Involuntary civil commitment may be necessary in some cases as a last resort to protect the health and safety of a person with a mental illness or those in contact with him/her. But the basic rationale of involuntary confinement is that the person is found to be dangerous to self or others at the time of the commitment, that he or she receives treatment and that the confinement is time-limited and paired with a course of treatment. None of these essential elements is present in the case of a sex offender committed after serving a prison sentence. Thus, sexual predator commitments are an abuse of civil commitment. (Mental Health America, 2011, para. 7)

Although reasonable people can differ on the legitimacy and efficacy of sexually violent predator laws, there can be little doubt that these laws serve a very different purpose than traditional civil commitment laws (Winick & LaFond, 2003). *Hendricks* and *Crane* transformed the civil commitment terrain in a palpable way. The basis of civil commitment statutes in the pre-*Hendricks* era was treatment. After *Crane* and *Comstock*, their primary purpose seems to have shifted to "the prevention of dangerousness, with treatment permissibly becoming an incidental and secondary objective" (Friedland, 1999, p. 112).

KEY TERMS

asylums

civil commitment

community mental health (CMH) movement

dangerousness

forensic risk assessment

gravely disabled

parens patriae

police power

sexually violent predator (SVP) laws

REVIEW QUESTIONS

1. Compare and contrast the first-, second-, and third-wave efforts to reform the criminal justice system's treatment of offenders with mental illness with the efforts of the community mental health movement. How were these efforts alike? How did they differ? Which, in your opinion, was the most successful? Why?
2. Using a minimum of four court cases, describe how due process protections have evolved for people facing civil commitment. Critique the current state of civil commitment law using one or two high-profile news stories of crimes committed by people who were clearly mental ill and dangerous but who were not involuntarily confined for inpatient treatment in spite of attempts to have them civilly committed.
3. Trace the evolution of the four generations of risk assessment for mentally ill people who may be "dangerous" within the meaning of civil commitment law. What are major limitations of each generation of risk assessment instruments?
4. How do the terms "mental illness" and "mental abnormality," as used in civil commitment legislation, differ from the meaning of the term "mental disease or defect" as used in the context of an insanity defense? Analyze the different ways in which state laws governing civil commitment use the term "mental illness." Which approach do you think is the best? Explain your reasoning.
5. Explain what "dangerousness" means in the civil commitment context. How has the concept of dangerousness evolved in the context of traditional civil commitment as compared to in context of the indefinite confinement of persons adjudicated as sexually violent predators?

13

Epilogue on Mental Illness and Criminal Justice Policy

In Chapters 3 through 10, we presented a synthesis of the historically relevant and current leading research linking particular mental disorders to crime. In Chapter 11 and 12, we addressed three of the most vexing issues courts face when dealing with people who present with serious mental illnesses (SMIs): competency to stand trial, the insanity defense, and involuntary civil commitment. In this final chapter, we look at how justice policies have shaped, for better and for worse, the current landscape of the intersection between mental illness and crime. In doing so, we offer some public policy suggestions that could improve societal responses to dealing with those who suffer from SMIs and come in contact with justice personnel.

Deinstitutionalization's Effect on Correctional Institutions

The community mental health (CMH) movement (see Chapter 12) was successful in getting Congress to include incentives for moving patients out of psychiatric hospitals and into community-based treatment—a process referred to as **deinstitutionalization**. Most notably, Medicaid and Medicare legislation passed in 1965 "purposefully excluded payments to 'institutions for the treatment of mental diseases' because the programs were not designed to supplant state control and financing of psychiatric facilities" (Harcourt, 2011, p.67). This exclusion gave states an incentive to move psychiatric patients out of their hospitals and into communities where they became eligible for "Supplemental Security Income . . . Medicaid, food stamps, and other federal benefits" (p. 67).

Deinstitutionalization caused the resident population of state mental hospitals to decline by more than 75% between 1955 and 1980, while more than 700 CMH centers were created (Morrissey, 1982; Morrissey & Goldman, 1986). As a result, state mental hospitals were closed across the country. But rather than receiving

Authors' Note: Portions of this chapter (those with headings marked by an asterisk) are from Fradella, H. F., & Smith-Casey, R. (2013). Criminal justice responses to the mentally ill. In S. A. Mallicoat & C. Gardiner (Eds.), *Criminal justice policy* (pages 201–224). Thousand Oaks, CA: Sage.

community-based care, those with SMIs were largely ignored because adequate funding was not provided to communities to support the needs of these patients upon their release from mental hospitals (Bassuk & Gerson, 1978).

> Deinstitutionalized patients encountered the hostility and rejection of the general public and the reluctance of community mental health and welfare agencies to assume responsibility for their care. Tens of thousands ended up in rooming houses, foster homes, nursing homes, run-down hotels, and on the streets. (Morrissey & Goldman, 1986, pp. 21–22)

The population in state mental hospitals peaked at more than 558,200 patients in 1955; that number stands in sharp contrast to the fewer than 70,000 patients with SMIs who were housed in public psychiatric hospitals in the mid-1990s (The Sentencing Project, 2002). By 2006, there were only 228 state psychiatric hospitals operating 49,000 beds, nearly a third of which were occupied by forensic patients—those "committed by the criminal courts because their competency to stand trial has been questioned, they have been found incompetent and have not regained competency, or they were adjudicated as not guilty by reason of insanity" (Fisher, Geller, & Pandiani, 2009, p. 679).

The overly optimistic CMH movement left tens of thousands of former patients "homeless or living in substandard housing, often without treatment, supervision, or social support" (Goldman & Morrissey, 1985, p. 729). Sadly, this state of affairs largely continues today; many communities currently have no services in place to assist those with SMIs. Largely as a function of these deficiencies, the mentally ill are often arrested for so-called "nuisance crimes," which leads to prolonged contact with the criminal justice system, especially for people who are unable to conform their behaviors to the rules of society due to their severe and chronic psychiatric issues.

On the other end of the spectrum, lack of access to quality mental health services has dire consequences, as it appears to have had for the Aurora movie theater victims in the James Holmes case (see Box 13.1). In the wake of Adam Lanza's school massacre in Newtown, Connecticut, President Obama stated, "We are going to need to work on making access to mental health care at least as easy as access to getting a gun." This is a tall order because, between 2009 and 2012, states cut more than $4.35 billion in public mental health spending, or about 12% of the total budget; as a result, more than 3,200 psychiatric hospital beds, or 6% of the total, have disappeared, and another 1,249 beds are in danger of being lost (Glober, Miller, & Sadowski, 2012).

In contrast to 1955, the height of mental hospitalizations, when there was one public psychiatric bed for every 300 people in the United States, currently there is one bed in both public and private facilities for every 3,000 people (Torrey, Kennard, Eslinger, Lamb, & Pavle, 2010). In other words, in 1955, those with mental illnesses were 10 times more likely to find space available in public psychiatric hospitals *alone* than their counterparts at the start of the twenty-first century are likely to find at general hospitals, public psychiatric hospitals, and private psychiatric facilities *combined* (Torrey, et al., 2010). Conversely, there are more than three times as many people with mental illnesses incarcerated in correctional institutions today than there are in psychiatric hospitals; thus, "America's jails and prisons have become our new mental hospitals" (Torrey, et al., 2010, p. 3).

Estimates of Mentally Ill Inmates

This book emphasizes the increased prevalence of individuals with mental illness among incarcerated populations; indeed, literally dozens of jail and prison prevalence rate studies are listed in the tables of Chapters 3 through 10. To contextualize those studies, consider that approximately 7.1 million adults were under the supervision of state or federal correctional authorities in the United States at the end of 2010 (Glaze, 2011)—the most recent year for which official statistics were available to the authors. Of these people, roughly 2.26 million were incarcerated in prisons and jails (p. 2). A sizable proportion of this population suffers from SMIs.

One study concluded that up to 17.5% of inmates in state prisons had schizophrenia, bipolar disorder, or major depression (Veysey & Bichler-Robertson, 2002). Another found that 16.6 percent of inmates in five jails met the diagnostic criteria for SMIs that included schizophrenia, schizophrenia spectrum disorder, schizoaffective disorder, bipolar disorder, brief psychotic disorder, delusional disorder, and psychotic disorder not otherwise specified (Steadman, Osher, Robbins, Case, & Samuels, 2009). And a 2006 survey conducted by the U.S.

BOX 13.1 PREVENTING PEOPLE WITH SMIS FROM COMMITTING GUN-RELATED CRIMES

The Second Amendment to the U.S. Constitution states, "A well regulated Militia, being necessary to the security of a free State, the right of the people to keep and bear Arms, shall not be infringed." In *District of Columbia v. Heller* (2008), the U.S. Supreme Court invalidated a ban on handgun possession in Washington, D.C., reasoning that Second Amendment rights are exercised individually. The Court went on to say, though, that "nothing in our opinion should be taken to cast doubt on longstanding prohibitions on the possession of firearms by felons and the mentally ill" (p. 626). Two years later in *McDonald v. City of Chicago* (2010), the Court extended *Heller*'s holding to the states.

Federal law has prohibited people with SMIs from possessing firearms since at least 1968, when the Federal Gun Control Act was adopted. As amended over the years, it provides that "it shall be unlawful for any person who has been adjudicated as a mental defective or who has been committed to a mental institution" to purchase or possess a firearm. Such adjudication occurs when someone has been declared legally incompetent, has undergone involuntary civil commitment, or has been adjudicated legally insane; in contrast, this law does not reach people in mental institutions either for observation or as a function of voluntary admission (Vars & Young, 2013). Although some states have no laws on point, most either mirror federal legislation or have more stringent prohibitions on gun ownership or possession by people with mental illnesses, including those without any history of commitment. "For example, Hawaii prohibits gun possession by anyone who 'is or has been diagnosed as having a significant behavioral, emotional, or mental disorder. . . . '" (p. 12). These laws, however, did not prevent the tragedies in Tucson, AZ; Virginia Tech; Aurora, CO; and Newtown, CT. Adam Lanza used guns his mother had purchased legally. Jared Loughner, James Holmes, and Seung Hui Cho each purchased "the firearms they used for the murders they committed from federally licensed firearms dealers" even though all three of them had shown signs of SMI (McCreary, 2013, p. 813). Similarly, Russell Weston shot and killed two police officers at the U.S. Capitol Building in 1998 to "prevent the United States from being annihilated by disease and legions of cannibals" (p. 829). Weston had purchased the gun he used from a firearms store in Illinois, even though he had been involuntarily hospitalized in Montana—a commitment Montana seemingly had never reported.

In the wake of the Virginia Tech shooting, Congress enacted the National Instant Check System (NICS) Improvement Amendments Act (McCreary, 2013, p. 836). The law required state and federal agencies to report information about people who were prohibiting from possessing firearms to the U.S. Attorney General who, in turn, would enter the data in a searchable electronic database that firearms' dealers need to check before selling a gun. The law authorized the withholding of certain federal funds to states that failed to comply. Yet, after the deadline for compliance had come and gone, at least nine states had failed to provide any information and the threatened loss of funds has never been imposed (McCreary, 2013).

Even if NICS were fully implemented and working properly, there are reasons to doubt that it would be effective in preventing mass shootings by those with SMIs. First and foremost, only federally licensed firearm stores are required to use NICS. In contrast, no background checks occur for the roughly 40% of all U.S. firearm sales that occur either between private sellers or at gun shows. Second, even if universal background checks were required, neither Jared Loughner nor James Holmes had been committed. Hence, a NICS search would have failed to prevent either of them from having obtained the weapons they used in their respective massacres.

As this book makes clear, psychiatric terms such as "mental illness" and "mental disorder" do not map well onto the language that is used in federal gun control laws, such "mental defect." Which mental illnesses render people significantly "mentally defective" such that they forfeit their Second Amendment rights? And who would make this determination? Should a formal adjudication be necessary, or should the types of behaviors exhibited by Seung Hui Cho while a student at Virginia Tech or by Jared Loughner while a student at Pima Community College trigger restrictions on the ability to obtain firearms legally?

1. Which of the following changes in law and public policy do you support to reduce gun violence while preserving Second Amendment rights?
   - Closing the "gun show loophole" by requiring universal background checks?
   - Requiring mental health professionals to report a patient to county governments if they believe the patient is "likely to engage in conduct that would result in serious harm to self or others," as the State of New York does?
   - Barring a person from purchasing firearms for five years, as California does, after being placed on a 72-hour psychiatric hold in a facility?
   - Restricting gun sales not only for those involuntarily committed but also for those who voluntarily admit themselves to inpatient psychiatric care, as Georgia and Mississippi both do?
   - Insisting that anyone who wants to purchase a gun be required to prove his or her medical and mental health fitness to do so by obtaining a permit based on a physician's approval, as suggested by law professor Jana McCreary (2013)?
2. What other ideas do you have to keep firearms out of the hands of people with SMIs?

Source: Fradella (in press).

Department of Justice concluded that upwards of 24% of inmates in certain metropolitan jails evidenced symptomology of a psychotic disorder (James & Glaze, 2006).

> Studies show that the number of persons with SMIs in the prison system has risen from 7% in 1982 to 10–19% of jail populations, 18–27% of state prison populations, and 16–21% of federal prison populations. To put these prevalence estimates into perspective, the current rate of SMIs in jails and prisons is two to four times higher than rates of SMIs found among the general public. (Litschge & Vaughn, 2009, p. 542 [internal citations omitted]; see also Skeem, Manchak, & Peterson, 2010)

Based on these studies and on official reports from many states, Torrey and colleagues (2010) concluded that we "have thus effectively returned to conditions that last existed in the United States in the 1840s" when Dorothea Dix first began her campaign against imprisoning the mentally ill in jails. This conclusion is supported by the fact that the largest psychiatric facility in the United States is New York City's Rikers Island, which is estimated to hold 3,000 mentally ill offenders at any given time (Stephey, 2007).

In addition to the high rates of those with serious mental illnesses in correctional institutions designed to punish offenders rather than provide treatment, it is important to note that substance abuse is high among this population of offenders. It is estimated that between 50 and 75% of all mentally ill offenders in jails have co-occurring substance abuse problems (Skeem et al., 2010). This high rate may be due, in part, to those with SMIs self-medicating with alcohol or illicit drugs to help them relieve the unpleasant or painful symptoms of their disorders (e.g., Dixon, 1999; Khantzian, 1997; Modestin, Nussbaumer, Angst, Scheidegger, & Hell, 1997; Robinson, Sareen, Cox, & Bolton, 2009; Strakowski & DelBello, 2000).

Explanations for the High Prevalence of Inmates With Serious Mental Illnesses

One key thrust of this book is to examine the relationship between mental illness and crime as indicated by the intersection of evidence from a large number of studies. These studies have demonstrated (1) higher prevalence rates of mental illness within many types of criminal populations relative to those for noncriminals and the general population and (2) increased rates of criminal, violent, and antisocial behavior among those with mental illness compared to those without. We acknowledge that the relationship between mental illness and criminal and violent behavior is most likely complex and multilayered and requires many more years of replicated high-quality empirical work to understand and quantify. Furthermore, it would be naïve to neglect consideration of the numerous societal and public policy issues that most certainly are in play in this relationship. Those will be discussed here.

There are several possible explanations as to why there are so many people with SMIs in correctional facilities. First, much research has demonstrated that police frequently arrest the mentally ill with whom they come into contact (Borum, Swanson, Swartz, & Hiday, 1997; Steadman, Cocozza, & Melick, 1978; Torrey, et al., 1992). To some, the most obvious explanation for this high incidence of arrest is that the police do not understand the behaviors exhibited by people with SMIs and, therefore, make arrests based on misconceptions (e.g., Hylton, 1995). In landmark studies conducted in the 1980s, Teplin (1984, 1990a) found that police were more likely to arrest people displaying psychiatric symptoms than those who may be engaging in similar nuisance behaviors but do not outwardly show any signs of mental illness. But other research has questioned these findings. For example, after controlling for variables linked to police decision making, such as noncompliance and the relationship between the victim and offender, Engel and Silver (2001) found that police were actually less likely to arrest offenders with mental illnesses. The differences in results may be a function of methodology. Teplin used clinical definitions while Engel and Silver relied on officer's perceptions of mental illness.

Second, in many U.S. jurisdictions, especially those in which police departments subscribe to "broken windows" policing (i.e., the maintenance of order through cracking down on blight and nuisance crimes), formal criminal justice enforcement has emerged as a significant—if not the preferred—response to disorderly people (Kelling & Coles, 1996). People with SMIs, especially those who are homeless, loud, or otherwise disorderly, often face formal arrests in these locales (Goldman & Morrissey, 1985; Lamb & Lamb, 1990; Torrey, et al., 2010).

Third, it is clear that police often arrest the mentally ill to help them obtain services. Teplin and Pruett (1992) reported that police often make so-called **mercy bookings** to ensure that arrestees have a place to sleep, especially in extreme weather conditions, and are fed two or three meals each day. Torrey and colleagues (1992) similarly found that police arrested people with SMIs to keep them in a relatively safe environment until treatment space became available at mental health facilities.

Fourth, research suggests that many people with SMIs are arrested and incarcerated because mental health alternatives are not available—even through such an alternative would have been preferable (Dupont & Cochran, 2000; Lurigio, Snowden, & Watson, 2006). Indeed, well-trained officers often recognize when the people they encounter need mental health services; nonetheless, these officers make arrests either because community resources are completely unavailable or are so inadequate that frustration leads them to doubt the feasibility of any public health option (Engel & Silver, 2001; Hails & Borum, 2003; Thompson, Reuland, & Souweine, 2003).

Finally, the high prevalence rates of inmates with SMIs call into question the fairness of the criminal justice system's treatment of mentally ill. Mentally ill offenders who commit minor crimes are the "frequent flyers" of local and county jail systems (Torrey, et al., 2010). Largely due to the high frequency of these arrests and the lack of coordination between the criminal justice and mental health systems, these offenders typically receive little or no aftercare treatment upon their release from jail, which, in turn, can lead them to decompensate and be rearrested (see Solomon, Osborne, LoBuglio, Mellow, & Mukamal, 2008).

People with SMIs who commit serious offenses often fare no better. One reason is public hostility to defenses of excuse. Traditionally, as explored in Chapter 11, the doctrine of competency to stand trial and the insanity defense were both designed to prevent those with SMIs from being subjected to criminal prosecution and punishment. But several factors described in detail in Chapter 11 have collectively contributed to the "sharp increase in the number of mentally ill people in prisons" since the mid-1980s (Fradella, 2008, p. 120)—namely, the low standard for adjudicative competency, the severe restriction or even abolition of the insanity defense, judicial and juror hostility to diminished capacity defenses, and the U.S. Supreme Court's decision *in Clark v. Arizona* (2006). Prisoners with SMIs cost more to incarcerate (Torrey, et al., 2010), cause significant management problems for correctional officials and the courts (Fradella, 2003), and frequently decompensate to the point that roughly half of them attempt to commit suicide (Goss, Peterson, Smith, Kalb, & Brodey, 2002).

In summary, though a relationship between mental illness and crime is suggested by the increased prevalence rates of crime among the mentally ill and mental disorders among criminals populations, a wide range of factors contribute to the high incarceration rates of the mentally ill, including the failure of many CMH initiatives in the wake of mass deinstitutionalization, decreased funding for public psychiatric services, tight restrictions on the involuntary civil commitment of the mentally ill, and policies that get tough on crime and disorder, policies ranging from "broken windows" policing to the narrowing of criminal defenses of excuse. Collectively, these factors have led many to conclude that people with SMIs have been "criminalized"—a phenomenon often referred to as the **criminalization of the mentally ill** or the criminalization of mental illness (see Abramson, 1972; Fisher, Silver, & Wolff, 2006; PrisonPolicy.org, 2011; Slate & Johnson, 2008; Torrey, et al., 2010). In essence, behaviors caused by mental illness that were once managed in the mental health system have now become behaviors that are referred to the criminal justice system.

It should be noted that some scholars have questioned the criminalization hypothesis, arguing that the criminal behavior exhibited by only a small, albeit important minority of offenders (estimated at just under 10%) is a direct result of either psychosis or survival crimes related to poverty (Junginger, Claypoole, Laygo, & Crisanti, 2006; Peterson, Skeem, Hart, Vidal, & Keith, 2010). But these studies suffer from some methodological limitations insofar as they focus primarily on those convicted of only serious offenses and on those with SMIs. The researchers readily acknowledge that less serious offenses are often driven by hostility, disinhibition, and emotional reactivity that might be exacerbated by mental illnesses not labeled "serious" (i.e., those that do not involve psychosis). For example, Junginger and colleagues (2006) concluded that co-occurring substance abuse disorders led to a sizable minority of offenses in the population they studied. Thus, although there are limited data to suggest that SMIs have not been "criminalized" *per se*, there is little doubt that mentally ill offenders are in need of treatment that can not only reduce recidivism but also promote successful community reentry for this population of offenders. Consider that, upon release from prison, mentally ill offenders recidivate at high rates (e.g., Messina, Burdon, Hagopian, & Prendergast, 2004). In fact, parolees with mental illness are nearly twice as likely than their counterparts who are not mentally ill to return to prison within one year of release (Eno-Louden

& Skeem, 2011), and between 39 and 70% reoffend within 27 to 55 months, depending on the type of crime for which they were originally convicted (Case, Steadman, Dupuis, & Morris, 2009; Lovell, Gagliardi, & Peterson, 2002; Theurer & Lovell, 2008).

Policy Efforts to Improve the Plight of the Mentally Ill in the Criminal Justice System*

Conforming to one of the primary goals of the criminal justice system, a number of initiatives have attempted to reduce recidivism among mentally ill offenders. Many of these initiatives have been funded by a federal grant program established under the **Mentally Ill Offender Treatment and Crime Reduction Act (MIOTCRA)** of 2004.

MIOTCRA was signed into law in 2004 by President George W. Bush. The law created the Justice and Mental Health Collaboration Program (JMHCP) to assist state and local governments in creating collaborative efforts between the criminal justice and mental health systems. Congress reauthorized the act in 2008 for an additional period of five years and expanded opportunities for training. These were aimed at assisting law enforcement in the identification of and response to those with mental illness, as well as in the assessment of the mental-health and substance-abuse treatment needs of those in custody.

Under the Act's grant program, $50 million has been available for state and local government use. The grant requires law enforcement or criminal justice agencies and mental health services to collaborate and focus on the intersection of the two systems for the purpose of dealing effectively with deviant behaviors that occur as a result of mental illness. According to the Council of State Governments (2012), this grant money has been used to develop and implement training programs for law enforcement, mental health courts, and a variety of corrections-based treatment initiatives. Evaluation research on a number of these programs suggests that some are more effective than others. Before we explore this research, it should be noted that MIOTCRA has been criticized because grant money for diversion programs is available only to initiatives that serve *nonviolent* criminal offenders; money to assist people with serious mental illnesses who have committed violent offenses is available only to correctional-based treatments in jails or prisons or to reentry programs after release (e.g., Danjczek, 2007).

Skeem, Manchak, and Peterson (2010) conducted a meta-analysis of the effectiveness of a number of programs aimed at reducing the recidivism rates of mentally ill offenders. They focused on six types of programs. Four employ criminal justice models: jail diversion, mental health courts, specialty mental health probation or parole programs, and aftercare or reentry programs. Two utilize mental health models: forensic assertive community treatment (FACT) programs and forensic intensive case management (FICM) programs. Overall, they found mixed evidence that these programs reduce recidivism; the programs based on mental health models and the jail-diversion programs showed little to no effectiveness in reducing recidivism. They speculated that this finding might be due, in part, to these programs' heavy reliance on case management services. In contrast, three of the programs based on criminal justice models demonstrated varying levels of success.

Mental Health Courts

Generally, evaluation research has indicated that mental health courts have achieved significant levels of success when it comes to reducing recidivism among mentally ill offenders, at least in comparison to most other policies with this aim. Perhaps because evaluation research has generally indicated that **mental health courts** have achieved significant levels of success when it comes to reducing recidivism among mentally ill offenders, at least in comparison to most other policies with this aim, these specialty courts have grown in use and popularity since the first one was established in 1997. By 2013, some 300 mental health courts had been established, and that number is consistently growing. These courts are staffed by personnel experienced in working with mentally ill offenders and are based on therapeutic jurisprudence rather than adversarial justice (Council of State Governments Justice Center, 2013; Mann, 2011). The mental health courts typically include judges, social workers, probation officers, and attorneys who have received special training regarding mental illness, psychotropic medication, and substance abuse, in direct contrast to the "mixed bag" of training and education that would be found in traditional adjudication.

Mental health courts are remarkably diverse. The clinical diagnoses that qualify arrestees for participation in mental health court vary significantly across the country, as do court procedures and completion requirements (Mann, 2011; Redlich, Hoover, Summers, & Steadman, 2010). The types of cases mental health courts adjudicate also vary; 85% accept misdemeanor cases and 75% handle felony cases, although only 20% accept violent felony cases and only 1% handle seriously violent felony cases (Mann, 2011).

Technically, participation in mental health court programs is supposed to be voluntary. Upon agreeing to participate, new participants are required to sign contracts that typically include commitments to take prescribed medications, attend and engage in treatment appointments, return to the court for status review hearings, come to court on time, meet with case managers or probation officers, and follow any other individual requirements deemed necessary (Mann, 2011; Redlich et al., 2010). The use of sanctions to enforce these provisions varies significantly across mental health courts. Redlich and colleagues (2010), however, found that although between 65 and 76% of mental health court participants reported that they chose to enroll in the programs, most indicated that they did not know the court was voluntary, had not been informed of the program requirements prior to enrolling, and were unaware that they could stop participation if they so desired.

Empirical evaluations of mental health courts have generally found them to be effective at reducing recidivism (Herinckx, Swart, Ama, Dolezal, & King, 2005; McNeil & Binder, 2007; Moore & Hiday, 2006; Trupin & Richards, 2003). For example, Dirks-Linhorst and Linhorst (2012) found that the rearrest rate of 351 defendants who successfully completed a mental health court program was 14.5%, as compared to with 38% among defendants negatively terminated from the program and 25.8% among defendants who chose not to participate. But at least two studies have concluded that there is little difference in reoffending levels between mental health court graduates and those who do not complete such programs (Christy, Poythress, Boothroyd, Petrila, & Mehra, 2005; Cosden, Ellens, Schnell, & Yamini-Diouf, 2005). The intense variations in mental health court policies and programs may be responsible for these divergent findings.

Specialty Mental Health Probation

More than 100 U.S. jurisdictions have created programs that see probation officers manage specialized, reduced-size caseloads in which they work directly with treatment providers for mentally ill probationers (Eno-Louden, Skeem, Camp, Vidal, & Peterson, 2012). These specialty probation officers "more frequently discussed probationers' general mental health than any individual criminogenic need"; "chiefly questioned, directed, affirmed, and supported (rather than confronted) probationers"; and "relied more heavily on neutral strategies and positive pressures (e.g., inducements) rather than negative pressures (e.g., threats of incarceration) to monitor and enforce compliance" (p. 109). Consequently, specialty probationers were modestly less likely to be rearrested or have their probation revoked over a one-year period than offenders assigned to tradition probation. But given the modest levels of success associated with most of the specialty probation programs that have been evaluated empirically, the third option for which Skeem and colleagues (2010) found support—reentry and aftercare programs—might be a better option.

Prisoner Reentry and Aftercare Programs

The first year after release from jail or prison is a particularly salient time for monitoring offenders with serious mental illnesses because 77% of reoffending occurs within this time (Lovell, et al., 2002). High rates of reoffending can be tied to a number of factors, including medication noncompliance, lack of treatment services, a return to disorganized community settings, and poor support services. Accordingly, a number of jurisdictions have formed collaborative programs between correctional and mental health services to provide some continuity of care, many of which have been effective at reducing recidivism rates, even for those with co-occurring substance abuse disorders (Kesten et al., 2012; Sacks, Chaple, Sacks, McKendrick, & Cleland, 2012). Sacks, Sacks, McKendrick, Banks, and Stommel (2004), for example, found that mentally ill offenders receiving **prisoner reentry and aftercare services** were three times less likely to be reincarcerated within a year than those who received no such treatment interventions (5% vs. 16%). Similarly, a comprehensive jail aftercare and reentry program in Harris County, Texas, was found by Held and colleagues (2012) to reduce the total number of rearrests significantly for both felonies and misdemeanors.

The most promising reentry and aftercare programs are those that combine "interagency collaboration, housing support, and intensive, integrated clinical attention to mental health and substance abuse problems" (Theurer & Lovell, 2008, p. 400). As the Council of State Governments (2002) stated, "Without housing that is integrated with mental health, substance abuse, employment, and other services, many people with mental illness end up being homeless, disconnected from community supports, and thus more likely to . . . become involved with the criminal justice system" (p. 8). It should come as no surprise that such comprehensive programs can be quite expensive, reaching an annual cost of approximately $20,000 per person in some jurisdictions (Frisman, Swanson, Marín, & Leavitt-Smith, 2010). However, given that the average cost of incarcerating an inmate ranges between $18,000 to $50,000 per year with an average of $36,000 (*The Economist*, 2010), such reentry programs represent a solid investment from a cost-benefit standpoint. Moreover, even in jurisdictions in which the cost of reentry programs exceed those of incarceration costs, such an investment protects the public from future crime associated with untreated mental illness while simultaneously providing "a better set of mental health and justice outcomes for people with mental health problems and their communities" (Wolff, Bjerklie, & Maschi, 2005, p. 38).

Unintended Consequences of Contemporary Criminal Justice Policy

The comparative effectiveness of several of these previously discussed criminal justice interventions, which leverage access to much-needed community services, can inadvertently increase police willingness to make "mercy bookings." In other words, the structured treatment that mental health courts and reentry and aftercare programs offer can create incentives for police to arrest those with serious mental illnesses in order to get them the services they need (Bazelon Center for Mental Health, 2012). At first blush, one might be tempted to conclude that because the humanitarian motivations underlying such mercy arrests result in people with SMIs obtaining the services they need, justice system involvement is not necessarily a bad thing. But using the criminal justice system to address the public health needs of people with SMIs has numerous and serious unintended consequences.

First, several negative consequences stem directly from arrest and incarceration. These traumas can aggravate the symptoms of many SMIs, causing not only an unnecessary increase in suffering for the affected person but also the manifestation of behaviors that lead to violence, which can injure those with serious mental illnesses, police officers, innocent bystanders, correctional officers, and other inmates in jails and prisons (see Gur, 2010). And arrests have collateral social consequences as well, which range from "stigmatization based on a criminal record" to the "resulting denial of housing or employment or treatment services—even if charges are dropped" (Bazelon Center for Mental Health, 2003, p. 2).

Second, because police often serve as the first responders to situations involving people with SMIs, significant resources must be devoted to training police to interact with this population to avoid unnecessary victimization. Today, many police departments have established a **crisis invention team (CIT)** to avoid situations in which officers mistake the symptoms of SMIs and respond using unnecessary levels of force, which sometimes result in preventable deaths (Gur, 2010; Stephey, 2007). But CIT programs are not cure-alls. Certainly, it costs a significant amount of money to establish these programs and then train officers. But perhaps more importantly, we do not know if CITs actually reduce the violent and victimization experiences of both police and people with SMIs during encounters between the two, nor has it been established that CIT programs are actually effective in reducing the arrests of persons with SMIs (see Watson, Ottati, Morabito, Draine, Kerr, & Angell, 2010).

Third, using the criminal justice system as the "front door to access mental health care" (p. 2) has placed enormous financial burdens on state and local governments, which have been forced to increase budgets to accommodate the expenditures required in dealing with these complex problems. According to Johnson (2011), states with large populations of prisoners must commit large portions of their state budgets to operating criminal justice services. The implications of these increasing criminal justice budgets are cuts to other programs in the state; ironically, at times, these cuts are to public health or housing programs that may help prevent some of the offenses leading to incarceration.

State and citywide expenditures continue to rise as more and more offenders requiring psychiatric treatment are relegated to the care and custody of jails and prisons. For instance, the Los Angeles County Jail spent $10 million on psychiatric medication in 2001, and the State of Ohio in 2005 was treating 8,371 mentally ill offenders at a cost of $67 million a year. In Florida the number of mentally ill inmates in jails and prisons is believed to outnumber those in state-run psychiatric facilities by 5 to 1; yet, the minimum cost to care for a mentally ill person is in excess of $40,000 in a Florida jail and $60,000 in a Florida prison, compared to the roughly $20,000 cost of providing intensive CMH treatment to those with serious mental illnesses (PrisonPolicy.org, 2012). Overall, imprisoning mentally ill offenders costs the United States roughly $9 billion per year (Slate & Johnson, 2008).

Fourth, mentally ill inmates create enormous problems for the corrections system. The three largest providers of psychiatric care in the United States are New York's Rikers Island Jail, the Cook County Jail in Illinois, and California's Los Angeles Jail (Slate & Johnson, 2008). The fact that so many mentally ill offenders are being held in our jails and prisons means that many of these prisoners are in daily contact with corrections officers who have not received proper training in dealing with psychiatric populations effectively and safely (Gur, 2010). This lack of training and understanding can lead to increases in conflicts, physical altercations, and injuries, for both corrections officers and inmates (Steadman et al., 2009). Indeed, people with SMIs are often victimized while incarcerated (Gur, 2010; Human Rights Watch, 2009). Failing to provide incarcerated inmates with a constitutionally minimum level of medical care, as well as failing to protect these inmates from foreseeable victimization while they are incarcerated, further adds to the budgetary strain local and state governments experience as a result of the criminalization of mental illness. "Perhaps the best example of this is Sheriff Joe Arpaio who, claiming to be the toughest sheriff in the country, has cost taxpayers of Phoenix millions of dollars in lawsuit settlements for violating the civil rights of inmates with mental and medical needs" (Johnson, 2011, p. 19).

At great cost, some larger correctional facilities have special units devoted to housing "special needs" populations. Their staff receives at least some training in working with the mentally ill. But even in these units, those with SMIs face a number of risks, not the least of which is **decompensation**, or a functional deterioration in response to stress accompanied by an increase in the severity of the mental illness or its associated symptoms. The incarceration environment is one in which inmates with SMIs "are more likely to violate rules or be injured in fights" (Gur, 2010, p. 228; James & Glaze, 2006).

Finally, the funding consequences linked with the criminalization of mental illness offenders have produced an untenable situation—funds are no longer available to support public mental health outside of the correctional setting in some U.S. jurisdictions. As a result, some states, such as Iowa, have turned to recommitting offenders with SMIs back into the prison system from which they were released after serving their sentences because the state has no other facility to which they can be referred (Fuller, 2011). The beginning of 2011 saw 75 mentally ill offenders committed to the prisons under this arrangement, some of whom had been civilly committed to the prison for a period of several years (Fuller, 2011). In essence, citizens who have served their sentences are still being remanded to prison as the result of their mental illness because there are no adequate mental health treatment facilities left in which they can be civilly committed for treatment. This situation is the purest example of our jails and prisons becoming *de facto* psychiatric facilities, and it raises the question of whether the due process rights of these mentally ill offenders are being violated by virtue of the fact that they have "served their time" and yet are not being released from prison.

Suggestions for Policy Reform

There is no shortage of calls for changes in policy to address the many problems with the revolving-door cycle of incarcerating those with mental illnesses in jails and prisons and then releasing them only to have them return to the criminal justice system (e.g., Torrey et al., 2010; Vitiello, 2010). In the final section of this chapter, we explore some of the most common recommendations.

Legislative Changes to Address Financial Problems

Two legislative changes could go a long way toward improving policies to assist mentally ill offenders. First, as noted earlier, MIOTCRA limits its funding of diversion programs to those that serve only nonviolent criminal offenders. If MIOTCRA were amended to fund diversion programs that reached violent offenders as well, more people with mental illnesses could benefit from mental health court supervision.

Second, the statutory restriction for using Medicaid funds to support mentally ill individuals in "institutions for mental diseases" should be lifted. This ban encourages states "to empty hospitals, even if the patients end up in jails or homeless" (Torrey, et al., 2010, p. 12). Moreover, "there are no fiscal incentives to follow up and make sure the patients receive care once they leave the hospitals" (p. 12). Accordingly, this restriction on Medicaid use should be repealed.

Increased Diversion Efforts by Expanding the Number and Scope of Mental Health Courts

As previously summarized, most studies evaluating the effectiveness of mental health courts find them to be effective at reducing recidivism (Dirks-Linhorst & Linhorst, 2012; Herinckx, et al. 2005; Moore & Hiday, 2006; McNiel & Binder, 2007; Trupin & Richards, 2003) and at improving mental health functioning (Boothroyd, Poythress, McGaha, & Petrila, 2003). But there are many communities that do not have this option available. It would therefore appear to be good public policy to increase the number of mental health courts. But care must be taken to insure that these courts are properly staffed and funded, lest the courts become so backlogged and unable to provide services that their effectiveness is compromised. Also, court resources deemed adequate for traditional populations will not be sufficient because the success or failure of any mental health court program depends "on the ability of the mental health system to treat effectively those diverted from the criminal justice system" (Litschge & Vaughn, 2009, p. 550). Thus, as discussed more fully below, inadequacies in the mental health system must also be addressed.

Regardless of the availability of mental health courts, there is a question of whether any criminal justice system involvement is necessary at all, especially in many misdemeanor cases. Consider that Fisher and colleagues (2006) noted that a review of the records of mentally ill offenders arrested for nuisance crimes and referred to the forensic evaluation unit of a state hospital in Massachusetts found that many of these offenders would have met criteria for an involuntary hospitalization if the police had not arrested them but had instead taken them for psychiatric emergency services. If that's the case, does the criminal justice system need to be involved at all? As Skeem and colleagues (2010) suggest, providing psychiatric treatment to those with mental illnesses *before* they violate the criminal law could prevent the criminal justice system from even being involved with people who should be treated as patients rather than offenders. Thus, the best public policy options may lie outside the criminal justice system, one of the most promising of which involves reforming the civil commitment process.

Reform Civil Commitment Laws

Torrey and colleagues (2010) call for significant changes in civil commitment laws. Specifically, they seek the statutory authority to commit those who need treatment without regard to their dangerousness. "Many times, it is this very dangerousness standard that necessitates law enforcement involvement. Mentally ill individuals should be able to access treatment before they become dangerous or commit a crime, not after" (p. 12). At first blush, this proposal seems logical and warranted. But two concerns threaten its viability.

First, as previously explained in Chapter 12, lax due process protections in the civil commitment arena were one of the reasons that civil liberties activists championed the tightening of these laws in the 1960s and 1970s. Legislators would need to vote to loosen these laws over the objections of both civil libertarians and advocates for the mentally ill who oppose involuntary hospitalization. Moreover, when such laws are challenged in the courts, judges would have to decide not only that the autonomy and privacy rights of the individual were outweighed by societal interests in caring for the mentally ill against their wishes but also that statutes provide sufficient safeguards to guarantee due process. Meeting these two standards is not, however, a difficult task. Several states, most notably New York, appear to have done so quite successfully (see Litschge & Vaughn, 2009; New York State Office of Mental Health, 2005).

Second, even if better laws could be enacted that eased dangerousness criteria for commitment while still honoring due process rights, increasing the number of civil commitments will not be possible until there are sufficient beds in psychiatric facilities to care for patients civilly committed to them. Given how few beds are available and in light of the incredible budgetary pressures on most states since the Great Recession of 2008, it is highly unlikely that most states could afford to expand the number of psychiatric beds available to accommodate need. Moreover, although there is an argument to be made that the funds currently used to pay for the incarceration of mentally ill offenders in jails and prisons could be shifted out of the criminal justice system and into the public health system to pay for these beds, the politics of doing so would likely be a significant obstacle. Consider that many other social services, most notably education, have been cut as public budgets have shrunk. Reasonable arguments can certainly be made that education and other services need to be funded before expanded access to psychiatric hospital beds.

There may, however, be a middle ground. In the past few years, many states have modified their civil commitment laws to allow for the *outpatient civil commitment* of mentally ill people in crisis (Slate, 2009, p. 21). Outpatient civil commitment is more commonly referred to as **assisted outpatient treatment (AOT)**. AOT "requires selected seriously mentally ill persons to take medication under court order as a condition for living in the community" (Torrey, et al., 2010, p. 12). According to the Treatment Advocacy Center (2012), 44 states have laws that authorize AOT. Empirical studies of AOT lend significant support to this policy recommendation, as AOT has been demonstrated not only to reduce dramatically the arrest rate of the mentally ill (Litschge & Vaughn, 2009; New York State Office of Mental Health, 2005; Swanson, Swartz, Borum, Hiday, Wagner, & Burns, 2000) but also to significantly decrease their use of alcohol and drugs, psychiatric rehospitalizations, homelessness, suicides, and violent behaviors (Fernandez & Nygard, 1990; Munetz, Grande, Kleist, & Peterson, 1996; Phelan, Sinkewicz, Castille, Huz, Muenzenmaier, & Link, 2010; Rohland, 1998; Swartz, et al., 2010; Zanni & deVeau, 1986). Moreover, there is evidence that several of these positive outcomes continue even after court supervision ends (Van Dorn, et al., 2010).

Improve Services for the Mentally Ill Within and Beyond the Criminal Justice System

Offenders with mental illnesses generally fall into three categories: those arrested for "simply displaying the signs and symptoms of mental illness in public"; those who commit petty, nuisance, or survival crimes; and those who commit serious crimes, including violent ones (Lurigio, 2011, p. 12). People in the first group do not belong in the criminal justice system at all. They need psychiatric services offered through an improved public health system. When police encounter such an individual, they should be able to take him or her for treatment without ever making a formal arrest. The aforementioned improvements in outpatient civil commitment laws vis-à-vis AOT would give police the authority to do so and would improve the public health outcomes for the mentally ill without ever involving them in the criminal justice system.

The second group of offenders should be diverted to mental health courts. But we need to conceptualize the primary purpose of these specialized courts as serving a public health function not a criminal justice role. Measures of success need to go beyond mere recidivism statistics. Indeed, the myth that treating psychiatric symptoms can improve recidivism rates must be dispelled. There are no studies empirically demonstrating that alleviating psychiatric symptoms—in and of itself—affects recidivism among offenders with SMIs (Lurigio, 2011). Thus, improvements that address only the treatment of psychiatric symptoms are not likely to reduce recidivism. To accomplish that goal, psychiatric treatments need to be paired with other interventions aimed at criminogenic factors (Skeem, et al., 2010), such as substance abuse, lack of education, lack of employment, and community disorganization. Toward that end, mental health courts need to pair offenders with a variety of social service agencies in much the same way that prison parolees are paired in the comprehensive reentry and aftercare programs that have demonstrated so much success at rehabilitating the whole person. Doing so would not only help these people "get back on their feet" but also help them avoid subsequent involvement in the criminal justice system (Council of State Governments, 2002; Kesten et al., 2012; Sacks, et al., 2004; Sacks, et al., 2012; Skeem, et al., 2010; Theurer & Lovell, 2008; Wolff, et al., 2005).

The third group of offenders—those who commit serious crimes—pose the most significant policy challenges. To be sure, those who are imprisoned need treatment while incarcerated, and, after release, they must be placed into comprehensive reentry and aftercare programs that help them comply with the rules governing their release, thereby avoiding probation and parole violations and reducing the incidence of new offenses. But treatment, reentry, and aftercare programs based in correctional institutions do not address the true problem of incarcerating offenders with mental illnesses in jails or prisons in the first place. Three changes to law and policy could make a significant difference in reducing the number of people with mental illnesses in correctional institutions, the final one of which might even reduce the commission of crime by this population.

First, the narrowing of defenses of excuse that began in the 1970s and accelerated dramatically in the wake of John Hinckley Jr.'s case must be revisited (see Fradella, 2007). In *Clark v. Arizona* (2006), the U.S. Supreme Court upheld the authority of states to limit severely a mentally ill criminal defendant from offering some of the most probative evidence concerning his or her guilt. To prove that Eric Clark committed murder, the prosecution in the *Clark* case introduced evidence that the defendant spoke of wanting to kill police and then argued that, to carry out this plan, the defendant lured police to the scene by blaring music from his truck while circling a block in a residential neighborhood. The defendant, however, was barred from introducing largely undisputed evidence about the nature of paranoid schizophrenia and how the disease caused or could have caused his actions. Specifically, the trial court was barred from considering expert testimony that people with schizophrenia often play music loudly to drown out the voices in their heads, which would have directly undercut the assertion that Clark did so to lure police officers to his car. The unworkable evidentiary framework upheld in *Clark* prevented the defense from arguing what should have been a straightforward defense, namely, that the defendant "did not commit the crime with which he was charged" because he lacked the requisite *mens rea* (*Clark v. Arizona*, 2006, p. 801, Kennedy, J., dissenting). The Supreme Court must revisit this misguided result and hold that barring the admissibility of such evidence violates due process (Fradella, 2007). Of course, dangerous people with serious mental illnesses like Eric Clark do not belong on the streets where they are free to maim or kill. But they do not belong in prisons either where they burden the correctional system and receive little or no treatment. Rather, such defendants should be remanded for treatment in secure psychiatric hospitals.

Second, the jurisdiction of mental health courts should be expanded to include the authority to adjudicate violent felony offenses. As Mann (2011) points out, 80% of mental health court systems do not accept any violent felony cases and only 1% handle those involving serious crimes of violence. If defendants who commit crimes such as robbery and aggravated assault as a function of their mental illnesses had their cases handled through a system that subscribed to a therapeutic jurisprudence model, these offenders could get the comprehensive help they need while being monitored for compliance in ways that help to increase public safety.

Finally, and most important, we must make improvements to the mental health system and related social services so that people with mental illnesses do not commit serious crimes in the first place. Significantly expanded use of AOT can help to effectuate this desirable outcome. Those with mental illnesses need both psychiatric care (including access to psychotropic medications, when appropriate) and interventions aimed at criminogenic factors, such as job training, substance abuse treatment, and housing assistance (Skeem, et al., 2010). Such multimodal services are likely to bring significant secondary benefits largely unrelated to the narrow metric of recidivism. Providing better treatment for the mentally ill would likely reduce psychiatric symptoms in ways that would allow the mentally ill to "become sober and employed, find and retain stable housing, develop better self-control, return to school, [and] mend relationships with family" (Lurigio, 2011, p. 15). These benefits, in turn, would reduce calls to police and correspondingly reduce the number of inmates with SMIs because mentally ill people receiving appropriate treatment and adequate social services will be better able to follow societal rules—they will not run afoul of the law in the first place.

KEY TERMS

assisted outpatient treatment (AOT)

criminalization of the mentally ill

crisis invention team (CIT)

decompensation

deinstitutionalization

mental health courts

Mentally Ill Offender Treatment and Crime Reduction Act (MIOTCRA)

mercy bookings

prisoner reentry and aftercare services

REVIEW QUESTIONS

1. What are the primary reasons offered to explain why there are so many people with serious mental illness in U.S. correctional facilities?
2. Explain the criminalization hypothesis. What evidence supports it? What evidence calls it into question?
3. In your opinion, which two of the four criminal justice programs aimed at reducing recidivism rates of mentally ill offenders are the most promising? Evaluate the effectiveness of these programs using empirical evidence. How might these programs be expanded to further reduce recidivism rates of mentally ill offenders?
4. What policy outside of the criminal justice system would, if implemented, most effectively improve services for people with serious mentally illnesses? Explain your reasoning.

Glossary

Accidental conditioning—A proposed behavioral explanation for some sexual deviations, referring to an unintended associative pairing of erotic pleasure with some form of nonsexualized behavior (e.g., spanking for the purposes of punishment), which results in sexual deviancy (e.g., a spanking fetish, or—in some cases—sadism or masochism).

Actus reus—Latin for "guilty act." It is the conduct element of crime, the specific act prohibited by a particular criminal law.

Addictive behaviors—Any compulsive habit pattern in which the individual seeks a state of immediate gratification. Gratification may be in the form of relief from discomforts, such as tension, negative mood, or withdrawal states, or it may involve the introduction of pleasure or euphoria. Addictive behaviors include excessive use of psychoactive substances (drugs that affect thought, emotion, and behavior) or excessive, unhealthy levels of other behaviors with compulsive characteristics, such as gambling, eating, or sexual acts. Addiction involves continued involvement with the behavior despite adverse consequences and attempts to stop.

Affective—Affect is a general term for feelings and emotions. Affective disorders are those characterized by disturbance of mood (currently conceptualized as disorders such as depressive and bipolar disorders).

ALI/MPC affective test—The American Law Institute (ALI) developed a Model Penal Code (MPC) in 1962, and its formulation of the insanity defense is usually referred to as the ALI/MPC affective test. According to the ALI/MPC affective test, a person is not responsible for criminal conduct if, at the time of the offense, the defendant suffered from a mental disease or defect (other than antisocial personality disorder or any other abnormality manifested only by repeated criminal or otherwise antisocial conduct) that caused the defendant to lack either the substantial capacity to appreciate the criminality (wrongfulness) of his or her conduct or the substantial capacity to conform his conduct to the requirements of law.

Amygdala—A component of the limbic system thought to be associated with memory, processing emotions, and aggression. It is an almond-shaped body located in both the right and left hemispheres of the brain, deep within the medial temporal lobes.

Anaclitic depression—A subtype of depression (proposed by Sydney Blatt) characterized by a vulnerability to perceived losses in relationships with others (i.e., a dependency upon the judgments of others for self-esteem). "Anaclitic" is a term originally coined to describe the state of depression, withdrawal, and listlessness into which infants fall when separated from their mothers.

Anal phase—Proposed by Freud, an early stage of psychosexual development in which the anus and defecation are the major source of sensuous pleasure and form the center of the infant's self-awareness. Fixation—or failure to progress through this stage—may result in an anal character (personality), which is typified by traits such as obstinacy, orderliness, parsimony, or their opposites (compulsive pliancy, untidiness, or generosity).

Anterior—A directional term meaning—in the brain and spinal cord—toward the front (or face).

Anthropophagy—A paraphilia associated with lust murder marked by an intense desire to eat the flesh or body parts of another.

Antisocial personality disorder—A personality disorder characterized by a pervasive pattern of disregard for or violation of the rights of others, beginning in childhood or early adolescence and continuing into adulthood. There may be a decreased moral sense or conscience and a history of crime, legal problems, impulsivity, and aggression.

Anxiety—Commonly defined as a diffuse, vague, and extremely unpleasant feeling of fear and apprehension. Physiological symptoms of anxiety may include combinations of rapid heart rate, shortness of breath, diarrhea, loss of appetite, fainting, dizziness, sweating, sleepiness, frequent urination, and tremors.

Approximate simultaneity—A theory on the relationship between drug use and crime. Proponents argued that, over the span of the addiction career, increased levels of drug use and crime appear to be somewhat episodic and sporadic (i.e., rarely lasting more than one or two years at a time) but vary directly with one another—likely reflecting increased income-generating criminality motivated by the need to purchase drugs during addicted periods.

Asperger's disorder—An autism spectrum disorder characterized by significant difficulties in social interaction and nonverbal communication, along with restricted and repetitive patterns of behavior and interests. It is considered among the higher functioning of the autism spectrum disorders and lacks the delays in cognitive development and language characteristic of autism.

Assessment—The collection of information for the purposes of making an informed decision. Assessment tools include life records, interviews, psychological tests, observations, and biological measures.

Assisted outpatient treatment (AOT)—Also known as "outpatient civil commitment." AOT refers to a mental health law that allows courts to issue orders for the compulsory outpatient treatment of persons with mental illnesses as a condition of living in the community. Such court orders typically include provisions for taking psychotropic medication. AOT is considered a less restrictive alternative than involuntary civil commitment and has been shown to reduce the incidence and duration of hospitalizations, homelessness, and incarcerations.

Asylums—Institutions established to provide treatment and care for the mentally ill. Prior to the establishment of asylums, the mentally ill were often confined in jails and prisons under inhumane conditions.

Asymmetry—Lacking symmetry. Regarding the brain, asymmetry indicates differences in structure or function in one side compared to the other.

Attention-deficit/hyperactivity disorder (ADHD)—A psychiatric disorder characterized by significant problems of attention and/or hyperactivity and impulsive behavior that are not appropriate for an individual's age.

Autistic disorder (autism)—A condition marked by social communication and interaction deficits as well as restricted repetitive patterns of behavior, interests, and activities.

Automatic thoughts—Thoughts that occur automatically in response to a given situation. These thoughts are "automatic" in that the interpretive process and even the thoughts themselves may be outside of the individual's awareness—leaving only the emotional consequence of the thought known to the individual. Cognitive and cognitive-behavioral therapies work to change negative automatic thoughts into more rational responses. Automatic thoughts are thought to be manifestations of deeper underlying maladaptive assumptions.

Autonomous depression—One of two types of depression proposed by Beck (1983), autonomous depression is marked by a focus on achievement and independence.

Avoidant personality disorder—A personality disorder characterized by a pervasive, inflexible, and enduring pattern of inhibited social interactions, feelings of inadequacy, and hypersensitivity to criticism or rejection.

Behavior genetics—The study of genetic influences on behavior aimed at understanding the combined influences of nature and nurture on normal and abnormal behavior (sometimes called behavioral genetics). Currently, a new generation of neurogenetic studies is beginning to identify specific genes that predispose an individual to adult antisocial behavior when combined with negative environmental influences such as child abuse.

Biological determinism—The hypothesis that biological factors such as an organism's individual genes (as opposed to social or environmental factors) completely determine how that organism will behave or change over time.

Bipolar I disorder—As defined in the DSM, bipolar I disorder is characterized by one or more manic or mixed episodes, usually accompanied by major depressive episodes.

Bipolar II disorder—As defined in the DSM, bipolar II disorder is characterized by one or more major depressive episodes accompanied by at least one hypomanic episode.

Borderline personality disorder—A personality disorder characterized by a pervasive, inflexible, and enduring pattern of instability in relationships with others, self-image, and emotions, along with significant impulsivity.

Capgras syndrome—The belief that familiar persons have been replaced by physically identical imposters. Capgras syndrome is a delusion of misidentification.

Catathymic crisis—A sudden release and potentially violent expression of suppressed emotion.

Catatonic behavior—A positive symptom of schizophrenia, catatonic behaviors occur when an individual moves or behaves in a disorganized manner, such as remaining completely still in unusual positions, moving in ways that do not serve a purpose, mimicking the speech or behaviors of others, or refusing to talk or respond to others.

Central nervous system—The part of the nervous system consisting of the brain and spinal cord.

Cerebral cortex—The 1.5 to 4.5 mm layer of gray matter that covers the surface of each cerebral hemisphere.

Civil commitment—An exercise of state power by which the government can hospitalize mentally ill persons against their will in order to prevent them from harming themselves or others. The procedures for involuntarily committing someone are civil procedures not criminal ones.

Classical conditioning—Rooted in the work of Ivan Pavlov (1849–1936), classical conditioning describes behavior based on reflexes that are automatically elicited by the environment. In his famous experiment with dogs, Pavlov repeatedly paired an *unconditioned stimulus* such as food, which elicits a reflexive (or *unconditioned response*) such as salivation, with a neutral stimulus such as a tone. Eventually, the neutral stimulus became a *conditioned stimulus* that elicited salivation as a *conditioned response*; the dogs learned to salivate in response to the tone.

Clinical psychology—A branch of psychology devoted to the study of psychopathology and to providing psychological diagnostic and treatment services to patients.

Cluster A—In regard to personality disorders, the DSM-IV-TR and DSM-5 outline a clustering system (Cluster A, Cluster B, and Cluster C) based on descriptive similarities. Cluster A includes the paranoid, schizoid, and schizotypal personality disorders (individuals described as odd or eccentric). It must be noted that this clustering system has serious limitations and has not been consistently validated and that individuals may often present with coexisting personality disorders from different clusters.

Cluster B—In regard to personality disorders, the DSM-IV-TR and DSM-5 outline a clustering system (Cluster A, Cluster B, and Cluster C) based on descriptive similarities. Cluster B includes the antisocial, borderline, histrionic, and narcissistic personality disorders (i.e., individuals often appearing dramatic, emotional, or erratic).

Cluster C—In regard to personality disorders, the DSM-IV-TR and DSM-5 outline a clustering system (Cluster A, Cluster B, and Cluster C) based on descriptive similarities. Cluster C includes the avoidant, dependent, and obsessive-compulsive personality disorders (i.e., individuals often appearing anxious or fearful).

Cognitive—Referring or related to a group of mental processes including attention, memory, producing and understanding language, learning, reasoning, problem solving, and decision making. Cognitive therapy is a form of psychotherapy that seeks to help patients overcome difficulties by identifying and changing dysfunctional thinking, behavior, and emotional responses.

Cognitive errors—Mistakes in thinking such as all-or-none thinking, arbitrary inferences, selective abstraction, magnification and minimization, and inexact labeling. Cognitive errors are caused by maladaptive assumptions, which drive automatic thoughts.

Cognitive inflexibility—Difficulties with the mental ability to switch between thinking about two different concepts and to think simultaneously about multiple concepts.

Command hallucinations—Auditory hallucinations ordering either violent or nonviolent action. Compliance with auditory command hallucinations may depend upon a variety of different factors and upon various personal, situational (e.g., outside versus inside hospital setting), and clinician variables.

Community mental health (CMH) movement—The third wave of major reforms to the ways in which society treats people with mental illnesses. The movement was ushered in by advances in psychiatry in the 1950s and 1960s, most notably the advent of psychotropic medication that allowed the mentally ill to lead lives outside the walls of institutions. During this era, the federal government enacted a series of laws that established the National Institute of Mental Health and created far-reaching policies to foster mental health in the United States.

Comorbidity—The coexistence of mental disorders in one individual. Comorbidity can be considered either in terms of a lifetime or at a single point in time.

Competency—A legal term referring to the possession of sufficient mental faculties to understand certain types of problems or situations and make rational decisions regarding the resolution of those problems.

Competency to stand trial—Competency to stand trial concerns itself with a criminal defendant's mental state at the time of trial. In order to stand trial, criminal defendants must be able to understand the nature of the charges against them and assist counsel in their own defense. The determination of competency to stand trial is purely a legal determination—not a clinical one. Competency to stand trial is an essential part of due process and may be raised at any time in the criminal process, even after conviction.

Complication model—In regard to the multiaxial diagnostic nature of the DSM-IV-TR, it is known that personality disorders (i.e., Axis II) may coexist with other mental disorders (i.e., Axis I). One explanation of the relationship between the two types of disorders, the complication model posits that the Axis I disorder creates a predisposition for personality change.

Compulsions—As defined in the DSM-IV-TR, compulsions are repetitive behaviors or mental acts that are employed to prevent or diminish anxiety, tension, or distress. This definition has conceptually remained relatively unchanged in the DSM-5. Compulsive behaviors are not goal oriented or rewarding in and of themselves. They may be linked functionally to obsessive thoughts but usually are not realistically connected to the source of the distress. Common and frequently reported compulsive behaviors include repetitive washing, checking, repeating rituals, ordering and arranging behaviors, hoarding, and cognitive compulsions.

Computed tomography (CT) scanning—Uses highly focused x-ray beams that delineate the distribution of tissue structures based on regional radio density to take images from multiple angles around a central point. These multiple images are then reconstructed by a computer to form a composite three-dimensional image of the brain. CT scans reveal the gross features of the brain, but do not reveal its structure well. Currently, CT scanning is one of the leading structural neuroimaging modalities used to map the anatomical architecture of the brain.

Conduct disorder—A disorder of childhood or adolescence characterized by a repetitive and persistent pattern of behavior that violates the basic rights of others or major age-appropriate norms.

Connectivity—A pattern of anatomical links between distinct units (i.e., individual or groups of neurons or brain regions) within the nervous system.

Criminalization of the mentally ill—Criminalizing the behaviors of those with serious mental illnesses (SMIs). As a result, behaviors caused by mental illness that were once managed in the mental health system have now become behaviors that are referred to the criminal justice system.

Crisis intervention team (CIT)—Used by many police departments, crisis intervention teams are specially trained to respond to situations involving people with serious mental illnesses (SMIs). Crisis intervention teams are specifically trained to avoid victimization of individuals with SMIs.

Cross-tolerance—Occurs when tolerance to one drug has developed and more of any drug in that class is necessary to produce comparable effects because of the similar organic structure of their active ingredients and the nervous system's response.

"Cycle of violence" theory—A theory regarding the association between PTSD and violence. It suggests that the experience of violent trauma may contribute to the commission of future violent acts.

Cyclothymic disorder—A disorder defined by numerous periods of hypomanic symptoms that do not meet criteria for a hypomanic episode and numerous periods of depressive symptoms that do not meet criteria for a major depressive episode.

Dangerousness—The traditional approach to the determination of dangerousness in the civil commitment context uses one or more of three distinct dangerousness criteria: the type of danger, the immediacy of the danger, and the likelihood of the danger.

Death instinct [Thanatos]—Proposed by Freud, a drive or wish to dissolve or annihilate oneself. According to Freud, the purpose of the death instinct was to oppose the **life instinct [Eros]** and drive individuals to return to the inorganic state.

Decompensation—An increase in the severity of the mental illness or the associated symptoms.

Defense mechanisms—As proposed by Freud, defense mechanisms—which are mostly unconscious—are employed by the ego to relieve the anxiety, guilt, and other unpleasant emotional problems occurring when unconscious desires and impulses approach consciousness. Defense mechanisms require significant mental energy and can ultimately fail. If they do fail, the person retreats (or regresses) to even more primitive, immature behaviors reminiscent of early childhood.

Deficient empathy—Referring to a reduced ability or incapacity for recognizing the emotional experiences of others.

Deficits—A term used to indicate comparative weaknesses in areas of biological, psychological, or social functioning. Cognitive deficits refer to any characteristic that acts as a barrier to cognitive performance while structural deficits refer to abnormalities (such as reductions in gray or white matter volume) in specific areas or structures in the brain.

Deinstitutionalization—The process of moving patients out of psychiatric hospitals and into community-based treatment. Deinstitutionalization was a product of the community mental health (CMH) movement that began in the 1950s. As a result, the resident population of state mental hospitals declined by more than 75% between 1955 and 1980, and state mental hospitals were closed across the country. However, rather than receiving community-based care, those with SMIs were largely ignored because adequate funding was not provided to communities to support the needs of these patients upon their release from mental hospitals.

Delusion—As defined in the DSM-IV-TR, a delusion is a "false belief based on an incorrect inference about external reality that is firmly sustained despite what almost everyone else believes and despite what constitutes incontrovertible and obvious proof of evidence to the contrary." In the DSM-5, delusions are defined as "fixed beliefs not amenable to change in light of conflicting evidence."

Delusions of misidentification—Delusions such as Capgras syndrome, Doppelgänger syndrome, Fregoli syndrome, and intermetamorphosis. Misidentification syndromes, in general, are associated with anger and suspiciousness toward the misidentified other.

Dependent personality disorder—A personality disorder characterized by a pervasive, inflexible, and enduring pattern of submissiveness, clinging behavior, and excessive need to be cared for.

Diagnosis—The classification of mental disorders by determining which of several possible descriptions best fits the nature of the problems.

***Diagnostic and Statistical Manual of Mental Disorder* (DSM)**—The primary tool used in the United States to define and diagnose mental illnesses. The DSM was created by the American Psychiatric Association (APA) in 1952 and is currently in its fifth edition (DSM-5).

Diathesis—A biological or psychological predisposition to disorder. According to the **diathesis-stress model**, abnormality is the product of two interacting factors: the diathesis and stressors arising from the family, environment, or the person's own behavior that translates the diathesis into an actual disorder. A diathesis can make people more likely to encounter stressors, and a stressor can intensify a diathesis.

Diathesis-stress model—See **Diathesis**.

Diminished capacity—Though there is no standard definition for the doctrine of diminished capacity, it deals with the admissibility of evidence concerning the accused's mental state. A defendant invoking the diminished capacity doctrine asserts that his or her mental state prevented him or her from forming the requisite *mens rea* for the crime.

Diminished responsibility—Diminished responsibility is concerned with the propriety of punishment. Diminished responsibility allows either a jury or a judge to mitigate the punishment of a defendant who is not legally insane but who, as a result of some mental illness or disability, is morally less culpable than someone who commits the same criminal act in the absence of psychiatric impairment.

Disorganization syndrome—One of three syndromes in a proposed theoretical model of schizophrenia based on reality distortion, disorganization, and psychomotor poverty. Prominent characteristics are disorganized behavior and speech and flat or inappropriate experiences of expressions of emotion.

Disorganized speech—A positive symptom of schizophrenia, disorganized speech patterns reflect disrupted and unorganized thoughts and may be characterized by jumping "off track" during conversations, speaking with random and jumbled words, and the use of words that do not make sense to others. Disorganized speech is also referred to by some as thought disorder.

Dissociation [dissociated]—A term in psychology describing varying degrees of detachment from immediate surroundings, physical and emotional experience, and reality.

Dissociative identity disorder (DID)—A mental disorder characterized by at least two distinct and relatively enduring identities or dissociated personality states that alternately control a person's behavior and accompanied by memory impairment for important information not explained by ordinary forgetfulness. This disorder was first introduced as multiple personality in the DSM-III, subsequently renamed multiple personality disorder in the DSM-III-R, and finally conceptualized as DID in the DSM-IV. The DID process is thought to begin before the age of five and to have resulted from overwhelming trauma that the mind of the child cannot tolerate.

Doppelgänger syndrome—The belief that one has a double or impersonator. Dopplegänger syndrome is a delusion of misidentification.

Dorsal [dorso-]—A directional term meaning—in the brain—toward the top. (In the spinal cord, dorsal means toward the back).

***Durham* rule**—A test for insanity developed by the U.S. Court of Appeals for the District of Columbia Circuit in response to dissatisfaction with the *M'Naghten* rule. Under the *Durham* rule, a defendant could not be held criminally responsible if the criminal act resulted from a mental defect. The D.C. Court of Appeals overruled the *Durham* rule in 1972 in *United States v. Brawner.*

Dyscontrol—A term referring to a reduced ability or capacity for control, usually applied to psychological or neurological processes or principles.

Dysthymic disorder—A disorder characterized by a prolonged period of depressed mood accompanied by additional depressive symptoms that do not meet criteria for a major depressive episode.

Early starters—Hodgins (2008) proposed three distinct subtypes of violent offenders with schizophrenia based upon the age of onset of antisociality and violence. In early starters, antisocial behavior emerges in childhood or adolescence, well before the onset of schizophrenia, and remains stable throughout the individual's lifespan.

Ego—One of the three mental "structures" identified in Sigmund Freud's psychoanalytic theory, the ego is the collection of regulatory functions that constrains the impulses of the id by acting as a sort of mediator. The ego is a theoretical concept, not an actual physical component of the brain.

Electroencephalography (EEG)—A technique for observing brain function in which electrodes placed on the scalp directly measure electrical responses of a large number of neurons inside the brain. Developed in the 1920's, this technique is one of the earliest methods for observing brain function.

Enslavement theory—A theory on the relationship between drug use and crime, the enslavement theory argues that opiate addiction enslaves otherwise law-abiding individuals to the point that they must commit crimes to support their drug use.

Epilepsy—A common and diverse group of chronic neurological disorders characterized by seizures.

Erotophonophilia—A paraphilia in which sexual excitement is derived from sexual homicide or lust murder.

Exhibitionism—A paraphilia in which the focus is the exposure of one's genitals to a stranger.

Extraversion—A trait (on a continuum with introversion) that is a central dimension of human personality theories. Extraversion tends to be manifested in outgoing, talkative, and energetic behavior.

Fagan's approach—A theoretical explanation for the linkages among drugs, alcohol, and violence, Fagan's approach proposes that intoxication influences aggression by impacting cognitive functioning, which is moderated by the context in which behavior occurs.

Fear—A basic element of human survival, fear is an emotional response to dangerous and threatening stimuli. Fear and anxiety appear to be interrelated on several different levels; however, it is generally held that individuals experiencing fear are easily able to articulate what they are afraid of, and those experiencing anxiety are not.

Fear avoidance theory—A theory proposing that some PTSD individuals may be characterized by feelings of anger and avoid intrusive, fear-related thoughts and feelings activated by reminders of the trauma through the expression of physical aggression.

Fetishism—A paraphilia involving the sexualization of inanimate or nonliving objects (the "fetish"), which commonly include women's undergarments, stockings, shoes, boots, other types of clothing and apparel, or a nongenital body part. The fetish is usually required or strongly preferred for sexual arousal, and males may experience erectile dysfunction in its absence.

Flagellationism—A paraphilia associated with lust murder marked by an intense desire to beat, whip, or club someone.

Forensic behavioral science—Fields of science that employ the scientific application of methods, procedures, and techniques to investigate human behavior relevant to problems found in criminal law and, to a lesser degree, civil law. These scientific fields include but are not limited to forensic psychology, forensic psychiatry, and forensic neuroscience.

Forensic risk assessment—Determining the likelihood that a person poses a particular type of recognized threat, such as the threat of committing a future act of violence. Forensic risk assessment instruments retain their highest rates of predictive accuracy when evaluating the populations upon which they were validated.

Fregoli syndrome—The belief that another person has changed his or her physical identity while his or her psychological identity remains the same. Fregoli syndrome is a delusion of misidentification.

Frontal [fronto-]—Related to, pertaining to, or situated in the frontal lobe, which is an area in the brain of mammals located at the front of each cerebral hemisphere.

Frontal lobe—The most anterior lobe of each cerebral hemisphere. The frontal lobes are involved in executive functions and play an important role in retaining some types of long-term memories.

Frotteurism—A paraphilia in which the focus is touching and rubbing against a nonconsenting person. Often the behavior occurs in crowded places, which allow the frotteur to easily conceal his rubbing behavior under the pretext of navigating through a large crowd and to more easily escape detection and arrest.

Functional brain imagining—One of two broad categories of brain imaging methods. Collected information on brain function, using methods such as functional magnetic resonance imaging (fMRI), single-photon emission computed tomography (SPECT), and positron emission tomography (PET), has suggested a link between violence and frontal dysfunction.

Functional magnetic resonance imaging (fMRI)—A technique for observing and recording brain function that is based on the concept of neural coupling—the fact that increased neuronal activity in a brain region is followed by a local increase in blood flow through the region. This response leads to an increase in the ratio of oxygenated to deoxygenated hemoglobin, which can be detected because the magnetic resonance of blood differs slightly depending upon the level of oxygen within it. This hemodynamic effect can be recorded using a special magnetic resonance pulse signal called BOLD (blood oxygen level dependent) contrast, which is used to form images of activity within the brain. Compared to CT and PET, fMRI has better spatial resolution, offers increased temporal resolution, and is noninvasive.

Generalized anxiety disorder (GAD)—A mental disorder marked by persistent and excessive anxiety and worry in various domains, including work and school performance, that the individual finds difficult to control.

Genital phase—Proposed by Freud, the genital phase is the final stage of psychosexual development, which begins in adolescence when physical maturity is nearly complete and continues through adulthood. Pleasure is focused once again on the genital area, but, if earlier development has gone well, the pursuit of pleasure is not characterized by the selfishness of the phallic stage. Rather, sexuality is fused with love for another and finds expression within a long-term relationship.

Goldstein's tripartite framework—A theoretical explanation for the linkages among drugs, alcohol, and violence, Goldstein's tripartite framework consists of *psychopharmacological violence* (stemming from properties of the drug itself), *economic compulsive violence* (associated with the high costs of the use of illicit drugs and the need or desire to obtain drugs that produce strong physical and psychological dependencies, such as opiates and cocaine), and *systemic violence* (associated with the traditionally aggressive interactions related to drug distribution and use).

Gravely disabled—As defined by the American Psychiatric Association, a gravely disabled person is someone who is substantially unable to provide for some of his or her basic needs, such as food, clothing, shelter, health, and safety, or a person who will, if not treated, suffer or continue to suffer severe and abnormal mental, emotional, or physical distress—also, this distress must be associated with significant impairment of judgment, reason, or behavior causing a substantial deterioration of the individual's previous ability to function on his or her own.

Gray matter—A major component of the central nervous system that is composed of neural cell bodies, other types of cells and unmylenated cellular structures (see **white matter**), and capillaries.

Guilty but mentally ill (GBMI)—First enacted in Michigan in 1975, the guilty but mentally ill verdict allowed juries to acquit those defendants who were insane under a traditional not guilty by reason of insanity (NGBRI) verdict but also provided jurors a "middle ground" verdict to convict those who were not insane but who did suffer from a mental illness at the time of the commission of a criminal offense. Under the Michigan GBMI scheme, a defendant so adjudicated would be sentenced just as if he or she had been found guilty of the crime, with one exception: a court must make a determination if the GBMI defendant needs treatment.

Guilty except insane (GEI)—The guilty except insane (GEI) verdict holds the person responsible (i.e., "guilty") but simultaneously exempts the legally insane from criminal punishment.

Gyrus—A ridge on the folded and convoluted surface of the cerebral hemispheres; the plural is **gyri**.

Hallucination—A hallucination is sensory perception without actual sensory input. Hallucinations may occur along any sensory modality—sight (visual), hearing (auditory), smell (olfactory), touch (tactile), and taste (gustatory). Auditory hallucinations are the most common type.

Harrison Narcotic Tax Act—Passed in the United States in 1914, The Harrison Narcotic Tax Act was a federal law regulating and taxing the production, importation, and distribution of opiates. This legislation marked a major governmental attempt to make psychoactive substances illegal and served to solidify and propel a popular social reform movement that labeled drug use as both a form of criminality and a common cause of violence and bizarre behavior.

Hemispheres—In relation to the brain, the cerebral cortex is divided into two hemispheres (right and left "halves"), which are thought to be individually associated with different aspects of broader cognitive abilities.

Histrionic personality disorder—A personality disorder characterized by a pervasive, inflexible, and enduring pattern of excessive emotionality and seeking of attention.

Hormones—Chemical messengers secreted by the endocrine system.

Humanism—Referring to a philosophy and movement that flourished in the Italian Renaissance in which the value and agency of human beings were emphasized, and individual thought and evidence were preferred over established doctrine or faith.

Hyperactivity—A physical state in which a person is abnormally active. Hyperactivity is one of the diagnostic criteria for attention-deficit/hyperactivity disorder.

Hypomanic episode—A less-severe variant of a manic episode with identical symptomatology, but a four-day versus a seven-day threshold for symptom duration.

Id—One of the three mental "structures" identified in Sigmund Freud's psychoanalytic theory, the id is the reservoir of raw, unstructured, impulsive energies seeking immediate gratification of its needs, desires, and impulses. The id is a theoretical concept not an actual physical component of the brain.

Impairment—A condition or its symptoms that make an individual weaker or less effective. According to the DSM, to be considered a mental disorder, the condition and its symptoms must cause significant difficulties in one or more major areas of an individual's life.

Impulsivity—A term reflecting a tendency to act on a whim, engaging in behavior characterized by little or no forethought, reflection, or consideration of the consequences. Impulsivity is one of the diagnostic criteria for attention-deficit/hyperactivity disorder.

Inattention—A term reflecting a lack of attention, notice, or regard. Inattention is one of the diagnostic criteria for attention-deficit/hyperactivity disorder.

Incidence—The number of people who develop a condition or symptom during a specific time period, such as a year.

Inferior—A directional term meaning—in the brain and spinal cord—below or toward the bottom (or feet).

Information processing theory—A neurobiological theory incorporating the concept of neural or memory networks. These are networks of interrelated elements or nodes that provide structure to the ways in which we think about and observe the world around us.

Inhibitory control—One of the brain's executive functions, reflecting the ability to stop or inhibit a response or not act on an impulse. Inhibitory control is necessary for moral conduct and moral cognitive development.

Insanity—A legal term referring to the defendant's state of mind at the time of the offense in which a **mental disease or defect** caused the person to lack the substantial capacity to appreciate the wrongfulness or criminality of her or his acts. Insanity must generally be asserted by the defendant, usually through defense counsel, in a timely manner in order to be litigated as a criminal defense at trial.

Insanity Defense Reform Act of 1984 (IDRA) -With the enactment of the IDRA, Congress codified the federal insanity defense for the first time and legislatively overruled the application of the ALI/MPC insanity test in all federal cases. According to the IDRA, a person is not responsible for criminal conduct if, at the time of acts constituting the offense, the defendant suffered from a severe **mental disease or defect** that caused the defendant to be unable to appreciate either the nature and quality of his or her acts or the wrongfulness of his or her acts.

Intelligence quotient (IQ)—A score derived from one of standardized neuropsychological tests used to assess intelligence.

Intermetamorphosis—The belief others have undergone radical physical and psychological changes to become persecutors. Intermetamorphosis is a delusion of misidentification.

Intermittent explosive disorder—A disorder characterized by a pattern of recurrent, unplanned outbursts of verbal or physical aggression, which are disproportionately intense relative to the situation and cause significant distress or have markedly deleterious consequences in the individual's life. Assaults occurring within these episodes may be verbal, destructive or nondestructive against property, or injurious or non-injurious against people.

Intracortical and **intercortical**—Terms used by scientists referring to neuronal connections within the cerebral cortex (or within the same area of the cerebral cortex) or between different parts of the cerebral cortex.

Introjective/self-critical depression—A subtype of depression (proposed by Sydney Blatt) characterized by vulnerability to self-criticism, failing to meet one's own unrealistically high standards (which are "introjected" or internalized mental representations of or from the parents), and later acceptance of external negative evaluations.

Kleptomania—A disorder characterized by the repeated inability to resist the impulsive stealing of objects (even though they are not needed by the individual or are of trivial monetary value), in which the thefts are preceded by an increasing sense of tension and followed by subsequent relief.

Latency phase—Proposed by Freud, a later stage of psychosexual development that occurs at age five or six as the turmoil of resolving the Oedipus complex subsides. During this phase, children spend several years focusing on academic skills and same-sex friendships.

Lateral—A directional term meaning—in the brain—toward the side.

Lesions—Abnormalities in brain tissue (in layman's terms, "damage"), usually caused by disease or trauma.

Life instinct [Eros]—Proposed by Freud, the life instinct includes both sexual and self-preservative instincts and opposes the **death instinct [Thantos]**—the drive to return to the inanimate state.

Limbic system—A claw-shaped network of smaller structures located toward the center of the brain and important in emotional responses, drive-related behavior, and memory. The limbic system includes the hippocampus, amygdala, anterior thalamic nuclei, septum, habenula, limbic cortex, and fornix.

Lobe—An anatomical term indicating a clear division or extension of an organ (e.g., the brain) that can be determined at the gross anatomy level without using a microscope.

Low-fear hypothesis—According to this hypothesis, certain types of psychopaths, known as "primary" psychopaths, are characterized by attenuated experiences of anxiety and fear; because of their "below average endowment of innate fearfulness," they are more difficult to socialize using conventional parenting methods, which are based on a child's motivation to avoid punishment. The hypothesis is derived from studies of psychopathy and other antisocial personalities.

***M'Naghten* rule**—A test for insanity enacted by the House of Lords of the United Kingdom in 1843. Still in use in several states within the United States, the *M'Naghten* rule provides that a person is not responsible for criminal conduct if, at the time of the offense, the defendant suffered from a **mental disease or defect** that caused the defendant either not to know the nature and quality of the act he or she committed or, knowing both, not to know that the act was wrong.

Magnetic resonance imaging (MRI)—Use of a powerful magnetic field along with radiofrequency stimuli to construct images that contrast different types of brain tissue (gray matter, white matter, and cerebrospinal fluid) due to the unique proton density of each tissue. Currently, MRI is one of the leading structural neuroimaging modalities used to map the anatomical architecture of the brain.

Magnetoencephalography (MEG)—A method used to observe brain function that measures the magnetic fields produced by electrical brain activity. Because the electrical activity measured by EEG has different physical properties than the magnetic waves MEG measures, MEG provides different information that can complement EEG data. It is primarily used to localize areas in which seizure activity occurs, as well as to identify areas of normal brain functioning in patients about to undergo brain surgery.

Major depressive disorder—As defined in the DSM, major depressive disorder is characterized by one or more **major depressive episodes**.

Major depressive episode—A period of depressive symptoms that lasts at least two weeks and causes significant impairment in important areas of an individual's life. A major depressive episode is the basic conceptual unit for a diagnosis of major

depressive disorder or, in combination with one or more hypomanic episodes, **bipolar II disorder**.

Maladaptive assumptions—From a cognitive psychology perspective, basic interpretive rules that drive automatic thoughts and lead to critical **cognitive errors** in everyday functioning. More generally, maladaptive assumptions are deeply held thoughts or beliefs about oneself that are too narrow, too broad, too severe, or simply inaccurate and that, consequently, contribute to psychological dysfunction.

Manic episode—A period of elevated mood symptoms and increased goal-directed activity or energy that lasts at least one week and causes significant impairment in important areas of an individual's life. A manic episode is the basic conceptual unit for a diagnosis of bipolar I disorder and is the portion of this disorder characterized by elevated, expansive, or irritable moods.

Medial [medio-]—A directional term meaning—in the brain—toward the middle.

Medical model—One approach to theoretically conceptualizing certain types of substance-related disorders, the medical model of addiction attributes the addiction and relapse to physiological factors (e.g., family history of addiction or pathological metabolism) beyond the individual's control, thus alleviating blame and encouraging addicts to seek professional help. This is the most common view in the United States.

Medicalization—The process by which medicine, especially psychiatry, creates diagnoses for a range of human behaviors and labels them as disorders.

Mens rea—Latin for "guilty mind." It refers to the defendant's mental state concerning his or her level of intentionality at the time of the commission of a criminal act (an *actus reus*).

***Mens rea* approach**—In jurisdictions that have abolished the insanity defense, a defendant may still attempt to escape criminal liability by demonstrating that a mental illness prevented him or her from forming the requisite *mens rea* associated with a particular crime. This approach is problematic for defendants with psychotic disorders who form criminal intent as a result of delusional beliefs.

Mental disease or defect—The legal term for mental disorders that qualify for particular legal standards. The term often has different meanings in different legal contexts. For example, the disorders that qualify as mental diseases or defects for insanity defense purposes vary from those that might form the basis of a diminished capacity defense. The mental disorders that qualify as mental diseases or defects for certain civil legal standards, such as involuntary civil commitment, also vary from those that are applicable in criminal law contexts.

Mental health courts—First established in 1997, these courts are staffed by specially trained personnel experienced in working with mentally ill offenders and are based on a therapeutic jurisprudence model rather than on an adversarial justice approach. The mental health courts typically include judges, social workers, probation officers, and attorneys who have received special training regarding mental illness, psychotropic medication, and substance abuse. Technically, participation in mental health court programs is supposed to be voluntary.

Mental retardation—A generalized disorder appearing before adulthood that is characterized by significantly impaired cognitive functioning and deficits in two or more adaptive behaviors. It has historically been defined as an intelligence quotient score under 70. Mental retardation has been replaced with "intellectual disability (intellectual developmental disorder)" in the DSM-5, which now includes both a component relating to mental functioning and one relating to individuals' functional skills in their environment (as opposed to previous definitions, which have focused almost entirely on cognition).

Mentalizing—See **Theory of mind (ToM)**.

Mentally Ill Offender Treatment and Crime Reduction Act (MIOTCRA)—Signed into law in 2004 by President George W. Bush, the law created the Justice and Mental Health Collaboration Program (JMHCP) to assist state and local governments in creating collaborations between the criminal justice and mental health systems. Grant money that has been made available under the JMHCP to state and local governments has been used to develop and implement training programs for law enforcement, mental health courts, and a variety of corrections-based treatment initiatives.

Mercy bookings—Refers to the act of police arresting the mentally ill in order to help them obtain services. Mercy bookings, especially those made in extreme weather conditions, ensure that arrestees have a safe place to sleep and are fed two or three meals each day.

Mesial [mesio-]—See **Medial [medio-]**.

Mesolimbic reward pathway—A critical brain circuit that connects areas of the frontal cortex with the nucleus accumbens and ventral tagmental area in the limbic system. A variety of neurotransmitters, including dopamine, serve this circuit. The rewarding effects of many psychoactive substances have been associated with the mesolimbic reward pathway.

Mindblindness—The relative inability to estimate the cognitive, perceptual, and emotional experiences of others as well as of one's self.

Moral model—One approach to theoretically conceptualizing certain types of substance-related disorders, the moral model of addiction proposes that addiction and relapse are signs of character or moral weakness for which the individual is responsible and which must be overcome by willpower. This approach can foster guilt as the addict takes on the blame for the addiction's initial development and for his or her failure to change.

Multiple personality disorder—See **Dissociative identity disorder (DID)**.

Narcissistic personality disorder—A personality disorder characterized by a pervasive, inflexible, and enduring pattern of grandiosity, need for admiration, and lack of empathy for others.

Narcissistic rage—One of two forms of aggression proposed by Heinz Kohut (the other being competitive aggression), narcissistic rage is directed toward selfobjects that threaten or are perceived to threaten the self and represent a need for avenging a previous narcissistic injury. (Selfobjects are people that we experience early in our lives as part of ourselves and later in life in terms of the functions or services they originally performed.) Although competitive aggression dissipates immediately after the barrier is removed, narcissistic rage persists long after the threat is eliminated and may endure and even increase with the passage of years.

Necrophilia—A paraphilia in which sexual excitement is derived from sexual contact with a dead body.

Necrosadism—A paraphilia associated with lust murder in which sexual excitement is derived from mutilating or otherwise inflicting damage to a corpse.

Negative reinforcement—In terms of operant conditioning, the disappearance of something unpleasant (e.g., an electric shock or an annoying sound), which makes behavior more likely to occur on appropriate occasions in the future.

Negative symptoms—Schizophrenia is characterized by a cluster of symptoms categorized into positive symptoms and negative symptoms. Negative symptoms, which include affective flattening, alogia, and avolition, represent ways of thinking, feeling, and behaving that suggest something is missing or has been taken away from a person's normal experience.

Neuropsychiatric developmental model (NDM) for serial murder—This model takes into account five causative components: neuropsychiatric development (i.e., autism spectrum disorders such as Asperger's disorder), psychopathy, aggressive behavior, sexual psychopathology (i.e., fetishism such as partialism or necrophilia), and environmental stressors.

Neuropsychology—A branch of psychology concerned with measuring the indirect expression of brain dysfunction, generally through behaviors observed and paper-and-pencil tests.

Neurotic—An adjective derived from the term "neurosis" (a term used historically for disorders with purely psychological causes). Neurotic is used to indicate that a particular phenomenon is not healthy (normal), not organic (physical), not psychotic, and is capable of psychological explanation.

Neuroticism—A fundamental personality trait characterized by anxiety, moodiness, worry, envy, and jealousy.

Neurotransmitters—Chemicals that form the basis of the transmission of information throughout the brain. Neurotransmitters are stored in the synaptic vesicles of communicating nerve cell axons. Neurotransmitters bind to receptor sites after crossing the synapses between nerve cells during the transmission of neuronal signals.

Nosology—A term meaning a classification system containing a set of categories of disorder and rules for categorizing disorders based on the signs and symptoms that appear.

Obsessions—As defined in the DSM-IV-TR, obsessions are persistent ideas, thoughts, impulses, or images that are experienced as intrusive and inappropriate and that cause marked anxiety or distress. This definition has remained largely consistent in the DSM-5. Obsessions are primarily *ego-dystonic*—meaning that the individual senses the obsession's content to be alien, outside of his or her control, and uncharacteristic of him or her. Repeated thoughts about becoming contaminated, repeated doubts, orderliness, impulses to commit aggressive or horrifying acts, and recurrent sexual imagery are among the most commonly reported obsessions.

Obsessive-compulsive disorder (OCD)—A mental disorder characterized by the presence of obsessions (recurrent and persistent thoughts, urges, or images that are experienced as intrusive and unwanted) and compulsions (repetitive behaviors or mental acts that an individual feels driven to perform in response to an obsession or according to rules that must be applied rigidly).

Obsessive-compulsive personality disorder—A personality disorder characterized by a pervasive, inflexible, and enduring pattern of concern for orderliness, perfectionism, and control.

Occipital—Related to, pertaining to, or situated in the occipital lobe.

Occipital lobe —The most posterior lobe of each cerebral hemisphere and the visual processing center of the brain.

Oedipus complex—See **Phallic phase**.

Operant conditioning—According to operant conditioning, all behavior is learned as a function of the antecedent conditions in which it is displayed and the consequences that follow it. Thus, behavior can be explained by looking at the functional relationships between operant behavior—acts that "operate" on the environment—and its observable antecedents and consequences. Behavior is strengthened through reinforcement, that is, when positive consequences follow the behavior. Additionally, behavior is less likely to occur when it is followed by negative consequences—a process called punishment. Behavior can also be made less likely to occur through extinction, or the absence of any notable consequences. Reinforcements and punishments may be external or internally, self-produced consequences, which can serve to motivate and inform future behavior.

Oppositional defiant disorder—A disorder of childhood characterized by an ongoing pattern of anger-guided disobedience, hostility, and defiant behavior toward authority figures that is outside the scope of normal childhood behavior.

Oral phase—Proposed by Freud, the first stage of psychosexual development, which occurs during the first year. During this phase, eating, sucking, and biting are the main sources of pleasure. According to Freud, oral fixation is reflected in habitual smoking, overeating, intemperate drinking, and excessive talking.

P300 ERP amplitude—A positive (in terms of voltage) electrophysiological waveform occurring approximately 300 milliseconds after the onset of a presented stimulus. ERP stands for "event-related potential," a measured brain response resulting from a specific sensory, cognitive, or motor event. The P300 (or P3) has consistently been found in antisocial and aggressive individuals and may reflect a form of cognitive deficit.

Paranoid personality disorder—A personality disorder characterized by a pervasive, inflexible, and enduring pattern of distrust and suspiciousness of others.

Paraphilia—Literally means "abnormal love." According to the DSM-IV-TR, the essential features of a paraphilia are recurrent, intense sexually arousing fantasies, sexual urges, or behaviors that occur over a period of at least six months and generally involve 1) nonhuman objects, 2) the suffering or humiliation of oneself or one's partner, or 3) children or other nonconsenting persons. Paraphilias include exhibitionism, fetishism, frotteurism, pedophilia, sexual masochism, sexual sadism, and transvestic fetishism.

Parasympathetic nervous system—One of two parts of the autonomic nervous system. Whereas the sympathetic nervous system prepares the body for action by increasing physiological and psychological arousal, usually by stimulating heart rate and increasing blood pressure and respiration as preparation for fighting or fleeing a threat, the parasympathetic nervous system decreases arousal in order to conserve the body's energy and resources. This system balances the sympathetic system by slowing heart rate and decreasing blood pressure and respiration.

Parens patriae—Latin for the "state as parent." This doctrine provides the state with the ability to impinge upon the autonomy rights of minors and incompetent people because such people are ostensibly incapable of engaging in the rational decision-making processes in which the law presumes people engage.

Parietal—Related to, pertaining to, or situated in the parietal lobe.

Parietal lobe—The part of the brain positioned above the occipital and temporal lobes and behind the frontal lobe. Areas of the parietal lobe are involved in integrating different types of sensory information, language comprehension, and determining spatial sense and navigation.

Parker's selective disinhibition approach—A theoretical explanation for the linkages among drugs, alcohol, and violence, Parker's selective disinhibition approach proposes that internalized norms against violence may become disinhibited in certain situations and contexts.

Pathogenic—Disease causing.

Pathological gambling (gambling disorder)—A problematic pattern of persistent and repeated gambling behavior leading to disruptions in personal, family, or vocational endeavors.

Pathologies—A synonym for "diseases."

Pathoplasty model—In regard to the multiaxial diagnostic nature of the DSM-IV-TR, it is known that personality disorders (i.e., Axis II) may coexist with other mental disorders (i.e., Axis I). One explanation of the relationship between the two types of disorders, the pathoplasty model, posits that personality influences the course of an Axis I disorder without itself disposing toward the development of the disorder.

Pedophilia—A paraphilia in which sexual excitement stems from sexual activity with a prepubescent child, usually 13 years of age or younger. To be diagnosed with pedophilia, an individual must be 16 years of age or older and at least 5 years older than the child. As pedophilia is generally ego-syntonic (i.e., psychologically compatible with the self), those with this disorder do not often experience significant distress.

Peripheral nervous system—The part of the nervous system consisting of the nerves and ganglia outside of the brain and spinal cord.

Persecutory delusions—As classified in the DSM-5, persecutory delusions refer to the belief that one is going to be harmed, harassed, and so forth by an individual, organization, or other group.

Personality disorders—Inflexible, pervasive, and enduring patterns of thoughts, feelings, interpersonal behavior, and impulse control that lead to significant distress or impairment in important areas of an individual's life.

Personality traits—Enduring patterns of perceiving, relating to, and thinking about the environment and self that are present across a wide range of contexts and situations. These traits represent *disorders* once they become inflexible and maladaptive, causing significant functional impairment or subjective distress.

Phallic phase—Proposed by Freud, a later stage of psychosexual development that occurs during the third or fourth year.

During this phase, the genitals become the focus of pleasure. Freud argued that, at this time, young boys begin to feel sexual desires for their mothers and wish to eliminate their fathers as sexual competitors (which he called the **Oedipus complex** due to its recapitulation of the plot of the Greek tragedy, *Oedipus Rex*). The boy fears that his desires will be discovered and that his father will punish him with castration; and the boy normally resolves the conflict and reduces his anxiety by repressing his sexual urges and forming an identification with his father. Freudians see fixation at the phallic stage as responsible for many adult problems, especially those dealing with parents and other authority figures, confusion about sex roles, and sexual dysfunctions.

Phobia—An anxiety disorder marked by fear. The term is derived from the Greek word "*phobos*," defined as flight, panic, fear, or terror.

Physical dependence—The physiological adaptation of the body to prolonged exposure to a substance.

Physiological symptoms—The body's physical reactions and responses to anxiety. Physiological symptoms of anxiety may include combinations of rapid heart rate, shortness of breath, diarrhea, loss of appetite, fainting, dizziness, sweating, sleepiness, frequent urination, and tremors.

Piquerism—A paraphilia marked by the intense desire to stab, wound, or cut the flesh of another person. Often these stab wounds are inflicted near the genitals or breasts in the act of lust killing.

Police power—The authority of the state to confine those who endanger society.

Polythetic approach—The approach utilized by the *Diagnostic and Statistical Manual of Mental Disorder* (DSM) to diagnose mental disorders. According to this approach, a person must meet a particular number of criteria out of a larger set of possible criterion symptoms in order to be diagnosed with a mental disorder.

Positive reinforcement—In terms of operant conditioning, any type of reinforcement (e.g., the appearance of something pleasant, such as food or praise) that makes behavior more likely to occur on appropriate occasions in the future.

Positive symptoms—Schizophrenia is characterized by a cluster of symptoms that are categorized into positive symptoms and negative symptoms. Positive symptoms, which include delusions, hallucinations, disorganized speech, and catatonic behavior, represent ways of thinking and behaving that indicate something has been added to the way a person normally thinks and behaves.

Positivism—A philosophy of science stating that the only authentic knowledge is that which allows verification and assumes that the only valid knowledge is scientific.

Positron emission tomography (PET)—A technique for observing and recording brain function that measures changes in regional blood flow and metabolism associated with changes in neural activity. Generally, this technique involves the presentation of a visual or auditory stimulus and the subsequent measurement of the brain's functional response as indicated by regional blood flow or glucose metabolism after the stimulus, which, in turn, indicates different levels of neural activity in those regions. Specifically, PET involves injecting a radioactive tracer compound bound to glucose (F-labeled fluorodeoxyglucose, or FDG) into the bloodstream. The brain metabolizes glucose to support neural activity, so wherever the glucose goes the radioactive material also goes. A scanner is able to pick up the brain regions where glucose is metabolized, indicating brain activity.

Posterior—A directional term meaning—in the brain and spinal cord—toward the back (or back of the head).

Postpartum depression (PPD)—A form of clinical depression affecting women (and less often men) typically occurring after childbirth.

Post-traumatic stress disorder (PTSD)—An anxiety disorder and characterized by the reexperiencing of an extremely traumatic event accompanied by symptoms of increased arousal and by avoidance of stimuli associated with the trauma.

Potentiation—Refers to the additive or synergistic effects of multiple drugs of the same class administered simultaneously, which can result in an overdose.

Prefrontal cortex—The part of the frontal lobe anterior to (in front of) the premotor and supplementary motor areas. Important for working memory, planning, and choosing appropriate responses to social and life situations.

Prevalence—In the context of this book, total number of people who suffer from a disorder in a specific population or the total number of people with a specific disorder who engage in criminal or violent behavior.

Prisoner reentry and aftercare services—Programs that provide continuity of care to mentally ill offenders following their release from incarceration. A primary goal of such programs is to reduce recidivism among mentally ill offenders, so these programs are often collaborations between correctional and mental health services.

Psychological dependence—Refers to users' perceptions that they need a substance to feel or function optimally.

Psychopathy—A personality disorder that manifests early in life and persists throughout life. Psychopathic individuals have been traditionally described as individuals who are lacking in empathy, loyalty, and guilt and who engage in persistent antisocial, impulsive, and irresponsible behavior. Such individuals typically do not evidence impaired intelligence but appear unable to make use of their intelligence to learn from mistakes. Psychopathy was the first personality disorder to be recognized in psychiatry.

Psychopathy Checklist—Revised (PCL-R)—Developed in 1980 by Canadian psychologist Robert Hare, the PCL-R is now considered the "gold standard" of psychopathy measures. The standard PCL-R assessment procedure consists of a semi-structured interview, along with a review of available file and collateral information. The PCL-R is based on a numerical scoring system in which each of its 20 items is assigned a value of 0–2 based on the "goodness of fit" of that item to the individual being assessed. Scores for all items are summed, and a PCL-R Total Score 30 out of a possible 40 points is considered the diagnostic threshold for psychopathy. Although it was initially developed in Canadian offender populations, it has since demonstrated sound psychometric properties (i.e., good reliability and validity) in a multitude of sample types in locations around the world.

Psychophysiology—An area of neuroscience defined as the study of brain-behavior relationships in the framework of central and peripheral physiological responses. Psychophysiology addresses how mental events (e.g., emotions and thoughts) may affect bodily processes (e.g., heart rate, respiration, pupil dilation, perspiration, and the electrical activity of the brain).

Psychosexual stages—Refers to a developmental sequence proposed by Freud based upon the anatomical structure most associated with pleasurable sensations at any given age. Freud suggested that a "fixation," or failure to advance developmentally through any one stage, could result in one reverting back to behavioral patterns characteristic of that stage during times of stress or crisis later in life. The stages are the oral stage, the anal stage, the phallic stage, the latency stage, and the genital stage.

Psychotic disorders—A class of illnesses characterized by delusions and hallucinations.

Punishment—In relation to operant conditioning, behavior is *less* likely to occur when it is followed by negative consequences—*punishment.* Negative consequences can take two forms: the appearance of something unpleasant, such as pain (positive), or the loss of something valued, such as privileges (negative). Punishments may be external or internally, self-produced consequences that serve to motivate and inform future behavior.

Pyromania—A disorder characterized by repeated, deliberate, and purposeful fire setting through which the individual experiences tension and emotional arousal before the act and pleasure or relief afterwards.

Restricted repetitive patterns of behavior, interests, and activities—One component of the diagnostic criteria for DSM-5 autism spectrum disorder, consisting of stereotyped or repetitive motor movements, use of objects, or speech; insistence on sameness, inflexible adherence to routines, or ritualized patterns of verbal or nonverbal behavior; highly restricted, fixated interests that are abnormal in intensity or focus; and hypereactivity or hyporeactivity to sensory input or unusual interest in the sensory aspects of the environment.

Reticular formation—A region in the brainstem involved in the regulation of the sleep-wake cycle and in filtering incoming stimuli to discriminate irrelevant background stimuli.

Schizoid personality disorder—A personality disorder characterized by a pervasive, inflexible, and enduring pattern of social detachment and by a limited range of emotional expression.

Schizophrenia—One of the larger group of psychotic disorders, characterized by a distinct cluster of symptoms conceptualized as *positive* (i.e., delusions, hallucinations, disorganized speech and behavior) and *negative* (i.e., comparative "absences" of emotion, thought, or goal-directed behavior). Schizophrenia may develop gradually or rapidly and can begin at any point in one's life, though it is typically first seen between the late teens and the mid-30s. Schizophrenia rarely occurs alone as a diagnosis: depression, anxiety disorders, or substance abuse often accompany schizophrenia.

Schizotypal personality disorder—A personality disorder characterized by a pervasive, inflexible, and enduring pattern of intense discomfort in close relationships, distorted thinking and perceptions, and eccentric behavior.

Serious mental illnesses (SMIs)—Although an oversimplification, this catch-all phrase generally refers to mental disorders that seriously impair the ability to care for oneself or the ability to function within the boundaries of reality. According to the National Alliance on Mental Illness, the serious mental illnesses include major depression, schizophrenia, bipolar disorder, obsessive-compulsive disorder, panic disorder, post-traumatic stress disorder, and borderline personality disorder.

Sexual masochism—A paraphilia in which sexual excitement is derived from acts involving being humiliated, restrained, beaten, or enduring other forms of suffering.

Sexual sadism—A paraphilia in which sexual excitement is derived from behaviors involving the physical or psychological suffering (including humiliation) of the victim. Sadistic fantasies or behaviors may involve dominance, restraint, blindfolding, and physical violence. Severe forms of this paraphilia, especially when combined with antisocial personality disorder, are associated with the serious injury and death of victims.

Sexually violent predator (SVP) laws—Laws targeting those who, after serving a prison sentence for certain types of sex offenses, are determined to be at high risk for reoffending.

Signal anxiety—According to Freud, anxiety represents the result of conflict between the id's unconscious sexual or aggressive wishes and the superego's corresponding threats of punishment. Signal anxiety refers to Freud's understanding that anxiety is a signal indicating danger within the unconscious. In response to signal anxiety, the ego marshals its defensive resources to prevent unacceptable thoughts and feelings from entering conscious awareness. Failure to do so results in intense, more persistent anxiety or other neurotic symptoms.

Single-photon emission computed tomography (SPECT)—A technique for observing and recording brain function that measures the changes in regional blood flow and metabolism that are associated with changes in neural activity. Generally, this technique involves the presentation of a visual or auditory stimulus and the subsequent measurement of the brain's functional response as indicated by regional blood flow or glucose metabolism after the stimulus, which, in turn, indicates different levels of neural activity in those regions. Specifically, SPECT is similar to PET, but uses a tracer that emits only a single photon. SPECT can produce a three-dimensional representation of regional cerebral blood flow in the brain.

Social communication and interaction deficits—Persistent deficits in social communication and social interaction across multiple contexts, as manifested by deficits in social-emotional reciprocity; deficits in the nonverbal communicative behaviors used for social interaction; and deficits in developing, maintaining, and understanding relationships. Social communication and interaction deficits are one component of the diagnostic criteria for autism spectrum disorder in DSM-5.

Social control—Social control refers to one of the primary purposes of law, which is to control the behaviors of members of society. Criminal law, for example, is designed to control behavior by deterring crime through the threat of punishment and then actually punishing those who commit offenses.

Sociopathy—An antiquated term, lacking in clear scientific definition, for a disorder characterized by a cluster of personality and behavioral traits similar to what is now referred to as "psychopathy." The term "sociopathy" was first coined in 1914 by German psychiatrist Karl Birnbaum, who attributed the causes of this disorder to societal forces.

Sociotropic depression—One of two types of depression proposed by Beck (1983), sociotropic depression refers to the dependency upon interpersonal relationships for positive self-evaluation.

South Oaks Gambling Screen—A measure utilized in pathological gambling studies, it calculates a score based on gambling-related behaviors such as chasing losses, lying about winning, losing time from school or work because of gambling, and borrowing money for gambling from one's household, relatives, financial institutions, and other sources.

Spectrum model—An explanation of the relationship between Axis II and Axis I disorders. In regard to the multiaxial diagnostic nature of the DSM-IV-TR, it is known that personality disorders (i.e., Axis II disorders) may coexist with other mental disorders (i.e., Axis I disorders). The spectrum model proposes a continuum of increasing trait or symptom severity (normal personality, subclinical traits, and Axis I disorders), wherein the entire personality is organized around subclinical traits.

Spiritual model—One approach to theoretically conceptualizing certain types of substance-related disorders, the spiritual model of addiction proposes that addiction and relapse are attributable to spiritual weakness and must be overcome by admission of helplessness over the problem and submission to a "higher power"; as well, addicts are thought to be aided by social supports (i.e., group meetings). These meetings, although advantageous, may alienate individuals who are not spiritual, and they utilize peers or paraprofessionals with addiction histories rather than addiction-trained professionals.

State anxiety—Reflects an individual's level of anxiety over shorter periods of time (compared to trait anxiety). State anxiety is considered transient.

Structural brain imaging—One of two broad categories of brain imaging methods. Structural neuroimaging modalities use computers and select imaging devices to map the anatomical architecture of the brain. The two leading technologies for doing so are computed tomography (CT) and magnetic resonance imaging (MRI). The basic premise of structural imaging is to make inferences about the brains of different groups using comparisons with normative individuals.

Subcortical—The portion of the brain immediately below the cerebral cortex.

Subjective doubles—See **Doppelgänger syndrome**

Substance abuse—A clinical disorder diagnosis of the DSM-IV-TR that requires fulfilling specific criteria. Substance abuse refers to a condition involving continued use of a mind-altering substance despite problems caused by such use.

Substance dependence—A clinical disorder diagnosis of the DSM-IV-TR that requires fulfilling specific criteria. Substance dependence implies an addiction to the drug.

Sulcus [*plural* **sulci**]—Grooves between the ridges on the folded and convoluted surface of the cerebral hemispheres.

Superego—One of the three mental "structures" identified in Sigmund Freud's psychoanalytic theory, the superego is the set of moral values and self-critical attitudes, internalized primarily from the parents, which assumes the role of stern taskmaster. The superego is a theoretical concept not an actual physical component of the brain.

Superior—A directional term meaning—in the brain and spinal cord—above or toward the top of the head.

Survivor mode theory—A theory suggesting that post-traumatic stress disorder (PTSD) individuals have a reduced threshold for the perception of situations as threatening, so any perception of threat activates a biological survival response possibly accompanied by anger regulation deficits.

Sympathetic nervous system—One of the two parts of the autonomic nervous system. The sympathetic nervous system prepares the body for action by increasing physiological and psychological arousal—usually by stimulating heart rate and increasing blood pressure and respiration as preparation for fighting or fleeing a threat (known as the fight-or-flight response). Conversely, the parasympathetic nervous system decreases arousal in order to conserve the body's energy and resources. The sympathetic system is balanced by the parasympathetic system, which slows heart rate and decreases blood pressure and respiration.

Synapses—The points of contact at which neurons influence one another; A synapse may be electrical but most are chemical.

Synaptic vesicles—Organelles in which neurotransmitters—the chemicals that form the basis of the transmission of information throughout the brain—are stored.

Synthetic competency—A term referring to the process of using antipsychotic drugs to restore competency. Synthetically restoring competency raises legal policy concerns of constitutional dimensions.

Temporal—Typically used to refer to matters of time but, in forensic behavioral science, the term usually describes something related to, pertaining to, or situated in the temporal lobe.

Temporal lobe—The lowest lobe of each hemisphere, located on the side of the brain under the parietal lobe (by the ear). The temporal lobes are involved in various forms of memory and in emotion, processing sensory input, and comprehending language.

Theory of mind (ToM)—The ability to estimate the cognitive, perceptual, and emotional experiences of others as well as those of one's self. Theory of mind deficits are often cited as causal mechanisms in the criminal and violent behavior of Asperger's disordered individuals.

Thought disorder—A primary feature of the disorganization syndrome. See also **Disorganized speech**.

Threat/control-override (TCO) symptoms—Specific delusions that have shown associations with violence, including perceptions of threat or harm from others and mind control or thought insertion.

Tolerance—Cellular and metabolic adaptations in response to the continued presence of a substance. As tolerance develops, more of the drug is necessary to obtain the desired effects, and use becomes more frequent.

Trait anxiety—Refers to either an individual's general vulnerability or predisposition to becoming anxious or that person's typical anxiety level. Trait anxiety is considered long lasting (compared to state anxiety).

Transvestic fetishism—A paraphilia in which sexual excitement is derived from cross-dressing in women's clothing. Traditionally, transvestism is described only in males.

Trichotillomania [hair-pulling disorder]—A disorder characterized by the impulsive and repeated pulling out of one's hair to the point that hair loss becomes noticeable. For diagnosis, significant distress or impairment must also result from the hair pulling. Trichotillomania often presents with other comorbid impulse control disorders.

Triple vulnerability theory—Explaining the psychological and biological predispositions that enhance an individual's vulnerability to acquiring fear, the triple vulnerability theory includes (1) genetics and temperament (the biologically based "fear of fear"), (2) anxiety sensitivity (the belief that anxiety causes negative physical, social, and psychological consequences beyond the immediate physical discomfort experienced during a panic or anxiety episode), and (3) early learning experiences focusing anxiety on particular areas of concern.

Unconscious guilt—Proposed by psychoanalytic theorists as a precursor to criminalty. According to this theory, individuals first experience guilt (attributed possibly to the Oedipus complex) outside of their awareness, which motivates them to then commit crime in order to have something tangible to which the guilt may be attached. When the unconscious need for punishment is satisfied, the individual is relieved from the feelings of guilt.

Unconscious processes—Referring to mental processes (e.g., drives, instincts, motivations, and defense mechanisms) of which the individual is not aware.

Ventral [ventro-]—A directional term meaning—in the brain—toward the bottom (in the spinal cord, ventral means toward the stomach).

Voyeurism—A paraphilia in which the focus is the act of observing others (usually strangers) who are nude, undressing, or engaging in sexual activity. Generally, no sexual interaction with the observed other is sought—the act of observation ("peeping") alone is enough for sexual gratification. In severe forms of voyeurism, peeping becomes the sole form of sexual behavior.

Vulnerability model—An explanation related to the multiaxial diagnostic nature of the DSM-IV-TR, it describes the coexistence of personality disorders (i.e., Axis II disorders) with other mental disorders (i.e., Axis I disorders). The vulnerability model considers personality as the equivalent of an immune system, with personality disorders predisposing an individual—via limited or impoverished coping responses—to the development of an Axis I disorder such as anxiety or depression.

White matter—A major component of the central nervous system consisting mostly of glial cells and myelinated axons (i.e., a part of the nerve cell coated or sheathed in a layer of electrically insulating material) that transmit signals from one region of the brain to another.

Withdrawal—Experienced when the administration of a substance to a physically dependent organism is halted. Characteristic withdrawal syndromes ensue, depending on the drug class used, and the withdrawal syndromes tend to involve opposite symptoms from the intoxication effects of the substance.

References

Abbott, M. W., & McKenna, B. G. (2000). *Gambling and problem gambling among recently sentenced women prisoners in New Zealand.* Wellington, NZ: Department of Internal Affairs.

Abbott, M. W., McKenna, B. G., & Giles, L. (2000). *Gambling and problem gambling among recently sentenced males in four New Zealand prisons.* Wellington: Department of Internal Affairs.

Abbott, M. W., & Volberg, R. A. (1991). *Gambling and problem gambling in New Zealand.* Research Series No. 12. Wellington, NZ: Department of Internal Affairs.

Abbott, M. W., & Volberg, R. A. (1996). The New Zealand national survey of problem and pathological gambling. *Journal of Gambling Studies, 12*(2), 143–160.

Abraham, K. (1927). A short study of the development of the libido, viewed in light of mental disorders. In *Selected papers on psycho-analysis* (pp. 418–501). London: Hogarth. Original work published 1924.

Abrahamsen, D. (1973). *The murdering mind.* New York: Harper & Row.

Abrahamsen, D. (1985). *Confessions of Son of Sam.* New York: Columbia University Press.

Abram, K. M., & Teplin, L. A. (1991). Co-occurring disorders among mentally ill jail detainees: Implications for public policy. *American Psychologist, 46*(10), 1036–1045.

Abramson, M. F. (1972). The criminalization of mentally disordered behavior: Possible side-effect of a new mental health law. *Hospital and Community Psychiatry, 23*, 101–107.

Abu-Akel, A., & Abushua'leh, K. (2004). "Theory of mind" in violent and nonviolent patients with paranoid schizophrenia. *Schizophrenia Research, 69*, 45–53.

Acklin, M. W. (2012). The forensic clinician's toolbox I: A review of competency to stand trial (CST) instruments. *Journal of Personality Assessment, 94*(2), 220–222.

Adam Walsh Child Safety and Protection Act, Pub. L. No. 109–248, *codified as amended at* 42 U.S.C. §§16911 et seq. (July 27, 2006).

Addington v. Texas, 441 U.S. 418 (1979).

Adkins, D. E., Åberg, K., McClay, J. L., Bukszár, J., Zhao, Z., Jia, P., Stroup, T. S., Perkins, D., McEvoy, J. P., Lieberman, J. A., Sullivan, P. F., & van den Oord, E. J. (2011). Genomewide pharmacogenomic study of metabolic side effects to antipsychotic drugs. *Molecular Psychiatry, 16*, 321–332.

Adler, G. (1982). Recent psychoanalytic contributions to the understanding and treatment of criminal behavior. *International Journal of Offender Therapy and Comparative Criminology, 26*, 281–287.

Aggrawal, A. (2009). *Forensic and medico-legal aspects of sexual crimes and unusual sexual practices.* Boca Raton, FL: CRC Press.

Agnew, R. (1992). Foundation for a general strain theory. *Criminology, 30*(1), 47–87.

Aichhorn, A. (1935). *Wayward youth.* New York: Viking Press.

Akers, R. L. (1973). *Deviant behavior: A social learning approach.* Belmont, CA: Wadsworth Publishing Company, Inc.

Alarcón, R. D., Becker, A. E., Lewis-Fernandez, R., Like, R. C., Desai, B., Foulks, E., et al., for the Cultural Psychiatry Committee of the Group for the Advancement of Psychiatry. (2009). Issues for DSM-V: The role of culture in psychiatric diagnosis. *Journal of Nervous and Mental Disease, 197*(8), 559–660.

Alexander, F., & Healy, W. (1969). *Roots of crime: Psychoanalytic studies.* Montclair, NJ: Patterson Smith.

Alexander, F., & Staub, H. (1931). *The criminal, the judge, and the public: A psychological analysis* (G. Zilboorg, Trans.). New York: The Macmillan Company.

Alexander, R. T., Green, F. N., O'Mahony, B., Gunaratna, I. J., Gangadharan, S. K., & Hoare, S. (2010). Personality disorders in offenders with intellectual disability: A comparison of clinical, forensic and outcome variables and implications for service provision. *Journal of Intellectual Disability Research, 54*(7), 650–658.

Alish, Y., Birger, M., Manor, N., Kertzman, S., Zerzion, M., Kotler, M., & Strous, R. D. (2007). Schizophrenia sex offenders: A clinical and epidemiological comparison. *International Journal of Law and Psychiatry, 30*, 459–466.

Allen v. Illinois, 478 U.S. 364 (1986).

Allen, L. B., McHugh, R. K., & Barlow, D. H. (2008). Emotional disorders: A unified protocol. In D. H. Barlow (Ed.), *Clinical handbook of psychological disorders* (4th ed., pp. 216–249). New York: The Guilford Press.

Almvik, R., & Woods, P. (2003). Short-term risk prediction: The Bröset Violence Checklist. *Journal of Psychiatric & Mental Health Nursing, 10*(2), 236–238.

American Bar Association. (1989). *Criminal justice mental health standards.* Chicago: Author. (See especially Part IV Competence to Stand Trial, Standard 7–4.1)

American Psychiatric Association. (1952). *Diagnostic and statistical manual: Mental disorders.* Washington, DC: Author.

American Psychiatric Association (1968). *Diagnostic and statistical manual of mental disorders* (2nd ed.). Washington, DC: Author.

American Psychiatric Association (1980). *Diagnostic and statistical manual of mental disorders* (3rd ed.). Washington, DC: Author.

American Psychiatric Association. (1983). Guidelines for legislation on the psychiatric hospitalization of adults. *American Journal of Psychiatry, 140*(5), 672–679.

American Psychiatric Association (1987). *Diagnostic and statistical manual of mental disorders* (3rd ed., revised). Washington, DC: Author.

American Psychiatric Association (1994). *Diagnostic and statistical manual of mental disorders* (4th ed.). Washington, DC: Author.

American Psychiatric Association (2000). *Diagnostic and statistical manual of mental disorders* (4th ed., text revision). Washington, DC: Author.

American Psychiatric Association (2013). *Diagnostic and statistical manual of mental disorders* (5th ed.). Washington, DC: Author.

Anand, S., & Malhi, G. S. (2009). Why DSM-V needs to address anger. *Journal of Clinical Psychiatry, 70*(10), 1478.

Anckarsäter, H. (2005). Clinical neuropsychiatric symptoms in perpetrators of severe crimes against persons. *Nordic Journal of Psychiatry, 59*(4), 246–252.

Anckarsäter, H. (2006). Central nervous system changes in social dysfunction: Autism, aggression, and psychopathy. *Brain Research Bulletin, 69,* 259–265.

Anderson, D. B. (1999). Problem gambling among incarcerated male felons. *Journal of Offender Rehabilitation, 29*(3–4), 113–127.

Andreasen, N. C. (1979). Thought, language, and communication disorders: I. Clinical assessment, definition of terms, and evaluation of their reliability. *Archives of General Psychiatry, 36,* 1315–1321.

Andrews, D. A., & Bonta, J. (1995). *Level of Service Inventory–Revised.* Toronto, ON: Multi-Health Systems.

Andrews, D. A., Bonta, J., & Wormith, J. S. (2004). *The Level of Service/Case Management Inventory (LS/CMI).* Toronto, ON: Multi-Health Systems.

Andrews, J. (2010a). From stack-firing to pyromania: Medico-legal concepts of insane arson in British, US and European contexts, c. 1800–1913. Part 1. *History of Psychiatry, 21*(3), 243–260.

Andrews, J. (2010b). From stack-firing to pyromania: Medico-legal concepts of insane arson in British, US and European contexts, c. 1800–1913. Part 2. *History of Psychiatry, 21*(4), 387–405.

Anglin, M. D., & Perrochet, B. (1998). Drug use and crime: A historical review of research conducted by the UCLA Drug Abuse Research Center. *Substance Use & Misuse, 33*(9), 1871–1914.

Anthony, H. S. (1968). The association of violence and depression in a sample of young offenders. *British Journal of Criminology, 8,* 346–365.

Anwar, S., Långström, N., Grann, M., & Fazel, S. (2011). Is arson the crime most strongly associated with psychosis?—A national case-control study of arson risk in schizophrenia and other psychoses. *Schizophrenia Bulletin, 37*(3), 580–586.

Appelbaum, K. L. (2011). Stimulant use under a prison treatment protocol for attention-deficit/hyperactivity disorder. *Journal of Correctional Health Care, 17*(3), 218–225.

Appelbaum, P. S., Robbins, P. C., & Monahan, J. (2000). Violence and delusions: Data from the MacArthur Violence Risk Assessment Study. *American Journal of Psychiatry, 157,* 566–572.

Appelbaum, P. S., Robbins, P. C., & Roth, L. H. (1999). Dimensional approach to delusions: Comparison across types and diagnoses. *American Journal of Psychiatry, 156*(12), 1938–1943.

Arango, C., Barba, A. C., Gonzáles-Salvador, T., & Ordóñez, A. C. (1999). Violence in inpatients with schizophrenia: A prospective study. *Schizophrenia Bulletin, 25*(3), 493–503.

Arenella, P. (1982). Reflections on current proposals to abolish or reform the insanity defense. *American Journal of Law and Medicine, 8*(3), 271–284.

Arens, R. (1974). *Insanity defense.* New York, NY: Philosophical Library.

Argersinger v. Hamlin, 407 U.S. 25 (1972).

Arieti, S. (1977). Psychotherapy of severe depression. *The American Journal of Psychiatry, 134*(8), 864–868.

Arieti, S., & Bemporad, J. R. (1980). The psychological organization of depression. *The American Journal of Psychiatry, 137*(11), 1360–1365.

Arieti, S., & Schreiber, F. R. (1981). Multiple murders of a schizophrenic patient: A psychodynamic interpretation. *Journal of the American Academy of Psychoanalysis, 9*(4), 501–524.

Ariz. Rev. Stat. Ann. § 13-3994 (1997).

Arnsten, A. F. T. (2004). Andrenergic targets for the treatment of cognitive deficits in schizophrenia. *Psychopharmacology, 174,* 25–31.

Aromäki, A. S., Lindman, R. E., & Eriksson, C. J. P. (1999). Testosterone, aggressiveness, and antisocial personality. *Aggressive Behavior, 25,* 113–123.

Arrigio, B. A. (1992/1993). Paternalism, civil commitment and illness politics: Assessing the current debate and outlining a future direction. *Journal of Law and Health, 7*(2), 131–168.

Arrigo, B. A., & Purcell, C. E. (2001). Explaining paraphilias and lust murder: Toward an integrated model. *International Journal of Offender Therapy and Comparative Criminology, 45*(1), 6–31.

Arrigo, B. A., & Shipley, S. (2001). The confusion over psychopathy (I): Historical considerations. *International Journal of Offender Therapy and Comparative Criminology, 454*(3), 325–344.

Arsenault, L., Moffitt, T. E., Caspi, A., Taylor, P. J., & Silva, P. A. (2000). Mental disorders and violence in a total birth cohort: Results from the Dunedin Study. *Archives of General Psychiatry, 57,* 979–986.

Ascher-Svanum, H. A., Nyhuis, A. W., Faries, D. E., Ball, D. E., & Kinon, B. J. (2010). Involvement in the US criminal justice system and cost implications for persons treated for schizophrenia. *BMC Psychiatry, 10*(11), 1–10.

Asnis, G. M., Kaplan, M. L., van Praag, H. M., & Sanderson, W. C. (1994). Homicidal behaviors among psychiatric outpatients. *Hospital and Community Psychiatry, 45*(2), 127–132.

Athanasiadis, L. (1999). Drugs, alcohol and violence. *Current Opinion in Psychiatry, 12,* 281–286.

Auerhahn, K. (2004). California's incarcerated drug offender population, yesterday, today, and tomorrow: Evaluating the war on drugs and proposition 36. *Journal of Drug Issues, 34*(1), 95–120.

Australian National University Centre for Gambling Research (ANUCGR). (2003). *Gambling and clients of ACT corrections: Final report.* Australian Capital Territory, Australia: Author.

Babiak, P., & Hare, R. D. (2006). *Snakes in suits: When psychopaths go to work.* New York: HarperCollins Publishers.

Babiak, P., Neumann, C. S., & Hare, R. D. (2010). Corporate psychopathy: Talking the walk. *Behavioral Sciences and the Law, 28*(2), 174–193.

Baillargeon, J., Black, S. A., Contreras, S., Grady, J., & Pulvino, J. (2001). Anti-depressant prescribing patterns for prison inmates with depressive disorders. *Journal of Affective Disorders, 63,* 225–231.

Baillargeon, J., Black, S. A., Pulvino, J., & Dunn, K. (2000). The disease profile of Texas prison inmates. *Annals of Epidemiology, 10,* 74–80.

Baltes, P. B., & Staudinger, U. M. (2000). Wisdom: A metaheuristic (pragmatic) to orchestrate mind and virtue toward excellence. *American Psychologist, 55*(1), 122–136.

Bandura, A. (1974). Behavior theory and the models of man. *American Psychologist, 29*(12), 859–869.

Bandura, A., & Huston, A. C. (1961). Identification as a process of incidental learning. *Journal of Abnormal and Social Psychology, 63*(2), 311–318.

Bandura, A., Ross, D., & Ross, S. A. (1961). Transmission of aggression through imitation of aggressive models. *Journal of Abnormal and Social Psychology, 63*(3), 575–582.

Bandura, A., Ross, D., & Ross, S. A. (1963). Vicarious reinforcement and imitative learning. *Journal of Abnormal and Social Psychology, 67*(6), 601–607.

Bankier, B., Lenz, G., Gutierrez, K., Bach, M., & Katschnig, H. (1999). A case of Asperger's syndrome first diagnosed in adulthood. *Psychopathology, 32,* 43–46.

Barker, A. (1994). Arson: A review of the psychiatric literature. *Maudsley Monographs, 35,* 1–98.

Baron-Cohen, S. (1988). An assessment of violence in a young man with Asperger's syndrome. *Journal of Child Psychology and Psychiatry, 29*(3), 351–360.

Barrett, E. L., Mills, K. L., & Teesson, M. (2011). Hurt people who hurt people: Violence among individuals with comorbid substance use disorder and post traumatic stress disorder. *Addictive Behaviors, 36*, 721–728.

Barron, P., Hassiotis, A., & Banes, J. (2002). Offenders with intellectual disability: The size of the problem and therapeutic outcomes. *Journal of Intellectual Disability Research, 46*(6), 454–463.

Barron, P., Hassiotis, A., & Banes, J. (2004). Offenders with intellectual disability: A prospective comparative study. *Journal of Intellectual Disability Research, 48*(1), 69–76.

Barry-Walsh, J. B., & Mullen, P. B. (2004). Forensic aspects of Asperger's Syndrome. *The Journal of Forensic Psychiatry and Psychology, 15*(1), 96–107.

Bartol, C. R., & Bartol, A. M. (2008). *Introduction to forensic psychology: Research and application* (2nd ed.). Los Angeles: Sage Publications.

Bartol, C. R., & Bartol, A. M. (2011). *Criminal behavior: A psychosocial approach* (9th ed.). Upper Saddle River, NJ: Prentice Hall, Inc.

Bartol, C. R., & Bartol, A. M. (2012). *Introduction to forensic psychology: Research and application*. Thousand Oaks, CA: Sage.

Barzman, D. H., DelBello, M. P., Fleck, D. E., Lehmkuhl, H., & Strakowski, S. M. (2007). Rates, types, and psychosocial correlates of legal charges in adolescents with newly diagnosed bipolar disorder. *Bipolar Disorders, 9*, 339–344.

Bassuk, E., & Gerson, S. (1978). Deinstitutionalization and mental health services. *Scientific American, 238*, 46–53.

Batts, S. (2009). Brain lesions and their implications in criminal responsibility. *Behavioral Sciences and the Law, 27*, 261–272.

Bauman, M. L. (1996). Brief report: Neuroanatomic observations of the brain in pervasive developmental disorders. *Journal of Autism and Developmental Disorders, 26*(2), 199–203.

Baumer, E., Lauritsen, J. L., Rosenfeld, R., & Wright, R. (2006). The influence of crack cocaine on robbery, burglary, and homicide rates: A cross-city, longitudinal analysis. In M. S. Kelley (Ed.), *Readings on drugs and society: The criminal connection* (pp. 89–101). New York: Pearson Education, Inc.

Baxter, H., Duggan, C., Larkin, E., Cordess, C., & Page, K. (2001). Mentally disordered parricide and stranger killers admitted to high-security care. 1: A descriptive comparison. *Journal of Forensic Psychiatry, 12*(2), 287–299.

Baxter, R. (1997). Violence in schizophrenia and the syndrome of disorganisation. *Criminal Behaviour and Mental Health, 7*, 131–139.

Bazelon Center for Mental Health Law, The. (2003). *Criminalization of people with mental illnesses: The role of mental health courts in system reform*. Washington, DC: Author. Retrieved from http://www.pbpp.state.pa.us/portal/server.pt/document/1037939/doc115_bazelon_2003_pdf.

Bazelon Center for Mental Health Law, The. (2012). Mental health courts. *Where we stand: Access to services*. Retrieved from http://www.bazelon.org/Where-We-Stand/Access-to-Services/Diversion-from-Incarceration-and-Reentry-/Mental-Health-Courts.aspx.

Bearden, C. E., Hoffman, K. M., & Cannon, T. D. (2001). The neuropsychology and neuroanatomy of bipolar affective disorder: A critical review. *Bipolar Disorders, 3*, 106–150.

Beck, J. S. (1995). *Cognitive therapy: Basics and beyond*. New York: The Guilford Press.

Becker, J. V., Kaplan, M. S., Tenke, C. E., & Tartaglini, A. (1991). The incidence of depressive symptomatology in juvenile sex offenders with a history of abuse. *Child Abuse and Neglect, 15*, 531–536.

Beetz, A. M. (2004). Bestiality/zoophilia: A scarcely investigated phenomenon between crime, paraphilia, and love. *Journal of Forensic Psychology Practice, 4*(2), 1–36.

Beigel, A., & Murphy, D. L. (1971). Assessing clinical characteristics of the manic state. *American Journal of Psychiatry, 128*(6), 688–694.

Bender, L. (1959). Children and adolescents who have killed. *American Journal of Psychiatry, 116*, 510–513.

Benedetti, F., Yeh, P. H., Bellani, M., Radaelli, D., Nicoletti, M. A., Poletti, S., Falina, A., Dellaspezia, S., Columbo, C., Scotti, G., Smeraldi, E., Soares, J. C., & Brambilla, P. (2011). Disruption of white matter integrity in bipolar depression as a possible structural marker of illness. *Biological Psychiatry, 69*, 309–317.

Benezech, M., Yesavage, J. A., Addad, M., Bourgeois, M., & Mills, M. (1984). Homicide by psychotics in France: A five-year study. *Journal of Clinical Psychiatry, 45*, 85–86.

Bennett, D. J., Ogloff, J. R. P., Mullen, P. E., Thomas, S. D. M., Wallace, C., & Short, T. (2011). Schizophrenia disorders, substance abuse and prior criminal offending in a sequential series of 435 homicides. *Acta Psychiatrica Scandinavica, 124*, 226–233.

Berman, L., & Osborne, Y. (1980). Attorneys' referrals for competency to stand trial evaluations: Comparisons of referred and nonreferred clients. *Behavioral Science and Law, 5*(3), 373–380.

Bernabeu, E. P. (1958). Underlying ego mechanisms in delinquency, USA. *Psychoanalytic Quarterly, 27*(3), 383–396.

Bernat, E. M., Hall, J. R., Steffen, B. V., & Patrick, C. J. (2007). Violent offending predicts P300 amplitude. *International Journal of Psychophysiology, 66*, 161–167.

Beyer, K. R., & Beasley, J. O. (2004). Nonfamily child abductors who murder their victims.: Offender demographics from interviews with incarcerated offenders. *Journal of Interpersonal Violence, 18*(10), 1167–1188.

Bibring, E. (1953). The mechanism of depression. In Phyliss Greenacre (Ed.), *Affective disorders: Psychoanalytic contributions to their study* (pp.13–48). Oxford: International Universities Press.

Biederman, J., Faraone, S. V., Hatch, M., Mennin, D., Taylor, A., & George, P. (2007). Conduct disorder with and without mania in a referred sample of ADHD children. *Journal of Affective Disorders, 44*, 177–188.

Bihan, P. L., & Bénézech, (2004). Degré d'organisation du crime de parricide pathologique: Mode opératoire, profil criminologique. À propos de 42 observations. *Annales Médico-Psychologiques, 162*(8), 615–625.

Binder, R. L., & McNiel, D. E. (1988). Effects of diagnosis and context on dangerousness. *American Journal of Psychiatry, 145*, 728–732.

Birbaumer, N., Veir, R., Lotze, M., Erb, M., Hermann, C., Grodd, W., & Flor, H. (2005). Deficient fear conditioning in psychopathy: A functional magnetic resonance imaging study. *Archives of General Psychiatry, 62*(7), 799–805.

Bjorkly, S. (2002a). Psychotic symptoms and violence toward others—a literature review of some preliminary findings. Part 1. Delusions. *Aggression and Violent Behavior, 7*, 617–631.

Bjorkly, S. (2002b). Psychotic symptoms and violence toward others—a literature review of some preliminary findings. Part 2. Hallucinations. *Aggression and Violent Behavior, 7*, 605–615.

Black, D. L. (1984). *Towards a general theory of social control: Vol. 1 Fundamentals*. San Diego, CA: Academic Press/ Elsevier.

Black, D. L. (1993). *Sociological justice*. New York, NY: Oxford University Press.

Blackburn, I. M. (1974). The pattern of hostility in affective illness. *British Journal of Psychiatry, 125*, 141–145.

Blackburn, R. (1979). Cortical and autonomic response arousal in primary and secondary psychopaths. *Psychophysiology, 16*, 143–150.

Blackburn, R. (2000). Treatment or incapacitation? Implications of research on personality disorders for the management of dangerous offenders. *Legal and Criminological Psychology, 5*, 1–21.

Blackman, J. S. (2004). *101 defenses: How the mind shields itself.* New York: Brunner-Routledge.

Blackshaw, A. J., Kinderman, P., Hare, D. J., & Hatton, C. (2001). Theory of mind, causal attribution and paranoia in Asperger syndrome. *Autism, 5*(2), 147–163.

Bland, R. C., Newman, S. C., Dyck, R. J., & Orn, H. (1990). Prevalence of psychiatric disorders and suicide attempts in a prison population. *Canadian Journal of Psychiatry, 35*, 407–413.

Blatt, S. J. (1974). Levels of object representation in anaclitic and introjective depression. *The Psychoanalytic Study of the Child, 29*, 7–157.

Blau, G. L., & Pasewark, R. A. (1994). Statutory changes and the insanity defense: Seeking the perfect insane person. *Law and Psychology Review, 18*, 69–108.

Blitz, C. L., Wolff, N., & Shi, J. (2008). Physical victimization in prison: The role of mental illness. *International Journal of Law and Psychiatry, 31*, 385–393.

Blum, E. M. (1966). Psychoanalytic views of alcoholism: A review. *Quarterly Review of Studies on Alcohol, 27*(2), 259–299.

Bo, S., Abu-Akel, A., Kongerslev, M., Haahr, U. K., & Simonsen, E. (2011). Risk factors for violence among patients with schizophrenia. *Clinical Psychology Review, 31*(5), 711–726.

Bobes, J., Fillat, O., & Arango, C. (2009). Violence among schizophrenia out-patients compliant with medication: Prevalence and associated factors. *Acta Psychiatrica Scandinavica, 119*, 218–225.

Boddy, C. R. (2011). Corporate psychopaths, bullying and unfair supervision in the workplace. *Journal of Business Ethics, 100*, 367–379.

Boden, J. M., Fergusson, D. M., & Horwood, L. J. (2007). Anxiety disorders and suicidal behaviours in adolescence and young adulthood: Findings from a longitudinal study. *Psychological Medicine, 37*, 431–440.

Boer, D. P., Hart, S. D., Kropp, P. R., & Webster, C. D. (1997). *Manual for the Sexual Violence Risk-20. Professional guidelines for assessing risk of sexual violence.* Burnaby, BC: Simon Fraser University, Mental Health, Law, and Policy Institute.

Bohne, A., & Stevens, S. (2009). Treatment model for cognitive behavior therapy of kleptomania. *Verhaltenstherapie, 19*(1), 40–46.

Bonnie, R. J. (1993). The competence of criminal defendants: Beyond *Dusky* and *Drope. University of Miami Law Review, 47*, 539–601.

Bonnie, R. J., & Grisso, T. (2000). Adjudicative competence and youthful offenders. In T. Grisso & R. G. Schwartz, (Eds.), *Youth on trial: A developmental perspective on juvenile justice* (pp. 73–103). Chicago, IL: University of Chicago Press.

Bonta, J., Law, M., & Hanson, K. (1998). The prediction of criminal and violent recidivism among mentally disordered offenders: A meta-analysis. *Psychological Bulletin, 123*, 123–142.

Boothroyd, R., Poythress, N., McGaha, A., & Petrila, J. (2003). The Broward Mental Health Court: Process, outcomes and service utilization. *International Journal of Law and Psychiatry, 26*, 55–71.

Boots, D. P., & Heide, K. M. (2006). Parricides in the media: A content analysis of available reports across cultures. *International Journal of Offender Therapy and Comparative Criminology, 50*(4), 418–445.

Borum, R., Bartel, P., & Forth, A. (2002). *Manual for the structured assessment of violence risk in youth* (SAVRY). Tampa, FL: University of South Florida.

Borum, R., & Fulero, S. (1999). Empirical research on the insanity defense and attempted reforms: Evidence toward informed policy. *Law and Human Behavior, 23*(3), 375–393.

Borum, R., Swanson, J., Swartz, M., & Hiday, V. (1997). Substance abuse, violent behavior and police encounters among persons with severe mental disorder. *Journal of Contemporary Criminal Justice, 13*(3), 236–50.

Bos, A. E. R., Kanner, D., Muris, P., Janssen, B., & Mayer, B. (2009). Mental illness stigma and disclosure: Consequences of coming out of the closet. *Issues in Mental Health Nursing, 30*(8), 509–513.

Bouchard, J. P., & Bachelier, A. S. (2004). Schizophrénie et double parricide: À propos d'une observation clinique. *Annales Médico-Psychologiques, 162*(8), 626–633.

Bourget, D., Gagné, P., & Labelle, M. E. (2007). Parricide: A comparative study of matricide versus patricide. *Journal of the American Academy of Psychiatry and the Law, 35*, 306–312.

Bowlby, J. (1944). Forty-four juvenile thieves: Their characters and home life. *International Journal of Psychoanalysis, 25*, 19–52, 107–127, 121–124.

Bowlby, J. (1969). *Attachment and loss: Vol. 1. Attachment.* New York: Basic Books.

Bowlby, J. (1973). *Attachment and loss: Vol. 2. Separation: Anxiety and anger.* New York: Basic Books.

Bowlby, J. (1980). *Attachment and loss: Vol. 3. Loss—Sadness and depression.* New York: Basic Books.

Bradford, J. M. W., Firestone, P., & Ahmed, A. G. (2007). The paraphilias and psychopathy. In A. Felthous & H. Saß (Eds.), *The international handbook of psychopathic disorders and the law: Volume I* (pp. 275–290). Hoboken, NJ: John Wiley & Sons, Ltd.

Bradley, R., Conklin, C. Z., & Westen, D. (2007). Borderline personality disorder. In W. O'Donohue, K. A. Fowler, & S. O. Lilienfeld (Eds.), *Personality disorders: Toward the DSM-V* (pp. 167–201). Los Angeles: Sage.

Braham, L. G., Trower, P., & Birchwood, M. (2004). Acting on command hallucinations and dangerous behavior: A critique of the major findings in the last decade. *Clinical Psychology Review, 24*, 513–528.

Braun, C., Leveille, C., & Guimond, A. (2008). An orbitofrontostriatopallidal pathway or morality: Evidence from postlesion antiosocial and obsessive-compulsive disorder. *Cognitive Neuropsychiatry, 13*(4), 296–337.

Brennan, P. A., & Alden, A. (2006). Schizophrenia and violence: The overlap. In A. Raine (Ed.), *Crime and schizophrenia: Causes and cures* (pp. 15–27). New York: Nova Science Publishers, Inc.

Brennan, P. A., Mednick, S. A., & Hodgins, S. (2000). Major mental disorders and criminal violence in a Danish birth cohort. *Archives of General Psychiatry, 57*(5), 494–500.

Brennan, T., & Oliver, W. L. (2000). *Evaluation of reliability and validity of COMPAS scales: National aggregate sample.* Traverse City, MI: Northpointe Institute for Public Management.

Brinkley, C. A., Newman, J. P., Widiger, T. A., & Lynam, D. R. (2004). Two approaches to parsing the heterogeneity of psychopathy. *Clinical Psychology: Science & Practice, 11*(1), 69–94.

Britton, K. R. (1998). Medroxyprogesterone in the treatment of aggressive hypersexual behaviour in traumatic brain injury. *Brain Injury, 12*(8), 703–707.

Bromberg, W. (1951). A psychological study of murder. *International Journal of Psycho-Analysis, 32*, 117–127.

Bromberg, W., & Thompson, C. B. (1937). The relation of psychosis, mental defect and personality types to crime. *Journal of Criminal Law and Criminology, 28*, 70–88.

Bronfenbrenner, U. (1979). *The ecology of human development: Experiments by design and nature.* Cambridge, MA: Harvard University Press.

Brooks, W. M. (2010). The tail still wags the dog: The pervasive and inappropriate influence by the psychiatric profession on the civil commitment process. *North Dakota Law Review, 86*, 259–319.

Brown, R. (1998). Problem gambling among people on community corrections. In *Compulsive Gambling Society of New Zealand. Proceedings of the National Workshop on Treatment For Problem Gambling.* Auckland, NZ: Compulsive Gambling Society of New Zealand.

Buchanan v. Kentucky, 483 U.S. 402 (1987).

Buchanan, A., Reed, A., Wessley, S., Garety, P., Taylor, P., Grubin, D., & Dunn, G. (1993). Acting on delusions. II: The phenomenological correlates of acting on delusions. *British Journal of Psychiatry, 163*(1), 77–81.

Bullock, J. L., & Arrigo, B. A. (2006). The myth that mental illness causes crime. In R. M. Bohm & J. T. Walker (Eds.), *Demystifying crime and criminal justice* (pp. 12–19). Los Angeles: Roxbury Publishing Company.

Bunker, H. A. (1941). Mother-murder in myth and legend. *Psychoanalytic Quarterly, 13*, 198–207.

Burgess, A. W., Commons, M. L., Safarik, M. E., Looper, R. R., & Ross, S. N. (2007). Sex offenders of the elderly: Classification by motive, typology, and predictors of severity of crime. *Aggression and Violent Behavior, 12*, 582–597.

Burgess, A. W., Hartman, C. R., Ressler, R. K., Douglas, J. E., & McCormack, A. (1986). Sexual homicide: A motivational model. *Journal of Interpersonal Violence, 13*(3), 251–272.

Burgess, R., & Akers, R. L. (1966). A differential association-reinforcement theory of criminal behavior. *Social Problems, 14*, 363–383.

Burke, E. (2012). Only as strong as the missing link: The unsteady constitutionality of the Adam Walsh Act. *Suffolk University Law Review, 45*, 427–464.

Bursik, R. J. (1988). Social disorganization and theories of crime and delinquency: Problems and prospects. *Criminology, 26*, 519–551.

Bursztajn, H. J., Hamm, R. M., & Gutheil, T. G. (1997). Beyond the black letter of the law: An empirical study of an individual judge's decision process for civil commitment hearings. *Journal of the American Academy of Psychiatry and Law, 25*(1), 79–94.

Burton, P. S., McNiel, D. E., & Binder, R. L. (2012). Firesetting, arson, pyromania, and the forensic mental health expert. *Journal of the American Academy of Psychiatry and the Law, 40*(3), 355–365.

Byers, K. A. (1994). Incompetency, execution, and the use of antipsychotic drugs. *Arkansas Law Review, 47*, 361–391.

Caffrey, M. (2005). A new approach to insanity acquittee recidivism: Redefining the class of truly responsible recidivists. *University of Pennsylvania Law Review, 154*, 399–423.

Calef, V., & Weinshel, E. M. (1972). On certain neurotic equivalents of necrophilia. *International Journal of Psycho-Analysis, 53*, 67–75.

Callahan, L. A., Mayer, C., & Steadman, H. J. (1987). Insanity defense reform in the United States—post-Hinckley. *Mental and Physical Disability Law Reporter, 11*, 54–59.

Callahan, L. A., Steadman, H .J., McGreevy, M.A., & Robbins, P. C. (1991). The volume and characteristics of insanity defense pleas: An eight-state study. *Bulletin of the American Academy of Psychiatry and Law, 19*(4), 331–338.

Campbell, M. A., French, S., & Gendreau, P. (2009). The prediction of violence in adult offenders: A meta-analytic comparison of instruments and methods of assessment. *Criminal Justice and Behavior, 36*(6), 567–590.

Campion, J., Cravens, J. M., Rotholc, A., Weinstein, H. C., Covan, F., & Alpert, M. (1985). A study of 15 matricidal men. *American Journal of Psychiatry, 142*(3), 312–317.

Cannon, M., Huttunen, M. O., Tanskanen, A. J., Arseneault, L., Jones, P. B., & Murray, R. M. (2002). Perinatal and childhood risk factors for later criminality and violence in schizophrenia. *British Journal of Psychiatry, 180*, 496–501.

Canter, D., & Fritzon, K. (1998). Differentiating arsonists: A model of firesetting actions and characteristics. *Legal and Criminological Psychology, 3*, 73–96.

Cantor, J. M., Blanchard, R., Christbanensen, B. K., Dickey, R., Klassen, P. E., Beckstead, A. L., Blak, T., & Kuban, M. E. (2004). Intelligence, memory, and handedness in pedophilia. *Neuropsychology, 18*(1), 3–14.

Cantor, J. M., Klassen, P. E., Dickey, R., Christensen, B. K., Kuban, M. E., Blak, T., Wiliams, N. S., & Blanchard, R. (2005). Handedness in pedophilia and hebephilia. *Archives of Sexual Behavior, 34*(4), 447–759.

Carlisle, A. L. (1991). Dissociation and violent criminal behavior. *Journal of Contemporary Criminal Justice, 7*(4), 273–285.

Carlson, G. A., & Goodwin, F. K. (1973). The stages of mania: A longitudinal analysis of the manic episode. *Archives of General Psychiatry, 28*, 221–228.

Carroll, A., Pantelis, C., & Harvey, C. (2004). Insight and hopelessness in forensic patients with schizophrenia. *Australian and New Zealand Journal of Psychiatry, 38*, 169–173.

Carter, A. S., Pauls, D. L., & Leckman, J. F. (1995). The development of obsessionality: Continuities and discontinuities. In D. Cicchatti & D. S. Cohen (Eds.), *Developmental psychopathology, Vol. 2: Risk, disorder, and adaptation* (pp. 609–632). Wiley series on personality process. Oxford, England: John Wiley & Sons.

Carter, L. H., & Burke, T. F. (2010). *Reason in law* (8th ed.). Upper Saddle River, NJ: Pearson.

Case, B., Steadman, H. J., Dupuis, S. A., & Morris, L. S. (2009). Who succeeds in jail diversion programs for persons with mental illness? A multi-site study. *Behavioral Science and Law, 22*, 661–674.

Cassani, F., Cadioli, G., Fazzari, G., Lescovelli, M., Malagrinò, E., & Micheletti, V. (1985). Parricidio e matricidio nella malattia mentale maschile e femminile. *Rivista Sperimentale di Freniatria e Medicina Legale delle Alienazioni Mentali, 109*(1), 100–114.

Cassity, J. H. (1941). Personality study of 200 murderers. *Journal of Criminal Psychopathology, 2*, 296–304.

Catanesi, R., Carabellese, F., Troccoli, G., Candelli, C., Grattagliano, I., Solarino, B., & Fortunato, F. (2011). Psychopathology and weapon choice: A study of 103 perpetrators of homicide and attempted homicide. *Forensic Science International, 209*(1–3), 149–153.

Chang, J., Berg, C. L., Saltzman, L. E., & Herndon, J. (2005). Homicide: A leading cause of injury deaths among pregnant and postpartum women in the United States, 1991–1999. *American Journal of Public Health, 95*(3), 471–477.

Chapple, B., Chant, B., Nolan, P., Cardy, S., Whiteford, H., & McGrath, J. (2004). Correlates of victimisation amongst people with psychosis. *Social Psychiatry and Psychiatric Epidemiology, 39*, 836–840.

Chemtob, C. M., Novaco, R. W., Hamada, R. S., Gross, D. M., & Smith, G. (1997). Anger regulation deficits in combat-related posttraumatic stress disorder. *Journal of Traumatic Stress, 10*(1), 17–36.

Chen, C. C., Chen, L. S., Yen, M. F., Chen, H. H., & Liou H. H. (2012). Geographic variation in the age- and gender-specific prevalence and incidence of epilepsy: Analysis of Taiwanese National Health Insurance-based data. *Epilepsia, 53*(2), 283–290.

Chen, P. S., Chen, S. J., Yang, Y. K., Yeh, T. L., Chen. C. C., & Lo, Y. L. (2003). Asperger's disorder: A case report of repeated stealing and the collecting behaviours of an adolescent patient. *Acta Psychiatrica Scandinavica, 107*, 73–76.

Chen, Y., Arria, A. M., & Anthony, J. C. (2003). Firesetting in adolescence and being aggressive, shy, and rejected by peers: New epidemiologic evidence from a national sample survey. *Journal of the American Academy of Psychiatry and the Law, 31*(1), 44–52.

Chesterman, P., & Rutter, S. C. (1993). Case report: Asperger's syndrome and sexual offending. *The Journal of Forensic Psychiatry, 4*(3), 555–562.

Chesterman, P., & Sahota, K. (1998). Mentally ill sex offenders in a regional secure unit. I: Psychopathology and motivation. *Journal of Forensic Psychiatry, 9*(1), 150–160.

Cheung, P., Schweitzer, I., Crowley, K., & Tuckwell, V. (1997). Violence in schizophrenia: Role of hallucinations and delusions. *Schizophrenia Research, 26*(2–3), 181–190.

Chinese Society of Psychiatry. (2001). *The Chinese Classification and Diagnostic Criteria of Mental Disorders Version 3* (CCMD-3). Jinan: Author.

Chiswick, D. (1981). Matricide. *British Medical Journal, 283*, 1279.

Christy, A., Poythress, N. G., Boothroyd, R. A., Petrila, J., & Mehra, S. (2005). Evaluating the efficiency and community safety goals of the Broward County mental health court. *Behavioral Sciences and the Law, 22*, 227–243.

Chuang, H. T., Williams, R., & Dalby, J. T. (1987). Criminal behavior among schizophrenics. *Canadian Journal of Psychiatry, 32*(4), 255–258.

Clark v. Arizona, 548 U.S. 735 (2006).

Clarke, M., Whitty, P., Browne, S., McTigue, O., Kinsella, A., Waddington, J. L., Larkin, C., & O'Callaghan, E. (2006). Suicidality in first episode psychosis. *Schizophrenia Research, 86*, 221–225.

Cleckley, H. (1941). *The mask of sanity*. London: Henry Kimpton.

Cleckley, H. (1976). *The mask of sanity*. St. Louis, MO: C.V. Mosby.

Cleckley, H. (1988). *The mask of sanity* (5th ed.). St. Louis, MO: C.V. Mosby.

Coccaro, E. F. (2012). Intermittent explosive disorder as a disorder of impulsive aggression for DSM-5. *The American Journal of Psychiatry, 169*(6), 577–588.

Coccaro, E. F., Kavoussi, R. J., Hauger, R. L., Cooper, T. B., & Ferris, C. F. (1998). Cerebrospinal fluid vasopressin levels: Correlates with aggression and serotonin function in personality-disordered subjects. *Archives of General Psychiatry, 55*(8), 708.

Cochrane, R., Grisso, T., & Frederick, R. (2001). The relationship between criminal charges, diagnoses, and psycholegal opinions among federal pretrial defendants. *Behavioral Sciences and the Law, 19*(4), 565–582.

Cohen, A. K. (1955). *Delinquent boys: The culture of the gang*. Glencoe, IL: The Free Press.

Cohen, B. J., Bonnie, R. J., & Monahan, J. (2009). Understanding and applying Virginia's new statutory civil commitment criteria. *Developments in Mental Health Law, 28*, 127–139.

Cohen, L. H., & Freeman, H. (1945). How dangerous to the community are state hospital patients? *Connecticut State Medical Journal, 9*, 697–700.

Cohen, L. J., & Galynker, I. I. (2002). Clinical features of pedophilia and implications for treatment. *Journal of Psychiatric Practice, 8*, 276–289.

Cohen, M. M., Schei, B., Ansara, D., Gallop, R., Stuckless, N., & Stewart, D. E. (2002). History of personal violence and postpartum depression: Is there a link? *Archives of Women's Mental Health, 4*, 83–92.

Cohen-Bendahan, C. C., Buitelaar, J. K., van Goozen, S. M., Orlebeke, J. F., & Cohen-Kettenis, P. T. (2005). Is there an effect of prenatal testosterone on aggression and other behavioral traits? A study comparing same-sex and opposite-sex twin girls. *Hormones And Behavior, 47*(2), 230–237.

Coid, B., Lewis, S. W., & Revelry, A. M. (1993). A twin study of psychosis and criminality. *British Journal of Psychiatry, 162*, 87–92.

Coid, J. W., & Ullrich, S. (2010). Antisocial personality disorder is on a continuum with psychopathy. *Comprehensive Psychiatry, 51*, 426–433.

Coid, J. W., Wilkins, J., & Coid, B. (1999). Fire-setting, pyromania and self-mutilation in female remanded prisoners. *Journal Of Forensic Psychiatry, 10*(1), 119–130.

Coid, J. W., Yang, M., Ullrich, S., Zhang, T., Sizmur, S., Farrington, D., & Rogers, R. (2011). Most items in structured risk assessment instruments do not predict violence. *The Journal of Forensic Psychiatry & Psychology, 22*(1), 3–21.

Collins, J. J., & Bailey, S. L. (1990a). Relationship of mood disorders to violence. *Journal of Nervous and Mental Disease, 178*(1), 44–47.

Collins, J. J., & Bailey, S. L. (1990b). Traumatic stress disorder and violent behavior. *Journal of Traumatic Stress, 3*(2), 203–220.

Collins, V. L. (2009). Camouflaged legitimacy: Civil commitment, property rights, and legal isolation. *Howard Law Journal, 52*, 407–458.

Colman, A. M. (1999). *What is psychology?* (3rd ed.). London, UK: Routledge.

Compton, A. (1992). The psychoanalytic view of phobias. Part I: Freud's theories of phobias and anxiety. *Psychoanalytic Quarterly, 61*(2), 206–229.

Compton, J. K. (1997). Note: Expert witness testimony and the diminished capacity defense. *American Journal of Trial Advocacy, 20*, 381–407.

Conrad, P., & Schneider, J. W. (1992). *Deviance and medicalization: From badness to sickness* (expanded ed.). Philadelphia, PA: Temple University Press.

Cooke, D. J. (2001). Psychopathy, sadism, and serial killing. In A. Raine & J. Sanmartín (Eds.), *Violence and psychopathy* (pp. 123–137). New York: Kluwer Academic/Plenum Publishers.

Cooke, D. J., & Michie, C. (2001). Refining the construct of psychopathy: Towards a hierarchical model. *Psychological Assessment, 13*, 171–188.

Cooke, D. J., Michie, C., & Skeem, J. (2007). Understanding the structure of the Psychopathy Checklist—Revised: An exploration of methodological confusion. *British Journal of Psychiatry, 190*(suppl. 49), s39–s50.

Coolidge, F. L., & Segal, D. L. (1998). Evolution of personality disorder diagnosis in the *Diagnostic and Statistical Manual of Mental Disorders. Clinical Psychology Review, 18*(5), 585–599.

Coons, P. M. (1991). Iatrogenesis and malingering of multiple personality disorder in the forensic evaluation of homicide defendants. *Psychiatric Clinics of North America, 14*(3), 757–768.

Cooper v. Oklahoma, 517 U.S. 348 (1996).

Cooper, A. J., Swaminath, S., Baxter, D., & Poulin, C. (1990). A female sex offender with multiple paraphilias: A psychologic, physiologic (laboratory sexual arousal) and endocrine case study. *Canadian Journal of Psychiatry, 35*, 334–337.

Cooper, S. A., Mohamed, W. N., & Collacott, R. A. (1993). Case report: Possible Asperger's syndrome in a mentally handicapped transvestite offender. *Journal of Intellectual Disability Research, 37*, 189–194.

Corder, B. F., Ball, B. C., Haizlip, T. M., Rollins, R., & Beaumont, R. (1976). Adolescent parricide: A comparison with other adolescent murder. *American Journal of Psychiatry, 133*(8), 957–961.

Cornell, D. G., Benedek, E. P., & Benedek, D. M. (1987). Characteristics of adolescents charged with homicide: Review of 72 cases. *Behavioral Sciences and the Law, 5*(1), 11–23.

Cornell, D. G., & Hawk, G. L. (1989). Clinical presentation of malingerers diagnosed by experienced forensic psychologists. *Law and Human Behavior, 13*(4), 375–383.

Cornell, D. G., Warren, J., Hawk, G., Stafford, E., Oram, G., & Pine, D. (1997). Psychopathy in instrumental and reactive violent offenders. *Journal of Consulting and Clinical Psychology, 64*(4), 783–790.

Cornwell, J. K. (1998). Understanding the role of the police and *parens patriae* powers in involuntary civil commitment before and after *Hendricks. Psychology, Public Policy, and Law, 4*, 377–413.

Corrigan, P. W. (2005). *On the stigma of mental illness*. Washington, DC: American Psychological Association.

Corrigan, P. W., Mueser, K. T., Bond, G. R., Drake, R. E., & Solomon, P. (2008). *Principles and practice of psychiatric rehabilitation: An empirical approach*. New York, NY: Guilford Press.

Corrigan, P. W., & Watson, A. C. (2005). Findings from the National Comorbidity Survey on the frequency of violent behavior in individuals with psychiatric disorders. *Psychiatry Research, 136*(2–3), 153–162.

Cosden, M., Ellens, J., Schnell, J., & Yamini-Diouf, Y. (2005). Efficacy of a mental health treatment court with assertive community treatment. *Behavioral Sciences and the Law, 23*, 199–214.

Cosgrove, L., & Krimsky, S. (2012). A comparison of DSM-IV and DSM-5 panel members' financial associations with industry: A pernicious problem persists. *PLoS Medicine, 9*(3), 1–4.

Coté, G., & Hodgins, S. (1990). Co-occurring mental disorders among criminal offenders. *Bulletin of the American Academy of Psychiatry and the Law, 18*(3), 271–281.

Coté, G., & Hodgins, S. (1992). The prevalence of major mental disorders among homicide offenders. *International Journal of Law and Psychiatry, 15*, 89–99.

Council of State Governments. (2002). *Final report of the Criminal Justice/Mental Health Consensus Project.* New York, NY: Author. Retrieved from http://issuu.com/csgjustice/docs/the_consensus_project_report_032513.

Council of State Governments. (2012). *Mentally Ill Offender Treatment and Crime Reduction Act: Fact Sheet.* New York, NY: Author. Retrieved from http://csgjusticecenter.org/wp-content/uploads/2012/12/MIOTCRA_Fact_Sheet_2_21_12.pdf.

Council of State Governments. (2013). *Mental health.* Retrieved from http://csgjusticecenter.org/mental-health/.

Cox, M. L., & Zapf, P. A. (2004). An investigation of discrepancies between mental health professionals and the courts in decisions about competency. *Law & Psychology Review*, 28, 109–132.

Craissati, J., & Hodes, P. (1992). Mentally ill sex offenders: The experience of a regional secure unit. *British Journal of Psychiatry, 161*, 846–849.

Crane, L. R. (1999). Interdisciplinary combined-degree and graduate law degree programs: History and trends. *John Marshall Law Review, 33*, 47–80.

Craske, M. G., & Barlow, D. H. (2008). Panic disorder and agoraphobia. In D. H. Barlow (Ed.), *Clinical handbook of psychological disorders: A step-by-step treatment manual* (4th ed., pp. 1–64). New York: The Guilford Press.

Cravens, J. M., Campion, J., Rotholc, A., Covan, F., & Cravens, R. A. (1985). A study of 10 men charged with patricide. *American Journal of Psychiatry, 142*(9), 1089–1092.

Crockford, D. N., Goodyear, B., Edwards, J., Quickfall, J., & el-Guebaly, N. (2005). Cue-induced brain activity in pathological gamblers. *Biological Psychiatry, 58*(10), 787–795.

Cruise, K. R., & Rogers, R. (1998). An analysis of competency to stand trial: An integration of case law and clinical knowledge. *Behavioral Sciences and the Law, 16*, 35–50.

Cunningham, M. D., Sorensen, J. R., & Reidy, T. J. (2009). Capital jury decision-making: The limitations of predictions of future violence. *Psychology, Public Policy, and Law, 15*(4), 223–256.

Curschmann, H. (1894). *Klinische Abbildungen.* Berlin: Julius Springer.

Cuthbert, T. M. (1970). A portfolio of murders. *British Journal of Psychiatry, 116*, 1–10.

D'Souza, W. J., Quinn, S. J., Fryer, J. L., Taylor, B. V., Ficker, D. M., O'Brien, T. J., Pearce, N., & Cook, M. J. (2012). The prevalence and demographic distribution of treated epilepsy: A community-based study in Tasmania, Australia. *Acta Neurologica Scandinavica, 125*, 96–104.

Daftary-Kapur, T., Groscup, J. L., O'Connor, M., Coffaro, F., & Galietta, M. (2011). Measuring knowledge of the insanity defense. Scale construction and validation. *Behavioral Sciences and the Law, 29*, 40–63.

Damasio, A. (1994). *Descartes' error: Emotion, reason, and the human brain.* New York: GP Putnam's Sons.

Daniel, A. E., & Harris, P. W. (1981). Female offenders referred for pre-trial psychiatric examination. *Bulletin of the American Academy of Psychiatry and Law, 9*, 40–47.

Danjczek, L. J. (2007). The mentally ill offender treatment and crime reduction act and its inappropriate non-violent offender limitation. *Journal of Contemporary Health Law and Policy, 24*, 69–117.

Darke, S. (2010). The toxicology of homicide offenders and victims: A review. *Drug and Alcohol Review, 29*, 202–215.

Darke, S., Torok, M., Kaye, S., Ross, J., & McKetin, R. (2010). Comparative rates of violent crime among regular methamphetamine and opioid users: Offending and victimization. *Addiction, 105*, 916–919.

Davis, F. J. (1962). Law as a type of social control. In F. J. Davis, H. H. Foster Jr., C. R. Jeffery, & E. E. Davis (Eds.), *Society and the law: New meanings for an old profession* (pp. 17–32). New York, NY: The Free Press.

Davis, J., & Lauber, K. (1999). Criminal behavioral assessments of arsonists, pyromaniacs, and multiple firesetters. *Journal of Contemporary Criminal Justice,15*(3), 273–290.

Davoli, J. I. (2005). Reconsidering the consequences of an insanity acquittal. *New England Journal on Criminal and Civil Confinement, 31*, 3–13.

De Pauw, K. W., & Szulecka, T. K. (1988). Dangerous delusions: Violence and the misidentification syndromes. *British Journal of Psychiatry, 152*, 91–96.

Dean, K., Walsh, E., Moran, P., Tyrer, P., Creed, F., Byford, S., Burns, T., Murray, R., & Fahy, T. (2006). Violence in women with psychosis in the community: Prospective study. *British Journal of Psychiatry, 188*, 264–270.

DeJong, J., Virkkunen, M., & Linnoila, M. (1992). Factors associated with recidivism in a criminal population. *Journal of Nervous and Mental Disease, 180*(9), 543–550.

Del Bove, G., & Mackay, S. (2011). An empirically derived classification system for juvenile firesetters. *Criminal Justice and Behavior, 38*(8), 796–817.

DelBello, M. P., Soutullo, C. A., Zimmerman, M. E., Sax, K. W., Williams, J. R., McElroy, S. L., & Strakowski, S. M. (1999). Traumatic brain injury in individuals convicted of sexual offenses with and without bipolar disorder. *Psychiatry Research, 89*, 281–286.

DeLia, D. The Achilles complex: Preoedipal trauma, rage, and repetition. *Psychoanalytic Review, 91*(2), 179–199.

Dell, S., & Smith, A. (1983). Changes in the sentencing of diminished responsibility homicides. *British Journal of Psychiatry, 142*, 20–34.

Dell'Osso, B., Altamura, A. C., Allen, A., Marazziti, D., & Hollander, E. (2006). Epidemiologic and clinical updates on impulse control disorders: A critical review. *European Archives of Psychiatry and Clinical Neuroscience, 256*, 464–475.

Delville, Y., Mansour, K., & Ferris, C. (1996). Serotonin blocks vasopressin-facilitated offensive aggression: Interactions within the ventrolateral hypothalamus of golden hamsters. *Physiology and Behavior, 59*(4), 813–816.

Dempster, R. J. (1998). *Prediction of sexually violent recidivism: A comparison of risk assessment instruments.* Unpublished master's thesis, Simon Fraser University.

DeMatteo, D., Batastini, A., Foster, E., & Hunt, E. (2010). Individualizing risk assessment: Balancing idiographic and nomothetic data. *Journal of Forensic Psychology Practice, 10*, 360–371.

Department of Veterans Affairs. Mental Health Services. Suicide Prevention Program. *Suicide data report, 2012* (A report by J. Kemp & R. Bossarte). Retrieved 5 July 2013 from the Office of Public and Intergovernmental Affairs website: http://www.va.gov/opa/docs/Suicide-Data-Report-2012-final.pdf.

DeRiver, J. P. (1951). *The sexual criminal: A psychoanalytic study* (3rd rev. printing). Springfield, IL: Charles C. Thomas.

Dershowitz, A. M. (1994). *The abuse excuse and other cop-outs, sob stories, and evasions of responsibility*. New York, NY: Little, Brown, & Co.

Deutsch, A. (1944). The history of mental hygiene. In J. K. Hall, G. Zilboorg, & H. A. Bunker (Eds.) *One hundred years of American psychiatry* (pp. 325–365). New York, NY: Columbia University Press.

Devaux, C., Petit, G., Perol, Y., & Porot, M. (1974). Inquiry into parricide in France. *Annales Médico-Psychologiques, 1*(2), 161–168

Diamantis, A., Sidiropoulou, K., & Magiorkinis, E. (2010). Epilepsy during the Middle Ages, the Renaissance and the Enlightenment. *Journal of Neurology, 257*, 691–698.

Digiusto, E., Shakeshaft, A. P., Ritter, A., Mattick, R. P., White, J., Lintzeris, N., Bell, J., Saunders, J. B., & the NEPOD Research Group (2006). Effects of pharmacotherapies for opioid dependence on participants' criminal behavior and expenditure. *The Australian and New Zealand Journal of Criminology, 39*(2), 171–189.

Dirks-Linhorst, P. A., & Linhorst, D. M. (2012). Recidivism outcomes for suburban mental health court defendants. *American Journal of Criminal Justice, 37*, 76–91.

District of Columbia v. Heller, 554 U.S. 570 (2008).

Dix, D. L. (1975). *On behalf of the insane poor: Selected reports 1842–1862*. New York: Ayer Co. Publishers, Inc.

Dixon, L. (1999). Dual diagnosis of substance abuse in schizophrenia: Prevalence and impact on outcomes. *Schizophrenia Research, 35*(Suppl. 1), S93–S100.

Dolan, M., McEwan, T. E., Doley, R., & Fritzon, K. (2010). Risk factors and risk assessment in juvenile fire-setting. *Psychiatry, Psychology & Law, 18*(3), 378–394.

Dolan, M. C., & Rennie, C. E. (2007). Is juvenile psychopathy associated with low anxiety and fear in conduct-disordered male offenders? *Journal of anxiety disorders, 21*(8), 1028–1038.

Dorman, D. (2006). Dante's cure: Schizophrenia and the two-person journey. In K. J. Schneider (Ed.), *Existential-integrative psychotherapy: Guideposts to the core of practice* (pp. 236–245). New York: Routledge.

Dorn, L. D., Kolko, D. J., Susman, E. J., Huang, B., Stein, H., Music, E., & Bukstein, O. G. (2009). Salivary gonadal and adrenal hormone differences in boys and girls with and without disruptive behavior disorders: Contextual variants. *Biological Psychology, 81*(1), 31–39.

Douglas, J. E., Burgess, A. W., Burgess, A. G., & Ressler, R. K. (1992). Arson. In J. Douglas, A. Burgess, A. Burgess, & R. Ressler (Eds.), *Crime classification manual* (pp. 163–169). New York: Lexington Books.

Douglas, K. S., & Skeem, J. L. (2005). Violence risk assessment: Getting specific about being dynamic. *Psychology, Public Policy, and Law, 11*(3), 347–383.

Douglas, K. S., Vincent, G. M., & Edens, J. F. (2006). Risk for criminal recidivism: The role of psychopathy. In C. J. Patrick (Ed.), *Handbook of psychopathy* (pp. 533–554). New York: The Guilford Press.

Douglas, M. (Producer), Zaentz, S. (Producer), & Forman, M. (Director). (1975). *One flew over the cuckoo's nest* [Motion picture]. United States of America: Fantasy Films and United Artists.

Draine, J., Wilson, A., & Pogorzelski, W. (2007). Limitations and potential in current research on services for people with mental illness in the criminal justice system. *Journal of Offender Rehabilitation, 45*, 159–177.

Drake, C. R., & Pathé, M. (2004). Understanding sexual offending in schizophrenia. *Criminal Behavior and Mental Health, 14*(2), 108–120.

Dressler, J. (1995). *Understanding criminal law* (2nd ed.). St. Paul, MN: Thomson/West.

Drope v. Missouri, 420 U.S. 162, 178–83 (1975).

Dubber, M. D. (2005). *The police power: Patriarchy and the foundations of American government*. New York, NY: Columbia University Press.

Dudeck, M., Spitzer, C., Stopsack, M., Freyberger, H. J., & Barnow, S. (2007). Forensic inpatient male sexual offenders: The impact of personality disorder and childhood sexual abuse. *Journal of Forensic Psychiatry & Psychology, 18*(4), 494–506.

Dumais, A., Potvin, S., Joyal, C., Allaire, J., Stip, E., Lesage, A., Gobbi, G., & Côté. G. (2011). Schizophrenia and serious violence: A clinical-profile analysis incorporating impulsivity and substance-use disorders. *Schizophrenia Research, 130*, 234–237.

Duncan, J. W., & Duncan, G. M. (1971). Murder in the family: A study of some homicidal adolescents. *American Journal of Psychiatry, 127*(11), 74–78.

Dunsieth, N. W., Nelson, E. B., Brusman-Lovins, L. A., Holcomb, J. L., Beckman, D., Welge, J. A., et al. (2004). Psychiatric and legal features of 113 men convicted of sexual offenses. *Journal of Clinical Psychiatry, 65*, 293–300.

Dupont, R., & Cochran, S. (2000). Police response to mental health emergencies—barriers to change. *The Journal of the American Academy of Psychiatry and the Law, 28*(3), 338–44.

Durham v. United States, 214 F.2d 862 (D.C. Cir. 1954), overruled by *United States v. Brawner*, 471 F.2d 969, 981 (D.C. Cir. 1972).

Durrant, R., & Thakker, J. (2003). *Substance use and abuse: Cultural and historical perspectives*. Thousand Oaks, CA: Sage Publications, Inc.

Duschinsky, R., & Chachamu, N. (2013). Sexual dysfunction and paraphilias in the DSM-5: Pathology, heterogeneity, and gender. *Feminism & Psychology, 23*(1), 49–55.

Dusky v. United States, 362 U.S. 402 (1960).

Ebejer, J. L., Medland, S. E., van der Werf, J., Gondro, C., Henders, A. K., Lynskey, M., Martin, N. G., & Duffy, D. L. (2012). Attention deficit hyperactivity disorder in Australian adults: Prevalence, persistence, conduct problems and disadvantage. *PloS One, 7*(10), 1–10.

Economist, The. (2010, July 22). Rough justice in America: Too many laws, too many prisoners—Never in the civilized world have so many been locked up for so little. *The Economist*. Retrieved from http://www.economist.com/node/16636027

Elbogen, E. B., & Johnson, S. C. (2009). The intricate link between violence and mental disorder results from the National Epidemiologic Survey on Alcohol and Related Conditions. *Archives of General Psychiatry, 66*, 152–161.

Elbogen, E. B., Johnson, S. C., Newton, V. M., Straits-Troster, K., Vasterling, J. J., Wagner, H. R., & Beckham, J. C. (2012). Criminal justice involvement, trauma, and negative affect in Iraq and Afghanistan War era veterans. *Journal of Consulting and Clinical Psychology, 80*(6), 1097–1102.

Elkins, B. E. (1994). Idaho's repeal of the insanity defense: What are we trying to prove? *Idaho Law Review, 31*, 151–171.

Engel, R. S., & Silver, E. (2001). Policing mentally disordered suspects: A re-examination of the criminalization hypothesis. *Criminology, 39*, 225–252.

Eno-Louden, J., & Skeem, J. L. (2011). Parolees with mental disorder: Toward evidence-based practice. *UC Irvine Center for Evidence-Based Corrections Bulletin, 7*(1), 1–9.

Eno-Louden, J., Skeem, J. L., Camp, J., Vidal, S., & Peterson, J. (2012). Supervision practices in specialty mental health probation: What happens in officer–probationer meetings. *Law and Human Behavior, 36*(2), 109–119.

Erb, M., Hodgins, S., Freese, R., Müller-Isberner, R., & Jöckel, D. (2001). Homicide and schizophrenia: Maybe treatment does have a preventative effect. *Criminal Behaviour and Mental Health, 11*, 6–26.

Eriksson, Å., Romelsjö, A., Stenbacka, M., & Tenström, A. (2011). Early risk factors for criminal offending in schizophrenia: A 35-year longitudinal cohort study. *Social Psychiatry and Psychiatric Epidemiology, 46*, 925–932.

Erlich, E. (1975). *Fundamental principles of the sociology of law.* (W. L. Moll, Trans.). New York, NY: Arno Press. (Original work published 1936)

Eronen, M., Hakola, P., & Tiihonen, J. (1996). Mental disorders and homicidal behavior in Finland. *Archives of General Psychiatry, 53*, 497–501.

Eronen, M., Tiihonen, J., & Hakola, P. (1996). Schizophrenia and homicidal behavior. *Schizophrenia Bulletin, 22*, 83–90.

Estelle v. Smith, 451 U.S. 454 (1981).

Estroff, S. E., Swanson, J. W., Lachiotte, W. S., Swartz, M., & Bolduc, M. (1998). Risk reconsidered: Targets of violence in the social networks of people with serious psychiatric disorders. *Social Psychiatry and Psychiatric Epidemiology, 33*, S95–S101.

Everall, I. P., & LeCouteur, A. (1990). Firesetting in an adolescent boy with Asperger's syndrome. *British Journal of Psychiatry, 157*, 284–287.

Evseeff, G. S., & Wisniewski, E. M. (1972). A psychiatric study of a violent mass murderer. *Journal of Forensic Sciences, 17*(3), 371–376.

Eysenck, H. J., & Eysenck, M. W. (1985). *Personality and individual differences: A natural science approach.* New York: Plenum.

Fabian, J. (2012). The Adam Walsh Child Protection and Safety Act: Legal and psychological aspects of the new civil commitment law for federal sex offenders. *Cleveland State Law Review, 30*, 307–364.

Falk, C. E. (1995). *State v. Phipps*: The Tennessee Court of Criminal Appeals accepts "diminished capacity" evidence to negate *mens rea*. *University of Memphis Law Review, 26*, 373–392.

Fals-Stewart, W. (2003). The occurrence of partner physical aggression on days of alcohol consumption: A longitudinal diary study. *Journal of Consulting and Clinical Psychology, 71*, 41–52.

Fals-Stewart, W., Golden, J., & Schumacher, J. (2003). Intimate partner violence and substance use: A longitudinal day-to-day examination. *Addictive Behaviors, 28*, 1555–1574.

Faretta v. California, 422 U.S. 806, 823 (1975).

Farrington, D. P. (2006) Family background and psychopathy. In C. J. Patrick (Ed.), *Handbook of psychopathy* (pp. 229–250). New York: The Guilford Press.

Faust, D., & Ziskin, J. (1988). The expert witness in psychology and psychiatry. *Science, 241*, 31–35.

Fazel, S., Buxrud, P., Ruchkin, V., & Grann, M. (2010). Homicide in discharged patients with schizophrenia and other psychoses: A national case-control study. *Schizophrenia Research, 123*, 263–269.

Fazel, S., Grann, M., Carlström, E., Lichtenstein, P., & Långström, N. (2009a). Risk factors for violent crime in schizophrenia: A national cohort study of 13,806 patients. *Journal of Clinical Psychiatry, 70*(3), 362–369.

Fazel, S., Gulati, D., Linsell, L., Geddes, J. R., & Grann, M. (2009b). Schizophrenia and violence: Systematic review and meta-analysis. *PLoS Med, 6*(8), 1–15.

Fazel, S., Långström, N., Hjern, A., Grann, M., & Lichtenstein, P. (2009c). Schizophrenia, substance abuse, and violent crime. *JAMA: The Journal of the American Medical Association, 301*(19), 2016–2023.

Fazel, S., Lichtenstein, P., Grann, M., Goodwin, G. M., & Långström, N. (2010). Bipolar disorder and violent crime: New evidence from population-based longitudinal studies and systematic review. *Archives of General Psychiatry, 67*(9), 931–938.

Feighner, J. P., Robins, E., Guze, S. B., Woodruff, R. A., Winokur, G., & Munoz, R. (1972). Diagnostic criteria for use in psychiatric research. *Archives of General Psychiatry, 26*, 57–63.

Feinman, J. M. (1998). The future history of legal education. *Rutgers Law Journal, 29*, 475–485.

Feldmann, T. B. (2001). Bipolar disorder and violence. *Psychiatric Quarterly, 72*(2), 119–129.

Felix, A., Herman, D., & Susser, E. (2008). Housing instability and homelessness. In K. T. Mueser & D. V. Jeste (Eds.), *Clinical handbook of schizophrenia* (pp. 411–423). New York: The Guilford Press.

Felthous, A. R. (2010). Psychopathic disorders and criminal responsibility in the USA. *European Archives of Psychiatry and Clinical Neuroscience, 260*(2), S137–S141.

Felthous, A. R. (2011). Competence to stand trial should require rational understanding. *Journal of the American Academy of Psychiatry and Law, 39*(1), 19–30.

Felthous, A. R., Lake, S. L., Rundle, B. K., & Stanford, M. S. (2013). Pharmacotherapy for impulsive aggression: A quality comparison of controlled studies. *International Journal of Law and Psychiatry, 36*, 258–263.

Fenichel, O. (1933). Outline of clinical psychoanalysis. *Psychoanalytic Quarterly, 2*, 562–591.

Ferdico, J. N., Fradella, H. F., & Totten, C. (2013). *Criminal procedure for the criminal justice professional* (11th ed.). Belmont, CA: Wadsworth/Cengage.

Feresin, E. (2009). Lighter sentence for murderer with 'bad genes.' Italian court reduces jail term after tests identify genes linked to violent behaviour. *Nature*. Retrieved from http://www.nature.com/news/2009/091030/full/news.2009.1050.html.

Ferguson, M., & Ogloff, J. R. P. (2011). Criminal responsibility evaluations: Role of psychologists in assessment. *Psychiatry, Psychology and Law, 18*(1), 79–94.

Fergusson, D. M., Boden, J. M., & Horwood, L. J. (2010). Classification of behavior disorders in adolescence: Scaling methods, predictive validity, and gender differences. *Journal of Abnormal Psychology, 119*(4), 699–712.

Fernandez, G. A., & Nygard, S. (1990). Impact of involuntary outpatient commitment on the revolving-door syndrome in North Carolina. *Hospital and Community* Psychiatry, *41*, 1001–1004.

Ferreira, C. (2000). Serial killers—Victims of compulsion or masters of control? In D. H. Fishbein (Ed.), *The science, treatment, and prevention of antisocial behaviors: Application to the criminal justice system* (pp. 15-1–15-18). Kingston, NJ: Civic Research Institute.

Ferris, C. E. (2008). The search for due process in civil commitment hearings: How procedural realities have altered substantive standards. *Vanderbilt Law Review, 61*, 959–981.

Fersch, E. L. (2006). *Thinking about psychopaths and psychopathy: Answers to frequently asked questions with case examples.* New York: iUniverse Inc.

Fincham, D., Grimsrud, A., Corrigall, J., Williams, D. R., Seedat, S., Stein, D. J., & Myer, L. (2009). Intermittent explosive disorder in South Africa: Prevalence, correlates and the role of traumatic exposures. *Psychopathology, 42*(2), 92–98.

Finkel, N. J. (1989). The Insanity Defense Reform Act of 1984: Much ado about nothing. *Behavioral Science and the Law, 7*, 403–419.

Finkel, N. J. (1995). *Commonsense justice: Jurors' notions of the law.* Cambridge, MA: Harvard University Press.

Finkel, N. J., Shaw, R., Bercaw, S., & Koch, J. (1985). Insanity defenses: From the jurors' perspective. *Law and Psychology Review, 9*, 77–92.

Firestone, P., Bradford, J. M., Greenberg, D. M., & Larose, M. R. (1998). Homicidal sex offenders: Psychological, phallometric, and diagnostic features. *Journal of the American Academy of Psychiatry and the Law, 26*(4), 537–552.

Firestone, P., Bradford, J. M., McCoy, M., Greenberg, D. M., Larose, M. R., & Curry, S. (1999). Prediction of recidivism in incest offenders. *Journal of Interpersonal Violence, 14*(5), 511–531.

First, M. B., & Hanlon, R. L. (2008). Use of DSM paraphilia diagnoses in sexually violent predator commitment cases. *Journal of the Academy of Psychiatry and the Law, 36*, 443–454.

Fisher, W. H., Geller, J. L., & Pandiani, J. A. (2009). The changing role of the state psychiatric hospital. *Health Affairs, 28*(3), 676–684.

Fisher, W. H., Silver, E., & Wolff, N. (2006). Beyond criminalization: Toward a criminologically informed framework for mental health policy and services research. *Administration and Policy in Mental Health and Mental Health Services Research, 33*, 544–557.

Fitzgerald, P. B., de Castella, A. R., Filia, K. M., Filia, S. M., Benitez, J., & Kulkarni, J. (2005). Victimization of patients with schizophrenia and related disorders. *Australian and New Zealand Journal of Psychiatry, 39*, 169–174.

Flannery, R. B., Penk, W. E., Irvin, E. A., & Gallagher, C. (1998). Characteristics of violent versus nonviolent patients with schizophrenia. *Psychiatric Quarterly, 69*(2), 83–93.

Flor, H. (2007). Cognitive correlates. In A. Felthous & H. Saβ (Eds.), *International handbook on psychopathic disorders and the law* (pp. 103–116). West Sussex, England: John Wiley & Sons Ltd.

Foley, H. A., & Sharfstein, S. S. (1983). *Madness and government: Who cares for the mentally ill?* Arlington, VA: American Psychiatric Press.

Foucault, M. (1965). *Madness and civilization: A history of insanity in the age of reason*. New York: Vintage Books.

Foucha v. Louisiana, 504 U.S. 71 (1992).

Fougere, A., Potter, S., & Boutilier, J. (2009). Psychopathy and offence severity in sexually aggressive and violent youth. *Criminal Behaviour & Mental Health, 19*(4), 247–252.

Fowles, D. C. (1993). Electrodermal activity and antisocial behavior: Empirical findings and theoretical issues. In J. C. Roy, W. Bouscein, D. C. Fowles, & J. H. Gruzelier (Eds.), *Progress in electrodermal research* (pp. 223–237). New York: Plenum Press.

Fox, R. P. (1974). Narcissistic rage and the problem of combat aggression. *Archives of General Psychiatry, 31*, 807–811.

Fradella, H. F. (2003). Faith, delusions, and death: A case study of the death of a psychotic inmate as a call for reform. *Journal of Contemporary Criminal Justice, 19*, 98–113.

Fradella, H. F. (2004). A content analysis of federal judicial views of the social science "researcher's black arts." *Rutgers Law Journal, 35*, 103–170.

Fradella, H. F. (2005). Competing views on the quagmire of synthetically restoring competency to be executed. *Criminal Law Bulletin, 41*(4), 447–451.

Fradella, H. F. (2007). *Mental illness and criminal defenses of excuse in contemporary American law*. Bethesda, MD: Academica Press.

Fradella, H. F. (2008). *Forensic psychology: The use of behavioral sciences in civil and criminal justice* (2nd ed.). Belmont, CA: Wadsworth/Cengage.

Fradella, H. F. (in press). *Guns, mental illness, and public policy*. Manuscript submitted for publication.

Fradella, H. F., Fogarty, A., & O'Neill, L. (2003). The impact of *Daubert* on the admissibility of behavioral science testimony. *Pepperdine Law Review, 30*, 403–444.

Fradella, H. F., & Smith-Casey, R. (2013). Criminal justice responses to the mentally ill. In S. A. Mallicoat & C. Gardiner (Eds.), *Criminal justice policy* (pp. 201–224) Thousand Oaks, CA: Sage.

Frances, A. F., & Ross, R. (2001). *DSM-IV-TR case studies: A clinical guide to differential diagnosis*. Washington, DC: American Psychiatric Publishing, Inc.

Frances, Allen J. (2012, Dec. 2). DSM-5 is guide, not bible—Ignore its ten worst changes: APA approval of DSM-5 is a sad day for psychiatry. *Psychology Today*. Retrieved May 31, 2013 from http://www.psychologytoday.com/blog/dsm5-in-distress/201212/dsm-5-is-guide-not-bible-ignore-its-ten-worst-changes

Frankle, W. G., Lombardo, I., New, A. S., Goodman, M., Talbot, P. S., Huang, Y., et al. (2005). Brain serotonin transporter distribution in subjects with impulsive aggression: A positron emission study with [11C]McN 5652. *American Journal of Psychiatry, 162*, 915–923.

Franklin, K. (2008). Malingering as a dichotomous variable: Case report on an insanity defendant. *Journal of Forensic Psychology Practice, 8*(1), 95–107.

Franklin, M. E., & Foa, E. B. (2008). Obsessive-compulsive disorder. In D. H. Barlow (Ed.), *Clinical handbook of psychological disorders: A step-by-step treatment manual* (4th ed., pp. 164–215). New York: The Guilford Press.

Frazier, S. H. (1974). Murder—single and multiple. *Research Publications. Association for Research in Nervous and Mental Disease, 52*, 304–312.

Freedman, D. (2009). When is a capitally charged defendant incompetent to stand trial? *International Journal of Law and Psychiatry, 32*(3), 127–133.

Fresán, A., Apiquian, R., García-Anaya, M., de la Fuente-Sandoval, C., Nicolini, H., & Graff-Guerrero, A. (2007). The P50 auditory evoked potential in violent and non-violent patients with schizophrenia. *Schizophrenia Research, 97*, 128–136.

Freud, A. (1946). *The ego and the mechanisms of defense*. New York: International Universities Press, Inc. (Original work published 1936)

Freud, A. (1966). *The ego and the mechanisms of defense* (revised edition). New York: International Universities Press. (Original work published 1936)

Freud, S. (1950). *Totem and taboo* (J. Strachey, Ed. and Trans.). New York: W. W. Norton & Company. (Original work published 1913)

Freud, S. (1961). *Beyond the pleasure principle* (J. Strachey, Ed. and Trans.). New York: W. W. Norton & Company. (Original work published 1920)

Freud, S. (1961). *Civilization and its discontents* (J. Strachey, Ed. and Trans.). New York: W. W. Norton & Company. (Original work published 1930)

Freud, S. (1961). The dissolution of the Oedipus complex. In J. Strachey (Ed. and Trans.), *The standard edition of the complete psychological works of Sigmund Freud* (Vol. 19, pp. 173–179). London: Hogarth Press. (Original work published 1924)

Freud, S. (1961) Dostoevsky and parricide. In J. Strachey (Ed. and Trans.), *The standard edition of the complete psychological works of Sigmund Freud* (Vol. 21, pp. 177–196). London: Hogarth Press. (Original work published 1928)

Freud, S. (1961). *The ego and the id* (J. Strachey, Ed. and Trans.). New York: W. W. Norton & Company. (Original work published 1923)

Freud, S. (1961). Some character-types met with in psychoanalytic work: Criminals from a sense of guilt. In J. Strachey (Ed. and Trans.), *The standard edition of the complete psychological works of Sigmund Freud* (Vol. 14, pp. 332–333). London: Hogarth Press. (Original work published 1916)

Freud, S. (1962). The neuro-psychoses of defence. In J. Strachey (Ed. and Trans.), *The standard edition of the complete psychological works of Sigmund Freud* (Vol. 3, pp. 48–62). London: Hogarth Press. (Original work published 1894)

Freud, S. (1962). *Three essays on the theory of sexuality* (J. Strachey, Ed. and Trans.). New York: Basic Books. (Original work published 1905)

Freud, S. (1963). Mourning and melancholia. In J. Strachey (Ed. and Trans.), *The standard edition of the complete psychological works of Sigmund Freud* (Vol. 14, pp. 237–260). London: Hogarth Press. (Original work published in 1917)

Freud, S. (1964). New introductory lectures on psycho-analysis. In J. Strachey (Ed. and Trans.), *The standard edition of the complete psychological works of Sigmund Freud* (Vol 22, pp. 1–182). London: Hogarth Press. (Original work published 1933)

Freud, S. (1966). Fixation to traumas: The unconscious. In J. Strachey (Ed. and Trans.), *Introductory lectures on psycho-analysis* (Lecture XVIII, pp. 338–353). New York: W. W. Norton & Company. (Original work published 1917)

Freud, S. (2003). *Analysis of a phobia in a five-year-old boy ["Little Hans"].* In L. A. Huish (Trans.), *The "Wolfman" and other cases*. New York: Penguin Books. (Original work published 1909)

Frick, P. J., Cornell, A. H., Bodin, S. D., Dane, H. E., Barry, C. T., & Loney, B. R. (2003). Callous-unemotional traits and developmental pathways to severe conduct problems. *Developmental Psychology, 39*(2), 372–378.

Fridell, M., Hesse, M., Jæger, M. M., & Kühlhorn, E. (2008). Antisocial personality disorder as a predictor of criminal behaviour in a longitudinal study of a cohort of abusers of several classes of drugs: Relation to type of substance and type of crime. *Addictive Behaviors, 33*, 799–811.

Friedland, S. I. (1999). On treatment, punishment, and the civil commitment of sex offenders. *University of Colorado Law Review, 70*, 73–154.

Friedlander, K. (1947). *The psychoanalytic approach to juvenile delinquency*. New York: International Universities Press.

Frisman, L. K., Swanson, J., Marín, M. C., & Leavitt-Smith, E. (2010). Estimating costs of reentry programs for prisoners with severe mental illnesses. *Correctional Health Care Report, 11*(6), 81–95.

Frith, C. D., & Corcoran, R. (1996). Exploring "theory of mind" in people with schizophrenia. *Psychological Medicine, 26*(3), 521–530.

Fromm, E. (1973). *The anatomy of human destructiveness*. New York: Holt, Rinehart & Winston.

Fukunaga, K. K., Pasewark, R. A., Hawkins, M., & Gudeman, H. (1981). Insanity plea: Interexaminer agreement and concordance of psychiatric opinion and court verdict. *Law and Human Behavior, 5*, 325–328.

Fuller, D. A. (2011). To fix "broken" jails—Fix treatment laws for mental illness. *Sheriff, 63(7)*, 30–31.

Fullerton, R. A. (2007). Psychoanalyzing kleptomania. *Marketing Theory, 7*(4), 335–352.

Gabbard, G. O. (2005). *Psychodynamic psychiatry in clinical practice* (4th ed.). Washington, DC: American Psychiatric Publishing, Inc.

Gacono, C. B. (1992). Sexual homicide and the Rorschach: A Rorschach case study of sexual homicide. *British Journal of Projective Psychology, 37*, 1–21.

Gacono, C. B. (1997). Borderline personality organization, psychopathy, and sexual homicide: The case of Brinkley. In I. B. Weiner (Ed.), *Contemporary Rorschach interpretation* (pp. 217–237). Mahwah, NJ: Lawrence Erlbaum Associates.

Galli, V., McElroy, S. L., Soutullo, C. A., Kizer, D., Raute, N., Keck Jr., P. E., & McConvile, B. J. (1999). The psychiatric diagnoses of twenty-two adolescents who have sexually molested other children. *Comprehensive Psychiatry, 40*(2), 85–88.

Gao, Y., Raine, A., & Schug, R. A. (2012). Somatic aphasia: Mismatch of body sensations with autonomic stress reactivity in psychopathy. *Biological Psychiatry, 90*, 228–233.

Garety, P. A., Kuipers, E., Fowler, D., Freeman, D., & Bebbington, P. E. (2001). A cognitive model of the positive symptoms of psychosis. *Psychological Medicine, 31*, 189–195.

Garner, B. A. (Ed.) (2004). *Black's law dictionary* (8th ed.). St. Paul, MN: Thomson/West.

Garno, J. L., Gunawardane, N., Goldberg, J. F. (2008). Predictors of trait aggression in bipolar disorder. *Bipolar Disorders, 10*, 285–292.

Gaynor, J. (1996). Fire-setting. In M. Lewis (Ed.), *Child and adolescent psychiatry: A comprehensive textbook* (pp. 601–611). Baltimore, MD: Williams & Wilkins.

Geberth, V. J. (1996). *Practical homicide investigation: Tactics, procedures, and forensic techniques* (3rd ed.). Boca Raton, Florida: CRC Press.

Geberth, V. J., & Turco, R. N. (1997). Antisocial personality disorder, sexual sadism, malignant narcissism, and serial murder. *Journal of Forensic Sciences, 42*(1), 49–60.

Gelhorn, H., Hartman, C., Sakai, J., Mikulich-Gilbertson, S., Stallings, M., & Young, S. (2009). An item response theory analysis of DSM-IV conduct disorder. *Journal of the American Academy of Child and Adolescent Psychiatry, 48*, 42–50.

Gendle, K., & Woodhams, J. (2005). Suspects who have a learning disability: Police perceptions toward the client group and their knowledge about learning disabilities. *Journal of Intellectual Disabilities, 9*(1), 70–81.

Gendreau, P., Goggin, C., French, S., & Smith, P. (2006). Practicing psychology in correctional settings. In I. B. Weiner & A. K. Hess (Eds.), *The handbook of forensic psychology* (3rd ed., pp. 722–750). Hoboken, NJ: John Wiley & Sons, Inc.

Ghaziuddin, M. (2010). Brief report: should the DSM V drop Asperger syndrome? *Journal of Autism & Developmental Disorders, 40*(9), 1146–1148.

Ghaziuddin, M., Tsai, L., & Ghaziuddin, N. (1991). Brief report: Violence in Asperger syndrome, a critique. *Journal of Autism and Developmental Disorders, 21*(3), 349–354.

Gibson, L. E., Holt, J. C., Fondacaro, K. M., Tang, T. S., Powell, T. A., & Turbitt, E. L. (1999). An examination of antecedent traumas and psychiatric comorbidity among male inmates with PTSD. *Journal of Traumatic Stress, 12*(3), 473–484.

Gideon v. Wainwright, 372 U.S. 335 (1963).

Gillies, H. (1965). Murder in the west of Scotland. *British Journal of Psychiatry, 111*, 1087–1094.

Gintis, H. (2007). A framework for the unification of the behavioral sciences. *Behavioral and Brain Sciences, 30*, 1–61.

Giovannoni, J., & Gurel, L. (1967). Socially descriptive behavior of ex-mental patients. *Archives of General Psychiatry, 17*, 146–153.

Glaze, L. E. (2011). *Correctional population in the United States, 2010*. Washington, DC: U.S. Department of Justice, Office of Justice Programs, Bureau of Justice Statistics. Retrieved from http://bjs.ojp.usdoj.gov/content/pub/pdf/cpus10.pdf

Glenn, A. L., & Raine, A. (2009). Psychopathy and instrumental aggression: Evolutionary, neurobiological, and legal perspectives. *International Journal of Law and Psychiatry, 32*, 253–258.

Glober, R. W., Miller, J. E., Sadowski, S. R. (2012). *Proceedings on the state budget crisis and the behavioral health treatment gap: The impact on public substance abuse and mental health treatment systems*. Washington, DC: National Association of State Mental Health Program Directors. Retrieved from http://www.nasmhpd.org/docs/Summary-Congressional Briefing_March 22_Website.pdf

Gobert, J. J., (1973). Competency to stand trial: A pre-and-post *Jackson* analysis. *Tennessee Law Review, 40*, 659–688.

Goffman, E. (1961). *Asylums*. New York, NY: Doubleday.

Goldberg, D. S. (2012). Against reductionism in law and neuroscience. *Houston Journal of Health Law & Policy, 11*, 321–346.

Goldenson, R. M. (1970). *The encyclopedia of human behavior: Psychology, psychiatry, and mental health*. Garden City, NY: Doubleday.

Goldman, H. H., Adams, N. H., & Taube, C. A. (1983). Deinstitutionalization: The data demythologized. *Hospital and Community Psychiatry, 34*(2), 129–134.

Goldman, H. H., & Morrissey, J .P. (1985). The alchemy of mental health policy: Homelessness and the fourth cycle of reform. *American Journal of Public Health, 75*(7), 727–731.

Goldney, R. D. (1977). Family murder followed by suicide. *Forensic Science, 9*, 219–228.

Goldstein, P. (1998). Drugs, violence, and federal funding: A research odyssey. *Substance Use & Misuse, 33*(9), 1915–1936.

Golenkov, A., Large, M., Nielssen, O., & Tsymbalova, A. (2011). Characteristics of homicide offenders with schizophrenia from the Russian federation. *Schizophrenia Research, 133*, 232–237.

Good, M. I. (1978). Primary affective disorder, aggression, and criminality: A review and clinical study. *Archives of General Psychiatry, 35*, 954–960.

Goodwin, R., & Hamilton, S. (2003). Lifetime comorbidity of antisocial personality disorder and anxiety disorders among adults in the community. *Psychiatry Research, 117*, 159–166.

Gosden, N. P., Kramp, P., Gabrielsen, G., Andersen, T. F., & Sestoft, D. (2005). Violence of young criminals predicts schizophrenia: A 9-year register-based followup of 15- to 19-year-old criminals. *Schizophrenia Bulletin, 31*(3), 759–768.

Goss, J. R., Peterson, K., Smith, L. W., Kalb, K., & Brodey, B. B. (2002). Characteristics of suicide attempts in a large urban jail system with an established suicide prevention program, *Psychiatric Services, 53*, 574–579.

Gothelf, D., Furfaro, J., Hoeft, F., Eckert, M., Hall, S., O'Hara, R., Erba, H. W., Ringel, J., Hayashi, K. M., Patnaik, S., Golianu, B., Kraemer, H. C., Thompson, P. M., Piven, J., & Reiss, A. (2008). Neuroanatomy of fragile X syndrome is associated with aberrant behavior and the fragile x mental retardation protein (FMRP). *Annals of Neurology, 63*(1), 40–51.

Gottfredson, M. R., & Hirschi, T. (1990). *A general theory of crime*. Stanford, CA: Stanford University Press.

Gottfredson, M., & Hindelang, M. (1979). A study of the behavior of law. *American Sociological Review, 44*, 3–18.

Gottlieb, P., Gabrielsen, G., & Kramp, P. (1987). Psychotic homicides in Copenhagen from 1959 to 1983. *Acta Psychiatrica Scandinavica, 76*, 285–292.

Gowensmith, W. N., Murrie, D. C., & Boccaccini, M. T. (2012). Field reliability of competence to stand trial opinions: How often do evaluators agree, and what do judges decide when evaluators disagree?. *Law and Human Behavior, 36*(2), 130–139.

Graber, B., Hartmann, K., Coffman, J. A., Huey, C. J., & Golden, C. J. (1982). Brain damage among mentally disordered sex offenders. *Journal of Forensic Sciences, 27*(1), 125–134.

Grachek, J. E. (2006). The insanity defense in the twenty-first century: How recent United States Supreme Court case law can improve the system. *Indiana Law Journal, 81*, 1479-1501.

Grafman, J., Schwab, K., Warden, D., Pridgen, A., Brown, H. R., & Salazar, A. M. (1996). Frontal lobe injuries, violence, and aggression: a report of the Vietnam Head Injury Study. *Neurology, 46*, 1231–1238.

Grann, M., Långström, N., Tengström, A., & Kullgren, G. (1999). Psychopathy (PCL-R) predicts violent recidivism among criminal offenders with personality disorders in Sweden. *Law and Human Behavior, 23*(2), 205–217.

Grant, B. F., Hasin, D. S., Stinson, F. S., Dawson, D. A., Chou, S. P., Ruan, W.J., & Huang, B. (2005). Co-occurrence of 12-month mood and anxiety disorders and personality disorders in the US: Results from the national epidemiologic survey on alcohol and related conditions. *Journal of Psychiatric Research, 39*, 1–9.

Grant, J. E. (2003). Family history and psychiatric comorbidity in persons with kleptomania. *Comprehensive Psychiatry, 44*, 437–441.

Grant, J. E. (2004). Co-occurrence of personality disorders in persons with kleptomania: A preliminary investigation. *Journal of the American Academy of Psychiatry and the Law, 32*, 395–398.

Grant, J. E. (2006). SPECT imaging and treatment of pyromania. *Journal of Clinical Psychiatry, 67*(6), 998.

Grant, J. E., Correia, S., & Brennan-Krohn, T. (2006). White matter integrity in kleptomania: A pilot study. *Psychiatry Research: Neuroimaging, 147*(2–3), 233–237.

Grant, J. E., & Kim, S. W. (2007). Clinical characteristics and psychiatric comorbidity of pyromania. *Journal of Clinical Psychiatry, 68*, 1717–1722.

Grant, J. E., Kim, S. W., & Odlaug, B. L. (2009). A double-blind, placebo-controlled study of the opiate antagonist, naltrexone, in the treatment of kleptomania. *Biological Psychiatry, 65*, 600–606.

Grant, J. E., & Odlaug, B. L. (2008). Kleptomania: Clinical characteristics and treatment. *Revista Brasileira de Psiquiatria, 30*, S11–S15.

Grant, J. E., Odlaug, B. L., Davis, A. A., & Kim, S. (2009). Legal consequences of kleptomania. *Psychiatric Quarterly, 80*(4), 251–259.

Grant, J. E., Odlaug, B. L., Schrieber, L. R. N., Chamberlain, S. R., & Kim, S. W. (2013). Memantine reduces stealing behavior and impulsivity in kleptomania: A pilot study. *International Clinical Psychopharmacology, 28*(2), 106–111.

Grant, J. E., Odlaug, B. L., & Wozniak, J. R. (2007). Neuropsychological functioning in kleptomania. *Behaviour Research and Therapy, 45*, 1663–1670.

Grant, J. E., & Potenza, M. N. (2008). Gender-related differences in individuals seeking treatment for kleptomania. *CNS Spectrums, 13*, 235–245.

Green, C. M. (1981). Matricide by sons. *Medicine, Science, and the Law, 21*(3), 207–214.

Greenberg, G., Rosenheck, R. A., Erickson, S. K., Desai, R. A., Stefanovics, E. A., Swartz, M., Keefe, R. S. E., McEvoy, J., Stroup, T. S., & other CATIE investigators (2011). Criminal justice system involvement among people with schizophrenia. *Community Mental Health Journal, 47*, 727–736.

Greene, E., & Heilbrun, K. (2011). *Wrightsman's psychology and the legal system* (7th ed.) Belmont, CA: Wadsworth.

Grella, C., Greenwell, L., Prendergast, M., Sacks, S., & Melnick, G. (2008). Diagnostic profiles of offenders in substance abuse treatment programs. *Behavioral Sciences and the Law, 26*, 369–388.

Gresham, A. C. (1993). The insanity plea: A futile defense for serial killers. *Law and Psychology Review, 17*, 193–208.

Grisso, T. (2003). *Evaluating competencies: Forensic assessments and instruments* (2nd edition). New York: Kluwer Academic/Plenum Publishers.

Grisso, T., & Tomkins, A. J. (1996). Communication violence risk assessments. *American Psychologist, 51*(9), 928–930.

Grob, G. N. (1966). *The state of the mentally ill.* Chapel Hill, NC: University of North Carolina Press.

Grob, G. N. (1973). *Mental institutions in America: Social policy to 1875.* New York, NY: Free Press.

Grob, G. N. (1994). *The mad among us: A history of the care of America's mentally ill.* Cambridge, MA: Harvard University Press.

Grossman, L. S., & Cavanaugh Jr., J. L. (1990). Psychopathology and denial in alleged sex offenders. *Journal of Nervous and Mental Disease, 178*(12), 739–744.

Grossman, L. S., & Wasyliw, O. E. (1988). A psychometric study of stereotypes: Assessment of malingering in a criminal forensic group. *Journal of Personality Assessment, 52*(3), 549–563.

Grove, W. M., Zald, D. H., Lebow, B. S., Snitz, B. E., & Nelson, C. (2000). Clinical versus mechanical prediction: A meta-analysis. *Psychological Assessment, 12*, 19–30.

Gudjónsson, G. H. (1990). Psychological and psychiatric aspects of shoplifting. *Medicine, Science, and the Law, 30*(1), 45–51.

Gudjónsson, G. H., & Pétursson, H. (1982). Some criminological and psychiatric aspects of homicide in Iceland. *Medicine, Science, and the Law, 22*(2), 91–98.

Gur, O. M. (2010). Persons with mental illness in the criminal justice system: Police interventions to prevent violence and criminalization. *Journal of Police Crisis Negotiations, 10*, 220–240.

Gurley, J. R., & Marcus, D. K. (2008). The effects of neuroimaging and brain injury on insanity defenses. *Behavioral Sciences and the Law, 26*, 85–97.

Gutheil, T. G., & Appelbaum, P. S. (1983). "Mind control," "synthetic sanity," "artificial competence," and genuine confusion: Legally relevant effects of antipsychotic medication. *Hofstra Law Review, 12*, 77–120.

Guze, S. B., Woodruff, R. A., & Clayton, P. J. (1974). Psychiatric disorders and criminality. *JAMA: The Journal of the American Medical Association, 227*(6), 641–642.

Haapasalo, J., & Hämäläinen, T. (1996). Childhood family problems and current psychiatric problems among young violent and property offenders. *Journal of the American Academy of Child and Adolescent Psychiatry, 35*, 1394–1401.

Hafemeister, T. L., Garner, S. G., Bath, V. E. (2012). Forging links and renewing ties: Applying the principles of restorative and procedural justice to better respond to criminal offenders with a mental disorder. *Buffalo Law Review, 60*, 147–223.

Häfner, H., & Böker, W. (1982). *Crimes of violence by mentally abnormal offenders: A psychiatric and epidemiological study in the Federal German Republic*. London, UK: Cambridge University Press.

Hails, J., & Borum, R. (2003). Police training and specialized approaches to respond to people with mental illnesses. *Crime & Delinquency, 49*(1), 52–61.

Häkkänen, H., & Laajasalo, T. (2006). Homicide crime scene behaviors in a Finnish sample of mentally ill offenders. *Homicide Studies, 10*(1), 33–54.

Häkkänen-Nyholm, H., & Hare, R. D. (2009). Psychopathy, homicide, and the courts: Working the system. *Criminal Justice and Behavior, 36*(8), 761–777.

Hall, J. R., & Benning, S. D. (2006). The "successful" psychopath: Adaptive and subclinical manifestations of psychopathy in the general population. In C. J. Patrick (Ed.), *Handbook of psychopathy* (pp. 459–478). New York: The Guilford Press.

Hall, P. D. (1989). Multiple personality disorder and homicide: Professional and legal issues. *Dissociation, 2*(2), 110–115.

Hall, W., Hando, J., Darke, S., & Ross, J. (1996). Psychological morbidity and route of administration among amphetamine users in Sydney, Australia. *Addiction, 91*(1), 81–87.

Hallahan, B., Newell, J., Soares, J. C., Brambilla, P., Strakowski, S. M., Fleck, D. E., Kieseppä, T., Altshuler, L. L., Fornito, A., Malhi, G. S., McIntosh, A. M., Yurgelun-Todd, D. A., Labar, K. S., Sharma, V., MacQueen, G. M., Murray, R. M., & McDonald, C. (2011). Structural magnetic resonance imaging in bipolar disorder: An international collaborative mega-analysis of individual patient data. *Biological Psychiatry, 69*, 326–335.

Haney, C. (1980). Psychology and legal change: On the limits of a factual jurisprudence. *Law and Human Behavior, 4*, 147–199.

Haney, C. (1993). Psychology and legal change: The impact of a decade. *Law and Human Behavior, 17*, 371–398.

Hanlon, R. E., Coda, J. J., Cobia, D., & Rubin, L. H. (2012). Psychotic domestic murder: Neuropsychological differences between homicidal and nonhomicidal schizophrenic men. *Journal of Family Violence, 27(2)*, 105–113.

Hanlon, R. E., Rubin, L. H., Jensen, M., & Daoust, S. (2010). Neuropsychological features of indigent murder defendants and death row inmates in relation to homicidal aspects of their crimes. *Archives of Clinical Neuropsychology, 25*, 1–13.

Hanson, R. K., & Harris, J. R. (2000). Where should we intervene? Dynamic predictors of sexual assault recidivism. *Criminal Justice and Behavior, 27*, 6–35.

Hanson, R. K., & Thornton, D. (1999). *Static-99: Improving actuarial risk assessments for sex offenders* (User Report 99-02). Ottawa, ON: Department of the Solicitor General of Canada.

Harcourt, B. E. (2011). Reducing mass incarceration: Lessons from the deinstitutionalization of mental hospitals in the 1960s. *Ohio State Journal of Criminal Law, 9*, 53–88.

Hare, D. J., Gould, J., Mills, R., & Wing, L. (2000). *A preliminary study of individuals with autistic spectrum disorders in three special hospitals in England*. Bromley, Kent: National Autistic Society.

Hare, R. D. (1993) *Without conscience: The disturbing world of the psychopaths among us*. New York: Pocket Books.

Hare, R. D. (1996). Psychopathy: A clinical construct whose time has come. *Criminal Justice and Behavior, 23*, 25–54.

Hare, R. D. (2003). *The Hare Psychopathy Checklist-Revised* (2nd ed.). Toronto, ON: Multi-Health Systems.

Harkavy-Friedman, J. M., Keilp, J. G., Grunebaum, M. F., Sher, L., Printz, D., Burke, A. K., Mann, J. J., & Oquendo, M. (2006). Are BPI and BPII suicide attempters distinct neuropsychologically? *Journal of Affective Disorders, 94*, 255–259.

Harrang, C. (2012). Psychic skin and narcissistic rage: Reflections on Almodóvar's *The Skin I Live In*. *The International Journal of Psychoanalysis, 93*, 1301–1308.

Harrer, G., & Kofler-Westergren, B. (1986). Depression and criminality. *Psychopathology, 19*(suppl. 2), 215–219.

Harris, G. T., & Rice, M. E. (2006). Treatment of psychopathy: A review of empirical findings. In C. J. Patrick (Ed.), *Handbook of psychopathy* (pp. 555–572). New York: The Guilford Press.

Harris, G. T., Rice, M. E., & Quinsey, V. L. (1993). Violent recidivism of mentally disordered offenders: The development of a statistical prediction instrument. *Criminal Justice and Behavior, 20*, 315–335.

Harris, V., Rafii, R., Tonge, S., & Uldall, K. (2002). Rearrest: Does HIV serostatus make a difference? *AIDS Care, 14*(6), 839–849.

Hart, S. D., & Hare, R. D. (1992). Predicting fitness to stand trial: The relative power of demographic, criminal, and clinical variables. *Forensic Reports, 5*, 53–65.

Hart-Kerkhoffs, L., Vermeiren, R., Jansen, L., & Doreleijers, T. (2011). Juvenile sex offenders: Mental health and reoffending. *European Psychiatry, 26* (Supp. 1), 2077–2077.

Harvard Law Review. (2008). Developments in the law—the law of mental illness: *Sell v. United States*: Forcibly medicating the mentally ill to stand trial. *Harvard Law Review, 121*, 1121–1133.

Harvard Mental Health Letter (2011, Jan). *Mental illness and violence*. Cambridge, MA: Harvard Medical School. Retrieved from http://www.health.harvard.edu/newsletters/Harvard_Mental_Health_Letter/2011/January/mental-illness-and-violence

Haskins, B. G., & Silva, J. A. (2005). Letter to the editor. *Journal of the American Academy of Psychiatry and the Law, 33*(3), 417–418.

Haskins, B. G., & Silva, J. A. (2006). Asperger's disorder and criminal behavior: Forensic-psychiatric considerations. *Journal of the American Academy of Psychiatry and the Law, 34*, 374–384.

Hastings, M, Krishnan, S., Tangney, J., & Stuewig, J. (2011). Predictive and incremental validity of the violence risk appraisal guide scores with male and female inmates. *Psychological Assessment, 23*(1), 174–183.

Hawes, S. W., Boccaccini, M. T., & Murrie, D. C. (2013). Psychopathy and the combination of psychopathy and sexual deviance as predictors of sexual recidivism: Meta-analytic findings using the Psychopathy Checklist—Revised. *Psychological Assessment, 25*(1), 233–243.

Hayes, S. (2007). Missing out: Offenders with learning disabilities and the criminal justice system. *British Journal of Learning Disabilities, 35*, 146–153.

Hayes, S. (2009). Brief report: The relationship between childhood abuse, psychological symptoms and subsequent sex offending. *Journal of Applied Research in Intellectual Disabilities, 2*, 96–101.

Haznedar, N. M., Buchsbaum, M. S., Hazlett, E. A., Shihabuddin, L., New, A., & Siever, L. J. (2004). Cingulate gyrus volume and metabolism in the schizophrenia spectrum. *Schizophrenia Research, 71*, 249–262.

Heide, K. M. (1992). *Why kids kill parents: Child abuse and adolescent homicide*. Columbus, OH: Ohio State University Press.

Heide, K. M., & Petee, T. A. (2007). Parricide: An empirical analysis of 24 years of U. S. data. *Journal of Interpersonal Violence, 22*(11), 1382–1399.

Heilbrun Jr., A. B. (1979). Psychopathy and violent crime. *Journal of Consulting and Clinical Psychology, 47*(3), 509–516.

Heinrichs, R. W., & Sam, E. P. (2012). Schizophrenia and crime: How predictable are charges, convictions, and violence? *International Journal of Mental Health and Addiction, 10*(1), 122–131.

Heitzeg, N. A. (1996). *Deviance: Rulemakers and rulebreakers*. Minneapolis, MN: West.

Held, M. L., Brown, C. A., Frost, L. E., Hickey, J. S., Buck, D. S. (2012). Integrated primary and behavioral health care in patient-centered medical homes for jail releasees with mental illness. *Criminal Justice & Behavior, 39*(4), 533–551.

Hellerstein, D., Frosch, W., & Koenigsberg, H. W. (1987). The clinical significance of command hallucinations. *American Journal of Psychiatry, 144*, 219–221.

Henderson, D. C., & Doraiswamy, P. M. (2008). Prolactin-related and metabolic adverse effects of atypical antipsychotic agents. *Journal of Clinical Psychiatry, 69*(1), 32–44.

Hendricks, P. S., Clark, C. B., Johnson, M. W., Fontaine, K. R., & Cropsey, K. L. (2014). Hallucinogen use predicts reduced recidivism among substance-involved offenders under community corrections supervision. *Journal of Psychopharmacology, 28*(1), 62–66.

Hendricks, S. E., Fitzpatrick, D. F., Hartmann, K., Quaife, M. A., Stratbucker, R. A., & Graber, B. (1988). Brain structure and function in sexual molesters of children and adolescents. *Journal of Clinical Psychiatry, 49*, 108–112.

Herinckx, H. A., Swart, S. C., Ama, S. M., Dolezal, C. D., & King, S. (2005). Rearrest and linkage to mental health services among defendants of the Clark County mental health court program. *Psychiatric Services, 56*(7): 853–857.

Herseth, S. M. (1996). Competency to stand trial. *Georgetown Law Journal, 84*, 1066–1076.

Hervé, H. F., Mitchell, D., Cooper, B. S., Spidel, A., & Hare, R. D. (2004). Psychopathy and unlawful confinement: An examination of perpetrator and event characteristics. *Canadian Journal of Behavioural Science, 36*(2), 137–145.

Herz, M. I., & Marder, S. R. (2002). *Schizophrenia: Comprehensive treatment and management*. Philadelphia, PA: Lippincott, Williams & Wilkins.

Hiatt, K. D., & Newman, J. P. (2006). Understanding psychopathy: The cognitive side. In C. J. Patrick (Ed.), *Handbook of psychopathy* (pp. 334–352). New York: Guilford Press.

Hickey, E. (1991). *Serial murderers and their victims*. Pacific Grove, CA: Brooks/Cole.

Hickey, E. (1997). *Serial murderers and their victims* (2nd ed.). Belmont, CA: Wadsworth.

Hickey, J. D., Tysinger, A. K., & Mims, W. C. (2007/2008). A new era begins: Mental health law reform in Virginia. *Richmond Journal of Law and the Public Interest, 11*, 101–125.

Hill, J., & Nathan, R. (2008). Childhood antecedents of serious violence in adult male offenders. *Aggressive Behavior, 34*, 329–338.

Hillbrand, M. (2001). Homicide-suicide and other forms of co-occurring aggression against self and against others. *Professional Psychology: Research and Practice, 32*(6), 626–635.

Hillbrand, M., Alexandre, J. W., Young, J. L., & Spitz, R. T. (1999). Parricides: Characteristics of offenders and victims, legal factors, and treatment issues. *Aggression and Violent Behavior, 4*(2), 179–190.

Hirose, S. (1979). Depression and homicide: A psychiatric and forensic study of four cases. *Acta Psychiatrica Scandinavica, 59*, 211–217.

Hiscoke, U. L., Langström, N., Ottosson, H., & Grann, M. (2003). Self-reported personality traits and disorders (DSM-IV) and risk of criminal recidivism: A prospective study. *Journal of Personality Disorders, 17*(4), 293–305.

Hoaken, P. N. S., & Stewart, S. H. (2003). Drugs of abuse and the elicitation of aggressive behavior. *Addictive Behaviors, 28*, 1533–1554.

Hodgins, S. (2004). Criminal and antisocial behaviours and schizophrenia: A neglected topic. In W. F. Gattaz & H. Häfner (Eds.), *Search for the causes of schizophrenia* (Vol. 5, pp. 315–341). New York: Springer-Verlag.

Hodgins, S. (2008). Violent behavior among people with schizophrenia: A framework for investigations of causes, and effective treatment, and prevention. *Philosophical Transactions of the Royal Society, 363*, 2505–2518.

Hodgins, S., Calem, M., Shimel, R., Williams, A., Harleston, D., Morgan, C., Dazzan, P., Fearon, P., Morgan, K., Lappin, J., Zanelli, J., Reichenberg, A., & Jones, P. (2011). Criminal offending and distinguishing features of offenders among persons experiencing a first episode of psychosis. *Early Intervention in Psychiatry, 5*, 15–23.

Hodgins, S., De Brito, S. A., Chhabra, P., & Côté, G. (2010). Anxiety disorders among offenders with antisocial personality disorders: A distinct subtype? *Canadian Journal of Psychiatry, 55*(12), 784–791.

Hodgins, S., & Hébert, J. (1984). Une etude de relance auprès de malades mentaux ayant commis des actes criminels. *Revue Canadienne de Psychiatrie, 29*, 669–675.

Hodgins, S., Mednick, S. A., Brennan, P. A., Schulsinger, F., & Engberg, M. (1996). Mental disorder and crime: Evidence from a Danish birth cohort. *Archives of General Psychiatry, 53*(6), 489–496.

Hodgins, S., Tiihonen J., & Ross D. (2005) The consequences of conduct disorder for males who develop schizophrenia: Associations with criminality, aggressive behavior, substance use, and psychiatric services. *Schizophrenia Research, 78*, 323–335.

Holmes, R. M. (1991). *Sex crimes*. Newbury Park, CA: Sage.

Holmes, R. M., & Holmes, S. T. (1998). *Serial murder* (2nd ed.). Thousand Oaks, CA: Sage.

Honkonen, T., Henriksson, M., Koivisto, A. M., Stengård, E., & Salokangas, R. K. R. (2004). Violent victimization in schizophrenia. *Social Psychiatry and Psychiatric Epidemiology, 39*, 606–612.

Hoptman, M. J., Volavka, J., Weiss, E. M., Czobor, P., Szeszko, P. R., Gerig, G., Chakos, M., Blocher, J., Citrome, L. L., Lindenmayer, J. P., Sheitman, B., Lieberman, J. A., & Bilder, R. M. (2005). Quantitative MRI measures of orbitofrontal cortex in patients with chronic schizophrenia or schizoaffective disorder. *Psychiatry Research: Neuroimaging, 140*, 133–145.

Horley, J., & Bowlby, D. (2011). Theory, research, and intervention with arsonists. *Aggression and Violent Behavior, 16*, 241–249.

Howells, J. G., & Osborn, M. L. (1984). *A reference companion to the history of abnormal psychology*. Westport, CT: Greenwood Press.

Hubbard, K. L., Zapf, P. A., & Ronan, K.A. (2003). Competency restoration: An examination of the differences between defendants predicted restorable and not restorable to competency. *Law and Human Behavior, 27*, 127–139.

Huchzermeier, C., Geiger, F., Bruß, E., Godt, N., Köhler, D., Hinrichs, G., & Aldenhoff, J. B. (2007). The relationship between DSM-IV cluster B personality disorders and psychopathy according to Hare's criteria: Clarification and resolution of previous contradictions. *Behavioral Sciences & the Law, 25*(6), 901–911.

Hucker, S., Langevin, R., Dickey, R., Handy, L., Chambers, J., Wright, S., Bain, J., & Wortzman, G. (1988). Cerebral damage and dysfunction in sexually aggressive men. *Annals of Sex Research, 1*, 33–47.

Huebner, T., Vloet, T. D., Marx, I., Konrad, K., Fink, G. R., Herpertz, S. C., & Herpertz-Dahlmann, B. (2008). Morphometric brain abnormalities in boys with conduct disorder. *Journal of the American Academy of Child and Adolescent Psychiatry, 47*(5), 540–547.

Hugdahl, K. (1995). *Psychophysiology: The mind-body perspective*. Cambridge, MA: Harvard University Press.

Hughes, D. T. (1992). *Lullaby and goodnight*. New York: Pocket Books.

Human Rights Watch. (2009). Mental illness, human rights, and US prisons: Human Rights Watch statement for the record to the Senate Judiciary Committee Subcommittee on Human Rights and the Law, September 22, 2009. New York, NY: Author. Retrieved from http://www.hrw.org/news/2009/09/22/mental-illness-human-rights-and-us-prisons

Humphrey v. Cady, 405 U.S. 504 (1972).

Humphreys, M. S., Johnstone, E. C., MacMillan, J. F., & Taylor, P. J. (1992). Dangerous behaviour preceding first admissions for schizophrenia. *British Journal of Psychiatry, 161*, 501–505.

Husted, J. R., & Nehemkis, A. (1995). Civil commitment viewed from three perspectives: Professional, family, and police. *Bulletin of the American Academy of Psychiatry & the Law, 23*(4), 533–546.

Hylton, J. H. (1995). Care or control: Health or criminal justice options for the long-term seriously mentally ill in a Canadian province. *International Journal of Law and Psychiatry, 18*, 45–59.

In re Crane, 7 P.3d 285 (Kan. 2000), *vacated*, 534 U.S. 407 (2002).

In re Oakes, 8 Law Rep. 122 (Mass. 1845).

Incham, D., Grimsrud, A., Corrigall, J., Williams, D., Seedat, S., Stein, D. J., & Myer, L. (2009). Intermittent explosive disorder in South Africa: Prevalence, correlates, and the role of traumatic exposures. *Psychopathology, 42*(2), 92–98.

Inciardi, J. A., & Pottieger, A. E. (1998). Drug use and street crime in Miami: An (almost) 20-year retrospective. *Substance Use & Misuse, 33*(9), 1839–1870.

Inciardi, J. A., & Surratt, H. L. (2001). Drug use, street crime, and sex-trading among cocaine-dependent women: Implications for public health and criminal justice policy. *Journal of Psychoactive Drugs, 33(4)*, 379–389.

Indira, R. (1987). The psychoanalytic theory as a basis for understanding criminal behavior. *Indian Journal of Behaviour, 11*(1), 29–32.

Ingle, M. P. (2002). Law on the rocks: The intoxication defenses are being eighty-sixed. *Vanderbilt Law Review, 55*, 607–645.

Inman, L. N. (1989). Mental impairment and *mens rea*: North Carolina recognizes the diminished capacity defense in *State v. Shank* and *State v. Rose*. *North Carolina Law Review, 67*, 1293–1315.

Insanity Defense Reform Act of 1984. Pub. L. No. 91–190, 98 Stat. 1837 (1984), *codified as amended at* 18 U.S.C. § 17 (2012).

Ishikawa, S. S., & Raine, A. (2003). The neuropsychiatry of aggression. In Schiffer, R. B., Rao, S. M., & Fogel, B. S. (Eds.), *Neuropsychiatry* (2nd ed., pp. 660–678). Philadelphia: Lippincott Williams & Wilkins.

Ishikawa, S. S., Raine, A., Lencz, T., Bihrle, S., & Lacasse, L. (2001). Autonomic stress reactivity and executive functions in successful and unsuccessful criminal psychopaths from the community. *Journal of Abnormal Psychology, 110*(3), 423–432.

Isir, A. B., Dai, A. I., Nacak, M., & Gorucu, S. (2010). Study: The lack of significant association of the catechol-*O*-methyl transferase (COMT) gene polymorphism in violent offenders with mental retardation. *Journal of Forensic Sciences, 55*(1), 225–228.

Jackson v. Indiana, 406 U.S. 715 (1972).

Jakupcak, M., Conybeare, D., Phelps, L., Hunt, S., Holmes, H. A., Felker, B., Klevens, M., et al. (2007). Anger, hostility, and aggression among Iraq and Afghanistan War veterans reporting PTSD and subthreshold PTSD. *Journal of Traumatic Stress, 20*(6), 945–954.

James, D. J., & Glaze, L. E. (2006). *Mental health problems of prison and jail inmates*. Washington, DC: U.S. Department of Justice, Bureau of Justice Statistics.

Janofsky, J. S., & Taburell, A. C. (2006). Diversion to the mental health system: Emergency psychiatric evaluations. *Journal of the American Academy of Psychiatry and Law, 34*(3), 283–291.

Janofsky, J. S., Vandewalle, M. B., & Rappeport, J. R. (1989). Defendants pleading insanity: An analysis of outcome. *Bulletin of the American Academy of Psychiatry and Law, 17*, 203–211.

Janowsky, D. S., El-Yousef, M. K., & Davis, J. M. (1974). Interpersonal maneuvers of manic patients. *American Journal of Psychiatry, 131*(3), 250–255.

Janus, E. S., & Meehl, P. E. (1997). Assessing the legal standard for predictions of dangerousness in sex offender commitment proceedings. *Psychology, Public Policy, and Law, 3*, 33–64.

Jeffrey, R. W., Pasewark, R. A., & Bieber, S. (1988). Insanity plea: Predicting not guilty by reason of insanity adjudications. *Bulletin of the American Academy of Psychiatry and the Law, 16*, 35–39.

Johns, J. H., & Quay, H. C. (1962). The effect of social reward on verbal conditioning in psychopathic and neurotic military offenders. *Journal of Consulting Psychology, 26*(3), 217–220.

Johnson, D. M., Zlotnick, C., & Perez, S. (2008). The relative contribution of abuse severity and PTSD severity on the psychiatric and social morbidity of battered women in shelters. *Behavior Therapy, 39*(3), 232–241.

Johnson, E. A. (2005). Criminal liability for loss of a chance. *Iowa Law Review, 91*, 59–130.

Johnson, W. W. (2011). Rethinking the interface between mental illness, criminal justice and academia. *Justice Quarterly, 28(1)*, 15–22.

Jones v. United States, 463 U.S. 354 (1983).

Jones, G., Huckle, P., & Tanaghow, A. (1992). Command hallucinations, schizophrenia and sexual assaults. *Irish Journal of Psychological Medicine, 9*, 47–49.

Jones, M. J., Van den Bree, M., Ferriter, M., & Taylor, P. J. (2010). Childhood risk factors for offending before first psychiatric admission for people with schizophrenia: A case-control study of high security hospital admissions. *Behavioral Sciences and the Law, 28*, 351–365.

Joyal, C. C., Black, D. N., & Dassylva, B. (2007). The neuropsychology and neurology of sexual deviance: A review and pilot study. *Sexual Abuse: A Journal of Research and Treatment, 19*, 155–173.

Joyal, C. C., Côté, G., Meloche, J., & Hodgins, S. (2011). Severe mental illness and aggressive behavior: On the importance of considering subgroups. *The International Journal of Forensic Mental Health, 10*(2), 107–117.

Joyal, C. C., Putkonen, A., Mancini-Marïe, A., Hodgins, S., Kononen, M., Boulay, L., Pihlajamaki, M., Soininen, H., Stip, E., Tiihonen, J., & Aronen, H. J. (2007). Violent persons with schizophrenia and comorbid disorders: A functional magnetic resonance imaging study. *Schizophrenia Research, 91*, 97–102.

Joyal, C. C., Putkonen, A., Paavola, P., & Tiihonen, J. (2004). Characteristics and circumstances of homicidal acts committed by offenders with schizophrenia. *Psychological Medicine, 34*, 433–442.

Juhász, C., Behen, M. E., Muzik, O., Chugani, D. C., & Chugani, H. T. (2001). Bilateral medial prefrontal and temporal neocortical hypometabolism in children with epilepsy and aggression. *Epilepsia, 42*, 991–1001.

Junginger, J. (1990). Predicting compliance with command hallucinations. *American Journal of Psychiatry, 147*(2), 245–247.

Junginger, J. (1995). Command hallucinations and the prediction of dangerousness. *Psychiatric Services, 46*(9), 911–914.

Junginger, J. (2006). "Stereotypic" delusional offending. *Behavioral Sciences and the Law, 24*, 295–311.

Junginger, J., Claypoole, K., Laygo, R., & Crisanti, A. (2006). Effects of serious mental illness and substance abuse on criminal offense. *Psychiatric Services, 57*, 879–882.

Juodis, M., Woodworth, M., Porter, S., & Ten Brinke, L. (2009). Partners in crime: A comparison of individual and multiperpetrator homicides. *Criminal Justice and Behavior, 36*(8), 824–839.

Jurek v. Texas, 428 U.S. 262 (1976).

Kachaeva, M., Dmitrieva, T., Satianova, L., & Rusina, V. (2010). Battered women who kill their children: The cycle of violence. *European Psychiatry, 25* (Supp. 1), 685–685.

Kafka, M. P., & Hennen, J. (2002). A DSM-IV Axis I comorbidity study of males (n = 120) with paraphilias and paraphilia-related disorders. *Sex Abuse, 14*, 349–366.

Kafka, M. P., & Prentky, R. (1998). Attention-deficit/hyperactivity disorder in males with paraphilias and paraphilia-related disorders: A comorbidity study. *Journal of Clinical Psychiatry, 59*(7), 388–396.

Kahn, M. W. (1971). Murderers who plead insanity: A descriptive factor-analytic study of personality, social, and history variables. *Genetic Psychology Monographs, 84*, 275–360.

Kaminski, R. J., Koons-Witt, Barbara A., Thompson, Stewart N., & Weiss, D. (2010). The impacts of the Virginia Tech and Northern Illinois University shootings on fear of crime on campus. *Journal of Criminal Justice, 38*, 88–98.

Kansas v. Crane, 534 U.S. 407 (2002).

Kansas v. Hendricks, 521 U.S. 346 (1997).

Kaplan, J., Papajohn, G., & Zorn, E. (1990). *The murder of innocence: The tragic life and final rampage of Laurie Dann*. New York: Warner Books.

Karpman, B. (1926). Psychoses in criminals: Clinical studies in the psychopathology of crime. *Journal of Nervous and Mental Disease, 64*, 331–351.

Karpman, B. (1951). A psychoanalytic study of a case of murder. *Psychoanalytic Review, 38*(2), 139–157, 245–270.

Kelling, G. L., & Coles, C. M. (1996). *Fixing broken windows: Restoring order and reducing crime in our communities*. New York, NY: Touchstone.

Kemeny, M. E., & Shestyuk, A. (2005). Emotions, the neuroendocrine and immune systems, and health. In M. Lewis, J. M. Haviland-Jones, & L. F. Barrett (Eds.), *Handbook of emotions* (3rd ed., pp. 661–675). New York: The Guilford Press.

Kemp, D. E., Hirschfeld, R. M. A., Ganocy, S. J., Elhaj, O., Slembarski, R., Bilali, S., Conroy, C., Pontau, J., Findling, R. L., & Calabrese, J. R. (2008). Screening for bipolar disorder in a county jail at the time of criminal arrest. *Journal of Psychiatric Research, 42*, 778–786.

Kemshall, H. (1996). *A review of research on the assessment and management of risk and dangerousness: Implications for policy and practice in the probation service*. Birmingham, UK: Home Office Research and Statistics Directorate.

Kendell, R., & Jablensky, A. (2003). Distinguishing between the validity and utility of psychiatric diagnoses. *American Journal of Psychiatry, 160*(1), 4–12.

Kennedy, H. G., & Grubin, D. H. (1990). Hot-headed or impulsive? *British Journal of Addiction, 85*, 639–643.

Kerber, L. (2001a). *Substance use among male inmates, Texas Department of Criminal Justice—State Jail Division: 1998*. Austin: Texas Commission on Alcohol and Drug Abuse.

Kerber, L. (2001b). *Substance use among female inmates, Texas Department of Criminal Justice—State Jail Division: 1998*. Austin: Texas Commission on Alcohol and Drug Abuse.

Kerber, L., & Harris, R. (2001). *Substance use among female inmates, Texas Department of Criminal Justice—Institutional Division: 1998*. Austin: Texas Commission on Alcohol and Drug Abuse.

Kerber, L., Maxwell, J. C., & Wallisch, L. S. (2001). *Substance use among offenders entering the Texas Department of Criminal Justice, Substance Abuse Felony Punishment Facilities: 1998–2000*. Austin: Texas Commission on Alcohol and Drug Abuse.

Kernberg, O. F., Selzer, M. A., Koenigsberg, H. W., & Applebaum, A. (1989). *Psychodynamic psychotherapy of borderline patients*. New York: Basic Books.

Kerridge, B. (2009). Sociological, social psychological, and psychopathological correlates of substance use disorders in the U.S. jail population. *International Journal of Offender Therapy and Comparative Criminology, 53*(2), 168–190.

Kesten, K. L., Leavitt-Smith, E., Rau, D. R., Shelton, D., Zhang, W., Wagner, J., & Trestman, R. L. (2012). Recidivism rates among mentally ill inmates: Impact of the Connecticut Offender Reentry Program. *Journal of Correctional Health Care, 18*(1), 20–28.

Khalsa, M. K. K., Salvatore, P., Hennen, J., Baethge, C., Tohen, M., & Baldessarini, R. J. (2008). Suicidal events and accidents in 216 first-episode bipolar I disorder patients: Predictive factors. *Journal of Affective Disorders, 106*, 179–184.

Khantzian, E. J. (1997). The self-medication hypothesis of substance use disorders: A reconsideration and recent applications. *Harvard Review of Psychiatry, 4*, 231–244.

Kieffer, C. C. (2003). How group analysis cures: An exploration of narcissistic rage in group treatment. *Psychoanalytic Inquiry, 23(5)*, 734–749.

King, J. D. (2008). Candor, zeal, and the substitution of judgment: Ethics and the mentally ill criminal defendant. *American University Law Review, 58*, 207–266.

Kingston, D., Firestone, P., Seto, M., & Bradford, J. (2010). Comparing indicators of sexual sadism as predictors of recidivism among adult male sexual offenders. *Journal of Consulting and Clinical Psychology, 78*(4), 574–584.

Kirschner, D. (1992). Understanding adoptees who kill: Dissociation, patricide, and the psychodynamics of adoption. *International Journal of Offender Therapy and Comparative Criminology, 36*(4), 323–333.

Kirschner, S. M., & Galperin, G. J. (2001). Psychiatric defenses in New York County: Pleas and results. *The Journal of the American Academy of Psychiatry and the Law, 29*(2), 194–201.

Klaf, F. S., & Davis, C. A. (1960). Homosexuality and paranoid schizophrenia: A survey of 150 cases and controls. *American Journal of Psychiatry, 116*, 1070–1075.

Klein, D. W. (2012). When coercion lacks care: Competency to make medical treatment decisions and *parens patriae* civil commitments. *University of Michigan Journal of Law Reform, 45*, 561–593.

Klein, M. (1975). Mourning and its relation to manic-depressive states. In M. Klein and R. E. Money-Kyrle (Eds.), *The writings of Melanie Kein: Vol. 1. Love, guilt, and reparation and other works, 1921–1945* (pp. 334–369). New York: Free Press. (Original work published in 1940)

Kleinplatz, P. J., & Moser, C. (2005). Politics versus science: An addendum and response to Drs. Spitzer and Fink. *Journal of Psychology and Human Sexuality, 17*(3/4), 135–139.

Klostermann, K., Kelley, M. L., Mignone, T., Pusateri, L., & Fals-Stewart, W. (2010). Partner violence and substance abuse: Treatment interventions. *Aggression and Violent Behavior, 15*, 162–166.

Knoll, J. L., & Resnick, P. J. (2008). Insanity defense evaluations: Toward a model for evidence-based practice. *Brief Treatment and Crisis Intervention, 8*(1), 92–110.

Kobau, R., Zahran, H., Grant, D., Thurman, D. J., Price, P. H., & Zack, M. M. (2007). Prevalence of active epilepsy and health-related quality of life among adults with self-reported epilepsy in California: California Health Interview Survey, 2003. *Epilepsia, 48*(10), 1904–1913.

Kocsis, R. N. (2004). Psychological profiling in serial arson offenses: An assessment of skills and accuracy. *Criminal Justice and Behavior, 31*, 341–361.

Kocsis, R. N. (2006). Criminal profiling of serial arson offenders. In R. Kocsis (Ed.), *Criminal profiling: International theory, research and practice* (pp. 153–174).Totowa, NJ: Humana Press.

Kohn, Y., Fahum, T., Ratzoni, G., & Apter, A. (1998). Agression and sexual offense in Asperger's syndrome. *The Israeli Journal of Psychiatry and Sciences, 34*(4), 293–299.

Kohut, H. (1972). Thoughts on narcissism and narcissistic rage. *The Psychoanalytic Study of the Child, 27*, 360–400.

Kohut, H., & Wolf, E. S. (1978). The disorders of the self and their treatment: An outline. *International Journal of Psycho-Analysis, 59*, 413.

Kondo, N. (2008). Mental illness in film. *Psychiatric Rehabilitation Journal, 31*(3), 250–252.

Kotler, M., Barak, P., Cohen, H., Averbuch, I. E., Grinshpoon, A., Gritsenko, I., Nemanov, L., & Ebstein, R. P. (1999). Homicidal behavior in schizophrenia associated with a genetic polymorphism determining low *catechol O-methyltransferase (COMT)* activity. *American Journal of Medical Genetics, 88*, 628–633.

Kovacs, M., & Pollock, M. (1995). Bipolar disorder and comorbid conduct disorder in childhood and adolescence. *Journal of the American Academy of Child and Adolescent Psychiatry, 34*, 714–723.

Kraanen, F. L., Scholing, A., & Emmelkamp, P. M. G. (2010). Substance use disorders in perpetrators of intimate partner violence in a forensic setting. *International Journal of Offender Therapy and Comparative Criminology, 54*(3), 430–440.

Kraepelin, E. (2002). *Dementia praecox and paraphrenia* (G. M. Robertson, Ed., and R. M. Barclay, Trans.). Bristol, UK: Thoemmes Press. (Original work published 1919)

Krafft-Ebing, R. V. (1965). *Psychopathia sexualis: A medico-forensic study* (F. S. Klaf, Trans.). New York: Arcade Publishing. (Original work published 1886)

Krakowski, M. (2005). Schizophrenia with aggressive and violent behaviors. *Psychiatric Annals, 35*(1), 45–49.

Kramer, U., & Zimmerman, G. (2009). Fear and anxiety at the basis of adolescent externalizing and internalizing behaviors. *International Journal of Offender Therapy and Comparative Criminology, 53*(1), 113–120.

Kretschmer, E. (1925). *Physique and character: An investigation of the nature of constitution and of the theory of temperament* (W. J. H. Sprott, Trans.). New York: Harcourt, Brace & Company, Inc.

Kretschmer, E. (1945). *Physique and character: An investigation of the nature of constitution and the theory of temperament* (2nd ed. Rev.). London: Kegan Paul, Trench, Trubner & Co., Ltd.

Kring, A. M., Davison, G. C., Neale, J. M., & Johnson, S. J. (2007). *Abnormal psychology* (10th ed.). Hoboken, NJ: John Wiley & Sons, Inc.

Kring, A. M., Johnson, S., Davison, G. C., & Neale, J. M. (2012). *Abnormal psychology* (12th ed.) Hoboken, NJ: Wiley.

Kropp, P. R., Hart, S. D., Webster, C. D., & Eaves, D. (1995). *Manual for the Spousal Assault Risk Assessment Guide* (2nd ed.). Vancouver, BC: British Columbia Institute of Family Violence.

Kruesi, M. J. P., Casanova, M. F., Mannheim, G., & Jonson-Bilder, A. (2004). Reduced temporal lobe volume in early onset conduct disorder. *Psychiatry Research: Neuroimaging, 132*, 1–11.

Kulynych, J. (1997). Psychiatric neuroimaging evidence: A high-tech crystal ball? *Stanford Law Review, 49*, 1249–1270.

Kumar, S., & Simpson, A. I. F. (2005). Application of risk assessment for violence methods to general adult psychiatry: A selective literature review. *Australian and New Zealand Journal of Psychiatry, 39*, 328–335.

Kumari, V., Aasen, I., Taylor, P., Ffytche, D. H., Das, M., Barkataki, I., Goswami, S., O'Connell, P., Howlett, M., Williams, S. C. R., & Sharma, T. (2006). Neural dysfunction and violence in schizophrenia: An fMRI investigation. *Schizophrenia Research, 84*, 144–164.

Kunkle Jr., W. J. (1997). Counter-point: *Gacy v. Dahmer*: An informed response. *John Marshall Law Review, 30*, 331–336.

Laajasalo, T., & Häkkänen, H. (2004). Background characteristics of mentally ill homicide offenders—a comparison of five diagnostic groups. *Journal of Forensic Psychiatry and Psychology, 15*(3), 451–474.

Laajasalo, T., & Häkkänen, H. (2006). Excessive violence and psychotic symptomatology among homicide offenders with schizophrenia. *Criminal Behaviour and Mental Health, 16*, 242–253.

Laajasalo, T., Salenius, S., Lindberg, N., Repo-Tiihonen, E., & Häkkänen-Nyholm, H. (2011). Psychopathic traits in Finnish homicide offenders with schizophrenia. *International Journal of Law and Psychiatry, 34*, 324–330.

Lachman, H. M., Nolan, K. A., Mohr, P., Saito, T., & Volavka, J. (1998). Association between *catechol O-methyltransferase* genotype and violence in schizophrenia and schizoaffective disorder. *American Journal of Psychiatry, 155*, 835–837

Lachman, M., Brzek, A., Mellan, J., Hampl, R., Starka, L., & Motlik, K. (1991). Recidivous offense in sadistic homosexual pedophile with karyotype 48, XXXY after testicular pulpectomy. *Experimental and Clinical Endocrinology, 98*(2), 171–174.

LaFave, W. R. (2011). *Substantive criminal law* (West's Criminal Practice Series 2nd ed.). St. Paul, MN: Thomson/West.

Lafrance, M. N., & Mckenzie-Mohr, S. (2013). The DSM and its lure of legitimacy. *Feminism & Psychology, 23*(1), 119–140.

Lamb, H. R., & Lamb, D. (1990). Factors contributing to homelessness among the chronically and severely mentally ill. *Hospital and Community Psychiatry, 41*, p. 301–305.

Lamberg, L. (1988). Mental illness and violent acts: Protecting the patient and the public. *JAMA: The Journal of the American Medical Association, 280*, 407–408.

Lamontagne, Y., Boyer, R., Hétu, C., & Lacerte-Lamontagen, C. (2000). Anxiety, significant losses, depression, and irrational beliefs in first-offence shoplifters. *Canadian Journal of Psychiatry, 45*, 63–66.

Lamparello, A. (2011). Using cognitive neuroscience to predict future dangerousness. *Columbia Human Rights Law Review, 42*, 481–539.

Lamparello, A. (2011–2012). Neuroscience, brain damage, and the criminal defendant: Who does it help and where in the criminal proceeding is it most relevant? *Rutgers Law Record, 39*, 161–180.

Lande, G. (2003). Whole blood serotonin levels among pretrial murder defendants. *The Journal of Psychiatry and Law, 31*(3), 287–303.

Lane, C. (2007). Shyness: How normal behavior became a sickness. New Haven, CT: Yale University Press.

Langevin, R. (2003). A study of the psychosexual characteristics of sex killers: Can we identify them before it is too late? *International Journal of Offender Therapy and Comparative Criminology, 47*(4), 366–382.

Langevin, R., & Curnoe, S. (2010). A comparison of psychopathy, attention deficit hyperactivity disorder, and brain dysfunction among sex offenders. *Journal of Forensic Psychology Practice, 10*, 177–200.

Langevin, R., Curnoe, S., Fedoroff, P., Bennett, R., Langevin, M., Peever, C., Pettica, R., & Sandhu, S. (2004). Lifetime sex offender recidivism: A 25-year follow-up study. *Canadian Journal of Criminology and Criminal Justice/La Revue canadienne de criminologie et de justice pénale, 46*(5), 531–552.

Langevin, R., Paitich, D., Orchard, B., Handy, L., & Russon, A. (1982). Diagnosis of killers seen for psychiatric assessment. *Acta Psychiatrica Scandinavica, 66*, 216–228.

Långström, N., & Lindblad, F. (2000). Young sex offenders: Background, personality, and crime characteristics in a Swedish forensic psychiatric sample. *Nordic Journal of Psychiatry, 54*(2), 113–120.

Large, M., & Nielssen, O. (2007). Treating the first episode of schizophrenia earlier will save lives. *Schizophrenia Research, 92,* 276–277.

Laurell, J., & Dåderman, A. M. (2005). Recidivism is related to psychopathy (PCL-R) in a group of men convicted of homicide. *International Journal of Law and Psychiatry, 28,* 255–268.

Lave, T. R. (2011). Throwing away the key: Has the Adam Walsh Act lowered the threshold for sexually violent predator commitments too far? *University of Pennsylvania Journal of Constitutional Law, 14,* 391–428.

Leckman, J. F., Goodman, W. K., Riddle, M. A., Hardin, M. T., & Anderson, M. T. (1990). Low CSF 5HIAA and obsessions of violence: Report of two cases. *Psychiatry Research, 33,* 95–99.

Lehrman, P. R. (1939). Some unconscious determinants in homicide. *Psychiatric Quarterly, 13*(4), 605–621.

Lejoyeux, M., Kerner, L., Thauvin, I., & Loi, S. (2006). Study of impulse control disorders among women presenting nicotine dependence. *International Journal of Psychiatry in Clinical Practice, 10*(4), 241–246.

Lemert, E. M. (1951). *Social pathology.* New York, NY: McGraw-Hill.

Lennings, C. J. (2002). Children who kill family members: Three case studies from Australia. *Journal of Threat Assessment, 2*(2), 57–72.

Leonard, K., Quigley, B., & Collins, R. (2003). Drinking, personality, and bar environmental characteristics as predictors of involvement in barroom aggression. *Addictive Behaviors, 28,* 1681–1700.

Lesieur, H. R. (1993). Female pathological gamblers and crime. In W. Eadington & J. Cornelius (Eds.), *Gambling behavior and problem gambling* (pp. 495–515). Reno: Institute for the Study of Gambling and Commercial Gaming, University of Nevada.

Lesieur, H. R., & Blume, S. B. (1987). The South Oaks Gambling Screen (SOGS): A new instrument for the identification of pathological gambling. *American Journal of Psychiatry, 144,* 1184–1188.

Lessard v. Schmidt, 349 F. Supp. 1078 (E.D. Wis. 1972), *vacated,* 414 U.S. 473 (1974), *on reh'g,* 379 F. Supp. 1376 (E.D. Wis. 1974), *vacated,* 421 U.S. 957 (1975), *reinstated,* 413 F. Supp. 1318 (E.D. Wis. 1976).

Leue, A., Borchard, B., & Hoyer, J. (2004). Mental disorders in a forensic sample of sexual offenders. *European Psychiatry, 19,* 123–130.

Leukefeld, C., Gallego, M., & Farabee, D. (1997). Drugs, crime, and HIV. *Substance Use and Misuse, 32*(6), 749–756.

Levenson, J., & Morin, J. (2006). Factors predicting selection of sexually violent predators for civil commitment. *International Journal of Offender Therapy and Comparative Criminology, 50(6),* 609–629.

Levy, K. N., Reynoso, J. S., Wasserman, R. H., & Clarkin, J. F. (2007). Narcissistic personality disorder. In W. O'Donohue, K. A. Fowler, & S. O. Lilienfeld (Eds.), *Personality disorders: Toward the DSM-V* (pp. 233–277). Los Angeles: Sage.

Levy, R. M., Rubenstein, L. S., Ennis, B. J., & Friedman, P. R. (1996). *The rights of people with mental disabilities: The authoritative ACLU guide to the rights of people with mental illness and mental retardation.* Carbondale, IL: Southern Illinois University Press.

Lewinsohn, P. M. (1974). A behavioral approach to depression. In R. M. Friedman & M. M. Katz (Eds.), *The psychology of depression: Contemporary theory and research* (pp. 157–185). New York: Wiley.

Lewis, C. F. (2011). Substance use and violent behavior in women with antisocial personality disorder. *Behavioral Sciences and the Law, 29,* 667–676.

Lewis, C. F., Baranowski, M. V., Buchanan, J. A., & Benedek, E. P. (1998). Factors associated with weapon use in maternal filicide. *Journal of Forensic Science, 43,* 613–618.

Lewis, D. O., Pincus, J. H., Bard, B., Richardson, E., Prichep, L. S., Feldman, M., & Yeager, C. (1988). Neuropsychiatric, psychoeducational, and family characteristics of 14 juveniles condemned to death in the United States. *American Journal of Psychiatry, 145*(5), 584–589.

Lewis, D. O., Shankok, S. S., & Pincus, J. H. (1979). Juvenile male sexual assaulters. *American Journal of Psychiatry, 136*(9), 1194–1196.

Lewis, D. O., Yeager, C. A., Blake, P., Bard, B., & Strenziok, M. (2004). Ethics questions raised by neuropsychiatric, neuropsychological, educational, developmental, and family characteristics of 18 juveniles awaiting execution in Texas. *Journal of the American Academy of Psychiatry and the Law, 32,* 408–429.

Lewis, D. O., Yeager, C. A., Swica, Y., Pincus, J. H., & Lewis, M. (1997). Objective documentation of child abuse and dissociation in 12 murderers with dissociative identity disorder. *American Journal of Psychiatry, 154*(12), 1703–1710.

Lewis, N. O. C., & Yarnell, H. (1951). *Pathological firesetting (pyromania).* Nervous and Mental Disease Monographs no. 82. New York: Coolidge Foundation.

Lezak, M. D., Howieson, D. B., Loring, D. W., Hannay, H. J., & Fischer, J. S. (2004). *Neuropsychological assessment* (4th ed.). Oxford: Oxford University Press.

Liddle, P. F. (1987). The symptoms of chronic schizophrenia. A re-examination of the positive-negative dichotomy. *The British Journal of Psychiatry, 151*(2), 145–151.

Liebert, J. A. (1985). Contributions of psychiatric consultation in the investigation of serial murder. *International Journal of Offender Therapy and Comparative Criminology, 29,* 187–200.

Liettu, A., Säävälä, H., Hakko, H., Räsänen, P., & Joukamea, M. (2009). Mental disorders of male parricidal offenders: A study of offenders in forensic psychiatric examination in Finland during 1973–2004. *Social Psychiatry and Psychiatric Epidemiology, 44,* 96–103.

Lijffijt, M., Moeller, F. G., Boutros, N. N., Burroughs, S., Steinberg, J. L., Lane, S. D., & Swann, A. C. (2009). A pilot study revealing impaired P50 gating in antisocial personality disorder. *Journal of Neuropsychiatry and Clinical Neurosciences, 21*(3), 328–331.

Lindberg, N., Holi, M. M., Tani, P., & Virkkunen, M. (2005). Looking for pyromania: Characteristics of a consecutive sample of Finnish male criminals with histories of recidivist fire-setting between 1973 and 1993. *BMC Psychiatry, 5*(1), 47.

Lindberg, N., Tani, P., Virkkunen, M., Porkka-Heiskanen, T., Appelberg, B., Naukkarinen, H., & Salmi, T. (2005). Quantitative electroencephalographic measures in homicidal men with antisocial personality disorder. *Psychiatry Research, 136,* 7–15.

Lindgren, M., Jensen, J., Dalteg, A., Meurling, A. W., Ingvar, D. H., & Levander, S. (2002). Dyslexia and AD/HD among Swedish prison inmates. *Journal of Scandinavian Studies in Criminology and Crime Prevention, 3,* 84–95.

Lindqvist, P., & Allebeck, P. (1990). Schizophrenia and crime: A longitudinal follow-up of 644 schizophrenics in Stockholm. *British Journal of Psychiatry, 157,* 345–350.

Lindsay, W. R., Taylor, J. L., Hogue, T. E., Mooney, P., Steptoe, L., & Morrissey, C. (2010). Relationship between assessed emotion, personality, personality disorder and risk in offenders with intellectual disability. *Psychiatry, Psychology and Law, 17*(3), 385–397.

Link, B. G., Andrews, H., & Cullen, F. T. (1992). The violent and illegal behavior of mental patients reconsidered. *American Sociological Review, 57,* 275–292.

Link, B. G., Monahan, J., Steuve, A., & Cullen, F. T. (1999). Real in their consequences: A sociological approach to understanding the association between psychotic symptoms and violence. *American Sociological Review, 64,* 316–332.

Link, B. G., Stueve, A., & Phelan, J. (1998). Psychotic symptoms and violent behaviors: Probing the components of "threat/control-override" symptoms. *Social Psychiatry and Psychiatric Epidemiology, 33*, S55–S60.

Linn, L. (1961). *Frontiers in general hospital psychiatry*. New York: International University Press.

Lipson, C. T. (1986). A case report of matricide. *American Journal of Psychiatry, 143*(1), 112–113.

Lipton, D., & Johnson, B. (1998). Smack, crack, and score: Two decades of NIDA-funded drugs and crime research at NDRI 1974–1994. *Substance Use & Misuse, 33*(9), 1779–1815.

Litschge, C. M., & Vaughn, M. G. (2009). The Mentally Ill Offender Treatment and Crime Reduction Act of 2004: Problems and prospects. *The Journal of Forensic Psychiatry & Psychology, 20*(4), 542–558.

Littlejohns, C. S., Clarke, D. J., & Corbett, J. A. (1990). Tourette-like disorder in Asperger's syndrome. *British Journal of Psychiatry, 156*, 430–433.

Lockhart v. McCree, 476 U.S. 162 (1986).

Logan, T., & Leukefeld, C. (2000). Violence and HIV risk behavior among male and female crack users. *Journal of Drug Issues, 30*(2), 261–282.

Lombroso, C. (2006). *Criminal man* (M. Gibson & N. H. Rafter, Trans.). London: Duke University Press. (Original work published 1876)

Lombroso-Ferrero, G. (1972). *Criminal man: According to the classification of Cesare Lombroso*. Montclair, NJ: Patterson Smith. (Original work published 1911)

Lopez-Ibor, J. (1990). Impulse control in obsessive-compulsive disorder: A biopsychopathological approach. *Progress in Neuro-Psychopharmacology and Biological Psychiatry, 14*, 709–718.

Lovell, D., Gagliardi, G. J., & Peterson, P. D. (2002). Recidivism and use of services among persons with mental illness after release from prison. *Psychiatric Services, 53(1)*, 1290–1296.

Low Jr., P. W., Jeffries, J. C., & Bonnie, R. J. (1986). *The trial of John W. Hinckley, Jr.: A case study in the insanity defense.* Mineola, NY: Foundation Press.

Lowenstein, L. F. (1992). The psychology of the obsessed compulsive killer: *The Criminologist, 16*, 26–38.

Loza, W., Neo, L. H., Shahinfar, A., & Loza-Fanous, A. (2005). Cross-validation of the Self-Appraisal Questionnaire: A tool for assessing violent and nonviolent recidivism with female offenders. *International Journal of Offender Therapy and Comparative Criminology, 49*(5), 547–560.

Lurigio, A. J. (2011). Examining prevailing beliefs about people with serious mental illness in the criminal justice system. *Federal Probation, 75*(1), 11–18.

Lurigio, A. J., Snowden, J., & Watson, A. (2006). Police handling of the mentally ill: Historical and research perspectives. *Law Enforcement Executive Forum, 6*, 87–110.

Lykken, D. T. (1957). A study of anxiety in the sociopathic personality. *Journal of Abnormal and Social Psychology, 9*, 6–10.

Lykken, D. T. (1995). *The antisocial personalities*. Hillsdale, New Jersey: Lawrence Erlbaum Associates, Publishers.

Lykken, D. T. (2000). The causes and costs of crime and a controversial cure. *Journal of Personality, 68*(3), 559–605.

Lyon, D. R., & Ogloff, R. P. (2000). Legal and ethical issues in psychopathy assessment. In C. B. Gacono (Ed.), *The clinical and forensic assessment of psychopathy* (pp. 139–173). Mahwah, NJ: Lawrence Erlbaum Associates, Publishers.

Lyons, J., McClelland, G., & Jordan, N. (2010). Fire setting behavior in a child welfare system: Prevalence, characteristics and co-occurring needs. *Journal of Child & Family Studies, 19*(6), 720–727.

M'Naghten, 8 Eng. Rep. 718 (H.L. 1843).

Maas, R. L., Prakash, R., Hollender, M. H., & Regan, W. M. (1984). Double parricide—matricide and patricide: A comparison with other schizophrenic murders. *Psychiatric Quarterly, 56*(4), 286–290.

MacCulloch, M. J., Snowden, P. R., Wood, P. J. W., & Mills, H. E. (1983). Sadistic fantasy, sadistic behavior, and offending. *British Journal of Psychiatry, 143*, 20–29.

Macdonald, J. M. (1986). *The murderer and his victim* (2nd ed.). Springfield, IL: Charles C. Thomas.

Mack, J. E., Scherl, D. J., & Macht, L. B. (1973). Children who kill their mothers. In E. J. Anthony & C. Koupernik (Eds.), *The child in his family: The impact of disease and death* (pp. 319–332). New York: John Wiley & Sons.

MacKay, S., Feldberg, A., Ward, A. K., & Marton, P. (2012). Research and practice in adolescent firesetting. *Criminal Justice and Behavior, 39*, 842–864.

Maden, T., Swinton, M., & Gunn, J. (1992). Gambling in young offenders. *Criminal Behaviour and Mental Health, 2*, 300–308.

Maeder, T. (1985). *Crime and madness: The origins and evolution of the insanity defense.* New York, NY: Harper and Row.

Magiorkinis, E., Sidiropoulou, K., & Diamantis, A. (2010). Hallmarks in the history of epilepsy: Epilepsy in antiquity. *Epilepsy & Behavior, 17*, 103–108.

Malloy, P., Cimino, C., & Westlake, R. (1992). Differential diagnosis of primary and secondary Capgras delusions. *Neuropsychiatry, Neuropsychology, and Behavioral Neurology, 5*(2), 83–96.

Malmquist, C. (1995). Depression and homicidal violence. *International Journal of Law and Psychiatry, 18*, 145–162.

Mann, J. (2011). Delivering justice to the mentally ill: Characteristics of mental health courts. *Southwest Journal of Criminal Justice, 8*(1), 44–58.

Mann, R. E., Hanson, R. K., & Thornton, D. (2010). Assessing risk for sexual recidivism: Some proposals on the nature of psychologically meaningful risk factors. *Sexual Abuse: A Journal of Research and Treatment, 22*(2), 191–217.

Marcus, D. K., Poythress, N. G., Edens, J. F., Lilienfeld, S. O. (2010). Adjudicative competence: Evidence that impairment in "rational understanding" is taxonic. *Psychological Assessment, 22*(3), 716–722.

Markowitz, F. E. (1998). The effects of stigma on the psychological well-being and life satisfaction of persons with mental illness. *Journal of Health and Social Behavior, 39*, 335–347.

Markowitz, F. E. (2011). Mental illness, crime, and violence: Risk, context, and social control. *Aggression and Violent Behavior, 16*(1), 36–44.

Marks, I. M. (1969). *Fears and phobias*. New York: Academic Press.

Marleau, J. D. (2002). Parricide et caractéristiques de la fratrie des agresseurs. *Canadian Journal of Criminology, 44*, 77–96.

Marleau, J. D. (2003). Methods of killing employed by psychotic parricides. *Psychological Reports, 93*(2), 519–520.

Marleau, J. D., Auclair, N., & Millaud, F. (2006). Comparison of factors associated with parricide in adults and adolescents. *Journal of Family Violence, 21*, 321–325.

Marleau, J. D., Millaud, F., & Auclair, N. (2003). A comparison of parricide and attempted parricide: A study of 39 psychotic adults. *International Journal of Law and Psychiatry, 26*, 269–279.

Maroney, T. A. (2006). Emotional competence, "rational understanding," and the criminal defendant. *American Criminal Law Review, 43*, 1375–1435.

Marshall, M., Balfour, R., & Kenner, A. (1998). *Pathological gambling: Prevalence, type of offense, comorbid psychopathology and demographic characteristics in a prison population* (Submission to the Australian Productivity Commission). Retrieved October 15, 2012, from http://www.pc.gov.au/inquiry/gambling/subs/sublist.html.

Martell, C. R., Addis, M. E., & Jacobson, N. S. (2001). *Depression in context: Strategies for guided action*. New York: Norton.

Martin, G., Bergen, H. A., Richardson, A. S., Roeger, L., & Allison, S. (2004). Correlates of firesetting in a community sample of young adolescents. *Australian and New Zealand Journal of Psychiatry, 38*(3), 148–154.

Martins de Barros, D., & de Pádua Serafim, A. (2008). Association between personality disorder and violent behavior pattern. *Forensic Science International, 179*, 19–22.

Mataró, M., Jurado, M. A., Garcia-Sanchez, C., Barraquer, L., Costa-Jussa, F. R., & Junqué, C. (2001). Long-term effects of bilateral frontal brain lesion. *Archives of Neurology, 58*, 1139–1142.

Mathieu, C., Hare, R. D., Jones, D. N., Babiak, P., & Neumann, C. S. (2013). Factor structure of the B-Scan 360: A measure of corporate psychopathy. *Psychological Assessment, 25*(1), 28–293.

Mavissakalian, M., & Barlow, D. H. (1981). Phobia: An overview. In M. Mavissakalian & D. H. Barlow (Eds.), *Phobia: Psychological and pharmacological treatment* (pp. 1–33). New York: The Guilford Press.

Mawson, D., Grounds, A., & Tantam, D. (1985). Violence and Asperger's syndrome: A case study. *British Journal of Psychiatry, 147*, 566–569.

Maxwell, J. C., & Wallisch, L. S. (1998). *Substance use and crime among probationers in three Texas counties: 1994–1995*. Austin: Texas Commission on Alcohol and Drug Abuse.

McBride, D. C., & McCoy, C. B. (2006). The drugs-crime relationship: An analytical framework. In M. S. Kelley (Ed.), *Readings on drugs and society: The criminal connection* (pp. 9–21). New York: Pearson Education, Inc.

McBurnett, K., Lahey, B. B., Rathouz, P. J., & Loeber, R. (2000). Low salivary cortisol and persistent aggression in boys referred for disruptive behavior. *Archives of General Psychiatry, 57*, 38–43.

McCabe, P. J., Christopher, P. P., Druhn, N., Roy-Bujnowski, K. M., Grudzinskas, A. J., & Fisher, W. H. (2012). Arrest types and co-occurring disorders in persons with schizophrenia or related psychoses. *Journal of Behavioral Health Services & Research, 1*, 1–13.

McCarthy, J. B. (1978). Narcissism and the self in homicidal adolescents. *American Journal of Psychoanalysis, 38*, 19–29.

McCleskey v. Kemp, 481 U.S. 279 (1987).

McClintock, K., Hall, S., & Oliver, C. (2003). Risk markers associated with challenging behaviours in people with intellectual disabilities: A meta-analytic study. *Journal of Intellectual Disability Research, 47*(6), 405–416.

McCloskey, M. S., Lee, R., Berman, M. E., Noblett, K. L., & Coccaro, E. F. (2008a). The relationship between impulsive verbal aggression and intermittent explosive disorder. *Aggressive Behavior, 34*(1), 51–60.

McCloskey, M. S., Noblett, K. L., Deffenbacher, J. L., Gollan, J. K., & Coccaro, E. F. (2008b). Cognitive-behavioral therapy for intermittent explosive disorder: A pilot randomized clinical trial. *Journal of Consulting and Clinical Psychology, 76*(5), 876–886.

McConaghy, N. (1998). Paedophilia: A review of the evidence. *Australian and New Zealand Journal of Psychiatry, 32*, 252–265.

McCord, W., & McCord, J. (1964). *The psychopath: An essay on the criminal mind*. New York: Van Nostrand Reinhold.

McCorkle, R. C. (2002). *Pathological gambling in arrestee populations*. Washington, DC: U.S. Department of Justice.

McCreary, J. R. (2013). "Mentally defective" language in the Gun Control Act. *Connecticut Law* Review, *45*, 813–864.

McCully, R. S. (1978). The laugh of Satan: A study of familial murder. *Journal of Personality Assessment, 42*(1), 81–91.

McDermott, S. (2006). A 38-year-old man with anxiety, intrusive violent thoughts. *Psychiatric Annals, 36*, 10–28.

McDonald v. City of Chicago, 130 S. Ct. 3020 (2010).

McElroy, S. L., Pope Jr., H. G., Hudson, J. I., Keck Jr., P. E., & White, K. L. (1991). Kleptomania: A report of 20 cases. *American Journal of Psychiatry, 148*, 652–657.

McElroy, S. L., Soutullo, C. A., Taylor Jr., P., Nelson, E. B., Beckman, D. A., Brusman, L. A., Ombaba, J. M., Strakowski, S. M., & Keck Jr., P. E. (1999). Psychiatric features of 36 men convicted of sexual offenses. *Journal of Clinical Psychiatry, 60*(6), 414–420.

McFall, M., Fontana, A., Raskind, M., & Rosenheck, R. (1999). Analysis of violent behavior in Vietnam combat veteran psychiatric inpatients with posttraumatic stress disorder. *Journal of Traumatic Stress, 12*(3), 501–517.

McFarlane, A., Schrader, G., Bookless, C., & Browne, D. (2006). Prevalence of victimization, posttraumatic stress disorder and violent behaviour in the seriously mentally ill. *Australian and New Zealand Journal of Psychiatry, 40*, 1010–1015.

McGuire, R. J., Carlisle, J. M., & Young, B. G. (1965). Sexual deviations as conditioned behavior: A hypothesis. *Behaviour Research and Therapy, 2*, 185–190.

McHugh, P. R. (2005) Striving for coherence: Psychiatry's efforts over classification. *JAMA: The Journal of the American Medical Association, 293*(20), 2526–2528.

McKnight, C. K., Mohr, J. W., Quinsey, R. E., & Erochko, J. (1966). Matricide and mental illness. *Canadian Psychiatric Association Journal, 11*(2), 99–106.

McNiel, D. E. (1994). Hallucinations and violence. In J. Monahan & H. J. Steadman (Eds.), *Violence and mental disorder* (pp. 183–202). Chicago: University of Chicago Press.

McNiel, D. E., & Binder, R. L. (2007). Effectiveness of a mental health court in reducing criminal recidivism and violence. *American Journal of Psychiatry, 164*(9), 1395–1403.

McNiel, D. E., Binder, R. L., & Greenfield, T. K. (1988). Predictors of violence in civilly committed acute psychiatric patients. *American Journal of Psychiatry, 145*, 965–970.

McWilliams, N. (1995). *Psychoanalytic diagnosis: Understanding personality structure in the clinical process*. New York: The Guilford Press.

Medina v. California 505 U.S. 437, 452 (1992).

Medlicott, R. W. (1955). Paranoia of the exalted type in a setting of *folie a deux*. A study of two adolescent homicides. *British Journal of Medical Psychology, 28*, 205–223.

Medlicott, R. W. (1976). Psychiatric aspects of murder and attempted murder. *New Zealand Medical Journal, 83*(555), 5–9.

Melançon, R. (1998). Note, Arizona's insane response to insanity. *Arizona Law Review, 40*, 287–317.

Melcher, R. K. (2012). There ain't no end for the "wicked": Implications of and recommendations for § 4248 of the Adam Walsh Act after *United States v. Comstock*. *Iowa Law Review, 97*, 629–664.

Meloy, J. R., & Shiva, A. (2007). A psychoanalytic view of the psychopath. In A. R. Felthous & H. Saß (Eds.), *International handbook of psychopathic disorders and the law* (Vol. 1, pp. 335–346). West Sussex, UK: John Wiley & Sons, Ltd.

Melton, G. B. (1992). The law is a good thing (psychology is, too): Human rights in psychological jurisprudence. *Law and Human Behavior, 16*, 381–398.

Melton, G. B., Petrila, J., Poythress, N. G., & Slobogin, C. (1987). *Psychological evaluations for the courts: A handbook for mental health professionals and lawyers*. New York, NY: Guildford Press.

Melton, G. B., Petrila, J., Poythress, N. G., & Slobogin, C. (2007). *Psychological evaluations for the courts: A handbook for mental health professionals and lawyers* (3rd ed.). New York, NY: The Guilford Press.

Menninger, W. W. (2007). Uncontained rage: A psychoanalytic perspective on violence. *Bulletin of the Menninger Clinic, 71*(2), 115–131.

Mental Health America. (2011). *Position statement 55: Confining sexual predators in the mental health system.* Alexandria, VA: Author. Retrieved from http://www.mentalhealthamerica.net/go/position-statements/55

Mentally Ill Offender Treatment and Crime Reduction Act (MIOTCRA) of 2004. Pub. L. 108–414, 118 Stat. 2327 (2004), amended by Pub. L. 110–416, 122 Stat. 4352 (2008), codified as amended in 42 U.S.C. § 3797aa (2008).

Mentally Ill Offender Treatment and Crime Reduction Act, 118 Stat. 2327, Pub. L. 108–414 (2004), *reauthorized by* 122 Stat. 4352, Pub. L. 110–416 (2008).

Mercado, C. C., Bornstein, B. H., & Schopp, R. F. (2006). Decision-making about volitional impairment in sexually violent predators. *Law and Human Behavior, 30,* 587–602.

Merton, R. K. (1968). *Social theory and social structure* (enlarged edition). New York, NY: The Free Press.

Messina, N., Burdon, W., Hagopian, G., & Prendergast, M. (2004). One year return to custody rates among co-disordered offenders. *Behavioral Sciences and the Law, 22,* 503–518.

Meyers, A. B. (1997). Supreme Court review: Rejecting the clear and convincing evidence standard for proof of incompetence. *Journal of Criminal Law and Criminology, 87,* 1016–1039.

Mich. Comp. Laws § 768.36(1) (1975).

Mickenberg, I. (1987). A pleasant surprise: The guilty but mentally ill verdict has both succeeded in its own right and successfully preserved the traditional role of the insanity defense. *University of Cincinnati Law Review, 55,* 943–996.

Millaud, F., Auclair, N., & Meunier, D. (1996). Parricide and mental illness: A study of 12 cases. *International Journal of Law and Psychiatry, 19*(2), 173–182.

Miller, B. L., Cummings, J. L., McIntyre, H., Ebers, G., & Grode, M. (1986). Hypersexuality or altered sexual preference following brain injury. *Journal of Neurology, Neurosurgery, and Psychiatry, 49,* 867–873.

Miller, R. D. (2003). Hospitalization of criminal defendants for evaluation of competence to stand trial or for restoration of competence: Clinical and legal issues. *Behavioral Sciences and the Law, 21*(3), 369–391.

Miller, W. (1958). Lower class culture as a generating milieu of gang delinquency. *Journal of Social Issues, 14*(3), 5–20.

Millon, T., & Davis, R. D. (1996). *Disorders of personality: DSM-IV and beyond* (2nd ed.). New York: John Wiley & Sons, Inc.

Millon, T., & Davis, R. D. (1998) Ten subtypes of psychopathy. In T. Millon, E. Simonsen, M. Birket-Smith, & R. D. Davis (Eds.), *Psychopathy: Antisocial, criminal, and violent behavior* (pp. 161–170). New York: The Guilford Press.

Millon, T., Simonsen, E., & Birket-Smith, M. (1998). Historical conceptions of psychopathy in the United States and Europe. In T. Millon, E. Simonsen, M. Birket-Smith, & R. D. Davis (Eds.), *Psychopathy: Antisocial, criminal, and violent behavior* (pp. 3–31). New York: The Guilford Press.

Milton, J., Duggan, C., Latham, A., Egan, V., & Tantam, D. (2002). Case history of co-morbid Asperger's syndrome and paraphilic behavior. *Medicine, Science and the Law, 42*(3), 237–244.

Minshew, N. J. (1996). Brief report: Brain mechanisms in autism: Functional and structural abnormalities. *Journal of Autism and Developmental Disorders, 26*(2), 205–209.

Miraglia, R., & Hall, D. (2011). The effect of length of hospitalization on re-arrest among insanity plea acquittees. *The Journal of the American Academy of Psychiatry and the Law, 39*(4), 524–534.

Mitchell, J., Brown, E., & Rush, A. (2007). Comorbid disorders in patients with bipolar disorder and concomitant substance dependence. *Journal of Affective Disorders, 102,* 281–287.

Mitchell, S. A., & Black, M. J. (1995). *Freud and beyond: A history of modern psychoanalytic thought.* New York: Basic Books.

Mitelman, S. A., Brickman, A. M., Shihabuddin, L., Newmark, R., Chu, K. W., & Buchsbaum,, M. (2004). Correlations between MRI-assessed volumes of the thalamus and cortical Brodman's areas in schizophrenia. *Schizophrenia Research, 75,* 265–281.

Mnukhin, S. S., & Isaev, D. N. (1975). On the organic nature of some forms of schizoid or autistic psychopathy. *Journal of Autism and Childhood Schizophrenia, 5*(2), 99–108.

Modestin, J., & Ammann, R. (1996). Mental disorder and criminality: Male schizophrenia. *Schizophrenia Bulletin, 22,* 69–82.

Modestin, J., Hug, A., & Ammann, R. (1997). Criminal behavior in males with affective disorders. *Journal of Affective Disorders, 42,* 29–38.

Modestin, J., Nussbaumer, C., Angst, K., Scheidegger, P., & Hell, D. (1997). Use of potentially abusive psychotropic substances in psychiatric in-patients. *European Archives of Psychiatry and Clinical Neuroscience, 247,* 146–153.

Mohr, J. W., & McKnight, C. K. (1971). Violence as a function of age and relationship with special reference to matricide. *Canadian Psychiatric Association Journal, 16*(2), 29–32.

Monahan, J. (1981). *The clinical prediction of violent behavior.* Washington, DC: National Institute of Mental Health/Government Printing House.

Monahan, J. (2000). Violence risk assessment: Scientific validity and evidentiary admissibility. *Washington and Lee Law Review, 57,* 901–918.

Monahan, J. (2002). The scientific status of research on clinical and actuarial predictions of violence. In D. L. Faigman, D. H. Kaye, M. J. Saks, & J. Sanders (Eds.). *Science and the law: Social and behavioral sciences issues* (pp. 90–112). St. Paul, MN: West Group.

Monahan, J., & Steadman, H. (Eds.). (1994). *Violence and mental disorder: Developments in risk assessment.* Chicago, IL: University of Chicago Press.

Monahan, J., Steadman, H., Appelbaum, P., Grisso, T., Mulvey, E., Roth, L. et al. (2005). *COVR Classification of Violence Risk.* Lutz, FL: Psychological Assessment Resources.

Money, J. (1990). Forensic sexology: Paraphilic serial rape (biastophilia) and lust murder (erotophonophilia). *American Journal of Psychotherapy, 44*(1), 26–36.

Moore, M. E., & Hiday, V. A. (2006). Mental health court outcomes: A comparison of re-arrest and re-arrest severity between mental health court and treatment court participants. *Law and Human Behavior, 30,* 659–674.

Moore, M. S. (1984). *Law and psychiatry: Rethinking the relationship.* Cambridge, UK: Cambridge University Press.

Moran, P., & Hodgins, S. (2004). The correlates of comorbid antisocial personality disorder in schizophrenia. *Schizophrenia Bulletin, 30*(4), 791–802.

Moran, R. (1981). *Knowing right from wrong: The insanity defense of Daniel M'Naghten.* New York, NY: Macmillan/Free Press.

Moran, R. (1985). The origin of insanity as a special verdict: The trial for treason of James Hadfield. *Law and Society Review, 19*(3), 487–519.

Morgan, J. P., & Kagan, D. (1980). The dusting of America: The image of phencyclidine (PCP) in the popular media. *Journal of Psychedelic Drugs, 12*(3–4), 195–204.

Morohn, R. C. (1987) John Wesley Hardin, adolescent killer: The emergence of a narcissistic behavior disorder. *Adolescent Psychiatry, 14,* 271–296.

Morris, G. H. (1997). Placed in purgatory: Conditional release of insanity acquittees. *Arizona Law Review, 39,* 1061–1114.

Morris, G. H. (2009). "Let's do the time warp again": Assessing the competence of counsel in mental health conservatorship proceedings. *San Diego Law Review, 46*, 283–342.

Morris, G. H., & Haroun, A. (2001). "God told me to kill": Religion or delusion? *San Diego Law Review, 38*, 973–1049.

Morrison, A. P. (2008). Cognitive-behavioral therapy. In K. T. Mueser & D. V. Jeste (Eds.), *Clinical handbook of schizophrenia* (pp. 226–239). New York: The Guilford Press.

Morrison, H. L. (1979). Psychiatric observations and interpretations of bite mark evidence in multiple murders. *Journal of Forensic Sciences, 24*(2), 492–502.

Morrissey, J. P. (1982). Deinstitutionalizing the mentally ill: Process, outcomes, and new directions. In W. Gove (Ed.), *Deviance and mental illness* (pp. 147–176). Beverly Hills, CA: Sage.

Morrissey, J. P., & Goldman, H. H. (1986). Care and treatment of the mentally ill in the United States: Historical developments and reforms. *Annals of the American Academy of Political and Social Science, 484*, 12–27.

Morse, S. J. (1984). Undiminished confusion in diminished capacity. *Journal of Criminal Law and Criminology, 75*, 1–55.

Morse, S. J. (1994). Culpability and control. *University of Pennsylvania Law Review, 142*, 1587–1660.

Morse, S. J. (2002). Uncontrollable urges and irrational people. *Virginia Law Review, 88*, 1025–1078.

Morse, S. J. (2003). Diminished rationality, diminished responsibility. *Ohio State Journal of Criminal Law, 1*, 289–308.

Mossman, D., Schwartz, A. H., Elam, E. R. (2012). Risky business versus overt acts: What relevance do "actuarial," probabilistic risk assessments have for judicial decisions on involuntary psychiatric hospitalization? *Houston Journal of Health Law and Policy, 11*, 365–453.

Mouridsen, S. E., Rich, B., Isager, T., & Nedergaard, N. J. (2008). Pervasive developmental disorers and criminal behavior: A case control study. *International Journal of Offender Therapy and Comparative Criminology, 52*(2), 196–205.

Mouridsen, S. E., & Tolstrup, K. (1988). Children who kill: A case study of matricide. *Journal of Child Psychology and Psychiatry, 29*(4), 511–515.

Mukaddes, N. M., & Topcu, Z. (2006). Case report: Homicide by a 10-year-old girl with autistic disorder. *Journal of Autism and Developmental Disorders, 36*(4), 474–474.

Mullen, P. E., Burges, P., Wallace, C., Palmer, S., & Ruschena, D. (2000). Community care and criminal offending in schizophrenia. *Lancet, 355*, 614–617.

Müller, A., Rein, K., Kollei, I., Jacobi, A., Rotter, A., Schütz, P., Hillemacher, T., & de Zwaan, M. (2011). Impulse control disorders in psychiatric inpatients. *Psychiatry Research, 188*, 434–438.

Müller, J. L., Sommer, M., Wagner, V., Lange, K., Taschler, H., Röder, C. H., Schuierer, G., Klein, H. E., & Hajak, G. (2003). Abnormalities in emotion processing within cortical and subcortical regions in criminal psychopaths: Evidence from a functional magnetic resonance imaging study using pictures with emotional content. *Biological Psychiatry, 54*, 152–162.

Munetz, M. R., Grande, T., Kleist, J., & Peterson, G. A. (1996). The effectiveness of outpatient civil commitment. *Psychiatric Services, 47*, 1251–1253.

Murphy, D. (2006). Theory of mind in Asperger's syndrome, schizophrenia and personality disordered forensic patients. *Cognitive Neuropsychiatry, 11*(2), 99–111.

Murphy, J. M. (1976). Psychiatric labeling in cross-cultural perspective: Similar kinds of disturbed behavior appear to be labeled abnormal in diverse cultures. *Science, 191*(4231) 1019–1028.

Murray-Close, D., Ostrov, J. M., Nelson, D. A., Crick, N. R., & Coccaro, E. F. (2010). Proactive, reactive, and romantic relational aggression in adulthood: Measurement, predictive validity, gender differences, and association with intermittent explosive disorder. *Journal of Psychiatric Research, 44*(6), 393–404.

Murrie, D. C., Boccaccini, M., Zapf, P. A., Warren, J. I., & Henderson, C. E. (2008). Clinician variation in findings of competence to stand trial. *Psychology, Public Policy, & Law, 14*, 177–193.

Murrie, D. C., Warren, J. I., Kristiansson, M., & Dietz, P. E. (2002). Asperger's syndrome in forensic settings. *International Journal of Forensic Mental Health, 1*(1), 59–70.

Myers, W. C., & Blashfield, R. (1997). Psychopathology and personality in juvenile sexual homicide offenders. Journal *of the American Academy of Psychiatry and the Law, 25*(4), 497–508.

Myers, W. C., Burket, R. C., Lyles, B., Stone, L., & Kemph, J. P. (1990). DSM-III diagnoses and offenses in committed female juvenile delinquents. *Bulletin of the American Academy of Psychiatry and the Law, 18*(1), 47–54.

Myers. W. C., & Kemph, J. P. (1990), DSM-III-R classification of murderous youth: Help or hindrance? *Journal of Clinical Psychiatry, 51*, 239–242.

Myers, W. C., Reccoppa, L., Burton, K., & McElroy, R. (1993). Malignant sex and aggression: An overview of serial sexual homicide. *Bulletin of the American Academy of Psychiatry and Law, 21*(4), 435–451.

Myers, W. C., Scott, K., Burgess, A. W., & Burgess, A. G. (1995). Psychopathology, biopsychosocial factors, crime characteristics, and classification of 25 homicidal youths. *Journal of the American Academy of Child and Adolescent Psychiatry, 34*(11), 1483–1489.

Nafekh, M., & Motiuk, L. L. (2002). *The statistical information on recidivism – Revised 1 (SIR-R1) Scale: A psychometric examination.* Ottawa, ON: Correctional Service of Canada, Research Branch.

National Council on Crime and Delinquency. (2004). *Correctional assessment and intervention system*. Oakland, CA: Author.

National Institutes of Health. (2010). *Behavioral and social sciences (BSSR) definition*. Bethesda, MD: Office of Behavioral and Social Sciences Research, Office of the Director. Retrieved from http://obssr.od.nih.gov/about_obssr/BSSR_CC/BSSR_definition/definition.aspx

Naudts, K., & Hodgins, S. (2006). Schizophrenia and violence: A search for neurobiological correlates. *Current Opinion in Psychiatry, 19*, 533–538.

Neller, D. J., Denney, R. L., Pietz, C. A., & Thomlinson, R. P. (2006). The relationship between trauma and violence in a jail inmate sample. *Journal of Interpersonal Violence, 21*, 1234–1241.

Netherton, S. D., & Walker, C. E. (1999). Brief history of DSM-IV and ICD-10. In S.D. Netherton, D. Holmes, & C.E. Walker (Eds.), *Child and adolescent psychological disorders: A comprehensive textbook* (pp. 1–5). London: Oxford University Press.

Neubauer, D. W., & Fradella, H. F. (2013). *America's courts and the criminal justice system* (11th ed.). Belmont, CA: Wadsworth Cengage Learning.

New York State Office of Mental Health. (2005). *Kendra's law: Final report on the status of assisted outpatient treatment.* Albany, NY: Author. Retrieved from http://bi.omh.ny.gov/aot/files/AOTFinal2005.pdf

New York State Office of Mental Health (2007). *Legally Oriented Forensic Tracking System (LOFTS).* Albany, NY: Author.

New York Times, The. (1900, July 16). The first insane asylum: To Virginia belongs the credit in this country. *New York Times.* Retrieved from http://query.nytimes.com/mem/archive-free/pdf?res=F00A10F73D5B11738DDDAF0994DF405B808CF1D3

Newhill. C. E. (1991). Parricide. *Journal of Family Violence, 6*(4), 375–394.

Newman, J. P. (1998). Psychopathic behavior: An information-processing perspective. In D. J. Cooke, A. E. Forth, & R. Hare (Eds.), *Psychopathy: Theory, research, and implications for society* (pp. 81–X104). Dordrecht, The Netherlands: Kluwer Academic Publishers.

Newman, S. S., & Ghaziuddin, M. (2008). Violent crime in Asperger syndrome: The role of psychiatric comorbidity. *Journal of Autism and Developmental Disorders, 38*, 1848–1852.

Newton, M. (2000). *The encyclopedia of serial killers*. New York: Checkmark Books.

Nichita, E. C., & Buckley, P. F. (2007). Comorbidities of psychopathy and antisocial personality disorder: Prevalence and implications. In A. Felthous & H. Saβ (Eds.), *International handbook on psychopathic disorders and the law* (Vol. 1, pp. 251–274). New York: John Wiley & Sons, Ltd.

Nicholson R. A., Kugler K. E. (1991). Competent and incompetent criminal defendants: A quantitative review of comparative research. *Psychological Bulletin, 109*, 355–370.

Nickerson, A., Aderka, I. M., Bryant, R. A., & Hofmann, S. G. (2012). The relationship between childhood exposure to trauma and intermittent explosive disorder. *Psychiatry Research, 197*, 128–134.

Nicolas, J. D., Consoli, A., Périsse, D., Cohen, D., & Mazet, P. (2005). Bipolar disorder and hypersexuality in adolescents: Therapeutic and forensic implications. *Neuropsychiatric de L'enfance et de L'adolescence, 53*, 142–148.

NICS Improvement Amendments Act of 2007, Pub. L. No. 110–180, 121 Stat. 2559, *codified as amended in* 18 U.S.C. § 922 (2008).

Nielssen, O. B., Malhi, G. S., & Large, M. M. (2012). Mania, homicide, and severe violence. *Australian and New Zealand Journal of Psychiatry, 46*(4), 357–363.

Nielssen, O. B., Westmore, B. D., Large, M. M., B., & Hayes, R. A. (2007). Homicide during psychotic illness in New South Wales between 1993 and 2002. *Medical Journal of Australia, 186*(6), 301–304.

Nietzel, M. T., Speltz, M. L., McCauley, E. A., & Bernstein, D. A. (1997). *Abnormal psychology*. Needham Heights, MA: Allyn & Bacon.

Nijman, H., Cima, M., & Merckelbach, H. (2003). Nature and antecedents of psychotic patients' crimes. *Journal of Forensic Psychiatry & Psychology, 14*(3), 542–553.

Noffsinger, S. G. (2001). Restoration to competency practice guidelines. *International Journal of Offender Therapy and Comparative Criminology, 45*, 356–362.

Nolen, S., McReynolds, L., DeComo, R., John, R., Keating, J., & Wasserman, G. (2008). Lifetime suicide attempts in juvenile assessment center youth. *Archives of Suicide Research, 12*, 111–123.

Nordström, A., & Kullgren, G. (2003). Victim relations and victim gender in violent crimes committed by offenders with schizophrenia. *Social Psychiatry and Psychiatric Epidemiology, 38*, 326–330.

Nordström, A., Dahlgren, L., & Kullgren, G. (2006). Victim relations and factors triggering homicides committed by offenders with schizophrenia. *The Journal of Forensic Psychiatry & Psychology, 17*(2), 192–203.

Nordström, A., Kullgren, G., & Dahlgren, L. (2006). Schizophrenia and violent crime: The experience of parents. *International Journal of Law and Psychiatry, 29*, 57–67.

Novaco, R., & Taylor, J. (2008). Ander and assualtiveness of male forensic patients with developmental disabilities: Links to volatile parents. *Aggressive Behavior, 34*(4), 380–393.

Nuffield, J. (1989). The 'SIR Scale': Some reflections on its applications. *Forum on Corrections Research, 1*, 19–22.

Nurco, D. (1998). A long-term program of research on drug use and crime. *Substance Use and Misuse, 33*(9), 1817–1837.

O'Connell, B. A. (1963). Matricide. *The Lancet, 1*, 1083–1084.

O'Connor v. Donaldson, 422 U.S. 563 (1975).

O'Connor, S. (2003). Violent behavior in chronic schizophrenia and inpatient psychiatry. *Journal of the American Academy of Psychoanalysis and Dynamic Psychiatry, 31*(1), 31–44.

O'Keefe, M. (1998). Posttraumatic stress disorder among incarcerated battered women: A comparison of battered women who killed their abusers and those incarcerated for other offenses. *Journal of Traumatic Stress, 11*(1), 71–85.

O'Toole, M. E. (2007). Psychopathy as a behavior classification system for violent and serial crime scenes. In H. Hervé & J. C. Yuille (Eds.), *The psychopath: Theory, research, and practice* (pp. 301–325). Mahwah, NJ: Lawrence Erlbaum Associates.

Oberdalhoff, H. E. (1974). Matricide in a schizophrenic psychosis: A case report. *Confinia Psychiatrica, 17*(2), 122–131.

Ogloff, J. R. P. (1991). A comparison of insanity defense standards on juror decision making. *Law and Human Behavior, 15*, 509–531.

Ogunwale, A., & Abayomi, O. (2012). Matricide and schizophrenia in the 21st century: A review and illustrative cases. *African Journal of Psychiatry, 15*, 55–57.

Okasha, A., Sadek, A., & Moneim, S. A. (1975). Psychosocial and electroencephalographic studies of Egyptian murderers. *British Journal of Psychiatry, 126*, 34–40.

Olivera, R. L. (2002). Intermittent explosive disorder: Epidemiology, diagnosis and management. *CNS Drugs, 16*(8), 517–526.

Olver, M. E., & Wong, S. (2011). Predictors of sex offender treatment dropout: Psychopathy, sex offender risk, and responsivity implications. *Psychology, Crime & Law, 17*(5), 457–471.

Olza-Fernández, I., Palanca-Maresca, I., Jiménez-Fernández, S., & Cazorla-Calleja, M. (2012). Trichotillomania, bipolar disorder and white matter hyperintensities in a six-year old girl. *Journal of the Canadian Academy of Child and Adolescent Psychiatry, 21*(3), 213–215.

Oquendo, M. A., & Mann, J. J. (2000). The biology of impulsivity and suicidality. *Psychiatric Clinics of North America, 23*(1), 11–25.

Ornstein, A. (1998). The fate of narcissistic rage in psychotherapy. *Psychoanalytic Inquiry: A Topical Journal for Mental Health Professionals, 18*(1), 55–70.

Otto, R. K. (1994). On the ability of mental health professionals to "predict dangerousness": A commentary on interpretations of the "dangerousness" literature. *Law and Psychology Review, 18*, 43–68.

Otto, R. K. (2006). Competency to stand trial. *Applied Psychology in Criminal Justice, 2*(3), 82–113.

Pajer, K., Tabbah, R., Gardner, W., Rubin, R. T., Czambel, R. K., & Wang, Y. (2006). Adrenal androgen and gonadal hormone levels in adolescent girls with conduct disorder. *Psychoneuroendocrinology, 31*, 1245–1256.

Pakhomou, S. M. (2006). Methodological aspects of telephone scatologia: A case study. *International Journal of Law and Psychiatry, 29*, 178–185.

Palermo, G. B. (1997). The Berserk syndrome: A review of mass murder. *Aggression and Violent Behavior, 2*(1), 1–8.

Palermo, G. B. (2007). New vistas on personality disorders and criminal responsibility. *International Journal of Offender Therapy and Comparative Criminology, 51*, 127–129.

Palermo, G. B., & Knudten, R. D. (1994). The insanity plea in the case of a serial killer. *International Journal of Offender Therapy and Comparative Criminology, 38*, 3–16.

Palermo, M. T. (2004). Pervasive developmental disorders, psychiatric comorbidities, and the law. *International Journal of Offender Therapy and Comparative Criminology, 48*, 40–48.

Paone, T. R., & Douma, K. B. (2009). Child-centered play therapy with a seven-year-old boy diagnosed with intermittent explosive disorder. *International Journal of Play Therapy, 18*(1), 31–44.

Parker, R. N., & Auerhahn, K. (1998). Alcohol, drugs, and violence. *Annual Review of Sociology, 24*, 291–311.

Parrott, D., Drobes, D., Saladin, M., Coffey, S., & Dansky, B. (2003). Perpetration of partner violence: Effects of cocaine and alcohol dependence and posttraumatic stress disorder. *Addictive Behaviors, 28*, 1587–1602.

Parry-Jones, W. L. (1988). Asylum for the mentally ill in historical perspective. *The Psychiatrist/Psychiatric Bulletin, 12*, 407–410.

Pasewark, R., Pantle, M., & Steadman, H. J. (1982). Detention and rearrest rates of persons found not guilty by reason of insanity and convicted felons. *American Journal of Psychiatry, 139*, 892–897.

Pate v. Robinson, 383 U.S. 375 (1966).

Patel, B. D., & Barzman, D. H. (2013). Pharmacology and pharmacogenetics of pediatric adhd with associated aggression: A review. *Psychiatric Quarterly, 84*, 407–415.

Pawlik, K., & Rosenzweig, M. R. (2002). *The international handbook of psychology*. Thousand Oaks, CA: Sage.

PDM Task Force (2006). *Psychodynamic diagnostic manual*. Silver Springs, MD: Alliance of Psychoanalytic Organizations.

People v. Bieber, 856 P.2d 811 (Colo. 1993).

People v. Carpenter, 627 N.W.2d 276 (2001).

People v. Low, 732 P.2d 622 (Colo. 1987).

People v. White, 117 Cal. App.3d 270, 172 Cal. Rptr. 612 (1981).

Perälä, J., Suvisarri, J., Saarni, S., Kuoppasalmi, K., Isometsä, E., Pirkola, S., et al. (2007). Lifetime prevalence of psychotic and bipolar I disorders in a general population. *Archives of General Psychiatry, 64*, 19–28.

Perlin, M. L. (1985). The things we do for love: John Hinckley's trial and the future of the insanity defense in the federal courts. *New York Law School Law Review, 30*, 857–875.

Perlin, M. L. (1990). Unpacking the myths: The symbolism mythology of insanity defense jurisprudence. *Case Western Reserve Law Review, 40*, 599–731.

Perlin, M. L. (1997). The borderline which separated you from me: The insanity defense, the authoritarian spirit, the fear of faking, and the culture of punishment. *Iowa Law Review, 82*, 1375–1426.

Pescosolido, B. A., Monahan, J., Link, B. G., Stueve, A., & Kikuzawa, S. (1999). The public's view of the competence, dangerousness, and need for legal coercion of persons with mental health problems. *American Journal of Public Health, 89*, 1339–1345.

Peterson, J., Skeem, J., Hart, E., Vidal, S., & Keith, F. (2010). Analyzing offense patterns as a function of mental illness to test the criminalization hypothesis. *Psychiatric Services, 61*, 1217–1222.

Pétursson, H., & Gudjónsson, G. H. (1981). Psychiatric aspects of homicide. *Acta Psychiatrica Scandinavica, 64*, 363–372.

Pfeffer, A. (2008). "Imminent danger" and inconsistency: The need for national reform of the "imminent danger" standard for involuntary civil commitment in the wake of the Virginia Tech tragedy. *Cardozo Law Review, 30*, 277–315.

Pfeiffer, E., Eisenstein, R. B., & Dabbs, E. G. (1967). Mental competency evaluation for the federal courts: I. Methods and results. *Journal of Nervous and Mental Disease, 144*(4), 320–328.

Pham, T. H., & Saloppé, X. (2010). PCL-R psychopathy and its relation DSM Axis I and II disorders in a sample of male forensic patients in a Belgian security hospital. *The International Journal of Forensic Mental Health, 9*(3), 205–214.

Phelan, J. C., Sinkewicz, M., Castille, D. M., Huz, S., Muenzenmaier, K., & Link, B. G. (2010). Effectiveness and outcomes of assisted outpatient treatment in New York State. *Psychiatric Services, 61*, 137–143.

Philip, R. C. M., Dauvermann, M. R., Whalley, H. C., Baynham, K., Lawrie, S. M., & Stanfield, A. C. (2012). A systematic review and meta-analysis of the fMRI investigation of autism spectrum disorders. *Neuroscience and Biobehavioral Reviews, 36*, 901–942.

Phillips, M. R., Wolf, A. S., & Coons, D. J. (1988). Psychiatry and the criminal justice system: Testing the myths. *American Journal of Psychiatry, 145*(5), 605–610.

Phillips, S. L., Heads, T. C., Taylor, P. J., & Hill, G. M. (1999). Sexual offending and antisocial sexual behavior among patients with schizophrenia. *Journal of Clinical Psychiatry, 60*, 170–175.

Philo, G., Secker, J., Platt, S., Henderson, L., McLaughlin, G., & Burnside, J. (1994). Impact of the mass media on public images of mental illness: Media content and audience belief. *Health Education Journal, 53*, 271–281.

Picot, M. C., Baldy-Moulinier, M., Daurès, J. P., Dujols, P., & Crespel, A. (2008). The prevalence of epilepsy and pharmacoresistant epilepsy in adults: A population-based study in a Western European country. *Epilepsia, 49*(7), 1230–1238.

Pierson, J. (2012). Construing *Crane*: Examining how state courts have applied its lack-of-control standard. *University of Pennsylvania Law Review, 160*, 1527–1559.

Pinals, D. A. (2005). Where two roads meet: Restoration of competence to stand trial from a clinical perspective, *New England Journal on Criminal and Civil Confinement, 31*, 81–108.

Pincus, A. L., & Lukowitsky, M. R. (2010). Pathological narcissism and narcissistic personality disorder. *Annual Review of Clinical Psychology, 6*, 421–426.

Pincus, W. H. (1995). Civil commitment and the "great confinement" revisited: Straightjacketing individual rights, stifling culture. *William and Mary Law Review, 36*, 1769–1817.

Pirelli, G., Gottdiener, W. H., & Zapf, P. A. (2011). A meta-analytic review of competency to stand trial research. *Psychology, Public Policy, and Law, 17*(1), 1–53.

Planansky, K., & Johnston, R. (1977). Homicidal aggression in schizophrenic men. *Acta Psychiatrica Scandinavica, 55*, 65–73.

Plaut, V. L. (1983). Punishment versus treatment of the guilty but mentally ill. *Journal of Criminal Law and Criminology, 74*(2), 428–456.

Pliszka, S. R., Sherman, J. O., Barrow, M. V., & Irick, S. (2000). Affective disorder in juvenile offenders: A preliminary study. *American Journal of Psychiatry, 157*(1), 130–132.

Pollock, P. H. (1995). A case of spree serial murder with suggested diagnostic opinions. *International Journal of Offender Therapy and Comparative Criminology, 39*(3), 258–268.

Popma, A., & Raine, A. (2006). Will future forensic assessment be neurobiologic? *Child and Adolescent Psychiatric Clinics of North America, 15*, 429–444.

Popper, K. (1989). *Conjectures and refutations: The growth of scientific knowledge* (5th ed.). New York, NY: Basic Books.

Porter v. McCollum, 130 S. Ct. 447 (2009).

Porter, S., Birt, A. R., & Boer, D. P. (2001). Investigation of the criminal and conditional release histories of Canadian federal offenders as a function of psychopathy and age. *Law & Human Behavior, 25*, 647–661.

Porter, S., ten Brinke, L., & Wilson, K. (2009). Crime profiles and conditional release performance of psychopathic and non-psychopathic sexual offenders. *Legal and Criminological Psychology, 14*, 109–118.

Porter, S., & Woodworth, M. (2006). Psychopathy and aggression. In C. J. Patrick (Ed.), *Handbook of psychopathy* (pp. 481–494). New York: Guilford Press.

Porter, S., & Woodworth, M. (2007). "I'm sorry I did it . . . but he started it": A comparison of the official and self-report homicide descriptions of psychopaths and non-psychopaths. *Law & Human Behavior, 31*(1), 91–107.

Porter, S., Woodworth, M., Earle, J., Drugge, J., & Boer, D. (2003). Characteristics of sexual homicides committed by psychopathic and nonpsychopathic offenders. *Law & Human Behavior, 27*(5), 459–470.

Pound, R. (1953). *The lawyer from antiquity to modern times*. St. Paul, MN: West Publishing Co.

Pratt, T. C., Cullen, F. T., Blevins, K. R., Daigle, L., & Unnever, J. D. (2002). The relationship of attention deficit hyperactivity disorder to crime and delinquency: A meta-analysis. *International Journal of Police Science & Management, 4*(4), 344–360.

Premack, D., & Woodruff, G. (1978). Does the chimpanzee have a theory of mind? *The Behavioral and Brain Sciences, 1*, 515–526.

Prentky, R. A., & Knight, R. A. (1991). Identifying critical dimensions for discriminating among rapists. *Journal of Counseling and Clinical Psychology, 59*(5), 643–661.

Preston-Baecht, L. A. (2009). Federal courts' interpretations of *Sell v. U.S. Journal of Psychiatry & Law, 37*, 413–430.

Pridmore, S. (2006). *Psychiatry*. Retrieved from http://eprints.utas.edu.au/287.

Prins, H., Tennant, G., & Trick, K. (1985). Motives for arson (fire raising). *Medicine, Science and the Law, 25*, 275–278.

PrisonPolicy.org. (2011). *From prisons to hospitals and back: The criminalization of mental illness*. Northampton, MA: Prision Policy Initiative. Retrieved from http://www.prisonpolicy.org/scans/menbrief.html

Pustilnik, A. C. (2005). Prisons of the mind: Social value and economic inefficiency in the criminal justice response to mental illness. *Journal of Criminal Law and Criminology, 96*, 217–265.

Putkonen, H., Collander, J., Honkasalo, M. L., & Lönnqvist, J. (2001). Personality disorders and psychoses form two distinct subgroups of homicide among female offenders. *The Journal of Forensic Psychiatry, 12*(2), 300–312.

Quanbeck, C. D., Frye, M. A., & Altshuler, L. L. (2003). Mania and the law in California: Understanding the criminalization of the mentally ill. *American Journal of Psychiatry, 160*(7), 1245–1250.

Quanbeck, C. D., Stone, D. C., McDermott, B. E., Boone, K., Scott, C. L., & Frye, M. A. (2005). Relationship between criminal arrest and community treatment history among patients with bipolar disorder. *Psychiatric Services, 56*, 847–852.

Quanbeck, C. D., Stone, D. C., Scott, C. L., McDermott, B. E., Altshuler, L. L., & Frye, M. A. (2004). Clinical and legal correlates of inmates with bipolar disorder at time of criminal arrest. *Journal of Clinical Psychiatry, 65*, 198–203.

Queensland Government. (2002). *Problem Gambling Prevalence Survey 2002*. Brisbane, Australia: Department of Corrective Services.

Quinney, R. (1970). *The problem of crime*. New York, NY: Dodd, Mead, and Co.

Quinsey, V. L., Harris, G. T., Rice, M. E., & Cormier, C. A. (2006). *Violent offenders: Appraising and managing risk* (2nd ed.). Washington, DC: American Psychological Association.

Rabkin, J. G. (1979). Criminal behavior of discharged mental patients: A critical appraisal of the research. *Psychological Bulletin, 86*(1), 1–27.

Raine, A. (1986). Psychopathy, schizoid personality, and borderline/schizotypal personality disorders. *Personality and Individual Differences, 7*(4), 493–501.

Raine, A. (1987). Effects of early environment on electrodermal and cognitive correlates of schizotypy and psychopathy in criminals. *International Journal of Psychophysiology, 4*, 277–287.

Raine, A. (1992). Schizotypal and borderline features in psychopathic criminals. *Personality and Individual Differences, 13*(6), 717–721.

Raine, A. (1993). Features of borderline personality disorder and violence. *Journal of Clinical Psychology, 49*(2), 277–281.

Raine, A. (2006). Pursuing a second generation of research on crime and schizophrenia. In A. Raine (Ed.), *Crime and schizophrenia: Causes and cures* (pp. 3–12). New York: Nova Science Publishers, Inc.

Raine, A. (2013). *The anatomy of violence*. New York: Pantheon Books.

Raine, A., Bihrle, S., Venables, P. H., Mednick, S. A., & Pollock, V. (1999). Skin-conductance orienting and increased alcoholism in schizotypal criminals. *Journal of Abnormal Psychology, 108*(2), 299–306.

Raine, A., Buchsbaum, M., & LaCasse, L. (1997). Brain abnormalities in murderers indicated by positron emission tomography. *Biological Psychiatry, 42*, 495–508.

Raine, A., Ishikawa, S. S., Arce, E., Lencz, T., Knuth, K. H., Bihrle, S., Lacasse, L., & Colletti, P. (2004). Hippocampal structural asymmetry in unsuccessful psychopaths. *Biological Psychiatry, 55*, 185–191.

Raine, A., Lai-chu Fung, A., Lam, B. Y. H. (2011). Peer victimization partially mediates the schizotypy-aggression relationship in children and adolescents. *Schizophrenia Bulletin, 37*(5), 937–945.

Raine, A., Lencz, T., Bihrle, S., Lacasse, L., & Colletti, P. (2000). Reduced prefrontal gray matter volume and reduced autonomic activity in antisocial personality disorder. *Archives of General Psychiatry, 57*, 119–127.

Raine, A., Lencz, T., Taylor, K., Hellige, J. B., Bihrle, S., Lacasse, L., Lee, M., Ishikawa, S., & Colletti, P. (2003). Corpus callosum abnormalities in psychopathic antisocial individuals. *Archives of General Psychiatry, 60*, 1134–1142.

Raine, A., Liu, J., Venables, P., & Mednick, S. A. (2006). Preventing crime and schizophrenia using early environmental enrichment. In A. Raine (Ed.), *Crime and schizophrenia: Causes and cures* (pp. 249–265). New York: Nova Science.

Raine, A., Meloy, J. R., Bihrle, S., Stoddard, J., Lacasse, L., & Buchsbaum, M. S. (1998). Reduced prefrontal and increased subcortical brain functioning assessed using positron emission tomography in predatory and affective murderers. *Behavioral Sciences and the Law, 16*, 319–332.

Raine, A., & Venables, P. H. (1984). Electrodermal nonresponding, antisocial behavior, and schizoid tendencies in adolescents. *Psychophysiology, 21*(4), 424–433.

Raine, A., & Venables, P. H. (1990). Evoked potential augmenting-reducing in psychopaths and criminals with impaired smooth-pursuit eye movements. *Psychiatry Research, 31*(1), 85–98.

Raine, A., & Yang, Y. (2006). The neuroanatomical bases of psychopathy: A review of brain imaging findings. In C. J. Patrick (Ed.), *Handbook of psychopathy* (pp. 278–295). New York: The Guilford Press.

Raizen, K. H. (1960). A case of matricide and patricide. *British Journal of Delinquency, 10*(4), 277–294.

Ran, M. S., Chen, P. Y., Liao, Z. G., Chan, C. L. W., Chen, E. Y. H., Tang, C. P., Mao, W. J., Lamberti, J. S., & Conwell, Y. (2010). Criminal behavior among persons with schizophrenia in rural China. *Schizophrenia Research, 122*, 213–218.

Randall, J., & Cunningham, P. (2003). Multisystematic therapy: A treatment for violent substance-abusing and substance-dependent juvenile offenders. *Addictive Behaviors, 28*, 1731–1739.

Rath, N. M., & Dash, B. (1990). A study on insanity related homicide. *Indian Journal of Psychiatry*, 32(1), 69–71.

Raymond, N. C., Coleman, E., Ohlerking, F., Christenson, G. A., & Miner, M. (1999). Psychiatric comorbidity in pedophilic sex offenders. *American Journal of Psychiatry, 156*, 786–788.

Read, S., & Rendall, M. (2007). An open-label study of risperidone in the improvement of quality of life and treatment of symptoms of violent and self-injurious behaviour in adults with intellectual disability. *Journal of Applied Research in Intellectual Disabilities, 20*, 256–264.

Realmuto, G. M., & Ruble, L. A. (1999). Sexual behaviors in autism: Problems of definition and management. *Journal of Autism and Developmental Disorders, 29*(2), 121–127.

Redlich, A. D., Hoover, S., Summers, A., & Steadman, H. J. (2010). Enrollment in mental health courts: Voluntariness, knowingness, and adjudicative competence. *Law and Human Behavior, 34*, 91–104.

Reevy, G. M., Malamud Ozer, Y., & Ito, Y. (2010). *Encyclopedia of emotion*. Santa Barbara, CA: Greenwood.

Rehm, L. P., Wagner, A. L., & Ivens-Tyndal, C. (2001). In P. B. Sutker & H. E. Adams (Eds.), *Comprehensive handbook of psychopathology* (3rd ed., pp. 277–308). New York: Kluwer Academic/Plenum Publishers.

Reich, J., & Wells, J. (1985). Psychiatric diagnosis and competency to stand trial. *Comprehensive Psychiatry, 26*(5), 421–432.

Reichard, S., & Tillman, C. (1950). Murder and suicide as defenses against schizophrenic psychosis. *Clinical Psychopathology, 11*(4), 149–163.

Reisner, R., Slobogin, C., & Rai, A. (2009). *Law and the mental health system: Civil and criminal aspects* (4th ed). St. Paul, MN: West Group.

Rendell, J. A., Huss, M. T., & Jensen, M. L. (2010). Expert testimony and the effects of a biological approach, psychopathy, and juror attitudes in cases of insanity. *Behavioral Sciences & the Law, 28*(3), 411–425.

Repo, E., & Virkkunen, M. (1997). Criminal recidivism and family histories of schizophrenic and nonschizophrenic fire setters: Comorbid alcohol dependence in schizophrenic fire setters. *Journal of the American Academy of Psychiatry and the Law, 25*(2), 207–215.

Report of the Virginia Tech Review Panel (2007). *Mass shootings at Virginia Tech: Report of the review panel*. Richmond, VA: Office of the Governor. Retrieved from http://www.governor.virginia.gov/tempcontent/techPanelReport-docs/FullReport.pdf.

Resick, P. A., Monson, C. M., & Rizvi, S. L. (2008). Posttraumatic stress disorder. In D. H. Barlow (Ed.), *Clinical handbook of psychological disorders: A step-by-step treatment manual* (4th ed., pp. 65–122). New York: The Guilford Press.

Resnick, P. J., & Harris, M. R. (2002). Retrospective assessment of malingering in insanity defense cases. In R. I. Simon & D. W. Shuman (Eds.), *Retrospective assessment of mental states in litigation: Predicting the past* (pp. 101–134). Arlington, VA: American Psychiatric Publishing, Inc.

Ressler, R. K., Burgess, A. W., & Douglas, J. E. (1988). *Sexual homicide: Patterns and motives*. New York: The Free Press.

Reuter, J., Raedler, T., Rose, M., Hand, I., Gläscher, J., & Büchel, C. (2005). Pathological gambling is linked to reduced activation of the mesolimbic reward system. *Nature Neuroscience, 8*(2), 147–148.

Revitch, E., & Schlesinger, L. B. (1981). *The psychopathology of homicide*. Springfield, IL: Charles C. Thomas.

Revitch, E., & Schlesinger, L. B. (1989). *Sex murder and sex aggression: Phenomenology, psychopathology, psychodynamics and prognosis*. Springfield, IL: Charles C. Thomas.

Rex v. Arnold, Y.B. 10 Geo. 1 (1724).

Rice, M. E., & Harris, G. T. (1990). The predictors of insanity acquittal. *International Journal of Law and Psychiatry, 13*, 217–224.

Richards, H., & Jackson, R. (2011). Behavioral discriminators of sexual sadism and paraphilia nonconsent in a sample of civilly committed sexual offenders. *International Journal of Offender Therapy and Comparative Criminology, 55*(2), 207–227.

Riggins v. Nevada, 504 U.S. 127 (1992).

Riggs, D. S., Dancu, C. V., Gersguny, B. S., Greenberg, D., & Foa, E. B. (1992). Anger and post-traumatic stress disorder in female crime victims. *Journal of Traumatic Stress, 5*(4), 613–625.

Roberts, A. L., & Coid, J. W. (2010). Personality disorder and offending behaviour: Findings from the national survey of male prisoners in England and Wales. *Journal of Forensic Psychiatry & Psychology, 21*(2), 221–237.

Robertson, G. (1988). Arrest patterns among mentally disordered offenders. *British Journal of Psychiatry, 153*, 313–316.

Robin, G. (1997). The evolution of the insanity defense. *Journal of Contemporary Criminal Justice, 13*(3), 224–235.

Robins, L. N. (1980). The natural history of drug abuse. *Acta Psychiatrica Scandinavica, 62*(s284), 7–20.

Robinson, J., Sareen, J., Cox, B. J., & Bolton, J. (2009). Self-medication of anxiety disorders with alcohol and drugs: Results from a nationally representative sample. *Journal of Anxiety Disorders, 23*, 38–45.

Roesch, R., & Golding, S. L. (1980). *Competency to stand trial*. Urbana: University of Illinois Press.

Roesch, R., Zapf, P. A., Golding, S. L., & Skeem, J. L. (1999). Defining and assessing competency to stand trial. In A. K. Hess & I. B. Weiner (Eds.), *The handbook of forensic psychology* (2nd ed., pp. 327–349). New York: John Wiley & Sons, Inc.

Rogers, J., Viding, E., Blair, R. J., Frith, U., & Happé, F. (2006). Autism spectrum disorder and psychopathy: Shared cognitive underpinnings or double hit? *Psychological Medicine, 36*, 1789–1798.

Rogers, J. L., Bloom, J. D., & Manson, S. M. (1984). Insanity defenses: Contested or conceded? *American Journal of Psychiatry, 141*, 885–888.

Rogers, M. A., Kasai, K., Koji, M., Fukuda, R., Iwanami, A., Nakagome, K., Fukuda, M., & Kato, N. (2011). Executive and prefrontal dysfunction in unipolar depression: A review of neuropsychological and imaging evidence. *Neuroscience Research, 50*, 1–11.

Rogers, R., Gillis, R. R., McMain S., & Dickens S. E. (1988). Fitness evaluations: A retrospective study of clinical, legal and sociodemographic variables. *Canadian Journal of Behavioral Science, 20*, 192–199.

Rogers, R. L. (1984). *Rogers Criminal Responsibility Assessment Scale (R-CRAS) and test manual*. Odessa, FL: Psychological Assessment Resources.

Rogers, R. L., & Cavanaugh, J. L. (1981). Application of the SADS diagnostic interview to forensic psychiatry. *Journal of Psychiatry and Law, 9*, 329–344.

Rohland, B. M. (1998). *The role of outpatient commitment in the management of persons with schizophrenia*. Iowa City, IA: Iowa Consortium for Mental Health, Services, Training, and Research.

Romito, P., Pomicino, L., Lucchetta, C., Scrimin, F., & Turan, J. M. (2009). The relationships between physical violence, verbal abuse, and women's psychological distress during the postpartum period. *Journal of Psychosomatic Obstetrics and Gynecology, 30*(2), 115–121.

Roncero, C. C., Rodríguez-Urrutia, A. A., Grau-López, L. L., & Casas, M. M. (2009). Antiepileptic drugs in the control of the impulses disorders. *Actas Españolas De Psiquiatría, 37*(4), 205–212.

Ronningstam, E. F. (Ed.). (2000). *Disorders of narcissism: Diagnostic, clinical, and empirical implications* (1st softcover ed.). Washington, DC: American Psychiatric Press.

Roos, A., Fouche, J., Stein, D. J., & Lochner, C. (2013). White matter integrity in hair-pulling disorder (trichotillomania). *Psychiatry Research: Neuroimaging, 211*(3), 246–250.

Root, C. C., MacKay, S. S., Henderson, J. J., Del Bove, G. G., & Warling, D. D. (2008). The link between maltreatment and juvenile firesetting: Correlates and underlying mechanisms. *Child Abuse & Neglect, 32*(2), 161–176.

Rosen, M. (1999). Insanity denied: Abolition of the insanity defense in Kansas. *Kansas Journal of Law & Public Policy, 8*, 253–262.

Rosenbaum, G. (1969). Schizophrenia as a "put-on." *Journal of Consulting and Clinical Psychology, 33*(6), 642–645.

Rosenbaum, M., & Bennett, B. (1986). Homicide and depression. *American Journal of Psychiatry, 143*(3), 367–370.

Rosenberg, R. S. (2013, Apr. 12). Abnormal is the new normal. Why will half of the U.S. population have a diagnosable mental disorder? *Slate*. Retrieved May 31, 2013 from http://www.slate.com/articles/health_and_science/medical_examiner/2013/04/diagnostic_and_statistical_manual_fifth_edition_why_will_half_the_u_s_population.html.

Rosenhan, D. L. (1973, Jan. 19). On being sane in insane places. *Science, 179*(4070), 250–258.

Rosinia, N. (2012). How "reasonable" has become unreasonable: A proposal for rewriting the lasting legacy of *Jackson v. Indiana*. *Washington University Law Review, 89*, 673–699.

Rösler, M., Retz, W., Retz-Junginger, P., Hengesch, G., Schneider, M., Supprian, T., Schwitzgebel, P., Pinhard, K., Dovi-Akue, N., Wender, P., & Thome, J. (2004). Prevalence of attention-deficit/hyperactivity disorder (ADHD) and comorbid disorders in young male prison inmates. *European Archives of Psychiatry and Clinical Neuroscience, 254*, 365–371.

Rosner, R., Wiederlight, M., Horner-Rosner, M. B., & Wieczorek, R. R. (1979). Adolescents accused of murder and manslaughter: A five-year descriptive study. *Bulletin of the American Academy of Psychiatry and the Law, 7*(4), 342–351.

Ross, E. R. (1901). *Social control: A survey of the foundations of order*. New York, NY: MacMillian.

Rothman, D. (1970). *The discovery of the asylum*. Boston, MA: Little Brown.

Rozycka, M., & Thille, Z. (1972). The psychopathological aspect of parricide. *Psychiatria Polska, 6*(2), 159–168.

Ruddell, R. (2006). Jail interventions for inmates with mental illnesses. *Journal of Correctional Health Care, 12*(2), 118–131.

Russell, D. H. (1965). A study of juvenile murderers. *Journal of Offender Therapy, 9*(3), 55–86.

Russell, D. H. (1984). A study of juvenile murderers of family members. *International Journal of Offender Therapy and Comparative Criminology, 28*, 177–192.

Rycroft, C. (1995). *A critical dictionary of psychoanalysis* (2nd ed.). New York: Penguin Books.

Sachdev, P. S. (2013). Is DSM-5 defensible? *Australian and New Zealand Journal of Psychiatry, 47*(1), 10–11.

Sacks, S., Chaple, M., Sacks, J. Y., McKendrick, K., & Cleland, C. (2012). Randomized trial of a reentry modified therapeutic community for offenders with co-occurring disorders: Crime outcomes. *Journal of Substance Abuse Treatment, 42*(3), 247–259.

Sacks, S., Sacks, J., McKendrick, K., Banks, S., & Stommel, J. (2004). Modified therapeutic community for MICA offenders: Crime outcomes. *Behavioral Sciences and the Law, 22*, 477–501.

Sadoff, S. (1982). Adolescent parricide in abusive families. *Child Welfare, 61*(7), 445–455.

Saha, S., Chant, D., Welham, J., & McGrath, J. (2005). A systematic review of the prevalence of schizophrenia. *PLoS Medicine, 2*(5), 413–433.

Sahota, K., & Chesterman, P. (1998a). Mentally ill sex offenders in a regional secure unit. II: Cognitions, perceptions and fantasies. *Journal of Forensic Psychiatry, 9*(1), 161–172.

Sahota, K., & Chesterman, P. (1998b). Sexual offending in the context of mental illness. *Journal of Forensic Psychiatry, 9*(2), 267–280.

Saladin, M., Drobes, D., Coffey, S., Dansky, B., Brady, K., & Kilpatrick, D. (2003). PTSD symptom severity as a predictor of cue-elicited drug craving in victims of violent crime. *Addictive Behaviors, 28*, 1611–1629.

Saleh, F. M., Malin, H. M., Grudzinskas, A. J., & Vitacco, M. J. (2010). Paraphilias with co-morbid psychopathy: The clinical and legal significance to sex offender assessments. *Behavioral Sciences and the Law, 28*, 211–223.

Salekin, R. T. (2006). Psychopathy in children and adults: Key issues in conceptualization and assessment. In C. J. Patrick (Ed.), *Handbook of psychopathy* (pp. 389–414). New York: The Guilford Press.

Salkovskis, P. M. (1985). Obsessional-compulsive problems: A cognitive-behavioural analysis. *Behavioural Research and Therapy, 23*(5), 571–583.

Samandari, G., Martin, S. L., & Schiro, S. (2010). Homicide among pregnant and postpartum women in the United States: A review of the literature. *Trauma, Violence, and Abuse, 11*(1), 42–54.

Sandler, J., & Joffe, W. G. (1965). Notes on childhood depression. *International Journal of Psychoanalysis, 46*, 88–96

Sansone, R. A., & Sansone, L. A. (2009). Borderline personality and criminality. *Psychiatry, 6*(10), 16–20.

Sansone, R. A., & Sansone, L. A. (2010). Fatal attraction syndrome: Stalking behavior and borderline personality. *Psychiatry, 7*(5), 42–46.

Saranson, I. G., & Saranson, B. R. (2002). *Abnormal psychology: The problem of maladaptive behavior* (10th ed.). Upper Saddle River, NJ: Prentice Hall.

Sareen, J., Houlahan, T., Coz, B. J., & Asmundson, G. J. G. (2005). Anxiety disorders associated with suicidal ideation and suicide attempts in the National Comorbidity Survey. *Journal of Nervous and Mental Disease, 193*(7), 450–454.

Sareen, J., Stein, M. B., Cox, B. J., & Hassard, S. T. (2004). Understanding comorbidity of anxiety disorders with antisocial behavior: Findings from two large community samples. *Journal of Nervous and Mental Disease, 192*(3), 178–186.

Sartorius, A., Ruf, M., Kief, C., Demirakca, T., Bailer, J., Ende, G., Henn, F. A., Meyer-Lindenberg, A., & Dressing, H. (2008). Abnormal amygdala activation profile in pedophilia. *European Archives of Psychiatry and Clinical Neuroscience, 258*, 271–277.

Sato, T., Bottlender, R., Kleindienst, N., & Möller, H. J. (2002). Syndromes and phenomenological subtypes underlying acute mania: A factor analytic study of 576 manic patients. *American Journal of Psychiatry, 159*, 968–974.

Savitz, J. B., Nugent, A. C., Bogers, W., Roiser, J. P., Bain, E. E., Neumeister, A., Zarate Jr., C. A., Manji, H. K., Cannon, D. M., Marrett, S., Henn, F., Charney, D. S., & Drevets, W. C. (2011). Habenula volume in bipolar disorder and major depressive disorder: A high-resolution magnetic resonance imaging study. *Biological Psychiatry, 69*, 336–343.

Savolainen, J., Hurtig, T. M., Ebeling, H. E., Moilanen, I. K., Hughes, L. A., & Taanila, A. M. (2010). Attention deficit hyperactivity disorder (ADHD) and criminal behaviour: The role of adolescent marginalization. *European Journal of Criminology, 7*, 442–459.

Schaefer, G. J. (1994/1995). Drug-induced alteration of psychotic behavior: Who benefits? *Journal of Law and Health, 9*, 43–68.

Scherl, D. J., & Mack, J. E. (1966). A study of adolescent matricide. *Journal of the American Academy of Child Psychiatry, 5*(2), 569–593.

Scherr, A. (2003). Daubert & danger: The "fit" of expert predictions in civil commitments. *Hastings Law Journal, 55*, 1–90.

Schienle, A., Hettema, J. M., Cáceda, R., & Nemeroff, C. B. (2011). Neurobiology and genetics of generalized anxiety disorder. *Psychiatric Annals, 41*(2), 113–123.

Schiffer, B., Gizewski, E., & Kruger, T. (2009). Reduced neuronal responsiveness to visual sexual stimuli in a pedophile treated with long-acting LH-RH agonist. *Journal of Sexual Medicine, 6*, 892–894.

Schiffer, B., Krueger, T., Paul, T., de Greiff, A., Forsting, M., Leygraf, N., Schedlowski, M., & Gizewski, E. (2008). Brain response to visual sexual stimuli in homosexual pedophiles. *Journal of Psychiatry and Neuroscience, 33*(1), 23–33.

Schiffer, B., & Vonlaufen, C. (2011). Executive dysfunctions in pedophilic and nonpedophilic child molesters. *Journal of Sexual Medicine, 8*(7), 1975–1984.

Schipkowensky, N. (1968). Affective disorders: Cyclophrenia and murder. In A. V. S. de Reuck & R. Porter (Eds.), *The mentally abnormal offender* (pp. 59–75). Boston: Little, Brown and Company.

Schlesinger, L. B. (1999). Adolescent sexual matricide following repetitive mother-son incest. *Journal of Forensic Sciences, 44*(4), 746–749.

Schmitz, J. (2005). The interface between impulse-control disorders and addictions: Are pleasure pathway responses shared neurobiological substrates? *Sexual Addiction & Compulsivity, 12*(2/3), 149–168.

Schuckit, M. A., Herrman, G., & Schuckit, J. J. (1977). The importance of psychiatric illness in newly arrested prisoners. *Journal of Nervous and Mental Disease, 165*(2), 118–125.

Schug, R. A. (2009). Biopsychosocial and forensic clinical correlates of schizophrenia and homicide. *Dissertation Abstracts International, 70*(7), UMI no. 3368644.

Schug, R. A. (2011). Schizophrenia and matricide: An integrative review. *Journal of Contemporary Criminal Justice, 27*(2), 204–229.

Schug, R. A., Gao, Y., Glenn, A. L., Peskin, M., Yang, Y., & Raine, A. (2010). The developmental evidence base: Neurobiological research and forensic applications. In G. Towl & D. Crighton (Eds.), *Forensic psychology* (pp. 73–94). West Sussex, UK: Blackwell Publishing Ltd.

Schug, R. A., & Raine, A. (2009). Comparative meta-analyses of neuropsychological functioning in antisocial schizophrenic persons. *Clinical Psychology Review, 29*, 230–242.

Schug, R. A., Raine, A., & Wilcox, R. R. (2007). Psychophysiological and behavioural characteristics of individuals with both antisocial personality disorder and schizophrenia-spectrum personality disorder. *British Journal of Psychiatry, 191*, 408–414.

Schug, R. A., Yang, Y., Raine, A., Han, C., & Liu, J. (2010). Structural and psychosocial correlates of birth order anomalies in schizophrenia and homicide. *Journal of Nervous and Mental Disease, 198*(12), 870–875.

Schug, R. A., Yang, Y., Raine, A., Han, C., Liu, J., & Li, L. (2011). Resting EEG deficits in accused murderers with schizophrenia. *Psychiatry Research: Neuroimaging, 194*, 85–94.

Schwade, E. D., & Geiger, S. G. (1953). Matricide with electroencephalographic evidence of thalamic or hypothalamic disorder. *Diseases of the Nervous System, 14*, 18–20.

Schwartz, R. C., Petersen, S., & Skaggs, J. L. (2001). Predictors of homicidal ideation and intent in schizophrenia: An empirical study. *American Journal of Orthopsychiatry, 71*(3), 379–384.

Scott, D. W. (1985). Asperger's syndrome and non-verbal communication: A pilot study. *Psychological Medicine, 15*, 683–687.

Scragg, P., & Shah, A. (1994). Prevalence of Asperger's syndrome in a secure hospital. *British Journal of Psychiatry, 158*, 55–62.

Scull, A. (1991). Psychiatry and social control in the nineteenth and twentieth centuries. *History of Psychiatry, 2*, 149–169.

Scurich, N., & John, R. S. (2011). The effect of framing actuarial risk probabilities on involuntary civil commitment decisions. *Law and Human Behavior, 35*, 83–91.

Segal, S. P. (2012). Civil commitment law, mental health services, and U.S. homicide rates. *Social Psychiatry and Psychiatric Epidemiology, 47*(9), 1449–1458.

Sell v. United States, 539 U.S. 166 (2003).

Seltzer, A., & Langford, M. A. (1984). Forensic psychiatric assessment in the Northwest Territories. *Canadian Journal of Psychiatry, 29*, 665–668.

Sentencing Project, The. (2002). *Mentally ill offenders in the criminal justice system: An analysis and prescription*. Washington, DC: Author.

Serin, R. C. (1991). Psychopathy and violence in criminals. *Journal of Interpersonal Violence, 6*(4), 423–431.

Seto, M. C. (2004). Pedophilia and sexual offenses against children. *Annual Review of Sex Research, 15*, 321–361.

Sexually Violent Predator Act, K.S.A. §§ 59–29a01 et seq. (1994).

Shapiro, D. (1999). *Neurotic styles*. New York: Basic Books.

Sharkey, J. (1999, Dec. 19). Word for word/mental disorders: Defining the line between behavior that's vexing and certifiable. *The New York Times*. Retrieved June 1, 2013 from http://www.nytimes.com/1999/12/19/weekinreview/word-for-word-mental-disorders-defining-line-between-behavior-that-s-vexing.html.

Shaw, C. R., & McKay, H. D. (1942). *Juvenile delinquency and urban areas: A study of rates of delinquents in relation to differential characteristics of local communities in American cities*. Chicago, IL: University of Chicago Press.

Shawyer, F., Mackinnon, A., Farhall, J., Sims, E., Blaney, S., Yardley, P., Daly, M., Mullen, P., & Copolov, D. (2008). Acting on harmful command hallucinations in psychotic disorders. *Journal of Nervous and Mental Disease, 196*, 390–398.

Shenal, B. V., Harrison, D. W., & Demaree, H. A. (2003). The neuropsychology of depression: A literature review and preliminary model. *Neuropsychology Review, 13*(1), 33–42.

Shepherd, M. (1961). Morbid jealousy: A psychiatric syndrome. *Journal of Mental Science, 107*, 687–753.

Shipley, S., & Arrigo, B. A. (2001). The confusion over psychopathy (II): Implications for forensic (correctional) practice. *International Journal of Offender Therapy and Comparative Criminology, 45*(4), 407–420.

Shoal, G. D., Giancola, P. R., & Kilrillova, G. P. (2003). Salivary cortisol, personality, and aggressive behavior in adolescent boys: A 5-year longitudinal study. *Child and Adolescent Psychiatry and Mental Health, 42*, 1101–1107.

Shore, D., Filson, C. R., & Rae, D. S. (1990). Violent crime arrest rates of White House case subjects and matched control subjects. *American Journal of Psychiatry, 147*, 746–750.

Short, T. B., Thomas, S., Luebbers, S., Mullen, P., & Ogloff, J. R. (2013). A case-linkage study of crime victimization in schizophrenia-spectrum disorders over a period of deinstitutionalization. *BMC Psychiatry, 13*(1), 66.

Sidiropoulou, K., Diamantis, A., & Magiorkinis, E. (2010). Hallmarks in 18th- and 19th-century epilepsy research. *Epilepsy & Behavior, 18*, 151–161.

Siegel, D. M. (2008). Involuntary psychotropic medication to competence: No longer an easy sell. *Michigan State University Journal of Medicine & Law, 12*, 1–16.

Silva, J. A., Ferrari, M. M., & Leong, G. B. (2002). The case of Jeffrey Dahmer: Sexual serial homicide from a neuropsychiatric developmental perspective. *Journal of Forensic Sciences, 47*(6), 1–13.

Silva, J. A., Ferrari, M. M., & Leong, G. B. (2003). Asperger's disorder and the origins of the Unabomber. *American Journal of Forensic Psychiatry, 24*(2), 5–43.

Silva, J. A., Leong, G. B., & Ferrari, M. M. (2004). A neuropsychiatric developmental model of serial homicidal behavior. *Behavioral Sciences and the Law, 22*, 787–799.

Silva, J. A., Leong, G. B., Smith, R. L., Hawes, E., & Ferrari, M. M. (2005). Analysis of serial homicide in the case of Joel Rifkin using the neuropsychiatric developmental model. *American Journal of Forensic Psychiatry, 26*(4), 25–55.

Silver, E., Cirincione, C., & Steadman, H. J. (1994). Demythologizing inaccurate perceptions of the insanity defense. *Law and Human Behavior, 18*, 63–70.

Silver, H., Goodman, C., Knoll, G., Isakov, V., & Modai, I. (2005). Schizophrenia patients with a history of severe violence differ from nonviolent schizophrenia patients in perception of emotions but not cognitive function. *Journal of Clinical Psychiatry, 66*, 300–308.

Simblett, G. J., & Wilson, D. N. (1993). Asperger's syndrome: Three cases and a discussion. *Journal of Intellectual Disability Research. 37*, 85–94.

Simon, R. J. (1967). *The jury and the defense of insanity*. Boston, MA: Little, Brown.

Simourd, D. J., & Malcolm, P. B. (1998). Reliability and validity of the Level of Service Inventory-Revised among federally incarcerated sex offenders. *Journal of Interpersonal Violence, 13*(2), 261–274.

Simpson, G., Blaszczynski, A., & Hodgkinson, A. (1999). Sex offending as a psychosocial sequel of traumatic brain injury. *Journal of Head Trauma Rehabilitation, 14*(6), 567–580.

Simpson, M. (2003). The relationship between drug use and crime: A puzzle inside an enigma. *International Journal of Drug Policy, 14*, 307–319.

Singh, J. P., Grann, M., & Fazel, S. (2011). A comparative study of violence risk assessment tools: A systematic review and metaregression analysis of 68 studies involving 25,980 participants. *Clinical Psychology Review, 31*(3), 499–513.

Singh, J. P., Grann, M., Lichtenstein, P., Långström, N., & Fazel, S. (2012). A novel approach to determining violence risk in schizophrenia: Developing a stepped strategy in 13,806 discharged patients. *PLoS ONE, 7*(2), e31727.

Siponmaa, L., Kristiansson, M., Jonson, C., Nydén, A., & Gillberg, C. (2001). Juvenile and young adult mentally disordered offenders: The role of child neuropsychiatric disorders. *Journal of the American Academy of Psychiatry and the Law, 29*, 420–426.

Skeem, J. L., Manchak, S., & Peterson, J. K. (2010). Correctional policy for offenders with mental illness: Creating a new paradigm for recidivism reduction. *Law and Human Behavior, 35*, 110–126.

Slate, R. N. (2009). Seeking alternatives to the criminalization of mental illness. *American Jails, 23*(1), 20–28.

Slate, R. N., & Johnson, W. W. (2008). *The criminalization of mental illness: Crisis and opportunity for the justice system*. Durham, NC: Carolina Academic Press.

Slate, R. N., Roskes, E., Feldman, R., & Baerga, M. (2003). Doing justice for mental illness and society: Federal probation and pretrial services officers as mental health specialists. *Federal Probation, 67(3)*, 13–19.

Sloan, K. (2011, Nov. 28). New York Law and John Jay to offer joint degree in law and forensic psychology. *National Law Journal.* Retrieved from http://www.law.com/jsp/nlj/PubArticleNLJ.jsp?id=1202533681232.

Slobogin, C. (1985). The guilty but mentally ill verdict: An idea whose time should not have come. *George Washington Law Review, 53*, 494–527.

Slobogin, C. (2000). An end to insanity: Recasting the role of mental disability in criminal cases. *Virginia Law Review, 86*, 1199–1247.

Slobogin, C. (2003a). The interactionist alternative to the insanity defense: Reflections on the exculpatory scope of mental illness in the wake of the Andrea Yates trial. *American Journal of Criminal Law, 30*, 315–341.

Slobogin, C. (2003b). Rethinking legally relevant mental disorder. *Ohio Northern University Law Review, 29*, 497–530.

Slobogin, C. (2006). *Minding justice*. Cambridge, MA: Harvard University Press.

Smallbone, S., & Wortley, R. (2004). Criminal diversity and paraphilic interests among adult males convicted of sexual offenses against children. *International Journal of Offender Therapy and Comparative Criminology, 48*(2), 175–188.

Smith, A. D. (1999). Aggressive sexual fantasy in men with schizophrenia who commit contact sex offences against women. *Journal of Forensic Psychiatry, 10*(3), 538–52.

Smith, A. D. (2000). Motivation and psychosis in schizophrenic men who sexually assault women. *Journal of Forensic Psychiatry, 11*(1), 62–73.

Smith, A. D., & Taylor, P. J. (1999a). Serious sex offending against women by men with schizophrenia. *British Journal of Psychiatry, 174*, 233–237.

Smith, A. D., & Taylor, P. J. (1999b). Social and sexual functioning in schizophrenic men who commit serious sex offences against women. *Criminal Behaviour and Mental Health, 9*, 156–167.

Smith, G. A., & Hall, J. A. (1982). Evaluating Michigan's guilty but mentally ill verdict: an empirical study. *University of Michigan Journal of Law Reform, 16*, 77–114.

Smith, R. S. (1976). Voyeurism: A review of the literature. *Archives of Sexual Behavior, 5*(6), 585–608.

Solomon, A., Osborne, J., LoBuglio, S., Mellow, J., & Mukamal, D. (2008, May). *Life after lockup: Improving reentry from jail to the community*. Washington, DC: Urban Institute, Justice Policy Center. Retrieved from http://www.ncjrs.gov/pdffiles1/bja/220095.pdf.

Solomon, P. L., Cavanaugh, M. M., & Gelles, R. J. (2005). Family violence among adults with severe mental illness. *Trauma, Violence, and Abuse, 6*, 40–54.

Solomon, P. L., & Draine, J. (1999). Explaining lifetime criminal arrests among clients of a psychiatric probation and parole service. *Journal of the Academy of Psychiatry and the Law, 27*(2), 239–251.

Sommers, I., Baskin, D., & Baskin-Sommers, A. (2006). Methamphetamine use among young adults: Health and social consequences. *Addictive Behaviors, 31*, 1469–1476.

Sonsteng, J. O., Ward, D., Bruce, C., & Petersen, M. (2007). A legal education renaissance: A practical approach for the twenty-first century. *William Mitchell Law Review, 34*, 303–472.

Sorensen, J. R., Cunningham, M. D., Vigen, M. P., & Woods, S. O. (2011). Serious assaults on prison staff: A descriptive analysis. *Journal of Criminal Justice, 39*, 143–150.

Soriano-Mas, C., Hernández-Ribas, R., Pujol, J., Urretavizcaya, M., Deus, J., Harrison, B. J., Ortiz, H., López-Solà, M., Menchón, J. M., & Cardoner, N. (2011). Cross-sectional and longitudinal assessment of structural brain alterations in melancholic depression. *Biological Psychiatry, 69*, 318–325.

Soyka, M., Graz, C., Bottlender, R., Dirschedl, P., & Schoech, H. (2007). Clinical correlates of later violence and criminal offences in schizophrenia. *Schizophrenia Research, 94*, 89–98.

Spaans, M., Barendregt, M., Haan, B., Nijman, H., & de Beurs, E. (2011). Diagnosis of antisocial personality disorder and criminal responsibility. *International Journal of Law and Psychiatry, 34*(5), 374–378.

Spalletta, G., Troisi, A., Alimenti, S., di Michele, F., Pau, F., Pasini, A., & Caltagirone, C. (2001). Reduced prefrontal cognitive activation associated with aggression in schizophrenia. *Schizophrenia Research, 50*(1–2), 134–135.

Speltz, M. L., DeKlyen, M., Calderon, R., Greenberg, M. T., & Fisher, P. A. (1999). Neuropsychological characteristics and test behaviors of boys with early onset conduct problems. *Journal of Abnormal Psychology, 108*(2), 315–325.

Spunt, B., Brownstein, H., Goldstein, P., Fendrich, M., & Liberty, H. J. (1995). Drug use by homicide offenders. *Journal of Psychoactive Drugs, 27*(2), 125–134.

Stambor, Z. (2006). Psychology's prescribing pioneers. *Monitor on Psychology, 37*, 30–33.

Stanfield, A. C., McIntosh, A. M., Spencer, M. D., Philip, R., Gaur, S., & Lawrie, S. M. (2008). Towards a neuroanatomy of autism: A systematic review and meta-analysis of structural magnetic resonance imaging findings. *European Psychiatry, 23*, 289–299.

State v. Bethel, 66 P.3d 840 (Kan. 2003).

State v. Breakiron, 532 A.2d 199 (N.J. 1987).

State v. Crenshaw, 659 P.2d 488 (Wash. 1983).

State v. Galloway, 628 A.2d 735 (N.J. 1993).

State v. Herrera, 895 P.2d 359 (Utah 1995).

State v. Korell, 690 P.2d 992 (Mont. 1984).

State v. Phipps, 883 S.W.2d 138 (Tenn. Crim. App. 1994).

State v. Searcy, 798 P.2d 914 (Idaho 1990).

State v. Worlock, 569 A.2d 1314 (N.J. 1990).

Steadman, H. J., Cocozza, J. J., & Melick, M. E. (1978). Explaining the increased arrest rates among mental patients. *American Journal of Psychiatry, 135*, 816–820.

Steadman, H. J., Monahan, J., Duffee, B., Hartstone, E., & Robbins, P. C. (1993). *Before and after Hinckley: Evaluating insanity defense reform.* New York: The Guildford Press.

Steadman, H. J., Osher, F. C., Robbins, P. C., Case, B., & Samuels, S. (2009). Prevalence of serious mental illness among jail inmates. *Psychiatric Services, 60*, 761–765.

Stein, M. L., Schlesinger, L. B., & Pinizzotto, J. (2010). Necrophilia and sexual homicide. *Journal of Forensic Sciences, 55*(2), 443–446.

Stein, N. L., Hernandez, M. W., & Trabasso, T. (2008). Advances in modeling emotion and thought: The importance of developmental, online, and multilevel analysis. In M. Lewis, J. M. Haviland-Jones, & L. F. Barrett (Eds.), *Handbook of emotions* (3rd ed., pp. 574–586). New York: Guilford.

Steinwachs, D. M., Kasper, J. D., & Skinner, E. A. (1992). Family perspectives on meeting the needs for care of severely mentally ill relatives: A national survey. Arlington, VA: National Alliance for the Mentally Ill.

Stelmack, R. M., & Stalikas, A. (1991). Galen and the humour theory of temperament. *Personality and Individual Differences, 12*(3), 255–263.

Stephey, M. J. (2007, August 16). De-criminalizing mental illness. *Time*. Retrieved from http://www.time.com/time/health/article/0,8599,1651002,00.html.

Steury, E. H., & Choinski, M. (1995). "Normal" crimes and mental disorder: A two-group comparison of deadly and dangerous felonies. *International Journal of Law and Psychiatry, 18*(2), 183–207.

Stevens, E. H., & Pullen, R. L. (2005). Access to civil commitment proceedings and records in Alabama: Balancing privacy rights and the presumption of openness. *Jones Law Review, 9*, 1–35.

Stinson, J. D., Becker, J. V., & Tromp, S. (2005). A preliminary study on findings of psychopathy and affective disorders in adult sex offenders. *International Journal of Law and Psychiatry, 28*, 637–649.

Stokes, M., & Newton, N. (2004). Autistic spectrum disorders and stalking. *Autism, 8*, 337–339.

Stone, E. M. (Ed.). (1988). *American psychiatric glossary* (6th ed.). Washington, DC: American Psychiatric Press.

Stone, M. H. (1989). Murder. *Psychiatric Clinics of North America, 12*, 643–651.

Stone, M. H. (1990). *The fate of borderline patients.* New York: Guilford Press.

Stone, M. H. (1998). The personalities of murderers: The importance of psychopathy and sadism. In A. E. Skodol (Ed.), *Psychopathology and violent crime* (pp. 29–52). Washington DC: American Psychiatric Press, Inc.

Strakowski, S. M., & DelBello, M. P. (2000). The co-occurrence of bipolar and substance use disorders. *Clinical Psychological Review, 20*(2), 191–206.

Strakowski, S. M., DelBollo, M. P., & Adler, C. M. (2005). The functional neuroanatomy of bipolar disorder: A review of neuroimaging findings. *Molecular Psychiatry, 10*, 105–116.

Strakowski, S. M., Eliassen, J. C., Lamy, M., Cerullo, M. A., Allendorfer, J. B., Madore, M., Lee, J. H., Welge, J. A., DelBollo, M. P., Fleck, D. E., & Alder, C. M. (2011). Functional magnetic resonance imaging brain activation in bipolar mania: Evidence for disruption of the ventrolateral prefrontal-amygdala emotional pathway. *Biological Psychiatry, 69*, 381–388.

Strous, R. D., Bark, N., Parsia, S. S., Volavka, J., & Lachman, H. M. (1997). Analysis of a functional catechol-*O*-methyltransferase gene polymorphism in schizophrenia: Evidence for association with aggressive and antisocial behavior. *Psychiatry Research, 69*, 71–77.

Strubel, A. (2007). Jeffrey Dahmer: His complicated, comorbid psychopathologies and treatment implications. *The New School Psychology Bulletin, 5*(1), 41–58.

Stuart, G. L., Moore, T. M., Coop Gordon, K., Ramsey, S. E., & Kahler, C. W. (2006). Psychopathology in women arrested for domestic violence. *Journal of Interpersonal Violence, 21*(3), 376–389.

Stuart, G. L., Moore, T. M., Ramsey, S. E., & Kahler, C. W. (2003). Relationship aggression and substance use among women court-referred to domestic violence intervention programs. *Addictive Behaviors, 28*, 1603–1610.

Stuart, H. L., & Arboleda-Flórez, J. E. (2001). A public health perspective on violent offenses among persons with mental illness. *Psychiatric Services, 52*(5), 654–659.

Sugai, K. (1999). A case of schizophrenia with a "dream occurrence" episode as "arrest coloring" in a prisoner after committing matricide. *Seishin Igaku (Clinical Psychiatry), 41*(4), 429–431.

Sullivan, E. A., & Kosson, D. S. (2006). Ethnic and cultural variations in psychopathy. In C. J. Patrick (Ed.), *Handbook of psychopathy* (pp. 437–458). New York: The Guilford Press.

Sullivan, J. T. (2000). The culpability or *mens rea* "defense" in Arkansas. *Arkansas Law Review, 53*, 805–884.

Sullivan, S., Brown, R., & Skinner, B. (2008). Pathological and subclinical problem gambling in a New Zealand prison: A comparison of the Eight and SOGS gambling screens. *International Journal of Mental Health And Addiction, 6*(3), 369–377.

Surette, R. (2011). *Media, crime, and criminal justice: Images, realities, and policies.* 4th ed. Belmont, CA: Thomson Wadsworth.

Sutherland, E. (1947). *Principles of criminology* (4th ed). New York, NY: Harper & Row, Publishers, Inc.

Swann, A. C. (1999). Treatment of aggression in patients with bipolar disorder. *Journal of Clinical Psychiatry, 60*(Suppl. 15), 25–28.

Swann, A. C., Stokes, P. E., Secunda, S. K., Maas, J. W., Bowden, C. L., Berman, N., & Koslow, S. H. (1994). Depressive mania versus agitated depression: Biogenic amine and hypothalamic-pituitary-adrenocortical function. *Biological Psychiatry, 35*, 803–813.

Swann, S. C., Gambone, L. J., Fields, A. M., Sullivan, T. P., & Snow, D. L. (2005). Women who use violence in intimate relationships: The role of anger, victimization, and symptoms of posttraumatic stress and depression. *Violence and Victims, 20*(3), 267–285.

Swanson, J. W. (1994). Mental disorder, substance abuse, and community violence: An epidemiological approach. In J. Monahan & H. Steadman (Eds.), *Violence and mental disorder: Developments in risk assessment* (pp. 101–136). Chicago, IL: University of Chicago Press.

Swanson, J. W., Borum, R., Swartz, M. S., & Monahan, J. (1996). Psychotic symptoms and disorders and risk of violent behaviour in the community. *Criminal Behaviour and Mental Health, 6*, 309–329.

Swanson, J. W., Holzer, C. E., III, Ganju, V. K., & Jono, R. T. (1990). Violence and psychiatric disorder in the community: Evidence from the epidemiological catchment area surveys. *Hospital and Community Psychiatry, 41*, 761–770.

Swanson, J. W., Swartz, M. S., Borum, R., Hiday, V. A., Wagner, H. R., & Burns, B. J. (2000). Involuntary out-patient commitment and reduction of violent behaviour in persons with severe mental illness. *The British Journal of Psychiatry, 176*, 324–331.

Swanson, J. W., Swartz, M. S., Van Dorn, R. A., Elbogen, E. B., Wagner, H. R., Rosenbeck, R. A., Stroup, T. S., McEvoy, J. P., & Lieberman, J. A. (2006). A national study of violent behavior in persons with schizophrenia. *Archives of General Psychiatry, 63*, 490–499.

Swartz, M. S., Wilder, C. M., Swanson, J. W., Van Dorn, R. A., Robbins, P. C., Steadman, H. J., Moser, L. L., Gilbert, A. R., & Monahan, J. (2010). Assessing outcomes for consumers in New York's assisted outpatient treatment program. *Psychiatric Services, 61*(10), 976–981.

Szabo, L. (2013, Jan. 7). Committing a mentally ill adult is complex. *USA Today*. Retrieved from http://www.usatoday.com/story/news/nation/2013/01/07/mental-illness-civil-commitment/1814301/

Szasz, T. S. (1961). *The myth of mental illness: Foundations of a theory of personal conduct*. New York, NY: Paul B. Hoeber.

Szasz, T. S. (1994). Mental illness is still a myth. *Society, 31*(May-June), 34–39.

Szondi, L. (1968). A letter to Theodor Reik (1968). *American Imago, 25*(1), 21–26.

Szymusik, A. (1972). Studies on the psychopathology of murderers. *Polish Medical Journal, 11*(3), 752–757.

Taft, C. T., Vogt, D. S., Marshall, A. D., Panuzio, J., & Niles, B. L. (2007). Aggression among combat veterans: Relationships with combat exposure and symptoms of posttraumatic stress disorder, dysphoria, and anxiety. *Journal of Traumatic Stress, 20*(2), 135–145.

Talbot, J., & Riley, C. (2007). No one knows: Offenders with learning difficulties and learning disabilities. *British Journal of Learning Disabilities, 35*, 154–161.

Talbott, J. A. (1982). Twentieth-century developments in American psychiatry. *Psychiatric Quarterly, 54*, 207–219.

Talih, F. R. (2013). Kleptomania and potential exacerbating factors: A review and case report. *Innovations in Clinical Neuroscience, 8*(10), 35–39.

Tanay, E. (1973). Adolescents who kill parents: Reactive parricide. *Australian and New Zealand Journal of Psychiatry, 7*(4), 263–277.

Tanay, E. (1976). Reactive parricide. *Journal of Forensic Sciences, 21*(1), 76–82.

Tanielian, T., & Jaycox, L. H. (2008). *Invisible wounds of war: Psychological and cognitive injuries, their consequences, and services to assist recovery*. Santa Monica, CA: RAND Corporation.

Tannenbaum, F. (1938). *Crime and the community*. New York, NY: Columbia University Press.

Tantam, D. (1988a). Lifelong eccentricity and social isolation. I. Psychiatric, social, and forensic aspects. *British Journal of Psychiatry, 153*, 777–782.

Tantam, D. (1988b). Lifelong eccentricity and social isolation. II. Asperger's syndrome or schizoid personality disorder? *British Journal of Psychiatry, 153*, 783–791.

Tapert, S. F., Tate, S. R., & Brown, S. A. (2001). Substance abuse: An overview. In P. B. Sutker & H. E. Adams (Eds.), *Comprehensive handbook of psychopathology* (3rd ed., pp. 559–594). New York: Kluwer Academic/Plenum Publishers.

Tardiff, K. (1984). Characteristics of assaultive patients in private hospitals. *American Journal of Psychiatry, 141*, 1232–1235.

Tardiff, K. (1999). Prediction of violence. In K. Tardiff (Ed.), *Management of the violent patient* (pp. 201–218). New York: Marcel Dekker.

Tardiff, K. (2007). Violence: Psychopathology, risk assessment and lawsuits. In A. R. Felthous & H. Saß (Eds.), *International handbook of psychopathic disorders and the law* (Vol. 1, pp. 117–133). West Sussex, England: John Wiley & Sons, Ltd.

Tardiff, K., & Koenigsberg, H. W. (1985). Assaultive behavior among psychiatric outpatients. *American Journal of Psychiatry, 142*, 960–963.

Tardiff, K., Marzuk, P., Lowell, K., Portera, L., & Leon, A. (2002). A study of drug abuse and other causes of homicide in New York. *Journal of Criminal Justice, 30*, 317–325.

Taylor, P. J. (1985). Motives for offending among violent and psychotic men. *British Journal of Psychiatry, 147*, 491–498.

Taylor, P. J. (1986). Psychiatric disorder in London's life-sentenced offenders. *British Journal of Criminology, 26*(1), 63–78.

Taylor, P. J. (1993). Schizophrenia and crime: Distinctive patterns in association. In S. Hodgins (Ed.), *Mental disorder and crime* (pp. 63–85). Newbury Park, CA: Sage.

Taylor, P. J. (1998). Disorders of volition: Forensic aspects. In C. Williams & A. Simms (Eds.), *Disorders of volition and action in psychiatry* (pp. 66–84). Leeds: Leeds University Press.

Taylor, P. J. (2006). Delusional disorder and delusions: Is there a risk of violence in social interactions about the core symptom? *Behavioral Sciences and the Law, 24*, 313–331.

Taylor, P. J., Garety, P., Buchanan, A., Reed, A., Wessely, S., Ray, K., Dunn, G., & Grubin, D. (1994). Delusions and violence. In J. Monahan & H. Steadman (Eds.), *Violence and mental disorder: Developments in risk assessment* (pp. 161–182). Chicago: Chicago University Press.

Taylor, P. J., & Gunn, J. (1984). Violence and psychosis: I—Risk of violence among psychotic men. *British Medical Journal, 288*, 1945–1949.

Taylor, P. J., & Gunn, J. (1999). Homicides by people with mental illness: Myth and reality. *British Journal of Psychiatry, 174*, 9–14.

Taylor, P. J., Leese, M., Williams, D., Butwel, M., Daly, R., & Larkin, E. (1998). Mental disorder and violence: A special (high security) hospital study. *British Journal of Psychiatry, 172*(3), 218–226.

Taylor, S., Lambeth, D., Green, G., Bone, R., & Cahillane, M. A. (2012). Cluster analysis examination of serial killer profiling categories: A bottom-up approach. *Journal of Investigative Psychology and Offender Profiling, 9*, 30–51.

Teasdale, B. (2009). Mental disorder and violent victimization. *Criminal Justice and Behavior, 36*(5), 513–535.

Templer, G. I., Kaiser, G., & Siscoe, K. (1993). Correlates of pathological gambling propensity in prison inmates. *Comprehensive Psychiatry, 34*, 347–351.

Tengström, A., Hodgins, S., Grann, M., Langström, N., & Kullgren, G. (2004). Schizophrenia and criminal offending: The role of psychopathy and substance use disorders. *Criminal Justice and Behavior, 31*(4), 367–391.

Teplin, L. A. (1984). Managing disorder: Police handling of the persons with mental illnesses. In L. Teplin (Ed.), *Mental health and criminal justice* (pp. 157–175). Beverly Hills, CA: Sage.

Teplin, L. A. (1990a). Criminalizing mental disorder: The comparative arrest rate of the mentally ill. *American Psychologist, 39*, 794–803.

Teplin, L. A. (1990b). The prevalence of severe mental disorder among male urban jail detainees: Comparison with the Epidemiologic Catchment Area Program. *American Journal of Public Health, 80*(6), 663–669.

Teplin, L. A. (1994). Psychiatric and substance abuse disorders among male urban jail detainees. *American Journal of Public Health, 84*(2), 290–293.

Teplin, L. A., Abram, K. M., McClelland, G. M., Dulcan, M. K., & Mericle, A. A. (2002). Psychiatric disorders in youth in juvenile detention. *Archives of General Psychiatry, 59*, 1133–1143.

Teplin, L. A., & Pruett, N. S. (1992). Police as street corner psychiatrist: Managing the mentally ill. *International Journal of Law and Psychiatry, 15*,139–156.

Thapar, A., van den Bree, M., Fowler, T., Langley, K., & Whittinger, N. (2006). Predictors of antisocial behavior in children with attention deficit hyperactivity disorder. *European Child and Adolescent Psychiatry, 15*, 118–125.

Theurer, G., & Lovell, D. (2008). Recidivism of offenders with mental illness released from prison to an intensive community treatment program. *Journal of Offender Rehabilitation, 47*(4), 385–406.

Thompson, M., Osher, F. C., & Tomasini-Joshi, D. (2008). *Improving responses to people with mental illnesses: The essential elements of a mental health court.* New York, NY: Council of State Governments Justice Center.

Thompson, M. D., Reuland, M., & Souweine, D. (2003). Criminal justice/mental health consensus: Improving responses to people with mental illness. *Crime & Delinquency, 49*(1), 31–50.

Thorneloe, W. F., & Crews, E. L. (1981). Manic depressive illness concomitant with antisocial personality disorder: Six case reports and review of the literature. *Journal of Clinical Psychiatry, 42*(1), 5–9.

Tiffin, P., Shah, R., & le Coutieur, A. (2007). Diagnosing pervasive developmental disorder in a forensic adolescent mental health setting. *The British Journal of Forensic Practice, 9*(3), 31–40.

Tiihonen, J., Isohanni, M., Raesaenen, P., Koiranen, M., & Moring, J. (1997). Specific major mental disorders and criminality: A 26-year prospective study of the 1996 Northern Finland Birth Cohort. *American Journal of Psychiatry, 154*, 840–845.

Tomkins, A. J., & Ogloff, J. R. P. (1990). Training and career options in psychology and law. *Behavioral Sciences & the Law, 8*(3), 205–216.

Torrey, E. F. (2011). Criminalization of individuals with severe psychiatric disorders. *Mental Illness Policy Org.* Retrieved from http://mentalillnesspolicy.org/consequences/criminalization.html.

Torrey, E. F., Kennard, A. D., Eslinger, D., Lamb, R., & Pavle, J. (2010). *More mentally ill persons are in jails and prisons than hospitals: A survey of the states.* Arlington, VA: National Sheriffs' Association, Treatment Advocacy Center. Retrieved from http://treatmentadvocacycenter.org/storage/documents/final_jails_v_hospitals_study.pdf.

Torrey, E. F., Stieber, J., Ezekiel, J., Wolfe, S. M., Sharfstein, J., Noble, J. H., & Flynn, L. M. (1992). *Criminalizing the seriously mentally ill.* Washington, DC: National Alliance for the Mentally Ill and Public Citizen Health Research.

Treatment Advocacy Center. (2012). Assisted outpatient treatment laws. *Treatment Advocacy* Center. http://www.treatmentadvocacycenter.org/solution/assisted-outpatient-treatment-laws.

Trestman, R., Ford, J., Zhang, W., & Wiesbrock, V. (2007). Current and lifetime psychiatric illness among inmates not identified as acutely mentally ill at intake in Connecticut's jails. *Journal of the American Academy of Psychiatry and the Law, 35*, 490–500.

Trupin, E., & Richards, H. (2003). Seattle's mental health courts: Early indicators of effectiveness. *International Journal of Law and Psychiatry, 26*(1), 33–53.

Tsalicoglou, F. (1988). Le matricide, paradis perdu du psychotique. *Revue Internationale de Criminologie et de Police Technique. 41*(3), 332–344.

Tsesis, A. (2011). Due process in civil commitments. *Washington and Lee Law Review, 68*, 253–307.

Turkat, D., & Buzzell, V. (1983). The relationship between family violence and hospital recidivism. *Hospital and Community Psychiatry, 34*(6), 552–553.

Turner, S. M., Beidel, D. C., Stanley, M. A., & Heiser, N. (2001). Obsessive-compulsive disorder. In P. B. Sutker & H. E. Adams (Eds.), *Comprehensive handbook of psychopathology* (3rd ed., pp. 155–182). New York: Kluwer Academic/Plenum Publishers.

Turvey, B. E. (2008). *Criminal profiling: An introduction to behavioral evidence analysis* (3rd ed.). New York: Elsevier.

Tyler, N., & Gannon, T. A. (2012). Explanations of fire setting in mentally disordered offenders: A review of the literature. *Psychiatry, 75*(2), 150–166.

United States v. Barajas-Torress, 2004 WL 1598914 (W. D. Tex. 2004).

United States v. Bilyk, 29 F.3d 459 (8th Cir. 1994).

United States v. Brawner, 471 F.2d 969, 981 (D.C. Cir. 1972).

United States v. Comstock, 560 U.S. 126 (2010).

United States v. Evans, 404 F.3d 227, 237 (4th Cir. 2005).

United States v. Garthus, 652 F.3d 715 (7th Cir. 2011).

United States v. Gomes, 387 F.3d. 157 (2nd Cir. 2004).

United States v. Kourey, 276 F. Supp. 2d. 580 (S.D. W.Va. 2003).

United States v. Loughner, 672 F.3d 731 (9th Cir. 2012).

United States v. Loyola-Dominguez, 125 F.3d 1315 (9th Cir. 1997).

United States v. Lyons, 731 F.2d 243 (5th Cir.), *cert. denied*, 469 U.S. 930 (1984).

United States v. McBroom, 124 F.3d 533 (3d Cir. 1997).

United States v. Murdoch, 98 F.3d 472 (9th Cir. 1996), *cert. denied*, 521 U.S. 1122 (1997).

United States v. Prescott, 920 F.2d 139 (2d Cir. 1990).

United States v. Salava, 978 F.2d 320 (7th Cir. 1992).

United States v. Shlater, 85 F.3d 1251 (7th Cir. 1996).

United States v. Tracy, 36 F.3d 187 (1st Cir. 1994).

United States v. Valenzuela-Puentes, 479 F.3d 1220 (10th Cir. 2007).

Unites States v. White, 620 F.3d 401 (4th Cir. 2010).

Vachon, D. D., Lynam, D. R., Widiger, T. A., Miller, J. D., McCrae, R. R., & Costa, P. T. (2013). Basic traits predict the prevalence of personality disorder across the lifespan: The example of psychopathy. *Psychological Science, 24*(5), 698–705.

Vago, S. (2009). *Law and society* (9th ed.). Upper Saddle River, NJ: Prentice Hall.

Van Dorn, R. A., Swanson, J. W., Swartz, M. S., Wilder, C. M., Moser, L. L., Gilbert, A. R., Cislo, A. M., & Robbins, P. C. (2010). Continuing medication and hospitalization outcomes after assisted outpatient treatment in New York. *Psychiatric Services, 61*(10), 982–987.

Van Dorn, R. A., Volavka, J., & Johnson, N. (2012). Mental disorder and violence: Is there a relationship beyond substance use? *Social Psychiatry and Psychiatric Epidemiology, 47*(3), 487–503.

Vandermeersch, P. (1991). The victory of psychiatry over demonology: The origin of the nineteenth-century myth. *History of Psychiatry, 2*, 351–363.

Varma, L. P., & Jha, B. K. (1966). Characteristics of murder in mental disorder. *American Journal of Psychiatry, 122*(11), 1296–1298.

Vars, F. E., & Young, A. A. (2013). Do the mentally ill have a right to bear arms? *Wake Forest Law Review, 48*, 1–24.

Venables, P. H., Raine, A., Dalais, C., Liu, J., & Mednick, S. A. (2006). Malnutrition, cognitive ability and schizotypy. In A. Raine (Ed.), *Crime and schizophrenia: Causes and cures* (pp. 131–150). New York: Nova Science Publishers, Inc.

Verheul, R. (2012). Personality disorder proposal for DSM-5: A heroic and innovative but nevertheless fundamentally flawed attempt to improve DSM-IV. *Clinical Psychology & Psychotherapy, 19*(5), 369–371.

Verona, E., & Vitale, J. (2006). Psychopathy in women: Assessment, manifestations, and etiology. In C. J. Patrick (Ed.), *Handbook of psychopathy* (pp. 415–436). New York: The Guilford Press.

Veysey, B. M., & Bichler-Robertson, G. (2002). Prevalence estimates of psychiatric disorders in correctional settings. In C. A. Hornung, B. Jaye Anno, R. B. Greifinger, S. Gadre (Eds.), *The health status of soon-to-be-released inmates: A report to Congress* (Vol. 2, pp. 57–80). Chicago, IL: National Commission on Correctional Health Care. Retrieved from http://www.ncchc.org/filebin/Health_Status_vol_2.pdf.

Viljoen, J. L., MacDougall, E. A. M., Gagnon, N. C., & Douzes, K. S. (2010). Psychopathy evidence in legal proceedings involving adolescent offenders. *Psychology, Public Policy, and Law, 16*(3), 254–283.

Viney, W., & Zorich, S. (1982). Contributions to the history of psychology XXIX: Dorothea Dix. *Psychological Reports, 50*, 211–218.

Virkkunen, M. (1974). On arson committed by schizophrenics. *Acta Psychiatrica Scandinavica, 50*, 152–160.

Vitacco, M. J., Caldwell, M. F., Van Rybroek, G. J., & Gabel, J. (2007). Psychopathy and behavioral correlates of victim injury in serious juvenile offenders. *Aggressive Behavior, 33*, 537–544.

Vitacco, M. J., & Rogers, R. (2009). The assessment of psychopathy and response styles in sex offenders. In F. M. Saleh, A. J. Grudzinskas, J. M. Bradford, & D. J. Brodsky (Eds.), *Sex offenders: Identification, risk assessment, treatment, and legal issues* (pp. 130–143). New York: Oxford University Press, Inc.

Vitale, J. E., & Newman, J. P. (2001). Using the Psychopathy Checklist-Revised with female samples: Reliability, validity, and implications for clinical utility. *Clinical Psychology: Science & Practice, 8*, 117–132.

Vitiello, M. (2010). Addressing the special problems of mentally ill prisoners: A small piece of the solution to our nation's prison crisis. *Denver University Law Review, 88*, 57–71.

Volavka, J. (1999). The neurobiology of violence: An update. *The Journal of Neuropsychiatry and Clinical Neurosciences, 11*(3), 307–314.

Volavka, J., & Citrome, L. (2011). Pathways to aggression in schizophrenia affect results of treatment. *Schizophrenia Bulletin, 37(5)*, 921–929.

Wahl, O. F. (1995). *Media madness: Public images of mental illness*. New Brunswick, NJ: Rutgers University Press.

Wahlund, K., & Kristiansson, M. (2006). Offender characteristics in lethal violence with special reference to antisocial and autistic personality traits. *Journal of Interpersonal Violence, 21*(8), 1081–1091.

Wakefield, J. C. (1992). The concept of mental disorder: On the boundary between biological facts and social values. *American Psychologist, 47*(3), 373–388.

Waldman, I. D., & Rhee, S. H. (2006). Genetic and environmental influences on psychopathy and antisocial behavior. In C. J. Patrick (Ed.), *Handbook of psychopathy* (pp. 205–228). New York: The Guilford Press.

Waldorf, D. (1998). Misadventures in the drug trade. *Substance Use & Misuse, 33*(9), 1957–1991.

Walker, L. E. A. (2009). *The battered woman syndrome* (3rd ed.). New York, NY: Springer Publishing Co.

Wallace, C., Mullen, P., Burgess, P., Palmer, S., Ruschena, D., & Browne, C. (1998). Serious criminal offending and mental disorder. *British Journal of Psychiatry, 172*, 477–484.

Wallisch, L. S., & Kerber, L. (2001). *Substance use and delinquency among youths entering Texas Youth Commission facilities, 2000–2001*. Austin: Texas Commission on Alcohol and Drug Abuse.

Walsh, A., & Wu, H. H. (2008). Differentiating antisocial personality disorder, psychopathy, and sociopathy: Evolutionary, genetic, neurological, and sociological considerations. *Criminal Justice Studies, 21*(2), 135–152.

Walsh, E., Buchanan, A., & Fahy, T. (2002). Violence and schizophrenia: Examining the evidence. *British Journal of Psychiatry, 180*, 490–495.

Walsh, Z., & Kosson, D. S. (2007). Psychopathy and violent crime: A prospective study of the influence of socioeconomic status and ethnicity. *Law and Human Behavior, 31*, 209–229.

Walters, G. D. (1997). Problem gambling in a federal prison population: Results from the South Oaks Gambling Screen. *Journal of Gambling Studies, 13*, 7–24.

Walters, G. D. (2012). Psychopathy and crime: Testing the incremental validity of PCL-R-measured psychopathy as a predictor of general and violent recidivism. *Law and Human Behavior, 36*(5), 404–412.

Walters, G. D., & Contri, D. (1998). Outcome expectancies for gambling: Empirical modeling of memory network in federal prison inmates. *Journal of Gambling Studies, 14*, 173–191.

Warner, T., & Kramer, J. (2009). Closing the revolving door? Substance abuse treatment as an alternative to traditional sentencing for drug-dependent offenders. *Criminal Justice and Behavior, 36*(1), 89–109.

Warren v. Schriro, 162 Fed. Appx. 705 (9th Cir. 2006).

Warren, J. I., Burnette, M. L., South, S. C., Chauhan P., Bale, R., & Friend, R. (2002). Personality disorders and violence among female prison inmates. *Journal of the American Academy of Psychiatry and the Law, 30*, 502–509.

Warren, J. I., Burnette, M. L., South, S. C., Chauhan P., Bale, R., Friend, R., & Van Patten, I. (2003). Psychopathy in women: Structural modeling and comorbidity. *International Journal of Law and Psychiatry, 26*, 223–242.

Warren, J. I., Murrie, D. C., Steskal, W., Colwell, L. H., Morris, J., Chauhan, P., & Dietz, P. (2006). Opinion formation in evaluating the adjudicative competence and restorability of criminal defendants: A review of 8,000 evaluations. *Behavioral Sciences and the Law, 24*(2), 113–132.

Warren, J. I., & South, S. C. (2006). Comparing the constructs of antisocial personality disorder and psychopathy in a sample of incarcerated women. *Behavioral Sciences and the Law, 24*, 1–20.

Washington v. Harper, 494 U.S. 210 (1990).

Watkins, J. G. (1984). The Bianchi (L.A. Hillside Strangler) case: Sociopath or multiple personality? *International Journal of Clinical and Experimental Hypnosis, 32*(2), 67–101.

Watson, A. C., Ottati, V. C., Morabito, M. S., Draine, J., Kerr, A. N., & Angell, B. (2010). Outcomes of police contacts with persons with mental illness: The impact of CIT. *Administration & Policy in Mental Health & Mental Health Services Research, 37*(4), 302–317.

Watson, J. B., & Rayner, R. (1920). Conditioned emotional reactions. *Journal of Experimental Psychology, 3*(1), 1–14.

Weber, M. (1954). *Law in economy and society*. (M. Rheinstein & E. Shils, Eds. & Trans.). Cambridge, MA: Harvard University Press.

Webster, C. D., Douglas, K. S., Eaves, D., & Hart, S. D. (1997). Assessing risk of violence to others. In C. D. Webster & M. A. Jackson (Eds.) *Impulsivity: Theory, assessment, and treatment* (pp. 251–177). New York, NY: Guildford Press.

Webster, C. D., Harris, G. T., Rice, M. E., Cormier, C., & Quinsey, V. L. (1994). *The violence prediction scheme – Assessing dangerousness in high risk men*. Toronto, ON: Centre of Criminology, University of Toronto.

Wechsler, H. (1955). The criteria of criminal responsibility. *University of Chicago Law Review, 22*, 367–376.

Weinstein, J. (1999). Coming of age: Recognizing the importance of interdisciplinary education in law practice. *Washington Law Review, 74*, 319–366.

Weizmann-Henelius, G., Sailas, E., Viermö, V., & Eronen, M. (2002). Violent women, blame attribution, crime, and personality. *Psychopathology, 35*, 355–361.

Wertham, F. (1937). The catathymic crisis: A clinical entity. *Archives of Neurology and Psychiatry, 37*(4), 974–978.

Wertham, F. (1941). The matricidal impulse. *Journal of Criminal Psychopathology, 2*, 455–464.

Wertham, F. (1949). *The show of violence*. Garden City, NY: Doubleday & Company, Inc.

Wertham, F. (1950). *Dark legend*. Garden City, NY: Doubleday & Company. (Original work published 1941)

Wessely, S., Buchanan, A., Reed, A., Cutting, J., Everitt, B., Garety, P., & Taylor, P. J. (1993). Acting on delusions I: Prevalence. *British Journal of Psychiatry, 163*, 69–76.

West, D. J. (1966). *Murder followed by suicide*. Cambridge, MA: Harvard University Press.

Westen, D. (1999). The scientific status of unconscious processes: Is Freud really dead? *Journal of the American Psychoanalytic Association, 47*, 1061–1106.

White, M. D., Mulvey, P., Fox, A. M., & Choate, D. (2012). A hero's welcome? Exploring the prevalence and problems of military veterans in the arrestee population. *Justice Quarterly, 29*(2), 258–286.

Whitman, T. A., & Akutagawa, D. (2004). Riddles in serial murder: A synthesis. *Aggression and Violent Behavior, 9*, 693–703.

Widiger, T. A. (1993). The DSM-III-R categorical personality disorder diagnoses: A critique and an alternative. *Psychological Inquiry, 4*(2), 75–90.

Wieter v. Settle, 193 F. Supp. 318 (W.D. Mo. 1961).

Wilcox, D. E. (1985). The relationship of mental illness to homicide. *American Journal of Forensic Psychiatry, 6*, 3–14.

Wilcox, D. E. (1987). Characteristics of seventy-one convicted murderers. *American Journal of Forensic Psychiatry, 7*, 48–52.

Wilkinson, D., Jones, T., & Caulfield, L. (2011). Time to reason about crime: Assessing the impact of schizotypal tendencies on a crime-based reasoning task. *The Howard Journal, 50*(4), 393–405.

Williams, R. J., Royston, J., & Hagen, B. F. (2005). Gambling and problem gambling within forensic populations: A review of the literature. *Criminal Justice and Behavior, 32*(6), 665–689.

Williamson, G. L. (1993). Postpartum depression syndrome as a defense against criminal behavior. *Journal of Family Violence, 8*(2), 151–165.

Williamson, S. E., Hare, R. D., & Wong, S. (1987). Violence: Criminal psychopaths and their victims. *Canadian Journal of Behavioral Science, 19*, 454–462.

Wilson, A. (2010). Disinhibition and narrative in the paraphilias. *Progress in Neuro-Psychopharmacology & Biological Psychiatry, 34*, 431.

Wilson, J. Q., & Herrnstein, R. (1985). *Crime and human nature*. New York: Simon and Schuster.

Wilt, J., Oehlberg, K., & Revele, W. (2011). Anxiety in personality. *Personality and Individual Differences, 50*, 987–993.

Wing, L. (1981). Asperger's syndrome: A clinical account. *Psychological Medicine, 11*, 115–119.

Winick, B. J. (1992). On autonomy: Legal and psychological perspectives. *Villanova Law Review, 37*, 1705–1777.

Winick, B. J. (1993). New directions in the right to refuse mental health treatment: The implications of *Riggins v. Nevada*. *William & Mary Bill of Rights Journal, 2*, 205–238.

Winick, B. J. (1995a). Ambiguities in the legal meaning and significance of mental illness. *Psychology, Public Policy, and Law, 1*, 534–611.

Winick, B. J. (1995b). Criminal law: Reforming incompetency to stand trial and plead guilty: A restated proposal and a response to Professor Bonnie. *Journal of Criminal Law and Criminology, 85*, 571–624.

Winick, B. J. (1999). Therapeutic jurisprudence and the civil commitment hearing. *Journal of Contemporary Legal Issues, 10*, 37–60.

Winick, B. J., & LaFond, J. Q. (2003). *Protecting society from sexually dangerous offenders: Law, justice, and therapy*. Washington, DC: American Psychological Association.

Wittels, F. (1937). The criminal psychopath in the psychoanalytic system. *Psychoanalytic Review, 24*(1), 276–291.

Wolff, N., Bjerklie, J. R., & Maschi, T. (2005). Reentry planning for mentally disordered inmates: A social investment perspective. *Journal of Offender Rehabilitation, 41*(2), 21–42.

Wolff, S. (1992). Psychiatric morbidity and criminality in 'schizoid' children grown up: A records survey. *European Child and Adolescent Psychiatry, 1*(4), 214–221.

Wolff, S., & Cull, A. (1986). "Schizoid" personality and antisocial conduct: A retrospective case note study. *Psychological Medicine, 16*, 677–687.

Wong, M. T. H., Fenwick, P. B. C., Lumsden, J., Fenton, G. W., Maisey, M. N., Lewis, P., & Badawi, R. (1997). Positron emission tomography in male violent offenders with schizophrenia. *Psychiatry Research: Neuroimaging Section, 68*, 111–123.

Wong, S. C. P., & Gordon, A. (2006). The validity and reliability of the Violence Risk Scale: A treatment-friendly violence risk assessment tool. *Psychology, Public Policy, and Law, 12*(3), 279–309.

Woo, B. K. P., Sevilla, C. C., & Obrocea, G. V. (2006). Factors influencing the stability of psychiatric diagnoses in the emergency setting. *General Hospital Psychiatry, 28*, 434–436).

Woodbury-Smith, M. R., Clare, I. C. H., Holland, A. J., & Kearns, A. (2006). High functioning autistic spectrum disorders, offending and other law-breaking: Findings from a community sample. *The Journal of Forensic Psychiatry and Psychology, 17*(1), 108–120.

Woodbury-Smith, M. R., Clare, I. C. H., Holland, A. J., Kearns, A., Staufenberg, E., & Watson, P. (2005). A case-control study of offenders with high functioning autistic spectrum disorders. *The Journal of Forensic Psychiatry and Psychology, 16*(4), 747–763.

Woodruff, R. A., Goodwin, D. W., & Guze, S. B. (1974). *Psychiatric diagnosis*. New York: Oxford University Press.

Woodworth, M., & Porter, S. (2002). In cold blood: Characteristics of criminal homicides as a function of psychopathy. *Journal of Abnormal Psychology, 111*(3), 436–445.

Wright, J. L. (2004). Protecting who from what, and why, and how?: A proposal for an integrative approach to adult protective proceedings. *Elder Law Journal, 12*, 53–118.

Wulach, J. S. (1983). Mania and crime: A study of 100 manic defendants. *Journal of the American Academy of Psychiatry and the Law, 11*(1), 69–75.

Yang, M., Wong, S. C. P., & Coid, J. (2010). The efficacy of violence prediction: A meta-analytic comparison of nine risk assessment tools. *Psychological Bulletin, 136*(5), 740–767.

Yang, Y., Glenn, A. L., & Raine, A. (2008). Brain abnormalities in antisocial individuals: Implications for the Law. *Behavioral Sciences and the Law, 26*, 65–83.

Yang Y., & Raine A. (2006) Functional and structural brain imaging research on psychopathy. In A. Felthous & H. Sass (Eds.), *International Handbook on Psychopathic Disorders and the Law* (pp. 69–82). West Sussex, England: John Wiley & Sons Ltd.

Yang, Y., Raine, A., Han, C., Schug, R. A., Toga, A. W., & Narr, K. L. (2010). Reduced hippocampus and parahippocampal volumes in murderers with schizophrenia. *Psychiatry Research: Neuroimaging, 182*, 9–13.

Yang, Y., Raine, A., Lencz, T., Bihrle, S., Lacasse, L., & Colletti, P. (2005a). Prefrontal structural abnormalities in liars. *British Journal of Psychiatry, 187*, 320–325.

Yang, Y., Raine, A., Lencz, T., Bihrle, S., Lacasse, L., & Colletti, P. (2005b). Volume reduction in prefrontal gray matter in unsuccessful criminal psychopaths. *Biological Psychiatry, 57*, 1103–1108.

Yarvis, R. M. (1990). Axis I and axis II diagnostic parameters of homicide. *Bulletin of the American Academy of Psychiatry and Law, 18*(3), 249–269.

Yates, K. F., Kunz, M., Khan, A., Volavka, J., & Rabinowitz, S. (2010). Psychiatric patients with histories of aggression and crime five years after discharge from a cognitive-behavioral program. *The Journal of Forensic Psychiatry and Psychology, 21*(2), 167–188.

Yee, N. Y. L., Large, M. M., Kemp, R. I., & Nielssen, O. B. (2011). Severe non-lethal violence during psychotic illness. *Australian and New Zealand Journal of Psychiatry, 45*, 466–472.

Yesavage, J. A. (1983). Bipolar illness: Correlates of dangerous inpatient behavior. *British Journal of Psychiatry, 143*, 554–557.

Yoshimasu, K., & Kawakami, N. (2011). Epidemiological aspects of intermittent explosive disorder in Japan; Prevalence and psychosocial comorbidity: Findings from the World Mental Health Japan Survey 2002–2006. *Psychiatry Research, 186*, 384–389.

Yung, C. R. (2011). Sex offender exceptionalism and preventive detention. *Journal of Criminal Law and Criminology*, *101*, 969–1003.

Zagar, R., Arbit, J., Hughes, J. R., Busell, R. E., & Busch, K. (1989). Developmental and disruptive behavior disorders among delinquents. *Journal of the American Academy of Child and Adolescent Psychiatry, 28*(3), 437–440.

Zanni, G., & deVeau, L. (1986). Inpatient stays before and after outpatient commitment. *Hospital and Community Psychiatry*, *37*, 941–942.

Zapf, P. A., Hubbard, K. L., Galloway, V. A., Cox, M., & Ronan, K. A. (2004). Have the courts abdicated their responsibility for determinations of competency to stand trial to clinicians? *Journal of Forensic Psychology Practice*, *4*, 27–44.

Zapf, P. A., & Roesch, R. (1998). Fitness to stand trial: Characteristics of remands since the 1992 criminal code amendments, *Canadian Journal of Psychiatry*, *43*, 287–293.

Zhou, S. Y., Suzuki, M., Hagino, H., Takahashi, T., Kawasaki, Y., Matsui, M., Seto, H., & Kurachi, M. (2005). Volumetric analysis of sulci/gyri-defined in vivo frontal lobe regions in schizophrenia: Precentral gyrus, cingulated gyrus, and prefrontal region. *Psychiatry Research: Neuroimaging, 139*, 127–139.

Ziff, K. (2004) Asylum and community: connections between the Athens Lunatic Asylum and the village of Athens, 1867–1893. Unpublished dissertation, Ohio University, Athens, USA.

Zilboorg, G. (1943). *Mind, medicine, & man.* New York, NY: Harcourt, Brace.

Zimmerman, M. (2012). Is there adequate empirical justification for radically revising the personality disorders section for DSM-5? *Personality Disorders: Theory, Research, and Treatment*, *3*(4), 444–457.

Zinermon v. Burch, 494 U.S. 113 (1990).

Zweben, J., Cohen, J., Christian, D., Galloway, G., Salinardi, M., Parent, D., & Iguchi, M. (2004). Psychiatric symptoms in methamphetamine users. *American Journal on Addiction, 13,* 181–190.

Index

Photo Credits

Chapter 1

Image source: AP Photo/NBC News, File *page 1*

Chapter 2

Image source: AP Photo *page 25*

Image source: iStock *page 30*

Image source: The Mayo Clinic *page 39*

Chapter 3

Image source: http://murderpedia.org/male.R/r/rifkin-joel-photos.htm *page 53*

Chapter 4

Image source: http://murderpedia.org/male.K/k/kasso-ricky.htm *page 154*

Chapter 5

Image source: http://en.wikipedia.org/wiki/Herbert_Mullin *page 161*

Images source: Pridmore (2006) *page 166, Box 5.1*

Image sources: Kraepelin (1919/2002); Curschmann (1894) *page 166, Box 5.2*

Image sources: (left) Freud (1923/1961); (right) http://medlibes.com/entry/dejerine-roussy-syndrome *page 169*

Chapter 6

Image source: ©AP Photo/Ventura Police Department *page 216*

Image source: © AP Photo/File *page 261*

Chapter 7

Image sources: (top) http://commons.wikimedia.org/wiki/File:Freud_hans.jpg; (bottom) http://cogpsy.info/learning/finding-little-albert/ *page 280*

Image source: AP Photo/Arkansas Department of Correction, File *page 297*

Chapter 8

Image source: AP Photo/Mark Elias *page 303*

Image sources: (A) http://en.wikipedia.org/wiki/Henry_Lee_Lucas; (B) http://www.allstarpics.net/pic-gallery/gordon-northcott-pics.htm; (C) http://en.wikipedia.org/wiki/Ottis_Toole; (D) http://law2.umkc.edu/faculty/projects/ftrials/manson/manson.html *page 319*

Image sources: (left) AP Photo/Michael Probst; (right) AP Photo/Polizei, HO *page 330*

Chapter 9

Image source: AP Photo *page 350*

Chapter 10

Image source: AP Photo *page 363*

Chapter 11

Image source: AP Photo/Pima County Sheriff's Dept. via *The Arizona Republic,* File *page 433*

Chapter 12

Image source: http://www.nsopw.gov *page 470*

About the Authors

Dr. Robert A. Schug earned a BA in psychology and an MS in forensic psychology at California State University, Los Angeles, and a second master's degree and PhD in psychology from the University of Southern California. He is currently Assistant Professor of Criminal Justice and Forensic Psychology in the Department of Criminal Justice at California State University, Long Beach. His area of specialization is the biology and psychology of the criminal mind. His research interests are predominantly focused upon understanding the relationship between extreme forms of psychopathology and antisocial, criminal, and violent behavior from a biopsychosocial perspective—with the application of advanced neuroscience techniques from areas such as neuropsychology, psychophysiology, and brain imaging. He is particularly interested in the etiological mechanisms, risk factors, and developmental progression of antisocial behavior within major mental disorders such as psychopathy and schizophrenia, as well as in the ability to predict antisocial behavioral outcomes within mentally ill individuals. It is his hope that a better understanding of the relationship between these disorders and antisociality will have important implications in research, treatment, and forensic arenas and will help to reduce the negative stigma often associated with mentally ill individuals who are not criminal or violent, while contributing to more effective treatment and management strategies for those who are. A seasoned writer, Dr. Schug has published numerous articles in prominent psychiatric, psychological, criminal justice, and neuroscience journals. And he has both authored and co-authored book chapters for several successful texts in forensic psychology, criminology, and the neurosciences.

Henry F. Fradella earned a BA in psychology from Clark University, a master's in forensic science and a law degree from The George Washington University, and a PhD in interdisciplinary justice studies from Arizona State University. He is currently a professor in and associate director of the School of Criminology and Criminal Justice at Arizona State University. His area of specialization is the social scientific study of courts and law. This includes research and teaching on the historical development of substantive, procedural, and evidentiary criminal law (including the courtroom acceptability of forensic and social scientific evidence, especially forensic psychological/psychiatric testimony); evaluation of law's effects on human behavior; the dynamics of legal decision making; and the nature, sources, and consequences of variations and changes in legal institutions or processes. He is the author or co-author of 8 books and 75 articles, reviews, and scholarly commentaries that have appeared in various periodicals, including *American Journal of Criminal Law*, *Criminal Justice Policy Review*, *Criminal Law Bulletin*, *Journal of Contemporary Criminal Justice*, *Journal of Criminal Justice Education*, *Journal of Ethnicity in Criminal Justice*, *Journal of Law and Public Policy*, *Journal of Law and Sexuality*, *The Justice Systems Journal*, *Law and Psychology Review*, *The Prison Journal*, and *Western Criminology Review*.

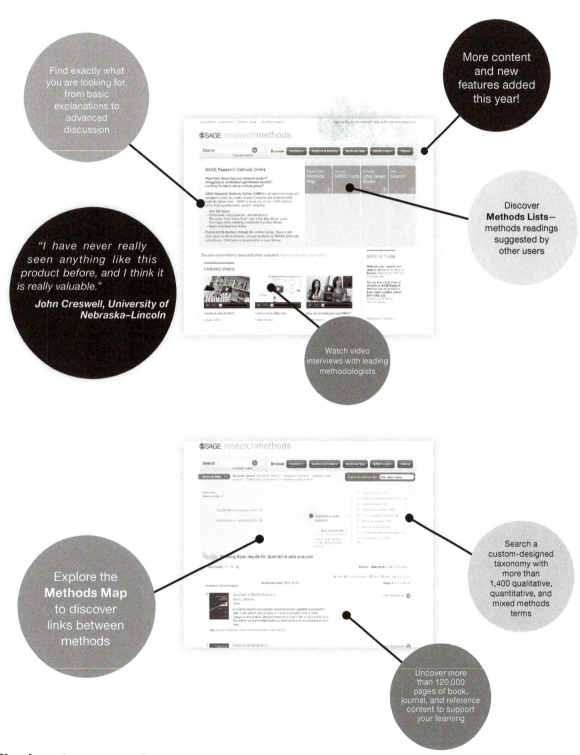

CPSIA information can be obtained
at www.ICGtesting.com
Printed in the USA
LVHW062203211218
601425LV00001B/1/P

9 781412 987073